THE CARTULARY OF PRÉMONTRÉ

Medieval Academy Books, No. 118

The Cartulary of Prémontré

Edited by Yvonne Seale and Heather Wacha

PUBLISHED FOR THE MEDIEVAL ACADEMY OF AMERICA BY
UNIVERSITY OF TORONTO PRESS 2023
Toronto Buffalo London

University of Toronto Press
Toronto Buffalo London
utorontopress.com

ISBN 978-1-4875-4483-6 (cloth) ISBN 978-1-4875-4542-0 (EPUB)
ISBN 978-1-4875-4543-7 (PDF)

Library and Archives Canada Cataloguing in Publication

Title: The cartulary of Prémontré / edited by Yvonne Seale and Heather Wacha.
Names: Seale, Yvonne, editor. | Wacha, Heather Gaile, editor. | Bibliothèque municipale de Soissons. Manuscript. 7.
Series: Medieval Academy books ; no. 118.
Description: Series statement: Medieval Academy books ; 118 | Includes bibliographical references and index.
Identifiers: Canadiana (print) 20220244561 | Canadiana (ebook) 20220244723 | ISBN 9781487544836 (hardcover) | ISBN 9781487545420 (EPUB) | ISBN 9781487545437 (PDF)
Subjects: LCSH: Abbaye de Prémontré – Charters. | LCSH: Abbaye de Prémontré – History – Middle Ages, 600–1500 – Sources. | LCSH: Premonstratensians – France – Prémontré – History – Middle Ages, 600–1500 – Sources. | LCSH: Bibliothèque municipale de Soissons. Manuscript. 7. | LCSH: Monasticism and religious orders – France – Prémontré – History – Middle Ages, 600–1500 – Sources. | LCSH: Prémontré (France) – Church history – Sources.
Classification: LCC BX2615.P74 C37 2023 | DDC 271/.19–dc23

Cover design: Liz Harasymczuk
Cover image: + SIGILL'. ABBATIS ET ECCLIE. PREMONSTRATI. D - Douet d'Arcq, Inventaire des Sceaux des Archives de l'Empire. SIGILLA.

We wish to acknowledge the land on which the University of Toronto Press operates. This land is the traditional territory of the Wendat, the Anishnaabeg, the Haudenosaunee, the Métis, and the Mississaugas of the Credit First Nation.

University of Toronto Press acknowledges the financial support of the Government of Canada, the Canada Council for the Arts, and the Ontario Arts Council, an agency of the Government of Ontario, for its publishing activities.

Canada Council for the Arts | Conseil des Arts du Canada

Funded by the Government of Canada | Financé par le gouvernement du Canada

CONTENTS

ABBREVIATIONS

AASS	*Acta Sanctorum quotquot toto orbe coluntur*, ed. Society of Bollandists. 68 vols. Brussels, 1643–present.
AD	Archives départementales
add.	addition
AN	Archives nationales de France
Barthélemy, *LDA*	Dominique Barthélemy. *Les deux âges de la seigneurie banale: pouvoir et société dans la terre des Sires de Coucy (milieu XIe–milieu XIIIe siècle).* Université de Paris IV, Série Histoire Ancienne et Médiévale 12. Paris: Publications de la Sorbonne, 1984.
BM	Bibliothèque municipale
BnF	Bibliothèque nationale de France
Bréquigny, *Table chronologique*	Louis-Georges de Bréquigny. *Table chronologique des diplômes, chartes, titres et actes imprimés, concernant l'histoire de France.* 8 vols. Paris, 1769–1876.
BVMM	Bibliothèque virtuelle des manuscrits médiévaux
Dufour-Malbezin, *Actes*	Annie Dufour-Malbezin. *Actes des évêques de Laon des origines à 1151.* Paris: CNRS Editions, 2001.
eras.	erasure
GC	*Gallia Christiana in Provincias Ecclesiasticas Distributa.* Ed. P. Piolin. 16 vols. Paris, 1715–65.

Guyotjeannin, *Episcopus*	Olivier Guyotjeannin. *Episcopus et comes: affirmation et déclin de la seigneurie épiscopale au nord du royaume de France (Beauvais-Noyon, Xe–début XIIIe siècle).* Mémoires et documents 30. Geneva: Librairie Droz, 1987.
homeo.	homeoteleuton
Hugo, *Annales*	Charles Louis Hugo. *Sacri et Canonici Ordinis Praemonstratensis annales*. 2 vols. Nancy, 1734–6.
Hugo, *prob.*	Charles Louis Hugo. *Sacri et Canonici Ordinis Praemonstratensis annales, probationes.* 2 vols. Nancy, 1734–6.
IRHT	Institut de recherche et d'histoire des textes
J	Philipp Jaffé. *Regesta Pontificum Romanorum ab condita ecclesia ad an*num post Christum natum MCXCVIII. Berlin, 1851.
JL	Philipp Jaffé and Samuel Löwenfeld. *Regesta Pontificum Romanorum ab condita ecclesia ad annum post Christum natum MCXCVIII.* 2nd ed. Vol. 1. Leipzig, 1885–8.
Le Paige, *Bibliotheca*	Jean Le Paige. *Bibliotheca Praemonstratensis ordinis.* 2 vols. Paris, 1633.
margo.	marginal addition
Melleville, *DH*	Maximilien Melleville. *Dictionnaire historique du département de l'Aisne.* 2nd ed. 2 vols. Laon, 1865.
MGH SS	*Monumenta Germaniae Historica, Scriptores.* 77 vols. Munich, 1826–present.
MP	Norbert Backmund, *Monasticon Praemonstratense id est, Historia circariarum atque canoniarum candidi et canonici Ordinis Praemonstratensis.* 3 vols. Straubing: Cl. Attenkofersche Buchdruckerei, 1949.
Newman, *Hombličres*	William Mendel Newman. *The Cartulary and Charters of Notre-Dame of Hombličres.* Ed. Theodore Evergates and Giles Constable. Cambridge, MA: Medieval Academy of America, 1990.

Newman, *Seigneurs*	William Mendel Newman. *Les seigneurs de Nesle en Picardie (XIIe–XIIIe siècle), leurs chartes et leur histoire; étude sur la noblesse régionale ecclésiastique et laïque.* 2 vols. Memoirs of the American Philosophical Society 91. Philadelphia: American Philosophical Society, 1971.
om.	omitted
PL	*Patrologiae cursus completus, series Latina.* Ed. J.-P. Migne. 221 vols. Paris, 1844–64.
Potthast, *Regesta*	August Potthast. *Regesta Pontificum Romanorum inde ab anno post Christum natum 1198 ad annum 1304.* 2 vols. Berlin, 1874–5.
Pycke and Vleeschouwers, *Actes*	Jacques Pycke and Cyriel Vleeschouwers. *Les actes des évêques de Noyon-Tournai (7e siècle–1146/48).* Episcopalis officii sollicitudo I. Louvain-la-Neuve: CIACO, 2015.
SAHSS	Société Archéologique, Historique et Scientifique de Soissons
superscr.	interlinear superscript addition
transp.	transposition
Wyard, *Saint-Vincent*	Robert Wyard. *Histoire de l'abbaye de Saint-Vincent de Laon.* Saint-Quentin, 1858.

MAPS, FIGURES, TABLES, AND CHART

MAPS

FIGURES

TABLES AND CHART

ACKNOWLEDGMENTS

Many individuals and institutions have given us invaluable assistance over the course of this project.

We thank the archivists, librarians, and staff of the Archives départementales de l'Aisne; the Archives départementales de l'Oise; the Archives départementales de la Somme; the Archives nationales, Paris; the Archives municipales de Metz; the Bibliothèque municipale, Soissons; the Bibliothèque nationale, Paris; the Institut de recherche et d'histoire des textes, Paris; Milne Library, SUNY Geneseo; the Société archéologique historique et scientifique de Soissons; the University of Iowa Main Library; and the University of Wisconsin-Madison Library. We especially thank M. Jean-Christophe Dumain of the Archives départementales de l'Aisne; Mme. Monique Judas-Urschel, formerly of the Société archéologique historique et scientifique de Soissons; and M. Frédéric Rèche of the Bibliothèque municipale de Soissons.

We thank Renate Blumenfeld-Kosinski, Lisa Fagin Davis, Eric Goldberg, and Sally Spence, of the Medieval Academy of America; Suzanne Rancourt of University of Toronto Press; and Samuel Huskey of the Digital Latin Library of the University of Oklahoma; for their assistance with bringing this project to fruition. We thank Bruce Venarde and an anonymous reviewer for their helpful and thorough feedback. We thank Laura Napier for her wonderful work as the indexer of this project.

Amy Livingstone (University of Lincoln) and Miriam Shadis (Ohio University) provided invaluable feedback and guidance, while Rosemary Sands (St. Norbert College) was a wonderful cheerleader. We thank Constance Hoffman Berman, our former advisor, for introducing us to the world of cartulary studies.

Heather is especially grateful to Sylvie and Duncan McEachern and Laure Augustins, who provided accommodation during several summers of research in Picardy and in Paris.

Yvonne thanks her parents for providing space at their dining room table to transcribe a lot of Latin over several summers; Catherine Denial (Knox College) and Anna Kaufman for their support; and all her helpful SUNY Geneseo colleagues.

Research for this project was partially supported through the Computational Analysis Cluster award to SUNY Geneseo from the State University of New York (SUNY) Expanded Investment and Performance Fund, and an Incentive Grant from the Faculty Research Subcommittee of the Geneseo Foundation Research Council.

THE CARTULARY OF PRÉMONTRÉ

INTRODUCTION[1]

While the Premonstratensian Order may be less well known today than other medieval reformed monastic orders such as the Cistercians, during the High Middle Ages its mother abbey exerted a strong influence across a broad swathe of what is now northern France. Its institutional links stretched further still, from Ireland east to Jerusalem and from Sweden south to Spain.[2] It is therefore perhaps surprising that this is the first published edition of the thirteenth-century cartulary of the abbey of Prémontré – now catalogued as Bibliothèque municipale de Soissons, MS 7.[3] Prémontré's cartulary is an important source for both the socio-economic and the religio-institutional history of the abbey and the order as a whole, as well as for the history of the Picardy region. A deeper engagement with this manuscript – together with the many other cartularies produced by the Premonstratensians – has the potential to further greatly our understanding of the order's development over the course of the Middle Ages.[4] We hope that this project will spur the study of a monastic order which has been comparatively understudied by Anglophone scholars, particularly given that the Premonstratensian Order has just celebrated its nine hundredth anniversary.[5]

TOWARDS A FEMINIST EDITION

We have been inspired by much recent work in the fields of cartulary studies and text-encoding studies to attempt what we have dubbed a "feminist" edition of the cartulary of Prémontré. This does not mean simply that we have chosen to highlight the presence of women within the cartulary – although, as we will discuss below, we have found within its pages many examples of medieval women's agency, authority, and activity. Rather, inspired by feminist insights into the nature of power, we have produced both the print and digital versions of this edition with a keen awareness of the ways in which gender, class, and other forms of social power have shaped both how the manuscript was produced in the thirteenth century and how successive generations of readers and scholars have interacted with it through to the present day.

We work from two interconnected premises. First, that a cartulary is not a neutral object. It is a constructed one, composed of acts deliberately chosen and then copied out in a specific sequence to meet a particular purpose. Second, that it is through the framing of an editor's summarizing, indexing, and formatting (and markup, in a digital edition) that an edition is accessed and processed by the reader – one of many reasons why an edition can never be treated as a straightforward facsimile of a manuscript or other text. As literary scholar Laurie Maguire put it, editing a text "is subjective in part and political in total," an undertaking carried out within larger social and political structures by someone who has been shaped by those very structures.[6]

Our awareness of our own non-neutrality as editors has, for instance, informed how we constructed the summaries which precede, and therefore frame, our transcription of each act. It has also spurred us to be very explicit as to how and why we engaged with the text as editors. As we wrote each summary, we consciously reflected on which of its actors should be referenced in that summary. Who should be described as an active participant, and who as a passive one? These may seem like small matters. Yet there is a world of difference between summarizing an act as "The bishop confirms a gift to the monastery" and "Marie makes a gift to the monastery, which the bishop acknowledges." The former phrasing privileges the bishop as the principal actor in the record based on his social standing and his role in confirming the transaction, while the latter places the emphasis on the person whose actions created a need for the charter in the first place. What an editor chooses to focus on in a summary – what actions and entities they choose to highlight – is a statement about what that editor considers important and relevant to the edition's user. These assumptions then guide the reader, who generally uses the summaries to help orient themselves with respect to a new text, and to decide which parts may be relevant to their own work.

We recognize, too, that long before we began work on this edition, the Prémontré cartulary manuscript was already framed by scholarly decisions. Our work was greatly facilitated by catalogues, finding aids, and existing transcriptions of individual charters from the abbey – but while these are useful resources, they are not neutral ones. For example, the volumes of the *inventaire-sommaire* compiled by the archivist Auguste Matton for the *archives départementales* of the Aisne in the 1880s are still the primary means by which researchers orient themselves to that archive's holdings.[7] One such volume summarizes an act issued in 1218 by Anselme de Mauny, bishop of Laon, as follows:

> A charter of Anselme, bishop of Laon, attesting that Guillaume de Monthiémont ceded to the abbey [of Prémontré] three *muids* minus one *setier* of *vinage* in exchange for sixteen Laonnois pounds.[8]

However, the editors of this edition have chosen to summarize that act (**101**) as:

> Anselme, bishop of Laon, makes known that Guillaume de Monthiémont sold to the church of Prémontré three *modii* of *vinagium*, less one *sextarius*, on the lands located at *Hormesellum* for the price of 16 *librae Laudunensium*. Mathilde, wife of Guillaume, approved the sale after receiving compensation for her *dos* on the vineyard at Fresne; Oudard, brother of Guillaume and fief lord, approved the sale also.

A document is summarized and catalogued according to what the summarizer and cataloguer take to be its key historical importance. The first summary foregrounds two of the men involved in the transaction recorded in the charter; the second summary acknowledges all of the people whose actions and consent were needed for the transaction documented in the act to occur. The first summary assumes the self-evident importance of Anselme's and Guillaume's respective roles. Yet while Anselme provided an additional layer of approving authority to the transaction, it could never have occurred without Mathilde's consent. That consent was needed because of Mathilde's established legal rights, and was surely only granted after some process of negotiation. Including Mathilde and the fief lord Oudard in the summary better reflects the complexity of the land holdings and social relationships which the charter captures. Yet the researcher looking through Matton's inventory while on the trail of evidence about medieval women's ability to negotiate, or how they exercised their property rights, might well overlook this charter.

A brief survey of the many volumes of the *inventaire-sommaire* series produced for each of the French *archives départementales* reveals similar examples.[9] Such issues are not unique to the *inventaire-sommaire* series, however; they appear in many such finding aids. How two representative, roughly contemporary acts from the region have been inventoried over time is instructive. One such summary for an 1147 charter from Prémontré that records a donation to the abbey by husband and wife Hugues IV, lord of Gournay, and Mélisende de Coucy, and that was made by a nineteenth-century archivist, describes it as a charter "containing a donation to the church of Prémontré by Hugues de Gournay and Millessende his wife."[10] However, the charter text makes clear that the gift came from Mélisende's *dos*, rather than from joint marital property. Similarly, a 1250 charter, now at the Archives nationales, was summarized by a nineteenth-century archivist as a land "acquisition by

Baudouin le Franc," which omits the fact that Odeline, widow of Manier; her son, Odin; and Colin, son of Denis le Cherequel, sold the land to him.[11]

This reductive summarization is not confined merely to archival inventories or finding aids. For example, in his 1875 edition of the Premonstratensian cartulary of Tinselve, Louis-Victor Pécheur summarized one act from 1211 as follows:

> A charter from Aymard, bishop of Soissons, concerning the alms gift of a vineyard at *Quercum* and a field in front of *Felcieras* that Egald de Margival gave to the church of Prémontré in alms.[12]

This is not an inaccurate summary, strictly speaking, but it is an incomplete one and therefore slightly misleading. Pécheur elides the fact that Egald made his gift with the assent of his wife Eringarde and his daughter Elisabeth, and that both women renounced all of their rights to the property in question. The women too were active participants in the making of this gift, and in the legal arrangements which accompanied it, and indeed were essential to it in a way that Aymard was not. Constructing a summary that includes Aymard and Egald but omits Eringarde and Elisabeth makes assumptions about the social implications of rank and gender, which the text does not necessarily support.

Our positioning of this as a feminist edition, however, is not an implicit argument that the cartulary of Prémontré reveals a hidden Golden Age for women in twelfth- and thirteenth-century Picardy, or that any of the actions undertaken by the women named within its pages were made in defiance of society in general or patriarchy in particular. The acts preserved in the cartulary show that women were certainly capable of being active participants in their society: buying, selling, and inheriting rights and properties; engaging with people and institutions as patrons, mediators, parishioners, and even antagonists. Yet the fact that these actions were recorded in the cartulary shows that they were, to a certain extent, normative. These women acted largely in accordance with the gendered norms of the time, though perhaps to a greater or lesser degree of social approval. They were not exceptional for their era, even if in the contemporary popular imagination medieval women are largely defined by an assumed passivity.[13] Moreover, while engaging in an act of recovery of women's voices and women's actions in the Middle Ages is important, it is insufficient if we are not sensitive to the ways in which those women helped to constitute and to maintain patriarchal and class-based systems of power.[14]

We posit a feminist edition of a medieval cartulary as one which does three things: it allows for more inclusive readings by revealing the structures of power underpinning the acts it includes; it imagines a broad and varied audience; and it avoids as much as possible the imposition of interpretations on the text for that audience. We do not claim to have produced a work which is entirely neutral or disinterested. We have made decisions and brought certain assumptions to our work. However, in line with digital media scholar Jacqueline Wernimont, we hope that this edition can provide a "generative" model of the cartulary manuscript rather than attempting to be the "sole authoritative" version.[15] After all, feminisms and various modes of feminist thought are not simply "about women" – to put things crudely but as feminist praxes are often popularly understood – but rather are liberatory modes of engagement which of necessity must grapple with ideas about power, authority, and inequity.

We consider this edition to be a feminist one also because, through the availability of an open-access digital version of this text, we can make the cartulary of Prémontré available not only to medievalists who have the use of a specialized research library but also to independent scholars of more limited resources, and even to members of the general public who possess a curiosity about the Middle Ages and an internet connection. As we conclude work on this edition, amid the COVID-19 pandemic and all its associated societal, economic, and pedagogical upheaval, increasing access seems ever more imperative. In making this work available in an open-access digital form, we are acknowledging the fact that the primary goal of a feminist edition of a text is not to produce "the definitive version" but rather to deepen existing scholarly conversations and create spaces for new ones. It is the editors' aim that our edition, particularly in its digital format, will lend itself to scholarly and classroom use with an ease that has not previously been possible. We also hope that the edition will encourage interest in further engagement with the materiality of the cartulary, which, as we show below, is a topic ripe for sustained study. However, we are mindful that a digital edition, while helpful in expanding access to a text, cannot replicate a manuscript's full materiality or the experience of physical engagement with it.[16] In particular, we hope that this will help to amplify the voices of those who have been marginalized in the historical record – however faint those voices, however scant the references to an unnamed wife or a solitary *conversa* may be.

TOWARDS MATERIAL ANALYSIS AS A METHODOLOGICAL APPROACH TO THE STUDY OF CARTULARIES

The study of the material make-up of any medieval document also amplifies the voices of a different set of actors: those of the makers who constructed it. A material analysis approach to the study of the book – where the researcher uses material clues not only to answer existing questions but also to ask new ones – allows for the embrace of the whole book as an artifact. The structure of the book, as much as the text that it contains, is a source for historical inquiry and examination. By digging into the processes of manuscript construction, this edition posits a more inclusive understanding of the cartulary of Prémontré's history, its makers, its place of origin, its historical context, and its survival into the twenty-first century.[17]

In the nineteenth century, a new interest in the Middle Ages across western Europe led to the publication of many important medieval charter collections and cartularies.[18] In France, the establishment of the École nationale des chartes in Paris in 1821 and the rise of regional scholarly societies reflected a burgeoning popular interest in the nation's archival *patrimoine*, while also formalizing methodologies for and creating publication venues focused on the study of charters and cartularies. The École des chartes saw itself not only as providing a pedagogical framework founded upon the work of earlier diplomatists such as the seventeenth-century Benedictine monk Jean Mabillon, but also as a means to rediscovering France's medieval heritage.[19] Scholar-librarians Léopold Delisle (1826–1910), who catalogued and described an enormous number of medieval charters and cartularies in the Bibliothèque nationale de France, and Lucien Broche (1877–1958), archivist for the Département de l'Aisne in the early decades of the twentieth century, were both graduates of the École des chartes, where they received the prestigious diploma of *archiviste paléographe*.[20] At a more local and often amateur level, members of scholarly societies – such as the Société des antiquaires de Picardie (founded in 1836), the SAHSS (founded in 1847), and the Société académique de Laon (founded in 1850) – devoted themselves to uncovering and studying hidden treasures held in municipal and departmental archives and libraries.[21] Indeed, the SAHSS's *Bulletin de la Société archéologique, historique et scientifique de Soissons* contains many of the first scholarly editions of medieval charter texts concerning the abbey of Prémontré and its surrounding area.[22]

While nineteenth-century editions did a great service in opening up historical study to a wider audience, twentieth- and twenty-first-century scholars have recognized the problems of their positivist editorial practices.[23] In early editions the charter, not the cartulary, occupied a place of primacy as the fundamental unit of historical inquiry. For example, the editor of the cartulary of the cathedral of Angoulême, Jean Nanglard, stated in his preface to his 1900 edition of that manuscript that "[a] cartulary is only, as we know, a collection of copies of charters."[24] Equally, the editor of the cartulary of Saint-Corneille de Compiègne, Émile Morel, felt no qualms about rearranging the medieval cartulary's original sequence of charters, which was based on geographical location, into one based on chronology.[25] Moreover for Morel, textual analysis took priority over material analysis. Morel's description of the cartulary includes only the manuscript's format, size, and script.[26] Pierre Chastang attributed this kind of approach to the "tenacious positivism that came out of the nineteenth century," which made it "difficult for cartularies, which are dependent on this heritage, to shed their status of simple collections of charters in order to become objects for study, restoring their function as … a *document-monument*."[27]

The 1993 publication of the edited collection *Les Cartulaires* marked a turning point in the field of cartulary studies, as it helped to set the benchmark for understanding the cartulary as a genre in its own right, deserving of both contextual study and historical inquiry.[28] Together, the essays in the collection present both case and comparative studies of English and French cartularies that demonstrate how the construction of these manuscripts was tied to the political, social, and economic contexts of their respective makers.[29] Many cartulary editors working in the later twentieth and twenty-first centuries have adopted the approach argued for in *Les Cartulaires*, seeking to preserve the cartularies' textual content and charter sequence in their publications. In this edition, we too have embraced the idea of the cartulary as a self-contained work and have incorporated the idea of the cartulary as "whole artifact" into the treatment of the individual cartulary acts themselves. We recognize the text of the cartulary copy as the primary content for this edition, and therefore note any textual variants found in surviving originals in the footnotes.[30] While acknowledging the significance of extant original charters as historical and diplomatic sources in their own right, we have approached them as sources that have the potential to tell us something about the cartulary.

Recent scholarly work on monastic cartularies as constructed documents has demonstrated how institutions selected and organized the content for the cartularies that they produced in line with specific agendas. Robert Berkhofer, Constance Bouchard, and Theodore Evergates, among others, have shown how cartularies functioned as vehicles for creating institutional memory and identity, as well as documenting administrative accountability and networking.[31] Paul Bertrand, Olivier Guyotjeannin, and Joanna Tucker have emphasized how changes in political and institutional circumstances could alter a cartulary's function.[32] For instance, Tucker argues that the use of two cartularies belonging to the cathedral chapter of Glasgow changed as multiple scribes engaged with the text over the years and created "space for people within the community to add material, mainly text for their archive that they wanted to be easily accessible for reading and studying [... revealing] hitherto unrecognized aspects of institutional identity."[33] The growing scholarly consensus is that cartularies cannot be seen as static objects reflecting a single motive or moment; rather we must consider them as fluid, active documents which were added to and used in different ways over time.

This edition is a conscious attempt to consider the cartulary of Prémontré as an object that was first created in the mid-thirteenth century – what we term its *noyau primitif* – and that continued to serve its home institution for more than five hundred years. By engaging with the manuscript's materiality as much as with its textual content, and by considering the actors and the processes behind its construction, we can better understand both the document and the history of the abbey of Prémontré. To fully engage with the materiality of the cartulary manuscript – with the script, content, organization, revision, and materials used to construct the book – is to undertake more than a paleographical or codicological study. It is to adopt a holistic approach to a manuscript that emphasizes careful observation and analysis, letting the materiality of a manuscript give rise to questions about its historical contexts. More broadly, we argue that the field of cartulary studies would benefit from examining these books not only as the product of specific institutions but also as the representation of a constructed process that discloses the voices, actions, and agendas of numerous makers.

THE ABBEY OF NOTRE-DAME ET SAINT-JEAN-BAPTISTE DE PRÉMONTRÉ

The foundation of an abbey is a process that unfolds over time, rather than a single discrete event. This is doubly true when it comes to the foundation of the abbey of Prémontré, which headed up an entire monastic order. Both the religious community at Prémontré and the Premonstratensian Order itself coalesced from some of the followers of a wandering preacher, Norbert of Xanten (ca. 1075–1134), although the processes by which this occurred, and the degree to which there was ever a singular Premonstratensian order in the Middle Ages, are still a matter of scholarly discussion.[34] Born in the Rhineland, Norbert of Xanten was an aristocratic career cleric who underwent a spiritual conversion in mid-life. He became a wandering preacher known for his charismatic rhetoric and attracted a large number of followers.[35] Norbert was one of a number of reform-focused church figures in the twelfth century who sought a *sancta novitas*, a renewal of sanctity, in the lives of Christians.[36] In 1120, Norbert helped to found a new community at Prémontré which it was hoped would create just such a renewal for those drawn to the religious life. Norbert did so with the encouragement of the reforming bishop of Laon, Barthélemy de Jur (ca. 1080–1158), and the assistance of his companion, Hugues de Fosses (ca. 1093–1164).[37]

Prémontré was an ideal location for a new monastery. A flat-bottomed, shallow valley in the forests which lay a short distance to the west of the prosperous cathedral town of Laon, it was yet at something of a remove from the most pressing concerns of the secular world. The valley of Prémontré was far from an untamed wilderness, however. Before Norbert's arrival, the valley was home to at least one structure – a small chapel dedicated to John the Baptist, which was originally dependent on the Benedictine house of Saint-Vincent de Laon – while on the far side of the low hills surrounding the valley were several farming hamlets such as Saint-Gobain, Faucoucourt, and Septvaux.[38] Prémontré was also located near a conjunction of various transportation routes that had been heavily travelled since Gallo-Roman times.[39]

The surviving medieval narratives make little note of such mundane considerations, however. They stress instead the spiritual pull of the site: that following a night spent in prayer in the chapel of John the Baptist, Norbert declared his intention to build a religious community on the opposite side of the valley.[40] Indeed, Philip of Harvengt (d. 1183), abbot of the Premonstratensian monastery of Bonne-Espérance, saw in the roughly cruciform shape of the valley of Prémontré a physical reflection of the motivating drive of the followers of Norbert: a place where they could go to spiritually "crucify" themselves through the observance of a devout and ascetic way of life.[41] The new abbey was to be embedded in a landscape which recalled the traditions of the Desert Fathers and evoked one of Christianity's most central symbols. The highly influential antiquarian studies of the Premonstratensians and their documentary records produced in the seventeenth and eighteenth centuries by Jean Le Paige, prior of the order's college in Paris, and Charles-Louis Hugo, abbot of Étival, also worked to support this view of Prémontré's origins.[42]

The first group of fourteen Premonstratensian brothers settled at the site by Easter 1120, and professed their vows on Christmas Day, 1121.[43] Many women figured among the early followers of Norbert, and a number of them entered into the religious life at Prémontré, although we do not know whether they also arrived at the site in 1120, what proportion of the community they formed in its early years, or the exact timeline for their ultimate departure from the abbey.[44] The fledgling order received papal confirmation of its way of life and its possessions from Pope Honorius II in 1126 (**52**). That same year, Norbert travelled east to become archbishop of Magdeburg in what is today central Germany, but the community at Prémontré continued in his absence. The form of life established at the new abbey was an attractive one in the twelfth century, at once "primitivist and innovative."[45] It combined the Augustinian Rule with a communal priestly life, evangelization, and pastoral care in what was seen as an *imitatio Christi*, which combined the best parts of the biblical figures of Mary (the *vita activa*) and Martha (the *vita contemplativa*).[46] Over the course of the Middle Ages, almost one hundred Premonstratensian houses were established in what is now France alone, with approximately two-thirds of them located north of the Loire (**map 1**).[47]

It is difficult for a visitor today to get a true sense of what the abbey would have looked like either in its earliest decades of existence or at the height of Prémontré's power and influence during the High Middle Ages. Most of the abbey's medieval structures have vanished over time. Some were lost to fires, warfare, or lack of funds for upkeep: Prémontré was abandoned from roughly 1414 to 1421, while in 1445, the abbot was forced to put out a call for funds for reconstruction.[48] Other buildings at Prémontré were demolished during a deliberate process of destruction and rebuilding on a grand scale which was carried out by many French Premonstratensian houses in the seventeenth

Map 1: Houses in predominantly Francophone Premonstratensian circaries.

and eighteenth centuries.[49] We know, however, that there was a program of construction undertaken at Prémontré in the second quarter of the thirteenth century, during the time of abbot Conrad (1220–33), which involved the expansion of the dormitory and refectory, and the development of the library and scriptorium.[50] An engraving produced in 1656 is one of the few surviving testaments to what the abbey looked like at the very end of the Middle Ages (**fig. 1**). Another tantalizing possible glimpse of the fabric of the medieval abbey remains, preserved in a piece of early seventeenth-century stained glass from the Premonstratensian abbey of Parc, which Ellen Shortell has argued shows Prémontré's western façade as it would have looked in the later Middle Ages.[51] A written description from the 1620s describes the abbey's dormitories as one of the grandest in France, the chapter house as one of the most notable in the order, and the refectory as "one of the most remarkable buildings of Prémontré in size, beauty, and structure."[52]

Within these buildings, generations of brothers lived, worked, and prayed. Although the Premonstratensians of France expressed a strong contemplative bent, the order as a whole was drawn to pastoral work, and their communities

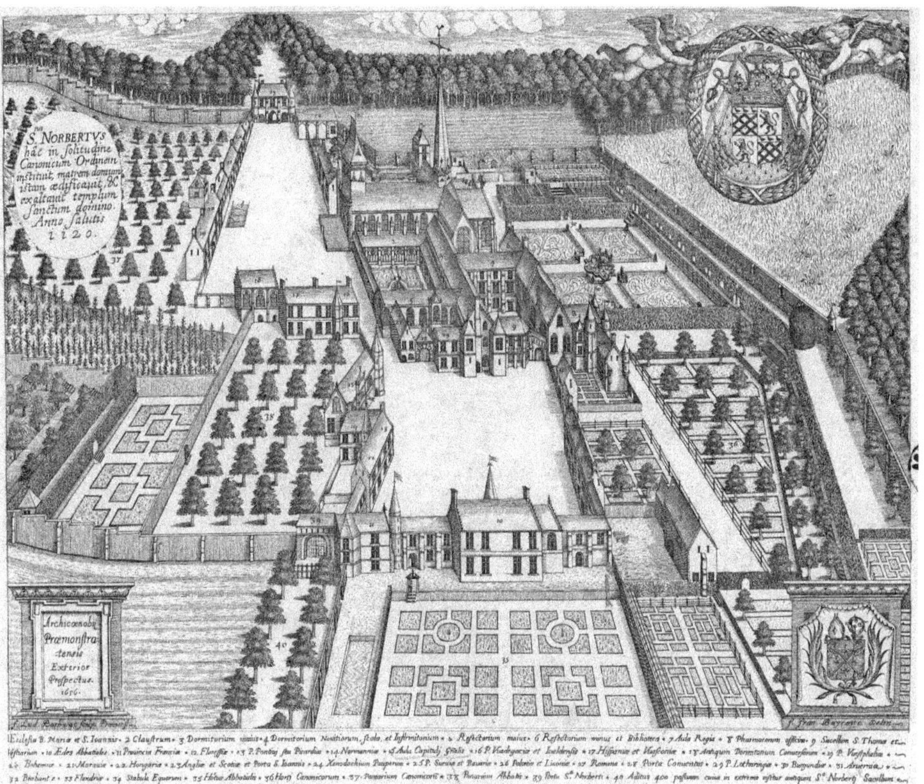

Fig. 1: Louis Barbaran and François Buyrette, *Vue cavalière du Prémontré*. Laon, ca. 1656. Reproduced by permission of the AD Aisne.

were never cut off from the laity. This was certainly true at Prémontré. As stated above, the earliest community there in the 1120s and 1130s consisted of both men and women, with the sisters under the command of Ricuère, lady of Clastres (**449**), staffing the *xenodochium*: part inn for travellers and pilgrims, part hospital for the sick.[53] Some of the physical remains of the *xenodochium* survived into the later nineteenth century, but were finally destroyed by fire in 1879.[54] Remains excavated at the site in recent years provide some clues as to the kind of people who may have travelled to Prémontré in search of care and perhaps a cure, given the presence of both male and female remains from a range of ages. However, given the lack of continuity in the site's occupancy, this conclusion can only be speculative.[55]

The Premonstratensian Order's occupation of the site came to an end amid the upheaval of the French Revolution. Throughout his period in office, the last abbot of Prémontré, Jean-Baptiste L'Écuy (1740–1834), had sought to promote both cohesion within the order and erudition among its members. He invested a substantial sum in expanding the library at Prémontré and trying as best he could to reconstitute its medieval library holdings.[56] However, he left in the 1790s never to return; the abbey's buildings were soon turned to secular purposes and its library holdings dispersed. An explosion in the early nineteenth century caused the abbey's church to collapse.[57] While there was an attempt in the mid-nineteenth century to restore religious life at Prémontré, it was unsuccessful.[58] The surviving buildings on the site are nowadays used to house a psychiatric hospital and are largely inaccessible to the general public, although the modern village of Prémontré runs right up to the edge of the property. The ruins of the twelfth-century church of Saint-Jean-Baptiste stand between them, the lone tangible and readily accessible testament to the medieval abbey's existence for most visitors.[59]

PAR EULX ET LEURS GENS: PRÉMONTRÉ AND ITS PLACE IN THE SOCIAL, ECONOMIC, AND RELIGIOUS LANDSCAPE

The contents of the cartulary of Prémontré provide material for the study of many aspects of the social, political, religious, and economic landscape of Picardy, together with other parts of western Europe, during the twelfth and thirteenth centuries. An essay of this length cannot hope to comprehensively cover all these aspects. Rather, in this section we gesture towards some of the kinds of histories which can be written using the cartulary as source material, and some of the preliminary conclusions which can be drawn from it. We focus in particular on what the acts selected for inclusion in the cartulary, their contents and arrangement, can tell us about the people who helped to create the world in which the abbey of Prémontré existed in this period: how they cultivated the soil beneath their feet, how they maintained relationships (or failed to do so), and when they thought it was important to take a stand. Charters provide a glimpse of aspects of people's lived experiences which were often not captured in contemporary narrative sources such as chronicles or romances.

Undergirding all this analysis, however, is the awareness that the cartulary was a text constructed to bolster a narrative in service of Prémontré. Moreover, the acts were largely written in a linguistic register (whether Latin or Middle French) that may not necessarily reflect how people tended to speak on a regular basis, or that may mask the true complexity of a given legal transaction. The acts which comprise the cartulary are heavily mediated records of moments in the life of the abbey and its surrounding communities and are not uncomplicated sources of social history.

Social Networks and Patronage

The very structure of the cartulary, as discussed in more detail below, reflects a keen awareness of existing political and dynastic power structures: acts are ordered according to social rank, with pre-eminence granted to those issued by popes, bishops, and the upper echelons of the nobility.[60] Charters issued by the lesser nobility and non-nobles followed. The lands, rights, and privileges which these elites granted to Prémontré, and which they helped the abbey to maintain, formed the foundations of the community's success. In return, these patrons helped to satisfy their own spiritual needs and support their own political and economic interests; this was especially the case with regional lay patrons. These reciprocal relationships were not static ones, as Els De Paermentier and Steven Vanderputten have pointed out: alliances could be unstable, new people could succeed to a lordship, or interests could diverge on a sometimes ad hoc basis.[61] The acts preserved within the cartulary show how these interpersonal dynamics shifted over time.

Alongside this evidence of lay power, there is an intentional narrative of institutional power crafted in the cartulary. By choosing to include certain acts issued by certain people – particularly when the cartulary makers selected just one act relating to a specific concern or transaction from among several relevant ones issued by various people – and by arranging them in a certain configuration, the brothers of Prémontré made a statement as to their relationships with varying forms of institutional authority, and as to which relationships they most valued. The cartulary, in other words, was constructed to form a narrative about power and identity which spoke back to the abbey's inhabitants as much as, if not more than, it addressed the wider world.

Members of the local aristocracy loom large in the cartulary, particularly those from what are now the Picard regions of the Laonnois, Soissonnais, and Noyonnais, and to a lesser extent the regions of Tardenois, Thiérache, and Vermandois (**map 2**). These nobles, whether of comital rank or lesser nobles who exercised power over smaller geographical areas, were the ones who forged the strongest relationships with the abbey, relationships which helped to constitute both their family's respective power bases and the presence of the Premonstratensian Order across the Picardy region. While Prémontré interacted with the French royal family over the course of the twelfth and early thirteenth centuries, the connection was never particularly strong, and the patronage that the abbey received from them was never as lavish as that which the Capetians bestowed first on the Cistercians and later on the Franciscans.[62] The monarchy was a presence which may have been esteemed but which was not ultimately essential to Prémontré's existence – much as was the case with the powerful comital families whose territories lay to the north and south of Picardy, such as the counts of Flanders and Hainaut (**1**, **2**, **7**, **424**) and of Troyes and Champagne

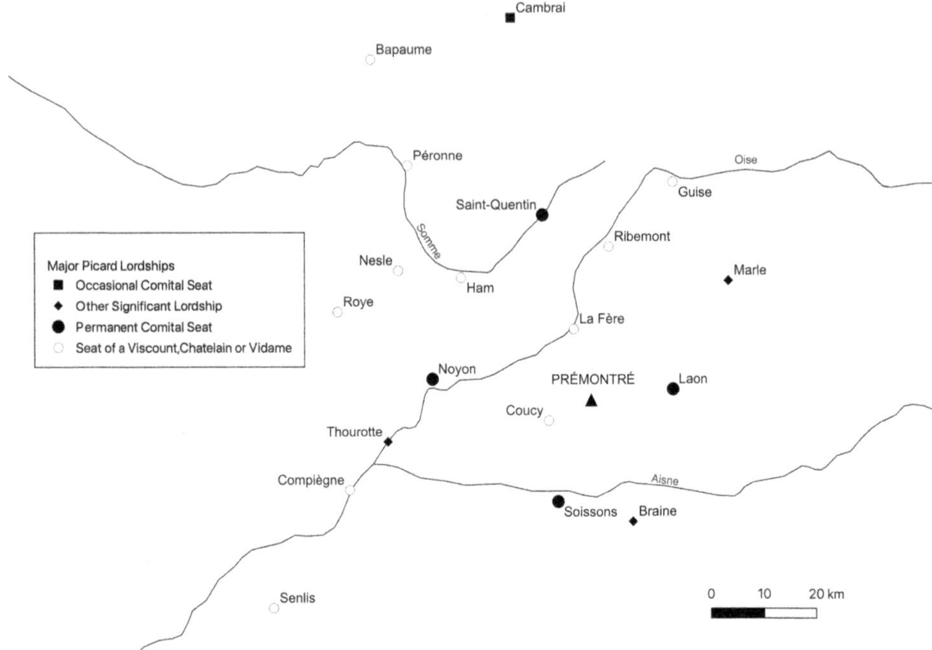

Map 2: Major lordships in eastern Picardy.

(**123**, **124**, **127**). However, Prémontré could not have flourished without the support of the local Picard aristocracy. After all, without land and a certain degree of both financial stability and social capital, it was difficult to ensure the survival of a fledgling monastic community.

Some families, such as the lords and ladies of Coucy, clearly formed a closer relationship with the abbey than did others. One of the dynastic success stories of the age, the Coucy family grew in standing over the course of the twelfth century.[63] When ground was broken for the construction of Prémontré's church in the early 1120s, at least two members of the Coucy family were present: Thomas de Marle (ca. 1073–1130) and his son Enguerrand II de Coucy (1110–1149).[64] Before his departure for Jerusalem in 1138, Enguerrand II made over rights of *vinagium* and *naulum* on his lands to the abbey (**5**). When Enguerrand II's namesake son was baptized in the early 1140s, the ceremony seems to have taken place in Prémontré's church (**98**).[65] The baptism was performed by Barthélemy de Jur, bishop of Laon, who was a great champion of the early Premonstratensians and who had forged close relationships with many of the local nobility. Successive lords of Coucy, Raoul I (**78**, **79**, **203**) in the 1170s, Enguerrand III in the first third of the thirteenth century (**80–5**, **88**, **89**, **166**), and Enguerrand IV in its latter half (**87**, **147**, **148**), together with their spouses such as Mélisende de Crécy-sur-Serre in 1138 (**5**) and Alix de Dreux in 1207 (**86**), supported, traded with, and occasionally disagreed with the abbots of Prémontré. This is not surprising. With their main seat located approximately eight kilometres to the southwest of Prémontré, the Coucy were well placed to become one of the abbey's most important patron families. Indeed, the abbey's main church would serve as the Coucy family's preferred burial place well into the sixteenth century.[66]

Like the Coucy, with whom they intermarried, the powerful noble family of Braine and Dreux also supported the Premonstratensian Order from its inception.[67] In one of the longest single entries in Prémontré's obituary, Agnès, lady of Braine (b. ca. 1080), and her husband André de Baudement (d. ca. 1142) were commemorated for their gifts of land and money, and for their help in founding a number of early Premonstratensian communities through their "zeal and expense" (*studio et impensis*).[68] Towards the end of her life, Agnès even joined the Premonstratensians at the *curtis* of Fontenille, not far from Prémontré. This property had been given to the abbey by Barthélemy, bishop of Laon, because of the "spiritual affection" in which he held Agnès.[69] Agnès and André's widowed daughter-in-law Aelide also made a gift to Prémontré (**503**). Yet unlike with the Coucy, the tenor of this family's connection to the abbey changed after that first generation.

Agnès and André's granddaughter – also called Agnès, who would become the wife of Robert I, count of Dreux – was certainly a vigorous supporter of the order, was likewise commemorated in Prémontré's obituary, and appears in the cartulary as a mediator on the abbey's behalf (**126**).[70] Yet the younger Agnès (ca. 1130–1204) was far more closely associated with the Premonstratensian community which her family had helped to establish near to their family seat at Braine than she was with the mother abbey some thirty kilometres away. In Braine, she helped to rebuild the abbey's church in grand style and to establish that building as a necropolis for her descendants.[71] Association with the abbey of Prémontré was beneficial to both the Coucy and the Braine and Dreux families. It allowed them to display their wealth and power while providing them with an outlet for their piety, helped to ensure their salvation, and offered the opportunity to form reciprocal affective bonds. Yet the divergent development of their associations with Prémontré, even as they retained ties with the Premonstratensian Order as a whole, shows that a patronage relationship had to be consciously maintained over time. While the Coucy family clearly did so when it came to Prémontré, over time the lords and ladies of Braine turned their attentions to Premonstratensian interests closer to home.

To these prominent noble families could be added many others which were lower down the medieval social hierarchy. Their names appear only once or twice within the cartulary, but they may regardless have nurtured connections with the abbey which were just as enduring as the connection between the Coucy and Prémontré – even if these families are less visible in the historical record. For instance, Robert de Royaucourt, *janitor* of the bishop of Laon, his wife Berthe, and their son Hugues appear in the cartulary only in relation to a gift in perpetual alms made to the abbey in 1227 (**220**). Husband and wife Nicolas and Aelide, *bourgeois* of Coucy, make their sole appearance in a 1207 act concerning their alms gift to Prémontré of three vineyards at Verneuil (**90**). We know nothing about these transactions apart from the information contained in the acts, and we have been unable to find any other trace of Robert, Berthe, Hugues, Nicolas, or Aelide in the historical record relating to Prémontré. Their brief appearance in the cartulary may accurately reflect the peripheral nature of their relationship with the abbey, but equally it may be misleading, a generations-long pious attachment to the community hidden from our view because it was not associated with a number of land transactions and therefore has not left a paper trail.

It should also be noted that the number of times a family appears in the cartulary does not imply a close or untroubled relationship with the abbey, or necessarily act as a proxy for the nature of a continuous social relationship. Changing economic or social circumstances could cause a family's relationship with the abbey to become more tenuous or fraught over time. A kin group consisting of members of the extended de Bucy and de la Chaine families appears in nineteen of the thirty-four charters in the Soissons section of the cartulary. Three sisters – Mathilde, Asceline, and Helvide, daughters of Lisiard, viscount of Bucy – were important early patrons of Prémontré. The extended family donated vineyards to the abbey (**266**, **268**), while Lisiard's sister Emmeline provided the resources needed to found the Premonstratensian *curtis* at Bucy.[72] Helvide entered the religious life at Prémontré in 1124 together with her husband and their children, while the widowed Mathilde entered the community in 1149 together with her daughters (**268**, **270**). The sisters' descendants (by their husbands Bérard de la Porte, Garnier de Neuville, and Yves de la Chaine, respectively) maintained an association with the abbey over successive generations (**270**).[73] Tracing their history of connection with the abbey shows how a family group – in this instance, the one founded on the sororal relationship of Mathilde, Asceline, and Helvide – could initially provide Prémontré with political and economic support while also bolstering their own family's social standing. However, the cartulary also reminds us that rank was not static. The first Lisiard in the family whom we encounter, in the early twelfth century, was a viscount; by the time of the death of his namesake descendant in 1219 (**289**), that Lisiard's descendants are described as clerics, a candlemaker, and an illuminator. While far from destitute, like many others in the first few decades of the thirteenth century, the Chaine family appears to have declined in socio-economic status, from the nobility to tradespeople. Their shifting fortunes caused an alteration in their relationship with Prémontré. As the family's economic standing slipped, so too did their perception of the social and spiritual benefits accruing to them from their ancestors' gifts to the abbey. This led the family to contest the abbey's possession of the properties it had once owned.

The cases explored above are representative of the numerous ways in which women from local families interacted with the abbey through gifts, sales, and patronage, in manners comparable to those of their male peers. Moreover, the cartulary also documents several women who joined Prémontré during the community's early years. Many women brought land with them on their entry into the religious life, such as Adéle, daughter of Hugues, castellan of Péronne, who entered in 1138 (**95**); Frédeburge *Domez*, who entered Prémontré as a *conversa* that same year (**299**); or Adélaïde, widow of Gervin, who entered sometime before 1155 (**302**). There were of course men who made gifts of land or rights to the abbey on their entry to the religious life, like Renaud, a *bourgeois* of Crépy who joined the community at Prémontré before 1212 (**152**), but women predominate among this kind of charter. The reason for this is unclear. Were women more likely to bring property rather than cash or gifts in kind when entering the religious life? Or were women's gifts more likely to be subsequently challenged, creating the need for the kind of paper trail which we now see in the manuscript? The acts transcribed in the cartulary of Prémontré show the consciously constructed, but also at times unconsciously shifting, nature of the social relationships between the abbey's community and the laity of the surrounding area.

Economic Life and the *Curtes* Network

Prémontré lay at the heart of a network of *curtes*, a network which formed what Robert-Henri Bautier termed an "organizational model of ecclesiastical patrimony."[74] These *curtes* (sing. *curtis*, the term habitually used by the brothers of Prémontré) seem to have been, broadly speaking, equivalent to the *grangia* of other medieval monastic orders: outlying farms or smaller-scale dependent communities, frequently inhabited by brothers or sisters of the order, which helped to sustain the mother abbey economically.[75] The *curtes*, together with their associated lands and rights, in addition to some urban properties, were acquired by Prémontré over the course of the twelfth and thirteenth centuries. The acquisition of these *curtes*, and moderate capital investments such as might have been needed for the digging of a canal (**483**), the construction of mills (**112**, **123**), or the creation of fishponds (**97**), helped to build a key part of the foundation of the abbey's economy.[76] Though perhaps only 2–3 per cent of the Picard population in the twelfth century were vowed religious, Robert Fossier has argued that members of canonical orders like the Premonstratensians in particular were drivers of economic activities in the region.[77]

While many *curtis* buildings no longer survive intact – their medieval footprints hidden beneath modern farms, the sites badly damaged or destroyed in later warfare, or simply abandoned over the centuries – some structures still survive to give us a sense of what the various *curtes* of Prémontré would have looked like during the Middle Ages. The tithe barns associated with the Premonstratensian abbeys of Ardenne (Calvados) and Lieu-Restauré (Oise) are particularly significant examples. The Ardenne barn, now restored following a bombing in the Second World War, was fifty metres long and capable of holding some eighty thousand sheaves of wheat; the one at Lieu-Restauré, while slightly smaller, is still a substantial structure.[78] Equally, it is often difficult to locate with any precision where Prémontré's townhouses were located, or to know what they looked like (**21**, **294**). However, we know that these buildings could generate rental income, and also perhaps served as a hub for Premonstratensian urban economic and social activity: to hold wares intended for market, or to serve as places for an abbot to stay when visiting a town.[79]

The economic strategies pursued by French Premonstratensian houses were shaped by their immediate surroundings. Clairfontaine, for instance, in what is now the western part of the Aisne, was heavily involved in glass production during the latter part of the Middle Ages because of its large woodlands and local sandy deposits.[80] The immediate area in which Prémontré was located was forested, but to the north, the Oise valley was home to rich arable land, while to the south and southeast, Laon's hinterland was known for its viticulture. Numerous acts document the payment of quantities of grain (referred to as *frumentum* or *triticum*), and less frequently of oats and peas, giving a sense of the staples of the local diet in this period. Other agricultural produce is also mentioned, such as grapes, as when in 1208 one Philippe de Soupir relinquished his right to receive annual baskets of grapes (*quosdam panerios racemorum*, **115**) from some of Prémontré's holdings. Such payments were often made – whether as part of a tithe or some other payment owed to Prémontré, or whether owed by the abbey to another party – at one of Prémontré's *curtes* or other dependent properties. These payments were made at fixed times of the year, generally on religious feast days such as the Feast of St. Remi (January 13), Easter, the Nativity of St. John the Baptist (June 24), the Nativity of the Virgin (September 8), St. Martin's Day (November 11), or the Octave of Christmas (December 25–January 1). For example, in the early fourteenth century, the widow Marie de Vézaponin gave Prémontré a mill and its appurtenances in return for the payment of an annual *cens*. All payments concerning the mill would continue to be made twice a year at the Premonstratensian *curtis* of Trosly-Loire, half at St. Martin's Day and half at Easter (**258**).[81]

Grain and grapes both needed to be processed, whether in mills or in wine presses (*torcularia*). Water mills, the rights to use them, and the rights over the waters which powered them were valued and much-disputed properties of the abbey. These disputes reflected the value of these water mills. Mills reduced the amount of human and animal labour needed to grind produce while potentially generating income. Yet this came at the cost of conflict over land and access rights should the mill's capacity ever need to be expanded.[82] Prémontré and the Augustinian abbey at Ham had a long-running quarrel in the early fourteenth century over the rights to fish and the responsibilities for sluice repair concerning the Premonstratensians' mills at Eppeville (**23**), while the presence of brothers Raoul and Renier in an 1140 charter (**372**) concerning the mills of Hamel reminds us that milling could be a family affair, and that economic concerns were always embedded in social relationships.

Prémontré was adept at exploiting other natural resources. For example, the abbey held many tracts of woodland. These woodlands often came with valuable associated rights – such as to clear the land as at Collezy (**485**), or to collect dead wood and to pasture animals as in the forest of Vois (**87**) – which provided the brothers of Prémontré with income, fuel, timber, and the opportunity to expand their arable and pasture lands. The sandstone quarried at Thury (**458–60**) could equally be used for construction at the abbey or sold to generate income.

Like the cardinal points of a compass, Prémontré was circled by the major market towns of Saint-Quentin, Laon, Soissons, and Noyon, which must have been ready outlets for the produce of its *curtes* and other holdings.[83] Laon in particular, approximately twenty kilometres to the east of Prémontré, was a significant node in the trade networks of the twelfth and thirteenth centuries.[84] The scope of the regional economic contact enjoyed by Prémontré is demonstrated by the range of coinages in which payments mentioned in the cartulary are denominated: Beauvais, Laon, Noyon, Paris, Provins, Soissons, Tours, and Vermandois.[85] The rights of access and transportation needed to get goods to those markets, and indeed the ability to do so, were also valuable – as was exemption from taxation on goods being transported. In 1216, Hugues, lord of Guny, permitted the brothers of Prémontré to use resources on his land whenever needed to repair the canal they had constructed across it to allow for river traffic up and down the Oise (**483**). Successive counts of Flanders exempted the abbey from paying dues such as *theloneum*, *pedagium*, *wionagium*, or *traversum* (**1**, **2**, **7**), while Denis de Valavergny exempted Prémontré from the *rotagium* owed at Lizy so that the brothers could transport wines for their own use (**102**).

Exactly how much income the abbey enjoyed annually is difficult to ascertain. The cartulary's evidence is fragmentary, telling us only what the brothers could expect to receive from a given property in a given year. It is also unclear how much of Prémontré's possessions were part of a *curtis* and its subsidiary holdings, and how much existed outside of the *curtis* network. There are few other surviving sources which can supplement our picture, and they mostly date

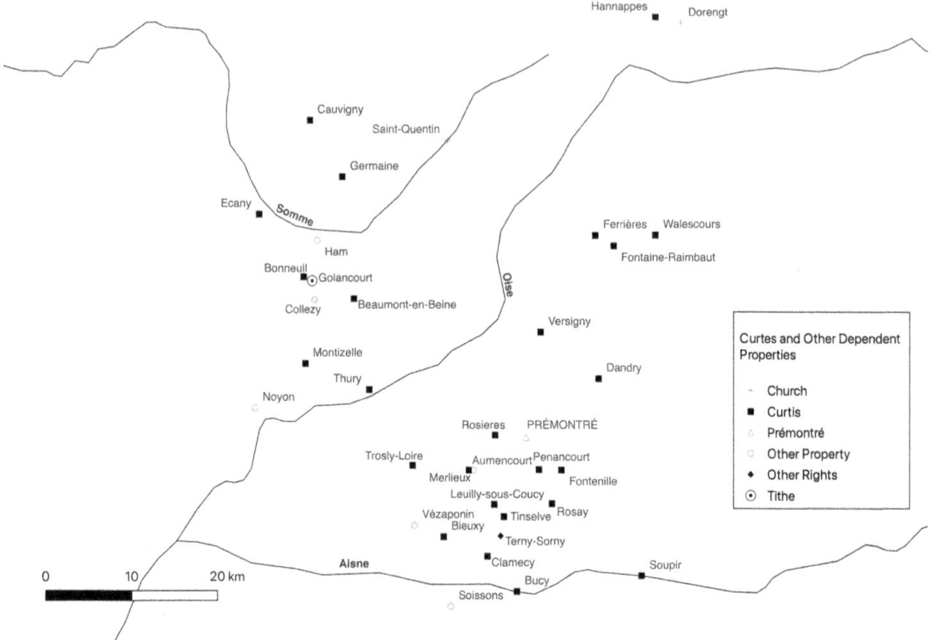

Map 3: *Curtes* and dependent properties of Prémontré, 1188.

to the later medieval or early modern periods.[86] Our best picture of the scale of Prémontré's holdings during its first century or so of existence, and how they were added to over time, comes from a series of papal confirmations, which foreground the *curtes*. An act issued by Pope Eugene III in 1147 attests that the abbey had acquired at least twenty-five *curtes* over roughly the first quarter-century of its existence (**50**). The cartulary preserves acts documenting the foundation of eleven of those twenty-five *curtes*.[87] By 1188, according to a confirmation act of Clement III, Prémontré had twenty-six *curtes* (**48**, **map 3**). It is difficult to ascertain the size of the holdings of any of these *curtes*, although Dietrich Lohrmann has argued that, at least initially, the *curtes* of Prémontré were relatively small.[88]

Many of these lands were worked by tenant farmers, some of whose names are preserved in the cartulary's acts. We know almost nothing about these people, although the litany of their names hints at the unrecoverable richness of their lives: what earned an early thirteenth-century woman the nickname "the Huntress" (*Maria dicta Venatrix*, **490**), or gave another a second name by which she was more commonly known (*Adeluia, que et Sarracena dicebatur*, **400**)? How did the abbey come to have a meadow named for a Mohammed

(*Mahumet*, **115**) in the early thirteenth century?[89] While the fact that a field in the early thirteenth century was known as "At the Sandpit" (*A La Sabloniere*, **223**) seems straightforward, the fact that the next field named in a list of properties was locally called "Where Big Stephen Died" (*Ubi Stephanardus Mortuus Fuit*, **223**) may give the reader pause.[90] Such place names also serve as a reminder that the *curtes* system, and other systems of geographical organization which appear in the cartulary, such as diocesan or seigneurial boundaries, were constructed ones, and often ones which were imposed on pre-existing farms and settlements by a literate elite. What we see in the cartulary may reflect local lay understandings of and practices around the land, but equally it may not.

Confraternity and Conflict: Relationships with Other Religious Communities

The cartulary text also tells us something of how the inhabitants of the abbey of Prémontré in the mid-thirteenth century understood the origins of their community, its rights, and its contemporary relationship with the rest of the *ordo Praemonstratensis*. None of these things were so clearly demarcated then as they may appear now, with the hindsight of several centuries.[91] Prémontré's institutional understanding of itself as the first among a network of religious communities ideally united by a common charism, rule, and liturgy was not a static thing. It changed over time, due both to internal catalysts and to external pressures. Ecclesiastical figures outside the order expressed concerns about the Premonstratensians' unity and clarity of charism from an early date, and even questioned the order's right to exist. For instance, Gautier, bishop of Maguelonne (1103–29), criticized the rule which Norbert initially adopted for use at Prémontré.[92] Gautier thought it was too short and obscure to be practical, and moreover that it did not accurately reflect the rule on which it was based, that of Augustine of Hippo. The Benedictine theologian Rupert of Deutz (ca. 1075–ca. 1129) criticized Norbert's leadership and qualifications.[93] Pope Honorius II issued a bull in 1126 (**52**) stressing that the Premonstratensians should seek liturgical unity and thereby endorsing the order, perhaps in an attempt to quell these arguments.[94] This decree was not a cure-all; disagreements at Prémontré in its early years became heated enough that some members argued for the abbey's dissolution and further papal intervention was needed.[95] While these conflicts are not directly referenced in the cartulary, having to defend the validity of their way of life from such an early date undoubtedly shaped how the first generation of Premonstratensians understood their identity. They may also have helped those at Prémontré to develop a clearer sense of the primacy of their community among the followers of Norbert.

The latter sense is one that does come through strongly in the cartulary, perhaps in large part because the institutional unity urged by the papacy was more easily mandated than achieved. In 1126, Norbert of Xanten left the abbey of Prémontré to become archbishop of Magdeburg. Before his death in 1134, he oversaw the reform of a number of religious communities in his new diocese, the most prominent of which, Unser Lieben Frauen, was located in Magdeburg itself. These brothers – perhaps better termed Norbertines than Premonstratensians – wore black rather than white habits, observed the liturgy of the cathedral of Magdeburg rather than the church of Prémontré, and evidently felt little affinity with their nominal confreres to the west.[96] A chronicle written at the German abbey of Ilfeld around 1300 described an *ordo Magdeburgensis* as well as an *ordo Praemonstratensis*, a distinction which likely reflected both the struggle which Prémontré faced in asserting its authority over houses which lay far outside of northern France and deep disagreements over what it meant to be a follower of Norbert.[97] Which should be stressed more in the order's way of life: the *vita activa* or the *vita contemplativa*? How should they dress? What liturgies should they use and was *abbas* or *praepositus* the more appropriate term to use when identifying those in charge of a community? These differences did not necessarily always result in conflict; some degree of "live and let live" probably prevailed, even if begrudgingly. Various popes and papal legates sought to address the ongoing tensions between Prémontré and some northeastern German houses, particularly Magdeburg, throughout the twelfth and thirteenth centuries. Their resulting acts, now preserved in the cartulary, granted or confirmed rights to Prémontré as mother abbey of all the houses founded by Norbert (**13**, **14**, **24–43**, **46–70**).

Even once an agreement of 1224 formalized a rapprochement in the often fractious relationship between Prémontré and Magdeburg (**14**), in actuality, as Walter Froese has put it, this "formal unity allowed the continuity of their actual separateness."[98] More wrangling about the institutional structure took place in the 1230s, with the bishop of Paris writing in 1239 about in-person negotiations scheduled to take place at Prémontré (**15**). Three further acts issued that same year (**16**, **17**, **18**) record the outcome of the meeting, a compromise in which Magdeburg agreed to send representatives to the General Chapter meetings at Prémontré on a triennial basis.[99] The agreement explicitly frames Prémontré as superior to Magdeburg.[100] Yet despite all the time and effort spent on achieving unity by parties in France, Germany, and Italy, the chronicler of Ilfeld still did not seem to recognize the existence of a singular Premonstratensian order when he sat down to write some seventy-five years later. While the issuing of these acts shaped the nature of Prémontré's relationship with Magdeburg and with other abbeys, for the chronicler in 1300 there was still a visible difference between the *ordo Magdeburgensis* and the *ordo Praemonstratensis*.

Despite, or perhaps because of, this ongoing wrangling with Magdeburg during the twelfth and thirteenth centuries, the abbots of Prémontré were keen to exert their authority over other regions at the same time. We can see this in abbot Hugues II's decree of 1182, mandating the attendance of English and Scottish Premonstratensian abbots at the order's annual General Chapter meeting (**501**), or in abbot William II's decree of 1233, which instituted a similar agreement for the abbots of Premonstratensian houses in Italy (**44**). The degree to which these decrees ever reflected reality is uncertain, however, and their effectiveness may have declined over time. Throughout the fourteenth century, there was a steady devolution in authority from Prémontré to English Premonstratensian houses and a weakening in ties between those houses and the mother abbey.[101]

The cartulary provides us with some clues as to how, even at Prémontré, ideas about what it meant to be a Premonstratensian shifted over time. It also shows that there were moments when those ideas changed more rapidly than others. One such moment was the second quarter of the thirteenth century. The reforming pope Gregory IX, seeking to encourage greater uniformity across the order, mandated a reform of the Premonstratensian governing statutes. Placide Lefèvre dated this revision of the statutes – one of a number to occur during the Middle Ages – to 1236–8.[102] In other words, these new statutes were written at roughly the same time that the cartulary project was being conceived at Prémontré. It is possible therefore to see both the cartulary and the statutes as reflecting a distinct reforming impulse which then animated the abbey. Also around the same time, following the Premonstratensian General Chapter meeting of 1240, abbot Hugues III d'Hirson issued a charter which reformed the way of life of the sisters of the dependent house of Bonneuil (**508**). This charter limited their number to twenty and forbade the female head of the community to style herself a *priorissa* since she was not permitted to exercise the *cura animarum*.[103]

The abbey of Prémontré was defined not just by its relationships with other Premonstratensian houses, however, but also by those which it maintained with religious communities from other orders (**maps 4, 5**). Most of them were located relatively near to Prémontré, such as the Benedictine abbey of Saint-Vincent de Laon – which had previously held part of the valley of Prémontré (**71**, **72**) and with which Prémontré established an act of confraternity in 1185 (**19**) – or the Augustinian canons of Ham (**23**, **369**, **370**, **377**, **404**, **406**, **414**, **495**). The abbey also interacted with other Benedictine and Augustinian houses, with nearby Cluniac communities such as the priory of Lihons (**359**), with the hospital of Noyon (**313–15**, **318**, **319**), with the Knights Hospitaller (**495**), and with the cathedral chapters of Laon, Soissons, and Le Puy en Velay (**500**).

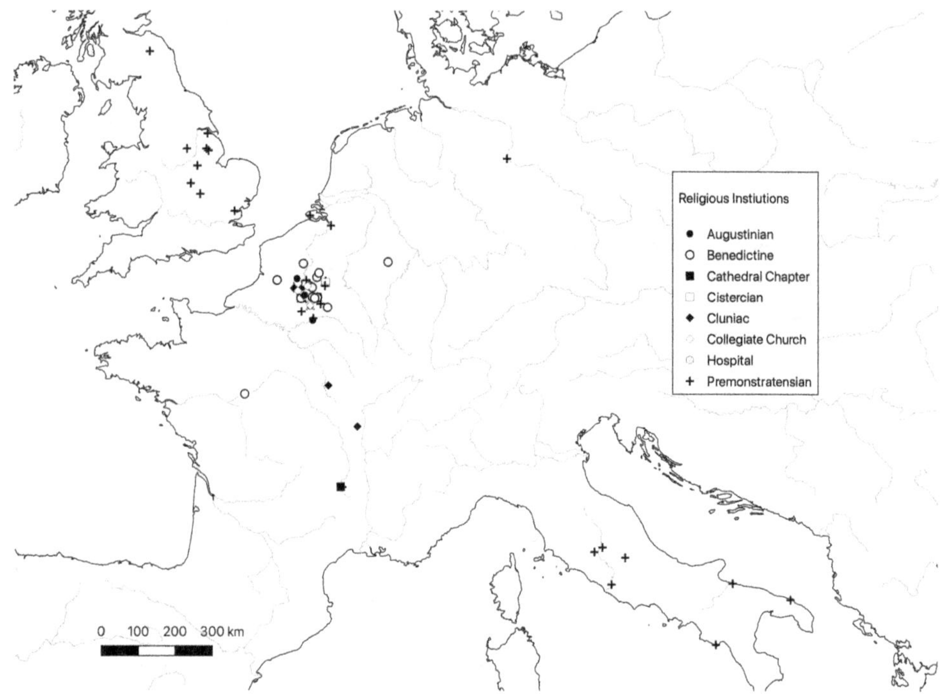

Map 4: Other religious institutions mentioned in the cartulary of Prémontré.

Many of the acts contained within the cartulary record instances of disputes, or at least the resolutions of these disputes, as individual religious communities clashed in their attempts to maintain their status or their valued connections with the laity. The Benedictine priory of Nogent-sous-Coucy – perhaps best known today as the home of the author Guibert de Nogent (ca. 1055–1124) – often found itself at loggerheads with its near neighbour, Prémontré. Both communities had close ties with the noble family of Coucy, and jockeyed for local pre-eminence (**222**, **223**, **224**, **412**).[104] An illustrative example is the dispute which occurred between Prémontré and Nogent in 1221 concerning the right to bury one Mathilde, a woman from Coucy. Nogent had long claimed the burial rights for the parishioners of Coucy, but Mathilde had expressed a desire to be buried at the abbey of Prémontré. Following arbitration by the abbots of the Premonstratensian houses of Saint-Martin de Laon and Valsecret over a period of several months (**225**), a compromise was reached according to which Mathilde's body would remain interred at Nogent, on the condition that Nogent not prevent any parishioners of Coucy from being buried at Prémontré in the future if they so wished (**226**). This dispute arose despite an agreement

Map 5: Other religious institutions mentioned in the cartulary, regional close-up.

of *societas* which had been made in the 1180s between the abbeys of Prémontré and Nogent, a reminder that acts often reflect a desire for certain kinds of behaviour rather than a guarantee that such behavioural standards were met (**222**).[105] However, the cartulary contains acts showing that Prémontré often tried to avoid conflict with other religious communities. The manuscript contains transcriptions of an agreement of confraternity made between the Premonstratensians and Cistercians in 1142 and renewed in 1153 (**497**, **498**), while a similar *conpositio* was reached between the Cluniacs and the Premonstratensians in the second quarter of the twelfth century (**499**).[106]

The abbey of Prémontré also interacted with the institutional church. Even more than the papal acts discussed above, episcopal charters abound within the pages of the cartulary. The archbishops of Magdeburg (**14**), Rouen (**504**), and Reims (**8**, **75**, **77**, **114**, **192**, **199**, **212**, **415**), together with the bishops of Amiens (**406**), Cambrai (**239**, **244**, **502**), Laon, Meaux (**377**, **406**), Noyon, Paris (**15**), Senlis (**275–7**, **281**, **377**, **406**), and Soissons (**21**, **121**, **125**, **262**, **264–71**, **280**, **288**), all make appearances in the cartulary (**map 6**). The acts in which they appear often have to do with the maintenance of order. For instance, according

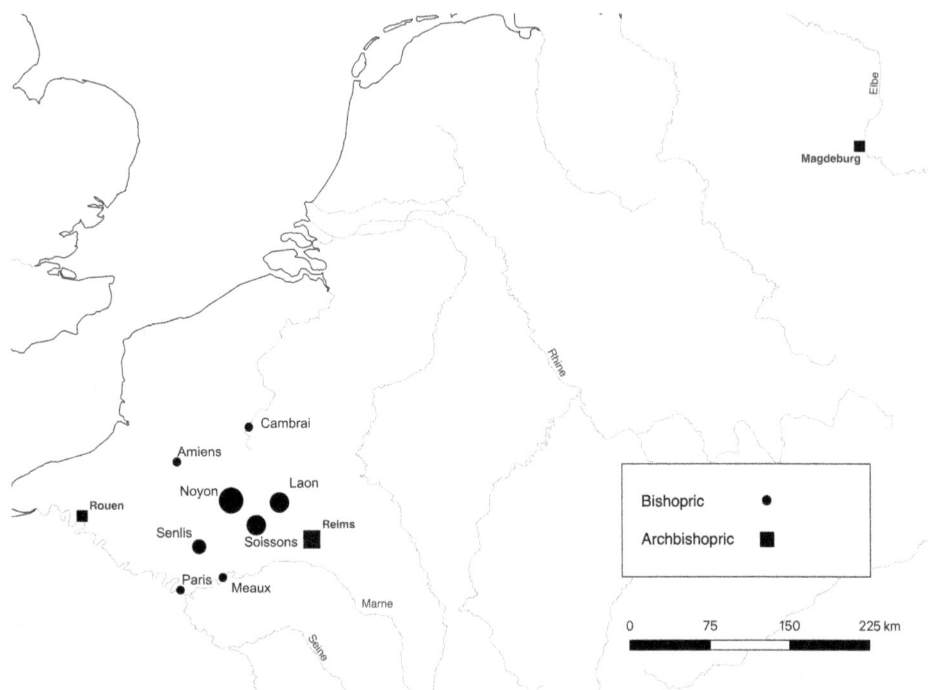

Map 6: Bishoprics and archbishoprics mentioned in the cartulary.

to an 1132 act, persistently unruly Premonstratensian abbots in the diocese of Cambrai could be disciplined by its bishop and chapter (**502**).[107] However, the order was broadly exempt from episcopal oversight, at least in principle, being under papal protection (**24**, **48**, **50**).[108] That Prémontré held the vast majority of its properties in the three dioceses of Noyon, Laon, and Soissons may explain the prominence in the cartulary text of the bishops of Noyon and Laon.[109] These acts show the bishops of Noyon and Laon by turns supporting, arguing with, and advocating for the brothers and sisters of Prémontré throughout the twelfth and thirteenth centuries, while also lending their authority to many acts which concerned the abbey. Some acts, while not authored by a bishop, were drawn up in their residences, as when in 1217 Baudouin, lord of Soupir, approved a gift to Prémontré in the bishop's chapel at Laon (**117**), or when Louis VI of France gave a tithe to the abbey in the bishop's palace at Soissons (**150**).

While these acts preserve only a partial picture of Prémontré's relationships with local bishops during the Middle Ages, they nonetheless point towards the richness and complexity of such relationships. In this, these acts parallel the way that the cartulary's other acts let us explore aspects of the religious, social, and economic life of Prémontré – individually fragmentary but capable of being placed in a collage which shows us a glimpse of the abbey's prominent role in a long-ago world.

MUNIMINE ROBORARE: THE CARTULARY OF PRÉMONTRÉ

If we were to contradict the common saying and judge a book by its cover, the cartulary of the abbey of Prémontré might well garner little respect or interest from readers, despite its great age. The exterior of the manuscript is visually underwhelming and the interior rather uniformly nondescript (**figs. 2** and **3**). However, when we study the cartulary of Prémontré in terms of the deliberate decisions that shaped it, we can see how vibrant a material historical source it is about the individuals who made it and the methods they used, regardless of its aesthetics. Studying the cartulary of Prémontré, in other words, requires the study of processes as much as of the final product. To truly understand how a medieval manuscript like the cartulary of Prémontré came into being requires connecting the book's present construction with what we can reconstruct of its past. In doing so, we can gain a new appreciation of the local institutional expectations, agendas, and practices which shaped the manuscript's production.

The cartulary of Prémontré contains copies of 509 acts that were selected from the abbey's archives, organized into separate sections, and then transcribed into the cartulary. As a thirteenth-century artifact, the cartulary is at the centre of a recursive interplay between human agency then and now. Then, the voices of those who generated the need to record the cartulary's content in the first place were affirmed in both the textual content and the material struc ture. Now, as a monument to the abbey's image of itself in the Middle Ages, the manuscript waits for scholars to dig into questions of where, when, how, and why the book was made in order to access the material evidence it holds, and bring an immediacy to the individual actors – men and women, noble and non-noble, religious and secular – who participated in the construction of the cartulary's textual content and the culture of the abbey.

The cartulary of Prémontré was held in the abbey's archives until after the French Revolution, at which time the monastery was dissolved and the cartulary was transferred some twenty kilometres away to the Bibliothèque municipale de Soissons.[110] The newly established government found itself in possession of hundreds of thousands of medieval charters, cartularies, and other documents, many of them formerly belonging to religious institutions. This did not occur by chance. In December 1798, the state's Conseil de conservation des objets des sciences et d'arts issued an order for monastic cartularies, together with other registers and similar materials, to be collected.[111] In line with this dictate, the charters from the original archives of Prémontré

Fig. 2: Cartulary of Prémontré, front cover. Reproduced by permission of the Bibliothèque municipale, Soissons.

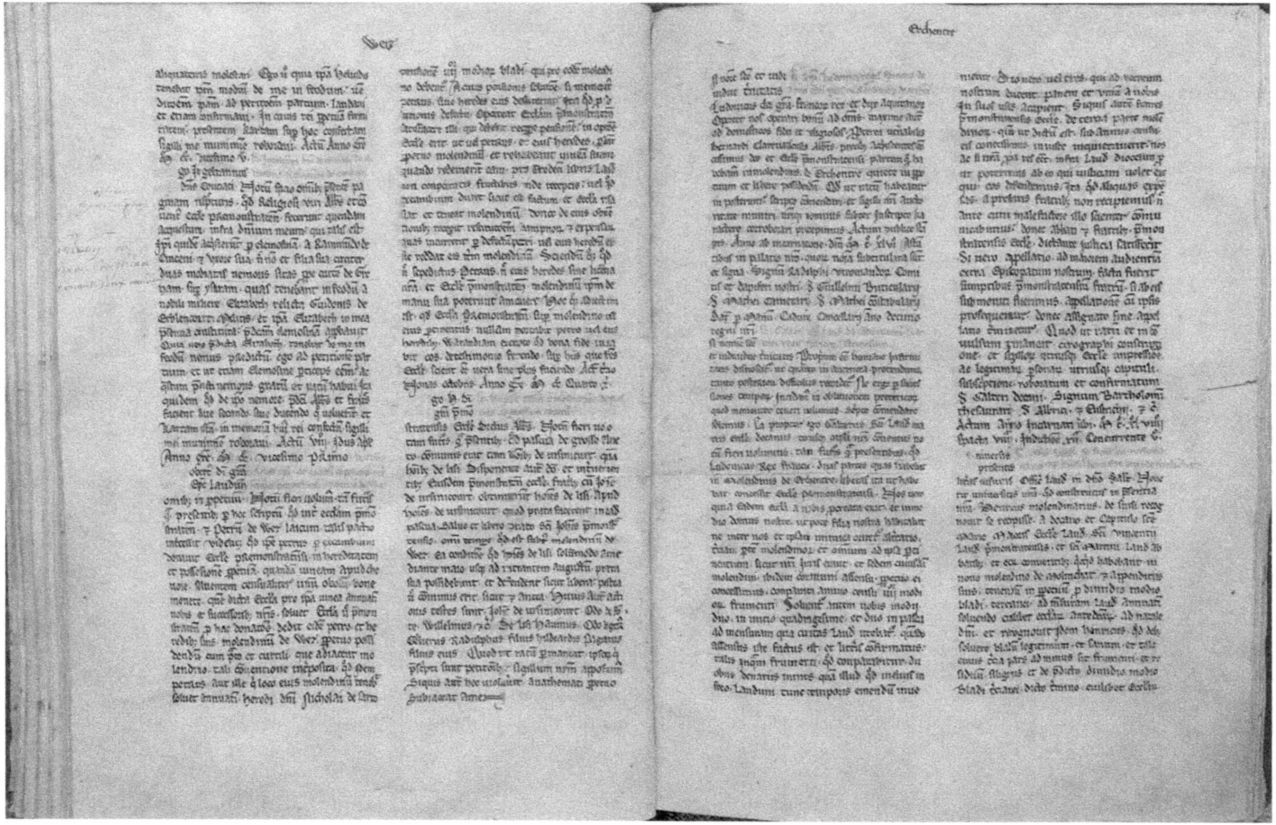

Fig. 3: Cartulary of Prémontré, fol. 41r. Reproduced by permission of the Bibliothèque municipale, Soissons.

were sent to the relevant regional repositories, and the cartulary and other manuscripts to the municipal library of Soissons.[112]

The Manuscript and Its Maker

The construction of a cartulary like that of Prémontré often involved many artisans – scribes, rubricators, correctors, illuminators, and binders – each of whom was needed for their individual technical expertise. In addition to these artisans, whose work is visible or tangible, we must add the anonymous person, or group of persons, who intentionally selected certain charters from the abbey's archives for transcription into the cartulary of Prémontré, and who came up with an organizational schema before that process began. It remains unclear whether this anonymous person or persons (the overseer) was the same person who transcribed the charter contents into the cartulary (the cartulary maker). We cannot assume that the overseer was a single individual, nor can we assume that the overseer and the cartulary maker were one and the same. It is clear, however, that only one person, the Prémontré cartulary maker, executed the tasks of charter transcription, rubrication, divisional tables of contents, and corrections of the *noyau primitif*, or initial core of the cartulary. We should note here that we will use male pronouns to refer to Prémontré's cartulary makers, because while both female and male Premonstratensian communities existed in the twelfth and thirteenth centuries, and while women often participated in the intellectual and technical creation of medieval manuscripts, during the period when Prémontré's cartulary was under construction, there were almost certainly only brothers resident at the abbey.[113]

In preparing this edition, we looked at the cartulary from the perspective of those who constructed it, applying a material studies approach that used what we know about medieval manuscript production in general to help us better identify those areas in the cartulary where typical practices were transgressed. Moments of digression from normal practice point to intentional interventions on the part of makers and raise questions as to how and why the departure from the norm occurred. In the first part of this section, we provide a general material description of the cartulary of Prémontré as it currently exists. In the second part, we address the cartulary's organizational schema, provide a general overview of the cartulary's content, and demonstrate how both material and textual anomalies suggest that the brothers of Prémontré's intended plan for the cartulary was never fully realized. In the third section, we discuss those clues left by the cartulary maker's hand that provide us with insight into his character, his decision-making processes, and his daily workflow practices.[114]

When considered together, the organization and execution of Prémontré's cartulary reveal the abbey's desire to create a monolithic manuscript that would function for its readers as a textual and tangible representation of a flourishing religious institution. The reality of a fragmented administrative structure at the abbey and simple human imperfection, however, impeded the full realization of the abbey's aspirations.

A Brief Description of the Cartulary's Material Aspects

The cartulary of Prémontré measures 291 mm (11.45 inches) by 402 mm (15.8 inches), and comprises 113 parchment folios numbered 1–12, and 12bis–112.[115] The parchment itself is of an inconsistent quality. A medieval manuscript maker had options when choosing parchment folios for their book. High-quality folios could be cut with precise measurements from the central area of a dried and processed animal skin, whereas lower-quality cuts might contain evidence of the slight curvature found on the outside edges of a prepared skin. Similarly, a maker could choose folios with no flaws, or take lower-quality pieces of parchment that contained small holes or cuts. While only a handful of the Prémontré cartulary's 113 folios show evidence of curvature at the edges, approximately 30 per cent contain flaws or holes, as well as evidence of attempted repairs with needle and thread (**figs. 4** and **5**). The number of lower-quality folios present in the cartulary of Prémontré suggests that the abbey was taking measures to use as much of a single prepared skin as possible in order to economize.[116]

Once the parchment folios were cut to size, they were pricked and ruled in preparation for receiving text. In the cartulary of Prémontré, pricking was performed on both inner (spine side) and outer margins (fore-edge side) of the text block to guide the maker in drawing horizontal lines for the text (**fig. 6**). Pricking is also visible along top and bottom margins marking the width of the columns. The practice of pricking both the inner and outer margins of the manuscript suggests that the maker ruled the folios after they had been folded and gathered into sections. Pricking marks are no longer visible where folios were later cropped in preparation for binding, or perhaps rebinding.[117] Ruled in lead point, the thirteenth-century folio layout of Prémontré's cartulary contains two columns of forty-five lines each (**fig. 3**).[118] The text is written in black ink, almost certainly iron gall. The short summaries that precede each act's text are rubricated, written in red ink likely made from red lead, and most folios have running titles pertinent to content along the top margin, in either red or black ink. The consistent folio layout and design in the thirteenth-century cartulary provides explicit material evidence that distinguishes this *noyau primitif* from later additions or alterations.

To keep track of the quire sequence, the cartulary of Prémontré was organized and arranged using a series of Roman numerals that appear on the verso

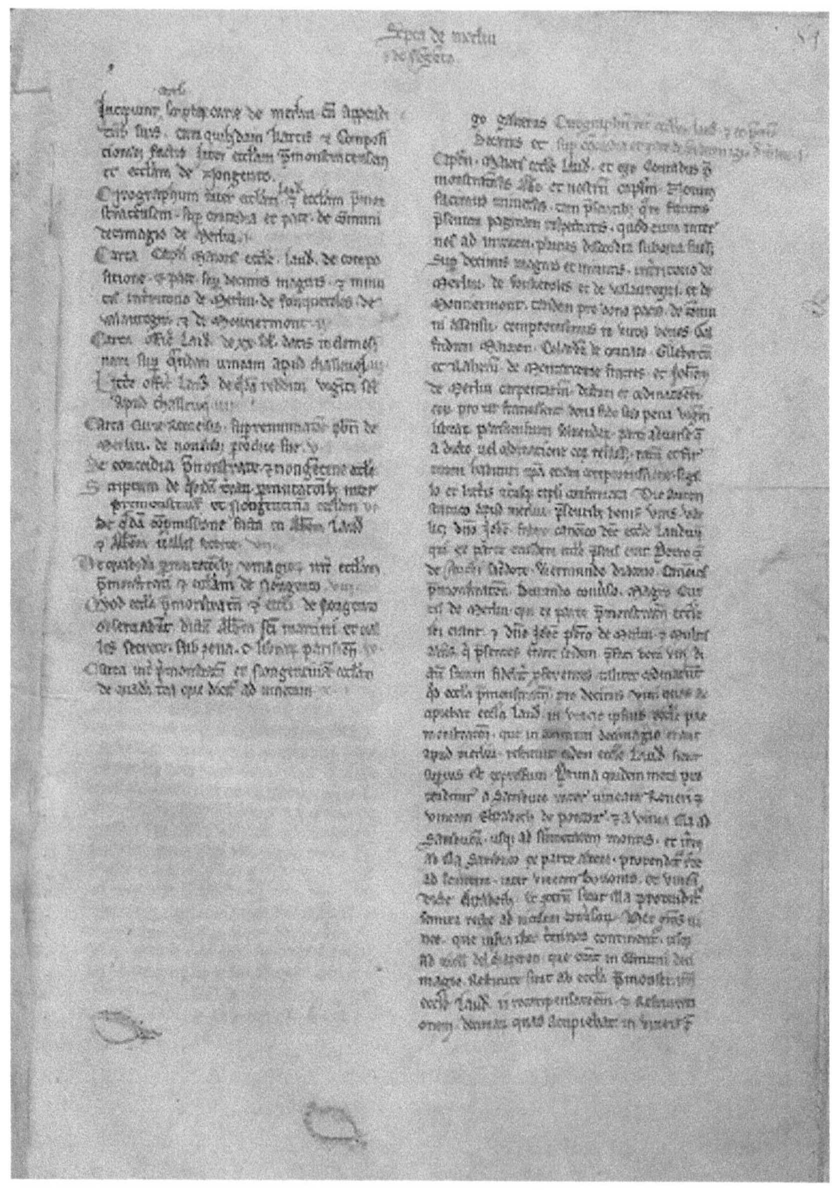

Fig. 4: Cartulary of Prémontré, fol. 54r, parchment holes. Reproduced by permission of the Bibliothèque municipale, Soissons.

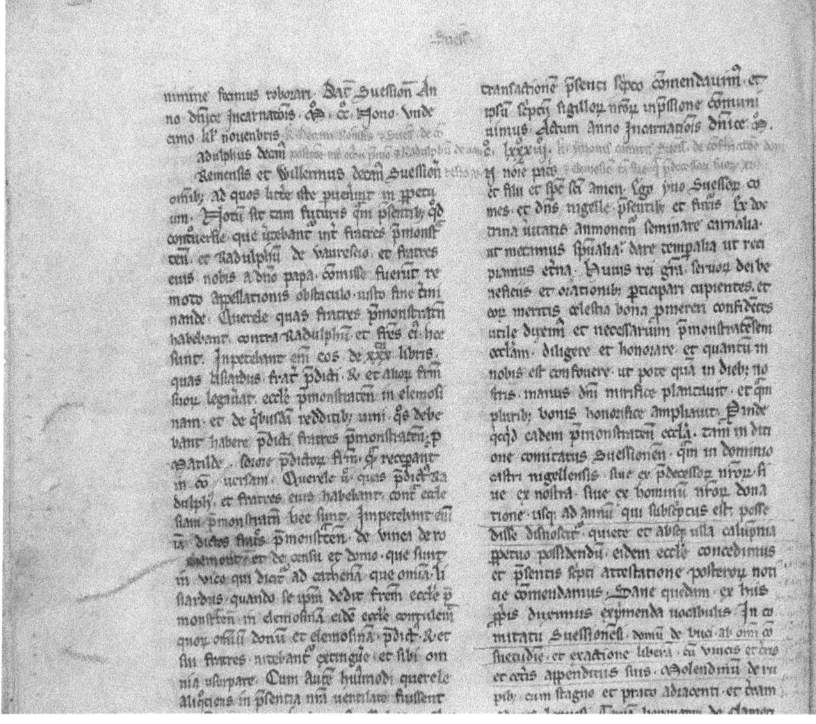

Fig. 5: Cartulary of Prémontré, fol. 67v, parchment repairs. Reproduced by permission of the Bibliothèque municipale, Soissons.

side of each quire's last folio.[119] For example, there is a carefully embellished roman numeral one (I) found at the centre of the bottom margin on the verso of the first quire's last folio (**fig. 7**). Quires two and three are marked in a similar manner, likewise quires nine through fifteen. The absence of these Roman numerals can indicate later quire alterations, such as in quires four through eight in the cartulary manuscript, which are discussed in more detail below. The Arabic numerals in the upper right corner of each folio were added in the seventeenth century.[120]

A second numbering system helped ensure the correct sequence of folios within a single quire. As per a common medieval practice, the bottom right corner of the first four folios in a quire often holds a minuscule letter and Roman numeral, for example: "ai, aii, aiii, aiiii." In the cartulary of Prémontré, this labelling continues alphabetically throughout the manuscript, *a* through *q*.[121]

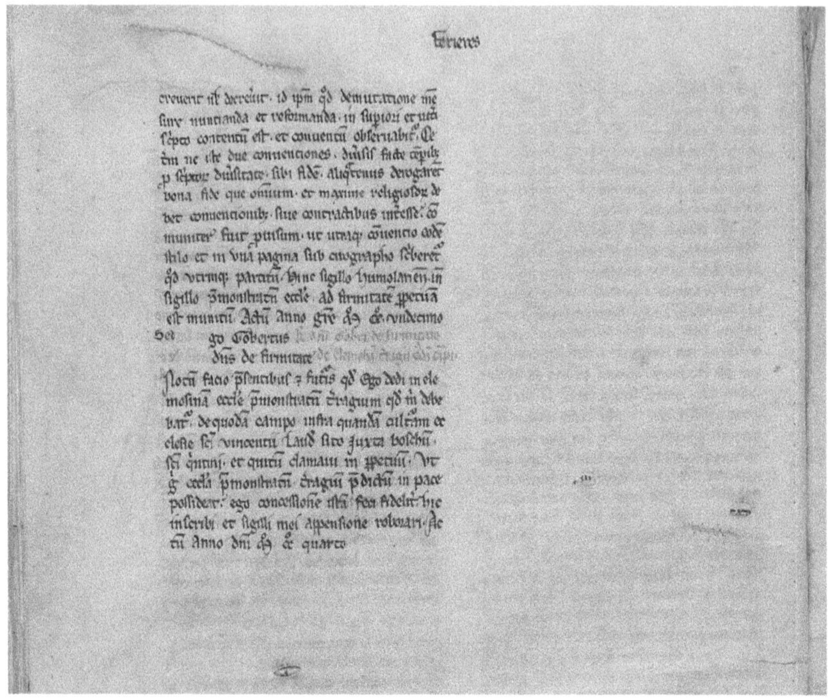

Fig. 6: Cartulary of Prémontré, fol. 47v, pricking. Reproduced by permission of the Bibliothèque municipale, Soissons.

The absence of these signatures or their non-sequential order can also indicate later alterations in a manuscript's collation.[122]

The cartulary of Prémontré's fifteen quires were sewn and bound together at some point after the completion of the transcription, likely in the mid- to late thirteenth century. In the late sixteenth or early seventeenth century, a previous binding, perhaps the thirteenth-century one, was removed, and the cartulary was rebound in its current binding, a stamped brown leather covering over pasteboards.[123] Roughly two hundred years later in the late nineteenth century, a conservation effort replaced the worn pieces of leather found on the cartulary's spine and cover corners.[124]

While the material analysis that follows pertains predominantly to the period of cartulary construction at the abbey of Prémontré, a duration perhaps of ten years (1230–40), we must be careful not to assume that the cartulary was a static object after the completion of the *noyau primitif.* Later codicological alterations to the document and textual emendations in the margins confirm

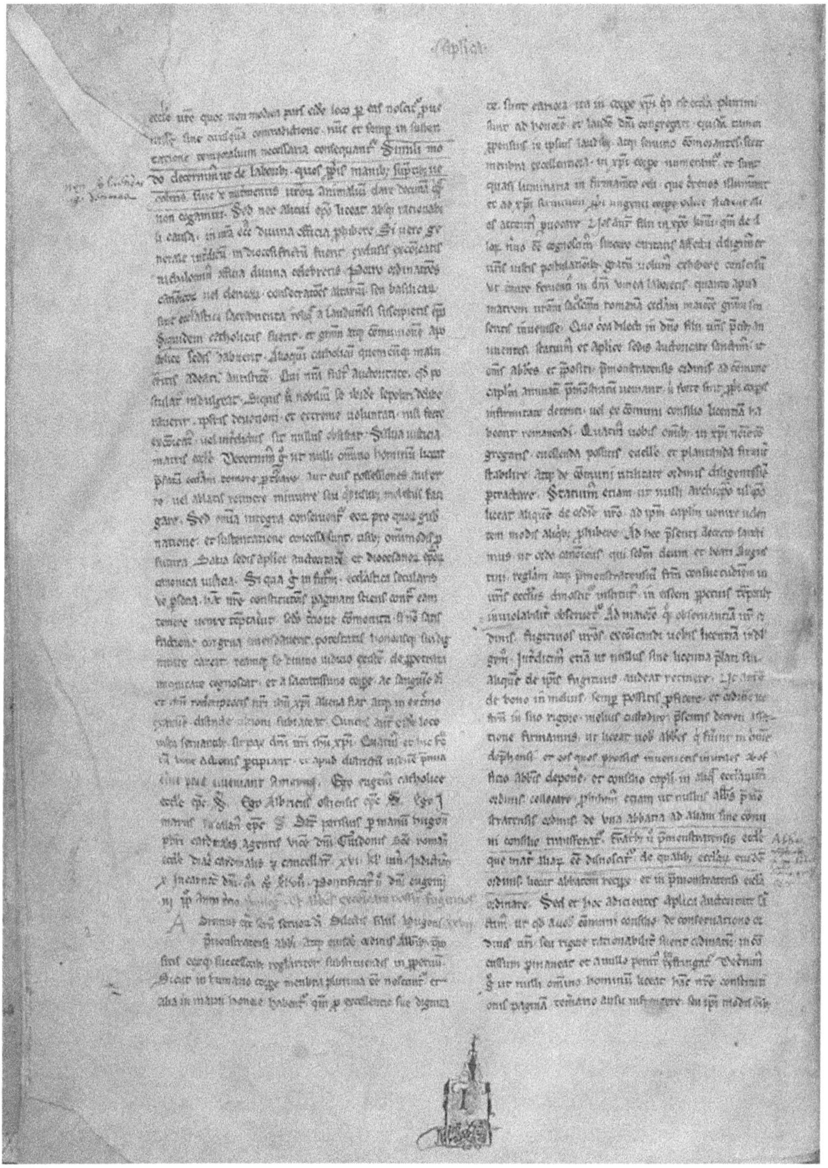

Fig. 7: Cartulary of Prémontré, fol. 12bisv, Roman numeral in bottom centre margin representing the end of the first quire. Reproduced by permission of the Bibliothèque municipale, Soissons.

that the cartulary of Prémontré continued to be an active document for the abbey and its community.[125]

The Conceptual Design and Organizational Schema

Incipit privilegium magnum de dignitate abbatis Premonstrato et tocius ordinis. (**24**)[126]
[Here begins the great privilege concerning the excellence of the abbot at Prémontré and all the order.]
The anonymous maker of the Cartulary of Prémontré

The inside of the cartulary of Prémontré is as visually underwhelming as its exterior. Behind the generally uniform aesthetic of its 113 folios, however, lies an organizational schema that exposes the abbey's understanding of its place and position within a local and regional political landscape. Whoever selected and organized the textual content of the cartulary of Prémontré – whether abbot, librarian, cartulary maker, or someone else altogether – did so as a representative of the abbey. The selection of cartulary content and organizational structure underscores a conceptualized set of preferences on the part of the abbey, which sought to create a document that readers could access through clearly separated cartulary divisions and naming protocols. The title of each division assumes hierarchies of social privilege and preferred spatial understandings. As a general rule when considering cartularies, the highest position of status and respect in the cartulary is accorded to those acts copied into the front of the manuscript. The first section of the cartulary, for example, whether original or a later addition, holds greater status than the last. Likewise, within sections, the first charter of each section usually holds a position of primacy over others in the same section. The quotation above, which prefaces Pope Innocent III's 1198 confirmation (**24**) of the regulations of the Premonstratensian order and which was witnessed by no less than nine cardinals, was the first line of the thirteenth-century cartulary and underscores the abbey's desire to recognize the papacy as the highest authority.

In addition to revealing the abbey's understanding of its place within a broad landscape, the cartulary's organizational tools, or reading aids, provide material and textual evidence as to the abbey's own documentary and administrative practices. Organizational tools such as titled sections, articulated divisions, and tables of contents support the abbey's aspiration to create a well-structured cartulary that would have been both useful and accessible to its readers. Approximately 80 per cent of the cartulary's charters pertain to its possessions, and the rights thereof, in the dioceses of Laon, Soissons, and Noyon. The organizational treatment of each of these divisions and subsequent subdivisions not only provides insight into the arrangement of the archives of original charters at Prémontré from which cartulary content was drawn, but also suggests that in the abbey's first 120 years, Prémontré relied heavily on the administrative organization of its *curtes*.[127] As we shall see, the inconsistent use of these organizational tools within and between the divisional sections, however, means that the abbey's aspirations did not always manifest themselves in reality.

The cartulary of Prémontré comprises eight divisional units, which on the whole contain charter records of privileges and possessions enjoyed by the abbey. The marked divisions help the reader grasp both what the abbey considered important to include in its cartulary and its implicit recognition of hierarchies within that content (**table 1**). On the one hand, it could be said that the cartulary and its contents served as a comprehensive document meant to legitimize or affirm the extent of Prémontré's holdings. On the other hand, the intentional arrangement of the eight divisions reveals Prémontré's preference for placing its highest-status patrons and their gifts before those of lesser- and non-noble local patrons.

The thirteenth-century cartulary originally began with the section of papal bulls, now fols. 6r–16v. The first three cartulary sections, therefore, privileged an organizing principle based on important religious and secular authorities: popes, bishops, and local lords and ladies. The following three sections of the manuscript contain records of Prémontré's temporal possessions within the boundaries of three medieval dioceses: Laon, Soissons, and Noyon. That the abbey of Prémontré itself was located in the diocese of Laon explains why this section appears before the other two dioceses. Indeed, the properties Prémontré acquired and held within the bishopric of Laon would have been those closest to the abbey in terms of proximity and affinity.

As shown in Table 1, two sections – the first and last quires of the current cartulary structure – contain charters that address certain of Prémontré's rights and privileges. In the original thirteenth-century cartulary, however, the current first section, an intact quire of three bifolia, figured as part of what is now the final section and quire (a single bifolium). Material evidence confirms that at some point after cartulary completion, the abbey separated the final quire and moved six of its folios to the beginning of the cartulary. Fol. 1r has a folio signature in the bottom right corner, *qii*, indicating that it originally belonged to quire *q*, which came after quire *p*, at the end of the cartulary.[128] Given that fols. 2r and 3r contain continuous content, they too belonged in the final *q* quire. Originally, this final quire held thirty-six charters. These acts focus primarily on the abbey's rights of *wionagium* and *pedagium*, the rights to traverse by wagon or foot those lands held by local gentry, exempt from the normal taxation. The quire also contains three royal charters, as well as treaties with English and German Premonstratensian abbeys. When the final quire was separated, the three outside bifolia and their content were moved to the front of the cartulary, a place of greater status, leaving the single inside bifolium at the

Table 1 Organizational layout of the cartulary of Prémontré by section.

	1120–49	1150–99	1200–39	1240–99	1300–1586	Undated	Total
General Rights and Privileges (fols. 1r–5v; Acts 1–22)	2	5	12	0	3	1	23
Papal Bulls (fols. 6r–16v; Acts 24–70)	6	18	23	0	0	0	47
Episcopal Charters (fols. 17r–21r; Acts 71–77)	4	3	0	0	0	0	7
Seigneurial Charters (fols. 21r–26r; Acts 78–105)	5	5	15	1	0	2	28
Diocese of Laon (fols. 26r–66v; Acts 106–263)	21	42	72	6	13	4	158
Diocese of Soissons (fols. 67r–75r; Acts 264–97)	9	5	17	0	3	0	34
Diocese of Noyon (fols. 75v–110v; Acts 298–496)	37	58	98	0	5	1	199
General Rights and Privileges, Continued (fols. 111r–112v; Acts 497–509)	7	3	1	1	1	0	13
TOTAL	**91**	**139**	**238**	**8**	**25**	**8**	**509**

Table indicating the order of sections in the cartulary of Prémontré today. The numbers of charters for each section have been further divided into thirty- and fifty-year periods. The thirty-year period 1120–49 comprises the period between the abbey's foundation and the middle of the twelfth century. This period saw several founding donations, and the majority of *curtes* were established. 1200–39 represents the period with the greatest charter activity and leads up to cartulary completion. Those charters dating 1240–99 and later show the addition of charters after the cartulary's initial iteration had been completed.

end of the manuscript. The reasoning for this move, discussed in detail below, provides key evidence for determining the date of cartulary completion.[129]

Equipped with a better understanding of the general organizational schema of Prémontré's cartulary, we can now explore the abbey's underlying intentions and assumptions about both the manuscript and its sense of institutional identity. Prémontré hoped to construct a document that would reflect a positive image to contemporary and future readers. First, the grouping of the cartulary's 509 acts into separate divisions – organized according to people and geographic locations – reinforces the abbey's sense of identity as the composite whole of those parts. For example, the titles given to the different divisions suggest that the abbey maintained and wanted to maintain amicable and appropriately respectful relationships with popes, bishops, and local seigneurial families, as well as with local patrons who interacted with the *curtes* in the dioceses of Laon, Soissons, and Noyon. Second, the tables of contents that occur before most divisions both articulate and facilitate the reader's access to the recorded evidence of Prémontré's numerous possessions, and by extension its wealth and status.

The cartulary's organizational schema also suggests that the abbey primarily intended the document to be used as a resource within its own walls, since the use of such a schema assumes that a reader would have the insider knowledge needed to understand it. For example, if a medieval reader wanted to find the cartulary charter that recorded Prémontré's acquisition of the mill at Barthel in 1125, they would first need to know that Barthélemy, bishop of Laon (1113–51), had given Barthel to the abbey. Only a reader equipped with this kind of institutional knowledge would know to look for the charter at the beginning of the section of episcopal charters, rather than in the geographical section associated with the mill's location, the diocese of Laon (**73**).

Yet as previously stated, while the organizational schema of Prémontré's cartulary may at first glance appear well executed, closer scrutiny reveals irregularities in the treatment of charter content within and between divisions. One of the most visual and overt of these appears in the Laon section of the cartulary. This section contains clearly articulated subdivisions, one for each of the *curtes* held in the diocese (**table 2**). Moreover, each subdivision is preceded by its own table of contents. The diocese of Laon is the only geographical section to be presented in such detail. This doubly preferential treatment of the diocese, both in its positioning before other geographical sections and in the presence of articulated subdivisions, demonstrates its primacy within the three geographical sections. The status of the Laon section likely derived partly from the fact that the abbey of Prémontré was located within the boundaries of the diocese of Laon, and partly from the fact that the abbey owed much to the influence of the bishop of Laon. As noted above, the foundation of Prémontré and

Table 2 Organizational layout of the Laon section of the cartulary, by *curtes*.

Diocese of Laon: *Curtis* Name	**1120–49**	**1150–99**	**1200–39**	**1240–99**	**1300–1586**	**Undated**	**Total**
Soupir (fols. 26r–35v; Acts 106–49)	8	12	17	5	2	0	44
Crépy (fols. 36r–42v; Acts 150–77)	7	4	14	0	1	2	28
Versigny (fols. 42r–43v; Acts 178–81)	2	1	1	0	0	0	4
Ferrières (fols. 44v–47v; Acts 182–95)	1	4	8	0	0	1	14
Valécourt (fols. 48r–53r; Acts 196–217)	2	8	10	0	2	0	22
Merlieu and Nogent (fols. 54r–57v; Acts 218–32)	0	2	9	0	3	1	15
Hannape (fols. 58r–66v; Acts 233–63)	1	10	14	1	5	0	31
TOTAL	**21**	**41**	**73**	**6**	**13**	**4**	**158**

Order of *curtes* within the Laon section of the cartulary of Prémontré. The numbers of charters for each section have been divided into thirty- and fifty-year periods.

several of the abbey's earliest acquisitions were due to the will and generosity of Barthélemy de Jur, bishop of Laon at the time of Prémontré's founding.

From an archival perspective, the sequential order of the Laon *curtes* within the manuscript also suggests a link between the organizational schema of the cartulary and the abbey's archives of original charters. The person who selected the charters for the Laon section drew them from an archive that may have already been organized, or even reorganized, by about 1159. In 1154, Gautier de Mortagne, bishop of Laon, challenged the legitimacy of donations of episcopal lands that his two predecessors – Barthélemy de Jur and Gautier de Saint Maurice – had made to Prémontré (**75**). It is reasonable to imagine that before the trial was called into session in 1158, the librarians or archivists at

Prémontré rigorously searched their archives to find and present in person the relevant original charters as proof positive of their possession of said properties during the legal proceedings in the chapter house at the cathedral of Laon. The trial, after all, was so prominent an event that Louis VII, king of France, the archbishop of Reims, the bishops of Soissons and Noyon, and the entire cathedral chapter of Laon were in attendance. When the dispute was resolved, the resolution was set out in a charter. Decades later, when the abbey decided to construct its cartulary, the person who selected its content had at his disposal an already built-in organization for the Laon section. This organization did not follow the sequence of properties as stated in the papal inventories – as can be the case with other cartularies – but rather followed the sequence as stated in the 1158 charter resolving the dispute between Gautier de Mortagne and Prémontré.[130] The order of *curtes* mentioned in the 1158 charter is almost identical to that in which the *curtes* appear in the cartulary, perhaps suggesting that both mirrored the organization of the abbey's archives.[131]

A study of the organization of the Laon section also emphasizes the fact that neither the Soissons nor the Noyon section received such detailed treatment. Neither of the latter has separate subdivisions for its *curtes*, suggesting that at the time of cartulary construction, one of two things may have been true: Prémontré's archive may not have included the original charters for all of the abbey's *curtis* holdings, or the cartulary maker was not familiar enough with the *curtes* in those areas that he felt confident about arranging them into subdivisions. One of the most notable organizational asymmetries in the cartulary is the low number of charters in the Soissons section (**table 1**), which contains only 34 charters total compared to the 158 in the Laon section and the 199 in the Noyon section. Moreover, the acts in the Soissons section primarily concern the two houses Prémontré held in the town of Soissons itself, as the section title indicates: *Scripta domum Suessionensis* (Charters of the houses in Soissons). The cartulary does not include any acts from the Soissons *curtes*, despite the survival of original charters pertaining to three of Prémontré's *curtes* from the area: Trosly-Loire, Tinselve, and Valpriez.[132] One plausible, yet admittedly speculative, explanation for their absence from the cartulary would be that these charters were kept at the *curtes* themselves, not at the abbey of Prémontré, and either were never within the scope of the cartulary project or simply were brought to Prémontré too late for inclusion in it.

This may also have been the case for the Noyon section of the cartulary, as it displays yet another type of organizational treatment. The Noyon section contains the largest number of charters of any of the cartulary sections, 199 acts; however, it is not subdivided. One extensive table of contents precedes the entire section and comprises the synopses of all 199 acts over six folios. Whoever selected the Noyon charters for inclusion in the cartulary made little attempt to organize them in such a way as to facilitate access within such a large grouping. It may be that the cartulary maker was not entirely familiar with the properties in the Noyon diocese, perhaps because the original charters were not held at the mother abbey itself. Although Prémontré had multiple properties in the diocese of Noyon, the Noyon section of the cartulary is titled after the diocese's principal *curtis*, Bonneuil, which lay approximately fifty kilometres northwest of the abbey. Perhaps Bonneuil had its own archives and sent the charters to Prémontré en masse for transcription. The exact nature of the administrative relationship between the abbey of Prémontré and its *curtis* of Bonneuil remains unclear. It may be that Bonneuil served as the administrative hub for the abbey's holdings in the diocese of Noyon and so exercised greater independence than did the *curtes* that Prémontré oversaw in the diocese of Laon and nearby Soissons.

Examining the material and textual evidence on the backs, or dorsals, of surviving original charters confirms that different archival notational practices were in use at the abbey of Prémontré compared to its *curtis* of Bonneuil.[133] The backs of original charters which were once held at Prémontré frequently contain a *curtis* name, written in a twelfth- or thirteenth-century hand and located along the bottom margin to the left or the right of the seal strip.[134] The Bonneuil charters display a different dorsal notation system (**figs. 8** and **9**). If a *curtis* name is written on the back of the original, it is invariably that of Bonneuil in Latin, *Bonolium* or *Bonolii*, but the notation is not consistently located along the bottom margin on either side of the seal strip – as occurs in the charters for the diocese of Laon, which were presumably housed at Prémontré – but rather in a position higher up from the bottom margin of the original charter.[135] While a more extensive quantitative evaluation of Prémontré's original charters is required to confirm that different notational systems were at work and when, preliminary observations suggest that the abbey's original twelfth- and thirteenth-century charters may have been held in different archives for at least part of the Middle Ages. This may partially explain the lack of a consistent organizational treatment between the cartulary's geographical sections.

While the abbey of Prémontré wanted its cartulary to be readily consultable and easily used as a resource, an analysis of the physical artifact illuminates the failure of the abbey to carry out its intentions in a consistent manner. Irregularities and discrepancies in the organizational treatment of different sections suggest that although Prémontré saw itself as the administrative centre for its *curtes*, certain *curtes* outside the diocese of Laon may have kept their own archives and possibly exercised a certain degree of administrative independence.

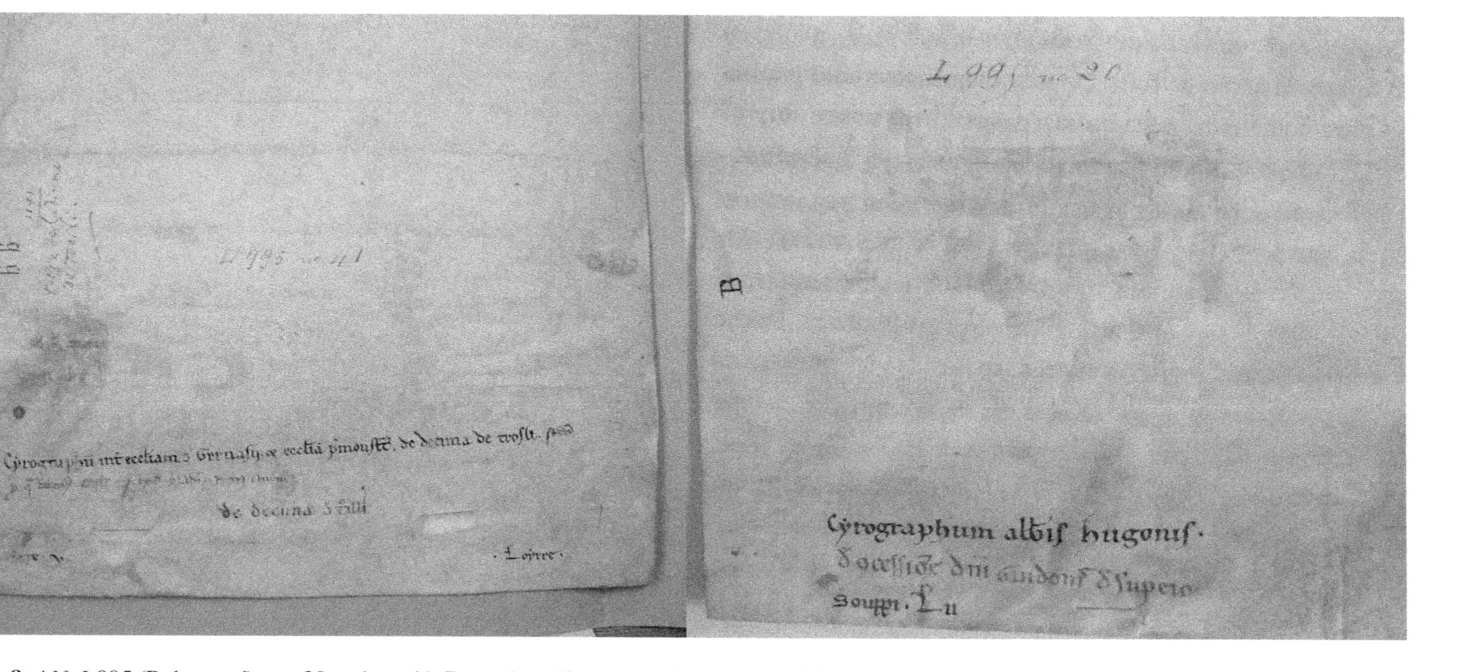

Fig. 8: AN, L995 (Prémontré), no. 20 and no. 41. Reproduced by permission of the Archives nationales.

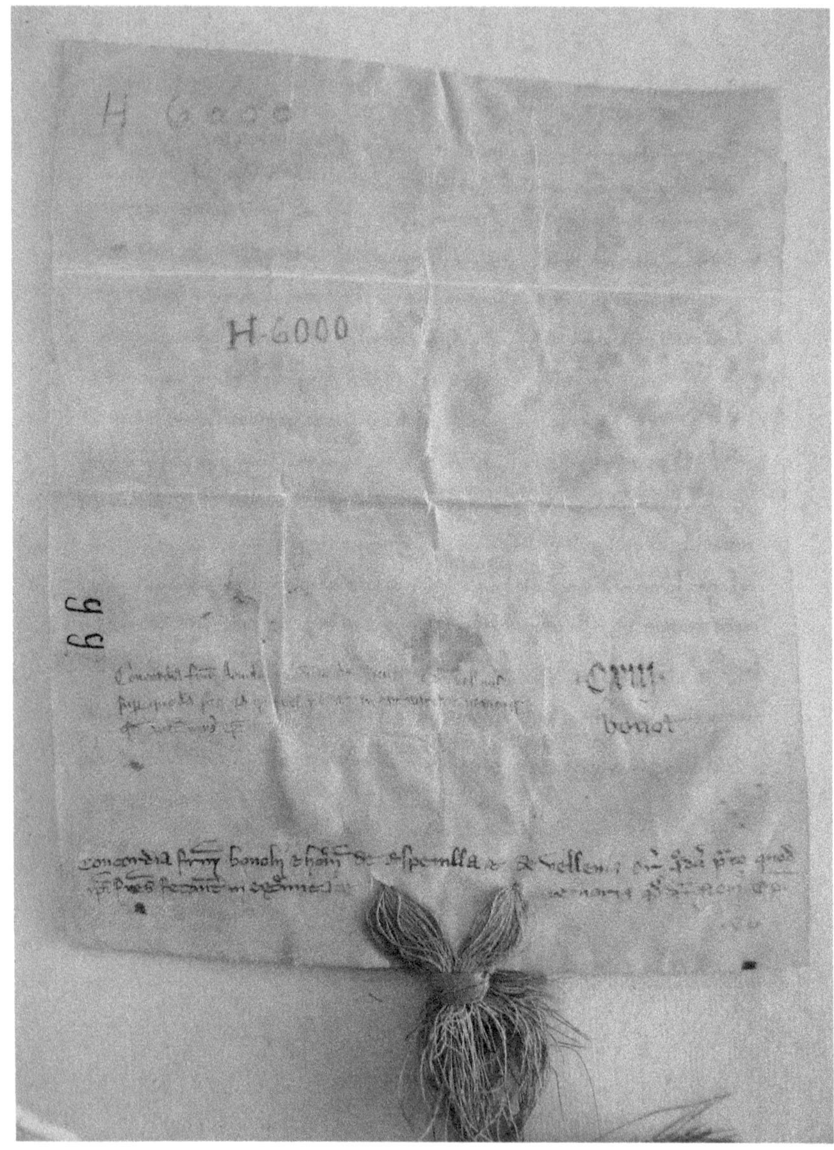

Fig. 9: AD Oise (Bonneuil), H 6000 (1215). Reproduced by permission of AD Oise.

The Practical Design: The Cartulary Maker's Workflow and Practices

> *Iste litere scripte sunt in precedenti quaterno versus finem verbo ad verbum et ideo hii non scribuntur.* [The contents of this charter are written in the preceding quaternion near the end, word for word, and therefore they are not written here.] (**136**)
>
> *Karta ista in precedenti pagina habetur verbo ad verbum et ideo non scripsi illam et habemus duas kartas super his confectas.* [This charter is found on the preceding page, word for word, and therefore I have not written it here; and we have two charters that were made to record the same thing.] (**370**)
>
> *The anonymous maker of the Cartulary of Prémontré*

A careful look at the writing on a folio of the cartulary of Prémontré is an invitation to journey back through time to the cartulary maker's thirteenth-century work environment and to follow his skilled hand as he dips his quill in an ink pot and places ink on the piece of parchment that lies in front of us. Few medieval scribes have left accounts of their workspace or workflows. What is known comes primarily from art historical and archaeological evidence, as well as from the rare instances when scribes have noted in a colophon their working conditions or how long it took for them to complete their task. The cartulary maker of Prémontré clearly took pains to construct a uniform and formulaic document, although he left a few traces of his personal agency in the textual content. The quotations above display two of the three moments where the cartulary maker alludes to personal intervention in the cartulary's construction.[136] With little other documentary evidence to help us assess how the cartulary of Prémontré came into existence, the manuscript's materiality provides an excellent opportunity to gain an understanding of the cartulary maker's character and his workflow practices (**fig. 3**).

First, a close analysis of the cartulary's text provides a glimpse into the character of Prémontré's cartulary maker. One hand, that is one person, wrote most of the thirteenth-century cartulary. He copied the charter texts, provided a summary for each charter, and constructed the tables of contents. An examination of the cartulary's 113 folios reveals the consistent care the cartulary maker applied to writing in a steady, uniform Gothic book hand and to maintaining the strict layout of each folio. This suggests an individual possessed of a focused sense of attention to detail and visual harmony.

This same sense of conscientiousness appears in the accuracy with which the cartulary maker copied from other texts. By placing surviving original charters alongside their cartulary copies, we can evaluate with confidence the cartulary maker's transcription practices: how many mistakes he made, or not; how attentive he was to his task, or not. There is no doubt: he was meticulous. Where textual variants do occur between the original charter and the cartulary copy, it is usually because the cartulary maker had taken the initiative to update the names of people and places to what he considered a standardized contemporary spelling. For example, if a twelfth-century charter original included the name *Radulfus*, the cartulary maker almost invariably updated the spelling to the more usual contemporary one, *Radulphus*. Likewise, he often changed the Latin spellings of place names such as Coucy-la-Ville, from the typical twelfth-century *Coci Villa* to the thirteenth-century *Couci Villa*. In some instances, cartulary makers changed a charter's text as they copied it into a cartulary in order to better fit with what they considered more desired understandings. Examples of this practice include altering witness lists or constructing an updated version of a foundation narrative that conveniently resolved a contemporary conflict.[137] The Prémontré cartulary maker did not make this his practice. Rather, his diligent work ethic is reflected in the uniform and visually harmonious script, neither too sparse nor too extravagant, and in the accuracy of the cartulary copies.

The cartulary maker's familiarity with Prémontré's charters and with spelling changes for local toponyms gives rise to questions surrounding his position at the abbey. It may be that his knowledge of Prémontré's hinterland and his well-practised hand indicate that he was an older member of the community whose scribal training took place in the first quarter of the thirteenth century. He ruled and pricked each folio so that the first line of text for any given column was placed above the top line (**fig. 10**). This practice had become mostly obsolete in northern France by 1230, after which time scribes began to place their first line of text *below* the first ruled line, not above it.[138] That the Prémontré cartulary maker continued to practise this earlier method at the time of the cartulary's construction in the late 1230s suggests he may have been carrying over techniques he learned as a youth.[139] By 1240, when the cartulary was complete, our cartulary maker may have been a man in late middle age.

Since the cartulary maker left no explicit colophon at the end of the cartulary, we can use the layout and number of folios to estimate how long it might have taken him to complete his task. Once he had pricked and ruled the parchment folios in preparation for his quill and ink, he could begin in earnest the work of completing over two hundred parchment sides of ninety lines each (two columns of forty-five lines of text). While he would have had to stop – to acquire more ink, sharpen a quill, eat a meal, sleep, or even recover from illness – if we use the calculations of Michael Gullick, who proposes that scribes wrote on average one line per minute, we can estimate that, in an ideal world, Prémontré's cartulary maker could have finished his task in as little as three months, at a general rate of around four sides (two folios) per day.[140] This calculation represents the minimum length of time needed. When we examine the manuscript more closely, however, we can see how the equivalent of approximately three months' worth of sustained, focused work was in fact carried out over a much longer period of time, underscoring the differences between ideal and real-life circumstances.[141]

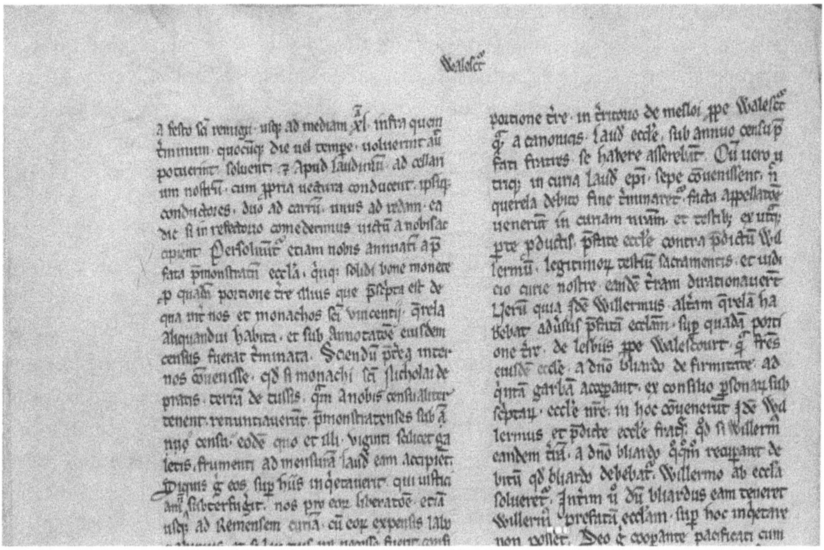

Fig. 10: Cartulary of Prémontré, fol. 49v close-up, ruling. Reproduced by permission of the Bibliothèque municipale, Soissons.

Paleographical and codicological analyses confirm the cartulary maker's day-to-day workflow. He worked in a linear progression, copying charters into the cartulary one after the other, from start to finish. On any given day, he began copying where he had left off on the previous day, adding folios and quires as needed. A comparison of the beginnings and ends of the titled cartulary sections and quires reveals that when one quire finishes, another begins, even if in the middle of a section and even if in the middle of a charter text.[142] The transition from quire one to quire two (both part of the papal charters section), for example, occurs in the middle of **51**, which begins on fol. 12bisv and finishes on fol. 13r, the first folio of the second quire. The cartulary's collation, or sequence of fifteen quires, was not to be disrupted by the conceptual divisions and subdivisions articulated in the organizational schema. In other words, the cartulary maker of Prémontré worked in sequential order and did not choose to complete the Noyon section of the cartulary before completing the preceding Laon and Soissons sections.

To the description of the cartulary maker as conscientious and meticulous, we can add methodical. Even when the cartulary's organizational schema makes the shift from highlighting important people to highlighting important places in the section titles, the cartulary maker maintains the continuity of transcribing one charter after the other. The shift from the section dedicated to charters issued by the lords and ladies of Coucy (persons of authority) to the

Laon section (geographical locations) takes place within the same quire. This consistent workflow continued throughout the cartulary. In the second quotation noted above – drawn from the Noyon section near the end of the cartulary – the cartulary maker is still making reference to his sequencing of one charter after another. Instead of copying the same charter for a second time, he notes in the text that "all the rest [of this text is] exactly as it appears in the previous charter" (**370**).[143]

Given the linear workflow of the cartulary maker, it is important for us to pause for a moment and recall that the cartulary was built section by section and that a table of contents precedes each section, including the seven subdivisions in the Laon section.[144] The tables of contents are written in the same hand as the charter texts, and their format suggests that the cartulary maker had either completed them prior to the copying of a charter section or, at a minimum, had left blank the same number of lines as charters, presumably to be filled in later. The tables of contents fit nicely into the spaces preceding each cartulary section. The cartulary maker never had to squeeze entries into too-small spaces where he was clearly running out of room, nor are there large gaps between a table of contents and the first charter of the section. If the tables of contents were at least conceptualized prior to the copying of each section, then the charters for each section must have also been pre-selected and organized *before* the cartulary maker began copying the section. In addition to creating a table of contents at the beginning of each section, the cartulary maker maintained an eye towards the future, leaving one or two blank folios at the end of every section, presumably for future entries.[145]

A final piece of material evidence, an ink stain, further shows that the cartulary maker worked in linear fashion and had arranged the original charters in sequential order before copying a section. Since we know the cartulary maker to be careful and conscientious, the following deviation from this understanding merits further scrutiny. In the Noyon section of the cartulary, **397–403** are repeated as **441–7**, but in a different order (**fig. 11**).[146] This is a unique anomaly in the manuscript. Moreover, that there is an ink spill in the cartulary on the very folio that contains the first set of repeated acts (**397–403**) raises suspicions of an accident. The ink spilled on cartulary fol. 96r blotches the middle of **400** and prompts the researcher to check for similar stains on any surviving originals that the cartulary maker would have been using in the scriptorium that day. Two original charters survive at the Archives départementales de l'Oise, those of cartulary acts **399** and **403**, and both display substantial ink stains, hinting that the spill was larger than the cartulary folio would indicate (**figs. 12** and **13**).[147] Closer scrutiny of the cartulary folios and the original charters confirms that Prémontré's cartulary maker had what might be called a very stressful day when he reached fol. 96r. The meditative act of copying one charter after the other was severely disrupted.

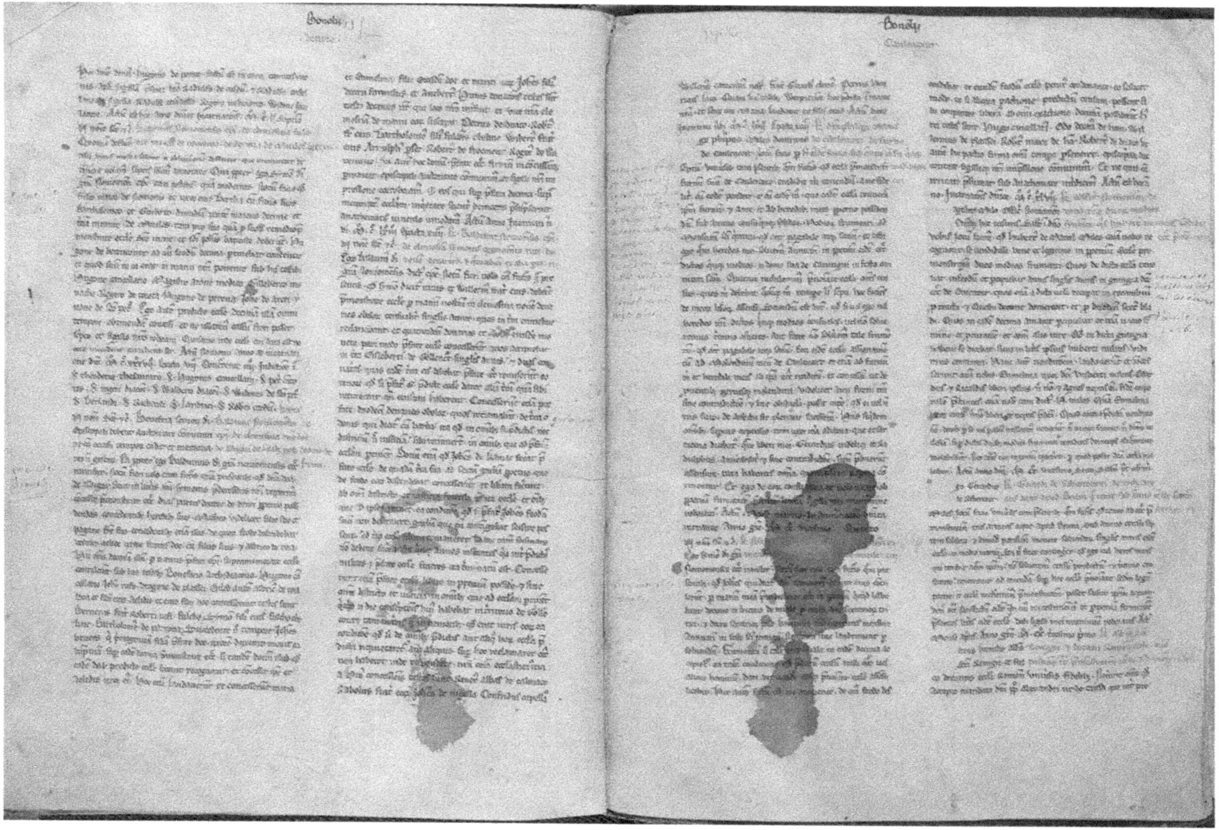

Fig. 11: Cartulary of Prémontré, fol. 96r, ink stain in the middle of **400**. Reproduced by permission of the Bibliothèque municipale, Soissons.

Fig. 12: AD Oise, H 6005, ink stain from ink spill. Reproduced by permission of AD Oise.

The task for the researcher is to take the material evidence, the set of seven charters repeated in different order, and attempt to reconstruct the scribe's process and discover the underlying factors behind the anomaly. This type of analysis provides insight into the cartulary maker's workflow nowhere visible in the textual content of the charters. On the day in question, the cartulary maker was in the process of copying a pile of charters that included **397–403**; these appear to be the only charters affected by the spill. A pile of uncopied charters, including the seven in question, was likely positioned to the left of the cartulary maker. Once he had copied a charter, he must have moved it to a "finished" pile on his right.[148] To the right of that pile was the ink pot, as suggested by the ink spill coming from the right on the original charters (**figs. 12** and **13**). Once the cartulary maker had finished copying **397–403**, the originals must have been sitting in a pile on his right, to the right of the cartulary folio when the ink spill occurred. Other original charters that had not yet been copied remained on

Fig. 13: AD Oise, H 6038, ink stain from ink spill. Reproduced by permission of AD Oise.

the cartulary maker's left, untouched by the ink spill. The ink pot was somehow knocked over and the ink splashed onto the pile of "already transcribed" charters, with some of the splashes reaching fol. 96r, the right side of the open cartulary folio. Reacting to the situation quickly, the cartulary maker likely gathered up the stained pile of originals he had used for cartulary **397–403** and dispersed them around the table or room in order to let them dry.

The repetition and reordering of the seven charters later in the same cartulary section took place when the original charters that had been stained were gathered back together after drying. As the charters dried, the cartulary maker continued his work. This he likely did for at least three days, since six cartulary folios (twelve sides) lie between the stained fol. 96r and the beginning of the set of repeated charters.[149] When the cartulary maker eventually gathered together the stained charters, he must have restacked them in a pile, but now in a different order.[150] With the workflow having been interrupted, the seven charters that had been stained and set aside somehow ended up back in the pile of original charters yet to be copied. At this point the cartulary maker

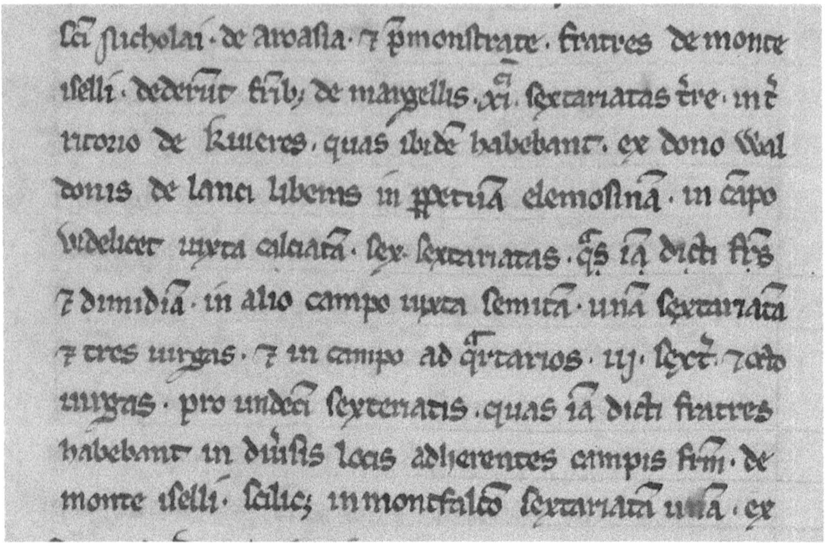

Fig. 14: Cartulary of Prémontré, fol. 78r, correction using sublinear dots. Reproduced by permission of the Bibliothèque municipale, Soissons.

copied all seven into the cartulary once again, this time as acts **441–7**. Had the accident not happened, the anomaly of the repeated charters in the cartulary would almost certainly not have occurred, and we would not be able to gain this insight into the cartulary maker's workflow and workspace.

The above example demonstrates that the cartulary maker was a human being after all and, like many of us, made inadvertent errors as he copied. This we can also see from evidence of three rounds of corrections, each made on a separate occasion. First, the cartulary maker made corrections as he was copying. He did this by striking through a word when he realized his mistake, and then carrying on with the correct word directly afterwards. These corrections appear in black ink and in line with the text, and they have been replicated in this edition. At the same time, the cartulary maker often placed sublinear dots under letters or phrases, a common medieval practice that indicated the reader should ignore the text directly above (**fig. 14**).[151] After this set of corrections was made, the cartulary maker undertook a second set of corrections when he went back through the cartulary to add the rubricated summaries, folio titles, and other reading aids.[152] At this point, he took the opportunity to further correct any errors in textual transcription using red ink (**fig. 15**).[153] This is seen when words that had been corrected with sublinear dots were then struck through in red ink.

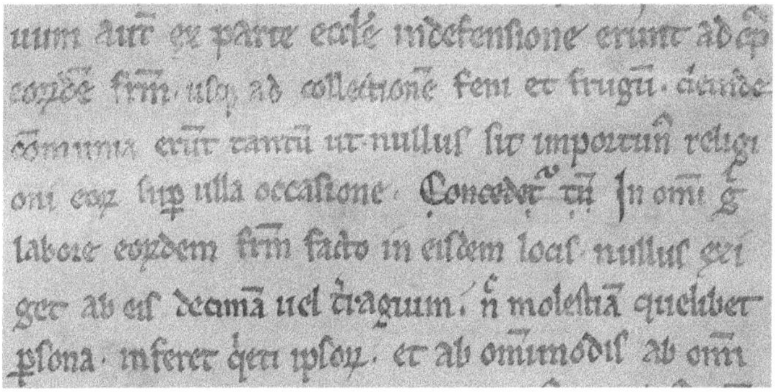

Fig. 15: Cartulary of Prémontré, fol. 17v, correction using sublinear dots and a strikethrough in red ink. Reproduced by permission of the Bibliothèque municipale, Soissons.

Fig. 16: Cartulary of Prémontré, fol. 99r, transposition as indicated by the use of apostrophes. Reproduced by permission of the Bibliothèque municipale, Soissons.

A final, third type of correction method appears in the cartulary, but it is not certain whether these corrections were made by the cartulary maker or, more likely, a later reader. At some point, someone went through the cartulary and compared the cartulary copies with their original charters in a type of proof-reading endeavour. The result is that certain words or phrases appear in the cartulary with marks similar to Anglophone quotation marks around them, made in black ink. These marks indicate words whose order the cartulary maker had inverted – perhaps inadvertently, perhaps intentionally – during the transcription process. For example, where an original charter may say *Robertus maritus eius*, the cartulary copy (**419**) says *maritus Robertus eius*. Quotation marks have been placed around the cartulary's *maritus* to indicate transposition (**fig. 16**). Because it remains unclear who inserted the quotation marks, it also remains uncertain when these corrections took place and what spurred them.

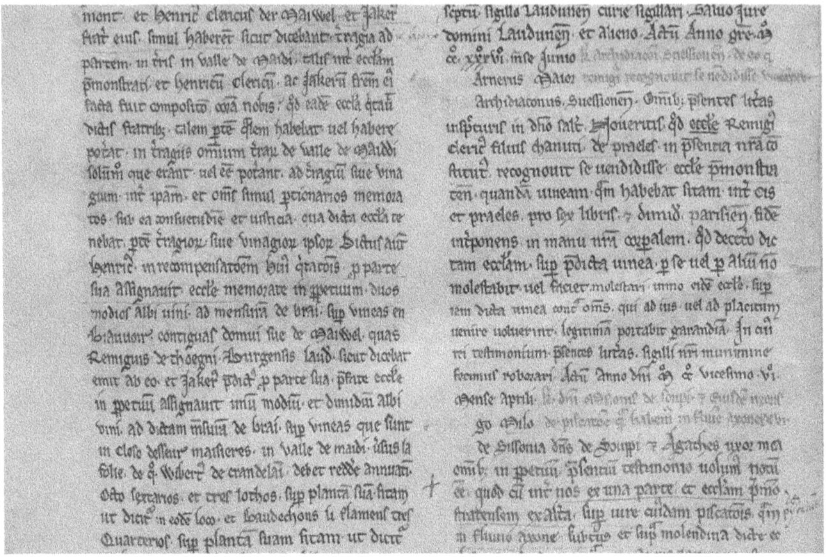

Fig. 17: Cartulary of Prémontré, fol. 30v, presence of two minuscule letters meant to guide the illuminator in creating the correct letter of the initial. Reproduced by permission of the AD Aisne.

Finally, one of the most intriguing pieces of material evidence in the cartulary is the absence of the first initial for each charter. After a transcription had been completed, decorated initials were traditionally inserted in alternating blue and red, as occurs in other contemporary northern French manuscripts. The absence of this typical decorative reading aid in the cartulary of Prémontré suggests an interruption in cartulary completion, perhaps due to lack of time, resources, personnel, or even interest on the part of the abbey. The cartulary maker clearly intended the initials to be added because he left a space for them, and may have provided a minuscule initial at various places (**fig. 17**). A cartulary with no initial letters is an unfinished cartulary, something that seems contrary to the cartulary maker's character, but also something that was likely out of his control.[154]

The material components of the cartulary of Prémontré provide visible clues as to the *noyau primitif*'s one maker, his conscientious nature, meticulous workflow patterns, and sequence of cartulary-making tasks. Despite the cartulary maker's aspirations to create a beautiful manuscript characteristic of his work habits and desired by the abbey, material analysis underscores the fact that we are all human. Strikethroughs, corrections, cancellations, ink spills, and the absence of decorated initials collapse eight centuries into one moment, and we realize that real life in the scriptorium mimics real life today.

The Date of Cartulary Construction and Completion

Between the moment the cartulary maker laid down his quill for the last time and today, a small number of charters have been added to the cartulary, and readers have made their own notes and marginal annotations. These later interventions, made into the sixteenth century and beyond, have opened up several possibilities as to the date of cartulary completion.[155] The cartulary's material evidence, however, argues that the cartulary maker completed the *noyau primitif* by 1239/40. First and foremost, separating the hand of the cartulary maker from the hands of later charter writers narrows down the possible timeframe of cartulary completion to no later than 1250. Evidence of quire alterations and latest charter dates, however, suggests that the cartulary maker had finished his work by 1240, and that the 1250 charters, if they are indeed in the hand of the first cartulary maker, were added as an afterthought.

In this section we examine the contexts in which the cartulary was constructed. First, we present the argument for a 1239/40 completion date in detail. With that date confirmed, we place the cartulary's construction within the abbey's historical context at the time of construction. The decade prior to cartulary completion was a period in which Prémontré strove to assert its status as the mother abbey of the Premonstratensian order, and the cartulary embodies Prémontré's satisfaction with the outcomes of those disputes in physical form.[156] Second, we situate the process of cartulary construction within the context of other documentary activity occurring in the abbey during the same period (1230s–early 1250s). An analysis of document production during these two decades shows Prémontré as an institution dynamic in its output and keen to present an outward image of itself as a reformed order with a new set of statutes created ca. 1236–8 and a new cartulary completed ca. 1239–40. Moreover, the abbey's cartulary production shows its desire to maintain an internal image as the administrative centre of the individual *curtes* in the dioceses of Laon, Soissons, and Noyon. Considering the cartulary's materiality within the broader context of other manuscripts produced at the abbey during this period and the abbey's later history highlights how difficult it could be to translate the ideals of document production into physical, tangible objects.

The Historical Context of Cartulary Construction

Evidence from Prémontré's original charter archives attests to the continual production of loose parchment charters throughout Prémontré's first century, but few of the abbey's early manuscripts or administrative ephemera survive.[157] Our picture of documentary production at the abbey becomes clearer in the thirteenth century, when a series of reform-minded, capable abbots encouraged document production both directly and indirectly. For instance, Gervais, abbot of Prémontré 1209–20 and later bishop of Séez, was a prolific letter writer whose correspondence shows his desire to drive reform at Prémontré and across the order as a whole.[158] Gervais set the stage for his immediate successor, abbot Conrad (1220–33), who was active in the repairing and building of new parts of the abbey, and in particular the stocking of the library.[159]

Manuscript production at Prémontré grew significantly during the 1230s. Not only was the abbey in the throes of rebuilding its library but, in 1235, Pope Gregory IX ordered the abbey of Prémontré to rewrite the order's statutes (**42**).[160] This request would have precipitated the production of copies of the new statutes to be disseminated to many other Premonstratensian houses.

The dates of the latest charters in each of Prémontré's cartulary sections confirm that its construction was also underway by 1235 or 1236 (**Chart 1**). Since we know that the cartulary maker worked in a sequential progression – from start to finish – it is significant that the first cartulary section of papal bulls contains charters that date no later than those issued by Gregory IX in 1235. While cartulary construction may have begun earlier, the papal section was not completed until sometime after February 20, 1235, the date of the latest papal bull.[161] The two following cartulary sections (the episcopal and seigneurial sections) contain charters dated no later than 1232 and thus do not challenge a beginning date for cartulary construction of ca. 1235. Even though the cartulary holds three charters dated 1236, none of them appear in the first three sections. The first of the three 1236 acts appears in the *curtis* subdivision of Soupir on fol. 30v (**129**).[162] Since the Soupir section directly follows the seigneurial section, it may be that the cartulary maker began work sometime in late 1235 and had arrived at fol. 30v in the Soupir subdivision by 1236. The next latest act is from 1237 (**409**) and appears on fols. 97r and 97v. No acts from 1238 appear in the cartulary, suggesting that the cartulary maker had finished the majority of his task by 1237.

The abbey continued to record transactions on loose parchment throughout this time period; several original charters from 1238 and early 1239 survive in regional archives today, but none were copied into the cartulary. Thus, the addition of a final cartulary quire with five charters from 1239 demonstrates two key things: first, that a hiatus of work occurred during 1238 and the first half of 1239, and second, that something happened at the end of 1239 of such importance that it required adding new entries to what was essentially a finished *noyau primitif* of the cartulary.[163]

The presence of four charters dated 1250, written in a hand that strongly resembles the cartulary maker's, might seem to cast doubt on a 1239 completion date.[164] Material and textual analysis, however, confirms that the 1250 charters were added after the cartulary maker had finished his work. All four 1250 charters appear on two folios at the end of the Soupir section in quire four. These two folios (fols. 34–5) are not original to the quire, but were tipped in, or pasted in, later to replace two original folios that had been cut out.[165]

Chart 1. Number of cartulary charters by year, 1230–40.

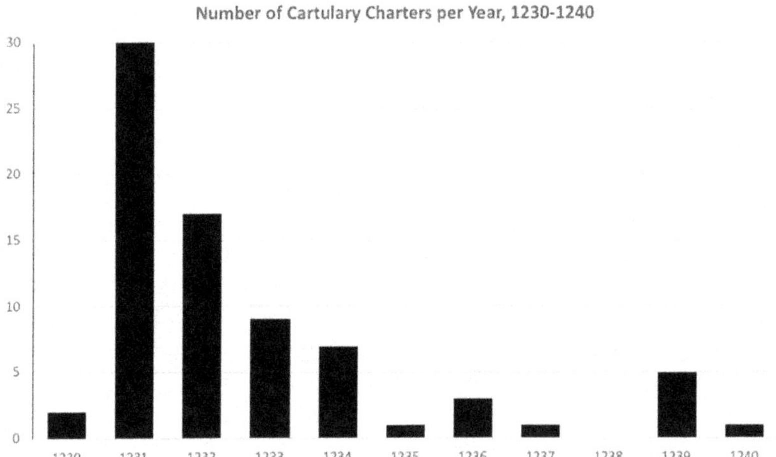

Moreover, fols. 34 and 35 are formatted differently from the rest of the cartulary. The colour of ink is a darker black and the folios have no titles at the top of the page. Each column has only forty-four lines as opposed to the cartulary maker's normal forty-five, and the top line of writing begins *below* the first ruled line rather than above it. Finally, the four additional Soupir charters do not appear as entries in the cartulary's Soupir table of contents. If the same cartulary maker indeed penned them, they remain later entries added a decade after the cartulary had essentially been completed.

Another folio substitution in the Merlieu-Nogent subdivision of the Laon section initially seems to point to a more precise *terminus post quem* of 1240, but a closer analysis shows that it can only provide speculative evidence. Upon first glance, **222**, an act of *societas* between the abbeys of Prémontré and Nogent-sous-Coucy, looks as if it is an integral part of both the Merlieu-Nogent section transcriptions and the quire. However, a comparison of the section's table of contents and the sequence of its charter copies suggests that the charter was added to the quire after its completion. Act **222** appears as the fifth charter transcription, but its summary is missing from the table of contents. While the table of contents displays one sequence of charter summaries, the charter transcriptions in the Merlieu-Nogent section have been rearranged to accommodate the late introduction of **222**.[166] After the cartulary maker had finished copying the Merlieu-Nogent texts into quire eight, he went back later to remove, rewrite, and reinsert the entire inside bifolium of the quire in order to include **222** as part of the section.

Unfortunately **222** is undated.[167] The antiquarian scholar Charles-Louis Hugo provides a version of the act which contains a clause not found in the cartulary of Prémontré that dates it to 1240.[168] Frustratingly, he does not provide a source for this text. Why the cartulary copy should be undated and the Hugo copy dated to 1240 is a mystery, as indeed is the question of why Hugo should date to 1240 an act whose internal evidence would seem to locate it in the 1180s. Were we to posit the 1240 date of the Hugo copy as a later *vidimus* of a charter from the 1180s, and **222** as an undated copy of that *vidimus*, then 1240 would provide a convenient *terminus post quem* for cartulary completion.[169] However, more research is needed before affirming an unsubstantiated date in a charter copy in Hugo's seventeenth-century printed work on the Premonstratensian Order. Instead, a more nuanced date for cartulary completion lies sometime after the addition of the 1239 charters into the final quire and the replacement of the bifolium in the Merlieu-Nogent section.

Five charters appear in the cartulary from 1239, with **455**, written in December 1239, the last chronologically. The date of this act provides us with our current best hypothesis for a *terminus post quem* for the cartulary's *noyau primitif.* Act **455** appears in the cartulary maker's hand and is located in the penultimate quire of the cartulary. Thus, we have stated 1239/40 as the most likely completion date of the cartulary because logic dictates a date after December 1239, while practical considerations may have required the cartulary maker to work into early 1240. Moreover, the cartulary presents no further material interventions or additional charters until 1250, when the Soupir charters discussed above were added.

The content of four of the five 1239 charters provides a historical explanation for their insertion into the cartulary's final fifteenth quire, most likely one and half years after the completion of the cartulary's previous fourteen quires.[170] In 1239, Prémontré reached an agreement with the community at Magdeburg, which sought to resolve the dispute between Prémontré and the houses of the Saxon circary (**15–18**).[171] An attempt had previously been made to resolve this longstanding conflict in 1224, through a resolution which outlined the houses' respective rights and relationships (**14**), but it had not worked.[172] Given the importance to Prémontré of settling the conflict once and for all, particularly when it came to acknowledging Magdeburg's promise to submit to the order's regulations, the abbey naturally wanted to include a copy of the resolution in the cartulary. One version would not do, so the cartulary maker copied three of the resolution charters, each issued by a different authority. The inclusion of four 1239 Magdeburg charters in the cartulary's final quire ensured the preservation of the charters' contents within the cartulary manuscript.[173] Moreover, it represented a moment in Prémontré's history when the abbey believed that it had avoided perhaps a potential schism within the order, and that in doing so it had asserted its status as mother abbey and its abbot as the order's supreme prelate.

The significance of the peaceful resolution with Magdeburg is reinforced by the fact that the five Magdeburg charters, including the four from 1239, currently appear in the first quire of the cartulary rather than in the last.[174] The cartulary's final bifolium containing fols. 111–12 originally sat inside three other bifolia, at present fols. 1–5, and the four bifolia together formed the final quire of the thirteenth-century cartulary. The separation of the final quire's folios suggests that the 1239 charters, which were originally placed at the end of the cartulary, were so significant to the abbey that they were intentionally moved from a position of lesser status to a position of the greatest status.

When examined as a physical artifact, the cartulary discloses the inextricable connection between the date of its construction and the events taking place at the abbey prior to cartulary construction during the 1220s and 1230s. The joint material and textual analysis provides us with a more nuanced understanding of when the cartulary maker began his work (sometime after 1235), reveals that a hiatus in construction took place ca. 1237–9, and strongly suggests the addition of a final quire sometime after the October General Chapter meeting of 1239 and December 1239. For the abbey of Prémontré, which had experienced disagreements with the community at Magdeburg for several decades, the crowning moment arrived in 1239 when three charters confirmed the apparently successful resolution of the dispute and promised the strengthening of Prémontré's asserted status as mother abbey of the Premonstratensian order.

The Context of Documentary Production at the Time of Cartulary Completion

The loss of much of the material produced at the abbey of Prémontré in the early to mid-thirteenth century makes it difficult to provide a quantitative assessment of its manuscript production activity, although there was certainly a need for it. The order's governing statutes, which were revised around 1236–8, assumed the use of a variety of books in a community's church, refectory, and infirmary. These books were to be kept under the custody of a librarian (*armarius*), who was also to correct or repair the manuscripts as needed.[175] Despite archival attrition, enough evidence survives to suggest that much documentary activity took place at the abbey during the period from the mid-1230s to 1250, the approximate period of the cartulary's construction. In addition to Prémontré's principal cartulary, three smaller thirteenth-century cartularies survive, each dedicated to one of Prémontré's *curtes*.[176] To avoid confusion when discussing these four cartularies, Prémontré's principal cartulary, the subject of this edition, will be referred to as Cartulary A for the remainder of this section. The three smaller cartularies will be referred to by the name of the *curtis* whose charters they contain: Valécourt, Tinselve, and Valpriez.[177] It is important to note that the three *curtis* cartularies were not produced independently of the abbey of Prémontré; rather they figure as part of a separate cartulary-making project that took place at Prémontré, broadly in conjunction with the construction of Cartulary A.[178] Although the *curtis* cartularies measure approximately half the size of Cartulary A, their overall presentation, complete with decorated initials and high-quality parchment, affords them a status not extended to Cartulary A.

These *curtis* cartularies raise questions as to what Prémontré, or its *curtes*, hoped to achieve by constructing both a principal cartulary, Cartulary A, and a set of smaller *curtis* cartularies. Contradictory material and textual evidence suggests that although Prémontré reified its central administrative role through creating documents such as Cartulary A, that same cartulary-making activity highlights the abbey's perception of its *curtes* as discrete units, each perhaps with a differing level of independence. Moreover, the disparity between the costs of labour and material directed towards the larger Cartulary A versus the smaller *curtis* cartularies is a reminder that size and scope are not necessarily indicative of a manuscript's perceived value or function.

While the cartularies of Valécourt (diocese of Laon), Tinselve (diocese of Soissons), and Valpriez (diocese of Soissons) reside today in separate French repositories, their physical and visual characteristics indicate they were once part of a single document-making endeavour.[179] All three *curtis* cartularies display identical characteristics (**figs. 18–20**), and are more aesthetically pleasing than Cartulary A. Where Cartulary A has no decorated initials, each of the *curtis* cartularies displays beautiful alternating blue and red initials at the beginning of each act. The folios of each *curtis* cartulary measure approximately half the size of a folio in Cartulary A and their text appears in one column.[180] The parchment used in the smaller cartularies shows no signs of holes or sewing repairs and the uniform script of all three smaller cartularies is from the same hand, which is different from that of Cartulary A's cartulary maker. Above the top line, scrolling ascenders rise into the margins. Likewise, the bottom line of text graces its margin with similar descenders. None of the *curtis* cartularies shows signs of heavy use, and they may have been made more as presentation copies.[181]

While the uniform hand and layout of the three small cartularies tie them together as part of one cartulary-making project, two anomalies give rise to questions about when they were constructed and the nature of their relationship to Cartulary A. First, we know that the three *curtes* cartularies were constructed by the same person, but the dates of the *curtis* cartulary charters vary significantly. While the Valécourt and Tinselve cartularies provide 1231 and 1232 respectively as the latest date of their charters, Valpriez's latest charter dates to 1251, two decades later. It may be that *curtis* cartulary-making began in the mid-1230s, but like Cartulary A experienced a workflow hiatus, and the project was only completed shortly after 1250, a decade after Cartulary A's completion. More likely however, all three cartularies were constructed at the

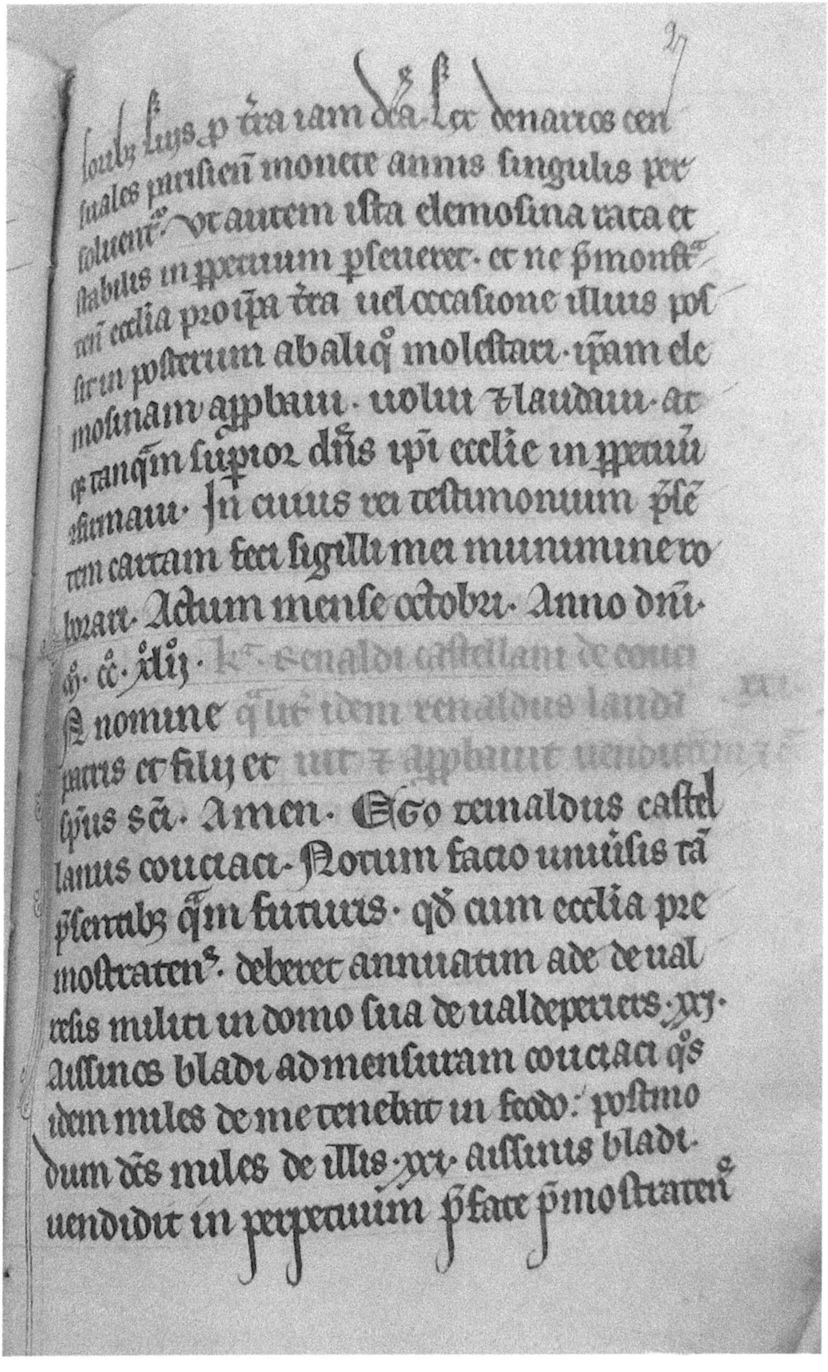

Fig. 18: Cartulary of Valpriez, fols. 10v–11r opening, decorated initials and layout. Reproduced by permission of the AD Aisne.

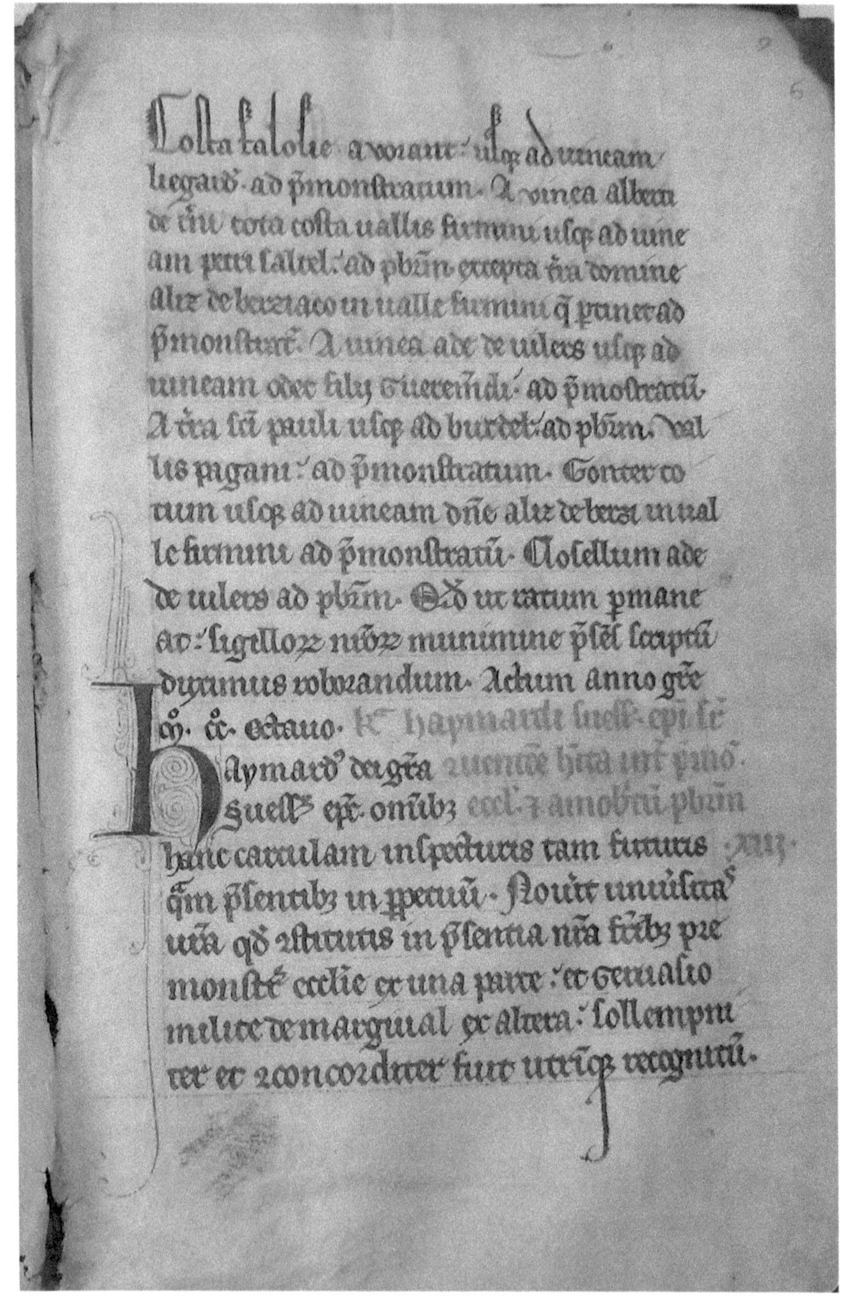

Fig. 19: Cartulary of Tinselve, fols. 4v–5r opening, decorated initials and layout. Reproduced by permission of SAHSS.

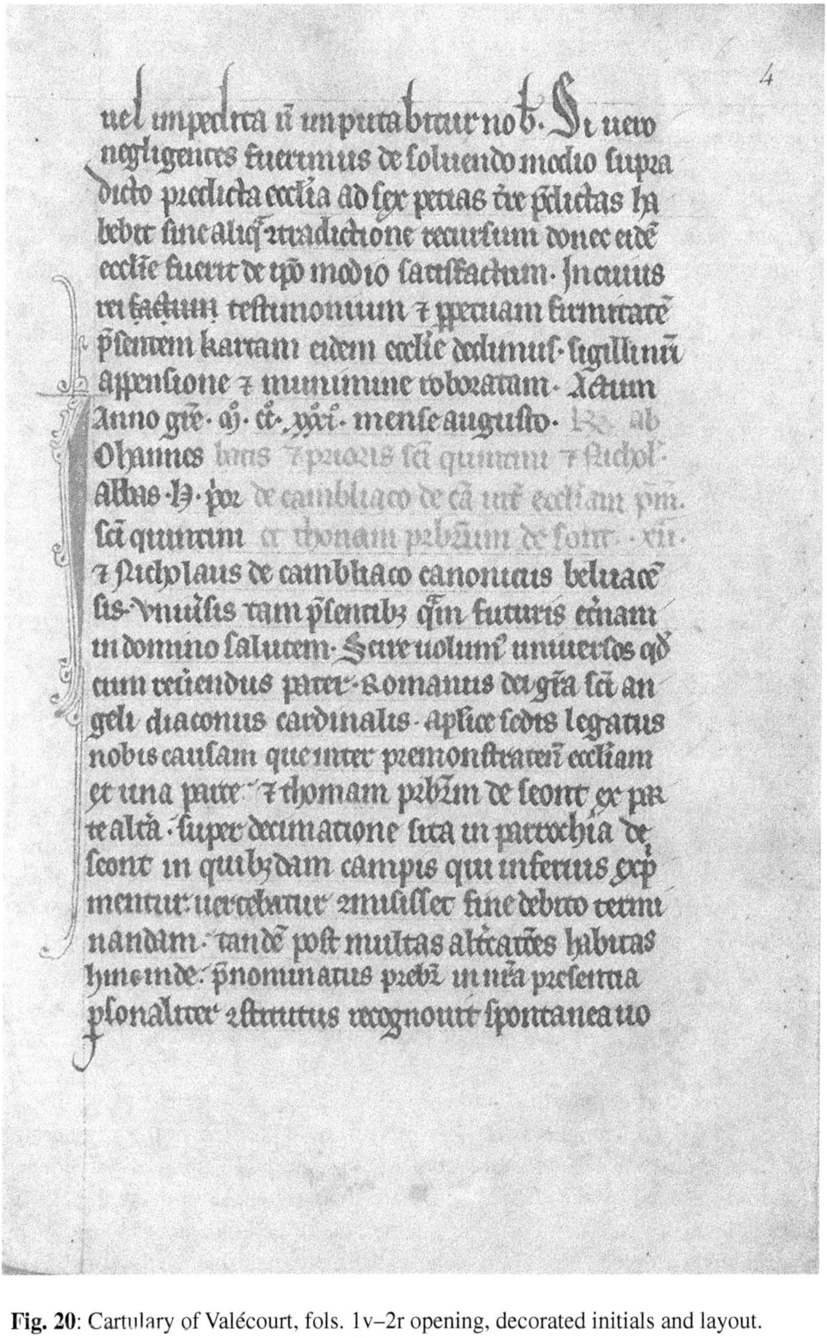

Fig. 20: Cartulary of Valécourt, fols. 1v–2r opening, decorated initials and layout. Reproduced by permission of the BnF.

same time in the 1250s. In support of this hypothesis, we know that Cartulary A received an intervention ca. 1250 (the addition of fols. 34 and 35) about the same time as the cartulary of Valpriez's latest charter date, 1251.[182]

Second, the content of the Valécourt cartulary provides a direct link between the *curtes* cartularies and Cartulary A and suggests that both projects were taking place at the abbey of Prémontré. The charter content found in the Valécourt cartulary appears word for word in Cartulary A. An examination of the textual variants between the Valécourt *curtis* cartulary and the Valécourt section in Cartulary A confirms that the two cartulary makers drew on the same set of organized original charters.[183] In other words, one scribe did not use the section of Valécourt charters in Cartulary A to create the Valécourt *curtis* cartulary, nor did the other use the Valécourt *curtis* cartulary to create the Valécourt section in Cartulary A. Both the cartulary maker for Cartulary A and the *curtis* cartulary maker must have used a pre-existing exemplar, likely a predetermined grouping of original charters, from which each made unique scribal errors.[184] Why none of the content found in the Tinselve cartulary, and little of the content from the Valpriez cartulary, appears in Cartulary A remains a frustrating mystery.[185] After all, both Tinselve and Valpriez were unambiguously *curtes* of Prémontré located in the diocese of Soissons, and the contents of their associated cartularies could have easily been part of the Soissons section of Cartulary A.

An examination of the material similarities and disparities between all four cartularies provides only partial answers as to when and why two cartulary projects were underway at the abbey of Prémontré at the same time. What is clear is that the construction of Cartulary A was broadly concurrent with the construction of the smaller cartularies associated with each of Prémontré's *curtes*, but with very different aesthetic outcomes, and presumably different functions.

The documentary activity described thus far points to a dynamic workplace at the abbey of Prémontré during the 1230s–1250s. Not only did the maker of Cartulary A complete his project, but the abbey's scriptorium was also in full production mode copying the new statutes requested by Pope Gregory IX in 1235. Additionally, a second *curtis* cartulary-making project was taking place at roughly the same time as that of Cartulary A and the copying of the new statutes.

Such an active scriptorium would have come at a cost, in terms of both materials and labour. Given that several projects were in progress at the same time, the abbey must have been well stocked with materials – such as parchment and ink – needed by the various scribes. Prémontré chose to make the *curtis* cartularies with consistently higher-quality cuts of parchment and to decorate the initials with blue and red pigments. That these materials were available at the abbey but not used for Cartulary A suggests that the abbey preferred to use what resources it had on the *curtis* cartulary project rather than on Cartulary

A. Perhaps Cartulary A was meant to be a "working" cartulary for the abbey's archivists and brothers; perhaps the *curtes* cartularies were meant more for show, or as gifts.[186] Either way, the trail of evidence appears to run dry. Until further information comes to light, the relationship between the cartulary projects remains unclear.

Yet the surviving manuscripts reflect a concerted effort on the part of the abbey to construct administrative documents. Moreover, the construction and subsequent preservation of the cartularies reflect the abbey's ongoing concern with consolidating its privileges and affirming the legitimacy of its temporal possessions both for its own community and for those who should ever question or challenge the abbey's holdings.[187] By undertaking the construction of Cartulary A and the surviving *curtis* cartularies, Prémontré used document production to demonstrate that by 1250 the abbey understood itself to have secured and validated its status within its religious and secular landscapes.

Later Readers

Readers and users throughout the centuries have continued to interact with the cartulary of Prémontré. Traces left by users post-1240 confirm that the cartulary served a long-term function for Prémontré and its community, although that function changed over time. Examining the relationship between the date of later entries and the nature of their content suggests that after 1400, the abbey shifted away from using the cartulary as a place to enter new charter content and legal precedent, and towards using it more as a source of institutional history.

Just as the cartulary maker envisioned when he left blank spaces for future charters at the end of certain sections, the brothers at Prémontré indeed added charter content after 1240 until about 1400. Twenty-five of the cartulary's charters are in late thirteenth- and fourteenth-century hands, and have been added to the manuscript at a point associated with their specific content, whether in the margins or in spaces previously left blank. This suggests that the abbey continued to respect the significance of the conceptual design of the cartulary, and that it implicitly assumed that, post-1240, new charter additions needed to be in the sections that readers would expect to find them. When one brother found no room in the appropriate geographical section for a 1346 charter concerning the Premonstratensian house in Ferrole (located in the diocese of Noyon), he wrote a short note at the bottom of a column on fol. 104r, next to other charters addressing that house. The note states: "Look for a new charter that concerns the rights of *justicia* on our house of Ferrole prior to the table of charter contents of the Noyon section at this sign" (**fig. 21**).[188] When readers follow these directions, they find the new charter entry on 75r, the folio just before the table of contents for the section of Bonneuil (Noyon), cross-referenced with the

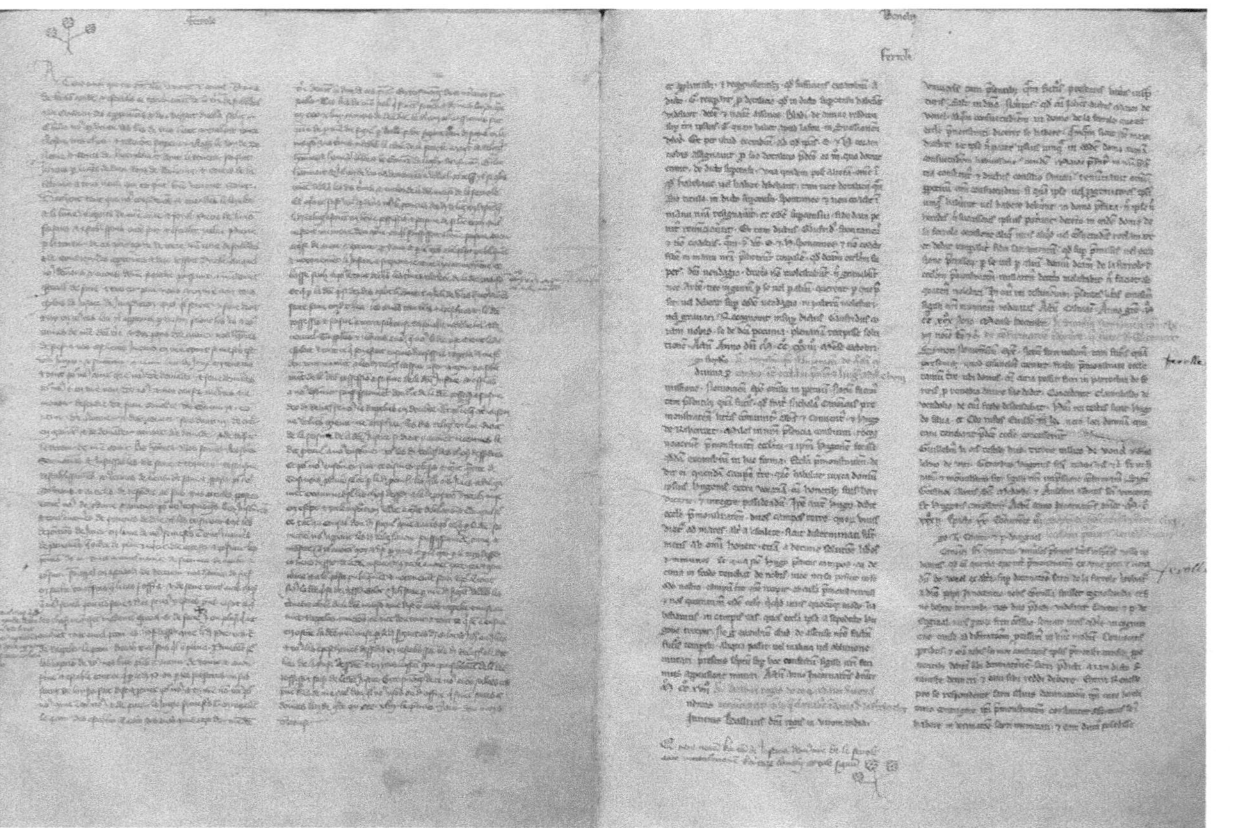

Fig. 21: Cartulary of Prémontré, fols. 75r and 104r. The floral sign used as a cross-referencing tool. Reproduced by permission of the Bibliothèque municipale, Soissons.

same floral sign (**297**). The need to include a floral sign as a tool for cross-referencing – rather than a note saying "see folio number X" – appears to confirm that, as of 1346, the cartulary had yet to receive foliation.

Prémontré continued to interact with its thirteenth-century cartulary after 1400, but a shift in the type of marginal notation being added reflects a shift in the abbey's use of the cartulary. Notes from fifteenth- to nineteenth-century readers provide signposts for quick access to certain charters concerning specific properties. In some charters, names of places and people have been underlined. In others, the place names, especially *curtis* names, have been extracted from the text and written in the margins, alongside the charter, for quick reference when skimming through the cartulary. The Noyon section of the cartulary, in particular, has several marginal notes written in a nineteenth-century hand that provide translations into French of the place names mentioned in the Latin charters. Further research and more accurate dating of the later scripts could potentially illuminate the relationship between the marginal notes and shifts in the use of certain of the abbey's properties between the Middle Ages and the time that the notes were written.

The cartulary contains no charters dated 1400–1586, which makes the addition of a single, and final, act in 1586 (**149**) all the more significant.[189] The 1586 date is broadly contemporary with the cartulary's late sixteenth-century or early seventeenth-century rebinding.[190] Two events important to the abbey of Prémontré might explain the decision to add one last charter and rebind the thirteenth-century cartulary during this time period; both involve the abbey's founder, Norbert of Xanten. The first event was Norbert's canonization, which took place in 1582. The second was the translation of Norbert's body in 1627 from Magdeburg, Germany, a Protestant enclave by the early seventeenth century, to Strahov Monastery, in Catholic Prague.[191] In either case, it would have been wholly appropriate for the abbey to revisit its most ancient documents and upgrade them in memoriam to its founder, now Saint Norbert.

The rebinding may also reflect an attempt on the part of Prémontré to assert its ancient primacy in the face of challenges both external and internal to the order that occurred during the sixteenth and seventeenth centuries. Both the Reformation and the Counter-Reformation caused issues for established religious orders, and members of those orders did not necessarily agree on how to face them. Premonstratensian houses in the Lorraine region in the sixteenth century undertook a program of reform.[192] This chipped away at Prémontré's authority, as did the fact that the Spanish Premonstratensian houses had broken away in 1573 to form a Hispanic Congregation.[193] Moreover, the ability of the abbots of Prémontré to respond effectively to these challenges was hampered by the imposition of a series of commendatory abbots.[194] Amid such instability, and with the order's most dynamic reform initiatives in France appearing to originate outside of Prémontré itself, the rebinding of the cartulary of

Prémontré may perhaps represent an attempt to reassert its now centuries-old rights and privileges.

Lastly, material and textual interventions for which no date can securely be suggested raise intriguing questions for future researchers. Several cartulary acts have x's or +'s written next to them, but the meaning of these symbols remains unclear. Closer analysis may produce connections between the original charter's contents and perhaps the selling off of these properties at a certain point in the abbey's history. Despite these lingering mysteries, the additions made to the cartulary of Prémontré post-1240 verify that the abbey considered the manuscript an active document, open for additional content and interpretation.[195] The abbey continued to respect the integrity of its early documents and history, long after the cartulary maker had laid his quill to rest.

CONCLUSION

Bishops and mill operators, widows and notaries, parish priests and tenant farmers populate the pages of the cartulary of Prémontré. The quarrels and aspirations of these women and men are told in the careful scribal hand that marches in neat rows across its pages, or in the cramped marginal scrawl of a later addition. In the fragmentary glimpses we get of their lives, we learn something of the agency, opportunities, and priorities of the people of northern France in the twelfth and thirteenth centuries. All of this makes the cartulary a rich source for contemporary socio-economic history, and a close reading of its texts cautions us against reductive assumptions about the Middle Ages. Contrary to later popular – and even some scholarly – perceptions, medieval women worked, prayed, and lived alongside men.

To this valuable history we can add something new when we "read" the cartulary's materiality as closely as we might its text. Exploring this materiality requires us to consider the human element of the manuscript's production. The comparatively poor quality of the principal cartulary's parchment and the neat handwriting, the never-completed decorated initials and the carefully spaced tables of contents, the ink spills and corrections: they all remind us of how large a gap can yawn between plans and reality, between intention and execution. This material analysis works in tandem with a close scrutiny of the handwriting, codicology, and production process. Together, they help us to date the manuscript's completion more precisely than ever before. Knowing that the bulk of the cartulary was written by 1240 allows us to view its production in relation to the other manuscripts produced at the abbey of Prémontré around the mid-century, a fraught period in the history of the Premonstratensian Order.

The object-driven approach of a material studies analysis, with its emphasis on how an artifact generates its own historical questions, lets us engage with the process of cartulary production in a different way. Paying attention to the organizational idiosyncrasies of the cartulary lets us ask new questions about the abbey's inner workings: might some dependent *curtes* have had their own archives? Was this a less than fully centralized administrative system? Ink spills on a page prompt us to picture a flustered scribe trying his best to restore a disrupted workflow; new leaves swapped in for old encourage us to consider what might have caused a change in the plan for the manuscript's organization. The reconstructed process becomes itself a historical source, one that tells us something about the conceptual and cultural beliefs and expectations of those who carried it out.

Working with a grounding in the fields of cartulary studies, feminist theory, and other forms of critical theory, we as editors have tried to combine certain conventional editorial principles with new ones that we believe better represent actors, makers, and constructed power structures past and present. Our edition is not intended to be the sole authoritative edition of the cartulary of Prémontré – it is no more definitive than the version of the manuscript that existed in 1240, or the framings of the cartulary's acts put forward by nineteenth-century cataloguers. Yet we have worked with an awareness of the subjectivities of medieval cartulary makers and modern editors, and with a questioning approach to the conventions that have long guided the production of scholarly editions. In other words, this is an edition that seeks to consciously recognize all of the varied human contributions to the manufacture, use, and study of the cartulary over the almost eight centuries of its existence. As editors, we hope that this edition will be a means of spurring new conversations about the cartulary of Prémontré, the abbey that made it, and the people who study it.

EDITORIAL PRINCIPLES AND METHODOLOGY

The original text is predominantly written in Latin, but certain acts are in contemporary regional dialects of French. As a general principle, the transcription strives to be as accurate a representation of what is present on the cartulary page as possible; the cartulary manuscript, as our object of study, is the *A* text and is always privileged as such throughout the edition. The transcription at times therefore includes obvious scribal errors, corrections, or strikethroughs; all variants noted in the footnotes indicate deviations from the cartulary text.

Principles of Transcription

We have constructed a set of semi-normalized cartulary transcription principles that preserves the cartulary's original orthography. We have used modern punctuation sparingly in service of reader comprehension, and employ paragraph breaks only when present in the cartulary. Place names, personal names (except in the case of "le" or "de" in family names), titles or epithets, and feast days in both Latin and vernacular texts are capitalized according to Anglophone norms. This means that all recognized place names are capitalized and we have included apostrophes in names such as *d'Espeville* (**49**) and *d'Ostel* (**496**). Abbreviations have been silently expanded. While the scribal use of abbreviations was inconsistent, we have tried to expand them in a consistent manner, e.g., *Prem.* being generally expanded to *Premonstratensis* where it makes grammatical sense to do so, or *etc.* being expanded to *et cetera* or *et ceteri*, depending on the context. The transcription of *c* or *t*, letters that are often indistinguishable in the text, particularly in the middle of a word, has been carried out according to ecclesiastical Latin pronunciation. When acts are written in French, only the *accent aigu* is present, and only on the final *e* should its absence change the meaning of the word.[196] We do not note the *accent cédille.*

Act Structure

The transcription of each act includes the following elements: date, summary, bibliographic information, rubric, full transcription, textual variants based on surviving original charters, and other notes where applicable.

We have numbered the acts in numerical order as they stand in the cartulary now, including those acts that are written in the margins and/or are later additions.

In accordance with the cartulary acts, dates are given in the old style. We have not noted where there are inconsistencies between the calendar date and any given indiction or epact dates. When the date is conjectural, it is indicated as such via a question mark in square brackets and a relevant footnote; when we have not been able to date an act, it is described as "undated." When the cartulary scribe misdated an act, we have provided the correct date in the accompanying apparatus, and indicated our intervention in a footnote. When the location in which the original charter was written is securely known, it has been given, using the modern form of the place name, immediately after the date.

In our summaries, we have chosen to represent the actors of the original transaction and the actors involved in recording the transaction (including principals, co-principals, and other relevant individuals) but for reasons of space have omitted witnesses unless they otherwise participate in a transaction. Witnesses do appear, however, in the charter texts. Summaries are given in English. We render names in the summary in the modern standardized form of the appropriate vernacular, with some exceptions. The names of popes are given according to their modern English equivalents. Where certain individuals are best known in the literature by a particular vernacular form of their name, even if that is not the standardized form that we have adopted elsewhere in the cartulary, we have continued to use the well-known form to avoid confusion (for example, Aelide de Dreux or de Coucy is more commonly referred to in the modern historiography as Alix de Coucy, and so we refer to her as Alix in the act summaries).

Information useful in identifying a particular individual which is not supplied by the charter text has been expanded in square brackets, e.g., "Simon [I de Vermandois], bishop of Noyon." Place names are rendered in the modern vernacular name where known; otherwise they are given in Latin or the medieval vernacular, which appears non-italicized within an italicized summary. Measurements and units of currency are given in Latin or the vernacular according to the language used in the act and appear in the glossaries below. Where there is ambiguity about the meaning of a term or title in Latin or the vernacular, we have elected to use the original word in the summary and also placed it in the glossaries below (see Appendices 2 and 3). If there are related acts, their number is given in parentheses at the end of the summary. If an act has a duplicate, this is stated by noting "duplicate" in conjunction with the related act number. A duplicate is an act that is identical in every way. We have also noted acts that are near-duplicates, i.e., the act is essentially a duplicate, but contains some textual variants.

Each act is preceded by a section which provides bibliographic information. Within it, *A* points the user to the relevant folio(s) in the cartulary manuscript (Soissons, Bibliothèque municipale, MS 7), and *B* to any known surviving original charter(s) generally associated with Prémontré's thirteenth-century archives. The description of all charters listed under *B* includes an archival reference and any mode or traces of sealing, if known. In the case of a chirograph where both parts survive, they are indicated by the letters B^1 and B^2. Other loose parchment copies are also noted, including both contemporary copies of an act which have a clear provenance not originating from Prémontré and other medieval manuscript copies such as those found in cartularies from other Premonstratensian houses, papal registers, or other documents. We also list where acts have been noted in any published editions or registers, to the best of our knowledge.

We have either provided the rubric of each charter as given in the cartulary in bold text before the body of each act, or indicated if an act has no rubric. We have preserved the cartulary's presentation of witness lists as much as possible. We use [illegible] in the transcription to indicate where text is present but unreadable; we use [lacuna] to indicate where the page has been damaged and the text is absent.

Footnotes are used to provide further biographical or geographical information about a topic, to point the reader to other relevant manuscripts, to provide information about the folio condition where applicable, or to indicate variations between the cartulary text and any known original texts. In the latter case, all variant readings are given in relation to the cartulary text; that is, the cartulary text is always the *A* text, while the original charters (as *B*, B^1, or B^2)

are always presented in comparison to it. For example, in **4**, when the name "Clarenbaldus" is footnoted "Clarembaldus *B*," this indicates that the cartulary text spells the name Clarenbaldus, while the *B* text, the original charter, spells it Clarembaldus. In **71**, when "super ulla occasione" is footnoted "*Om.* Concedetur tamen rusticis qui sunt in vicina colligere de silva que est in iugis montium colligere materiam ad opus capitis seu scepi aratri sive axis *A.*", this means that the cartulary scribe omitted this phrase, but that the phrase appears in the original act, or *B* text. In **19**, at a point when the cartulary scribe included a word in the cartulary text that was absent from the original charter, the footnote reads "*Add.* congruam *A.*"

NOTES

1 Françoise Muret, *archiviste-paléographe* and *ingénieure de recherche* at the Centre national de la recherche scientifique, Orléans, began work on an edition in the 1980s. While Muret's project was never completed, the typescript of her transcriptions and some other notes are preserved at the Institut de recherche et d'histoire des textes (IRHT), Paris. This edition owes a great debt to Muret's pioneering work, although it diverges from it in several respects, particularly in that it does not follow the act numbering system which she adopted.

2 For the geographical growth of the order, see Bond, "The Premonstratensian Order." For a fuller listing of Premonstratensian houses in France and elsewhere, see Ardura, *Abbayes, prieurés et monastères de l'ordre de Prémontré en France des origines à nos jours*; Backmund, *MP.*

3 A digitized copy of BM Soissons, MS 7, can be consulted at the IRHT's Bibliothèque virtuelle des manuscrits médiévaux (BVMM) website, https://bvmm.irht.cnrs.fr/mirador/index.php?manifest=https://bvmm.irht.cnrs.fr/iiif/24600/manifest, accessed July 1, 2020. Almost no scholarship has taken the cartulary of Prémontré as its primary focus object of study, although in the mid-nineteenth century the antiquarian Joseph-Épiphane Darras wrote that "[o]n peut affirmer, sans crainte d'exagération, que ce précieux volume renferme l'histoire la plus complète et la plus authentique du monastère aux trois premiers siècles de son existence, c'est-à-dire pendant l'époque la plus glorieuse et la plus féconde que présentent les annales de cette maison chef d'ordre" ("[w]e can say without the least fear of exaggeration that this invaluable volume comprises the most complete and authentic history of the abbey's first three centuries of existence, that is to say during the most glorious and fruitful period that the annals present of this motherhouse"). Darras, "Observations sur le cartulaire de Prémontré (XIIIe siècle)," 13. Unless otherwise stated, all translations from French and Latin in this volume are those of the present editors.

4 Only a small proportion of the order's surviving medieval cartularies has been made available in a modern print edition. For print editions of French Premonstratensian

cartularies, see Barthélemy, "Cartulaire de l'abbaye de Bucilly"; Beaurain, *Le cartulaire de l'abbaye de Selincourt 1131–1513*; Gaubin, *Abbaye de La Case-Dieu*; Guyotjeannin, *Le chartrier de l'abbaye prémontrée de Saint-Yved de Braine (1134–1250)*; Haigneré, "Les chartes de Notre-Dame de Licques, 1078–1311"; Lalanne, *Le cartulaire de Valpriez, 1135–1250*; Lalore, *Collection des principaux cartulaires du diocèse de Troyes: Cartulaire de l'Abbaye de Basse-Fontaine*; Lalore, *Collection des principaux cartulaires du diocèse de Troyes: Cartulaire de l'Abbaye de la Chapelle-aux-Planches*; Lecocq, *Histoire de l'abbaye Notre-Dame de Vermand*; and Pécheur, "Cartulaire de Tinselve." For a fuller list of Premonstratensian cartularies produced both in France and elsewhere in Europe, see Seale, "Handlist of Premonstratensian Cartularies," while for French cartularies more generally, Stein, *Bibliographie générale des cartulaires français ou relatifs à l'histoire de France* has not been surpassed, though see also *CartulR*, accessed July 1, 2020.

5 Norbert's first followers to settle at Prémontré did so in 1120, while the order was formally incorporated in 1121. Both 2020 and 2021 therefore can lay claim to being the nine hundredth anniversary year.

6 Maguire, "Feminist Editing and the Body of the Text," 78.

7 Auguste Matton (1819–1905) was a founder member of the Société historique de Haute-Picardie, and the *archiviste départemental* of the Aisne, 1848–89. As well as compiling the many volumes of the archive's inventories, he also wrote a number of monographs, including *La Commune de Laon au XIIIe siècle* (1866), *Dictionnaire topographique du département de l'Aisne* (1871), *Histoire de la ville et des environs de Guise* (1898), and *Les anciennes papeteries de l'Aisne* (1903). Comité des travaux historiques et scientifiques, "MATTON, Auguste," *Annuaire prosopographique: la France savante*, 2006, https://cths.fr/an/savant.php?id=100.

8 "Charte d'Anselme, évêque de Laon, attestant que Guillaume de Monthiémont a cédé, à ladite abbaye [Prémontré], 3 muids moins un setier de vinage moyennant 16 livres de la monnaie de Laon." Summary of AD Aisne, H 745. Matton, ed., *Inventaire sommaire des Archives départementales antérieures à 1790: Archives ecclésiastiques. Séries G et H*, vol. 3, 111.

9 This largely nineteenth-century series (the *Inventaire-sommaire des archives départementales antérieures à 1790*) remains the starting point for users of the French *archives départementales* who are interested in the history of medieval or Ancien Régime France. The online inventories of individual ADs, or meta-inventories such as France Archives (www.francearchives.fr), are generally digitized versions of these older works.

10 The summary is written on a piece of paper which is wrapped around the charter. AD Oise, H 6036. While this act does not appear in the cartulary, a related act of Hugues III, archbishop of Rouen, does (**504**).

11 AN, L 732, Dossier 2, no. 51. This summary is written on a small scrap of paper included in the dossier which holds this charter.

12 "Karta Haymardi, Suessionensis episcopi, super elemosinam vinee ad Quercum et campo ante Felcieras, quos Egaldus de Margival contulit in elemosinam ecclesie Premonstrati." Pécheur, "Cartulaire de Tinselve," 230.

13 For a recent state-of-the-field overview on the history and historiography of women's history, power, and exceptionalism, see Tanner, ed., *Medieval Elite Women and the Exercise of Power, 1100–1400.*

14 In trying to think more critically about both the roles played by these women in their society and our own responses to those women, we are indebted to the feminist theories first advanced by Kimberlé Crenshaw, which are attentive to the intersectional nature of oppressions. See Crenshaw, *On Intersectionality.*

15 Wernimont, "Whence Feminism?"

16 But see Green, "Digital Manuscripts as Sites of Touch," for a discussion of how digital or digitized manuscripts can be presented as dynamic objects that function as "haptic intermediaries."

17 There is no single definition of a cartulary in use in the field of cartulary studies, but a widely accepted one appeared in 1984, when the Commission internationale de diplomatique defined a cartulary as "un recueil de copies de ses propres documents, établi par une personne physique ou morale, qui, dans un volume ou plus rarement dans un rouleau, transcrit ou fait transcrire intégralement ou parfois en extraits, des titres relatif à ses biens et à ses droits et des documents concernant son histoire ou son administration, pour en assurer la conservation et en faciliter la consultation" ["a collection of copies of its [i.e., the producing institution's] own documents, drawn up by a person or a body, who, in a volume, or more rarely in a scroll, transcribes or causes to have transcribed in full or sometimes in extracts, deeds relating to its possessions and its rights, and documents concerning its history or its administration, to ensure their conservation and facilitate consultation"]. Cárcel Ortí, ed., *Vocabulaire international de la diplomatique*, 36.

18 A directory of various charter collections and cartularies, published in 1904 for the Library of Congress, includes hundreds of then recently published editions, many of which came from presses associated with French and Belgian local and regional scholarly societies. Griffin, *List of Cartularies (Principally French) Recently Added to the Library of Congress with Some Earlier Accessions.* Interest in these medieval sources was not universal, however. Many continued to be lost to neglect, incompetence, or indifference, as was the case with the unknown number of northern French charters which were used as wadding for practice shots at the artillery school at Metz. Brunel, "Les parchemins de la collection Salis aux archives historiques de la ville de Metz," 351–2.

19 "Missions et projets," École nationale des chartes, April 1, 2015, http://www.chartes.psl.eu/fr/rubrique-ecole/missions-et-projets.

20 Comité des travaux historiques et scientifiques, "DELISLE, Léopold Victor," *Annuaire prosopographique: la France savante*, 2006, https://cths.fr/an/savant.php?id=792; Comité des travaux historiques et scientifiques, "BROCHE, Lucien

Albert Etienne," *Annuaire prosopographique: la France savante*, 2006, https://cths.fr/an/savant.php?id=1707. More recent scholar-historians who were also trained at the École des chartes – including Robert-Henri Bautier, Robert Fossier, Ghislain Brunel, and Annie Dufour-Malbezin – have promoted the use of charters and cartularies through their studies of medieval social and economic history, including studies of the region of Picardy, where Prémontré is located.

21 The Société académique de Laon was succeeded by the Société historique de Haute-Picardie in 1914.

22 Attal, "Les Riches Heures de La Société."

23 These early printed editions continue to shape how we access and use cartularies as sources today, whether that is approaching them with an uncritical acceptance, imagining them as simply the print version of a handwritten manuscript, or assuming that a cartulary's textual contributions outweigh its material ones. Tucker, "Understanding Scotland's Medieval Cartularies." See also Geary, *Phantoms of Remembrance*.

24 "Un cartulaire n'est, comme on le sait, qu'un recueil de copies de chartes." Nanglard, *Cartulaire de l'église d'Angoulême*, xvii.

25 Saint-Corneille, founded in 876, was first a community of canons and later a Benedictine abbey. Émile Morel published three initial volumes of his edition beginning in 1894, followed by an expanded edition in three volumes beginning in 1904. The third volume of that revised edition was to have been published in 1918, but, in an incident which must surely inspire a pang of empathy in the heart of any scholar, the volume had only been partly printed when it and the printer's premises were destroyed during the burning of Montdidier in the last months of the First World War. Partial proofs and a partial manuscript of the edition alone survived, which Louis Carolus-Barré used to finally finish the edition in the 1970s. Morel, *Cartulaire de l'abbaye de Saint-Corneille de Compiègne*; Morel and Carolus-Barré, eds., *Cartulaire de l'abbaye de Saint-Corneille de Compiègne*.

26 Morel, *Saint-Corneille de Compiègne,* vol. 1, vi–vii; Morel and Carolus-Barré, eds., *Saint-Corneille de Compiègne*, vol. 1, ix–x.

27 "… en la matière, le positivisme issu du XIXe siècle est tenace et les cartulaires, tributaires de cet héritage, ont bien du mal à se débarrasser de leur statut de 'recueils de chartes' pour devenir objet d'études qui restitueraient leur fonction de document-monument …" Chastang, *Lire, écrire, transcrire*, 15.

28 Guyotjeannin, Morelle, and Parisse, eds., *Les cartulaires*. For examples of recent cartulary editions, see Amt, ed., *The Latin Cartulary of Godstow Abbey*; Lalanne, *Le cartulaire de Valpriez*; Redford, ed., *The Cartulary of Alvingham Priory*; Stucky Skinner, "The Cartulary of Clairmarais, a Monastery of Cistercian Nuns at Reims, France, c. 1220–1460."

29 For example, Patrick Geary argues that Freising Abbey's ninth-century cartulary was undertaken to honour the abbey's early clerical leaders. Geary, "Entre Gestion et Gesta." Similarly, Dietrich Lohrmann argues that the placement and emphasis

on royal and imperial charters in the *Liber aureus d'Echternach* reveal the abbey's efforts to retain its status as an imperial abbey. Lohrmann, "Évolution et organisation internes des cartulaires rhénans du moyen âge."

30 This is a major point of divergence from Françoise Muret's approach. In her unpublished and unfinished draft transcription of the cartulary of Prémontré, Muret chose to transcribe those surviving original charters of which she was aware instead of the copy of the act as contained in the cartulary.

31 See Berkhofer, *Day of Reckoning*; Bouchard, "Monastic Cartularies: Organizing Eternity," 25; Geary, *Phantoms of Remembrance*; Kosto, *Making Agreements in Medieval Catalonia*; Lohrmann, "Évolution et organisation interne des cartulaires rhénans du Moyen Âge"; Evergates, *Aristocracy in the County of Champagne, 1100–1300*; Bouchard, *Rewriting Saints and Ancestors*.

32 Bertrand and Hélary, "Constructions de l'espace dans les cartulaires"; Guyotjeannin, "La fabrique du Cartulaire Blanc"; Tucker, *Reading and Shaping Medieval Cartularies*.

33 Tucker, *Reading and Shaping Medieval Cartularies*, 25.

34 The degree to which allegiance to Prémontré and its General Chapter indicated a Premonstratensian identity in the twelfth and early thirteenth centuries, or what was understood by a Premonstratensian identity, deserve further investigation. Rothe, "Zwischen *contemplatio* und *vita apostolica*"; Van de Perre, "Die ältesten Klostergesetzgebungen von Prémontré, Oigny, Cîteaux, Klosterrath und Arrouaise und ihre Beziehungen zueinander"; Wolbrink, "Noble Pursuits," 36–7, 60–9.

35 There is no scholarly biography of Norbert of Xanten in English, though see Grauwen, *Norbertus, aartsbisschop van Maagdenburg (1126–1134)*, together with Van Engen, "Norbert of Xanten," and the essays in Elm, ed., *Norbert von Xanten*. For Norbert's medieval *vitae*, see *PL* 170, cols. 1257–1343; *MGH SS*, 12. These have been partly translated in Antry and Neel, eds., *Norbert and Early Norbertine Spirituality*, 126–92.

36 For an overview of the role of Norbert and the Premonstratensians in the twelfth-century reform movement, see Constable, *The Reformation of the Twelfth Century*. On contemporary responses to Norbert and his followers, see Van Engen, *Rupert of Deutz*, 270, 311–12, 324, 337–41.

37 Barthélemy would go on to be a major figure in the order's early history, and has a reasonable claim to be considered one of its co-founders along with Norbert. Tétart, "Barthélemy, évêque de Laon, moine cistercien de Foigny." See **5**, **71–4**, **91**, **95**, **96**, **98**, **99**, **106**, **112**, **140**, **141**, **161**, **164**, **178**, **179**, **184**, **233**. So too does Hugues de Fosses, who would become Prémontré's first abbot. Elm, ed., "Hugo von Fosses, Erster Abt von Prémontré und Organisator des Prämonstratenserordens"; Lamy, *Vie du bienheureux Hugues de Fosses*.

38 Plouvier, "L'abbaye de Prémontré (Aisne)," 512.

39 Ibid.

40 *PL* 156, col. 992; Herman of Tournai, *Les miracles de Sainte Marie de Laon*, 206–7.

41 "Quae vallis non humano molimine sed naturali opera quoddammodo crucifixa, quid monet vel praemonet nisi ut eam confluentes mundo vivere jam non curent, sed se illi, imo Christo crucifixione congrua configurent?" *PL* 203, col. 238.

42 Jean Le Paige (d. ca. 1650) professed at Prémontré as a young man. In 1601, he accompanied the abbot-general François de Longpré and Servais de Lairuelz in their visits to the various houses of the order, which would have afforded Le Paige ample opportunity to examine the manuscript holdings of the Premonstratensians' various houses. In 1607, he was installed as the prior of the Premonstratensian college at Paris. His *Bibliotheca Praemonstratensis ordinis* (1633) preserves many important early documents concerning the order's history. Ardura, *Abbayes, prieurés et monastères de l'ordre de Prémontré en France des origines à nos jours*, 37–8; Le Paige, *Bibliotheca*. Charles-Louis Hugo (1667–1739) entered the Premonstratensian abbey of Pont-à-Mousson in 1683 and received his doctorate from the University of Bourges in 1691. In 1700, he was appointed to lead the Premonstratensian community at Nancy, and remained there until 1713, when he moved to Étival. *MP* 3: 67–71. Hugo spent the next decade gathering material for his two great works on the order, the *Sacræ Antiquitatis* and the *Annales*. Hugo's many notebooks, containing the research for the *Annales* (which was not completed before his death), are currently held at the Bibliothèque municipale de Nancy, MS 1752. Hugo, *Sacrae antiquitatis monumenta historica, dogmatica, diplomatica, notis illustrata* and *Sacri et Canonici Ordinis Praemonstratensis annales*.

43 Petit, "Pourquoi saint Norbert a choisi Prémontré."

44 The two medieval *vitae* of Norbert are largely silent about his interactions with women generally or his women followers in particular. More work remains to be done on the presence of sisters at Prémontré, the roles women played in the Premonstratensian Order in the Middle Ages, the regional differences in such roles, and the extent to which prescriptive texts were representative of the lives of the Premonstratensian sisters. See Neel, "The Premonstratensian Project," 203–4; Seale, "'Ten Thousand Women.'"

45 Neel, "The Premonstratensian Project," 193.

46 Dereine, "Les origines de Prémontré."

47 The geographical concentration depicted in this map, with Premonstratensian houses located primarily in what is now northern and northeastern France, with two subsidiary clusters in Normandy and far southwestern France, may reflect the influence of the treaty agreed between the Cistercians and the Premonstratensians concerning minimum distances to be observed between houses of their respective orders (**497**).

48 *MP* 2: 523; Bondéelle-Souchier, *Bibliothèques de l'Ordre de Prémontré dans la France d'Ancien Régime*, vol. 2, 229.

49 Bonnet, *Les constructions de l'ordre de Prémontré en France aux XVIIe et XVIIIe siècles*.

50 Plouvier, "L'abbaye," 514.

51 Shortell, "An Image of the Abbey Church of Prémontré under Construction." Some archaeological excavations have taken place on the site in recent years, primarily between 2008 and 2012 by the Pôle archéologique du Conseil département de l'Aisne under the direction of Thierry Galmiche. See Galmiche et al., Excavation Reports. Code Patriarche: 9414, Code Patriarche: 9596, Code Patriarche: 10007, Code Patriarche: 10038. The findings of these excavations remain as yet largely unstudied by historians, although they show that archaeologists have been able to ascertain the position of the west and north walls of the later medieval abbey church. Some preliminary articles have been published. See Galmiche and Buccio, "Les ardoises gravées de l'abbaye de Prémontré (Aisne)."

52 AD Yvelines, 46 H 1. Sadly, a description of the abbey written in the mid-1660s by one of its canons now survives only in excerpts, which refer to foundations of now-vanished medieval buildings which were unearthed whenever anyone dug in the vicinity of the abbey.

53 Le Paige, *Bibliotheca*, vol. 1, 438; *AASS*, October 13, 51–3.

54 "Tout à fait au nord, au fond de la basse-cour actuelle, l'on voyait, il y a trois ans, des constructions remontant [… aux] restes du Xenodochium élevé par le Saint, et quelques débris du monastère des Religieuses Norbertines … Un violent incendie consuma, en 1879, ces restes précieux" ["At the far north, at the end of the current inner courtyard, three years ago, we could see constructions dating back [… to] the remains of the *xenodochium* erected by the saint, and some remains of the monastery of the Norbertine Nuns … A violent fire consumed, in 1879, these precious remains"]. Madelaine, *L'abbaye de Prémontré en 1882*, 10–11. In the later Middle Ages, the *xenodochium* moved from Prémontré to Saint-Quentin. Ardura, *The Order of Prémontré*, 31.

55 Excavations carried out at Prémontré in the early twenty-first century uncovered about one hundred burials, with approximately 10 per cent of those whose sex could be established being osteologically female. The female remains have been tentatively identified as representing *xenodochium* patients, members of the patron Coucy family, or members of the order. Galmiche et al., Excavation Reports; Plouvier, *L'abbaye de Prémontré: du service de Dieu au soin des hommes*, 22. However, demographic conclusions based on these modern excavations must be treated with care, owing to the large-scale destruction of burial sites at the abbey during the nineteenth century. Godefroid Madelaine wrote that during the construction of accommodations for psychiatric patients in the nineteenth century, hundreds of remains, presumably belonging to members of the order, were dug up. "Il y a quelques années, lorsque l'on construisit les sections, on déterra des centaines de têtes et des monceaux d'ossements; c'étaient les anciens Prémontrés dont on remuait les cendres" ["A few years ago, when the sections were being built, hundreds of heads and piles of bones were dug up; these were the ancient Premonstratensians whose ashes were being stirred"]. Madelaine, *L'abbaye*, 10.

56 Bondéelle-Souchier, *Bibliothèques de l'Ordre*, vol. 2, 229. For L'Écuy's role in the expansion of the library collection at Prémontré and his own personal collection, see Hennezel d'Ormois, *Les bibliophiles du pays Laonnois*, vol. 1, 171–81.

57 Between the Revolution and their conversion to a hospital, the buildings were used first as a glassworks and then as an orphanage run by the Daughters of Wisdom of Saint-Laurent-sur-Sèvres. A glass oven constructed inside the church during the former period exploded, leading to the structural collapse. Ardura, *The Order of Prémontré*, 430.

58 Paul-Armand de Cardon de Garsignies, bishop of Soissons, purchased the site in 1855 with the intention of re-establishing the Premonstratensian Order there, but the restoration failed. Ardura, "De conciles en réformes," 241–2.

59 Sheila Bonde and Clarke Maines carried out a small-scale excavation on the site in 1988 and believe it to be the remains of the first church built there; Michelle Steger refutes this on stylistic grounds. Bonde and Maines, "Note sur la fouille de l'église de saint Norbert à Prémontré"; Steger, "L'église de Saint-Jean-Baptiste de Prémontré est-elle l'église construite en 1121 sous la direction de saint Norbert?"

60 See below, pp. 38–44.

61 De Paermentier and Vanderputten, "Aristocratic Patronage, Political Networking and the Shaping of a Private Sanctuary," 319–20.

62 The cartulary contains acts recording gifts and confirmations to the abbey of Prémontré from Louis VI, Louis IX, Philippe IV, Philippe V, Philippe VI (**147**, **150**, **259**, **505–7**, **509**), and especially Louis VII (**75**, **77**, **151**, **160**, **169**). Another tangential royal presence comes from an act issued by a deputy of John, King of Bohemia, less than a month before that ruler's death at the Battle of Crécy (**297**). While the cartulary's structure generally foregrounds acts issued by those of high social rank, those acts issued by royalty are not assigned the primacy one would expect based on comparable cartularies.

63 For fuller discussion of the Coucy family's history, see Dominique Barthélemy, *Les deux âges de la seigneurie banale*; Leson, "'Partout la figure du lion.'"

64 *MGH SS* 23, 823.

65 Enguerrand (d. ca. 1174), son of Enguerrand II, lord of Coucy, and Agnès de Beaugency. Du Chesne, *Histoire généalogique des maisons de Guines*, 348. This Enguerrand was mentioned in the abbey's obituary. Van Waefelghem, *L'Obituaire*, 158.

66 For instance, Enguerrand III was buried there in 1242, and the *Lignages de Coucy* (written 1303) recorded that many of Enguerrand's children who had died in infancy were buried there as well. Du Chesne, *Histoire généalogique des maisons de Guines*, 385. See also Barthélémy, *Les deux âges de la seigneurie banale*, 130–1.

67 As noted above, Raoul I of Coucy's second wife was Alix de Dreux, while his daughter Yolande became the second wife of Robert II, Count of Dreux (and thus her stepmother's sister-in-law). Guyotjeannin, *Le chartrier*, 195. No sustained

scholarly study of the counts of Braine and Dreux has appeared since André Du Chesne's antiquarian study in the early seventeenth century. Du Chesne, *Histoire généalogique de la maison royale de Dreux*.

68 Evers, "L'obituaire de l'Abbaye de Prémontré," 30.

69 "ob spiritualis dilectionis affectum quem habueram erga dominam Agnetem, uxorem domini Andree de Baldimento, que Christo servitura, eisdem sororibus se conjunxerat, apud prefatam curtem Fontenellam, constructo eis ex sumptibus meis monasterio" (**96**).

70 Van Waefelghem, *L'Obituaire*, 205. For a fuller account of the association of the two Agnèses with the Premonstratensians, see Seale, "Well-Behaved Women?"

71 Agnès's contributions to the abbey church of Braine were long overlooked. See Caviness, "Writing Women."

72 "Preterea Emmelina, filia Godesbur, soror praedicti Lisiardi, prefate ecclesie dedit domum de Buciaco ubi fratres commorantur et vineam de Hardilleres pro qua solvitur modium vini et vi sexteriis habet in alodio vineamque de vico de Vals solvente xii sexteriis vini …" AD Aisne, H 761.

73 For more on the genealogical connections and a fuller analysis of these acts, see Wacha, "La Puissance du Choix," 117ff.

74 "… modèle d'organisation du patrimoine ecclésiastique." Bautier, "Les 'courts' de l'Ordre de Prémontré au XIIe siècle," 216.

75 Ghislain Brunel, "Agriculture et équipement agricole à Prémontré (XIIe–XIIIe s.)." More research needs to be done to establish to what extent, if any, Prémontré's *curtis* system was employed by other Premonstratensian houses, and the degree to which the Premonstratensians used the Cistercians' grange system as a template. It is not clear to what extent regional differences in vocabulary about landholdings indicate differences in practice. For instance, the term *grangia* was used very rarely by the brothers of Prémontré, and may have indicated properties with a solely agricultural usage. Bautier, "Les 'courts,'" 218. (See, however, **64**, where the body of a papal confirmation refers to the *grangia* of Fontaine-Raimbaut, but the scribe of Prémontré rubricates the act as concerning the *curtis* of Fontaine-Raimbaut.) Yet the most commonly used terms in the *chartrier* of Sainte-Marie-et-Saint-Yved de Braine (containing documents dating roughly 1135–1250) are *grangia* and *curia*, with *curtis* used just twice. Braine is located thirty kilometres from Prémontré. Guyotjeannin, *Le chartrier*. In the southern Premonstratensian house of La Casedieu, the term *grangia* is used almost exclusively in its surviving documentation, with a dozen examples of the word *domus* also used to describe monastic farms. The term *curtis* is entirely absent from documents produced at La Casedieu. Abadie, "Un temporel monastique dans l'espace médiéval gascon," 153–6. Johannes Mol has suggested that there was a Premonstratensian model which originated at Prémontré but which was subject to adaptation, pointing to the fact that the Premonstratensians of Mariëngaarde (Friesland) and Wittewierum (Groningen) used the term *grangia* rather than *curtis* or *curia* in their thirteenth-century chronicles. Mol, "The Cistercian Model?," 224.

76 For a study of another major Premonstratensian abbey, that of Floreffe, see the work of Georges Despy. He argues that the abbots of Floreffe in the twelfth and thirteenth centuries followed "une politique à long terme … d'investissements délibérés … permettent à une abbaye de Prémontré de tirer parti, en une localité soigneusement choisie, de l'expansion économique" ["a long-term policy … of deliberate investments … permitting a Premonstratensian abbey to take part in economic expansion in a carefully chosen locality"]. Despy, "Les richesses de la terre," 74.

77 Fossier, "La Société Picarde au Moyen Âge," 155.

78 David-Roy, "Les granges monastiques en France aux XIIe et XIIIe siècles," 54; François, "Trois granges médiévales méconnues dans le canton de Crépy-en-Valois (Oise)," 17–19.

79 For a study of Dutch Premonstratensians' townhouses, see Van Bavel, "Schakels tussen abdij en stad."

80 Palaude, "La politique de défrichement de la terre par le verre."

81 "en leur maison de Loirre chascun doit à tous jours perpetuelment la moitié de la Saint Martin d'iver et l'autre moitié à la Pasque" (**258**).

82 Berman, "Later Monastic Economies," in *The Cambridge History of Medieval Monasticism in the Latin West*, vol. 2, 839–40.

83 Fossier, "Première exploitation des ressources picardes," 125.

84 For the social and economic history of Laon and its hinterland during this period, see Saint-Denis, *Apogée d'une cité*.

85 Acts also sometimes specify that payments be made in *bone monete* (good money), *solidi blancorum* (blank or plain *solidi*), or *solidi nigrorum* (debased *solidi*).

86 A statute enacted at the General Chapter of 1290 mandated that all Premonstratensian abbeys should send an annual sum to Prémontré to meet the order's expenses, but these payments often fell into arrears. Lefèvre, *Les statuts de Prémontré réformés*, 91; Knowles, *The Religious Orders in England*, vol. 2, 141–2. In the 1640s, through his position as commendatory abbot of Prémontré, Cardinal Richelieu received an annual income of 8,000 *livres*, roughly a third of the amount he received from the similar benefice he held at Cîteaux. Bergin, *Cardinal Richelieu*, 308.

87 Wacha, "La Puissance du Choix," 287.

88 Lohrmann, "Répartition et création de nouveaux domaines monastiques au XIIe siècle," 243.

89 Following the Seventh Crusade, Louis IX settled a number of people in Laon who were originally from North Africa or the Levant and who had converted from Islam to Christianity. However, this happened roughly fifty years after this act was written. Jordan, *The Apple of His Eye*, 68.

90 Stephanardus appears to be an augmentative form of Stephen. Ménage and Jault, *Dictionnaire etymologique de la langue françoise*, vol. 1, 80.

91 The term "order" is being used here to refer to the Premonstratensians as a discrete subset of monasticism, with its own sense of distinct identity and a set of legal and institutional structures which set it apart from other such subsets of monasticism. The question of when *ordo* began to take on something like this meaning in the Middle Ages, and of precisely what should be understood by terms like *ordo* and *religio* according to the period and the perspective of the author, is one which lies outside the scope of this edition, but see Constable, *Three Studies in Medieval Religious and Social Thought*, 249–341.

92 For Gautier's critique, see Dereine, "Le premier ordo de Prémontré," 87; Dereine, "Saint-Ruf et ses coutumes au XIe et XII siècles."

93 Rupert criticized what he saw as the unseemly haste of Norbert's ordination and his lack of qualifications to preach, although he did praise his preaching ability. *PL* 170: 490, 492, 539–40. For further discussion of Rupert's interactions with Norbert, see Van Engen, *Rupert of Deutz*, 270, 311–12, 324, 337–41.

94 Ardura, *The Order of Prémontré*, 47–8.

95 *PL* 170, cols. 1328–9; Placide Lefèvre, "Deux bulles pontificales," 69.

96 For a fuller discussion of the development of the Premonstratensian houses of what is now northeastern Germany and the semi-independent nature of the circary of Saxony, see Froese, "The Early Norbertines."

97 *MGH SS* 25: 587–9.

98 Froese, "The Early Norbertines," 203.

99 "Cum causa verteretur inter abbatem et ordinem Premonstratensem ex una parte et prepositum Sancte Marie Magdeburgensis [et al. …] ex altera, super eo videlicet quod eidem abbas et ordo Premonstratensis, prepositos prenominatos … asserebant debere convenire ad generale capitulum Premonstratense, et communibus institutionibus ordinis obedire … secundum quod inferius est expressum: videlicet quod omne prepositi supradicti tenebuntur accedere ad generale capitulum Premonstratense de triennio in triennium, et ibidem facere obedientiam domino abbati Premonstatensi" [When the case was resolved between the abbot and order of Prémontré on one hand, and the *prepositus* of Saint Mary of Magdeburg on the other, namely that the abbot and order of Prémontré asserted that the aforesaid *prepositi* must convene at the General Chapter meeting at Prémontré, and obey the community's institutions of the order … following which it was resolved: namely that all the aforesaid *prepositi* promise to come to the General Chapter meeting at Prémontré every three years, and there make obedience to the lord abbot of Prémontré] (**14**). It is clear that this did not happen, since by 1239 neither Prémontré nor Magdeburg was satisfied with what had been happening.

100 "[U]t unusquisque nostrum atque successorum nostrorum succesive in perpetuum quolibet triennio semel veniremus Premonstratum ad capitulum generale … et ibi faciant … obedientiam manualem" [So that each one comes to us and to our successors in perpetuity in whatsoever place it pleases once every three

years to the General Chapter meeting at Prémontré … and there let them make manual obedience) (**16**). The question of how the brothers of Unser Lieben Frauen Magdeburg positioned the agreements within their documentary record is sadly more difficult to answer. At least two cartularies were made there during the Middle Ages and were attested in the sixteenth century, but they and the vast majority of the community's archives have since been lost. When editing a collection of sources relating to the monastery in the late nineteenth century, Gustav Hertel drew on the publications of the antiquarian Charles-Louis Hugo for the text of those acts reproduced in the cartulary of Prémontré as **15–18**. Hertel, ed., *Urkundenbuch des Klosters Unser Lieben Frauen zu Magdeburg*, vii–x, 112–16.

101 Gribbin, *The Premonstratensian Order in Late Medieval England*, 14. While there have been some studies of individual houses, the development of the Premonstratensians as an order in Italy remains largely unassessed, but see Backmund, "Ordo Praemonstratensis in Italia."

102 Lefèvre, *Les statuts de Prémontré réformés*, xviii. These statutes only survive in later copies. A full account of the development of Premonstratensian statutes over time lies outside of the scope of this study, but see Lefèvre and Grauwen, eds., *Les Statuts de Prémontré au milieu du XIIe siècle*; Oberste, "Règle, coutumes et statuts"; Thomas, "Une version des statuts de Prémontré au debut du XIIIe siècle"; Valvekens, "Le chapitre général de Prémontré et les nouveaux statuts de 1505"; Perre, "Die ältesten Klostergesetzgebungen von Prémontré, Oigny, Cîteaux, Klosterrath und Arrouaise und ihre Beziehungen zueinander"; Van Waefelghem, "Les premiers statuts de l'Ordre de Prémontré."

103 The extent to which the changes mandated at Bonneuil can be extrapolated out to other communities of Premonstratensian women is far from certain. For more discussion on the community of Bonneuil and the continued presence of sisters in the Premonstratensian Order into the later thirteenth century and beyond, see Seale, "'Ten Thousand Women,'" 109–11, 309–15.

104 See Dominique Barthélemy, "Monachisme et aristocratie au XIIe siècle."

105 **222** is undated and a later insertion into the cartulary, but based on internal evidence we believe it dates to the 1180s. For further discussion of its relevance to the dating of the manuscript, see p. 60 and p. 452 n. 1.

106 See Gerits, "Les actes de confraternité de 1142 et de 1153 entre Cîteaux et Prémontré."

107 This act was later cancelled and the name of its issuing bishop, Liétard, deliberately erased, perhaps because of his deposition at the Council of Reims, 1134.

108 There are of course exceptions to every rule. The thirteenth-century archbishop of Rouen, Eudes Rigaud, conducted a number of visitations of Premonstratensian houses in Normandy. Davis, *The Holy Bureaucrat*, 69.

109 We might expect to see the bishops of Soissons in the list of most prominent ones, since Prémontré held properties in this diocese as well. Soissons's *curtes* properties, however, are not included in the cartulary. The Laon and Noyon sections of the cartulary contain 158 and 199 charters respectively, but the Soissons section contains only 34 charters.

110 The full nature of Prémontré's medieval manuscript holdings prior to the French Revolution remains frustratingly opaque. Although the cartulary and other administrative documents appear to have remained in its library until Prémontré's dissolution in 1789, Anne Bondéelle-Souchier has noted that the majority of Prémontré's original medieval library, including most of its twelfth- and thirteenth-century scholarly and liturgical manuscripts, was burned in the fifteenth century, likely when the abbey's residents abandoned Prémontré and moved to Floreffe in 1445 due to war. The reconstructed library then burned again in the seventeenth century. A new library was built 1718–28 and the abbey sought to reassemble some of its original manuscripts in the eighteenth century, but these efforts were not wholly successful. Bondéelle-Souchier, *Bibliothèques de l'Ordre*, vol. 2, 195, 229. Given that the cartulary and the bulk of the charter archives survived both fires, they were likely located somewhere in the abbey other than the library, avoiding the worst of the damage. However, it may be that Prémontré's original papal charters were kept in the library and thus destroyed during one of the fires, since we have been unable to locate originals for any of the papal acts included in the cartulary.

111 This order was, however, unevenly observed, and led to further dispersal and loss of archival materials. Delisle, *Le cabinet des manuscrits de la Bibliothèque nationale*, vol. 2, 29. Even once a manuscript was transferred to a library or archive, its survival was not secured. In his 1885 description of the holdings of the Bibliothèque municipale de Soissons, Auguste Molinier noted that a number of manuscripts from Prémontré which had been catalogued there in the 1820s had since vanished. Molinier, *Catalogue général des manuscrits des bibliothèques publiques de France*, vol. 3, 70.

112 More than 500 loose parchment charters survive from the abbey's original archive. The majority are AD Aisne, H 737–H 845, and AD Oise, H 5887–H 6004. A number of them, however, can also be found in AN L 995, 1–150; BnF Collection Picardie 290, 1–56; SAHSS, nos. 1–28 and 193–7; AM Metz, Salis II, nos. 241–8; and AD Somme, 20 H_SC_1–20 H_SC_19, 20 H 5–20 H 19. Since more than 500 original charters survive, 237 of which appear in the cartulary, we can say that on average, for every surviving original charter included in the cartulary, another surviving charter was omitted. Since the cartulary has 507 charters, approximately 270 charters no longer survive, and thus we can add this number to the existing 500+ that do. At a minimum, Prémontré's archives most likely contained more than 750 loose parchment charters in the 1230s.

113 The sisters associated with Prémontré lived at other dependent houses such as Bonneuil. For more on women scribes in the Middle Ages, see Beach, *Women as Scribes*; Blanton, O'Mara, and Stoop, eds., *Nuns' Literacies in Medieval Europe: The Hull Dialogue*; Blanton, O'Mara, and Stoop, eds., *Nuns' Literacies in Medieval Europe: The Kansas City Dialogue*; Blanton, O'Mara, and Stoop, eds., *Nuns' Literacies in Medieval Europe: The Antwerp Dialogue*; Cyrus, *The Scribes for Women's Convents in Late Medieval Germany*; Radini et al., "Medieval Women's Early Involvement in Manuscript Production Suggested by Lapis Lazuli Identification in Dental Calculus."

114 As scribe, rubricator, and corrector, the person who executed the writing of Prémontré's cartulary is henceforth referred to as the cartulary maker. See pp. 44–56.

115 The folio following fol. 12 has been numbered fol. 12bis since it was skipped in the original foliation.

116 Holes appear in folios throughout the cartulary, from fol. 18 to fol. 112. Two-thirds of the holes appear in the second half of the cartulary.

117 The rebinding of the cartulary of Prémontré is discussed below on pp. 69–70.

118 Ruling lines were made using drypoint in the early medieval period. For this method, a stylus with a dull point at one end created a visible indentation in the folio as it was dragged along a straightedge. After the eleventh century, many manuscripts were ruled in lead point, or graphite. After the thirteenth century, ink became a common material for ruling manuscripts. Clemens and Graham, *Introduction to Manuscript Studies*, 16–17.

119 Most quires in the cartulary of Prémontré consist of four pieces of parchment, called bifolia. Folded in half, these four bifolia make eight folios, each with a recto and verso side. The foliation that appears in the cartulary of Prémontré mostly dates to shortly before the early seventeenth century, sometime before the manuscript received its current binding. Arabic numerals appear in black ink in the upper right corner of the recto of all folios until about fol. 55, after which point the foliation is written in a nineteenth- or early twentieth-century hand. The later rewriting of folio numbers 55–112bis is likely due to those folios having been cropped during the rebinding process and losing their original numbering.

120 IRHT, "Notice, Cartulaire de Prémontré," 1.

121 See below pp. 39–40 for how the lettered numbering system of folios inside quire *q* helps to ascertain the date of cartulary completion.

122 The reordering of the quires is discussed on pp. 44–56.

123 The reasoning for the rebinding is discussed in more detail on pp. 69–70. IRHT, "Notice, Cartulaire de Prémontré," 1.

124 IRHT, "Notice, Cartulaire de Prémontré," 4.

125 Arguments for the date of completion of the *noyau primitif* and evidence of later readers can be found on pp. 44–56 and 67–70.

126 BM Soissons, fols. 6r–7r. The first act of the original thirteenth-century cartulary is now **24**, due to a later reorganization and rebinding of the manuscript.

127 For discussion of the *curtes*, see pp. 19–20.

128 The signatures for *qiii* and *qiiii* are not visible because their right corners have been cut. Fol. 111r remains at the end of the cartulary, in its original position. Its content carries on from the end of fol. 3v, and thus it originally sat inside the final quire. It appears that the folio holding the signature *qi* is missing from the cartulary. If so, then the final quire originally consisted of five folios, which would be unusual for the cartulary of Prémontré. Future codicological work may help clarify the anomaly in the first folio's signature.

129 This is argued in more detail on pp. 57–61.

130 Prémontré's cartulary contains copies of four papal inventories, one each for Honorius II, Celestine II, Eugene III, and Clement III. All of these inventories list and confirm Prémontré's possessions in a similar order. Instead of following the order of properties as stated in these inventories, however, the cartulary of Prémontré's Laon section follows a slightly different one, one that mirrors the sequence of *curtes* as noted in the 1158 charter. The 1158 charter lists Prémontré's properties in Soupir, Crépy, Versigny, Ferrières, Valécourt, Coucy-la-Ville, Nogent, and Hannape. The sequence is almost precisely replicated in the cartulary section for the diocese of Laon: Soupir, Crépy, Versigny, Ferrières, Valécourt, Merlieu, Nogent, and Hannape. For more on the internal structure of a cartulary, see Berkhofer, "Inventaires de biens et proto-comptabilités dans le nord de la France (XIe–début XIIe siècle)."

131 The cartulary of Saint-Denis likewise mirrors the sequence of its original charter archives. "La répartition et la numérotation des actes dans le Cartulaire blanc suivent bien l'ordre qui a été donné au chartrier dans les décennies précédents la compilation …" [The distribution and numbering of the acts in the *Cartulaire blanc* follow the archival order which was created in the decades before the [*cartulary*] compilation …]. Guyotjeannin, "La tradition de l'ombre," 89.

132 For surviving charters from Trosly-Loire, see AD Aisne, H 832; for Tinselve, see SAHSS, no. 194; from Valpriez, see AD Aisne, H 754.

133 Most of the original charters relevant to Prémontré's Laonnois properties are at the AD Aisne and the AN; those from the Noyonnais are mostly held at the AD Oise. Although the majority of original charters from Bonneuil are held at the AD Oise, the original *curtis* of Bonneuil is now located just over the border in the modern-day department of the Somme.

134 The numbering system that appears on the back of archival charters does not correspond with the numbering system used to sequence charters in the cartulary's tables of contents.

135 The few exceptions indicate one charter with *Hamiaus* noted on the back, AD Oise, H 6000 (1195), and three with *Noion*: AD Oise, H 6052 (1142); AD Oise, 6053 (twelfth century), AD Oise, 6053 (1178).

136 In the third instance, the scribe notes that the same charter existed in two locations, but was written in one (**298**). The original is AD Oise, Hs 1368. Another copy is AD Oise, H 5987, but it is not identical and contains phrases found neither in the B text nor in the cartulary.

137 The comparison of original charters and cartulary copies shows that while the Prémontré cartulary maker may have abridged a witness list for the purposes of saving time and space, he never added or falsified information in the cartulary copy. For more, see Berkhofer, *Day of Reckoning*, 11–53; Heidecker, "30 June 1047," 87; Framond, "Chartes et notices relatives à la fondation de Saint-Sauveur de Séverac et sa donation à Saint-Chaffre-du-Monastier."

138 Ker, "From 'above Top Line' to 'below Top Line.'"

139 See the section below where the date of cartulary completion is argued to be 1239/40, pp. 57–67.

140 This calculation assumes ideal working conditions, i.e., six days a week at least six hours a day, which would be a challenge given the number of feast days in the liturgical calendar and required participation in prayer cycles. With a scribe completing approximately one line per minute, as suggested by Michael Gullick, the cartulary of Prémontré would have taken a total of fifty-six days, each with an average of six hours' work. This does not include filling ink pots, pricking and ruling pages, binding, and other necessary components. Gullick, "How Fast Did Scribes Write?" It is possible that the Prémontré cartulary maker copied into the early evening using candlelight, as there is evidence of wax residue on fol. 36r, but this may have just as well come from a reader who was reading after dark in the centuries that followed.

141 See pp. 57–67.

142 There are three subdivisions in the Laon section (the *curtes* of Versigny, Valécourt, and Hannape) where the subdivision starts on the first folio of a new quire. Two of them occur in quires 4–8, which show multiple signs of later interventions. It is quite possible that in their original format, these two subdivisions began with a new quire; but it is equally possible that they did not.

143 There is another occasion where the scribe notes two copies of the same charter (**298**). See note 136.

144 There is no table of contents, however, for the cartulary's papal section or the seigneurial section.

145 Given the varying amount of space left at the end of each section, it is interesting to ponder how far into the future the cartulary maker envisioned this cartulary would serve. Perhaps he envisioned that another cartulary would be constructed after two to three decades. If indeed another medieval cartulary was constructed, it no longer survives, nor does any secondary evidence that alludes to it. However, there is an eighteenth-century register, BM Laon, MS 518, "Cartulaire de l'abbaye de Prémontré, par Louis de Vinay, religieux; divisé en trois parties, avec des tables," as well as some extracts and notes made ca. 1700 by the antiquarian Étienne Baluze, BnF Coll. Baluze 51, fols. 132r–143r.

146 **397–403** appear on fols. 95v–96r; **441–7** appear on fols. 102r–102v.

147 AD Oise, H 6038 (**399**); AD Oise, H 6005 (**403**). Original charters for **397**, **398**, **400**, **401**, and **402** also survive, but are held today in two different repositories. These originals show no stains and were almost certainly not those being used in the thirteenth-century scriptorium for cartulary transcription. It was common medieval practice to make at least two copies of a given charter, one for each party involved. The collections held at the BnF and AM Metz are likely original charters that did not stay at Prémontré, but went with the other party or were held at other Premonstratensian communities. This is supported by the fact that two surviving charters relate to the cartulary act **389**: AD Oise, H 6003, which has a stain and was issued by the abbot and chapter of Prémontré, and AM Metz, Salis II.245, no. 11, which has no stain and was issued by the lord in question, Jean de Bethancourt. BnF, Coll. Picardie 290, no. 1 (**397**); BnF, Coll. Picardie 290, no. 8 (**398**); BnF, Coll. Picardie 290, no. 36 (**400**); AM Metz, Salis II.247, no. 1 (**401**); AM Metz, Salis II.248, no. 9 (**402**).

148 This is supported by the fact that **441–7** appear mostly in the reverse order of **397–403**.

149 The number of days is based on Michael Gullick's calculation that it took a scribe approximately one minute to write one line of text. See p. 48 and note 140.

150 The table of contents for the Noyon section includes rubrics for both sets of the seven charters and must have been filled in after the section was finished. In this case, the number of lines were left blank before the cartulary maker began copying the charters of the lengthy section. The cartulary maker filled them in after the section transcriptions were complete.

151 The four dots underneath the phrase "quas iam dicti fratres" indicate to the reader that these four words do not belong in the text.

152 **211** is the only act where the scribe left room for the rubric, but no rubric was added. Given that the space appears to be squeezed between two charters, it may be that the scribe simply overlooked it.

153 Additional material evidence confirms that rubrication took place after all the charter content had been copied, in line with normal practice. Two interesting charters from the final quire of the cartulary have both been cancelled in red ink. In other words, both have a red X placed across their entire contents, and neither has a rubricated summary. It appears that as the cartulary maker was rubricating the last quire, he realized that these two charters were erroneously included in the cartulary and cancelled them instead of providing them with a rubric. The first of these is a letter to Hugues [I/II?], abbot of Prémontré, from the chapter of the Benedictine abbey of Saint-Pierre de la Tour du Puy (**500**). The abbot and chapter ask to affiliate Saint-Pierre's church at La Doue with the Premonstratensian order. It is not clear why this act was cancelled. The reasoning behind cancelling the second charter (**502**) is more apparent. Liétard, bishop of Cambrai, who

issued the charter in 1132, was deposed at the Council of Reims in 1134 on the basis of charges of serious misconduct. Ott, "'Both Mary and Martha,'" 157. Not only has the charter been cancelled, but Liétard's name and the charter date have also been entirely erased.

154 We know that the cartulary maker still intended to add the decorated initials, even after 1250. Each of the four charters on fols. 34–5 – additions made in 1250 or shortly thereafter – has a space reserved for its initial. For more on these four charters, see pp. 58–60.

155 The IRHT dates the cartulary to 1239–50 (https://telma-repertoires.irht.cnrs.fr/cartulr/notice/8368), while the BM Soissons dates it to 1266–87 (https://ccfr.bnf.fr/portailccfr/ark:/06871/004D09020008).

156 See pp. 23–5 above.

157 There may be several reasons for this, not least the two fires that occurred in the abbey, one in the fifteenth century and the other in the seventeenth century. See note 110.

158 Gervais's Latin rhetorical skills were admirable enough for his secretary or amanuensis to copy some 150 of his letters. This register and the originals of Gervais's letters have all been lost, but a later medieval manuscript copy and two seventeenth-century print editions survive. The letters have not received much scholarly attention. For details of Gervais's career, see Cheney, "Gervase, Abbot of Prémontré."

159 Plouvier, *L'Abbaye de Prémontré aux XVIIe et XVIIIe siècles*, 35–8; Le Paige, *Bibliotheca*, vol. 2, 929.

160 See note 102.

161 Six papal bulls issued by Pope Gregory IX in 1234 and 1235 appear in the cartulary (**28**, **42**, **43**, **45**, **46**, **59**). Two of the six (**28**, **42**) are dated in the cartulary text to 1234, per old style dating when the New Year began at Easter, but date to 1235 in the new style.

162 The other two acts dated to 1236 appear in the Soissons section (**293**) and in the Noyon section (**460**).

163 The hiatus corresponds exactly with work on the revised statutes. The content of these charters and its significance are discussed below. See pp. 60–1.

164 These four 1250 charters are likely the reason behind the IRHT's suggestion of a possible completion date as late as 1250.

165 It may be that the addition of the two new folios expunged existing content, although it is uncertain what that content would have been. All charters noted in the Soupir section appear in their correct sequence in the section. More likely, it may be that in a first attempt either the wrong charters were added to the end of the quire or their transcription went badly, so much so that the two original folios were simply cut out and replaced with new ones and pristine transcriptions. In either case, the desire to copy the four charters into the cartulary would have precipitated the intervention ca. 1250.

166 For more detail, see Wacha, "The Cartulary of the Abbey of Prémontré," 131–2.

167 We argue that **222** dates to the 1180s, based on the dates of the abbatiate of one of the act's co-principals, Hélie of Nogent-sous-Coucy. See also the later copy in the seventeenth-century cartulary-chronicle of Nogent-sous-Coucy, AD Aisne, H 325, fols. 45–45v, which likewise suggests an 1180s date.

168 "… huic chirographum curavimus annotari … anno Domini 1240." Hugo, *Annales*, vol. 4, col. 31.

169 A second charter, **508**, is dated 1240, but it was copied into the cartulary after 1240 and in a cursive script. Its date of original composition therefore cannot definitively narrow down the date of completion for the cartulary's *noyau primitif.*

170 **16**, **17**, and **18** (fols. 2v–3v), all dated October 1239. A fourth 1239 charter, dating to December (**455**; fol. 104r), confirms Prémontré's possession of a house at La Ferrole. It remained in the final bifolium at the end of the cartulary and was never moved to the front.

171 The substance of the following argument also appears in Wacha, "The Cartulary of the Abbey of Prémontré."

172 See above for a fuller discussion of the history of Magdeburg and Prémontré, pp. 23–5.

173 The four 1239 charters include the three copies of the resolution (**16–18**), as well as the letter sent from the bishop of Paris in anticipation of the resolution (**15**).

174 The December 1239 charter, which addresses Prémontré's house at Ferrole, was not moved to the front of the cartulary and remains in the final bifolium at the end of the cartulary.

175 "Ad armarium pertinet libros custodire, et, si sciverit, emendare, armarium librorum cum necesse fuerit claudere et aperire, lectiones si ad hoc ydoneus fuerit terminare; quid in ecclesia legendum, et quando incipiende sunt hystorie cum cantore, si necesse fuerit, concordare, et quod ibi minus legitur legentibus in refectorio demonstrare; libros mutuo accipere, cum necesse fuerit, et nostros querentibus accomodare, sed non sine licentia abbatis et memoriali competenti. Debet etiam notitiam habere et numerum, quantum potest, librorum qui sunt ei ad custodiendum commissi." Lefèvre, *Les statuts de Prémontré réformés*, 49–50. See also Gerits, "A propos de l'organisation des bibliothèques médiévales de l'Ordre de Prémontré en Angleterre et en Allemagne"; Lefèvre, "L'ancienne bibliothèque de l'abbaye d'Averbode d'après les sources d'Archives." The abbey must also have produced copies of these revised statutes, but no contemporary manuscript copies survive. Apart from the administrative documents addressed in this edition, we know of no surviving manuscripts that can be traced with certainty to Prémontré's thirteenth-century scriptorium. The thirteenth-century manuscripts attributed to Prémontré and held at the Bibliothèque municipale de Soissons may or may not have been part of the abbey's original library. For a list of these, see Appendix 1.

176 These cartularies are those of Valécourt (BnF, MS nouv. acq. lat. 938), Tinselve (SAHS, no. 193), and Valpriez (AD Aisne, H 753). That the three cartularies are

held today in separate locations indicates that when they were dispersed after the French Revolution they likely ended up in the hands of different people. The Valécourt cartulary at one time belonged in the Thomas Phillipps collection. Phillipps was a nineteenth-century English bibliophile and book collector. The BnF acquired the manuscript in 1908. Omont, *Catalogue des manuscrits latins et français de la collection Phillipps acquis en 1908 pour la Bibliothèque nationale*, 40. The Tinselve cartulary was presumably donated to the SAHS by an antiquarian member, perhaps the Abbé Pécheur who wrote a description for the *Bulletin de la Société archéologique de Soissons*: Pécheur, "Cartulaire de Tinselve." The Valpriez cartulary was in private hands until 1870, when a certain Monsieur F. Le Sérurier donated it to the AD Aisne.

177 The modern place name is Valécourt, but the BnF has catalogued the cartulary under a medieval spelling, Walescours.

178 We know that the *curtis* cartularies were made at the abbey of Prémontré because of a flyleaf in the cartulary of Tinselve, a piece of scrap paper that must have come from the abbey of Prémontré since it lists the summaries of letters sent to various Premonstratensian affiliates from the abbot of Prémontré. Seale and Wacha, "Spare No Scrap." For more on cartulary creation and production, see Berkhofer, *Day of Reckoning*, 73–89; Tucker, *Reading and Shaping Medieval Cartularies*, 13–25.

179 All cartularies appear to have been written by one scribe. Today, the Valécourt cartulary has 8 folios. It would have originally contained 17 acts, but the table of contents is missing, as well as Act 1 through the beginning of Act 6. The cartulary only contains the end of Act 6 through Act 17. The Tinselve cartulary has 14 folios but is missing its second quire. The cartulary would have originally held a table of contents and 18 acts, but today Acts 1 through the beginning of act 10 are missing. The Valpriez cartulary is complete. It has 34 folios and holds 29 charter texts, but only 28 acts, as one was duplicated. For a digitized copy, see the BVMM: https://bvmm.irht.cnrs.fr/mirador/index.php?manifest=https://bvmm.irht.cnrs.fr/iiif/32644/manifest. All three cartularies have the number of the act noted in the rubric, either at the end of the rubric or in the margin.

180 The three cartularies are all in octavo format. Valécourt measures 225/235 × 160 mm; Tinselve measures 210 × 145 mm; Valpriez measures 210/220 × 150/170 mm. Columns in the Tinselve and Valpriez cartularies contain 23 lines each; the columns in the Valécourt cartulary contain 25 lines. All of the cartularies are ruled in lead point.

181 The Valécourt cartulary has no later charter additions, and has only one place name written in the margins on fol. 3r. The cartulary of Tinselve contains two added folios at the end, in a late thirteenth- or early fourteenth-century hand, that list fourteen of the *curtis*'s revenues. Any marginalia in this cartulary is from a nineteenth-century archivist making reference to original charters. The Valpriez cartulary, held in the AD Aisne, refers to two originals from the same archives, but in a nineteenth-century hand. The word *dixme* is written in the margins

of three separate folios and the only evidence of contemporary marginalia is a fourteenth-century note on fol. 3r that clarifies the charter content. No later charter transcriptions appear.

182 See pp. 58–9.

183 The first quire is missing from the Valécourt cartulary today, however, which contained copies of its first five and half charters. BnF, nouv. acq. lat. 938.

184 Because the Tinselve and Valécourt cartularies contain no charters dated between 1232 and 1250, it may be that the *curtis* cartulary maker copied these two cartularies shortly after 1232, or perhaps constructed them alongside the Valpriez cartulary after 1251, but used an exemplar that had been prepared in the 1230s for the construction of Cartulary A.

185 As noted, all charters of the Valécourt cartulary appear in the Valécourt section of Cartulary A. No charters from the Tinselve cartulary appear in Cartulary A. Three charters concerning Valpriez appear in both Cartulary A and Valpriez's cartulary; two are original to the Valpriez cartulary but are fourteenth-century additions to Cartulary A: **263** and **296**. The third charter figures among those grouped under the diocese of Soissons in Cartulary A: **280**. Of the twenty-eight acts present in Valpriez's cartulary, only one appears in Prémontré's original thirteenth-century Cartulary A. Lalanne, *Le Cartulaire de Valpriez*, 11.

186 Unfortunately, we do not know exactly where the *curtis* cartularies were kept after they were completed. They may have stayed at the abbey or been distributed to their respective *curtes*.

187 See pp. 19–25.

188 "Quere novam kartam de justicia domus nostre de le Ferrole ante intitulationem kartaram Bonolii ad tale signum." BM Soissons, MS 7, fol. 104r.

189 This act concerns the charging of one Antoine Voulcet with collecting the tithe at Prémontré's *curtis* of Crépy. While placed at the very end of the Soupir section in the diocese of Laon on fol. 35v, the act directly precedes the section for Crépy that begins on fol. 36r, once again showing an attempt to maintain a certain locational integrity in the cartulary's three geographical sections.

190 Another important Premonstratensian house, that of Saint-Paul de Verdun, produced a cartulary (BM Verdun, MS 751) ca. 1246–55 during a period of major reconstruction at that abbey following a devastating fire, and rebound and reorganized the manuscript, ca. 1640–6/7. Whether these chronological similarities with the cartulary project at Prémontré are more than mere coincidence requires further study. Évrard, "Écrire à Verdun au XIIIe siècle," 201–3.

191 Petit, *La spiritualité*, 98.

192 This reform, known as the reform of the *Antique* (or *Ancien*) *Rigueur*, which sought to return the order's practices to a more austere twelfth-century model and which eventually led to internal cleavages in the order, was championed by the abbot of Sainte-Marie-au-Bois, Servais de Lairuelz (1560–1631), and was given permanence in 1617 when, despite the objections of Prémontré's abbot,

Pope Paul V issued a bull establishing an autonomous Congregation of Ancient Observance within the Premonstratensian Order. For more on the reforms pioneered by de Lairuelz, see Delcambre, *Servais de Lairuelz et la réforme des prémontrés*.

193 This was largely the result of pressure imposed by Philip II of Spain. See Alcina-Rossello, "Les Prémontrés en Espagne au XVIe siècle: réforme et sécession"; Gaztambide, "La reforma de los Premonstratenses españoles del siglo XVI."

194 Rather than being elected by the community, commendatory abbots were appointed by the king to administer a religious house's temporal holdings. Even if they were members of the clergy, commendatory abbots were seldom members of the houses over which they ruled, and were largely absent. Between 1535 and 1572, Prémontré was governed by two such commendatory abbots, to whom a nineteenth-century historian would refer as the abbey's scourges (*les fléaux de Prémontré*). Taïée, "Prémontré," 210. A return to free elections in 1572 installed the reform-minded and prudent Jean des Pruets as abbot. Van Dijck, "L'état général de l'ordre de Prémontré au XVIe siècle," 44–61. His two immediate successors were also directly elected, but in 1636 Cardinal Richelieu was made Prémontré's commendatory abbot.

195 For more on cartularies as active documents, see Tucker, *Reading and Shaping Medieval Cartularies*.

196 We have largely accorded with the system suggested in Vieillard and Guyotjeannin, eds., *Conseils pour l'édition des textes médiévaux, Fascicule 1*, 48.

THE CARTULARY OF PRÉMONTRÉ

1

March, 1202. Le Quesnoy.

Baudouin,[1] *count of Flanders and Hainaut, exempts the brothers of the Premonstratensian Order from paying* theloneum *or* wionagium *on any goods they bring to buy or sell in his lands.*

A. Cartulary of Prémontré, fol. 1r.
B. Original not found.
EDITION: Le Paige, *Bibliotheca*, 761.
REGISTER: Bréquigny, *Table chronologique*, vol. 3, 326.

Karta Balduini Flandrensis comitis de elemosina quam fecit ecclesie super wionagiis.

[E]go Balduinus, Flandrensis et Hainonensis comes. Notum fieri volo tam futuris quam presentibus quod pro salute anime mee et Marie karissime uxoris mee, et antecessorum meorum ac deinceps successorum, omnes fratres Premonstratensis ordinis de omnibus rebus suis propriis, quas vendendas duxerint vel quas ad usus suas emptas reduxerint in terra mea, quantum ad me pertinet, ab omni theloneo et wionagio per totam terram meam ubique liberos [sint]. Ut autem hoc ratum et stabile maneat in perpetuum, eisdem fratribus presentem contuli paginam sigilli mei appensione munitam. Actum apud Haimmonis Quercetum, anno dominice incarnationis M° CC° secundo, mense martio.

1 Baudouin VI of Hainaut/IX of Flanders (1172–ca. 1205), son of Baudouin V of Hainaut and Marguerite I of Flanders, and later first Latin emperor of Constantinople.

2

August, 1190.

Philippe,[1] *count of Flanders and Vermandois, exempts the brothers of the church of Prémontré from payment of* theloneum, pedagium, *and* traversum *for all goods that they might transport by land or by water through his lands for their own use, on condition that after the death of the count and his wife Mahaut [Teresa of Portugal],*[2] *the abbey will annually celebrate a service in their memory. (See 7.)*[3]

A. Cartulary of Prémontré, fol. 1r.
B. Original not found.
EDITION: Le Paige, *Bibliotheca*, 760–1.
REGISTER: Bréquigny, *Table chronologique*, vol. 3, 127.

Karta comitis Flandrensis Philipi et Viromandensis de wionagiis.

[E]go Philippus, Flandrensis et Viromandensis comes. Notum fieri volo quod pro salute anime mee et antecessorum meorum ac deinceps successorum ecclesiam Premonstrati liberam dimisi et quitavi per universam terram meam, ab omni consuetudine et exactione thelonei, pedagii, et traversi, ex hiis dumtaxat, que ad usum fratrum ibidem Deo servientium deferentur tam per terram quam per aquam, ea videlicet conditione quod fratres ecclesie Premonstrati, audito obitu meo et uxoris mee Mehadis, pro nobis servitium celebrabunt, et singulis annis memoriam habebunt. Ut igitur hec ecclesie inmunitas et concessa libertas rata semper et inconvulsa permaneat, presentem ipsi concessi paginam, tam sigilli mei impressionem quam testium subnotatione munitam. S. G.,[4] Brugensis et Sancti Audemari prepositi ac Flandrensis cancellarii. S. G.,[5]

---

1 Philippe I d'Alsace (1143–1191), count of Flanders, son of Thierry d'Alsace, count of Flanders, and his second wife Sibylle d'Anjou.

2 Teresa of Portugal (d. 1218), daughter of Afonso I of Portugal and Mathilde de Savoie.

3 This act was confirmed by *vidimus* in 1454. SAHSS, *casier* 1, no. 17.

4 Gérard d'Alsace (d. 1206), illegitimate son of Thierry d'Alsace, count of Flanders, was *prepositus* at Bruges and chancellor of Flanders. Verhulst and de Hemptinne, "Le chancelier de Flandre sous les comtes de la maison d'Alsace (1128–1191)," 303–4.

5 Gérard de Messines was notary and *sigillarius comitis* of the count of Flanders, 1169–81, and *prepositus* of Lille, ca. 1183–ca. 1191. Reusens, "Les chancelleries inferieures en Belgique depuis leur origins jusqu'au XIIIe siècle," 111; Verhulst and de Hemptinne, "Le chancelier de Flandre sous les comtes de la maison d'Alsace (1128–1191)," 308.

prepositi Insule. S. G.,[6] abbatis Sancti Martini Laudunensis. S. W.,[7] abbatis de Viromandensis. Actum anno Domini M° C° XC°, mense augusto.

3

February, 1222.

Raoul,[1] *count of Soissons, grants in alms to the church of Prémontré an exemption from paying* pedagium *and* wionagium *on his land for the passage of wine and other goods up to the amount of 60* solidi Suessionensium. *If the* pedagium *and* wionagium *surpass this amount, Prémontré will pay the difference. In return for these exemptions, Prémontré will celebrate a service on the anniversary of the death of Raoul and the countess Ada, his wife.*[2] *(See duplicate* ***282; 496****.)*

A. Cartulary of Prémontré, fol. 1r.
B. Original not found.

Karta Radulphi comitis Suessionensis de libertate wionagiorum per terram suam usque ad LX[a] solidorum.

[E]go Radulphus, comes Suessionensis, tam presentibus quam futuris. Notum facio quod ego divine remunerationis intuitu et ob salutare remedium anime mee et illustris mulieris Ade comitisse Suessionensis uxoris mee, et antecessorum meorum necnon et liberorum meorum ecclesie Premonstratensis quam sincera dilectione conplector, nomine elemosine concessi et dedi quod ipsa ecclesia de propriis vinis suis et propriis rebus suis cum propriis vecturis suis annuatim poterit ducere per wionagia mea usque ad summam sexaginta solidorum monete Suessionensis absque aliqua pedagii vel wionagii solutione. Et si contigerit quod eadem ecclesia per wionagia mea de propriis vinis suis vel de propriis rebus suis duxerit plus quam summa prenotata sexaginta solidorum contineat, dicta ecclesia de supercrescenti pedagium vel wionagium suum persolvet. Predictis siquidem est addendum quod memorata ecclesia mihi et

6 Guy (or Gautier) d'Epernay, abbot of the Premonstratensian abbey of Saint-Martin de Laon, 1189–91. *MP* II, 509.

7 Gilbert II, abbot of the Premonstratensian abbey of Vermand, 1181–4. *MP* II, 427.

1 Raoul I, count of Soissons (d. 1235), son of Raoul, castellan of Nesle and Bruges, and Gertrude, *neptis* of Thierry, count of Flanders. Newman, *Seigneurs*, vol. 1, 64.

2 Ada d'Avesnes (d. aft. 1249), daughter of Jacques I, lord of Avesnes, Leuze, and Condé, and Adèle de Guise.

prenominate uxori mee, divine pietatis mediante intuitu, concessit anniversaria nostra annis singulis facienda. Quod ut ratum habeatur, presentem paginam sigilli mei munimine tradidi communitam. Actum anno gratie M° CC° XX° II°, mense februario.

4

1178

Clérembaud[1] *de Vendeuil confirms the gift made in alms to the church of Prémontré by his father (also named Clérembaud) of an exemption from payment of all* wionagium *that he would normally receive within his lands.*

A. Cartulary of Prémontré, fol. 1r.
B. Original, AN, L 995, no. 40, previously sealed.

Karta Clarenbaldi de Vendolio de wionagio per totam terram suam et dominium suum.

[E]go Clarenbaldus[2] de Vendolio.[3] Notum fieri volo tam presentibus quam futuris quod Clarenbaldus,[4] pater meus, ob remedium anime sue et predecessorum suorum contulit in elemosinam ecclesie Premonstratensis wionagium per totam terram et dominium suum liberum quod ab aliis accipere solebat. Ego vero, cupiens bonum quod pater meus incepit pia devotione manutenere, firma perseveratione similiter ob remedium anime mee et predecessorum meorum, idem wionagium eidem ecclesie recognovi et concessi. Quod ut ratum permaneat et inconvulsum, scripto commendare et sigilli mei impressione munire curavi. Huius rei testes sunt: dominus Radulphus[5,6] de Couciaco,[7] Johannes Rivarz, Gerardus maior, Hugo de Quinci,[8] Petrus[9] de Gondran,[10] Willelmus[11]

1 Likely Clérembaud IV, lord of Vendeuil, son of Clérembaud III, lord of Vendeuil. Melleville, *DH*, vol. 2, 412; Larive, *Essai historique sur la commune de Vendeuil*, 40–1.

2 Clarembaldus *B*.

3 Venduil *B*.

4 Clarembaldus *B*.

5 Radulfus *B*.

6 Raoul I, lord of Coucy (d. 1191), son of Enguerrand II, lord of Coucy, and Agnès de Beaugency.

7 Cociaco *B*.

8 Quincy, cant. Coucy-le-Château, https://dicotopo.cths.fr/places/P34442927.

9 One of a number of members of the seigneurial family of Condren (cant. Chauny, https://dicotopo.cths.fr/places/P28107866) by that name. Newman, *Seigneurs*, vol. 2, 203–4.

10 Gundran *B*.

11 Guillaume, knight of Montescourt-Lizerolles (cant. Saint-Simon, https://dicotopo.cths.fr/places/P52353952), is attested in the 1190s–1200s. Melleville, *DH*, vol. 2, 121.

de Montescurt, Walbertus Crassus, Hugo primo natus Muillier,[12] Radulfus maior. Actum anno incarnati verbi M° C° LXX° octavo.[13]

5

1138. Choir of the church at Prémontré.

Barthélemy,[1] *bishop of Laon, confirms an act in which Enguerrand [II de Coucy]*[2] *on the day of his departure for Jerusalem gave to the church of Prémontré the payments of* vinagium *and* naulum *that he receives from property transfers within his lands, except on those transfers intended for resale. Enguerrand's mother Mélisende, his brother Robert, and his sister Mélisende consent.*

A. Cartulary of Prémontré, fols. 1r–1v.

B. Original, SAHSS, *casier* 1, no. 5, previously sealed with a double strip of parchment.

EDITION: Dufour-Malbezin, *Actes*, 284–5; Slack, *Crusade Charters, 1138–1270*, 2–3; *Chartae Galliae*, no. 208327, http://telma.irht.cnrs.fr/outils/chartae-galliae/charte208327/; "Charter of Enguerran II de Coucy, 1138," Independent Crusaders Project, https://independentcrusadersproject.ace.fordham.edu/items/show/2321.

Karta episcopi Laudunensis de confirmatione et testimonio elemosine wionagii et nauli que dedit Ingelrannus, filius Thome de Couci, ecclesie Premonstrati.

[I]n nomine sancte et individue Trinitatis. Ego Bartholomeus, Dei gratia Laudunensis episcopus. Notum fieri volo tam futuris quam presentibus quod Ingelrannus, filius Thome de Couci,[3] ob remedium anime sue et patris et matris sue et predecessorum suorum Premonstrate ecclesie perpetuo remisit winagium et naulum in omni loco terre sue ubi ab alienis accipiebatur, nisi de re que ematur ut iterum venalis exponenda deferatur. Facta est autem ista concessio anno incarnati verbi M° C° XXX° octavo,[4] epacta VII[a], indictione prima,[5] concurrente

12 Muilliez *B*.

13 VIII° *B*.

1 Barthélemy de Jur (d. 1158), son of Conon, lord of Grandson and La Sarraz, and Ada de Roucy; first subdeacon and then treasurer of Reims, later bishop of Laon, 1113–51.

2 Enguerrand II de Coucy (d. ca. 1149), son of Thomas de Marle, lord of Coucy, and his third wife, Mélisende de Crécy-sur-Serre.

3 Coci *B*.

4 VIII° *B*.

5 I[a] *B*.

V°, in choro eiusdem Premonstrate ecclesie ea die qua ad peregrinandum exiit Jherusalem,[6] astante fratre suo, Roberto, et matre sua, Milissende, et sorore eiusdem nominis Milissende, quorum voluntate et assensu hoc donum factum est, astantibus etiam multis hominibus et de suis nobilioribus de quibus quosdam annotare curavimus. Quorum ista sunt nomina: Wido[7] Castellanus, Ado[8] de Guni, et Iterus[9] frater eius, Robertus[10] Vitulus, Joiffridus et frater eius Sarracenus,[11,12] Gerardus Auris.[13] Quod ut ratum et inconvulsum permaneat, sigilli nostri impressione corroboravimus. Et tam nostram quam domini Pape excommunicationem predicto Ingelranno favente, apposuimus ut scilicet quicumque contra hoc venire temptaverit, secundo terciove commonitus, nisi resipuerit, reum se divino judicio existere de perpetrata iniquitate cognoscat et a sacratissimo corpore et sanguine Dei et Redemptoris nostri Jhesu Christi alienus fiat, atque in extremo examine districte ulteriori subiaceat. Connservatoribus[14] autem ~~in extremo examine~~ sit pax Domini nostri Jhesu Christi quatinus et hic fructum bone actionis percipiant et apud districtum judicem premia eterne pacis inveniant. Amen.

6

1231

Jean [II],[1] *castellan of Noyon and Thourotte, makes known that he gave and conceded to the church of Prémontré in perpetual alms his part of the right of* traversum *on the 50* dolia *of wine that the church owed him annually.*

---

6 Jerusalem *B*.

7 Guy II, castellan of Coucy (d. 1165); husband of Théophanie. Barthélemy, *LDA*, 506–7.

8 Adon de Guny, son of Guy I, lord of Guny, and Elizabeth, and nephew of Guy II, castellan of Coucy. Newman, *Seigneurs*, vol. 2, 96; Barthélemy, *LDA*, 150–5.

9 Itier de Guny, son of Guy I, lord of Guny, and Elizabeth, and nephew of Guy II, castellan of Coucy. Newman, *Seigneurs*, vol. 2, 96; Barthélemy, *LDA*, 150–5.

10 Robert *Vitulus* (or le Veau), a knight of Coucy, also appears in **184** and **452**. Barthélemy, *LDA*, 155–6.

11 Sarrazenus *B*.

12 Sarracin, castellan of La Fère (from 1133) and of Laon (from 1166); brother of Geoffroi de Condren, knight, and Hugues *le Captif* de Vendeuil, husband of Helvide. Newman, *Seigneurs*, vol. 2, 203–4.

13 Gérard *l'Oreille* was part of the seigneurial family of Housset (cant. Sains, https://dicotopo.cths.fr/places/P27336521), and frequently appeared in charters issued by the Coucy family in the 1130s–60s. Barthélemy, *LDA*, 521.

14 *Sic A*.

---

1 Jean II (d. ca. 1235), lord of Thourotte (cant. Ribécourt, https://dicotopo.cths.fr/places/P28703302) and castellan of Noyon; son of Jean I, lord of Thourotte and castellan of Noyon, and Alix de Dreux, and husband of Odette de Dampierre.

A. Cartulary of Prémontré, fol. 1v.
B. Original, AD Oise, H 6074, previously sealed with a double strip of parchment.

Karta Johannis castellani Noviomi et Thorote de elemosina in transverso de Thorota super quinquaginta doliis vini.

[E]go Johannes castellanus Noviomi et Thorote. Notum facio universis presentibus et futuris quod ego, ob remedium anime mee et antecessorum meorum, dedi et concessi in perpetuam elemosinam ecclesie et fratribus Premonstratensibus libere et absolute, sine aliqua exactione et consuetudine, partem illam que me contingit in traverso de Thorota super quinquaginta doliis vini de collectione vinearum suarum annuatim, quando duxerint vina sua per transversum antedictum, ita quod dicta ecclesia nichil possit petere in posterum occasione dicti transversi[2] ab heredibus Willermi dilecti, quondam filii mei, neque ab hominibus qui a me aliquid de traverso tenere in feodo dinoscuntur, neque per hoc eis aliquod prejudicium generetur. Et ne ista elemosina possit in posterum aliquatenus pertubari vel per aliquorum maliciam revocari, ego presentem kartam in confirmationem predicte elemosine factum feci sigilli mei munimine roborari. Actum anno gratie M° CC° tricesimo primo.

7

August, 1190.

A[nselme],[1] *bishop of Laon, confirms by* vidimus *an act of Philippe [I], count of Flanders and Vermandois, that grants the abbey an exemption from payment of* pedagium, theloneum, *and* traversum *on his lands for all goods that the brothers of the church of Prémontré might transport, either by land or by water, for their own use, on condition that upon the announcement of the death of Philippe and Mahaut [Teresa of Portugal] his wife, the abbey will annually celebrate a service in their memory. (See* ***2****.)*

A. Cartulary of Prémontré, fol. 1v.
B. Original not found.

2 traversi *B*.

1 Anselme de Mauny (or de Bercenay), bishop of Laon, 1215–38.

Karta episcopi Laudunensis super eo quod se perhibet vidisse kartam comitis Flandrensis de wionagiis.

A., miseratione divina Laudunensis episcopus, universis fidelibus Christi presentes litteras inspecturis salutem in Domino. Noveritis quod nos kartam nobilis recordationis Ph[hilippus], quondam Flandrensis et Viromandensis comitis, ecclesie Premonstratensi concessam inspeximus in hec verba: Ego Ph[ilippus], Flandrensis et Viromandensis comes. Notum fieri volo quod, pro salute anime mee et antecessorum meorum ac deinceps successorum, ecclesiam Premonstrati liberam dimisi et quitam per universam terram meam ab omni consuetudine et exactione pedagii, thelonei, et traversi, ex hiis dumtaxat que ad usum fratrum ibidem Deo servientium deferentur, tam per terram quam per aquam, ea videlicet conditione quod fratres ecclesie Premonstrati, audito obitu meo et uxoris mee Mehaldis, pro nobis servitium celebrabunt et singulis annis memoriam habebunt. Ut igitur hec ecclesie immunitas et concessa libertas rata semper et inconvulsa permaneat, presentem ipsi concessi paginam tam sigilli mei inpressione quam testium subnotatione munitam: S. G. [2] Brugensis et Sancti Audomari, prepositi ac Flandrensis cancellarii. S. G. [3] prepositi Insule. S. G.[4] abbatis Sancti Martini Laudunensis. S. W.[5] abbatis de Viromandensis. Actum anno Domini M° centesimo nonagesimo, mense augusto.

8

1227–40.[1]

Henri, archbishop of Reims, makes known his confirmation of the preceding act. (See 7.)

A. Cartulary of Prémontré, fol. 1v.[2]
B. Original not found.

---

2 Gérard d'Alsace (d. 1206), illegitimate son of Thierry d'Alsace, count of Flanders, was *prepositus* at Bruges and chancellor of Flanders. Verhulst and de Hemptinne, "Le chancelier de Flandre sous les comtes de la maison d'Alsace (1128–1191)," 303–4.

3 Gérard de Messines was notary and *sigillarius comitis* of the count of Flanders, 1169–81, and *prepositus* of Lille, ca. 1183–ca. 1191. Reusens, "Les chancelleries inferieures en Belgique depuis leur origins jusqu'au XIIIe siècle," 111; Verhulst and de Hemptinne, "Le chancelier de Flandre sous les comtes de la maison d'Alsace (1128–1191),".

4 Guy (or Gautier) d'Epernay, abbot of the Premonstratensian abbey of Saint-Martin de Laon, 1189–91. *MP* II, 509.

5 Gilbert II, abbot of the Premonstratensian abbey of Vermand, 1181–4. *MP* II, 427.

---

1 Henri de Dreux (ca. 1193–1240), son of Robert II, count of Dreux, and his second wife Yolande de Coucy, was archbishop of Reims, 1227–40.

2 This act appears in its entirety in the left margin next to **9**.

Karta archiepiscopi unde supra precedenti.

Henricus, Dei gratia Remorum archiepiscopus, universis fidelibus Christiani presentes litteris inspecturis, salute in Domino. Noveritis quod nos kartam nobilis recordationis Philippi quondam Flandrensis sicut in p[recede]nti karta habere [illegible] ad libere.

9

July 20, 1223.

Gosuin,[1] *lord of Menin-sur-la-Lys, provides an exemption from payment of* passagium, calceiagium, *and* wionagium *throughout his lands on all goods belonging to the church of Mont-Saint-Martin,*[2] *as well as all churches of the Premonstratensian Order. His wife Yusilie, children, friends, and relatives consent.*

A. Cartulary of Prémontré, fol. 1v.

B. Original not found.

Other Manuscript Copies: Cartulary of Mont-Saint-Martin, BnF, MS lat. 5478, fol. 29v (13th c.).

REGISTER: Alphonse Wauters, "Exploration de chartes et de cartulaires existants à la Bibliothèque nationale, à Paris," *Compte Rendu des Séances de la Commission Royale d'Histoire*, Fourth Series, vol. 3 (1876), 82.

Karta domini de Menin de quitatione passagii, wionagii, et calceagii per totam terram suam tocius ordinis.

[E]go Gossuinus, dominus de Menin super aquam que vocatur Li Lis. Scire volo presentes et futuros quod ego, de voluntate et consensu Yusilie, conjugis mee, liberorum et amicorum meorum ad me linea consanguinitatis pertinentium, pro salute et remedio animarum nostrarum, mee scilicet et uxoris mee, predecessorum et successorum meorum concedo, remitto et quito in perpetuum ecclesie Montis Sancti Martini et omnibus eclesiis[3] ordinis Premonstrati passagium, calceiagium et wionagium omnium rerum suarum in tota terra mea, dominio et districto. Actum anno gratie M° CC° XXIII°, mense julio, die Margarete Virginis.

---

1 Gosuin and/or Yusilie, lord and lady of Menin-sur-la-Lys, are also attested in acts concerning the abbeys of Ourscamp (1203) and Froidmont (1223). Deladreue, "Notice sur l'abbaye de Froidmont: 1re partie," 531; Peigné-Delacourt, *Cartulaire de l'Abbaye de Notre-Dame d'Ourscamp de l'ordre de Cîteaux, fondée en 1129 au diocèse de Noyon*, 475.

2 The Premonstratensian abbey of Mont-Saint-Martin. *MP* II, 417–20.

3 *Sic A*.

10

April, 1224.

Roger,[1] *lord of Chimay, grants in perpetual alms an exemption from payment of* passagium *and* wionagium *to the church of Prémontré, but not to its daughter houses, on iron acquired in his lands. (See* ***11****.)*

A. Cartulary of Prémontré, fol. 1v.
B. Original not found.

Karta domini de Cimaco de elemosina quam contulit ecclesie Premonstratensis passagii ac wionagii.

[E]go Rogerus, dominus de Cimaco. Notum facio universis presentes litteras inspecturis quod contuli in perpetuam elemosinam Premonstratensi ecclesie passagium ac wionagium tocius ferri quod [fratres] eiusdem ecclesie ement in terra mea pro usibus ecclesie memorate. In hac vero donatione filias sepedicte ecclesie non intelligo comprehendi sed eas excludo, ne super hoc in posterum questionis vel dubitationis scrupulus oriatur. Ut autem premissa donatio perpetuum robur optineat firmitatis, in huius rei testimonium presentes litteras emisi sigilli mei confirmatas. Actum anno Domini M° CC° XX° IIII°, mense aprili.

11

April, 1229.

Jean,[1] *eldest son of [Raoul] count of Soissons, and Marie his wife,*[2] *lord and lady of Chimay and Thour, grant in perpetual alms an exemption from payment of* passagium *and* wionagium *to the church of Prémontré, excluding its daughter houses, for all the iron that the religious acquire in his lands. (See* ***10****.)*

A. Cartulary of Prémontré, fol. 1v.
B. Original not found.

---

1 Roger I, lord of Chimay (arr. Thuin, Hainaut), son of Alard, lord of Chimay. Hagemans, *Histoire du pays de Chimay*, vol. 1, 119–20.

---

1 Jean II, count of Soissons (d. ca. 1270), son of Raoul I, count of Soissons, and his second wife Yolande. Newman, *Seigneurs*, vol. 1, 67–8.
2 Marie du Thour et du Chimay (d. ca. 1241), daughter of Roger I, lord of Chimay, and Agnès, lady of Thour. Ibid., vol. 1, 68.

Karta Johannis comitis Suessionensis, domini de Cimaco et Marie, uxoris eius, unde supra.[3]

[N]os Johannes, comitis Suessionensis primogenitus, dominus de Cimaco et de Turno, et Maria uxor eius, notum facimus universis quod, pro salute animarum nostrarum necnon et pro remedio animarum predecessorum nostrorum atque successorum, dedimus et concessimus ecclesie Premonstratensis in elemosinam perpetuam passagium ac wionagium tocius ferri quod fratres eiusdem ecclesie ement in terra nostra pro usibus ecclesie memorate. In hac vero donatione filias ecclesie sepedicte non intelligimus nec volumus comprehendi, ne super hoc in posterum dubitatio aliqua oriatur. Ut autem predicta donatio rata et firma permaneat, nos presentes litteras fecimus sigillorum nostrorum munimine confirmari. Actum anno Domini M° CC° vicesimo nono, mense aprili.

12

1182. Cloister of Saint-Martin de Tournai.

Évrard [III] Radoul,[1] princeps *of Tournai, with the assent of his son, Baudouin,*[2] *and following the example of his father, grants in alms to the religious at the church of Prémontré the free right of* passagium *and* wionagium *on his land, by road and by waterway, to come and go, sell and buy at will.*

A. Cartulary of Prémontré, fols. 1v–2r.
B. Original not found.
EDITION: Herbomez, "Une charte des chatelains de Tournai"; *Diplomata Belgica*, no. 11076, https://www.diplomata-belgica.be/charter_details_en.php?dibe_id=11076.

Karta Evrardi Radoul principis de Tornaco de quitatione passagii et wionagii per totam terram suam.

[C]um priorum memoria solet oblivione deleri, necessario scripto commendatur quod in posterum memoriter retinendum est. Ea propter ego Evrardus

3 The rubric reflects the fact that, in 1235, Jean inherited the county of Soissons from his father, Raoul.

1 Evrard III Radoul (d. ca. 1189), castellan of Tournai and lord of Mortagne, son of Evrard II Radoul and Richilde of Hainaut. Herbomez, *Histoire des châtelains de Tournai de la maison de Mortagne*, vol. 1, 64–5.

2 Baudouin (d. aft. 1208), son of Evrard III Radoul, castellan of Tournai and lord of Mortagne, and his second wife Gertrude, *neptis* of Thierry, count of Flanders. Ibid.

Radous, princeps Tornacensis, notum fieri volo tam presentibus quam futuris quod assensu filii mei, Balduini, ad instar et exemplum patris mei, concessi in elemosinam in perpetuum ob remedium anime mee et predecessorum meorum, per totam terram meam, tam in terris quam in aquis, ecclesie Premonstratensis passagium liberum a[c] wionagio et omni consuetudine quantum spectat ad jus et dominium meum. Volo itaque ut omnes fratres ad ecclesiam Premonstratensem pertinentes per totam terram meam liberam facultatem habeant eundi et redeundi, vendendi et emendi sine omni vexatione, sicut prelibatum est. Ut autem firmiter et inconvulse in posterum teneatur presens scriptum, sigilli nostri appositione et testium annotatione munire curavimus. Testes itaque sunt: dominus Yvo[3] abbas Sancti Martini Tornacensis, Symon supprior, Oretus[4] prepositus, Walterus de Orca,[5] Ascricus de Sancto Piato,[6] Dei Amicus, Roscellus, Balduinus cantor, Johannes de Orca miles. Actum anno incarnationis dominice M° C° LXXX° II°, in claustro Sancti Martini Tornacensis, presentibus abbate Premonstratense,[7] abbate Sancti Foillani,[8] abbate de Alnuic,[9] et multis aliis tam clericis quam aliis.

13

June 28, 1125. Noyon.

Cardinal Pietro Pierleoni[1] and Gregorio,[2] cardinal deacon of Sant'Angelo in Pescheria, both legates of the Holy See, grant to all followers of Norbert the blessings of the Holy See, affirm the validity of their present state of life, and forbid those who have professed canonical vows to leave the cloister without the authorization of their abbot and community.

---

3 Yves, abbot of the Benedictine abbey of Saint-Martin de Tournai, 1160–84. Berlière, *Monasticon belge*, vol. 1, 278–9.

4 Oretus is also attested in 1193. Herbomez, *Chartes de l'abbaye de Saint-Martin de Tournai*, vol. 1, 170.

5 Orcq, comm. Tournai.

6 Saint-Python, cant. Caudry.

7 Hugues II de Douai, abbot of the Premonstratensian abbey of Cuissy, 1161–5, and abbot of Prémontré, 1174–89. *MP* II, 497.

8 Nicholas II, abbot of the Premonstratensian abbey of Saint-Feuillien du Rœulx, 1170–1205. *MP* II, 396.

9 (Richard?), abbot of the Premonstratensian abbey of Alnwick. *MP* II, 33.

---

1 Pietro Pierleoni, cardinal priest of Santa Maria in Trastevere, 1120–30, and antipope as Anacletus II, 1130–8.

2 Gregorio Papareschi, cardinal deacon of Sant'Angelo in Pescheria, 1116–30, and pope as Innocent II, 1130–43.

A. Cartulary of Prémontré, fol. 2r.

B. Original not found.

Other Manuscript Copies: Cartulary of Grimbergen Abbey, Abdij van Grimbergen Oud Archief, Klas II, 1, fol. 1v (13th c.); Cartulary of Park Abbey, Archief van de Abdij van Park te Heverlee, MS VII 24, fol. 136r (13th c.); Cartulary of Saint-Augustin-lès-Thérouanne, Brussels, KBR, MS 4132, fol. 165r (13th c.); Cartulary of Park Abbey, Archief van de Abdij van Park te Heverlee, MS VII 26, fol. 49r (15th c.); Cartulary of Averbode Abbey, Archief van de abdij van Averbode, Sectie IV, no. 109, fol. 1r (15/16th c.).

EDITION: Wichmans, *Brabantia Mariana Tripartita*, 674–5; Le Paige, *Bibliotheca*, 390–1; Hertoghe *Religio canonicorum ordinis Praemonstratensis*, 123–5 (partial); Hugo, *La vie de S. Norbert, Archevêque de Magdebourg*, 227–9; Saulnier, "Confirmatio Prima Canonici Ordinis, a Sanctissimo Patre Norberto Fundati," in *Statuta Candidi et Canonici Ordinis Praemonstratensis Renovata ac Anno 1630*; Hugo, *Vita Sancti Norberti, Sacri Ordinis Praemonstratensium Canonicorum Regularium Patriarchae*, 175–7; Hugo, *prob.* 1, col. viii–ix.

REGISTER: Grauwen, "Lijst van oorkonden waarin Norbertus wordt genoemd," 144.

Privilegium Gregorii Sancti Angeli diaconi cardinalis ne quis vadat ad aliam religionem etiam districti omnie sine consensu abbatis et capituli.

[Pe]trus Leonis presbiter et Gregorius Sancti Angeli diaconus, Dei gratia Sedis Apostolice cardinales et legati, venerabili fratri Norberto ceterisque fratribus canonicam sub eo vitam professis salutem et benedictionem. Omnipotenti Deo cuius misericordia super vitas gratias agimus, quia vos estis qui sanctorum patrum vitam probabilem renovatis et apostolice ~~sed~~ instituta doctrine, primordiis ecclesie sancte inolita, sed et crescente ecclesia iam pene deleta, instinctu Sancti Spiritus suscitatis. Due enim ab ecclesie sancte primordiis vite eius sunt filiis institute: una qua infirmorum debilitas detinetur, altera qua fortiorum virtus beata proficitur; una remanens in Segor parvula, altera ad montis altiora conscendens; una lacrimis et elemosinis cotidiana peccata redimens, altera per cotidiana instituta merita eterna conquirens; alteram tenentes inferiorem bonis terrenis utuntur, alteram sequentes superiorem bona terrena despiciunt et relinqu[u]nt. Hec autem que a terrenis divino fervore divertitur, in duas unius pene eiusdemque propositi dividitur portiones, canonicorum scilicet et monachorum; harum secunda per divinam misericordiam frequentato iam satis secundo universo elucet. Prima vero, licet decalescente fervore fidelium aliquantum pene defluxerit, nostris tamen temporibus divina inspirante clementia, vigere plurimum cepit. Hanc Urbanus pontifex et martyr instituit, hanc Augustinus suis ordinavit regulis, hanc Jeronimus suis epistolis informavit. Non minoris itaque estimandum est meriti vitam hanc primitive ecclesie, aspirante ac prosequente Domini Spiritu suscitare, quam florentem monachorum religionem eiusdem Spiritus perseverantia custodire. Vestrum ergo propositum Sedis Apostolice, cuius legatione fungimur, auctoritate firmamus et firmos vos stare in eo adhortamur et tamquam Deo per nos exhortante obsecramus. Quamobrem omnibus in vestris cenobiis vitam canonicam secundam huius tenorem ordinis profitentibus et in ea, adjuvante Domino, permanentibus, nos apostolorum Petri et Pauli benedictionem et peccatorum suorum absolutionem concedimus, constituentes ne cuiquam omnino liceat hunc vestri ordinis statum commutare, cuius tantus in tot terrarum partibus fructus exuberat ut plures vestri saporis dulcedine condiantur; statuimus etiam ne professionis canonice quispiam, postquam Dei vice super capud si hominem imposuerit, alicuius levitatis instinctu, et districtioris religionis obtentu, ex eisdem claustris audeat, sine abbatis totiusque congregationis permissione, discedere; discedentem vero, ut nullus abbatum vel episcoporum, nullus monachorum, sine communium literarum cautione suscipiat interdicimus. Vos ergo, filii in Christo karissimi, dilectionis nostre studiis semper promptioribus respondentes, strenue quod Deo promisistis implere satagite. Luceat lux vestra coram hominibus, ut videant opera vestra bona et glorificent patrem vestram qui in celis est, cuius Patris, ut hec firma permaneant et Filii et Spiritus Sancti virtute sanctimus. Siquis autem contra huius pagine sanctionem sciens venire temptaverit, nisi secundo terciove commonitus satisfecerit, canonica ultione plectatur. Ego Petrus, Sedis Apostolice presbiter cardinalis et legatus. Ego Gregorius, Sancti Angeli diaconus cardinalis et legatus. Scriptum Noviomi, IIII kalenda julii, anno incarnationis dominice M° C° XXV°, pontificatus autem domini Kalixti II Pape sexto.

14

December 1, 1224. Metz.

Konrad,[1] *cardinal bishop of Porto e Santa Rufina and papal legate, confirms an agreement reached in the presence of H., cantor of Metz, his co-judges, and* magister *Louis, prosecutor for the archbishop of Magdeburg, between the abbey of Prémontré and the Premonstratensian Order on the one hand, and the abbey of Unser Lieben Frauen Magdeburg*[2] *and its affiliated houses on the other hand. This agreement determines the institutional relationship between the abbey of Prémontré and the houses associated with Magdeburg, as well as the respective rights of the abbeys and of the archbishopric of Magdeburg.*

1 Konrad von Urach (d. 1227), son of Egino IV, count of Urach, and Agnes von Zähringen, was successively abbot of Villers, 1209, abbot of Clairvaux, 1214, abbot of Cîteaux, 1217, and cardinal bishop of Porto e Rufina, 1219–27.

2 The Premonstratensian abbey of Magdeburg. *MP* I, 232–5.

A. Cartulary of Prémontré, fols. 2r–2v.
B. Original not found.
Other Manuscript Copies: Landeshauptsarchiv Sachsen-Anhalt, Abt. Magdeburg, U 4a Stifter und Klöster im Erzstift Magdeburg, Kloster Gottesgnaden, no. 18, sealed; "Liber statutorum necnon et de institutione sive de origine candidi ordinis scilicet Premonstratensis," Koninklijke Bibliotheek van Nederland, MS 128 G 21, fols. 76r–76v (1445).
EDITION: Hugo, *prob.* 1, cols. xxiii–xxv; Gercken, *Ausführliche Stifts-Historie von Brandenburg*, 425–7; Riedel, *Codex diplomaticus Brandenburgensis*, 138–9; *Mecklenburgisches Urkundenbuch*, vol. 1, 296–8; Klempin, *Pommersches Urkundenbuch*, vol. 1, 169–70; Heinemann, *Codex diplomaticus Anhaltinus*, vol. 2, 57–9; Hertel, *Urkundenbuch des Klosters Unser Lieben Frauen zu Magdeburg*, 95–6.
REGISTER: Bréquigny, *Table chronologique*, vol. 5, 232; Mülverstedt, *Regesta Archiepiscopatus Magdeburgensis*, vol. 2, 330–2; Dobenecker, *Regesta diplomatica necnon epistolaria historiae Thuringiae*, vol. 2, 388; Wölfing, *Das Prämonstratenserkloster Veßra, Urkundenregesten 1130–1573*, 66.

Scriptum de compositione Premonstratensis et Magdeburgensis tempore domini Conradi abbatis terminata.

[I]n nomine patris et cetera. Conradus, miseratione divina Portuensis et Sancte Rufine episcopus, Apostolice Sedis legatus, omnibus in perpetuum. Cum causa verteretur inter abbatem et ordinem Premonstratensem ex una parte, et prepositum Sancte Marie Magdeburgensis, de Gratia Dei,[3] de Liereka,[4] de Brandeburg,[5] de Havelbeg,[6,7] de Raceburg,[8] de Jericho,[9] de Colebeke,[10] de Rothe,[11] de Quetelingeburg,[12] de Wida,[13] de Poleke,[14] de Grammerewe[15] et de Temeniz[16] prepositos, ab ecclesia Sancte Marie Magdeburgensis descendentes ex parte

3 The Premonstratensian abbey of Gottesgnaden. *MP* I, 218–20.
4 The Premonstratensian abbey of Leitzkau. *MP* I, 230–2.
5 The Premonstratensian abbey of Brandenburg. *MP* I, 215–17.
6 *Sic A.*
7 The Premonstratensian abbey of Havelberg. *MP* I, 223–5.
8 The Premonstratensian abbey of Ratzeburg. *MP* I, 241–3.
9 The Premonstratensian abbey of Jerichow. *MP* I, 225–7.
10 The Premonstratensian abbey of Kölbigk. *MP* I, 228–30.
11 The Premonstratensian abbey of Klosterrode. *MP* I, 227–8.
12 The Premonstratensian abbey of Quedlinburg. *MP* I, 239–40.
13 The Premonstratensian abbey of Mildenfurt. *MP* I, 235–7.
14 The Premonstratensian abbey of Pöhlde. *MP* I, 237–9.
15 The Premonstratensian abbey of Gramzow. *MP* I, 221–2.
16 A little-known Premonstratensian community, possibly now Ciemnik, Poland. *MP* I, 245–6.

altera, super eo videlicet quod iidem abbates et ordo Premonstratensis, prepositos prenominatos a prima plantatione religionis ordinis Premonstratensis, asserebant debere ~~convertere~~ convenire ad generale capitulum Premonstratense, et communibus institutionibus ordinis obedire; partibus super hoc dissentientibus, cum a Sede Apostolica diverse super hoc littere ad diversos judices emanassent, tandem presentibus et spontanee consentientibus viris discretis H., cantore, et suis conjudicibus Metensibus, necnon et viro venerabili magistro Lodovico, procuratore Reverendi patris Dei gratia Magdeburgensis archiepiscopi ad conponendum specialiter destinato, placuit partibus in hanc formam pacis et concordie, amicabiliter in nostra presentia convenire, secundam quod inferius est expressum: videlicet quod omnes prepositi supradicti tenebuntur accedere ad generale capitulum Premonstratense de triennio in triennium, et ibidem facere obedientiam domino abbati Premonstratensi, excepto preposito Sancte Marie Magdeburgensis de quo inferius est aliter ordinatum, ita tamen, quod obedientia illa non ligabit eos ad recedendum a consuetudinibus seu juribus, observationibus seu constitutionibus quas antea habuerunt, nec per abbatem Premonstratensem, neque per capitulum conpellentur recedere ab eisdem; immo suis conscientiis relinquentur donec fuerit eis divinitus inspiratum, quod per omnia se velint ordini conformare. Si autem predicti prepositi, vel aliquis eorum ea que predicta sunt, non observaverint, dominus Premonstratensis abbas ipsos per suspensionis et excommunicationis sentencias puniet, si voluerit, et dominus prepositus Sancte Marie Magdeburgensis ipsas sentencias observabit et faciet observari, nec eis, si super hoc voluerint se deffendere, aliquid auxilium et consilium exibebit. Prepositus siquidem Sancte Marie Magdeburgensis non tenebitur facere obedienciam sed prepositus de Gratia Dei obedienciam faciet manualem sicut alii prepositi supradicti. De cohertione autem istorum duorum prepositorum, videlicet Sancte Marie Magdeburgensis et de Gratia Dei, ita ordinatum est, quod si ad capitulum ambo vel alter eorum non venerint, sicut supradictum est dominus abbas Premonstratensis significabit venerando patri Dei gratia Magdeburgensi archiepiscopo, per litteras suas, ut puniat per sentencias suspensionis et excommunicationis eosdem; quod si non fecerit idem archiepiscopus infra tres menses a receptione litterarum abbatis vel capituli Premonstratensis, extunc abbas Premonstratensis ipsos puniet, sicut supradictum est de cohercione aliorum prepositorum, ita tamen quod propter hoc, videlicet pro eo quod non venerint, dictos duos prepositos vel alios prelatos a prelatione vel amministratione amovere non possit. Hoc autem adjectum est et conventum, quo quamdiu fuerint tam ipse prepositus Sancte Marie Magdeburgensis quam etiam omnes prepositi supradicti circa Premonstratum ad tres dietas, sive eundo ad capitulum, sive redeundo a capitulo, sive alio modo moram fecerint circa Premonstratum ad tres dietas, conformes erunt ceteris professoribus ordinis in habitu et in victu. Et hoc nichilominus condictum fuit a partibus et statutum, quod si aliquam ecclesiam Premonstratensis ordinis intraverint, citra Renum, versus Premonstratum, ibidem manentibus se in victu et habitu conformabunt. Si que autem ecclesie in posterum a predictis vel sub predictis ecclesiis plantate fuerint et fundate, prelati ipsarum ecclesiarum sub ipsa forma compositionis qua prelati alii a prepositis Sancte Marie Magdeburgensis et de Gratia Dei comprehendentur. Si vero abbas vel capitulum Premonstratense ab ista compositione resilierint, tam prepositus Sancte Marie Magdeburgensis quam omnes alii prepositi supradicti ac eorum eorum[17] ecclesie ab omni subjectione et impetione abbatis vel capituli Premonstratensis erunt in perpetuum penitus absoluti; et si prepositus Sancte Marie Magdeburgensis vel alii prelati ecclesiarum supradictarum ab hac compositione resilierint, abbati et ordini Premonstratensi, sicut et alii abbates et professores eiusdem ordinis erunt omnino subjecti, et in observantiis ordinis uniformes. Preterea notandum est, quod prepositus Sancte Marie Magdeburgensis omni juri, quod habebat vel habere poterat in Vescerensi[18] et Arnestennensi[19] ecclesiis renunciavit omnino et quantum in eo est abbati et capitulo Premonstratensi remisit. Partes etiam omnibus instrumentis litis supradicta causa optentis renuntiaverunt ex toto. Hanc igitur compositionem, initam de bona partium voluntate, auctoritate nostra et ex injuncto nobis legationis officio confirmamus. Et ne super hoc in posterum aliqua possit dubietas suboriri, sigilli nostri impressione et sigillis duorum judicum, quorum etiam auctoritas intercessit, tercio per suas literas excusato, presentem paginam fecimus communiri. Acta sunt hec Metis in kalendis decembris, anno incarnationis dominice M° CC° vicesimo quarto.

15

October 5, 1239.

Guillaume,[1] bishop of Paris, writes to Hugues [III],[2] abbot of Prémontré, with a letter of recommendation for the prepositus *of Unser Lieben Frauen Magdeburg,[3] who will shortly arrive at Prémontré in order to conclude an agreement between the abbey of Prémontré, Magdeburg, and other churches in its circary. Guillaume excuses his unintended absence and sends his wishes for a successful agreement, offering to help in any way that he can.*

---

17 *Sic A*; *rep.* eorum.

18 The Premonstratensian abbey of Veßra. *MP* I, 138–40.

19 The Premonstratensian abbey of Arnstein. *MP* I, 151–4.

---

1 Guillaume d'Auvergne was a canon of Notre-Dame de Paris by 1223, a professor of theology at the University of Paris by 1225, and bishop of Paris, 1228–49.

2 Hugues III d'Hirson, perhaps a descendant of the lords of Hirson and/or a relative of the lords of Guise, was abbot of Prémontré, 1238–42. Le Long, *Histoire ecclésiastique et civile du diocèse de Laon, et de tout le pays contenu entre l'Oise et la Meuse, l'Aisne et la Sambre*, 516; *GC* IX, cols. 649–50; Goovaerts, *Ecrivains, artistes et savants de l'ordre de Prémontré*, vol. 3, 129–30.

3 The Premonstratensian abbey of Magdeburg. *MP* I, 232–5.

A. Cartulary of Prémontré, fol. 2v.
B. Original not found.
EDITION: Le Paige, *Bibliotheca*, 929–30; Hugo, *prob.* 1, cols. xxvii–xxviii; Hertel, *Urkundenbuch des Klosters Unser Lieben Frauen zu Magdeburg*, 112.
REGISTER: Bréquigny, *Table chronologique*, vol. 5, 558.

Littere domini episcopi Parisiensis ad abbatem Premonstratensis pro conpositione Magdeburgensis.

[V]iro religioso et amico semper in Christo karissimo H[ugoni], Dei gratia Premonstratensi abbati, G[uillermus], permissione divina Parisiensis ecclesie minister indignus, salutem et sincere vinculum caritatis. Cum vir venerabilis et nobilis ob prestanciam meritorum quibus apud Dominum et homines claret, clarissimus prepositus Sancte Marie Magdeburgensis, de consilio vestro et etiam ad vocationem vestram, specialiter autem propter confidentiam quam de benignitate vestra gerit, et nos cum eo, Premonstratum venerit pro emendanda, immo, quod verius est, pro facienda compositione inter ecclesiam Premonstratensem et ecclesiam suum, et alias quasdam quarum nomina nescimus, religiositatem vestram rogamus et requirimus affectu quo possumus ampliori, quatinus ad eandem conpositionem amore Dei et ipsarum ecclesiarum et nostro, diligenter intendere curetis. Multas enim formas compositionis vobis proposuit merito acceptandas, quoniam per eas periculis animarum in primis occurritur multiplicibus, deinde corporum atque rerum; et propter hoc personaliter ad capitulum vestrum generale accedere proposueramus, sed arduissima atque inevitabilia negotia nos hoc facere non permittunt. Quod si forte, quod avertat Deus, bonum compositionis istius hac vice non provenerit, rogamus tota affectione qua possumus, quatinus vobis et aliquibus de abbatibus vestris eam retineatis potestatem ut vobiscum et cum eis fieri possit. Intendimus enim et volumus modis omnibus ad hoc vobiscum et cum illis loco et tempore quibus vobis placuerit post instans provincie vestre concilium laborare. Bene et diu valeatis. Datum anno Domini M° CC° XXX° nono, die mercuri ante festum Sancti Dyonesi.

16

October, 1239.

The text of the letters sent to Johannes [II],[1] prepositus *of Unser Lieben Frauen of Magdeburg, and to the* prepositi *of the associated churches in that circary, to which they are asked to affix their seals in acknowledgment of the agreement*

1 Johann II, *prepositus* of Magdeburg, 1230–46. *MP* I, 234.

reached between the abbey of Prémontré and the church of Magdeburg concerning attendance at the annual General Chapter at Prémontré.

A. Cartulary of Prémontré, fols. 2v–3r.
B. Original not found.
EDITION: Le Paige, *Bibliotheca*, 931–2; Hugo, *prob.* 1, cols. xxix–xxx; Hertel, *Urkundenbuch des Klosters Unser Lieben Frauen zu Magdeburg*, 114–16.
REGISTER: Bréquigny, *Table chronologique*, vol. 5, 559.

Conpositio facta de novo inter ecclesiam Premonstratensem et Magdeburgensem secundum formam antiquam.

[H]ec est forma litterarum quas debent sigillare vir religiosus frater Johannes, prepositus Sancte Marie Magdeburgensis, et prepositi aliarum ecclesiarum ad suam ecclesiam pertinencium. Notum facimus universis quod, cum venerabiles pater Hugo,[2] abbas totumque generale capitulum Premonstratense ad piam instanciam consiliumque bonorum nobis hanc gratiam gratissimam fecissent propter animarum pericula necnon et gravia laborum et expensarum dispendia ut unusquisque nostrum atque successorum nostrorum successive in perpetuum quolibet triennio semel veniremus Premonstratum ad capitulum generale, cum alias omnes simul venire ad idem capitulum quolibet triennio teneremur, nos tante gratie nolentes remanere ingrati, in perpetuam memoriam eiusdemque gratie signumque nostre devotionis ac reverentie quam habemus et habere semper volumus erga ecclesiam Premonstrati, concessimus et ordinavimus nos inter ut ille de nobis vel successoribus nostris qui vice omnium nostrum vel successorum nostrorum venerit Premonstratum ad capitulum generale, offeret ecclesie Premonstrati ornamentum vel ornamenta pro que in eadem diurnum officium decoretur ita quod precium ornamenti vel ornamentorum illorum non sit minus viginti librarum Parisiensium. Emenda sunt ornamentum vel ornamenta predicta de consilio abbatis, prioris vel provisoris. Premonstratensis infra triduum capituli generalis, si ibi sufficientia poterunt inveniri. Alioquin dentur ille viginti libri Parisienses priori et preposito Premonstratensi, qui bona fide et in periculo animarum suarum infra mensem convertent illas, de consilio abbatis, in ornamenta predicta, ita quod non poterunt in alios usus expendi. Volumus etiam et concessimus ut idem litteras patentes habeat et mandatum

2 Hugues III d'Hirson, perhaps a descendant of the lords of Hirson and/or a relative of the lords of Guise, was abbot of Prémontré, 1238–42. Le Long, *Histoire ecclésiastique et civile du diocèse de Laon, et de tout le pays contenu entre l'Oise et la Meuse, l'Aisne et la Sambre*, 516; *GC* IX, cols. 649–50; Goovaerts, *Ecrivains, artistes et savants de l'ordre de Prémontré*, vol. 3, 129–30.

omnium prepositorum qui mutati fuerunt, tempore nobis indulto quo ad capitulum non tenemur convenire de facienda, nomine et vice eorum, obediencia domino Premonstratensi abbati donec memorati prepositi in ordine vicis sue veniant ad capitulum memoratum et ibi faciant nichilominus per se ipsos obedientiam manualem, excepto preposito Magdeburgensi qui, cum venerit in ordine vicis sue, secum adducet canonicum sufficienter instructum qui, vice mutatorum prepositorum faciet obedientiam manualem. Quod si aliquo impedimento destinatus sic prepositus ad generale capitulum Premonstratum venire non poterit, per canonicum qui cum eo veniet cum patentibus literis suis hoc ipsum dicto Premonstratensi abbati significare tenebitur et capitulo generali, dans in eisdem literis dicto canonico potestatem de jurando in animam suam super illo impedimento; utrum autem illud impedimentum legitimum sit necne, Premonstratensis abbatis arbitrio relinquetur. Quod si forte minus legitimum illud impedimentum abbas judicaverit, vindicandum erit pena in antiqua compositione contenta. Idem vero canonicus omnia facere tenebitur que ille prepositus, si presens esset, facere teneretur; prepositus autem vel canonicus, pro omnibus missus, debet secum deferre litteras patentes omnium conprepositorum suorum continentes; mittunt illum loco sui ad generale capitulum Premonstrati. Ad faciendum omnia que ipsi, si presentes essent, facere tenerentur. Sciendum vero est quod hec omnia nobis concessa sunt et indulta salva in omnibus et per omnia quantum ad omnes alios articulos conpositione antiqua. Quod si venerimus contr[a] [lacuna] vel aliquod premissorum tenebimur omnes simul [lacuna] venire Premonstratum ad capitulum [lacuna]qua. Quod si non ita venerimus [lacuna] contenta videlic[et] [lacuna] et ordini Premonstratensi sicut alii abbates et professores eiusdem ordinis omnino subjecti et in observantiis ordinis uniformes. Quam autem hec acta sunt nobis Guillermo Parisiensis episcopo,[3] presentibus[4] in horum testimonium et robur sigillum nostrum presentibus litteris appendendum. Actum anno gratie M° CC° tricesimo nono, mense octobris.

17

October, 1239.

Hugues [III],[1] *abbot of Prémontré, having examined the text of a decree issued by the General Chapter of the order of Prémontré, and being authorized by that*

3 Guillaume d'Auvergne was a canon of Notre-Dame de Paris by 1223, a professor of theology at the University of Paris by 1225, and bishop of Paris, 1228–49.

4 *Sic A.*

1 Hugues III d'Hirson, perhaps a descendant of the lords of Hirson and/or a relative of the lords of Guise, was abbot of Prémontré, 1238–42. Le Long, *Histoire ecclésiastique et civile du diocèse de Laon, et de tout le pays contenu entre l'Oise et la Meuse, l'Aisne et la Sambre*, 516; *GC* IX, cols. 649–50; Goovaerts, *Ecrivains, artistes et savants de l'ordre de Prémontré*, vol. 3, 129–30.

body to negotiate an agreement between the order and Unser Lieben Frauen of Magdeburg,[2] *and to use the General Chapter's seal to that end, makes known that together with the abbots of the communities of Cuissy*[3] *and Lieu-Restauré*[4] *he has granted to the* prepositi *of Magdeburg and its affiliated houses the right to attend the General Chapter meetings at Prémontré once every three years, and to take turns doing so.*

A. Cartulary of Prémontré, fols. 3r–3v.

B. Original not found.

EDITION: Le Paige, *Bibliotheca*, 930–1; Hugo, *prob.* 1, cols. xxviii–xxix; Hertel, *Urkundenbuch des Klosters Unser Lieben Frauen zu Magdeburg*, 112–14.

REGISTER: Bréquigny, *Table chronologique*, vol. 5, 559.

Negotium comissum domino Hugoni abbati Premonstratensis de compositione inter Magdeburgensem et ordinem.

[U]niversis presentes litteras inspecturis frater Hugo, Dei patientia abbas Premonstratensis, salutem in Domino, noveritis nos literas nostri generalis capituli recepisse in hac forma: Universis Christi fidelibus presentes literas inspecturis, abbatum Premonstratensis ordinis capitulum generale salutem in omnium salvatore. Universitati vestre volumus esse notum quod nos venerabili patri nostro in Christo, domino Hugoni, Premonstratensi abbati, de communi consilio et consensu commisimus negotium compositionis inter ordinem nostrum et Magdeburgensem ut de consilio abbatum sui ordinis quos duxerit advocandos, componat cum ipse secundum quod viderit expedire; et volumus quod in isto tantum modo negotio utatur sigillo capituli generalis, ratum habituri et gratum quicquid super premissi modo predicto duxerit faciendum. Datum Premonstrati, in capitulo generali, anno gratie M° CC° XXX° IX°. Auctoritate igitur tam nostra quam literarum illarum, vocatis nobiscum venerabilibus in Christo fratribus Cuissiaci et Loci Restaurati abbatibus et dilecto filio fratre priore nostro, attendentes in primis animarum pericula deinde labores corporum rerumque dispendia que viri religiosi et venerabiles prepositus Sancte Marie Magdeburgensis aliarumque ecclesiarum ad eius ecclesiam pertinentium prepositi incurrebant, et incurrere poterant veniendo ad nostrum capitulum generale, de causa remotis partibus et ad propria redeundo, ad piam instantiam consiliumque bonorum, eis indulsimus de gratia speciali,

2 The Premonstratensian abbey of Magdeburg. *MP* I, 232–5.

3 Conrad the Swabian was prior of Weissenau, 1203–17, abbot of Valsecret, 1218–20, abbot of Prémontré, 1220–33, and abbot of Cuissy, aft. 1235–41. *MP* I, 89; *MP* II, 497, 527, 536.

4 R. (?), abbot of the Premonstratensian abbey of Lieu-Restauré. *MP* II, 514.

quod in quolibet anno triennio unius solus eorum pro omnibus successive in perpetuum ad capitulum veniat memoratum, munitus litteris patentibus omnium aliorum, continentibus quod ab aliis missus sit idem prepositus ad faciendum in nostro generali capitulo quicquid illi, si presentes essent, facere tenerentur; quod si fortasis destinatus prepositus aliquo impedimento detentus ad capitulum non veniret, canonicus qui cum eo venturus erat, pro eo venie[t] [lacuna] -dedictas deferens et litteras eiusdem prepositi pat-[lacuna] [lacuna]-bitur quod pro eo veniet et mandatum et [lacuna]-di juramentum super huiusmodi [lacuna] canonicum sit seu l-[lacuna] [lacuna]-tinebit [lacuna][5] continentes mandatum eorum expressum mutatorum sic prepositorum ut eorum vice et nomine abbati Premonstratensi obedientiam faciant manualem, excepto preposito Magdeburgensis, qui cum venerit in ordine vicis sue, et secum adducet canonicum sufficienter instructum, qui vice mutatorum prepositorum faciet obedientiam manualem. Nichilominus tamen ipsimet, videlicet mutati prepositi, prout in ordine vicis sue unusquisque illorum, prout, dictum est, venerint, eam par se ipsos personaliter facere tenebuntur. Et hec omnia indulsimus atque concessimus duodecim prepositis predictis, duobus aliis scilicet de Gremmerewe[6] et de Temeniz[7] prepositis in ipso numero minime computatis, salva in omnibus et per omnia antiqua compositione et in nullo ei quantum ad alios articulos penitus derogato. Sciendum vero quod si contra permissa, vel aliquid premissorum, quod Deus avertat, venerint, tenebuntur secundum antiquam compositionem venire de triennio in triennium ad capitulum generale. Quod si non venerint, punientur pena in antiqua compositione contenta, videlicet quod cadent a causa et erunt nobis omnino subjecti et in observantiis ordinis uniformes. In cuius rei testimonium presentibus litteris nostrum et coabbatum nostrorum videlicet Cuissiaci et Loci Restaurati sigilla duximus appendenda. Actum anno Domini M° CC° XXX° IX°, mense octobri.

5 The cartulary fol. 3r has been cut diagonally along its bottom right corner. While no original survives for this act, per Hugo, *prob.* 1, cols. 28–9, it should read: patentes illas deferens simul et eiusdem prepositi litteras, quibus sibi committatur ut pro illo veniat et mandatum datur speciale in animam illius, quodcumque licitum prestandi juramentum super impedimenti hujusmodi veritate; quod quidem an canonicum sit seu legitimum, abbas Premonstratensis judicabit. Prepositus autem seu canonicus qui pro omnibus missi fuerint, habebunt litteras a prepositis quos tempore indulto non veniendi ad capitulum generale contigerit mutatos esse, continentes mandatum eorum expressum mutatorum sic prepositorum ut eorum vice et nomine abbati Premonstratensi obedientiam.

6 The Premonstratensian abbey of Gramzow. *MP* I, 221–2.

7 A little-known Premonstratensian community, possibly now Ciemnik, Poland. *MP* I, 245–6.

18

October, 1239.

Hugues [III],[1] *abbot of Prémontré, makes known that he will affix the official seal of the General Chapter of the order of Prémontré to the agreement he concluded with the* prepositus *of Unser Lieben Frauen Magdeburg*[2] *and his fellow* prepositi, *when the latter have sealed and sent to him their agreements in turn. The agreement will begin in 1240.*

A. Cartulary of Prémontré, fol. 3v.
B. Original not found.
EDITION: Le Paige, *Bibliotheca*, 931; Hugo, *prob.* 1, col. xxix; Hertel, *Urkundenbuch des Klosters Unser Lieben Frauen zu Magdeburg*, 114.
REGISTER: Bréquigny, *Table chronologique*, vol. 5, 559.

Karta abbatis Premonstratensis de triennio de quo fit fit mentio in litteris conpositionis.

[U]niversis fidelibus Christi presentes litteras inspecturis, frater Hugonis, abbas Premonstratensis, salutem in Domino. Cum generale capitulum ordinis nostri ratum habeat quicquid cum venerabilibus fratribus preposito Sancte Marie Magdeburgensis et conprepositis suis, duxerimus faciendum per compositionem, prout in literis eiusdem capituli super hoc confectis evidenter apparet, per sigillum ipsius generalis capituli faciemus compositionem ipsam firmari, cum dictus prepositus et conprepositi sui sigillaverint et miserint nobis litteras compositionis, articulos et seriem continentes. Triennium autem de quo fit mentio in literis compositionis illius, incipiet computari anno gratie M° CC° XL°. In cuius rei testimonium presentes litteras emisimus sigilli nostri appensione munitas. Datum mense octobri, anno gratie M° CC° XXX° nono.

19

1185

An agreement of confraternity reached between the Benedictine abbey of Saint-Vincent de Laon and the church of Prémontré.

1 Hugues III d'Hirson, perhaps a descendant of the lords of Hirson and/or a relative of the lords of Guise, was abbot of Prémontré, 1238–42. Le Long, *Histoire ecclésiastique et civile du diocèse de Laon, et de tout le pays contenu entre l'Oise et la Meuse, l'Aisne et la Sambre*, 516; *GC* IX, cols. 649–50; Goovaerts, *Ecrivains, artistes et savants de l'ordre de Prémontré*, vol. 3, 129–30.

2 The Premonstratensian abbey of Magdeburg. *MP* I, 232–5.

A. Cartulary of Prémontré, fols. 3v and 111r.
B. Original, AD Aisne, H 121, previously sealed with four seals (of which one survives as a fragment) attached with a double strip of leather.

Conpositione inter ecclesiam Premonstratensem et ecclesiam Sancti Vincenti Laudunensis de pace et concordia tenenda.

[Lacuna] et cetera. Ca-[lacuna] vinculo irrefragrabili ligare non de-[lacuna] emerserit manu devote [lacuna] satagit revocare [lacuna]-pitulum [lacuna][1] audientiam questio referetur sed abbas Sancti Vincentii providebit duos canonicos in conventu ecclesie Premonstratensis, similiter et abbas Premonstratensis accipiet duos monachos in conventu Sancti Vincentii qui, in unum convenientes et rem sufficienti inquisitione addicentes, infra quadraginta[2] dies sua ipsorum industria, si fieri potest, amicabili compositione querelam terminabunt. Quod si querela gravis eis visa fuerit et nodosa adeo ut alieno suffragio se egere cognoverint, consilium requirent simul et, prout eis visum fuerit post acceptum consilium, compositione vel judicio eam terminabunt et utraque ecclesia nostra irrefragabiliter tenebit quod ab illis quatuor audierit. Ut igitur hec sancta confederatio rata sit et nulla interpolatione valeat infirmari, quia providimus in bono pacis quietem corporum et concordiam animorum, visum est aliquid addiciendum esse ad salutem animarum et preter antiquas sollemnitates quas vivis et defunctis ad invicem inpendebamus, communi decreto sancitum est quod abbas Sancti Vincentii aut prior cum duobus aut tribus monachis, si abbas non poterit, singulis annis festo natalis Beati Johannis interesse non omittent. Similiter et abbas Premonstratensis aut prior et duo vel tres cum eo canonici festo Sancti[3] Vincentii annuatim intererunt. Sed et decedente altero fratrum

1 Due to damage to this folio in the cartulary manuscript, we reproduce here the entirety of the beginning of the *B* text: In nomine sancte et individue Trinitatis, amen. Caritas que patiens est et benigna filios obedientie vinculo irrefragabili ligare non desistit et si quid inter eos indebita subreptione emerserit, manu devote sollicitudinis et caute provisionis ad pacem et concordiam satagit revocare. Inde est quod ego Hugo, ecclesie Sancti Vincentii Laudunensis abbas, et capitulum et ego Hugo, ecclesie Premonstratensis abbas, et capitulum nostrum memorie posterorum volumus commendari quod omnem dissentiendi sive litigandi occasionem de omnibus querelis que decetero emerserint inter utramque ecclesiam nostram hoc modo communi assensu statuimus in perpetuum amputari. Convenit igitur inter nos et communi assensu firmatum est in utroque capitulo nostro quod de omni questione que emerserit inter utramque ecclesiam nostram, nulla secularis sive ecclesiastica persona requiretur nec ad alienam.

2 XL[a] *B*.

3 Beati *B*.

alterius ecclesie et obitu eius alteri ecclesie nuntiato vigilia[4] et missa et commendatio in conventu pro eo celebrabuntur[5] et semel in anno, in natali videlicet Sancti Valentini, pro defunctis omnibus ad utramque ecclesiam pertinentibus plenarium sicut in presentia fratris defuncti servitium sollempniter persolvetur et a die illa cotidie missa pro eisdem celebrabitur[6] in utraque ecclesia usque ad diem tricesimum. Abbatum autem utriusque ecclesie dies anniversarius singulis annis persolvetur. Sane his[7] decrevimus annectendum quod ad fomentum ampliorius[8] dilectionis utrinque, concessum est videlicet quod in omnibus querelis et in omnibus audientiis coram omnibus personis tam per nos quam per subditos nostros fraterna compassione nos invicem fovebimus constanter adjuvabimus et omnia nostra quotiens expedierit vinculo caritatis et debito pactionis partiemur. Ne igitur consensus personarum presentium utriusque capituli temeraria presumptione succendentium valeat annullari,[9] in utroque capitulo sub interminatione anathematis prohibuimus ne quis huic pactioni pro bono pacis facte contendat obviare et, siquis inde contentiose agere presumpserit, in utriusque capitulo congruam[10] satisfactionem cogatur exhibere. Ut igitur hec pactio karitatis[11] rata semper existat, presentem kartam[12] sigillorum nostrorum appositione et [lacuna][13] qui affuerunt annotatione roborari fecimus. Signum Wi- [lacuna] -is supprioris, Gualteri, Herberti, Henrici, [lacuna] Thome, Gerardi, Johannis, Richardi, [lacuna]-orum Sancti Vincentii. Signum [lacuna] -onis, Raineloni, He- [lacuna] -is, Joscelini. [lacuna][14] Radulphi, Roberti, Gerardi, Symonis, canonicorum Premonstratensis ecclesie. Actum anno incarnati verbi M° C° octogesimo quinto.[15]

4 vigilie *B*.

5 *Transp. A*; celebrabuntur pro eo *B*.

6 *Transp. A*; celebrabitur pro eisdem *B*.

7 hiis *B*.

8 amplioris *B*.

9 adnullari *B*.

10 *Add.* congruam *A*.

11 caritatis *B*.

12 cartam *B*.

13 eorum *B*.

14 The cartulary text continues after this point on fol. 111r.

15 Due to damage to this folio in the cartulary manuscript, we reproduce here the entirety of the witness list from *B*: Signum Wiboldi prioris, S. Bovonis supprioris, S. Gualteri, S. Herberti, S. Henrici, S. Balduini, S. Raineri, S. Radulfi, S. Thome, S. Gerardi, S. Johannis, S. Richardi, S. Berengeri, S. Lamberti, monachorum Sancti Vincentii. Signum Eustachii, prioris. S. Egidii, supprioris. S. Harmonis, S. Remelmi, S. Helvini, S. Gualteri, S. Lietoldi, S. Wermundi, S. Danielis, S. Joscelini, S. Radulfi, S. Roberti, S. Gerardi, S. Symonis, canonicorum Premonstratensis ecclesie. Actum anno incarnati verbi millesimo centesimo octogesimo quinto.

20

March 27, 1338. Bonneuil.

Jean de Châtillon,[1] *abbot of Prémontré, bought 28* sextariae *of land situated near Bonneuil*[2] *and Caulaincourt,*[3] *which Colard* Briques *held in fief from Jean and the church of Prémontré. Jean then resold the land and fief to Pierre* Waingnart *and Geoffroi* Hazart *de Caulaincourt in exchange for an annual and perpetual payment of two modii of grain (*bladus*).*

A. Cartulary of Prémontré, fol. 4r.
B. Original not found.

NO RUBRIC. LATER ADDITION.

Anno Domini millesimo CCC° XXXVIII°. Nos Johannes de Castellione, abbas Premonstratensis, acquisivimus et emisimus de pecunia nostra XX[ti] et octo sextariis terre sitos prope Bonolium et Caulaincourt, quos tenebat a nobis et ecclesia nostra in feodo Colardus dictus Briques armiger, morans tunc a Villerserve, quam terram et quem feodum vendidentes seu [illegible][4] Petro dicto Waingnart et Gaufrido dicto Hazart, de Caulaincourt, sub conditionibus infrascriptis: videlicet [quod dicta terra in duas] dividetur et quilibet eorum habebit medietatem et pro dicta terra quilibet eorum erit homo noster et ecclesie [feodalis, sicut in dicto] loco ab aliis nostris hominibus feodalibus fuit et est consuetum, et quod etiam quilibet eorum et illi qui sibi succedent, nobis et ecclesie nostre pro dicta terra duos modios bladi modiagii secundum estimationem et valorem modiagiorum ville de Caulaincourt [annis] singulis perpetuo in octava nativitatis Domini reddere et solvere tenebuntur pro nostro anniversario faciendo. Et [his] premissis conditionibus dicti Petrus et Gaufridus nobis fidelitatem et homagium prestiterunt cum juramento in modo consueto. Acta fuerunt hec apud Bonolium, feria quinta post Letare Jherusalem, anno suprascripto [illegible] presentibus fratribus Jacobo de Sains,[5] magistro dicte domus, J. Maubert magistro de Germanis,[6] Jacobo de Hennecourt, Guerrico furnario Premonstratensi, J. Boumyn, J. Sergant tunc capellano regis,[7] Thoma Kanel

1 Jean de Châtillon, first prior and then abbot of Prémontré, ca. 1333–40. *GC*, IX, col. 653.
2 Bonneuil, cant. Ham, https://dicotopo.cths.fr/places/P66750585.
3 Caulaincourt, cant. Vermand, https://dicotopo.cths.fr/places/P02972526.
4 The upper right corner of this folio is extremely faded; the text in brackets indicates a best guess at a reading.
5 Sains, arr. Vervins, https://dicotopo.cths.fr/places/P35898483.
6 Germaine, cant. Vermand, https://dicotopo.cths.fr/places/P36636067.
7 *Superscr.* tunc capellano regis *A*.

maiore nostro, J. de Wesignicourt,[8] J. de Sains, G. Marescallo, Collino Coquo, et aliis pluribus tam familiaribus nostris quam aliis secularibus fidedignis super hoc evocatis.

21

January 1, 1363.

Simon,[1] *bishop of Soissons, makes known that he amortizes and places in mortmain a grange and adjoining open space, which had belonged to Robert de Bruyères,*[2] *bordered on one side by the house in Chaine belonging to the church of Prémontré and on the other side by the lane leading to the town walls of Soissons. Simon retains the right of* justicia *over the property.*

A. Cartulary of Prémontré, fol. 4r.
B. Original not found.

NO RUBRIC. LATER ADDITION.

A tous ceulz qui ces presentes lettres verront et orront, Symons par la grace de Dieu evesques de Suessons, salut en Nostre Seigneur. Savoir faisons a tous presens et advenir que pour l'amour et bonne affection que nous avons a nos bien amés les religieux, abbet et couvent de l'eglise de Premonstré et aussis en recompensacion de aucuns proufis fais par culz au proufit de [nostre] dicte eveschié admorti admortissons et mettons en main morte au proufit des diz religieux de Premonstré a tousjours perpetuelment une grange et place joingnant a ycelle seulement qui fu Robert de Bruieres, seant en nostre quartier et justice de Soissons, tenant d'une part au courtil de la maison condit en la Chaine, maison des diz religieux, et d'autrepart a la voie au les des murs de la ville de Soissons et volons et expressement consentons et accordonz que la dicte grange et place joingnant a ycelle soient admorties a tousjours et tenues quittement et en pais et mainmorte sans ce que li diz religieux puissent estre contrains par nous ou par nos successeurs a les vendre ou aultrement mettre hors de leur main. Toutevoies nous avons retenu et retenons pour nous et nos successeurs toute la justice es dictes grange et place; et aussis lesdiz religieux

8 Wissignicourt, cant. Anizy-le-Château, https://dicotopo.cths.fr/places/P16285342.

1 Simon de Bucy, son of Simon de Bucy, president of the *parlement* of Paris, and his wife Nicolle Taupin, was bishop of Soissons, 1362–1404. Brun, "Note sur les Simon de Bucy et le vieux château de Bucy-le-Long," 394–5.

2 A Robert de Bruyères, *bourgeois* of Soissons, made a bequest to the chapter of Notre-Dame-des-Vignes de Soissons in 1369. AD Aisne G 706.

pour [ce paieront] a nous et a nos successeurs tous les ans au jour de la Sainct Remy deulz solz et demi de Pairisis a loi et a amende tant pour [illegible] que la dicte grange et place nous doit come pour cens, rentes, censeives et pour toutes aultres choses que la dicte maison de la Chaine nous peuvent devoir. En tesmoing de la quelle chose nous avons scellées ces presentes lettres de nostre seel, qui furent faites et données l'an de grace mil CCC trois cens[3] soissante et trois, le jour de la Circoncision Nostre Seigneur.

22

After ca. 1200.[1]

A note that pertains to the election procedures for the Premonstratensian and Cistercian orders based on the writings of Bernardus Compostellanus.

A. Cartulary of Prémontré, fol. 4v.
B. Original not found.

NO RUBRIC. LATER ADDITION.

Istud pertinet ad electionem nostre ecclesie Premonstrati et specialiter hoc notatur extra de consuetudine capitulo, cum veniet per hoc et Bernardum Compostella in versiculo *unde quidem*, et cetera; per hec verba *unde quidem* sic Cisterciensis et Premonstratensis habent privilegium quod sine confirmatione administrent, si sunt clerici, in concordia et quod pro prelatis se gerent nec confirmatione indigent vel quod sine inquisitione confirmantur. Istud pertinet ad electionem in nostre ecclesie.

23

June, 1316.

Adam,[1] abbot of Prémontré, and the community on the one hand, and Hugues [II],[2] abbot of Ham and that monastery on the other hand, desiring to avoid future disputes, reach an agreement about certain mills' fishing rights and the repair of the sluices that lie between Ham and its mills.

---

3 *Sic A.*

---

1 The two canonists known as Bernardus Compostellanus were active in the early to mid-thirteenth century, and so this act must be contemporary with or post-date their period of activity.

---

1 Adam I de Crécy, abbot of Prémontré, 1304–27. *MP* II, 528.
2 Hugues II, abbot of the Augustinian abbey of Notre-Dame de Ham, 1310s. *GC* IX, col. 1123.

A. Cartulary of Prémontré, fols. 4v–5r.
B. Original not found.

NO RUBRIC. LATER ADDITION.

A tous chiaus qui chez presentes lettres verront. Nous Adans par le souffrance de Diu abbés de le eglise de Premonstré en l'eveschié de Loon, et tous li couvens de ce meisme lieu; et nous Huez, par icele souffrance abbés de le eglise de Ham en Vermendois en l'eveschié de Noion, et tous li couvens de che meisme liu, salut en Nostre Signur. Sachent tout que comme contens, descors et debas fuissent meux entre nous abbé et couvent de l'eglise de Premonstré d'une part, et nous abbé et couvent de l'eglise de Nostre Dame de Ham d'autre, et peussent en tamps a venir plus grant esmovoir, seur le peskerie de dedens le martelee des molins d'Espevile[3] et sur les boutures des escluses de l'iaue qui est entre Ham et lesdiz molins, nous abbés et couvens de l'eglise de Premonstré et nous abbés et couvens de l'eglise Nostre Dame de Ham dessus nommé sur lesdis contens, descors et debas, pour bien de pais, par conseil de bonnes gens et pour no pourfit et le pourfit de no dites eglises apparant et pour le damage de nous et chascun de nous et de nos eglises eskiver, nous acordons et sommes acordé par certain traitié et certainne deliberation ewe sur ce de nous et de chascun de nous en nos plains capitles en le maniere qui s'ensuit: Premierement que le pesquerie dedens le martelee des molins d'Espevile tant seulement est et demourra a tous jours entierement et pour le tout en tous pourfis a l'eglise de Premonstré dessus dite, et ni deverons ne porrons nous abbés et couvens de Ham ne autres pour nous dedens le dite martelee peskier ne faire peskier par nous ne par autrui en tamps nul. Item nous abbés et couvens de Premonstré porrons rompre ou faire rompre a no volenté, repenre et faire repenre a nos volentés pour le pourfit de nos molins les escluses entre le vile de Ham et les molins d'Espevile ou les devers le mares toutes fois que il nous plaira. Et toutes fois que nous meterons nouvel mannier es dis molins nous li ferons une fois faire sairement en le presence chiaus de le eglise de Ham, se estre et venir leur plaist as dis molins, que il ne romp[e] les dites escluses fors en cas de necessité; et quant il ara fait le rompture ou elle peut faite par chiaus de no eglise de Premonstré, nous de Premonstré le repenrons ou li ferons repenre le dicte rompture au plus tost que on porra, bonnement a no coust du tout et plus ne ferons a faire ne plus n'en porrons ne deverons nous abbés et couvens de l'eglise de Ham requerre ne demander. Item se li dite [~~eglise~~] escluse rompoit ou estoit rompté par cas d'aventure de fortune ou par forche d'iaue ou deslanasse ou par autrui que de aucun de nous de Premonstré

3 Eppeville, cant. Ham, https://dicotopo.cths.fr/places/P94171781.

et de Ham dessus dis, en teil cas, nous de Premonstré ferons refaire le ronpture et meterons les II pars au refaire et nous de Ham et le tierche partie, et seroit refaite le dite ronpture au plus tost que on porroit bonnement. Item en cas que autre personne que une de nous deus eglises dessus nommées ou de par nous aroit ronpu et on voloit plaidier pour ravoir le damage contre cheli ou chiaus qui aroient faite le ronture et pour le cause du plait que on feroit, il convenroit metres cous et frais li eglise a cui instance ou commencheroit le plait et meteroit les II pars et li autre le tierch ou dit plait maintenir et raroient chascune eglise a l'avenant de che que ele i meteroit de ce que on porroit conquester a ravoir du plait. Et deveroit estre li plais qui de che naisteroit, commenchiés de bone foy sans hainne et sans fraude, et pour che ne demourroit mie que nous de Premonstré ne deussiens faire rependre le ronture et refaire dou plus tost que on porroit bonement et i meteriemmes les II pars, et nous de l'eglise de Ham le tierche. Item nous abbés et couvens de l'eglise de Premonstré dessus dit avons rechu et reconnu puis avoir recheu de l'eglise de Ham dessus dite XV livres Parisis pour le bordel que nous avons fait faire dessus les molins dessus dis, et ne deverons dorenavant nous de Ham ne en refaire ne en retenir le dit bordel metre riens, mais retenir le deverons nous de Premonstré dessus dis a nos frais et a nos cous du tout. Che sauf a nous de Premonstré que se oster nous plaist ledit bordel ou laissier aler aval, oster ou laissier aler aval, le porrons toutes fois que il nous plaira ne riens ne leur en porrons demander nous de Ham dessus dit ne requerre que nous de Premonstré en devons ou soions tenu de respondre a chiaus de Ham ou cas ou nous ariemmes ostei ledit bordel ou laissier aler aval, du tout fors tant seulement que nous de Premonstré ou cas dessus dit ferons bien et souffisamment une fois refaire le trou ou l'ovreture ou aroit esteit li diz bourdiaus, si ostei le aviemmes ou laissier aler aval si comme dit est, et a no coust du tout et le trau du bourdel refait ainsi comme dit est. Se par cas d'aventure de fortune ou par forche d'iaue ou deslanasse ou par autrui que de aucun de nous de Premonstré et de Ham dessus dit novele ronture venoit, en teis cas nous de Premonstré meteriemmes lez II pars au refaire et nous de Ham le tierche partie, si comme dessus est dit. Et se nous de Premonstré ou nos gens rompiemmes ou fasiemmes ronpre pour nos volentés pour le pourfit de nos dis molins ou dit liu refait, nous de Premonstré le feriemmes refaire au plus tost que on porroit bonnement a nos cous, si comme dit est, ou cas lau nous rompons ou faisons rompre par nous ou par nos gens et ou cas lau nous de Premonstré ariemmes osteit ou fait osteir ou laissiet aler aval ledit bourdel du tout et refait le trau si comme dessus est contenu, se il plaisoit a nous de Premonstré apres refaire bourdel a leurs faire le ~~porrons~~ porriemmes et a nos cous du tout. Et aussi le seriemmes tenu a retenir du tout a nos cous, sauf chou que li eglise de Ham i fust de riens tenue au metre ni au retenir. Et nous de Ham ne leur porriemmes ne deveriemmes debatre mais que il le fessissent du tout a leur coust et retenissent, si comme dit est. Et toutes les choses dessus dites nous abbés et couvens de l'eglise de Premonstré d'une part et nous abbés et couvens de l'eglis de Ham d'autre part et chascuns de nous proumetons et avons proumis a tenir et warder fermement et amiaulement a tousjours de point en point, de article en article, sans venir jamais de riens encontre par nos sairemens seur ce bailliés de nous et de chascun de nous en nos plains capitles. Et a toutes les choses dessus dites tenir fermement et warder et remplir a tous jours sans ja venir encontre, si comme devant est dit, avons nous obligié et aloyé, et obligons nous et aloyons nous et chascun de nous, nos eglises dessus dictez et chascune d'iceles nos successeurs et tous nos biens temporeus et les biens de chascun de nous quelz que il soient et ou que il soient et porront estre trouvé presens et a venir a prendre, saisir, lever, detenir seur le partie de chelui de nous qui encontre les choses dessus dites ou aucune d'iceles venroit ou ne warderoit fermement et entierement, si comme dit est, a pourfit de l'autre partie de nous qui les choses dessus dites warderoit et vauroit tenir et warder, par quelconque juge ou justice que il plaira sans riens opposer a l'encontre. Et renonchons et avons renonchiet nous et chascuns de nous par nos sairmens en ce cas a toutes exceptions de mal et de bordie, de fraude et de lezion, de deception quele qu'ele soit a exception de chose qui n'ait mie esteit ainsi faite et acordée comme deseure est dit et devisé, a exception de circunvention que nous ou li aucune partie de nous puissons dire ou pourposeir en tamps a venir, que nous ou li aucune partie de nous aions esté ou soions circumvenu ou decheu es choses dessus dites ou aucune d'icelez a benefice de restitution en terme a toutez barrez et cauissations a toutes aywes de fait et de droit et de loy a tous usages, estaulisemens et coustumez et generaument a toutez autres exceptions et raisons qui contre ces presentes lettres et contre les choses dessus dites ou aucune d'iceles porroient estre proposées, alleguiés et mises au contraire, et qui a l'une ou aucune partie de nous ou tamps a venir porroient nuire, et grever et a l'autre partie pourfiter. Et volons, greons et otroions tout ensamble et chascun a parlui que ceste generaus renonciations vaile et s'estende a toutez exceptions et a tous cas qui sus general renonciation pueent estre comprises et entendues et qui porroient estre expressées escriptes et mises en cez presentes lettres et pour ce que toutes ches chozes dessus dites, devisées et ordenées soient fermes et estaubles a tous jours, nous abbés et couvens de l'eglise de Premonstré et nous abbés et couvens de l'eglise de Nostre Dame de Ham dessus nommé, avons ce presentes lettres faites de nous seur lez choses dessus dites et par nos grés acordées et scelées de nos seaulz et avons requis et depriié, requerons de deprions a sages hommes et honnestes le prevost et les hommes de le court le Roy a Chauny,[4] devant lezquelz nous avons par nos procureurs seur ce souffisamment instruis, estaulis et fondeis, proumises, reconnutes et fait reconnoistre et

4 Chauny, arr. Laon, https://dicotopo.cths.fr/places/P32247131.

proumetre lez choses dessus dites que il welent les choses dessus dictes faites et reconnutes de nous et par nous, si comme dite est, confremer et ~~esprouver~~ approuver par leurs lettres et par leurs sciaulz mises et fichiés en chestes nostres presentes lettres seelées de nos sciaulz en tesmoingnage de verité et en confermement de ces choses dessus dites. Che fu fait en l'an de grace mil CCC et XVI, ou mois de joing.

24

August 27, 1198. Rieti.

Pope Innocent [III] writes to Pierre [I],[1] *abbot of Prémontré, and to the other abbots and canons of the order, in confirmation of the rules of the order of Prémontré and principally of provisions relative to its abbots.*[2]

A. Cartulary of Prémontré, fols. 6r–7r.

B. Original not found.

Other Manuscript Copies: AD Haute-Marne, F 523, previously sealed with a strip of parchment (ca. 1198); AD Aube, 1 H 5, no. 1 (ca. 1210); Cartulary of Easby Abbey, British Library, MS Egerton 2827, fol. 311r (ca. 1281); Cartulary of Braine, AN, LL 1583, 28–37 (early 13th c.); "Formulae curiae," Real Colegio de España, Bologna, Cod. 275, pp. 24–8 (13th c.); Cartulary of Silly, BnF, MS lat. 11059, fols. 31v–34v (13th c.); Cartulary of Notre-Dame de Vicoigne, AD Nord, 59 H 95, fols. 4r–8r (13th c.); "Liber Cancellariae Apostolicae," BnF, MS lat. 4169, fols. 26v–29v (1380); Archiwum Państwowe we Wrocławiu, Rep. 67, no. 2 (3) (14th c.); Cartulary of Wincentego na Ołbinie we Wroclawiu, Archiwum Państwowe we Wrocławiu, Rep. 136 D 90 a, fol. 195r–198r (late 15th c.).

EDITION: Sirleto, *Innocentii tertii, pontificis maximi decretalium, atque aliarum epistolarum tomus*, vol. 1, 156–158b; Le Paige, *Bibliotheca*, 645; Baluze, *Epistolarum Innocentii III*, vol. 1, 185–8; Cocquelines, *Bullarum privilegiorum ac diplomatum romanorum pontificum*, vol. 3, 72–4; Spottiswoode, *Liber S. Marie de Dryburgh*, 183–90; *PL* 214, cols. 297–302; Hertel, *Urkundenbuch des Klosters Unser Lieben Frauen zu Magdeburg*, 72–7; Lalore, *Collection des principaux cartulaires du diocèse de Troyes*, vol. 3, 143–55; Erler, *Der Liber Cancellariae Apostolicae vom Jahre 1380*, 49–55; Tangl, *Die päpstlichen Kanzleiordnungen von 1200–1500*, 234–9; Hageneder and Haidacher, *Die Register Innocenz' III*, vol. 1, 481–7; Guyotjeannin et al., *Le chartrier de l'abbaye Prémontrée de Saint-Yved*

1 Pierre I de Saint-Médard, abbot of the Premonstratensian abbeys of Saint-Just en Chaussée, 1184–95, Prémontré, 1195–1201, and Cuissy, 1210–17. *MP* II, 497, 527, 565.

2 This act follows the form of ones previously issued by Popes Clement III and Lucius III, and was later reissued in largely similar form by Pope Innocent III. See Cheney and Cheney, *The Letters of Pope Innocent III (1198–1216) Concerning England and Wales*, 177–8.

de Braine, 154–9; *Chartae Galliae*, no. 204263, http://telma.irht.cnrs.fr/chartes/chartae-galliae/charte204263/.

REGISTER: Reg. Vat. 4, fols. 87v–89v; Potthast, *Regesta*, no. 334; Bréquigny, *Table chronologique*, vol. 3, 239; Grünhagen, *Codex Diplomaticus Silesiae*, vol. 7, 59–60; Cheney and Cheney, *The Letters of Pope Innocent III (1198–1216) Concerning England and Wales*, 7; Grauwen, "Lijst van oorkonden waarin Norbertus wordt genoemd," 176–7.

Incipit privilegium magnum de dignitate abbatis Premonstratensis tocius ordinis.

[I]nnocentius episcopus, servus servorum Dei, dilectis filiis Petro, abbati Premonstratensi, et ceteris abbatibus et canonicis Premonstratensis ordinis tam presentibus quam futuris regularem vitam professis in perpetuum. In eminenti Apostolice Sedis specula, licet inmeriti, disponente Domino, constituti pro singulorum statu solliciti esse compellimur et ea sincere tenemur amplecti que ad incrementum religionis pertinent et ad virtutum spectant ornatum. Quatinus religiosorum quies ab omni sit perturbatione secura et a jugo mundane oppressionis servetur illesa, cum apostolica fuerit tuitione munita, attendentes itaque quomodo religio et ordo vester, multa refulgens gloria meritorum et gratia redolens sanctitatis, palmites suos a mari usque ad mare extenderit, ipsum ordinem et universas domos eiusdem ordinis apostolice protectionis presidio duximus confovendas et presenti privilegio muniendas. Eapropter, dilecti in Domino filii, vestris justis postulationibus benignius annuentes, ad exemplar felicis recordationis Alexandri, Lucii, Urbani, et Clementis, predecessorum nostrorum Romanorum pontificum, universas regulares institutiones et dispositiones quas de communi consensu vel maioris et sanioris partis fecistis, sicut inferius denotantur, auctoritate apostolica roboramus et presentis scripti privilegio communimus videlicet ut ordo canonicus quemadmodum in Premonstratensi ecclesia secundum Beati Augustini regulam et dispositionem recolende memorie Norberti, quondam Premonstratensis ordinis institutoris, et successorum suorum in candido habitu, institutus esse disnoscitur, per omnes eiusdem ordinis ecclesias perpetuis temporibus inviolabiliter observetur. Et eedem penitus observantie idem quoque libri qui ad divinum officium pertinent ab omnibus eiusdem ordinis uniformiter teneatur nec aliqua vel persona ecclesia ordinis vestri adversus communia ipsius ordinis instituta privilegium aliquod postulare vel obtentum audeat quomodolibet retinere. Nulla etiam ecclesiarum ei quam genuit, quamlibet terreni commodi exactionem imponat, sed tantum pater abbas curam de profectu tam filii abbatis quam fratrum domus illius habeat et potestatem habeat secundum ordinem corrigendi que in ea noverit corrigenda et illi ei tamquam patri reverentiam filialem humiliter exhibeant et devote. Abbas autem Premonstratensis ecclesie que mater esse disnoscitur aliarum, non solum in hiis ecclesiis quas instituit, sed etiam in omnibus aliis eiusdem ordinis, et dignitatem et officium patris obtineat et ei ~~tam~~ ab omnibus, tam abbatibus quam fratribus, debita patri obedientia impendatur. Preterea omnes abbates ordinis vestri singulis annis ad generale capitulum Premonstratense, postposita omni occasione, conveniant allis[3] solis exceptis quos a labore vie retardaverit infirmitas, qui tamen ydoneum pro se delegare debent nuntium per quem necessitas et causa remorationis sue capitulo valeat nuntiari. Hii autem qui in remotioribus partibus habitantes sine gravi difficultate, singulis annis, se nequiverint capitulo presentare, in eo termino conveniant qui in ipso eis capitulo fuerit constitutus. Si vero quilibet abbatum aut prepositorum per contumatiam vestrum capitulum frequentare desierint, liceat abbati Premonstratensi, consilio sui capituli, eos usque ad dignam satisfactionem sententia percellere regulari, et sententiam quam prefatus abbas Premonstratensis sive in generali capitulo, sive extra capitulum consilio coabbatum ~~suorum~~ in prelatos et subditos totius ordinis vestri canonice tulerit, nulli archiepiscoporum seu episcoporum, nisi forte de mandato Romani pontificis, liceat relaxare. In generali igitur vestro capitulo, presidente abbate Premonstratensi ceterisque considentibus et in Spiritu Dei cooperantibus, de hiis que ad edificationem animarum, ad instructionem morum et ad informationem virtutum atque incrementum regularis discipline spectabunt, sermo diligens habeatur. Porro de omnibus questionibus et querelis tam spiritualibus quam temporalibus que in ipso capitulo preposite fuerint, illud teneatur irrefragabiliter et servetur quod abbas Premonstratensis cum hiis qui sanioris consilii et magis ydonei apparuerint, juste ac provide judicabit. Sane si abbas aliquis vestri ordinis infamis vel inutilis aut ordinis sui prevaricator inventus fuerit, et prius, per patrem suum abbatem aut per nuntios eius ammonitus, suum corrigere et emendare delictum neglexerit aut cedere, si amovendus fuerit, sponte noluerit, auctoritate generalis capituli deponatur, et depositus sine dilatione ad domum unde exivit seu ad aliam eiusdem ordinis quam elegerit sine ulla conditione temporalis commodi revertatur, in obedientia abbatis, sicut ceteri fratres ipsius domus, firmiter permansurus. Idipsum etiam alio tempore si necesse fuerit et capitulum sine scandalo vel periculo expectari nequiverit, per abbatem Premonstratensem et patrem abbatem et alios abbates quos vocaverit fieri licebit. Quod si depositus in se date sententie contumaciter contraire temptaverit, tam ipse quam principales eius qui de ordine vestro fuerint in sua contumacia fautores ab abbate Premonstratensi et ceteris abbatibus censure ecclesiastica, donec satisfaciat, arceantur. Verum cum aliqua ecclesiarum vestrarum abbate proprio fuerit destituta vel cum ibi abbatis electio non fuerit celebrata, sub patris abbatis potestate ac dispositione consistat et cum eiusdem consilio, qui

3 *Sic A*, *read* aliis.

eligendus fuerit, a canonicis eligatur. Electo autem fratres ecclesie statim obedientiam promittant, qui non quasi absolutus a potestate patris abbatis vel ordinis sui archiepiscopo vel episcopo in cuius diocesi fuerit presentetur plenitudinem ab eo officii percepturus, ita tamen quod post factam archiepiscopo vel episcopo suo professionem occasione illa non transgrediatur constitutiones ordinis sui nec in aliquo eius prevaricator existat. Siquis etiam ex vobis canonice electus in abbatem diocesano episcopo. Semel et iterum per abbates vestri ordinis presentatus, benedictionem ab eo non potuerit obtinere, ne ecclesia ad quam vocatur est, destituta consilio periclitetur, officio et loco abbatis plenarie secundum ordinem fungatur in ea tam in exterioribus providendis quam in interioribus corrigendis, donec autem interventu generalis capituli vestri, aut precepto Romani pontificis seu metropolitani, benedictionem suam obtineat. Porro nulla persona ecclesiastica pro crismate aut consecrationibus et ordinationibus aut pro sepultura precium aut pro benedicendo abbate et deducendo in sedem suam palefridum aut aliquod aliud a vobis exigere, nullus etiam vestrum, si exigatur, dare presumat, quia et exigentem et dantem nota et periculum symoniace pravitatis involvit. Ceterum si aliqua ecclesiarum vestrarum pastoris solatio destituta inter fratres de substituendo abbate discordia fuerit vel scissura suborta, et ipsi facile ad concordiam vel unitatem revocari nequiverint, pater abbas consilio coabbatum suorum eis ydoneam provideat personam et illi eam sine contradictione recipiant in abbatem. Quam si recipere contempserint, sententie subjaceant quam pater abbas cum consilio coabbatum suorum in eos duxerit auctoritate ordinis promulgandam. Ad hec quoniam Premonstratensis ecclesia prima mater est omnium ecclesiarum tocius ordinis et patrem super se alium non habet, sicut ad cautelam et custodiam ordinis, statutum est per tres primos abbates, Laudunensem,[4] Floreffiensem,[5] Cussiacensem;[6] annua ibidem visitatio fiat et si quid in ipsa domo corrigendum fuerit absque maiori per eos audientia corrigatur. Quod si abbas in corrigendo tepidus et fratres sepius moniti incorrigibiles permanserint, ad generale capitulum referantur et sicut melius visum fuerit consilio generalis capituli emendetur et sententia in hac parte capituli sine retractione aliqua observetur. Quotiens vero ecclesia Premonstratensis sine abbate fuerit, ad prefatos tres abbates eius cura respiciat et a canonicis ipsius ecclesie cum eorum consilio persona ydonea in abbatem eligatur, ad consilium suum quatuor aliis abbatibus ad eandem ecclesiam pertinentibus pariter advocatis, quos ipsi canonici providerint advocandos. Liceat quoque unicuique matri ecclesie ordinis vestri cum consilio abbatis Premonstratensis de abbatibus ecclesiarum que ab ea processisse noscuntur sive etiam de alia eiusdem ordinis inferiore ecclesia,

4 The Premonstratensian abbey of Saint-Martin de Laon. *MP* II, 509–13.

5 The Premonstratensian abbey of Floreffe. *MP* II, 373–8.

6 The Premonstratensian abbey of Cuissy. *MP* II, 495–9.

sibi quemcumque voluerit, si tamen ydoneus extiterit, in abbatem assumere. Personam autem de alio ordine nulla ecclesiarum vestrarum sibi eligat in abbatem nec vestri ordinis aliqua in abbatem monasterii alterius ordinis nisi de auctoritate Romane ecclesie ordinetur. Nulli etiam canonicos vel conversos vestros sine licentia abbatum suorum recipere aut susceptos liceat retinere. Sane nulli ecclesie vestri ordinis liceat ad aliquam aliam professionem temeritate qualibet se transferre, si que vero ecclesie canonicorum alterius ordinis habeant sine refragatione respectum in qua vestrum noscuntur ordinem assumpsisse. Preterea si inter aliquas ecclesias vestri ordinis de temporalibus questio emerserit non extra ordinem ecclesiastica vel secularis audientia requiratur, sed mediante Premonstratensi abbate et ceteris quos vocaverit aut caritative inter eas conponatur aut, auditis utrinque rationibus, eadem controversia justo judicio terminetur. Ad maiorem quoque ordinis vestri pacem conservandam districtis prohibemus ne aliquis prelatorum vel subditorum vestrorum in hiis que ad disciplinam et instituta ordinis spectant audeat, prout statutum est in Lateranensi concilio appellare, sed si quisquam appellare temptaverit, nichilominus illi quorum interest regularem disciplinam exercere debebunt. De cetero quoniam, a streptitu et tumultu secularium remoti, pacem et quietem diligitis, grangias vestras et curtes sicut et atria ecclesiarum a pravorum incursu et violentia libera fore sanctimus, prohibentes ut nullus ibi hominem capere, spoliare, verberare, seu interficere aut furtum aut rapinam committere audeat. Ob evitandas vero secularium virorum frequentias liberum sit vobis, salvo jure diocesanorum episcoporum, oratoria in grangiis et curtibus vestris construere et in ipsis vobis et familie vestra divina officia, cum necesse fuerit, celebrare et ipsam familiam, nisi aliqui sint qui in vicinia habeant propria domicilia, ad confessionem, communionem et sepulturam cum ordinis vestri honestate suscipere. Liceat quoque vobis personas liberas et absolutas, e seculo fugientes ad conversionem recipere et eas cum rebus suis sine contradictione aliqua retinere. Infirmos quoque absolutos qui in extrema voluntate ad vos se transferri aut apud vos sepeliri deliberaverint, nullus impedire seu res earum legitimas detinere presumat, salva tamen heredum legitima portione et canonica justicia illarum ecclesiarum a quibus mortuorum corpora assumuntur. Ad maiorem etiam ordinis vestri reverentiam et regularis discipline observantiam vobis, filii abbates, subjectos vestros ligandi et solvendi plenam concedimus facultatem. Quia vero singula que ad religionis profectum et animarum salutem ordinastis, presenti abreviationi nequiverunt annecti, nos cum hiis que scripta sunt, consuetudines vestras quas inter vos, religionis intuitu, regulariter statuistis et deinceps, auctore Domino, statuetis, auctoritate apostolica roboramus et vobis vestrisque successoribus et omnibus qui ordinem vestrum professi fuerint perpetuis temporibus inviolabiliter observandas decernimus nec alique littere habeant firmitatem que tacito nomine Premonstratensis ordinis contra libertates vobis ab Apostolica Sede indultas fuerint impetrate. Sane laborum vestrorum quos propriis manibus aut sumptibus colitis de possessionibus habitis ante concilium generale, sive de ortis et virgultis, pratis, pascuis et piscationibus vestris vel de nutrimentis animalium vestrorum seu etiam de novalibus nullus a vobis decimas exigere vel extorquere presumat. Interdicimus vero episcopis et aliarum ecclesiarum prelatis, nisi servato evectionis numero in Lateranensi concilio constituto, in vestris monasteriis hospitari. Ad grangias autem vestras et ad curtes, hospitandi gratia, non nisi in magna necessitate, divertant et tunc condenti sint ipsarum mansionum cibariis consuetis cum honestate atque caritate exhibitis. Nulli autem seculari persone vel ecclesiastice in aliqua domorum vestrarum liceat carnibus vesci nisi manifeste egritudinis causa et hoc in solis monasteriis conventualibus vestris. Prohibemus insuper ne aliqua persona fratres ordinis vestri audeat ad secularia judicia provocare; sed siquis adversus eos aliquid sibi crediderit de jure competere, sub ecclesiastici examine judicii experiendi habeat facultatem. Licitum preterea vobis sit in causis vestris fratres vestros ydoneos ad testificandum adducere et eorum testimonio, sicut rectum fuerit, et propulsare violentiam et justiciam vendicare. Prohibemus quoque ne cuilibet ecclesiastice vel seculari persone fas sit in ecclesiis vestris contra statuta Lateranensis concilii tallias exercere vel quaslibet alias vobis ineptas et iniquas exactiones imponere. Interdicimus etiam vobis ne feras, aves, canes sive cetera huiusmodi curiositatis animalia a quolibet ad nutriendum sive custodiendum in detrectatione ordinis vestri suscipere presumatis. Porro ut quietius Deo servire possitis et discurrendi a vobis necessitas auferatur, presenti scripto duximus indulgendum ut si, episcopis vestris aut maliciose differentibus vel pro justo impedimento non valentibus, ordinationes et cetera ecclesiastica ministeria vobis conferre aliquem episcopum de cuius ordinatione et officio plena sit vobis notitia, hospitem vos habere contigerit, liberum sit vobis ab eo ordinationem suscipere et cetera sacramenta dum tamen prejudicium dyocesano episcopo non debeat genare. Preterea, postulatione vestra clementius inclinati, presenti pagina duximus inhibendum ne quis archiepiscopus vel episcopus aut eorum officiales ecclesias vestras seu regulares personas earum absque manifesta et rationabili causa interdicere seu suspendere presumat, sed, si quid in eis fuerit corrigendum, ad audientiam generalis capituli Premonstratensis referatur et ibi, prout justicie et honestati congruerit, emendetur. Porro si qui episcopi aut eorum officiales in personas vestras aut ecclesias sententiam aliquam contra libertatem eisdem a predecessoribus nostris vel a nobis indultam promulgaverint, eamdem sententiam tamquam contra Apostolice Sedis indulta prolatam statuimus irritandam. Decernimus ergo ut nulli omnino hominum liceat prefatam ecclesiam temere perturbare aut earum possessiones auferre vel[7] ablatas

7 *Superscr.* vel *A.*

retinere, minuere seu quibuslibet vexationibus fatigare sed omnia integra conserventur eorum pro quorum[8] gubernatione ac sustentatione concessa sunt usibus omnimodis pro futura salva Sedis Apostolice auctoritate. Si qua igitur in futurum ecclesiastica secularisve persona hanc nostre constitutionis paginam sciens contra eam temere venire temptaverit, secundo ve tercio commonita nisi reatum suum digna congrua[9] satisfactione correxerit potestatis honorisque sui careat dignitate reamque se divino judicio existere de perpetrata iniquitate cognoscat et a sacratissimo Corpore ac Sanguine Dei et Domini Redemptoris nostri Jhesu Christi aliena fiat atque in extremo examine districte ultioni subjaceat. Cunctis autem eidem loco sua jura servatibus sit pace Domini Nostri Jhesu Christi. Quatinus et hic fructum bone actionis percipiant et apud districtum judicem premia eterne pacis inveniant, amen.

Ego Petrus[10] tituli Sancte Cecilie presbiter cardinalis
Ego Jordanus[11] Sancte Pudenciane tituli Pastoris presbiter cardinalis
Ego Guido[12] Sancte Marie Transtiberim tituli Calixti presbiter cardinalis
Ego Hugo[13] presbiter cardinalis Sancti Martini tituli equitii
Ego Soffredus[14] tituli Sancte Praxedis presbiter cardinalis
Ego Gerardus[15] Sancti Adriani diaconus cardinalis
Ego Gregorius[16] Sancte Marie in Aquiro diaconus cardinalis
Ego Gregorius[17] Sancti Georgii ad Velum Aureum diaconus cardinalis.
Ego Petrus[18] Sancte Marie in Via Lata diaconus cardinalis

Datum Reatum per manum Renaldi[19] domini Pape notarii, cancelarii vicem agentis sexto kalendas augusti, indictione prima, anno dominice incarnationis M° C° XC° VIII°, pontificatus vero domini Innocentii Pape III anno primo.

---

8 *Superscr.* pro quorum *A*.
9 *Superscr.* congrua *A*.
10 Pietro Diana (d. 1208), cardinal priest of Santa Cecilia in Trastevere from 1188.
11 Giordano di Ceccano (d. 1206) was abbot of the Cistercian abbey of Fossanova and cardinal priest of Santa Pudenziana from 1188.
12 Guy Paré (d. 1206), abbot of Cîteaux, 1186–9, cardinal priest of Santa Maria in Trastevere, 1190–9, and archbishop of Reims, 1204–6.
13 Ugo Bobone, cardinal priest of San Martino ai Monti, 1190–1206.
14 Soffredo (d. 1210), cardinal deacon of Santa Maria in Via Lata from 1182, and cardinal priest of Santa Prassede from 1193.
15 Gerardo Allucingoli (d. 1208), cardinal deacon of Sant'Adriano al Foro from 1182 and nephew of Pope Lucius III.
16 Gregorio Crescenzi (d. ca. 1207), cardinal deacon of Santa Maria in Aquiro from 1188.
17 Gregorio Carelli (d. 1211), cardinal deacon of San Giorgio in Velabro from 1190.
18 Pietro Capuano (d. 1214), cardinal deacon of Santa Maria in Via Lata from 1193.
19 Rainaldo, vice-chancellor of the papal chancellery, ca. 1198, and archbishop of Acerenza, 1198–9. Delisle, "Mémoire sur les actes d'Innocent III," 44.

25

January 27, 1233–4. Lateran.

Pope Gregory [IX] grants to the abbot of Prémontré certain rights to hear the confessions of his order's religious and conversi *and to absolve them from excommunication. He also grants to the abbot the right to tonsure novices, to bless religious ornaments, and, in the absence of a bishop, to give benediction at the end of chapter meetings.*[1]

A. Cartulary of Prémontré, fols. 7r–7v.
B. Original not found.
EDITION: Le Paige, *Bibliotheca*, 657 (partial).

Privilegio domino Premonstratensi concessum super tonsura clericali facienda et cetera.

[G]regorius episcopus, servus servorum Dei, dilecto filio abbati Premonstratensi salutem et apostolicam benedictionem. Cum sis pater omnium qui Premonstratensem ordinem sunt professi et abbatias ipsius ordinis tenearis ex debito visitare, tibi ad executionem officii tui apostolicum volumus indulgere favorem. Inde est quod, tuis precibus annuentes, presentibus tibi literis indulgemus ut fratribus et conversis eiusdem ordinis, si qui tibi peccata sua confiteri voluerint, penitenciam injungendi et absolvendi eos, etiam si forte vinculo sint excommunicationis astricti, nisi eorum fuerit tam gravis et enormis excessus quod pro absolucionis beneficio obtinendo merito essent ad Sedem Apostolicam transmittendi ac dispensandi cum eis si ante absolutionem obtentam vel sacros susceperint ordines vel fuerint iam susceptis, et tonsuras tuis novitiis clericis faciendi, dummodo presbiter sis, benedicendi quoque vestimenta sacerdotalia et pallas altaris et, convenientibus abbatibus, cum episcopus absens fuerit, benedictionem in conclusione capituli proferendi liberam habeas facultatem. Nulli ergo omnino hominum liceat hanc paginam nostre concessionis infringere vel ei ausu temerario contraire. Siquis autem hoc attemptare presumpserit, indignationem omnipotentis Dei et beatorum Petri et Pauli apostolorum eius se noverit incursum. Datum Laterani, quinto kalendas februarii, pontificatus nostri anno septimo.

1 This act reissues one given by Alexander III in 1171. Le Paige, *Bibliotheca*, 630; *PL* 200, col. 1288.

26

June 6, 1232. Alatri.

Pope Gregory [IX] excuses the priors and subpriors of the order of Prémontré from being required to be aware of cases involving the Premonstratensian Order that are discussed in letters issued by the Holy See, except when specifically instructed to do so, in order to permit them to devote themselves more fully to their religious duties.[1]

A. Cartulary of Prémontré, fol. 7v.
B. Original not found.
Other Manuscript Copies: Cartulary of Cockersand Abbey, British Library, Add. MS 37769, fols. 5v–6r (1268).
EDITION: Farrer, *The Chartulary of Cockersand Abbey of the Premonstratensian Order*, vol. 1, part 1, 38–9.

Indulgentia domini Pape communis ordini [*margo*: quod priores et suppriores non teneantur cognoscere de causis.]

[G]regorius episcopus, servus servorum Dei, dilectis filiis universis prioribus et supprioribus ordinis Premonstratensis salutem et apostolicam benedictionem. Cum ad hoc postposueritis universa ut in claustrali silentio possitis liberius Domino famulari, indecens esse videtur vos secularibus negotiis inmiscere; hinc est igitur quod nos, vestris supplicationibus inclinati, auctoritate vobis presentium indulgemus ut nostrarum commissionum obtentu non teneamini cognoscere de causis vobis ab Apostolica Sede commissis, nisi forte in litteris commissionum ipsarum de hac indulgentia specialem fecerimus mentionem. Nulli ergo omnino hominum liceat hanc paginam nostre concessionis infringere vel ei ausu temerario contraire. Siquis autem hoc attemptare presumpserit, indignationem omnipotentis Dei et beatorum Petri et Pauli apostolorum eius se noverit incursurum. Datum Alatri VIII° idus junii, pontificatus nostri anno sexto.

1 This act reissues one given by Honorius III in 1222. Le Paige, *Bibliotheca*, 654; Honorius III, *Honorii III Romani Pontificis opera omnia quae exstant*, vol. 4, col. 185.

27

January 20, 1201. Lateran.

Pope Innocent [III] grants to the religious of the order of Prémontré the privilege of bringing their suits before judges from their own order at the exclusion of all other judges.[1]

A. Cartulary of Prémontré, fol. 7v.

B. Original not found.

Other Manuscript Copies: Bayerische Hauptstaatsarchiv München, Literalien des Klosters Schäftlarn, no. 2, fol. 56r (14th c.).

EDITION: Le Paige, *Bibliotheca*, 646–7; Joester, *Urkundenbuch der Abtei Steinfeld*, 35–6.

REGISTER: Bréquigny, *Table chronologique*, vol. 4, 287; Potthast, *Regesta*, no. 1247; Weissthanner, *Die Urkunden und Urbare des Klosters Schäftlarn*, 263.

Indulgentia domini Pape communis toti ordini [*margo*: quod ad extraneos judices nisi de ordine commitatur aliqua causa.]

[I]nnocentius episcopus, servus servorum Dei, dilectis filiis abbatibus et universis fratribus ordinis Premonstratensis, salutem et apostolicam benedictionem. Et si nemo militans Deo litibus se debeat inmiscere, cum servum Domini litigare non deceat sed ad omnes secundum apostolum esse mittem, quia tamen inimicus homo ibi messi dominice zizania dolo suis superseminare conatur, unde dolet fertiliores manipulos in horrea congregari, sollicite nos convenit precavere ut incentivum litis quod non potest penitus sepeliri, quoniam necesse est, ut scandala veniant, sopiatur et per eos regularium virorum cause, presertim que vertuntur super spiritualibus, decidantur qui in spiritu humilitatis et in anima contrita Domino famulantes constitutiones et observantias norunt plenius regulares. Paci ergo et quieti vestri paterna volentes sollicitudine providere, in favorem religionis canonice vobis vel potius ordini vestro concedimus ut quotiens inter abbates vel fratres vestros qui Premonstratensis ecclesie magisterium recognoscunt, ad audientiam Apostolice Sedis super spiritualibus cause quecumque fuerint delate, si commitende fuerint, ad viros vestri ordinis remittantur. Ita quod si ad alios judices, huius indulgentie non habita mentione, commissio de cetero apparuerit impetrata, robore careat firmitatis. Ad hec

1 This act was confirmed by *vidimus* in the fourteenth century. Hauptsstaatsarchiv Düsseldorf, Steinfeld, no. 5. Clement VI confirmed it by *vidimus* in 1343. Le Paige, *Bibliotheca*, 697.

vobis auctoritate presentium indulgemus, ut, cum generale interdictum terre fuerit, liceat vobis in ecclesiis vestris que a populari sunt habitatione remote, divina officia celebrare sollempniter, dummodo excommunicati et interdicti procul absistant ut ea non possint audire. In aliis autem exclusis, excommunicatis et interdictis, non pulsatis campanis, suppressa voce, clausis januis a vestris fratribus celebretur. Nulli ergo omnino hominum liceat hanc paginam nostre concessionis infringere vel ei ausu temerario contraire. Siquis autem hoc attemptare presumpserit, indignationem omnipotentis Dei et beatorum Petri et Pauli apostolorum eius se noverit incursurum. Datum Laterani, XIII kalendas februarii, pontificatus nostri anno tercio.

28

January 17, 1234. Lateran.[1]

Pope Gregory [IX] grants to Premonstratensian abbeys the right to disregard letters obtained from the Holy See if those letters do not mention the Premonstratensian Order. Gregory also states that the Premonstratensians cannot convene meetings about papal letters which do not explicitly mention their order. (See duplicate ***45****.)*

A. Cartulary of Prémontré, fol. 7v.

B. Original not found.

Other Manuscript Copies: Cartulary of Cockersand Abbey, British Library, Add. MS 37769, fol. 6(b)v (1268); Bayerische Hauptstaatsarchiv München, Literalien des Klosters Schäftlarn, no. 2, fols. 56r–56v (14th c.); Stiftsarchiv Wilten, Lade 8 M, 54–5 (early 15th c.).

EDITION: Le Paige, *Bibliotheca*, 658–9; Sanders, *Chorographia sacra Brabantiae*, vol. 1, 172–3; Smet, *Corpus chronicorum Flandriae*, vol. 2, 883–4; Farrer, *The Chartulary of Cockersand Abbey of the Premonstratensian Order*, vol. 1, part 1, 39–40.

REGISTER: Reg. Vat. 17, fol. 131r; Bréquigny, *Table chronologique*, vol. 5, 312; Potthast, *Regesta*, no. 8107; Auvray, *Les registres de Grégoire IX*, vol. 1, col. 944; Weissthanner, *Die Urkunden und Urbare des Klosters Schäftlarn*, 270–1.

Concessionis indulgentia de eo quod non possimus conveniri per illam clausulam *quidam alii*.

[G]regorius episcopus, servus servorum Dei, dilectis filiis abbati Premonstratensi et coabbatibus suis salutem et apostolicam benedictionem. Licet

1 This act is transcribed again as **45**, where it is dated to the 17th rather than the 16th Kalends.

vobis, sicut asseritis, a Sede Apostolica sit indultum ut littere contra vos a Sede Apostolica impetrate non valeant, nisi de ordine vestro fecerint mentionem, nos tamen quieti vestre volentes consultius providere, auctoritate vobis presentium indulgemus, ut per illam clausulam generalem *Quidam alii*[2] non possitis aliquatenus conveniri, nisi littere apostolice expressam de Premonstratensi ordine fecerint mentionem. Nulli ergo omnino hominem liceat hanc paginam nostre concessionis infringere, vel ei ausu temerario contraire. Siquis autem hoc attemptare presumpserit, indignationem omnipotentis Dei et beatorum Petri et Pauli apostolorum eius se noverit incursurum. Datum Laterani, XVI° kalendas februarii, pontificatus nostri anno septimo.

29

1138–43.[1] Lateran.

Pope Innocent [II] confirms that all those who have taken vows in the Premonstratensian Order are obliged to stability of life, and grants to Hugues [I],[2] *abbot of Prémontré, and to the order's other abbots the privilege that no religious can be moved from a Premonstratensian community without the order's permission and that a sentence of excommunication can only be lifted from a fugitive Premonstratensian religious on their return to their original community.*

A. Cartulary of Prémontré, fol. 7v.

B. Original not found.

Other Manuscript Copies: "Statuta Praemonstratensia," Bayerische Staatsbibliothek München, Clm 17174, fol. 42v (late 12th c.); Bayerische Staatsbibliothek München, Clm 1031, fols. 172–172v (late 12th c.); Cartulary of Grimbergen Abbey, Oud Archief, Abdij van Grimbergen, fol. 6r (13th c.); Cartulary of Saint-Augustin-lès-Thérouanne, Brussels, KBR, MS 4132, fol. 149r (13th c.); Brussels, KBR, MS 1251, fol. 134r (13th c.); Bayerische Hauptstaatsarchiv München, Literalien des Klosters Schäftlarn, no. 2, fol. 32v (14th c.); Stiftsarchiv Wilten, Lade

2 For further discussion of *quidam alii* and *rebus aliis*, see Linehan and Bertram, "Bermerkungen zu einer Extravagante Gregors IX. und zu ihrer Verwendung im Lorvãn-Prozeß," 373–5.

1 This act must date to the period of overlap in the tenures of Innocent II (1130–43) and Hugues I de Fosses, abbot of Prémontré (1128–61). On the basis of a 1379 *vidimus* act, which states "Datum Laterani, XII kalendas aprilis," Olivier Guyotjeannin dates this act to March 21, 1138–43, since Innocent II was only resident in the Lateran during those years. Guyotjeannin et al, *Le chartrier de l'abbaye Prémontrée de Saint-Yved de Braine*, 298–9. However, Le Paige dates the act to 1138. Le Paige, *Bibliotheca*, 421.

2 Hugues I de Fosses (ca. 1093–1164), first abbot of Prémontré.

8 M, 8–9 (early 15th c.); Cartulary of Beaurepart, Bibliothèque du Séminaire Episcopal de Liège, G IV 7, fol. 12v (15th c.); Cartulary of Park Abbey, Archief van de Abdij van Park te Heverlee, MS VII 26, fol. 43v (15th c.); Cartulary of Averbode Abbey, Archief van de abdij van Averbode, Sectie IV, no. 109, fol. 3r (15/16th c.); Cartulary of Park Abbey, Archief van de Abdij van Park te Heverlee, fol. 4v (15/16th c.).

EDITION: Le Paige, *Bibliotheca*, 421, 623 (partial); *PL* 179, 350–1.

REGISTER: JL no. 7878 (J: 5625); Weissthanner, *Die Urkunden und Urbare des Klosters Schäftlarn*, 254–5.

Indulgentia quod non liceat alicui retinere canonicum seu conversum nostrum nisi invitis.

[I]nnocentius episcopus, servus servorum Dei, dilectis filiis Hugoni Premonstrate ecclesie et aliis eiusdem professionis abbatibus et religiosis viris salutem et apostolicam benedictionem. Quemadmodum ea que semel Deo dicata sunt, ad usus seculares redire non possunt, ita qui se Deo in locis vestris servire voverunt atque se ipsos professionis vinculo astrinxerunt ad alia loca sine licentia prelati sui transire non possunt. Nulli ergo episcopo abbati, priori liceat professos vestros, canonicos sive conversos, absque libera licentia prelati sui, suscipere. Et id ipsum auctoritate apostolica prohibemus ne quis attemptet professionis vestre aliquos, vobis invitis, ausu temerario retinere. Preterea potestatem attribuimus vobis fugitivos vestros, usque dum redeuntes satisfaciant, excommunicationis sentencia innodare. Datum Laterani.

30

March 16, 1228. Lateran.

Pope Gregory [IX] forbids the requirement of a palfrey or any other thing for the installation of an abbot of the Premonstratensian Order.

A. Cartulary of Prémontré, fol. 8r.

B. Original not found.

Other Manuscript Copies: Bayerische Hauptstaatsarchiv München, Literalien des Klosters Schäftlarn, no. 2, fol. 58r (14th c.); Stiftsarchiv Wilten, Lade 8 M, 55 (early 15th c.).

EDITION: Le Paige, *Bibliotheca*, 654–5.

REGISTER: Potthast, *Regesta*, no. 8146; Weissthanner, *Die Urkunden und Urbare des Klosters Schäftlarn*, 270.

Ne aliquis requirat palefridum sui aliud pro installatione abbatum.

[G]regorius episcopus, servus servorum Dei, dilectis filiis abbati Premonstratensi et ceteris abbatibus Premonstratensis ordinis, salutem et apostolicam benedictionem. Volentes utilitati vestre consulere et obviare que in perisque inolevit locis et ecclesiis corruptele, auctoritate presencium districtius inhibemus ne pro installatione abbatum ordinis vestri, deducti fuerint postquam vel antequam deducantur ad sedem, aliquis palefridum vel aliquid aliud exigere vel extorquere presumat. Nulli ergo omnino hominum liceat hanc paginam nostre inhibitionis infringere vel ei ausu temerario contraire. Siquis autem hoc attemptare presumpserit, indignationem omnipotentis Dei et beatorum Petri et Pauli apostolorum eius se noverit incursurum. Datum Laterani, XVII kalendas aprilis, pontificatus nostri anno primo.

31

July 24, 1225. Rieti.

Pope Honorius [III] renews the privilege granted to the order of Prémontré by his predecessor Innocent [III], which forbids archbishops and bishops in the dioceses that hold Premonstratensian grangiae *to exert any rights whatsoever on the said* grangiae, *except in the case of hospitality when necessary. (See* ***32****.)*[1]

A. Cartulary of Prémontré, fol. 8r.

B. Original not found.

Other Manuscript Copies: Bayerische Hauptstaatsarchiv München, Literalien des Klosters Schäftlarn, no. 2, fols. 57r–57v (14th c.); Stiftsarchiv Wilten, Lade 8 M, 60 (early 15th c.).

EDITION: Le Paige, *Bibliotheca*, 654; Honorius III, *Honorii III Romani Pontificis opera omnia quae exstant*, vol. 4, cols. 899–901.

REGISTER: Potthast, *Regesta*, no. 7448; Weissthanner, *Die Urkunden und Urbare des Klosters Schäftlarn*, 269–70.

Privilegium domini Pape [*margo*: ne archiepiscopi sive episcopi hospitentur in grangiis nostre ordinis.]

[H]onorius episcopus, servus servorum Dei, venerabilibus fratribus universis archiepiscopis et episcopis in quorum diocesibus grangie fratrum

1 The act of Innocent III, dating to 1200, reproduced within this one, is Le Paige, *Bibliotheca*, 647; Potthast, *Regesta*, no. 1051.

Premonstratensis ordinis sunt site, salutem et apostolicam benedictionem. Si veri Christiane religionis amatores et cultores essetis, religiosis viris in personis vel rebus nullam molestiam inferretis, quorum potius tenemini gravaminibus obviare. Unde, conquerentibus dilectis filiis abbate ac fratribus ordinis Premonstratensis, nostris est auribus intimatum, quod licet in eorum privilegiis inhibitum sit expresse, ne quis archiepiscopus vel episcopus nisi in manifesta necessitate in eorum grangiis hospitentur, quidam vestrum in singulis grangiis eorumdem fratrum, in suis diocesibus constitutis, procurationes exigunt annuatim, que si eis aliquando forte negantur, ministri eorum de animalibus eorumdem fratrum predas violenter abducunt, quas vel pignori obligant, vel alienant omnino, nec fratribus ipsis restituunt, donec pro requisita procuratione certa pecunia persolvatur; qui ut avaritiam suam et exactionem excusent, frivolas exigende procurationis, causas assignant, vel quod in grangiis illis decime colligantur, vel quod canonici qui parrochialem ecclesiam, in vicinis locis obtinere noscuntur, aliquando commorantur in grangiis, vel quod in eis claustrum sororum habetur, que potius ex accessu vestro materiam dissolutionis accipiunt, dum confabulantur cum clericis et per officinas discurrunt, quam doctrinam recipiant salutarem. Quia vero cause huius frivole sunt, nec earum occasione fratres ipsos in exhibendis procurationibus credimus esse cogendos, fraternitati vestre ad exemplar felicis recordationis Innocentii Pape, predecessoris nostri, per apostolica scripta mandamus et districte precipimus. Quatinus fratres ipsos contra indultam sibi a Sede Apostolica libertatem, nec in predictis nec in aliis aggravetis nec exactiones aliquas illis imponere presumatis. Alioquin non poterimus sub dissimulatione transire, quin eorum indempnitati contra exactiones vestras paterna sollicitudine consulamus. Datum Reatum, IX kalendas augusti, pontificatus nostri anno X°.

32

February 7, 1230. Lateran.

*Pope Gregory [IX] renews the preceding privilege granted to the order of Prémontré by Popes Innocent [III] and Honorius [III]. (See **31**.)*[1]

A. Cartulary of Prémontré, fol. 8r.

B. Original not found.

EDITION: Le Paige, *Bibliotheca*, 656.

REGISTER: Potthast, *Regesta*, no. 8658.

1 The act of Innocent III, dating to 1200, reproduced within this one, is Le Paige, *Bibliotheca*, 647; Potthast, *Regesta*, no. 1051.

Item unde supra.

[G]regorius episcopus, servus servorum Dei, venerabilibus fratribus universis archiepiscopis et episcopis in quorum diocesibus grangie fratrum Premonstratensis ordinis sunt site salutem et apostolicam benedictionem. Si veri Christiane religionis amatores et cultores essetis, religiosis viris in personis et rebus nullam molestiam inferretis, quorum tenemini gravaminibus obviare. Verum, conquerentibus dilectis filiis abbate et fratribus ordinis Premonstratensis, nostris est auribus intimatum quod, licet in eorum privilegiis inhibitum sit expresse ne quis archiepiscopus vel episcopus nisi in manifesta necessitate in eorum grangiis hospitetur, quidam vestrum in singulis grangiis eorumdem fratrum in suis diocesibus constitutis procurationes indebitas exigunt annuatim, que si aliquando eis forte negantur, ministri eorum de animalibus eorumdem fratrum predas violenter abducunt quas vel pignori obligant, vel alienant omnino, nec fratribus ipsis restituunt donec pro requisita procuratione certa pecunia persolvatur, qui, ut avariciam suam excusent, frivolas exigende procurationis causas assignant vel quid in grangiis illis decime colligantur, vel quod canonici qui aliquando commorantur in grangiis et vicinis locis noscuntur parrochialem ecclesiam obtinere. Quia vero cause huiusmodi frivole sunt nec earum occasione fratres ipsos in exhibendis procurationibus credimus esse cogendos fraternitati vestre ad exemplar felicis recordationis Innocentii et Honorii, Romanorum pontificum, predecessorum nostrorum, per apostolica scripta mandamus et districte precipimus quatinus fratres ipsos contra indultam sibi a Sede Apostolica libertatem nec in predictis nec in aliis aggravetis nec exactiones aliquas illis imponere presumatis. Alioquin non poterimus sub dissimulatione transire quin eorum indempnitati contra exactiones vestras paterna sollicitudine consulamus. Datum Laterani, VII idus februarii, pontificatus nostri anno quarto.

33

August 21, 1173. Anagni.

Pope Alexander [III] grants to the abbot and religious of Prémontré the privilege of imposing penance and giving the communion host to those who serve them and live from their table.

A. Cartulary of Prémontré, fols. 8r–8v.

B. Original not found.

Other Manuscript Copies: Cartulary of Grimbergen Abbey, Abdij van Grimbergen Oud Archief, Klas II, 1, fol. 2v (13th c.); Cartulary of Saint-Augustin-lès-Thérouanne, Brussels, KBR, MS 4132, fol. 153v (13th c.); Cartulary of Park Abbey, Archief van de Abdij van Park te Heverlee, MS VII 24, fol. 130r (13th c.);

Cartulary of Beaurepart, Bibliothèque du Séminaire Episcopal de Liège, G IV 7, fol. 22r (15th c.); Cartulary of Park Abbey, Archief van de Abdij van Park te Heverlee, MS VII 26, fol. 44r (15th c.); Cartulary of Averbode Abbey, Archief van de abdij van Averbode, Sectie IV, no. 109, fol. 5v (15/16th c.); Cartulary of Park Abbey, Archief van de Abdij van Park te Heverlee, MS VII 35, fol. 19r (15/16th c.).

EDITION: Le Paige, *Bibliotheca*, 630–1.

REGISTER: JL no. 12621 (J: 8403).

***Margo*: Quod liceat nobis penitenciam dare et comunicare famulos nostros.**

[A]lexander episcopus, servus servorum Dei, dilectis filiis abbati et fratribus Premonstratensis salutem et apostolicam benedictionem. Apostolice Sedis auctoritate inducimur et nostri officii debito provocamur preces filiorum ecclesie, que rationi concordant, et ab ecclesiastica non dissonant honestate, clementer admittere et eas utili effectu prosequendo complere. Inde est quod vestris precibus benignius annuentes, vobis auctoritate apostolica indulgemus, ut servientibus vestris, qui de mensa vestra vivunt, vobis absque alicuius contraditione penitenciam dare et Corpus dominicum in statutis temporibus tradere liceat. Decernimus ergo ut nulli hominum liceat hanc paginam nostre concessionis constitutionis infringere vel ei aliquatenus contraire. Siquis autem hoc attemptare presumpserit indignationem omnipotentis Dei et beatorum Petri et Pauli apostolorum eius se noverit incursurum. Datum Anagnie, XII° kalendas septembrii.

34

December 21, 1138–43.[1] Lateran.

Pope Innocent [II] grants to Hugues [I],[2] abbot of Prémontré, and all the abbots and prepositi *of the order of Prémontré, the authorization to depose and replace abbots who have committed a serious offence or have showed themselves incapable of fulfilling their duties.*

A. Cartulary of Prémontré, fol. 8v.

B. Original not found.

1 This act must date to the period of overlap in the tenures of Innocent II (1130–43) and Hugues I de Fosses, abbot of Prémontré (1128–61). The editors of the *Patrologia Latina* dated this to 1138, while Le Paige dated it to 1141; neither offer a rationale for this. *PL* 179, col. 387; Le Paige, *Bibliotheca*, 624. However, Innocent II was only resident in the Lateran 1138–43.

2 Hugues I de Fosses (ca. 1093–1164), first abbot of Prémontré.

Other Manuscript Copies: Cartulary of Grimbergen Abbey, Abdij van Grimbergen Oud Archief, Klas II, 1, fol. 6v (13th c.); Cartulary of Saint-Augustin-lès-Thérouanne, Brussels, KBR, MS 4132, fol. 154r (13th c.); Cartulary of Park Abbey, Archief van de Abdij van Park te Heverlee, MS VII 24, fol. 130r (13th c.); Bayerische Hauptstaatsarchiv München, Literalien des Klosters Schäftlarn, no. 2, fol. 56v (14th c.); Cartulary of Beaurepart, Bibliothèque du Séminaire Episcopal de Liège, G IV 7, fol. 12v (15th c.); Cartulary of Park Abbey, Archief van de Abdij van Park te Heverlee, MS VII 26, fol. 41v (15th c.); Cartulary of Averbode Abbey, Archief van de abdij van Averbode, Sectie IV, no. 109, fol. 2r (15/16th c.); Cartulary of Park Abbey, Archief van de Abdij van Park te Heverlee, MS VII 35, fol. 4r (15/16th c.).

EDITION: Le Paige, *Bibliotheca*, 624; *PL* 179, col. 387.

REGISTER: JL no. 7928 (J: 5657); Weissthanner, *Die Urkunden und Urbare des Klosters Schäftlarn*, 255–6.

NO RUBRIC.

Innocentius[3] episcopus, servus servorum Dei, dilecto filio suo Hugoni, abbati Premonstratensi, necnon ceteris abbatibus et prepositis eiusdem ordinis atque professionis salutem et apostolicam benedictionem. Qui divina disponente clementia locum pastoris obtinere meretur, necesse habet non solum de sua, sed etiam de fratrum suorum salute sollicite cogitare, certus existens quod sicut pro bonis operibus, tam suis quam eorum, qui sibi committuntur, retributionem a Domino et benedictionem accipiet. Ita econtrario, si quod absit, vel ipse oberraverit, vel subditos suos exorbitare promiserit, sententiam dampnationis incurret, quem etiam oportet medici vicem agere, ut que cognoverit fovenda confoveat, et que viderit amputanda, ferro discretionis abscidat. Hoc nimirum intuitu constituimus, ut si aliquis abbatum vestri ordinis atque professionis, sive Premonstrate ecclesie, sive alterius loci, quod Deus avertat, in crimine fuerit deprehensus, aut prorsus inutilis in suo officio apparuerit, communi omnium vestrum, vel etiam maioris et sanioris partis consilio, huiuscemodi deponendi, et loco eius alium subrogandi ex nostra concessione habeatis liberam facultatem. Datum Laterani, XII kalendas januarii.

35

January 25, 1231. Lateran.

Pope Gregory [IX], considering the lamentable state of the monastery of Sant'Alessio all'Aventino[1] *in Rome and the good reputation of the order of*

3 The initial letter has been added at a later, possibly post-medieval date.

1 The Premonstratensian abbey of Sant'Alessio all'Aventino. *MP* I, 387–8.

Prémontré, cedes Sant'Alessio and its dependencies to Prémontré, while retaining its census *and preserving the monastic freedom of Sant'Alessio.*

A. Cartulary of Prémontré, fol. 8v.
B. Original not found.
EDITION: Le Paige, *Bibliotheca*, 656–7; Nerini, *De templo et coenobio sanctorum Bonifacii et Alexii Historica Monumenta*, 242–3.
REGISTER: Bréquigny, *Table chronologique*, vol. 5, 387.

Privilegium de ecclesia Sancti Alexii nostro ordine collata.

[G]regorius episcopus, servus servorum Dei, dilectis filiis abbati et conventui Premonstratensi salutem et apostolicam benedictionem. Officii nostri credimus laudabiliter prosequi actionem, cum nos, quibus omnium ecclesiarum est sollicitudo commissa, de hiis que ad jus et ad proprietatem Beati Petri pertinere noscuntur, specialiter cogitamus, sicut earum necessitati et utilitati disnoscitur expedire. Attendentes ergo non modicum lapsum monasterii Sancti Alexii de urbe Sedis Apostolice specialis positi in loco qui Mons Aventinus vocatur, et cupientes illud in spiritualibus et temporalibus, sicut indiget, in melius reformari, cum religio vestra longe lateque cuius bonus odor diffunditur, Deo sit et hominibus gratiosa, de fratrum nostrorum consilio, monasterium ipsum cum omnibus ecclesiis, possessionibus, juribus, et pertinenciis suis, salvo censu ecclesie Romane debito ac servata ipsius monasterii libertate, vobis, vestris successoribus presenti privilegio duximus concedendum. Ita quod abbas, canonici et conversi eiusdem ~~ordinis~~ qui pro tempore fuerint, regulam et ordinem Premonstratensem tenere debeant inviolabiliter et servare; ac tu, fili abbas, et successores tui visitandi corrigendi et reformandi secundum ordinis Premonstratensis statuta, plenam habeatis ibidem et liberam potestam. Nulli ergo omnino hominum liceat hanc paginam nostre concessionis infringere, vel ei ausu temerario contraire. Siquis autem hoc attemptare presumpserit, indignationem omnipotentis Dei et beatorum Petri et Pauli apostolorum eius se noverit incursurum. Datum Laterani, VIII kalendas februarii, pontificatus nostri anno IIII°.

36

July 14, 1220. Orvieto.

Pope Honorius [III] authorizes the abbots of the order of Prémontré to have their liturgical vessels, vestments, and altars blessed by any visiting bishop known to them who is in favour with the Holy See, and to permit that bishop to ordain canons.

A. Cartulary of Prémontré, fol. 8v.

B. Original not found.

Other Manuscript Copies: Bayerische Hauptstaatsarchiv München, Literalien des Klosters Schäftlarn, no. 2, fols. 55v–56r (14th c.); Book of Privileges, Osterhofen Abbey, Bayerische Hauptstaatsarchiv München, Clm 9903, fols. 22r–22v (early 14th c.) Stiftsarchiv Wilten, Lade 8 M, 23–4 (early 15th c.).

EDITION: Le Paige, *Bibliotheca*, 652 (partial); Honorius III, *Honorii III Romani Pontificis opera omnia quae exstant*, vol. 3, col. 478.

REGISTER: Reg. Vat . 4, fol. 205r; Potthast, *Regesta*, no. 6303; Weissthanner, *Die Urkunden und Urbare des Klosters Schäftlarn*, 268–9.

Privilegium quod liceat nobis ordines recipere ab extraneis episcopis.

[H]onorius episcopus, servus servorum Dei, dilectis filiis abbatibus Premonstratensis ordinis salutem et apostolicam benedictionem. Vestris et ordinis vestri ecclesiarum conmoditatibus providentes, auctoritate vobis presentium indulgemus ut si quem episcopum communionem et gratiam Sedis Apostolice habentem, et de quo plenam noticiam habeatis, per vos transire contigerit, cum non semper propriorum episcoporum copiam habeatis, liceat vobis ab eo recipere benedictionem vasorum et vestium, consecrationes altarium ac ordinationes canonicorum, qui ad sacros fuerint ordines promovendi. Nulli ergo omnino hominum liceat hanc paginam nostre concessionis infringere vel ei ausu temerario contraire. Siquis autem hoc attemptare presumpserit, indignationem omnipotentis Dei et beatorum Petri et Pauli apostolorum eius se noverit incursurum. Datum apud Urbem Veterem, II idus julii, pontificatus nostri anno quarto.

37

May 25, [1198?].[1] Saint Peter's, Rome.

Pope Innocent forbids the lifting of any interdictions or excommunications levelled against those who have caused harm to the religious of Prémontré or

1 G.M. van der Velden attributes this act to Innocent IV in 1244, but offers no rationale for this. Van der Velden, "Documenten betreffende de orde van Prémontré, verzameld door Merselius van Macharen in 1445," 80–1. This act, however, does not appear in the registers covering the first five years of Innocent IV's papacy. See Berger, *Les registres d'Innocent IV, publiés ou analysés d'après les manuscrits originaux du Vatican et de la Bibliothèque nationale*, vol. 1. The current editors suggest this act was most likely issued during the first year of Innocent III's papal tenure, along with other acts such as **69**.

dishonestly possessed goods belonging to the church of Prémontré for as long as they continue to do so.

A. Cartulary of Prémontré, fol. 8v.

B. Original not found.

Other Manuscript Copies: "Liber statutorum necnon et de institutione sive de origine candidi ordinis scilicet Premonstratensis," Koninklijke Bibliotheek van Nederland, MS 128 G 21, fol. 92r (1445).

Edition: Van der Velden, "Documenten betreffende de orde van Prémontré, verzameld door Merselius van Macharen in 1445," 80–1.

Quod nullus absolvat excommunicatos a nobis nisi prius nobis satisfactum.

[I]nnocentius episcopus, servus servorum Dei, dilectis filiis ~~Dei~~ abbati et universo conventui Premonstratensi salutem et apostolicam benedictionem. Religiosis viris annuere eorumque intendere commodis et augmentis et officium nostrum exigit et debitum postulat caritatis. Eapropter auctoritate vobis presentium duximus indulgendum ut nullus malefactores vestros vel rerum ecclesia vestre male fidei possessores, cum fuerint interdicto vel excommunicatione notati, absolvere aliqua ratione attemptet donec excessum suum, prout possibile fuerit, corrigant et emendent et vobis ab eis fuerit satisfactum. Nulli ergo omnino hominum liceat hanc paginam nostre concessionis infringere, vel ei ausu temerario contraire. Siquis autem hoc attemptare presumpserit, indignationem omnipotentis Dei et beatorum Petri et Pauli apostolorum eius se noverit incursurum. Datum Rome apud Sanctum Petrum, VIII kalendas junii, pontificatus nostri anno primo.

38

May 22, 1222. Alatri.

Pope Honorius [III] authorizes the abbots and the religious of Prémontré to imprison the canons and conversi of the order who have carried out or are planning to carry out any criminal acts against them.

A. Cartulary of Prémontré, fols. 8v–9r.

B. Original not found.

Edition: Le Paige, *Bibliotheca*, 653; Honorius III, *Honorii III Romani Pontificis opera omnia quae exstant*, vol. 4, cols. 359–60.

Register: Reg. Vat. 6, fol. 243r; Potthast, *Regesta*, no. 7026.

Quod liceat nobis incarcerare maleficiores canonicos vel conversos.

[H]onorius episcopus, servus servorum Dei, dilectis filiis abbatibus et fratribus universis ordinis Premonstratensis, salutem et apostolicam benedictionem. Cum, sicut ex parte vestra fuit propositum coram nobis, non nulli post professionem ab eis ordini vestro factam, diabolica fraude seducti, ab ecclesiis suis malivole recedentes, domos vestras incendere ac alias graviter vos dampnificare presumant, nos indempnitati vestre paterna volentes sollicitudine providere, presentium vobis auctoritate concedimus, ut vestros canonicos et conversos si in hiis presumptores vel rebelles extiterint, quamdiu in sua malicia perdurarint, sub ea possitis custodia detinere, quod vobis aut domibus vestris molestias inferre nequeant vel jacturas. Nulli ergo omnino hominum liceat hanc paginam nostre concessionis infringere vel ei ausu temerario contraire. Siquis autem hoc attemptare presumpserit, indignationem omnipotentis Dei et beatorum Petri et Pauli apostolorum eius se noverit incursurum. Datum Alatri, X kalendas junii, pontificatus nostri anno sexto.

39

May 13, 1198. Saint Peter's, Rome.

Pope Innocent [III] writes to Pierre [I],[2] *abbot of Prémontré, to confirm the decision taken by the abbots of the Premonstratensian Order in a General Chapter meeting to no longer be required to accept women as sisters or* conversae, *and also to forbid any abbot or monastery of the order to sell or exchange their possessions without the consent of the General Chapter or the authorization of the father abbot.*

A. Cartulary of Prémontré, fol. 9r.

B. Original not found.

Other Manuscript Copies: Bayerische Hauptstaatsarchiv München, Literalien des Klosters Schäftlarn, no. 2, fols. 46v–47r (14th c.); Stiftsarchiv Wilten, Lade 8 M, 49–50 (early 15th c.).

EDITION: Sirleto, *Innocentii tertii, pontificis maximi decretalium, atque aliarum epistolarum tomus*, vol. 1, 92; Middendorp, *D. Innocentii Pontificis Maximi Eivs Nominis III*, vol. 2, 119; Le Paige, *Bibliotheca*, 644–5; Baluze, *Epistolarum Innocentii III*, vol. 1, 107; *PL* 214, cols. 173–4; Hageneder and Haidacher, *Die Register Innocenz' III*, vol. 1, 286–7.

---

2 Pierre I de Saint-Médard, abbot of the Premonstratensian abbeys of Saint-Just en Chaussée, 1184–95, Prémontré, 1195–1201, and Cuissy, 1210–17. *MP* II, 497, 527, 565.

REGISTER: Reg. Vat. 4, fol. 50v; Bréquigny, *Table chronologique*, vol. 4, 231; Potthast, *Regesta*, no. 168; Weissthanner, *Die Urkunden und Urbare des Klosters Schäftlarn*, 261–2.

Privilegium quod non recipiamus decetero mulieres.

[I]nnocentius episcopus, servus servorum Dei, dilectis filiis Petro, abbati et ceteris abbatibus eiusdem ordinis salutem et apostolicam benedictionem. Cum a nobis petitur quod justum est et honestum, tam vigor equitatis quam ordo exigit rationis, ut id per sollicitudinem officii nostri ad debitum perducatur effectum, significastis siquidem nobis, quod ad implendum illud apostolicum, "ab omni specie mala abstinete vos"[3] et ad reprimendum os loquentium iniqua, qui in detractionibus gloriantur et opinionem justorum nituntur multipliciter infamare, olim in communi capitulo statuistis et postmodum sub interminatione gravis pene sepius innovastis, ut nullam decetero in sororem teneamini recipere vel conversam, presertim cum ex hoc aliquando incommoda fueritis multa perpessi. Nos igitur institutionem ipsam sicut de communi consilio abbatum, ad commune capitulum convenientium, provide facta fuit et recepta, auctoritate apostolica confirmamus et presentis scripti patrocinio communimus. Ad hec adicimus, ne aliquis abbas vel conventus possessiones ecclesiarum vestri ordinis, preter assensum generalis capituli, vendere audeat, vel sine patris abbatis licentia commutare. Nulli ergo omnino hominum liceat hanc nostre paginam confirmationis et inhibitionis infringere vel ei ausu temerario contraire. Siquis autem hoc attemptare presumpserit, indignationem omnipotentis Dei et beatorum Petri et Pauli apostolorum eius se noverit incursurum. Datum Rome apud Sanctum Petrum, III idus maii, pontificatus nostri anno primo.

40

December 21, 1138–40.[1] Lateran.

Pope Innocent [II] forbids any bishop, ecclesiastic, or lay person to demand tithes on anything that is the product of the labour of Premonstratensian religious and necessary for their nourishment, or to disturb the peace for any reason.[2]

---

3 1 Thessalonians 5:22.

---

1 Jaffé dates this to 1138, while Le Paige dates it to 1140. J: 5655; Le Paige, *Bibliotheca*, 624.

2 Both this act and **69** were confirmed at the Council of Basel in 1437. *Monumenta Boica*, vol. 21, 491–6. This act was also confirmed by *vidimus* in the late twelfth century (Archief van de abdij van Tongerlo, no. 35) and 1436 (Staatsarchiv Antwerp, Fonds S. Michiels in Antwerpen, no. 2).

A. Cartulary of Prémontré, fol. 9r.

B. Original not found.

Other Manuscript Copies: Bayerische Staatsbibliothek München, Clm 1031, fol. 173r (late 12th c.); Cartulary of Saint-Augustin-lès-Thérouanne, Brussels, KBR, MS 4132, fol. 155r (13th c.); Cartulary of Park Abbey, Archief van de Abdij van Park te Heverlee, MS VII 24, fol. 131r (13th c.); Cartulary of Ninove, Archives de l'Archevêché de Malines-Bruxelles, Fonds Prémontrés Ninove, MS 1, fol. 128v (14th c.); Bayerische Hauptstaatsarchiv München, Literalien des Klosters Schäftlarn, no. 2, fols. 33Br–33Bv (14th c.); Stiftsarchiv Wilten, Lade 8 M, 1 (early 15th c.); Cartulary of Beaurepart, Bibliothèque du Séminaire Episcopal de Liège, G IV 7, fol. 13r (15th c.); Cartulary of Park Abbey, Archief van de Abdij van Park te Heverlee, MS VII 26, fol. 45r (15th c.); Cartulary of Averbode Abbey, Archief van de abdij van Averbode, Sectie IV, no. 109, fol. 2v (15/16th c.); Cartulary of Park Abbey, Archief van de Abdij van Park te Heverlee, MS VII 35, fol. 5r (15/16th c.); Cartulary of Parc Abbey, Parc Abbey Archives, VII 31, fol. 13v (15th–18th c.).

EDITION: Le Paige, *Bibliotheca*, 624; Fejér, *Codex diplomaticus Hungariae ecclesiasticus ac civilis, studio et opera*, vol. 2, 115–16.

REGISTER: JL no. 7927 (J: 5656); Weissthanner, *Die Urkunden und Urbare des Klosters Schäftlarn*, 255.

Quod non liceat alicui exigere a nobis decimas de aliquo.

[I]nnocentius episcopus, servus servorum Dei, dilectis filiis abbatibus, prepositis ac reliquis fratribus Premonstratensis ordinis atque professionis tam presentibus quam futuris in perpetuum. Decimas a populo sacerdotibus atque levitis esse solvendas divine legis sancxit auctoritas. Ceterum a canonicis sive clericis communi vita viventibus nulla ratio finit, ut episcopi vel persone quelibet ecclesiastice seu mundane decimas de ipsorum laboribus propriis, vel nutrimentis accipiant, beato scilicet Gregorio Magno et egregio doctore attestante atque dicente: Communi vita viventibus de faciendis elemosinis et exhibenda hospitalitate nobis quid erit dicendum, cum omne quod superest in piis causis debeant erogare.[3] Quodam[4] ob rem presentis scripti pagina sanctimus et auctoritate apostolica constituimus, ut nulli episcopo, nulli ecclesiastice, secularive persone licentia pateat, de laboribus quos propriis manibus sumptibusve colligitis vel etiam de nutrimentis vestris, decimas a vobis exigere, nec quietem vestram occasione aliqua perturbare. Sed potius, ab huiusmodi vexationibus expediti, divino servitio diebus ac noctibus libera mente vacetis. Siquis

3 This is a close paraphrase of Gregory I the Great's Letter 64. *PL* 77, col. 1186.

4 *Sic A*, *read* quod.

autem ausu temerario contra hoc venire temptaverit nisi presumptionem suam satisfactione congrua emendaverit, indignationem omnipotentis Dei et beatorum Petri ac Pauli apostolorum eius incurrat. Datum Laterani, XII kalendarum januarii.

41

February 18, 1219. Lateran.

Pope Honorius [III] forbids anyone to demand of the religious of Prémontré the noval tithe on lands cultivated at the time of the Fourth Lateran Council (1215) and on those lands that the religious cultivate afterwards either by their own hand or at their own cost. (See near-duplicate ***55****.)*

A. Cartulary of Prémontré, fol. 9r.

B. Original not found.

Other Manuscript Copies: Cartulary of Leiston Abbey, British Library, Cotton MS Vespasian E XIV, fols. 26r–26v (1st half of 13th c.); Cartulary of Cockersand Abbey, British Library, Add. MS 37769, fols. 11r–11v (1268); Bayerische Hauptstaatsarchiv München, Literalien des Klosters Schäftlarn, no. 2, fols. 57v–58r (14th c.); Stiftsarchiv Wilten, Lade 8 M, 60 (early 15th c.).

EDITION: Le Paige, *Bibliotheca*, 650–1; Lalore, *Collection des Principaux Cartulaires du diocèse de Troyes*, vol. 3, 159–60; Honorius III, *Honorii III Romani Pontificis opera omnia quae exstant*, vol. 3, col. 127–8; Farrer, *The Chartulary of Cockersand Abbey of the Premonstratensian Order*, vol. 1, part 1, 23–35; Mortimer, *Leiston Abbey Cartulary and Butler Priory Charters*, 70.

REGISTER: Bréquigny, *Table chronologique*, vol. 5, 103; Potthast, *Regesta*, no. 5991; Weissthanner, *Die Urkunden und Urbare des Klosters Schäftlarn*, 267.

Privilegium [*margo*: ne aliquis male interpretetur privilegia.]

[H]onorius episcopus, servus servorum Dei, dilectis filiis abbati Premonstratensi et universis coabbatibus suis et fratribus sub eodem ordine Deo servientibus, salutem et apostolicam benedictionem. Contingit interdum quod nonnulli propriis inconbentes[1] affectibus, dum sanctionum sensum legitimum ad sua ~~commoda~~ vota non habent accomodum, superadducunt adulterum intellectum, in temporali compendio eternum dispendium non timentes. Sane, quia, sicut audivimus, quidam suo nimis inherentes ingenio, nimiumque voluntarii, concilii generalis interpres de novalibus postidem concilium acquisitis, a vobis

1 *Sic A, read* incumbentes.

intendunt decimas extorquere, ne super hiis vos contingat in debita molestacione vexari, nos interpretationem illorum intellectui constitutionis predicti concilii super Premonstratensis decimis edite, asserimus peregrinam. In ipsa quidem expresse cavetur, ut de alienis terris et amodo acquirendis, si eas propriis manibus aut sumptibus colueritis, decimas persolvatis ecclesiis, quibus ratione prediorum antea solvebantur. Unde si a prope positum atiem[2] discretionis extenderent, advertentes nichilominus de quibus novalibus Apostolica Sedes intelligat, indulgentiam super talibus piis locis concessam, non sic circa novalia nove interpretationis ludibria ingenia fatigarent. Inhibemus igitur auctoritate presentium ut nullus a vobis de novalibus a tempore concilii excultis vel in posterum propriis manibus aut sumptibus excolendis, decimas exigere vel extorquere presumat. Nulli ergo omnino hominum liceat hanc paginam nostre inhibitionis infringere vel ei ausu temerario contraire. Siquis autem hoc attemptare presumpserit, indignationem omnipotentis Dei et beatorum Petri et Pauli apostolorum eius se noverit incursurum. Datum Laterani, XII kalendas martii, pontificatus nostri anno tercio.

42

January 26, 1234. Lateran.

Pope Gregory [IX], through the Premonstratensian abbots of Sant'Alessio all'Aventino,[1] *Sint-Michielsabdij,*[2] *and Onze-Lieve-Vrouwe Abdij,*[3] *mandates a reform of the order's statutes and requests that abbot [Conrad] of Prémontré implement these throughout the order.*[4]

A. Cartulary of Prémontré, fols. 9r–9v.

B. Original not found.

EDITION: Manrique, *Cisterciensium seu verius* ecclesiasticorum annalium *a condito Cistercio*, vol. 4, 459; Le Paige, *Bibliotheca*, 660.

REGISTER: Reg. Vat. 17, fol. 136r; Bréquigny, *Table chronologique*, vol. 5, 446; Potthast, *Regesta*, no. 9379; Auvray, *Les registres de Grégoire IX*, vol. 1, col. 954.

---

2 *Sic A, read* aciem.

---

1 The Premonstratensian abbey of Sant'Alessio all'Aventino, Rome. *MP* I, 387–8.

2 The Premonstratensian abbey of Sint-Michielsabdij, Antwerp. *MP* II, 265–9.

3 The Premonstratensian abbey of Onze-Lieve-Vrouwe Abdij, Middelburg. *MP* II, 306–11.

4 For a related act by Gregory IX, see Potthast, *Regesta*, no. 9137; Auvray, *Les registres de Grégoire IX*, vol. 1, cols. 683–4.

Privilegium de amotione visitatorum quorundam de ordine nostro.

[G]regorius episcopus, servus servorum Dei, dilecto filio abbati Premonstratensi salutem et apostolicam benedictionem. Sicut in nostra proposuisti presentia constitutus, cum olim pro reformatione tui ordinis statuta quedam de fratrum nostrorum consilio fecissemus, dilectis filiis Sancti Alexii de Urbe,[5] Sancti Michaelis de Antverpia[6] et de Mildebourc[7] abbatibus eiusdem ordinis litteris nostris injunximus ut ad generale Premonstratense capitulum accedentes statutis ipsis ibidem sollempniter publicatis ea servarent, et ab aliis facerent inviolabiliter observari corrigendo et reformando tam in capite quam in membris, que correctionis et reformationis officio noscerent indigere. Sed tandem quia predicti abbates, propter quandam appellationem ad Sedem Apostolicam interjectam ultra publicationem statutorum ipsorum minime processerunt et idem abbas Sancti Alexii ab ecclesia sua abesse non poterat, dilectos filios Fulcardi Montis[8] et Frigidi Montis[9] abbates, Cisterciensis ordinis loco subrogantes ipsius, eisdem et prefatis Sancti Michaelis et de Mildeborch abbatibus nostris dedimus litteris in mandatis, ut appellatione huiusmodi non obstante, mandatum apostolicum exequi procurarent juxta priorum continentiam litterarum, quicquid inde facerent, nobis usque ad festum Beati Andree proximo preteritum fideliter rescripturi, qui super premissis cum diligentia processerunt, prout in ipsorum litteris nobis exhibitis plenius continetur. Quare nobis humiliter supplicasti, ut cum dicti abbates iam sint officio suo functi, ac penes te, tamquam caput tui ordinis, in premissis et aliis, que ad correctionem et reformationem dicti ordinis pertinent, videatur remansisse potestas, providere tam tibi super hoc quam toti ordini salubriter dignaremur. Licet igitur ad correctionem membrorum tuorum procedere ex officio tuo possis, ut tamen melius et efficatius correctioni eorum valeas inminere quia plus timeri solet, quod specialiter indulgetur, quam quod generali concluditur sponsione, presentium tibi auctoritate mandamus. Quatinus iam dicta statuta omnino faciens observari, circa correctionem subditorum tuorum, tam auctoritate nostra quam tua libere officii tui debitum exequaris non obstantibus litteris ad eundem abbatem Sancti Michelis suosque collegas a Sede Apostolica destinatis. Contradictores per censuram ecclesiasticam appellatione postposita compescendo. Sciturus pro certo quod si statuta ipsa non fuerint

5 Angelo?, abbot of the Premonstratensian abbey of Sant'Alessio all'Aventino, ca. 1235. *MP* I, 388.

6 Arnold II, abbot of the Premonstratensian abbey of Sint-Michielsabdij, Antwerp, 1230/1–9. *MP* II, 268.

7 Theobald, abbot of the Premonstratensian abbey of Middelburg, 1231–7. *MP* II, 310.

8 The Cistercian abbey of Foucarmont.

9 The Cistercian abbey of Froidmont.

inviolabiliter observata, cogemur, licet inviti, alter de ipso ordine cogitare. Datum Laterani, VII kalendas februarii, pontificatus nostri anno septimo.

43

February 19, 1234. Lateran.

At the request of [William II] abbot of Prémontré,[1] *Pope Gregory [IX] grants the right to interpret the recent modifications of the order's statutes to suit local circumstances, including circumstances under which the laity can enter the cloisters of Premonstratensian men or women.*

A. Cartulary of Prémontré, fol. 9v.

B. Original not found.

EDITION: Le Paige, *Bibliotheca*, 660–1; Auvray, *Les registres de Grégoire IX*, vol. 1, cols. 984–5.

REGISTER: Bréquigny, *Table chronologique*, vol. 5, 448; Potthast, *Regesta*, no. 9412.

Privilegium de quibusdam verbis a domino Pape expositis.

[G]regorius episcopus, servus servorum Dei, dilecto filio abbati Premonstratensi salutem et apostolicam benedictionem. Olim intellecto quod illa Premonstratensis ordinis vinea Domini gratiosa, que flores odoris et fructus producere consuevit honestatis, esset adeo deformata, quod spinas et tribulos germinabat, ad reformationem ordinis et observantiam regularem de fratrum nostrorum consilio intendentes, quedam super hoc duximus statuenda, quibusdam ad observantiam eorum exequutoribus deputatis. Sed cum eisdem exequutoribus officio suo functis, tua videretur occasione huiusmodi juridictio[2] impediri, ac per hoc ad reformationem ordinis et correctionem excessuum intendi non poterat cum effectu, devotioni tue nostris dedimus litteris in mandatis, ut statuta premissa faciens inviolabiliter observari, circa reformationem ordinis et correctionem excessuum predictorum, officii tui debitum exequi procurares. Verum quia sicut in nostra proposuisti presentia constitutus, quedam inter cetera continentur in eis, que vel est difficile observari, vel observata in gravem redundarent tocius ordinis lesionem, nos tuis precibus inclinati, ne videamur imponere onera humeris aliorum, que tolerari vix possint, sic ea ubi sunt difficilia temperamus. Ubi dicitur quod "quolibet anno

1 William II of Dale was abbot of Dale Abbey, 1231–3, and abbot of Prémontré, 1233–8. Colvin, "The Internal History of Dale Abbey," 31.

2 *Sic A*, *read* jurisdictio.

in generali capitulo diffinitores et visitatores mutentur, novis qui religione ac discretione premineant veteribus subrogatis" [3] ita quod visitatores ipsi de una circaria ad aliam assumantur sic intelligi volumus, exceptis videlicet, illis provinciis, in quibus pauce sunt abbatie, quas circatores aliarum provinciarum non poterunt commode visitare. Et ubi prohibetur abbati, canonico vel converso habere servientem, equitem, secularem, necessitatem manifestam et evidentem excipimus, in quo casu per abbatem Premonstratensem, vel per generale capitulum concedimus dispensari. Ubi vero interdicitur, ut nullus regularis vel secularis presumat domos sororum eiusdem ordinis introire, illud firmiter volumus observari, nisi evidens necessitas interdum aliud exigat, vel aliquid fabrilis operis intercedat. Ceterum cum sit mulieribus interdictum generaliter, ne ipsarum aliqua claustrum, refectorium, dormitorium, et infirmitorium canonicorum omnino permittatur intrare; ab hoc subducimus domorum dicti ordinis fundatrices, quibus intrare claustrum, dumtaxat sine scandalo fieri poterit, concedatur. Et quia periculum sequi possit, si abbates residentes pro tempore quantitatem receptorum et expensarum, summam quoque debitorum et nomina creditorum, causas etiam propter quas contracta sunt debita, et in quas utilitates conversa, in suo capitulo bis in anno, et ipsi exponant, et sibi faciant diligenter exponi, prout in statutis continetur eisdem, volumus ad periculum evitandum ut premissa coram officialibus solummodo et senioribus domum fiant. Ad hec quia tempus ad uniformitatem librorum ubique servandam tam in cantu quam in lectionibus et regularibus institutis nimium in statutis ipsis causabaris artari de circumspectione tua plenam in Domino fiduciam optinentes, discretioni tue commitimus ut ad hoc exequendum prefigere possis tempus, prout consideratis circumstantiis negotii videris expedire. Tu autem sicut vir discretus et prudens sic predicta et alia que providentie tue commisimus exequi studeas inoffense quod prudentiam tuam merito commendantes contra te moveri merito non possimus. Datum Laterani, XII kalendas martii, pontificatus nostri anno septimo.

44

January 7, 1233. Lateran.

William [II], abbot of Prémontré,[1] *clarifies that the abbots of the Italian Premonstratensian houses of San Samuele di Barletta,*[2] *Santa Maria del Ponte*

3 This is a reference to a previous bull of Gregory IX's. See Cocquelines, ed., *Bullarium privilegiorum ac diplomatum romanorum pontificum amplissima collectio*, vol. 3, 272–4. The text was later incorporated into Premonstratensian statutes. See Lefèvre, *Les statuts de Prémontré réformés sur les ordres de Grégoire IX et d'Innocent IV au XIIIe siècle*, 89.

1 William II of Dale was abbot of Dale Abbey, 1231–3, and abbot of Prémontré, 1233–8. Colvin, "The Internal History of Dale Abbey," 31.

2 The Premonstratensian abbey of Barletta. *MP* I, 379–81.

Parvo di Brindisi,[3] *San Pietro di Camerota,*[4] *Santi Quirico e Giulitta ad Antrodoco,*[5] *Santi Severo e Martirio di Orvieto,*[6] *Sant'Alessio all'Aventino,*[7] *and San Leucio di Todi*[8] *will attend the order's General Chapter meetings, each in his turn, and that a given year's delegate will have visited the other Italian abbeys during that year. William clarifies the process of making a formal complaint about such visitations, as well as the procedure for electing a new abbot.*

A. Cartulary of Prémontré, fols. 9v–10r.
B. Original not found.
EDITION: Le Paige, *Bibliotheca,* 927–8; Hugo, *prob.* 1, cols. xxv–xxvii.

Quomodo debeant venire ad capituli illi qui sunt ultra montes.

[W]illermus, Dei patientia dictus abbas Premonstratensis, venerabilibus fratribus Sancti Samuelis de Barolo, Sancte Marie de Parvo Ponte Brundusii, Sancti Petri de Camerota, Sancti Quirici de Introduco, Sancti Severi de Urbe Veteri, Sancti Alexii de Urbe, Sancti Leutii de Turdertinensis,[9] abbatibus Premonstratensis ordinis, tam presentibus quam futuris in domino. Quia sicut ex visitationis defectu perniciosius ordinem tepescere et observantias regulares negligi quandoque contingit, sic ex studio visitationis et lima correctionis ordo validius convalescit, nos qui ad profectum ordinis vigilare tenemur, diligentius attendentes quod raro hactenus visitati, rarius generale capitulum visitastis, de consilio quorundam cardinalium et aliorum bonorum virorum, ita de visitando a nobis nostro capitulo generali, et visitandis etiam ecclesiis vestris duximus ordinandum, quod vos de Sancto Leutio Tudertinensis visitetis instans capitulum generale, vos de Sancto Severo anno proxime succedenti, vos de Santo Alexio proxime post eundem, vos de Sancto Quirico post ipsum, deinde vos de Sancto Samuele, postremo vos Sancti Marie de Parvo Ponte Brundisii et vos Sancti Petri de Camerota simul venietis ad capitulum memoratum, et sic servato ordine vicis vestre, quolibet anno quilibet vestrum, quolibet tamen sexto anno duo vestrum, sicut dictum est, venietis ad capitulum generale. Hoc proviso, quod quilibet vestrum anno quo venturus est vel venturi sunt ad capitulum, visitet vel visitent diligenter tam visitatoris ecclesiam et tunc assumpto

3 The Premonstratensian abbey of Santa Maria del Ponte Parvo di Brindisi. *MP* I, 381–2.
4 The Premonstratensian abbey of San Pietro di Camerota. *MP* I, 383–4.
5 The Premonstratensian abbey of Santi Quirico e Giulitta ad Antrodoco. *MP* I, 378–9.
6 The Premonstratensian abbey of Santi Severo e Martirio di Orvieto. *MP* I, 386–7.
7 The Premonstratensian abbey of Sant'Alessio all'Aventino. *MP* I, 387–8.
8 The Premonstratensian abbey of San Leucio di Todi. *MP* I, 391–3.
9 *Sic A*, *read* Tudertinensis.

secum aliquo vestrum, quam alias ecclesias vestras, statum earum tam super spiritualibus quam temporalibus rebus, mobilibus et inmobilibus diligentissime describentes, duo scripta super hoc eiusdem continentie faciendo, quorum unum remaneat in ecclesia visitata, anno quolibet in visitatione annua renovandum et alterum generali capitulo presentetur per visitatorem eundem, sive unus fuerit, sive duo, et eadem scripta sigillentur, tam proprii abbatis ecclesie visitate, quam visitatoris sigillis, ut sic ecclesiarum nostrarum status generali capitulo plenius innotescat, ita etiam quod visitationes ille fiant non inutiliter, vel in vanum, sed cum timore divino et animarum salute et secundum instituta Domini Pape, que necnon et observantias et consuetudines approbatas ordinis, a vobis volumus et precipimus inviolabiliter observari; precipiendo districte, ut visitator sive unus fuerit, sive duo super hiis devotus, sollicitus, intentus ac discretus zelator existat, diligentissime inquirendo si libri consuetudinum et ordinarius et ceteri libri qui ad divinum pertinent officium, habeantur cum ecclesia Premonstratensi, et secundum usum eiusdem ecclesie uniformes, et utrum sollicite conserventur in legendo, et cantando et ceteras constitutiones et observantias conservando et corripiantur graviter, qui super hec fuerint negligentes. Porro si aliquam ecclesiam vestram vacare contingat, ne occasione remotionis vel absentie patris abbatis diu remaneat consilio destituta, abbas qui tempore visitationis visitator, vel circator fuerit eo anno, vice nostra electionem regat in ecclesia sive ecclesiis, que vacaverint ipso anno. Electio vero que sine visitatore anni illius fuerit celebrata, robore careat firmitatis, cum visitator vices nostras gerat in hac parte, et ecclesie vestre, nostre sint filie speciales, nisi factum fuerit de nostra licentia speciali, quod de mandato nostro sub aliis electio celebretur. Volumus autem ut recturus electionem, aliquem de vobis, quem habere commodius potuerit, secum assumat, ut in provisione vacatis ecclesie consilium eo sanius habeatur, quo adjuvante gratia Spiritus Sancti, plures fuerint in eius nomine congregati. Preterea si a prelatis contra subditos, vel forsitan econverso, sicut ex humano defectu contingere solet, interdum alique mota fuerint questiones, coram illius anni circatore caritative et fideliter proponantur, cum dilectione hominum et odio vitiorum et ipse secundum Deum et ordinem, salvo capitis statu usque ad discussionem nostram corrigendo et reformando ea que correctione et reformatione indiguerint, faciat quod viderit expedire, contradictores et rebelles per censuram ecclesiasticam cohercendo. Ut autem ea que scripta sunt firmius observentur, vobis universis et singulis in virtute obedientie duximus injungendum. Quatinus hec ordinatio nostra, annis singulis die prima circationis annue, in capitulo coram fratribus sollempniter recitetur, salva tam in hoc quam in omnibus premissis auctoritate nostra et capituli generalis, revocationem enim correctionem, additionem et mutationem ordinationis istius nobis duximus retinendam. Valete universi et singuli in Domino Jhesu Christo. Datum Laterani, VII° idus januarii, anno gratie M° CC° tricesimo tercio, pontificatus ~~nostri anno~~ vero domini Pape Gregorii noni anno septimo.

45

January 16, 1234. Lateran.

*Pope Gregory [IX] grants to Premonstratensian abbeys the right to disregard letters obtained from the Holy See if those letters do not mention the Premonstratensian Order. Gregory also states that the Premonstratensians cannot convene meetings about papal letters which do not explicitly mention their order. (See duplicate **28**.)*

A. Cartulary of Prémontré, fol. 10r.

B. Original not found.

Other Manuscript Copies: Cartulary of Cockersand Abbey, British Library, Add. MS 37769, fol. 6(b)v (1268); Bayerische Hauptstaatsarchiv München, Literalien des Klosters Schäftlarn, no. 2, fols. 56r–56v (14th c.); Stiftsarchiv Wilten, Lade 8 M, 54–5 (early 15th c.).

EDITION: Le Paige, *Bibliotheca*, 658–9; Sanders, *Chorographia sacra Brabantiae*, vol. 1, 172–3; Smet, *Corpus chronicorum Flandriae*, vol. 2, 883–4; Farrer, *The Chartulary of Cockersand Abbey of the Premonstratensian Order*, vol. 1, part 1, 39–40.

REGISTER: Reg. Vat. 17, fol. 131r; Bréquigny, *Table chronologique*, vol. 5, 312; Potthast, *Regesta*, no. 8107; Lucien Auvray, *Les registres de Grégoire IX*, vol. 1 (Paris, 1896), col. 944; Weissthanner, *Die Urkunden und Urbare des Klosters Schäftlarn*, 270–1.

Privilegium que ultra duas dietas non possimus conveniri.

[G]regorius episcopus, servus servorum Dei, dilectis filiis abbati Premonstratensi et coabbatibus suis salutem et apostolicam benedictionem. Licet vobis, sicut asseritis, a Sede Apostolica sit indultum, ut littere contra vos a Sede Apostolica impetrare non valeant, nisi de ordine vestro fecerint mentionem, nos tamen quieti vestre volentes consultius providere, auctoritate vobis presentium indulgemus, ut per illam clausulam generalem *Quidam alii*[1] non possitis

1 For further discussion of *quidam alii* and *rebus aliis*, see Linehan and Bertram, "Bermerkungen zu einer Extravagante Gregors IX. und zu ihrer Verwendung im Lorvão-Prozeß," 373–5.

aliquatenus conveniri, nisi littere apostolice expressam de Premonstratensi ordine fecerint mentionem. Nulli ergo omnino hominum liceat hanc paginam nostre concessionis infringere, vel ei ausu temerario contraire. Siquis autem hoc attemptare presumpserit, indignationem omnipotentis Dei et beatorum Petri et Pauli apostolorum eius se noverit incursurum. Datam Laterani XVII kalendas februarii, pontificatus nostri anno septimo.

46

February 20, 1234. Lateran.

Pope Gregory [IX] instructs the abbots of the Benedictine abbeys of Saint-Jean de Laon and Saint-Vincent de Laon, as well as the prior of the Benedictine abbey of Nogent, to protect the religious of Prémontré against those who would attack them, and to bring the miscreants to trial.

A. Cartulary of Prémontré, fols. 10r–10v.
B. Original not found.

Privilegium unde supra cum additamento.

[G]regorius episcopus, servus servorum Dei, dilectis filiis Sancti Johannis et Sancti Vincentii abbatibus et priori de Nongento Laudunensis diocesis salutem et apostolicam benedictionem. Qui non solum sua verum etiam semetipsos salubriter abnegantes, carnem suam cum vitiis et concupiscentiis crucifigunt in castris claustralibus se claudendo sunt non immerito gratis attolendi favoribus et congruis presidiis muniendi ut eo devotius quo quietius Domino famulantes sibi per vite meritum et aliis proficiant per exemplum. Cum itaque, sicut dilecti filii abbates et conventus ecclesie Premonstratensis Laudunensis diocesis nobis conquerendo monstravit, ecclesia ipsa a nonnullis qui nomen Domini recipere in vacuum non formidant multipliciter molestetur. Nos et eorundem abbatis et conventus providere quieti et molestantium maliciis obviare volentes, discretioni vestre per apostolica mandamus. Quatinus eidem monasterio contra perversorum audatiam efficaciter assistentes non permittatis eos contra indulta Sedis Apostolice ab aliquibus indebite molestari. Molestatores huius per censuram ecclesiasticam appellatione postposita conpescendo, non obstante constitutione de duabus dietis edita in concilio generali dummodo ultra terciam vel quartam extra suam diocesim per literas apostolicas aliqui non trahantur presentibus ultra quinquennium minime valituris. Quod si non omnes hiis exequendis potueritis interesse, duo vestrum ea nichilominus exequantur. Datum Laterani, X° kalendas martii, pontificatus nostri anno septimo.

47

May 30, 1158.[1] Tuscolo.

Pope Adrian [IV] confirms an agreement between Gautier [II],[2] bishop of Laon, and Hugues [I],[3] abbot of Prémontré, under the auspices of Louis [VII] of France and Samson,[4] archbishop of Reims, and other bishops. This agreement confirms all of Prémontré's possessions that were previously disputed by bishop Gautier, namely those acquired during the tenure of the previous bishops of Laon, Barthélémy[5] and Gautier [I].[6] In exchange, bishop Gautier receives 300 librae Proveniensium, *50 ewes, 20 cows, 12 mares, and seven sows from Prémontré. (See* **77**.*)*

A. Cartulary of Prémontré, fols. 10v–11r.
B. Original not found.
Other Manuscript Copies: Cartulary of Park Abbey, Archief van de Abdij van Park te Heverlee, MS VII 35, fol. 25v (15/16th c.).
EDITION: Le Paige, *Bibliotheca*, 433–5; *PL* 188, cols. 1632–5; Florival, *Étude historique sur le XIIe siècle*, 267 (partial).
REGISTER: JL no. 10572 (J: 7120).

Privilegium Adriani Pape de confirmatione pacis inter episcopum Laudunensis et ecclesiam Premonstrati.

[A]drianus episcopus, servus servorum Dei, dilectis filiis ~~Dei~~ Hugoni, abbati et fratribus Premonstratensis ecclesie, salutem et apostolicam benedictionem. Ea que conpositione vel concordia mediante inter viros ecclesiasticos rationabiliter statuuntur, in sua debent stabilitate consistere et ad maiorem in posterum firmitatem habendam Apostolice Sedis presidio eadem necesse est communiri. Eapropter, dilecti in Domino filii, vestris justis postulationibus gratum impertientes assensum, concordiam que inter vos et venerabilem fratrem Galterum,

1 The cartulary dates this charter to May 30, 1158, but to Adrian IV's fifth pontifical year, which began December 4, 1158. Based on the place of issuing (Tuscolo), we believe the charter was more likely issued in 1159.
2 Gautier de Mortagne was dean of Laon, ca. 1142–55, and bishop of Laon, 1155–74.
3 Hugues I de Fosses (ca. 1093–1164), first abbot of Prémontré.
4 Samson de Mauvoisin, son of Raoul III le Barbu de Mauvoisin, lord of Rosny-sur-Seine, and his first wife Odeline, was archdeacon and provost of Chartres, and archbishop of Reims, 1140–61.
5 Barthélemy de Jur (d. 1158), son of Conon, lord of Grandson and La Sarraz, and Ada de Roucy; first subdeacon and then treasurer of Reims, later bishop of Laon, 1113–51.
6 Gautier de Saint-Maurice was abbot of the Premonstratensian abbey of Saint-Martin de Laon, 1124–51, and bishop of Laon, 1151–3. *MP* II, 512.

Laudunensem episcopum, super subscriptis possessionibus, mediantibus karissimo filio nostro Ludovico, illustri rege Francorum, et venerabili fratre nostro Sansone, Remensi archiepiscopo, Apostolice Sedis legato, et aliis quibusdam episcopis et principibus ex utriusque partis assensu rationabili providentia facta est, auctoritate apostolica confirmamus et presentis scripti patrocinio communimus. Hec autem concordia sicut in scripto exinde facto contineri disnoscitur huiusmodi est: Pastoralis officii est religiosorum paci et quieti providere que rationabiliter acta sunt attestari et ne aliquo oblivionis nubilo obfuscari possint vel infirmari scripto commendare et posterorum noticie transmittere. Eapropter ego Galterus, Dei gratia Laudunensis vocatus episcopus, notum fieri volumus tam futuris quam presentibus quod temporibus nostris inter nos et Hugonem, abbatem, et fratres Premonstrate ecclesie querela emersit super possessionibus inferius annotatis, pro eo quod minus ordinate bona episcopalia nobis distracta viderentur tandem vero mediante rege Francorum et archiepiscopo Remensi et [erasure] episcopis et principibus hoc modo controversia illa conpositionis finem accepit. Fratres quidem Premonstratenses ut salvis privilegiis et possessionibus suis firmam et perpetuam pacem possent adipisci, trecentas libras Proveniensium ad instaurationem curtis nobis nostrisque successoribus in perpetuum permansure, cum quingentis ovibus, vaccis XX^ti^, jumentis XII et suibus septem nobis tradiderunt. Nos autem eis omnia de quibus querela emerserat, que temporibus predecessorum nostrorum, Bartholomei et Galteri, tenuerant, deinceps libere et quiete possidenda concessimus et, communi assensu capituli nostri, presentis scripti auctoritate confirmavimus. Que etiam vocabulis propriis sigillatis duximus exprimenda: Vallem, videlicet, Premonstrati in qua sita est ecclesia, liberam ab omni exactione persone cuiuslibet absolutam, cum vineis, terris, silvis, pascuis, pratis, rivis, et molendinis que ibidem construxerunt, et proclivia montium ex omni parte cum vallibus adjacentibus a rivo versus Voiz[7] usque ad Hunberti Pontem[8] et usque Molnant Voisin et usque ad Vallem Rohardi et ad Halierpre, in quibus videlicet terminis pro ea parte in qua prius [ultra] rivum versus Molnant Voisin communis erat pascua, nunc autem stagnis et molendinis occupatur, solvuntur nobis ab ipsis fratribus duo solidi censualiter in festo Sancti Remigii. Curtem de Fontenellis[9] liberam, exceptis sex denariis qui solvuntur pro minuta decima canonicis Sancte Marie Laudunensis, et carrucatam unam ex dono episcopali et terram quatuordecim galetos sementis capientem ex elemosina fratris Udonis cum modio frumenti parve mensure ad molendinum de Taterel.[10] Aliam quoque terram tam ad Belmont quam juxta Rothecen capientem circiter duos modios et

7 Forest of Vois, https://dicotopo.cths.fr/places/P93994197.

8 Hubertpont, comm. Prémontré, https://dicotopo.cths.fr/places/P71559674.

9 Fontenille, comm. Wissignicourt, https://dicotopo.cths.fr/places/P36537367.

10 Taterel, cant. Anizy-le-Château, https://dicotopo.cths.fr/places/P91053037.

dimidium sementis Laudunensis mensure solventem nobis censualiter XIII denarios et obolum, que collecta est ex quorumdam elemosinis, scilicet, Harduini, Gerardi Rufi, Emehardi, et Thome fratris eius, Dodonis, Raineri, Harduini, Gaufridi de Guez. Campum etiam ad modum sementis solventem Hermentrudi de Firmitate duos solidos. Novem prata circiter XII falcas capientia, duo videlicet prata fratris Udonis in Bruil, duo prata eiusdem versus Pinon,[11] item in Bril, duo prata a Bertrada et a Radulpho Cholet, et pratum Hugonis Lupi. Pratum quoque Gelrici de Montemunt[12] et pratum fratris Hugonis ad Testam sub Baretel.[13] Pratum Hugonis de Montarcem,[14] duas partes molendini de Baretel et de Tercia quintam partem pro custodia eiusdem molendini, cum adjacenti vivario et prato. Molendinum de Guez et stagnum quod dedit Ermengardis sub censu quatuor modiorum parve mensure et ortum solventem nobis obolum et pratum solvens duos denarios ecclesie Sancti Johannis de Burg. Curtem de Panencourt[15] ad septem modios sementis Laudunensis mensure que ex multorum elemosinis collecta est, scilicet Amisardi, Alde, Gelrici, Constantii, Galteri, Hermundi, Widelonis, Odonis, Roberti, Berengeri, Gerlici, Roberti, Hugonis, Dodonis, Thome, Roberti, Elvidis, Bernardi, Bernuidis, Hauwini, Anselmi, Dude, Terrici, vineas quoque adjacentes in Gislenval, vineam Elvini, vineam Legardis, in loco qui dicitur Ad Duos Campos, vineam Hersendis, vineam Renoldi in Ocemont, vineam Theodrici ad torcular, vineam que collecta est ex elemosinis Bernuidis, Radulphi Spaillart, Dude, Riche, Hugonis, Reinaldi, Rollandi, Ysenberti, Hermene, Hermundi, Brunelli, Walteri et Alde. In Solario vineam Hauwini et Rollandi, in Rahier vineam Dodonis, in Marval III[es] vineas Roberti et Gelrici et vineam collectam ex elemosinis Warneri, Thome, Roberti, Hugonis prepositi, Gerardi Rufi, Balduini, Matildis, Widelonis, Emehardi et Thome fratrum, Roberti Aggei, Reineri, Odonis et Gerardi fratrum, Odonis Aggei, Anselmi et Odonis, in Fossa, vineam Alde, in quartariis vineam Radulphi et Hugonis, in Larriz vineam Gerlici et Roberti, in Longprei vineam Aggei, in Larriz vineam Thome, desuper fontem vineam Roberti et Gerlici, ad Salicem, vineam Rascendis et filiorum Roberti Cordele, in Warpunval vineam Radulphi, in Gerardon vineam Hermundi, in Larriz medietatem vinee que fuit Ydonis, in Cantaplora vineam Odonis, in Buimont duas vineas Terrici et Hugonis, duodecim pratorum particulas, scilicet super Aquilam prata duo Pagani et fratris Roberti, ad Pontem pratum Roberti Tanier, ad Toluci duo prata fratris Ydonis et pratum Odonis filii Aveline, ad Communpre et ad Bu[16]

11 Pinon, cant. Anizy-le-Château, https://dicotopo.cths.fr/places/P22218866.

12 Monthiémont, comm. Merlieux-et-Fouquerolles, https://dicotopo.cths.fr/places/P83003256.

13 Barthel, comm. Lizy, https://dicotopo.cths.fr/places/P65460297.

14 Montarcène, comm. Montbavin, https://dicotopo.cths.fr/places/P24202828.

15 Penancourt, comm. Anizy-le-Château, https://dicotopo.cths.fr/places/P36114519.

16 But, comm. Crépy, https://dicotopo.cths.fr/places/P31280705.

duas partes pratorum Alde et Roberti Cati, in Buimont pratum Stephani, ad Escorni pratum fratris Gelrici, ad Nodam Auram duo prata Roberti Cordele. Nemus extra Broiencourt[17] de quo videlicet cum duabus vineis et prato solvuntur nobis novem denarii et obolus bone monete et duodecim sextarii vini, dimidium modium vini viros et III[es] a Radulpho Spaillart, dimidium etiam modium in Larre a filiis Aggei. Curtem de Merli[18] et vineas appendentes, vineam scilicet de Biars, vineam de Coart, vineam in Letolt, vineam in Petra Hadue cum campo et nemore de Balescans et campo ad quararium et nemore ad Nodam que fuerunt fratris Ligeri et heredum eius in Premonstratensi ecclesia conversorum. Clausum de Lisi[19] et Descapholt liberum quod tam elemosina quam emptione acquisitum est ecclesie. In Escorni duas vineas ex elemosina fratris Udonis, vineam Balduini, vineam Aggei, vineam Albrici de Rua, vineam Johannis Albi, in Cesseroi[20] vineam Gisleberti, in Caperon vineam Burdini, in Petra Hadue vineam Bernuidis et vineam Albrici de Rua, in La Perche vineam Udonis, tres vineas Gerardi, una in Valarcenois, aliam in Buteni, terciam in Biars, item in Biars vineam collectam ex elemosinis Ermengardis, Gerardi, Ydonis, Radulphi, in valle de Val Aurigni[21] vineam Racendis, ad Fulcheroles[22] vineam Dude, in Sola Valle in vineam Roberti, in valle de Monbaven[23] vineam Hermundi, prata circiter VI falces capientia, scilicet in Bruil pratum Gerardi de Merli solvens nobis denarium, ad novum molendinum duas partes pratorum solventes nobis VI denarium et obolum et dimidiam sedem molendini a fratre Roberto de Montarcen,[24] in Bullipre pratum fratris Hugonis ad Testam, ad Cavetel pratum Odonis militis. Campum unum de Lisi, duas partes camporum in valle de Merli,[25] curtem de Vercigni[26] liberam et carrucatam unam terre quam primitus contulit eis Bartholomeus episcopus. Alias quoque circiter duas quas crescente numero fratrum idem ipse partim de culta, partim de inculta cum prato sub censu duorum solidorum super addidit ubi et ecclesiam cum atrio ad habendam sui et successorum suorum memoriam edificari precepit. Aliud quoque novale quod more ceterorum incolarum fratres ipsi fecerunt sub censu duorum solidorum. Molendinum de Acheri[27] et piscationem in aqua quandocumque vel quomodocumque volunt et mansum unum

17 Brancourt, cant. Anizy-le-Château, https://dicotopo.cths.fr/places/P91051513.
18 Merlieux-et-Fouqerolles, cant. Anizy-le-Château, https://dicotopo.cths.fr/places/P92396813.
19 Lizy, cant. Anizy-le-Château, https://dicotopo.cths.fr/places/P40948829.
20 Cessières, cant. Anizy-le-Château, https://dicotopo.cths.fr/places/P02167711.
21 Valavergny, comm. Merlieux, https://dicotopo.cths.fr/places/P74214194.
22 Fouquerolles, comm. Merlieux-et-Fouquerolles, https://dicotopo.cths.fr/places/P88868999.
23 Montbavin, cant. Anizy-le-Château, https://dicotopo.cths.fr/places/P47211476.
24 Montarcène, comm. Montbavin, https://dicotopo.cths.fr/places/P24202828.
25 Merlieux, cant. Anizy-le-Château, https://dicotopo.cths.fr/places/P92396813.
26 Versigny, cant. La Fère, https://dicotopo.cths.fr/places/P17885640.
27 Achery, cant. La Fère, https://dicotopo.cths.fr/places/P61820808.

terre censualiter pro modio frumenti Laudunensis mensure nobis persolvendo et curtem ab omni exactione liberam absque fure et duello, carrucatam unam terre in monte de Capriniaco[28] ex dono episcopali, tres vineas ad Brai, duo prata in valle Capriniaco, duos modios vinagii in monte Nantolio, terram Albrici et Beatricis de Bertolcourt in monte de Brai, terram Hersendis de Brai et filiorum suorum, duas partes molendini de Aquila sub censu decem solidorum bone monete qui solvuntur thesaurario Sancte Marie Laudunensis ecclesie. Ut igitur hec omnia robur perpetue firmitatis optineant, auctoritate Apostolice Sedis ea duximus roboranda et presentis scripti patrocinio munienda. Decernimus ergo ut nulli omnino hominum liceat hanc paginam nostre con~~e~~firmationis infringere vel ei aliquatinus contraire. Siquis autem hoc attemptare presumpserit secundo tertiove commonitus presumptionem suam satisfactione congrua non correxerit indignationem omnipotentis[29] et beatorum Petri et Pauli apostolorum eius incurrat et excommunicationis eum vinculo statuimus subjacere. Amen. Amen. Datum Tusculani, per manu Hermanni,[30] domini Pape subdiaconi et scriptoris, III kalendas junii, indictione VII, incarnationis dominice anno M° C° LVIII°, pontificatus vero domini Adriani Pape IIII anno quinto.

48

April 1, 1188. Lateran.

Pope Clement [III], like his predecessors, Popes Adrian [IV], Alexander [III] and Urban [III], takes the church of Prémontré under his protection, and confirms the possessions of the church and some of the abbot's privileges.

A. Cartulary of Prémontré, fols. 11r–12r.

B. Original not found.

Other Manuscript Copies: Cartulary of Saint-Paul de Verdun, BM Verdun, MS 751, pp. 5–6 (13th c.); Cartulary of Drongen Abbey, Rijksarchief te Gent, K9–8, fol. 33r (14th c.); Cartulary of Drongen Abbey, Rijksarchief te Gent, K9–9, fol. 8r (14th c.); "Privilegia a Romanis Pontificibus ordini Praemonstratensi concessa," BnF, MS lat. 4394, fol. 83r (14th c.); Cartulary of Beaurepart, Bibliothèque du Séminaire Episcopal de Liège, G IV 7, fol. 19v (15th c.); Cartulary of Averbode Abbey, Archief van de abdij van Averbode, Sectie IV, no. 109, fol. 9r (15/16th c.); Cartulary of Park Abbey, Archief van de Abdij van Park te Heverlee, MS VII 35, fol. 27v (15/16th c.).

EDITION: Le Paige, *Bibliotheca*, 641–3; *PL* 204, cols. 1333–4 (partial).

---

28 Chevregny, cant. Anizy-le-Château, https://dicotopo.cths.fr/places/P06529464.

29 *Om.* Dei *A*.

30 Ermanno, vice-chancellor of the Apostolic Chancery, 1159–66, and cardinal priest of Santa Susanna, 1165–ca. 1170.

REGISTER: Bréquigny, *Table chronologique*, vol. 3, 95; JL no. 16188 (J: 10063); Pfaff, "Papst Clemens III," 290; Böhmer and Schmidt, *Regesta Imperii IV*, vol. 4, 103–4.

Privilegium Clementis Pape de confirmatione canonicarum possessionum et cetera.

[C]lemens episcopus, servus servorum Dei, dilectis filiis Hugoni, abbati Premonstratensis ecclesie, eiusque fratribus tam presentibus quam futuris regularem vitam professis in perpetuum. Religiosam vitam professis apostolicum convenit adesse presidium ne forte cuiuslibet temeritatis incursus aut eos a proposito revocet aut robur quod absit sacre religionis infringat. Eapropter, dilecti in Domino filii, vestris justis postulationibus ~~annuentes~~ clementer annuimus et prefatam Premonstratensem ecclesiam in qua divino estis obsequio mancipati, ad instar felicis recordationis Adriani, Alexandri et Urbani, predecessorum nostrorum Romanorum pontificum, sub Beati Petri et nostra protectione suscipimus et presentis scripti privilegio communimus. Statuentes ut quascumque possessiones, quecumque bona ecclesia eadem in presentiarum juste et canonice possidet, aut in futurum concessione pontificum, largitione regum vel principium, oblatione fidelium seu aliis justis modis prestante Domino poterit adipisci, firma vobis vestrisque successoribus et illibata permaneant. In quibus hec propriis duximus exprimenda vocabulis, locum ipsum in quo prefata ecclesia sita est cum omnibus pertinentiis suis: Totam, videlicet, vallem Premonstratensem inmunem et liberam ab omni exactione et consuetudine et valles eidem valli adjacentes et proclivia montium sicut valles proportant et nemus quod est in eis ad opus edificiorum et necessitatum vestrarum, et usuarium de mortuo nemore in foresta de Vois[1] et pascua animalibus vestris, sicut hec omnia de concessione bone memorie Bartholomei,[2] quondam Laudunensis episcopi, et Thome,[3] domini de Couciaco, rationabiliter possidetis; universa etiam que a Radulpho, eiusdem Thome nepote, et de feudatis et aliis hominibus eius, de concessione eiusdem Radulphi tenetis, ita ut ob recognitionem horum et concessionem, justiciam quam in villa de Sorni[4] habuistis libere dimitatis eidem Radulpho; stagna etiam et molendina predictarum vallium ab omni decimatione et exactione libera, silvam in vestros usus ab Halierpre usque ad Humberti Pontem,[5] et ex alia parte per mediam vallem Rohardi usque ad

1 Forest of Vois, https://dicotopo.cths.fr/places/P93994197.

2 Barthélemy de Jur (d. 1158), son of Conon, lord of Grandson and La Sarraz, and Ada de Roucy; first subdeacon and then treasurer of Reims, later bishop of Laon, 1113–51.

3 Thomas de Marle, lord of Coucy and Marle (ca. 1073–1130), son of Enguerrand I, lord of Coucy, and Adèle de Marle.

4 Sorny, cant. Vailly, https://dicotopo.cths.fr/places/P79681466.

5 Hubertpont, comm. Prémontré, https://dicotopo.cths.fr/places/P71559674.

Monandi vicinum; curtem de Fontenellis[6] cum appenditiis suis et duas partes molendini de Baretel[7] cum stagno; curtem de Panencourt[8] cum vineis et ceteris appenditiis suis; curtem de Merliu[9] cum vineis et appenditiis suis; partem decime ipsius ville; vinagia de Burguino[10] et census de Poilli;[11] duas partes molendini de Aquila;[12] molendinum de Weiz;[13] molendinum de Rupibus;[14] molendinum de Proisel; curtem de Souppi[15] cum appenditiis suis et molendina in Axona; curtem de Hanapiis[16] in alodio cum decima et appenditiis suis; curtem de Firmitate cum appenditiis suis; curtem de Walescourt[17] cum silva de Mesloi[18] et altaribus et decimis ad ea pertinentibus, cum ceteris appenditiis suis sicut a canonicis Sancte Marie Laudunensis censualiter accepta firmastis; curtem de Vercigni[19] cum appenditiis suis; molendina de Erchentre;[20] duas partes decime de Crespi[21] que dedit vobis rex Ludovicus; molendinum de Acheri[22] cum terra quam a Gilberto de Chili emistis; curtem de Daneri[23] cum appenditiis suis; curtem de Roseriis[24] cum appenditiis suis; vineas et vinagia et terragia et duo molendina cum stagno ad Couci Villam et vineas ad Couci Castrum; quandam partem in decimis et terragiis de Vergium et de Agneis; partem decime de Chaun;[25] molendinum de Cinceni;[26] molendinum de Courchum;[27] in episcopatu Suessionensi extra muros eiusdem civitatis, domum, vineas et torcularia cum ceteris appenditiis suis; vinagia et census apud Pomiers; curtem de Buci cum vineis torcularibus et ceteris appenditiis suis; curtem Clameci[28] cum vineis et

6 Fontenille, comm. Wissignicourt, https://dicotopo.cths.fr/places/P36537367.

7 Barthel, comm. Lizy, https://dicotopo.cths.fr/places/P65460297.

8 Penancourt, comm. Anizy-le-Château, https://dicotopo.cths.fr/places/P36114519.

9 Merlieux, cant. Anizy-le-Château, https://dicotopo.cths.fr/places/P92396813.

10 Bourguignon-sous-Montbavin, cant. Anizy-le-Château, https://dicotopo.cths.fr/places/P25732714.

11 Pouilly, cant. Crécy-sur-Serre, https://dicotopo.cths.fr/places/P77273113.

12 Aile, comm. Royaucourt-et-Chailvet, https://dicotopo.cths.fr/places/P82381255.

13 Huet, comm. Lizy, https://dicotopo.cths.fr/places/P74654387.

14 Les Roches, comm. Bucy-le-Long, https://dicotopo.cths.fr/places/P20402237.

15 Soupir, cant. Vailly, https://dicotopo.cths.fr/places/P62600159.

16 Hannape, cant. Wassigny, https://dicotopo.cths.fr/places/P37303056.

17 Valécourt, comm. Chevresis-Monceau, https://dicotopo.cths.fr/places/P14207928.

18 Mesloy, comm. Chevresis-Monceau , https://dicotopo.cths.fr/places/P54953574.

19 Versigny, cant. La Fère, https://dicotopo.cths.fr/places/P17885640.

20 Archantré, comm. Remies, https://dicotopo.cths.fr/places/P18258469.

21 Crépy, cant. Laon, https://dicotopo.cths.fr/places/P85331504.

22 Achery, cant. La Fère, https://dicotopo.cths.fr/places/P61820808.

23 Dandry, comm. Crépy, https://dicotopo.cths.fr/places/P99162453.

24 Rozières, cant. Oulchy-le-Château, https://dicotopo.cths.fr/places/P75685266.

25 Champs, cant. Coucy-le-Château, https://dicotopo.cths.fr/places/P17397889.

26 Sinceny, cant. Chauny, https://dicotopo.cths.fr/places/P29595722.

27 Courson, comm. Landricourt, https://dicotopo.cths.fr/places/P39892049.

28 Clamecy, cant. Vailly, https://dicotopo.cths.fr/places/P24475745.

appenditiis suis; molendina juxta Margival; curtem de Tinselva[29] cum appenditiis suis, vineas et vinagia et quosdam census ad Sorni;[30] molendinum de Curcellis; curtem de Luilli[31] cum appenditiis suis; curtem de Buici cum appenditiis suis; duas partes decime de Athiei et ibidem domum, terras et vineas; curtem in monte de Troisli[32] et aliam in valle cum appenditiis suis et ibidem decimam laborum vestrorum; molendinum de Corblencort; duas partes decime de Vassen[33] in annona et vino; duas partes decime vini ad Terni;[34] curtem de Rosel cum appenditiis suis; partem decime de Pinum[35] et ibidem partem cuiusdam molendini; in episcopatu Noviomensi in suburbio eiusdem civitatis domum, terras vineas cum appenditiis suis, silvam quam ab episcopo eiusdem civitatis censualiter accepistis; curtem de Bonolio[36] cum altari et decima et pertinentiis suis; curtem de Montisel[37] cum appenditiis suis, et terram de Homencourt;[38] curtem de Germaniis[39] cum appenditiis suis et quamdam partem de Leher Wez; curtem de Calveni[40] cum appenditiis suis et duas partes eiusdem decime ville et duas partes decime de Coulencort;[41] curtem de Alodio cum appenditiis suis et quandam partem decime de Cuissi; curtem de Escanli[42] cum molendino et appenditiis; molendinum de Hameals;[43] molendinum de Oufoiz[44] et quandam partem decime eiusdem; molendinum de Espevile[45] et duas partes decime eiusdem ville et de Muile;[46] quandam partem decime de ~~Buci~~ Duri; quandam partem decime de Lanci[47] et ibidem terram Odonis conversi, duas partes decime de Estoilli;[48] decimam de Divisa[49] et de Esclui; decimam Sancte Radegundis de Perona, decimam de Perona; decimam de Bechincourt;[50]

29 Tinselve, comm. Leuilly, https://dicotopo.cths.fr/places/P54510057.
30 Sorny, cant. Vailly, https://dicotopo.cths.fr/places/P79681466.
31 Leuilly, cant. Coucy-le-Château, https://dicotopo.cths.fr/places/P91541747.
32 Trosly-Loire, cant. Coucy-le-Château, https://dicotopo.cths.fr/places/P24780558.
33 Vassens, cant. Coucy-le-Château, https://dicotopo.cths.fr/places/P82223652.
34 Terny-et-Sorny, cant. Vailly, https://dicotopo.cths.fr/places/P98869464.
35 Pinon, cant. Anizy-le-Château, https://dicotopo.cths.fr/places/P22218866.
36 Bonneuil, cant. Ham, https://dicotopo.cths.fr/places/P66750585.
37 Montizel, cant. Ham, https://dicotopo.cths.fr/places/P16235568.
38 Aumencourt, comm. Auffrique-et-Nogent, https://dicotopo.cths.fr/places/P03934228.
39 Germaine, cant. Vermand, https://dicotopo.cths.fr/places/P36636067.
40 Cauvigny, comm. Trefcon, https://dicotopo.cths.fr/places/P87955155.
41 Caulaincourt, cant. Vermand, https://dicotopo.cths.fr/places/P02972526.
42 Canny-lès-Voyennes, cant. Nesle, https://dicotopo.cths.fr/places/P44415541.
43 Hamel-lès-Corbie, cant. Corbie, https://dicotopo.cths.fr/places/P37197765.
44 Offoy, cant. Ham, https://dicotopo.cths.fr/places/P14011159.
45 Eppeville, cant. Ham, https://dicotopo.cths.fr/places/P94171781.
46 Muille-Villette, cant. Ham, https://dicotopo.cths.fr/places/P77128677.
47 Lanchy, cant. Vermand, https://dicotopo.cths.fr/places/P51978975.
48 Estouilly, cant. Ham, https://dicotopo.cths.fr/places/P96663971.
49 Devise, cant. Ham, https://dicotopo.cths.fr/places/P85212875.
50 Becquincourt, cant. Bray, https://dicotopo.cths.fr/places/P53738864.

decimam de Falevi; decimam de Gricourt;[51] decimas de Buici; decimam de Chisencourt;[52] terram quam dedit nobis Ermenricus de Nigella; curtem de Bolmont[53] cum appenditiis suis; curtem de Toiri[54] cum molendino et appenditiis suis; decimam de Sonmet; duas partes decime de Kartigni;[55] capellam Sancti Nicolai apud Sanctum Quintinum; terram de Omencourt quam dedit vobis Agnes, soror Alardi de Bonolio;[56] domum apud Castrum Hami; partem decime de Goslencourt terram quoque de Apponi[57] quam de manu Iteri[58] de Espaigni ad garbam suscepistis; terram de Colesi[59] quam ab Odone, domino Hamensi, conparastis; census quos in eodem castro habetis et census de Boengni; ecclesiam Sancti Petri de Dorenc[60] cum omnibus prebendis decimis, terragiis, censibus et cum omnibus aliis redditibus et pertinentiis suis, in ea libertatis integritate in qua eam seculares canonici ante vos tenuisse et per manum Bartholomei, Galteri et Walteri, Laudunensium episcoporum, Rogerus castellanus de Perona et Odo clericus frater eius, annuente matre ipsorum fratribus et sororibus, vobis confirmasse noscuntur cum grangia que dicitur Fons Raimbaldi,[61] cum carrucis et omnibus pertinentiis suis. Apostolica auctoritate sanctimus ut nullus ecclesiasticorum prelatorum ipsam ecclesiam vestram aut oratoria eius, in quibus cura parrochialis non est, nisi per expressum Apostolice Sedis mandatum divinorum interdicto supponat, sed cum generale interdictum terre fuerit, liceat vobis clausis januis, non pulsatis campanis, exclusis excommunicatis et interdictis, suppressa voce divina officia celebrare. Concedimus etiam tibi, fili abbas, ut cum ecclesias quaslibet ordinis tui duxeris visitandas, liceat tibi confessionem fratrum, qui tibi delictorum suorum secreta voluerint confiteri recipere, et eis penitencie atque absolutionis remedium impertiri: Ut vestimenta etiam sacerdotalia et pallas altaris benedicere valeas et convenientibus abbatibus, cum episcopus absens fuerit, in conclusione capituli benedictionem proferre devotioni tue presenti pagina indulgemus. Ad hec quotiens diocesanum episcopum abesse contingeret, vel esse in presentia sua negligentem, in correctione malefactorum vestrorum, incendiariorum atque predonum, liceat tibi, fili abbas, si

51 Grécourt, cant. Nesle, https://dicotopo.cths.fr/places/P84842582.

52 Cizancourt, cant. Nesle, https://dicotopo.cths.fr/places/P70322720.

53 Beaumont-en-Beine, cant. Chauny, https://dicotopo.cths.fr/places/P18685379.

54 Thury, comm. Marest-Dampcourt, https://dicotopo.cths.fr/places/P84789655.

55 Cartigny, cant. Péronne, https://dicotopo.cths.fr/places/P86731604.

56 Alard de Bonneuil, possibly a son of Alard I de Ham (or de la Porte), knight of Ham, and Helvide. He also appears in **360**.

57 Vézaponin, cant. Vic-sur-Aisne, https://dicotopo.cths.fr/places/P00069317.

58 Itier, lord of Épagny (Épagny, cant. Vic-sur-Aisne, https://dicotopo.cths.fr/places/P39948319); husband of Elizabeth. Melleville, *DH*, vol. 1, 353; Newman, *Seigneurs*, vol. 2, 120.

59 Collezy, comm. Berlancourt, https://dicotopo.cths.fr/places/P68465476.

60 Dorengt, cant. Nouvion, https://dicotopo.cths.fr/places/P90882005.

61 Near La Ferté-Chevresis, cant. Ribemont, https://dicotopo.cths.fr/places/P15499504.

episcopus eos infra quadraginta dies postquam ei conquesti fueritis, neglexerit emendare, ipsos maleficos, incendiarios, predones rerum vestrarum, in coabbatum vestrorum collegio excommunicationis pena ferire, quos episcoporum nullus, citra dignam satisfactionem, absolvat. Volumus etiam ut liberum tibi sit fugitivos aut ejectos ordinis vestri, post statutam penitenciam injunctam, propriis restituere domibus, nisi forte tales existant quos enormitas criminis evidens ab ordine debeat sequestrare. Sed et hoc caritatis intuitu precipimus, ut nullus de laboribus vestris, quos propriis manibus vel sumptibus colitis, sive de nutrimentis vestrorum animalium, decimas a vobis exigere vel extorquere presumat. Licet fundorum dominis pro rei proprietate aliquem censum, vel quotamlibet partem frugum reddatis, in parrochialibus autem ecclesiis quas habetis liceat vobis quatuor vel tres de canonicis vestris ponere, quorum unum diocesano episcopo presentetis, qui ei de spiritualibus vobis autem de temporalibus et de ordinis observancia debeat respondere. Inhibemus etiam, ne ecclesias aut terras seu aliquod beneficium ecclesie vestre collatum, liceat alicui personaliter dari, sive aliquo modo alienari sine consensu totius capituli, vel maioris et sanioris partis eiusdem. Sique vero donationes vel alienationes aliter, quam dictum est, facte fuerint, eas irritas esse censemus. Ad hec autem adicimus ne aliqui canonici seu conversi sub potestate domus vestre astricti, sine consensu abbatis et maioris partis capituli vestri, pro aliquo fidejubeant, vel ab aliquo pecuniam mutuo accipiant ultra precium capituli vestri providentia provisum, nisi propter domus vestre manifestam utilitatem. Quod si facere presumpserint, non teneatur conventus, sine cuius licentia et consensu hoc egerant, pro his aliquatenus respondere. Decernimus ergo ut nulli omnino hominum liceat prefatam ecclesiam temere perturbare aut eius possessiones auferre vel ablatas retinere, minuere seu quibuslibet vexationibus fatigare, sed omnia integra et illibata serventur eorum pro quorum gubernatione ac sustentatione concessa sunt omnimodis usibus profutura, salva Sedis Apostolice auctoritate et diocesani episcopi canonica justicia. Siqua igitur in futurum ecclesiastica secularisve persona hanc nostre constitutionis paginam sciens contra eam temere venire temptaverit, secundo terciove commonita nisi reatum suum congrua satisfactione correxerit, potestatis honorisque sui careat dignitate reamque se divino judicio existere de perpetrata iniquitate cognoscat et a sacratissimo corpore et sanguine Dei et Domini Redemptoris nostri Jhesu Christi aliena fiat atque in extremo examine districte ultioni subjaceat. Cunctis autem eidem loco sua jura servantibus sit pax Domini nostri Jhesu Christi. Quatinus et hic fructum bone actionis percipiant et apud districtum judicem premia eterne pacis inveniant. Amen. + Ego Clemens Catholice Ecclesie episcopus sanctus + Ego Theobaldus[62] Hostiensis et Velletrensis episcopus SS. ego Jacobus,[63] diaconus

62 Thibaut de Vermandois, cardinal priest of Santa Croce in Gerusalemme, 1171–8, abbot of Cluny, 1180–3/4, and cardinal bishop of Ostia e Velletri, 1183/4–8.

63 Jacopo, cardinal deacon of Santa Maria in Cosmedin from 1178.

cardinalis Sancte Marie in Cosmydin SS. Ego Bovo,[64] Sancti Angeli diaconus cardinalis SS. Ego Soffredus[65] in Via Lata, diaconus cardinalis SS. Ego Johannes,[66] presbiter cardinalis titulo Sancti Marci SS. Ego Laborans,[67] presbiter cardinalis Sancte Marie Trans Tiberim SS. Ego Albinus[68] titulo Sancte Crucis in Jerusalem, presbiter cardinalis SS. Data Laterani, per manum Moysi,[69] Sancte Romane Ecclesie subdiaconi vicem agentis cancelarii kalendas aprili, indictione sexta, incarnationis dominice M° C° LXXX° VIII°, pontificatus vero domini Clementis Pape tercii anno primo.

49

December 6, 1143. Lateran.

Pope Celestine [II] confirms the possessions of the church of Prémontré and certain of its privileges.

A. Cartulary of Prémontré, fols. 12r–12v.

B. Original not found.

Other Manuscript Copies: Cartulary of Averbode Abbey, Archief van de abdij van Averbode, Sectie IV, no. 109, fol. 3v (15/16th c.); Cartulary of Park Abbey, Archief van de Abdij van Park te Heverlee, MS VII 35, fol. 23v (15/16th c.).

EDITION: Le Paige, *Bibliotheca*, 428; Hugo, *prob*. 1, col. xiv; *PL* 179, cols. 778–81.

REGISTER: JL no. 8450 (J: 5989); Grauwen, "Lijst van oorkonden waarin Norbertus wordt genoemd," 167.

Privilegium Celestini Pape de confirmatione canonicarum nostrarum possessionum et dignitatum abbatis et ecclesie.

[C]elestinus episcopus, servus servorum Dei, dilectis filiis Hugoni Premonstratensi abbati eiusque fratribus tam presentibus quam futuris regulariter substituendis in perpetuum. Justis votis assensum prebere et religiosorum preces benignis auribus exaudire, apostolice convenit dignitati. Nec dubium quod si

64 Boson d'Arles was cardinal deacon of Sant'Angelo in Pescheria, 1187–8, cardinal deacon of S. Giorgio in Velabro, 1188–9, and cardinal priest of S. Anastasia, 1189–90.

65 Soffredo (d. 1210), cardinal deacon of Santa Maria in Via Lata from 1182, and cardinal priest of Santa Prassede from 1193.

66 Giovanni (Conti? d. 1196?), cardinal priest of San Marco.

67 Laborante da Panormo (d. ca. 1190), elected cardinal bishop of Santa Maria in Trastevere from ca. 1180.

68 Albino da Milano (d. ca. 1199), cardinal bishop of Santa Croce in Gerusalemme from 1185.

69 Moyses, datary to the papacy ca. 1187–94. Cheney, "The Office and Title of the Papal Chancellor, 1187–1216," 370–1.

servorum Dei petitionibus benigne concurrimus, nostris oportunitatibus clementem dominum reperimus ut quemadmodum divina providentia patres in Dei populo dicimur, ita etiam affectu prosequente operis, salubriter precesse fidelibus mereamur. Cum igitur universis personis ecclesiasticis nos oporteat generaliter providere, erga illos tamen propensiori cura nos convenit esse sollicitos, quos constat maiori studio cunctipotentis Dei servitio inhiare et acriori religione ac morum honestate clarescere. Hoc profecto intuitu, dilecti in Domino filii, vestre devotionis precibus debita benignitate inpertimur assensum et Premonstratensem ecclesiam in qua divino mancipati estis obsequio cum omnibus ad eam pertinentibus presentis privilegii pagina communimus. Statuentes ut quascumque possessiones, quecumque bona idem venerabilis locus in presentiarum juste et canonice possidet aut in futurum concessione pontificum, largitione regum vel principum, oblatione fidelium seu aliis justis modis, Deo propitio, acquirere poteritis, firma vobis vestrique successoribus et illibata permaneant. In quibus hec propriis duximus exprimenda nominibus: ambitum scilicet ipsius vallis Premonstratensis sicut in vestris scriptis continetur et certis terminis diffinitur, ab omni videlicet exactione liberum tam terragii quam decime sive census; curtem quoque de Fontenellis[1] cum vivario et duabus partibus molendinorum subjacentium ceterisque appenditiis suis; curtem de Panencourt[2] cum vineis et ceteris appenditiis suis; curtem de Merliu[3] cum vineis suis; curtem de Roseriis[4] cum pertinentiis et appenditiis suis; curtem de Vercigni[5] cum appenditiis suis; curtem de Soupi[6] cum molendinis subjacentibus in flumine quo dicitur Axona ceterisque appenditiis et pertinentiis suis; duas partes decime de Crespi;[7] terciam partem decime de Chauns;[8] apud Valaurigni[9] decem modios vini de decima eiusdem ville; decimam cum terragio de Vervin et terragia de Couci Villa exceptis duobus modiis que inde persolvi debent ecclesie Beate Marie Nongenti; vivarium etiam et molendinum juxta eandem villam, sicut hec ipsa habuerat in suo dominio Engelrannus,[10] filius Thome de Marla in predictis duabus villis; census de Poisli;[11] molendinum de Rochis,[12]

1 Fontenille, comm. Wissignicourt, https://dicotopo.cths.fr/places/P36537367.

2 Penancourt, comm. Anizy-le-Château, https://dicotopo.cths.fr/places/P36114519.

3 Merlieux, cant. Anizy-le-Château, https://dicotopo.cths.fr/places/P92396813.

4 Rozières, cant. Oulchy-le-Château, https://dicotopo.cths.fr/places/P75685266.

5 Versigny, cant. La Fère, https://dicotopo.cths.fr/places/P17885640.

6 Soupir, cant. Vailly, https://dicotopo.cths.fr/places/P62600159.

7 Crépy, cant. Laon, https://dicotopo.cths.fr/places/P85331504.

8 Champs, cant. Coucy-le-Château, https://dicotopo.cths.fr/places/P17397889.

9 Valavergny, comm. Merlieux, https://dicotopo.cths.fr/places/P74214194.

10 Enguerrand II de Coucy (d. ca. 1149), son of Thomas de Marle, lord of Coucy, and his third wife, Mélisende de Crécy-sur-Serre.

11 Pouilly, cant. Crécy-sur-Serre, https://dicotopo.cths.fr/places/P77273113.

12 Les Roches, comm. Bucy-le-Long, https://dicotopo.cths.fr/places/P20402237.

molendinum de Proesel; molendinum de Acheri;[13] molendinum de Courchun;[14] molendinum de Cinceni;[15] vinagia de Bourguinum;[16] terram de Carenni;[17] duas partes molendini de Aquila;[18] vineas de Broiencourt,[19] Ursinicourt,[20] Bruinmunt, Lisi, Vallaureni,[21] Montarcene[22] et de Montbavain,[23] vineas de Couci Castello et de Couci Villa; vinagia et vineas de Nova Villa; in Suessionensi episcopatu, in suburbio civitatis, curtem et locum torcularium et vineas; apud Pomerias vinagia, census denariorum Brane Castri et Branelle Ville; curtem de Buci cum vineis et vinagiis ceterisque pertinentiis suis; molendinum de Rupibus[24] quod sub eadem villa est; curtem de Clameci[25] cum torculari, vineis et aliis pertinentiis; apud Sorni[26] duo torcularia, vineas et alios redditus; curtem de Tinselva[27] cum pertinentiis suis; curtem de Luilli[28] et dimidium molendinum cum ceteris pertinentiis; apud Bethencourt[29] vinagia et alios redditus; apud Pinon quendam censum et tertiam partem minute decime de Atrio et sextam partem cuiusdam molendini et decimam quam Josbertus ibidem habuit; capellam et curtem de Rosel cum molendino, vivario, torculari, vineis et omnibus pertinentiis suis; in monte de Trosli[30] curtem unam et in valle aliam cum terris, vineis et aliis pertinentiis suis et partem eiusdem ville cum suis appenditiis quam Andreas[31] de Baldimento nobis contulit, sicut eam in dominio suo tenebat, et quedam alia ab aliis Dei fidelibus oblata; curtem de Biuci cum pertinentiis suis; curtem de Atechi et duas partes decime, vineas cum ceteris appenditiis; apud Cauvigni censum et vinagia; in villa que dicitur Pons Sancti Medardi[32] quandam partem decime; apud Margival dimidium molendinum;

13 Achery, cant. La Fère, https://dicotopo.cths.fr/places/P61820808.
14 Courson, comm. Landricourt, https://dicotopo.cths.fr/places/P39892049.
15 Sinceny, cant. Chauny, https://dicotopo.cths.fr/places/P29595722.
16 Bourguignon-sous-Montbavin, cant. Anizy-le-Château, https://dicotopo.cths.fr/places/P25732714.
17 Likely Craonne, comm. Coucy-la-Ville, https://dicotopo.cths.fr/places/P01212484.
18 Aile, comm. Royaucourt-et-Chailvet, https://dicotopo.cths.fr/places/P82381255.
19 Brancourt, cant. Anizy-le-Château, https://dicotopo.cths.fr/places/P91051513.
20 Wissignicourt, cant. Anizy-le-Château, https://dicotopo.cths.fr/places/P16285342.
21 Valavergny, comm. Merlieux, https://dicotopo.cths.fr/places/P74214194.
22 Montarcène, comm. Montbavin, https://dicotopo.cths.fr/places/P24202828.
23 Montbavin, cant. Anizy-le-Château, https://dicotopo.cths.fr/places/P47211476.
24 Les Roches, comm. Bucy-le-Long, https://dicotopo.cths.fr/places/P20402237.
25 Clamecy, cant. Vailly, https://dicotopo.cths.fr/places/P24475745.
26 Sorny, cant. Vailly, https://dicotopo.cths.fr/places/P79681466.
27 Tinselve, comm. Leuilly, https://dicotopo.cths.fr/places/P54510057.
28 Leuilly, cant. Coucy-le-Château, https://dicotopo.cths.fr/places/P91541747.
29 Béthancourt, comm. Crécy-au-Mont, https://dicotopo.cths.fr/places/P52359541.
30 Trosly-Loire, cant. Coucy-le-Château, https://dicotopo.cths.fr/places/P24780558.
31 André de Baudement (d. ca. 1146), lord of Baudement and La Fère-en-Tardenois, was the seneschal of Thibaut II, count of Champagne.
32 Pont-Saint-Mard, cant. Coucy-le-Château, https://dicotopo.cths.fr/places/P93612418.

medietatem castanearum de Vausaillum;[33] in episcopatu Noviomensi, altare et curtem de Bonolio[34] cum pertinentiis suis; curtem de Bolmont,[35] curtem de Calveni; alodium de Germaines;[36] curtem de Montisel;[37] curtem de Toiri; curtem de Landricourt;[38] curtem de Landrimont[39] et in suburbio Noviomensi terras, vineas et prata; curtem cum hiis que ad eandem spectant; molendina d'Espevile[40] et dimidiam partem decime eiusdem ville; duas partes decime de Stoilli;[41] sextam partem decime de Duri; molendina de Offois[42] et duas partes decime eiusdem ville; terciam partem decime de Creci; dimidiam sedem cuiusdam molendini apud Divisam[43] et medietatem decime de eiusdem ville; duas partes decime de Sancta Radegunde; duas partes decime de Calveni; terciam partem decime de Caullaincourt;[44] duas partes decime de Gricourt;[45] tres partes dimidie partis decime de Leher Wez; tertiam partem decime de Lanci;[46] decimam de Kiures;[47] terram apud Omencourt;[48] terram de Liencourt et de Curci; tria jugera apud Greuni;[49] cappellam Sancti Nicholai libera apud Sanctum Quintinum; curtem Alodiorum cum suis appenditiis; curtem de Voiana cum appenditiis; curtem de Hanapiis[50] in alodio cum decima; duas partes decime de Bethincourt;[51] duas partes decime de Cartigni; totam decimam de Falevi excepta minuta; quartam partem de Aldeni; molendina de Escanli[52] cum appenditiis suis; molendina de Hamel;[53] sedes cuiusdam molendini apud Pieton.[54] Illud etiam humanitatis ratione perspeximus et presenti decreto in perpetuum valituro sanctimus ut sorores que per laborem fratris nostri Norberti, bone memorie Magdeburgensis archiepiscopi, et vestram exhortationem ad omnipotentis

33 Vauxaillon, cant. Anizy-le-Château, https://dicotopo.cths.fr/places/P32329338.
34 Bonneuil, cant. Ham, https://dicotopo.cths.fr/places/P66750585.
35 Beaumont-en-Beine, cant. Chauny, https://dicotopo.cths.fr/places/P18685379.
36 Germaine, cant. Vermand, https://dicotopo.cths.fr/places/P36636067.
37 Montizel, cant. Ham, https://dicotopo.cths.fr/places/P16235568.
38 Landricourt, cant. Coucy-le-Château, https://dicotopo.cths.fr/places/P66354305.
39 Landrimont, comm. Noyon, https://dicotopo.cths.fr/places/P74301629.
40 Eppeville, cant. Ham, https://dicotopo.cths.fr/places/P94171781.
41 Estouilly, cant. Ham, https://dicotopo.cths.fr/places/P96663971.
42 Offoy, cant. Ham, https://dicotopo.cths.fr/places/P14011159.
43 Devise, cant. Ham, https://dicotopo.cths.fr/places/P85212875.
44 Caulaincourt, cant. Vermand, https://dicotopo.cths.fr/places/P02972526.
45 Grécourt, cant. Nesle, https://dicotopo.cths.fr/places/P84842582.
46 Lanchy, cant. Vermand, https://dicotopo.cths.fr/places/P51978975.
47 Possibly Quivières, cant. Ham, https://dicotopo.cths.fr/places/P53835780.
48 Aumencourt, comm. Auffrique-et-Nogent, https://dicotopo.cths.fr/places/P03934228.
49 Grouches, cant. Roye, https://dicotopo.cths.fr/places/P04293263.
50 Hannape, cant. Wassigny, https://dicotopo.cths.fr/places/P37303056.
51 Bethencourt-sur-Somme, cant. Nesle, https://dicotopo.cths.fr/places/P85791062.
52 Canny-lès-Voyennes, cant. Nesle, https://dicotopo.cths.fr/places/P44415541.
53 Hamel-lès-Corbie, cant. Corbie, https://dicotopo.cths.fr/places/P37197765.
54 Pithon, cant. Saint-Simon, https://dicotopo.cths.fr/places/P56020430.

Dei servitium accesserunt et semetipsas Domino obtulerunt de bonis ecclesie vestre quorum non modica pars eidem loco noscitur pervenisse sine cuiusquam contradictione nunc et semper in sustentationem temporalium necessaria consequantur: Simili modo quoque decernimus ut de laboribus quos propriis manibus sumptibusve colligitis dare decimam cuiquam non cogamini. Sed nec alicui episcopo liceat qualibet occasione in vestra ecclesia divina officia celebrare. Si vero generale interdictum in diocesi factum fuerit, exclusis excommunicatis divina nichilominus officia celebretis. Porro ordinationes clericorum vel canonicorum, consecrationes altarium et basilicarum seu reliqua ecclesiastica sacramenta a Laudunensi suscipietis episcopo, si quidem catholicus fuerit et gratiam atque communionem Apostolice Sedis habuerit. Alioquin catholicum quemcumque malveritis adeatis antistitem. Qui nostra fultus auctoritate, quod postulatur indulgeat. Siquis vero nobilium se ibidem sepeliri ~~desiderat~~ deliberaverit ipsius devotioni et extreme voluntati, nisi forte excommunicatus sit, nullus obsistat, salva justicia matris ecclesie. Decernimus ergo ut nulli omnino hominum liceat prefatam ecclesiam temere perturbare aut eius possessiones auferre vel ablatas retinere minuere seu quibuslibet molestiis fatigare. Sed omnia integra conserventur eorum pro quorum gubernatione et sustentatione concessa sunt usibus omnimodis profutura. Siquis sane ausu temerario huic nostre constitutioni scienter contraire presumpserit, secundo terciove commonitus si non presumptionem suam congrua emendatione correxerit excommunicationi subjaceat. Conservantes autem hec omnipotentis Dei et beatorum Petri et Pauli apostolorum eius gratiam consequantur. Amen. Ego Celestinus catholice ecclesie episcopus SS. Ego Conradus[55] Sabinensis episcopus SS et ceteri. Datum Laterani, per manum Gerardi[56] Sancte Romane ecclesie cardinalis ac bibliotecarii, VIII idus decembris, indictione VII^{a}, incarnationis dominice anno M^{o} C^{o} XLIII°, pontificatus nostri anno primo.

50

May 17, 1147. Paris.

Pope Eugene [III], like his predecessor, Pope Celestine [II], takes the abbey of Prémontré under his protection and confirms its goods and privileges.

A. Cartulary of Prémontré, fols. 12bisr–12bisv.

B. Original not found.

EDITION: Le Paige, *Bibliotheca*, 428–9; Hugo, *prob.* 1, cols. xv–xvi; *PL* 180, cols. 1217–20.

55 Corrado della Suburra (ca. 1073–1154), cardinal bishop of Sabina, 1127/8–53, and pope as Anastasius IV, 1153–4.

56 Gerardo Caccianemici dell'Orso (d. 1145), papal *bibliothecarius* from 1141 and pope as Lucius II, 1144–5.

REGISTER: JL no. 9050 (J: 6310); Grauwen, "Lijst van oorkonden waarin Norbertus wordt genoemd," 170.

Privilegium domini Pape Eugenii de confirmatione possessionum.

[E]ugenius episcopus, servus servorum Dei, dilectis filiis Hugoni Premonstratensi abbati, eiusque fratribus tam presentibus quam futuris regulariter substituendis in perpetuum. Cum universis personis ecclesiasticis nos oporteat generaliter providere, erga illos tamen propensiori cura non convenit esse sollicitos, quos constat maiori studio cunctipotentis Dei servitio inhiare et acriori religione ac morum honestate clarescere. Hoc nimirum caritatis intuitu, dilecti in Domino filii, vestre devotionis precibus debita benignitate impertimur assensum, et Premonstratensem ecclesiam in qua divino mancipati estis obsequio ad exemplar predecessoris nostri felicis memorie, Pape Celestini, cum omnibus ad ipsam pertinentibus sub Beati Petri et nostra protectione suscipimus, et presentis scripti privilegio communimus. Statuentes ut quascumque possessiones, quecumque bona idem venerabilis locus in presentiarum juste et canonice possidet, aut in futurum concessione pontificum, largitione regum vel principum, oblatione fidelium seu aliis modis, Deo propitio, poterit adipisci firma vobis vestrisque successoribus et illibata permaneant. In quibus hec propriis duximus exprimenda vocabulis: ambitum scilicet ipsius vallis Premonstratensis sicut in vestris scriptis continetur et certis terminis diffinitur, ab omni videlicet exactione liberum tam terragii quam decime sive census; curtem quoque de Fontenellis[1] cum vivario et duabus partibus molendinorum subjacentium ceterisque appenditiis suis; curtem de Panencourt[2] cum vineis et ceteris appenditiis suis; curtem de Merliu[3] cum vineis, et decimam quam Odo[4] de Abbatia in illa potestate tenebat; curtem de Rosieres[5] cum pertinentiis suis; decimam cum terragio de Vervin; terragia de Couci Villa et vivarium cum molendino juxta eandem villam; curtem de Vercigni[6] cum appenditiis suis; curtem juxta

1 Fontenille, comm. Wissignicourt, https://dicotopo.cths.fr/places/P36537367.

2 Penancourt, comm. Anizy-le-Château, https://dicotopo.cths.fr/places/P36114519.

3 Merlieux, cant. Anizy-le-Château, https://dicotopo.cths.fr/places/P92396813.

4 Eudes de l'Abbaye (comm. Bucilly, https://dicotopo.cths.fr/places/P35628143) was either the son or nephew of Raoul de l'Abbaye and Amaltrude. He and his wife Bertrade appear as witnesses in a number of episcopal acts in the 1110s–ca. 1150. Dufour-Malbezin, *Actes*, 137, 197. He was probably from a *lieu dit* called L'Abbaye about a kilometre southeast of Bucilly. Melleville, *DH*, vol. 1, 167; Saint-Denis, *Apogée d'une cité*, 211–15.

5 Rozières, cant. Oulchy-le-Château, https://dicotopo.cths.fr/places/P75685266.

6 Versigny, cant. La Fère, https://dicotopo.cths.fr/places/P17885640.

Firmitatem cum pertinentiis suis; curtem de Crespi[7] cum pertinentiis suis et duabus partibus decime; curtem de Hanapiis[8] in alodio cum decima et ceteris pertinentiis suis; terciam partem decime de Chauns;[9] molendinum de Acheri[10] et duas partes molendinorum de Erchentre;[11] duas partes molendini de Aquila;[12] molendinum de Curcoun;[13] molendinum de Cinceni;[14] vinagia de Bourguino;[15] vineas de Couci Castello et de Couci Villa molendinum et vineas et vinagia de Nova Villa; quartam partem de Aldeni; curtem de Soupi[16] cum molendinis subjacentibus in flumine quod dicitur Axona ceterisque appenditiis suis et terram de Capriniaco[17] monte; in Suessionensi episcopatu in suburbio civitatis, domum et torcularia et vineas; apud Pomerias vinagia, census denariorum Brane Castri et Branele ville; curtem de Buci cum vineis, vinagiis et pertinentiis suis et molendino de Rupibus[18] quod est sub eadem villa; curtem de Clameci[19] cum vineis et pertinentiis suis, curtem de Tinselva[20] cum pertinentiis suis; curtem de Luili[21] et dimidium molendinum cum pertinentiis suis; apud Betencourt[22] vinagia et alios redditus; apud Pinon[23] quendam censum et tertiam partem minute decime de Atrio et sextam partem cuiusdam molendini et decimam quam Joisbertus de Noviomo ibi habuit; curtem de Rosel cum omnibus pertinentiis suis; in monte de Troisli[24] curtem unam et in valle aliam cum pertinentiis suis et partem eiusdem ville cum appenditiis suis et ad Sorni[25] torcularia, vineas, terram et alios redditus; curtem de Buci cum pertinentiis suis; curtem de Atheci cum duabus partibus decime et vineis ceterisque appenditiis suis; apud Chaveni censum et vinagia; apud Margival molendinum; in episcopatu Noviomensi altare et curtem de Bonolio cum omnibus pertinentiis suis; curtem de Bolmont cum pertinentiis suis; curtem de Cauvigni cum

7 Crépy, cant. Laon, https://dicotopo.cths.fr/places/P85331504.
8 Hannape, cant. Wassigny, https://dicotopo.cths.fr/places/P37303056.
9 Champs, cant. Coucy-le-Château, https://dicotopo.cths.fr/places/P17397889.
10 Achery, cant. La Fère, https://dicotopo.cths.fr/places/P61820808.
11 Archantré, comm. Remies, https://dicotopo.cths.fr/places/P18258469.
12 Aile, comm. Royaucourt-et-Chailvet, https://dicotopo.cths.fr/places/P82381255.
13 Courson, comm. Landricourt, https://dicotopo.cths.fr/places/P39892049.
14 Sinceny, cant. Chauny, https://dicotopo.cths.fr/places/P29595722.
15 Bourguignon-sous-Montbavin, cant. Anizy-le-Château, https://dicotopo.cths.fr/places/P25732714.
16 Soupir, cant. Vailly, https://dicotopo.cths.fr/places/P62600159.
17 Chevregny, cant. Anizy-le-Château, https://dicotopo.cths.fr/places/P06529464.
18 Les Roches, comm. Bucy-le-Long, https://dicotopo.cths.fr/places/P20402237.
19 Clamecy, cant. Vailly, https://dicotopo.cths.fr/places/P24475745.
20 Tinselve, comm. Leuilly, https://dicotopo.cths.fr/places/P54510057.
21 Leuilly, cant. Coucy-le-Château, https://dicotopo.cths.fr/places/P91541747.
22 Béthancourt, comm. Crécy-au-Mont, https://dicotopo.cths.fr/places/P52359541.
23 Pinon, cant. Anizy-le-Château, https://dicotopo.cths.fr/places/P22218866.
24 Trosly-Loire, cant. Coucy-le-Château, https://dicotopo.cths.fr/places/P24780558.
25 Sorny, cant. Vailly, https://dicotopo.cths.fr/places/P79681466.

appenditiis suis; alodium de Germaines;[26] curtem de Montisel[27] cum pertinentiis suis; curtem de Toiri[28] cum molendinis et pertinentiis suis; curtem de Landrimunt[29] cum vineis ceterisque appenditiis suis; molendina d'Espevile[30] et dimidiam partem decime eiusdem ville et duas partes minute; decimam de Gollancourt[31] excepta minuta; duas partes decime de Buici et de Cisencourt[32] et de Stoilli;[33] sextam partem decime de Duri; molendina de Offois[34] et duas partes decime eiusdem ville et partem Johannis Mosun; tertiam partem decime de Creci; dimidiam sedem cuiusdam molendini apud Divisam[35] et medietatem decime eiusdem ville; duas partes decime de Sancta Radegunde; duas partes de Calveni; terciam partem decime de Collancourt;[36] duas partes decime de Gricourt[37] et de Curti; capellam Sancti Nicholai liberam apud Sanctum Quintinum; curtem Alodiorum cum appenditiis suis; terram de Voana; duas partes decime de Bechincourt;[38] decimam totam de Falevi excepta minuta; duas partes decime de Cartigni; molendina de Escanli[39] cum appenditiis suis; molendina de Hamiaus; apud Pieton[40] sedem cuiusdam molendini; quartam partem decime de Leher Weiz; terciam partem decime de Lanci;[41] terram de Liencourt et de Curti. Illud etiam humanitatis ratione perspeximus et presenti decreto in perpetuum valituro sanctimus, ut sorores que per laborem fratris nostri Norberti, bone memorie Magdeburgensis archiepiscopi, et vestram exhortationem ad omnipotentis Dei servitium accesserunt et semetipsas Domino obtulerunt, de bonis ecclesie vestre, quorum non modica pars eidem loco per eas noscitur provenisse, sine cuiusquam contradictione nunc et semper in sustentatione temporalium necessaria consequantur. Simili modo decernimus ut de laboribus quos propriis manibus sumptibusve colitis, sive de nutrimentis vestrorum animalium dare decimam cuiquam non cogamini. Sed nec alicui episcopo liceat absque rationabili causa in vestra ecclesia divina officia prohibere. Si vero generale interdictum in diocesi factum fuerit, exclusis excommunicatis,

26 Germaine, cant. Vermand, https://dicotopo.cths.fr/places/P36636067.
27 Montizel, cant. Ham, https://dicotopo.cths.fr/places/P16235568.
28 Thury, comm. Marest-Dampcourt, https://dicotopo.cths.fr/places/P84789655.
29 Landrimont, comm. Noyon, https://dicotopo.cths.fr/places/P74301629.
30 Eppeville, cant. Ham, https://dicotopo.cths.fr/places/P94171781.
31 Golancourt, cant. Guiscard, https://dicotopo.cths.fr/places/P75999303.
32 Cizancourt, cant. Nesle, https://dicotopo.cths.fr/places/P70322720.
33 Estouilly, cant. Ham, https://dicotopo.cths.fr/places/P96663971.
34 Offoy, cant. Ham, https://dicotopo.cths.fr/places/P14011159.
35 Devise, cant. Ham, https://dicotopo.cths.fr/places/P85212875.
36 Caulaincourt, cant. Vermand, https://dicotopo.cths.fr/places/P02972526.
37 Grécourt, cant. Nesle, https://dicotopo.cths.fr/places/P84842582.
38 Becquincourt, cant. Bray, https://dicotopo.cths.fr/places/P53738864.
39 Canny-lès-Voyennes, cant. Nesle, https://dicotopo.cths.fr/places/P44415541.
40 Pithon, cant. Saint-Simon, https://dicotopo.cths.fr/places/P56020430.
41 Lanchy, cant. Vermand, https://dicotopo.cths.fr/places/P51978975.

nichilominus officia divina celebretis. Porro ordinationes canonicorum vel clericorum, consecrationes altarium seu basilicarum sive ecclesiastica sacramenta reliqua a Laudunensi suscipietis episcopo. Siquidem catholicus fuerit et gratiam atque communionem Apostolice Sedis habuerit, alioquin catholicum quemcumque malueritis adeatis antistitem, qui nostra fultus auctoritate quod postulatur indulgeat. Siquis vero nobilium se ibidem sepeliri deliberaverit ipsius devotioni et extreme voluntati, nisi forte excommunicatus vel interdictus sit, nullus obsistat, salva justicia matris ecclesie. Decernimus ergo ut nulli omnino hominum liceat prefatam ecclesiam temere perturbare aut eius possessiones auferre vel ablatas retinere, minuere seu quibuslibet molestiis fatigare, sed omnia integra conserventur eorum pro quorum gubernatione et sustentatione concessa sunt usibus omnimodis profutura, salva Sedis Apostolice auctoritate et diocessanorum episcoporum canonica justicia. Si qua igitur in futurum ecclesiastica secularisve persona hanc nostre constitutionis paginam sciens contra eam temere venire temptaverit, secundo terciove commonita, si non satisfactione congrua emendaverit, potestatis honorisque sui dignitate careat, reamque se divino judicio existere de perpetrata iniquitate cognoscat, et a sacratissimo corpore ac sanguine Dei et Domini Redemptoris nostri Jhesu Christi aliena fiat, atque in extremo examine districte ultioni subjaceat. Cunctis autem eidem loco justa servantibus sit pax Domini nostri Jhesu Christi. Quatinus et hic functum bone actionis percipiant et apud districtum judicem premia eterne pacis inveniant, amen. Ego Eugenius catholice ecclesie episcopus SS. Ego Albricus[42] Ostiensis episcopus. SS. Ego Imarus[43] Tuscalanus[44] episcopus SS. Datum Parisius, per manum Hugonis[45] presbiteri cardinalis, agentis vicem domini Guidonis Sancte Romane ecclesie diaconi cardinalis et cancellarii, XVI kalendas junii, indictione X, incarnationis Domini M° Cϵ° XL° VII°, pontificatus vero domini Eugenii III Pape anno tercio.

51

January 3, 1154. Saint Peter's, Rome.

Pope Adrian [IV] grants to the order of Prémontré certain privileges concerning the General Chapter meetings, the excommunication of members of the

42 Albéric, abbot of the Benedictine abbey of Vézelay, 1131–8, and cardinal bishop of Ostia, 1138–48.

43 Imar/Icmar, cardinal bishop of Tusculum from 1142.

44 *Sic A*, *read* Tusculanus.

45 Ugo Misini (or Misani) (d. 1150), first prior of the monastery of S. Prassede and then cardinal priest of San Lorenzo in Lucina from 1144, served as a substitute for Cardinal Guido da Vico as chancellor of the Roman Church, 1147–8.

order, the deposition of abbots and the designation of the abbot at the mother abbey of Prémontré, and compliance with the decisions of the General Chapter.

A. Cartulary of Prémontré, fols. 12bisv–13r.

B. Original not found.

Other Manuscript Copies: Cartulary of Grimbergen Abbey, Abdij van Grimbergen Oud Archief, Klas II, 1, fol. 2r (13th c.); Cartulary of Saint-Augustin-lès-Thérouanne, Brussels, KBR, MS 4132, fol. 163r (13th c.); Cartulary of Park Abbey, Archief van de Abdij van Park te Heverlee, MS VII 24, fol. 136v (13th c.); Cartulary of Beaurepart, Bibliothèque du Séminaire Episcopal de Liège, G IV 7, fol. 21r (15th c.); Cartulary of Park Abbey, Archief van de Abdij van Park te Heverlee, MS VII 26, fol. 50r (15th c.); Cartulary of Averbode Abbey, Archief van de abdij van Averbode, Sectie IV, no. 109, fol. 4v (15/16th c.); Cartulary of Park Abbey, Archief van de Abdij van Park te Heverlee, MS VII 35, fol. 25r (15/16th c.).

EDITION: Hanegraaf, *Compendio della vita, miracoli, et instituto del glorioso patriarcha S. Norberto*, 185–6 (partial); Le Paige, *Bibliotheca*, 627–8; Hertoghe, *Religio canonicorum ordinis Praemonstratensis*, 91–2 (partial); Hugo, *prob.* 1, cols. xviii–xix; *PL* 188, cols. 1373–5.

REGISTER: JL no. 9970 (J: 6829).

Privilegium quod abbates excommunicare possint fugitivos.

Adrianus[1] episcopus, servus servorum Dei, dilectis filiis Hugoni, Premonstratensi abbati, atque eiusdem ordinis abbatibus, prepositis eorumque successoribus regulariter substituendis in perpetuum. Sicut in humano corpore menbra plurima esse noscuntur, et alia in maiori honore habentur, quoniam pro excellentie sue dignitate sunt cariora, ita in corpore Christi quod est ecclesia, plurimi sunt ad honorem et laudem Domini congregati, quidam tamen propensius in ipsius laudibus atque servitio commorantes, sicut menbra excellentiora in Christi corpore numerantur, et sunt quasi luminaria in firmamento celi que terrenos illuminant et ad Christi servitium proprii ungenti ~~corpore~~ odore student alios attentius provocare. Vos autem filii in Christo karissimi, quoniam de illorum numero esse cognoscimus, sincero caritatis affectu diligimus et vestris justis postulationibus gratum volumus exhibere consensum ut tanto ferventius in Domini vinea laboretis, quanto apud matrem vestram Sacrosanctam Romanam Ecclesiam maiorem gratiam senseritis invenisse. Quo circa dilecti in Domino filii, vestris precibus annuentes, statuimus et Apostolice Sedis auctoritate sanctimus, ut omnes abbates et prepositi Premonstratensis ordinis ad

1 The initial letter has been added at a later, possibly post-medieval date.

commune capitulum annuatim Premonstratum veniant, nisi forte sint proprii corporis infirmitate detenti, vel ex communi consilio licentiam habeant remanendi. Quatinus vobis omnibus in Christi nomine congregatis, evellenda possitis evellere, et plantanda firmiter stabilire, atque de communi utilitate ordinis diligentissime pertractare. Statuimus etiam ut nulli archiepiscopo vel episcopo liceat aliquem de ordine vestro ad ipsum capitulum venire volentem, modis aliquibus prohibere. Ad hec presenti decreto sanctimus, ut ordo canonicus qui secundum Deum et Beati Augustini regulam atque Premonstratensum fratrum consuetudinem in vestris ecclesiis dinoscitur institutus, in eisdem perpetuis temporibus inviolabiliter observetur. Ad maiorem quoque observantiam vestri ordinis, fugitivos vestros excommunicandi vobis licentiam indulgemus. Interdicimus etiam ut nullus sine licentia prelati sui aliquem de ipsis fugitivis audeat retinere. Ut autem de bono in melius semper possitis proficere, et ordinem vestrum in suo rigore melius custodire, presentis decreti assertione firmamus, ut liceat vobis abbates qui fuerint in crimine deprehensi, et eos quos prorsus invenietis inutiles, ab officio abbatis deponere et consilio capituli in aliqua ecclesiarum vestri ordinis collocare. Prohibemus etiam ut nullus abbas Premonstratensis ordinis de una abbatia ad aliam sine communi consilio transferatur. Fratribus vero Premonstratensis ecclesie que mater aliarum esse dinoscitur, de qualibet ecclesiarum eiusdem ordinis liceat abbatem recipere et in Premonstratensi ecclesia ordinare. Sed et hoc adicientes apostolica auctoritate sanctimus, ut quod a vobis communi consilio de conservatione ordinis vestri, seu rigore rationabiliter fuerit ordinatum, in concussum permaneat, et a nullo penitus ~~re~~infringatur. Decernimus ergo ut nulli omnino hominum liceat hanc nostre constitutionis paginam temerario ausu infringere, seu ipsi modis omnibus, contraire, salva Sedis Apostolice auctoritate. Siqua igitur in futurum ecclesiastica secularisve persona, hanc nostram constitutionem sciens, contra eam temere venire temptaverit, secundo tertiove commonita, si non reatum suum congrua satisfactione correxerit, potestatis, honorisque sui dignitate careat, reamque se divino judicio existere de perpetrata iniquitate cognoscat et a sacratissimo corpore ac sanguine Dei et Domini redemptoris nostri Jhesu Christi aliena fiat atque in extremo examine districte subjaceat. Amen. Adrianus, catholice ecclesie episcopus. Ego Hugo,[2] Hostiensis episcopus. Ego Gregorius,[3] Sabinensis episcopus SS. Ego Guido,[4] presbiter cardinalis tituli. SS.[5]

2 Hugues de Châlons, abbot of the Cistercian abbey of Trois-Fontaines, 1147–50, and cardinal bishop of Ostia, 1150–8.

3 Gregorio della Suburra, cardinal bishop of Sabina in 1154–ca. 1163.

4 Guido di Bellagio, cardinal priest of San Crisogono, 1138–58.

5 Here the scribe uses SS to indicate a truncated witness list. See Le Paige, *Bibliotheca*, 628, for the full list.

Datum Rome apud Sanctum Petrum, per manum Rollandi[6] Sancte Romane Ecclesie presbiteri cardinalis et cancelarii, III° nonas januarii, indictione III, incarnationis dominice anno M° C° LIIII°, pontificatus vero domini Adriani Pape IIII[ti] anno primo.

52

February 16, 1126. Lateran.

Pope Honorius [II] confirms the new order founded by Norbert according to the rule of Saint Augustine and forbids anyone to modify the order thus established. He also forbids bishops to evict members of the order from their churches and forbids Premonstratensians to break claustration without authorization of the community. He confirms the possessions of the said order.

A. Cartulary of Prémontré, fol. 13r.

B. Original not found.

Other Manuscript Copies: Cartulary of Grimbergen Abbey, Abdij van Grimbergen Oud Archief, Klas II, 1, fol. 1r (13th c.); Cartulary of Park Abbey, Archief van de Abdij van Park te Heverlee, MS VII 24, fol. 135v (13th c.); Cartulary of Saint-Augustin-lès-Thérouanne, Brussels, KBR, MS 4132, fol. 148r (13th c.); Book of Privileges, Osterhofen Abbey, Bayerische Hauptstaatsarchiv München, Clm 9903, fol. 62 (early 14th c.); Bayerische Hauptstaatsarchiv München, Literalien des Klosters Schäftlarn, no. 2, fols. 28r–29r (14th c.); "Liber statutorum necnon et de institutione sive de origine candidi ordinis scilicet Premonstratensis," Koninklijke Bibliotheek van Nederland, MS 128 G 21, fol. 82v (1445); Stiftsarchiv Wilten, Lade 8 M, 3–4 (early 15th c.); Cartulary of Beaurepart, Bibliothèque du Séminaire Episcopal de Liège, G IV 7, fol. 17r (15th c.); Cartulary of Park Abbey, Archief van de Abdij van Park te Heverlee, MS VII 26, fol. 49r (15th c.); Cartulary of Averbode Abbey, Archief van de abdij van Averbode, Sectie IV, no. 109, fol. 1v (15/16th c.).

EDITION: Le Mire, *Ordinis Praemonstratensis chronicon*, 36–8; Le Paige, *Bibliotheca*, 392–3; Dubal, *Vida apostolica, muerte y translacion de N.P. y Patriarca S. Norberto, fundador del orden candido y canonico premonstratense*, 72–3; Hugo, *La vie de S. Norbert, Archevêque de Magdebourg*, 238–40; Saulnier, "Confirmatio instituti Ordinis Praemonstratensis per Sanctissimum D.N. Honorium PP. II," in *Statuta Candidi et Canonici Ordinis Praemonstratensis Renovata ac Anno 1630*, partial; Launoy, *Opera Omnia*, vol. 3, part 1, 497 (partial); Hugo, *prob.* 1, cols. ix–x; Kuen, *Collectio Scriptorum Rerum Historico-Monastico Ecclesiasticarum*

6 Rolando Bandinelli, chancellor of the Roman Church, 1153–9, and pope as Alexander III, 1159–81.

Variorum Religiosorum Ordinum, vol. 6, 10; *PL* 166, cols. 1249–51; Madelaine, *Histoire de saint Norbert, fondateur de l'ordre de Prémontré et archevêque de Magdebourg*, 534–5; *DiplomataBelgica*, no. 517, https://www.diplomata-belgica.be/charter_details_en.php?dibe_id=517.

REGISTER: Bréquigny, *Table chronologique*, vol. 2, 540; JL no. 7244 (J: 5232); Weissthanner, *Die Urkunden und Urbare des Klosters Schäftlarn*, 251–2; Grauwen, "Lijst van oorkonden waarin Norbertus wordt genoemd," 148–9.

Privilegium de confirmatione quarundam abbatiarum et possessiones.

Honorius[1] episcopus, servus servorum Dei, dilectis filiis Norberto Fratri in Christo et canonicis Premonstrate ecclesie Sancte Marie, eorumque successoribus regularem vitam professis in perpetuum. Apostolice discipline sectantes vestigia mundanis quidem ponpis[2] et possessionibus abrenuntiant, et Domino totis annisibus famulantur. Isti ergo si bonum quod inceperint, consumaverint, in extremi examine judicis sunt immortalitatis stolam et perpetuam gloriam adepturi. Quia igitur vos religiose vivere et canonicam vitam secundum Beati Augustini institutionem ducere, inspirante superna gratia, decrevistis, propositum vestrum Sedis Apostolice auctoritate firmamus et firmos vos in remissionem peccatorum vestrorum in eo persistere adhortamur. Statuimus itaque, ut in ecclesiis vestris, in quibus fratres vitam canonicam professi degunt, nulli omnino hominum liceat secundum Beati Augustini regulam ibidem constitutum ordinem commutare. Nullus etiam episcoporum futuris temporibus audeat eiusdem religionis fratres de ecclesiis vestris expellere, nec professionis canonice quispiam ex eisdem ecclesiis aut claustris audeat sine communi congregationis permissione discedere, discedentem vero nullus episcoporum, nullus abbatum, nullus monachorum sine communium litterarum cautione suscipere. Bona etiam et possessiones quas juste et legitime possidetis, presentis scripti nostri pagina confirmamus, in quibus hec propriis nominibus duximus exprimenda: ecclesiam videlicet Sancti Martini[3] in Laudunensi episcopatu, Vivariensem[4] ecclesiam Sancte Marie in Suessionensi episcopatu, Floreffie[5] ecclesiam Sancte Marie in Leodiensi, Capenberg[6] ecclesiam Sancte

1 The initial letter has been added at a later, possibly post-medieval date.
2 *Sic A*, *read* pompis.
3 The Premonstratensian abbey of Saint-Martin de Laon. *MP* II, 509–13.
4 The Premonstratensian community founded at Vivières in 1124/6 moved to Valsery in 1153. *MP* II, 537–9.
5 The Premonstratensian abbey of Floreffe. *MP* II, 373–8.
6 The Premonstratensian abbey of Cappenberg. *MP* I, 158–60.

Marie et Beatorum Petri et Pauli in Monasteriensi, Varlar[7] ecclesiam Sancte Marie in eodem episcopatu, Elostat[8] ecclesiam Sancte Marie in Magontiensi, ecclesiam Sancti Arnualis[9] in Metensi, Antverpie[10] ecclesiam Sancti Michaelis in Cameracensi. Ambitum eiusdem vallis a loco qui dicitur Helierpre usque ad vallem Rohardi, cum tribus adjacentibus vallibus et a rivo versus Voiz,[11] sicut valles proportant; duas partes decime quas in villa de Crespi[12] per Laudunensem episcopum habetis, et cetera que in eadem villa largitione dilecti filii nostri Ludovici, regis Francie, possidetis; alodium Clari Fontis; alodium Ramengeis cum molendino; tres mansos apud Bolmunt;[13] Anisi[14] mansum unum cum molendino; Fraisne[15] mansum unum; Vercigni[16] mansum unum; Soupi[17] tres mansos et dimidium; totum alodium quod dicitur Bonvel; Suessione domum unam cum vineis et terris; vineas in Laudunensi pago, in villa que dicitur Broiencourt[18] et Ursinicourt[19] et Arcenne. Quecumque preterea in futurum, concessione pontificum, liberalitate regum vel principum, vel aliis justis modis canonice poteritis adipisci, firma vobis vestrisque successoribus in sancte religionis proposito permansuris, et illibata serventur. Decernimus ergo ut nulli omnino hominum liceat easdem ecclesias temere perturbare, aut earum possessiones auferre, vel ablatas retinere, minuere, vel temerariis vexationibus fatigare, sed omnia integra conserventur, regularium fratrum et pauperum usibus profutura, salva diocesanorum episcoporum canonica justicia. Siqua igitur in futurum ecclesiastica secularisve persona hanc nostre constitutionis paginam sciens, contra eam venire temptaverit, secundo terciove commonita, si non satisfactione congrua emendaverit, potestatis honorisque sui careat dignitate, reamque se divino judicio existere de perpetrata iniquitate cognoscat, et a sacratissimo corpore et sanguine Dei et Domini redemptoris nostri Jhesu Christi aliena fiat atque in extremo examine districte ultioni subjaceat. Cunctis autem eisdem ecclesiis justa servantibus sit pax Domini nostri Jhesu Christi. Quatinus et hic fructum bone actionis percipiant et apud districtum judicem premia eterne pacis inveniant, amen. Ego Honorius, catholice ecclesie episcopus SS.

---

7 The Premonstratensian abbey of Varlar. *MP* I, 197–9.
8 The Premonstratensian abbey of Ilbenstadt. *MP* I, 101–3.
9 Likely the collegiate church of Sankt Arnual, today in Saarbrücken.
10 The Premonstratensian abbey of Sint-Michielsabdij, Antwerp. *MP* II, 265–9.
11 Forest of Vois, https://dicotopo.cths.fr/places/P93994197.
12 Crépy, cant. Laon, https://dicotopo.cths.fr/places/P85331504.
13 Beaumont-en-Beine, cant. Chauny, https://dicotopo.cths.fr/places/P18685379.
14 Anizy-le-Château, arr. Laon, https://dicotopo.cths.fr/places/P86940236.
15 Fresne, cant. Coucy-le-Château, https://dicotopo.cths.fr/places/P35697386.
16 Versigny, cant. La Fère, https://dicotopo.cths.fr/places/P17885640.
17 Soupir, cant. Vailly, https://dicotopo.cths.fr/places/P62600159.
18 Brancourt, cant. Anizy-le-Château, https://dicotopo.cths.fr/places/P91051513.
19 Wissignicourt, cant. Anizy-le-Château, https://dicotopo.cths.fr/places/P16285342.

Datum Laterani, per manum Almourici,[20] Sancte Ecclesie Romane diaconi cardinalis et cancellarii, XIIII kalendas martii, indictione IIII, anno dominice incarnationis M° C° XXVI°, pontificatus autem domini Honorii Pape II anno secundo.

53

April 19, 1225. Lateran.

Pope Honorius [III] confirms the agreement reached in the presence of the pontifical legate, K[onrad of Urach],[1] *bishop of Porto e Rufina, between the abbot of Prémontré and the* prepositi *of abbeys associated with the abbey of Magdeburg, concerning the obligation for the said* prepositi *to attend the annual General Chapter and to obey all of the order's statutes.*

A. Cartulary of Prémontré, fols. 13r–13v.
B. Original not found.
EDITION: Le Paige, *Bibliotheca*, 926; Hugo, *prob.* 1, col. xxv; Klempin, *Pommersches Urkundenbuch*, vol. 1, 172–3; Heinemann, *Codex diplomaticus Anhaltinus*, vol. 2, 62–3; Hertel, *Urkundenbuch des Klosters Unser Lieben Frauen zu Magdeburg*, 97–8.
REGISTER: Reg. Vat. 9, fol. 48r; Bréquigny, *Table chronologique*, vol. 5, 249; Potthast, *Regesta*, no. 7399.

Privilegium de confirmatione pacis inter ecclesiam Premonstratensem et Magdeburgensem.

Honorius[2] episcopus, servus servorum Dei, dilecto filio abbati Premonstratensi, salutem et apostolicam benedictionem. Ea que pro ecclesiarum utilitate ac pace proinde ordinantur, apostolico sunt munimine roboranda, ut inpensiori diligentia observentur. Ex parte siquidem tua fuit propositum coram nobis, quod cum inter te ex parte una, et Sancte Marie Magdeburgensis,[3] de Gratia

---

20 Aimeric de la Châtre, cardinal deacon of Santa Maria Nuova from 1120 and papal chancellor, ca. 1123–41.

---

1 Konrad von Urach (d. 1227), the son of Egino IV, count of Urach, and Agnes von Zähringen, was successively abbot of Villers, 1209, abbot of Clairvaux, 1214, abbot of Cîteaux, 1217, and cardinal bishop of Porto e Rufina, 1219–27.

2 The initial letter has been added at a later, possibly post-medieval date.

3 The Premonstratensian abbey of Magdeburg. *MP* I, 232–5.

Dei,[4] de Liezebeca,[5] de Brandeburg,[6] de Havelberg,[7] de Rasceburg,[8] de Jherico,[9] de Colebeche,[10] de Rothe,[11] de Querelingeburg,[12] de Widda,[13] de Polethe,[14] de Granmorwe[15] et de Temenis[16] prepositos ex altera, questio verteretur super eo quod asserebas prefatos prepositos debere annis singulis Premonstratum convenire ad generale capitulum et omnibus communibus institutionibus ordinis obedire, pluresque super hoc littere a Sede Apostolica emanassent tandem mediantibus cantore Metensis suisque collegis, super hoc negotio delegatis a nobis, tu fili abbas et pars adversa, in certam concordie formam coram venerabili fratre nostro Conrado, Portuensi episcopo, Apostolice Sedis legato, sponte ac amicabiliter convenistis, quam apostolico postulasti munimine roborari. Nos igitur tuis precibus benignum impertientes assensum, concordiam ipsam sicut sine pravitate provide facta est et a partibus sponte recepta, et hactenus pacifice observata, atque in ipsius episcopi et dictorum judicum literis inde confectis plenius continetur auctoritate apostolica confirmamus, et presentis scripti patrocinio communimus. Nulli ergo hominum omnino liceat hanc paginam nostre confirmationis infringere vel ei ausu temerario contraire. Siquis autem hoc attemptare presumpserit, indignationem omnipotentis Dei et beatorum Petri et Pauli apostolorum eius se noverit incursurum. Datum Laterani, XIIII kalendas maii, pontificatus nostri anno nono.

54

March 5, 1219.

Pope Honorius [III] recommends to the archbishops, bishops, and prelates that they continue to support the papal privileges and indulgences that have been granted to the Premonstratensian Order, while keeping in mind the changes made by the Fourth Lateran Council (1215) concerning tithes.

A. Cartulary of Prémontré, fol. 13v.

B. Original not found.

---

4 The Premonstratensian abbey of Gottesgnaden. *MP* I, 218–20.
5 The Premonstratensian abbey of Leitzkau. *MP* I, 230–2.
6 The Premonstratensian abbey of Brandenburg. *MP* I, 215–17.
7 The Premonstratensian abbey of Havelberg. *MP* I, 223–5.
8 The Premonstratensian abbey of Ratzeburg. *MP* I, 241–3.
9 The Premonstratensian abbey of Jerichow. *MP* I, 225–7.
10 The Premonstratensian abbey of Kölbigk. *MP* I, 228–30.
11 The Premonstratensian abbey of Klosterrode. *MP* I, 227–8.
12 The Premonstratensian abbey of Quedlinburg. *MP* I, 239–40.
13 The Premonstratensian abbey of Mildenfurt. *MP* I, 235–7.
14 The Premonstratensian abbey of Pöhlde. *MP* I, 237–9.
15 The Premonstratensian abbey of Gramzow. *MP* I, 221–2.
16 A little-known Premonstratensian community, possibly now Ciemnik, Poland. *MP* I, 245–6.

Other Manuscript Copies: Cartulary of Leiston Abbey, British Library, Cotton MS Vespasian E XIV, fols. 24v–26r (1st half of 13th c.); Bayerische Hauptstaatsarchiv München, Literalien des Klosters Schäftlarn, no. 2, fols. 58r–58v (14th c.); Stiftsarchiv Wilten, Lade 8 M, 59 (early 15th c.).

EDITION: Le Paige, *Bibliotheca*, 651–2; Saulnier, "Aliquot Summorum Pontificum de Ordine Praemonstratensi Elogia," in *Statuta Candidi et Canonici Ordinis Praemonstratensis Renovata ac Anno 1630*, partial; Sanders, *Chorographia sacra Brabantiae*, vol. 1, 174–5; Honorius III, *Honorii III Romani Pontificis opera omnia quae exstant*, vol. 3, col. 153–4; Mortimer, *Leiston Abbey Cartulary and Butler Priory Charters*, 69.

REGISTER: Potthast, *Regesta*, no. 6002; Weissthanner, *Die Urkunden und Urbare des Klosters Schäftlarn*, 268.

Ne aliquis archiepiscopi sive episcopi audeat infringere sive male interpretavi privilegia nostra.

[H]onorius episcopus, servus servorum Dei, venerabilibus fratribus archiepiscopis et episcopis et dilectis filiis aliis ecclesiarum prelatis ad quos litere iste pervenerint salutem et apostolicam benedictionem. Benefaciens Dominus bonis et rectis corde, dilectos filios fratres Premonstratensis ordinis in via mandatorum ipsius inoffense currentes, tamquam populum acceptabilem sibi numero et merito ampliavit, eisque de rore celi et terre pinguedine benedicens, dilatavit locum tentorii eiusdem ordinis et pelles tabernaculorum eius extendit. Sed quod dolentes referimus in via hac quam ambulant superbi, contra eos laqueos extendentes, immo velut torrentes iniquitatis irruentes in eos, ipsos bonis suis, que soli Domino sunt dicata, non solum nequiter defraudare cum filii huius seculi prudentiores filiis Lucis in generatione sua sint verum etiam iniquitate potentes violenter spoliare nituntur et quod gravius est, non nulli de hiis qui eos debuerunt in Christi visceribus carius amplexari et favorabilius confovere, ipsos immanius persequentes privilegia que ipsis a Sede Apostolica, suis exigentibus meritis, sunt indulta, gestiunt penitum enervare dicendo illa fuisse omnino in generali concilio revocata, vel alias intellectum privilegiorum ipsorum ita maligna interpretatione ad libitum pervertendo, quod nisi os iniqua loquentium obstruatur, nil restet quin predicti fratres privilegiorum suorum pene penitus fructu frustentur[1] per quod illi non tam eisdem fratribus, quam nobis injuriari probantur, dum contra Sedis Apostolice indulgentias memoratos fratres temere perturbare presumunt, molientes contra nostre plenitudinem potestatis, dum indulta nostra irreverenter impugnant. Nos igitur qui predictos fratres speciali prerogativa dilectionis et gratie amplexamur, ut pote qui

1 *Sic A*, *read* frustrentur.

Domino jugiter offerentes suorum vitulos labiorum, non solum nobis sed etiam universali ecclesie piis intercessionibus incomparabiliter suffragantur, nolentes huiusmodi vexationibus eorum sabbati amaricari quietem, quos potius tenemur omnimodis consolari, universitatem vestram monemus et hortamur attente. Ac per apostolica scripta precipiendo mandamus, quatinus supradictos fratres ob reverentiam divinam et nostram habentes in visceribus caritatis eis privilegia et indulgentias Apostolice Sedis eisdem concessas inviolabiliter conservetis, et faciatis ab aliis conservari, salva moderatione concilii generalis, videlicet, ut de alienis terris a tempore predicti concilii acquisitis et de cetero acquirendis, exsolvant decimas ecclesiis quibus ratione prediorum antea solvebantur, nisi aliter cum eis duxerint componendum. Alias quoque dictos fratres ab incursibus malignorum taliter deffendatis, quod defensores justicie ac pietatis probemini amatores, Deumque vobis propitium, et nos reddatis, exinde favorabiles et benignos. Datum Laterani, III nonas martii, pontificatus nostri anno tercio.

55

February 18, 1219. Lateran.

*Pope Honorius [III] forbids anyone to demand of the religious of Prémontré the noval tithe on lands cultivated at the time of the Fourth Lateran Council (1215) and on those lands that the religious cultivate afterwards by their own hand or at their own cost. (See near-duplicate **41**.)*

A. Cartulary of Prémontré, fols. 13v–14r.

B. Original not found.

Other Manuscript Copies: Cartulary of Leiston Abbey, British Library, Cotton MS Vespasian E XIV, fols. 26r–26v (1st half of 13th c.); Cartulary of Cockersand Abbey, British Library, Add. MS 37769, fols. 11r–11v (1268).

EDITION: Le Paige, *Bibliotheca*, 650–1; Lalore, *Collection des principaux cartulaires du diocèse de Troyes*, vol. 3, 159–60; Honorius III, *Honorii III Romani Pontificis opera omnia quae exstant*, vol. 3, col. 127–8; Farrer, *The Chartulary of Cockersand Abbey of the Premonstratensian Order*, vol. 1, part 1, 23–35; Mortimer, *Leiston Abbey Cartulary and Butler Priory Charters*, 70.

REGISTER: Bréquigny, *Table chronologique*, vol. 5, 103; Potthast, *Regesta*, no. 5991.

Privilegium ut nullus exigat a nobis decimas de novalibus prius concilium generale excultis sive excolendis.

[H]onorius episcopus, servus servorum Dei, dilectis filiis abbati Premonstratensi et universis coabbatibus eius et fratribus sub eodem ordine Deo servientibus salutem et apostolicam benedictionem. Contigit interdum quod non nulli propriis incumbentes affectibus, dum sanctionum sensum legitimum ad sua vota non habent accommodum, superadducunt adulterum intellectum, in temporali compendio eternum dispendium non timentes. Sane sicut audivimus, quidam suo nimis inherentes ingenio, nimium que voluntarii, concilii generalis interpretes, de novalibus post idem concilium acquisitis, a vobis intendunt decimas extorquere. Ne super hiis vos contingat in debita molestatione vexari, nos interpretationem illorum intellectui constitutionis predicti concilii super Premonstratensibus decimis edite asserimus peregrinam. In ipsa quidem expresse cavetur, ut de alienis terris et amodo acquirendis, si eas propriis manibus aut sumptibus colueritis, decimas persolvatis ecclesiis, quibus ratione prediorum antea solvebantur. Unde si ad prope positum atiem[1] discretionis extenderent, advertentes nichilominus de quibus novalibus Apostolica Sedes intelligat, indulgentiam super talibus piis locis concessam, non sic circa novalia nove interpretationis ludibrio ingenia fatigarent. Inhibemus igitur auctoritate presentium, ut nullus a vobis de novalibus a tempore concilii excultis, vel in posterum propriis manibus aut sumptibus excolendis, decimas exigere vel extorquere presumat. Nulli ergo omnino hominum liceat hanc paginam nostre inhibitionis infringere vel ei ausu temerario contraire. Siquis autem hoc attemptare presumpserit, indignationem omnipotentis Dei et beatorum Petri et Pauli apostolorum eius se noverit incursurum. Datum Laterani, XII kalendas martii, pontificatus nostri anno tercio.

56

July 21, 1220. Orvieto.

Pope Honorius [III] forbids archbishops and bishops to hold against the will of Premonstratensian abbots any of the order's canons who serve as parish priests, or who have been recalled to their cloister to be disciplined; he also forbids archbishops and bishops to demand a fine in order to lift excommunication from a Premonstratensian canon.

A. Cartulary of Prémontré, fol. 14r.

B. Original not found.

EDITION: Le Paige, *Bibliotheca*, 652–3; Sanders, *Chorographia sacra Brabantiae*, vol. 1; Honorius III, *Honorii III Romani Pontificis opera omnia quae exstant*, vol. 3, col. 482–3.

1 *Sic A*, *read* aciem.

Privilegium ut liceat abbatibus illos qui manent in parochiis revocare ad claustrum quandocumque voluerint.

[H]onorius episcopus, servus servorum Dei, venerabilibus fratribus universis archiepiscopis et episcopis ad quos littere iste pervenerint salutem et apostolicam benedictionem. Dilecti filii abbas Premonstratensis ac alii abbates ordinis sui coram nobis exponere curaverunt, quod cum canonici eiusdem ordinis commorantes in parrochialibus ecclesiis ad ipsos spectantibus aliquo casu delinquunt, ita quod expediret eos ad claustrum suum recepturos disciplinam ordinis revocari, quidam vestrum indignum favorem inpendentes eisdem, ipsos retinere conantur in locis, in quibus nequeunt absque scandalo et ecclesiarum ipsarum dispendio commorari. Ad hec cum in eorum aliquos, propter suos excessus, excommunicationis sentenciam promulgatis, relaxare non vultis eandem, nisi pena pecuniaria precedente. Ideoque universitatem vestram rogandam duximus et monendam per apostolica scripta mandantes, quatinus cum dicti abbates, tales ad claustrum propter scandalum et ecclesiarum dispendium evitandum, seu etiam pro disciplina monastica circa delinquentes huiusmodi exercenda duxerint revocandos, non obsistatis eisdem, nec illis favorem indebitum impendatis sed instituentes, prout ad vos pertinet, in ipsis ecclesiis alios vobis presentatos ab ipsis delinquentes revocari ad claustrum libere permittatis, disciplinam ordinis recepturos, ne aliter faciendo tribuatis eis audaciam detractandi obedientie jugum et ipsorum abbatum potestatem quodammodo enervetis. Illud autem districtius inhibemus, ne pro relaxandis excommunicationis sententiis promulgatis in ipsos, penam pecuniariam exigatis, cum nec habeant proprium ne illorum culpa debeat in ecclesie sue dispendium redundare. Datum apud Urbem Veterem, XII kalendas augusti, pontificatus nostri anno quarto.

57

May 23, 1222. Alatri.

Pope Honorius [III] forbids members of the order of Prémontré to act as procurator in cases that do not directly involve their order.

A. Cartulary of Prémontré, fol. 14r.

B. Original not found.

Other Manuscript Copies: Bayerische Hauptstaatsarchiv München, Literalien des Klosters Schäftlarn, no. 2, fol. 58r (14th c.); Stiftsarchiv Wilten, Lade 8 M, 60 (early 15th c.).

EDITION: Le Paige, *Bibliotheca*, 653; Hugo, *Sacrae antiquitatis monumenta historica, dogmatica, diplomatica*, vol. 1, 482; Honorius III, *Honorii III Romani Pontificis opera omnia quae exstant*, vol. 4, col. 359.

REGISTER: Potthast, *Regesta*, no. 6863; Weissthanner, *Die Urkunden und Urbare des Klosters Schäftlarn*, 269.

Ne aliquis existat procurator in causis alienis privilegium.

[H]onorius episcopus, servus servorum Dei, dilectis filiis abbatibus et fratribus universis ordinis Premonstratensis, salutem et apostolicam benedictionem. Cum relictis seculi vanitatibus, ei soli inpendere teneamini famulatum, cui servire regnare est, indecens constat esse, ut cum debetis orationibus vigilare, involvatis vos questionibus alienis. Quocirca universitati vestre auctoritate presentium inhibemus, ne quisquam vestrum in pertractandis alienis causis presumat existere procurator. Nulli ergo omnino hominum liceat hanc paginam nostre inhibitionis infringere, vel ei ausu temerario contraire. Siquis autem hoc attemptare presumpserit, indignationem omnipotentis Dei et cetera. Datum Alatri, X kalendas junii, pontificatus nostri anno sexto.

58

January 16, 1233. Lateran.

Pope Gregory [IX] authorizes the abbot of Prémontré to establish, with the consent of the General Chapter, a procurator in the Roman Curia.

A. Cartulary of Prémontré, fol. 14r.
B. Original not found.
EDITION: Le Paige, *Bibliotheca*, 657.
REGISTER: Reg. Vat. 17, fol. 131r; Bréquigny, *Table chronologique*, vol. 5, 445; Potthast, *Regesta*, no. 9369; Auvray, *Les registres de Grégoire IX*, vol. 1, col. 944.

Ut liceat abbati Premonstratensis habere procuratorem in Curia Romana.

[G]regorius episcopus, servus servorum Dei, dilecto filio abbati Premonstratensi salutem et apostolicam benedictionem. Devotionis tue precibus benignum impertientes assensum, auctoritate tibi presentium indulgemus, ut liceat tibi pro ecclesiis tui ordinis, cum consensu generalis capituli tui, procuratorem ad impetrandum et contradicendum in Romana Curia constituere generalem. Nulli ergo, et cetera. Siquis, et cetera. Datum Laterani, XVII kalendas februarii, pontificatus nostri anno VII°.

59

September 5, 1234. Spoleto.

Pope Gregory [IX] confirms the decision taken by the abbot of Prémontré, in accordance with the other abbots and religious of the order, to require all conversi *to wear gray hoods and not white ones in order to distinguish themselves from canons.*

A. Cartulary of Prémontré, fol. 14r.

B. Original not found.

EDITION: Le Paige, *Bibliotheca*, 661–2.

REGISTER: Reg. Vat. 17, fol. 207r; Bréquigny, *Table chronologique*, vol. 5, 464; Potthast, *Regesta*, no. 9696; Auvray, *Les registres de Grégoire IX*, vol. 1, col. 1127.

Privilegium de confirmatione caparum grisearum.

[G]regorius episcopus, servus servorum Dei, dilecto filio abbati Premonstratensi, Laudunensis diocesis, salutem et apostolicam benedictionem. Justis petentium desideriis dignum est nos facilem prebere consensum et vota que a rationis tramite non discordant, effectu prosequente, complere. Significasti siquidem nobis quod cum tu tam auctoritate nostra, quam tua, in monasteriis Premonstratensis ordinis tue jurisdictioni subjectis, de coabbatum et fratrum tuorum consilio, ad reformationem ipsius ordinis duxeris statuendum, ut conversi commorantes in ipsis, quorum quidam cappis albis, et alii griseis utebantur, cappas griseas ad differentiam canonicorum, prout in eisdem monasteriis habebatur, de antiqua consuetudine deportarent, ut sibi essent invicem uniformes, nobis humiliter suplicasti ut statutum huiusmodi apostolico dignaremur munimine roborare. Nos igitur tuis precibus inclinati statutum ipsum, sicut provide factum esse disnoscitur, auctoritate apostolica confirmamus, et presentis scripti patrocinio communimus. Nulli ergo omnino hominum liceat hanc paginam nostre concessionis infringere vel ei ausu temerario contraire. Siquis autem hoc attemptare presumpserit, indignationem omnipotentis [Dei] et beatorum Petri et Pauli apostolorum eius se noverit incursurum. Datum Spoleti, nonas septembris, pontificatus nostri anno octavo.

60

February 13, 1164–71.[1] Genoa.

Pope Alexander [III] invites Abbot Ph[ilippe I][2] *and the chapter of Prémontré to welcome back to the Church the schismatics of their order and to force*

---

1 This act must date to the overlap of the pontificate of Alexander III (1159–81), the anti-pontificate of Victor IV/Ottaviano de' Monticelli (1164–8), and the abbatiate of Philippe I (1161–71).

2 Philippe I de Reims, abbot of Prémontré, 1161–71.

them to renounce under oath [the Antipope Victor IV], under penalty of excommunication.

A. Cartulary of Prémontré, fols. 14r–14v.

B. Original not found.

Other Manuscript Copies: Bayerische Hauptstaatsarchiv München, Literalien des Klosters Schäftlarn, no. 2, fol. 61r (14th c.); Stiftsarchiv Wilten, Lade 8 M, 56 (early 15th c.); Cartulary of Beaurepart, Bibliothèque du Séminaire Episcopal de Liège, G IV 7, fol. 22v (15th c.); Cartulary of Averbode Abbey, Archief van de abdij van Averbode, Sectie IV, no. 109, fol. 5r (15/16th c.); Cartulary of Park Abbey, Archief van de Abdij van Park te Heverlee, MS VII 35, fol. 20r (15/16th c.).

EDITION: Hanegraaf, *Compendio della vita, miracoli, et instituto del glorioso patriarcha S. Norberto*, 186–7 (partial); Le Paige, *Bibliotheca*, 629–30; Saulnier, "Aliquot Summorum Pontificum de Ordine Praemonstratensi Elogia," in *Statuta candidi et Canonici Ordinis Praemonstratensis Renovata ac Anno 1630* (partial); Hugo, *prob.* 1, col. xxi; *PL* 200, cols. 130–1; Bouquet and Delisle, *Recueil des historiens des Gaules et de la France*, vol. 15, 774.

REGISTER: JL no. 10697 (J: 7185); Weissthanner, *Die Urkunden und Urbare des Klosters Schäftlarn*, 258–9.

Ut liceat abbatibus excommunicare scismaticos.

[A]lexander episcopus, servus servorum Dei, dilectis filiis Ph. abbati et universo capitulo Premonstratensi salutem et apostolicam benedictionem. Omnipotenti Deo a quo universa bona procedunt, gratiarum referimus actiones, quod vos in unitate catholica conservavit, et non permisit scismatica pollui pravitate. Licet enim scismaticorum presumptio, diversis nos calliditatibus et mandatus a devotione Beati Petri et nostra retrahere niteretur, vestra tamen discretio illorum iniquitatem studuit evitare, et unitatem catholicam conservare. Quod siquidem gratum et acceptum tenentes, et vestre fidei constantiam et sinceritatis affectum in Domino plurimum commendantes, gratias quas debemus vobis referimus, firmum propositum et promptam voluntatem habentes, personas et ecclesiam vestram mera cordis affectione diligere, et interne dilectionis brachiis amplexari, et jura ipsius illesa et integra conservare. Ceterum quoniam non sufficit bene incipere, nisi quod bene inceptum est, optime consumationis finem debeat invenire, devotionem vestram per apostolica scripta rogamus, monemus et exhortamur in Domino, quatinus bono principio potiora augmenta addatis, et ad honorem et exaltationem atque augmentum Sancte Romane Ecclesie ac nostrum totis viribus aspiretis, scismaticos quoque ordinis vestri ad unitatem et sinum Matris Ecclesie et mandatum nostrum diligenti ammonitione studeatis propensius revocare et scismatici, Octaviano heresiarce,[3] sub

3 Ottaviano dei Crescenzi Ottaviani di Monticelli (1095–1164), cardinal priest of San Nicola in Carcere from 1138, cardinal priest of Santa Cecilia in 1151, and a Ghibelline antipope, 1159–64.

jure jurando abrenuntiare. Si autem juxta commonitionem ab iniquitate sua redire contempserint, illos excommunicationis sententia innodetis et eorum consortium propensius evitetis. Datum Janue, idus februarii.

61

June 15, 1173. Anagni.

Pope Alexander [III], having learned that certain bishops granted their clergy the presbyteries in parishes where Premonstratensian brothers and sisters reside, proscribes all bishops from introducing any secular clergy into those places.

A. Cartulary of Prémontré, fol. 14v.

B. Original not found.

Other Manuscript Copies: Cartulary of Park Abbey, Archief van de Abdij van Park te Heverlee, MS VII 24, fol. 138r (13th c.); Bayerische Hauptstaatsarchiv München, Literalien des Klosters Schäftlarn, no. 2, fols. 60v–61r (14th c.); "Privilegia a Romanis Pontificibus ordini Praemonstratensi concessa," BnF, MS 4394, fols. 85v–86v (14th c.); Stiftsarchiv Wilten, Lade 8 M, 56 (early 15th c.); Cartulary of Park Abbey, Archief van de Abdij van Park te Heverlee, MS VII 26, fol. 51r (15th c.); Cartulary of Park Abbey, Archief van de Abdij van Park te Heverlee, MS VII 35, fol. 19v (15/16th c.).

EDITION: Le Paige, *Bibliotheca*, 631; Fejér, *Codex diplomaticus Hungariae ecclesiasticus ac civilis, studio et opera*, vol. 2, 187.

REGISTER: JL no. 12583 (J: 8392); Weissthanner, *Die Urkunden und Urbare des Klosters Schäftlarn*, 259.

Privilegium qui non licet episcopis dare altaria nostra clericis secularibus.

[A]lexander episcopus, servus servorum Dei, venerabilibus fratribus universis episcopis in quorum episcopatibus ecclesie ac possessiones Premonstratensium fratrum consistunt, salutem et apostolicam benedictionem. Quanto religio predictorum fratrum et ordo gratior Deo existit, tanto pro conservatione et augmento ipsius amplius debemus esse solliciti et paci ipsorum et quieti propensiori cura intenti. Accepimus autem quod quidam vestrum presbiteratus altarium, in quibus aliquando ville fuerint, et modo grangie sunt fratrum et sororum Premonstratensium clericis suis concedunt, et sic eorum interrumpere otium et quietem presumunt. Unde quoniam indignum est, ut tantus ordo molestias et gravamina sustineat, que temporibus predecessorum vestrorum minime noscitur sustinuisse, fraternitati vestre per apostolica scripta percipiendo mandamus, quatinus in locis, ubi fratres vel sorores predicti ordinis habitant, nullos seculares clericos introducere, nec aliquid eis concedere presumatis, nec fratribus vel sororibus aliquam in hiis infferatis molestiam vel gravamen quod hactenus non consueverunt perferre. Datum Anagnie, XVII kalendas julii.

62

March 14, 1176–March 14, 1181.[1] Tuscolo.

Pope Alexander [III] invites N[ivelon I], bishop of Soissons,[2] R[oger], bishop of Laon,[3] and R[enaud],[4] bishop of Noyon to excommunicate all those in their respective dioceses who have harmed the Premonstratensian canons and who have not yet made amends.

A. Cartulary of Prémontré, fol. 14v.

B. Original not found.

Other Manuscript Copies: Cartulary of Beaurepart, Bibliothèque du Séminaire Episcopal de Liège, G IV 7, fol. 24v (15th c.); Cartulary of Averbode Abbey, Archief van de Abdij van Averbode, 4. Abt. no. 109, fol. 43v (15/16th c.).

EDITION: Wiederhold, "Papsturkunden in Frankreich," 160–1; Lohrmann, *Papsturkunden in Frankreich. Neue Folge*, vol. 7, 668.

Privilegium que episcopi excommunicent malefactores nostros [*margo*: sibi subditos] si ad ipsos querela deferatur.

[A]lexander episcopus, servus servorum Dei, venerabilibus fratribus N[iveloni] Suessionensi, R[ogeri] Laudunensi et R[enaldi] Noviomensi episcopis salutem et apostolicam benedictionem. Apostolice Sedis auctoritas nos inducit et debitum postulat caritatis viros religiosos oculo benigno respicere et eos contra malignorum hominum insolentiam apostolice defensionis clipeo communire ut tanto securius susceptum religionis officium exequantur quanto se viderint fortius apostolica protectione suffultos. Ea propter fraternitati vestre per apostolica scripta mandamus percipiendo quatinus si dilecti filii nostri

1 This act must date to the overlap in the tenures of Alexander III (1159–81), Nivelon (1175–1207), Roger (1175–1207), and Renaud (1175–88).

2 Nivelon I de Quierzy (or Chérizy), son of Gérard II, lord of Quierzy, and Agnès de Longpont, bishop of Soissons, 1175/6–1207.

3 Roger de Rozoy, son of Clérembaud, lord of Rozoy, and Elizabeth de Namur, was bishop of Laon, 1175–1207.

4 Renaud, bishop of Noyon, 1175–88.

Premonstratenses canonici de parrochianis vestris malefactoribus suis, quod eis res suas abstulerint, in vestra presentia deposuerint questionem monere curetis eos et diligenter inducere ut dampna data resarciant, ablata restituant et de injuriis illatis satisfaciant congruenter. Quod si monitis vestris non adquieverint, ipsos, non obstante gratia vel timore, donec res ipsas reddiderint vel eis satisfecerint, appellatione remota, excommunicationis vinculo astringatis. Qui si nec sic resipuerint in locis in quibus presentes fuerint, divina prohibeatis obsequia celebrari, providentes ne excommunicationis vel interdicti sentencia, nisi cum volun~~in~~tate illorum, sine satisfactione congrua relaxetur ut ipsi per vos sentiant sibi sua jura servari et vos possitis de zelo justicie merito commendari. Datum Tusculani, II idus martii.

63

1175–81.[1] Ferrara.

*Pope Alexander [III] confirms the possession of the church of Saint-Pierre de Dorengt[2] and all its appurtenances, as they were held during the episcopacies of Barthélemy,[3] Gautier [I],[4] and Gautier [II][5] of Laon. (See **64**.)*

A. Cartulary of Prémontré, fol. 14v.
B. Original not found.
EDITION: Le Paige, *Bibliotheca*, 629.
REGISTER: JL no. 12819 (J: 8479).

Privilegium ecclesie de Dorenc cum pertinentiis suis.

[A]lexander episcopus, servus servorum Dei, dilectis filiis Hugoni, abbati et fratribus Premonstratensis ecclesie, salutem et apostolicam benedictionem. Et si universorum votis, que rationi conveniunt, prompto animo teneamur annuere, vota tamen religiosorum virorum, que ad religionem respiciunt, et ad ecclesiasticam pertinent honestatem, specialius promovere nos convenit, et ut dignum

1 Alexander III was pope, 1159–81, while the last-named bishop of Laon referenced in the text, Gautier II de Mortagne, died July 7, 1174. See Martinet, "Un évêque bâtisseur: Gautier de Mortagne," 89. Since the charter is dated to the third kalends of May, the earliest possible year for this act must be 1175. Le Paige dates this act to 1177 but provides no evidence.

2 Dorengt, cant. Nouvion, https://dicotopo.cths.fr/places/P90882005.

3 Barthélemy de Jur (d. 1158), son of Conon, lord of Grandson and La Sarraz, and Ada de Roucy; first subdeacon and then treasurer of Reims, later bishop of Laon, 1113–51.

4 Gautier de Saint-Maurice was abbot of the Premonstratensian abbey of Saint-Martin de Laon, 1124–51, and bishop of Laon, 1151–3. *MP* II, 512.

5 Gautier de Mortagne was dean of Laon, ca. 1142–55, and bishop of Laon, 1155–74.

sortiantur effectum, pastoralem sollicitudinem adhibere. Ea propter dilecti in Domino filii, vestris justis postulationibus annuentes, ecclesiam Sancti Petri de Dorenc cum prebendis, decimis, terragiis, et cum aliis omnibus redditibus et pertinentiis suis quemadmodum tam ecclesiam quam grangiam ipsam rationabiliter possidetis, in ea libertate in qua eandem ecclesiam cum pertinentiis suis temporibus ~~suis~~ trium episcoporum Laudunensium videlicet Bartholomei, Walteri et alterius Walteri tenuistis, vobis et per vos ecclesie vestre et successoribus vestris auctoritate apostolica confirmamus et presentis scripti patrocinio communimus. Statuentes ut nulli omnino ecclesiastice secularive persone liceat hanc paginam nostre concessionis infringere vel ei aliquatenus contraire. Siquis autem hoc attemptare presumpserit, indignationem omnipotentis Dei et beatorum Petri et Pauli apostolorum eius se noverit incursurum. Datum Ferrarie, IIIº kalendas maii.

64

July 21, 1186. Verona.

Pope Urban [III], like his predecessor Alexander [III], confirms Saint-Pierre de Dorengt[1] *and the* grangia *of Fontaine-Raimbaut*[2] *as Prémontré's possessions. (See* ***63****.)*

A. Cartulary of Prémontré, fols. 14v–15r.

B. Original not found.

Other Manuscript Copies: Cartulary of Park Abbey, Archief van de Abdij van Park te Heverlee, MS VII 35, fol. 18v (15/16th c.).

EDITION: Le Paige, *Bibliotheca*, 640; Ramackers, *Papsturkunden in den Niederlanden*, vol. 2, 440–1 (partial).

REGISTER: JL no. 15900 (J: 9930).

Item privilegium Urbani Pape unde supra cum confirmatione curtis Raimbaldi Fontis.

[U]rbanus episcopus, servus servorum Dei, dilectis filiis Hugoni abbati et fratribus Premonstratensis ecclesie, salutem et apostolicam benedictionem. Et si universorum votis, que rationi conveniunt prompto animo teneamur annuere, vota tamen religiosorum virorum que ad religionem respiciunt et ad ecclesiam pertinent honestatem, specialius promovere nos convenit et ut dignum sortiantur effectum pastoralem sollicitudinem adhibere. Ea propter, dilecti in Domino

1 Dorengt, cant. Nouvion, https://dicotopo.cths.fr/places/P90882005.

2 Near La Ferté-Chevresis, cant. Ribemont, https://dicotopo.cths.fr/places/P15499504.

filii, vestris justis petitionibus annuentes, ecclesiam Sancti Petri de Dorenc cum prebendis, decimis, terragiis et cum aliis omnibus redditibus et pertinentiis suis et cum grangia que dicitur Fons Rainboldi et cum carrucis et ceteris pertinentiis suis, quemadmodum tam ecclesiam quam grangiam ipsam rationabiliter possidetis, in ea libertate in qua eandem ecclesiam cum pertinentiis suis temporibus trium episcoporum Laudunensium, videlicet Bartholomei,[3] Walteri,[4] et alterius Walteri[5] tenuistis, ad instar recordationis felicis predecessoris nostri Alexandri Pape, vobis et per vos ecclesie vestre et successoribus vestris auctoritate apostolica confirmamus et presentis scripti patrocinio communimus. Statuentes ut nulli omnino hominum liceat hanc paginam nostre confirmationis infringere vel ei ausu temerario contraire. Siquis autem hoc attemptare presumpserit, indignationem et cetera. Datum Verone, XII kalendas augusti.

65

March 9, 1160–81.[1] Tuscolo.

Pope Alexander [III] authorizes the abbot and the canons of Prémontré to receive secular clergy and their possessions into their monastery, in accordance with the canonical regulations of the place in which they first entered the religious life.

A. Cartulary of Prémontré, fol. 15r.

B. Original not found.

Other Manuscript Copies: "Liber statutorum necnon et de institutione sive de origine candidi ordinis scilicet Premonstratensis," Koninklijke Bibliotheek van Nederland, MS 128 G 21, fol. 19r (1445); Cartulary of Beaurepart, Bibliothèque du Séminaire Episcopal de Liège, G IV 7, fol. 122r (15th c.); Cartulary of Averbode

---

3 Barthélemy de Jur (d. 1158), son of Conon, lord of Grandson and La Sarraz, and Ada de Roucy; first subdeacon and then treasurer of Reims, later bishop of Laon, 1113–51.

4 Gautier de Saint-Maurice was abbot of the Premonstratensian abbey of Saint-Martin de Laon, 1124–51, and bishop of Laon, 1151–3. *MP* II, 512.

5 Gautier de Mortagne was dean of Laon, ca. 1142–55, and bishop of Laon, 1155–74.

---

1 Alexander III was pope September 1159–August 1181. Dietrich Lohrmann dates this act to 1181, given Alexander III's known movements. Lohrmann, *Papsturkunden in Frankreich. Neue Folge*, vol. 7, 667. G.M. van der Velden attributes a truncated version of this act to Alexander IV and dates it to 1258, without offering a rationale. Van der Velden, "Documenten betreffende de orde van Prémontré, verzameld door Merselius van Macharen in 1445," 82–3. The registers for Alexander IV, however, contain only one act issued by him to the abbot of Prémontré, and it is not this one. La Roncière, Loye, Cenival, and Coulon, *Les registres d'Alexandre IV; recueil des bulles de ce pape publiées ou analysées d'après les manuscrits originaux des archives du Vatican*, vol. 2, 816–17.

Abbey, Archief van de Abdij van Averbode, 4. Abt. no. 109, fol. 5v (15/16th c.); Cartulary of Park Abbey, Archief van de Abdij van Park te Heverlee, MS VII 35, fol. 19v (15/16th c.).

EDITION: Wiederhold, "Papsturkunden in Frankreich," 160; Lohrmann, *Papsturkunden in Frankreich. Neue Folge*, vol. 7, 667; Van der Velden, "Documenten betreffende de orde van Prémontré, verzameld door Merselius van Macharen in 1445," 82–3 (partial).

Privilegium que liceat nobis clericos recipere cum rebus suis.

[A]lexander episcopus, servus servorum Dei, dilectis filiis abbati et canonicis Premonstratensibus, salutem et apostolicam benedictionem. Cum sitis operibus pietatis ~~dedin~~ et divinis obsequiis mancipati, ordo juris expostulat et caritas ordinata requirit ut vestris justis postulationibus facilem prebeamus assensum et intendamur libenter vestris commodis et augmentis. Ea propter, dilecti in Domino filii, auctoritate vobis presentium indulgemus ut liceat vobis clericos seculares cum rebus suis ad vestrum monasterium venientes, nullius contradictione obstante, recipere, salva tamen illarum ecclesiarum canonica justicia in quibus primo fuerint conversati. Nulli ergo, et cetera. Siquis autem, et cetera. Datum Tusculani, VII idus martii.

66

February 28–9, 1174–February 27–8, 1178.[1] Anagni.

Pope Alexander [III] exempts the abbot and the religious of Prémontré from paying the minor tithe on oils, fruits, and meadows.

A. Cartulary of Prémontré, fol. 15r.

B. Original not found.

Other Manuscript Copies: Cartulary of Beaurepart Abbey, Bibliothèque du Séminaire Episcopal de Liège, G IV 7, fol. 22v (15th c.); Cartulary of Averbode Abbey, Archief van de Abdij van Averbode, 4 Abt. no. 109, fol. 37r (15/16th c.).

EDITION: Wiederhold, "Papsturkunden in Frankreich," 141–2; Lohrmann, *Papsturkunden in Frankreich. Neue Folge*, vol. 7, 665–6.

1 Alexander III was pope September, 1159–August, 1181. Dietrich Lohrmann favours a date of 1174–8 for this act, given its subject matter. Lohrmann, *Papsturkunden in Frankreich. Neue Folge*, vol. 7, 665–6.

Privilegium quod non tenemus solvere minutas decimas alicui.

[A]lexander episcopus, servus servorum Dei, dilectis filiis abbati et fratribus Premonstratensis ecclesie, salutem et apostolicam benedictionem. Justis petentium desideriis dignum est nos facilem prebere consensum et vota que a rationis tramite non discordant, effectu sunt prosequen~~da~~te complenda. Ea propter, dilecti in Domino filii, vestris justis postulationibus grato concurrentes assensu, auctoritate vobis apostolica indulgemus ut minutas decimas oleorum, fructuum et pratorum nulli solvere teneamini sed libere de cetero habeatis sicut usque modo noscimini habuisse; statuentes ut nulli omnino hominum liceat hanc paginam, et cetera. Siquis autem, et cetera. Datum Anagnie, II kalendas martii.

67

May 12, 1198. Saint Peter's, Rome.

In a letter to Pierre [I],[1] *abbot of Prémontré, Pope Innocent [III] confirms the decision by the Premonstratensian abbots not to wear a mitre or gloves, and further states that no exceptions be made for anyone entering the Premonstratensian Order from another religious order, and that no Premonstratensian travelling to or from Rome may wear secular clothing except in case of absolute necessity.*

A. Cartulary of Prémontré, fol. 15r.

B. Original not found.

EDITION: Guglielmo Sirleto, *Innocentii tertii, pontificis maximi decretalium, atque aliarum epistolarum tomus*, vol. 1, 91b; Middendorp, *D. Innocentii Pontificis Maximi Eivs Nominis III*, vol. 2, 118–19; Le Paige, *Bibliotheca*, 644; Baluze, *Epistolarum Innocentii III*, vol. 1, 107; Launoy, *Opera Omnia*, vol. 3, part 1, 247 (partial), 467; *PL* 214, col. 173; Hageneder and Haidacher, *Die Register Innocenz' III*, vol. 1, 285–6.

REGISTER: Reg. Vat. 4, fols. 50r–50v; Bréquigny, *Table chronologique*, vol. 3, 230; Potthast, *Regesta*, no. 162; Pearson, *Pope Innocent III*, 6.

Privilegium ut nullus abbatis vocatur pontificalibus et que nullus incedat in habitu seculari.

[I]nnocentius episcopus, servus servorum Dei, dilectis filiis ~~Dei~~ Petro abbati Premonstratensi et eiusdem ordinis abbatibus, salutem et apostolicam benedictionem.

1 Pierre I de Saint-Médard, abbot of the Premonstratensian abbeys of Saint-Just en Chaussée, 1184–95, Prémontré, 1195–1201, and Cuissy, 1210–17. *MP* II, 497, 527, 565.

Que in favorem religionis ad subtrahendam dissolutionis materiam sunt provide instituta, firma debent et illibata servari, et ne infringi valeant apostolico presidio communiri. Significastis siquidem nobis, quod communi consilio abbatum vestri ordinis statuistis, quod nullus abbatum vestrorum mitra vel cirothecis utatur, ne forsan ex ipsis supercilium elationis assumat, aut sibi videatur sublimis, cum hiis uti se viderit, que pontificibus et maioribus ecclesiarum prelatis a Sede Apostolica sunt concessa. Nos igitur ~~co~~institutionem ipsam, sicut a vobis provide facta est et recepta, auctoritate apostolica confirmamus et presentis scripti patrocinio communimus. Statuentes ut siqua forsan ecclesia laxioris ordinis vestram voluerit regulam profiteri, huius pontificalibus, etiam si ea prius habuerit, ulterius non utatur, immo potius humilitatem servet, et in ea statuta vestri ordinis imitetur. Presenti quoque institutioni ~~institimus~~ adicimus quod nullus fratrum vestrorum ad Apostolicam Sedem accedens, vel recedens ab ipsa, vel alias incedat in habitu seculari, nisi evidens hoc necessitas postularit. Inhibemus preterea, ne quis contra statuta generalis capituli, sive in habitu, sive in uniformitate officii, seu etiam in temporalibus, temere venire presumat. Quod siquis presumpserit, regulariter puniatur. Nec aliquis assumat honorem, ad quem fuerit forsan electus, sine licentia vel precepto illius, cui obedire tenetur nisi forte ipse sibi eam malitiose presumpserit denegare, ut tandem pro licentia optinenda maiori liceat supplicari. Nulli ergo et omnino hominum licitum sit hanc nostre paginam confirmationis, institutionis et inhibitionis infringere vel ei ausu temerario contraire. Siquis autem hoc attemptare presumpserit, indignationem et cetera. Datum Rome apud Sanctum Petrum, IIII idus maii, pontificatus nostri anno primo.

68

June 10, 1187. Verona.

Pope Urban [III] exempts the order of Prémontré from paying noval tithes.

A. Cartulary of Prémontré, fols. 15r–15v.

B. Original not found.

Other Manuscript Copies: Cartulary of Grimbergen Abbey, Abdij van Grimbergen Oud Archief, Klas II, 1, fol. 2v (13th c.); Cartulary of Park Abbey, Archief van de Abdij van Park te Heverlee, MS VII 24, fol. 138r (13th c.); Cartulary of Saint-Paul de Verdun, BM Verdun, MS 751, p. 8 (13th c.); "Privilegia a Romanis Pontificibus ordini Praemonstratensi concessa," BnF, MS lat. 4394, fols. 73r–74v (14th c.); Bayerische Hauptstaatsarchiv München, Literalien des Klosters Schäftlarn, no. 2, fols. 58v–59r (14th c.); Stiftsarchiv Wilten, Lade 8 M, 60–1 (early 15th c.); Cartulary of Beaurepart, Bibliothèque du Séminaire Episcopal de Liège, G IV 7, fol. 21v (15th c.); Cartulary of Park Abbey, Archief van de Abdij van Park te Heverlee, MS VII 26, fol. 51v (15th c.); Cartulary of Averbode Abbey, Archief van de abdij van Averbode, Sectie IV, no. 109, fol. 9r (15th/16th c.); Cartulary of Park Abbey, Archief van de Abdij van Park te Heverlee, MS VII 35, fol. 18r (15/16th c.).

EDITION: Le Paige, *Bibliotheca*, 639–40; *PL* 202, cols. 1520–1.

REGISTER: Reg. Lat. IV, 4, 4, 3, no. 825; Bréquigny, *Table chronologique*, vol. 3, 90; JL no. 15989 (J: 9967); Weissthanner, *Die Urkunden und Urbare des Klosters Schäftlarn*, 261.

Privilegium ut nullus exigat a nobis decimas novalium et que nullus appellet.

[U]rbanus episcopus, servus servorum Dei, Hugoni Premonstratensi et coabbatibus eius et fratribus, tam futuris[1] regulariter instituendis in perpetuum. Cum ex injuncto nobis a Deo apostolatus officio, universis Dei fidelibus existamus in promovendis eorum justis petitionibus debitores religiosorum petitiones tanto libentius debemus admittere ac providere, que ad pacem eorum pertinent ac quietem, quanto magis ex vita ipsorum Christi adornatur ecclesia, et qui in seculo morantur addiscunt qualiter in via recta per opera fidei gradiantur. Sane propositum est nobis per venerabilem fratrem nostrum Concordum,[2] Enactunensis episcopum, quod quidam ex clero vel ex ordine monachorum eo vos intuitu super novalibus decimarum exactione fatigant, quod hominibus illis, a quibus exstirpanda nemora, vel alia loca inculta recipitis excolenda, censum seu partem aliquam frugum, pro rei proprietate confertis, et ex eo libertatem ab Ecclesia Romana nobis indultam, que vos a decimis novalium prestandis absolvit, infringere moliuntur. Quia igitur talis eorum instancia ratione non utitur, auctoritate apostolica interdicimus ut quisquam vos ex huiusmodi causa, super decimis vestrorum novalium, que propriis manibus vel sumptibus colitis, audeat infestare. Ut autem firma inter vos disciplina servetur presenti capitulo inhibemus, ne contra canonicam disciplinam claustralis quisquam appellare presumat et correctionem suorum eludere prelatorum. Quod si facere forte temptaverit, nichilominus exerceatur in eum correctio ~~secularis~~ regularis. Et ordini quidem est et saluti cont~~e~~rarium, ut qui ex voto regulari et prelati sui se supposuit voluntati, sub appellationis obtentu ad motum animi sui sequendum redire sinatur, et dissolutionis licentia vim proveniat unde correctio debet procedere delictorum. Preterea quia tollenda est a religiosis discurrendi necessitas et convenit eis que ad salutem pertinent sine difficultate

1 *Sic A*, *read* tam futuris quam presentibus.

2 Conn ua Mellaig (d. 1220) was bishop of Annaghdown in western Ireland. He witnessed an 1192 charter as *Concorde, Enachdunensi episcopo*. Gilbert, *Chartularies of St. Mary's Abbey, Dublin*, vol. 1, 143.

conferri hoc etiam de apostolica benignitate duximus indulgendum ut si episcopis vestris aut non valentibus aut nolentibus ordines celebrare aliquem vos episcopum habere contigerit de cuius officio et potestate sit vobis plena noticia, liberum sit vobis ab eo et ordines et ecclesiastica sacramenta dum tamen talis sit de quo propriis episcopus nullum sibi debeat prejudicium formidare. Decernimus ergo ut nulli omnino hominum liceat hanc paginam nostre constitutionis infringere vel ei ausu temerario contraire. Siqua igitur in futurum ecclesiastica secularisve persona huius constitutionis paginam sciens contra eam temere venire temptaverit secundo terciove commonita nisi presumptionem suam congrua satisfactione correxerit potestatis honorisque sui careat dignitate reamque se divino judicio existere de perpetrata iniquitate cognoscat et a sacratissimo corpore et sanguine Dei et Domini redemptoris nostri Jhesu Christi aliena fiat atque in extremo examine districte ultioni subjaceat. Cunctis autem eam servantibus sit pax Domini nostri Jhesu Christi. Quatinus et hic fructum bone actionis percipiant et apud districtum judicem premia eterne pacis inveniant, amen. Ego Urbanus, catholica ecclesie episcopus S. Ego Henricus,[3] Albanensis episcopus SS. Ego Paulus,[4] Prenestinus episcopus SS. Ego Theobaldus,[5] Hostiensis et Velletrensis episcopus SS. Ego Laborans,[6] presbiter cardinalis Sancte Marie Trans Tiberni titulo Calixti SS. Ego Jacinctus,[7] Sancte Marie in Cosmidim diaconus cardinalis SS. Ego Radulphus,[8] Sancti Georgii ad Velum Aureum diaconus cardinalis SS. Datum Verone per manum Alberti,[9] Sancte Romane Ecclesie presbiteri cardinalis et cancellarii, IIII° idus junii, indictione quinta, incarnationis dominice anno M° C° LXXX° VII°, pontificatus nostri anno secundo.

---

3 Henri de Marcy (or de Marsiac) was abbot of the Cistercian abbey of Hautecombe, 1160–76, abbot of Clairvaux, 1176–9, and cardinal bishop of Albano, 1179–89.

4 Paolo Scolari (ca. 1130–1191), son of Giovanni Scolari and Maria, was cardinal bishop of Palestrina, 1180–7, and pope as Clement III, 1187–91.

5 Thibaut de Vermandois, cardinal priest of Santa Croce in Gerusalemme, 1171–8, abbot of Cluny, 1180–3/4, and cardinal bishop of Ostia e Velletri, 1183/4–8.

6 Laborante da Panormo (d. ca. 1190), elected cardinal bishop of Santa Maria in Trastevere from ca. 1180.

7 Giacinto di Pietro di Bobone was cardinal deacon of Santa Maria in Cosmedin from 1144, and pope as Celestine III, 1191–8.

8 Ridolfo Nigelli was cardinal deacon of San Giorgio in Velabro, 1185–8, and cardinal priest of Santa Prassede, 1188–9.

9 Alberto di Morra was cardinal deacon of Sant'Adriano from 1156, cardinal priest of San Lorenzo in Lucina from 1158, chancellor of the Roman Church from 1178, and pope as Gregory VIII in 1187. He may have been a Premonstratensian. Petit, *Spirituality of the Premonstratensians*, 92, fn. 6.

69

June 22, 1198. Saint Peter's, Rome.

Pope Innocent [III] invites all clergy and prelates to excommunicate or ban all those who harm Premonstratensians or their possessions.[1]

A. Cartulary of Prémontré, fol. 15v.

B. Original not found.

Other Manuscript Copies: Cartulary of Leiston Abbey, British Library, Cotton MS Vespasian E XIV, fols. 3r–4r (1st half of 13th c.); Cartulary of Notre-Dame de Vicoigne, AD Nord, 59 H 95, fol. 3v (13th c.); "Liber statutorum necnon et de institutione sive de origine candidi ordinis scilicet Premonstratensis," Koninklijke Bibliotheek van Nederland, MS 128 G 21, fol. 72 (1445); "Register of Richard Redman," Bodleian Library, MS Ashmole 1519, fol. 57v (15/16th c.).

EDITION: Sirleto, *Innocentii tertii, pontificis maximi decretalium, atque aliarum epistolarum tomus*, vol. 1, 94–94b; Middendorp, *D. Innocentii Pontificis Maximi Eivs Nominis III*, vol. 2 (Cologne, 1575), 122; Le Paige, *Bibliotheca*, 647–8; Baluze, *Epistolarum Innocentii III*, vol. 1, 110; Fejér, *Codex diplomaticus Hungariae ecclesiasticus ac civilis, studio et opera*, vol. 2, 341–3; Suckling, *The History and Antiquities of the Hundreds of Blything and Part of Lothingland in the County of Suffolk*, 436–7 (variant); *PL* 214, col. 178; *PL* 217, cols. 138–40; Hageneder and Haidacher, *Die Register Innocenz' III*, vol. 1, 293–4; Mortimer, *Leiston Abbey Cartulary and Butler Priory Charters*, 55–6; Guyotjeannin et al., *Le chartrier de l'abbaye Prémontrée de Saint-Yved de Braine*, 153–4 (variant); Rodríguez de Diego, *Colección Diplomática de Santa María de Aguilar de Campoo (852–1230)*, 203–4 (variant).

REGISTER: Reg. Vat. 4, fols. 51v–52r; Bréquigny, *Table chronologique*, vol. 3, 288; Potthast, *Regesta*, no. 179; Wymans, *Inventaire des archives de l'abbaye de Saint-Feuillien du Roeulx*, 149–50.

Privilegium de illis qui iniciunt manus in canonicos.

[I]nnocentius episcopus, servus servorum Dei, venerabilibus fratribus archiepiscopis, episcopis et dilectis filiis abbatibus, prioribus et ceteris ecclesiarum prelatis, ad quos litere iste pervenerint, salutem et apostolicam benedictionem. Non absque dolore cordis et plurima turbatione didicimus quod ita in plerisque

---

1 This act was confirmed by *vidimus* by *Magister* Gabriel, canon and *officialis* of Cambrai, in the thirteenth century, and by Johannes, abbot of the Premonstratensian abbey of Osterhofen, in August 1476. Wymans, *Inventaire des archives de l'abbaye de Saint-Feuillien du Roeulx*, 271; Pichler, *Urkundenbuch des Stiftes Schlägl: die Rechts- und Geschichtsquellen der Cisterce Slage und des Prämonstratenserchorherrenstiftes Schlägl von den Anfängen bis zum Jahr 1600*, 512–17. Innocent III issued an almost identical privilege to the Templars on May 27, 1198. AN, L 236, no. 7.

partibus ecclesiastica censura dissolvitur, et canonice sententie severitas enervatur, ut viri religiosi, et hii maxime qui per Sedis Apostolice privilegia maiori donati sunt libertate, passim a malefactoribus suis injurias sustineant et rapinas, dum vix invenitur qui congrua illis protectione subveniat, et pro fovenda pauperum innocentia murum se defensionis opponat. Specialiter autem dilecti filii nostri abbas et fratre Premonstratenses, et ceteri ordinem ipsorum professi, tam de frequentibus suis injuriis quam de ipso cotidiano defectu justicie conquerentes, universitatem vestram per literas petierunt apostolicas excitari, ut ita, videlicet, eis in tribulationibus suis contra malefactores eorum prompta debeatis magnanimitate consurgere quod ab angustiis, quas sustinent et pressuris, vestro possint presidio respirare. Ideoque universitati vestre per apostolica scripta mandamus atque precipimus, quatinus illos qui in aliquem de predictis fratribus, instigante diabolo, manus violentas injecerint, sive possessiones, vel res, seu domos Premonstratenses aut aliorum fratrum ipsius ordinis vel hominum suorum irreverenter invaserint, aut ea que predictis fratribus e testamento decedentium relinquuntur, contra justiciam detinuerint, seu in ipsos fratres contra Apostolice Sedis indulta, sentenciam excommunicationis aut interdicti proferre presumpserint, vel decimas laborum seu nutrimentorum suorum, spretis privilegiis Apostolice Sedis extorserint, si laici fuerint, publice candelis accensis, excommunicationis sentencia percellatis. Clericos autem canonicos, sive monachos, appellatione remota, ab officio et beneficio suspendatis neutram relaxaturi sentenciam, donec predictis fratribus plenarie satisfaciant, et hii precipue qui pro violenta manuum injectione vinculo fuerint anathematis innodati, cum diocesani episcopi literis ad Sedem Apostolicam venientes, ab eodem vinculo mereantur absolvi, nisi forte monachi vel canonici regulares per abbates, vel priores suos post satisfactionem congruam, secundum ordinis disciplinam fuerint absoluti. Villas autem in quibus bona predictorum fratrum seu hominum suorum per violentiam detenta fuerint, quamdiu ibi sunt interdicti sentencie supponatis. Datum Rome, apud Sanctum Petrum, X° kalendas julii, pontificatus nostri anno primo.

70

March 17, 1188. Lateran.

Pope Clement [III] excuses the order of Prémontré from paying noval tithes, and includes a specific confirmation of the exemption on the woodland at La Ferté given to Prémontré by Gobert de la Ferté.[1]

1 Gobert, lord of La Ferté-Chèvresis (or La Ferté-Blihard; cant. Ribemont, https://dicotopo.cths.fr/places/P35438398), son of Bliard, lord of La Ferté-Chevresis, and Brémonde, became a vassal of the lords of Coucy between 1182 and 1184 and married Marguerite, a niece of Raoul I, lord of Coucy. Barthélemy, *LDA*, 112; Melleville, *DH*, vol. 1, 382.

A. Cartulary of Prémontré, fol. 16r.

B. Original not found.

Other Manuscript Copies: Cartulary of Drongen Abbey, Rijksarchief te Gent, K9–8, fol. 34r (14th c.); Cartulary of Beaurepart, Bibliothèque du Séminaire Episcopal de Liège, G IV 7, fol. 20v (15th c.); Cartulary of Averbode Abbey, Archief van de abdij van Averbode, Sectie IV, no. 109, fol. 10r (15/16th c.); Cartulary of Park Abbey, Archief van de Abdij van Park te Heverlee, MS VII 35, fol. 28v (15/16th c.).

EDITION: Le Paige, *Bibliotheca*, 641; *Le privilège pour les dixmes novalles, concedé, maintenu et conservé*, 54; Hugo, *prob*. 1, col. xxiii; *PL* 204, cols. 1326–7.

REGISTER: Bréquigny, *Table chronologique*, vol. 4, 94; JL no. 16178 (J: 10056); Weissthanner, *Die Urkunden und Urbare des Klosters Schäftlarn*, 261; Böhmer and Schmidt, *Regesta Imperii IV*, vol. 4, 82.

Privilegium de novalibus maiores de Firmitate.

[C]lemens episcopus, servus servorum Dei, dilectis filiis ~~Dei~~ abbati et fratribus Premonstratensibus salutem et apostolicam benedictionem. Justis petentium desideriis facilem nos convenit prebere consensus et vota que a rationis tramite non discordant, effectu sunt prosequente complenda. Ea propter, dilecti in Domino filii, vestris justis postulationibus grato concurrentes assensu, ne de cetero alicui de novalibus vestris que propriis manibus aut sumptibus colitis, decimas persolvatis, auctoritate apostolica vobis vestrisque successoribus indulgemus, firmiter prohibentes ne quis eas amodo a vobis exigat, vel extorquere presumat. Decimas quoque novalium vestrorum vobis clementer annuimus, que habetis infra parrochiam de Firmitate in nemore quod vobis Gobertus de Firmitate, dimidia fructuum parte, exceptis messorum garbis, sibi et heredibus suis retenta, misericorditer contulit et ea ad exemplar domini Urbani predecessoris nostri, auctoritate apostolica confirmamus, et presentis scripti patrocinio communimus. Statuentes ut nulli omnino hominum liceat prefatam paginam nostre indulgentie et confirmationis infringere vel ei ausu temerario contraire. Siquis autem hoc attemptare presumpserit, indignationem omnipotentis Dei et beatorum Petri et Pauli apostolorum eius se noverit incursurum. Datum Laterani, XVII kalendas aprilis, pontificatus nostri anno primo.

TABLE OF CONTENTS: BISHOPS OF LAON

A. Cartulary of Prémontré, fol. 17r.

Incipiunt karte et confirmationes episcoporum Laudunensium de valle Premonstratensis cum appenditiis suis cum quibusdam scriptis heredum de Couci.

I Karta Bartholomei episcopi de terminis et decimis et pascuis Premonstrati loci.

II Karta domini Bartholomei episcopi de concessione vallis Premonstrati domino Norberto.

III Karta domini Bartholomei episcopi de molendino et vivario de Baretel.

IIII Item karta Bartholomei episcopi de pratis et molendinis.

V Karta de compositione Galteri Laudunensis episcopi posterioris.

VI Karta Walteri episcopi de Premonstrata valle et pertinentiis suis.

VII Karta conpositionis inter Premonstratensem et Laudunensem ecclesiam.

VIII Karta domini Radulphi de Couci.

Nota de domo de Rosel in Firmitate.[1]

71

1121. Chapter house of Sainte-Marie de Laon.

Barthélemy,[1] *bishop of Laon, gives Norbert [of Xanten] land at Prémontré previously held by the Benedictine abbey of Saint-Vincent de Laon. Saint-Vincent had given it to Barthélemy for the purpose of this gift. Barthélémy adds to this lands and rights over an allod at Hubertpont,*[2] *and the entire donation is confirmed by Louis VI of France.*

A. Cartulary of Prémontré, fols. 17r–17v.

B. Original, AN, K 22, no. 13, previously sealed.

EDITION: Le Paige, *Bibliotheca*, 373–4; Delancy, *Historia Fusniacensis Coenobii, Ordinis Cisterciensis*, 87 (partial); Hugo, *prob*. 1, cols. vi–viii; *PL* 170 1359–62; Madelaine, *Histoire de saint Norbert, fondateur de l'ordre de Prémontré et archevêque de Magdebourg*, 532–4; Dufour-Malbezin, *Actes*, 172–4.

REGISTER: Bréquigny, *Table chronologique*, vol. 2, 502; Tardif, *Monuments Historiques*, 214; Grauwen, "Lijst van oorkonden waarin Norbertus wordt genoemd," 142–3.

---

1 Later addition. For the original act that attests to Prémontré's acquisition of this house, see BnF, Coll. Picardie 290, no. 2 (1140).

---

1 Barthélemy de Jur (d. 1158), son of Conon, lord of Grandson and La Sarraz, and Ada de Roucy; first subdeacon and then treasurer of Reims, later bishop of Laon, 1113–51.

2 Hubertpont, comm. Prémontré, https://dicotopo.cths.fr/places/P71559674.

Karta domini Bartholomei episcopi Laudunensis de valle Premonstrati cum appenditiis.

[I]n nomine sancte et individue Trinitatis. Notum fieri volumus tam presentibus quam futuris quod ego Bartholomeus, Laudunensis episcopus, viro reverendo et spectabilis religionis temporibus nostris Norberto et successoribus eius in sancto proposito viventibus, dederim locum qui nostri juris erat, totum liberum ab omni exactione cuiuslibet persone absolutum apud Hunberti Pontem, a loco qui dicitur Halierprei,[3] usque ad Vallem Rohardi, cum tribus adjacentibus vallibus, totum in alodium,[4] a rivo versus Voiz,[5] sicut[6] valles dividunt et perportant, ad ecclesiam Dei[7] et Sancte Genitricis Dei Marie construendam,[8] et sicut totum possidemus in allodium, ita omnimodis libere possidendum eis concedimus. Pascua vero, seu prata, a Ponte Hunberti usque ad Monnandi Vicinum, et citra et ultra rivum, animalibus eorum communia erunt omni tempore. Ultra rivum autem ex parte ecclesie in defensione erunt ad opus eorumdem fratrum usque ad collectionem feni et frugum. Deinde vero communia erunt tantum, ut nullus inportunus sit religioni eorum super ulla occasione.[9] In omni igitur labore eorumdem fratrum facto in hisdem locis, nullus exiget ab eis nec decimam, nec terragium, nec molestiam quelibet persona inferet quieti ipsorum et omnimodis ab omni parrochia absolutos omnesque eis subjectos heremitas permanere censemus. Volumus etiam notum fieri quod ecclesia Premonstratensis et locus eiusdem a predecessore meo Helenando[10] data et confirmata fuit ecclesie Sancti Vincentii, sicut etiam in privilegio eorum continetur; modo vero, quia penitus in solitudinem universa ibidem erant redacta, abbas Segefridus[11] et conventus eiusdem ecclesie Sancti Vincentii utile duxerunt esse consilium in nostram manum reddere et ad nostram dispositionem pendere. Quod et factum est unde nichil[12] melius esse considerantes in hoc negotio, eandem ecclesiam cum omnibus que monachi predicti ibidem possidebant, eidem Norberto venerabili viro et successoribus eius in sancto proposito viventibus similiter

3 Haliepreit *B.*

4 allodium *B.*

5 Forest of Vois, https://dicotopo.cths.fr/places/P93994197.

6 sicuti *B.*

7 ad ecclesiam in honore Dei *B.*

8 et sancte Dei genetricis construendam *B.*

9 *Om.* Concedetur tamen rusticis qui sunt in vicina colligere de silva que est in iugis montium colligere materiam ad opus capitis seu scepi aratri sive axis *A.*

10 Elinand, bishop of Laon, 1052–98. Martinet, "Elinand, évêque de Laon méconnu (1052–1098)."

11 Seifroy, abbot of the Benedictine abbey of Saint-Vincent de Laon, 1120–8. Wyard, *Histoire de l'abbaye de Saint-Vincent*, 580.

12 nihil *B.*

ab omni exactione libere condonavimus perpetuo possidenda, ita ut[13] nullos conventus laicorum secum adhibeant, nisi tantum personas que sub eodem proposito vivant. Et ut liberius ista possideant, ad molendinum nostrum quod dicitur Burdellum,[14] censum frumenti sex galetarum constituimus predictis monachis per singulos annos. Fratres vero de Premonstratensi[15] ecclesia nichil[16] amodo super hoc respondebunt eis; et canonicis de Sancto Johanne Laudunensi, ad quos decima Premonstratensis[17] ecclesie pertinebat, ad idem molendinum quatuor galetas frumenti divisimus et fratres Premonstratensis[18] ecclesie in nullo, que ad decimam parrochie eorum pertinent, amodo respondebunt eis. Totum etiam sicut valles perportant circumiacentes Premonstratensis[19] loco et proclivia montium ex omni parte eisdem fratribus religiose viventibus perpetuo possidenda libere, sicut alodium[20] ratum esse censemus, et nulla circumiacentium parrochiarum vel in decimis, vel in aliqua inquietudine molestiam ingerat eorum religioni. Factum est autem hoc, assensu et voluntate Thome, de cuius feodo due partes decime descendebant, quas ipse et illi qui ab eo tenebant, in nostras manus ad opus predictorum fratrum reddiderunt; quicquid etiam juris vel consuetudinum ipse Thomas et sub eo forestarii eius, scilicet Girelmus de Valsalione[21] et Radulphus[22] de Quinciaco[23] et Radolfus, maior de Couciaco[24] Villa, habebant, totum ad opus predictorum fratrum[25] reddidit. Preterea nos dedimus predictis ~~viris~~ fratribus tres carrucatas terre, unam apud villam nostram Anisiacum,[26] aliam apud Verciniacum,[27] terciam apud Capriniacum,[28] supra montem, ultra rivum Aquilam, absque decimis earumdem carrucarum. Quicumque hanc nostre institutionis paginam et institutum infringere vel

13 *Superscr.* ut *A.*

14 Barthel, comm. Lizy, https://dicotopo.cths.fr/places/P65460297.

15 Premonstrata *B.*

16 nihil *B.*

17 Premonstrate *B.*

18 Premonstrate *B.*

19 Premonstrato *B.*

20 allodium *B.*

21 Vauxaillon, cant. Anizy-le-Château, https://dicotopo.cths.fr/places/P32329338.

22 Radolfus *B.*

23 Quincy, cant. Coucy-le-Château, https://dicotopo.cths.fr/places/P34442927.

24 Cociaco *B.*

25 *Om. and homeo.* fratrum liberum et quietum donaverunt. Ipse etiam Thomas apud locum Rosiers carrucatam terre predictis fratribus dedit. Viam etiam quam viciniacole per mediam vallem Premonstrate ecclesie ire consueverant, omnibus volentibus obstrui fecimus. Robertus etiam de Anlerio allodium, quod in contigua silva habebat, in nostra manu ad opus predictorum fratrum *A.*

26 Anizy-le-Château, arr. Laon, https://dicotopo.cths.fr/places/P86940236.

27 Perhaps Versigny, cant. La Fère, https://dicotopo.cths.fr/places/P17885640.

28 Chevregny, cant. Anizy-le-Château, https://dicotopo.cths.fr/places/P06529464.

inquietare temptaverit, anathema sit et iram omnipotentis Dei incurrat in die judicii. Actum est hoc anno dominice incarnationis M° C° XXI°, indictione XIIII, epacta nulla, concurrente quinto. Signum Bartholomei, Laudunensis episcopi. Signum Widonis,[29] decani et archidiaconi. Signum Radulphi,[30,31] archidiaconi. Signum Sifridi,[32] abbatis Sancti Vincentii. Signum Simonis,[33] abbatis Sancti Nicholai de Silva.[34] Signum Bliardi,[35] cantoris. Signum Drogonis, presbiteri. Signum Herberti, presbiteri. Signum Ebali, diaconi. Signum Godefridi, diaconi. Signum Ebali, subdiaconi. Signum Widonis,[36] subdiaconi. Signum Roberti, acoliti. Signum Roberti, decani Sancti Johannis. Signum Jufridi,[37] cantoris. Signum Hemmonis, thesaurarii. Signum Henrici.[38] S. Valerii. S. Gundranni. S. Hugonis. S. Roberti, prepositi ecclesie Sancti Martini. S. Helberti, propositi[39] vicedomini. S. Clarembaldi[40] de Foro.[41] S. Nicholai, castellani.[42] Actum Lauduni, in capitolio[43] Beate Marie Laudunensis ecclesie, anno dominice incarnationis M° C° XXI°, indictione XIIII, epacta nulla, concurrente V°, regnante rege Francorum Ludovico,[44] qui fratri Norberto et ceteris fratribus in supradicto loco religiose viventibus concessit habendum in perpetuum

29 Guy de Pierrepont, son of Roger, lord of Pierrepont, and Ermengarde, lady of Montaigu, was first treasurer, archdeacon, and dean of the chapter of Laon, and later bishop of Châlons, 1144–7.

30 Radulfi *B.*

31 Raoul de Laon (d. 1133), brother of the theologian Anselm de Laon, was archdeacon of Laon, 1117–26, and chancellor of Laon, 1117–33. Dufour-Malbezin, *Actes*, 29.

32 Seifridi *B.*

33 Symonis *B.*

34 Simon, abbot of the Benedictine abbey of Saint-Nicolas-aux-Bois, 1120–34. Duval, "Histoire de l'abbaye bénédictine de Saint-Nicolas-aux-Bois, diocèse de Laon, première partie," 174–81.

35 Blihardi *B.*

36 Vuidonis *B.*

37 Jusfridi *B.*

38 Heinrici *B.*

39 *Add.* propositi *A.*

40 Clarebaldi *B.*

41 Clérembaud I du Marché, lord of Bruyères and Barenton-Bugny, marshal of the Laonnois. He was a relation of Barthélemy de Jur, bishop of Laon, and of the comital Roucy family. Mellevile, *DH*, vol. 1, 164; Hidé, "L'administration et la juridiction municipale de la commune de Bruyères, du XIIe au XVIIIe siècle," 68.

42 Nicolas, castellan of Laon, son of Guinemar, castellan of Laon. Saint-Denis, *Apogée d'une cité*, 80. He also appears with his wife Beatrice and son Raoul in an 1149 charter of Barthélemy, bishop of Laon, confirming donations made to the Templars, and is mentioned in the writings of Guibert de Nogent. Guibert of Nogent, *A Monk's Confession*, 192; Dufour-Malbezin, *Actes*, 431–7.

43 *Sic A, read* capitulo.

44 Ludvico *B.*

quicquid datur et dabitur eis, quod pertineat ad suum feodum. Ego Radulphus,[45] cancellarius, scripsi et subscripsi.[46]

72

1121. Chapter house of Sainte-Marie de Laon.

Barthélemy,[1] bishop of Laon, gives Norbert [of Xanten] land at Prémontré previously held by the Benedictine abbey of Saint-Vincent de Laon. Saint-Vincent had given it to Barthélemy for the purpose of this gift. Barthélémy adds to this lands and rights over an allod at Hubertpont.[2]

A. Cartulary of Prémontré, fols. 17v–18r.

B. Original, AN, L 995, no. 1, damaged at top and bottom.[3]

EDITION: Florival, *Étude historique sur le XIIe siècle*, 291–5; Dufour-Malbezin, *Actes*, 172–4.

REGISTER: Bréquigny, *Table chronologique*, vol. 2, 502.

Karta Bartholomei episcopi Laudunensis de concessione vallis Premonstrati donatione Norberto.

[I]n nomine sancte et individue Trinitatis. Notum fieri volumus tam presentibus quam futuris quod ego Bartholomeus Laudunensis episcopus viro reverendo et spectabilis religionis temporibus nostris Norberto et successoribus eius in sancto proposito viventibus, dederim locum qui nostri juris erat totum liberum ab omni exactione cuiuslibet persone apud Humberti Pontem, a loco qui dicitur Halierpreit[4] usque ad vallem Rohardi, cum tribus adjacentibus vallibus, totum in alodium,[5] a rivo versus Vois,[6] sicuti valles dividunt et perportant, ad ecclesiam in honorem Dei et Sancte Dei genitricis Marie[7] construendam et, sicut totum possidemus in alodium,[8] ita omnimodis libere possidendum eis

45 Rodulfus *B*.
46 scribsi et subscribsi *B*.

1 Barthélemy de Jur (d. 1158), son of Conon, lord of Grandson and La Sarraz, and Ada de Roucy; first subdeacon and then treasurer of Reims, later bishop of Laon, 1113–51.
2 Hubertpont, comm. Prémontré, https://dicotopo.cths.fr/places/P71559674.
3 Due to conservation concerns, the original was not available to the editors. Variants noted here therefore follow those noted by Françoise Muret.
4 Halipreit *B*.
5 allodium *B*.
6 Forest of Vois, https://dicotopo.cths.fr/places/P93994197.
7 *Add.* Marie *A*.
8 allodium *B*.

concedimus. Pascua vero seu prata a Ponte Humberti usque ad Monnandi vicinum et citra et ultra rivum animalibus eorum communia erunt omni tempore; ultra rivum autem ex parte ecclesie in defensione erunt ad opus eorumdem fratrum usque ad collectionem feni et frugum, deinde communia erunt tantum ut nullus sit[9] importunus religioni eorum super ulla occasione. ~~Concedetur tamen.~~[10] In omni igitur labore eorumdem fratrum facto in eisdem locis nullus exiget ab eis decimam vel terragium nec molestiam quelibet persona inferet quieti ipsorum et ab[11] omnimodis ab omni parrochia absolutos permanere censemus. Volumus etiam notum fieri quod ecclesia Premonstratensis[12] et locus eiusdem a predecessore meo Helinando[13] data et confirmata fuit ecclesie Sancti Vincentii, sicut etiam in privilegio eorum continetur. Modo vero quia penitus in solicitudinem universa ibidem erant redacta, abbas Seifridus[14] et conventus eiusdem ecclesie Sancti Vincentii utile duxerunt esse consilium in nostram manum reddere et ad nostram dispositionem pendere. Quod et factum est. Unde nichil melius esse considerantes in hoc negotio eandem ecclesiam cum omnibus que monachi predicti ibidem possidebant eidem venerabili viro Norberto et successoribus eius similiter ab omni exactione libera condonavimus perpetuo possidenda et ut liberius ista possideant, ad molendinum nostrum quod dicitur Burdellum,[15] censum frumenti sex galetarum constituimus predictis monachis per singulos annos. Fratres vero de Premonstratensi[16] ecclesia nichil amodo super hoc respondebunt eis et canonicis de Sancto Johanne Laudunensi ad quos decima Premonstratensis[17] ecclesie pertinebat ad idem molendinum IIII[or] galetas frumenti divisimus et fratres Premonstratensis[18] ecclesie in nullo que ad decimam parrochie eorum pertinent amodo respondebunt eis. Totum etiam sicut valles perportant circumjacentes Premonstratensi[19] loco et proclivia montium ex omni parte eisdem fratribus religiose viventibus perpetuo possidenda libere sicut alodium[20] ratum esse censemus et nulla parrochia vel in decimis vel in aliqua inquietudine molestiam eis ingerat. Factum est autem hoc assensu et voluntate Thome de cuius feodo due partes decime descendebant, quas ipse

9 *Add.* sit *A.*

10 *Om.* rusticis quis sunt in vicinia colligere materia de silva que est in jugis montium ad opus capitis seu scepi aratri sive axis *A.*

11 *Add.* ab *A.*

12 Premonstrata *B.*

13 Elinand, bishop of Laon, 1052–98. Martinet, “Elinand, évêque de Laon méconnu (1052–1098).”

14 Seifroy, abbot of the Benedictine abbey of Saint-Vincent de Laon, 1120–8. Wyard, *Saint-Vincent*, 580.

15 Barthel, comm. Lizy, https://dicotopo.cths.fr/places/P65460297.

16 Premonstrate *B.*

17 Premonstrate *B.*

18 Premonstrate *B.*

19 Premonstrato *B.*

20 allodium *B.*

et illi qui ab eo tenebant, in manus nostras ad opus predictorum fratrum reddiderunt. Quicquid etiam juris vel consuetudinum ipse Thomas et sub eo forestarii eius, scilicet Girelmus de Valssallione[21,22] et Radulphus de Quinciaco[23] et Radulphus maior de Couciaco[24] Villa habebant, liberum et quietum ad opus fratrum donaverunt. Ipse vero Thomas ob remedium anime sue et suorum concessit eisdem fratribus usuarium suum in nemore, excepta quercu et fago, sed et pascua animalibus suis et carrucatam terre apud Rosieres dedit eis. Robertus etiam de Anlerio alodium[25] quod in contigua silva habebat in manu nostra ad opus fratrum reddidit. Preterea nos dedimus predictis fratribus tres carrucatas terre, unam apud Anisiacum,[26] aliam apud Verciniacum,[27] terciam supra montem Capriniaci[28] ultra rivum Aquilam. Actum Lauduni in capitulo Beate Marie, anno incarnati verbi M° C° XX° I°, indictione XIIII[a], epacta nulla, concurrente quinto, regnante rege Francorum Ludovico qui fratri Norberto et fratribus de Premonstrato concessit habendum in perpetuum quicquid datur et dabitur eis quod pertineat ad suum feodum quicumque igitur hanc nostre institutionis paginam infringere vel inquietare temptaverit, anathema sit. Signum mei ipsius Bartholomei, Laudunensis episcopi. SS. Widonis,[29] decani et archidiaconi. SS. Radulphi,[30,31] archidiaconi. SS. Seifridi, abbatis Sancti Vincentii. SS. Simonis,[32] abbatis Sancti Nicolai de Silva. SS. Bliardi,[33] cantoris. SS. Drogonis et Herberti, presbiterorum. SS. Ebali et Godefridi, diaconorum. SS. Ebali et Widonis, subdiaconorum. Item SS. Roberti, decani Sancti Johannis. SS. Joiffridi,[34] cantoris. SS. Hemmonis, thesaurarii. SS. Henrici, Gundranni, Hugonis. S. Roberti, prepositi Sancti Martini. S. Helberti, vicedomini. SS. Clarenbaldi[35] de Foro.

---

21 Valsalione *B*.

22 Vauxaillon, cant. Anizy-le-Château, https://dicotopo.cths.fr/places/P32329338.

23 Quincy, cant. Coucy-le-Château, https://dicotopo.cths.fr/places/P34442927.

24 Cociaco *B*.

25 allodium *B*.

26 Anizy-le-Château, arr. Laon, https://dicotopo.cths.fr/places/P86910236.

27 Perhaps Versigny, cant. La Fère, https://dicotopo.cths.fr/places/P17885640.

28 Chevregny, cant. Anizy-le-Château, https://dicotopo.cths.fr/places/P06529464.

29 Guy de Pierrepont, son of Roger, lord of Pierrepont, and Ermengarde, lady of Montaigu, was first treasurer, archdeacon, and dean of the chapter of Laon, and later bishop of Châlons, 1144–7.

30 Radulfi *B*.

31 Raoul de Laon (d. 1133), brother of the theologian Anselm de Laon, was archdeacon of Laon, 1117–26, and chancellor of Laon, 1117–33. Dufour-Malbezin, *Actes*, 29.

32 Simon, abbot of the Benedictine abbey of Saint-Nicolas-aux-Bois, 1120–34. Duval, "Histoire de l'abbaye bénédictine de Saint-Nicolas-aux-Bois, diocèse de Laon, première partie," 174–81.

33 Blihardi *B*.

34 Joffridi *B*.

35 Clérembaud I du Marché, lord of Bruyères and Barenton-Bugny, marshal of the Laonnois. He was a relation of Barthélemy de Jur, bishop of Laon, and of the comital Roucy family. Mellevile, *DH*, vol. 1, 164; Hidé, "L'administration et la juridiction municipale de la commune de Bruyères, du XIIe au XVIIIe siècle," 68.

S. Nicolai,[36] castellani. Ego Radulphus[37] ecclesie Laudunensis[38] cancellarius scripsi et subscripsi.[39]

73

October 13, 1125. Laon.

Barthélemy, bishop of Laon, gives to Prémontré the mill at Barthel[1] *that he recently constructed on a piece of land adjacent to a Premonstratensian* curtis, *retaining the rights of the bishops of Laon over the usage of the neighbouring fishpond.*

A. Cartulary of Prémontré, fol. 18r.

B. Original, AD Aisne H 806, previously sealed with a double strip of parchment.

EDITION: Le Paige, *Bibliotheca*, 230 (partial); Florival, *Étude historique sur le XIIe siècle*, 307–8; Dufour-Malbezin, *Actes*, 190–1; *Chartae Galliae*, no. 208164, http://telma.irht.cnrs.fr/outils/chartae-galliae/charte208164/.

REGISTER: Grauwen, "Lijst van oorkonden waarin Norbertus wordt genoemd," 148.

Karta Bartholomei episcopi Laudunensis de molendino de Baretel et vivario.

[I]n nomine sancte et individue Trinitatis. Ego Bartholomeus, Dei gratia sancte Laudunensis ecclesie minister indignus. Pars religionis est religiosorum virorum conversationem sanctam ac virtutum insignia diligere, eorumque necessitatibus, pie devotionis studio, subvenire atque id in aliis venerari et laudare ad cuius imitationem, fragilitatis tue titubante defectu, nequeas aspirare. Siquidem, temporibus nostris, in diocesi[2] nostra, in Vosagi silva[3] apud Premonstratum locum, religiosorum virorum assensu atque auxilio[4]

36 Nicolas, castellan of Laon, son of Guinemar, castellan of Laon. Saint-Denis, *Apogée d'une cité*, 80. He also appears with his wife Beatrice and son Raoul in an 1149 charter of Barthélemy, bishop of Laon, confirming donations made to the Templars, and is mentioned in the writings of Guibert de Nogent. Guibert of Nogent, *A Monk's Confession*, 192; Dufour-Malbezin, *Actes*, 431–7.

37 Radulfus *B*.

38 *Transp. A*; Laudunensis ecclesie *B*.

39 Because of a tear in the parchment, these last words are missing in *B*.

1 Barthel, comm. Lizy, https://dicotopo.cths.fr/places/P65460297.

2 dyocesi *B*.

3 Forest of Vois, https://dicotopo.cths.fr/places/P93994197.

4 *Om.* nostro *A*.

fratrisque Norberti illustris viri et, quantum corporeus censet intuitus Deo hominibusque probati cura, novus ordo institutus est, qui in clericali habitu, secundum regulam Beati Augustini Domino famulantes, heremiticam vitam ducerent et de labore manuum sibi necessaria providerent. Nos ergo, sanctitati eorum fragilitatem nostram commendare cupientes, atque et in huius seculi fluctuante salo et post decessum nostrum intercessionum ipsorum fulciri presidio desiderantes, ad cetera que eis[5] prout facultas suppetebat feceramus bona, hoc etiam, gratuita benignitate, adjecimus ut novum molendinum nostrum de Baretel, quod nuper propria opera et expensa construxeramus, ad usum sancti illius conventus atque ad supplementum curtis quam in contiguo habebant, devote contraderemus, annuentes ut, si forte eis congruum visum fuerit, aliud in decursu aque molendinum sibi construant. Vivarium autem unde ad ipsum molendinum aqua dirivatur,[6] nostro et successorum nostrorum usui retinuimus, id sollicite precaventes ne pro piscium captura aliqua disceptatio possit oboriri, per quam elemosine ad famulorum Dei subsidium collate donum aliquatenus valeat infirmari. Ut igitur hec donatio nostra in perpetuum firma et inconvulsa permaneat, hoc privilegium eis scribi precepimus, quod etiam legitimarum personarum testimonio subscripto firmari, atque ad maioris auctoritatis prerogativam, sigilli nostri impressione roborari mandavimus. Signum Bartholomei, episcopi, qui hoc privilegium fieri jussit. S. Guidonis, [7] decani. S. Radulphi,[8,9] archidiaconi. S. Bliardi,[10] cantoris. S. Benedicti, sacerdotis. S. Radulphi,[11] sacerdotis.[12] S. Rogeri, diaconi.[13] S. Johannis, subdiaconi et ceteri.[14] Actum Lauduni,[15] anno dominice incarnationis M°C°XX°V°, indictione IIII[a], epacta XXV[a],[16] concurrente IIII°.[17] Ego Radulphus,[18] Sancte Marie cancellarius, relegi.

---

5 *Om.* iam *A*.

6 derivatur *B*.

7 Guy de Pierrepont, son of Roger, lord of Pierrepont, and Ermengarde, lady of Montaigu, was first treasurer, archdeacon, and dean of the chapter of Laon, and later bishop of Châlons, 1144–7.

8 Radulfi *B*.

9 Raoul de Laon (d. 1133), brother of the theologian Anselm de Laon, was archdeacon of Laon, 1117–26, and chancellor of Laon, 1117–33. Dufour-Malbezin, *Actes*, 29.

10 Blihardi *B*.

11 Radulfi *B*.

12 *Om.* S. Roberti, sacerdotis *A*.

13 *Om.* S. Petri, diaconi. S. Bonefacii, diaconi *A*.

14 *Add.* et ceteri *A*; S. Ebali, subdiaconi. S. Milonis subdiaconi *B*.

15 *Om.* III idus octobris, feria III, luna XII *A*.

16 XXV *B*.

17 IIII *B*.

18 Radulfus *B*.

74

1132

Barthélemy,[1] *bishop of Laon, makes known the resolution of a dispute between the religious of Prémontré and the inhabitants of Brancourt*[2] *concerning certain rights, and also confirms a list of Premonstratensian possessions.*

A. Cartulary of Prémontré, fol. 18v.

B. Original not found.

EDITION: Dufour-Malbezin, *Actes*, 234–5; *Chartae Galliae*, no. 208197, http://telma.irht.cnrs.fr/outils/chartae-galliae/charte208197/.

REGISTER: Grauwen, "Lijst van oorkonden waarin Norbertus wordt genoemd," 156.

Karta Bartolomei episcopi de confirmatione curiarum et possessionum in episcopatu Laudunensis.

[I]n nomine sancte et individue Trinitatis. Ego Bartholomeus, Dei gratia Sancte Marie Laudunensis ecclesie minister indignus. Quia ex officii nobis injuncti, licet indignis, debito in ovilis Dominici cura, ipso opitulante, laboramus, licet omnibus in commune fidelibus pro capacitate singulorum mensuram tritici in tempore erogandam susceperimus, precipuam tamen illorum laboribus atque negotiis compassionis ac supportationis vicem debemus qui ut Deo soli jocundo beate contemplationis studio vacarent mundi sarcinam penitus abjecerunt. Eis autem ita interne vitalis anime pabula providere debemus ut fictilis et lutee domus in qua interior homo a Deo peregrinatur ruinam terreni stipendii adminiculo fulcire minime negligamus. Oportet ergo ut et de nostro, si facultas suppetit, eorum necessitatibus concurramus et aliorum erga ipsos munificentiam benigno favore comprobemus et episcopalis officii auctoritate roboremus. Notum igitur fieri volumus tam futuris quam presentibus de multis bonis que facere debuimus, pauca quedam que potuimus, que apud Premonstratensem ecclesiam per nos data, facta et concessa sunt, tempore domini Norberti, nostris temporibus viri spectabilis religionis, quomodo valles ibidem sibi et fratribus suis Deo famulantibus et proclivia montium data et confirmata fuerint a rivo qui est versus Vois[3] usque ad Hunberti Pontem[4] et usque Monandi vicinum et usque ad vallem Rohardi et Halierpre, sicut in primo ipsorum privilegio a nobis confirmato continetur. Succedentibus vero temporibus, ampliato fratrum et sororum parvulorum et debilium numero,

1 Barthélemy de Jur (d. 1158), son of Conon, lord of Grandson and La Sarraz, and Ada de Roucy; first subdeacon and then treasurer of Reims, later bishop of Laon, 1113–51.

2 Brancourt, cant. Anizy-le-Château, https://dicotopo.cths.fr/places/P91051513.

3 Forest of Vois, https://dicotopo.cths.fr/places/P93994197.

4 Hubertpont, comm. Prémontré, https://dicotopo.cths.fr/places/P71559674.

cum vir prefatus recessisset et, loco eius, abbas Hugo nomine, a nobis consecratus, successisset, ipse tante tamque infirme multitudini in posterum providere volens, infra prefatos terminos quecumque in silvis et campis, pratis, stagnis et molendinis ipsorum usibus profutura vidit ad habendum cepit edificare. Videntes autem quidam indigene de Broiencourt in illa parte que est versus Monandi vicinum, quia ipsis cum fratribus in paludibus illis ultra rivum communis erat pascua a nobis quidem concessa, ceperunt molestare eos. Nos autem quia nostri juris erat quod utrique a nobis acceperant, de pascuis et omnibus controversiis querimoniam ita terminavimus videlicet ut partes illas quas stagna et molendina et vivariorum aque occupaverant, ob remedium anime nostre et predecessorum nostrorum, fratres quiete et libere possiderent, ita tamen ut ecclesia Premonstratensis nobis et successoribus nostris duos solidos currentis in Laudunensi pago monete quot annis in festo Sancti Remigii persolveret et sic nostrum jus retineretur et fratrum inopia sustentaretur. Insuper quia pro eorum sustentanda proposite paupertatis necessitate parvas habebant possessiones, Dei et nostra auctoritate qui hanc ecclesiam susceperamus providendam, precepimus ne futuris temporibus abbas quilibet eiusdem ecclesie vel fratres quorumcumque rogatu vel cuiusquam bone voluntatis pretextu sine pari ~~conditione~~ commutatione qualibet sua possessione suis stipendiis deputata privare audeat. Quarum inferius adnotata sunt nomina: vallis videlicet Premonstrati; curie etiam cum suis appenditiis Soupi,[5] Bolmunt,[6] Anisi,[7] Fraisne,[8] Vercini,[9] Bonul, Troissi,[10] Sorni,[11] Luli;[12] alie etiam possessiones in villa de Crespi,[13] due partes decime cum curia; Cauvini similiter due partes decime cum curia et terris; Li Hiri Weiz septima pars decime; ad Duri sexta pars decime; Cresci tercia pars decime; Suessionis domus una cum vineis et terris; Clameci[14] domus una cum vineis et terris; Buci vinee et terre in pago Laudunensi vinee; ad Broiencourt, Apanencourt,[15] domus cum vineis, terris et pratis; Sinnicourt vinee et terre; Marcilli vinea que vocatur Bolmunt cum adjacenti prato; Montarcenne[16] vinee; in Valla Urini terre et prata; in Castro Couci et Villa vinee; in Jamarcourt[17] vinea una; in Nova Villa vinee,

5 Soupir, cant. Vailly, https://dicotopo.cths.fr/places/P62600159.
6 Beaumont-en-Beine, cant. Chauny, https://dicotopo.cths.fr/places/P18685379.
7 Anizy-le-Château, arr. Laon, https://dicotopo.cths.fr/places/P86940236.
8 Fresne, cant. Coucy-le-Château, https://dicotopo.cths.fr/places/P35697386.
9 Versigny, cant. La Fère, https://dicotopo.cths.fr/places/P17885640.
10 Trucy, cant. Craonne, https://dicotopo.cths.fr/places/P86532867.
11 Sorny, cant. Vailly, https://dicotopo.cths.fr/places/P79681466.
12 Leuilly, cant. Coucy-le-Château, https://dicotopo.cths.fr/places/P91541747.
13 Crépy, cant. Laon, https://dicotopo.cths.fr/places/P85331504.
14 Clamecy, cant. Vailly, https://dicotopo.cths.fr/places/P24475745.
15 Penancourt, comm. Anizy-le-Château, https://dicotopo.cths.fr/places/P36114519.
16 Montarcène, comm. Montbavin, https://dicotopo.cths.fr/places/P24202828.
17 Jumencourt, cant. Coucy-le-Château, https://dicotopo.cths.fr/places/P89535611.

terre cum pomerio; Anslers[18] pratum unum; Anisi due partes molendini quod dicitur Barethel[19] cum adjacenti prato; Alisi prata cum terris. Quecumque preterea legitime et justis modis poterunt supradicte ecclesie fratres adipisci suis usibus profutura, ipsis suisque successoribus in sancte religionis preposito permansuris firma et illibata serventur nisi quod in datione ad abbatiam faciendam determinatum fuerit. Et ut ratum et inconvulsum permaneat, sigilli nostri inpressione et testium subscriptione subsignamus, addentes ut siqua in futurum ecclesiastica secularisve persona hoc nostrum decretum infringere presumpserit, secundo terciove commonita; si non emendaverit, anathematis rea in extremo examine districte ultioni subjaceat. Cunctis autem servantibus sit pax in eterna beatitudine. Amen. S. Bartholomei, episcopi qui hoc scriptum fieri jussit. S. Guidonis, decani.[20] S. Herberti, sacerdotis. S. Letoldi, archidiaconi.[21] S. Roberti, capellani. S. Bliardi, cantoris. S. Dei Amici, sacerdotis. S. Nicholai, subdiaconi. S. Nicholai, castellani.[22] S. Gilelmi de Apia.[23] S. Ursionis de Soupi. Actum anno dominice incarnationis M° C° XXX° II°, indictione X[a], epacta XII[a], concurrente quinto.

75

Before September, 1153–September 1158.[1]

Gautier [II],[2] bishop of Laon – at the request of Louis [VII], king of France, Samson,[3] archbishop of Reims and legate of the Holy See, Anscoul,[4] bishop

---

18 Aulers, comm. Bassoles, https://dicotopo.cths.fr/places/P60632746.

19 Barthel, comm. Lizy, https://dicotopo.cths.fr/places/P65460297.

20 Guy de Pierrepont, son of Roger, lord of Pierrepont, and Ermengarde, lady of Montaigu, was first treasurer, archdeacon and dean of the chapter of Laon, and later bishop of Châlons, 1144–7.

21 Létaud, archdeacon of Laon, attested 1126–33. Dufour-Malbezin, *Actes,* 195, 243.

22 Nicolas, castellan of Laon, also appears with his wife Beatrice and son Raoul in an 1149 charter of Barthélemy, bishop of Laon, confirming donations made to the Templars. Dufour-Malbezin, *Actes*, 431–7.

23 Guillaume I, lord of Eppes (cant. Laon, https://dicotopo.cths.fr/places/P60931308). Melleville, *DH*, vol. 1, 358.

---

1 This must date after the beginning of Gautier II de Mortagne's episcopacy in 1153, and before the death of Ansculphe de Pierrefonds, bishop of Soissons, on September 19, 1158. It most likely dates to around 1158, however; see **47**, **77**.

2 Gautier de Mortagne was dean of Laon, ca. 1142–55, and bishop of Laon, 1155–74.

3 Samson de Mauvoisin, son of Raoul III le Barbu de Mauvoisin, lord of Rosny-sur-Seine, and his first wife Odeline, was archdeacon and provost of Chartres, and archbishop of Reims, 1140–61.

4 Anscoul de Pierrefonds, son of Nivelon II, lord of Pierrefonds, and Hawide (de Montmorency?), was archdeacon of Soissons, 1101–25/9, *prepositus* of Soissons, 1129–52, and bishop of Soissons, 1152–8.

of Soissons, and Baudouin [II],[5] *bishop of Noyon – resolves the dispute between himself and the church of Prémontré concerning certain properties that Prémontré claimed as its own. Gautier confirms that Prémontré indeed holds all the properties that it possessed within the bishopric of Laon at the time of his episcopal predecessors Barthélemy*[6] *and Gautier [I].*[7] *(See **47**, 77.)*

A. Cartulary of Prémontré, fols. 19r–19v.
B. Original not found.

Karta Galteri Laudunensis episcopi de compositione inter nos et ecclesiam Laudunensem super quibusdam rebus.

[I]n nomine sancte et individue Trinitatis, Patris et Filii et Spiritus Sancti, amen. Cum pro debito pastoralis officii piis omnium votis et necessitatibus nos oporteat concurrere, speciali tamen cura religiosos fovere et que ipsis a fidelibus Dei conferuntur, firmare debemus et tueri et que a nobis rationabiliter acta sunt, fideliter attestari. Ea propter ego Galterus, Dei gratia Laudunensis vocatus episcopus, notum fieri volumus tam futuris quam presentibus quod querela super quibusdam possessionibus inter nos et ecclesiam Premonstratensem emersit, que tandem precibus domini Ludovici, regis Francorum, et Sansonis, Remensis archiepiscopi et Apostolice Sedis legati, necnon etiam episcoporum Ansculphi Suessionensis, Balduini Noviomensis et procerum curie regalis bono compositionis fine sopita est ita quod quecumque eiusdem ecclesie fratres temporibus predecessorum nostrorum, Bartholomei et Galteri, infra terminos episcopatus nostri tenuerunt, pietatis intuitu a nobis confirmanda concessimus. Unde presenti scripto eadem omnis libere et quiete in perpetuum eis possidenda confirmamus, propriisque vocabulis sigillatim duximus exprimenda: curtem de Soupi[8] quam dedit eis Balduinus[9] et Guido, filius eius, liberam excepta decima que solvitur canonicis Sancte Marie Laudunensis cum tribus carrucatis terre et omnibus aisentiis et nemus et vineam subjacentem domui quam in novalibus fratres plantarunt; quartam quoque carrucatam tam in

5 Baudouin II de Boulogne, abbot of the Augustinian abbey of Saint-Eloi-Fontaine, ca. 1130–ca. 1139, and bishop of Noyon, 1148–67. *GC* IX, col. 1126.

6 Barthélemy de Jur (d. 1158), son of Conon, lord of Grandson and La Sarraz, and Ada de Roucy; first subdeacon and then treasurer of Reims, later bishop of Laon, 1113–51.

7 Gautier de Saint-Maurice was abbot of the Premonstratensian abbey of Saint-Martin de Laon, 1124–51, and bishop of Laon, 1151–3. *MP* II, 512.

8 Soupir, cant. Vailly, https://dicotopo.cths.fr/places/P62600159.

9 Baudouin I, lord of Soupir. Wacha, "La Puissance du Choix," 116.

territorio de Soupi quam de Brai[10] et de Maidi[11] quam tenent ad manum firmam a Guidone de Soupi et Renaldo Curello et Nicholao de Monte Acuto, Radulpho de Lobrai,[12] et Willermo de Sarni; campum etiam Guidonis de Loisi;[13] terram Radulphi et Herberti; campum Adam de Toslis; campum Guidonis de Soupi super lapidem de Hostel;[14] nemus de Silvella cuius unam partem tenent a Guidone de Soupi, aliam a Renaldo Curello, terciam a Nicholao de Monte Acuto, quartam a Radulpho de Lobrai sub censu VI denariorum; molendina de Soupi in Axona quorum medietatem dedit eis comes Theobaldus, aliam Balduinus de Soupi; molendinum etiam de Ribaudon[15] quod dedit eis Reinaldus Curellus pro duabus filiabus suis conversis, annuentibus fratribus suis Reinero, Guidone, Willelmo, cum aisentiis canonicorum Sancte Marie Laudunensis pro quibus XVI denarii censualiter eis a fratribus persolvuntur et terram quam ibidem dedit eis Guido de Soupi ad pomerium et vivarium faciendum, et conductum aque a castro suo usque in ipsum vivarium, sub censu duodecim denariorum; prata in valle de Maidi ad octo falces, vineam et nemus et tres campos ad Moissi;[16] terram quoque arabilem Radulphi de Rohuniis et duos modios vini et falcem prati et pascua et aisentias quas habebat in valle de Maidi sub censu duodecim ~~XII~~ denariorum; in Subarcourt[17] vineam Bartholomei cum duabus partibus pomerii; ad Cessarias[18] duas vineas Tierrici et vineam Ermentei et vineam Franconis cum pomerio; apud Panencourt[19] sex modios et sex sextarios vini a Radulpho Cane;[20] item ibidem IIII^{or} modios et dimidium vini a Renaldo Bellehere; duas partes decime de Merli[21] et de Vallaureni[22] quam Odo[23] de Abbatia dedit in elemosinam pro remedio anime sue et filie sue ibidem

10 Braye-en-Laonnois, cant. Craonne, https://dicotopo.cths.fr/places/P35162562.

11 Le Metz, comm. Moussy-sur-Aisne, https://dicotopo.cths.fr/places/P31678789.

12 Perhaps Lobray, comm. Quincy-Basce, https://dicotopo.cths.fr/places/P80666531.

13 Perhaps Loizy, cant. Laon, https://dicotopo.cths.fr/places/P33210650.

14 Ostel, cant. Vailly, https://dicotopo.cths.fr/places/P14381512.

15 Ribaudon, comm. Soupir, https://dicotopo.cths.fr/places/P28661536.

16 Moussy-sur-Aisne, cant. Craonne, https://dicotopo.cths.fr/places/P63059874.

17 Sebacourt, comm. Suzy, https://dicotopo.cths.fr/places/P94766735.

18 Cessières, cant. Anizy-le-Château, https://dicotopo.cths.fr/places/P02167711.

19 Penancourt, comm. Anizy-le-Château, https://dicotopo.cths.fr/places/P36114519.

20 Raoul Chien (d. ca. 1191), son of Gautier de la Tournelle and Agnès, appears in episcopal acts from the 1140s and was particularly associated with the lords of Coucy. Barthélemy, *LDA*, 160; Morelle, "Une charte nuptiale laonnoise de 1158 conservée en original," 223, fn. 69.

21 Merlieux, cant. Anizy-le-Château, https://dicotopo.cths.fr/places/P92396813.

22 Valavergny, comm. Merlieux, https://dicotopo.cths.fr/places/P74214194.

23 Eudes de l'Abbaye (comm. Bucilly, https://dicotopo.cths.fr/places/P35628143) was either the son or nephew of Raoul de l'Abbaye and Amaltrude. He and his wife Bertrade appear as witnesses in a number of episcopal acts in the 1110s–ca. 1150. Dufour-Malbezin, *Actes*, 137, 197. He was probably from a *lieu dit* called L'Abbaye about a kilometre southeast of Bucilly. Melleville, *DH*, vol. 1, 167; Saint-Denis, *Apogée d'une cité*, 211–15.

converse; ad Burguinon[24] XII modios vini, IIII[or] sextarios minus et XVII denarios bone monete et galetum avene ab Hugone de Sailli et Adelide de Vallaureni; ab hisdem de Panencourt et Broiencourt[25] XVI modios vini et duos solidos census et IIII[or] galetas avene; ab hisdem ad Poilli[26] XI solidos bone monete et IIII[or] obsonia ad Monciaus IIII solidos census a Marga; in Vaus a Simone Crasso vineam unam et XIII[cim] denarios bone monete et mansum unum solventem Premonstratensi ecclesie VII capones et XII sextarios vini; apud Vercini[27] campum terre a Radulpho Despourdon sub censu VI denariorum; apud Acheri[28] carrucatam terre quam dedit Gillebertus de Cheri sub censu quinque solidorum et redditum unum IIII[or] panum et IIII[or] sextariorum vini et IIII[or] sextariorum avene et IIII[or] denariatarum carnis de feodo Clarenbaldi[29] de Vendueil; molendinum de Rochis[30] cum orto et duobus alnetis sub censu trium solidorum et octo denariorum et stagnum adjacens sub censu XII denariorum solvendorum castellano; carrucatam terre apud Omencourt[31] quam commutavit ecclesia Premonstratensis pro alia terra ecclesie Sancte Marie de Nongento; curtem de Firmitate ab omni exactione liberam cum quinque carrucatis sicut in privilegio ipsorum continetur; terram Sancte Marie Humolariensis[32] quam censualiter acceperunt et sedem molendini ad Lehericourt; terram etiam Wichardi de Firmitate, sicut metis positis divisa est; curtem de Walescourt[33] et quicquid canonici Sancte Marie Laudunensis habebant in silva de Mesloi[34] cum altaribus et decimis ad ea pertinentibus sicut ab eisdem canonicis censualiter accepta firmarunt; curtem de Daneri[35] cum tribus carrucatis quam ad censum et terragium a rege acceperunt; duas partes decime de Crespi[36] tam maioris quam minoris ex elemosina eiusdem regis; duas partes molendini de Erchentre[37] ex elemosina ipsius regis, terciam ex censu canonicorum Sancte Marie Laudunensis; curtem de Roseriis[38]

24 Bourguignon-sous-Montbavin, cant. Anizy-le-Château, https://dicotopo.cths.fr/places/P25732714.

25 Brancourt, cant. Anizy-le-Château, https://dicotopo.cths.fr/places/P91051513.

26 Pouilly, cant. Crécy-sur-Serre, https://dicotopo.cths.fr/places/P77273113.

27 Versigny, cant. La Fère, https://dicotopo.cths.fr/places/P17885640.

28 Achery, cant. La Fère, https://dicotopo.cths.fr/places/P61820808.

29 Likely Clérembaud III, lord of Vendeuil, ca. 1130–ca. 1153. Newman, *Homblières*, 120, fn. 3; Melleville, *DH*, vol. 2, 412.

30 Les Roches, comm. Bucy-le-Long, https://dicotopo.cths.fr/places/P20402237.

31 Aumencourt, comm. Auffrique-et-Nogent, https://dicotopo.cths.fr/places/P03934228.

32 Homblières, cant. Saint-Quentin, https://dicotopo.cths.fr/places/P24870893.

33 Valécourt, comm. Chevresis-Monceau, https://dicotopo.cths.fr/places/P14207928.

34 Mesloy, comm. Chevresis-Monceau, https://dicotopo.cths.fr/places/P54953574.

35 Dandry, comm. Crépy, https://dicotopo.cths.fr/places/P99162453.

36 Crépy, cant. Laon, https://dicotopo.cths.fr/places/P85331504.

37 Archantré, comm. Remies, https://dicotopo.cths.fr/places/P18258469.

38 Rozières, cant. Oulchy-le-Château, https://dicotopo.cths.fr/places/P75685266.

quam dedit Thomas[39] de Marla et filius eius Ingelrannus[40] cum tribus carrucatis terre quarum una a predictis Thoma et Ingelranno, due ab hominibus eorum assensu et benivolentia ipsorum collate sunt; totum etiam terragium de dominio eiusdem Ingelranni quod tempore messis ad Couci Villam adducitur terram Bovonis sellarii, vineas ad Couci, vineam scilicet de Trubercourt[41] ex elemosina Otberti, vineam fratris Guidonis ad vivarium, vineam Petronille matris Guidonis Castellani; ad Couci Villam vineam de Rengart ex elemosina Roberti Crassi et Henrici, vineam Roberti, filii Aelidis, duas vineas Sigeberti, ad Puilliers vineam Reineri de Mivilla et Odonis Manensac, duas vineas Harduini Divitis, unam ad Praellam, alteram ad Quercum, in valle de Menchi vineam Belli Hominis, duas vineas Lamberti filii Haimonis, in Walmont vineam Rollandi, in Rochefort vineam Roberti Cementarii et Soffridi, vineam alterius Roberti filii Fulconis et eiusdem Soffridi, vineam Enmeline cum pomerio, vineam filie Reneri de Mivilla, vineam Reneri filii Udeline sub Watencourt; pratum Reneri de Mivilla et Belli Hominis, ad Foulenbrai[42] pratum eiusdem Belli Hominis, ad Coucivillam pratum Harduini Divitis; molendinum de Couci Villa cum vivario et mansione ex dono Ingelranni de Couci et Guidonis de Vaussaillon[43] et Radulphi de Coucivilla et heredum eius et Theoderici, cognomine Salderbos, et heredum eius; molendinum de Novavilla quod Richa et Ermengardis filia eius venientes ad conversionem dederunt assensu Roberti de Chaum,[44] fratris eiusdem Riche; sex modios vinagii ab Henrico; quinque modios a Lamberto Gruel; decem sextarios a Bertranno Bataille; in decima de Chaun terciam partem frumenti et sextam avene post messem presbiteri et collectam tercio anno et culturam unam in Fermeli; in decima de Duellet dimidium modium frumenti et dimidium avene a Beatrice, uxore Simonis de Quinci, ad mensuram de Duellet, ita quod si de uno defuerit, de alio supplebitur; campum de Quinci et tres galetos ~~terre~~ avene ab Albrico cognomine Stulto; molendinum de Courcon[45] ex elemosina fratris Guidonis et censu Radulphi de Quinci et heredum eius ad duos modios frumenti et piscationem in aqua sicut inter Premonstratensem et Nongentinam ecclesiam determinatum est; molendinum de Cinceni;[46] partem decime et terragii de Vervin[47] et de Agneis que a sepe fa~~c~~to Ingelranno de Couci

39 Thomas de Marle, lord of Coucy and Marle (ca. 1073–1130), son of Enguerrand I, lord of Coucy, and Adèle de Marle.

40 Enguerrand II de Coucy (d. ca. 1149), son of Thomas de Marle, lord of Coucy, and his third wife, Mélisende de Crécy-sur-Serre.

41 Trébecourt, comm. Jumencourt, https://dicotopo.cths.fr/places/P13724068.

42 Folembray, cant. Coucy-le-Château, https://dicotopo.cths.fr/places/P36108248.

43 Vauxaillon, cant. Anizy-le-Château, https://dicotopo.cths.fr/places/P32329338.

44 Champs, cant. Coucy-le-Château, https://dicotopo.cths.fr/places/P17397889.

45 Courson, comm. Landricourt, https://dicotopo.cths.fr/places/P39892049.

46 Sinceny, cant. Chauny, https://dicotopo.cths.fr/places/P29595722.

47 Vervins, arr. Vervins, https://dicotopo.cths.fr/places/P65564790.

collata; winagium quoque et naulum de omni terra Ingelranni ab eodem Ingelranno et patre eius remissum; curtem de Hanapia[48] in alodio cum omnibus appenditiis suis quam dederunt Albricus et filii eius Petrus et Robertus, assensu Buchardi de cuius feodo descendit, et altare cum pertinentiis quod dedit Nicholaus Dericus et filii eius, Johannes et Albertus, per manum Bartholomei episcopi et quod reliquum est decime ab Enmelina et filia et duobus filiis suis ibidem conversa per manum eiusdem episcopi; ecclesia de Dorenc[49] cum altari et decima et omnibus appenditiis suis, quam dedit Odo clericus per manum Galteri episcopi, annuente matre sua Fredeburge et fratribus Rogero et Balduino et sororibus suis Ermengarde et Adelide qui ante eum laica manu ipsam tenuerant assensu etiam Buchardi de cuius feodo descendit. Ut igitur hec omnia rata et inconvulsa permaneant et nullam molestiam pauperes Christi sub hiis que juste possident sustineant, tam sigilli nostri inpressione quam legitimorum testium annotatione presentem paginam communiri fecimus et ne quis temerario usu super hiis ecclesiam inquietare presumat episcopali auctoritate interdicimus. Signum Lisiardi, decani Laudunensis.[50] S. abbatis Galteri Sancti Vincentii.[51] S. Brunonis, abbatis Sancti Johannis.[52] Signum Radulphi, abbatis Vallis Clare.[53] Signum Guarini, abbatis Sancti Martini.[54] S. Guntheri. S. Galteri, S. Fulberti, presbiterorum. S. Odonis de Capriniaco.[55] S. Gerardi, subthesaurarii.[56] S. magistri Hugonis, S. magistri Petri, diaconorum. S. Manasse. Signum Renaldi. Signum Haimonis, S. Johannis, subdiaconorum Sancte Marie Laudunensis. S. Hectoris. S. Guidonis de Appia.[57] S. Joisberti, fratris eius. S. Simonis de Vaus. S. Guidonis de Chermisi.[58] S. Willermi de Sarni.[59] S.

48 Hannape, cant. Wassigny, https://dicotopo.cths.fr/places/P37303056.

49 Dorengt, cant. Nouvion, https://dicotopo.cths.fr/places/P90882005.

50 Lisiard, dean of Laon, ca.1153–ca.1168.

51 Gautier, abbot of the Benedictine abbey of Saint-Vincent de Laon, 1155/6–74. *GC* IX, col. 579; Wyard, *Saint-Vincent*, 416–21.

52 Bruno, abbot of the Benedictine abbey of Saint-Jean de Laon, 1152–61. Taïée, "L'abbaye de Saint-Jean de Laon," 211–16

53 Raoul, abbot of the Cistercian abbey of Vauclair, 1156–78. *GC* IX, col. 634.

54 Guérin, abbot of the Premonstratensian abbey of Saint-Martin de Laon, 1151–71. *MP* II, 512.

55 Eudes de Chevregny, a cathedral canon of Laon, appears as a witness in episcopal acts ca. 1143–60s. Morelle, "Une charte nuptiale laonnoise de 1158 conservée en original," 221, fn. 56.

56 Gérard, subtreasurer of Laon, is a witness to episcopal acts from 1145. Dufour-Malbezin, *Actes*, 372.

57 Guy I, lord of Eppes, son of Guillaume I, lord of Eppes (cant. Laon, https://dicotopo.cths.fr/places/P60931308), and either his first wife Béatrice or his second wife Amaltrude. Melleville, *DH*, vol. 1, 358.

58 Guy I, lord of Chermizy (cant. Craonne, https://dicotopo.cths.fr/places/P58073186). Melleville, *DH*, vol. 1, 237.

59 Guillaume, lord of Cerny-lès-Bucy (cant. Laon, https://dicotopo.cths.fr/places/P99577961), ca. 1158–77. Melleville, *DH*, vol. 1, 195.

Bartholomei, vicecomitis.[60] S. Malonis. S. Anselmi de Vaus. S. Dionisii, prepositi.[61] S. Odonis de Abbatia.[62] S. Radulphi Canis. S. Willelmi, filii Odonis.[63] S. Guidonis de Brissi[64] et fratris eius Balduini de Gonessa.[65] S. Bernardi. S. Deusleuvart. S. Radulphi de Porta Sancti Georgii.[66] Signum Drogonis, camerarii.[67] Actum anno incarnati verbi M° C° LVIII°, indictione septima, epacta nulla, concurrente II°. Agothus cancellarius relegit, scripsit et subscripsit.

76

1151

At the request of abbot Hugues [I][1] *and the religious of Prémontré, Gautier [I],*[2] *bishop of Laon, confirms the properties that Prémontré had acquired at the time of bishop Barthélemy.*

A. Cartulary of Prémontré, fols. 19v–20r.

B. Original, SAHSS, *casier* 1, no. 7, previously sealed.

EDITION: Le Paige, *Bibliotheca*, 430; Hugo, *prob*. 1, cols. xvii–xviii.

REGISTER: Grauwen, "Lijst van oorkonden waarin Norbertus wordt genoemd," 172; *Studium Baldwin*, fiche 2203.

---

60 Barthélemy, viscount of Laon in 1152, was a nephew of Guillaume de la Ferté. Saint-Denis, *Apogée d'une cité*, 218.

61 Denis, son of Guillaume Bouche and Helvide la Prévote, was *prepositus* of Laon, 1152–1217, and a cousin of Barthélemy, viscount of Laon. Ibid., 220.

62 Eudes de l'Abbaye (comm. Bucilly, https://dicotopo.cths.fr/places/P35628143) was either the son or nephew of Raoul de l'Abbaye and Amaltrude. He and his wife Bertrade appear as witnesses in a number of episcopal acts in the 1110s–ca. 1150. Dufour-Malbezin, *Actes*, 137, 197. He was probably from a *lieu dit* called L'Abbaye about a kilometre southeast of Bucilly. Melleville, *DH*, vol. 1, 167; Saint-Denis, *Apogée d'une cité*, 211–15.

63 Guillaume de Monceau (or de Moncel), son of Eudes de l'Abbaye and Bertrade, was a knight of Laon, 1150–68. Ibid., 212–13.

64 A Guy de Brissy also appears as a witness in an 1153 act of Gautier, bishop of Laon. AD Aisne, H 375.

65 Baudouin de Gonesse also appears as a witness in **77**.

66 Raoul de la Porte Saint-Georges was perhaps the mayor of Laon in 1165. Saint-Denis, "Maires et jurés de Laon aux premiers temps de la commune (1128–1297)," 170. The St. George Gate was a gate on the east side of the city walls of Laon. It was walled up in the 1870s but was recently rediscovered by archaeologists. "À Laon, la porte Saint-Georges retrouvée sous terre," *L'Union*, December 1, 2018.

67 Dreux, the chamberlain of Laon, is attested in acts 1158–73. Saint-Denis, "Maires et jurés de Laon aux premiers temps de la commune (1128–1297)," 171–3.

---

1 Hugues I de Fosses (ca. 1093–1164), first abbot of Prémontré.

2 Gautier de Saint-Maurice was abbot of the Premonstratensian abbey of Saint-Martin de Laon, 1124–51, and bishop of Laon, 1151–3. *MP* II, 512.

Karta episcopi Laudunensis de confirmatione possessionum et quarundam curiarum nostrarum.

[I]n nomine sancte et individue Trinitatis. Dignitas episcopalis officii est semper lucere, semper bonis operibus insudare, subditorum quieti et utilitatibus providere, bene gestis preteritorum patrum inherere, presentia diligenter ordinare, futura ut memoriter teneantur, dignis assertionibus commendare. Ea propter ego Gualterus, Dei gratia Laudunensis[3] episcopus, notum fieri volo tam futuris quam presentibus quod ecclesia Premonstratensis[4] a predecessore nostro bone memorie Bartholomeo episcopo plantata et constructa fuit per manum cuiusdam viri nostris temporibus spectabilis religionis nomine Norberti, sicut ubique terrarum in vestigiis successorum ipsius patet, que per momenta temporum crevit et dilatata est multis et magnis temporalium rerum possessionibus, sicut in privilegiis eorum tam apostolica quam episcopali auctoritate roboratis continetur. Quia vero per decursus labentium temporum et oblivionem succedentium hominum res geste solent inminui, Hugo abbas et fratres eiusdem ecclesie que apud eos gesta et eis collata fuerant innovari et prout rationabiliter poterant augmentari expetierunt. Necesse enim videbatur ut, ubi creverat fidelium multitudo, ibi etiam fieret rerum augmentatio. Nos igitur justis eorum peticionibus acquiescentes, quicquid a prefato predecessore nostro eis collatum et confirmatum est, denuo confirmamus et approbamus: vallem videlicet in qua sita est ecclesia et omnes aisentias in circuitu ipsorum que nostri juris sunt in silvis, terris, pascuis, rivis, pratis,[5] et molendinis que ibi construxerunt; curtem de Fontenellis[6] cum pertinentiis suis et molendinum de Baretel[7] cum adjacenti vivario; curtem de Vercigni[8,9] cum pertinentiis suis; molendinum de Acheri[10] cum pertinentiis suis; curtem de Firmitate cum pertinentiis suis; carrucatam terre in Monte Caprino; curtem de Soupi[11] cum pertinentiis suis que de feodo nostro descendit; curtem de Roseriis[12] cum pertinentiis suis; elemosinam Adelidis[13] converse de Homencourt;[14,15] molendinum

3 Laudunensium vocatus *B.*

4 Premonstrata *B.*

5 *Transp. A*; pratis, rivis *B.*

6 Fontenille, comm. Wissignicourt, https://dicotopo.cths.fr/places/P36537367.

7 Barthel, comm. Lizy, https://dicotopo.cths.fr/places/P65460297.

8 Vercini *B.*

9 Versigny, cant. La Fère, https://dicotopo.cths.fr/places/P17885640.

10 Achery, cant. La Fère, https://dicotopo.cths.fr/places/P61820808.

11 Soupir, cant. Vailly, https://dicotopo.cths.fr/places/P62600159.

12 Rozières, cant. Oulchy-le-Château, https://dicotopo.cths.fr/places/P75685266.

13 Adhelidis *B.*

14 Homencurt *B.*

15 Aumencourt, comm. Auffrique-et-Nogent, https://dicotopo.cths.fr/places/P03934228.

de Aquila;[16] Panencourt[17,18] cum pertinentiis suis; Merli[19] cum pertinentiis suis; similiter molendina de Vadis, de Proisel, de Rochis,[20] de Curchun;[21,22] duo etiam molendina ad Coucivillam[23] cum vivario, terragio et vineis; partem quoque decime et terragii de Vervin[24] que ab Ingelranno filio Thome, domino de Couci,[25] ob remedium anime sue et predecessorum suorum eis collata sunt. Quod ut ratum et inconvulsum permaneat tam sigilli nostri impressione quam legitimorum testium annotatione consignare curavimus. S. Jordani,[26] Romane ecclesie presbiteri cardinalis. S. Willelmi, abbatis de Sancto Vincentio.[27] S. Gisleberti, abbatis Sancti Nicholai de Silva.[28] S. Richardi, abbatis Sancti Nicholai de Pratis.[29] S. Bartholomei, thesaurarii.[30] S. Balduini, archidiaconi.[31] S. magistri Petri. S. magistri Angoti. S. Roberti, cognomine Comedonis. S. Gerardi, subthesaurarii.[32] S. magistri Hugonis. S. Letoldi de Foro. S. Reinaldi,[33] filii Manasse. S. Fulberti, presbiteri. S. Walteri, presbiteri de Vercigni.[34] Quicumque ergo prescripta beneficia imminuere vel perturbare presumpserit nisi

16 Aile, comm. Royaucourt-et-Chailvet, https://dicotopo.cths.fr/places/P82381255.

17 Pendencurt *B.*

18 Penancourt, comm. Anizy-le-Château, https://dicotopo.cths.fr/places/P36114519.

19 Merlieux, cant. Anizy-le-Château, https://dicotopo.cths.fr/places/P92396813.

20 Les Roches, comm. Bucy-le-Long, https://dicotopo.cths.fr/places/P20402237.

21 Curchuin *B.*

22 Courson, comm. Landricourt, https://dicotopo.cths.fr/places/P39892049.

23 Cocivillam *B.*

24 Vervinz *B.*

25 Coci *B.*

26 Giordano Bobone (d. 1165), cardinal priest of Santa Susanna from 1145. He drew the ire of both John of Salisbury and Bernard of Clairvaux for his activities during his legation in France. Robinson, *The Papacy, 1073–1198*, 163–4, 254.

27 This act may date to the latter half of 1151, since Wyard notes that the abbacy of Guillaume, abbot of the Benedictine abbey of Saint-Vincent de Laon, began "environ l'année 1152." Wyard, *Saint-Vincent*, 405.

28 Gilbert, abbot of the Benedictine abbey of Saint-Nicolas-aux-Bois, 1134–ca. 1157. Duval, "Histoire de l'abbaye bénédictine de Saint-Nicolas-aux-Bois, diocèse de Laon, première partie," 181–96.

29 Richard II, abbot of the Benedictine abbey of Saint Nicolas des Prés sous Ribemont, 1186–97. *GC* IX, col. 617.

30 Barthélemy de Montcornet (d. 1175), son of Hugues de Montcornet and Béatrice de Reynel, was archdeacon and treasurer of Laon from ca. 1133 and later archdeacon of Reims. Guyotjeannin, *Episcopus*, 131.

31 Baudouin de Rumigny, son of Nicolas II, lord of Rumigny, and Aleide van Hainaut, is attested as archdeacon of Laon 1148–51. Dufour-Malbezin, *Actes*, 421, 445.

32 Gérard, subtreasurer of Laon, is a witness to episcopal acts from 1145. Dufour-Malbezin, *Actes*, 372.

33 Rainaldi *B.*

34 Vercini *B.*

commonitus satisfecerit anathema sit. Actum est hoc[35] incarnati verbi M° C° LI°, indictione XIIII[a].

77

1158. Laon.

At the request of [Louis VII], king of France, [Samson],[1] archbishop of Reims, and several other bishops and dignitaries, Gautier [II],[2] bishop of Laon, resolves his dispute with abbot Hugues [I][3] and the religious of Prémontré concerning certain properties. He confirms Prémontré's possession of said properties, held at the time of the previous bishops, Barthélemy[4] and Gautier [I],[5] and receives from Prémontré 300 librae Proveniensium, *50 ewes, 20 cows, 12 mares, and seven sows. (See **47**, **75**.)*[6]

A. Cartulary of Prémontré, fols. 20r–21r.

B. Original, SAHSS, *casier* 1, no. 8, previously sealed with a double strip of parchment.

EDITION: Le Paige, *Bibliotheca*, 432–3; *PL* 188, cols. 1632–5; Florival, *Étude historique sur le XIIe siècle*, 264–5.

Karta Galteri Laudunensis episcopi super quadam compositione inter ipsam et ecclesiam Premonstratam.

[I]n nomine sancte et individue Trinitatis, amen.[7] Pastoralis officii est religiosorum paci et quieti providere, que rationabiliter acta sunt attestari et ne aliquo

35 *Om.* anno *A*.

1 Samson de Mauvoisin, son of Raoul III le Barbu de Mauvoisin, lord of Rosny-sur-Seine, and his first wife Odeline, was archdeacon and provost of Chartres, and archbishop of Reims, 1140–61.

2 Gautier de Mortagne was dean of Laon, ca. 1142–55, and bishop of Laon, 1155–74.

3 Hugues I de Fosses (ca. 1093–1164), first abbot of Prémontré.

4 Barthélemy de Jur (d. 1158), son of Conon, lord of Grandson and La Sarraz, and Ada de Roucy; first subdeacon and then treasurer of Reims, later bishop of Laon, 1113–51.

5 Gautier de Saint-Maurice was abbot of the Premonstratensian abbey of Saint-Martin de Laon, 1124–51, and bishop of Laon, 1151–3. *MP* II, 512.

6 Gautier, bishop of Laon, wrote to Pope Adrian IV informing him of this agreement. Le Paige, *Bibliotheca*, 433; Bouquet and Delisle, eds., *Recueil des historiens des Gaules et de la France*, vol. 15, 689.

7 *Add.* In nomine sancte et individue Trinitatis, amen. *A*; Domino et patri suo Adriano, dei gratia summo pontifici, Galterus Dei misericordia Laudunensis ecclesie humilis minister, salutem et integram cum devotione in omnibus obedientiam. Paternitati vestre notum facimus, consilio domini nostri Ludovici regis Francorum et domini Samsonis Remensis archiepiscopi Apostolice Sedis legati, consilio etiam episcoporum Ansculfi Suessionensis, Balduini

oblivionis nubilo obfuscari possint vel infirmari, scripto commendare et posterorum noticie transmittere. Ea propter ego Galterus, Dei gratia Laudunensium vocatus episcopus, notum fieri volumus tam futuris quam presentibus, quod temporibus nostris inter nos et Hugonem, abbatem et fratres Premonstrate ecclesie querela emersit super possessionibus inferius annotatis, pro eo quod minus ordinate bona episcopalia nobis distracta viderentur. Tandem vero, mediante rege Francorum et archiepiscopo Remensi et episcopis et principibus subnotatis, hoc modo controversia[8] compositionis finem accepit. Fratres quidem Premonstratenses, ut salvis privilegiis et possessionibus suis firmam et perpetuam pacem possent adipisci, trecentas libras Proveniensium ad instaurationem curtis nobis nostrisque successoribus in perpetuum permansure cum quingentis ovibus, vaccis XX, jumentis XII et suibus VII nobis tradiderunt, nos autem eis omnia de quibus querela emerserat, que temporibus predecessorum nostrorum Bartholomei et Galteri[9] tenuerant, deinceps libere et quiete possidenda concessimus et communi assensu capituli nostri presentis scripti auctoritate confirmavimus. Que etiam vocabulis propriis singillatim duximus exprimenda: vallem videlicet Premonstrati in qua sita est ecclesia, liberam et ab omni exactione cuiuslibet persone absolutam, cum vineis, terris, silvis, pascuis, pratis, rivis et molendinis que ibidem construxerunt, et proclivia montium ex omni parte cum vallibus adiacentibus a rivo versus Voiz[10,11] usque ad Hunberti[12] Pontem[13] et usque Molnnant[14] Voisin et usque ad Vallem Rohardi et ad Halierpre[15] in quibus videlicet terminis pro ea parte in qua prius ultra rivum versus Molnant Voisin communis erat pascua nunc autem stagnis et molendinis occupatur, solvuntur ab ipsis fratribus nobis[16] duo solidi censualiter in festo Sancti Remigii, curtem de Fontenellis[17] liberam, exceptis sex[18] denariis qui pro minuta decima solvuntur[19] canonicis Sancte Marie Laudunensis, et carrucatam unam ex dono

Noviomensis, et assensu capituli nostri inter nos et ecclesiam Premonstratensem de querelis in presentia vestra tractatis compositionem factam esse et sigillo tam nostro quam ecclesie nostre confirmatam, sicut in subscripta pagina continetur. Ea propter sanctitatis vestre dulcedinem attentius exoramus ut quod a nobis tanto consilio factum est et ratum esse volumus prout voluntati vestre placuerit confirmare dignemini. Omnipotens Deus sanctitatem vestram ecclesie sue sancte conservet incolumem *B*.

8 *Om.* illa *A*.

9 Gualteri *B*.

10 Vehoz *B*.

11 Forest of Vois, https://dicotopo.cths.fr/places/P93994197.

12 Humberti *B*.

13 Hubertpont, comm. Prémontré, https://dicotopo.cths.fr/places/P71559674.

14 Molnant *B*.

15 Halerpre *B*.

16 nobis ab ipsis fratribus *B*.

17 Fontenille, comm. Wissignicourt, https://dicotopo.cths.fr/places/P36537367.

18 VI *B*.

19 solvuntur pro minuta decima *B*.

episcopali et terram XIIII^cim[20] galetos sementis capientem ex elemosina fratris Udonis cum modio frumenti parve mensure ad molendinum de Taterel,[21] aliam quoque terram tam ad Belmont quam juxta Rothecen capientem circiter duos modios et dimidium sementis Laudunensis[22] mensure, solventem nobis censualiter XIII denarios et obolum, que collecta est ex elemosinis quorumdam,[23] scilicet Harduini, Gerardi Rufi, Emehardi et Thome fratris eius, Dodonis, Reineri, Harduini, Gaufridi de Guez, campum etiam ad modium sementis, solventem Ermentrudi de Firmitate duos solidos, novem prata circiter duodecim[24] falces capientia, duo videlicet prata fratris Udonis in Bruil, duo prata eiusdem versus Pinun,[25] item in Bruil duo prata a Bertrada et Radulpho[26] Cholet[27] et pratum Hugonis Lupi, pratum quoque Gelrici de Montemont et pratum fratris Hugonis ad Testam sub Baretel,[28,29] pratum Hugonis de Montarcen,[30] duas partes molendini de Baretel[31] et de tercia quintam partem pro custodia eiusdem molendini cum adiacenti vivario et prato, molendinum de Guez[32] et stagnum quod dedit Ermeniardis[33] sub censu IIII^or modiorum parve mensure et ortum solventem nobis obolum et pratum solvens duos denarios ecclesie Sancti Johannis de Burgo, curtem de Panencourt[34,35] et terram adiacentem inter Burdel[36] et Viviers[37] et Panencourt[38] ad septem[39] modios sementis Laudunensis[40] mensure, que ex multorum elemosinis collecta est, scilicet Amisardi, Alde, Gelrici,[41] Constantii, Galteri,[42] Hermundi, Widelonis, Odonis, Roberti, Berengeri, Gelrici[43] et Roberti, Hugonis, Dodonis, Thome, Roberti, Helvidis, Beroardi,

20 XIIII *B.*
21 Taterel, cant. Anizy-le-Château, https://dicotopo.cths.fr/places/P91053037.
22 Laudunsis *B.*
23 ex quorumdam elemosinis *B.*
24 XII^cim *B.*
25 Pinon, cant. Anizy-le-Château, https://dicotopo.cths.fr/places/P22218866.
26 Radulfo *B.*
27 Colet *B.*
28 Barethel *B.*
29 Barthel, comm. Lizy, https://dicotopo.cths.fr/places/P65460297.
30 Montarcène, comm. Montbavin, https://dicotopo.cths.fr/places/P24202828.
31 Barethel *B.*
32 Huet, comm. Lizy, https://dicotopo.cths.fr/places/P74654387.
33 Ermengardis *B.*
34 Pendencurt *B.*
35 Penancourt, comm. Anizy-le-Château, https://dicotopo.cths.fr/places/P36114519.
36 Barthel, comm. Lizy, https://dicotopo.cths.fr/places/P65460297.
37 Vivers *B.*
38 Pendencurt *B.*
39 VII *B.*
40 Laudunsis *B.*
41 Gerlici *B.*
42 Gualteri *B.*
43 Gerlici *B.*

Bernuidis, Hauwini,[44] Anselmi, Dude, Tierrici,[45] vineas quoque adiacentes in Gislenval,[46] vineam Elvini et vineam Liegardis,[47] in loco qui dicitur Ad Duos Campos vineam Hersendis et vineam Renoldi,[48] in Ochemont vineam Theoderici,[49] ad Torcular vineam que collecta est ex elemosinis ~~Garneri~~ Bernuidis, Radulphi[50] Spaillart,[51] Dude, Riche, Hugonis, Renoldi,[52] Rollandi, Ysemberti,[53] Hermene, Hermundi, Brunelli, Galteri,[54] Alde, in Solariolo vineam Havini[55] et Rollandi, in Raher vineam Dodonis, in Marval tres[56] vineas Roberti et Gelrici[57] et vineam collectam ex elemosinis Garneri,[58] Thome, Roberti, Hugonis Prepositi, Gerardi Rufi, Balduini, Matildis,[59] Widelonis, Emehardi, et Thome fratrum Roberti Aggei, Reneri,[60] Odonis et Gerardi fratrum Odonis Aggei, Anselmi et Odonis, in Fossa vineam Alde, in Quartariis vineam Radulphi[61] et Hugonis, in Larriz[62] medietatem vinee que fuit Udonis, in Cantaplora vineam Odonis, in Buimont duas vineas Tierrici[63] et Hugonis, duodecim[64] particulas pratorum,[65] scilicet super Aquilam prata duo Pagani et fratris Roberti, ad Pontem pratum Roberti Taisnier,[66] ad Tolum duo prata fratris Udonis et pratum Odonis filii Aveline, ad Communpre et ad Bu[67] duas partes pratorum Alde et Roberti Cati, in Buimont pratum Stephani, ad Escorni pratum fratris Gelrici,[68] ad Nodam Aurain

44 Hawini *B*.
45 Terrici *B*.
46 Geneva, comm. Chaourse, https://dicotopo.cths.fr/places/P73454738.
47 Legardis *B*.
48 Reinoldi *B*.
49 Teoderici *B*.
50 Radulfi *B*.
51 Spallart *B*.
52 Reinoldi *B*.
53 Isemberti *B*.
54 Walteri *B*.
55 Hawini *B*.
56 IIIes *B*.
57 Gerlici *B*.
58 Warneri *B*.
59 Mathildis *B*.
60 Reineri *B*.
61 Radulfi *B*.
62 *Om. and homeo.* vineam Gerlici et Roberti, in Lonpre vineam Aggei, in Larriz vineam Thome de Super Fontem vineam Roberti et Gerlici, ad Salicem vineam Rascendis et filiorum Roberti Cordele, in Warpunval vineam Radulfi, in Gerardon vineam Hermundi in Larriz *A*.
63 Terrici *B*.
64 XII^{cim} *B*.
65 pratorum particulas *B*.
66 Tainer *B*.
67 But, comm. Crépy, https://dicotopo.cths.fr/places/P31280705.
68 Gerlici *B*.

duo prata Roberti Cordele, nemus extra Broiencourt,[69,70] de quo videlicet cum duabus vineis et prato solvuntur nobis novem[71] denarii et obolus bone monete et duodecim[72] sextarii vini, dimidium modium vini in Roszui a Radulpho[73] Spaillart,[74] dimidium etiam modium in Larriz a filiis Aggei, curtem de Merli et vineas appendentes, vineam scilicet de Biars, vineam de Conart,[75] vineam in Letolt, vineam in Petra Hadue, cum campo et nemore de Baleschans[76] et campo ad quarrariam et nemore ad Nodam que fuerunt fratris Ligeri et heredum eius in Premonstratensi[77] ecclesia conversorum, clausum de Lisi et de Scaphot[78] liberum, quod tam elemosina quam emptione acquisitum est ecclesie, in Escorni duas vineas ex elemosina fratris Udonis, vineam Balduini, vineam Aggei, vineam Albrici de Ruha,[79] in Laperche vineam Udonis, tres vineas Gerardi, unam in Valarcenois, aliam in Butigni,[80] terciam in Biars, item in Biars vineam collectam ex elemosinis Ermengardis, Gerardi, Udonis, Radulphi,[81] in valle de Vallaureni[82] vineam Rascendis, ad Fulcheroles[83] vineam Dude, in Sola Valle vineam Roberti,[84] in valle de Monbaven[85] vineam Hermundi, prata circiter sex[86] falces capientia, scilicet in Bruil pratum Gerardi de Merli, solvens nobis denarium, ad novum molendinum duas partes pratorum solventes nobis sex[87] denarios et obolum et dimidiam sedem molendini a fratre Roberto de Montarcenne,[88,89] in Bullipre[90] pratum fratris Hugonis ad Testam, ad Kavetel pratum Odonis militis,

69 Broiencurt *B*.
70 Brancourt, cant. Anizy-le-Château, https://dicotopo.cths.fr/places/P91051513.
71 IX *B*.
72 XII *B*.
73 Radulfo *B*.
74 Spallart *B*.
75 Coart *B*.
76 Balescans *B*.
77 Premonstrata *B*.
78 Scaphoit *B*.
79 *Om. and homeo.* vineam Johannis Albi in Cesseroi, vineam Gilleberti, in Caperon vineam Burdini, in Petra Hadue vineam Bernuidis, vineam Albrici de Ruha *A*.
80 Buteni *B*.
81 Radulfi *B*.
82 Valavergny, comm. Merlieux, https://dicotopo.cths.fr/places/P74214194.
83 Fouquerolles, comm. Merlieux-et-Fouquerolles, https://dicotopo.cths.fr/places/P88868999.
84 Roiberti *B*.
85 Montbavin, cant. Anizy-le-Château, https://dicotopo.cths.fr/places/P47211476.
86 VI *B*.
87 VI *B*.
88 Montarcen *B*.
89 Montarcène, comm. Montbavin, https://dicotopo.cths.fr/places/P24202828.
90 Busilipre *B*.

campum unum in monte[91] de Lisi,[92] duas partes camporum in valle de Merli,[93] curtem de Vercigni[94,95] liberam et carrucatam unam terre quam primitus eis contulit Bartholomeus episcopus, alias quoque circiter duas quas crescente numero fratrum, idem ipse partim de culta, partim de inculta cum prato sub censu duorum solidorum superaddidit ubi et ecclesiam cum atrio ad habendam sui et successorum memoriam suorum[96] edificari precepit, aliud quoque novale quod more ceterorum incolarum fratres ipsi fecerunt sub censu duorum solidorum, molendinum de Acheri[97] et piscationem in aque quandocumque vel quomodocumque voluerint et mansum unum terre censualiter pro modio frumenti Laudunensis mensure nobis persolvendo et curtem ab omni exactione liberam absque fure et duello, carrucatam unam terre in monte de Capriniaco[98] ex dono episcopali, tres vineas ad Brai, duo prata in valle de Capriniaco, duos modios vinagii in Monte Nantolio, terram Albrici et Beatricis de Bertoncourt[99] in monte de Brai, terram Hersendis de Brai et filiorum suorum, duas partes molendini de Aquila sub censu decem solidorum bone monete qui solvuntur thesaurario Sancte Marie Laudunensis ecclesie. Que omnia ut absque ulla reclamatione vel perturbatione Premonstratensi ecclesie perpetua firmitate consistant tam sigilli nostri quam ecclesie Laudunensis impressione presentem paginam communire curavimus. Et ne quis deinceps ecclesiam super hiis[100] inquietare presumat, episcopali auctoritate interdicimus. Actum publice Lauduni et recitatum in capitulo Sancte Marie Laudunensis, presente et cooperante domino Ludovico rege Francorum et domino Sansone[101] Remensi archiepiscopo et Apostolice Sedis legato astantibus quoque nonnullis episcopis et principibus et abbatibus et multis aliis quorum nomina subsignata sunt: Signum Ansculphi[102] Suessionensis.[103] S. Balduini[104] Noviomensis episcoporum.

91 *Add.* in monte *A*.

92 Lizy, cant. Anizy-le-Château, https://dicotopo.cths.fr/places/P40948829.

93 Merlieux, cant. Anizy-le-Château, https://dicotopo.cths.fr/places/P92396813.

94 Vercenni *B*.

95 Versigny, cant. La Fère, https://dicotopo.cths.fr/places/P17885640.

96 suorum memoriam *B*.

97 Achery, cant. La Fère, https://dicotopo.cths.fr/places/P61820808.

98 Chevregny, cant. Anizy-le-Château, https://dicotopo.cths.fr/places/P06529464.

99 Bertolcurt *B*.

100 his *B*.

101 Samsone *B*.

102 Ansculfi *B*.

103 Anscoul de Pierrefonds, son of Nivelon II, lord of Pierrefonds, and Hawide (de Montmorency?), was archdeacon of Soissons, 1101–25/9, *prepositus* of Soissons, 1129–52, and bishop of Soissons, 1152–8.

104 Baudouin II de Boulogne, abbot of the Augustinian abbey of Saint-Eloi-Fontaine, ca. 1130–ca. 1139, and bishop of Noyon, 1148–67. *GC* IX, col. 1126.

Et de curia domini regis. S. Yvonis[105,106] Suessionensis comitis. S. Roberti[107] comitis, fratris eiusdem regis. S. Hugonis[108] cancellarii eiusdem regis. S. Drogonis de Pierrefons.[109,110] S. Guidonis,[111] buticularii regis. S. Theoderici[112] Waleran. S. Guidonis de Garlanda.[113] S. Federici. S. Ade,[114] cubicularii regis, et de capitulo Laudunensi. S. Lisiardi decani.[115] S. Richardi, archidiaconi.[116] S. Bartholomei, thesaurarii.[117] S. Balduini, archidiaconi.[118] S. Milonis, cantoris.[119] S. Guntheri. S. Josberti.[120] S.[121] Dei Amici. S.[122] Fulberti, S. Gualteri, presbiterorum. S. Odonis de Capriniaco.[123] S.[124] Gerardi,[125] subthesaurarii. S.[126] magistri Hugonis.[127] S.[128]

---

105 Ivonis *B.*

106 Yves II de Nesle (d. ca. 1178), lord of Nesle and count of Soissons, son of Raoul, lord of Nesle, and Raintrude. Newman, *Seigneurs*, vol. 1, 61.

107 Robert I, count of Dreux (ca. 1125–1188), son of Louis VI of France and Adélaïde of Savoy.

108 Hugues II de Champfleury (d. 1175), was first archdeacon of Arras, ca. 1131–9, 1157–9, then archdeacon of Ostrevant, 1141/2–54, chancellor of France, 1150–72, and bishop of Soissons, 1158/9–75.

109 Petrefonz *B.*

110 Dreux, lord of Pierrefonds (d. 1160), son of Nivelon II, lord of Pierrefonds, and Hawide. Newman, *Seigneurs*, vol. 1, 187–9.

111 Guy III de Senlis (d. 1188), lord of Chantilly and butler of France, son of Guillaume le Loup de Senlis, lord of Chantilly and butler of France, and Adèle. Voillemier, "Note sur la maison des Bouteiller de Senlis," 40–2.

112 Teoderici *B.*

113 Guy III de Garlande (d. aft. 1186), lord of La Houssaye-en-Brie, son of Gilbert (or Gautier?) de Garlande and Eustacie de Possesse; brother of Manassès de Garlande, bishop of Orléans.

114 Adam de Beaumont-Gâtinais, lord of Villemomble, chamberlain of the king, son of Josselin II de Beaumont-Gâtinais. Lewis, "The Career of Philip the Cleric, Younger Brother of Louis VII," 126, fn. 66.

115 Lisiard, dean of Laon, ca. 1153–ca. 1168.

116 Richard, archdeacon of Laon, ca. 1145–ca. 1158. Wyard, *Saint-Vincent*, 34.

117 Barthélemy de Montcornet (d. 1175), son of Hugues de Montcornet and Béatrice de Reynel, was archdeacon and treasurer of Laon from ca. 1133 and later archdeacon of Reims. Guyotjeannin, *Episcopus*, 131.

118 Baudouin de Rumigny, son of Nicolas II, lord of Rumigny, and Aleide van Hainaut, is attested as archdeacon of Laon 1148–51. Dufour-Malbezin, *Actes*, 421, 445.

119 Milon, cantor of Laon, ca. 1146–ca. 1158. Wyard, *Saint-Vincent*, 37.

120 Jolberti *B.*

121 *Om.* S. *B.*

122 *Om.* S. *B.*

123 Eudes de Chevregny, a cathedral canon of Laon, appears as a witness in episcopal acts ca. 1143–60s. Morelle, "Une charte nuptiale laonnoise de 1158 conservée en original," 221, fn. 56.

124 *Om.* S. *B.*

125 Gérard, subtreasurer of Laon, is a witness to episcopal acts from 1145. Dufour-Malbezin, *Actes*, 372.

126 *Om.* S. *B.*

127 Hugues de Mortagne (d. ca. 1180), later prior of the Benedictine abbey of Saint-Martin de Sées, appears as a witness in episcopal acts from 1149. Morelle, "Une charte nuptiale laonnoise de 1158 conservée en original," 221, fn. 57.

128 *Om.* S. *B.*

Herberti Peleel.[129] S.[130] Odonis de Petraponte,[131,132] diaconorum. S. Gualteri de Mauritania. S. Guidonis de Montcornet.[133] S.[134] Alexandri. S.[135] Bretali.[136] S.[137] Manasse. S.[138] Rainaldi. S.[139] Petri filii Willelmi, subdiaconorum. S. Ingravi,[140] abbatis Sancti Medardi. S. Galteri,[141,142] abbatis Sancti Vincentii. S. Brunonis, abbatis Sancti Johannis. S. Johannis,[143] abbatis Sancti Michaelis. S. Richardi,[144] abbatis Sancti Nicholai de Prato. S. Ingelranni,[145] abbatis de Nongento. S. Roberti,[146] abbatis Fusniaci. S. Radulphi,[147,148] abbatis de Valle Clara. S. Garini,[149,150] abbatis Sancti Martini. S. Guidonis,[151] abbatis[152] Cussiacensis. S. Albrici[153]

---

129 Herbert Peleel, canon and dean of Laon, appears as a witness to episcopal charters ca. 1115–ca. 1147. Herbomez, *Chartes de l'abbaye de Saint-Martin de Tournai*, vol. 1, 24, 68, 69; Dufour-Malbezin, *Actes*, 329, 359, 408, 411.

130 *Om.* S. *B.*

131 Petrefonte *B.*

132 The deacon Eudes de Pierrepont also appears as a witness in an 1162 act for the Premonstratensian abbey of Braine. Guyotjeannin et al., *Le chartrier de l'abbaye prémontrée de Saint-Yved de Braine (1134–1250)*, 245.

133 A Guy is attested as lord of Montcornet, ca. 1162–78. Through his sister Elizabeth he was the brother-in-law of Gossuin, castellan of Pierrepont. Melleville, *DH*, vol. 2, 119.

134 *Om.* S. *B.*

135 *Om.* S. *B.*

136 Bretelli *B.*

137 *Om.* S. *B.*

138 *Om.* S. *B.*

139 *Om.* S. *B.*

140 Ingramm was abbot of the Benedictine abbey of Saint-Médard de Soissons, 1148–77. Poquet, *Pélerinage à l'ancienne abbaye de Saint-Médard-lès-Soissons*, 41.

141 Walteri *B.*

142 Gautier, abbot of the Benedictine abbey of Saint-Vincent de Laon, 1155/6–74. *GC* IX, col. 579; Wyard, *Saint-Vincent*, 416–21.

143 Jean, abbot of the Benedictine abbey of Saint-Michel en Thiérache, 1142–60. *GC* IX, col. 600.

144 Richard I, abbot of the Benedictine abbey of Saint-Nicolas-des-Prés sous Ribemont, ca. 1150–ca. 1170. *GC* IX, col. 618.

145 Enguerrand, abbot of the Benedictine abbeys of Nogent-sous-Coucy, 1157–ca. 1160, and of Saint-Jean de Laon, 1161–82. *GC* IX, col. 607; Taïée, "L'abbaye de Saint-Jean de Laon," 217.

146 Robert I (de Coucy?), abbot of the Cistercian abbey of Foigny, 1148–69. *GC* IX, col. 630.

147 Radulfi *B.*

148 Raoul, abbot of the Cistercian abbey of Vauclair, 1156–78. *GC* IX, col. 634.

149 Guarini *B.*

150 Guérin, abbot of the Premonstratensian abbey of Saint-Martin de Laon, 1151–71. *MP* II, 512.

151 Guy, abbot of the Premonstratensian abbey of Cuissy, 1155–9. *MP* II, 497.

152 *Add.* abbatis *A.*

153 Aubry, abbot of the Premonstratensian abbey of Thenailles, 1158–62. *MP* II, 401.

Thenoliensis.[154] S. Radulphi[155,156] Branensis. S. Gisleberti,[157] Viromandensis abbatum. S. Johannis,[158] abbatis Belli Loci. S. Gisleberti,[159,160] abbatis de Monte Sancti Martini. S. Geroldi,[161] abbatis de Viconia. S. Radulphi[162] vicedomini.[163] S. Hectoris. S. Bartholomei.[164] S. Guidonis,[165] castellani de Couci.[166] S. Joifridi[167] et Sarraceni fratris eius. S. Bliardi[168,169] de Firmitate et Guidonis de Soupi[170] fratris eius. S. Bartholomei de Bolmont.[171,172] S. Radulphi[173] Canis.[174] S. Dionisii,[175] prepositi. S. Balduini de Gonessa.[176] Actum anno incarnati verbi M° C° LVIII°,[177] indictione septima,[178] epacta nulla, concurrente secundo.[179] Angotus cancellarius relegit, scripsit et subscripsit.

154 Tenoliensis *B*.

155 Radulfi *B*.

156 Raoul, abbot of the Premonstratensian abbey of Braine, 1150–63. *MP* II, 486.

157 Gilbert I, abbot of the Premonstratensian abbey of Vermand, 1152–66. *MP* II, 427.

158 Jean I de Brienne, abbot of the Premonstratensian abbey of Beaulieu, 1156–82. *MP* II, 482.

159 Gilleberti *B*.

160 Gillebert, abbot of the Premonstratensian abbey of Mont-Saint-Martin, 1151–74. *MP* II, 419.

161 Gérard, abbot of the Premonstratensian abbey of Vicogne, 1151–8. *MP* II, 436.

162 Radulfi *B*.

163 Raoul, vidame of Laon (d. 1187), son of Sarrasine and Hector. Saint-Denis, *Apogée d'une cité*, 206–7.

164 Bartholomei vicecomitis *B*.

165 Guy II, castellan of Coucy (d. 1165); husband of Théophanie. Barthélemy, *LDA*, 506–7.

166 Coci *B*.

167 Joffridi *B*.

168 Blihardi *B*.

169 Bliard de La Ferté-Chevresis, son of Baudouin de Soupir and Cécile, and brother or half-brother of Guy de Soupir. Morelle, "Une charte nuptiale laonnoise de 1158 conservée en original," 222, fn. 64.

170 Supi *B*.

171 Bolmunt *B*.

172 Barthélemy de Montchâlons, lord of Bosmont, son of Aubry I, lord of Montchâlons and Bosmont. He appears as a witness in episcopal acts, 1130–ca. 1150. Melleville, *DH*, vol. 1, 131; Dufour-Malbezin, *Actes*, 215, 456.

173 Radulfi *B*.

174 Raoul Chien (d. ca. 1191), son of Gautier de la Tournelle and Agnès, appears in episcopal acts from the 1140s and was particularly associated with the lords of Coucy. Barthélemy, *LDA*, 160; Morelle, "Une charte nuptiale laonnoise de 1158 conservée en original," 223, fn. 69.

175 Denis, son of Guillaume Bouche and Helvide la Prévote, was *prepositus* of Laon, 1152–1217, and a cousin of Barthélemy, viscount of Laon. Saint-Denis, *Apogée d'une cité*, 220.

176 A Baudouin de Gonesse also appears as a witness in **75**, where he is described as the brother of another witness, Guy de Brissy.

177 LVIII *B*.

178 VII^a^ *B*.

179 II° *B*.

78

1178. Laon.

Raoul [I],[1] *lord of Coucy, confirms all the donations that Thomas [de Marle],*[2] *his grandfather, and Enguerrand [II de Coucy],*[3] *his father, gave to the religious of the church of Prémontré, including, among other things, the rights for the religious of Prémontré to freely transport their goods over certain roads, in exchange for the rights of* advocatus *of Sorny under the condition that he and his heirs never alienate them. (See **80**.)*

A. Cartulary of Prémontré, fols. 21r–21v.

B. Original, SAHSS, *casier* 2, no. 13, sealed with green wax on a double strip of leather.

EDITION: Du Chesne, *Histoire genealogique des maisons de Guines, d'Ardres, de Gand, et de Coucy*, 349–50 (partial); Hugo, *prob.* 1, col. xxii; Slack, *Crusade Charters, 1138–1270*, 66–9.

Karta Domini Radulphi de Couci de confirmatione elemosine predecessorum suorum.

[I]n nomine Patris et Filii et Spiritus Sancti, amen. Ego Radulphus[4] dominus Couciaci,[5] notum fieri volo tam presentibus quam futuris quod, amore Dei ductus et desiderio salutis mee et predecessorum pariterque heredum meorum, recognovi et concessi in perpetuum elemosinas et aisentias quas avus meus Thomas et Ingelrannus, pater meus, contulerunt fratribus Premonstrate ecclesie perpetuo possidendas, videlicet quicquid juris vel consuetudinis habebat avus meus predictus in loco qui Premonstratus dicitur, remisit fratribus ibidem Deo servientibus et servituris. Valles etiam omnes Premonstrato adjacentes et proclivia montium, sicut valles perportant, ex quibus fratres partim sartaverant et residuum se posse sartare asserebant, sed obtinui apud eos, quod deinceps in eis sartabitur non,[6] sed nemus vallium et pendentium ad opus edificiorum suorum et aliarum necessitatum suarum reservabunt. Concessit etiam idem avus

1 Raoul I, lord of Coucy (d. 1191), son of Enguerrand II, lord of Coucy, and Agnès de Beaugency.

2 Thomas de Marle, lord of Coucy and Marle (ca. 1073–1130), son of Enguerrand I, lord of Coucy, and Adèle de Marle.

3 Enguerrand II de Coucy (d. ca. 1149), son of Thomas de Marle, lord of Coucy, and his third wife, Mélisende de Crécy-sur-Serre.

4 Radulfus *B*.

5 Cociaci *B*.

6 *Transp. A*; non sartabitur *B*.

meus eis usuarium de mortuo nemore in foresta de Voiz[7,8] et pascua animalibus suis. Dedit quoque ipsis locum qui Rosieres dicitur, et de propria terra sua unam carrucatam; que omnia predicte ecclesie fratres in diebus eiusdem avi mei et in diebus patris mei quiete possederunt. Cum autem locus prefatus ampliari cepisset, et per universos fines tocius orbis dilatari, pater meus qui locum illum plurimum dilexit, paterne liberalitatis emulator concessit eiusdem loci fratribus terragium et decimam de Vervin, terragium de Aegnies,[9] terragium de Couci[10] Villa exceptis duobus modiis hiemalis annone qui persolvuntur ecclesie Beate Marie de Nongento;[11] vivarium etiam cum molendino juxta eandem villam videlicet Couci,[12] feodum quoque et partem decime de Vassen. Remisit etiam eis wionagium in omni loco terre sue ubi ab alienis accipiebatur, nisi de re que ematur ut iterum venalis exponenda deferatur. Ego itaque qui beneficia et elemosinas avi mei, sive patris mei minuere non appeto, neque servientes Deo super elemosinis sibi collatis vexari desidero, ea que predicta sunt, benigne eis recognovi et concessi et quod eis in pace facerem possidere promisi. Unde volo quod servientes mei et heredum meorum de hiis omnibus pacem eis ferant. Quod si pro quacumque occasione wagia eorum ceperint vel ad me ea deferant sive adducant apud Couciacum[13] vel in vicinia, si presens fuero, aut eis recredant usque ad reditum meum et tunc res mihi notificabitur et ut res pacifice et rationabiliter valeat terminari, mittam, si voluero, ad veritatem cognoscendam. Volo enim ut pax eis conservetur et ut a servientibus meis non inquietentur. Quia vero moleste ferebam quod tot nove vie vel ab ipsis vel ab aliis fiebant in foresta mea, vias eis assignari feci per quas bona eorum libere et quiete adduci poterunt et reduci; videlicet viam per Anleirs,[14] viam per longum Buellum, viam juxta Rosieres,[15] viam per Septem Valles, viam que ducit Crispiacum, et que ducit ad Sanctum Nicholaum et que ducit per Broiencourt,[16,17] et que ducit versus Anisiacum.[18] Has vias concedo liberas et quitas karris eorum et karretis. Quia igitur et ea que predicta sunt et omnia que de feodatis et hominibus meis in omni posse meo, tempore huius scripti, tenebant benigne eis

7 Voois *B.*
8 Forest of Vois, https://dicotopo.cths.fr/places/P93994197.
9 Aengnies *B.*
10 Coci *B.*
11 Beate Marie Nogenti *B.*
12 Coci *B.*
13 Cociacum *B.*
14 Anlers *B.*
15 Rozières, cant. Oulchy-le-Château, https://dicotopo.cths.fr/places/P75685266.
16 Broiencurt *B.*
17 Brancourt, cant. Anizy-le-Château, https://dicotopo.cths.fr/places/P91051513.
18 Anizy-le-Château, arr. Laon, https://dicotopo.cths.fr/places/P86940236.

concessi, ipsi versa vice dederunt mihi advocatiam suam de Sorni,[19] salvis redditibus et possessionibus eorum et omnibus que ibidem habent preter justiciam eiusdem ville. Ita sane quod eum quem sibi maiorum in eadem villa constituent per singulos annos ad querendos et recipiendos redditus suos, liberum habebunt ab omni tallia, ab omni exactione et requisitione et si forifecerit, per abbatem Premonstratensem emendabit aut si nollet per me michi emendaret. Convenit autem inter me et ipsos quod advocatia illa numquam alienabitur a domino de Couci,[20] sed qui erit dominus de Couci[21] erit advocatus de Sorni. Ut igitur hec concessio predecessorum meorum et mea rata et inconcussa perpetuo prefate Premonstrate ecclesie permaneat presenti scripto et sigilli mei ~~annotatione~~ appositione et hominum meorum qui interfuerunt annotatione feci roborari. Actum Lauduni anno incarnationis dominice M° C° LXX° VIII°, presentibus hominibus meis Radulpho[22] de Hussel,[23] Radulpho[24] Cane,[25] Hectore,[26] Simone[27] de Amigni,[28,29] Petro camerario,[30] Guidone[31] de Sancto Paulo.[32] Postmodum autem cum presens scriptum facerem confirmari recognovi iterum apud Couciacum[33] coram istis: Petro capellano meo, Renardo[34] de Foro, Roberto[35] maiore de Couci[36] et Mauberto, servientibus meis. Ex parte autem

19 Sorny, cant. Vailly, https://dicotopo.cths.fr/places/P79681466.

20 Coci *B.*

21 Coci *B.*

22 Radulfo *B.*

23 Raoul I, lord of Housset (cant. Sains, https://dicotopo.cths.fr/places/P27336521), appears as a witness to acts, primarily of the lords of Coucy, between 1147 and 1187. Barthélemy, *LDA*, 519–20.

24 Radulfo *B.*

25 Raoul Chien (d. ca. 1191), son of Gautier de la Tournelle and Agnès, appears in episcopal acts from the 1140s and was particularly associated with the lords of Coucy. Barthélemy, *LDA*, 160; Morelle, "Une charte nuptiale laonnoise de 1158 conservée en original," 223, fn. 69.

26 Likely Hector, son of Gile, lady of Aulnois, and husband of Marguerite, who appears in a number of mid-twelfth-century acts as *miles, dominus et civis Lauduni* and who was *maior* of the commune of Laon in 1158 and 1164. Saint-Denis, *Apogée d'une cité*, 221.

27 Symone *B.*

28 Amegni *B.*

29 Simon I, lord of Amigny (cant. Chauny, https://dicotopo.cths.fr/places/P65669952), ca. 1178–84. Melleville, *DH*, vol. 1, 21.

30 Pierre, chamberlain of Raoul I de Coucy, appears as a witness in acts 1166–90. Barthélemy, *LDA*, 393.

31 Gwidone *B.*

32 Likely Saint-Paul-aux-Bois, cant. Coucy-le-Château, https://dicotopo.cths.fr/places/P45354298.

33 Cociacum *B.*

34 Reinardo *B.*

35 Robert is the earliest attested mayor of Coucy-la-Ville. Mabire La Caille, "Château, bourg castral, Villeneuve," 167.

36 Coci *B.*

domini Hugonis[37] Premonstrati abbatis, affuerunt cum eo Willelmus[38] abbas de Cartovoro,[39] Ellebaudus[40] abbas Loci Restaurati, Simon,[41] Hermannus, Willelmus fratres Premonstrati et sacerdotes.

79

1173

Raoul [I],[1] *lord of Coucy, gives in alms to the church of Prémontré 20* solidi Proveniensium *to be received annually on the Feast of the Circumcision of Christ (January 1), to be collected from his* vinagium *at Coucy. (See* ***88****.)*

A. Cartulary of Prémontré, fol. 21v.

B. Original not found.

EDITION: Du Chesne, *Histoire genealogique des maisons de Guines, d'Ardres, de Gand, et de Coucy*, 347 (partial); Hugo, *prob.* 1, cols. xxi–xxii.

Karta Radulphi de Couci super elemosina XX[ti] solidorum Proveniensium.

[E]go Radulphus, dominus de Couciaco, notum fieri volo tam futuris quam presentibus quod, ob remedium anime uxoris mee Agnetis et antecessorum meorum, dedi in elemosinam ecclesie de Premonstrato viginti solidos Proveniensium hereditate perpetua, quos fratres de Premonstrato singulis annis accipient in Circuncisione Domini apud Couciacum de winagio meo. Ut autem irrefragabiliter hec elemosina permaneat et sine calumpnia persolvatur, sigilli mei impressione et legitimorum testium astipulatione presentem kartem muniri feci. S. Ingravi,[2] abbatis Sancti Medardi. S. Ingelranni,[3] abbatis

37 Hugues II de Douai, abbot of the Premonstratensian abbey of Cuissy, 1161–5, and abbot of Prémontré, 1174–89. *MP* II, 497.

38 Guillaume Hennepaix, abbot of the Premonstratensian abbey of Cuissy, 1170–4, of the Premonstratensian abbey of Bucilly, 1176–8, and of the Premonstratensian abbey of Chartreuve, 1178–85. *MP* II, 366, 494, 497.

39 Cartavoro *B*.

40 Erlebaud, abbot of the Premonstratensian abbey of Lieu-Restauré, 1172–9. *MP* II, 514.

41 Symon *B*.

1 Raoul I, lord of Coucy (d. 1191), son of Enguerrand II, lord of Coucy, and Agnès de Beaugency.

2 Ingramm, abbot of the Benedictine abbey of Saint-Médard de Soissons, 1148–77. Poquet, *Pélerinage à l'ancienne abbaye de Saint-Médard-lès-Soissons*, 41.

3 Enguerrand, abbot of the Benedictine abbeys of Nogent-sous-Coucy, 1157–ca. 1160, and of Saint-Jean de Laon, 1161–82. *GC* IX, col. 607; Taïée, "L'abbaye de Saint-Jean de Laon," 217.

Sancti Johannis Laudunensis. S. Willelmi,[4] abbatis Sancti Nicholai. S. Johannis castellani.[5] S. Hectoris vicedomini Laudunensis.[6] S. Simonis de Couciaco. S. Warneri. S. Hugonis, clerici. S. Petri, camerarii.[7] S. Petri, cancellarii mei.[8] Actum anno verbi incarnati millesimo centesimo septuagesimo tercio.

80

1207

*Enguerrand [III],[1] lord of Coucy, confirms gifts made by his father, Raoul [I],[2] his grandfather, Enguerrand [II, lord of Coucy],[3] and his great-grandfather, Thomas [de Marle].[4] (See **78**.)*

A. Cartulary of Prémontré, fol. 21v.[5]

B. Original not found.

EDITION: Du Chesne, *Histoire genealogique des Maisons de Guines, d'Ardres, de Gand, et de Coucy*, 358; Le Paige, *Bibliotheca*, 923; Hugo, *prob.* 1, col. xxiii.

REGISTER: Bréquigny, *Table chronologique*, vol. 3, 412.

NO RUBRIC. LATER ADDITION.

Ego Ingelrannus, dominus Couciaci, notifico per hoc scriptum presentibus et futuris quod bone memorie Radulphus, pater meus, recognovit, cum adhuc

---

4 Guillaume I, abbot of the Benedictine abbey of Saint-Nicolas-aux-Bois, ca. 1168–ca. 1180. Duval, "Histoire de l'abbaye bénédictine de Saint-Nicolas-aux-Bois, diocèse de Laon, première partie," 198–200.

5 Jean I, castellan of Noyon and Thourotte, son of Guy II, castellan of Coucy, and Théophanie, is attested 1150s–1170s. Barthélemy, *LDA*, 508–9.

6 Likely Hector, son of Gile, lady of Aulnois, and husband of Marguerite, who appears in a number of mid-twelfth-century acts as *miles, dominus et civis Lauduni* and who was *maior* of the commune of Laon in 1158 and 1164. Saint-Denis, *Apogée d'une cité*, 221.

7 Pierre, chamberlain of Raoul I de Coucy, appears as a witness in acts 1166–90. Barthélemy, *LDA*, 393.

8 Pierre, chancellor of Raoul I de Coucy, appears as a witness in acts 1170–91. Barthélemy, *LDA*, 393.

---

1 Enguerrand III de Boves, lord of Coucy (ca. 1182–1242), son of Raoul I, lord of Coucy, and Alix de Dreux.

2 Raoul I, lord of Coucy (d. 1191), son of Enguerrand II, lord of Coucy, and Agnès de Beaugency.

3 Enguerrand II de Coucy (d. ca. 1149), son of Thomas de Marle, lord of Coucy, and his third wife, Mélisende de Crécy-sur-Serre.

4 Thomas de Marle, lord of Coucy and Marle (ca. 1073–1130), son of Enguerrand I, lord of Coucy, and Adèle de Marle.

5 This act is written in the lower margin of the folio.

viveret, et concessit in perpetuum elemosinas et aisentias quas avus suus Thomas et Ingelrannus, pater suus, contulerunt fratribus Premonstrate ecclesie perpetuo possidendas et redegit in scripto auctentico per hec verba: In nomine Patris et Filii et Spiritus sancti, amen. Ego Radulphus et ceteris in supra verbo ad verbum et infra. Post mortem denique predicti patris mei. Ego Ingelrannus ad quem ratione primogeniti ipsius devoluta est hereditas requisitus a prefate ecclesie abbate et fratribus omnes prescriptas elemosinas et aisentias ad exemplar felicis memorie. Radulphi patris mei benigne recognovi concessi et confirmavi Premonstrate ecclesie possidendas ut autem concessio et confirmatio huius firma et stabilis perseveret presenti scripto in perpetuum valituro sigillum meum feci inprimi et apponi. Actum anno ab incarnatione Domini M° CC° septimo.

81

July, 1221.

Enguerrand [III],[1] *lord of Coucy, makes known that the abbot and brothers of Prémontré purchased land at Ferrières rendering about 18* galeti *of seed grain, measure of La Ferté, from Anselme de Fay,*[2] *who held it from knight Guillaume de la Ferté,*[3] *who in turn held it in fief from Enguerrand.*

A. Cartulary of Prémontré, fol. 22r.

B. Original, AD Aisne, H 800, previously sealed with a double strip of parchment.

Karta Ingelranni de Couci de terra Anselmi de Fai quam emimus.

[E]go Ingelrannus, dominus de[4] Couciaco,[5] notum facio universis tam presentibus quam futuris quod dilecti et familiares mei abbas et fratres Premonstratenses acquisierunt per emptionem ab Anselmo de Fai quandam terram sitam in territorio suo de Fericres, circiter decem et octo galetos sementis, capientem, ad mensuram Firmitatis. Quia vero eandem terram tenebat dictus

1 Enguerrand III de Boves, lord of Coucy (ca. 1182–1242), son of Raoul I, lord of Coucy, and Alix de Dreux.

2 Anselme, lord of Fay-le-Noyer, attested 1210s–20s. Melleville, *DH*, vol. 1, 374. He and his wife Elizabeth (or Isabel) also made a gift to the abbey of Saint-Nicolas-des-Prés de Ribemont in 1218. Stein, *Cartulaire de l'ancienne abbaye de Saint Nicolas des Prés sous Ribemont*, 127–8.

3 La Ferté-Chevresis, cant. Ribemont, https://dicotopo.cths.fr/places/P35438398.

4 *Add.* de *A*.

5 Cociaci *B*.

Anselmus de Willermo[6] de Firmitate milite in feodum et idem Willelmus de me, ego ad petitionem dictorum fratrum, ne aliquis possit contra eos in posterum malignari, super emptione prefata, concessi eis presentes literas[7] testimoniales, sigilli mei munimine roboratas. Actum mense julio, anno gratie M° CC° vicesimo primo.

82

May, 1232. Church of Prémontré.

Enguerrand [III],[1] *lord of Coucy, makes known that on the occasion of the dedication of a church at Prémontré, he gave in alms to the religious of Prémontré 100* solidi Parisiensium *to be collected annually from the* census *of Faucoucourt.*[2]

A. Cartulary of Prémontré, fol. 22r.
B. Original not found.

Karta Ingelranni de Couci de elemosine quam dedit ecclesie Premonstrato.

Ingelrannus,[3] dominus Couciaci, universis tam presentibus quam futuris in Domino salutem. Noverint universi quod, cum viri religiosi et karissimi mei in Christo Conradus, abbas, et conventus Premonstratensis, temporibus meis, per Dei gratiam ecclesiam suam fecissent, sicut decebat, sollempniter dedicari, nolentes ut eadem ecclesia que in dominio meo specialiter est fundata, in tanta sollempnitate liberalitatis mee munere privaretur ex speciali devotione et devota dilectione quam habeo erga ecclesiam supradictam, obtuli et dedi in puram, liberam et perpetuam elemosinam ad dotem ipsius ecclesie quiete et pacifice in perpetuum possidendos centum solidos Parisiensium percipiendos, annis singulis in perpetuum ab ecclesia eadem ad census meos de Foucaucort in festo Omnium Sanctorum; ita quod si dicti centum solidi forsitan, quod absit, negentur vel non reddantur termino constituto, tam ego quam heredes mei sicut de proprio censu meo compellere tenemur, tamquam superior dominus, eos

6 Willelmo *B*.
7 litteras *B*.

1 Enguerrand III de Boves, lord of Coucy (ca. 1182–1242), son of Raoul I, lord of Coucy, and Alix de Dreux.
2 Faucoucourt, cant. Anizy-le-Château, https://dicotopo.cths.fr/places/P22159528.
3 The initial letter has been added at a later, possibly post-medieval date.

qui dictos census debent ut prefatos centum solidos nodo predicto solvant et reddant integraliter ecclesie sepedicte. Ut autem hec oblatio et donatio rata et firma perpetuo perseveret, presentem kartam eidem ecclesie tradidi sigilli mei appensione munitam. Actum in ecclesia Premonstratensi, mense maio, anno gratie millesimo ducentesimo tricesimo secundo.

83

April 17, 1210.

Enguerrand [III, lord] of Coucy,[1] *having sold a part of his forest of Vois*[2] *to the king's* prepositus, *Guy de Béthisy,*[3] *to Soibert,*[4] *and to their associates the* bourgeois *of Laon, grants in recompense to the religious of Prémontré the same rights of usage of the dead wood at* Seignorimont *as they had held at Vois.*

A. Cartulary of Prémontré, fol. 22r.

B. Original not found.

Karta domini Ingelranni de usuario que habemus in foresta de Voiz.

Ego[5] Ingelrannus, dominus Couciaci, tam futuris quam presentibus notum facio per hoc scriptum quod, cum fratres ecclesie Premonstrati in foresta mea de Vooiz in mortuo nemore suum perpetuo haberent usuarium, quandam partem ipsius foreste pro mea necessitate vendidi preposito regis, Guidoni de Bestisi et Sigeberto et sociis suis, burgensibus Laudunensibus. Nolo igitur ut, occasione huius venditionis, processu temporis, dicti fratres in usuario suo detrimentum sustineant aut jacturam, sed omni tempore post venditionem factam burgensibus supradictis per forestam meam ad usuarium suum et ad pendentia sua quorum partem predicti burgenses inciderunt apud Seignorimont, supra

---

1 Enguerrand III de Boves, lord of Coucy (ca. 1182–1242), son of Raoul I, lord of Coucy, and Alix de Dreux.

2 Forest of Vois, https://dicotopo.cths.fr/places/P93994197.

3 Guy de Béthisy, king's *bailli* and *prepositus*, operated out of Laon with a sphere of activity extending from Noyon in the west to Reims in the southeast. Bouquet and Delisle, eds., *Recueil des historiens des Gaules et de la France*, vol. 24, part 1, 58; Baldwin, *The Government of Philip Augustus*, 130, 133.

4 Soibert, *bourgeois* of Laon, was a king's *bailli* from 1216. Bouquet and Delisle, eds., *Recueil des historiens des Gaules et de la France*, vol. 24, part 1, 53–6; Baldwin, *The Government of Philip Augustus*, 131, 133.

5 The initial letter has been added at a later, possibly post-medieval date.

campum ecclesie Premonstratensis qui est a latere Huberti Pontis,[6] liberum habeant recursum, prout tam in scripto meo quod penes se habent quam in antecessorum meorum auctenticis continetur. Quod ut perpetuis temporibus firmiter observetur, presens scriptum factum in testimonium huius rei sigilli mei impressione munivi. Actum quinto decimo kalendas maii, anno gratie millesimo ducentesimo decimo.

84

May, 1232. Church of Prémontré.

Enguerrand [III, lord] of Coucy,[1] *makes known that he gave in alms to the church of Prémontré 10* librae Parisiensium *to be collected annually from the* census *of Faucoucourt*[2] *for the celebration of his anniversary after his death.*

A. Cartulary of Prémontré, fol. 22r.
B. Original not found.

Karta Ingelranni de X[cem] libris post decessum suum.

[I]ngelrannus, dominus Couciaci, universis tam presentibus quam futuris in Domino salutem. Noverint universi quod, habens respectum ad dilectionem quam habeo specialiter erga karissimos meos fratres Premonstratensis ecclesie, ob remedium anime mee, contuli et dedi libere eidem ecclesie Premonstratensi in puram et perpetuum elemosinam pro anniversario meo, annis singulis, in eadem ecclesia faciendo decem libras Parisiensium accipiendos, annis singulis, in perpetuum post decessum meum ad census meos qui debentur michi apud Foukoucourt in festo Omnium Sanctorum; ita quod post decessum meum, quicquid de me contingat in futurum, eadem ecclesia Premonstratensis dictas decem libras percipiet in perpetuum in villa predicta termino supradicto, hoc adjecto quod si dicte decem libre forsitan, quod absit, eidem ecclesie negarentur vel non solverentur termino constituto, tam heredes mei quam servientes eorum tamquam de proprio censu suo tenerentur ad compellendum eos qui debent reddere dictos census ut dictas decem libras Parisiensium modo supradicto solvant et reddant annis singulis integraliter ecclesie sepedicte. In cuius rei testimonium et perpetuam firmitatem presentes literas eidem ecclesie

6 Hubertpont, comm. Prémontré, https://dicotopo.cths.fr/places/P71559674.

1 Enguerrand III de Boves, lord of Coucy (ca. 1182–1242), son of Raoul I, lord of Coucy, and Alix de Dreux.

2 Faucoucourt, cant. Anizy-le-Château, https://dicotopo.cths.fr/places/P22159528.

tradidi sigillo meo munitas. Actum mense maio, in ecclesia Premonstratensi, anno gratie M° CC° tricesimo secundo.

85

June, 1228.

Enguerrand [III, lord] of Coucy[1] *gives to the church of Prémontré an alder grove located between the causeway of the* leprosarium *at Basce*[2] *and the mill at Bassoles*[3] *to make into a meadow, since he had taken meadows Prémontré had held at Briquenay*[4] *and Saint-Lambert.*[5]

A. Cartulary of Prémontré, fols. 22r–22v.
B. Original, AD Aisne, H 818, previously sealed with a double strip of parchment.

Karta Ingelranni de restitutione quorundam pratorum.

Ego[6] Ingelrannus, dominus Couciaci,[7] notum facio[8] tam presentibus quam futuris quod, cum deberem prata restituere ecclesie Premonstratensi pro pratis suis que occupavi apud Brikenai et apud Sanctum Lambertum, ego, habito consilio et deliberatione, dedi in perpetuum ipsi ecclesie Premonstratensi ad omnimodas commoditates suas unum alnetum quod situm est inter calceatam domus leprosorum de Basce[9] et molendinum quod erat tempore huius scripti subtus villam de Baschole, sicut fossata et mete hinc inde posite se proportant, ad sartandum et ad faciendum inde pratum ita quod pratum ipsum de me et de meis warandire tenebor et per restitutionem istius prati quitavit me ecclesia predicta de omnibus pratis suis que occupaveram usque ad tempus presentium literarum. Sciendum est autem quod alneta, dumos et alias arbores sique vel ad presens vel in futurum excreverint vel pullulaverint infra ambitum tocius prati predicti, poterit ecclesia Premonstratensis demere, sartare, extirpare sine forisfacto et emenda et facere de eodem prato et de territorio prati sicut de suo

1 Enguerrand III de Boves, lord of Coucy (ca. 1182–1242), son of Raoul I, lord of Coucy, and Alix de Dreux.
2 Basce, comm. Quincy-Basce, https://dicotopo.cths.fr/places/P14475073.
3 Bassoles, cant. Anizy-le-Château, https://dicotopo.cths.fr/places/P97208516.
4 Briquenay, comm. Saint-Gobain, https://dicotopo.cths.fr/places/P47400428.
5 Saint-Lambert, comm. Fourdrain, https://dicotopo.cths.fr/places/P30848534.
6 The initial letter has been added at a later, possibly post-medieval date.
7 Cociaci *B*.
8 *Om.* universis *A*.
9 Basche *B*.

et sciendum quod pratum ipsum dedi ipsi ecclesie liberum ab omni censu et consuetudine. Que omnia ut in perpetuum rata sint et firma, presentem kartam super hoc confectam sigilli mei feci munimine roborari. Actum mense junio, anno gratie millesimo CC° vicesimo octavo.

86

1207

Alix,[1] *lady of Coucy, reaches an agreement with the religious of Prémontré, in the presence of Étienne [I],*[2] *bishop of Noyon, in which she concedes to Prémontré the free possession of a fishpond at Coucy-la-Ville; the woods of Tristre-de-Pinon*[3] *in exchange for an annual* census *of 10* librae, *5* solidi Suessionensium*; and the meadow of Garnier in exchange for an annual* census *of one* denarius. *She also authorizes those men who are neither obliged to pay her the* tallia *nor subject to the* assisia *to grind freely at the mill of Coucy-la-Ville; confirms a gift made by her husband Raoul [I, lord of Coucy]*[4] *for the soul of his first wife Agnès,*[5] *as well as a gift made by* magister *Pierre for Raoul's soul, both to be collected annually from the* wionagium *of Coucy; and acknowledges the established boundary between her land and Prémontré's.*

A. Cartulary of Prémontré, fol. 22v.

B. Original, AD Aisne, H 775, sealed with a partial fragment on blue and white linen thread.

Karta domine Aelidis de Couci de quadam pace inter nos et ipsam.

Ego[6] Aelidis,[7] domina Couciaci,[8] tam futuris quam presentibus, notum facio per hoc scriptum quod, cum inter me et fratres Premonstratenses super vivario

1 Alix de Dreux (ca. 1157–aft. 1217), daughter of Robert I, count of Dreux, and Agnès II, lady of Braine; second wife of Raoul I, lord of Coucy.

2 Étienne de Villebéon (or de Nemours), son of Gautier de Villebéon, lord of La Chapelle-Gauthier and Nemours, and Aveline, was bishop of Noyon, 1188–1221.

3 Comm. Pinon, https://dicotopo.cths.fr/places/P46620646.

4 Raoul I, lord of Coucy (d. 1191), son of Enguerrand II, lord of Coucy, and Agnès de Beaugency.

5 Agnès de Hainaut (d. ca. 1174), daughter of Baudouin IV, count of Hainaut, and Alix de Namur; first wife of Raoul I, lord of Coucy.

6 The initial letter has been added at a later, possibly post-medieval date.

7 Adelidis *B*.

8 Cochiaci *B*.

et molendino Couci[9] Ville et nemore del Tristre de Pinum[10] cum prato Garneri et terris de Roseriis[11] et quibusdam redditibus verteretur querela, ego tandem bonorum virorum usa consilio, presente et mediatore reverendo patre Stephano, Noviomensi episcopo, vivarium supradictum, sicut maritus meus Radulphus illis in elemosinam ex hereditario suo concesserat, ex dotalicio meo liberum eis concessi perpetuo possidendum. Quam concessionem a me factam postea in generali abbatum capitulo recognovi. Nemus quoque del Tristre secundum quod posite mete perportant, sub annuo censu ~~decem~~ XI[12] librarum Suessionensium monete quinque solidis minus illis concessi, similiter et pratum Garneri sub annuo censu unius denarii eiusdem monete. Volo etiam et benigne permitto ut homines qui de tallia et assisia mea non sunt ad molendinum ipsorum de Couci Villa[13] libere veniant ad molendum. Recognovi quoque eis viginti solidos Proveniensium quos eis pro domine Agnete, quondam uxore mariti mei Radulphi, debeo annuatim secundum formam scripti ipsius Radulphi. Recognovi quoque alios viginti solidos Laudunensium quos magister Petrus pro anima mariti mei Radulphi contulit ecclesie Premonstrati, accipiendos ad wionagia de Couci[14] in crastino Purificationis Beate Marie. Porro et metas, que proclivia montium adiacentium, Premonstrato ex parte nemoris mei distingunt, secundum quod eas posuerunt ministeriales mei et servientes filii mei Ingelranni cum fratribus ipsius ecclesie, ratas habeo et meo confirmo assensu pariter et sigillo. Omnes quoque querele quas usque in diem huius scripti adversus eosdem fratres habebam vel me habere credebam, per istam concordiam sunt sopite. Ipsi quoque fratres, si quid in eos ante deliqueram, michi, quantum ad eos attinet, indulserunt. Ut autem predicta omnia inviolabilia perseverent, presens scriptum sigilli mei impressione roboravi. Actum anno dominice incarnationis millesimo ducentesimo[15] septimo.

87

April, 1264.

Enguerrand [IV],[1] *lord of Coucy, Sissy, and Montmirail, concedes annually to Prémontré 21* galeti *of grain (*bladus*), measure of Coucy, in compensation*

9 Cocivilla *B*.
10 Pynun *B*.
11 Rozières, cant. Oulchy-le-Château, https://dicotopo.cths.fr/places/P75685266.
12 *Superscr. A*; undecim *B*.
13 Cocivilla *B*.
14 Coci *B*.
15 M° CC° *B*.

1 Enguerrand IV (d. 1310), lord of Coucy, son of Enguerrand III, lord of Coucy, and Marie de Montmirail.

for rights that were previously held by Prémontré but which Enguerrand then gave to the Benedictine abbey of Saint-Nicolas-aux-Bois, namely the rights to collect dead wood and to pasture animals in part of the forest of Vois.[2] *Enguerrand keeps the road through the forest that leads to Crépy*[3] *for Premonstratensian use and promises to maintain it.*

A. Cartulary of Prémontré, fol. 22v.[4]
B. Original not found.

NO RUBRIC. LATER ADDITION.

Ingelrannus, dominus Couciaci, Cisaci, et Montismirelli, notum facio presentibus et futuris quod, cum fratres ecclesie Premonstratensis habeant usuarium ad Mortuum Nemus in foresta de Vois et pascua animalibus, ut in litteris predecessorum nostrorum super hoc confectis plenius continetur, et ego dederim monachis Sancti Nicolai in Bosco decem modiatas vel circiter illius foreste prope pasturagia de Crespiaco ad locum [f]losse Brienoise et alibi, in qua parte dicti fratres Premonstratenses suum habebant usuarium, ut dictum est, nolens quod ipsi, occasione predicta, in aliquo dampnificentur vel sustineant detrimentum, concessi dictis Premonstratensibus et quictavi et [lacuna] pro dicto usuario quem habebant in dicto loco dato monachis predictis, in recompensationem usuarii predicti, XXI galetos bladi ad mensuram Cociaci quem[5] habebam et percipiebam singulis annis in curte ipsorum que vocatur [lacuna], salvo viam dictis Premonstratensibus, via illa que ducit apud Crespiacum per forestam, predictam sive per partem illius foreste dictis de Sancto Nicolao date, quam viam teneor eisdem Premonstratensibus deliberare ac warandire in perpetuum [lacuna/illegible] quod absit non potuero eis dictam viam deliberare sive warandire, ut dictum est, ego aliam viam assignabo dictis fratribus Premonstratensibus ad petitionem ipsorum in nemore meo sive in foresta predicta, per assensum [lacuna] ubi melius sibi viderint expedire. Insuper si occasione vie predicte vel etiam dicte recompensationis incurrerent aliqua dampna, teneor eis omnia dampna vel deperdita restituere. Et ad hec omnia observata firmiter [h]eredes meos et successores in perpetuum per presentes literas obligavi. In cuius rei testimonium presentes literas emisi sigilli mei munimine roboratas. Datum anno Domini M° CC° LXIIII°, mense aprili.

---

2 Forest of Vois, https://dicotopo.cths.fr/places/P93994197.

3 Crépy, cant. Laon, https://dicotopo.cths.fr/places/P85331504.

4 This charter is written in the bottom margin of the folio. Parts are illegible due to later cropping of the folio.

5 *Sic A, read* quos.

88

1207

Enguerrand [III] of Coucy[1] *confirms by* vidimus *the gift in alms made to the brothers of the church of Prémontré by Raoul [I], his father, in an act from 1178. (See* ***79****.)*

A. Cartulary of Prémontré, fols. 22v–23r.

B. Original, SAHSS, *casier* 2, no. 19, previously sealed with yellow and green silk thread.

EDITION: Hugo, *prob.* 1, col. xxiii.

Karta domini Ingelranni de Couci de confirmatione scriptorum predecessorum suorum.

[E]go Ingelrannus, dominus Couciaci,[2] notifico per hoc scriptum presentibus et futuris quod bone memorie Radulphus,[3] pater meus, recognovit, cum adhuc viveret, et concessit in perpetuum elemosinas et aisentias quas avus suus Thomas et Ingelrannus, pater suus, contulerunt fratribus Premonstrate ecclesie perpetuo possidendas et redegit in scripto auctentico per hec verba: In nomine Patris et Filii et Spiritus Sancti, amen. Ego Radulphus,[4] dominus Couciaci,[5] notum fieri volo tam presentibus quam futuris quod amore Dei ductus et desiderio salutis mee et predecessorum meorum[6] pariterque heredum meorum recognovi et concessi in perpetuum elemosinas et aisentias quas avus meus Thomas et Ingelrannus, pater meus, contulerunt fratribus Premonstrate ecclesie perpetuo possidendas, videlicet quicquid juris vel consuetudinis habebat avus meus predictus in loco, qui Premonstratus dicitur, remisit fratribus ibidem Deo servientibus et servituris, valles etiam omnes Premonstrato adjacentes et proclivia montium sicut valles perportant ex quibus fratres partim sartaverant et residuum se posse sartare asserebant sed optinui apud eos quod deinceps in eis non sartabitur sed nemus vallium et pendentium ad opus edificiorum suorum et aliarum necessitatum suarum reservabunt. Concessit etiam idem avus meus eis usuarium de mortuo nemore in foresta de Vooiz[7,8] et pascua

1 Enguerrand III de Boves, lord of Coucy (ca. 1182–1242), son of Raoul I, lord of Coucy, and Alix de Dreux.
2 Cociaci *B*.
3 Radulfus *B*.
4 Radulfus *B*.
5 Cociaci *B*.
6 *Add.* meorum *A*.
7 Voois *B*.
8 Forest of Vois, https://dicotopo.cths.fr/places/P93994197.

animalibus suis. Dedit quoque ipsis locum qui Rosieres[9] dicitur et de propria terra sua unam carrucatam que omnia predicte ecclesie fratres in diebus eiusdem avi mei et in diebus patris mei quiete possederunt. Cum autem locus prefatus qui Rosieres dicitur[10] ampliari cepisset et per universos fines tocius orbis dilatari, pater meus qui locum illum plurimum dilexit, paterne liberalitatis emulator, concessit eiusdem loci fratribus terragium et decimam de Vervin, terragium de Aegnies,[11] terragium de Couci[12] Villa exceptis duobus modiis hyemalis annone qui persolvuntur ecclesie Beate Marie Nongenti, vivarium etiam cum molendino juxta eandem villam videlicet Couci,[13] feodum quoque et partem decime de Vassen; remisit etiam eis winagium in omni loco terre sue ubi ab alienis accipiebatur nisi de re qua ematur ut iterum venalis exponenda deferatur. Ego itaque qui beneficia et elemosinas avi mei sive patris mei minuere non appeto neque servientes Deo super elemosinis sibi collatis vexari desidero, ea que predicta sunt benigne eis recognovi et concessi et quod eis in pace facerem possidere promisi. Unde volo quod servientes mei et heredum meorum de hiis omnibus pacem eis ferant. Quod si pro quacumque, occasione wagia eorum ceperint vel ad me ea deferant sive adducant apud Couciacum[14] vel in vicinia, si presens fuero, aut eis recredant usque ad reditum meum et tunc res michi notificabitur et ut res pacifice et rationabiliter valeat terminari mittam, si voluero, ad veritatem cognoscendam. Volo enim ut pax eius[15] conservetur et ut a servientibus meis non inquietentur. Quia vero moleste ferebam quod tot nove vie vel ab ipsis vel ab aliis fiebant in foresta mea, vias eis assignari feci per quas bona eorum libere et quiete adduci poterunt et reduci, videlicet viam per Anleirs,[16] viam per longum Buellum, viam juxta Rosieres, viam per Septem Valles,[17] viam que ducit Crispiacum[18] et que ducit ad Sanctum Nicholaum et que ducit per Broiencourt[19,20] et que ducit versus Anisiacum.[21,22] Has vias concedo liberas et quittas karris eorum et karretis. Quia igitur et ea que predicta sunt et omnia que de feodatis et hominibus meis in omni posse

---

9 Rozières, cant. Oulchy-le-Château, https://dicotopo.cths.fr/places/P75685266.

10 *Rep. and homeo.* qui Rosieres dicitur *A*.

11 Aengnies *B*.

12 Coci *B*.

13 Coci *B*.

14 Cociacum *B*.

15 eis *B*.

16 Anlers *B*.

17 Septvaux, cant. Coucy-le-Château, https://dicotopo.cths.fr/places/P39910999.

18 Crépy, cant. Laon, https://dicotopo.cths.fr/places/P85331504.

19 Broiencurt *B*.

20 Brancourt, cant. Anizy-le-Château, https://dicotopo.cths.fr/places/P91051513.

21 Anysiacum *B*.

22 Anizy-le-Château, arr. Laon, https://dicotopo.cths.fr/places/P86940236.

meo tempore huius scripti tenebant, benigne eis concessi, ipsi versa vice dederunt michi advocatiam suam de Sorni,[23] salvis redditibus et possessionibus eorum et omnibus que ibidem habent preter justiciam eiusdem ville. Ita sane quod eum quem sibi maiorem in eadem villa constituent per singulos annos ad querendos et recipiendos redditus suos liberum habebunt ab omni tallia, ab omni exactione et requisitione et, si forifecerit, per abbatem Premonstratensem emendabit aut, si nollet, per me michi emendaret. Convenit autem inter me et ipsos quod advocatia illa nonquam alienabitur a domino de Couci[24] sed qui erit dominus de Couci,[25] erit advocatus de Sorni. Ut igitur hec concessio predecessorum meorum et mea rata et inconcussa perpetuo prefate Premonstrate ecclesie permaneat presenti scripto et sigilli mei appositione et hominum meorum qui interfuerunt annotatione feci roborari. Actum Lauduni anno incarnationis dominice M° C° LXX° VIII° presentibus hominibus meis Radulpho[26] de Hussel,[27] Radulpho[28] Cane,[29] Hectore,[30] Simone[31] de Amigni,[32,33] Petro camerario,[34] Guidone de Sancto Paulo.[35] Postmodum autem cum presens scriptum facerem confirmari recognovi iterum apud Couciacum[36] coram istis Petro capellano meo, Reinardo de Foro, Roberto maiore de Couci[37,38] et Mauberto servientibus meis, ex parte autem domini Hugonis[39] Premonstrati abbatis affuerunt

23 Sorny, cant. Vailly, https://dicotopo.cths.fr/places/P79681466.

24 Coci *B*.

25 Coci *B*.

26 Radulfo *B*.

27 Raoul I, lord of Housset (cant. Sains, https://dicotopo.cths.fr/places/P27336521), appears as a witness to acts, primarily of the lords of Coucy, between 1147 and 1187. Barthélemy, *LDA*, 519–20.

28 Radulfo *B*.

29 Raoul Chien (d. ca. 1191), son of Gautier de la Tournelle and Agnès, appears in episcopal acts from the 1140s and was particularly associated with the lords of Coucy. Barthélemy, *LDA*, 160; Morelle, "Une charte nuptiale laonnoise de 1158 conservée en original," 223, fn. 69.

30 Likely Hector, son of Gile, lady of Aulnois, and husband of Marguerite, who appears in a number of mid-twelfth-century acts as *miles, dominus et civis Lauduni* and who was *maior* of the commune of Laon in 1158 and 1164. Saint-Denis, *Apogée d'une cité*, 221.

31 Symone *B*.

32 Amegni *B*.

33 Simon I, lord of Amigny (cant. Chauny, https://dicotopo.cths.fr/places/P65669952), ca. 1178–84. Melleville, *DH*, vol. 1, 21.

34 Pierre, chamberlain of Raoul I de Coucy, appears as a witness in acts 1166–90. Barthélemy, *LDA*, 393.

35 Saint-Paul-aux-Bois, cant. Coucy-le-Château, https://dicotopo.cths.fr/places/P45354298.

36 Cociacum *B*.

37 Coci *B*.

38 Robert is the earliest attested mayor of Coucy-la-Ville. Mabire La Caille, "Château, bourg castral, Villeneuve," 167.

39 Hugues II de Douai, abbot of the Premonstratensian abbey of Cuissy, 1161–5, and abbot of Prémontré, 1174–89. *MP* II, 497.

cum eo Willermus[40,41] abbas de Cartovoro, Ellebaudus[42] abbas Loci Restaurati, Symon, Hermannus, Willelmus, fratres Premonstrati et sacerdotes. Post mortem denique predicti patris mei ego Ingelrannus ad quem ratione primogeniti ipsius devoluta est hereditas requisitus a prefate ecclesie abbate et fratribus, omnes prescriptas elemosinas et aisentias ad exemplar felicis memorie R[adulphi] patris mei benigne recognovi, concessi et confirmavi Premonstrate ecclesie possidendas. Ut autem concessio et confirmatio huiusmodi firma et stabilis perseveret, presenti scripto in perpetuum valituro, sigillum meum feci inprimi[43] et apponi. Actum anno ab incarnatione Domini millesimo CC°[44] septimo.

89

July, 1212.

Enguerrand [III] of Coucy[1] *gives to Prémontré a hedge located near the field of Rozières*[2] *and all of the alder grove beneath the* Halipré *road to make a meadow, in exchange for having used two* falcae *of Prémontré's meadow when digging his pond below Barizis.*[3]

A. Cartulary of Prémontré, fol. 23r.
B. Original not found.

Karta domini Ingelranni de Couci de quodam excambio.

Ego,[4] Ingelrannus, dominus Couciaci, universis notum facio per hoc scriptum quod dedi ecclesie Premonstratensi, in excambium duarum falcium prati quas

40 Willelmus *B*.
41 Guillaume Hennepaix, abbot of the Premonstratensian abbey of Cuissy, 1170–4, of the Premonstratensian abbey of Bucilly, 1176–8, and of the Premonstratensian abbey of Chartreuve, 1178–85. *MP* II, 366, 494, 497.
42 Erlebaud, abbot of the Premonstratensian abbey of Lieu-Restauré, 1172–9. *MP* II, 514.
43 imprimi *B*.
44 ducentesimo *B*.

1 Enguerrand III de Boves, lord of Coucy (ca. 1182–1242), son of Raoul I, lord of Coucy, and Alix de Dreux.
2 Rozières, cant. Oulchy-le-Château, https://dicotopo.cths.fr/places/P75685266.
3 Barizis, cant. Coucy-le-Château, https://dicotopo.cths.fr/places/P70249408.
4 The initial letter has been added at a later, possibly post-medieval date.
5 *Sic A*, *read* disrumpendam.

ego absorbui in faciendo quodam vivario meo subtus Barisiacum, quandam parvam haiam disrunpendam[5] que erat juxta campum Roseriarum et totum alnetum quod est subtus viam de Haliprei, viam scilicet que ducit Laudunum et que est juxta pratum quod dicitur pratum Thome de Suisi[6] usque ad calciatam Huberti Pontis[7] similiter disrumpendum, sicut Bassaria vallis et marisci proportat, ad faciendum pratum et perpetuo libere possidendum. Ne igitur ecclesia ipsa possit super hoc excambio in posterum molestari, presens scriptum sigilli mei feci impressione muniri. Actum anno Domini millesimo ducentesimo decimo, mense julio.

90

December, 1217.[1]

Anselme [de Mauny],[2] bishop of Laon, makes known that husband and wife Nicolas and Adèle, bourgeois *of Coucy, gave in alms to the religious of Prémontré three vineyards located in Verneuil,[3] and that Prémontré in turn ceded to Nicolas and Adèle for life a vineyard called* Maucovens, *located in the valley below the church of Saint-Sauveur.*

A. Cartulary of Prémontré, fols. 23r–23v.
B. Original not found.

Karta episcopi Laudunensis de elemosina Nicholai.

Anselmus,[4] Dei gratia Laudunensis episcopus, omnibus presentem paginam inspecturis, salutem in omnium Salvatore. Quia ea que ex devotione fidelium religiosis locis in elemosina conferuntur auctoritate ordinarii judicis solent et debent per testimoniales literas confirmari notum fieri volumus per hoc scriptum presentibus et futuris quod Nicholaus, burgensis Couciaci, et Audelvia,

5 *Sic A*, *read* disrumpendam.
6 Suzy, cant. Anizy-le-Château, https://dicotopo.cths.fr/places/P75897317.
7 Hubertpont, comm. Prémontré, https://dicotopo.cths.fr/places/P71559674.

1 Although the cartulary dates this act to 1207, this is almost certainly a scribal error for 1217, as Anselme was not consecrated bishop until 1215.
2 Anselme de Mauny (or de Bercenay), bishop of Laon, 1215–38.
3 Verneuil-sous-Coucy, cant. Coucy-le-Château, https://dicotopo.cths.fr/places/P85264680.
4 The initial letter has been added at a later, possibly post-medieval date.

uxor eius, in nostra et fratrum Premonstratensium presentia constituti, recognoverunt sollempniter se predictis fratribus tres vineas ab eisdem de suo proprio acquisitas in elemosinam contulisse perpetuo ab ipsis fratribus possidendas. Hee autem tres vinee sunt in territorio de Vernuel, quarum due sunt site juxta ortum Petri de Mediavilla et tercia sita est in Vaucello. Preterea predicti Nicholaus et uxor eius, in nostra presentia constituti, publice protestati sunt et recognoverunt quod abbas et fratres Premonstratensis ecclesie quamdam vineam que vocatur Maucovens et sita est in valle subtus ecclesiam Sancti Salvatoris, concesserunt eisdem nomine Premonstratensis ecclesie quamdiu vixerint possidendam; ita quidem quod si alter eorum decesserit, superstes nichilominus ipsam vineam in proprios usus tenebit et post utriusque decessum eadem vinea ad Premonstratensem ecclesiam suam libere revertetur. Ut autem prefate elemosine collatio et possessionis vinee de Maucovent recognitio firma et stabilis habeatur, presentem kartulam in memoriam et testimonium huius rei confectam sigilli nostri munimine fecimus roborari. Actum anno gratie millesimo CC° septimo, mense decembri.

91

1142

Barthélemy,[1] *bishop of Laon, makes known that Boniface, former* prepositus *of Enguerrand [II] of Coucy, Helvide his wife, and their sons Simon, Raoul de Hollande,*[2] *Guy, and Dreux gave to abbot Hugues [I]*[3] *and the church of Prémontré a piece of land and woods contiguous to land near Rozières*[4] *that Thomas [de Marle]*[5] *had previously given to Prémontré.*

A. Cartulary of Prémontré, fol. 23v.

B. Original, AD Aisne, H 777, previously sealed with a double strip of parchment.

EDITION: Dufour-Malbezin, *Actes*, 332–3; *Chartae Galliae,* no. 208368, http://telma.irht.cnrs.fr/outils/chartae-galliae/charte208368/.

---

1 Barthélemy de Jur (d. 1158), son of Conon, lord of Grandson and La Sarraz, and Ada de Roucy; first subdeacon and then treasurer of Reims, later bishop of Laon, 1113–51.

2 Likely Hollande, comm. Ronchères, https://dicotopo.cths.fr/places/P77534604.

3 Hugues I de Fosses (ca. 1093–1164), first abbot of Prémontré.

4 Rozières, cant. Oulchy-le-Château, https://dicotopo.cths.fr/places/P75685266.

5 Thomas de Marle, lord of Coucy and Marle (ca. 1073–1130), son of Enguerrand I, lord of Coucy, and Adèle de Marle.

Karta Bartolomei episcopi Laudunensis de confirmatione elemosine.

[I]n nomine sancte et individue Trinitatis. Officii nostri est fidelium devotiones approbare, oblationes memorie commendare et ex episcopali auctoritate corroborare. Ea propter ego Bartholomeus, Dei gratia Laudunensis episcopus, notum fieri volo tam futuris quam presentibus quod Bonefacius[6] qui erat prepositus domini Ingelranni de Couci, et uxor eius Heluidis[7] et eorum filii Simon,[8,9] Radulphus[10] de Hollande, Wido, Drogo, ob remedium animarum suarum et predecessorum suorum contulerunt Premonstrate ecclesie et Hugoni abbati et fratribus eiusdem[11] ibidem Deo servientibus quandam terram et silvam usibus fratrum profuturam terre illi quam dominus Thomas de Couci[12] dederat juxta curiam de Rosieres[13] contiguam, concedente Ingelranno eiusdem Thome filio, de cuius feodo descendebat. Et ut hoc donum bene et devote factum non possit inmutari, sub annotatione[14] legitimorum testium oblatum est. Quorum hec sunt nomina: Symon de Ribemont,[15,16] Jofridus de Gontran,[17,18] Alardus[19,20] de Porta, Johannes de Aschit,[21] Helgoz de Chauni,[22] Martellus filius Martelli, et Johannes frater eius, et Gerardus[23] armiger ipsorum. Actum est anno dominice incarnationis M° C° XL° II°, indictione IIII[a], epacta III[a], concurrente III°. Quod ut ratum et inconvulsum permaneat in conservatoribus benedictionem, in eis autem qui auferre vel inminuere vel perturbare presumpserint,

---

6 Boniface de Coucy appears as a witness in acts of Enguerrand II de Coucy, 1131–47. Barthelemy, *LDA*, 401–2.

7 Helwidis *B*.

8 Symon *B*.

9 Simon I de Chavigny, son of Boniface de Coucy and Helvide. Barthélemy, *LDA*, 402.

10 Radulfus *B*.

11 eius *B*.

12 Coci *B*.

13 Rosires *B*.

14 annotacione *B*.

15 Ribelmont *B*.

16 Simon I, lord of Ribemont (d. aft. 1161), son of Geoffroi IV, lord of Ribemont. Melleville, *DH*, vol. 2, 277. He appears as a witness in acts of the Benedictine abbey of Homblières 1142–56. Newman, *Homblières*, 107, 111, 113, 126, 149.

17 Josfridus de Contran *B*.

18 Geoffroi de Condren, knight, brother of Sarracin, castellan of La Fère and Laon, and Hugues le Captif de Vendeuil. Newman, *Seigneurs*, vol. 2, 203, 205.

19 Adlardus *B*.

20 Alard I de Ham (or de la Porte), knight of Ham; husband of Helvide. He also appears in **298**, **334**, **385**, **415**, **452**, and **464**.

21 Assis-sur-Serre, cant. Crécy-sur-Serre, https://dicotopo.cths.fr/places/P13973127.

22 Calni *B*.

23 Gerhardus *B*.

dedimus anathematis maledictionem. Signum Bartholomei, thesaurarii.[24] S. Guidonis,[25] decani.[26] S. Roberti, capellani.[27] S. Roberti, presbiteri de Rouci.[28]

92

October, 1173. Laon.

Gautier [II],[1] bishop of Laon, cedes to Prémontré through an intermediary, brother Auger, land at Beaumont[2] that holds six galeti *of seed grain, in exchange for an annual* census *of six* denarii.

A. Cartulary of Prémontré, fol. 23v.

B. Original, AD Aisne, H 745, previously sealed with a double strip of parchment.

Karta Galteri Laudunensis episcopi de quadam terra.

[I]n nomine sancte et individue Trinitatis. Ego Gualterus[3] Dei gratia Laudunensis episcopus, illas nostras concessiones rationabiles, quas firmas in posterum volumus permanere, debemus fideliter attestari. Iccirco[4] notum facimus quos nos, fratri Augero et per eum ecclesie Premonstrati, concessimus de terra nostra ad sementem sex galetorum in monte Bellimontis sub annuo censu sex denariorum. Testes inde sunt: Custeblus maior, Guillelmus Brito cellerarius, Johannes decanus de Lisi,[5] Amisardus Scabinus, ministeriales nostri qui eidem fratri terram limitarunt. Herbertus etiam de Anisi hiis[6] interfuit. Actum dudum apud

24 Barthélemy de Montcornet (d. 1175), son of Hugues de Montcornet and Béatrice de Reynel, was archdeacon of Laon from 1133, treasurer of Laon from 1137, and chancellor of Laon, 1141–4; later archdeacon of Reims; and bishop of Beauvais, 1162–75. Guyotjeannin, *Episcopus*, 131; Dufour-Malbezin, *Actes*, 30.

25 Widonis *B*.

26 Guy de Pierrepont, son of Roger, lord of Pierrepont, and Ermengarde, lady of Montaigu, was first treasurer, archdeacon, and dean of the chapter of Laon, and later bishop of Châlons, 1144–7.

27 Robert, chaplain of Laon, appears as a witness to episcopal acts 1130–50. Dufour Malbezin, *Actes*, 215, 445.

28 Roucy, arr. Laon, https://dicotopo.cths.fr/places/P39468514.

1 Gautier de Mortagne was dean of Laon, ca. 1142–55, and bishop of Laon, 1155–74.

2 Likely Beaumont-en-Beine, cant. Chauny, https://dicotopo.cths.fr/places/P18685379.

3 Galterus *B*.

4 *Sic A*.

5 Lizy, cant. Anizy-le-Château, https://dicotopo.cths.fr/places/P40948829.

6 his *B*.

Anisi.[7] Scriptum postea Lauduni, anno incarnationis dominice M° C° LXX° III°, mense octobri. Guillermus[8,9] cancellarius noster scripsit.

93

1191

Roger,[1] bishop of Laon, makes known that Raoul Chien, with the consent of his wife Cécile, gave in alms to the church of Prémontré all that he possessed in the major and minor tithes of Brancourt.[2] After the death of Raoul, Jean, his son and sole heir, approves his parents' gift, and adds to it, with the consent of his unnamed wife, all the tithes of Basce[3] and Bassoles.[4]

A. Cartulary of Prémontré, fol. 23v.

B. Original, BnF, Coll. Picardie 290, no. 18, previously sealed.

REGISTER: Boghen, "Inventaire des actes épiscopaux originaux conservés à la Bibliothèque nationale (1121–1200)," 116.

Karta episcopi Laudunensis de confirmatione de decime de Broiencourt.

[E]go Rogerus, Dei gratia Laudunensis episcopus. Notum facimus presentibus et futuris quod Radulphus[5] Canis[6] ob remedium anime sue, annuente uxore sua Cecilia, contulit in elemosinam Premonstratensi ecclesie quicquid habebat in maiori et in minuta decima de Broiencourt.[7] Post decessum autem eiusdem Radulphi, filius suus Johannes, ad quem universa patris sui spectabat hereditas,

7 Anizy-le-Château, arr. Laon, https://dicotopo.cths.fr/places/P86940236.

8 Guillelmus *B*.

9 Guillaume, chancellor of the bishop of Laon, is attested 1173–1201. BnF, MS. lat. 11073, fol. 55r; BM Reims, MS 1843 (N. 863), fol. 112v.

1 Roger de Rozoy, son of Clérembaud, lord of Rozoy, and Elizabeth de Namur, was bishop of Laon, 1175–1207.

2 Brancourt, cant. Anizy-le-Château, https://dicotopo.cths.fr/places/P91051513.

3 Basce, comm. Quincy-Basce, https://dicotopo.cths.fr/places/P14475073.

4 Bassoles, cant. Anizy-le-Château, https://dicotopo.cths.fr/places/P97208516.

5 Radulfus *B*.

6 Raoul Chien (d. ca. 1191), son of Gautier de la Tournelle and Agnès, appears in episcopal acts from the 1140s and was particularly associated with the lords of Coucy. Barthélemy, *LDA*, 160; Morelle, "Une charte nuptiale laonnoise de 1158 conservée en original," 223, fn. 69.

7 Broiencurt *B*.

prescriptam elemosinam ea devotione et eo tenore quo a patre suo facta fuerat, coram nobis recognovit pariter et laudavit et eandem[8] elemosinam tam pro sua quam pro sui patris salute augmentare studens, totam decimam de Bacia et de Basciola[9] cum pertinentiis suis, assensu uxoris sue, ecclesie iamdicte contulit et ad perpetue stabilitatis memoriam nostro scripto auctentico[10] petiit roborari. Scriptum anno Domini M° C° nonagesimo secundo. Ego Willermus[11,12] cancellarius scripsi.

94

December, 1227.

The maior, jurati, *and the commune of Coucy declare that in their presence Itier de Vauxaillon,*[1] *knight, renounces his claims to 15* sextarii *of* vinagium *collected from the vineyard that Jean de Pont-Saint-Mard,*[2] bourgeois *of Coucy, had given to the religious of Prémontré.*

A. Cartulary of Prémontré, fols. 23v–24r.
B. Original not found.

Karta maioris et communie Couciaci.

[M]aior, jurati et tota communitas Couciaci universis tam presentibus quam futuris, salutem in Domino. Noverint universi quod vir nobilis Itherus de Vausaillon miles in nostra presentia personaliter constitutus publice recognovit quod vineam illam quam Johannes de Ponte Sancti Medardi, burgensis de Couciaco, tenebat de ipso per quindecim sextarios vinagii qui solvebantur ei et compartionariis suis, quitavit in perpetuum tam de ipso vinagio quam de omnibus aliis rebus ecclesie Premonstratensi, cui per excambium contulit ipsam vineam predictus Johannes. Et quia coram nobis recognovit hoc ipsum, nos recognitionem

8 eamdem *B*.
9 Baciola *B*.
10 autentico *B*.
11 Willelmus *B*.
12 Guillaume, chancellor of the bishop of Laon, is attested 1173–1201. BnF, MS. lat. 11073, fol. 55r; BM Reims, MS 1843 (N. 863), fol. 112v.

1 Itier I, lord of Vauxaillon (cant. Anizy-le-Château, https://dicotopo.cths.fr/places/P32329338). Melleville, *DH*, vol. 2, 409.
2 Pont-Saint-Mard, cant. Coucy-le-Château, https://dicotopo.cths.fr/places/P93612418.

ipsam in presentibus litteris comprehensam sigillo nostro duximus roborandam. Actum mense decembri, anno gratie millesimo ducentesimo XX° septimo.

95

1138

Barthélemy,[1] *bishop of Laon, makes known that Adèle, daughter of Hugues Péronne, became a* conversa *at Prémontré and that, with her father's consent, she gave to Prémontré and its abbot, Hugues [I],*[2] *a fief that she held hereditarily from Barthélemy. Moreover, the* vidame *Gerard [I]*[3] *abandoned all his rights over this fief, in favour of Prémontré.*

A. Cartulary of Prémontré, fol. 24r.

B. Original, BnF, nouv. acq. lat. 2309, no. 2, previously sealed.

EDITION: Dufour-Malbezin, *Actes*, 282–3; *Chartae Galliae*, no. 208325, http://telma.irht.cnrs.fr/outils/chartae-galliae/charte208325/.

REGISTER: Florival, *Étude historique sur le XIIe siècle*, 356; Boghen, "Inventaire des actes épiscopaux originaux conservés à la Bibliothèque nationale (1121–1200)," 112–13.

Karta Bartholomei episcopi.

[I]n nomine sancte et individue Trinitatis. Ego Bartholomeus, Dei patientia Laudunensis ecclesie minister humilis, Hugoni, Premonstratensis ecclesie abbati, eiusque successoribus canonice substituendis in perpetuum. Quia episcopalis est officii proprium saluti fidelium et ecclesiarum paci insudare, eo magis decet nos eorum quieti providere qui, abjectis pompis vite secularis, tantum vaccare[4] desiderant et videre celestium bonorum jocunditatem. Notum igitur fieri volumus tam futuris quam presentibus quod Aelidis, filia Hugonis de Perona, gratia conversionis, ecclesie Premonstratensi et eiusdem abbati Hugoni ad obediendum se reddidit, conferens ad usum fidelium inibi Deo servientium feodum quod de manu nostra hereditario jure habebat, assensu predicti patris sui Hugonis, annuente Gerardo vicedomino, qui quod in eo habebat

1 Barthélemy de Jur (d. 1158), son of Conon, lord of Grandson and La Sarraz, and Ada de Roucy; first subdeacon and then treasurer of Reims, later bishop of Laon, 1113–51.

2 Hugues I de Fosses (ca. 1093–1164), first abbot of Prémontré.

3 Gérard I de Picquigny, *vidame* of Amiens (d. 1178), son of Guermond II de Picquigny, *vidame* of Amiens, and Béatrice.

4 vacare *B*.

in manu nostra resignavit et ego prefate ecclesie perpetuo possidendum dedi. Feodum autem tale est viginti quatuor[5] modii vinatii apud Burguinum,[6,7] XII modii cum duodecim[8] denariis apud Panencourt[9,10] et Broiencourt,[11] alii XII modii apud Homuncourt,[12,13] terra et silva apud Poeli,[14] terra et census, sicut in utraque villa sepefatus Hugo, pater ipsius puelle, in suo in dominio tenuerat. Quod ut ratum firmumque permaneat, inviolatum sigilli nostri munimen apponimus. Si qua vero ecclesiastica secularisve persona[15] nostre concessionis simul et confirmationis donum ausu temerario auferre, minuere vel perturbare presumpserit, secundo terciove commonita,[16] nisi resipuerit, divine animadversioni in extremo examine subjaceat. Actum est hoc anno dominice incarnationis millesimo centesimo[17] XXX°[18] VIII°, epacta VII, concurrente quinto,[19] indictione XVª. S.[20] mei ipsius Bartholomei, episcopi. S. Ernaldi, archidiaconi. S. Roberti, capellani.[21] S. Arnulphi, clerici. S. Gerardi, vicedomini.[22] Sunt etiam testes: Ado de Valaverni,[23,24] Ado de Foukeroles,[25,26] Johannes de Ursinicourt,[27] Paganus de Foukeroles,[28] Foukuinus[29] cellerarius. Ego Ernaldus[30] cancellarius relegi.

---

5 IIII^or^ *B.*
6 Burgeinum *B.*
7 Bourguignon-sous-Montbavin, cant. Anizy-le-Château, https://dicotopo.cths.fr/places/P25732714.
8 XII *B.*
9 Pendendcurt *B.*
10 Penancourt, comm. Anizy-le-Château, https://dicotopo.cths.fr/places/P36114519.
11 Broincurt *B.*
12 Homuncurt *B.*
13 Aumencourt, comm. Auffrique-et-Nogent, https://dicotopo.cths.fr/places/P03934228.
14 Pouilly, cant. Crécy-sur-Serre, https://dicotopo.cths.fr/places/P77273113.
15 *Om.* hoc *A.*
16 submonita *B.*
17 M° C° *B.*
18 XXX^mo^ *B.*
19 V *B.*
20 Signum *B.*
21 Robert, chaplain of Laon, appears as a witness to episcopal acts 1130–50. Dufour Malbezin, *Actes*, 215, 445.
22 Gérard I de Clacy, *vidame* of Laon (d. 1140). Newman, *Seigneurs*, vol. 1, 180–1.
23 Vallaverni *B.*
24 Adon, lord of Valavergny. Melleville, *DH*, vol. 2, 396.
25 Fokeroles *B.*
26 Adon, lord of Fouquerolles. Mellevile, *DH*, vol. 1, 406.
27 Wissignicourt, cant. Anizy-le-Château, https://dicotopo.cths.fr/places/P16285342.
28 Fokeroles *B.*
29 Fokuinus *B.*
30 Ernaud, chancellor of Laon, 1133–41, and archdeacon of Laon, 1136/8–41. Dufour-Malbezin, *Actes*, 29.

96

1141

Barthélemy,[1] *bishop of Laon, makes known that after Norbert [of Xanten]'s elevation to the archbishopric [of Magdeburg], abbot Hugues [I]*[2] *decided to relocate the religious sisters who were living in the valley of Prémontré. Barthélemy expresses his wish for the sisters to live within the bishopric of Laon and his affection for Agnès,*[3] *wife of André de Baudement. Accordingly, Barthélemy permits Agnès, recently a Premonstratensian sister, and the other sisters to settle at Fontenille*[4] *in a* curtis *which he had given to Norbert, and grants them a neighbouring mill and fishpond, together with all the pertinent rights. Barthélemy also grants the sisters lands bordering the* curtis, *and provides an equal exchange of lands for the following* rustici*: Consteval, Thibault, Adon de Anizy and his brother Bovo, Anselme, Hugues, and Roger.*

A. Cartulary of Prémontré, fols. 24r–24v.

B. Original, AD Aisne, H 845, previously sealed with a double strip of leather.

EDITION: Le Paige, *Bibliotheca*, 422; Hugo, *La vie de S. Norbert, Archevêque de Magdebourg*, 448 (partial); Hugo, *prob.* 1, cols. cccxviii–cccxix; Melleville, *DH*, vol. 1, 403; Florival, *Étude historique sur le XIIe siècle*, 377–9; Dufour-Malbezin, *Actes*, 314–15; *Chartae Galliae*, no. 208352, http://telma.irht.cnrs.fr/outils/chartae-galliae/charte208352/.

REGISTER: Bréquigny, *Table chronologique*, vol. 3, 54; Grauwen, "Lijst van oorkonden waarin Norbertus wordt genoemd," 166–7.

Karta Bartholomei episcopi de curte nostra de Fontenilles cum quibusdam aliis.

[I]n nomine sancte et individue Trinitatis. Quia inter multimodas humane corruptele miserias, non ultimum sibi locum oblivio vendicat, huic non mediocriter medetur si pietatis opus ad posteritatis notitiam scripto commendetur. Ea propter ego Bartholomeus, Dei gratia Laudunensis episcopus, notum esse volo tam futuris quam presentibus quod domino Norberto, viro Deo hominibusque accepto eiusque fratribus in valle Premonstratensi Deo famulantibus, curtem Fontenellam et molendinum quod noviter juxta eandem curtem

---

1 Barthélemy de Jur (d. 1158), son of Conon, lord of Grandson and La Sarraz, and Ada de Roucy; first subdeacon and then treasurer of Reims, later bishop of Laon, 1113–51.

2 Hugues I de Fosses (ca. 1093–1164), first abbot of Prémontré.

3 Agnès I, lady of Braine (d. aft. 1144); wife of André de Baudement. She entered the Premonstratensian community at Fontenille.

4 Fontenille, comm. Wissignicourt, https://dicotopo.cths.fr/places/P36537367.

sumptibus meis construxeram, ob remedium anime mee et predecessorum meorum, veluti Christi pauperibus, perpetuo habendam concesserim. Igitur procedentibus temporibus, domno Norberto ad archiepiscopatus dignitatem promoto, dominoque Hugone ad predictorum fratrum curam subrogato, eidem visum est Hugoni, sorores suas que in eadem valle penes se morabantur, veluti nimis sibi propinquas removere et ad Deo serviendum longinquius relocare. Ego autem nolens eas ab episcopio meo exponi et precipue ob spiritualis dilectionis affectum, quem habueram erga dominam Agnetem, uxorem domini Andree de Baldimento,[5] que Christo servitura, eisdem sororibus se conjunxerat, apud prefatam curtem Fontenellam, constructo eis ex sumptibus meis monasterio, concessu predicti abbatis in vicinitate mea, me earum sperans apud Deum adjuvari suffragio[6] eas detinui et tunc demum vivarium predicto molendino adjacens, quod prius detinueram, in usus earumdem sororum attribui, quodque mei juris erat in donariis, hominum meorum que eisdem fratribus et sororibus per episcopium meum contulerunt, libere concessi et quasdam terras in confinio eiusdem curtis jacentes, a rusticis quibusdam quos nominabimus, data eis[7] eque bona, cambivimus ut fratribus essent viciniores et ad excolendum promptiores. Hec nomina rusticorum: Constevalus, Theobaldus,[8] Ado de Anisi et Bovo frater eius, Anselmus, Hugo, Rogerus. Quod ut ratum et inconvulsum perpetuo perseveret, sigilli[9] nostri impressione[10] signamus et malignorum proterviam ab huius doni nostri temeraria violatione data anathematis sentencia cohibemus. Actum est hoc anno incarnationis dominice M° C° XLI°, epacta XI^{a}, indictione IIII^{a}, concurrente secundo.[11] Signum domni Bartholomei, episcopi. S. Bartholomei, archidiaconi et thesaurarii.[12] S. Arnulphi,[13] clerici. S. Roberti, capellani.[14] Ego Bartholomeus cancellarius subscripsi.

5 Baldimente *B.*

6 *Transp. A*; suffragio adjuvari *B.*

7 *Om.* terra *A.*

8 Teobaldus *B.*

9 sygilli *B.*

10 inpressione *B.*

11 II° *B.*

12 Barthélemy de Montcornet (d. 1175), son of Hugues de Montcornet and Béatrice de Reynel, was archdeacon of Laon from 1133, treasurer of Laon from 1137, and chancellor of Laon, 1141–4; later archdeacon of Reims; and bishop of Beauvais, 1162–75. Guyotjeannin, *Episcopus*, 131; Dufour-Malbezin, *Actes*, 30.

13 Arnulfi *B.*

14 Robert, chaplain of Laon, appears as a witness to episcopal acts 1130–50. Dufour Malbezin, *Actes*, 215, 445.

97

1166. Laon.

Gautier [II],[1] *bishop of Laon, makes known that Sarracin,*[2] *castellan of Laon and La Fère, grants to the church of Prémontré all that is necessary to make a fishpond on its land located on the other side of the river at Hubertpont,*[3] *in exchange for an annual* census *of six* nummi Proveniensium. *Helvide, his wife, and their children, Hugues, Geoffroi, Raoul,*[4] *Nicholas,*[5] *and Pierre,*[6] *consent.*

A. Cartulary of Prémontré, fol. 24v.
B. Original, SAHSS, *casier* 1, no. 10, previously sealed.

Karta Laudunensis episcopi de terra Sarraceni.

[I]n nomine sancte et individue Trinitatis.[7] Ad nos pertinet que in presentia nostra ecclesiis rationabiliter conferuntur attestari, et ne oblivione depereant, litteris annotari[8] et posteris notum fieri. Ea propter ego Galterus, Dei gratia Laudunensium episcopus, notum facimus universis tam futuris quam presentibus quod Sarracenus, castellanus Laudunensis et Feriensis, contulit ecclesie Premonstratensi, ob remedium anime sue et predecessorum suorum, per manum nostram de terra quam habebat apud Hunberti[9] Pontem[10] ultra rivum, quantum scilicet opus fuerit ad faciendum vivarium, sub censu sex nummorum Proveniensium in festo Sancti Remigii annuatim persolvendorum. Hoc autem

1 Gautier de Mortagne was dean of Laon, ca. 1142–55, and bishop of Laon, 1155–74.
2 Sarracin, castellan of La Fère (from 1133) and of Laon (from 1166); brother of Geoffroi de Condren, knight, and Hugues *le Captif* de Vendeuil, husband of Helvide. Newman, *Seigneurs*, vol. 2, 203–4.
3 Hubertpont, comm. Prémontré, https://dicotopo.cths.fr/places/P71559674.
4 Raoul, lord of Sart, son of Sarracin, castellan of Laon and La Fère, and Helvide. Barthélemy, *LDA*, 180–2; Newman, *Seigneurs*, vol. 2, 204.
5 Nicolas du Sart, knight, son of Sarracin, castellan of Laon and La Fère, and Helvide. Barthélemy, *LDA*, 180–2; Newman, *Seigneurs*, vol. 2, 204.
6 Pierre (d. aft. 1207), son of Sarracin, castellan of Laon and La Fère, and Helvide, was castellan of La Fère in 1197. Barthélemy, *LDA*, 180–2; Newman, *Seigneurs*, vol. 2, 203–5.
7 *Om.* Amen *A*.
8 adnotari *B*.
9 Humberti *B*.
10 Hubertpont, comm. Prémontré, https://dicotopo.cths.fr/places/P71559674.

concessit uxor eiusdem Sarraceni, Helvidis, et filii eius Hugo, Gaufridus, Radulfus,[11] Nicholaus, Petrus. Hoc autem ut ratum et inconvulsum permaneat, sigilli nostri impressione et testium subscriptione muniri fecimus. Signum Galteri, Laudunensis thesaurarii.[12] S. Ingelranni, abbatis Sancti Johannis.[13] S. Garini, abbatis Sancti Martini.[14] S. Guidonis de Mont Cornet.[15] S. Hergoti de Brueriis.[16] S. Gerardi Zoquet.[17] S. Theobaldi,[18] nepotis eius. S. Drogonis, decani de Couci La Vile. S. Theoderici[19] del Sart, presbiteri. S. Hugonis, presbiteri de Verciniaco.[20] S. Willelmi, prepositi Sancti Nicolai.[21] S. Gepuini, militis de Noviant.[22] S. Petri de Cherec.[23] Actum Lauduni anno incarnati verbi M° C° LX° VI°. Angotus cancellarius relegit, scripsit, et subscripsit.

98

1142

Barthélemy,[1] bishop of Laon, makes known that on the day he baptized Enguerrand,[2] son of Enguerrand [II] of Coucy, he had made Raoul Chien[3] agree

---

11 *Transp. A*; Radulfus, Gaufridus *B*.

12 Gautier, treasurer of Laon, ca. 1162–ca. 1173. Per AD Aisne, G 171, a nephew of Gautier de Mortagne, bishop of Laon.

13 Enguerrand, abbot of the Benedictine abbeys of Nogent-sous-Coucy, 1157–ca. 1160, and of Saint-Jean de Laon, 1161–82. *GC* IX, col. 607; Taïée, "L'abbaye de Saint-Jean de Laon," 217.

14 Guérin, abbot of the Premonstratensian abbey of Saint-Martin de Laon, 1151–71. *MP* II, 512.

15 A Guy is attested as lord of Montcornet, ca. 1162–78. Through his sister Elizabeth he was the brother-in-law of Gossuin, castellan of Pierrepont. Melleville, *DH*, vol. 2, 119.

16 Bruyères-et-Montbérault, cant. Laon, https://dicotopo.cths.fr/places/P62433167.

17 Zoget *B*.

18 Teobaldi *B*.

19 Teoderici *B*.

20 Versigny, cant. La Fère, https://dicotopo.cths.fr/places/P17885640.

21 Likely the prior of the Benedictine abbey of Saint-Nicolas-aux-Bois.

22 Gebuin (or Gepuin), knight and lord of Nouvion-le-Comte, attested 1138–77. Melleville, *DH*, vol. 2, 174. He also appears as a witness in **138** and in Raoul I, lord of Coucy's 1163 grant of rights to Vervins. Mennesson, "Les chartes de Vervins," 22.

23 Chérêt, cant. Laon, https://dicotopo.cths.fr/places/P99149152.

---

1 Barthélemy de Jur (d. 1158), son of Conon, lord of Grandson and La Sarraz, and Ada de Roucy; first subdeacon and then treasurer of Reims, later bishop of Laon, 1113–51.

2 Enguerrand (d. ca. 1174), son of Enguerrand II, lord of Coucy, and Agnès de Beaugency. Du Chesne, *Histoire généalogique des maisons de Guines, d'Ardres, de Gand et de Coucy*, 348.

3 Raoul Chien (d. ca. 1191), son of Gautier de la Tournelle and Agnès, appears in episcopal acts from the 1140s and was particularly associated with the lords of Coucy. Barthélemy, *LDA*, 160; Morelle, "Une charte nuptiale laonnoise de 1158 conservée en original," 223, fn. 69.

to no longer trouble the religious of Prémontré concerning part of a tithe in the parish of Brancourt[4] *that he claimed to be part of his fief, in return for a payment of 60* solidi. *Raoul, on the point of leaving for Jerusalem, forfeited the tithe payment, seeking and obtaining pardon. (See **99**.)*

A. Cartulary of Prémontré, fol. 24v.

B. Original, BnF, Coll. Picardie 290, no. 3, previously sealed.

EDITION: Dufour-Malbezin, *Actes*, 333–4; Slack, *Crusade Charters, 1138–1270*, 12–13; *Chartae Galliae*, no. 208369, http://telma.irht.cnrs.fr/outils/chartae-galliae/charte208369/.

REGISTER: Du Chesne, *Histoire genealogique des maisons de Guines, d'Ardres, de Gand, et de Coucy*, 338; Grauwen, "Lijst van oorkonden waarin Norbertus wordt genoemd," 167; Boghen, "Inventaire des actes épiscopaux originaux conservés à la Bibliothèque nationale (1121–1200)," 113.

Karta Laudunensis episcopi de compositione Radulfi Canis.

[I]n nomine sancte et individue Trinitatis. Ego Bartholomeus, Dei gratia Laudunensis episcopus, notum fieri volo tam futuris quam presentibus quod domino Norberto, viro spectabilis religionis qui primo in Premonstrato loco ad commanendum se contulit et fratribus suis proximas[5] eidem loco circumiacentes, episcopali auctoritate, tam a decimis quam a ceteris consuetudinibus emancipavi ab omnibus qui jure hereditario aliquid ibi possidere videbantur, eo ordine quo a me ipso in ipsorum privilegiis sancitum est. Post longum vero temporis curriculum surrexit quidam Radulphus, Canis cognominatus, filius Walteri de Laturnela, qui inquietare voluit quod factum fuerat pro quadam particula decime que est in parrochia de Broiencourt,[6] quam de feodo suo esse dicebat. Quam inquietationem LX solidos donando ipsi Radulpho[7] sedavi ea die qua ad batizandum[8] Ingelrannum, domini Ingelranni de Couci[9] filium, veneram. Et quod inde abbati et ecclesie forisfecerat, Jherosolimam[10] iturus, veniam petiit et accepit. Et ut ecclesia

4 Brancourt, cant. Anizy-le-Château, https://dicotopo.cths.fr/places/P91051513.
5 *Om.* valles *A*.
6 Borincurt *B*.
7 Radulfo *B*.
8 baptizandum *B*.
9 Coci *B*.
10 Jehrusalam *B*.

predicta in perpetuum libere possideret ob remedium anime sue sibique attinentium concessit, me presente et aliis legitimis testibus: Roberto capellano,[11] Radulpho[12] presbitero de Rouci,[13,14] Widone de Loisi,[15] Malone[16] milite, Fulcuino cellerario, Drogone et Nichasio[17] famulis episcopi, Petro filio Arnulphi.[18] Ut autem hec nostre confirmationis pagina inviolatum robur obtineat, sigilli nostri impressione subsignavimus et in perturbatoribus nisi resipiscant, anathematis innodationem in perpetuum apponere curavimus. Actum est hoc anno incarnationis dominice M° C° XLII°,[19] indictione IIII[a],[20] epacta tercia,[21] concurrente tercio.[22] S.[23] Bartholomei, archidiaconi.[24] S. Widonis, decani.[25] S. Hoelis, vicedomini. S. Arnulphi,[26] clerici. S. Petri.[27] S. Willelmi Agasonis. S. Nicholai, clerici. S. Herberti de Broiencourt.[28,29] S. Odonis.[30]

11 Robert, chaplain of Laon, appears as a witness to episcopal acts 1130–50. Dufour Malbezin, *Actes*, 215, 445.

12 Radulfo *B*.

13 Roci *B*.

14 Roucy, arr. Laon, https://dicotopo.cths.fr/places/P39468514.

15 Loizy, cant. Laon, https://dicotopo.cths.fr/places/P33210650.

16 Walone *B*.

17 Nicasio *B*.

18 Arnulfi *B*.

19 M. C. XL. II *B*.

20 IIII *B*.

21 tercia *B*.

22 III *B*.

23 Signum *B*.

24 Barthélemy de Montcornet (d. 1175), son of Hugues de Montcornet and Béatrice de Reynel, was archdeacon of Laon from 1133, treasurer of Laon from 1137, and chancellor of Laon, 1141–4; later archdeacon of Reims; and bishop of Beauvais, 1162–75. Guyotjeannin, *Episcopus*, 131; Dufour-Malbezin, *Actes*, 30.

25 Guy de Pierrepont, son of Roger, lord of Pierrepont, and Ermengarde, lady of Montaigu, was first treasurer, archdeacon, and dean of the chapter of Laon, and later bishop of Châlons, 1144–7.

26 Arnulfi *B*.

27 *Superscr.* Berardi *B*.

28 Broincurt *B*.

29 Brancourt, cant. Anizy-le-Château, https://dicotopo.cths.fr/places/P91051513.

30 *Om.* de Fulkosi *A*.

99

1140

Barthélemy,[1] *bishop of Laon, declares a resolution to the dispute between Prémontré and Raoul Chien, confirming that Prémontré holds the tithe exemption in the parish of Brancourt*[2] *since, at the behest of Norbert [of Xanten], Raoul's mother Agnès had given the tithe to Prémontré in exchange for Thomas [de Marle, lord of Coucy]*[3] *returning the forfeited fief of her late husband, Gautier de la Tournelle. (See **98**.)*

A. Cartulary of Prémontré, fols. 24v–25r.

B. Original, AN, L 995, no. 9, previously sealed.

EDITION: Dufour-Malbezin, *Actes*, 305–6; *Chartae Galliae*, no. 208344, http://telma.irht.cnrs.fr/outils/chartae-galliae/charte208344/.

REGISTER: Grauwen, "Lijst van oorkonden waarin Norbertus wordt genoemd," 166.

Karta Bartholomei Laudunensis episcopi de quadam parte decime de Broiencurt.

[I]n nomine sancte et individue Trinitatis. Quoniam hominum brevis est vita labilisque memoria, res gestas scripturarum conmendare custodie decrevit antiquitas. Quam maiorum sollertiam ex multimoda utilitate approbans, ego Bartholomeus, Dei providentia Laudunensis episcopus, notum fieri volo tam futuri quam presentis evi hominibus quod domino Norberto, magne sanctitatis et sancte conversationis viro, Premonstratum locum in quo ad serviendum Deo se contulit, elegi et preoptavi proximasque valles eidem loco circumjacentes tam a decimis quam a censu seu terragio, sicut in primo[4] Premonstrate ecclesie privilegio continetur, liberas facere studui. Preterea partem decime que est in parrochia de Broiencurt[5] Walterus de la Tornele[6] a domino Thoma de Coci in feodo tenuerat, sed quoniam forefecerat, predictum feodum eodem tempore dominus Thomas in manu sua receperat. Post mortem vero Walteri, Thomas feodum reddere uxori eius, Agneti, et filio eorum, Radulpho,[7,8] qui Canis cognominatur, nullo modo

1 Barthélemy de Jur (d. 1158), son of Conon, lord of Grandson and La Sarraz, and Ada de Roucy; first subdeacon and then treasurer of Reims, later bishop of Laon, 1113–51.

2 Brancourt, cant. Anizy-le-Château, https://dicotopo.cths.fr/places/P91051513.

3 Thomas de Marle, lord of Coucy and Marle (ca. 1073–1130), son of Enguerrand I, lord of Coucy, and Adèle de Marle.

4 *Om.* eiusdem *A*.

5 Broincurt *B*.

6 Thornele *B*.

7 Radulfo *B*.

8 Raoul Chien (d. ca. 1191), son of Gautier de la Tournelle and Agnès, appears in episcopal acts from the 1140s and was particularly associated with the lords of Coucy. Barthélemy, *LDA*, 160; Morelle, "Une charte nuptiale laonnoise de 1158 conservée en original," 223, fn. 69.

voluit donec pro eis Norbertus, vir Deo plenus, interveniens rogavit. Cuius precibus Thomas, ut dignum fuerat, satisfaciens, predicte Agneti feodum tali conditione reddidit quod ipsa Premonstrate ecclesie decimam liberam in perpetuum remisit, fratre suo Goberto cum ceteris parentibus suis concedente et assensum prebente Radulphus[9] autem filius Agnetis puer adhuc erat[10] et ideo concedere vel contradicere, ut pote infra discretionis annos non valebat. Procedente vero tempore cum ad virilem provenisset etatem pro predicta decima Premonstratum venit, et quia habere eam non potuit ecclesie carrucas violenter rapuit. Unde in presentia nostra tam pro rapina, quam fecerat, quam pro pace quam violaverat ad causam vocatus et ordine judiciario a nobis superatus prevalere non potuit, sed rapinam quam tulerat prius reddidit et postea ut nobis pro pace quam infregerat satisfaceret inducias usque ad proximam Sancti Remigii sollempnitatem responsurus petiit. Determinavit etiam ut si ipsa die pro predicta decima in presentia nostra placitare vellet ecclesia Premonstratensis[11] quantum justicia dictaret ei satisfaceret. Si vero se nobis non presentaret ulterius inde ei ecclesia non responderet quia vero dies ab ipso constituta preteriit et se nobis non presentavit judicatum est. Ut quemadmodum ipse constituerat ecclesia ulterius ei inde non respondeat, sed decimam suam liberam in perpetuum possideat. Quod ut deinceps firmum permaneat auctoritate mea confirmo et inviolatum sigilli mei munimen appono. Si igitur predictus Radulphus[12] vel quilibet alius perditionis filius contra hoc venire temptaverit anathemati subjaceat donec de contemptu auctoritatis episcopalis et injuria ecclesie satisfaciat. Actum est hoc anno incarnationis dominice M° C° XL°, epacta XXX[a], indictione III[a], concurrente primo.[13] Signum mei ipsius Bartholomei episcopi. Testes autem huius rei sunt: Bartholomeus[14] archidiaconus et thesaurarius, Ernaldus[15] archidiaconus, Arnulphus[16] episcopus, Nicholaus[17] castellanus Laudunensis, Gerardus[18] qui Auris vocatur.

---

9 Radulfus *B*.

10 *Transp. A*; ad huc puer erat *B*.

11 Premonstrata *B*.

12 Radulfus *B*.

13 Io *B*.

14 Barthélemy de Montcornet (d. 1175), son of Hugues de Montcornet and Béatrice de Reynel, was archdeacon of Laon from 1133, treasurer of Laon from 1137, and chancellor of Laon, 1141–4; later archdeacon of Reims; and bishop of Beauvais, 1162–75. Guyotjeannin, *Episcopus*, 131; Dufour-Malbezin, *Actes*, 30.

15 Ernaud, chancellor of Laon, 1133–41, and archdeacon of Laon, 1136/8–41. Dufour-Malbezin, *Actes*, 29.

16 *Om.* qui vocatur *A;* Arnulfus *B*.

17 Nicolas, castellan of Laon, son of Guinemar, castellan of Laon. Saint-Denis, *Apogée d'une cité*, 80. He also appears with his wife Beatrice and son Raoul in an 1149 charter of Barthélemy, bishop of Laon, confirming donations made to the Templars, and is mentioned in the writings of Guibert de Nogent. Guibert of Nogent, *A Monk's Confession*, 192; Dufour-Malbezin, *Actes*, 431–7.

18 Gérard *l'Oreille* was part of the seigneurial family of Housset, and frequently appeared in charters issued by the Coucy family in the 1130s–60s. Barthélemy, *LDA*, 521.

100

February, 1220.

Gérard Ravars de Chevresis,[1] *knight, appears before [L.],*[2] *abbot of Saint-Crépin-en-Chaye, and his co-judges of Soissons, over his failure to pay the three* modii *of white wine that is owed every year to Prémontré on the vineyard of* Es Biars *because of a gift made by Marie, Gérard's wife, and Denis, Gérard's father-in-law, more than 30 years ago. Gérard recognizes the obligation and agrees to pay, as do Marie and their children, Jean, Gilon, Marguerite, Havide, Elizabeth, and Aelide. (See* ***102****.)*

A. Cartulary of Prémontré, fol. 25r.
B. Original not found.

Karta Gerardi Ravart de Chievresi[3]

[E]go Gerardus Ravars de Chievresi miles, notum facio tam presentibus quam futuris quod cum ecclesia Premonstratensis traxisset me in causam coram viris venerabilibus abbate Sancti Crispini in Cavea et conjudicibus suis Suessionensibus auctoritate apostolica super tribus modiis albi vini quos ipsa ecclesia dicebat sibi annuatim deberi in vinea mea que dicitur Es Biars, que contigua est domui fratrum Premonstratensum de Merliu[4] et collatos esse sibi a Dionisio, patre Marie uxoris mee, in perpetuam elemosinam et fuisse in possessione illius vini per triginta annos, tandem pro bono pacis, de assensu Marie uxoris mee et liberorum meorum videlicet Johannis, Gilonis, Margarete, Hauwidis, Elizabeth et Aelidis, predictam elemosinam et possessionem predicte ecclesie ob remedium anime mee et uxoris mee et liberorum meorum recognovi, concessi, et quitavi, fide mea et uxoris mee et liberorum meorum super hoc corporaliter interposita, quod videlicet ipsam in perpetuum ratam haberem et inviolabiliter observarem que premissa sunt et que secuntur universa. Assignavi insuper predicte ecclesie tres modios vini albi in prefata vinea percipiendos in perpetuum. Ut igitur predicta recognitio, concessio et quitatio et assignatio in perpetuum rata permaneat illesa presentes litteras sigilli mei appensione roboravi. Actum anno gratie M° CC° vicesimo, mense februario.

1 Gérard II *Ravars*, knight and lord of Chevresis-Monceau, attested 1210–20. He also appears in two acts dated 1210 and 1214 respectively in the cartulary of Foigny. BM Reims 1563 (N. Fonds), fols. 16r–16v, 18v.

2 L., attested as abbot of the Augustinian abbey of Saint-Crépin-en-Chaye, 1220s. *GC,* IX, col. 466.

3 Here, a marginal addition in red ink in a later medieval hand reads "Hic scriptum debet esse cum scriptis de Merliu."

4 Merlieux, cant. Anizy-le-Château, https://dicotopo.cths.fr/places/P92396813.

101

June, 1218.

Anselme,[1] *bishop of Laon, makes known that Guillaume de Monthiémont*[2] *sold to the church of Prémontré three* modii *of* vinagium, *less one* sextarius, *on several holdings located at* Hormesellum *for the price of 16* librae Laudunensium. *Mathilde, wife of Guillaume, approved the sale after receiving compensation for her* dos *on the vineyard at Fresne;*[3] *Oudard, brother of Guillaume and fief lord, approved the sale also.*

A. Cartulary of Prémontré, fols. 25r–25v.
B. Original, AD Aisne, H 745, previously sealed with a single strip of parchment.

Karta Anselmi episcopi Laudunensis de quadam recognitione facta coram ipso super tribus modiis vinagiorum.

[A]nselmus, Dei gratia Laudunensis episcopus, omnibus presentes literas inspecturis salutem in Domino. Noverit universitas vestra quod Guillermus de Montiermont coram nobis recognovit se vendidisse ecclesie Premonstratensi tres modios vinagiorum, unum sextarium minus, quos habebat super terras apud Hormesellum, unum modium ad Crucem, decem et octo sextaria; super terram Anselmi Brasier et ecclesie Premonstratensis quatuor sextaria; super terram ecclesie Premonstratensis et Guiardi des Cloches duo sextaria et duos tercius;[4] super campum ecclesie Premonstratensis situm secus viam de Broiencourt[5,6] quatuor sextaria; super campum ad Markais sex cathalanenses;[7] super campum ante portam curtis de Panencourt[8,9] tres cathalanenses; super campum qui fuit Roberti Menuel unum cathalanensem. Hec autem omnia vendidit dicte ecclesie pro precio sexdecim librarum Laudunensium, fidem interponens corporalem quod in hiis omnibus nichil de cetero reclamabit. Hoc etiam laudavit Matildis,[10] uxor eius, recepta reconpensatione dotis sue ad vineam

---

1 Anselme de Mauny (or de Bercenay), bishop of Laon, 1215–38.
2 Monthiémont, comm. Merlieux-et-Fouquerolles, https://dicotopo.cths.fr/places/P83003256.
3 Perhaps Fresne, cant. Coucy-le-Château, https://dicotopo.cths.fr/places/P35697386.
4 Terceus *B*.
5 Broiencort *B*.
6 Brancourt, cant. Anizy-le-Château, https://dicotopo.cths.fr/places/P91051513.
7 This is the only time this unit of measurement appears in the cartulary manuscript. It appears to be a unit of land measurement subsidiary to a sextarius.
8 Panencort *B*.
9 Penancourt, comm. Anizy-le-Château, https://dicotopo.cths.fr/places/P36114519.

de Fraisneto, fidem interponens quod super hoc nichil de cetero reclamabit et quod sufficientem habebat reconpensationem. Istud etiam laudavit Odardus de Montiermont, frater dicti Guillermi, de cuius feodo omnia predicta erant et feodum quitavit penitus in perpetuum, digna sibi reconpensatione facta, fidem interponens quod de cetero non reclamabit. In quorum omnium testimonium ad petitionem partium presentes literas emisimus sigilli nostri munimine roboratas. Actum anno Domini M° CC°[11] octavo decimo, mense junio.

102

July, 1212. Church of Prémontré.

Gilles de Valavergny,[1] prepositus *of* Laudunisio, *confirms the alms gift of three* modii *of white wine that his father Denis had made to Prémontré, which are to be collected from the vineyard called* Es Bihars, *contiguous to the Premonstratensians' house at Merlieux.*[2] *Égide also confirms that his father exempted the religious of Prémontré from the* rotagium *at Lizy*[3] *so that they could transport their wines for their own use, and also gave them the right to collect wood in the forest of Vois.*[4] *(See **100**.)*

A. Cartulary of Prémontré, fol. 25v.
B. Original, BnF, nouv. acq. lat. 2590, no. 45, previously sealed.

Karta Egidii prepositi de Valavreni de elemosina patris sui.

[E]go Egidius de Valavreni, prepositus de Laudunisio, tam futuris quam presentibus notum facio per hoc scriptum quod olim Dyonisius, pater meus, dedit in perpetuam elemosinam ecclesie Premonstratensis tres modios albi vini et

10 Mathildis *B*.
11 millesimo ducentesimo *B*.

1 The chronology and relationships of the *prepositi* of Laon – a minor official who was an assistant to Laon's *vidame* – and of the *prepositi* of the Laonnois is unclear. Melleville writes that Gilles de Valavergny "descendait sans aucun doute de la maison de Montchâlons-Mauregny," though his source for this assertion is unclear. Melleville, *DH*, vol. 2, 396. Per Alain Saint-Denis, Denis, brother of Alexander, canon of Notre-Dame de Laon, was *prepositus* of Laon, 1152–1217, although this clearly conflicts with this act, in which Denis is deceased by 1202. Saint-Denis, *Apogée d'une cité*, 220.
2 Merlieux, cant. Anizy-le-Château, https://dicotopo.cths.fr/places/P92396813.
3 Lizy, cant. Anizy-le-Château, https://dicotopo.cths.fr/places/P40948829.
4 Forest of Vois, https://dicotopo.cths.fr/places/P93994197.

quitavit in perpetuum fratribus ecclesie ipsius rotagium de Lisi ex vino quod in usus proprios fratrum ecclesie duceretur. Quitavit insuper eisdem fratribus in perpetuum quicquid juris vel forisfacti ei posset accidere quando circationem suam faceret in foresta de Voiz,[5] ita quod nec ipse nec heres eius eos vel eorum vecturas aliquatenus impediret. Ego vero Egidius, post obitum patris mei, veniens Premonstratum, predictam elemosinam et quitationem a patre meo factam in presentia fratrum ecclesie recognovi et meo confirmavi assensu. Sane quia a patre meo assignatus non fuerat certus locus ubi dicti fratres acciperent tres modios memoratos, ego ob remedium anime mee et ipsius patris mei assignavi supradictis fratribus illos tres modios accipiendos in perpetuum annuatim in vinea mea que dicitur Es Bihars[6] et est contigua domui eorum de Merliu. Ut igitur predicta concessio cum assignamento de tribus modiis vini facto futuris temporibus rata permaneat et illesa, ego presentes litteras super illa concessione et assignamento factas sigilli mei appensione munivi. Actum mense julio, anno gratie M° CC° XII°.

103

April 29, 1220.

Garnier,[1] *canon of Laon and* officialis *of the bishop of Laon, makes known that the knight Nivelon, [lord] of Septmonts,*[2] *relinquished all his rights on the tithe over vineyards within the tithe jurisdiction of Coucy-la-Ville to Prémontré, with the caveat that Béatrice, wife of Thomas,*[3] *knight of Pont-Saint-Mard,*[4] *retain her rights to the vineyards during her lifetime by right of* dotalicium. *Gérard, son of Nivelon, consents to this.*

A. Cartulary of Prémontré, fol. 25v.

B. Original not found.

REGISTER: *Studium Baldwin*, fiche 2294.

---

5 Voois *B*.

6 Esbiharz *B*.

---

1 Garnier, *officialis* of Laon, ca. 1219–ca. 1220. Wyard, *Saint-Vincent*, 37.

2 Nivelon (II?), knight and lord of Septmonts (cant. Soissons, https://dicotopo.cths.fr/places/P71270363). Melleville, *DH*, vol. 2, 321.

3 Thomas, lord of Pont-Saint-Mard, is attested 1207–24. Melleville, *DH*, vol. 2, 226.

4 Pont-Saint-Mard, cant. Coucy-le-Château, https://dicotopo.cths.fr/places/P93612418.

Karta officialis Laudunensis de resignatione decimationis Couci Ville.

[U]niversis Christi fidelibus presentes literas inspecturis, magister Garnerus, canonicus Laudunensis, officialis domini Laudunensis, salutem eternam in Domino. Notum facimus tam presentibus quam futuris, quod Nivelo de Septem Montibus, miles, de assensu Gerardi filii sui, resignavit in manum nostram quicquid juris habebat in decima vinearum quas ecclesia Premonstratensis tenebat in decimatione Couci Ville tempore huius scripti conferendum in elemosinam per manum nostram ecclesie Premonstrati. Hoc etiam expresse dicto, quod ipsa ecclesia post decessum Beatricis, uxoris Thome, militis de Ponte Sancti Medardi, habebit per hanc elemosinam portionem illam quam ipsa B[eatrix] tenebat per dotalicium in vineis Premonstratensibus eo tempore quo elemosina ista fuit facta. Nos autem qui vices gerebamus Domini nostri A[nselmi],[5] episcopi Laudunensis, qui absens erat pro quibusdam negotiis in Romana curia procurandis, ad petitionem predicti militis et filii eius recepimus resignationem de manu ipsorum et ecclesiam Premonstratensem per manum viri religiosi Gervasii,[6] eiusdem ecclesie abbatis, de ipsa decima investivimus et super hoc facto ut ratum futuris temporibus habeatur, emisimus presens scriptum sigilli curie Laudunensis appensione munitum. Actum tertio kalendas maii, anno gratie M^{o} CC^{o} vicesimo.

104

Twelfth Century[1]

Hugues [I de Fosses/II], abbot of Prémontré, makes known the agreement reached through an intermediary between the inhabitants of Wissignicourt[2] and Lizy[3] concerning the common grazing pastures of Gros Aulnois.[4] The inhabitants of Lizy will now use the pastures only from the middle of May until the first of August. (See duplicate ***168****.)*

5 Anselme de Mauny was bishop of Laon, 1215–38.

6 Gervais, abbot of the Premonstratensian abbeys of Saint-Just-en-Chaussée, 1199–1205, Thenailles, 1205–9, and Prémontré, 1209–20, and bishop of Séez, 1220–8. *MP* II, 401, 527, 565; Cheney, "Gervase, Abbot of Prémontré."

1 Hugues I de Fosses was abbot of Prémontré, 1128–64, while Hugues II was abbot, 1171–92.

2 Wissignicourt, cant. Anizy-le-Château, https://dicotopo.cths.fr/places/P16285342.

3 Lizy, cant. Anizy-le-Château, https://dicotopo.cths.fr/places/P40948829.

4 Probably in or near Aulnois-sous-Laon, cant. Laon, https://dicotopo.cths.fr/places/P03560401.

A. Cartulary of Prémontré, fol. 25v.
B. Original not found.

Karta super pascuis de Grosso Alneto.

[E]go Hugo, Dei gratia Premonstratensis ecclesie dictus abbas, notum fieri volo tam futuris quam presentibus quod pascua de Grosso Alneto communis erat tam hominibus de Ursinicourt quam hominibus de Lisi. Disponente autem Deo et intervenientibus eiusdem Premonstratensis ecclesie fratribus, cum Johanne de Ursinicourt, obtinuerunt homines de Lisi apud homines de Ursinicourt quod prata facerent in eadem pascua salvo et libero prato Sancti Johannis Premonstratensis omni tempore quod est subtus molendinum de Wez,[5] ea conditione quod homines de Lisi solummodo a mediante maio usque ad intrantem augustum prata sua possidebunt et defendent sicut libera, postea vero communis erit sicut et antea. Huius autem actionis testes sunt: Johannes de Ursinicourt, Odo de Fonte, Willelmus, Harduinus, Hugo de Fraxino,[6] Wibertus, Radulphus Gavele, Robertus Pratarius, Radulphus Mal Baillis. De Lisi: Havinus, Odo, Legierus, Gelierus, Radulphus filius Hildiardis, Paganus filius eius, Ansellus, Haimmericus, Hermundus, Constantius. Quod ut ratum permaneat, ipsorum qui prescripti sunt peticionibus sigillum nostrum apposuimus. Siquis autem hoc violaverit, anathemati subiaceat in etertum.[7] Amen.

105

1208–34[1]

R[enaud], castellan of Coucy, writes to the abbot of Prémontré to announce that he approves the donation of a vineyard given in alms to the abbey of Prémontré by archbishop Robert and asks the abbot to receive the archbishop as a brother.

A. Cartulary of Prémontré, fol. 26r.
B. Original not found.

5 Huet, comm. Lizy, https://dicotopo.cths.fr/places/P74654387.
6 Fresne, cant. Coucy-le-Château, https://dicotopo.cths.fr/places/P35697386.
7 *Sic A*, *read* eternum.

1 The only archbishops of French dioceses called Robert between 1120 and 1250 were Robert de La Tour du Pin of Vienne (1170–95); Robert III Poulain of Rouen (1208–22); and Robert of Lyon (1226/7–34). Two successive castellans of Coucy were called Renaud, one 1207–22 and the second 1222–61.

Karta castellani de Couci de concessione elemosine Roberti.

[P]atri suo reverendo domino Premonstratensi abbati et eiusdem toti conventui, R[adulphus] castellanus de Couci salutem et obsequium. Vestre notificamus sanctitati quod donationi vinee quam Robertus archiepiscopus domui contulit vestre sub elemosine nomine, libenti animo adquiescimus illamque et literis nostris et sigilli appensione roborando confirmamus, vos insuper devotius rogantes ut ipsum R[adulphum] in fratrem pietatis intuitu et nostro interventu recipiatis.

TABLE OF CONTENTS: SOUPIR

A. Cartulary of Prémontré, fol. 26r.

Incipiunt capitula scriptorum curie de Sopi cum appenditiis suis.
Carta Bartholomei episcopi de confirmatione elemosine de Soppi. **I**
Carta episcopi Laudunensis de confirmatione tocius decime de Soppi. **II**
Carta episcopi de confirmatione elemosine et venditionis terre Philipi. **III**
Confirmat episcopi venditionem cuiusdam terre Colardi prepositi de Soppi. **IIII**
Carta curie Laudunensis de resignatione decime maioris et minute. **V**
Scriptum capituli Laudunensis et decani de altari de Soppi et de decima eiusdem. **VI**
Item karta episcopi Laudunensis de confirmatione elemosine Balduini de Soppi. **VII**
Carta episcopi quod ecclesia Premonstratensi non tenetur ad reparationem ecclesie de Soppi. **VIII**
Carta Remensis archiepiscopi de quitatione Odonis de Sopi super quibusdam. **IX**
Carta episcopi de quitatione facta ecclesie Premonstratensis a Philipo de Sopi. **X**
Carta comitis Campanie de molendinis Axone. **XI**
Carta Balduini de elemosina et venditione terre Philippi de Maiel. **XII**
Carta episcopi Laudunensis de molendino de Ribaudon cum parte silvule. **XIII**
Carta officialis Suessionensis de quadam compositione inter ecclesiam Premonstratensis et Egidium militem. **XIV**
Carta domini Hamensis de quitatione Petri cognomento Bacheleir. **XV**
Carta Suessionensis episcopi de sex modiis vini qui debetur nobis apud Chavones. **XVI**
Carta Yvonis comitis de quadam compositione inter Johannem de Hostel et ecclesiam. **XVII**
Carta comitis Theobaldis de molendino Axone et de loco molendini. **XVIII**
Carta comitis Henrici de potestate quam habemus apud Cis, apud Praellam, apud Sanctum Medardum. **XIX**
Carta episcopi Suessionis de confirmatione nemoris de Hostel. **XX**
Carta comitisse de Brana de compositione et pace inter ecclesiam et Guidonem. **XXI**
Carta comitisse de Campania de confirmatione rerum quas ecclesia acquisivit ante ipsam. **XXII**
Carta Balduini et uxoris eius de elemosina qua Philipus fecit nobis. **XXIII**
Carta officialis Laudunensis de Henrico et Jakero fratre eius de Maiwel. **XXIIII**
Carta archidiaconi Suessionensis de quadam recognitione facta coram ipso. **XXV**
Carta Milonis de Soupi de piscatione qua habemus in Axona. **XXVI**
Carta curie Laudunensis de compositione inter Jakerum et ecclesiam Premontratensis super pascuis. **XXVII**
Carta curie Laudunensis de laude Milonis super compositione inter Jakerum et ecclesiam. **XXVIII**

106

1133

Barthélemy,[1] *bishop of Laon, approves and makes known that Baudouin de Soupir*[2] *gave in alms to the church of Prémontré all that he possessed between the roads leading from Soupir to Ostel*[3] *and to Chevregny;*[4] *that 12 of the inhabitants of Soupir who also possessed land there had committed to giving a part of their own lands to Prémontré; and that the said inhabitants, having begun the construction of a church at Soupir but being unable to finish it due to wars and other impediments, asked Hugues [I],*[5] *abbot of Prémontré, and his brothers to complete the construction in exchange for the land in question.*

A. Cartulary of Prémontré, fol. 26v.
B. Original, AD Aisne, H 826, previously sealed with a double strip of leather.
EDITION: Dufour-Malbezin, *Actes*, 248–9; *Chartae Galliae*, no. 208206, http://telma.irht.cnrs.fr/outils/chartae-galliae/chartc208206/.
REGISTER: Florival, *Étude historique sur le XIIe siècle*, 349; Grauwen, "Lijst van oorkonden waarin Norbertus wordt genoemd," 158.

---

1 Barthélemy de Jur (d. 1158), son of Conon, lord of Grandson and La Sarraz, and Ada de Roucy; first subdeacon and then treasurer of Reims, later bishop of Laon, 1113–51.
2 Baudouin I, lord of Soupir (cant. Vailly, https://dicotopo.cths.fr/places/P62600159). Wacha, "La Puissance du Choix," 116.
3 Ostel, cant. Vailly, https://dicotopo.cths.fr/places/P14381512.
4 Chevregny, cant. Anizy-le-Château, https://dicotopo.cths.fr/places/P06529464.
5 Hugues I de Fosses (ca. 1093–1164), first abbot of Prémontré.

Karta Bartholomei episcopi de confirmatione elemosine Balduini de Soupi.

[I]n nomine sancte et individue Trinitatis. Ego Bartholomeus, Laudunensis ecclesie[6] minister indignus. Notum sit tam futuris quam presentibus quod Balduinus de Soupi[7] in inicio Premonstratensis[8] ecclesie tempore domini Norberti, viri spectabilis nostris temporibus religionis, qui eam incepit, dedit illi ad usus fratrum in ea Deo servientium totam terram quam de ~~in~~dominio suo habebat supra montem de feodo meo inter duas vias que de Soupi[9] vadunt ad Hostel et ad Capriniacum, ob remedium anime sue et predecessorum suorum, me concedente; infra has duas vias habebant particulas terre homines de Soupi[10] et infra subnotatos terminos, scilicet a campo qui est juxta parvulam silvam predicti Balduini usque ad viam que precedit de fossa, que dicitur ab indigenis Fossa Richardi, ad crucem et sicut via perportat usque ad terminum ubi fixus est lapis qui dividit Laudunensem et Suessionensem episcopatum et usque ad Creci ubi dividuntur tres potestates et totam albam viam usque ad silvulam;[11] sed ex hiis quidam juste quidam injuste possidebant. Que contentio tandem sic sedata est: ex precepto domini sui Balduini juraverunt duodecim de hominibus suis quod dividerent unicuique partem suam et sic fecerunt. Quorum sub notata sunt nomina: Robertus[12] filius Ernoldi, Radulphus[13] frater eius, Bernardus Charlez,[14] Bernardus filius Tangreiz,[15] Albertus Malez, Tiebaldus filius Soroldi,[16] Tioldus de Vileirs,[17] Dodo filius Alberti, Albertus Rufus, Robertus[18] Columba, Robertus[19] filius Bosonis, Gozuinus. Succedente vero tempore, predicti homines cum in eadem villa, Soupi[20] videlicet, ecclesiam incepissent facere ad honorem Dei, ut bonorum parrochianorum mos est, et non possent eas perficere

6 *Om.* dei gratia *A.*
7 Sulpi *B.*
8 Premonstrate *B.*
9 Sulpi *B.*
10 Sulpi *B.*
11 selvulam *B.*
12 Rotbertus *B.*
13 Radulfus *B.*
14 Carlez *B.*
15 Tangrez *B.*
16 Seroldi *B.*
17 Vilers *B.*
18 Rotbertus *B.*
19 Rotbertus *B.*
20 Sulpi *B.*

propter werras et multas alias que tunc illis inerant inportunitates, per ipsum dominum suum Balduinum, petitione etiam ipsius, contulerunt se ad abbatem Premonstratensis[21] ecclesie Hugonem et fratres suos, quatinus ipsum opus prenominatum ad perficiendum susciperent eo siquidem tenore ut ipsas terre particulas quas inter suas terras habebant in monte, in predictis terminis, ecclesie Premonstratensis[22] et fratribus perpetuo habendas darent. Sicque factum est et partem suam singuli domino suo, Balduino reddiderunt. Ipse autem, quia de feodo meo erat, michi reddidit. Ego vero sepefacte ecclesie jure perpetuo possidendam concessi. Insuper sub excommunicationis annotatione quod fuerat factum confirmavi et sigilli mei inpressione subsignavi, et quia homines illi ob remedium[23] anime sue et predecessorum suorum opus illud et donum fecerant ut in perpetua memoria et in facti huius testimonio haberentur, ipsos eosdem qui suas contulerunt portiones subnotare precepi. Horum sunt nomina:[24] Jacobus et Gilius et Gervasius, Bernardus Ursio et Agnes et Hugo, Symon, Petrus

---

21 Premonstrate *B*.

22 Premonstrate *B*.

23 remidio *B*.

24 The *A* and *B* texts diverge substantially from this point on. For ease of reading, the remainder of the *B* text is reproduced here: Horum sunt nomina: Jacobus miles, et Gilius et Gervasius filii eius, Bernardus Carlez, Ursio miles et Agnes uxor eius, et Hugo, Symon, Petrus filii eorum, et gener suum Albricus miles, et Erma uxor eius, Hugo Scropha, Helvidis Rufa et filia eius, Boso miles, Bernardus frater eius, Boso, Warinus, filii eorum, Adelardus Strabo, Radulfus frater eius, Rotbertus filius Arnulfi, Radulfus Bernardus, Arnulfus fratres, Robertus, filius Bosonis et Emma uxor eius, Rotbertus Columba et sorores eius, Rotbertus et Milo frater eius, Tiebaldus, filius Geraldi, Bertrannus, Albertus, Rotbertus, Odo fratres, Dodo filius Alberti, Haduidis uxor eius, Hugo, Lantbertus filii Dodonis et sorores eorum, Boso filius Alberti, Haduidis uxor eius, Ursio et Petrus frater eius et sorores eorum, Lambertus serviens, Domizella uxor eius Drogo filius eorum et soror eius, Tiebaldus Frosarz, Elizabet uxor sua et Radulfus, Albertus filii eorum, Rotgerus Bridehar, Ermengardis uxor eius et Helduidis soror eius, Tiezo, Herbertus, Bernardus, Albertus, Laurentius fratres Goduinus Evaginatis Gladium, Helvidis uxor eius, Ursio filius eorum Gela Parvula, Hezelo, Balduinus filii eius, Bertrannus Dansul et Burga, uxor eius, et filie eorum, Burgo, Erardus, Martinus, Radulfus fratres et sorores eorum, Richardus Petrus Otiosus fratres et uxores eorum, Gerberga et filie eius, Johannes Aminus et uxor eius et filii eorum Hugo Paganus et uxor eius et filie eorum, Berta et Herbertus Sagitarius filius eius, Herbertus Encalceroi, Emma incisatrix, Alardus, Tiebaldus, Albertus filii eius, Emma mater Radulfi, Hermundi, Hugonis, Pagani filii Wederici, Rotberti, Ursio Boditi, Aia, David et filii eius et uxor eius, Hugo filius Wernir et uxor eius et filii eorum, Wibertus, Amolricus et uxor eius et filii eorum, Liduidus, Herbertus, Judit uxor eius et filii eorum, Hezelo, Does, Diez, Wido, Rothardus fratres Rufi, Rufus, Albertus Rufus et uxores et filii eorum, Tiebertus, Balduinus fratres, Haduidis uxor Radulfi de Musci et filie eius, Bernardus et uxor eius et filii eorum, Stephanus Harez et uxor eius et filii eorum, Aloz et filii eius omnes, Emma, Heinricus, Hugo Bernuinus, Ursio fratres, Haduidis Mala, Albertus Malez et uxor eius, Arnulfus, Radulfus, fratres et fratres eorum Albertus, conversus. Actum est hoc anno incarnationis dominice M° C° XXXIII°, epacta XII[a], indictione XI[a], concurrente VI°. Signum mei ipsius Bartholomei episcopi, Guidonis decani. Ego Arnoldus cancellarius relegi *B*.

filii eorum, et gener suus Albricus et Enma, Hugo, Helvidis et filia eius Boso, Bernardus frater eius, Boso Warinus filii eorum, Adelardus Radulphus frater eius, Robertus Radulphus et ceteri. Actum est hoc anno incarnationis dominice M° C° XXXIII°, epacta XII^{a}, indictione XI^{a}, concurrente VI°. Signum mei ipsius Bartholomei episcopi, Guidonis decani.[25] Ego Arnoldus[26] cancellarius relegi.

107

August 25, 1134. Laon.

Barthélémy,[1] bishop of Laon, makes known that Ursio, knight of Soupir,[2] together with Aubry and Lambert, his sons-in-law, exempts the church of Prémontré from two-thirds of the minor tithe owed at Soupir. Agnès, wife of Ursio; their sons Pierre, Hugues, and Simon; their daughters Emmeline, wife of Aubry, and Fréssende Doumisun, *wife of Lambert; and Fréssende and Lambert's children Dreux and Gile, all consent to this. The fief lords Létaud Galerne,[3] Renaud de Punchy,[4] and Robert de Montaigu[5] approve.*

A. Cartulary of Prémontré, fols. 26v–27r.

B. Original not found.

EDITION: Dufour-Malbezin, *Actes*, 254–5; *Chartae Galliae*, no. 208213, http://telma.irht.cnrs.fr/outils/chartae-galliae/charte208213/.

---

25 Guy de Pierrepont, son of Roger, lord of Pierrepont, and Ermengarde, lady of Montaigu, was first treasurer, archdeacon, and dean of the chapter of Laon, and later bishop of Châlons, 1144–7.

26 Ernaud, chancellor of Laon, 1133–41, and archdeacon of Laon, 1136/8–41. Dufour-Malbezin, *Actes*, 29.

---

1 Barthélemy de Jur (d. 1158), son of Conon, lord of Grandson and La Sarraz, and Ada de Roucy; first subdeacon and then treasurer of Reims, later bishop of Laon, 1113–51.

2 Soupir, cant. Vailly, https://dicotopo.cths.fr/places/P62600159.

3 Létaud Galerne (or Li Vialerne) also appears as a witness in other episcopal acts of 1134 and 1136. Dufour Malbezin, *Actes*, 253, 270.

4 Renaud de Punchy (cant. Rosières, https://dicotopo.cths.fr/places/P43010035) is attested 1115–36. Dufour-Malbezin, *Actes*, 146, 271.

5 Robert de Montaigu (or de Pierrepont), son of Roger, lord of Pierrepont, and Ermengarde,

Karta Bartolomei episcopi de confirmatione tocius minute decime de Sopi.

[I]n nomine sancte et individue Trinitatis. Ego Bartholomeus, Dei gratia sancte Laudunensis ecclesie minister indignus. Notum esse volumus tam posteris quam modernis quod Ursio, miles de Soupeio, annuente uxore eius Agnete cum filiis suis Petro, Hugone, Symone, et Albricus, gener ipsius Ursionis, concedente uxore eius Emmelina, Lambertus quoque, assensu uxoris eius Freessendis, que Doumisun dicitur, et filii eius Drogonis et filie eius Gile, duas partes tocius minute decime de curia Premonstratensis ecclesie que in Monte de Supeio sita est, eidem Premonstratensi ecclesie pro remedio animarum suarum jure perpetuo habendas concesserunt, ita scilicet quod Letaldus Galerne et Renaldus de Povenci, dominus etiam Robertus de Monte Acuto, de quorum feodo chasium ecclesie de Supeio habebant, intra cuius terminos curia hec est, elemosinam et donationem eorum assensu suo confirmaverunt et concessionis sue signum in manu nostra posuerunt. Quod ne aliqua in posterum occasione vel oblivione deleatur, presenti scripto firmari precepimus, testium quoque subscriptione et sigilli nostri impressione muniri curavimus. S. Barthomolei, episcopi qui hoc scriptum fieri jussit. S. Balduini de Supeio.[6] S. Roboldi. S. Theobaldi. S. Roberti. S. Radulphi. S. Frumentini. S. Alberti Malet.[7] S. Ernaldi. Actum Lauduni VIII kalendas septembris, anno dominice incarnationis M° C° XXX° IIII°, indictione XII^{a}, epacta XXIII^{a}, concurrente VII^{a}. Ego Ernaldus[8] Sancte Marie cancellarius relegi.

108

December 22, 1217. Bishop's chapel, Laon.

Anselme,[1] *bishop of Laon, makes known that Philippe de Soupir,*[2] *knight, gave half of the land he held at Soupir, less one* sextariata, *to the church of Prémontré and sold the rest to the same church, with the approval of his children Henri, Jacques, Bertrand, and Elizabeth, as well as of Ada, his wife, who was*

6 Baudouin I, lord of Soupir. Wacha, "La Puissance du Choix," 116.

7 Albert Malet (or Malez) also appears in an 1133 act as a *homo* of Baudouin I, lord of Soupir.

8 Ernaud, chancellor of Laon, 1133–41, and archdeacon of Laon, 1136/8–41. Dufour-Malbezin, *Actes*, 29.

1 Anselme de Mauny (or de Bercenay), bishop of Laon, 1215–38.

2 Philippe de Soupir (Soupir, cant. Vailly, https://dicotopo.cths.fr/places/P62600159), knight, son of Guy I, lord of Soupir; husband of Ada. Wacha, "La Puissance du Choix," 116.

compensated for her dotalicium *with vineyards between the millstream and the town of Moussy.*[3] *Baudouin, lord of Soupir and fief lord, also approved. (See* ***117*** *and* ***128****.)*

A. Cartulary of Prémontré, fol. 27r.
B. Original not found.

Karta episcopi Laudunensis de confirmatione elemosine et venditionis terre Philipi de Sopi.

Anselmus,[4] Dei gratia Laudunensis episcopus, presentibus et futuris in perpetuum. Per hoc scriptum auctenticum notum fieri volumus universis quod Philippus de Souppi, miles, in nostra et plurium tam ecclesiasticarum quam secularium personarum presentia constitutus, sollempniter et publice recognovit quod medietatem totius terre quam habebat in Monte de Souppi prope curtem Premonstratensis ecclesie une sexterlata minus contulerat in elemosinam eidem ecclesie et quod totum residuum ipsius terre eidem vendiderat sub certo precio. Huic autem recognitioni interfuerunt omnes liberi ipsius Philippi videlicet Henricus, Jacobus et Bertrannus, filii et Elizabeth, filia qui et elemosinam dicte terre et venditionem laudaverunt. Uxor etiam ipsius Philippi, nomine Ada, que de quadam parte predicte terre dotata fuerat, hoc ipsum laudavit, facta sibi et nominata coram nobis recompensatione dotalicii sui ad alia bona sui mariti, videlicet ad vineas que sunt inter rivum molendini et villam de Moissi, quam recompensationem astricta fidei sacramento asservit condignam esse, sicut credebat. Balduinus etiam, dominus de Soppi, a quo idem Philippus terram illam cum alia hereditate sua tenebat in feodum et Balduinus de nobis, elemosinam et venditionem laudavit et tam ipse Balduinus quam Philippus omni advocatie et justicie et omnimodo juri ac proprietati quam in ipsa terra habebant renunciantes, ipsam terram in manu nostra posuerunt et nos eam in manu viri venerabilis Gervasii, Premonstratensis abbatis, reponentes, ipsi et ecclesie sue eam contradidimus libere et perpetuo possidendam. Preterea Balduinus et Philippus et predicta uxor eius in manu nostra corporaliter fidem dederunt quod nichil amodo in terra illa reclamabunt. Dicti etiam liberi ipsius Philippi in capella nostra super sancta juraverunt quod nullam deinceps questionem movebunt sive molestiam inferent ecclesie Premonstrati super ipsa terra. Sciendum autem quod Balduinus et Philippus sub interpositione fidei promiserunt quod legitimam warandiam portabunt super illa terra contra omnes qui ad jus venire voluerint. Ut igitur omnia que in hac pagina continentur, perpetuam optineant

3 Moussy-sur-Aisne, cant. Craonne, https://dicotopo.cths.fr/places/P63059874.
4 The initial letter has been added at a later, possibly post-medieval date.

firmitatem, presens scriptum in testimonium et memoriam huius rei episcopali auctoritate confectum sigilli nostri munimine confirmamus. Actum Lauduni in capella nostra, undecimo kalendas januarii, anno incarnationis dominice millesimo ducentesimo septimo decimo.

109

January, 1230.

Anselme,[1] *bishop of Laon, approves as fief lord the sale made by Colard,*[2] prepositus *of Soupir, and Sybille,*[3] *husband and wife, to the church of Prémontré of a piece of land that has the capacity to support about five* sextarii *of seed grain, located next to the field of* Ad Spinum *on the Chavonne*[4] *pathway. Sybille received compensation for the sale of the said land since it figured as part of her* dos. *Husband and wife Milon [de Sissonne]*[5] *and Agathe*[6] *approve as fief lords of Soupir.*

A. Cartulary of Prémontré, fols. 27r–27v.
B. Original, AD Aisne, H 826, previously sealed with a double strip of parchment.

Confirmat Anselmus Laudunensis episcopus venditionem cuiusdam terre Colardi prepositi de Soppi.

[A]nselmus, Dei gratia Laudunensis episcopus, universis presentes litteras inspecturis salutem in Domino. Noverit universitas vestra quod Colardus, dictus prepositus de Souppi, vendidit ecclesie Premonstratensi quandam terram circiter quinque sextarios sementis capientem, que sita est ad semitam de Chavones juxta campum Ad Spinam, liberam ab omni censu vel redditu seu tallia, plenarie coram nobis recognoscens sibi esse satisfactum competenter de toto precio venditionis predicte, promittens etiam fideliter et firmiter,

1 Anselme de Mauny (or de Bercenay), bishop of Laon, 1215–38.
2 Colard, *prepositus* of Soupir, is also mentioned in acts of 1242/3 of the abbey of Saint-Aubert de Cambrai concerning transactions involving his sons, the cleric Pierre, Raoul, and Remi. AD Nord, 36 H 335; Jules De Laprairie, "Notes sur le village de Soupir," *Bulletin de la Société historique et archéologique de Soissons* 17 (1863), 256–7.
3 Sybille, likely sister of Simon de Passi. De Laprairie, "Notes sur le village de Soupir," 256.
4 Chavonne, cant. Vailly, https://dicotopo.cths.fr/places/P90566217.
5 Milon, lord of Sissonne (d. aft. 1248), son of Gobert, lord of Sissonne, and Agnès. Newman, *Seigneurs*, vol. 1, 170, 173.
6 Agathe, lady of Soupir (d. aft. 1248), daughter of Baudouin II, lord of Soupir, and Aelide. She inherited her lordship from her brother Baudouin III. Newman, *Seigneurs*, vol. 1, 170, 174; Wacha, "La Puissance du Choix," 116.

fide corporaliter prestita in manu nostra, quod contra venditionem predictam decetero non veniet nec dictam terram repetet aut repeti faciet nec predictam ecclesiam decetero super hoc molestabit aut faciet molestari. Dictam etiam venditionem laudavit et approbavit, fide corporaliter prestita, Sibilla, uxor eiusdem Colardi, predicta omnia plenarie in nostra presentia recognoscens, et quia eadem Sibilla dotata erat de terra predicta sicut dicebat, eadem quitavit spontanea et non coacta in nostra presentia predicte ecclesie quicquid juris habebat vel habere poterat tam nomine dotis quam alio quocumque modo vel titulo in terra predicta, promittens firmiter et fideliter fide corporali prestita quod ipsam terram decetero non reclamabit per se vel per alium nec ipsam ecclesiam super hoc decetero aliquatenus inquietabit. Dictus autem Colardus in recompensationem eiusdem venditionis assignavit eidem Sibille, uxori sue, terram aliam equevalentem quam in dote sua posuit, de qua terra eadem Sibilla coram nobis plenarie recognovit sibi esse competenter et sufficienter satisfactum. Et quia dicta terra vendita de feodo viri nobilis domini Milonis de Sissonia descendebat et movebat, idem Milo cum uxore sua, Agatha, de cuius etiam hereditate eadem terra movebat in nostra presentia constituti, dictam venditionem factam a dictis Colardo et Sibilla tanquam domini laudaverunt et approbaverunt et ratam habuerunt fide prestita corporali in manu nostra. Quitaverunt etiam et dederunt eidem ecclesie quicquid nomine feodi vel assisie aut hereditario jure seu quocumque alio modo vel titulo habebant vel habere poterant in terra predicta, promittentes fide prestita corporali quod de cetero nichil penitus in terra predicta reclamabunt aut facient reclamari, nec super ipsa venditione decetero Premonstratensem ecclesiam molestabunt vel facient molestari. Nos autem, quia dicta terra in dominio nostro erat et dictus Milo eandem a nobis tenebat in feodo, dictam venditionem factam, sicut superius est expressum, tamquam superior dominus, laudavimus et approbavimus et ratam habuimus et quitavimus etiam et dedimus eidem ecclesie quicquid nomine feodi seu dominii habebamus in terra predicta. In cuius rei testimonium, presentes literas patentes emisimus sigilli nostri munimine salvo jure nostro et alieno roboratas. Actum anno Domini M° CC° tricesimo, mense januario.

110

December 26, 1211.

Magister *Prieur,*[1] *canon of Laon and* officialis *for Robert,*[2] *bishop-elect of Laon, makes known that husband and wife Baudouin, knight of Montigny,*[3] *and*

1 Prieur, *officialis* of Laon, ca. 1210–ca. 1213. Wyard, *Saint-Vincent*, 36.

2 Robert de Châtillon, son of Guy II, lord of Châtillon and Alix de Dreux, bishop of Laon, 1210–15.

3 Perhaps Montigny-sur-Vesle, cant. Fismes, https://dicotopo.cths.fr/places/P59181065.

Emmeline relinquished to the church of Prémontré the major and minor tithes that they held in the territory of Soupir.[4] *Eustacie, Emmeline's daughter from a previous marriage, consented, as did Baudouin and Emmeline's other adult children Clérembaud, Albert, Mathilde, Cécile, Mélisende, and Elizabeth, and the fief lord Nicholas de Humont. The adult children also consented on behalf of two unnamed minor daughters. In addition, Baudouin and Emmeline received 120* librae Laudunensium *from Prémontré, 20 of which was set aside for Nicholas de Humont. (See **136**.)*

A. Cartulary of Prémontré, fol. 27v.
B. Original, AN, L 995, no. 57, previously sealed.

Karta curie Laudunensis de resignatione decime maioris et minute de Soupi [*margo*: quam Balduinus miles et uxor eius fecerunt in curia Laudunensis.]

[I]n nomine Patris et Filii et Spiritus Sancti, amen. Ego magister Prior, canonicus Laudunensis et officialis domini Laudunensis electi, omnibus huius carte inspectoribus tam presentibus quam futuris in perpetuum. Noverit universitas vestra quod Balduinus, miles de Montigni[5] et Enmelina, uxor eius, in Laudunensi curia cui, ex auctoritate domini nostri Roberti Laudunensis electi, presidentes specialiter ad exequendum subscriptum negotium, deputati eramus, coram nobis presentialiter constituti, totam decimam tam maiorem quam minutam, quam habebant vel aliquo jure habere poterant in territorio de Souppi[6] ad hoc ut Premonstratensi ecclesie ad quam in magna parte ex apostolico privilegio pertinebat in elemosinam perpetuo conferretur habenda in manum nostram absolute et sollempniter resignarunt et quia dicta decima de patrimonio uxoris ipsius Balduini quasi jure hereditario procedebat, filia uxoris eiusdem,[7] nomine Eustachia, quam de alio viro sustulerat, cum in nostra presentia similiter constituta interrogata fuisset a nobis utrum aliquid de prefata decima cum traderetur marito sibi collatum fuisset, publice confessa est et respondit quod nec matrimonii nec hereditatis jure quicquam in ipsa decima vendicabat quin potius resignationem quam eius mater et vitricus suus in manu nostra fecerant pro parte sua laudabat et ratam prorsus habebat. Preterea eandem resignationem liberi predictorum Balduini et Enmeline, videlicet Clarenbaldus et Albricus filii, Matildis, Cecilia, Milesendis et Elizabeth filie, sine aliqua reclamatione in posterum et presentialiter et pariter laudaverunt. Nicholaus etiam miles de

4 Soupir, cant. Vailly, https://dicotopo.cths.fr/places/P62600159.
5 Montegni *B*.
6 Suppi *B*.
7 *Transp. A*; eiusdem uxoris *B*.

Humont, de cuius feodo ipsa decima descendebat, idipsum laudavit ex parte sua et quicquid juris habebat vel poterat habere in feodo in manum nostram sine retentione aliqua resignavit Premonstratensi ecclesie conferendum. Ceterum omnes predicti tam principales videlicet resignatores quam etiam laudatores decime memorate, preter duas juvenculas filias a quibus pro eo, quod vix[8] decennes erant in sua laudatione nec requisitum fuit nec prestitum juramentum, et corporaliter et pariter juraverunt quod nec per se nec per alios quoslibet ope, arte, sive consilio Premonstratensem ecclesiam decetero super resignata predicto modo decima molestabunt vel facient molestari sed bona fide id quod ab eis et laudatum et juratum est, observantes contra omnes reclamatores vel molestatores qui ad curiam venire voluerint ecclesie Premonstratensi secundum legitimum suum posse et defensionis et warandie ferent auxilium. In huius autem resignationis gratiam, predictus Balduinus et uxor eius centum et quadraginta libras Laudunensium de caritate et beneficio Premonstratensis ecclesie habuerunt de quibus memoratus Nicholaus ad cuius feodum decima dicta pertinuerat, viginti libras fortium pro sua concessione et laudatione in partem suam disnoscitur habuisse. Nos igitur in hac parte vicem et auctoritatem domini nostri Laudunensis electi de ipsius mandato agentes, eadem decima virum venerabilem Gervasium, abbatem Premonstratensem nomine sue ecclesie curavimus sollempniter investire. Ut igitur translatio decime memorate prefato modo facta futuris temporibus inviolabiliter observetur, eam fideliter hic inscribi et inpressione sigilli curie Laudunensis fecimus communiri. Actum septimo kalendas januarii, anno incarnationis dominice M° CC°[9] undecimo.

111

August 25, 1134. Laon.

Dean Guy[1] *and the chapter of the cathedral of Laon on the one hand, and abbot Hugues [I]*[2] *and the canons of Prémontré on the other, make an arrangement concerning the altar of Soupir*[3] *and the disposition of its minor tithe.*

A. Cartulary of Prémontré, fols. 27v–28r.

B. Original not found.

8 *Om.* tunc *A*.

9 millesimo ducentesimo *B*.

1 Guy de Pierrepont, son of Roger, lord of Pierrepont, and Ermengarde, lady of Montaigu, was first treasurer, archdeacon, and dean of the chapter of Laon, and later bishop of Châlons, 1144–7.

2 Hugues I de Fosses (ca. 1093–1164), first abbot of Prémontré.

3 Soupir, cant. Vailly, https://dicotopo.cths.fr/places/P62600159.

Scriptum capituli Laudunensis et decani de altari de Soupi et de tercia parte decime maioris.

[I]n nomine sancte et individue Trinitatis. Ego, Guido decanus cum toto sancte Laudunensis ecclesie capitulo. Utile fuit litterarum insinuatione memorie commendari quod pro utilitate aliqua ad posterorum noticiam debuit transmitti. Notum ergo fieri volumus tam futuris quam presentibus, quia, cum altare de Soupeio et tercia pars decime pro altari ipso in partem nostram antiquo jure succederet, Hugo, abbas, et canonici Premonstrate ecclesie, intra terminos eiusdem parrochie curiam habentes, in hoc nobiscum convenerunt quod pro tercia parte totius minute decime de predicta curia singulis annis duodecim nummos persolverent, sex quidem presbitero eiusdem parrochie et alios sex pro conditione subjecta sibi retinerent. Pro tercia autem parte nostra decime que de agricultura carrucarum eiusdem curie nobis contigeret, si tres carrucas ibi haberent de tercia carruca modium melioris frumenti, quod ibi de labore suo habebunt et modium avene singulis annis nobis persolverent ita scilicet ut pro sex predictis nummis propria eorum vectura ad cellarium nostrum deferri facerent. Presbiter vero parrochie quod econtra sui juris erit de reliqua decima que in villa congregabitur, habebit. Porro si preter tres carrucas illas una vel due vel eo amplius superaddantur quantum pro tercia parte nostra nobis debet contingere, simili modo in frumento et avena a predictis canonicis ecclesie nostre decima persolvetur. Hanc autem conventionem ne aliqua in posterum occasione vel oblivione dissolvatur, presenti scripto firmari voluimus testium quoque subscriptione et sigillo ecclesie impresso muniri curavimus. Signum Guidonis, decani. Signum Bartholomei, archidiaconi.[4] S. Bliardi, cantoris.[5] S. Herberti, sacerdotis. S. Albrici, sacerdotis. S. Milonis, diaconi. S. Rogeri, diaconi.[6] S. Arnulphi, subdiaconi.[7] S. Widonis, subdiaconi.[8] S. Hugonis, acoliti. S. Balduini, acoliti. Actum Lauduni VIII kalendas septembris, anno dominice incarnationis M° C° XXX° IIII°, indictione XII[a], epacta XX[a] III[a], concurrente septimo. Ego Ernaldus[9] Sancte Marie cancellarius relegi.

4 Barthélemy de Montcornet (d. 1175), son of Hugues de Montcornet and Béatrice de Reynel, was archdeacon of Laon from 1133, treasurer of Laon from 1137, and chancellor of Laon, 1141–4; later archdeacon of Reims; and bishop of Beauvais, 1162–75. Guyotjeannin, *Episcopus*, 131; Dufour-Malbezin, *Actes*, 30.

5 Bliard, cantor of Laon, attested ca. 1113–ca. 1135. BM Reims, MS 1843 (N. 863), fols. 13r, 24v; BM Laon MS 532, fols. 24v–25r, 36r–37r; Wyard, *Saint-Vincent*, 37.

6 Roger, deacon of Laon, is a witness in episcopal acts 1125–34. Dufour-Malbezin, *Actes*, 188, 260.

7 Arnoul, subdeacon of Laon, is a witness to episcopal acts 1128–45. Dufour-Malbezin, *Actes*, 201, 371.

8 Guy, subdeacon of Laon, is a witness to episcopal acts 1115–36. Dufour-Malbezin, *Actes*, 144, 268.

9 Ernaud, chancellor of Laon, 1133–41, and archdeacon of Laon, 1136/8–41. Dufour-Malbezin, *Actes*, 29.

112

1135

Barthélemy,[1] bishop of Laon, confirms the augmentation of an alms gift by Baudouin de Soupir[2] to the church of Prémontré of land to build a mill on the river Aisne in the territory of Soupir at a place the brothers judge suitable. The site is to be exempt of taxes and customs, and will be constituted of as much land and water as can be encompassed by a bow shot.

A. Cartulary of Prémontré, fol. 28r.

B. Original, AD Aisne, H 826, previously sealed on braided threads of blue, yellow, and green silk.

EDITION: Dufour-Malbezin, *Actes*, 264–5; *Chartae Galliae*, no. 208221, http://telma.irht.cnrs.fr/outils/chartae-galliae/charte208221/.

Karta episcopi Laudunensis de confirmatione elemosine domini Balduini de Soupi.

[I]n nomine sancte et individue Trinitatis. Ego Bartholomeus, Dei gratia Laudunensis ecclesie minister humilis, notum fieri volo tam futuris quam presentibus quia, cum Balduinus de Supeio in Monte qui predicte ville preminet, pro remedio anime sue, de propria cultura Premonstratensi[3] ecclesie contulisset, ad augmentum elemosine sue in ripa fluminis quod Axona dicitur, ubi fratres ipsi oportunius sibi previderint, in territorio de Supi,[4] intra metas juris ipsius Balduini, locum ad construendum molendinum ab omni censu et consuetudine liberum, eidem ecclesie donavit et insuper ad ipsius molendini necessitatem et omnem aliam fratrum conmoditatem a loco ipsius quantum a parte superiori et inferiori et e transverso fluminis arcus jacere potest, in terra et aqua, concessit. Quoniam vero de feodo nostro descendebat prefatus Balduinus, hoc donum in manu nostra posuit et auctoritate nostra confirmari postulavit. Nos autem, ut omnis contradictio sopiatur, tam presenti scripto quam testium subscriptione necnon et sigilli nostri impressione, anathemate interposito, firmari precepimus.

1 Barthélemy de Jur (d. 1158), son of Conon, lord of Grandson and La Sarraz, and Ada de Roucy; first subdeacon and then treasurer of Reims, later bishop of Laon, 1113–51.

2 Baudouin I, lord of Soupir (Soupir, cant. Vailly, https://dicotopo.cths.fr/places/P62600159). Wacha, "La Puissance du Choix," 116.

3 Premonstrate *B*.

4 Supeio *B*.

S.[5] Guidonis decani.[6] S. Bliardi[7] cantoris.[8] S. Arnulphi,[9] clerici. S. Hugonis Poivre.[10,11] S. Herberti Poilevilain.[12] S. Haimonis Bretel[13] et ceteri.[14] Actum est hoc anno incarnationis dominice M° C° XXX° V°,[15] indictione XIII[a], epacta XV[a], concurrente primo.[16] Ego Ernaudus[17] Sancte Marie cancellarius relegi.

113

1162. Laon.

*Gautier [II],[1] bishop of Laon, recalls the conditions of the construction of the church of Soupir[2] (see **106**) and makes known that at the request of Guy [II],[3] lord of Soupir and the town's inhabitants, the church of Prémontré had also helped with the restoration of the bell tower. Gautier declares that in the future Prémontré will no longer be responsible for any restoration work concerning Soupir's church.*

A. Cartulary of Prémontré, fol. 28r.

B. Original, BnF, nouv. acq. lat. 2590, no. 37bis, previously sealed with a single seal.

REGISTER: Boghen, "Inventaire des actes épiscopaux originaux conservés à la Bibliothèque nationale (1121–1200)," 114.

---

5 Signum *B*.

6 Guy de Pierrepont, son of Roger, lord of Pierrepont, and Ermengarde, lady of Montaigu, was first treasurer, archdeacon and dean of the chapter of Laon, and later bishop of Châlons, 1144–7.

7 Blihardi *B*.

8 Bliard, cantor of Laon, attested ca. 1113–ca. 1135. BM Reims, MS 1843 (N. 863), fols. 13r, 24v; BM Laon MS 532, fols. 24v–25r, 36r–37r; Wyard, *Saint Vincent*, 37.

9 Arnulfi *B*.

10 Poyure *B*.

11 Hugues Poivre also appears as a witness in **141**.

12 Herbert Poilevilain appears as a witness in a number of episcopal acts dating 1134–5. Dufour-Malbezin, *Actes*, 256, 265, 266, 316.

13 Haimo Bretel also appears as a witness in episcopal acts of 1141 (**141**) and 1142 (Dufour-Malbezin, *Actes*, 329).

14 *Add.* et ceteri *A*, Signum Gerardi, vicedomini. S. Nicholai, castellani. S. Clarembaldi de Turricula. S. Hugonis Truie. S. Roberti Vinun. S. Roberti Vituli *B*.

15 M C XXX V, indictione XIIII, epacta V *B*.

16 I *B*.

17 Ernaud, chancellor of Laon, 1133–41, and archdeacon of Laon, 1136/8–41. Dufour-Malbezin, *Actes*, 29.

---

1 Gautier de Mortagne was dean of Laon, ca. 1142–55, and bishop of Laon, 1155–74.

2 Soupir, cant. Vailly, https://dicotopo.cths.fr/places/P62600159.

3 Guy II, lord of Soupir, son of Guy I, lord of Soupir; husband of Agnès. Wacha, "La Puissance du Choix," 116.

Karta episcopi Laudunensis quod ecclesia Premonstratensis non tenetur decetero ad reparationem ecclesie de Soupi.

[I]n nomine sancte et individue Trinitatis.[4] Ego Galterus, Dei gratia Laudunensis episcopus, notum facimus tam futuris quam presentibus quod Balduinus de Soupeio[5] et homines sui ecclesiam ceperant edificare ubi ad servitium Dei convenirent, quam, cum nullatenus per se possent perficere, venerunt ad Hugonem, abbatem Premonstratensem, obnixe expetentes quatinus ad preficiendam ecclesiam illam aliquod consilium daret. Postea vero habito consilio, communi assensu dederunt ecclesie Premonstratensi per manum domini Bartholomei, episcopi predecessoris nostri, quasdam terre particulas quas habebant ipsi infra culturas et extra per Montem de Supeio[6] ecclesie perpetuo habendas concesserunt et scripto firmaverunt. Et ob hoc ecclesia Premonstratensis ecclesiam inceptam perfecit et perfectam ex integro eis reddidit.[7] Longo post tempore clocarius cepit deficere, Guido, dominus de Suppeio, et homines sui venerunt ad ecclesiam Premonstratensem omnino expetentes, quatinus clocarium illum juvarent reficere. Ecclesia vero Premonstratensis petitionibus eorum obtemperans ex integro clocarium illum refecit. Postea vero petitionibus Premonstratensis ecclesie et assensui Guidonis de Supeio[8] et hominum suorum firmari impressione sigilli nostri fecimus sub anathemate ut quocumque modo pars eiusdem ecclesie vel tota ecclesia vel etiam ipse clocarius deinceps dirveretur, Premonstratenses amodo nichil restaurabunt. Unde sunt testes: Anselmus[9] decanus de Cerni, Petrus sacerdos de Suppi,[10] Simon[11] miles eiusdem ville, et ceteri.[12] Actum est hoc Lauduni, anno incarnati verbi M° C° sexagesimo secundo.[13] Angotus[14] cancellarius[15] scripsit et subscripsit.

4 *Om.* amen *A*.
5 Suppeio *B*.
6 Suppeio *B*.
7 *Transp. A*, reddidit eis *B*.
8 Suppeio *B*.
9 Ansel, dean of Cerny, ca. 1171–ca. 1178. Beauvillé, *Recueil de documents inédits concernant la Picardie*, vol. 4, 15; Herbomez, *Chartes de l'abbaye de Saint-Martin de Tournai*, vol. 1, 116.
10 Soupir, cant. Vailly, https://dicotopo.cths.fr/places/P62600159.
11 Symon *B*.
12 *Add.* ceteri *A*; Walterus prepositus, Herbertus carpentarius de Berlencurt, qui fecit eundem clocarium *B*.
13 II° *B*.
14 Angot, chancellor of Laon, ca. 1144–ca. 1170.
15 *Om.* relegit *A*.

114

1186

Guillaume,[1] *archbishop of Reims, titular cardinal of Santa Sabina, legate of the Holy See, makes known that Eudes de Soupir*[2] *relinquished to the Premonstratensian house at Soupir an oven, a press, and the* rotagium *that he claimed to hold there, under the condition that the holder of the lordship of Soupir will in future receive revenue from the* rotagium *in the places where they receive revenue from the* vinagium.

A. Cartulary of Prémontré, fols. 28r–28v.
B. Original not found.

Karta Remensis archiepiscopi de quitatione Odonis de Soupi super quibusdam rebus.

[G]uillermus, Dei gratia Remorum archiepiscopus, Sancte Romane Ecclesie titulo Sancte Sabine cardinalis, Apostolice Sedis legatus, omnibus ad quos littere iste pervenerint in Domino salutem. Noverint tam presentes quam futuris quod, constitutus in presentia nostra, Odo de Soupeio furnum, pressorium, rotagium, que clamabat in domo Premonstratensi de Supeio, omnino resignavit et nichil juris se in eis habere asseruit et nichil se deinceps reclamaturum fide interposita firmavit, excepto quod ubi dominus de Supeio winagium accipiet, ipse rotagium solummodo habebit. Adjecit autem predictus Odo quod legitimam warandiam portabit adversus omnes qui predictam concessionem impedire voluerint. Ut autem hec concessio in presentia nostra sollempniter facta et fidei interpositione firmata in posterum malignorum incursibus non possit infringi, scripto nostro et sigilli nostri auctoritate confirmamus, statuentes et sub anathemate prohibentes ne quis hanc nostre confirmationis paginam audeat infringere, salva in omnibus Apostolice Sedis auctoritate. Actum anno incarnationis dominice M° C° LXXX° sexto. Datum per manum Lambini cancellarii nostri.

---

1 Guillaume aux Blanches Mains (1135–1202), son of Thibaut II, count of Blois and Champagne, and Mathilde von Spanheim, was bishop of Chartres, 1164–76, archbishop of Sens, 1169–76, and archbishop of Reims, 1176–1202.

2 Soupir, cant. Vailly, https://dicotopo.cths.fr/places/P62600159.

115

February 27, 1208.

Renaud,[1] *bishop of Laon, makes known that Philippe de Soupir*[2] *relinquished to Prémontré the right to receive baskets of grapes from Prémontré's vineyards in the valley of Metz*[3] *annually. Philippe also relinquished the 26* denarii censuales *that Prémontré paid him annually on certain fields, meadows, and woods.*

A. Cartulary of Prémontré, fol. 28v.

B[1]. Original, BnF, nouv. acq. lat. 2590, no. 42, previously sealed with a single seal.

B[2]. Original, BnF, Coll. Picardie 290, no. 23, previously sealed with a single seal.

Karta Laudunensis episcopi de quitatione facta ecclesie Premonstratensis a domino Philippo de Soupi.

[E]go Rainaldus,[4] Dei gratia Laudunensis episcopus, notum facimus presentibus et futuris quod vir nobilis Philippus de Soupiaco,[5] coram nobis constitutus, quitavit in perpetuum ecclesie Premonstrati[6] quosdam panerios racemorum quos de consuetudine habere solebat annuatim in vineis eiusdem ecclesie in valle de Maidi constitutis. Quitavit etiam eidem ecclesie in perpetuum viginti sex denarios bone monete censuales quos sepedicta ecclesia eidem persolvere solebat, videlicet super silvulam VIII denarios, super campum Bardulfi IIII[or] denarios, super vineam Pautart II denarios, super campum Alarue[7] II denarios, super pratum Richeri Frestele II denarios, super pratum leprosorum I obolum, super pratum Mahumet[8] I obolum, super pratum Ermengardis[9] I obolum, super pratum Galteri maioris I denarium, super pratum Enmelini[10] II denarios, super boscum, fratris Mathei I denarium, super parvum boscum eiusdem Mathei I obolum, super campum ad Annesum[11] I denarium, super pratum juxta pratum Pasturel I denarium. Hanc autem quitationem coram nobis recognitam nostro confirmamus assensu et sigillum nostrum appendimus in testimonium et munimen. Actum anno Domini[12] M° CC° octavo, IIII[13] kalendas martii.

---

1 Renaud Surdelle, bishop of Laon, 1207–10.

2 Soupir, cant. Vailly, https://dicotopo.cths.fr/places/P62600159.

3 Le Metz, comm. Moussy-sur-Aisne, https://dicotopo.cths.fr/places/P31678789.

4 Renaldus *B*[1].

5 Sopiaco *B*[1], *B*[2].

6 Premonstratensis *B*[1].

7 A La Rue *B*[1], *B*[2].

8 Maumet *B*[1].

9 Hermengardis *B*[1].

10 Hemelini *B*[1], *B*[2].

11 Aunesun *B*[1], *B*[2].

12 *Add.* Domini *A*; incarnationis dominice *B*[1], *B*[2].

13 quarto *B*[1]; IIII° *B*[2].

116

1152–97.[1] Troyes.

Henri [I/II], count of Troyes [and of Champagne], commands B.,[2] seneschal of Oulchy[-le-Château], to respect the rights of the religious of Prémontré in their dispute with Guy de Soupir[3] and Barthélemy Ballene concerning mills on the River Aisne that Prémontré held in alms from Henri's father, lest the brothers feel the need to appeal again in front of count Henri.

A. Cartulary of Prémontré, fol. 28v.

B. Original not found.

EDITION: Benton and Bur, *Recueil des actes d'Henri le Libéral, Comte de Champagne*, vol. 1, 662–3.

Karta comitis Campanie de molendinis Axone.

[H]enricus, Trecensis ~~episcopus~~ comes, B. senescallo Ulcheiacensis omnibusque qui post ipsum fuerint senescallis salutem et dilectionem. Mando vobis et firmiter omnino precipio ut de querela que inter fratres Premonstratenses et Guidonem de Soupi et Bartholomeum Ballenam habetur, videlicet de molendinis de Axona qui de elemosina patris mei sunt, quotiens dicti fratres super hoc ad vos venerint, jus suum illis faciatis habere, ita ne pro defectu justicie sive rectitudinis eos ad me reverti oporteat; servientem etiam dictorum fratrum et equum cum omnibus hiis que ad usus dictorum molendinorum necessaria sunt, custodiatis et manu teneatis, ita ne quis ad ea manum apponere presumat. Valete. Testibus Marescallo et Ertaldo,[4] Trecis.

1 This date range is derived from the rule of Counts Henri I (1152–81) and Henri II (1181–97); and a Guy, lord of Soupir, who is attested ca. 1160s. On stylistic grounds, John Benton and Michel Bur date this act to 1158–81.

2 Possibly the Bernier, viscount of Oulchy, who appears in acts in the cartulary of Notre-Dame d'Igny in 1156. BnF, MS lat. 9904, fols. 88r–88v, 126v; Melleville, *DH*, vol. 2, 190.

3 Either Guy I, lord of Soupir (cant. Vailly, https://dicotopo.cths.fr/places/P62600159), or his son Guy II, lord of Soupir. Wacha, "La Puissance du Choix," 116.

4 Artaud de Nogent, a "citizen of Nogent" and chamberlain of the counts of Champagne, 1163–90. Joinville and Villehardouin, *Chronicles of the Crusades*, 186; Evergates, *Henry the Liberal*, 188.

117

December 22, 1217. Bishop's chapel, Laon.

*Baudouin [II],[1] lord of Soupir, approves as fief lord his uncle Philippe's[2] gift of half of a piece of land located at Soupir to the church of Prémontré, and the sale of the other half by Philippe to the same church. (See **108** and **128**.)*

A. Cartulary of Prémontré, fol. 28v.
B. Original, BnF, Coll. Picardie 290, no. 32, previously sealed.

Karta de elemosine et venditione terre domini Philippi de Maiel.[3]

[E]go Balduinus, dominus de Soupi,[4] notum facio presentibus et futuris quod Philippus, patruus meus, medietatem totius terre quam habebat in Monte de Soupi[5] prope curtem Premonstratensis ecclesie, una sexterlata minus contulit in elemosinam eidem ecclesie, et quod totum residuum ipsius terre eidem vendidit sub certo precio. Ego igitur Balduinus, a quo idem Philippus terram illam cum alia hereditate sua tenebat in feodum, elemosinam et venditionem dicte terre laudavi et tam ego quam ipse Philipus omni advocatie et justicie et omnimodo juri ac proprietati quam in ipsa terra habebamus renuntiantes, eam in manu venerabilis patris Anselmi,[6] Laudunensis episcopi, de cuius feodo terra illa principaliter descendebat, posuimus, et ipse dominus episcopus de nostro assensu et petitione ipsam terram in manu viri venerabilis Gervasii, Premonstratensis abbatis, reponens ipsi, et ecclesie sue eam contradidit libere et perpetuo possidendum.[7] Sciendum autem quod ego Balduinus et idem Philippus sub interpositione fidei nostre promisimus quod legitimam warandiam portabimus super illa terra contra omnes qui ad jus venire voluerint. Ut igitur ea que in hac cartula continentur perpetuam habeant firmitatem, eandem cartulam sigillo meo confirmo. Actum Lauduni in cappella domini episcopi undecimo kalendas januarii, anno incarnationis dominice M° CC°[8] septimo decimo.

---

1 Baudouin II, lord of Soupir (cant. Vailly, https://dicotopo.cths.fr/places/P62600159), son of Guy II, lord of Soupir, and Agnès. Wacha, "La Puissance du Choix," 116.
2 Philippe de Soupir, knight, son of Guy I, lord of Soupir; husband of Ada. Ibid.
3 Philippe de Maiel is otherwise referred to in this act as Philippe de Soupir.
4 Suppi *B*.
5 Suppi *B*.
6 Anselme de Mauny (or de Bercenay), bishop of Laon, 1215–38.
7 Posidendam *B*.
8 millesimo ducentesimo *B*.

118

1173

Gautier [II],[1] *bishop of Laon, makes known that Nicholas approved the gift that his uncle Renier* Curaus *made to Prémontré of the mill of Ribaudon*[2] *and a quarter part of a small wood. Nicholas also approved the gift of lands given by Robert de Bar and Guillaume de Fay, while fief lords Hugues de Pierrepont*[3] *and Clemence [de Rethel],*[4] *husband and wife, and their son Robert,*[5] *also conceded their rights. Bishop Gautier grants Prémontré the right to construct another town and church inside the parish of Hannape,*[6] *with the same rights of* altaria *as the first; Prémontré is to present its candidate for curate for the bishop's approval.*

A. Cartulary of Prémontré, fols. 28v–29r.
B. Original not found.
REGISTER: *Studium Baldwin*, fiche 2204.

Karta episcopi Laudunensis de molendino de Ribaudon [*margo:* altare de Hanapia ecclesie Premonstratensis.]

[I]n nomine sancte et individue Trinitatis. Ego Galterus, Dei gratia Laudunensis episcopus. Donum quod Renerus Curaus fecit ecclesie Premonstratensi de molendino de Ribaudon et de quarta parte silvelle, Nicholaus, nepos eius, laudavit ecclesie et quitum clamavit in perpetuum et terram de dono Roberti de Bar et terram de dono ~~Re~~ Guillelmi de Fai. Hec etiam concesserunt Hugo de Petreponte et Clementia uxor eius, et Robertus eorum filius, de quorum feodo hec descendunt. Testes inde sunt: Galterus thesaurarius, Britellus canonicus Laudunensis, magister Anglicus et magister Arnulphus, canonicus Sancti Petri in Foro. De cetero scimus quod altare de Hanapia est ecclesie Premonstrati. Propter quod si abbas et fratres Premonstrati novam aliquando infra terminos parrochie de Hanapia villam et ecclesiam construxerint, concedimus ut ipsi, sicut justum est, habeant ibi jus altaris, ita ut cum ibi presbiterum voluerint instituere, eum episcopo Laudunensi canonice representent ad suscipiendum regimen animarum, episcopali per omnia jure salvo. Unde testes fecimus hic

1 Gautier de Mortagne was dean of Laon, ca. 1142–55, and bishop of Laon, 1155–74.
2 Ribaudon, comm. Soupir, https://dicotopo.cths.fr/places/P28661536.
3 Hugues de Vanault, lord of Pierrepont (d. ca. 1190).
4 Clemence de Rethel (d. aft. 1191), daughter of Ithier, count of Rethel and castellan of Vitry, and Beatrix de Namur.
5 Robert de Pierrepont, lord of Pierrepont, son of Hugues, lord of Pierrepont, and Clémence de Rethel; husband of Eustacie, countess of Roucy, and count of Roucy *iure uxoris*.
6 Hannape, cant. Wassigny, https://dicotopo.cths.fr/places/P37303056.

inscribi: Galterum[7] thesaurarium, Guillermum[8] abbatem Quissiaci, Fulbertum canonicum Sancti Petri de Foro,[9] Simonem presbiterum de capella, et Guillermum[10] cancellarium nostrum qui hec scripsit. Actum anno Domini M° centesimo septuagesimo tercio.

119

February, 1229.

Geoffroi [II],[1] *canon and* officialis *of Soissons, makes known the resolution of a dispute between the church of Prémontré and Gilles [II],*[2] *knight, son of the lord of Marquaix. Gilles and his wife Béatrice de Soupir*[3] *relinquished to Prémontré all their rights over the fishponds, lands, and other possessions that Prémontré had previously acquired, and which had formed part of Béatrice's* dos.

A. Cartulary of Prémontré, fol. 29r.
B. Original not found.

Karta officialis Suessionensis de quadam compositione inter ecclesiam Premonstratensem et Egidium militem [*margo:* de piscaria molendinorum de Axona.]

[G]odefridus, canonicus et officialis Suessionensis, universis presentes litteras inspecturis salutem in Domino. Noverint universi quod cum inter

7 Gautier, treasurer of Laon, ca. 1162–ca. 1173. Per AD Aisne, G 171, a nephew of Gautier de Mortagne, bishop of Laon.
8 Guillaume Hennepaix, abbot of the Premonstratensian abbey of Cuissy, 1170–4, of the Premonstratensian abbey of Bucilly, 1176–8, and of the Premonstratensian abbey of Chartreuve, 1178–85. *MP* II, 366, 494, 497.
9 The collegiate church of Saint-Pierre-au-Marché in the Saint-Georges quarter, Laon.
10 Guillaume, chancellor of the bishop of Laon, is attested 1173–1201. BnF, MS. lat. 11073, fol. 55r; BM Reims, MS 1843 (N. 863), fol. 112v.

1 Geoffroi II, *officialis* of Soissons, ca. 1220–ca. 1239. Newman, *Seigneurs*, vol. 1, 282.
2 Gilles II, lord of Marquaix, son of Gilles I, lord of Marquaix, and Adèle de Guny. Newman, *Seigneurs*, vol. 2, 100.
3 Béatrice de Soupir (as *Madame Biatris de Marcais*) is mentioned in a 1261 act of Gérard, lord of Soupir (who also appears in **131**), and his wife Marie concerning her *doaire*. This suggests that she was a member of the seigneurial family of Soupir, perhaps an aunt or great-aunt of Gérard's, but the precise familial connection is unclear. AD Aisne, H 826.

ecclesiam Premonstratensem ex una parte et virum nobilem Egidium militem, filium domini Egidii, domini de Marchasio, discordia orta esset supra piscaria molendinorum eiusdem ecclesie que sita sunt in Axona et super terris et rebus aliis quas eadem ecclesia acquisierat in dominio dicti Egidii et uxoris sue, Beatricis nomine de Soupi, quod dominium Egidius tenebat ratione dicte uxoris sue que ipsum dominium in dote tenebat. Tandem idem Egidius, in nostra presentia constitutus, mediantibus bonis viris et consilio sano usus, dedit et quittavit eidem ecclesie Premonstratensi spontanea voluntate sua in perpetuam elemosinam quicquid juris habebat vel habere poterat tempore huius scripti in piscaria predicta et terris et rebus aliis in dicto dominio suo et uxoris sue predicte ab eadem ecclesia emptione vel elemosina sive quocumque modo alio acquisitis. Dicta vero Beatrix, uxor prefati Egidii, etiam in nostra presentia constituta, predicta omnia eidem ecclesie dedit, laudavit, approbavit et concessit in perpetuam elemosinam voluntate sua spontanea, non coacta et tam eadem Beatrix quam predictus Egidius, maritus suus, in manu nostra fidem corporaliter prestiterunt firmiter et fideliter, promittentes se premissa omnia inviolabiliter servaturos et quod nec per se nec per alios super premissis omnibus predictam ecclesiam decetero molestabunt vel facient aliquatenus molestari, sed adversus omnes qui voluerint juri stare super predictis omnibus legitimam warandiam portabunt quantum pertinet ad eos et quantum debebunt ecclesie supradicte. In quorum omnium testimonium, presentes litteras ad petitionem partium sigillo curie Suessionensis fecimus sigillari. Actum anno Domini M° C°XX° nono, mense februario.

120

June, 1215.

Eudes [IV],[1] *lord of Ham, makes known that Pierre* Bachelier, *brother of Geoffroi de Broche,*[2] *knight and Eude's* fidelis, *relinquished to the church of Prémontré all rights to the major and minor tithes of the* curtis *of Soupir*[3] *held by him or his unnamed wife. Eudes and Geoffroi confirm this by counterpledge.*

A. Cartulary of Prémontré, fol. 29r.

B. Original not found.

1 Eudes IV, lord of Ham (d. 1234), son of Eudes III, lord of Ham, and Elizabeth; husband of Elizabeth de Béthencourt.

2 Broche, comm. Beaumont-en-Beine, https://dicotopo.cths.fr/places/P93349423.

3 Soupir, cant. Vailly, https://dicotopo.cths.fr/places/P62600159.

Karta domini Hamensis de quitatione Petri cognomino Bacheleirs.

[E]go Odo, dominus Hamensis, notum facio universis presentes litteras inspecturis quod Petrus, cognomento Bacheleirs, frater dilecti et fidelis mei Gaufridi de Brochi militis, in mea presentia constitutus, quitavit ecclesie Premonstratensi quicquid juris habebat vel habere poterat, vel ex parte sua, vel ex parte uxoris sue, vel ex parte alterius, in tota decima curtis de Soupi, magna vel minuta, et de hac quitancia dedit ecclesie in plegium et in obsidem dictum Gaufridum et de assensu meo et eiusdem Gaufridi addidit in contraplegium quicquid tenebat de me vel de ipso Gaufrido vel de alio in tota castellania Hamensi si ab hac quitancia resiliret. Actum mense junio, anno gratie M° CC° quinto decimo.

121

January 2, 1206. Soissons.

Nivelon [I],[1] *bishop of Soissons, makes known that the children of Robert Foucher de Chavonne,*[2] *a deceased* conversus *of Prémontré, sought to reclaim the gift their father had given to the church of Prémontré: half of a house, three vineyards, and a small wood. Prémontré agrees that the four children, Égide, Raoul, Alix, and Eremburge, hold the properties in return for an annual payment of six* modii *of white wine, measure of Vailly.*[3]

A. Cartulary of Prémontré, fols. 29r–29v.
B. Original not found.

Karta Suessionensis episcopi de sex modiis albi vini qui debentur nobis apud Chavones.

[N]evelo, Dei gratia Suessionensis episcopus, omnibus Christi fidelibus in perpetuum. Universitati vestre notum facimus per hoc scriptum quod cum filii Roberti Fulcheri de Chavones, quondam conversi Premonstratensis, Egidius scilicet et Radulfus et sorores eorum, Aelis et Erenburgis, reclamantes requisissent ea que idem pater eorum Robertus, ipsis concedentibus, contulerat ecclesie Premonstratensi, videlicet medietatem domus sue et tres vineas et nemus quoddam parvum, inter illos et fratres Premonstratenses talis composito

1 Nivelon I de Quierzy (or Chérizy), son of Gérard II, lord of Quierzy, and Agnès de Longpont, bishop of Soissons, 1175/6–1207.
2 Chavonne, cant. Vailly, https://dicotopo.cths.fr/places/P90566217.
3 Vailly, arr. Soissons, https://dicotopo.cths.fr/places/P00798425.

facta fuit quod predicti filii Roberti et sorores eorum omnia ea super quibus reclamaverant, tenerent solventes pro eis ecclesie Premonstratensis annuatim sex modios albi vini ad mensuram de Vaisli accipiendos in cuppa. Cumque illa divisissent in IIIIor portiones, quisque per se, pro parte que eum contingerat, fecit fratribus Premonstratensibus assignationem vini quod debebat tam super ipsam portionem quam super aliam terram suam. Assignatio autem talis est: dictus Egidius debet unum modium super mansum suum totum et dimidium modium super vineam sub domo sua et decem sextarios super vineam En Val. Aelis, soror eius, et Balduinus, maritus ipsius, debent sex sextarios et tres quarterios super vineam En Ruissiaus et sex sextarios et tres quarterios super vineam En La Loe. Radulfus frater eorum, debet XII sextarios super vineam El Mares, V sextarios super domum Englateigni, IIII sextarios et I quarterium super vineam sub domo sacerdotis, IIII sextarios et I quarterium super plantam Es Osches, II sextarios En Ruissiaus super vineam que fuit Urselli. Erenburgis, soror eorumdem, et Herbertus, vir eius, debent XII sextarios super vineam et super nemus En Val et quinque sextarios super vineam En La Sentele et dimidium modium super vineam En Cerciaus. Preter hos modios taliter assignatos predictus Egidius debet predicte ecclesie VII sextarios vinagii super vineam En Cerciaus, Radulfus, frater eius debet, IIII sextarios et I quarterium vinagii super vineam sub domo sacerdotis, Albricus nepos eorum debet sex sextarios et terciam partem sextarii vinagii super vineam En Sarnuel. Hanc igitur compositionem coram prudentibus viris factam recognoverunt coram nobis sepedicti Egidius et Radulphus fratres, Herbertus et Balduinus mariti sororum eorum. Nos autem, ut hec conventio rata permaneat et illesa, eam sigilli nostri appensione munimus. Testes qui huic conventioni interfuerunt voluimus hic subscribi: Sigillum Alardi, decani presbiteri de Chavones. S. Radulfi, prepositi de Vaisli. S. Renaldi, filii Pagani. S. Odonis de Cerni, Urselli scabini, Richeri maioris, Arnulphi Cokenbart, Andree filii Theobaldi. Actum Suessioni, anno gratie M° CC° VI°, in octavis Beati Stephani martiris.

122

1174

Yves [II],[1] *count of Soissons and lord of Nesle, makes known the resolution of a dispute between the church of Prémontré and the knight Jean [I],*[2] *lord of*

1 Yves II de Nesle (d. ca. 1178), lord of Nesle and count of Soissons, son of Raoul, lord of Nesle, and Raintrude. Newman, *Seigneurs*, vol. 1, 61.

2 Jean I, lord of Ostel (d. bef. 1183), appears as a witness to episcopal acts from 1169, and was the *dapifer* to Yves II, count of Soissons. He was commemorated in the obituary of Prémontré on January 12. Van Waefelghem, *L'Obituaire de l'abbaye de Prémontré*, 27–8; Newman, *Seigneurs*, vol. 2, 143–4.

Ostel. The disputed land held by Prémontré from Yves will be divided into two parts. One part will go to Prémontré and the other to Jean. Jean will also cede to Prémontré a forest and the road leading to it so that the brothers may access their land. Marie, Jean's wife, and her father Bernier de Maissemy[3] approve.

A. Cartulary of Prémontré, fol. 29v.

B. Original not found.

EDITION: Newman, *Seigneurs*, vol. 2, 142–3; *Chartae Galliae*, no. 212850, http://telma.irht.cnrs.fr/outils/chartae-galliae/charte212850/.

Karta Yvonis comitis Suessionensis de quadam compositione inter Johannem de Hostel [*margo*: et ecclesiam Premonstratensis.]

[E]go Ivo, Dei gratia Suessorum comes et dominus Nigelle, notum fieri volo tam futuris quam presentibus quod querele que erant inter Premonstratensem ecclesiam et Johannem militem, dominum de Hostel, ita sedate sunt: mediantibus igitur nobis et aliis prudentibus viris, terra quedam quam prefata ecclesia diu tenuerat et de feodo nostro erat et unde querela fuerat, ita divisa est quod Johannes medietatem inde possidet, aliam vero medietatem ecclesia retinet. Nemus autem, quod Johannes calumpniabatur quitum clamavit et ecclesie prenominate in perpetuum possidere concessit, ita liberum et absque ulla calumpnia quod et servare et vendere et quicquid voluerit sicut de suo proprio inde facere poterit. Viam etiam ad nemus per terram et districtum suum fratribus eiusdem ecclesie concessit ita ut a dampno sibi caveant. Si vero casu aliquo dampnum intulerint, sine forisfacto restituent et per vicinos circummanentes emendabunt. Et ut inter ecclesiam et ipsum Johannem firma pax existeret deinceps, statutum est ab utriusque partis amicis quod de omnibus que predicta ecclesia tenebat, prefatus Johannes eam ulterius non inquietaret sed pacem ei de omnibus teneret. Pacem istam fide data se tenere spopondit et fidejussores inde dedit: Johannem castellanum Noviomensem,[4] Widonem de Erblencourt fratrem suum, Petrum de Ponte Sancti Medardi,[5] Drogonem de Viri,[6] Garnerum

3 Bernier, lord of Maissemy (cant. Vermand, https://dicotopo.cths.fr/places/P53328046), and his wife, Elizabeth, had a number of children, including Guy the cleric, Gobert, Philippe, Hesdiarde, and Marie. Newman, *Seigneurs*, vol. 2, 143–4; Melleville, *DH*, vol. 2, 3.

4 Jean I, castellan of Noyon and Thourotte, son of Guy II, castellan of Coucy, and Théophanie, is attested 1150s–70s. Barthélemy, *LDA*, 508–9.

5 Pierre de Pont-Saint-Mard (cant. Coucy-le-Château, https://dicotopo.cths.fr/places/P93612418) appears as a witness in acts associated with the Coucy family ca. 1163–ca. 1190. Newman, *Seigneurs*, vol. 2, 119.

6 Viry-Noureuil, cant. Chauny, https://dicotopo.cths.fr/places/P15709172.

de Juvigni[7] qui etiam inde testes sunt. Quod ut firmum in posterum permaneat, literis et sigilli mei impressione utriusque partis petitione roboravi et etiam testes cum predictis testibus super addere curavi. S. Jolendis,[8] comitisse Suessionensis. S. Simonis, buticularii de Perona.[9] S. Roberti de Chilli.[10] S. Albrici, militis de Nigella qui dicitur Gaians.[11] Factum est autem hoc assensu Berneri de Maissemi et Marie, ipsius Johannis de Hostel uxoris, filie predicti Berneri, anno incarnationis verbi M° C° LXX° IIII°.

123

1136. Vertus.

Count Thibaut [II][1] *of Champagne gave to the church of Prémontré all that he held both in land and water at the place where Hugues [I],*[2] *abbot of Prémontré, had built the mill of Cys.*[3]

A. Cartulary of Prémontré, fol. 29v.
B. AN, K 22, no. 9 (4).[4]
REGISTER: Tardif, *Monuments Historiques*, 232.

Karta comitis Theobaldi de molendino Axone cum sclusa et de loco ubi situm est molendinum.

[N]otum sit omnibus hominibus tam futuris quam presentibus quod Hugo, abbas Premonstratensis ecclesie, fecit quendam molendinum in fluvio Ethne juxta villam firmam comitis Theobaldi que Cis vocatur, et ripa illius fluvii in qua molendinus factaus fuit et quedam pars aque erant in terra comitis Theobaldi.

7 Juvigny, cant. Soissons, https://dicotopo.cths.fr/places/P97496070.
8 Yolande de Hainaut (d. aft. April 1202), daughter of Baudouin IV, count of Hainaut, and Alix de Namur. Yves II de Nesle, count of Soissons, was her first husband.
9 Simon, *buticularius* of Péronne, is attested in acts ca. 1172–ca. 1178. Newman, *Seigneurs*, vol. 2, 129, 133, 139, 151.
10 A Robert de Chilly (cant. Rosières, https://dicotopo.cths.fr/places/P80391731), knight, also appears as a witness in acts 1160s–80s. Newman, *Seigneurs*, vol. 2, 94.
11 Aubry *Gigas/Gaiant*, knight of Nesle and son of Robert *Gaianz*, appears as a witness in acts dated 1142–78. Newman, *Seigneurs*, vol. 2, 119.

1 Thibaut II, count of Champagne (IV of Blois and Chartres, d. 1152), son of Étienne II, count of Blois, and Adèle of Normandy.
2 Hugues I de Fosses (ca. 1093–1164), first abbot of Prémontré.
3 Cys-la-Commune, cant. Braine, https://dicotopo.cths.fr/places/P30360246.
4 Due to archival access restrictions in operation in 2020, the editors were unable to access this charter.

Prefatus vero comes Theobaldus dedit Deo et Sancte Marie et Sancto Johanni Baptiste et fratribus qui in Premonstratensi ecclesia Deo serviunt, quicquid habebat in terra illa et in aqua ubi molendinus ille situs est cum sclusa et cum omnibus que ad molendinum pertinent, pro remedio anime sue et uxoris et filiorum suorum et antecessorum ipsius, et ut hoc donum stabile et inconvulsum in perpetuum permaneret, comes Theobaldus hanc cartulam sigilli sui auctoritate confirmari precepit. Huius rei testes sunt: Radulphus[5] capellanus comitis Theobaldi, Ebrardus clericus, magister domini Henrici[6] filii prefati comitis, Gauterius de Bernon,[7] Balduinus Colomel, Drogo de Lachi,[8] Herluinus prepositus Sparnaci.[9] Actum est hoc apud Virtutem, anno incarnati verbi M° C° XXX° VI°, indictione XIIII^{a}, epacta XXVI^{a}, concurrente III°, regnante Ludovico rege Francorum, Bartholomeo episcopo Laudunensi cathedra residente.

124

1178. Château-Thierry.

*Henri [I],[1] count of Troyes, states that he had previously confirmed Prémontré in its possession of the land of Pierre de Courcelle,[2] and that after having taken the cross Henri visited Prémontré on another occasion and confirmed its possessions at Cys,[3] Saint-Mard,[4] Rhû,[5] and Presles,[6] and any future possessions they should acquire there.[7] (See **127**.)*

---

5 Raoul, chaplain of Thibaut II, count of Champagne, sealed most of his acts from 1129. Evergates, *Littere Baronum*, 28, n. 48.

6 Henri I the Liberal, count of Champagne and Brie (1127–1181), son of Thibaut II, count of Blois and Champagne, and Mathilde von Spanheim.

7 Gautier de Bernon, probably lord of Bernon (cant. Chaource, Aube), who appears as a witness in comital acts ca. 1134–ca. 1154. Jubainville, *Histoire des ducs et des comtes de Champagne, depuis le VIe siècle jusqu'à la fin du XIe*, vol. 3, 142.

8 Dreux de Lachy (cant. Sézanne, https://dicotopo.cths.fr/places/P60288542) also appears in the 1131 foundation charter of the Benedictine abbey of Notre-Dame-d'Andecy. Édouard de Barthélemy, "Le cartulaire de l'abbaye d'Andecy," 93.

9 The Augustinian abbey of Saint-Martin d'Épernay.

---

1 Henri I the Liberal, count of Champagne and Brie (1127–1181), son of Thibaut II, count of Blois and Champagne, and Mathilde von Spanheim.

2 Courcelles, cant. Braine, https://dicotopo.cths.fr/places/P98374204.

3 Cys-la-Commune, cant. Braine, https://dicotopo.cths.fr/places/P30360246.

4 Saint-Mard, cant. Braine, https://dicotopo.cths.fr/places/P95809628.

5 Rhû, comm. Cys-la-Commune, https://dicotopo.cths.fr/places/P95842496.

6 Presles-et-Boves, cant. Braine, https://dicotopo.cths.fr/places/P12121690.

7 This act was confirmed by *vidimus* by Garnier, bishop of Laon, in 1246. BnF, Coll. Picardie 290, no. 13.

A. Cartulary of Prémontré, fols. 29v–30r.
B. Original not found.[8]
EDITION: Jubainville, *Histoire des ducs et des comtes de Champagne*, vol. 3, 471; Slack, *Crusade Charters, 1138–1270*, 78; Benton and Bur, *Recueil des actes d'Henri le Libéral. Comte de Champagne (1152–1181)*, vol. 1, 577–8; "Charter of Henry the Liberal, 1178," Independent Crusaders Project, https://independentcrusadersproject.ace.fordham.edu/items/show/2293.

Karta comitis Henrici que concedit nobis retinens potestate quicquid potimus acquirere in terra sua elemosina dono sive emptione apud Cis, apud Sanctum Medardum, Ru et Praellem.

[E]go Henricus, Trecensium comes palatinus. Notum facio presentibus et futuris quod, cum domui et fratribus de Premonstrato terram Petri de Curcellis laudassem, postea signo dominice crucis assumpto, cum eosdem fratres et domum[9] visitaturus illuc venissem, eis laudavi quicquid apud Cis et in potestate de Cis et apud domnum Medardum et apud Ru et apud Praellam dono sive elemosina sive etiam emptione possent acquirere. Eorum etiam que acquisierint consuetudines, si quas ibi habuero, tam in terragiis, quam in censibus et vinagiis, eis concessi; et quicquid ibidem de feodo meo acquisierint unde hominum non amittam, laudavi. Quod ut notum permaneat et stabile teneatur in perpetuum, litteris annotatum sigilli mei impressione firmavi. Affuerunt autem huius rei testes: Henricus comes Grandis Prati,[10] Gaufridus frater eius,[11] Willermus marescallus,[12] Theobaldus Revelarz,[13] Ertaudus camerarius,[14] et Milo de Pruvino.[15] Actum anno incarnati verbi M° C° LXX° VIII°. Datum apud Castrum Theodrici, per manum Stephani cancellarii.

8 According to the research notes of Françoise Muret, "Cette pièce acquise par le département de la Moselle, avec un certain nombre d'autres provenant de la collection Cheltenham, doit être envoyée aux archives départementales de l'Aisne." However, neither the archivists of AD Moselle nor those of AD Aisne have a record of this charter.

9 Per the 1246 *vidimus* (BnF, Coll. Picardie 290, no. 13), here read "domum eorum."

10 Henri II, count of Grandpré (d. ca. 1190), son of Henri I, count of Grandpré, and Ermentrude de Joux (or de Grandson).

11 Geoffroi I de Grandpré (d. bef. 1185), lord of Balham and count of Château-Porcien, son of Henri I, count of Grandpré, and Ermentrude de Joux (or de Grandson).

12 William Rex Breban de Provins, marshal of Champagne, 1158–79. Evergates, *Henry the Liberal*, 188.

13 Thibaut Revelard, knight, appears as a witness in acts ca. 1171–9. Gassies, *Les Chartes de la commune de Meaux, 1179–1222*, 30.

14 Artaud de Nogent, a "citizen of Nogent" and chamberlain of the counts of Champagne, 1163–90. Joinville and Villehardouin, *Chronicles of the Crusades*, 186; Evergates, *Henry the Liberal*, 188.

15 Milo I Breban de Provins, treasurer of the counts of Champagne, 1165–86, son of William Rex Breban of Provins. Evergates, *Henry the Liberal*, 188.

125

1158

Anscoul,[1] bishop of Soissons, adjudicates and makes known that the church of Prémontré retains the woods and pastures in the valley of Ostel[2] that they had received in alms from Robert de Chivres,[3] husband and wife Gilbert de Sancy[4] and Rosza, and their son Hugues.

A. Cartulary of Prémontré, fol. 30r.
B. Original, AN, L 995, no. 26, previously sealed.

Karta episcopi Suessionensis de confirmatione nemoris de Hostel.

[I]n nomine sancte et individue Trinitatis. Ego Ansculphus,[5] Dei gratia Suessorum vocatus episcopus, notum fieri volo tam futuris quam presentibus quod ecclesia Premonstratensis[6] tenet in valle de Hostel ex latere de Vaisli[7] partem nemoris et pascua usque ad vivarium que dederunt in elemosinam eidem ecclesie Robertus de Chiure[8] et Gilebertus[9] de Salchio, assensu uxoris sue Rosze et filii sui Hugonis, sub censu duorum solidorum. Hominibus autem de Chavones[10,11] calumpniantibus et sibi violenter usurpantibus, ventum est ad causam in nostra presentia et audita utrimque ratione judicio totius ~~ecclesie~~ curie pars illa nemoris cum pascuis permansit ecclesie tuentibus elemosinam suam predicta Rosza et Hugone et Adone de Curlandum[12,13] qui partem Gilleberti tenebat. Cumque prefati homines a causa se decidisse viderent multis supplicationibus instituerunt ut nostram in eos temperaremus justiciam et ipsi pro arbitrio nostro satisfacerent ecclesie quod, nobis annuentibus, data fide spoponderunt Robertus, Paganus, Herbertus, Joifridus,[14] IIII^or^ videlicet pro

1 Anscoul de Pierrefonds, son of Nivelon II, lord of Pierrefonds, and Hawide (de Montmorency?), was archdeacon of Soissons, 1101–25/9, *prepositus* of Soissons, 1129–52, and bishop of Soissons, 1152–8.
2 Ostel, cant. Vailly, https://dicotopo.cths.fr/places/P14381512.
3 Chivres, cant. Vailly, https://dicotopo.cths.fr/places/P27495958.
4 Sancy, cant. Vailly, https://dicotopo.cths.fr/places/P02259780.
5 Ansculfus *B*.
6 Premonstrata *B*.
7 Vasli *B*.
8 Chiuire *B*.
9 Gillebertus *B*.
10 Chawnes *B*.
11 Chavonne, cant. Vailly, https://dicotopo.cths.fr/places/P90566217.
12 Curlandun *B*.
13 Courlandon, cant. Fismes, https://dicotopo.cths.fr/places/P10603857.
14 Josfridus *B*.

reliquis omnibus quod numquam decetero super hoc ecclesiam inquietarent nec ab aliquo inquietari permitterent. Quod ut ratum permaneat et sigilli nostri auctoritate roboramus et in perturbatores anathematis sentenciam promulgamus, legitimorum quoque testium nomina subsignamus: S. Nivelonis[15] et Johannis,[16] archidiaconi. S. Warneri, diaconi.[17] S. Bernardi et Walteri, sacerdotis. S. Guidonis.[18] S. Guidonis de Garlandum.[19] S. Pagani, prepositi.[20] S. Theodorici[21] de Buci.[22] S. Simonis[23] et Walteri de Soupi.[24,25] Actum anno incarnati verbi M° C° LVIII°, epacta XVIII^a^, indictione VII^a^, concurrente II°.

126

1175

Agnès,[1] countess of Braine, makes known that she and Simon de Montaigu, acting on the part of the king, adjudicated the dispute between the church of Prémontré and Guy[2] de Soupir concerning lands that Prémontré had possessed for many years in the lordship of Soupir. Guy, Agnès his wife, and their children, Baudouin, Guy, Philippe, Marsilie, Cécile, and Richance, agree to end the dispute, on the condition that Prémontré not acquire any land at Soupir in the future without the consent of Guy or his heirs. Countess Agnès, along with Oilard de Braine,[3] Simon de Neuville, and Mathieu, the king's ministeriales, *pledge to act as guarantors of the agreement.*

A. Cartulary of Prémontré, fol. 30r.

B. Original not found.

---

15 Nivelon I, archdeacon of Soissons, ca. 1129–ca. 1181. Newman, *Seigneurs*, vol. 1, 110, 115.

16 Jean, archdeacon of Soissons, ca. 1153–ca. 1167. Newman, *Seigneurs*, vol. 1, 110, 115.

17 decani *B*.

18 *Om.* de Supi *A*.

19 Garlandun *B*.

20 Payen, *prepositus* of Soissons, also known as Payen de Braine. Lewis, "Fourteen Charters of Robert I of Dreux (1152–1188)," 161, fn. 11.

21 Teoderici *B*.

22 Bucy-le-Long, cant. Vailly, https://dicotopo.cths.fr/places/P35759725.

23 Symonis *B*.

24 *Superscr.* de Soupi *B*.

25 Soupir, cant. Vailly, https://dicotopo.cths.fr/places/P62600159.

---

1 Agnès II, lady of Braine and countess of Dreux (d. 1204), daughter of Guy, lord of Baudement, and Alix; wife of Robert, count of Dreux.

2 Guy II, lord of Soupir (cant. Vailly, https://dicotopo.cths.fr/places/P62600159), son of Guy I, lord of Soupir; husband of Agnès. Wacha, "La Puissance du Choix," 116.

3 Likely Oilard, castellan of Braine, 1170s–80s. Prioux, *Monographie de l'ancienne abbaye royale Saint-Yved de Braine*, 41.

Karta Comitisse de Brana de compromissione et pace inter ecclesiam Premonstrati et Guidonem de Soupi.

[I]n nomine sancte et individue Trinitatis. Ego Agnes, comitissa Brane, notum facio tam futuris quam presentibus quod quedam querela inter ecclesiam Premonstrati et dominum Guidonem de Soupi super quibusdam terris et possessionibus agebatur, quas prefata ecclesia multis annis, sicut in scriptis et privilegiis eius continetur, legitime et quiete possederat. Tandem vero utriusque partis communi voluntate et assensu in nos et dominum Symonem de Monte Acuto, qui ex parte regis super eadem querela convenerat, ecclesia Premonstratensis et prefatus Guido super omnibus de quibus controversia vertebatur, compromiserunt. Nos, siquidem, ad honorem et commodum utriusque partis laborantes, sub tali compositionis et pacis forma processimus. In primis prefatus Guido et uxor eius predicte ecclesie privilegia que de prefatis terris conscripta erant, laudaverunt et de illatis injuriis ecclesie satisfecerunt. Omnes etiam querelas que eatenus emerserant, quitas clamaverunt, universas terras et possessiones quas eadem ecclesia in territorio sive dominio domini de Soupi usque ad diem illam possederat, abbati et fratribus eiusdem ecclesie libere et quiete perpetuo possidendas concesserunt, hac videlicet conditione interposita quod fratres in territorio eius sive districto sine assensu ipsius et successorum suorum in terris, pratis aut vineis ex hinc nichil acquirent. Deinde, dato fidei sacramento conventionis huius tenende, obsides et fidejussores dederunt, me videlicet et Oilardum de Brana, Simonem quoque de Nova Villa et Matheum, ministeriales regis, qui loco regis aderant, tam ex parte regis quam ex parte sua, quos etiam obsides atque fidejussores abbas et ecclesia dederunt. Et ut pax ista firmior haberetur, predictus abbas et fratres eius ipsi Guidoni et uxori eius, Agneti, atque eorum liberis consilio nostro de beneficio ecclesie dederunt. Actum est in curia fratrum de Soupi et ipsa die recognitum et laudatum in domo Guidonis de Soupi ab ipso Guidone et uxore eius, Agnete, et eorum liberis quorum ista sunt nomina: Balduinus, Guido, Philippus, Marsilia, Cecilia, Richancia. Ut igitur istud ratum permaneat, sigilli nostri appositione et cirographi conscriptione atque testium subnotatione presentem paginam munivimus. S. Bartholomei,[4] abbatis Laudunensis. S. Willelmi,[5] Cussiacensis abbatis. S. Balduini,[6] abbatis

4 Barthélemy de Mons, abbot of the Premonstratensian abbey of Saint-Martin de Laon, 1171–9. *MP* II, 512.

5 Guillaume Hennepaix, abbot of the Premonstratensian abbey of Cuissy, 1170–4, of the Premonstratensian abbey of Bucilly, 1176–8, and of the Premonstratensian abbey of Chartreuve, 1178–85. *MP* II, 366, 494, 497.

6 Baudouin, abbot of the Premonstratensian abbey of Braine, 1173–ca. 1177. *MP* II, 486.

Branensis. S. Erlebaldi,[7] abbatis Loci Restaurati. S. Simonis de Monte Acuto. S. Pagani, fratris eiusdem Simonis. S. Johannis de Hostel.[8] S. Balduini, nepotis eius. S. Petri. S. Radulfi, filii de Caprino. S. Mathei, prepositi regis.[9] S. Odonis de Brueriis. S. Alberti de Comi,[10] et ceteri. Actum est hoc incarnati verbi M° C° LXX° V°.

127

September 9, 1193. Château-Thierry.

*Marie,[1] countess of Troyes, concedes to the religious of Prémontré the peaceful possession of all that they had acquired up until this day, either by gift, alms, or purchase, at Cys,[2] Saint-Mard,[3] Rhû,[4] and Presles.[5] (See **124**.)*

A. Cartulary of Prémontré, fols. 30r–30v.
B. Original not found.[6]

Karta comitisse de Campania de confirmatione illarum rerum quas acquisivit ecclesia sub ipsa et ante ipsam.

[E]go Maria, Trecensis comitissa, notum facio presentibus et futuris quod fratribus de Premonstrato pacifice tenendum concessi in perpetuum quicquid

7 Erlebaud, abbot of the Premonstratensian abbey of Lieu-Restauré, 1172–9. *MP* II, 514.

8 Jean I, lord of Ostel (d. bef. 1183), appears as a witness to episcopal acts from 1169, and was the *dapifer* to Yves II, count of Soissons. He was commemorated in the obituary of Prémontré on January 12. Van Waefelghem, *L'Obituaire de l'abbaye de Prémontré*, 27–8; Newman, *Seigneurs*, vol. 2, 143–4.

9 Both an Eudes de Bruyères and a Mathieu are attested as king's *prepositus* at Laon in the 1170s. Gravier, *Essai sur les prévots royaux du XIe au XIVe siècle*, 178.

10 Likely Comin, comm. Bourg-et-Comin, https://dicotopo.cths.fr/places/P21306750.

1 Marie de France (1145–1198), daughter of Louis VII of France and Eleanor of Aquitaine; wife of Henri I, count of Troyes and Champagne.

2 Cys-la-Commune, cant. Braine, https://dicotopo.cths.fr/places/P30360246.

3 Saint-Mard, cant. Braine, https://dicotopo.cths.fr/places/P95809628.

4 Rhû, comm. Cys-la-Commune, https://dicotopo.cths.fr/places/P95842496.

5 Presles-et-Boves, cant. Braine, https://dicotopo.cths.fr/places/P12121690.

6 In the 1980s, Françoise Muret identified an original for this charter as "AD Moselle, Cheltenham, no. 1291." Neither the present editors nor the archivists of AD Moselle have been able to trace this reference. AD Moselle suggests that it and a number of other documents from the Cheltenham collection may have been sent to AD Aisne shortly after the First World War, but AD Aisne has no record of this. The variants noted for this act are therefore taken from Muret's notes.

usque in diem hodiernum apud[7] Cis,[8] et in potestate de Cis[9] et apud[10] donum[11] Medardum, et apud[12] Ru, et apud[13] Praellam dono, sive elemosina, sive etiam emptione adquisierunt. Quod ut ratum teneatur, litteris annotari et sigilli mei testimonio feci confirmari. Actum mense septembrio, in crastinum nativitatis Sancte Marie apud[14] Castrum Theoderici, anno ab incarnatione Domini M° C° nonagesimo tercio.[15] Datum[16] per manum Galteri[17] cancellarii.[18]

128

December, 1217.

Baudouin de Reims,[1] *lord of Gueux, and Aelide,*[2] *his wife, approve the sale and the gift in alms made by Philippe de Soupir, knight, to the church of Prémontré, of land in the territory of Soupir*[3] *next to the Premonstratensian house there. (See* ***108*** *and* ***117****.)*

A. Cartulary of Prémontré, fol. 30v.
B. Original not found.

Karta domini Balduini et uxoris eius de Soupi de elemosina quam Philipus fecit ecclesie Premonstrati.

[E]go Balduinus, dominus de Geus, dictus de Remis, notum facio presentibus et futuris quod ego et Aelidis, uxor mea, laudamus et quitamus venditionem

7 aput *B*.
8 Cys *B*.
9 Cys *B*.
10 aput *B*.
11 donnum *B*.
12 aput *B*.
13 aput *B*.
14 aput *B*.
15 millesimo centesimo *B*.
16 data *B*.
17 Gautier de Chappes, chancellor of Champagne, 1190–1207, son of Clérembaud III, lord of Chappes, and Ermengarde. Evergates, *Marie of France*, 103.
18 *Om.* Theoderici *A*.

1 Baudouin de Reims, lord of Gueux (cant. Ville-en-Tardenois, https://dicotopo.cths.fr/places/P43022382), d. bef. 1221.
2 In an April 1221 charter in the cartulary of Notre-Dame d'Igny, Aelide is described as the *relicta Balduini de Remis* and is remarried to a *Bertrannus miles*. BnF, MS lat. 9904, fols. 37v–38r.
3 Soupir, cant. Vailly, https://dicotopo.cths.fr/places/P62600159.

et elemosinam quam dilectus noster Philippus de Soupi, miles, fecit ecclesie Premonstratensi super quadam terra sita in territorio de Souppi juxta domum ecclesie Premonstratensis. In huius rei testimonium, presentes litteras patentes emisi sigilli mei munimine roboratas. Actum anno incarnationis dominice M° CC° septimo decimo, mense decembri.

129

June, 1236.

The officialis *of Laon makes known the agreement and exchange reached between the church of Prémontré and the inheritors of Maucrues and Humont on the one hand and Henri de Maiel*[1] *and his brother Jacquet on the other concerning the rights of* terragium *and* vinagium *in the valley of Metz.*[2] *(See* ***132, 133****, and* ***135****.)*

A. Cartulary of Prémontré, fol. 30v.
B. Original, AN, L 995, no. 84, previously sealed.

Karta officialis Laudunensis de Henrico de Maiel et Jakero fratre eius.

[U]niversis Christi fidelibus[3] tam presentibus quam futuris, officialis Laudunensis in Domino salutem. Noverint universi quod cum abbas et conventus Premonstratensis et heredes de Maucrues[4] et de Humont et Henricus, clericus der[5] Maiwel, et Jakerus, frater eius, simul haberent, sicut dicebant, terragia ad partem in terris in valle de Maidi, talis inter ecclesiam Premonstrati et Henricum clericum ac Jakerum, fratrem eius, facta fuit compositio coram nobis quod eadem ecclesia quitavit dictis fratribus talem partem qualem habebat vel habere poterat in terragiis omnium terrarum de valle de Maiddi[6] solummodo que erant vel esse poterant ad terragium sive vinagium inter ipsam et omnes simul partionarios memoratos sub ea consuetudine et justicia qua dicta ecclesia tenebat partem terragiorum sive vinagiorum ipsorum. Dictus autem Henricus in recompensationem huius quitationis pro parte sua assignavit[7] ecclesie memorate in perpetuum duos

1 Today Le Moulin Brûlé, comm. Braye-en-Laonnois, https://dicotopo.cths.fr/places/P59801482.
2 Le Metz, comm. Moussy-sur-Aisne, https://dicotopo.cths.fr/places/P31678789.
3 *Transp. A*; fidelibus Christi *B*.
4 Maucrwes *B*.
5 de *B*.
6 Maidi *B*.
7 *Transp. A*; assignavit sua *B*.

modios albi vini ad mensuram de Brai super vineas En Biauvoir[8] contiguas domui sue de Maiwel, quas Remigius de Thoegni,[9,10] burgensis Laudunensis, sicut dicebat, emit ab eo, et Jakerus predictus pro parte sua prefate ecclesie in perpetuum assignavit unum modium et dimidium albi vini ad dictam mensuram de Brai super vineas que sunt in Closo desseur Maisieres in valle de Maidi versus La Folie, de quo Wibertus de Crandelain[11] debet reddere annuatim octo sextarios et tres lothos super plantam suam sitam ut dicitur in eodem[12] loco[13] et Baudechons Li Flamens tres quarterios super plantam suam sitam, ut dicitur, in loco prefato de quibus tribus quarteriis accipiet dicta ecclesia dimidium modium dimidio sextario minus et Jakerus residuum, scilicet unum quarterium et dimidium sextarium possidebit et illos tres modios et dimidium vinagii memorati tenebit ecclesia supradicta ad usus et consuetudines sub quibus dicti fratres illud tenebant et habebit eadem ecclesia in ipso vinagio justicias usque ad septem solidos et dimidium bone monete cum omnibus venditionibus, que inde possent exire salvo tamen dictis fratribus manso dominico eorumdem. Porro sciendum est quod istud excambium factum fuit de illis vinagiis sive terragiis que erant in valle de Maiddi[14] tantummodo ad partem inter dictam ecclesiam et omnes simul partionarios superius nominatos, quia Premonstratensis ecclesia ut dicebat habet cum heredibus de Maucrues[15] et de Humont in territorio de Maiddi[16] vinagia antiqua ad partem que sua remanent sicut prius in quibus heredes de Maiwel sicut recognoverunt partionariam non habebant et de quibus nulla commutatio facta fuit. In cuius rei testimonium et perpetuam firmitatem ad petitionem partium, fecimus presens scriptum sigillo Laudunensis curie sigillari, salvo jure domini Laudunensis et alieno. Actum anno gratie M° CC° XXX° VI°,[17] mense junio.

---

8 Biauvooir *B*.

9 Thooegni *B*.

10 Likely Thony, comm. Pontavert, https://dicotopo.cths.fr/places/P63464231.

11 Crandelein *B*.

12 *Om.* eodem *B*.

13 *Om.* predicto et Hugo li doiens octo sextarios et tres lothos super plantam suam sitam in eodem loco ut dicitur *A*.

14 Maidi *B*.

15 Maucrwes *B*.

16 Maidi *B*.

17 millesimo ducentesimo tricesimo sexto *B*.

130

April, 1226.

Garnier,[1] maior *archdeacon of Soissons, makes known that in his presence, Rémi, cleric, son of Chanut de Presles,*[2] *declared having sold to the church of Prémontré for six and a half* librae Parisiensium *a vineyard located between Cys*[3] *and Presles.*

A. Cartulary of Prémontré, fol. 30v.
B. Original not found.

Karta archidiaconi Suessionensis de eo quod Remigius recognovit se vendidisse vineam.

[G]arnerus, maior archidiaconus Suessionensis, omnibus presentes litteras inspecturis in Domino salutem. Noveritis quod ~~ecclesie~~ Remigius clericus, filius Chanuti de Praeles, in presentia nostra constitutus, recognovit se vendidisse ecclesie Premonstratensi quandam vineam quam habebat, sitam inter Cis et Praeles, pro sex libris et dimidia Parisiensibus, fidem interponens in manu nostra corporalem quod decetero dictam ecclesiam super predicta vinea per se vel per alium non molestabit vel faciet molestari, inmo eidem ecclesie super iam dicta vinea contra omnes qui ad jus vel ad placitum venire voluerint, legitimam portabit garandiam. In cuius rei testimonium, presentes litteras sigilli nostri munimine fecimus roborari. Actum anno Domini M° CC° vicesimo VI°, mense aprili.

131

March, 1233.

Milon de Sissonne[1] *and Agathe,*[2] *lord and lady of Soupir, give annually to the church of Prémontré ten* modii *of white wine, measure of Soupir,*[3] *in exchange for the right to fish in the Aisne upstream and downstream from Prémontré's*

1 Garnier, archdeacon of Soissons, ca. 1215–ca. 1232. Newman, *Seigneurs*, vol. 1, 111, 119.
2 Presles-et-Boves, cant. Braine, https://dicotopo.cths.fr/places/P12121690.
3 Cys-la-Commune, cant. Braine, https://dicotopo.cths.fr/places/P30360246.

1 Milon, lord of Sissonne (d. aft. 1248), son of Gobert, lord of Sissonne, and Agnès. Newman, *Seigneurs*, vol. 1, 170, 173.
2 Agathe, lady of Soupir (d. aft. 1248), daughter of Baudouin II, lord of Soupir, and Aelide. She inherited her lordship from her brother Baudouin. Newman, *Seigneurs*, vol. 1, 170, 174; Wacha, "La Puissance du Choix," 116.
3 Soupir, cant. Vailly, https://dicotopo.cths.fr/places/P62600159.

mills at Soupir. Their eldest son, Gérard,[4] *along with other unnamed children, consents.*

A. Cartulary of Prémontré, fols. 30v–31v.

B. Original, AN, L 995, no. 145, previously sealed with two seals.

Karta domini Milonis de Soupi et eiusdem uxoris de piscatione quam habemus in flumine Axone.

[E]go Milo de Sissonis, dominus de Souppi, et Agathes, uxor mea, omnibus in perpetuum. Presentium testimonio volumus notum esse quod cum inter nos ex una parte et ecclesiam Premonstratensem ex altera super jure cuiusdam piscationis quam in fluvio Axone, subtus et supra molendina dicte ecclesie apud Souppi, quantum arcus jacere potest inferius et superius et ex transverso similiter eadem ecclesia vendicabat et petebat libere suam esse, questio verteretur et super hoc esset diutius litigatum, tandem bonorum virorum usi consilio de communi[5] composuimus in hunc modum quod nos predicte ecclesie dedimus annuatim in redditibus nostris de Souppi decem modios albi vini ad mensuram eiusdem ville super quasdam possessiones que a nobis ad vinagium tenebantur sub ea consuetudine atque jure quod si, tempore debito, solutum non fuerit vinagium memoratum, ipsa ecclesia auctoritate sua et sine clamore alicubi faciendo, nisi ei placuerit, poterit in possessionibus illis libere ac licite wagia capere et eadem tenere, donec sibi tam de vinagio debito quam de emenda fuerit plenius satisfactum. Quam siquidem emendam secundum terre illius consuetudinem, prout est judicata, ibidem capiet ecclesia memorata. Verum si processu temporis possessiones dicte ecclesie assignate vel ob sterilitatem earum vel propter ~~in~~cultorum incuriam[6] fuerint derelicte, easdem possessiones saisire poterit eadem ecclesia et pro debita sibi pensione aliis dare cultoribus excolendas nec auferri ab eis poterunt per aliam potestatem. Possessiones autem quas assignavimus ecclesie supradicte ad recipiendum decem modios vinagii supradictos nominatim duximus exprimendas et presenti pagine inserendas hoc modo: Petrus clericus debet unum modium de vinea sua retro Le Moncel et duos modios de vinea Es Noves; de vinea En Wederon unum quarterium; de vinea En Lambruel dimidium modium et de vinea El Fontenil duas partes dimidii modii; Hersendis Laukaint unum modium de vinea sua a Bolliant; Petrus de Muro unum modium de vinea sua En Malni et tres quarterios de vinea

4 Gérard de Sissonne, knight, lord of Soupir and La Selve (d. aft. 1265); son of Milon, lord of Sissonne, and Agathe, lady of Soupir. Newman, *Seigneurs*, vol. 1, 170, 174.

5 *Om.* consensu *A*.

6 *Transp. A*; incuriam cultorum *B*.

Au[7] Touc; Bernardus der[8] Moncel unum ~~quarterium~~ modium de vinea sua Es Noves et tres quarterios de vinea ad Nemus; Radulfus Baisselete[9] dimidium modium de vinea sua Al Touc et dimidium modium de vinea a Boulliant[10] et unum quarterium de La Faisse En Vaus et duos sextarios Del Quarrel; Tribous tres lotos Del Quarrel En Vaus. Porro ecclesia Premonstratensis pro huiusmodi redditibus sibi datis quitavit nobis et heredibus nostris in perpetuum piscationem predictam, sicut superius notata est et[11] descripta pariter, factis tamen quibusdam exactionibus[12] et statutis que a nobis et heredibus nostris debent in perpetuum firmiter observari, videlicet quod nullomodo circa molendina eiusdem ecclesie supra vel infra, a dextris vel a sinistris, poterimus sic piscari quod deterior vel infirmior possit inde fieri sclusa ecclesie supradicte, quod piscatio pauchorum molendini, que ipsius ecclesie libere ac pacifice esse debent, possit inutilis fieri vel aliquatenus impediri nec repentie[13] eiusdem ecclesie similiter quas sibi in aqua superiori libere retinet, ab aliquo valeant perturbari quo minus de ipsis eadem ecclesia ad suum commodum possit uti. Hoc etiam adjectum est pariter et firmatum quod in aqua superiori quantum arcus jacere potest neque nos neque aliqui successores nostri vel heredes facere poterimus vennam aliquam nec infra spatium illius parve insule que supra sclusam dicte ecclesie sita est et eidem libera remanet et quita ad faciendum omni modam voluntatem suam decetero piscari poterimus ullomodo nisi tantummodo ad tramallum et hoc etiam salva piscatione pauchorum et repentiarum eiusdem ecclesie, sicut superius est expressum. Illud quoque statutum est quod in aqua superiori vel inferiori vel in aliquo latere molendini nichil prorsus a nobis vel heredibus nostris fieri poterit ulla occasione vel causa per quod vel propter quod excludi valeant molendina vel suam perdere molituram nisi forte a fratribus dicte ecclesie ibidem commorantibus hoc nostris precibus aliquando potuerimus obtinere, hoc tamen salvo quod propter concessionem huiusmodi nullum eidem ecclesie in posterum debeat prejudicium generari. Jus etiam eundi ad molendinum et ab eo redeundi, navigandi supra et infra, prout sibi expedierit, plenissime ac liberrime retinuit ecclesia supradicta.[14] Et si forte processu temporis sclusa rupta fuerit in aliqua parte sui, dicta ecclesia poterit eam reficere et redintegrare et etiam palos figere in terram nostram et in utroque latere terram et lapides ponere et quicquid necessarium vel utile crediderit[15] scluse sue ibidem facere

7 al *B*.
8 del *B*.
9 Baisse Lece *B*.
10 Bolliant *B*.
11 *Add.* et *A*.
12 exceptionibus *B*.
13 repentye *B*.
14 sepedicta *B*.
15 *Om.* eadem ecclesia *A*.

poterit quotienscumque voluerit pleno jure. Nos igitur super hiis omnibus fideliter observandis, laudantibus et consentientibus omnibus liberis nostris tam Gerardo primogenito nostro quam aliis, prestitimus corporaliter in manu domini nostri episcopi Laudunensis fidei sacramentum promittentes firmiter bona fide sub sacramento predicto quod contra compositionem supradictam non veniemus decetero nec prefatam ecclesiam Premonstratensem super hiis omnibus per nos aut per alios molestabimus aut faciemus aliquatenus molestari sed adversus omnes qui juri et justicie parere voluerint legitimam warandiam portabimus tam nos quam heredes nostri ecclesie sepedicte de omnibus supradictis. Illud autem sciendum est quod superior justicia remanet nobis et heredibus nostris in possessionibus illis quas assignavimus ecclesie supradicte, salvo eo quod dictum est superius de wagiis capiendis, si solutum non fuerit debito tempore vinagium memoratum, prout superius plenius est expressum, ut autem predicta compositio, prout est ordinata et facta, tam a nobis quam ab heredibus nostris fideliter et firmiter in perpetuum observetur, nos presentem kartam sigillorum nostrorum fecimus appensione muniri. Datum anno gratie M° CC°[16] tricesimo tercio, mense martio.

132

November, 1232.

The officialis *of Laon*[1] *makes known that, before the king's* ballivus, *the church of Prémontré reached a resolution with the cleric Henri, his brother Jacquet de Maiel,*[2] *and R., wife of Jacquet, concerning their disagreement over grazing rights in the valley of Metz*[3] *and the surrounding area, and the mill at Ribaudon.*[4] *In return for the confirmation of their rights, Henri, Jacquet, and R. will give Prémontré three* modii *of wine annually. (See* ***129****,* ***133****, and* ***135****.)*

A. Cartulary of Prémontré, fol. 31v.

B. Original not found.

---

16 millesimo ducentesimo *B*.

---

1 Jean du Temple, *officialis* of Laon, is attested ca. 1231–ca. 1235. BM Reims 1563 (N. Fonds), fol. 170v; AD Aisne, H 873, fols. 172r–172v, 262r. His appointment as *officialis* was the subject of a long-running dispute with the cathedral chapter of Laon. Picó, "Membership in the Cathedral Chapter of Laon, 1217–1238," 5, 19.

2 Today Le Moulin Brûlé, comm. Braye-en-Laonnois, https://dicotopo.cths.fr/places/P59801482.

3 Le Metz, comm. Moussy-sur-Aisne, https://dicotopo.cths.fr/places/P31678789.

4 Ribaudon, comm. Soupir, https://dicotopo.cths.fr/places/P28661536.

Karte de conpositione inter Jakerum et Henricum, fratres de Maiwel et ecclesiam Premonstratensis super quibusdam pascuis.

[U]niversis fidelibus Christi tam presentibus quam futuris officialis Laudunensis salutem in Domino. Notum fieri volumus quod cum inter ecclesiam Premonstratensem ex una parte et Henricum clericum fratremque eius, Jakerum de Maiwel et R., uxorem eius, ex altera super quibusdam pascuis in tota Valle de Maidi et circa eandem vallem existentibus et super molendino de Ribaudon juxta Souppi[5] questio verteretur coram ballivo illustrissimi regis Francorum, tandem mediantibus bonis viris, qui ad pacem et concordiam partium fideliter laborarunt, de utriusque partis assensu, sic fuit ab eis sub sacramento fidei corporaliter prestito publice et sollempniter ordinatum quod Premonstratensis ecclesia inmittet ad pascendum omnia pecora domus sue de Sopeio et molendini de Ribaudon in tota Valle de Maidi et in toto manso dominico predictorum fratrum, Henrici scilicet et Jakeri, ac successorum eorumdem in perpetuum sicut protenditur a villa de Braio versus Souppeium et usque ad pontem de Arseio libere ac licenter quotiens, quomodo et quandocumque voluerit sine ulla contradictione et impedimento aliquo ab eisdem fratribus sive ab aliis ex parte ipsorum vel eorum nomine inferendo ita etiam quod dictus Jakerus vel successores ipsius vias vel semitas non poterunt impedire, quominus animalia de Souppi et de Riboudon in plenam possint pascuam introire. Habebunt quoque fratres de Souppi aisentias pascuorum in toto territorio predicto, excepto quodam grandi prato necnon et ortis et viridariis de Maiwel. Et quoniam uti licet unicuique jure suo, licet et licebit prefato Jakero terras suas proprias et heredibus suis ubi Premonstratenses nichil habent juris vel consuetudinis dare et conferre quibuscumque voluerint pro sue beneplacito voluntatis sed terras sive possessiones illas in quibus ecclesia Premonstratensis cum prefato Jakero et heredibus suis aliquid juris habet et habuit a temporibus retroactis, nulli conferre poterunt dictus Jakerus aut heredes eius ad aliquid faciendum in eis nisi salvo eo jure sive illa consuetudine quam prefata Premonstratensis ecclesia solet aut debet percipere in eisdem. Verum quia bonis ac religiosis se debet quisque favorabilem exhibere placuit eidem Jakero et uxori eius et concesserunt liberaliter ~~et~~ coram nobis ut ecclesia Premonstratensis habeat et possideat libere ac pacifice in perpetuum sub titulo elemosine tres modios vini annuos, scilicet tres modios uno quadrante minus super vineam A Laruele, que fuit Roberti Baccarii de Compendio,[6] et alium quadrantem super vineam Gobini, que dicitur A Busellon, quos modios eidem ecclesie legavit quorumdam fidelium devotio pro suarum salute animarum nec cogere poterunt sepedictus Jakerus vel heredes eius ecclesiam memoratam ad

5 Soupir, cant. Vailly, https://dicotopo.cths.fr/places/P62600159.

6 Compiègne, arr. Compiègne, https://dicotopo.cths.fr/places/P76061382.

distrahendum vel alienandum prefatos tres modios vini ex aliqua occasione vel causa sed eam permittent libere et pacifice possidere, retenta tamen[7] sibi justicia quam habere debent in talibus domini censuales. Et sciendum est quod omnes querele et controversie que mote fuerant inter ecclesiam Premonstratensem et fratres predictos antequam presens compositio facta esset per compositionem istam in bona pace et concordia remanserunt. Hec autem omnia, sicut superius sunt expressa, laudaverunt, approbaverunt et concesserunt, prestito coram nobis fidei sacramento corporaliter, prenominati H[enricus] clericus, Jakerus et uxor ipsius promittentes se compositionem istam fideliter et firmiter in perpetuum servaturos et obligaverunt se et heredes suos ad observandum omnia supradicta. Qui siquidem pro concessione et quitatione omnium predictorum sexaginta et quinque libras Parisiensium a fratribus Premonstratensis ecclesie receperunt. Et ut prefata concessio firma et stabilis in perpetuum perseveret, nos ad petitionem partium sigillo curie Laudunensis prefatam compositionem duximus confirmandam. Actum anno Domini M° CC° XXX° secundo, mense novembri.

133

After Christmas, 1232.

The officialis *of Laon*[1] *makes known that husband and wife Milon de Sissonne*[2] *and Agathe,*[3] *lord and lady of Soupir,*[4] *approve a dispute resolution in their capacity as fief lords. (See **129**, **132**, and **135**.)*

A. Cartulary of Prémontré, fols. 31v–32r.
B. Original not found.

---

7 *Superscr.* tamen *A*.

---

1 Jean du Temple, *officialis* of Laon, is attested ca. 1231–ca. 1235. BM Reims 1563 (N. Fonds), fol. 170v; AD Aisne, H 873, fols. 172r–172v, 262r. His appointment as *officialis* was the subject of a long-running dispute with the cathedral chapter of Laon. Picó, "Membership in the Cathedral Chapter of Laon, 1217–1238," 5, 19.

2 Milon, lord of Sissonne (d. aft. 1248), son of Gobert, lord of Sissonne, and Agnès. Newman, *Seigneurs*, vol. 1, 170, 173.

3 Agathe, lady of Soupir (d. aft. 1248), daughter of Baudouin II, lord of Soupir, and Aelide. She inherited her lordship from her brother Baudouin. Newman, *Seigneurs*, vol. 1, 170, 174; Wacha, "La Puissance du Choix," 116.

4 Soupir, cant. Vailly, https://dicotopo.cths.fr/places/P62600159.

Karta officialis Laudunensis de eo quod Milo de Soupi laudavit compositionem factam inter ecclesiam Premonstratensem et Jakerum.

[U]niversis Christi fidelibus presentes litteras inspecturis, officialis Laudunensis salutem in Domino. Noverint universi quod Milo de Sissonia, miles et dominus de Souppi, et Agathes, uxor eius, in nostra presentia constituti, laudaverunt, approbaverunt et concesserunt compositionem factam inter ecclesiam Premonstrati ex una parte et duos fratres, Henricum clericum et Jakerum de Maiwel[5] ac uxorem eiusdem Jakeri ex altera, que, inquam, compositio facta fuit super molendino de Ribaudon[6] et super pascuis in tota Valle de Maidi[7] et circa eandem vallem existentibus, de quibus ecclesiam inter prelibatam et fratres superius nominatos questio vertebatur; laudaverunt, inquam, dictus Milo de cuius feodo et dominio et Agathes, uxor eius, de cuius hereditate dicta pascua, sicut dicebant, descendunt et obligaverunt se et heredes suos ad observandam compositionem factam inter partes predictas, prestantes corporaliter fidei sacramentum quod ecclesiam Premonstratensem super compositione illa, sicut est in litteris Laudunensis curie conprehensa. Iidem[8] Milo et Agathes, uxor eius, per se vel per alios nullatenus molestabunt nec facient molestari. Acceptaverunt etiam et concesserunt predicti ~~et uxor~~ Milo et Agathes, uxor eius, elemosinam trium modiorum vini factam ecclesie Premonstrati ut eadem ecclesia dictos tres modios vini in perpetuum possideat libere et quiete. In cuius rei testimonium, presentes litteras fecimus sigillo curie Laudunensis muniri, salvo jure domini Laudunensis et alieno. Actum anno Domini M° CC° tricesimo secundo, post nativitatem Domini.

134

1232

Milon de Sissonne[1] *and Agathe,*[2] *lord and lady of Soupir,*[3] *confirm in their capacity as fief lords the church of Prémontré's acquisition of revenues worth about 10* modii *of wine every year, together with about 16* sextarii *of arable*

5 Today Le Moulin Brûlé, comm. Braye-en-Laonnois, https://dicotopo.cths.fr/places/P59801482.
6 Ribaudon, comm. Soupir, https://dicotopo.cths.fr/places/P28661536.
7 Le Metz, comm. Moussy-sur-Aisne, https://dicotopo.cths.fr/places/P31678789.
8 *Sic A.*

1 Milon, lord of Sissonne (d. aft. 1248), son of Gobert, lord of Sissonne, and Agnès. Newman, *Seigneurs*, vol. 1, 170, 173.
2 Agathe, lady of Soupir (d. aft. 1248), daughter of Baudouin II, lord of Soupir, and Aelide. She inherited her lordship from her brother Baudouin. Newman, *Seigneurs*, vol. 1, 170, 174; Wacha, "La Puissance du Choix," 116.
3 Soupir, cant. Vailly, https://dicotopo.cths.fr/places/P62600159.

land in various locations. Milon and Agathe's children, including their eldest son Gérard, consent.

A. Cartulary of Prémontré, fol. 32r.
B. Original, AN, L 995, no. 80, previously sealed with two seals.

Karta Milonis de Sissonia de confirmatione cuiusdam terre et de emptione decem modiorum vini.

[E]go Milo de Sissonia,[9] miles et dominus de Soupeio,[10] et Agathes, uxor mea, omnibus[11] presentium testimonio volumus notum esse quod cum ecclesia Premonstratensis in territorio de Souppi, quod de feodo et dominio nostro movet, tam per emptionem quam per elemosinam fideliter acquisisset circiter decem modios et dimidium vini annuos et circiter sexdecim[12] sextarios terre arabilis subsequenter nominatos hoc modo videlicet quinque sextarios de terra Gilonis Cervel,[13] sitos ad semitam de Ostel, novem sextarios de terra Hugonis, fratris domini Leodegarii presbiteri, sitos partim videlicet quinque sextarios in valle et partim videlicet quatuor sextarios in monte subtus spinam, tres quarterios de terra Albrici cognomento Doke, fratris Hugonis predicti, sitos in monte et similiter subtus spinam, unum aissinum de terra Pijon situm in valle juxta rivum et unum aissinum de terra Roberti Baccarii[14] de Compendio,[15] situm in valle juxta vivarium, nos intuitu Dei et ob remedium animarum nostrarum dictos decem modios et dimidium vini annuos et sexdecim[16] sextarios terre sementis superius nominatos concessimus et quitavimus dicte ecclesie Premonstrati perpetuo possidendos sine omni exactione, terragio et omni debito servitutis, ita quod nos aut heredes nostri ratione feodi sive ratione alterius juris in premissis omnibus nichil poterimus reclamare nec cogere ecclesiam memoratam ad distrahendum, vendendum vel alienandum ea que sunt superius nominata. Et ut ista quitatio et concessio[17] facta a nobis et heredibus nostris, firma et stabilis in perpetuum perseveret, ego Milo et dicta Agathes, uxor mea, necnon et liberi nostri, tam Gerardus primogenitus noster

9 Seissonia *B.*
10 Suppeio *B.*
11 *Om.* in perpetuum *A.*
12 sedecim *B.*
13 Servel *B.*
14 Bacari *B.*
15 Compiègne, arr. Compiègne, https://dicotopo.cths.fr/places/P76061382.
16 sedecim *B.*
17 *Om.* et quitatio *A.*

quam omnes alii, laudantes et approbantes quitationem factam super premissis prestitimus omnes corporaliter fidei sacramentum quod dictam ecclesiam super omnibus predictis per nos vel per alium nullatenus molestabimus nec faciemus aliquatenus molestari. In cuius rei testimonium et ob perpetuam firmitatem, ego Milo et Agathes dicta, de cuius hereditate feodum et dominium de Souppeio descendebat, presentem kartam fecimus sigillorum nostrorum munimine roborari. Actum anno gratie M° CC°[18] tricesimo secundo.

135

After Christmas, 1232.

Milon de Sissonne[1] *and Agathe,*[2] *lord and lady of Soupir,*[3] *approve the agreement reached between the church of Prémontré and the brothers Henri, cleric, and Jacquet de Maiel.*[4] *(See* ***129**, **132**, and **133**.)*

A. Cartulary of Prémontré, fols. 32r–32v.
B. Original, AN, L 995, no. 79, previously sealed.

Karta Milonis de Sissonia de compositione inter ecclesiam Premonstratensem et duos fratres Jakerum et Henricum de Maiwel.

[U]niversis fidelibus Christi presentem paginam inspecturis, Milo de Sissonia,[5] miles et dominus de Soupeio,[6] et Agathes uxor eius, salutem in Domino. Quoniam per largitionem temporalium quandoque acquiritur regnum Dei et mundanis celestia comparantur, placuit nobis pie ac liberaliter propter Deum concedere fratribus ecclesie Premonstrati quod stabilis et firma sit compositio que facta est inter eandem ecclesiam et duos fratres,

---

18 millesimo ducentesimo *B*.

---

1 Milon, lord of Sissonne (d. aft. 1248), son of Gobert, lord of Sissonne, and Agnès. Newman, *Seigneurs*, vol. 1, 170, 173.
2 Agathe, lady of Soupir (d. aft. 1248), daughter of Baudouin II, lord of Soupir, and Aelide. She inherited her lordship from her brother Baudouin. Newman, *Seigneurs*, vol. 1, 170, 174; Wacha, "La Puissance du Choix," 116.
3 Soupir, cant. Vailly, https://dicotopo.cths.fr/places/P62600159.
4 Today Le Moulin Brûlé, comm. Braye-en-Laonnois, https://dicotopo.cths.fr/places/P59801482.
5 Seissonia *B*.
6 Soppeio *B*.

Henricum clericum videlicet et Jakerum, quatinus omnia pecora domus sue de Soupi[7] et de Riboudon[8] inmittere valeant ad pascendum, prout voluerint, per totam vallem de Maidi et totum mansum dominicum predictorum fratrum Henrici clerici et Jakeri de Maiwel ac successorum eorumdem et habeant aisentias pascuorum in perpetuum liberrime et sine ullo debito servitutis in toto predicto territorio quod de feodo et dominio nostro movet, exceptis quodam grandi prato, ortis et viridariis de Maiwel. Cum enim de prefatis pascuis et molendino de Ribaudon[9] mota fuisset questio inter pretaxatam ecclesiam Premonstrati ex una parte et predictos fratres de Maiwel ex altera decisaque fuerit questio omnium predictorum per bonos viros qui compositionem amicabilem fecerunt inter ecclesiam memoratam et fratres de Maiwel superius nominatos, sicut in litteris curie Laudunensis super hoc confectis diffusius et apertius est expressum, nos compositionem illam expresse laudavimus, benigne acceptavimus, prestantes fidei corporaliter[10] sacramentum quod contra[11] compositionem illam minime veniemus sed eam nos et heredes nostri observare tenebimur in perpetuum illibatam. Acceptavimus etiam expresse quandam elemosinam trium modiorum vini factam ecclesie memorate ut eam liberrime et pacifice possideat in eternum salva tamen predictis fratribus de Maiwel ea justicia quam habere debent in talibus domini censuales. Ex illis autem tribus modiis vini assignati sunt tres modii uno quadrante minus super vineam A La Ruele que fuit Roberti Bacarii de conpendio et alius quadrans super vineam Gobini que dicitur A Busillon.[12] Et ut ista compositio prout est ordinata et facta in perpetuum fideliter et firmiter tam a nobis quam a nostris heredibus observetur presentem cartam[13] sigilli nostri munimine duximus roborandam. Et quia ego Agathes[14] sigillum proprium non habebam, sigillo domini mei usa sum pariter et contenta. Actum anno Domini M° CC° XXX° II° post nativitatem Domini.[15]

7 Souppi *B*.
8 Ribaudon, comm. Soupir, https://dicotopo.cths.fr/places/P28661536.
9 Ribodon *B*.
10 *Transp. A*; corporaliter fidei *B*.
11 *Superscr.* contra *A*.
12 Buscillon *B*.
13 kartam *B*.
14 Agates *B*.
15 millesimo ducentesimo tricesimo secundo *B*.

136

After December 26, 1211–15.[1]

Robert,[2] bishop of Laon, confirms by vidimus *an already executed act of* magister *Prieur, canon of Laon and* officialis, *concerning husband and wife Baudouin de Montigny,[3] knight, and Emmeline. (See **110**.)[4]*

A. Cartulary of Prémontré, fol. 32v.
B. Original not found.
REGISTER: *Studium Baldwin*, fiche 2434.

Karta officialis Laudunensis sicut in precedenti pagina continetur.

[I]n nomine sancte Trinitatis, amen. Ego Robertus, Dei gratia Laudunensis electus. Presentis scripti testimonio tam modernis quam posteris innotescat quod officialis noster magister Prior,[5] canonicus Laudunensis, vices nostras in hiis que subscripta eius cartula comprehendit de nostro speciali mandato prudenter fuit et fideliter executus. Cuius executionis processum et gratum et ratum habentes cartulam ipsam fecimus hic transcribi verba talia continentem: In nomine Patris et Filii et Spiritus Sancti, amen. Ego magister Prior, canonicus Laudunensis et officialis domini Laudunensis electi, omnibus karte huius inspectoribus tam presentibus quam futuris in perpetuum. Noverit universitas quod Balduinus de Montigni, miles, et Enmelina, uxor eius, et ceteri. Iste litere scripte sunt in precedenti quaterno versus finem verbo ad verbum et ideo hii non scribuntur.

137

1144

Hugues [I],[1] abbot of Prémontré, makes known that Hersende de Braye,[2] her sons Adon, Jean, and Baudouin, and their sisters Marie and Berthe, gave to

1 The act must have been written after **110** (December 26, 1211), to which this act refers, and before the end of Robert's episcopacy in 1215.
2 Robert de Châtillon, son of Guy II, lord of Châtillon and Alix de Dreux, bishop of Laon, 1210–15.
3 Perhaps Montigny-sur-Vesle, cant. Fismes, https://dicotopo.cths.fr/places/P59181065.
4 Rather than transcribing this act in full, the scribe refers the reader to another act in the previous quarternion.
5 Prieur, *officialis* of Laon, ca. 1210–ca. 1213. Wyard, *Saint-Vincent*, 36.

1 Hugues I de Fosses (ca. 1093–1164), first abbot of Prémontré.
2 Braye-en-Laonnois, cant. Craonne, https://dicotopo.cths.fr/places/P35162562.

the church of Prémontré a piece of land located at Soupir,[6] *in return for the* terragium *of every twelfth sheaf.*

A. Cartulary of Prémontré, fol. 32v.

B. Original (chirograph) on parchment, AD Aisne, H 826, previously sealed with a double strip of parchment. In the left margin and beginning at the top, the top half of the letters that form the word CHYROGRAPHUM.

Karta Hugonis Premonstratensis de cultura de Brai quam dedit Hersendis de Brai.

[I]n nomine sancte et individue Trinitatis. Ea que fiunt, cito a memoria hominum deciderent, nisi cartis annotata essent. Qua propter ego Hugo, Dei gratia Premonstratensis ecclesie abbas, notum fieri volo tam futuris quam presentibus quod Hersendis de Brai et filii eius Ado et Johannes et Balduinus cum sororibus suis, Maria et Berta, Premonstratensi ecclesie manufirma dederunt et super altare obtulerunt terram suam sicut metis terminata fuit testimonio vicinorum qui subscripti sunt, quam habebant juxta culturam eiusdem ecclesie de Sopi[7] pro duodecima garba terragii pro qua in campum venient et ibi eam recipient. Ab omnibus autem reclamato,[8] predicti viri eandem terram se liberaturos fore spoponderunt et terragium suum nemini dare nec inde alicui elemosinam facere, nisi ecclesie nostre pacti sunt. Quod si illud vendere vel in vadimonio ponere voluerint, primum fratribus nostris offerent qui, si voluerint accipere, nulli alii poterunt vendere vel in vadimonio ꝑ tradere. Sin autem voluerint,[9] de terragio suo facient quod eis utile fuerit. Huius rei testes fuerunt: Ansellus Lupus, Gerardus Gruinnarz,[10] Herbertus filius Haudewidis,[11] Letoldus, et ceteri.[12] Actum est hoc anno incarnationis dominice M° C° XLIIII°,[13] indictione VIIa, epacta XXVa, concurrente IIII°.

---

6 Soupir, cant. Vailly, https://dicotopo.cths.fr/places/P62600159.

7 Supi *B*.

8 reclamatoribus *B*.

9 noluerint *B*.

10 Grinnarz *B*.

11 Haduigis *B*.

12 *Add.* et ceteri *A*; Constanius decanus, Albuinus filius Wiburgis, et Hugo frater eius, Herbertus filius sacerdotis, Walterus carpentarius, Rogerus filius Odeline *B*.

13 XL° IIII° *B*.

138

1163. Laon.

Gautier [II],[1] *bishop of Laon, confirms the resolution of a dispute between Prémontré and Robert* Bretel *de Bruyères*[2] *on the one hand, and Robert's stepsons, Raoul de la Braye and the cleric Adon,*[3] *on the other. Robert and his unnamed wife, Raoul and Adon's mother, had given a piece of heathland which was part of her inheritance to the Premonstratensians at Soupir.*[4] *Raoul contested certain of the gift's conditions, claiming that he and his brother as minors had not been able to legally consent. Raoul and Adon now renounce their claims, while Aelide, Raoul's wife, and their sons Enguerrand and Raoul consent to this.*

A. Cartulary of Prémontré, fols. 32v–33r.
B. Original, AN, L 995, no. 29, previously sealed.
REGISTER: *Studium Baldwin*, fiche 2200.

Karta Galteri Laudunensis episcopi de confirmatione cuiusdam terre de Brai.

[I]n nomine sancte et individue Trinitatis. Quia nostrum est ea que bene gesta sunt, approbare et perturbata ad pacem revocare ac contentioni imponere finem, idcirco ego Galterus Dei gratia Laudunensis episcopum notum fieri volumus tam futuris quam presentibus quod Robertus de Brueriis,[5] cognomento Bretiaus,[6] victricus Radulphi[7] de la Brai et Adonis clerici, terram quandam[8] incultam et brueria plenam quam acceperat cum uxore sua, matre predicti Radulphi[9] et Adonis, uxore prius Pagani Pourcelet,[10] patris corumdem videlicet Radulphi[11] et Adonis, que jacet in Monte de Soupi,[12] dedit fratribus Premonstrate ecclesie in eodem monte de Supeio commorantibus ad

1 Gautier de Mortagne was dean of Laon, ca. 1142–55, and bishop of Laon, 1155–74.
2 Bruyères-et-Montbérault, cant. Laon, https://dicotopo.cths.fr/places/P62433167.
3 Adon de Braye is mentioned in an 1162 act concerning the Premonstratensian abbey of Braine. Guyotjeannin et al., *Le chartrier de l'abbaye prémontrée de Saint-Yved de Braine (1134–1250)*, 244–5.
4 Soupir, cant. Vailly, https://dicotopo.cths.fr/places/P62600159.
5 Bruieres *B*.
6 Bretel *B*.
7 Radulfi *B*.
8 *Transp. A*; quandam terram *B*.
9 Radulfi *B*.
10 Porceleth *B*.
11 Radulfi *B*.
12 Suppi *B*.

disrumpendam[13] et excolendam ad terciam decimam garbam, prius ejecta garba messoris et decima, hac autem interposita conventione ut pro qualibet parte terre illius que custodiretur et nutriretur in silvam sex[14] nummi bone monete ei singulis annis censualiter persolverentur. Si autem silva deinceps disrumperetur[15] et coleretur, census sex[16] nummorum decideret et terre rupte terragium acciperet sicut cetere terre culte. Ita etiam ut eandem conventionem quam idem Robertus cum fratribus prefate ecclesie habuit, filiastros suos et Odonem[17] Radulfum faceret concedere et ratam habere. Quod si fecerit aliquamdiu licet[18] indiscussum permanserit predictus Radulphus[19] postmodum miles factus de eadem terra terragium et eundem censum quia ei contigit eadem terra eo quod de patre suo movebat Pagano videlicet Pourcelet[20] quem Robertus prius receperat ipse perplures annos recipiens movit tandem et intulit huic prius habite conventioni calumpniam dicens quod, cum adhuc puer esset, eandem conventionem non concesserit nec frater eius Ado. Quam querelam predicti fratres pacificare volentes, et eundem Radulphum[21] super hac vexare nolentes, ipsum cum amicis suis convenerunt, ipse tandem rogatu et ammonitu tam amicorum suorum quam dono quod ei dederunt predicti fratres adhoc attractus et adductus est et frater eius Ado, conventionem a Roberto prius factam cum predictis fratribus Ado et Radulphus[22] annuerunt et postmodum coram multis astantibus tam clericis quam laicis in capitulo Laudunensi omnem querelam deponentes concesserunt ita et quod in hac carta corrigendum fuit presens capitulum correxit. Quod ut in perpetuum ratum permaneat nostre auctoritatis sigillo munimus et confirmamus sub anathemate ut si quelibet persona hanc conventionem violaverit vel deinceps violare temptaverit vel deinceps interruperit si ad satisfactionem non venerit hic et in eternum excommunicationi subiaceat et anathema sit. Hanc concessionem approbavit et concessit Aelidis, uxor predicti Radulphi.[23] Concesserunt etiam filii eius Ingelrannus, Radulphus.[24] Huius rei testes sunt: dominus Lisiardus[25] decanus, dominus Walterus[26] thesaurarius,[27]

---

13 dirrumpendam *B*.

14 VI *B*.

15 dirrumperetur *B*.

16 VI *B*.

17 *Transp. A*; Radulfum et Adonem *B*.

18 *Transp. A*; licet aliquamdiu *B*.

19 Radulfus *B*.

20 Porceleth *B*.

21 Radulfum *B*.

22 Radulfus *B*.

23 Radulfi *B*.

24 Radulfus *B*.

25 Lisiard, dean of Laon, ca. 1153–ca. 1168.

26 Gautier, treasurer of Laon, ca. 1162–ca. 1173. Per AD Aisne, G 171, a nephew of Gautier de Mortagne, bishop of Laon.

27 tesaurarius *B*.

Gerardus[28] subthesaurarius,[29] magister Hugo,[30] dominus Alexander, Willermus sacerdos, Abricus,[31] Johannes, Warnerius[32] conversi, Anselmus[33] decanus de Cerni, Gerbertus sacerdos de Nougent,[34] huius etiam compositor conventionis[35] et testis est Gelbuinus[36] de Nougent[37] avunculus Radulfi, uxor eius Cecilia, Ado de Brai, Johannes frater eius, Renerus,[38] Stephanus. Actum est hoc Lauduni,[39] anno incarnationis dominice M° C° LX° III°.[40] Magister Angotus[41,42] relegit, scripsit et subscripsit.

139

1156

Gautier [II],[1] bishop of Laon, makes known the confirmation made by Guy [I],[2] lord of Soupir, of an alms gift granted to the abbot and church of Prémontré by Baudouin, Guy's father. Guy also makes his own gift to the said church of the rights of easement on the mill of Ribaudon,[3] as well as various woods, land, and vineyards over which Guy retains rights of justicia*; this is in exchange for small payments from Prémontré. (See **141**.)*

28 Gérard, subtreasurer of Laon, is a witness to episcopal acts from 1145. Dufour-Malbezin, *Actes*, 372.

29 subtesaurarius *B*.

30 Hugues de Mortagne (d. ca. 1180), later prior of the Benedictine abbey of Saint-Martin de Sées, appears as a witness in episcopal acts from 1149. Morelle, "Une charte nuptiale laonnoise de 1158 conservée en original," 221, fn. 57.

31 Alricus *B*.

32 Varnerius *B*.

33 Ansel, dean of Cerny, ca. 1171–ca. 1178. Beauvillé, *Recueil de documents inédits concernant la Picardie*, vol. 4, 15; Herbomez, *Chartes de l'abbaye de Saint-Martin de Tournai*, vol. 1, 116.

34 Nugent *B*.

35 *Transp. A*; conventionis compositor *B*.

36 Gebuin (or Gepuin), knight and lord of Nouvion-le-Comte, attested 1138–77. Melleville, *DH*, vol. 2, 174. He also appears as a witness in **97** and in Raoul I, lord of Coucy's 1163 grant of rights to Vervins. Mennesson, "Les chartes de Vervins," 22.

37 Gebbuinue de Nugent *B*.

38 Reinerus *B*.

39 *Transp. A*; Lauduni hoc. *B*.

40 M C[mo] LX° III° *B*.

41 Andgodus cancellarius *B*.

42 Angot, chancellor of Laon, ca. 1144–ca. 1170.

1 Gautier de Mortagne was dean of Laon, ca. 1142–55, and bishop of Laon, 1155–74.

2 Guy I, lord of Soupir (cant. Vailly, https://dicotopo.cths.fr/places/P62600159), son of Baudouin I, lord of Soupir. Wacha, "La Puissance du Choix," 116.

3 Ribaudon, comm. Soupir, https://dicotopo.cths.fr/places/P28661536.

A. Cartulary of Prémontré, fol. 33r.
B. Original, AN, L 995, no. 24, previously sealed.
REGISTER: *Studium Baldwin*, fiche 2354.

Karta Galteri Laudunensis episcopi de confirmatione cuiusdam elemosine Balduini de Soupi.

[I]n nomine sancte et individue Trinitatis. Ego Galterus, Dei gratia Laudunensis[4] episcopus. Notum fieri volumus universis quod Guido, dominus de Souppi,[5] concessit domino Hugoni, Premonstratensis ecclesie abbati, et eiusdem ecclesie fratribus quicquid possidebant de elemosina Balduini, patris sui, in territorio et in Monte de Soupi,[6] sicut in ipsius ecclesie privilegiis continetur firmatum. In augmentum etiam elemosine addidit ob remedium anime sue et predecessorum suorum aisentias molendini de Ribaudon[7] et cursum aque de Supi manantem, ita tamen ut ad irriganda prata sua, cum necesse fuerit, eandem habeat aquam. Sed et ortum et vivarium, sicut suis consistunt terminis. Debentur autem inde ipsi Guidoni duodecim[8] nummi bone monete. Dedit etiam in elemosinam quartam partem silvule pro qua solvuntur octo[9] nummi bone monete. Districtum vero et justiciam eiusdem silvule ad hoc tamen retinuit ut arceret ecclesie dampna inferentes. Vineam quoque ultra puteum, sicut prefixis distenditur terminis, unde quatuor[10] persolvuntur nummi bone monete. Concessit nichilominus quicquid in valle de Soupi[11] et de Maidi[12] et in omni dominio suo antea tenuerant quiete deinceps possidendum, hoc tamen interposito quod amodo in omni districto suo nichil nisi ipso concedente acquirent. Testes sunt Lisiardus[13] decanus, Hugo[14] abbas Sancti Nicholai de Bosco, Garinus[15] Sancti Martini Laudunensis et Radulfus[16] Branensis abbates,

4 Laudunensium *B*.
5 Supi *B*.
6 Supi *B*.
7 Ribaudun *B*.
8 XII[cim] *B*.
9 VIII[to] *B*.
10 IIII[or] *B*.
11 Supi *B*.
12 Maedi *B*.
13 Lisiard, dean of Laon, ca. 1153–ca. 1168.
14 Hugues, abbot of the Benedictine abbey of Saint-Nicolas-aux-Bois, ca. 1156–ca. 1166. Duval, "Histoire de l'abbaye bénédictine de Saint-Nicolas-aux-Bois, diocèse de Laon, première partie," 196–8.
15 Guérin, abbot of the Premonstratensian abbey of Saint-Martin de Laon, 1151–71. *MP* II, 512.
16 Raoul, abbot of the Premonstratensian abbey of Braine, 1150–63. *MP* II, 486.

Galterus capellanus et Magister Hugo, Symon miles, Lambertus, Galterus prepositus, Hugo Cerviaus,[17] Radulfus Costars.[18] Actum anno incarnati verbi M° C° LVI°, indictione IIII[a]. Siquis igitur huic nostre confirmationi obviare presumpserit, donec resipiscat anathema sit. Ego Angotus[19] cancellarius relegi et subscripsi.

140

1124. Laon.

Barthélemy,[1] bishop of Laon, confirms as fief lord the gift from Baudouin [I][2] de Soupir to Norbert and the brothers of Prémontré of three carrucatae *of arable land in the parish of Soupir, as much land as will hold 45* modii *of seed grain, as well as pastures, all of which remains subject to rights of* justicia *and* advocatus.

A. Cartulary of Prémontré, fols. 33r–33v.

B. Original not found.

EDITION: Dufour-Malbezin, *Actes*, 186–7; *Chartae Galliae*, no. 208160, http://telma.irht.cnrs.fr/outils/chartae-galliae/charte208160/.

REGISTER: Florival, *Étude historique sur le XIIe siècle*, 305.

Karta Galteri Laudunensis episcopi de confirmatione doni et elemosine Balduini de Sopi.

[I]n nomine sancte et individue Trinitatis. Ego Bartholomeus, Dei gratia Laudunensis ecclesie minister indignus. Pars religionis est religiosorum virorum provectui pia devotione concurrere et, aliena bona tamquam propria amando, eorum fructum benivolo assensu et caritatis unanimitate sui profectus usui conciliare. Notum igitur esse volumus tam posteris quam modernis qualiter Balduinus de Sopeio, voluntate et assensu nostro, a quibus beneficium Soupeii tenet, concesserit domino Norberto, venerabili presbitero, et fratribus suis in Premonstrato loco Deo famulantibus eorumque successoribus in parrochia Soupeiensi terre arabilis carrucatas tres, videlicet quantum ad quadraginta

17 Cervels *B*.

18 Costarz *B*.

19 Angot, chancellor of Laon, ca. 1144–ca. 1170.

1 Barthélemy de Jur (d. 1158), son of Conon, lord of Grandson and La Sarraz, and Ada de Roucy; first subdeacon and then treasurer of Reims, later bishop of Laon, 1113–51.

2 Baudouin I, lord of Soupir (cant. Vailly, https://dicotopo.cths.fr/places/P62600159). Wacha, "La Puissance du Choix," 116.

quinque modios sementis sufficere possit, scilicet unam culturam desuper nemus et alteram culturam que dicitur cultura Roiboldi, que est desuper fossam de Brai, et de tercia cultura, que de Muinis dicitur, quantum sufficiat ad tres carrucatas explendas, vel totam eam si tota necessaria sit. Ipsam autem terram et curtem cum pascuis dominii sui et omnia tam intus quam extra ad usum fratrum pertinentia, ita ab omni seculari justicia vel advocaria libera et absoluta esse concessit, ut neque eo superstite neque post decessum eius, vel ipse vel aliqua alia secularis persona ad ea que ipsorum erunt manum mittere presumat. Nos ergo quia terra illa de beneficio nostro erat huic donationi, sicut prescripsimus, assensum prebentes, presenti eam scripto firmari precepimus necnon et sigilli nostri impressione atque anathematis interposi[3] ac testium subscriptione firma stabilitate corroborari curavimus. Signum Bartholomei, episcopi, qui hoc scriptum fieri jussit. S. Guidonis,[4] decani. Signum Radulphi, archidiaconi. S. Soifridi,[5] abbatis. S. Rainaldi,[6] abbatis, et ceteri. Actum Lauduni, dominice incarnationis anno M° C° XXIIII°, indictione XII[a], epacta XIIII[a], concurrente IIII°. Ego Radulphus, [7] Sancte Marie cancellarius, relegi et subscripsi.

141

1141. Laon.

Barthélemy,[1] *bishop of Laon, as fief lord confirms the gift from Baudouin I de Soupir*[2] *to Norbert and the brothers of Prémontré of three* carrucatae *of arable land in the parish of Soupir; a later augmentation of the gift to include land on which to build a mill; and the later confirmation of Baudouin's gifts by his son, Guy,*[3] *who confirms certain boundaries and concedes the easement to the*

3 *Sic A*, *read* interposui.

4 Guy de Pierrepont, son of Roger, lord of Pierrepont, and Ermengarde, lady of Montaigu, was first treasurer, archdeacon, and dean of the chapter of Laon, and later bishop of Châlons, 1144–7.

5 Seifroy, abbot of the Benedictine abbey of Saint-Vincent de Laon, 1120–8. Wyard, *Saint-Vincent*, 580.

6 Renaud, first abbot of the Cistercian abbey of Foigny, 1121–31. *GC* IX, cols. 629–30.

7 Raoul de Laon (d. 1133), brother of the theologian Anselm de Laon, was archdeacon of Laon, 1117–26, and chancellor of Laon, 1117–33. Dufour-Malbezin, *Actes*, 29.

1 Barthélemy de Jur (d. 1158), son of Conon, lord of Grandson and La Sarraz, and Ada de Roucy; first subdeacon and then treasurer of Reims, later bishop of Laon, 1113–51.

2 Baudouin I, lord of Soupir (cant. Vailly, https://dicotopo.cths.fr/places/P62600159). Wacha, "La Puissance du Choix," 116.

3 Guy I, lord of Soupir, son of Baudouin I, lord of Soupir. Ibid.

mill of Ribaudon.[4] *All lands remain subject to rights of* justicia *and* advocatus. *(See* ***139****.)*

A. Cartulary of Prémontré, fol. 33v.

B. Original, AD Aisne, H 826, previously sealed with a double strip of leather.

EDITION: Grauwen, "Twee onuitgegeven oorkonden over Norbert van Gennep," 283–5; Dufour-Malbezin, *Actes*, 315–17; *Chartae Galliae*, no. 208353, http://telma.irht.cnrs.fr/outils/chartae-galliae/charte208353/.

REGISTER: Grauwen, "Lijst van oorkonden waarin Norbertus wordt genoemd," 147.

Karta Bartholomei episcopi de tribus carrucatis quas dedit Balduinus ecclesie Premonstratensis.

[I]n nomine sancte et individue Trinitatis. Ego Bartholomeus, Dei gratia sancte Laudunensis ecclesie minister indignus. Pars religionis est religiosorum virorum provectui pia devotione concurrere et aliena bona tamquam propria amando eorum fructum benivolo assensu et caritatis unanimitate sui profectus usui conciliare. Notum igitur esse volumus tam posteris quam modernis qualiter Balduinus de Soupeio,[5] voluntate et assensu nostro, a quibus beneficium Supeii tenet, concesserit domino Norberto, venerabili presbitero, et eius fratribus in Premonstratensi loco Deo famulantibus, eorumque successoribus, in parrochia Supeiensi terre arabilis carrucatas tres, videlicet quantum ad quadraginta quinque modios sementis sufficere possit, scilicet unam culturam desuper nemus et alteram culturam, que dicitur cultura Roiboldi, que est desuper fossam de Brai, et de tertia cultura, que de Muinis dicitur, quantum sufficiat ad tres carrucatas explendas, vel totam eam, si tota sit necessaria. Ipsam autem terram et curtem cum pascuis dominii sui, et omnia, tam intus, quam extra, ad usum fratrum pertinentia, ita ab omni seculari justicia vel advocaria libera et absoluta esse concessit, ut neque eo superstite, neque post decessum eius, vel ipse vel alia aliqua[6] secularis persona ad ea que ipsorum erunt manum mittere presumat. Nos ergo quia terra illa de beneficio nostro erat, huic donationi sicut prescripsimus assensum prebentes, presenti eam scripto firmari precepimus, necnon et sigilli nostri impressione, atque anathematis interpositione, ac testium subscriptione, firma stabilitate, corroborari curavimus. Signum Bartholomei episcopi, qui hoc scriptum fieri jussit. Signum Guidonis, decani. S. Radulfi, archidiaconi. S. Soifridi, Rainaldi, Andree, Symonis, abbatum et ceteri.[7] Actum Lauduni, anno

4 Ribaudon, comm. Soupir, https://dicotopo.cths.fr/places/P28661536.

5 Supeio *B*.

6 *Transp. A*; aliqua alia *B*.

7 *Add.* et ceteri *A*; S. Gerardi, decani de Guysia. S. Lethaldi, Arnulfi, Ebali, subdiaconorum. S. Nicholai, castellani. S. Clarembaldi de Foro. S. Henrici, comitis. S. Arnulfi Calderun. S. Clarembaldi de Loisi. S. Wichardi de Auriniaco. S. Othonis. S. Albrici Pesleth. S. Alardi. S.

dominice incarnationis anno M° C° XXIIII°, indictione XII[a], epacta XIIII[a], concurrente IIII°. Succedente vero tempore, predictus Balduinus de Sopeio, ad augmentum elemosine sue, in ripa fluminis, quod Axona dicitur, ubi fratres ipsius supradicte Premonstratensis ecclesie oportunius sibi previderint, in territorio de Supeio intra metas juris ipsius Balduini, locum ad construendum molendinum, ab omni censu et consuetudine liberum, donavit et insuper ad ipsius molendini necessitatem et omnem aliam fratrum commoditatem, a loco ipsius, quantum a parte superiori et inferiori et e transverso fluminis arcus jacere potest, in terra et in aqua concessit. Quoniam vero de feodo nostro descendebat, prefatus Balduinus hoc donum in manu nostra posuit et auctoritate nostra confirmari postulavit. Nos autem, ut omnis contradictio sopiatur, tam presenti scripto quam testium subscriptione necnon et sigilli nostri impressione, anathemate interposito, firmari precepimus. Signum Guidonis, decani. Signum Blihardi, cantoris. S. Arnulphi, clerici. S. Hugonis Poivre,[8] et ceteri.[9] Actum est autem hoc, anno incarnationis dominice M° C° XXX° quinto, indictione XIII[a], epacta XV[a], concurrente primo.[10] Post decessum autem sepefati Balduini, Guido, filius eius, miles effectus, in honore patris sui intravit et prefatas donationes, quas pater eius fecerat, sicut bonus successor, Premonstratensi ecclesie benigne concessit; et ipse et milites eius et servientes eius circuierunt terras et posuerunt metas et vineam sub domo procalcaverunt, et vi~~ne~~am de domo ad molendinum, ubi non solebat esse via. Cuius rei testes fuerunt: Ursio de Roia,[11] Hugo filius eius, Symon frater eius, Albricus, Johiers, Lambertus de Aberlai[12] de Fontene,[13] Gualterus prepositus, Robertus filius Ernaldi, et tres fratres eius Radulphus Barduinus, Bernardus Sotus et Ernaldus, Warinus, Paganus de Bernot, Radulphus filius Bernardi, Hugo filius Herveri, Robodus. Nos igitur ex officii nostri debito, ecclesie paci providentes, ut omnia quiete possideat, tam post actam a Guidone concessionem, quam prius factam a patre eius elemosinam, sigilli nostri impressione munimus et in conservatores benedictionem, in perturbatores vero perpetui anathematis proferimus innodationem. Actum[14] est hoc, anno dominice incarnationis M° C° XLI°, indictione IIII[a], epacta XI[a], concurrente II°. Ego B.[15] relegi.

Odonis, filii Alardi de Bunuis. S. Roberti, castellani de Coci. S. Gerardi Dolleth. S. Petri de Brana. S. Adonis de Derci. S. Walteri Vituli. S. Walteri, camerarii *B*.

8 Hugues Poivre also appears as a witness in **112**.

9 *Add.* Et ceteri *A*; S. Herberti Poilevilain. S. Haimonis Bretel. S. Gerardi, vicedomini. S. Nicholai, castellani. S Clarembaldi de Turricula. S. Hugonis Truie. S. Roberti Vinun. S. Roberti Vituli *B*.

10 I° *B*.

11 Roye, cant. Roye, https://dicotopo.cths.fr/places/P52439933.

12 Perhaps L'Auberlaye, comm. Crouy, https://dicotopo.cths.fr/places/P30303401.

13 *Om.* Stephanus de Fontene *A*.

14 vero *B*.

15 Bartolomeus, cancellarius *B*.

142

1163. Laon.

Gautier [II],[1] bishop of Laon, makes known the agreement reached between the abbots of Prémontré and of [Marmoutier],[2] following a dispute over a house which Létaud de Braye[3] had partly sold, and partly given in alms, to Prémontré. Pierre, prior of Saint-Nicolas de Roucy,[4] on whose priory's land the house was located, had complained about Létaud's actions to his superior, the abbot of Marmoutier. The dispute was resolved when the brothers of Prémontré promised to pay an annual census *of two* nummi *in return for keeping the house.*

A. Cartulary of Prémontré, fol. 34r.
B. Original not found.

NO RUBRIC. CIRCA 1250 ADDITION.

[I]n nomine sancte et individue Trinitatis. Ego Galterus, Dei gratia Laudunensis episcopus, notum fieri volumus tam futuris quam presentibus quod Letaldus de Brai tenebat mansum unum terre de monachis Sancti Nicholai de Ruci sub censu annuali et debito, sicut et antecessores eius tenuerunt. Huius mansi terre particulam predictus Letaldus fratribus Premonstratensis ecclesie commorantibus in Monte de Suppeio dedit partim in elemosinam, partim emptione contulit. Deinde super elemosinam et venditionem quam Letaldus cum predictis fratribus fecerat, movit querelam dominus Petrus, prior Sancti Nicholai de Ruci, quia de Sancto Nicholao de Ruci terra illa movebat, coram abbate suo, videlicet Sancti Martini Turonensis, adversus abbatem Premonstratensem; verba in hunc modum intulit ut vel ipse eandem terram redderet, vel cum Petro, priore de Ruci, quoquomodo pacem faceret de eadem terra et terram sibi, pace facta, retineret. Tandem huius rei conquestio inter duos abbates, videlicet Turonensem et Premonstratensem, ad hoc perducta est quod abbas Turonensis huius querele negotium imposuit Petro, priori de Ruci, et concessit ratam esse quamcumque pactionem. Predictus prior de possessione huius terre, calumpniam, multis astantibus tam laicis quam clericis in curia Laudunensi, deposuit et dedit eam in proprium possidendam fratribus Premonstratensis ecclesie sub censu annuali duorum nummorum bone monete qui reddentur ad festum Sancti Remigii tali villico quem habebit Sanctus Nicholaus de Ruci in villa

1 Gautier de Mortagne was dean of Laon, ca. 1142–55 and bishop of Laon, 1155–74.
2 Either Robert IV Méguier, abbot of Marmoutier, 1155–63, or Robert V de Blois, abbot of Marmoutier, 1163–76.
3 Braye-en-Laonnois, cant. Craonne, https://dicotopo.cths.fr/places/P35162562.
4 The Benedictine priory of Saint-Nicolas de Roucy (arr. Laon, https://dicotopo.cths.fr/places/P39468514), a dependent house of Marmoutier.

de Brai. Ut istud in perpetuum ratum permaneat, nostri sigilli impressione et testium subscriptione muniri fecimus. Huius rei testes sunt: Abbas Hugo[5] Cuissiacensis, Walterus[6] thesaurarius, Gerardus[7] subthesaurarius, et ceteri. Actum est hoc Lauduni, anno M° C° LX° III°. Ansgotus cancellarius relegit, scripsit et subscripsit.

143

January 7, 1250.

Robert,[1] *treasurer of Noyon, canon of Laon, gives to the church of Prémontré, after his death, the vineyard that he bought from Roelier de Soupir,*[2] *at a place called* Ad Tiliam *near Soupir. The* magister *of the* curtis *of Soupir will perpetually hold the vineyard, and will give 60* solidi Parisiensium *a year from its proceeds to fund a pittance at Prémontré. (See* ***144****.)*

A. Cartulary of Prémontré, fol. 34r.

B. Original, AD Aisne, H 826, previously sealed with a double strip of parchment.

NO RUBRIC. CIRCA 1250 ADDITION.

[U]niversis presentes litteras visuris, Robertus, thesaurarius Noviomensis, canonicus Laudunensis, salutem in Domino. Noverit universitas vestra quod nos quandam vineam quam emimus a Roelerio de Soupiaco,[3] sitam in territorio eiusdem ville de Soupiaco[4] ad exitum eiusdem ville versus Vaisliacum,[5] loco qui dicitur Ad Tiliam, concessimus et dedimus ecclesie Premonstratensi tenendam ab eadem ecclesia post decessum nostrum, habendam et possidendam tanquam suam in perpetuum. Concessimus etiam et tradidimus ecclesie Premonstratensi predicte dictam vineam tenendam et habendam et excolendam

5 Hugues de Douai, abbot of the Premonstratensian abbey of Cuissy, 1161–5. *MP* II, 497.

6 Gautier, treasurer of Laon, ca. 1162–ca. 1173. Per AD Aisne, G 171, a nephew of Gautier de Mortagne, bishop of Laon.

7 Gérard, subtreasurer of Laon, is a witness to episcopal acts from 1145. Dufour-Malbezin, *Actes*, 372.

1 Robert de Roye (d. bef. 1252), first archdeacon of Senlis and later treasurer of Noyon; nephew of the chamberlain of France, Barthélemy de Roye. Picó, "Membership in the Cathedral Chapter of Laon, 1217–1238," 18.

2 Soupir, cant. Vailly, https://dicotopo.cths.fr/places/P62600159.

3 Souppiaco *B.*

4 Souppiaco *B.*

5 Vailly, arr. Soissons, https://dicotopo.cths.fr/places/P00798425.

ab ipsa ecclesia ad medietatem proventuum et exituum dicte vinee nobis reddendam ab ipsa ecclesia ad sumptus ipsius ecclesie ad domum nostram apud Laudunum singulis annis de anno in annum quamdiu vixerimus, et post obitum nostrum dicta vinea erit ipsius ecclesie in perpetuum. Post nostrum vero decessum, quicunque fuerit magister curtis Premonstratensis que dicitur Soupiacum,[6] tenebit dictam vineam et possidebit in perpetuum et pro eadem vinea reddet singulis annis conventui Premonstratensi sexaginta solidos Parisienses pro pitantia dicti conventus temporibus minutionum eiusdem conventus. In cuius rei testimonium, presentes litteras patentes emisimus sigilli nostri munimine roboratas. Datum anno Domini M°CC°L°,[7] mense januario, in crastino Epyphanie Domini.

144

January, 1250.

Magister *Guillaume de Viviers,*[1] officialis *of Laon, reiterates and reconfirms the preceding act. (See **143**.)*

A. Cartulary of Prémontré, fol. 34r.
B. Original, AD Aisne, H 826, previously sealed.

NO RUBRIC. CIRCA 1250 ADDITION.

[U]niversis presentes litteras visuris magister Guillermus de Vivariis, officialis Laudunensis, salutem in Domino. Noverit universitas vestra quod in nostra presentia constitutus, vir venerabilis R., thesaurarius Noviomensis, canonicus Laudunensis, recognovit se quandam vineam quam ipse dicebat se emisse a Roelerio de Soupiaco[2] sitam, ut dicebat in territorio de Soupiaco[3] ad exitum eiusdem ville versus Vaisliacum,[4] loco qui dicitur Ad Tiliam, concessisse et dedisse ecclesie Premonstratensi tenendam ab eadem ecclesia post decessum ipsius thesaurarii, habendam et possidendam tanquam suam in perpetuum. Recognovit etiam dictus thesaurarius coram nobis se concessisse et tradidisse

6 Souppiacum *B*.
7 quinquagesimo *B*.

1 *Magister* Guillaume de Viviers, *officialis* of Laon, ca. 1250–ca. 1252. Wyard, *Saint-Vincent*, 37.
2 Souppiaco *B*.
3 Souppiaco *B*.
4 Vailly, arr. Soissons, https://dicotopo.cths.fr/places/P00798425.

ecclesie dicte[5] Premonstratensis dictam vineam tenendam et habendam[6] et excolendam ab ipsa ecclesia ad medietatem proventuum et exituum dicte vinee reddendam ab ipsa ecclesia ad sumptus ipsius ecclesie ad domum ipsius thesaurarii apud Laudunum singulis annis de anno in annum quamdiu vixerit, ut dicebat, thesaurarius supradictus, volens et ordinans dictus thesaurarius quod post suum decessum quicumque fuerit magister curtis Premonstratensis, que dicitur Soupiacum,[7] teneat dictam vineam et habeat in perpetuum et pro eadem reddat singulis annis conventui Premonstratensi sexaginta solidos Parisiensium pro pitancia dicti conventus temporibus minutionum dicti conventus. In cuius rei testimonium, presentes litteras patentes emisimus salvo jure domini Laudunensis episcopi et alieno sigillo curie Laudunensis roboratas. Datum anno Domini M°CC° quinquaginta, mense januario.

145

December, 1250.

Guillaume de Viviers,[1] officialis *of Laon, makes known that husband and wife Martould de Soupir*[2] *and Isabelle, together with husband and wife Aubry de Soupir and Berte, made a gift and sale to the church of Prémontré of an annual* supercensus *over the house of Geoffroi de Chavonne*[3] *an attached courtyard, and a vineyard at Soupir.*

A. Cartulary of Prémontré, fols. 34r–34v.
B. Original, AN, L 995, no. 105, previously sealed.

NO RUBRIC. CIRCA 1250 ADDITION.

[U]niversis presentes litteras visuris, magister Guillermus de Vivariis, officialis Laudunensis, salutem in Domino. Noverit universitas vestra quod in jure coram nobis constituti Marthouldus de Soupi[4] et Ysabella eius uxor, Albricus de Soupi[5] alutarius et Berta, eius uxor, dicentes et asserentes se habere annuatim

5 *Transp. A*; dicte ecclesie *B*.
6 *Transp. A*; habendam et tenendam *B*.
7 Souppiacum *B*.

1 *Magister* Guillaume de Viviers, *officialis* of Laon, ca. 1250–ca. 1252. Wyard, *Saint-Vincent*, 37.
2 Soupir, cant. Vailly, https://dicotopo.cths.fr/places/P62600159.
3 Chavonne, cant. Vailly, https://dicotopo.cths.fr/places/P90566217.
4 Souppi *B*.
5 Souppi *B*.

supercensus subscriptos assignatos super domum Gaufridi de Chavones[6] piscatoris sitam apud Soupi[7] ad exitum ville versus Vaisliacum[8] et super curtillum dicte domui adiacentem et etiam super vineam ipsius Gaufridi sitam subtus dictam domum ex altera parte vie, videlicet dicti Martouldus et Ysabella decem solidos Parisienses et dicti Albricus et Berta quinque solidos Parisienses supercensuales singulis annis in perpetuum persolvendos dictis Martouldo, Ysabelle, Albrico et Berte et eorum heredibus sive successoribus in festo Beati Martini hyemalis, ut dicebant, de dictis supercensibus in puram et perpetuam elemosinam contulerunt et concesserunt et se contulisse et concessisse recognoverunt ecclesie Premonstratensis, videlicet dicti Martouldus et Ysabella duos solidos Parisienses supercensuales de dictis decem solidorum Parisiensium supercensualibus et dicti Albricus et Berta duodecim denarios Parisienses supercensuales de dictis quinque solidis Parisiensium supercensualibus modo predicto assignatis et persolvendis. Recognoverunt etiam dicti Martouldus et Ysabella, Albricus et Berta se vendidisse dicte ecclesie Premonstratensis residuum dictorum supercensuum videlicet dictus Martouldus et dicta Ysabella octo solidos Parisienses supercensuales residuos de dictis decem solidis Parisiensibus supercensualibus precio quatuor librarum Parisiensium de quibus recognoverunt sibi esse satisfactum ad plenum ab ipsa ecclesia Premonstratensis in pecunia numerata et dicti Albricus et Berta quatuor solidorum Parisiensium supercensuales residuos de dictis quinque solidis Parisiensibus supercensualibus precio quadraginta solidorum Parisiensium de quibus ipsi recognoverunt sibi esse satisfactum ad plenum in pecunia numerata ab ecclesia supradicta. Cesserunt etiam et concesserunt penitus et in perpetuum et se cessisse et concessisse recognoverunt dicti Martouldus et Albricus et etiam dicte uxores sue fide corporali ab ipsis prestita super hoc spontanee et non coacte, ut dicebant, ecclesie Premonstratensis predicte supercensus predictos et quicquid juris in eisdem habebant et habere poterant aut debebant sive ratione dotis sive alia quacumque[9] ratione vel titulo. Promiserunt etiam dicti Martoudus,[10] Ysabella, Albricus et Berta sub dicte fidei sue religione se legitimam portaturos garandiam in perpetuum dicte ecclesie Premonstratensi superdictis supercensibus videlicet dicti Martouldus et Ysabella super dictis decem solidorum Parisiensium supercensualibus et dicti Albricus et Berta super dictis quinque solidorum Parisiensium supercensualibus modo predicto assignatis et persolvendis contra omnes juri et justicie parere volentes se et sua et heredes suos et successores ad dictam garandiam portandam perpetuo obligantes et constituentes obligatos. Insuper cesserunt et concesserunt penitus et in perpetuum ecclesie memorate

6 Chavonnes *B*.

7 Souppi *B*.

8 Vailly, arr. Soissons, https://dicotopo.cths.fr/places/P00798425.

9 *Transp. A*; quacumque alia *B*.

10 *Sic A*.

omne jus et omnem actionem que habebant et habere poterant erga quoscumque super dictis supercensibus et occasione eorundem et sub dicta fide sua promittentes quod in eisdem supercensibus per se vel per alium aliquid non reclamabunt in futurum nec facient reclamari nec contra premissa sive contra aliquid de premissis venient decetero seu venire presument immo omnia et singula supradicta inviolabiliter observabunt. In cuius rei testimonium presentes litteras patentes emisimus salvo jure domini Laudunensis episcopi et alieno sigillo curie Laudunensis roboratas. Actum[11] anno Domini M° CC° L°,[12] mense decembri.[13]

146

March, 1250.

Magister *Aubry de Fontenoy,*[1] officialis *of Soissons, makes known that Isabelle, widow of Jean Morel, and the church of Prémontré reached an agreement. Isabelle, who held the mill of Ribaudon*[2] *from Prémontré for the duration of her life with an annual pension of 100* solidi, *agrees to relinquish that pension in exchange for a payment of nine* librae.

A. Cartulary of Prémontré, fol. 34v.
B. Original, BnF, Coll. Picardie 290, no. 49, previously sealed.

NO RUBRIC. CIRCA 1250 ADDITION.

[U]niversis presentes litteras inspecturis, magister Albricus de Fontene, officialis Suessionensis, in Domino salutem. Noverint universi quod Ysabella,[3] vidua relicta Johannis Morel, coram nobis propter hoc proposuit constituta quod quoddam molendinum ecclesie Premonstratensis[4] situm juxta Pontem Arseii, quod dicitur molendinum de Riboudon, habebat tenere et possidere cum eius appendiciis, quamdiu ipsa viveret, sub annua pensione centum solidorum fortium ab ea dicte ecclesie annis singulis, quoad viveret, solvendorum. Verum pacto inter eam et dictam ecclesiam interveniente super hoc, ipsa eidem ecclesie dictum,

---

11 Datum *B*.
12 millesimo ducentesimo L° *B*.
13 *Om*. I. Suessionensis *A*.

---

1 Aubrey de Fontenoy, *officialis* of Soissons, ca. 1249–ca. 1251. Newman, *Seigneurs*, vol. 1, 283.
2 Ribaudon, comm. Soupir, https://dicotopo.cths.fr/places/P28661536.
3 Isabella *B*.
4 Premonstrati *B*.

molendinum cum omni jure quod in eo et eius appenditiis competebat sibi et competere poterat, coram nobis remisit penitus et quitavit[5] mediantibus novem libris fortium sibi, ut dicebat, ab ipsa ecclesia propter hoc persolutis. Promisit autem dicta Ysabella,[6] fide data, quod in dicto molendino et eius appendiciis nichil juris per se aut per alium decetero reclamabit. Promisit nichilominus quod litteras, si que super concessione dicti molendini sibi olim et Johanni predicto marito quondam ipsius, facta fuerant tradite vel confecte, sive sub sigillo abbatis et conventus Premonstratensis sive alterius cuiuscumque, quibus ipsa ex nunc renunciat, penitus coram nobis eidem ecclesie, si eas invenire poterit, restituet atque traddet[7] nec eis voluit deinceps in aliquo se juvare. In cuius rei testimonium, presentibus litteris sigillum curie Suessionensis fecimus apponi. Datum[8] anno Domini M° CC° L°,[9] mense martio.[10]

147

September, 1311. Corbeil.

Philippe [IV the Fair], king of France, approves and confirms the bequests made by the late Enguerrand [IV],[1] lord of Coucy, to several religious institutions in certain places of his barony and lands of Coucy, La Fère,[2] and Marle,[3] including 12 librae Parisiensium *annually to Prémontré and the Benedictine abbey of Nogent for the purchase of clothes and shoes for the local poor, and 40* librae Parisiensium *to Prémontré and Nogent for pittances and building repairs. (See **148**.)*

A. Cartulary of Prémontré, fols. 34v–35r.

B. Original not found.

Other Manuscript Copies: AN, JJ 46, fols. 76r–76v.

EDITION: Hugo, *prob.* 1, cols. xxxii–xxxiv.

REGISTER: Fawtier, *Registres du trésor des chartes*, vol. 1, 266; Lalou, *Itinéraire de Philippe IV le Bel (1285–1314)*, vol. 2, 375.

5 quittavit *B*.
6 Isabella *B*.
7 tradet *B*.
8 Actum *B*.
9 quinquagesimo *B*.
10 martii *B*.

1 Enguerrand IV (d. 1310), lord of Coucy, son of Enguerrand III, lord of Coucy, and Marie de Montmirail.
2 La Fère, arr. Laon, https://dicotopo.cths.fr/places/P73165961.
3 Marle, arr. Laon, https://dicotopo.cths.fr/places/P68626104.

NO RUBRIC. LATER ADDITION.

Ph[ilippus], Dei gratia Francorum Rex, notum facimus universis tam presentibus quam futuris, quod cum bone memorie Ingerannus, dominus quondam Couciaci, in suo testamento, seu voluntate ultima, certos annuos et perpetuos redditus capiendos et percipiendos in certis locis baronie seu terre de Couciaco, de Fara et Marla certis personis et in certos pios usus convertendos, prout inferius continetur, perpetuo legaverit sub modis qui secuntur, prout in dicto testamento seu voluntate ultima plenius continetur: primo videlicet octies viginti libras Parisienses annui et perpetui redditus pro pannis laneis et calciaturis emendis pro vestiendis et calciendis anno quolibet pauperibus castellaniarum de Coucicaco, de Fara et de Marla; item duodecim libras Parisienses annui et perpetui redditus pro expensis priorum Premonstratensis et de Nogento qui pro tempore fuerint qui quidem priores pannos et calciamenta predicta debent anno quolibet dispertiri; item quadraginta libras Parisienses annui et perpetui redditus conventibus Premonstratensibus et de Nogento pro pitanciis, videlicet cuilibet conventui medietatem, ita tamen quod conventus de Nogento debet habere de illa medietate decem libras pro pitancia et decem libras pro fabrica ecclesie loci eiusdem; quas octies ~~ving~~ viginti libras annui redditus pro predictis pauperibus vestiendis et calciendis et dictas duodecim libras pro expensis dictorum priorum, ac quadraginta libras pro pitanciis dictorum conventuum, ut predicitur, ad eodem testatore legatas, capiendas, et percipiendas, de cetero anno quolibet idem testator in modum qui sequitur ordinavit: videlicet super vinagio seu pedagio de Petramanda,[4] sexaginta decem libras Parisienses; item super winagio seu pedagio pontis ad Buciacum et de Fara, sexaginta et duodecim libras; et super winagio seu pedagio Creciaci sexaginta decem libras Parisiensis; item conventui de Tenalliis quatuor libras Parisienses annui et perpetui redditus pro pitancia capiendas anno quolibet et etiam percipiendas super winagio de Marla; item ecclesie de Sauvoir[5] subtus Laudunum, quadraginta solidos Parisienses annui et perpetui redditus capiendos et percipiendos anno quolibet super winagio de Lauduno quod tenetur ab episcopo Laudunensi; item ecclesie de Sancto Gobano[6] viginti solidos Parisienses annui et perpetui redditus pro duabus torchiis anno quolibet faciendis in eadem ecclesia pro illuminando Corpori Christi in ecclesia memorata, capiendos et percipiendos anno quolibet super tallia de Sancto Gobano; item curato, monachis et capellanis de Sancto Gobano viginti solidos Parisienses annui et perpetui redditus, illis videlicet, qui anniversario anno quolibet ibidem celebrando intererint equaliter inter eos dividendos, capiendos et percipiendos de cetero anno quolibet super

4 Pierremande, cant. Coucy-le-Château, https://dicotopo.cths.fr/places/P72978208.

5 The Cistercian abbey of Notre-Dame du Sauvoir-sous-Laon.

6 Saint-Gobain, cant. La Fère, https://dicotopo.cths.fr/places/P81132050.

tallia de Sancto Gobano predicta; item ecclesie Sancti Jacobi de Semiliaco[7] viginti solidos Parisienses annui et perpetui redditus pro ~~pitancia~~ quadam lampade ardente de die et de nocte in dicta ecclesia habenda ~~in~~ perpetuo, capiendos super winagio de Lauduno; item monachis de Sancto Lanberto,[8] viginti solidos Parisienses annui et perpetui redditus capiendos et percipiendos annis singulis super venda vivarii de Sancto Lanberto; item a Laval[9] Sancti Petri quadraginta solidos Parisienses annui et perpetui redditus pro pitancia percipiendos et habendos super winagio de Vervino; item ecclesie Beate Marie de Lauduno, centum solidos Parisienses annui et perpetui redditus distribuendos canonicis et capellanis dicte ecclesie anno quolibet in die qua suum anniversarium celebrabunt capiendos et percipiendos anno quolibet, super winagio de Lauduno quod tenetur ab episcopo Laudunensi; item canonicis, curato et capellanis ecclesie de Fara; item conventui monasterii Sancti Eligii Noviomensis sexaginta solidos Parisienses annui et perpetui redditus pro pitantia habendas et percipiendas anno quolibet de cetero super winagio de Blerencourte;[10] item conventui Sancti Bartholomei Noviomensis sexaginta solidos Parisienses annui et perpetui redditus pro pitantia percipiendos et habendos annis singulis super winagio de Blerencourte; item conventui Sancte Ysabellis de Genliaco[11] quadraginta solidos Parisienses annui et perpetui redditus pro pitantia percipiendos et habendos anno quolibet pro pitancia predicta super winagio de Petramanda; item conventui de Gaudio[12] quadraginta solidos Parisienses annui et perpetui redditus pro pitancia percipiendos et habendos annis singulis super winagio Des Chainiaus; item conventui Sancti Stephani[13] justa[14] Suessionensis unum modium bladi ad mensura[15] Couciaci et annui et perpetui redditus pro pitantia, capiendum annis singulis super molendino de Juvengniaco.[16] Hos in hac parte ipsius testatoris piam voluntatem ac laudabilem commendantes predicta legal~~ia~~ta omnia et singula ab eodem testatore sub modis ~~super~~ suprascriptis facta rata habentes et grata ea volumus, laudamus, approbamus ac tenore presentium ex certa sciencia auctoritate regia confirmamus, volentes et concedentes expresse quod persone quibus predicti perpetui redditus a predicto testatore sunt legati sub modis quibus supradicitur eos possint tenere,

7 The parish church of Saint-Jacques de Semilly, Laon, https://dicotopo.cths.fr/places/P92470596.
8 The priory of Saint-Lambert, comm. Fourdrain, https://dicotopo.cths.fr/places/P30848534.
9 Likely Laval, cant. Anizy-le-Château, https://dicotopo.cths.fr/places/P09615337.
10 Blérancourt, cant. Coucy-le-Château, https://dicotopo.cths.fr/places/P84631594.
11 The abbey of Sainte-Élisabeth de Genlis (today Villequier-Aumont), cant. Chauny, https://dicotopo.cths.fr/places/P28265469.
12 The Cistercian abbey of Notre-Dame de la Joie, comm. Berneuil-sur-Aisne, https://dicotopo.cths.fr/places/P23569177.
13 The Augustinian abbey of Saint-Étienne de Soissons.
14 *Sic A, read* juxta.
15 *Sic A, read* mensuram.
16 Juvigny, cant. Soissons, https://dicotopo.cths.fr/places/P97496070.

percipere et habere pacifice perpetuo sine actione vendendi vel extra manum suam ponendi aut prestandi nobis seu ~~suss~~ successoribus nostris vel premissis financiam qualemcumque et dantes baillivo Viromandensis qui nunc est et qui pro tempore fuerit ceterisque justiciariis nostris tenore presentium in mandatis ut predictos annuos redditus annis singulis de cetero personis et locis quibus sunt legati persolvi faciant absque alterius expectatione mandati cum super hoc fuerint requisiti, prout ad eorum quemlibet noverint pertinere. Quod ut firmum et stabilem permaneat in futurum presentibus litteris nostrum fecimus apponi sigillum, salvo in aliis jure nostro et quolibet in omnibus alieno. Actum Corbolis, anno Domini M° CCC° undecimo, mense septembris.

148

December, 1290.

Enguerrand [IV],[1] *lord of Coucy, Oisy, and Montmirail, lists the alms that he has given for clothing and shoes for the poor of his lands of Coucy, La Fère,*[2] *and Marle,*[3] *and he charges the priors of Prémontré and the Benedictine abbey of Nogent or their representatives to distribute them annually. He also gives a sum of money to be used annually for pittances. (See **147**.)*

A. Cartulary of Prémontré, fols. 35r–35v.
B. Original not found.
Other Manuscript Copies: AN, JJ 62, 190.

NO RUBRIC. LATER ADDITION.

Je Engelrans, sires de Coucy, d'Oysi et de Montmirrail, fais asavoir a tous chiaus qui ces presentes lettres verront et orront que je ai laissiet et lais pour Diu et en ausmone VIII^{xx} livres de Parisis de rente chascun an a tousjours pour acater dras et chassementes pour vestir et chaucier les povres de me terre, chest a savoir es chasteleries de Coucy, de le Fere et de Marle, a recevoir et a departir cascun an a tousjours par les prieus de Nongeant et de Premonstré quicumques i soient prieus pour le tans ou par leur commandement. Et lais encore XII livres de Parisis de rente cascun an a tousjours pour les cous et pour les despens qu'il convenra faire en achater et en departir les dras et les solers devant dis chascun an; et s'il ni convenoit tous les douze livres Parisis pour les depens et pour les cous, je veul que li surplus soit convertis en l'aumone des devant dis povres

1 Enguerrand IV (d. 1310), lord of Coucy, son of Enguerrand III, lord of Coucy, and Marie de Montmirail.
2 La Fère, arr. Laon, https://dicotopo.cths.fr/places/P73165961.
3 Marle, arr. Laon, https://dicotopo.cths.fr/places/P68626104.

et pour les painnes qu'il aront dou requerre et du departir; et pour se que je veul que on face chascun an men anniversaire es couvens de Nongiant et de Premonstré, lais je et ai laissié a chascun des couvens devant dis XX livres de rente chascun an a tousjours en pitances et lais wit vins livres ~~ren~~ de Parisis devant dis pour les povres vestir et chaucier et les douze livres de Parisis de rente pour les cous et pour les despens et les XV livres de Parisis de rente que je lis et ai laissié au couvens de Nongent et de Premonstré ai je assignes et assenne a penre chascun an a tousjours apres mon trespas landemain de le Purification Nostre Dame a mes winaiges de Pierremande,[4] du Pont a Bucy,[5] de La Fere et de Crecy; c'est a savoir sur mes winaiges de Pierremande LXX livres de Parisis, a men winaige du Pont a Bucy et de Le Fere LXXII livres Parisis, a men winaige de Crecy LXX livres Parisis. Et a se oblige je especiaument tous les winaiges devant dis et pri pour Diu a chascun des couvens devant dis qu'il faichent en chascun de leur couvens une propre orison espicial cascun jour en une messe pour moi et pour Marguerite[6] ma chiere compaingne jadis ma femme et pour mes ~~ansisseurs~~ ancisseurs; et veul et devis que li dit priers devant dis ou leur certains commandemens soient present a recevoir chascun an a tousjours les wit vins XII livres de Parisis deseur dis. Je veul et devis que li abbés ou li couvens, s'il ni avoit point d'abbé, y envoit certain message toutes les fois que mestiers sera parmanablement pour toutes les choses devant dites faire et acomplir en antel point comme feroit li prieus soient y estant presens. Et se il avenoit en aucun temps que aucuns des devant dis prieus, des abbés ou des couvens, se il ni avoit point d'abbé, ne vousissent avoir le painne de requerre et de recevoir et de l'aumosne faire pars yaus ou par leur certain conmandement si comme il est deseure devisé. Je veul et ordonne que li prieus, li abbés et li couvens qui sera en defance de faire les choses deseur dites toutes les années qu'il en defaura, n'aist nules des XX livres de Parisis de rente que je leur ai laissié en pitances et veul que li prieus, li abbés ou li couvens, s'il ni avoit point d'abbé, qui les wit vins ~~livres~~ et XII livres Parisis recevera et l'aumosne fera ou fera faire, ensi com il est devant devisé, ait et recoive comme siens les XX livres Parisis de rente que cius deveront avoir qui seroit en defaute pour tant d'annees tant seulement comme cius seroit en defance, et veul que il les convertissent en pitances a leur couvens avec leurs autres XX livres et nient en autre usage, en tele menniere que il fassent pour l'arme demi en messes et en orisons autant comme cius qui defauroit, estoit tenus a faire par tout le tans que il receveront les vint livres de Parisis devant dis, et veul que chele aumosne devant dite soit faite chascun an a tous jours permanablement

4 Pierremande, cant. Coucy-le-Château, https://dicotopo.cths.fr/places/P72978208.

5 Pont-à-Bucy, cant. Crécy-sur-Serre, https://dicotopo.cths.fr/places/P91887862.

6 Margaretha van Gelre (d. ca. 1286), daughter of Otto II, count of Guelders, and of Margaretha van Kleef.

par les personnnes devant dites et s'en conseilleront au curet et a deus preudonnes de chascune parroche des chastelleries desur dites; et se il avenoit en aucun tans que aucune des rentes deseur dites ou toutes que je ai laissiés pour les povres de me terre des chastelleries desur dites vestir et chaucier et pour les despens pour nostre anniversaire faire, pour les painnes et pour les travaus que lie devant dis prieus ou leur certain commandemens auront en requerre et en departir les rentes dessur dites, ne fussent paiées et deliverées cascun an a tous jours au jour et au termes dessur devisés, je veul et ordonne que mi hoir et mi successeur qui tenront les choses seur quoi je ai les dites rentes assises, qui defauront de paier, soient tenus a rendre et a paier as devant dis prieus, abbés ou couvens ou a leur certains commandemens, ainsi comme il est devant dit, tous cous et tous damaiges que il auroient eus par ~~leur~~ le defaute de leur paiement en quelcunques menniere que ce fust et vint solz Parisis de painne pour chascun jour pour tant de jours comme il defauroient de paier les rentes dessur dites apres le terme devisé et assené, et doing plain pooir as personnes devant dites de ces eglises devant nommées et autorité de requerre et de demande et de recevoir les choses devant dites en jugement et hors jugement et de faire toutes les choses dessur dites en la menniere que il est contenu en ces presentes lettres. Et est a savoir que chascuns des prieus dessur dis ait une telle lettre et ne ~~feront~~ font les deus paire de lettres que une seule lettre quant a le rente et a toutes ches choses dessure dites fermement tenir a tous jours et garder toutes ensanble et chascune par li oblige je tous les winages dessur dis, mes hoirs et mes successeurs et pour le tanps a venir tenront les winages dessur dis. Et pour ce que toutes ces choses dessur dites soient fermes et estables a tous jours, je ai ces presentes lettres seelées de mon seel propre. Ce fu fait l'an de grace mil CC quatrevins et dis ou mois de decembre.

149

July 11, 1586.

Antoine Voulcet, collector of the tithes of Crépy,[1] *is charged with collecting from the inhabitants of Crépy every sixteenth sheaf as well as one* septier *per* pièce *of wine and four* septiers *per barrel. This act is signed by one Dagneaux.*

A. Cartulary of Prémontré, fol. 35v.

B. Original not found.

1 Crépy, cant. Laon, https://dicotopo.cths.fr/places/P85331504.

NO RUBRIC. LATER ADDITION.

L'unziesme jour de jullet mil cinq cens quatrevings et six seigné Dagneaux: Anthoine Voulcet nostre fermier des dixmes de Crespy a obtenu sentence avec nostre adjonction pour la cotte des dixmes de Crespy, que les habitants payeront la dixme au seziesme en gerbe et pour le regard du vin, ung septier pour la piece et quatre septiers pour le tonneau.

TABLE OF CONTENTS: CRÉPY

A. Cartulary of Prémontré, fol. 36r.

Capitula: Incipiunt scripta de Crespiaco et Daneri cum appenditiis suis, cum scriptis de molendino de Acheri.

I Karta regis Ludovici de duabus partibus decime.

II Item preceptum regis Ludovici junioris de duabus partibus decime de Crespi.

III Conpositio inter ecclesiam Premonstratensem et burgenses de Crespiaco et quod licet nobis in domo nostra de Crespi facere pressoria et omnis aisentias quas voluerimus.

IIII Scriptum inter ecclesiam Premonstratensem et ecclesiam Sancti Nicholai de Boscho super decimis de Crespi de Bris et de Furdren.

V Karta de monialibus de Santigni, confirmata ab abbatissa earumdem.

VI Scriptum domini Renaldi Laudunensis episcopi super compositione facta inter nos et presbyterum parrochialem de Crespi.

VII Karta domini Gualteri Laudunensis episcopi de dono Galteri Cuvout et uxoris eius apud Crespi.

VIII Conpositio inter ecclesiam Premonstratensem et conmuniam de Crespi de eo que debemus ei XX^{ti} solidorum alborum.

IX De decimatione curtis de Bus nobis adjudicata per R. cantorem et P. d'Orgival et V. cantorem Sancti Quintini.

X Karta regis Ludovici de domo de Daneri.

XI Karta Bartholomei episcopi Laudunensis de molendino d'Acheri.

XII Scriptum Galteri episcopi Laudunensis de Herberto d'Acheri.

XIII Conpositio inter nos et Johannem Direchon de molendino d'Acheri et super hic karta Rogeri episcopi Laudunensis.

XIIII Karta Bartholomei episcopi Laudunensis de Dionisio et molendinis de Acheri.

XV Karta domini Petri militis de Caumenchon de quodam modio frumenti apud Acheri.

XVI Confirmatio domini Ingelranni de Couci de duabus modiatis nemori que fuerunt Rainmundi de Cinceni.

XVII Carta episcopi Laudunensis de molendino de Weiz.

XVIII Privilegium Hugonis abbatis de prato de Weiz.

XIX Carta Ludovici regis Francorum de molendino d'Erchente.

XX Item cirographum capituli Laudunensis de molendino d'Erchente.

XXI Carta officialis Laudunensis de quodam dimidio modio bladi.

XXII Carta domini Radulphi de Sarto de quodam modio frumenti ad mensuram Lauduni.

XXIII Item karta domini de Sarto de quinque modiis vini.

XXIIII Confirmatio episcopi Laudunensis de Petro milite de Servai.

XXV Item carta alia eiusdem Petri.

XXVI Carta domini Radulphi de Sarto de quodam latere nemoris.

150

1125.[1] Bishop's palace, Soissons.

Louis [VI], king of France, gives to Norbert and the religious at Prémontré two parts of the tithe in the parish of Crépy.[2] *(See* ***151.****)*

A. Cartulary of Prémontré, fol. 36r.

B. Original destroyed.[3]

EDITION: Le Paige, *Bibliotheca*, 390; Hugo, *prob.* 1, col. ix; Pardessus, ed., *Ordonnances des rois de France de la troisième race. Supplément*, 214; Florival, *Étude historique sur le XIIe siècle*, 240 (partial); Beauvillé, *Recueil de documents inédits concernant la Picardie*, vol. 4, 2–3; Bautier and Dufour, *Recueil des actes de Louis VI, roi de France (1108–1137)*, vol. 1, 479–82.

REGISTER: Bréquigny, *Table chronologique*, vol. 2, 532; Luchaire, *Louis VI le Gros*, 165–6; Grauwen, "Lijst van oorkonden waarin Norbertus wordt genoemd," 144–5.

Karta regis Ludovici de duabus partibus decime de Crespi quas dedit ecclesie.

[I]n nomine sancte et individue Trinitatis. Ego Ludovicus, gratia Dei Francorum rex, notum fieri volo tam presentibus quam futuris quod, propter Deum per quem reges regnant, pro regni nostri protectione et remedio anime mee, seu conjugis, heredumque meorum incolumitate, viris Deum timentibus et valde religiosis domno Norberto et fratribus sub eo degentibus eorumque successoribus, in ecclesia Sancte Dei genitricis Marie, Sanctique Johannis Baptiste in loco qui dicitur Premonstratus, dedi duas partes decime de parrochia que dicitur Crispiacus, que nostri fuerant juris et possessionis, perpetuo possidendas. Quod ne cuiuslibet usurpatoris invidia minui posset vel infirmari, litterarum memorie commendari et nostri nominis caractere et sigillo signari et corroborari precepimus, viventibus in palatio nostro quorum nomina subtitulata sunt et signa. Signum Stephani tunc temporis dapiferi et cancellarii. S. Gisleberti, buticularii. S. Hugonis, constabularii. S. Albrici, camerarii. Actum est publice Suessionis in palatio episcopali, anno incarnati verbi M° C° XX° quinto, anno

1 Since the date of Louis VI's coronation was August 3, 1108, and this act was written "anno … consecrationis nostre XVI°," this act must have been before August 3, 1125.

2 This donation is mentioned in the obituary of Prémontré. "Commemoratio dom. Ludovici, regis, a quo habemus decimam de Crespi, et Adelidis, uxoris ejus ac liberorum, pro quibus plenarium fiet servitium." Van Waefelghem, *L'Obituaire de l'abbaye de Prémontré*, 153. Crépy, cant. Laon, https://dicotopo.cths.fr/places/P85331504.

3 This charter was in the possession of the de Beauvillé family at Montdidier, but "il y fut détruit, tout comme l'ensemble de la collection, lors de la WW1." Bautier and Dufour, *Recueil des actes de Louis VI, roi de France (1108–1137)*, vol. 1, 479, fn. 2.

quoque consecrationis nostre XVI°. Huius denique caritatis testimonium perhibent veritatis: Stephanus[4] episcopus Parisiensis, Petrus[5] episcopus Belvacensis, Radulphus[6] comes Vermandensis, Renaldus[7] comes Suessionensis, Drogo de Petraponte,[8] Walerannus[9] prepositus ecclesie, Ansculphus[10] archidiaconus, Ebalus[11] archidiaconus, Bernardus[12] decanus. Ego Stephanus,[13] regis notarius, dictando propria manu subscripsi.

151

1138. Royal palace, Paris.

Louis [VII] of France confirms his father, Louis VI's, donation to abbot Hugues [I][1] *and the brothers of Prémontré of the two parts of the tithe of Crépy.*[2] *(See **150**.)*

A. Cartulary of Prémontré, fols. 36r–36v.

B. Original, BnF, MS lat. 17062, no. 1, previously sealed with two seals on a double strip of parchment.

EDITION: Le Paige, *Bibliotheca*, 425; Hugo, *prob.* 1, col. xiv.

---

4 Étienne de Senlis (d. 1142), son of Guy I de Senlis, lord of Chantilly and Berthe, was bishop of Paris, 1123–42.

5 Pierre de Beauvais, son of Lancelin I de Beauvais, deacon of Beauvais, 1103–13, and bishop of Beauvais, 1114–33.

6 Raoul I, count of Vermandois, Amiens, and Valois (d. 1152), was the son of Hugues I le Grand, count of Vermandois and Valois, and Adélaïde de Vermandois, and served as seneschal of France, 1131–51.

7 Renaud III, count of Soissons (d. 1146), son of Jean I, count of Soissons, and Aveline de Pierrefonds.

8 Dreux, lord of Pierrefonds (d. 1160), son of Nivelon II, lord of Pierrefonds, and Hawide. Newman, *Seigneurs*, vol. 1, 187–9.

9 Galeran, *prepositus* of Soissons, by 1110–aft. 1125. AN, K 21 n° 1/11; Herbomez, *Chartes de l'abbaye de Saint-Martin de Tournai*, vol. 1, 38.

10 Anscoul de Pierrefonds, son of Nivelon II, lord of Pierrefonds, and Hawide (de Montmorency?), was archdeacon of Soissons, 1101–25/9, *prepositus* of Soissons, 1129–52, and bishop of Soissons, 1152–8.

11 Eble, archdeacon of Soissons, 1120s–aft. 1139. BnF, MS lat. 9904, fol. 94v; BnF, MS lat. 11004, fol. 36r; Jacquemin, "Annales de la vie de Joscelin de Vierzi, 57e évêque de Soissons (1126–1152)," 3.

12 Bernard, dean and chancellor of Soissons by 1110. Paulin Paris, ed., *Histoire littéraire de la France*, vol. 10, 268.

13 Étienne de Garlande (d. 1150), son of Guillaume I, lord of Garlande-en-Brie, and Havoise, was bishop of Beauvais, 1099–1103, and seneschal of France, 1108–27 and 1132–7.

---

1 Hugues I de Fosses (ca. 1093–1164), first abbot of Prémontré.

2 Crépy, cant. Laon, https://dicotopo.cths.fr/places/P85331504.

Item preceptum regis Ludovici junioris de duabus partibus decime de Crespi nobis solvendis.

[I]n nomine sancte et individue Trinitatis. Quoniam labente vita mortalium, etiam actus ipsorum labuntur a memoria, placuit scripto commendare quod successione temporum posset oblivio delere. Igitur ego Ludovicus, Dei gratia Francorum rex, spe regni melioris et corone, religiosis viris Hugoni, abbati Premonstratensis[3] ecclesie, et fratribus eius canonicis Deo servientibus, cui regnans servire volo, in pago Laudunensi, apud villam que Crispiacus nuncupatur, duas partes decime, que mei juris erant, perpetuo possidendas concedo, eo jure et ea liberatatis integritate qua pater meus rex Ludovicus[4] eas tenuit, qui easdem, me presente et cooperante, sub auctoritate privilegii eis ante concessit. Posterorum itaque paci providentes, precepto regali decernimus ut, sicut ad regalem graneam, patris mei tempore, duas partes decime tercia singulis annis sequebatur, eiusdem tercie partis assistente et collaborante custodia, sicut ministris tempore messium victus de communi providebatur granea de communi reparatur, decima de universis domibus indifferenter, tam in villa quam in atrio regi libere solvebatur; sic Premonstratensi ecclesie jura date elemosine in his omnibus integra et illesa serventur, salva nimirum dote altaris determinata et feodo sacerdotis. Quod ut ratum et inconcussum permaneat, sigilli nostri auctoritate et nominis nostri karactere[5] subtersignavimus. Actum Parisius in palatio nostro publice, anno incarnati verbi M° C° XXX° VIII°, regni nostri primo. Astantibus in palatio nostro quorum nomina subtitulata sunt et signa. S. Willelmi,[6] buticularii. Signum Mathie,[7] constabularii. S. Mathie,[8] camerarii. Dapifero nullo. Data per manum Algrini.[9,10]

---

3 Premonstrate *B.*

4 Lodovicus *B.*

5 caractere *B.*

6 Guillaume le Loup de Senlis, knight and lord of Chantilly, Ermenonville, Villepeinte and Bray, son of Guy de la Tour de Senlis, lord of Chantilly, Ermenonville, Derency, Villepeinte and Bray-sur-Aunette, and Berthe, was butler of France, ca. 1130–47. Voillemier, "Note sur la maison des Bouteiller de Senlis," 36–7.

7 Mathieu I, lord of Montmorency (d. 1160), son of Bouchard, lord of Montmorency, and Agnès de Beaumont, was constable of France from 1138.

8 Mathieu I, count of Beaumont-sur-Oise, chamberlain of France from 1135, son of Yves II, count of Beaumont, and Adélaïde (de Gournay?). Secousse et al., *Ordonnances des rois de France de la troisième race*, vol. 7, 415.

9 *Om.* cancellarii *A.*

10 Algrin was vice chancellor under Louis VI, chancellor of France under Louis VII, 1137–9, and chancellor of Notre-Dame de Paris, ca. 1124–ca. 1152. Luchaire, *Remarques sur la succession des grands officiers de la couronne qui ont souscrit les diplômes de Louis VI et de Louis VII (1108–1180)*, 33–4; Luchaire, *Histoire des institutions monarchiques de la France sous les premiers Capétiens (mémoires et documents)*, 52–4.

152

1212

Milo, maior *of Crépy,*[1] *and the* bourgeois *of the commune make known that, after a dispute with the church of Prémontré, an agreement was reached concerning Prémontré's possessions at Crépy. Prémontré will retain the house and* masura *given to it by the late Renaud,* bourgeois *of Crépy, on entering the religious life, in exchange for an annual* census *of one hen and a* galetus *of oats, measure of Crépy. However, Prémontré undertakes not to acquire any further property in Crépy for a year and a day.*

A. Cartulary of Prémontré, fol. 36v.
B. Original not found.

De quadam compositione inter ecclesiam Premonstratensem et burgenses de Crespiaco.

[E]go Milo, maior, et burgenses communie Crispiaci omnibus istam kartam visuris in perpetuum. Ad presentium et futurorum noticiam fecimus hic inscribi quod cum super quibusdam possessionibus quas apud Crispiacum ecclesia Premonstratensis habebat, dudum inter nos et ipsam mota fuisset querela, tandem de utriusque partis assensu, per compositionem gratuitam talis conventio intercessit, videlicet quod dicta ecclesia tenebit perpetuo domum et masuram quam dedit ei frater Renaldus, quondam burgensis Cripsiaci, quando habitum religionis,[2] sub annuo censu unius galline et unius galeti avene ad cumulum et ad mensuram Crispiaci, sine omni alia consuetudine preter justiciam quam nos burgenses habebimus in ea, sicut primitus habebamus. Licebit autem eidem ecclesie facere et in masura et in domo pressoria, de quibus recipiet pressoragia secundum consuetudinem aliorum pressoriorum ville et omnes alias aisentias de quibus utilitatem suam crediderit provenire. Porro, si ecclesia habuerit conducticios servientes in domo, qui non exerceant in villa mercimonia nec faciant aliud unde debeant burgoisiam, liberi erunt ab omni tallia et consuetudine salva justicia. Conventum est autem quod hec que acquisierat ipsa ecclesia in territorio Crispiaci ante elemosinam quam dederunt ei predictus Renaldus et Gregorius, filius eius, perpetuo, si voluerit, retinebit, sed nec per elemosinam nec alio modo infra pacem Crispiaci acquiret aliquid post tempus huius scripti quod non oporteat eam vendere infra annum et diem, nisi terminus vendendi per assensum nostrum fuerit prorogatus. Quod ut ratum sit et a neutra parte in posterum irritetur scriptum istud ad perpetuandam memoriam huius conventionis confectum communie nostre sigillo fecimus confirmari. Actum anno dominice incarnationis M° CC° duodecimo.

1 Crépy, cant. Laon, https://dicotopo.cths.fr/places/P85331504.
2 *Sic A*; the editors suggest adding "induit" here for a clearer reading.

153

June, 1234.

Renier,[1] *abbot of Saint Nicolas-aux-Bois and his chapter, on the one hand, and the church of Prémontré,*[2] *on the other, make known an agreement concerning the revenues from certain lands, vineyards, houses, and orchards which form the endowments of the altars of Crépy,*[3] *Brie,*[4] *and Fourdrain.*[5]

A. Cartulary of Prémontré, fols. 36v–37v.
B. Original not found.

Karta inter ecclesiam Premonstratensem et ecclesiam Sancti Nicholai super decimis de Crespi, de Bris, et de Fourdren.

[E]go Renerus, abbas Sancti Nicholai in Bosco, et capitulum nostrum, notum facimus universis tam presentibus quam futuris quod, cum questio esset orta super dote altaris de Crespi et de Bris et de Fourdrein inter nos ex una parte et ecclesiam Premonstratensem ex altera, tandem, mediantibus bonis viris, de utriusque partis assensu, fuit taliter ordinatum et ab utraque ecclesia finaliter acceptatum quod ecclesia nostra ratione et nomine dotis altaris, terrarum, vinearum, domorum et ortorum inferius expressorum totam decimam in perpetuum libere possidebit. Et hec sunt nomina terrarum, vinearum, domorum et ortorum qui sunt de dote altaris: campus videlicet ante portam de Bus, continens duos galetos sementis; campus ad fossam Deseur Bus, continens similiter duos galetos sementis; campus Desous Aurilmont, continens quatuor galetos; campus Au Boutonier, continens sex galetas; campus A l'Argent, continens quatuor galetas; campus A La Marliere ante Reinquenci, continens duos galetos; campus Au Buisson a Franfosse, continens tres galetos; campus in valle Sancti Petri, continens quatuor galetos et dimidium; campus retro domum Le Cardounier, continens unum galetum; campus A La Rue Le Cardonier, continens duos galetos; campus en Duedel, continens tres galetos; campus A La Maladerie, continens unum galetum; campus ad molendina ad

1 Renier de Mailly, abbot of the Benedictine abbey of Saint-Nicolas-aux-Bois, ca. 1230–51. Duval, "Histoire de l'abbaye bénédictine de Saint-Nicolas-aux-Bois, diocèse de Laon, première partie," 214–17.

2 William II of Dale was abbot of Dale Abbey, 1231–3 and abbot of Prémontré 1233–8. Colvin, "The Internal History of Dale Abbey," 31.

3 Crépy, cant. Laon, https://dicotopo.cths.fr/places/P85331504.

4 Brie, cant. La Fère, https://dicotopo.cths.fr/places/P40042593.

5 Fourdrain, cant. La Fère, https://dicotopo.cths.fr/places/P82755957.

Ventum, continens unum galetum; et campus En Taisi de la le[6] chemin versus Couveron,[7] continens tres galetos. Omnes campi prenotati siti sunt in territorio de Crispiaco. Isti adhuc campi sunt de dote altaris, videlicet: campus En Wegelin capiens unum galetum tam in terra quam in orto, quem excolunt Gilo Potiers et partionarii eius; et campus En Beeloi, continens duos galetos et dimidium tam in vinea quam in terra, quem excolunt Huardus de la Bruiere et partionarii eius. Hee vero sunt vinee de dote altaris, videlicet: vinea Wiberti de Vivaise; vinea Anselmi au P~~rer~~is; vinea Petri, cognomento Presbiteri, et Vaillandi sororii eius; vinea Garsilii la Vache; vinea Evrardi la Pouille; vinea Ade de Nemore; vinea Hugonis, cognomento Saint Martin; vinea Colardi Bele Maisnie; vinea Wedeline relicte Flamenc; vinea Huardi de Espourdon et vinea que fuit Richaldis Male Gueule, quam quatuor partionarii tenent. Omnes vinee predicte site sunt in loco qui dicitur Amerfosse inter metas istas, videlicet a meta sita in loco qui dicitur Au Novier, que fuit Petri quondam maioris, usque ad metam sitam inter vineam Olardi Blondel et vineam Gerardi Tannatoris, sicut via protenditur, et a meta sita inter vineam Odardi Blondel et Gerardi Tannatoris recte versus metam que protenditur usque ad vineam Isberti, patris Godonis Salenbien, et usque ad campum Gerberti Hurtebuef et a meta sita inter vineam Odardi Blondel et Gerardi directe versus metam sitam inter vineam Thome Bonefoi et vineam Evrardi la Pouille, per quam metam dividuntur vinagia domini regis et vinagia Sancti Nicholai, et a meta ista usque ad dictam metam sitam ad locum qui dicitur Au Novier, que fuit Petri maioris. Et sic inter quatuor metas predictas comprehenduntur vinee de Ameirfosse que sunt de dote altaris. Item iste vinee sunt de dote altaris, site in territorio de Bris, scilicet: vinea Henrici Gaillart, capiens unum aissinum sementis; vinea Milonis de Couveron, capiens unum aissinum; vinea Radulphi Goubart, capiens unum galetum; vinea Dodonis et Marie de Nemore, capiens unum aissinum in duabus petiis galetum; vinea Les Bautors, capiens duos;[8] vinea Rahieri et Petri Maugis, capiens unum galetum; vinea Herbini Bele Fuelle, capiens unum aissinum; terra Roberti Nigri, capiens unum aissinum in duabus petiis; terra Goberti Chauvel, Rahieri et Dodonis Nigri, capiens unum aissinum; campus domini Roberti presbiteri, capiens unum galetum tam in terra quam in vinea; terra Johannis Daubart et suorum partionariorum, capiens quindecim virgas facientes quartam partem unius aissini; vinee Les Goubars, capientes sex galetos; vinea Theobaldi Mutin et fratris eius, capiens unum aissinum; vinea Rahieri de Pressorio, Radulphi Gobart et Erardi Charlet, capiens tres

---

6 *Sic A.*

7 Couvron-et-Aumencourt, cant. Crécy-sur-Serre, https://dicotopo.cths.fr/places/P99401693.

8 *Sic A.*

quarterios; vinea dame Soible et familie sue, capiens unum quarterium; vinea Huardi de la Bruiere et Radulphi fratris cius, capiens unum aissinum; item vinea Theobaldi Mutin et suorum partionariorum, capiens unum aissinum; item vinea Rahieri de Pressorio, capiens unum aissinum; vinea Goberti dou Ru et Gilonis le Grant, capiens unum aissinum; vinea Petri de Sarto, capiens unum quarterium; item vinea Petri de Sarto, Stephani de Bautor et Petri Maugis, capiens unum aissinum; vinea Balduini Mouton, capiens unum aissinum et vinea Goberti dou Ru, capiens unum quarterium. Omnes vinee et terre prescripte site sunt En Tosteleu et En Vaus et En Soumeval, sicut mete inferius annotate proportant, scilicet a meta sita En Tosteleu in vinea Henrici Gaillart usque ad metam sitam inferius inter vineam eiusdem Henrici Gaillart et vineam Theobaldi Mutin et a meta ista usque ad metam sitam inter vineam Goberti Chauvel et vineam Wedeline, sororis eius, et a meta ista usque ad metam sitam inter vineam Erardi Charlet et vineam Wedeline, et a meta ipsa usque ad metam sitam inter terram Bertanni Troche et Erardi Charlet, et a meta ista usque ad metam sitam in campo Roberti Nigri En Sonmeval, et a meta ista usque ad metam sitam inter vineam Radulphi Eschaufe Estrein et vineam Radulphi Goubart; et sic inter metas predictas conprehenduntur vinee de Tosteleu et de Vaus et de Sonmeval que sunt de dote altaris. Isti autem mansi sunt de dote altaris scilicet: mansus Odardi Fauvel, mansus Mathei Lolier, mansus Petri Chevalier et Odonis, sororii eius, mansus Johannis Chevalier contiguus manso precedenti, mansus Evrardi Fauvel, mansus Johannis Goisel, campellus qui dicitur vulgariter La Faisse, contiguus manso Goisel, mansus Milonis de Couveron et Harduini, fratris eius, mansus Johannis Forrel et mansus Marie relicte Michaelis. Omnes mansi predicti siti sunt circa atrium de Crespiaco. Item est de dote altaris mansus Mabille de Bris, situs ante monasterium de Bris. Relique autem terre, vinee, domus et orti, de quibus decima solvitur vel debetur, communi decime integraliter remanabunt, cuius decime tam maioris quam minoris Premonstratensis ecclesia duas partes et nostra ecclesia terciam partem in perpetuum libere possidebunt, sub hac conditione quod Premonstratensis ecclesia de omnibus que pertinent ad supradictam dotem altaris nichil prorsus petere vel reclamare poterit in futurum nec ecclesia nostra ulla ratione in omnibus aliis que ad dictam dotem altaris non pertinent quicquam juris processu temporis poterit vendicare, excepto quod, si forte in territorio vel decimatione de Crespi aliqua fiant novalia, illic ubi jus erit, decima persolvatur. Ut autem ista compositio firma et stabilis in perpetuum perseveret et robur optineat firmitatis, presentem kartam fecimus sigillorum nostrorum munimine roborari. Actum anno gratie millesimo CC° tricesimo quarto, mense junio.

154

July, 1233.

A[va],[1] *abbess, and the Benedictine abbey of Berteaucourt, make known that the prioress and nuns of Berteaucourt's priory at Santigny*[2] *reached an agreement with the church of Prémontré and the Benedictine house of Saint Nicholas-aux-Bois concerning the tithe on lands, vineyards, and other possessions in the parish of Crépy,*[3] *held by the priory of Santigny.*

A. Cartulary of Prémontré, fols. 37v–38r.
B. Original not found.

Karta de monialibus de Santigni confirmata ab abbatissa earundem monialium.

[I]n nomine Patris et Filii et Spiritus Sancti, amen. Universis fidelibus Christi tam presentibus quam futuris A[va] dicta abbatissa de Bertoucourt et totus eiusdem loci conventus salutem in Domino. Noverint universi quod cum inter Premonstratensis et Sancti Nicholai in Boscho ecclesias, Laudunensis diocesis, ex una parte et dilectas priorissam et moniales nostras prioratus nostri de Santigni, eiusdem diocesis, ex altera discordia verteretur super tota decima terrarum et vinearum quas idem prioratus noster habet in parrochia de Crespi et super tota decima et reportagio terrarum, domus et territorii de Villari, curte ex eodem prioratu de Santigniaco dependente et super reportagio terrarum de Santigni et terrarum etiam quas excolit idem prioratus extra parrochiam de Crespi, in quibus decimis et reportagiis dicta Premonstratensis ecclesia duas partes et ecclesia Sancti Nicholai in Boscho terciam se habere dicebant, partibus super hoc dissentientibus, tandem pro bono pacis dicte priorissa et moniales ~~nobis volentibus et consentientibus~~ nostre de Santigni de nostro consilio et assensu in hoc unanimiter consenserunt, scilicet quod recognoverunt eedem priorissa et moniales, nobis volentibus et consentientibus, pertinere ad duas ecclesias supradictas totam decimam terrarum et vinearum quas in parrochia de Crespi habent vel sunt in posterum habiture, et tenentur reddere annis singulis eandem decimam predictis ecclesiis bona fide. Pro decima vero et reportagio terrarum pertinentium et dependentium a predicta

1 Ava, abbess of the Benedictine abbey of Notre-Dame de Berteaucourt-les-Dames (cant. Domart, https://dicotopo.cths.fr/places/P64988630), by 1225–bef. 1239. *GC* X, col. 1323.

2 Santigny (comm. Crépy, https://dicotopo.cths.fr/places/P69608848) was a priory dependent on the Benedictine abbey of Notre-Dame de Berteaucourt-les-Dames, 1144–1302. Becquet, "Abbayes et Prieurés," 229.

3 Crépy, cant. Laon, https://dicotopo.cths.fr/places/P85331504.

domo de Vileirs[4] necnon et omnium aliarum quas dictus noster prioratus habet in territorio de Vileirs vel est in posterum habiturus, reddent priorissa et moniales eiusdem prioratus annis singulis in grangia de Vilers decem et septem galetos bladi sani et pagabilis ad mensuram Laudunensem, duas partes ybernagii et terciam avene in festo Omnium Sanctorum ecclesiis supradictis. Pro decima vero et reportagio terrarum de Santigni quas habent et excolunt extra parrochiam de Crespi vel habiture vel exculture sunt in perpetuum extra eandem parrochiam moniales predicte, reddent eedem moniales prenominatis ecclesiis annuatim unum galetum bladi sani et pagabilis ad mensuram predictam loco et termino supradictis et, si forte deficerent in solutione bladi predicti, sicut superius est expressum, expectaretur ipsa solutio usque ad festum Sancti Johannis Baptiste proxime subsequens facienda et quacumque die solverint a dicto festo Omnium Sanctorum usque ad festum Sancti Johannis Baptiste solutionem earum dicte ecclesie recipere tenebuntur. Si autem nec in festo Omnium Sanctorum nec in festo Sancti Johannis Baptiste proxime subsequenti nec etiam medio tempore decem et octo galetos reddiderint supra dictos, ex tunc dicte due ecclesie totam decimam et reportagium percipient in perpetuum in locis omnibus supradictis nec amplius nostre moniales de Santigni nec nos etiam redire poterimus ad dictorum solutionem annuatim galetorum et nichilominus de eisdem decem et octo galetis bladi de quibus solvendis nostre moniales negligentes fuerint illo anno dictis ecclesiis satisfacere tenebuntur. Verum quamdiu priorissa et moniales nostre de Santigni, loco et tempore supradictis, decem et octo galetos bladi predictos solverint annuatim, eedem totam decimam magnam et minutam et reportagium terrarum quas habent in territorio de Vileirs et sunt in perpetuum habiture vel habiture et exculture ubicumque extra parrochiam de Crespi integre et libere possidebunt et dicte ecclesie de eisdem decima et reportagio tenebuntur ipsis monialibus portare legitimam warandiam adversus omnes qui voluerint juri stare secundum usus et consuetudines diocesis Laudunensis. Insuper etiam moniales nostre de Santigni tenentur reddere annuatim ecclesie Premonstrati in festo Sancti Remigii decem denarios censuales bone monete pro minutis decimis curtis nostre de Villari superius memorate. Predicte autem priorissa et moniales nostre de Santigni pacem istam inter se et ecclesias memoratas ex parte nostra fecerunt, nobis approbantibus, volentibus et ratam habentibus illam pacem. Et ut ea que premissa sunt, firmam et perpetuam obtineant, firmitatem presentem kartam fecimus sigillorum nostrorum munimine roborari. Actum anno domini M° CC° tricesimo tertio, mense julio.

4 Villers, cant. Laon, https://dicotopo.cths.fr/places/P72234458.

155

1209

Renaud,[1] *bishop of Laon, makes known that the churches of Prémontré and Saint Nicolas-aux Bois,*[2] *on the one hand, and R[obert],*[3] *priest of the parish of Crépy,*[4] *on the other, settled a dispute concerning the major and minor tithes of the three* carucatae *that R. received annually, two in the territory of Crépy and one in the territory of Brie.*[5]

A. Cartulary of Prémontré, fols. 38r–38v.

B. Original (chirograph), BnF, Coll. Picardie 290, no. 24, previously sealed. In the right margin and beginning at the top, the bottom half of the letters that form the word CYROGRAPHUM.

Scriptum domini Renaldi Laudunensis episcopi super compositione facta inter nos et presbiterum parochialem de Crespi.

[R]enaldus, Dei gratia Laudunensis episcopus, omnibus in perpetuum. Notum fieri volumus presentibus et futuris quod cum querela verteretur inter ecclesiam Premonstrati et ecclesiam Sancti Nicholai de Boscho[6] ex una parte et R[obertum], presbiterum parrochialem de Crispiaco, ex altera super magnis et minutis decimis trium carrucatarum quarum duas in territorio de Crispiaco et terciam in territorio de Bris idem presbiter singulis annis accipiebat et super prosecutione decimarum hominum de Fourdrein,[7,8] tandem de voluntate et consensu partium, assensu nostro, facta est conpositio in hunc modum quod certi nuntii predictarum ecclesiarum singulis annis infra quindecim dies ante festum Beati Johannis Baptiste et presbiter parrochialis apud Crispiacum convenient, ita quod predicte ecclesie pro una carrucata accipient primo tres modiatas terre honeratas ybernagio[9] ad mensuram Laudunensem in toto territorio Crispiaci, ubicumque voluerint, et tantumdem terre honerate marciagio, ita quod totum ibernagium accipient continue si ibi ubi accipient ibernagium, tantum fuerit ibernagii et si tantum ibi non fuerit, quod deficiet, accipient in loco proximiori habente ibernagium. Similiter ubi accipient marciagium, continue accipient et

1 Renaud Surdelle, bishop of Laon, 1207–10.
2 The Benedictine abbey of Saint-Nicolas-aux-Bois.
3 Likely the same Robert who appears in **157**.
4 Crépy, cant. Laon, https://dicotopo.cths.fr/places/P85331504.
5 Brie, cant. La Fère, https://dicotopo.cths.fr/places/P40042593.
6 Bosco *B*.
7 Fordrain *B*.
8 Fourdrain, cant. La Fère, https://dicotopo.cths.fr/places/P82755957.
9 ibernagio *B*.

siquid defuerit, in proximiori loco quod deficiet accipere tenebuntur. In acceptione autem tam ibernagii quam marciagii non computabuntur nisi terre ille quarum tota decima vadit ad communem decimam de Crispiaco. Accipient autem predicte ecclesie primo in tota villa Crispiaci parrochianum unum, quemcumque voluerint, pro vino et minutis decimis. Postea vero presbiter de Crispiaco in toto territorio Crispiaci, ubicumque voluerit, accipiet duas carrucatas pro utraque tantum terre honerate ibernagio et tantum terre honerate marciagio quantum ecclesie predicte et eodem modo quo ecclesie sepedicte et, si voluerit, ambas carrucatas continue accipere poterit et, si maluerit, in diversis locis ad instar ecclesiarum predictarum. Similiter in tota villa Crispiaci accipiet duos parrochianos, quoscumque voluerit, pro vino et minutis decimis. Pro tercia vero carrucata in toto territorio de Bris presbiter parrochialis accipiet, ubicumque voluerit, tantum terre honerate ~~marciagio~~ ibernagio et tantum terre honerate marciagio et eodem modo, sicut dictum est, de territorio Crispiaci et similiter accipiet in villa de Bris unum parrochianum, quemcumque voluerit, pro vino et minutis decimis. Residuum vero decimationum maiorum et minutarum de Crispiaco et de Bris ad ecclesias predictas pertinebit, salva tam maiori quam minuta decima presbitero parrochiali in vico de Bu[10] infra metas et divisiones assignatas, salva etiam presbitero parrochiali magna et minuta decima de Fourdrain[11] infra divisiones antiquas, hoc adjuncto quod decetero nulla erit prosecutio decimarum sive maiorum sive minutarum inter presbiterum parrochialem et ecclesias memoratas. Hanc igitur conpositionem sicut suprascripta est ad petitionem partium assensu etiam interveniente patroni auctoritate pontificali duximus confirmandam, et sub cirographo[12] sigilli nostri caractere muniendam. Actum anno dominice incarnationis M° CC° nono.

156

1166

Gautier [II],[1] *bishop of Laon, makes known that husband and wife Gautier Cuvous,*[2] *knight of Crépy,*[3] *and Mainsende, and their daughter Marguerite, gave to the church of Prémontré a meadow, a vineyard, and two parts of the tithes of* Roques *and* Proisel, *in exchange for an annual* census *of six* denarii Catalaunensium *to be*

10 But, comm. Crépy, https://dicotopo.cths.fr/places/P31280705.

11 Fordrain *B*.

12 cyrografo *B*.

1 Gautier de Mortagne was dean of Laon, ca. 1142–55, and bishop of Laon, 1155–74.

2 Gautier Cuvous, knight and lord of Crépy (cant. Laon, https://dicotopo.cths.fr/places/P85331504). Melleville, *DH*, vol. 1, 321.

3 Crépy, cant. Laon, https://dicotopo.cths.fr/places/P85331504.

paid to Gautier and his heirs. They also gave two parts of the tithe on a vineyard at Roques *in exchange for seven* solidi *and six* nummi censualibus.

A. Cartulary of Prémontré, fol. 38v.

B. Original, AD Aisne, H 782, previously sealed.

Karta Galteri Laudunensis episcopi de elemosina Galteri Cuvout, militis de Crespi.

[I]n nomine sancte et individue Trinitatis.[4] Ego Gualterus, Dei gratia Laudunensis[5] episcopus. Notum fieri volumus tam futuris quam presentibus quod Galterus Cuvous,[6] miles de Crespi, et uxor sua, Mainsendis, et filia eius, Margareta, pari consensu dederunt ecclesie Premonstratensi pro Deo et animarum suarum redemptione pratum unum ad Leguttele, quod est inter Fundren[7] et Tortoir,[8] sicut metis positis divisum est. Quod videlicet pratum fratres Premonstratenses qui ad Daneri[9] manebant, de nemore extraxerunt et sartaverunt ea conditione quod singulis annis in festo Sancti Johannis Baptiste septem[10] solidos Proveniensium prefato Gualtero et heredibus suis inde censualiter persolverent. Sed et eadem devotione idem Gualterus et uxor eius et filia tradiderunt in elemosinam predicte ecclesie vineam unam ad Crespi in loco qui dicitur ad Bu concesserunt, etiam eidem ecclesie duas partes minute decime de Roques[11] et de Proisel que ipsis jure hereditario provenerat, sub annuo censu VI denariorum Catalaunensium similiter in festo Sancti Johannis solvendorum. Insuper duas partes decime vinearum quas Premonstratenses faciunt vel facient ad Roques[12] infra terminos constitutos, que scilicet decima ad ipsum Gualterum pertinebat. Ipse Gualterus cum uxore et filia prefate ecclesie libere concessit eo tenore quod in anniversario matris sue conventus de vino decime illius refectionem habebit. Concesserunt etiam quod nec ipsi nec eorum heredes de supradictis septem[13] solidis et sex[14] nummis censualibus poterunt alicui homini

4 *Om.* amen *A.*
5 Laudunensium *B.*
6 Cuvolz *B.*
7 Fourdrain, cant. La Fère, https://dicotopo.cths.fr/places/P82755957.
8 Tordoir, comm. Saint-Nicolas-aux-Bois, https://dicotopo.cths.fr/places/P93371881.
9 Dandry, comm. Crépy, https://dicotopo.cths.fr/places/P99162453.
10 VII [tem] *B.*
11 Roches *B.*
12 Roches *B.*
13 VII *B.*
14 VI *B.*

vel ecclesie alteri elemosinam facere sed nec dare nec vendere neque in pignus ponere nisi Premonstratensi ecclesie. Hec autem omnia prefatus Galterus[15] et uxor eius et filia primo in ecclesia de Crespi publice coram omni multitudine concesserunt et donum super altare ad opus Premonstratensis ecclesie posuerunt. Postea ipse Gualterus, in presentia nostra Premonstratum veniens, donum quod fecerat, recognovit et in manum nostram posuit et nos abbati et ecclesie Premonstratensi perpetuo possidendum resignavimus. Unde testes sunt: Galterus[16] thesaurarius, Robertus cantor, Renerus capellanus, Guillelmus camerarius, Arnulfus filius Radulfi Canis. Deinde filia ipsius Gualteri, cum eodem patre suo apud Anisiacum[17] veniens, in presentia nostra, donum quod pater fecerat, concessit. Sub hiis testibus: Herberto decano, Renero[18] capellano, Anselmo sacerdote de Sancto Remigio,[19] Guillelmo camerario, Geraldo[20] de Subarcurt,[21] Fulcone de Pinum.[22,23] Novissime apud Laudunum Garinus, sacerdos de Crespi, et milites qui subscripti sunt venientes in presentia nostra, testimonium perhibuerunt quod uxor predicti Galteri cum ipso Gualtero et filia eius sicut suprascriptum est, in ecclesia de Crespi totum donum quod prescriptum est, libere concesserat. Hec autem nomina sunt[24] eorundem militum: Johannes et Symon frater eius, Rogerus et Rainaldus frater eius, Ivo vicecomes. Ut igitur hec omnia rata et inconvulsa in posteram permaneant, presentem paginam tam sigilli nostri inpressione quam testium inscriptione communiri precepimus et in omnes qui temerare aut perturbare presumpserint, donec resipiscentes satisfecerint, anathematis sententiam promulgamus. S.[25] Lisiardi,[26] decani. S. Gualteri,[27] thesaurarii. S. Gerardi,[28] subthesaurarii. S. Milonis, argentarii. Signum Reneldi[29] Belin, subdiaconorum. Actum[30] incarnati verbi M° C° LX° VI°. Angotus cancellarius relegit, scripsit, et subscripsit.

---

15 Gualterus *B*.
16 Gualterus *B*.
17 Anizy-le-Château, arr. Laon, https://dicotopo.cths.fr/places/P86940236.
18 Reinero *B*.
19 Likely the parish church of Saint-Rémy-au-Velours, Laon.
20 Geroldo *B*.
21 Sebacourt, comm. Suzy, https://dicotopo.cths.fr/places/P94766735.
22 Pinun *B*.
23 Pinon, cant. Anizy-le-Château, https://dicotopo.cths.fr/places/P22218866.
24 *Transp. A*; sunt nomina *B*.
25 Signum *B*.
26 Lisiard, dean of Laon, ca. 1153–ca. 1168.
27 Gautier, treasurer of Laon, ca. 1162–ca. 1173. Per AD Aisne, G 171, a nephew of Gautier de Mortagne, bishop of Laon.
28 Gérard, subtreasurer of Laon, is a witness to episcopal acts from 1145. Dufour-Malbezin, *Actes*, 372.
29 S. Rainaldi *B*.
30 *Om.* anno *A*.

157

February 15, 1206.

Michel, maior *of Crépy, and the commune of Crépy, make known that the arbiters Jean Garnier, canon of Saint-Jean de Laon, and* magister *Robert, priest of Crépy,*[1] *resolved the dispute between Crépy and the church of Prémontré concerning the* census, *use of, and access to woods near the Premonstratensian house of Dandry,*[2] *as well as the clearing of certain small hills nearby for cultivation.*

A. Cartulary of Prémontré, fols. 38v–39r.
B. Original not found.
REGISTER: *Studium Baldwin*, fiche 2451.

Karta maioris et commune de Crespi de quadam compromisione in quasdam super quibusdam.

[E]go Michael, maior, et conmunia de Crespi omnibus Christi fidelibus in perpetuum. Notum facimus universis tam presentibus quam futuris quod cum inter nos et ecclesiam Premonstrati super censu quodam et nemore juxta Daneri et monticulis quibusdam supra ipsum Daneri verteretur querela, et in viros venerabiles et discretos Johannem Garneri, canonicum Sancti Johannis Laudunensis, et magistrum Robertum, presbiterum de Crespi, esset ab utraque sub pena viginti librarum Parisiensium compromissum, dicti arbitri dixerunt sententialiter monticulos ipsos, dum jacent inculti et non sartati, tam ad pascua quam ad lapides ibidem sumendos quam etiam ad omnes aisentias nobis et Premonstratensibus debere esse communes, ita tamen quod non poterunt aliqui ipsos sartare nisi Premonstratenses qui, si illos sartare voluerint et excolere, excolent illos sicut alias terra suas, scilicet medietatem ad terragium et medietatem ad censum. Dum vero inculti sunt, nichil debent ex eis. Nemus vero parvum quod est in proclivi montis supra curtem de Daneri, juxta vineam intra metas positas, ipsum quidem nemus dixerunt esse fratrum Premonstratensium, ita quod dicti fratres ipsum nutrire poterunt usque ad quinque annos, in sexto anno oportet ut seccent illud, relictis ibi XX^{ti} arboribus quas ipsi volent, sive ad edificia sive ad alias conmoditates suas. Nemus vero fratrum vetus quod ascendit a via juxta curtem usque ad nemus dictum non oportebit secari nisi cum voluerint ipsi fratres, sed predictum nemus parvum tenentur fratres claudere ita quod aliquis non possit eques intrare vel exire. Si autem aliquo tempore terras fratrum prius cultas contigerit remanere incultas, alius ad illas

1 Crépy, cant. Laon, https://dicotopo.cths.fr/places/P85331504.
2 Dandry, comm. Crépy, https://dicotopo.cths.fr/places/P99162453.

colendas intrare non poterit nec debebit, sed pro eis solvent fratres medietatem terragii juxta estimationem bonorum virorum. Omnes autem terras incultas, ubicumque sint intra terminos suos site, licet eis sartare et, si vineam ibidem plantaverint, medietatem vinagii, si vero terram arabilem fecerint, medietatem census et medietatem terragii solvere tenebuntur. Pro omnibus autem terris super quibus vertebatur querela tam nemore supradicto quam etiam campello apud Reinquenci quam etiam aliis omnibus terris quas tenent infra metas suas, solvent ipsi viginti solidos alborum vel monete equivalentis. Ut autem hec conventio futuris temporibus rata permaneat atque firma eam sigilli nostri appensione duximus roborandam. Actum anno incarnationis dominice M° CC° VI°, XV°, kalendas martii.

158

Undated

Pierre Godon, curate of Crépy,[1] *and [Soibert?] pronounce a verdict against the churches of Prémontré and of Saint Nicolas concerning a* court *and its dependencies located behind the manor houses of the aforesaid churches at Crépy.*

A. Cartulary of Prémontré, fol. 39r.[2]
B. Original not found.

NO RUBRIC. LATER ADDITION.

Sachent tuit cil qui cest escript verront et orront que mesires Pierres Godons, curés de Nostre Dame de Crespy et [Soibers?] diz [illegible] de Crespy esleut arbitre ou amiable apaisenteur du descort qui estoit entre l'eglize de Premonstré d'une part et l'eglise de Saint Nicolas d'autre part, si comme il appert par leur compromis baillies des deus eglises, c'est a savoir du descort de la court et des appartenances court, laquele court siet derier les manoirs des dictes eglizes a Crespy prononcierent et prononcent li devant diz [illegible] en cette maniere leur dit, c'est a savoir que la grange et toute la terre wide derier la graingie et devant sauf les [contrediz?] [illegible] maisons masonnées desqueles maisons il ne dient nul dit demeurant es eglises la grange [illegible] …

1 Crépy, cant. Laon, https://dicotopo.cths.fr/places/P85331504.
2 The bottom part of this act has been cropped.

159

1198–1216.[1]

Cantor R., P. d'Orgeval,[2] and magister *V., canons of Saint-Quentin, having been tasked by Pope Innocent [III] to resolve the dispute concerning the division of the tithe of But[3] between the church of Prémontré on the one hand and the priest Martin and Robert de Colligis,[4] citizen of Laon, on the other, decide in favour of Prémontré and give them the right to divide the tithe.*

A. Cartulary of Prémontré, fols. 39r–39v.
B. Original, BnF, Coll. Picardie 290, no. 26, previously sealed with two seals.
REGISTER: *Studium Baldwin*, fiche 2135.

De diffinitione cuiusdam cause inter Premonstratensem et Martinum presbiterum et Robertum de Curlegis.

[E]go R. Cantor, P. de Orgeval[5] et magister V.[6], canonici Sancti Quintini, universos presentes litteras inspecturos nosse volumus quod cum querela que inter Premonstratensem ex una parte et Martinum, presbiterum, et Robertum de Curlegis, civem Laudunensem, ex altera super decimatione curtis de Bus vertebatur, a domino Papa Innocentio nobis commissa fuisset cognoscenda et sine debito terminanda, nos duo predicti, videlicet cantor et P. de Orgeval,[7] tercii college nostri excusatam habentes ~~cons~~absentiam et ex justa causa juris peritorum freti consilio, servato juris ordine in cognitione cause ac diffinitione[8] processimus in hunc modum. Convocatis partibus et coram nobis in jure constitutis ipsis Premonstratensibus proponentibus debitam sibi decimationem curtis prenominate a iamdictis Martino et Roberto, cive Laudunensi, injuste detineri et eam sibi reddi debere, econtra Martino pro se et pro ipso cive pro quo instructus venerat, respondente se de curte illa decimationem nec debere nec umquam reddidisse Premonstratensi ecclesie, ipsi Premonstratenses constanter asserentes se jus habere in decimatione memorate curtis de Bus et eam diutius possedisse et recepisse ratione decimagii ad curtim[9] suam de

1 A Pierre d'Orgeval was a canon of Saint-Quentin in 1226 (AD Aisne H 1654); this act therefore most likely dates to the papacy of Innocent III, 1198–1216. See **457**.
2 Orgeval, cant. Laon, https://dicotopo.cths.fr/places/P49065943.
3 But, comm. Andelain, https://dicotopo.cths.fr/places/P24052391.
4 Colligis, cant. Craonne, https://dicotopo.cths.fr/places/P74119641.
5 Orgival *B*.
6 W. *B*.
7 Orgival *B*.
8 difinitione *B*.
9 *Sic A, B*.

Rainquenci[10] pertinentis, in cuius decimagii territorio curtis de Bus contineri dinoscitur, id per legitimos testes indubitanter se probaturos promiserunt. Nobis igitur huic probationi diem prefigentibus, sepedictus Martinus tam juridictioni[11] nostre quam appellationi in literis apostolicis inhibite minime deferens, ad Sedem Apostolicam appellans, contumaciter recessit. Productis vero testibus ex Premonstratensium parte[12] coram nobis, die sibi prefixa, Martinus ibidem presens, data sibi copia dicendi in ipsos testes, si vellet, nichil in eos dicens, sed iterum appellans, indignanter nos deseruit. Testibus autem receptis sub forma juramenti expressa, examinatis diligenter et auditis eorumque attestationibus redactis in scriptum die statuto, partibus ad publicandas[13] attestationes[14] presentibus tam Premonstratensibus quam Martino coram positis attestationibus,[15] cum interrogaremus Martinum utrum in eas dicere vellet, ipso nolente eas inspicere vel audire sed appellante sicut prius et ita a nobis discedente, nos, publicatis[16] attestationibus,[17] lectis diligenter et recitatis in publico[18] accito[19] juris peritorum consilio, sepedicte decimationis possessionem Premonstratensi ecclesie, apostolica freti auctoritate,[20] adjudicavimus, firmiter statuentes ut ipsi eadem possessione libere gaudeant et quiete.

160

1145. Royal palace, Paris.

Louis [VII], king of France, gives to the church of Prémontré the land of Dandry,[1] *as marked out by Louis de Choisy and other royal servants, free from rights of* justicia *and* consuetudine, *with half of it subject to* terragium, *and half subject to* census.

A. Cartulary of Prémontré, fol. 39v.
B. Original not found.
EDITION: Le Paige, *Bibliotheca*, 425; Hugo, *prob.* 1, cols. xiv–xv.

10 Raincenci *B*.
11 *Sic A and B*, *read* jurisdictioni.
12 *Transp. A*; parte Premostratensium *B*.
13 apuplicandas *B*.
14 atestationes *B*.
15 atestationibus *B*.
16 puplicatis *B*.
17 atestationibus *B*.
18 puplico *B*.
19 ascito *B*.
20 actoritate *B*.

1 Dandry, comm. Crépy, https://dicotopo.cths.fr/places/P99162453.

Karta Ludovici regis Francorum de elemosina de Daneri.

[I]n nomine sancte et individue Trinitatis. Ludovicus, Dei gratia, rex Francorum et dux Aquitanorum. Digne nimirum munificentia regalis et pauperum Christi necessitudinibus pie subvenit et ecclesiarum possessiones tuetur et augmentat. Notum proinde facimus presentibus pariter atque futuris quod ecclesie Premonstratensi et fratribus inibi servientibus Deo terram de Daneri, prout a Ludovico[2] de Choisiaco et ceteris servientibus nostris certis designata est metis, donavimus medietatem quidem ad terragium et medietatem ad censum. Edificium autem ipsorum cum omni integritate sua et familia tota fratrum, perpetuo liberum ab omni justicia et consuetudine, prorsus esse statuimus sed in ceteris hominibus preter proprios fratrum justicias et forisfacta nobis ex integro retinemus. Quod ut perpetue stabilitatis optineat munimenta, scripto commendari, sigilli nostri auctoritate muniri nostrique nominis subter inscripto karactere corroborari precipimus. Actum publice Parisius, anno ab incarnatione Domini M° C° XL° V°, regni vero nostri VIIII°. Astantibus in palatio nostro quorum nomina subtitulata sunt et signa. Signum Radulphi,[3] Viromandorum comitis, dapiferi nostri. S. Guillelmi,[4] buticularii. S. Mathei,[5] camerarii. S. Mathei,[6] constabularii. Data per manum Cadurci,[7] cancelarii.

Additional Rubric

1239/1240

This is the only place in the manuscript where rubrication has been added that is not immediately followed by a single act. The full contents of the three acts

2 Louis de Choisy appears in the entourage of Adélaïde de Maurienne, queen of France, in 1153. Morel, *Cartulaire de l'abbaye de Saint-Corneille de Compiègne*, vol. 1, 132.

3 Raoul I, count of Vermandois, Amiens, and Valois (d. 1152), was the son of Hugues I le Grand, count of Vermandois and Valois, and Adélaïde de Vermandois, and served as seneschal of France, 1131–51.

4 Guillaume le Loup de Senlis, knight and lord of Chantilly, Ermenonville, Villepeinte and Bray, son of Guy de la Tour de Senlis, lord of Chantilly, Ermenonville, Derency, Villepeinte, and Bray-sur-Aunette, and Berthe, was butler of France, ca. 1130–47. Voillemier, "Note sur la maison des Bouteiller de Senlis," 36–7.

5 Mathieu I, count of Beaumont-sur-Oise, chamberlain of France from 1135, son of Yves II, count of Beaumont, and Adélaïde (de Gournay?). Secousse, ed., *Ordonnances des rois de France de la troisième race*, vol. 7, 415.

6 Mathieu I, lord of Montmorency (d. 1160), son of Bouchard, lord of Montmorency, and Agnès de Beaumont, constable of France from 1138.

7 Cadurc, chancellor of Louis VI, 1140–7. Luchaire, *Remarques sur la succession des grands officiers de la couronne qui ont souscrit les diplômes de Louis VI et de Louis VII (1108–1180)*, 37.

described in the compound rubric below follow accordingly, but each act also contains its own rubric.

A. Cartulary of Prémontré, fol. 39v.

Incipiunt scripta de Acheri cum appenditiis suis:
Karta Bartolomei episcopi de concessione molendinorum de Acheri.
Karta Galteri Laudunensis episcopi super quitatione facta a Herberto, maiore.
Karta Rogeri Laudunensis episcopi de compositionem quandam factam coram ipso.

161

1141

Barthélemy,[1] *bishop of Laon, gives to the brothers of Prémontré the site of the mills at Achery,*[2] *long in disrepair, so that the brothers can build new mills there, on the condition that they render an annual payment of one* modius *of grain (*annona*), measure of Laon, at Versigny.*[3] *Barthélemy adds to this the rights over a mill and a nearby* curtis, *including fishing rights, but reserves to himself the rights of* fur *and* duellum. *(See* ***164****.)*

A. Cartulary of Prémontré, fol. 39v.
B. Original not found.
EDITION: Dufour-Malbezin, *Actes*, 317; *Chartae Galliae*, no. 208354, http://telma.irht.cnrs.fr/outils/chartae-galliae/charte208354/.
REGISTER: Florival, *Étude historique sur le XIIe siècle*, 381.

Karta Bartholomei episcopi Laudunensis de concessione molendinorum de Acheri sub annuo censu.

[I]n nomine sancte et individue Trinitatis. Ego Bartholomeus, Dei gratia Laudunensis episcopus. Quia expedit scripto mandari que in posterum oblivione timentur deleri, commodum esse duximus litterarum auctoritate firmari que utilitas poposcerit diutina memoria retineri. Notum igitur sit omnibus tam presentibus quam futuris quod in villa, que Acheri dicitur, sedes molendinorum a longis retro nostris temporibus per incuriam neglectas habuimus, de quarum reparatione, quia parum nobis utiles esse videbantur, aut parva aut nulla penitus

1 Barthélemy de Jur (d. 1158), son of Conon, lord of Grandson and La Sarraz, and Ada de Roucy; first subdeacon and then treasurer of Reims, later bishop of Laon, 1113–51.
2 Achery, cant. La Fère, https://dicotopo.cths.fr/places/P61820808.
3 Versigny, cant. La Fère, https://dicotopo.cths.fr/places/P17885640.

cura fuit. Et quoniam fratribus Premonstrati oportunitate loci ad construenda molendina magis quam nobis apte fuere, predictas sedes eterno jure possidendas eis donavimus, tali conditione quod singulis annis in festivitate Omnium Sanctorum apud Vercenniacum, in domo nostri maioris, unum modium annone vectura sua adductum, ad mensuram Laudunensem, nobis persolvent. Que quidem annona talis dabitur, qualis de molitura molendinorum provenerit, ita tamen quod non sit neque de meliori, neque de peiori. Omnimodam vero piscationem ad proprios usus suos ipsis in eadem aqua concedimus. Curtem quoque unam inde haut longe sitam, omni libertate donata, cum molendinis supradictis eisdem fratribus confirmamus, excepto fure, si ibi forte deprehensus fuerit, excepto duello, si ibi aliqua de causa pullulaverit. Predicte ergo predicto modo facte donationes et concessiones, ne aliqua in posterum oblivione aut occasione possint dissolvi, presentem paginam tam sigilli nostri inpressione quam testium subscriptione muniri precepimus. Signum Bartholomei,[4] archidiaconi. S. Arnulphi, clerici. S. Roberti,[5] capellani. S. Nichasii. Signum Radulphi Milet. S. Dionisii. S. Drouet. Actum anno incarnationis dominice M° C° XL° I°, indictione IIII[a], epacta XI[a], concurrente II°. Si qua igitur ecclesiastica secularisve persona hanc nostre institutionis paginam infringere aut mutare presumpserit, si secundo terciove commonita non acquieverit et emendaverit, in extremo examine districte ultioni subjaceat. Ego Bartholomeus, cancellarius, relegi.[6]

162

1172. Bishop's residence, Laon.

Gautier [II],[1] *bishop of Laon, makes known that following a dispute with the church of Prémontré over lands at Achery,*[2] *Herbert,*[3] maior *of Achery,*

---

4 Barthélemy de Montcornet (d. 1175), son of Hugues de Montcornet and Béatrice de Reynel, was archdeacon of Laon from 1133, treasurer of Laon from 1137, and chancellor of Laon, 1141–4; later archdeacon of Reims; and bishop of Beauvais, 1162–75. Guyotjeannin, *Episcopus*, 131; Dufour-Malbezin, *Actes*, 30.

5 Robert, chaplain of Laon, appears as a witness to episcopal acts 1130–50. Dufour Malbezin, *Actes*, 215, 445.

6 In the margin below this charter are additions in two later medieval hands: "Aliam kartam de Acheri novam quare post kartas de Walescours" (hand 1) and "Magistri Johannis de Ribodimonte" (hand 2).

---

1 Gautier de Mortagne was dean of Laon, ca. 1142–55, and bishop of Laon, 1155–74.

2 Achery, cant. La Fère, https://dicotopo.cths.fr/places/P61820808.

3 Herbert, *maior* of Achery, also confirms an 1158 gift to the Benedictine abbey of Saint-Nicolas aux Bois. Caffiaux, *Trésor généalogique, ou extraits de titres anciens qui concernent les maisons & familles de France & des environs, connus en 1400 ou auparavant*, 15.

relinquished his claims and recognized Prémontré's free possession of these lands. Herbert's unnamed wife and children consent.

A. Cartulary of Prémontré, fol. 40r.
B. Original, AD Aisne, H 741, previously sealed.

Karta Galteri Laudunensis episcopi super quitatione terrarum de Acheri facta a Herberto, maiore.

[I]n nomine sancte et individue Trinitatis. Ego Galterus, Dei gratia Laudunensis episcopus: Herbertus, maior de Acheri, sepe et multum fatigaverat ecclesiam Premonstrati super quibusdam terris apud Acheri quas ipse sepius occupavit et sui juris esse dicebat. Verum postea resipiscens, destitit a querela et easdem terras, assensu uxoris sue et liberorum, quittas clamavit in perpetuum ecclesie supradicte, presentibus et hec audientibus Galtero[1] archidiacono, et Galtero[2] thesaurario, Widone[3] de Moncornet, magistro Gervasio et magistro Haimone[4] frater eius, canonicis Laudunensibus, et Johanne[5] decano de Marla. Willermus[6] etiam, abbas Cuissiacensis, et dominus Rogerus[7] de Roseto et dominus Renaldus frater eius similiter affuerunt. Ut igitur hoc stet immotum nostro illud sigillo communivimus. Actum anno incarnationis dominice M° C° LXX° II°, Lauduni, in logia[8] nostra ante salam. Willermus[9] cancellarius[10] scripsit.

1 Gautier, archdeacon of Laon, ca. 1172. Wyard, *Saint-Vincent*, 34.
2 Gautier, treasurer of Laon, ca. 1162–ca. 1173. Per AD Aisne, G 171, a nephew of Gautier de Mortagne, bishop of Laon.
3 A Guy is attested as lord of Montcornet, ca. 1162–78. Through his sister Elizabeth he was the brother-in-law of Gossuin, castellan of Pierrepont. Melleville, *DH*, vol. 2, 119.
4 Hamone *B*.
5 Jean, dean of Marle, ca. 1170–ca. 1205. Desilve, "Analyse d'un cartulaire de l'abbaye de la Valroy," 164; Édouard de Barthélemy, *Analyse du cartulaire de l'abbaye de Foigny*, 89. He had a brother, Syger, and a nephew, Droard, also a priest. Barthélemy, *LDA*, 348, fn. 392.
6 Guillaume Hennepaix, abbot of the Premonstratensian abbey of Cuissy, 1170–4, of the Premonstratensian abbey of Bucilly, 1176–8, and of the Premonstratensian abbey of Chartreuve, 1178–85. *MP* II, 366, 494, 497.
7 Roger (d. 1201) and his brother Renaud, lord of Rozoy-sur-Serre (d. bef. 1190), were the sons of Clérembaud, lord of Rozoy-sur-Serre (d. bef. 1158) and Elizabeth de Namur (d. aft. 1148).
8 loga *B*.
9 Guillaume, chancellor of the bishop of Laon, is attested 1173–1201. BnF, MS. lat. 11073, fol. 55r; BM Reims, MS 1843 (N. 863), fol. 112v.
10 *Om.* noster *A*.

163

1174–1207.[1]

Roger [I],[2] bishop of Laon, makes known that a certain Guy gave land at Achery[3] to the church of Prémontré in alms prior to his marriage and his departure to Jerusalem. Following a dispute over this land, his sons, Jean de Hirson,[4] Roger, Guy, and Anselme, recognize Prémontré's rightful possession.

A. Cartulary of Prémontré, fol. 40r.
B. Original not found.

Karta Rogeri Laudunensis episcopi de compositione quadam factam coram ipso.

[E]go Rogerus, Dei gratia Laudunensis episcopus, notum fieri volo presentibus et futuris quod Johannes de Yrechun et fratres eius, videlicet Rogerus, Guido, Anselmus moverunt querelam adversus fratres Premonstrate ecclesie super quadam terra quam eadem ecclesia possidebat in domo sua de Acheri, infra curiam et extra, quam videlicet terram Guido, pater eorum, eidem ecclesie Premonstratensi dederat in elemosinam, antequam matrem eorum duxisset in uxorem et etiam antequam Jherosolimam proficisceretur. Tandem predictus Johannes et predicti fratres eius, cognoscentes se injuste querelam adversus iamdictam ecclesiam movisse, in presentia nostra, eandem elemosinam recognoverunt et ad opus predicte ecclesie in manus nostras resignaverunt. Recognoverunt etiam se nichil habere requisitionis vel alicuius consuetudinis in domo illa, sed exitus et introitus de domo sufficientes habebunt predicti fratres et omnes aisentias in omnibus que ad predictum Johannem et fratres eius pertinent, absque calumpnia et reclamatione, sicut homines eiusdem ville habere noscuntur, ita quod si aliquis super hoc sepedictam ecclesiam inquietare voluerit, contra omnis qui ad justiciam venire voluerint warandiam portabunt.[5]

1 Date based on the tenure of Roger de Rozoy as bishop of Laon.
2 Roger de Rozoy, son of Clérembaud, lord of Rozoy, and Elizabeth de Namur, was bishop of Laon, 1174–1207.
3 Achery, cant. La Fère, https://dicotopo.cths.fr/places/P61820808.
4 Likely Hirson, comm. Dercy, https://dicotopo.cths.fr/places/P79543878.
5 The word "portabunt" appears as a contemporary addition in the bottom margin of the leaf.

164

1148. Laon.

Barthélemy,[1] *bishop of Laon, desiring that his gift of the mill of Achery*[2] *to Prémontré be respected in full, asks that his* prepositus *Denis*[3] *surrender any rights he might claim on that mill. Denis accedes to this request with the consent of Havide, his mother, and Alexandre and Gervais, his brothers. (See* ***161****.)*

A. Cartulary of Prémontré, fol. 40r.
B. Original not found.
EDITION: Dufour-Malbezin, *Actes*, 428; *Chartae Galliae*, no. 208808, http://telma.irht.cnrs.fr/outils/chartae-galliae/charte208808/.
REGISTER: Florival, *Étude historique sur le XIIe siècle*, 402.

Karta Bartholomei episcopi Laudunensis de libertate molendini de Acheri.

[I]n nomine sancte et individue Trinitatis. Ego Bartholomeus, Dei gratia Laudunensis episcopus. Notum fieri volo tam futuris quam presentibus quod in molendino de Acheri, quod censualiter ab omni alia exactione liberum Premonstrate ecclesie dedi, prepositus meus Dionisius quasdam consuetudines et exactiones et justicias inordinatas, scilicet tallias que nulli regularium conveniunt, habere volebat. Ego autem ut donum meum et elemosina, quam feceram, eiusdem molendini integra et libera inviolabiliter permaneret, sicut in privilegio eorum continetur, elaboravi ut totum quicquid illud erat, quod calumpniabatur, in manu mea resignaret. Et sic tandem amore Dei et petitionibus meis fecit; ego vero ecclesie reddidi, excepto duello et latrone, astante matre sua Hauwide et fratribus suis, Alexandro et Gervasio, volentibus et consentientibus. Hoc autem ne in posterum aliquatenus possit infirmari, et scripto commendari et sigilli nostri impressione et testium subscriptione precepimus consignari. S. Walteri,[4] abbatis Sancti Martini. S. Aschonis de Buciliis.[5] S. Hectoris,[6] vicedomini et ceteri. Actum est hoc Lauduni, anno incarnati verbi M° C° XLVIII°, epacta IX[a], indictione XII[a], concurrente IIII[o].

---

1 Barthélemy de Jur (d. 1158), son of Conon, lord of Grandson and La Sarraz, and Ada de Roucy; first subdeacon and then treasurer of Reims, later bishop of Laon, 1113–51.
2 Achery, cant. La Fère, https://dicotopo.cths.fr/places/P61820808.
3 Denis, son of Guillaume Bouche and Helvide la Prévote, was *prepositus* of Laon, 1152–1217, and a cousin of Barthélemy, viscount of Laon. Saint-Denis, *Apogée d'une cité*, 220.
4 Gautier de Saint-Maurice was abbot of the Premonstratensian abbey of Saint-Martin de Laon, 1124–51, and bishop of Laon, 1151–3. *MP* II, 512.
5 Bucilly, cant. Hirson, https://dicotopo.cths.fr/places/P91269366.
6 Hector, *vidame* of Laon, husband of Sarrasine. Saint-Denis, *Apogée d'une cité*, 206–7.

165

1225

The knight Pierre [II] de Viry,[1] *lord of Commenchon, approves and confirms as fief lord that Helvide de Mennessis*[2] *sold to the church of Prémontré the annual payment of one* modius *of grain (*frumentum*), measure of Saint-Quentin, that the church had paid her for use of the sluice and water channel that runs from below Vendeuil*[3] *to the mill at Achery.*[4] *Her children Gilon, Wiard, Fulcard, Guillaume, and Marge approve.*

A. Cartulary of Prémontré, fols. 40r–40v.

B. Original, AD Aisne, H 741, previously sealed on a double strip of parchment.

EDITION: Melleville, "Une charte où une femme, vassale d'un seigneur, est appelée *Homo mea*"; Martin-Marville, *Trosly-Loire ou le Trosly des conciles, ses chateaux, ses villas, ses fiefs et ses seigneurs*, 232.

Karta Petri militis de Viri domini de Caumencon de confirmatione unius modii frumenti.

[E]go Petrus de Viri,[5] dominus de Caumenchon, notum facio universis tam presentibus quam futuris quod nobilis mulier Helvidis de Manessies, homo mea, vendidit ecclesie Premonstratensis de spontaneo et voluntario assensu liberorum suorum Gilonis, Wiardi, Fulcardi, Willermi et Marge, unum modium frumenti ad mensuram Sancti Quintini quem ei debebat annuatim ipsa ecclesia in molendino suo de Acheri pro esclusa et conductu aque que descendit a fluvio subtus Vendolium ad predictum molendinum de Acheri, quem conductum aque cum esclusa tenentur tam ipsi quam heredes eorum in perpetuum warandire ipsi ecclesie Premonstratensis, sicut eadem ecclesia ipsum conductum aque cum esclusa tenuit usque ad hec tempora pacifice et quiete. Sciendum est autem quod tam ipsa Helvidis quam predicti liberi sui fidem in mea presentia corporaliter prestiterunt quod nec per se nec per alios molestabunt in posterum ipsam ecclesiam super dicto modio frumenti nec facient aliquatenus molestari. Ego vero quia ipsa Helvidis tenebat ipsum modium de me in feodum, venditionem ipsam ad petitionem partium laudavi et etiam confirmavi. In cuius rei perpetuam firmitatem presentem kartam super hoc confectam sigilli mei munimine roboravi. Actum anno gratie M° CC° vicesimo V°.[6]

---

1 Pierre II, lord of Viry and Commenchon (cant. Chauny, https://dicotopo.cths.fr/places/P45903373). Melleville, *DH*, vol. 1, 267.

2 Mennessis, cant. La Fère, https://dicotopo.cths.fr/places/P40987837.

3 Vendeuil, cant. Moy, https://dicotopo.cths.fr/places/P36797569.

4 Achery, cant. La Fère, https://dicotopo.cths.fr/places/P61820808.

5 *Om.* miles *A*.

6 quinto *B*.

166

April 6, 1221.

Enguerrand [III],[1] *lord of Coucy, approves the gift that Raymond de Sinceny,*[2] *his unnamed wife, and their unnamed daughter gave in alms to the church of Prémontré of about two* modiatae *of woodland, near the Premonstratensian* curtis *of Grehen.*[3] *Elizabeth,*[4] *widow of the knight Guy d'Arblincourt and the immediate fief lord, approves the gift.*

A. Cartulary of Prémontré, fol. 40v.
B. Original BnF, Coll. Picardie 290, no. 34, previously sealed.

Karta Ingelranni domini de Couciaco de elemosina Raimundi de Cinceni.

[E]go Ingelrannus, dominus Couciaci,[5] notum facio omnibus presentem paginam inspecturis quod religiosi viri abbas et conventus[6] ecclesie Premonstratensis[7] fecerunt quendam acquestum infra dominium meum qui talis est. Ipsi quidem acquisierunt per elemosinam a Rainmundo de Cinceni et uxore sua necnon et filia sua circiter duas modiatas nemoris sitas prope curtem de Greham super Ysaram, quas tenebant in feodum a nobili muliere Elizabeth, relicta Guidonis de Erblencourt[8] militis et ipsa Elizabeth, in mea presentia constituta, predictam elemosinam approbavit. Quia vero predicta Elizabeth tenebat de me in feodum nemus predictum, ego ad petitionem partium et, ut etiam elemosine particeps essem, acquestum predicti nemoris gratum et ratum habui, ita quidem quod de ipso nemore predicti abbas et fratres facient sive secando sive ducendo quo[9] voluerint et kartam istam in memoriam huius rei confectam sigilli mei munimine roboravi. Actum VIII° idus aprilis, anno gratie M°[10] CC° vicesimo primo.

1 Enguerrand III de Boves, lord of Coucy (ca. 1182–1242), son of Raoul I, lord of Coucy, and Alix de Dreux.
2 A *Raymond de Chincheni* (Sinceny, cant. Chauny, https://dicotopo.cths.fr/places/P29595722) appears in a 1221 act in the cartulary of the chapter of Saint-Quentin. BnF, MS lat. 11070, fols. 88r–88v.
3 Grehen, cant. Chauny, https://dicotopo.cths.fr/places/P96268330.
4 Elizabeth, daughter of Guy II, lord of Guny, and widow of Guy III, lord of Arblincourt. Newman, *Seigneurs*, vol. 2, 100; Barthelemy, *LDA*, 516.
5 Cociaci *B*.
6 fratres *B*.
7 *transp. A*; Premonstratensis ecclesie *B*.
8 Erblencort *B*.
9 quod *B*.
10 millesimo *B*.

167

October 5, 1214.

Robert [I],[1] *bishop of Laon, makes known that Pierre de Huet*[2] *gives Prémontré a vineyard at Chaillevois,*[3] *owing an annual* census *of one* obolus *to the bishops of Laon, in exchange for the mill of Huet with its associated meadow and courtyard. Prémontré will pay the one* obolus *to the bishops of Laon for the vineyard, and Pierre will pay the annual pension of four* modii *of grain (*frumentum*) to the heirs of lord Nicolas*[4] *du Sart for the mill.*

A. Cartulary of Prémontré, fol. 40v.
B. Original, AD Aisne, H 767, previously sealed.

Karta Roberti Laudunensis episcopi de quadam compositione inter ecclesiam Premonstratensem et Petrum de Wez.

[R]obertus, Dei gratia episcopus Laudunensis, omnibus in perpetuum. Notum fieri volumus tam futuris quam presentibus per hoc scriptum quod inter ecclesiam Premonstratensem et Petrum de Wez, laicum, talis pactio intercessit, videlicet quod ipse Petrus per excambium donavit ecclesie Premonstratensis in hereditatem et possessionem perpetuam quandam vineam apud Chevoie, solventem censualiter unum obolum bone monete, quem dicta ecclesia pro ipsa vinea annuatim nobis et successoribus nostris solvet. Ecclesia vero Premonstratensis pro hac donatione dedit eidem Petro et heredibus suis molendinum de Wez perpetuo possidendum cum prato et curtili que adiacent molendino, tali conventione interposita quod idem Petrus aut ille qui loco eius molendinum tenebit, solvet annuatim heredi domini Nicholai de Sarto pensionem IIII°[5] modiorum bladi qui pro eodem molendino debentur. A cuius pensionis solutione si memoratus Petrus sive heredes eius destiterint, ita quod pro solutionis defectu oporteat ecclesiam Premonstratensem satisfacere, illi qui debebit recipere pensionem in optione ecclesie erit ut vel Petrus et eius heredes perdant perpetuo molendinum et rehabeant vineam suam, quando redemerint eam pro tredecim libris Laudunensibus, non conputatis fructibus inde receptis, vel quod excambium duret, sicut est factum, et ecclesia resasiat et teneat molendinum,

1 Robert de Châtillon, son of Guy II, lord of Châtillon and Alix de Dreux, bishop of Laon, 1210–15.
2 Huet, comm. Lizy, https://dicotopo.cths.fr/places/P74654387.
3 Chaillevois, cant. Anizy-le-Château, https://dicotopo.cths.fr/places/P60386090.
4 Nicolas du Sart, knight, son of Sarracin, castellan of Laon and La Fere, and Helvide. Barthélemy, *LDA*, 180–2; Newman, *Seigneurs*, vol. 2, 204.
5 quatuor *B*.

donec de eius obventionibus receperit restitutionem dampnorum et expensarum quas incurrerit per defectum Petri vel eius heredum et sic reddat eis iterum molendinum. Sciendum quoque quod nec sepedictus Petrus nec eius heredes sine licentia nostra et ecclesie Premonstratensis molendinum ipsum de manu sua poterunt amovere. Hoc quoque adiectum est quod ecclesia Premonstratensis super molendino vel eius pertinentiis nullam portabit Petro vel eius heredibus warandiam excepto quod bona fide juvabit eos de testimonio ferendo super hiis que fratres ecclesie scient esse vera sine plus faciendo. Actum tercio nonas octobris, anno gratie M° CC° quarto X°.[6]

168

Twelfth Century[1]

Abbot Hugues [I/II] of Prémontré makes known an agreement concerning grazing rights at Gros Aulnois.[2] (See duplicate ***104****.)*

A. Cartulary of Prémontré, fol. 40v.
B. Original not found.

Karta Hugonis abbatis Premonstratensis de pascuis ad Grossum Alnetum.

[E]go H[ugo], Dei gratia Premonstratensis ecclesie dictus abbas, notum fieri volo tam futuris quam presentibus quod pascua de Grosso Alneto communis erat tam hominibus de Ursinicurt[3] quam hominibus de Lisi.[4] Disponente autem Deo et intervenientibus eiusdem Premonstratensis ecclesie fratribus cum Johanne de Ursinicourt, obtinuerunt homines de Lisi apud homines de Ursinicourt quod prata facerent in eadem pascua, salvo et libero prato Sancti Johannis Premonstratensis omni tempore, quod est subtus molendinum de Wez, ea conditione quod homines de Lisi solummodo a mediante maio usque ad intrantem augustum prata sua possidebunt et defendent sicut libera, postea vero communis erit sicut et antea. Huius autem actionis testes sunt: Johannes de Ursinicourt, Odo de Fonte, Willelmus et ceteri. De Lisi: Havinus, Odo,

6 millesimo ducentesimo quartodecimo *B*.

1 Hugues I de Fosses was abbot of Prémontré, 1128–64, while Hugues II was abbot, 1171–92.
2 Probably in or near Aulnois-sous-Laon, cant. Laon, https://dicotopo.cths.fr/places/P03560401.
3 Wissignicourt, cant. Anizy-le-Château, https://dicotopo.cths.fr/places/P16285342.
4 Lizy, cant. Anizy-le-Château, https://dicotopo.cths.fr/places/P40948829.

Ligerus, Gelierus, Radulphus filius Hildeardis, Paganus filius eius. Quod ut ratum permaneat, ipsorum qui prescripti sunt, petitionibus sigillum nostrum apposuimus. Siquis autem hoc violaverit, anathemati perpetuo subjaceat. Amen.

169

1146. Étampes.

Louis [VII], king of France, responding to a request of abbot Bernard of Clairvaux, cedes his two of three parts of the mills at Archantré[1] *to the church of Prémontré. (See **170**.)*

A. Cartulary of Prémontré, fol. 41r.

B. Original, AD Aisne, H 819, previously sealed with double strip of leather.

EDITION: Delancy, *Historia Fusniacensis Coenobii, Ordinis Cisterciensis*, 87–8; Hugo, *prob.* 1, col. xv.

Karta domini Ludovici regis Francorum de dono cuiusdam partis molendinorum de Erchentre.

[I]n nomine sancte et individue Trinitatis. Ludovicus, Dei gratia Francorum rex et dux Aquitanorum. Oportet nos operari bonum ad omnes maxime autem[2] ad domesticos fidei et religiosos. Propterea venerabilis Bernardi, Clarevallensis abbatis, precibus acquiescentes concessimus Deo et ecclesie Premonstratensi partem quam habebamus in molendinis de Erchentre[3] quiete in perpetuum et libere possidendam. Quod ut ratum habeatur in posterum scripto commendari et sigilli nostri auctoritate muniri nostrique nominis subter inscripto karactere corroborari precepimus. Actum publice Stampis, anno ab incarnatione Domini M° C° XL° VI°. Astantibus in palatio nostro quorum nomina subtitulata sunt et signa: Signum Radulphi,[4,5] Viromandorum comitis et dapiferi nostri.

1 Archantré, comm. Remies, https://dicotopo.cths.fr/places/P18258469.

2 maximeque *B*.

3 Herchentre *B*.

4 Radulfi *B*.

5 Raoul I, count of Vermandois, Amiens, and Valois (d. 1152), was the son of Hugues I le Grand, count of Vermandois and Valois, and Adélaïde de Vermandois, and served as seneschal of France, 1131–51.

S. Guillelmi,[6] buticularii. S. Mathei,[7] camerarii. S. Mathei,[8] constabularii. Data per manum Cadurci[9] cancellarii anno decimo[10] regni nostri.

170

1149

Dean Gautier[1] *and the chapter of Laon transfer to the church of Prémontré one of three parts of the mills of Archantré,*[2] *in exchange for an annual* census *of four* modii *of grain (*frumentum*), measure of Laon. Louis [VII], king of France, had already transferred to Prémontré his two parts of the mills. (See **169**.)*

A. Cartulary of Prémontré, fol. 41r.

B. Original (chirograph), AD Aisne, H 819, previously sealed with a double strip of parchment. In the right margin and beginning at the top, the lower half of the letters that form the word CYROGRAPHUM.

REGISTER: *Studium Baldwin*, fiche 2423.

Karta Galteri episcopi Laudunensis de confirmatione Ludovici regis Francorum elemosine.

I[]n nomine sancte et individue Trinitatis. Proprium esse humane infirmitatis disnoscitur, ut quanto in anteriora protenditur tanto posteriorum difficilius recordetur. Ne ergo per successiones temporum incidamus in oblivionem preteritorum, quod memoriter teneri volumus, scripto commendare solemus. Ea propter ego Galterus,[3] Sancte Laudunensis, matris ecclesie, decanus, totusque

6 Guillaume le Loup de Senlis, knight and lord of Chantilly, Ermenonville, Villepeinte and Bray, son of Guy de la Tour de Senlis, lord of Chantilly, Ermenonville, Derency, Villepeinte and Bray-sur-Aunette, and Berthe, was butler of France, ca. 1130–47. Voillemier, “Note sur la maison des Bouteiller de Senlis,” 36–7.

7 Mathieu I, count of Beaumont-sur-Oise, chamberlain of France from 1135, son of Yves II, count of Beaumont, and Adélaïde (de Gournay?). Secousse et al., *Ordonnances des rois de France de la troisième race*, vol. 7, 415.

8 Mathieu I, lord of Montmorency (d. 1160), son of Bouchard, lord of Montmorency, and Agnès de Beaumont, was constable of France from 1138.

9 Cadurc, chancellor of Louis VI, 1140–7. Luchaire, *Remarques sur la succession des grands officiers de la couronne qui ont souscrit les diplômes de Louis VI et de Louis VII (1108–1180)*, 37.

10 X° *B*.

1 Gautier de Mortagne was dean of Laon, ca. 1142–55, and bishop of Laon, 1155–74.

2 Archantré, comm. Remies, https://dicotopo.cths.fr/places/P18258469.

3 Walterus *B*.

capituli nostri conventus notum fieri volumus tam futuris quam presentibus quod Ludovicus, rex Francie, duas partes quas habebat in molendinis de Erchentre liberas, ita ut habebat, concessit ecclesie Premonstratensi. Nos vero quia eadem ecclesia a nobis procreata erat et in medio domus nostre, utpote filia nostra, habitabat, ne inter nos et ipsam inimica oriretur altercatio, terciam partem molendinorum et omnium ad ipsa pertinentium, sicut nostri juris erant, et sedem cuiusdam molendini ibidem, conmuni assensu, perpetuo ei concessimus comparata annuo censu IIII^or modiorum frumenti. Solventur autem nobis modii duo in initio Quadragesime et duo in Pasca,[4] ad mensuram qua civitas Laudunensis utebatur, quando assensus iste factus est et litteris confirmatus, talis, inquam, frumenti quod comparabitur duobus denariis minus quam illud quod melius in foro Lauduni tunc temporis emendum invenietur. Duo vero vel tres qui ad horreum nostrum ducent panem et vinum a nobis in suos usus accipient. Siquis autem fratres Premonstratensis ecclesie de tercia parte molendinorum quam, ut dictum est, sub annuo censu eis concessimus, injuste inquietaverit, nos ac si nostra propria res esset infra Laudunensem diocesim, prout poterimus, ab eo qui justiciam volet exequi, eos defendemus, ita quod aliquas expensas a prefatis fratribus non recipiemus nec ante cum malefactore illo scienter communicabimus, donec abbati et fratribus Premonstratensis ecclesie dictante justicia satisfecerit. Si vero appellatio ad maiorem audientiam extra episcopatum nostrum facta fuerit, sumptibus Premonstratensium fratrum, si ab eis submoniti fuerimus, appellationem cum ipsis prosequemur, donec assignato fine appellatio terminetur. Quod ut ratum et inconvulsum permaneat, cirographi[5] conscriptione et sigillorum utriusque ecclesie impressione ac legitimarum personarum utriusque capituli subscriptione roboratum et confirmatum.[6] S. Galteri,[7] decani. Signum[8] Bartholomei,[9] thesaurarii.[10] S. Albrici et Eustachii, et ceteri.[11] Actum anno incarnati verbi M° C° XL° VIIII°, epacta VIIII^a, indictione XII^a, concurrente V°.

---

4 pascha *B*.

5 cyrographi *B*.

6 *Om.* est *A*.

7 Signum Walteri *B*.

8 S. *B*.

9 Barthélemy de Montcornet (d. 1175), son of Hugues de Montcornet and Béatrice de Reynel, was archdeacon of Laon from 1133, treasurer of Laon from 1137, and chancellor of Laon, 1141–4; later archdeacon of Reims; and bishop of Beauvais, 1162–75. Guyotjeannin, *Episcopus*, 131; Dufour-Malbezin, *Actes*, 30.

10 *Om.* S. Richardi et Balduini, archidiaconorum. S. Milonis, cantoris. S. Gunteri et Roberti, presbiterorum. S. magistri Petri et Odonis, diaconorum. S. Lisiardi et Hawini, subdiaconorum. Item signum Hugonis, abbatis. S. Warheri, prioris. S. Johannis, subprioris. S. Haimonis, cantoris. S. Gozuini et Symonis, presbiterorum. S. Hugonis et Johannis, diaconorum. *A*.

11 *Add.* et ceteri *A;* subdiaconorum. S. Fulconis et Walteri, acolitorum. *B*.

171

March, 1235.[1]

In the presence of the officialis *of Laon, Henri, miller of Suzy,*[2] *declares that the chapter of Notre-Dame de Laon, and the abbots of Prémontré, the Premonstratensian abbey of Saint-Martin de Laon, and the Benedictine abbey of Saint-Martin de Laon surrendered their rights over the new mill at Molinchart,*[3] *in exchange for an annual payment of a half* modius *of grain (*bladus terciani*), measure of Laon, to be paid to each institution.*

A. Cartulary of Prémontré, fols. 41r–41v.
B. Original not found.
Other Manuscript Copies: Cartulary of the Cathedral Chapter of Notre-Dame de Laon, AD Aisne, G 1850, fol. 344v (13/14th c.).

Karta officialis Laudunensis de Henrico molendinario de Suisi de molendino de Molinchat.

[U]niversis presentes litteras visuris officialis Laudunensis in Domino salutem. Noverit universitas vestra quod, constitutus in presentia nostra, Henricus molendinarius de Suisi, recognovit se recepisse a decano et capitulo Sancte Marie Maioris ecclesie Laudunensis, Sancti Vincentii Laudunensis, Premonstratensis et Sancti Martini Laudunensis abbatibus et eorum conventibus quicquid habebant in novo molendino de Molinchat et appenditiis suis tenendum in perpetuum pro dimidio modio bladi tercianei ad mensuram Laudunensem annuatim solvendo cuilibet ecclesiarum antedictarum ad Natale Domini et recognovit idem Henricus quod debet solvere bladum legitimum et sanum et tale cuius tercia pars ad minus sit frumenti et residuum siliginis et de predicto dimidio modio bladi tercianei dicto termino cuilibet ecclesiarum antedictarum annuatim solvendo, fecit eis assignamentum dictus Henricus in perpetuum ad dictum molendinum et in hoc consensit dictus Henricus quod si ipse vel ille qui molendinum predictum teneret, deficeret in solutione dicti dimidii modii bladi dicto termino quolibet anno facienda, quelibet dictarum ecclesiarum pro suo dimidio modio bladi ex tunc sine contradictione et impedimento ipsius H[enrici] vel heredum suorum dictum molendinum saisire poterit libere et detinere, donec de dicto dimidio modio bladi et decem solidis Parisiensium, nomine emende, esset eidem plenarie satisfactum et recognovit dictus Henricus quod

1 The date is partly erased in the cartulary, but must be 1235, as the *officialité* of Laon emerges as an institution only in the early 1220s.
2 Suzy, cant. Anizy-le-Château, https://dicotopo.cths.fr/places/P75897317.
3 Molinchart, cant. Laon, https://dicotopo.cths.fr/places/P13555538.

dictum dimidium modium ecclesie Premonstratensis solvere tenetur singulis annis apud Roques [*eras.*] dicte ecclesie Premonstratensis. In cuius rei testimonium presentes litteras patentes emisimus sigillo curie Laudunensis, salvo jure domini Laudunensis et alieno roboratas. Actum anno Domini M° C° [*eras.*] tricesimo V°, mense martio.

172

September, 1215.

With the consent of his eldest son Guillaume, Raoul,[1] *lord of Sart, gave in alms to the church of Prémontré one* modius *of grain (*frumentum*), measure of Laon, to be taken annually from the mill of Sauvrezis,*[2] *and two* modii *of wine from his vineyards at Cessières,*[3] *in exchange for Masses to be said on the anniversary of his death.*

A. Cartulary of Prémontré, fol. 41v.

B. Original, BnF, nouv. acq. lat. 2590, no. 46, previously sealed with a single seal.

Karta domini Radulphi de Sarto super elemosina unius modii frumenti [*margo*: Sauvergi.]

[E]go Radulphus,[4] dominus de Sarto, notum facio tam presentibus quam futuris quod ob remedium anime mee, pro anniversario meo faciendo, concedente Willermo filio meo primogenito, dedi in perpetuam elemosinam ecclesie Premonstrati unum modium frumenti ad mensuram Lauduni, accipiendum annuatim in molendino de Sauvergi[5] in festo Omnium Sanctorum et duos modios vini accipiendos singulis annis in vinagiis meis apud Cessarias. Ut igitur hec elemosina a me facta perpetuam habeat firmitatem, presens scriptum super ea confectum sigilli mei testimonio roboravi. Actum mense septembri, anno Domini M° CC° quinto decimo.

1 Raoul, lord of Sart, son of Sarracin, castellan of Laon and La Fère, and Helvide. Barthélemy, *LDA*, 180–2; Newman, *Seigneurs*, vol. 2, 204.

2 Sauvrezis, comm. Cessières, https://dicotopo.cths.fr/places/P70800587.

3 Cessières, cant. Anizy-le-Château, https://dicotopo.cths.fr/places/P02167711.

4 Radulfus *B*.

5 Salvergi *B*.

173

1190

Raoul,[1] *lord of Sart, makes known that he gave in alms to the church of Prémontré five* modii *of wine, measure of Brie,*[2] *to be received annually after his death from his* vinagium *at Brie. Raoul's wife Havide, brothers Nicholas and Pierre, and kinsmen Guy [I],*[3] *lord of Faillouel, and his brother lord Jean*[4] *approved of the gift.*

A. Cartulary of Prémontré, fol. 41v.
B. Original not found.

Karta domini Radulphi de Sarto de elemosina quinque modiorum vini ad mensuram de Bris.

[E]go Radulphus, dominus de Sarto, notum facio tam futuris quam presentibus quod, pro remedio anime mee, in elemosinam dedi ecclesie Sancti Johannis Premonstratensis quinque modios vini ad mensuram de Bris, annuatim post obitum meum in eadem villa de vinagiis meis accipiendos. Hanc elemosinam et donum hoc uxor mea, Hauwidis, et fratres mei, Nicholaus et Petrus et dominus Guido de Foiluel et dominus Johannes frater eius, cognati mei, laudaverunt et stabiliter tenendum super sanctos juraverunt. Actum anno gratie millesimo centesimo nonagesimo.

174

1209

Renaud,[1] *bishop of Laon, after his episcopal consecration, reconfirms an act that he had confirmed at the time of his election and before his consecration; namely that in his presence Pierre,*[2] *knight of Servais, gave in alms one*

1 Raoul, lord of Sart, son of Sarracin, castellan of Laon and La Fère, and Helvide. Barthélemy, *LDA*, 180–2; Newman, *Seigneurs*, vol. 2, 204.
2 Brie, cant. La Fère, https://dicotopo.cths.fr/places/P40042593.
3 Guy I de Condren, lord of Faillouël, son of Geoffroi de Condren, knight. Newman, *Seigneurs*, vol. 2, 203–4.
4 Jean I de Condren, lord of Condren and Mondescourt (cant. Noyon, https://dicotopo.cths.fr/places/P60804459), son of Geoffroi de Condren, knight. Newman, *Seigneurs*, vol. 2, 203–4.

1 Renaud Surdelle, bishop of Laon, 1207–10.
2 Pierre, lord of Servais, ca. 1199–1223; son of Jean II, lord of Servais, and brother of Aelide. Melleville, *DH*, vol. 2, 328.

modius *of grain (*frumentum*), measure of La Fère, to the church of Prémontré. (See **175**.)* [3]

A. Cartulary of Prémontré, fol. 41v.

B. Original not found.

Karta Renaldi Laudunensis episcopi de elemosina Petri militis de Servai.

[E]go Renaldus, Dei gratia Laudunensis episcopus, omnibus in perpetuum. Notum facimus universis presentibus et futuris quod tempore electionis mee, videlicet ante consecrationem meam, Petrus, miles de Servai, in presentia nostra constitutus, recognovit se et heredes suos in perpetuum titulo elemosine debere ecclesie Premonstratensi modium unum frumenti ad mensuram de Fara quale ex molitura molendini de Selvai[4] provenerit, de eodem molendino annuatim a festo Sancti Remigii infra quindecim dies eiusdem ecclesie persolvendum. Nos autem de hac elemosina coram nobis sollempniter a dicto Petro recognita et in manu nostra resignata prefatam ecclesiam investivimus et ipsam elemosinam post consecrationem meam modis omnibus approbantes, nostris litteris confirmamus. Actum anno gratie M° CC° nono.

175

1207

Renaud,[1] *bishop-elect of Laon, and* magister *Gobert and Hector, canons of Laon, approve and confirm the agreement reached in their presence between the church of Prémontré and Pierre,*[2] *lord of Servais, according to which Prémontré cedes to the said Pierre the land that it claimed to hold from his unnamed sister, as well as 12* galeti *of grain (*frumentum*) to be taken annually from the mill of Servais.*[3] *(See **174**.)*

A. Cartulary of Prémontré, fols. 41v–42r.

B. Original not found.

---

3 An almost identical act – but dated to 1207, when Renaud was bishop-elect of Laon, rather than 1209 – is BnF, Coll. Picardie 290, no. 21.

4 *Sic A*, *read* Servai.

---

1 Renaud Surdelle, bishop of Laon, 1207–10.

2 Pierre, lord of Servais, ca. 1199–1223; son of Jean II, lord of Servais, and brother of Aelide. Melleville, *DH*, vol. 2, 328.

3 Servais, cant. La Fère, https://dicotopo.cths.fr/places/P42659145.

Karta Renaldi Laudundensis electi de quadam pace inter ecclesiam Premonstratensem et Petrum de Servai.

[R]enaldus Dei gratia Laudunensis electus, magister Gobertus et Hector, canonici Laudunenses omnibus ad quos littere iste pervenerint in Domino salutem. Noverit universitas vestra quod cum inter ecclesiam Premonstratensem ex una et Petrum, militem de Selvai,[4] ex altera super quadam elemosina, auctoritate apostolica, questio veteretur, fratribus eiusdem ecclesie asserentibus quod soror dicti Petri terram ad sex galetos seminis ad mensuram de Fara dicte ecclesie in ultimo testamento in elemosinam contulisset, prefato vero Petro in contrarium asserente, tandem partibus in presentia nostra constitutis, conpositum est in hunc modum: terram siquidem illam quam sibi titulo elemosine predicta ecclesia vendicabat, militi tenendam concessit, ita quod in recompensationem elemosine dictus Petrus miles quatuor galetos talis frumenti quale ex molitura de Selvai[5] molendini proveniet annuatim, a festo Sancti Remigii infra quindecim dies in perpetuum eidem ecclesie solvendos assignavit, et preterea octo galetos super idem molendinum eiusdem frumenti in eodem termino se et heredes suos in perpetuum debere recognovit. Ut autem hoc ratum permaneat, transactionem istam coram nobis legitime factam auctoritate apostolica approbamus et confirmamus et presentis scripti patrocinio communimus. Contradictores etiam et rebelles auctoritate qua fungimur, perpetuo anathematis vinculo innodamus. Actum anno gratie millesimo CC° septimo.

176

July 25, 1213.

Raoul,[1] [lord of] Sart, reaches an agreement with the church of Prémontré concerning woods that Prémontré held from him at Saint-Lambert;[2] although the Premonstratensians cleared some of the woodland in order to expand their adjacent meadow, Raoul continues to receive the annual census *owed at the current rate of four* solidi *and eight* denarii.

A. Cartulary of Prémontré, fol. 42r.

B. Original not found.

4 *Sic A*.

5 *Sic A*.

1 Raoul, lord of Sart, son of Sarracin, castellan of Laon and La Fère, and Helvide. Barthélemy, *LDA*, 180–2; Newman, *Seigneurs*, vol. 2, 204.

2 Saint-Lambert, comm. Fourdrain, https://dicotopo.cths.fr/places/P30848534.

Karta domini de Sarto super quadam compositione inter ecclesiam Premonstratensem et ipsum.

[E]go Radulphus de Sarto, notum facio per hanc cartulam presentibus et futuris quod cum ecclesia Premonstratensis traxisset me in causam coram judicibus a Sede Apostolica delegatis super quodam latere nemoris mei apud Sanctum Lambertum quod se extirpare et in pratum posse reducere asserebat ad dilatandum quoddam pratum eidem boscho contiguum, quod de me sub annuo censu quatuor solidorum et octo denariorum bone monete tenebat, tandem inter me et ipsam ecclesiam mediantibus bonis viris, talis conpositio intervenit quod ego concessi eidem ecclesie quandam partem illius lateris quod petebat, cum potuerit et voluerit, extirpandam et de me ac de heredibus meis cum prato contiguo sine predicti census augmentatione tenendam. Ne etiam inter me et sepedictam ecclesiam possit iterum questio suboriri, per mediatores huius compositionis, dominum videlicet Willermum, presbiterum de Vercigni,[3] et Walterum, militem ac commensalem meum, necnon et alios probos viros, inter partem illam quam concessi ecclesie et nemus meum feci lapideas metas poni, hoc adjecto quod si nemus vel frutices aliqui iterum recreverint ultra metas, licebit ecclesie extirpare eos lineariter de meta ad metam sine licentia mea et sine aliquo quod ad me vel heredes meos pertineat forisfacto. Quod ut ratum futuris temporibus habeatur presens scriptum super hoc factum sigilli mei feci appensione muniri. Actum octavo kalendas augusti, anno incarnationis dominice millesimo ducentesimo terciodecimo.

177

August, 1349.

Evrard, maior *of Crépy,*[1] *the* jurati, *and the commune of Crépy make known the agreement that they reached with Prémontré and the Benedictine abbey of Saint-Nicolas-aux-Bois concerning the wine that the town of Crépy owes as an annual tithe to the two churches.*

A. Cartulary of Prémontré, fols. 42r–42v.

B. Original not found.

---

3 Versigny, cant. La Fère, https://dicotopo.cths.fr/places/P17885640.

---

1 Crépy, cant. Laon, https://dicotopo.cths.fr/places/P85331504.

NO RUBRIC. LATER ADDITION.

Universis presentes litteras visuris, Everardus maior, jurati et tota communitas de Crespiaco in Laudunesio salutem in Domino. Noverit universitas vestra quod, cum discordia verteretur inter nos et singulos nostrum ex una parte, et ecclesias Premonstratensis et Sancti Nicholaii in Bosco ex altera super solutione et modo solutionis communis decime vini quam debemus eisdem ecclesiis annuatim, tandem inter nos et singulos nostrum ex una parte, et predictas ecclesias ex altera talis compositio intercessit quod quilibet nostrum cuiuscumque sexus de gutta vini vinearum dicte communis decimationis suam faciet voluntatem, aisinum vero eiusdem vini deferet vel faciet deferi fideliter ad pressorium et totum vinum quod exibit de singulis saccis aisini cuiuslibet ad illud pressorium insimul commistetur videlicet de quolibet sacco par se et de toto vino albo insimul commixto quilibet nostrum decimam commune quam dictus ecclesiis debebit solvet insimul nunciis dictarum ecclesiarum vel nuncio eorundem cuius vel quorum primo copiam habuerit vel cui eorum maluerit bona fide; et dicti nuncii sive nuncius eandem decimam recipiet ad illud pressorium, videlicet de singulis decem mensuris undecimam mensuram secundum quantitatem tocius vini habiti tam de tota gutta prehabita quam de toto vino illo quod exierit de aisino illo, de quo vino sic insimul commixto, nisi prius dicta decima, ut dictum est, fuerit persoluta, quicquam a dicto pressorio amovere non poterimus nisi divine pietatis intuitu vel ex mera curialitate ex quibus nec commodum nec premium nec spem remuneracionis quo ad temporalia expectemus vel percipiamus seu alicuius obligationis liberacionem consequimur, aliquid nos vel aliquem nostrum dare contiguit, hoc tamen salvo quod si aliquis nostrum cum pressoraverit aisinum alicuius, fata ipsi nuncio vel ipsis nunciis dictarum ecclesiarum illam decimam colligentibus nunciaverit vel nunciari fecerit infra villam de Crespiaco, ut decimam quam solvere voluerit, recipiant vel recipiat et ille vel illi non venerint seu venire distulerint ad illam decimam recipiendam, ille nostrum quicumque fuerit postquam nuncium vel nuncios predictos post dictam nunciatremus[2] tantum expectaverit quod rationabiliter potuisset venisse dicti nuncii vel nuncius ipse extunc decimam vini quam tunc soluturus esset nuncio vel nunciis predictis, si presentes essent, tradet pressorario sine pressore fidelibus illius pressorarii pro ecclesiis memoratis et nomine earumdem debitor autem decime dictis pressorario vel pressore persolvendo liberabitur de ea quantitate decime quam dicti pressorarii vel pressorarius asseruerint vel asseruerit per juramentum suum se a dicto debitore recepisse. Ceterum si denunciacione vel expectatione predictis orta fuerit questio debitoris decime in juramento super hiis si licet si dicat rationabiliter expectasse et nunciasse ut dictum est stabitur et credetur dicti autem pressorarii vel pressorarius decimam

---

2 *Sic A*, *read* nunciaremus.

vini eis vel ei ut dictum est solutam servare tenebuntur bene et legitime per juramentum suum et eam reddere nuncio vel nunciis dictarum ecclesiarum cum eorumdem vel alterius eorum copia habuerint hoc tamen salvo dictis pressorariis quod si aliquo casu decima vel pars decime eis ut dictum est soluta consumpta vel diminuta vel deteriorata fuerit et ipsi per juramentum suum dixerint per culpam aut negligenciam eorum factum non fuisse super hoc stabitur eorum juramento dicti siquidem pressoriarii singulis annis in principio vindemiarum dictis ecclesiis apud Crespiacum tenebuntur facere fidelitatem cuius fidelitatis forma talis est quod pressorarii omni pressore prescencium et futurorum apud Crespiacum jurabunt super sancta presentibus nunciis dictarum ecclesiarum apud Crespiacum, quod ipsi pressorarii bene et legitime servabunt decimas vini ipsis pro dictis ecclesiis et nomine earumdem tradendum et quod eas reddent bona fide nuncio vel nunciis dictarum ecclesiarum cum eorumdem vel alterius eorum copia habuerint et quod scienter non sustinebunt dampnum fieri dictis ecclesiis in decimis dictarum ecclesiarum sibi tradendum in pressoriis supradictis et quod nuncio vel nunciis dictarum ecclesiarum dicent in reddicione dictarum decimarum qui et quantum eis tradiderint de decimis predictis quam fidelitatem nos tenemur facere fieri singulis annis in principio vindemiarum nunciis dictarum ecclesiarum in dicta villa ab omnibus et singulis pressorariis quos inposterum pressoria de Crespiaco presentia et futura custodire contigerit, ita tamen quod si aliqui de dictis pressorariis ad requisitionem nostram fidelitatem predictam facere recusaverint debitor decime illi pressorario persolvendo non liberabitur. Adjectum est etiam quod si vinum exiens de aisino in pressorium posito ad decime solutionem in dictis ecclesiis pleniore faciendi non sufficeret vel si aliquis aisinum suum pressorari non faceret ille quicunque esset de equivalenti vino decimam dictis ecclesiis perfacere et solvere teneretur secundum quantitatem tocius vini quod exierit vel exire poterit bona fide de illo aisino et de tota gutta predicta quod si de valore vini de quo preficeretur solucio ut dictum est questio moveretur juramento vinum solucionis super dicto valore traderetur. Tenentur autem dicte ecclesie ponere singulis annis ad dictam decimam communiter recipiendo servienti ad sufficientem qui dictis ecclesiis singulis annis in principio vindemiarum apud Crespiacum fidelitatem facient maiore et duobus vel tribus de juratis de Crespiaco si interesse voluerint presentibus fore autem dicte fidelitatis tale erit quod ipsi servientes jurabunt super sancta quod bona fide expedient homines dicte ville de Crespiaco super receptione decimarum predictarum nec hoc dimittent gratia, odio vel timore. Hanc autem compositionem et pacem nos et singuli nostrum promittimus bene et fideliter nos observaturi imperpetuum et ad eandem composicionem et pacis observanciam nos successores et heredes nostros imperpetuum obligantes non obstante aliquo usu sive aliqua consuetudine precedente. In cuius rei testimonium presentes litteras sigilli communitatis nostre emisimus munimine roboratas. Actum anno Domini M° CCC° quadragesimo nono, mense augusto.

TABLE OF CONTENTS: VERSIGNY

A. Cartulary of Prémontré, fol. 43r.

178

1143

Barthélemy,[1] *bishop of Laon, after having recounted the circumstances of Norbert [of Xanten]'s foundation of Prémontré and the lands that Barthélemy had previously ceded to him, adds to his first gifts three* carrucatae *of cultivated and uncultivated land at Anizy,*[2] *Chevregny,*[3] *and Versigny,*[4] *in exchange for an annual* census *of two* solidi. *(See **179**.)*

A. Cartulary of Prémontré, fol. 43r.

B. Original, AD Aisne, H 841, previously sealed.

EDITION: Le Paige, *Bibliotheca*, 372–3; Delancy, *Historia Fusniacensis Coenobii, Ordinis Cisterciensis*, 85–6 (partial); Melleville, *DH*, vol. 2, 230–1; Florival, *Étude historique sur le XIIe siècle*, 387–8 (partial); Grauwen, "Lijst van oorkonden waarin Norbertus wordt genoemd," 168 (partial); Dufour-Malbezin, *Actes*, 337–8; *Chartae Galliae*, no. 208373, http://telma.irht.cnrs.fr/outils/chartae-galliae/charte208373/.

Karta Bartolomei episcopi Laudunensis de domo de Vercigni.

[I]n nomine sancte et individue Trinitatis. Ego Bartholomeus, Dei patientia Laudunensis ecclesie minister indignus. Sancte rectores ecclesie, quanto ceteris dignitate et honore videntur preminere tanto lucidius ac firmius que statuunt et disponunt debent diffinire. Notum igitur fieri volumus tam futuris quam

1 Barthélemy de Jur (d. 1158), son of Conon, lord of Grandson and La Sarraz, and Ada de Roucy; first subdeacon and then treasurer of Reims, later bishop of Laon, 1113–51.
2 Anizy-le-Château, arr. Laon, https://dicotopo.cths.fr/places/P86940236.
3 Chevregny, cant. Anizy-le-Château, https://dicotopo.cths.fr/places/P06529464.
4 Versigny, cant. La Fère, https://dicotopo.cths.fr/places/P17885640.

presentibus quod anno incarnationis dominice M° C° XX° vir spectabilis religionis Norbertum nomine per episcopatum nostrum transire contigerit cuius agnoscentes sanctitatem honestatem atque facundiam multis eum precibus coegimus ut apud nos hiemaret, quem quanto amplius loquentem audivimus et familiarem nobis astrinximus tanto magis boni odoris eius flagrantia referti sumus, deinde iam fere transacta hieme[5] cum vir ille sanctus a nobis vellet recedere, a personis ecclesie nostre et aquam pluribus episcopatus nostri nobilibus rogati sumus quamvis et hoc satis desideraremus, ut eum in nostra dyocesi[6] alicubi ad serviendum Deo collocaremus. Quod vix tandem divina gratia cooperante ab ipso impetravimus. Nostrarum igitur perlustrantes[7] possessionum ad locum valde desertum qui Premonstratus dicitur tunc temporis inhabitabilem venimus. Quem vir Domini considerans locum inquit video secundum cor meum a Deo michi ante omnia[8] preparatum. Hoc igitur audientes, gavisi sumus gaudio magno, et ipsum ibidem cum paucis Christiani pauperibus loco illi terminis inpositis, sicut in primo ipsorum privilegio continetur, ad commanendum ordinavimus. Volebat autem sepefatus vir cum fratribus suis ut de laboribus manuum suarum viveretur; quod nos, inpossibile considerantes, dedimus eis tres terre carrucatas, unam ad Anisi, aliam in Capriniaco Monte, terciam ad Vercigni.[9] Succedente vero tempore domino Norberto in episcopatum subrogato et domino Hugone Premonstrate ecclesie regimen adepto, ampliato fratrum numero ipsorum nimie paupertati conpatientes apud prefatum Verciniacum[10] aliam carrucatam partim de culta, maiori tamen parte de inculta sub censu duorum solidorum in festo Sancti Remigii mihi et successoribus meis persolvendorum superaddidimus. Hec superadditio facta est a nobis et confirmata anno dominice incarnationis M° C° XL° III°, epacta XXII[a], concurrente III°, indictione VI[a]. Signum mei ipsius Bartholomei episcopi, Widonis[11] decani, Bartholomei[12] et ceteri. Quicumque hanc nostre devotionis elemosinam auferre vel inminuere temptaverit nisi resipiscat anathema sit. Ego Bartholomeus[13,14] relegi.

5 hyeme *B*.

6 diocesi *B*.

7 terminos *B*.

8 *Om.* tempora *A*.

9 Vercini *B*.

10 Verceniacum *B*.

11 Guy de Pierrepont, son of Roger, lord of Pierrepont, and Ermengarde, lady of Montaigu, was first treasurer, archdeacon and dean of the chapter of Laon, and later bishop of Châlons, 1144–7.

12 thesaurarii et archidiaconi et cancellarii, Milonis cantoris, Roberti de Terigei, Odonis de Capriniaco, Henrici, Nicolai canonicorum *B*.

13 *Om.* cancellarius *A*.

14 Barthélemy de Montcornet (d. 1175), son of Hugues de Montcornet and Béatrice de Reynel, was archdeacon of Laon from 1133, treasurer of Laon from 1137, and chancellor of Laon, 1141–4; later archdeacon of Reims; and bishop of Beauvais, 1162–75. Guyotjeannin, *Episcopus*, 131; Dufour-Malbezin, *Actes*, 30.

179

1145

Barthélemy,[1] *bishop of Laon, gives to the church of Prémontré an annual* census *of two* solidi, *one* carrucata *of land at Versigny, and a meadow, part of which is in Versigny*[2] *and the other part in the pasture held by the inhabitants of Versigny, who consent to the gift along with Sarracin,*[3] *castellan of La Fère. (See* ***178****.)*

A. Cartulary of Prémontré, fols. 43r–43v.

B. Original, AD Aisne, H 841, previously sealed.

EDITION: Dufour-Malbezin, *Actes*, 364–5; *Chartae Galliae*, no. 208513, http://telma.irht.cnrs.fr/outils/chartae-galliae/charte208513/.

REGISTER: Florival, *Étude historique sur le XIIe siècle*, 391; Grauwen, "Lijst van oorkonden waarin Norbertus wordt genoemd," 170.

Item karta eiusdem episcopi de terris acquisitis apud Verciniacum.

[I]n nomine sancte et individue Trinitatis. Episcopalis officii est subjectorum sibi paci et quieti providere et res usibus eorum necessarias, ne ab aliquo in posterum minui possint, scripto commendare ac sigillis roborare. Iccirco ego Bartholomeus, Dei gratia Laudunensis episcopus, notum fieri volo tam futuris quam presentibus dedisse me Premonstratensi ecclesie, tempore domini Norberti, viri spectabilis religionis, carrucatam terre in territorio de Vercigni. Succedente vero tempore, multiplicati fratres, partim a silva purgando, partim ab hominibus qui eam hereditario jure possidebant emendo, assensu ac voluntate mea, tantum ibidem terre acquisierunt, quod circa tres carrucatas, adjuncta suprascripta carrucata, ibi possidere visi sunt. Dedi quoque quoddam pratum ecclesie supradicte, cuius pars in prenominata terra erat, pars vero in pascua hominum ville, concedentibus eisdem hominibus et Sarraceno, Ferie castellano, qui partem se in eo habere dicebat. Ministeriales autem mei iamdictam terram et pratum, presentibus nonnullis legitimis hominibus, bonnis terminaverunt et presbiter Walterus, in plena ecclesia, precepto meo, anathematis vinculo innodavit omnes qui easdem bonnas ultra removere auderent, et de

1 Barthélemy de Jur (d. 1158), son of Conon, lord of Grandson and La Sarraz, and Ada de Roucy; first subdeacon and then treasurer of Reims, later bishop of Laon, 1113–51.

2 Versigny, cant. La Fère, https://dicotopo.cths.fr/places/P17885640.

3 Sarracin, castellan of La Fère (from 1133) and of Laon (from 1166); brother of Geoffroi de Condren, knight, and Hugues *le Captif* de Venuil, husband of Helvide. Newman, *Seigneurs*, vol. 2, 203–4.

sepefata terra dampnum fratribus facere presumerent vel verbum inde, quod eis nocere posset, inciperent. Solventur vero michi et successoribus meis a fratribus pro superius memorata terra et prato duo solidi census in festo Sancti Remigii. Siquidem fratres, me volente, in curte sua, que ibi erat, capellam edificaverunt, ut in ea mei ac successorum meorum memoria in orationibus haberetur, quotiens ibidem vel missa celebraretur, vel alie orationes a fratribus fierent, in cuius dedicatione excommunicationem, quam presbiter fecerat, renovavi totamque terram, sicuti eam tenebant, quemadmodum iam feceram, iterum ecclesie concessi scripturequc tradi volui atque sigilli mei impressione signavi hominesque, qui ad hoc factum presentes fuerunt, subnotari precepi. Quorum hec sunt nomina: Bartholomeus[4] thesaurarius, Arnulphus[5] clericus cognomento Episcopus, Robertus capellanus, Petrus Berardus,[6] Walterus sacerdos de Vercigni,[7] et ceteri.[8] Actum anno gratie[9] M° C° XL° V°, epacta XV[a],[10] indictione VIII[a],[11] concurrente septimo.[12]

180

August, 1207.

Renaud,[1] *bishop-elect of Laon,* magister *Gobert, and Hector, canon of Laon, make known that in their presence Eudes, Raoul, and Robert conceded that the church of Prémontré received an alms gift of a house at La Fère*[2] *from Rohard and his unnamed wife. The three men take the house on an emphyteutic*[3] *lease for an annual* census *of 20* solidi Parisiensium.

4 Barthélemy de Montcornet (d. 1175), son of Hugues de Montcornet and Béatrice de Reynel, was archdeacon of Laon from 1133, treasurer of Laon from 1137, and chancellor of Laon, 1141–4; later archdeacon of Reims; and bishop of Beauvais, 1162–75. Guyotjeannin, *Episcopus*, 131; Dufour-Malbezin, *Actes*, 30.

5 Arnoul *Episcopus*, cleric and brother of Garnier, appears as a witness in episcopal acts, 1136–47. Dufour-Malbezin, *Actes*, 270, 459.

6 Pierre Berard is attested in episcopal acts, 1132–45. Dufour-Malbezin, *Actes*, 213, 365.

7 Vercenni *B*.

8 *Add.* et ceteri *A*; Hirbodo medicus, Robertus villicus de Vercenni, Falco decanus, Walbertus et Robertus et Gereverus et Wihardus scabini, Jozo villicus, Radulphi Canis, Henricus villicus de Rogercurt, Gerardus prepositus, Odo filius Leogardis, Amisardu[s] del Meis, multi etiam vicinorum de Vercenni et de Rogercurt *B*.

9 *Add.* gratie *A*; incarnationis dominice *B*.

10 XV *B*.

11 VIII *B*.

12 VII[a] *B*.

1 Renaud Surdelle, bishop of Laon, 1207–10.

2 La Fère, arr. Laon, https://dicotopo.cths.fr/places/P73165961.

3 A type of long-term lease agreement.

A. Cartulary of Prémontré, fol. 43v.
B. Original BnF, Coll. Picardie 290, no. 22, previously sealed.
REGISTER: *Studium Baldwin*, fiche 2341.

Quorum apud Faram debentur nobis XX^ti solidorum Parisiensium pro domo.

[R]enaldus,[4] Dei gratia Laudunensis electus, et magister Gobertus et Hector canonicus Laudunensis, omnibus presentes litteras inspecturis salutem in Domino. Noverit universitas vestra quod cum inter ecclesiam Premonstratensem et Odonem et Radulphum[5] et Robertum super quadam domo in Castro Fare sita, quam ex elemosina Rohardi et uxoris sue predicta ecclesia ad se pertinere proponebat, coram nobis auctoritate apostolica questio verteretur, tandem, partibus in nostra presentia constitutis, predicti homines elemosinam predicte ecclesie legitime factam in judicio recognoverunt et eam approbaverunt et siquid juris habebant, penitus quitaverunt, predictam domum sub pensione viginti solidorum Parisiensium singulis annis in festo Omnium Sanctorum eidem ecclesie persolvendorum, nomine enphitheosis perpetuo a predicta ecclesia recipientes. Insuper promiserunt contra omnes qui ad justiciam venire et juri parere voluerint, se legitimam warandiam perpetuis temporibus portaturos nec aliquam warandiam a predicta ecclesia sepedicti homines vel eorum heredes requirere poterunt, aut super hoc molestare. Adjectum est etiam in contractu prenominate enphitheosis quod si predicti viginti[6] solidi statuto termino non fuerint persoluti, sepedicti homines reddent pensionem et, lege qua vivunt, emendabunt. Quod si forte hoc facere neglexerint post monitionem et requisitionem ecclesie, sepedicta ecclesia ad predictam domum libere redire poterit et eam possidere. Ad hec ecclesia de consensu predictorum hominum retinet optionem utrum, eis cessantibus in solutione predicte pensionis, ad domum predictam velit habere recursum an ad res et possessiones eorumdem hominum velit se tenere de pensione singulis annis persolvenda. Ad hoc enim omnia bona sua predicte ecclesie obligarunt et in contravadium posuerunt. Ut autem hec rata et inconcussa permaneant, presentem paginam sigillorum nostrorum munimine duximus confirmandam. Actum anno verbi incarnati M^o CC^o VII,[7] mense augusto.

4 Reinaldus *B*.
5 Radulfum *B*.
6 XX^ti *B*.
7 VII° *B*.

181

1156

Gilbert,[1] *abbot of Saint-Nicolas-aux-Bois, concedes to the church of Prémontré land contiguous to Premonstratensian lands at Faisseleu*[2] *for a* census *of two* solidi. *Gilbert acknowledges also an exchange of land between Saint-Nicolas and Prémontré in which Saint-Nicolas receives land at But*[3] *next to one of its* curia, *in return for giving Prémontré two pieces of land near its* curia *at Versigny.*[4]

A. Cartulary of Prémontré, fol. 43v.

B. Original (chirograph), AD Aisne, H 841, previously sealed with a double strip of parchment. In the right margin and beginning at the top, the lower half of the letters that form the words CIROGRAPHU[M] PAX CHRISTI SIT SEMP[ER] NOBISCUM.

Concambium inter ecclesiam Premonstratensem et ecclesiam Sancti Nicholaum.

[I]n nomine sancte et individue Trinitatis. Notum sit tam futuris quam presentibus quod ecclesia Sancti Nicholai de Silva habebat de dote altaris de Verciniaco quandam terram, partim cultam, partim incultam, contiguam terre que dicitur de Faiseleu, quam episcopus Bartholomeus in elemosinam Premonstratensi dederat ecclesie. Hanc siquidem terram concessit Premonstrate ecclesie domnus[5] Gislebertus, abbas Sancti Nicholai, assensu capituli sui sub annotatione census duorum solidorum bone monete in nativitate Sancti Johannis Baptiste solvendorum. De qua etiam terra decima dabitur prefate ecclesie de eo quod in ea laboratum fuerit. Sed et concambium annotare studuimus quod inter utramque ecclesiam factum est de quadam terra quam habebat Premonstratensi[6] ecclesia juxta curiam Sancti Nicholai que dicitur Aldinbus[7] pro duabus particulis terre eiusdem Sancti Nicholai, que vicine erant curie Premonstratensis[8] apud Verciniacum. Cuius rei testes sunt: Fulco monachus de

1 Gilbert, abbot of the Benedictine abbey of Saint-Nicolas-aux-Bois, 1134–ca. 1157. Duval, "Histoire de l'abbaye bénédictine de Saint-Nicolas-aux-Bois, diocèse de Laon, première partie," 181–96.

2 Today Saint-Jean, comm. Versigny, https://dicotopo.cths.fr/places/P23491878.

3 But, comm. Andelain, https://dicotopo.cths.fr/places/P24052391.

4 Versigny, cant. La Fère, https://dicotopo.cths.fr/places/P17885640.

5 dompnus *B*.

6 Premonstrata *B*.

7 Aldimbus *B*.

8 Premonstrate *B*.

Aldinbus,[9] Robertus maior de Verciniaco, Falco decanus, Gualbertus et ceteri.[10] Et sic omnia quecumque habebant utreque ecclesie in territorio illo sub his testibus paccata sunt et discreta ut amodo quicumque custodes in curiis illis succedant, altercari non debeant nec inter utramque ecclesiam occasionem discordie ministrare. Actum anno Domini[11] M° C° LVI°.[12]

9 Aldimbus *B*.

10 *Add.* et ceteri *A*; Gerardus, Gervierus scabini, Henricus maior domini Sarraceni, Joszo maior Radulfi Canis, Geruldus et Amasardus *B*.

11 Actum ab incarnatione Domini anno *B*.

12 L° VI° *B*.

TABLE OF CONTENTS: FERRIÈRES

A. Cartulary of Prémontré, fol. 44v.

Incipiunt scripta de Ferieres cum appenditiis suis.

I Karta Rogeri episcopi Laudunensis de paccata controversia inter ecclesiam Premonstratensis et Gobertum de Firmitate.

II Item karta Rogeri episcopi de nemore eiusdem Goberti quod dicitur Taillegueule et de tribus modiis frumenti.

III Scriptum episcopi Laudunensis de libertate curie de Ferieres.

IIII Cirographum Hugonis abbatis Premonstratensis de Heslino.

V Carta Johannis militis de Kahaire.

VI Scriptum officialis Laudunensis de elemosina Roberti de Fai.

VII Item scriptum officialis Laudunensis de terra Johannis de Sartellis.

VIII Scriptum curie Laudunensis de terra Adam Coquel.

IX Carta domini Willermi de Wiege de terra Anselmi de Fai.

X De concambio quarundam terrarum inter nos et monachos Sancti Nicholai de Ribodimonte.

XI Privilegium Remensis archiepiscopi de decimis et terragiis ecclesie de Dorenc et de grangia Rainbaldi Fontis cum novalibus de Firmitate.

XII Item karta episcopi Laudunensis super desponsationibus sororis Goberti militis.

Cirographum inter ecclesiam Premonstratensis et Humolariensis.

Carta domini Goberti de Firmitate de elemosina terragii cuiusdam campi siti intra quandam culturam Sancti Vincentii.

182

1182

Roger,[1] *bishop of Laon, confirms that Gobert*[2] *de la Ferté agreed to resolve his dispute with the church of Prémontré, giving permission to Prémontré to increase its* curtis *at Ferrières*[3] *without prejudicing its access to the mill of Archantré.*[4] *Gobert's wife Marguerite*[5] *and daughter Brémunde approve of the resolution.*

---

1 Roger de Rozoy, son of Clérembaud, lord of Rozoy, and Elizabeth de Namur, was bishop of Laon, 1175–1207.

2 Gobert, lord of La Ferté-Chèvresis (or La Ferté-Blihard), son of Bliard, lord of La Ferté-Chevresis, and Brémonde, became a vassal of the lords of Coucy between 1182 and 1184 and married Marguerite, a niece of Raoul I, lord of Coucy. Barthélemy, *LDA*, 112; Melleville, *DH*, vol. 1, 382.

3 Ferrières, comm. La Ferté-Chevresis, https://dicotopo.cths.fr/places/P96262032.

4 Archantré, comm. Remies, https://dicotopo.cths.fr/places/P18258469.

5 Marguerite, niece of Raoul I, lord of Coucy. Barthélemy, *LDA*, 112.

A. Cartulary of Prémontré, fol. 44v.
B. Original (chirograph), AN, L 995, no. 42, previously sealed. In the left margin and beginning at the top, the upper half of letters that form the word CYROGRAPHUM.

Karta Rogeri episcopi Laudunensis de paccata controversia inter ecclesiam Premonstratensem et Gobertum de Firmitate.

[I]n nomine Domini. Ego Rogerus, Dei gratia Laudunensis episcopus, notum facimus per hoc scriptum quod Gobertus de Firmitate movit controversiam contra ecclesiam Premonstrati dicens quod fratres apud Ferieres[6] morantes curiam suam dilataverant ulterius quam pater eius ipsis concessisset, dicens quod eo invito et ultra concessionem patris sui terras in dominio suo acquisierant et eas colere presumebant, dicens etiam quod ad molendina eorum de Erchentre[7] jus habebat in ripis super quibus omnibus talem coram nobis concordiam inierunt. Clausuram curie de Ferieres,[8] sicut modo est, laudavit Gobertus in perpetuum ab omni exactione et consuetudine penitus absolutam. Claudere etiam poterunt curiam suam muro, X pedes de terra plana habente cum cumulo. Concessit quod omnes terras quas in dominio suo acquisierant usque modo in libera pace teneant in perpetuum. Remisit etiam nomine elemosine jus illud quod vendicabat in ripis ad predicta molendina de Erchentre[9] ita tamen quod aqua molendinorum consideratione fratrum et bonorum virorum loco domini Goberti qui in huius modi mensuris sunt periti, tenebitur eo modo quod sine inpedimento et dampno molendinorum parcatur, si fieri potest, pratis et pasturis. Si vero sine dampno molendinorum fieri non potuerit ita per eos ordinetur quod molendina remaneant sine dampno. Concessit etiam ecclesie Premonstratensi in elemosinam pasturas suas et aisentias pro curte de Walescourt[10,11] ita liberas sicut fratres de Ferieres[12] pro curte sua eas habere noscuntur. Remisit eis omnes querelas quas adversus eos usque modo habuerat et concessit quod omnes terras quas usque ad diem huius pacis acquisierant libere teneant in perpetuum. In dominio tamen eius nullas amodo terras acquirere poterunt sine eius assensu. Condictum est etiam inter eos quod siquis super hiis que in dominio eius habent querelam adversus eos

6 Ferrieres *B*.
7 Herchentré *B*.
8 Ferrieres *B*.
9 Herchentré *B*.
10 Walescurt *B*.
11 Valécourt, comm. Chevresis-Monceau, https://dicotopo.cths.fr/places/P14207928.
12 Ferrieres *B*.

moverit, venient ante eum per amorem ut componat inter eos si potuerit; si non potuerit ibunt libere ad justiciam quo debebunt. Et ipse Gobertus erit eis warandus et auxiliator bona fide. Omnia ista sicut supradicta sunt concessit ecclesie supradicte in elemosinam sollempniter coram nobis, assensu uxoris sue Margarete et filie sue Braimundis. Sub testimonio Roberti decani Laudunensis, Hugonis[13] abbatis Sancti Vincentii, Ingelranni[14] abbatis Sancti Johannis et ceteri.[15] Ut igitur concessiones iste firme permaneant, nos eas sigillo nostro et prescriptorum testimonio confirmamus; Gobertus etiam sigillum suum ad maius robur apposuit. Actum anno Domini M° C° LXXX° II°. Ego Willermus[16] cancellarius scripsi.

183

1184

Roger,[1] *bishop of Laon, makes known the arrangements by which Gobert [I],*[2] *lord of La Ferté-Chevresis, gave to the church of Prémontré his forest of Taillegueule, near Ferrières,*[3] *for the collection of wood, in exchange for half of what Prémontré clears and collects. Gobert also cedes to Prémontré three* modii *of grain (*frumentum*), measure of Ferrières, to be taken from his* terragium *at La Ferté-Chevresis. Gobert's wife Marguerite*[4] *and daughter Brémunde approve the gifts. Raoul [I], lord of Coucy, also consents. (See **193**.)*

A. Cartulary of Prémontré, fols. 44v–45r.

---

13 Hugues, abbot of the Benedictine abbey of Saint-Vincent de Laon, 1174–1205. *GC* IX, cols. 579–81.

14 Enguerrand, abbot of the Benedictine abbeys of Nogent-sous-Coucy, 1157–ca. 1160, and of Saint-Jean de Laon, 1161–82. *GC* IX, col. 607; Taïée, "L'abbaye de Saint-Jean de Laon," 217.

15 *Add.* et ceteri *A*; Radulfi abbatis Sancti Nicholai de Pratis, Johannis abbatis de Nongento, Walteri abbatis Sancti Martini Laudunensi, Gregorii abbatis Thenoliensis, Radulfi de Cociaco, Radulfi de Husel, Johannis fratris eius, Radulfi de Sarto, Arnulfi de Moncellis, Balduini de Cheri, et Willemi cognomento Monachi, Roberti de Rogiscurt, Guidonis de Husel *B*.

16 Willelmus *B*.

---

1 Roger de Rozoy, son of Clérembaud, lord of Rozoy, and Elizabeth de Namur, was bishop of Laon, 1175–1207.

2 Gobert I, lord of La Ferté-Chèvresis (or La Ferté-Blihard), son of Bliard, lord of La Ferté-Chevresis, and Brémonde, became a vassal of the lords of Coucy between 1182 and 1184 and married Marguerite, a niece of Raoul I, lord of Coucy. Barthélemy, *LDA*, 112; Melleville, *DH*, vol. 1, 382.

3 Ferrières, comm. La Ferté-Chevresis, https://dicotopo.cths.fr/places/P96262032.

4 Marguerite, niece of Raoul I, lord of Coucy. Barthélemy, *LDA*, 112.

B. Original (chirograph), AN, L 995, no. 45, previously sealed. In the right margin and beginning on the top, the lower half of the letters that form the word CYROGRAPHUM.

EDITION: Martin-Marville, *Trosly-Loire ou le Trosly des conciles, ses chateaux, ses villas, ses fiefs et ses seigneurs*, 230–1.

Karta eiusdem de nemore que dicitur Taillegeule et de tribus modiis frumenti.

I[]n nomine sancte et individue Trinitatis. Ego Rogerus, Dei gratia Laudunensis episcopus, notum fieri volo tam futuris quam presentibus quod Gobertus, dominus de Firmitate, nemus suum quod dicebatur Taillegueule[5] quod ex jure paterno habebat, juxta curiam de Ferrariis, per manum nostram dedit Premonstratensi ecclesie, ut fratres Premonstratenses illud sartarent et terram in qua nemus ipsum fuerat, sicut metis ipsius nemoris positis determinatum est, in perpetuum possiderent et excolerent, ea tamen conditione ut prefati fratres medietatem frugum predicte terre eidem Goberto redderent, separata primitus decime garba et garba messoris, partemque eiusdem Goberti vel apud Firmitatem vel apud Chievresi[6] vecturis suis transportari facerent. Tempore autem messis quando ipsius Goberti pars separanda erit ac reddenda, fratres nunciabunt ministeriali eius aut heredum ipsius apud Firmitatem ut veniat illuc et eam suscipiat. Qui si quacumque de causa venire distulerit, fratres sine omni forisfacto partem eius a sua juste ac fideliter separabunt et, ut iam dictum est, duci facient tam ei quam heredibus eius post eum. Siquis vero fratres Premonstrati super predicta terra inquietare presumpserit, ipse Gobertus et post eum heres eius Premonstratensi ecclesie warandiam contra omnes inquietantes exhibebit. Testes huius rei Bernardus sacerdos, Radulphus[7] de Hursel,[8] Arnulphus[9] de Montigni,[10] Renerus[11,12] de Monciaus,[13] Balduinus[14] de Cheri,[15] Guillermus le

5 Talliguele *B*.

6 Chirurisei *B*.

7 Raoul I, lord of Housset, appears as a witness to acts, primarily of the lords of Coucy, between 1147 and 1187. Barthélemy, *LDA*, 519–20.

8 Husel *B*.

9 Arnoul de Montigny, nephew of Blihard de la Ferté, second husband of Adélaïde de Guise. Barthélemy, *LDA*, 523–4.

10 Montinnei *B*.

11 Reinerus *B*.

12 Renier de Monceau, son of Anselme de Marle and Adélaïde de Guise. Barthélemy, *LDA*. 525

13 Monces *B*.

14 Baldwuinus *B*.

15 Chirei *B*.

Moines,[16] Robertus de Rogescurt.[17] Hoc etiam recognitum fuit apud Calniacum[18] in presentia nostra virorumque nobilium, Radulphi videlicet, domini de Couci[19] qui hoc concessit ac laudavit, nam hoc de feodo eius erat, et Simonis de Amini,[20,21] Petri[22] de Ponte Sancti Medardi, Guidonis de Juvigni,[23,24] Adam de Trosli[25,26] qui recognitionis huius testes existunt. Sepedictus etiam Gobertus, extrema vite huius agens, tam pro eorum que Premonstratensi ecclesie violenter abstulerat restauratione quam pro anime sue redemptione dedit singulis annis ipsi ecclesie tres modios frumenti ad mensuram de Firmitate accipiendos in terragiis suis que redduntur ei a fratribus de Ferrariis.[27] Si vero predicta terragia infra ipsam curiam non fuerint reposita, prefati tres modii in suis apud Firmitatem accipientur molendinis. Pro faciendo etiam in Premonstratensi ecclesia anniversario suo singulis annis dedit ipsi ecclesie piscatores duos una die in aquis suis. Hec omnia concessit pariter atque laudavit uxor eius Margareta et filia eius Bremunda. Testes horum Galterus abbas de Sancto Martino, Bernardus sacerdos de Firmitate, Radulphus dominus de Couci[28] et ceteri.[29] Ut autem cuncta hec Premonstratensi ecclesie rata semper atque inmota consistant inconvulsisque radicibus in perpetuum quieta permaneant dignum esse judicavimus ac necessarium et presentis cirographi[30] annotari[31] conscriptione et sigilli nostri monimento ad perpetuam stabilitatem muniri ac roborare. Actum est hoc anno incarnationis dominice M° C° LXXX° quarto.[32]

16 li Mones *B*.
17 Rogécourt, cant. La Fère, https://dicotopo.cths.fr/places/P89159573.
18 Chalneiacum *B*.
19 Cocei *B*.
20 Symonis de Amminnei *B*.
21 Simon I, lord of Amigny, ca. 1178–84. Melleville, *DH*, vol. 1, 21.
22 Pierre de Pont-Saint-Mard appears as a witness in acts associated with the Coucy family ca. 1163–ca. 1190. Newman, *Seigneurs*, vol. 2, 119.
23 Juvinnei *B*.
24 Juvigny, cant. Soissons, https://dicotopo.cths.fr/places/P97496070.
25 Troslei *B*.
26 Trosly-Loire, cant. Coucy-le-Château, https://dicotopo.cths.fr/places/P24780558.
27 *Om.* et hoc quando reponentur infra curiam de Ferrariis *A*.
28 Cocei *B*.
29 *Add.* et ceteri *A*; Radulphus de Husel, Arnulphus de Montinnei, Balduwinus de Chirei, Bernardus prepositus *B*.
30 cyrographi *B*.
31 adnotari *B*.
32 IIII° *B*.

184

1147

Barthélemy,[1] bishop of Laon, makes known that Bliard,[2] lord of La Ferté-Chevresis, transferred a piece of land for the construction of a free curia *with all the usual rights, including rights of sale, to the church of Prémontré. Bliard's wife Brémunde, daughters Ada and Elizabeth, son Raoul, and other heirs approve, as does Raoul [I], count of Vermandois.*

A. Cartulary of Prémontré, fols. 45r–45v.

B^1. Original (chirograph), AN, L 995, no. 13, previously sealed with a double strip of leather. In the left margin and beginning at the top, the upper half of the letters that form the word CYROGRAPHUM. (This charter likely belonged to Prémontré.)

B^2. Original (chirograph), AD Aisne, H 800, previously sealed. In the right margin and beginning at the top, the bottom half of the letters that form the word CYROGRAPHUM. (This charter likely belonged to either the Bishop of Laon or Bliard and Brémunde de la Ferté, based on dorsal annotations.)

EDITION: Bretonnier, *Oeuvres De M. Claude Henrys*, vol. 1, 112–13; Dufour-Malbezin, *Actes*, 397–8; *Chartae Galliae*, no. 208781, http://telma.irht.cnrs.fr/outils/chartae-galliae/charte208781/.

REGISTER: Florival, *Étude historique sur le XIIe siècle*, 397.

Scriptum episcopi Laudunensis de libertate curie de Ferieres.

[I]n nomine sancte et individue Trinitatis. Quia successu defluentium temporum facile prolabimur in oblivionem preteritorum, que memoriter retineri volumus, scripto commendare solemus. Igitur ego Bartholomeus, Dei gratia Laudunensis episcopus, notum facio futuris et presentibus quod Bliardus[3] de Firmitate quandam terram incultam hereditarie possidebat juxta eandem Firmitatem quam pro XXX[ta] libris bone monete Premonstratensi[4] ecclesie perpetuo dedit excolendam ad terragium pro nona[5] garba preter garbam decime et messoris. Est autem inter divisiones terre illius quedam terra culta de qua reddetur IIII[a]

1 Barthélemy de Jur (d. 1158), son of Conon, lord of Grandson and La Sarraz, and Ada de Roucy; first subdeacon and then treasurer of Reims, later bishop of Laon, 1113–51.

2 Bliard de La Ferté-Chevresis, son of Baudouin de Soupir and Cécile, and brother or half-brother of Guy de Soupir. Morelle, "Une charte nuptiale laonnoise de 1158 conservée en original," 222, fn. 64.

3 Blihardus B^1, B^2.

4 Premonstrate B^1, B^2.

5 IX[na] B^1, B^2.

garba. Utramque vero dedit liberam ab omni exactione sicut eam possidebat in dominio, quinque[6] carrucatas unamquamque habentem decem et octo[7] modios sementis ad mensuram de Firmitate, sed et terram quantum duobus[8] modiis seritur ad construendam curiam concessit liberam ab omni consuetudine, winagio, rotagio, theoloneo, districto omnique justicia et duas[9] lanceatas in circuitu ad munitionem curie. Quod si de quinque[10] carrucatis defuerit, juxta quod minus habebitur de terra predicta pecunia rehabebit ecclesia, ita quod non a Bliardo[11] recipietur sed a terragio. Si vero quinque[12] carrucatis dimidia superfuerit, solum terragium dabitur et nichil pecunie sed si usque ad unius vel plurium perfectionem excreverit et fratres habere voluerint eo tenore dabitur ut quantum pecunie et terragii datum est pro una vel pluribus tantum detur pro altera vel pluribus. Et siquis eos inde inquietaverit qui justiciam exequi velit, Bliardus[13] in episcopatu nostro pro ipsis placitabit. Quod si liberare nequiverit, de terra sua viciniore restaurabit. Qui vero a justicia subterfugerint, ipsos ipse sicut ecclesia persequetur. Tempore autem messis quam terragiam recipiendum erit, fratres nuntiabunt ministro domini Blihardi; qui si venire distulerit, fratres sine forisfacto terragium separabunt et ad Firmitatem ducent. Concessit etiam ipse Blihardus fratribus omnem in castro suo et terra sua libertatem in emendo et vendendo omnemque vicinitatem terre que sui juris est in pascuis, rivis, silvis et ceteris commoditatibus, que eis erunt necessarie sicut nobilibus et ignobilibus qui infra dominium eius et Firmitatem manent et manebunt et exitum sufficientem de curia usque ad publicam viam. Terram etiam Sancte Marie de Humolariis[14] concessit eis sed aliam terram cuiuscumque sancti vel sancte vel clerici aut que ad dominium castri de Firmitate appendat nisi assensu eius abbati vel fratribus eiusdem curie non licebit acquirere. Factum est autem hoc assensu uxoris sue Bremundis et filii sui Radulphi[15] et filiarum suarum Ade et Elizabeth et aliorum heredum. Concessit etiam Radulphus,[16,17] Viromandensis comes, astantibus legitimis viris Roberto[18] capellano eius,

6 V^{que} *B*^{1}, *B*^{2}.

7 X^{cem} VIII^{to} *B*^{1}, *B*^{2}.

8 II^{obus} *B*^{1}; II^{bus} *B*^{2}.

9 II^{as} *B*^{1}, *B*^{2}.

10 V^{que} *B*^{1}, *B*^{2}.

11 Blihardo *B*^{1}, *B*^{2}.

12 V^{que} *B*^{1}, *B*^{2}.

13 Blihardus *B*^{1}, *B*^{2}.

14 The Benedictine abbey of Notre-Dame de Homblières.

15 Radulfi *B*^{1}, *B*^{2}.

16 Radulfus *B*^{1}, *B*^{2}.

17 Raoul I, count of Vermandois, Amiens, and Valois (d. 1152), was the son of Hugues I le Grand, count of Vermandois and Valois, and Adélaïde de Vermandois, and served as seneschal of France, 1131–51.

18 Robert, chaplain of Laon, appears as a witness to episcopal acts 1130–50. Dufour Malbezin, *Actes*, 215, 445.

Drogone[19] de Nigella, Symone[20] de Ribodimonte[21] et ceteri.[22] Quod ne aliquis infringere presumat sub anathemate interdicimus et ut inconvulsum permaneat sigilli nostri impressione et cyrographi conscriptione et legitimorum testium annotatione roboramus. Huius rei testes sunt: Clarembaldus[23] dominus de Vendeuil,[24] Robertus Vitulus,[25] Nicholaus[26] de Courlandum,[27] Radulphus[28,29] Canis et ceteri.[30] Actum anno incarnati verbi M° C° XL° VII°, epacta VII^{a},[31] indictione X^{a}, concurrente II°.

185

Mid-Twelfth Century[1]

Hugues [I/II], abbot of Prémontré, makes known to his brothers that Hellin, cleric of Saint-Feuillien and canon of Fosses, bought from Guiscard de La Ferté, for the church of Prémontré, one carrucata *of land, with the condition that Prémontré annually pay him six* modii *of grain (*frumentum*), measure of Saint-Quentin, until his death.*

---

19 Dreux de Nesle, knight, son of Raoul, lord of Nesle, and Raintrude. Newman, *Seigneurs*, vol. 1, 62.

20 Possibly Simon I, lord of Ribemont (d. aft. 1161), son of Geoffroi IV, lord of Ribemont. Melleville, *DH*, vol. 2, 277. He appears as a witness in acts of the Benedictine abbey of Homblières 1142–56. Newman, *Homblières*, 107, 111, 113, 126, 149.

21 Riboumunt *B*[1], *B*[2].

22 *Add.* et ceteri *A*; Gaufrido le Malvus *B1*; Gaufrido LeMalveis *B*[2].

23 Clérembaud III, lord of Vendeuil, ca. 1130–ca. 1153. Newman, *Homblières*, 120, fn. 3; Melleville, *DH*, vol. 2, 412.

24 Vendoil *B*[1], *B*[2].

25 Robert *Vitulus* (or le Veau), a knight of Coucy, also appears in **5** and **452**. Barthélemy, *LDA*, 155–6.

26 A Nicolas de Courlandon (cant. Fismes, https://dicotopo.cths.fr/places/P10603857) and his brother Hugues appear in an 1148 act of Barthélemy de Jur, bishop of Laon, and Samson Mauvoisin, archbishop of Reims. Dufour Malbezin, *Actes*, 418–19.

27 Curlandun *B*[1], *B*[2].

28 Radulfus *B*[1], *B*[2].

29 Raoul Chien (d. ca. 1191), son of Gautier de la Tournelle and Agnès, appears in episcopal acts from the 1140s and was particularly associated with the lords of Coucy. Barthélemy, *LDA*, 160; Morelle, "Une charte nuptiale laonnoise de 1158 conservée en original," 223, fn. 69.

30 *Add.* et ceteri *A*; Reinerus Curels, Benscelina soror prefati Blihardi et Gislebertus maritus eius, Letaldus Caseus, Gaufridus et Sarracenus et Hugo Captivus, fratres, Geroldus dapifer, Walterius filius Escot, Isaac, Arnulfus Libret *B*[1], *B*[2].

31 XVII^{a} *B*[1], *B*[2].

---

1 A Guichard de la Ferté appears in an 1165 act in the cartulary of Saint-Martin de Laon, suggesting an approximately mid-century date for this act. BM Laon, MS 532, 5r–6r.

A. Cartulary of Prémontré, fol. 45v.
B. Original not found.

Cirographum Hugonis abbatis Premonstratensis de Hellino clerico Sancti Foillani.

[E]go Hugo, Dei gratia Premonstratensis ecclesie dictus abbas, notum facio fratribus meis tam presentibus quam futuris quod Hellinus, clericus Sancti Foillani, Fossensis ecclesie canonicus, emit Premonstratensis ecclesie carrucatam terre a Guicardo de Firmitate contiguam terre nostre quam ibidem habemus, ea siquidem conditione ut singulis annis in festo Sancti Remigii a predicta ecclesia Premonstratensi persolventur ei sex modii frumenti ad mensuram Sancti Quintini quamdiu ipse vixerit et sibi placuerit vel, eo jubente, frumentum illud vendetur et quod inde accipi poterit, usque Fossas ab ecclesia sibi transmittetur. Si autem, Deo disponente, de mundo migraverit vel alibi conversus fuerit, sex illi modii frumenti Premonstratensi ecclesie in perpetuum erunt sic tamen quod ecclesia in suos usus expendet sicut ipse Hellinus disponet. Ipse autem alibi dimittere non poterit nisi Premonstratensi ecclesie. Ne vero tale beneficium quod pro remedio anime sue et predecessorum suorum ecclesie contulit, oblivioni traderetur, ego sigilli mei et sigilli capituli mei inpressione subsignavi cum hiis testibus Hugone priore, Johanne subpriore, Johanne Calvo et ceteri.

186

April, 1232.

Jean[1] der Kahaire *d'Origny, knight, transfers to the church of Prémontré four pieces of land located in the territory of Ferrières,*[2] *able to hold 20* galeti *minus 12* virgae *of seed grain, in exchange for an annual payment of four* modii *of grain (*bladus*).*

A. Cartulary of Prémontré, fol. 45v.
B. Original not found.

1 Jean *der Kahaire*, knight, lord of Origny-Sainte-Benoîte (cant. Ribemont, https://dicotopo.cths.fr/places/P14935952), ca. 1232–ca. 1248. Jean and his wife Mathilde appear in another transaction concerning Prémontré, ca. 1245–8. AD Aisne H 800; Demay, *Inventaire des sceaux de l'Artois et de la Picardie*, 46.

2 Ferrières, comm. La Ferté-Chevresis, https://dicotopo.cths.fr/places/P96262032.

Karta Johannis militis de Cahaire.

[I]n nomine Patris et Filii et Spiritus Sancti, amen. Ego Johannes dictus der Kahaire, de Aurigniaco miles, notum facio universis tam presentibus quam futuris quod, habita conventione inter me et ecclesiam Premonstratensem, tradidi eidem ecclesie ad modiagium et ad manum firmam quatuor petias terre mee quas habebam in territorio de Ferieres, continentes viginti galetas sementis ad virgam de Firmitate, duodecim virgis minus, pro quatuor modiis bladi sani et pagabilis ad mensuram de Firmitate currentem tempore huius scripti solvendis michi in perpetuum annuatim in domo eiusdem ecclesie de Ferieres predicta infra festum Omnium Sanctorum, nec tenetur ipsa ecclesia ducere ipsum bladum pro me vel successoribus meis extra dictam domum suam de Ferieres. Si vero ego vel heredes mei infra festum Omnium Sanctorum neglexerimus aut noluerimus recipere ipsum bladum, ex tunc de dampno et periculo et pejoratione ipsius bladi eadem ecclesia non tenebitur nobis in aliquo respondere sed totum dampnum et periculum et pejoratio redundabit in nobis. Et tam ego quam successores mei qui habere voluerint dictum modiagium, tenemur predictam terram eidem ecclesie fideliter warandire adversus omnes qui voluerint juri stare. Sciendum est preterea quod preditos IIII^{or} modios bladi ego vel heredes mei non poterimus dare in elemosinam alii ecclesie quam ecclesie Premonstrati. Et si forte voluerimus ipsum bladum vendere, nulli poterimus vendere ipsum nisi ecclesie memorate, dum tamen tantumdem voluerit inde dare quantum alius. In cuius rei testimonium et perpetuam firmitatem, presentem kartam dedi sepedicte ecclesie sigilli mei munimine roboratam. Actum mense aprili, anno gratie M^{o} CC^{o} tricesimo secundo.

187

August, 1231.

Jean du Temple,[1] officialis *of Laon, makes known that Robert de Fai gave in perpetual alms to the church of Prémontré a piece of arable land situated at the place called* La Broche Bouherei,[2] *able to hold 11* galeti *minus 10* virgae *of seed grain, measure of La Ferté-Chevresis. Ada, wife of Robert, approves the gift and relinquishes her rights over the land, including that of* dos, *in exchange for compensation.*

---

1 Jean du Temple, *officialis* of Laon, is attested ca. 1231–ca. 1235. BM Reims 1563 (N. Fonds), fol. 170v; AD Aisne, H 873, fols. 172r–172v, 262r. His appointment as *officialis* was the subject of a long-running dispute with the cathedral chapter of Laon. Picó, "Membership in the Cathedral Chapter of Laon, 1217–1238," 5, 19.

2 Likely the modern Les Broches, comm. Bertaucourt-Épourdon, https://dicotopo.cths.fr/places/P12836498.

A. Cartulary of Prémontré, fols. 45v–46r.
B. Original, AD Aisne, H 800, previously sealed.

Scriptum officialis Laudunensis de elemosina Roberti de Fai.

[U]niversis presentes litteras visuris magister Johannes de Templo, officialis Laudunensis, in Domino salutem. Noverit universitas vestra quod, constitutus in presentia nostra, Robertus de Fai contulit in elemosinam perpetuam ecclesie Premonstratensi ob remedium anime sue et animarum patris et matris ipsius quandam petiam terre arabilis que proveniebat ex hereditate sua, sicut dicebat, sitam loco qui dicitur La Broche Bouherei,[3] contiguam culture dicte ecclesie Premonstratensi, continentem, sicut dicitur, undecim galetos terre sementis, decem virgis minus ad mensuram de Firmitate Bliardi. Ada etiam, uxor prefati Roberti, dictam collationem coram nobis laudavit et approbavit et quicquid juris habebat in dicta petia terre, vel habere poterat, sive nomine dotis, sive alio modo, prefate Premonstratensi ecclesie spontanea et non coacta, sicut eadem dicebat, penitus in perpetuum quitavit condigna reconpensatione dotis sibi facta a dicto Roberto, marito suo, sicut eadem dicebat, ~~penitus ad perpetuum~~ ad unam modiatam terre site in territorio de Firmitate Bliardi et tam dictus Robertus quam eadem Ada fidem interposuerunt corporalem quod contra dictam collationem nullo tempore per se vel per alium venire presument. Et ad maiorem securitatem fide corporali prestita promisit dictus Robertus se legitimam portaturum garandiam dicte ecclesie Premonstratensi super petia terre antedicta contra omnes juri et justicie parere volentes. In cuius rei testimonium presentes litteras patentes emisimus sigillo Laudunensis curie roboratas. Actum anno gratie M° CC°[4] tricesimo primo, mense augusto.

188

The Octave of Christmas, 1232.

The officialis[1] *of Laon makes known that husband and wife Jean de Certeau*[2] *and Mathilde gave to the church of Prémontré three* galeti *of land in alms. They also sold to the church eight* galeti *minus 12 ¼* virgae *of land located near the house of Ferrières*[3] *that formed part of the inheritance of Mathilde and her*

3 Buherei *B*.
4 millesimo ducentesimo *B*.

1 Jean du Temple, *officialis* of Laon, is attested ca. 1231–ca. 1235. BM Reims 1563 (N. Fonds), fol. 170v; AD Aisne, H 873, fols. 172r–172v, 262r. His appointment as *officialis* was the subject of a long-running dispute with the cathedral chapter of Laon. Picó, "Membership in the Cathedral Chapter of Laon, 1217–1238," 5, 19.
2 Certeau, comm. Autremencourt, https://dicotopo.cths.fr/places/P49988823.
3 Ferrières, comm. La Ferté-Chevresis, https://dicotopo.cths.fr/places/P96262032.

daughter Ada, for 24 librae *and three* solidi Parisiensium. *Jean and Mathilde also granted Prémontré two pieces of land able to hold about nine* galeti *of seed grain, located between Malval and La Ferté-Chevresis.*[4] *Wiard, husband of Ada, also consents.*

A. Cartulary of Prémontré, fol. 46r.
B. Original, AD Aisne, H 800, previously sealed with a double strip of parchment.

Scriptum officialis Laudunensis de terra Johannis Sartellis.

[U]niversis fidelibus Christi presentem paginam inspecturis, officialis Laudunensis salutem in Domino. Noverint universi quod Johannes de Sartellis et Matildis,[5] uxor eius, in nostra presentia personaliter constituti, recognoverunt se partim dedisse in elemosinam, videlicet tres galetas et partim vendidisse, videlicet octo galetas terre duodecim virgis et quarta parte unius virge minus ad virgam de Firmitate, dedisse inquam et vendidisse ecclesie Premonstrati quandam petiam terre sitam, ut dicitur, prope domum de Ferieres infra territorium eiusdem domus, laudantibus et concedentibus ipsam elemosinam et ipsam venditionem Ada filia eiusdem Matildis[6] et Wiardo, marito eius, de quarum videlicet Matildis et Ade hereditate, ut dicitur, dicta terra descendit et hii omnes fidem corporaliter prestiterunt quod nec per se nec per alios dictam ecclesiam super terra predicta aliquatenus molestabunt nec querent artem nec ingenium per se vel per alios per que possit in posterum super hoc dicta ecclesia molestari. Sciendum est insuper quod dicti Johannes et Matildis,[7] uxor eius, de ipsa terra tenentur eidem ecclesie portare legitimam warandiam adversus omnes qui voluerint juri stare. Et ut de ipsa warandia dicta ecclesia reddatur magis secura, dicti Johannes et Matildis, uxor eius, assignaverunt eidem ecclesie duas petias terre continentes circiter novem galetas sementis sitas, ut dicitur, inter Maleval et Firmitatem Bliardi ad saisiendum eas, sicut suas, si defecerint de warandia portanda. Recognoverunt in super dicti Johannes de Sarcellis[8] et Matildis,[9] uxor eius, sibi esse plenarie satisfactum ab ecclesia Premonstrati de precio eiusdem terre, videlicet de viginti quatuor libris et tribus solidis Parisiensium monete. In cuius rei testimonium presentes litteras sigillo curie Laudunensis ad petitionem partium fecimus communiri, salvo jure domini Laudunensis et alieno. Actum anno Domini M° CC°[10] tricesimo secundo, infra octavas nativitatis Domini.

4 La Ferté-Chevresis, cant. Ribemont, https://dicotopo.cths.fr/places/P35438398.
5 Mathildis *B*.
6 Mathildis *B*.
7 Mathildis *B*.
8 Sartellis *B*.
9 Mathildis *B*.
10 millesimo ducentesimo *B*.

189

February, 1231.

Magister *Jean du Temple,*[1] officialis *of Laon, makes known that husband and wife Adam* Cokiaus *of La Ferté*[2] *and Ava sold to the church of Prémontré approximately eight* galeti *of land located at a place called the Assart of Pierre de Brissy, near Ferrières,*[3] *for an unspecified sum of money. Ava surrendered her rights of* dos *and other rights of inheritance.*

A. Cartulary of Prémontré, fol. 46r.

B. Original, AD Aisne, H 800, previously sealed with a double strip of parchment.

Scriptum curie Laudunensis de terra Adam Coquel de Firmitate.

[M]agister Johannes de Templo, officialis Laudunensis, universis presentes litteras inspecturis in Domino salutem. Noverint universi quod Adam dictus Coquiaus[4] de Firmitate et Eva, uxor ipsius, in nostra presentia personaliter constituti, recognoverunt coram nobis se vendidisse ecclesie Premonstratensis octo galetos terre parum plus vel parum minus, ad mensuram de Firmitate, sitos in loco qui dicitur Sartus Petri de Brissi juxta Ferieres, domum ecclesie supradicte, pro quadam videlicet summa pecunie de qua recognoverunt coram nobis predicti A[dam]et E[va] sibi esse plenarie satisfactum, promittentes fide prestita corporali in manu nostra quod decetero dictam terram non repetent nec repeti facient. Dicta etiam Eva quitavit dicte ecclesie spontanea voluntate sua, non coacta, sicut dicebat, quicquid juris habebat vel habere poterat tam nomine dotis quam alio quocunque modo vel titulo in tota terra predicta. In cuius rei testimonium presentes litteras ad petitionem partium sigillo curie Laudunensis fecimus sigillari, salvo jure domini Laudunensi episcopi et alieno. Actum mense februario, anno Domini M° CC° XXX° I°.[5]

1 Jean du Temple, *officialis* of Laon, is attested ca. 1231–ca. 1235. BM Reims 1563 (N. Fonds), fol. 170v; AD Aisne, H 873, fols. 172r–172v, 262r. His appointment as *officialis* was the subject of a long-running dispute with the cathedral chapter of Laon. Picó, "Membership in the Cathedral Chapter of Laon, 1217–1238," 5, 19.

2 La Ferté-Chevresis, cant. Ribemont, https://dicotopo.cths.fr/places/P35438398.

3 Ferrières, comm. La Ferté-Chevresis, https://dicotopo.cths.fr/places/P96262032.

4 Cokiaus *B*.

5 tricesimo primo *B*.

190

August, 1221.

Guillaume,[1] *lord of Wiège, and his wife Ada*[2] *approve as fief lords the sale made by husband and wife Anselme*[3] *de Fay and Elizabeth to the church of Prémontré of 18* galeti *of land, measure of La Ferté, consisting of two pieces of land, one at a place called* Pincecon, *and another at a place called the Assart of the Converts (*Sartus Conversorum*).*

A. Cartulary of Prémontré, fols. 46r–46v.

B. Original, AD Aisne, H 800, previously sealed with two double strips of parchment.

Karta Willermi de Wiege de terra Anselmi de Fai.

[E]go Willermus miles, dominus de Wiege, et Ada, uxor mea notum facimus universis tam presentibus quam futuris quod Anselmus de Fageto et Elizabeth, uxor sua, vendiderunt ecclesie Premonstratensi decem et octo galetos terre ad mensuram de Firmitate que divisa est per duas petias terre[4] quarum una sita est in loco qui dicitur Pinecon, inter Ferrarias[5] et Firmitatem, alia vero sita est in loco qui dicitur Sartus Conversorum inter Ferrarias[6] et Fagetum.[7] Sciendum est[8] quod quia terram predictam tenebat de nobis in feodum idem Anselmus, nos ad petitionem fratrum ecclesie et suam approbavimus venditionem et eandem gratam habuimus atque ratam, ita quidem quod dicti fratres nec ratione feodi nec ratione huius[9] servitii nobis vel heredibus nostris, eidem Anselmo vel uxori sue aut etiam heredibus eorum in aliquo tenebuntur, sed terram predictam quitam et absolutam clamamus. Debent vero idem Anselmus et dicta uxor sua necnon et heredes eorum portare ecclesie legitimam warandiam adversus omnes qui voluerint juri stare. Ut igitur ista venditio rata futuris temporibus habeatur et firma, nos fecimus presentes literas in testimonium huius rei factas sigillorum nostrorum munimine roborari. Actum mense augusto, anno gratie M° CC° XX°[10] primo.

1 Guillaume, lord of Wiège (modern Wiège-Faty, cant. Sains, https://dicotopo.cths.fr/places/P99221859), son of Mathieu, lord of Wiège, and Brémonde, daughter of Gobert [I], lord of La Ferté-Chevresis, and Marguerite, niece of Raoul I, lord of Coucy. See **183**.

2 Ada, lady of Wiège (d. aft. 1229–bef. 1236). Newman, *Seigneurs*, vol. 1, 134.

3 Anselme, lord of Fay-le-Noyer (comm. Surfontaine-et-Fay-le-Noyer, https://dicotopo.cths.fr/places/P49852544), attested 1210s–20s. Melleville, *DH*, vol. 1, 374. He and his wife Elizabeth (or Isabel) also made a gift to the abbey of Saint-Nicolas-des-Prés de Ribemont in 1218. Stein, *Cartulaire de l'ancienne abbaye de Saint Nicolas des Prés sous Ribemont*, 127–8.

4 *Add.* terre *A*.

5 Ferrerias *B*.

6 Ferrerias *B*.

7 Fay-le-Noyer, comm. Surfontaine-et-Fay-le-Noyer, https://dicotopo.cths.fr/places/P49852544.

8 *Om.* autem *A*.

9 alicuius *B*.

10 vicesimo *B*.

191

1182

Hugues [II],[1] *abbot of Prémontré, and Raoul,*[2] *abbot of Saint-Nicolas-des-Près de Ribemont, make known an exchange of lands. Saint-Nicolas exchanged their land at Coucy, near Prémontré's* curtis *of Ferrières,*[3] *for a similar holding of Prémontré's, near Saint-Nicolas's* curtis *of Chevresis.*

A. Cartulary of Prémontré, fol. 46v.

B. Original (chirograph), AN, L 995, no. 43, previously sealed. In the left margin and beginning at the top, the upper half of letters that form the word CYROGRAPHUM.

Other Manuscript Copies: Cartulary of Saint-Nicolas-des-Près de Ribemont, AN, LL 1015, fol. 40v (13th c.).

EDITION: Stein, *Cartulaire de l'ancienne abbaye de Saint Nicolas des Prés sous Ribemont*, 84–5.

De concambio quarundam terrarum inter nos et monachos Sancti Nicholai de Ribodimonte.

[E]go Hugo, Dei gratia Premonstratensis ecclesie dictus abbas, ego quoque Radulphus, abbas ecclesie Sancti Nicholai de Ribodimonte, notum fieri volumus tam futuris quam presentibus quod ecclesia Beati Nicholai de Ribodimonte habebat quandam possessionem terre ab omni decimatione liberam que vocabatur Couchiebus, juxta curtem Premonstrati scilicet Ferieres, et fratres eiusdem curtis habebant aliam possessionem terre solventem decimam juxta curtem ecclesie Beati Nicholai de Chievresis,[4] quarum possessionum commutatio et concambium factum est assensu utriusque capituli utriusque ecclesie, facta equa mensuratione utriusque possessionis. Sed tamen facta est quedam emendatio de quodam agello tres galetos et dimidium continente ex parte Beati Nicholai erga fratres de Ferieres. Et notandum quod ecclesia Premonstrati et ecclesia Beati Nicholai debent ferre warandiam legitimam ad invicem super predictis possessionibus si aliquis contra ipsas violenter insurgere voluerit et si hoc inpossible[5] fore contingat, unusquisque ad suam redibit possessionem.

---

1 Hugues II de Douai, abbot of the Premonstratensian abbey of Cuissy, 1161–5, and abbot of Prémontré, 1174–89. *MP* II, 497.

2 Raoul, abbot of the Benedictine abbey of Saint-Nicolas-des-Près de Ribemont, ca. 1179–ca. 1184. Stein, *Cartulaire de l'ancienne abbaye de Saint Nicolas des Prés sous Ribemont*, 71, 84, 123, 156.

3 Ferrières, comm. La Ferté-Chevresis, https://dicotopo.cths.fr/places/P96262032.

4 Chevresis *B*.

5 impossible *B*.

Quod ut firmius habeatur in perpetuum, presens cirographum[6] sigillis utriusque ecclesie munimus et confirmamus et testes utriusque capituli subscribi fecimus: Ex parte Premonstrati Gerardus prior, Egidius supprior, Haimo[7] et Willermus prepositi et ceteri.[8] Actum est hoc anno incarnati verbi M° C° LXXX° II°.

192

1186

Guillaume,[1] archbishop of Reims, confirms the possessions and rights of the religious of Prémontré that were previously confirmed by Popes Alexander III and Urban III, namely the church of Dorengt,[2] its prebends, its tithes, its lands, and the grange of Fontaine-Raimbaut.[3]

A. Cartulary of Prémontré, fol. 46v.
B. Original not found.

Privilegium Remensis archiepiscopi de decimis et terragiis ecclesie et grangia Rainbaldi Fontis cum novalibus de Firmitate.

[G]uillermus, Dei gratia Remorum archiepiscopus, Sancte Romane Ecclesie tituli Sancte Sabine cardinalis, Apostolice Sedis legatus, omnibus Sancte Matris Ecclesie filiis ad quos littere iste pervenerint in Domino salutem. Vestre notum facimus universitati quod dominus papa, Urbanus, ad exemplar felicis memorie Alexandri, pape, antecessoris sui, dilectorum filiorum nostrorum H[ugonis], abbatis et fratrum Premonstrati justis postulationibus grato concurrens assensu, ecclesiam de Dorenc cum prebendis, decimis, terragiis et omnibus pertinentiis suis, grangiam quoque qui dicitur Fons Rainbaldi, cum pertinentiis eis confirmavit et scripti sui patrocinio communivit. Idem etiam dominus papa, Urbanus, quoniam prefati fratres a prestatione decimarum de novalibus suis

6 cyrographum *B*.
7 Haymo *B*.
8 *Add.* et ceteri *A;* Alulfus, Soibertus, Ernaldus, Alardus conversi; ex parte vero ecclesie Beati Nicholai, Herbertus prior, Adam Theobaldus, Robertus frater eius, Tivannus miles, Landrinus de Maimbencurt, Robertus Testa, Johannes Turpin *B*.

1 Guillaume *aux Blanches Mains* (1135–1202), son of Thibaut II, count of Blois and Champagne, and Mathilde von Spanheim, was bishop of Chartres, 1164–76, archbishop of Sens, 1169–76 and archbishop of Reims, 1176–1202.
2 Dorengt, cant. Nouvion, https://dicotopo.cths.fr/places/P90882005.
3 Near La Ferté-Chevresis, cant. Ribemont, https://dicotopo.cths.fr/places/P15499504.

que propriis manibus excolunt et sumptibus auctoritate Apostolice Sedis sunt exempti, nichilominus decimas novalium infra parrochiam de Firmitate in nemore quod G[obertus], dominus de Firmitate, fructuum sibi quadam parte retenta, pia devotione eisdem fratribus contulerat, auctoritate apostolica confirmavit. Nos itaque pari affectione predictorum filiorum nostrorum devotionem attendentes, omnia que superius annotata sunt eis presentis scripti patrocinio roboramus et sigilli nostri auctoritate confirmamus, statuentes et sub interminatione anathematis firmiter inhibentes ne quis hanc nostre confirmationis paginam audeat infringere vel ei in aliquo contraire, salva tamen in omnibus Apostolice Sedis auctoritate. Actum anno gratie M° C° octogesimo VI°. Datum per manum Lambini[4] cancellarii nostri.

193

1200

Roger,[1] *bishop of Laon, makes known that Mathieu de Wiège,*[2] *upon his betrothal to Brémonde, sister of the knight Gobert [II]*[3] *de La Ferté-Chevresis, undertakes to maintain an agreement reached between, on the one hand, Gobert [I] and Blihard, father and grandfather, respectively, of Gobert [II] and Brémonde, and, on the other hand, the Premonstratensian brothers of Ferrières.*[4] *The agreement states that the Premonstratensians will continue to cultivate about 24* modiatae *of land, measure of Guise, owing half the sheaves produced; about four* modiatae *of land owing a quarter of the sheaves produced; and about 50* modiatae *of land owing a ninth of the sheaves produced, excepting the sheaves reserved for the tithe and the reaper. (See* ***183****.)*

A. Cartulary of Prémontré, fols. 46v–47r.

B. Original (chirograph), AN, L 995, no. 51, previously sealed. In the left margin and beginning at the top, the top half of the letters that form the word CYROGRAPHUM.

4 Lambert (or Lambin) de Bruges, chancellor of the archbishop of Reims in the 1180s, then archdeacon of Thérouanne and Cambrai, then bishop of Thérouanne, 1191–1207.

1 Roger de Rozoy, son of Clérembaud, lord of Rozoy, and Elizabeth de Namur, was bishop of Laon, 1175–1207.

2 Mathieu, lord of Wiège (cant. Sains, https://dicotopo.cths.fr/places/P99221859), brother of Jean Bédous, lord of Puisieux and Marchais. Melleville, *DH*, vol. 2, 476.

3 Gobert II, lord of La Ferté-Chevresis, son of Gobert I, lord of La Ferté-Chevresis, and Marguerite, niece of Raoul I, lord of Coucy.

4 Ferrières, comm. La Ferté-Chevresis, https://dicotopo.cths.fr/places/P96262032.

Item karta episcopi Laudunensis super desponsationibus sororis Goberti militis de Firmitate.

[I]n nomine Domini. Ego Rogerus, Dei gratia Laudunensis episcopus, notum facimus per hoc scriptum presentibus et futuris quod Gobertus de Firmitate pro desponsatione sororis sue Braimundis,[5] quam Matheus de Wiege[6] in uxorem accepit, dedit eidem Matheo in feodum et in liberum hominium terram quam fratres Premonstratensis ecclesie apud Ferieres morantes a Bliardo[7] avo et a Goberto, patre predicti Goberti, susceperunt in perpetuum excolendam, partim ad frugum medietatem, partim ad quartam garbam et partim ad nonam, salva ubique garba decime et messoris de qua terra inter ecclesiam Premonstratensem et Gobertum scripta a tempore avi et patris sui facta et sub cirographo[8] divisa habentur, in quibus et de ipsa terra et de quibusdam rebus aliis plenius est expressum. Igitur ad petitionem predictorum Goberti et Mathei, tam ipsi quam dominus Petrus, abbas Premonstratensis, in nostra presentia constituti, exhibitis utrimque et lectis veteribus scriptis, in hoc concorditer ~~de~~convenerunt quod fratres de Ferieres supradicto Matheo de terra memorata tantum amodo facere tenebuntur quantum Goberto secundum eadem scripta facere tenebantur. Et idem Matheus vel heres eius tantum predictis fratribus pro ipsa terra faciet quantum Gobertus eis debebat facere, secundum veterum scriptorum tenorem, et hoc salvis ceteris omnibus que in ipsis scriptis veteribus continentur. Adiectum est autem quod terra prefata continet ad mensuram Guisie,[9] sicut dicitur, circiter viginti[10] modiatas terre[11] ad medietatem et circiter quatuor modiatas ad quartam garbam et circiter quinquaginta modiatas ad nonam garbam, sicut metis positis determinata est et signata. Quod si infra ipsas metas plus aut minus contineatur terre quam dictum est cuiuscumque sit territorii sive de Firmitate sive de Chievresi[12] seu aliunde totum erit Mathei nec ei vel heredi suo Gobertus vel heres eius nec etiam Premonstratensis ecclesia respondebit. Ut ea ergo[13] que superius scripta sunt sicut in presentia nostra recognitum est, perpetuam habeant firmitatem, presens scriptum sub cirographi[14] partitione divisum, salvis quantum ad alia scriptis veteribus sigilli nostri munimine roboramus. Actum anno ab incarnatione Domini M° CC°.[15]

5 Braymundi *B.*
6 Wege *B.*
7 Blihardo *B.*
8 cyrographo *B.*
9 Guysie *B.*
10 *Om.* quatuor *A.*
11 *Add.* terre *A.*
12 Chyevresi *B.*
13 *Transp. A*; ut ergo ea *B.*
14 cyrographi *B.*
15 millesimo ducentesimo *B.*

194

1211

The churches of Prémontré and Homblières[1] modify the terms of their 1146 agreement, the text of which is reproduced within, with regard to the payment of a census, *measured in modii of grain (*frumentum, avene*), for the land and mill of* Le Héricourt *due to a change in the calculation of the number of* sextarii *in a* modius, *measure of Saint-Quentin.[2]*

A. Cartulary of Prémontré, fols. 47r–47v.

B. Original (chirograph), AN, L 995, no. 58, previously sealed. In the left margin and beginning at the top, the top half of the letters that form the word CYROGRAPHUM in red.

EDITION: Newman, *Homblières*, 198–9; *Chartae Galliae*, no. 212321, http://telma.irht.cnrs.fr/outils/chartae-galliae/charte212321/.

Cyrographum inter ecclesiam Premonstratensem et ecclesiam Humolariensem.

[P]er hoc publicum instrumentum tam modernis quam posteris innotescat quod olim inter Humolariensem et Premonstratensem ecclesias scriptum autenticum factum fuit in quo continetur quedam censualis conventio in hec verba: In nomine sancte et individue Trinitatis. Notum sit omnibus quod ecclesia Premonstratensis[3] censualiter accepit ab ecclesia Humolariensi terram de Lehericourt[4] cultam et incultam in aquis, silvis, pratis et sedem molendini, in omnibus usibus in quibus melius ad suum conmodum[5] coli poterit. Census autem talis est: Decem modii ad modium Sancti Quintini octo sextarios continentem. Quod si forte mensura creverit, ecclesia Premonstrata nuntiabit ecclesie Humolariensi. Si vero decreverit, Humolariensis nuntiabit Premonstratensi[6] et mensura in id ipsum quod fuerat, reformabitur. Persolvetur autem a festo Sancti Remigii usque ad festum Sancti Martini et, quando recipiendum erit, fratres Premonstratensis[7] ecclesie nuntiabunt Humolariensi ecclesie ut mittat nuntios suos ad mensurandum. Quod si infra quindecim dies non venerint, et postea communi dampno, ut est incendium vel rapina, petierit,[8] eis non restau-

1 The Benedictine abbey of Notre-Dame de Homblières.

2 The original of which this is the *vidimus* is an 1146 act, AD Aisne, H 791.

3 Premonstrata *B*.

4 Lehericurt *B*.

5 commodum *B*.

6 Premonstrate *B*.

7 Premonstrate *B*.

8 perierit *B*.

rabitur. De frumento novem modii erunt et unus modius avene qui sexdecim[9] mensurabitur sextariis[10] et frumentum de eadem terra persolvetur de meliori post sementem. Quod si alibi accipiatur consimile ipsorum monachorum arbitrio persolvetur et aut ad Castellulum[11] aut ad Morecourt[12,13] eis deducetur a fratribus Premonstratensis[14] ecclesie. Quod si de hiis aliqua querimonia unde placitari oporteat, emerserit et ecclesia Premonstratensis[15] per se terminare nequiverit, abbas Humolariensis per se et per suos in querenda justicia Premonstratensem[16] ecclesiam juvabit quantum poterit sine sacramento et rerum suarum dispendio. Quod ut ratum permaneat assensu utriusque capituli sigillis utriusque ecclesie confirmatum est. Actum anno verbi incarnati M° centesimo quadragesimo[17] sexto.

Procedente vero tempore cum prescripta conventio per sexaginta[18] annos et eo amplius iam durasset, tandem occasione cuiusdam mensure veteris ad quam fratres Premonstratenses predictum censum se proponebant semper ab antiquo solvisse sed monachi Humolarienses ipsum amplius ad illam mensuram nolebant recipere, cum, secundum apostolum, sevos[19] Dei non oporteat litigare[20,21] de utriusque ecclesie assensu communi, nova quedam et amicabilis conventio, nullum complete iam prescriptioni factura prejudicium sed eidem potius continuanda, mediante bonorum et ad hoc electorum virorum arbitrio intercessit talis, videlicet quod, salvo quantum ad alia scripto veteri superius annotato pro censu predicto unus modius avene et novem modii frumenti a modo duobus sextariis minus ad mensuram Sancti Quintini eo tempore quo scriptum hoc ultimo factum fuit currentem perpetuo singulis annis solventur et, si deinceps mensura creverit vel decreverit, id ipsum quod demutatione mensure nuntianda et reformanda in superiori et veteri scripto contentum est et conventum observabitur. Ceterum ne iste due conventiones diversis facte temporibus pro scriptorum diversitate sibi fidem aliquatenus derogarent bona fide que omnium et maxime religiosorum debet conventionibus sive contractibus interesse, communiter fuit provisum ut utraque conventio eodem stilo et in una pagina sub

---

9 sedecim *B.*
10 *Transp. A.*; sextariis mensurabitur *B.*
11 Châtillon-sur-Oise, cant. Moy, https://dicotopo.cths.fr/places/P09388740.
12 Morocurt *B.*
13 Morcourt, comm. Flavigny-le-Grand-et-Beaurain, https://dicotopo.cths.fr/places/P16795067.
14 Premonstrate *B.*
15 Premonstrata *B.*
16 Premonstratam *B.*
17 C° XL° *B.*
18 LX^a^ *B.*
19 servos *B.*
20 *Transp. A*; litigare non oporteat *B.*
21 2 Timothy 2:24.

cirographo[22] scriberetur quod utrinque partitum hinc sigillo Humolariensis inde sigillo Premonstratensis ecclesie ad firmitatem perpetuam est munitum. Actum anno gratie M° CC° undecimo.

195

1204

Gobert, lord of la Ferté, makes known that he gave in alms to the church of Prémontré the terragium *due to him on a field near the woods of Saint-Quentin.*

A. Cartulary of Prémontré, fol. 47v.
B. Original not found.

Karta domini Goberti de Firmitate de elemosina terragii cuiusdam campi.

[E]go Gobertus, dominus de Firmitate, notum facio presentibus et futuris quod ego dedi in elemosinam ecclesie Premonstratensis terragium quod mihi debebatur de quodam campo infra quandam culturam ecclesie Sancti Vincentii Laudunensis, sito juxta boschum Sancti Quintini et quitum clamavi in perpetuum. Ut igitur ecclesia Premonstratensis terragium predictum in pace possideat, ego concessionem istam feci fideliter hic inscribi et sigilli mei appensione roborari. Actum anno Domini M° CC° quarto.

22 cyrographo *B*.

TABLE OF CONTENTS: WALESCOURS

A. Cartulary of Prémontré, fol. 48r.

Incipiunt scripta de Walescours cum appenditiis suis.

Capitula I arta[1] Galteri Laudunensis episcopi de alodio de Walescourt et de parte silve de Mesloy cum altaribus et decimis.

II Carta de quadam compositione inter ecclesiam Premonstratensem et Bliardum de Firmitate super quadam parte alodii de Walescours.

III Item carta Galteri Laudunensis episcopi, decani, et capituli de alodiis de Walescours cum appenditiis suis.

IIII Karta archiepiscopi Remensis de quadam conpositione inter ecclesiam Premonstratensem et dominum Willermum de Firmitate.

V Karta episcopi Laudunensis de decima de Walescours que fuit Eustachii, data ad trecensum IX modiorum bladi eidem ecclesie.

VI Karta abbatis Sancti Nicholai de Silva Vedogii de parte alodiorum de Moncellis super Perron.

VII Karta episcopi Laudunensis et Balduini archidiaconi Leodiensis de compositione inter ecclesiam Premonstratensem et Radulphum de Montiniaco.

VIII Karta domini Radulphi de Couciaco de quadam compositione inter ecclesiam Premonstrato et quosdam viros de territorio de Walescours.

IX Karta episcopi Laudunensis de terra quam vendidit Gerardus Paillars ecclesie Premonstrato.

X Karta ~~episcopi Laudunensis~~ Johannis de Hussello de resignatione cuiusdam modiagii.

XI Karta episcopi de elemosina Guidonis de Moncellis de novem portionibus minute decime Veteris Moncelli.

XII Karta abbatis de Fusniaco de quitatione quamdam quam fecit ecclesia Premonstratensis in territorio de Foucauzies.

XIII Karta abbatis et prioris Sancti Quintini et Nicholai de Camblicao de compositione inter ecclesiam Premonstratensem et Radulphum presbyterum de Sont.

XIIII Karta episcopi Laudunensis de compositione inter ecclesiam Premonstrato et presbyterum de Sont.

XV Karta abbatis et conventus Premonstratensis de elemosina presbyteri de Moncellis.

XVI Karta Anselli de Moncello Novo de resignatione minute decime Veteris Moncelli quam fecit Guido, frater meus, ecclesie Premonstrati.

XVII Karta archiepiscopi Remensis de dono Guidonis de Chermisi et cetera.

XVIII Karta abbatis Clarifontis de compositione inter ecclesiam Premonstratensem et Robertum militem de Autmont.

---

1 *Sic A*, *read* Karta.

XIX **K**arta Bartholomei episcopi Laudunensis de confirmatione elemosine quam fecit Ingelrannus filius Thome de Marla ecclesie Premonstrati.

XX **K**arta abbatis Thenoliensis de dote altaris que accepimus sub annua pensione octo galetarum frumenti de Murci.

196

1159

In 1153 Gautier [II],[1] *bishop of Laon, confirmed the resolution of a dispute between husband and wife Anselme*[2] *de Marle and Adélaïde*[3] *[de Guise] and the church of Prémontré, concerning a gift to Prémontré of woodland at Mesloy*[4] *by the canons of Notre-Dame de Laon. This gift had been made at the same time that Anselme and Adélaïde gave Prémontré allods at Valécourt with the assent of Adélaïde; Renier de Guise, her brother; Maurin and Pierre*[5] *de Rougeries, the maternal cousins of Adélaïde and Renier; and several others. In this charter, Adélaïde, her second husband Arnoul,*[6] *and her brother Renier first contest the previous gifts but then recognize their validity. Adélaïde's brother Renier and Sibille, his wife, give Prémontré easements of their territory at Monceau-le-Vieil.*[7] *Adélaïde's sons, Renier*[8] *and Robert,*[9] *together with Bliard*[10] *de La Ferté-Chevresis, his son Raoul, Raoul de Housset,*[11] *his brother Gérard,*[12] *and others, consent to this.*[13] *(See **198**.)*

1 Gautier de Mortagne was dean of Laon, ca. 1142–55, and bishop of Laon, 1155–74.

2 Anselme de Marle or de Monceau (d. bef. 1159), son of Doumissons, was the first husband of Adélaïde de Guise. Barthelemy, *LDA*, 523–4.

3 Adélaïde, daughter of Bouchard, lord of Guise, and Adèle; sister of Rénier, lord of Guise, and heiress of Monceau. Barthelemy, *LDA*, 523–4.

4 Mesloy, comm. Chevresis-Monceau, https://dicotopo.cths.fr/places/P54953574.

5 Pierre de Rougeries (cant. Sains, https://dicotopo.cths.fr/places/P34843917), possibly the son of an Ermentrude de Guise, sister of Bouchard. Melleville, *DH*, vol. 2, 293.

6 Arnoul de Montigny, nephew of Blihard de la Ferté, second husband of Adélaïde de Guise. Barthélemy, *LDA*, 523–4.

7 Monceau-le-Vieil, comm. Chevresis-Monceau, https://dicotopo.cths.fr/places/P61634471.

8 Renier de Monceau, son of Anselme de Marle and Adélaïde de Guise. Barthélemy, *LDA*, 525.

9 Robert de Montigny, son of Arnoul de Montigny and Adélaïde de Guise. Barthélemy, *LDA*, 525.

10 Bliard de La Ferté-Chevresis, son of Baudouin de Soupir and Cécile, and brother or half-brother of Guy de Soupir. Morelle, "Une charte nuptiale laonnoise de 1158 conservée en original," 222, fn. 64.

11 Raoul I, lord of Housset (cant. Sains, https://dicotopo.cths.fr/places/P27336521), appears as a witness to acts, primarily of the lords of Coucy, between 1147 and 1187. Barthélemy, *LDA*, 519–20.

12 Dominique Barthélemy suggests that Gerard, brother of Raoul I, lord of Housset, may be the same as Gerard *Auris* (**5, 99, 407**). Barthélemy, *LDA*, 521.

13 The companion act of Hugues I, abbot of Prémontré, survives in two chirograph copies, AN, L 995, no. 18 and no. 19.

A. Cartulary of Prémontré, fols. 48r–48v.
B. Original, AN, L 995, no. 27.[14]

Karta Galteri Laudunensis episcopi de alodio de Walescourt et de parte silve de Mesloi cum altaribus et decimis.

[I]n nomine sancte et individue Trinitatis, Patris et Filii et Spiritus Sancti, amen. Pastoralis officii est que rationabiliter ecclesiis Dei conferuntur et in presentia nostra conceduntur attestari et ne aliquo oblivionis nubilo obfuscata deleri possint aut infirmari scripto commendare et posterorum notitie transmittere. Ea propter ego Galterus,[15] Dei gratia Laudunensis[16] vocatus episcopus, notum fieri volumus tam futuris quam presentibus quod canonici Sancte Marie Laudunensis ecclesie alodia de Walescourt[17,18] et partem silve de Mesloi cum altaribus et decimis et terris appendentibus, que omnia de jure et fundo eorum erant, Premonstratensi ecclesie sub annuali censu perpetuo possidenda contulerunt, sicut in cyrographo ipsorum plenius continetur ubi, cum fratres eiusdem Premonstratensis[19] ecclesie habitare et terram colere cepissent, Anselmus de Marla qui ibidem districtum suum esse dicebat cum Adelaide, uxore sua, ad cuius precipue hereditatem pertinebat super pascuis et ceteris aisentiis suis et eadem silva de Mesloi, calumpniam movit et fratribus molestiam intulit, unde convenientibus et mediantibus multis et magnis viris in hunc modum conpositio provenit. De silva illa decretum est quod quando incidetur quod superius incisum fuerit, Anselmus vel successor eius habebit quod vero reliquum fuerit in terra et stipitibus et radicibus ecclesia possidebit et in suos usus quamdiu ante ligones invenerit eadem ecclesia de ipsa silva accipiet, et, si ibi non suffecerit, alibi in eadem silva ubi magis voluerit accipiet. Quod si usque ad quadraginta dies post incisionem ipse Anselmus vel successor eius quod suum est in lignis et ramusculis non receperit, ecclesia sine forisfacto in suos usus auferet vel conburet. Determinatum est etiam quod in eadem silva, in loco competenti, ecclesia, si ei placuerit, curtem construet spacio duorum modiorum sementis ad mensuram castri de Firmitate et in quocumque latere curtis voluerit, de ipsa nichilominus silva, quantum duo modii sementis capiunt, in suos usus retinebit. Ipsam vero curtem a consuetudine molendini et furni seu

14 Due to conservation concerns, the original was not available to the editors. Variants are noted in accordance with the 1980s transcription of Françoise Muret.

15 Gaulterus *B*.

16 Laudunensium *B*.

17 Valescurt *B*.

18 Valécourt, comm. Chevresis-Monceau, https://dicotopo.cths.fr/places/P14207928.

19 Premonstrate *B*.

thelonei et rotagii necnon ab omni decimatione et omni alia exactione liberam et omnes terre sue aisentias in pascuis, aquis, introitu vel exitu viarum et in omni districto suo idem Anselmus ob remedium anime sue et predecessorum suorum concessit, sed et mercennarios fratrum ubique liberos esse concessit qui, si quid forefecerint, abbas Premonstratensis justiciam tenebit, si per eum jus exequi voluerint; sin autem ad ipsum Anselmum vel successorem eius justicia pertinebit. Pro huius donationis et concessionis libertate constitutum est ut, singulis annis, prefata ecclesia sex modios frumenti ad mensuram castri de Firmitate tunc temporis currentem censualiter eidem Anselmo et heredibus eius persolvat; hec autem annona submonente ipso vel nuntio eius quindecim diebus, sive ante sive post festum Sancti Remigii, si necesse fuerit, ubi voluerit tribus leugis longe a villa de Monciaus[20] salva et quieta ei a fratribus ducetur, post quem videlicet terminum, si rogatu eius ab ipsis ad servandum retenta casu aliquo deperierit, deinceps ei ab ipsis fratribus non respondebitur. Hoc autem totum libere concessit predicta Adelaidis,[21] uxor Anselmi, et Renerus[22] de Guisia, frater eiusdem Adelaidis, necdum miles, effectus presentibus et concedentibus quibusdam consobrinis suis, Maurino et fratre eius, Petro de Rogeriis, Rohardo de Ostremoncourt,[23,24] Gerardo Raget,[25] Gilleberto de Cheri, astantibus quoque et testantibus quibusdam religiosis Hugone,[26] abbate Premonstratensis, Guarino,[27] abbate Sancti Martini, Elberto,[28] abbate Buciliensi, Hugone sacerdote.[29] Actum est hoc et approbatum et concessum in presentia capituli Sancte Marie Laudunensis ecclesie in die electionis nostre deinde recitatum et recognitum est in curte de Walescours[30] ab eisdem Anselmo et prefata uxore eius et Renero[31] et prefatis consobrinis suis, presente Bliardo[32] de Firmitate cum fratribus supranominatis, anno Domini[33] M° C° LIII°. Succedente vero tempore cum Anselmus obisset et Arnulphus,[34] nepos Blihardi de Firmitate, ~~cum fratribus~~ prefatam Adelaidem uxorem accepisset, tam ipse

20 Moncels *B.*

21 Adhelaidis *B.*

22 Reinerus *B.*

23 Ostrumoncurt *B.*

24 Autremencourt, cant. Marle, https://dicotopo.cths.fr/places/P04545373.

25 A Gerard Raget also appears in an 1198 act of Henri, dean of Guise. AD Aisne, H 659.

26 Hugues I de Fosses (ca. 1093–1164), first abbot of Prémontré.

27 Guérin, abbot of the Premonstratensian abbey of Vicogne, 1129–51, and of the Premonstratensian abbey of Saint-Martin de Laon, 1151–71. *MP* II, 436, 512.

28 Elbert (or Nelbert), abbot of the Premonstratensian abbey of Bucilly, ca. 1159–60. *MP* II, 366.

29 *Om.* Matheo, Gualtero, Alberto acolitis, Noe et Petro conversis *A.*

30 Valescurt *B.*

31 Reinero *B.*

32 Blihardo *B.*

33 dominice *B.*

34 Arnulfus *B.*

quam illa et prefatus Renerus, frater eiusdem Adelaidis, iam miles factus, ecclesiam denuo super hoc inquietare ceperunt sed postea tam ipse Arnulphus et uxor eius quam Renerus a quo feodum ipsum tenebant, et amicorum ratione et beneficiis ecclesie flexi, totum, sicut prius fecerant, recognoverunt et libere concesserunt et contra omnes inquietantes qui infra episcopatum Laudunensem justiciam exequi vellent, absque erogatione expensarum suarum et persecutione amicorum suorum ecclesiam tueri data fide spoponderunt. Hoc etiam concesserunt filii eiusdem Adelaidis, Renerus,[35] Robertus. Predictus quoque Renerus,[36] frater sepedicte Adelaidis, omnes aisentias suas in territorio de Monciaus[37] et citra et ultra aquam assensu Sibille[38] uxoris sue fratribus Premonstratensis[39] ecclesie libere concessit. Huic recognitioni et concessioni interfuerunt testes legitimi: Bliardus[40] de Firmitate et Radulphus[41] filius eius, Radulfus de Houssel[42] et Gerardus frater eius et ceteri.[43] Postea ut firmius staret huius conventionis concessio tam Arnulphus[44] cum predicta uxore sua quam ipse Renerus[45] ante presentiam nostram venerunt et quod prius fecerant recognoscentes, totum coram nobis libere concesserunt. Ne ergo quod factum est ulla deinceps valeat perturbatione cassari, precibus Premonstratensium fratrum acquiescentes, tam sigilli nostri impressione quam testium annotatione presentem paginam communiri precepimus. S. Galteri,[46] capellani. S. Gerardi, thesaurarii[47] et ceteri.[48] Siquis igitur conpositionem prescriptam et concessionem infringere vel inpugnare presumpserit, iram Dei omnipotentis incurrat. Actum anno incarnati verbi M° C° L° IX°, epacta nulla, indictione VII[a], concurrente III°. Angotus[49] cancellarius recognovit, relegit, scripsit, et subscripsit.

---

35 Reinerus *B*.
36 Reinerus *B*.
37 Monciels *B*.
38 Sybille *B*.
39 Premonstrate *B*.
40 Blihardus *B*.
41 Radulfus *B*.
42 Hussel *B*.
43 *Add.* et ceteri *A*; Gillebertus de Cheri, Escatus de Leheriis, Balduinus de Cher, Eustacius de Monteigni, Radulfus de Lobrai *B*.
44 Arnulfus *B*.
45 Reinerus *B*.
46 Gulteri *B*.
47 subthesaurarii *B*.
48 *Add.* et ceteri *A*; Signum Roberti de Lusarchis. Signum Herberti, decani de Anisciaco. Signum Gualteri, presbiteri de Moncels. Signum Fulberti, presbiteri de Purpriis. Signum Hugonis, prioris Premonstrate ecclesie. Signum Gosuini. Signum Haimonis, sacerdotum. Signum Fulconis; signum Mathei, acolitorum. Signum Dicti; signum Noe; signum Liberti; signum Balduini, conversorum *B*.
49 Angot, chancellor of Laon, ca. 1144–ca. 1170.

197

1164. Church at La Ferté.

Gautier [II],[1] bishop of Laon, makes known that after having contested the possession of part of the allod of Valécourt,[2] Bliard,[3] lord of La Ferté-Chevresis, and his wife, Brémunde, recognize the claims made by the church of Prémontré and return in full the land in question.

A. Cartulary of Prémontré, fols. 48v–49r.

B. Original (chirograph), BnF, Coll. Picardie 290, no. 9, previously sealed. In the right margin and beginning on the top, the lower half of the letters that form the word CYROGRAPHUM in red.

REGISTER: Boghen, "Inventaire des actes épiscopaux originaux conservés à la Bibliothèque nationale (1121–1200)," 114.

De quadam compositione inter ecclesiam Premonstratensem et Blihardum de Firmitate super quadam parte allodii de Walescurs.

[I]n nomine Patris et Filii et Spiritus Sancti, amen. Episcopalis officii est regulariter viventium quieti providere et paci ut tanto liberius divinis vacent obsequiis, quanto ferventius crucifixerunt se mundo et mundum sibi; ad id vero agendum nichil commodius invenitur quam si ea que memorie posterorum profutura sunt, scripto commendentur. Ea propter ego Galterus, Dei gratia Laudunensis vocatus episcopus, notum fieri volo tam futuris quam presentibus quod querela quedam emerserat inter Premonstratensem ecclesiam et dominum Bliardum[4] de Firmitate pro quadam parte alodii de Walescourt[5] quam idem Bliardus[6] suam esse asserebat; dicebat enim terram suam continuari usque ad publicam viam que venit de Parigniaco[7,8] et vadit versus Foucoziis[9,10] et eandem viam dividere terram suam et prefatum alodium supra

1 Gautier de Mortagne was dean of Laon, ca. 1142–55, and bishop of Laon, 1155–74.

2 Valécourt, comm. Chevresis-Monceau, https://dicotopo.cths.fr/places/P14207928.

3 Bliard de La Ferté-Chevresis, son of Baudouin de Soupir and Cécile, and brother or half-brother of Guy de Soupir. Morelle, "Une charte nuptiale laonnoise de 1158 conservée en original," 222, fn. 64.

4 Blihardum *B*.

5 Walescurt *B*.

6 Blihardus *B*.

7 Parregniaco *B*.

8 Pargny-lez-Bois, cant. Crécy-sur-Serre, https://dicotopo.cths.fr/places/P07132323.

9 Flucouziis *B*.

10 Faucousis, comm. Monceau-le-Neuf, https://dicotopo.cths.fr/places/P08023812.

grangiam de Walescort;[11] econtra fratres Premonstrati qui censualiter alodium illud ab ecclesia nostra, sub testimonio canonicorum nostrorum et legitimorum hominum circummanentium, ex bonnatum receperant, prefatum alodium ultra publicam viam transire asserebant usque ad quasdam bonnas antiquitus positas et, sicut verbis assercierunt, ita et sacramentis legitimorum hominum circummanentium et sacerdotum in presentia nostra et personarum ecclesie nostre probari fecerunt. Tandem vero, ut altercatio illa fine debito terminaretur, predictus Bliardus[12] et uxor eius, Bremundis,[13] cognita rei veritate, terram quam calumpniabantur, prefate ecclesie liberam sine ulla reclamatione remiserunt ita tamen quod fratres prefate ecclesie tantum terre ipsius Bliardi[14] que illi alodio erat contigua, quantum erat inter predictas bonnas et prefatam viam, acceperunt excolendum ad terragium pro quinta garba, excepta garba decime et garba messoris; sic enim dictum est de terragio omni[15] quod ei debent et de terra ista quam pretaxavimus et de alia terra que est apud grangiam ipsorum Ferieres,[16] quod excipientur garbe messorum et decime. Facta sunt hec assensu filiorum et filiarum ipsius Bliardi[17] et uxoris eius, Bremundis.[18] Siquis ergo fratres Premonstrati super predicta terra juxta alodium de Walescourt[19] inquietaverit, Bliardus[20] warandus eius erit in episcopatu Laudunensi contra omnes qui justiciam exequi voluerint; quod si eam liberare nequiverit, quicquid fratres posuerint in excolendo, terram illam Bliardus[21] eius restaurabit aut tantundem terre culte et ita valentis in vicino eis restituet qui, si[22] a justicia subterfugerint, persequetur eos sicut prefata ecclesia. Tempore autem messis quando terragium accipiendum erit, fratres nuntiabunt ministro domini Bliardi[23] apud Firmitatem. Qui si venire distulerit, fratres sine forisfacto terragium seperabunt et ad Firmitatem ducent tam ei quam heredibus eius post ipsum. Concessit etiam Bliardus[24] prefate ecclesie fratribus terram de feodo suo quam emerant a milite quondam de Firmitate, Wichardo. Hec compositio facta est actoribus et

11 Walescurt *B.*
12 Blihardus *B.*
13 Breimmudis *B.*
14 Blihardi *B.*
15 *Transp. A*; omni terragio *B.*
16 Ferrieres *B.*
17 Blihardi *B.*
18 Breimmundis *B.*
19 Walescurt *B.*
20 Blihardus *B.*
21 Blihardus *B.*
22 *Add.* si *A*; vero *B.*
23 Blihardi *B.*
24 Blihardus *B.*

mediantibus dilecto filio nostro Galtero[25,26] Sancti Vincentii abbate, Simone[27,28] de Ribemont,[29] Gaufrido[30] de Condram, et ceteri[31] in ecclesia de Firmitate ita esse recognovit. Hoc autem ut ratum et inconvulsum permaneat, sigilli nostri impressione et testium subscriptione sub cirographo[32] communiri fecimus. S.[33] Lisiardi,[34,35] decani. S. Roberti,[36] cantoris et ceteri.[37] Actum anno verbi incarnati M° C° LX° IIII°. Angotus[38] cancellarius relegit, scripsit, et subscripsit.

198

1153. Laon.

Gautier,[1] dean of the chapter of Notre-Dame de Laon, and the chapter cede to the church of Prémontré the allod of Valécourt[2] and its appurtenances, in exchange for an annual census. *(See **196**.)*

A. Cartulary of Prémontré, fols. 49r–49v.

B[1]. Original (chirograph), AN, L 995, no. 22, previously sealed with two seals. In the right margin and beginning at the top, the lower half of the letters that form the word + CYROGRAPHUM. (This chirograph belonged to the Cathedral Chapter of Laon, based on dorsal annotation.)

---

25 Gautero *B*.

26 Gautier, abbot of the Benedictine abbey of Saint-Vincent de Laon, 1155/6–74. *GC* IX, col. 579; Wyard, *Saint-Vincent*, 416–21.

27 Symone *B*.

28 Simon II, lord of Ribemont, 1150s–60s, son of Simon I, lord of Ribemont. Melleville, *DH*, vol. 2, 277.

29 Ribuomunt *B*.

30 Geoffroi de Condren, knight, brother of Sarracin, castellan of La Fère and Laon, and Hugues le Captif de Vendeuil. Newman, *Seigneurs*, vol. 2, 203, 205.

31 *Add.* et ceteri *A*; Sarracenno de Fara, Gisleberto de Cheri militibus, et ipse Blihardus coram uxore sua prefata, et filio suo Goberti et quibusdam militibus suis, Clarenbaudo de Abbatia, Poberto de Soon, Herberto Rivarz, Geroldo Dapifero, Johanne Sacerdote presentibus etiam prefato abbate, et abbate Premonstatensi *B*.

32 cyrographo *B*.

33 Signum *B*.

34 Laudunensis *B*.

35 Lisiard, dean of Laon, ca. 1153–ca. 1168.

36 Robert, cantor of Laon, ca. 1164–ca. 1168. Wyard, *Saint-Vincent*, 37.

37 *Add.* et ceteri *A*; S. Gauteri abbatis Sancti Vincentii. S. Ingelranni abbatis Sancti Johannis. S. Garini abbatis Sancti Martini. S. Johannis abbatis Buciliensis. S. Gerardi subthesaurarii. S. magister Hugonis. S. Herberti decani de Anisi *B*.

38 Angot, chancellor of Laon, ca. 1144–ca. 1170.

---

1 Gautier de Mortagne was dean of Laon, ca. 1142–55, and bishop of Laon, 1155–74.

2 Valécourt, comm. Chevresis-Monceau, https://dicotopo.cths.fr/places/P14207928.

B[2]. Original (chirograph), BnF, Coll. Picardie 290, no. 5, previously sealed with two seals. In the left margin and beginning at the top, the top half of the letters that form the word + CYROGRAPHUM. (This chirograph likely belonged to Prémontré.)

Other Manuscript Copies: Cartulary of the Cathedral Chapter of Notre-Dame de Laon, AD Aisne G 1850, fols. 342r–344r (13/14th c.).

EDITION: *PL* 156, cols. 1155–6.

REGISTER: *Studium Baldwin*, fiche 2201.

Karta Galteri decani Laudunensis et capituli de alodiis de Walescours cum appenditiis suis.

[I]n nomine sancte et individue Trinitatis, amen. Quia nature mutabilis exigente defectu generatio preterit et generatio advenit fitque ut vetustas oblivionem, oblivio confusionem pariat et contentionem necessarie mos inolevit, ut beneficia vel possessiones ecclesiarum scripto tradantur et transmittantur ad noticiam posterorum. Ea propter ego Galterus,[3] Dei gratia Sancte Marie Laudunensis ecclesie decanus, totusque capituli nostri conventus notum fieri volumus tam futuris quam presentibus quod contulimus ecclesie Premonstratensi sub annuo[4] censu alodia de Walescours[5] cum appenditiis suis, scilicet silva de Mesloi[6] et cultura que est in confinio de Landierfai[7,8] et ceteris omnibus pertinentiis, et altaria cum dotibus suis et decimis tam in territorio de Monciaus[9] quam de Murci[10] et de Walescourt[11] et in eisdem locis impositionem sacerdotum ydoneorum[12] quos videlicet, in presentia nostra, adducent ipsique fidelitatem nobis facient quod justicias nostras tam proprias quam communes pro posse suo tenebunt, ea siquidem conditione quod eadem Premonstratensis ecclesia persolvet nobis, singulis annis, circatas in sinodo de Murci et de Walescourt[13] et septem[14] modios et quatuor[15] galetos frumenti et modium unum pisorum ad mensuram in

3 Gualterus *B*[1], *B*[2].

4 annuali *B*[1], *B*[2].

5 Valescurt *B*[1], *B*[2].

6 Mesloy, comm. Chevresis-Monceau, https://dicotopo.cths.fr/places/P54953574.

7 Landerfai *B*[1], *B*[2].

8 Landifay-et-Bertaignemont, cant. Sains, https://dicotopo.cths.fr/places/P80498640.

9 Moncels *B*[1], *B*[2].

10 Murcy, comm. Monceau-le-Neuf, https://dicotopo.cths.fr/places/P08613211.

11 Valescurt *B*[1], *B*[2].

12 idonerorum *B*[1], *B*[2].

13 Valescurt *B*[1], *B*[2].

14 VII[tem] *B*[1], *B*[2].

15 IIII[or] *B*[1], *B*[2].

civitate Laudunensi eo tempore quo hec acta sunt currentem que utrimque sine diminutione vel augmentatione servabitur. Hoc autem frumentum tale solvitur quale in duobus vel tribus aut pluribus mercatis uno nummo minus valens cariore repperitur, pisa quoque denario uno minus valentia carioribus persolvuntur. Terminus[16] persolvendi est a festo Sancti Remigii usque ad mediam XL^{am}, infra quem terminum quocumque die vel tempore voluerint aut potuerint, solvent et apud Laudunum ad cellarium nostrum cum propria vectura conducent ipsique conductores duo ad carrum, unus ad redam ea die, si in refectorio comederimus, victum a nobis accipient. Persolvuntur etiam nobis annuatim a prefata Premonstratensi ecclesia quinque[17] solidi bone monete pro quadam portione terre illius que prescripta est, de qua inter nos et monachos Sancti Vincentii querela aliquandiu habita et sub annotatione eiusdem census fuerat terminata. Sciendum preterea inter nos convenisse quod si monachi Sancti Nicholai de Pratis terram de Tussis[18] quam a nobis censualiter tenent, renunciaverunt,[19] Premonstratenses sub ~~annuo~~ censu eodem[20] quo et illi, viginti[21] scilicet galetis frumenti ad mensuram Laudunensem, eam accipient. Siquis igitur eos super hiis inquietaverit, qui justiciam non[22] subterfugerit, nos pro eorum liberatione etiam usque ad Remensem curiam cum eorum expensis laborabimus et si longius ire necesse fuerit, consilium et auxilium sine expensis nostris exhibebimus. Si vero malefactor audientiam subterfugerit, nos cum eis eandem justiciam quam de propriis nostris redditibus[23] facere consuevimus, exequemur. Quod ut ratum et inconvulsum permaneat et prius quidem[24] predicta alodia sub presentia et testimonio circummanentium per nos[25] terminavimus et ecclesie Premonstratensi assignavimus quorum nomina hec sunt: Bernardus villicus de Monciaus,[26] Wibertus filius Constantii,[27] Paganus[28] de Derci[29] et ceteri[30] ac postmodum cirographi[31] conscriptione et legitimorum testium utriusque

16 *Om.* vero *A*.

17 V^{que} B^1, B^2.

18 Perhaps Torcy, comm. Parpeville, https://dicotopo.cths.fr/places/P92146153.

19 renuntiaverint B^1, B^2.

20 *Transp. A*; eodem censu B^1, B^2.

21 XX^{ti} B^1, B^2.

22 *Superscr.* non *A*.

23 reditibus B^1, B^2.

24 *Om.* per nos B^1.

25 *Add.* per nos B^1.

26 Moncels B^1, B^2.

27 *Om.* Siwart *A*.

28 A Païen de Dercy also appears as a witness in an 1144 act in the cartulary of Thenailles. BnF, MS Lat 5649, fol. 35v; Dufour-Malbezin, *Actes*, 259.

29 Dercy, cant. Crécy-sur-Serre, https://dicotopo.cths.fr/places/P47810688.

30 *Add.* et ceteri *A*; Odo Aldent, Herbertus de Bois vero et de Pareni, Odo miles, Robertus villicus, Richardus et filii eius, Terricus, Wascelinus B^1.

31 cyrographi B^1, B^2.

capituli annotatione[32] necnon etiam utriusque sigilli impressione presentem paginam communiri fecimus. S. Galteri,[33] Laudunensis episcopi. S. Rigardi[34,35] et Balduini,[36] archidiaconorum et ceteri.[37] Actum Lauduni anno incarnati verbi M° C° LIII°, indictione I[a], epacta XXIII[a], concurrente tercio.[38]

199

1165. Reims.

Henri,[1] archbishop of Reims, makes known the agreement reached between the church of Prémontré and Guillaume[2] Monachus *de La Ferté Chevresis concerning a portion of land in the territory of Mesloy[3] that Prémontré held in* census *from the canons of Laon.*

A. Cartulary of Prémontré, fol. 49v.
B. Original, AN, L 995, no. 33, previously sealed.
REGISTER: *Studium Baldwin*, fiche 1603.

Karta archiepiscopi Remensis de quadam conpositione inter ecclesiam Premonstratensem et Willermum de Firmatate.

[I]n nomine Patris et Filii et Spiritus Sancti. Ego Henricus, Dei gratia Remorum archiepiscopus, notum facio tam futuris quam presentibus quod Willermus de

32 adnotatione *B*[1], *B*[2].
33 Gualteri *B*[1], *B*[2].
34 Richardi *B*[1], *B*[2].
35 Richard, archdeacon of Laon, ca. 1145–ca. 1158. Wyard, *Saint-Vincent*, 34.
36 Baudouin de Rumigny, son of Nicolas II, lord of Rumigny, and Aleide van Hainaut, is attested as archdeacon of Laon 1148–51. Dufour-Malbezin, *Actes*, 421, 445.
37 *Add.* et ceteri *A*; S. Bartholomei thesaurarii. S. Milonis cantoris. S. Guntheri et Roberti presbiterorum. S. Odonis et Gerardi diaconorum. S. magistri Petri. S. magistri Hugonis. S. Roberti de Tireniaco. S. Angoti. S. Reineri, S. Manasses subdiaconorum. S. Hugonis, abbatis Premonstratensis. S. Gisleberti prioris. S. Honorati supprioris. S. Gozuini. S. Grimberti presbiterorum. S. Elberti. S. Hugonis, S. Johannis, S. Albrici diaconorum, S. Walcheri, S. Roberti, S. Ade subdiaconorum *B*[1], *B*[2].
38 III° *B*[1], *B*[2].

1 Henri de France (1121–1175), son of Louis VI of France and Adélaïde of Savoy, was bishop of Beauvais, 1149–62, and archbishop of Reims, 1162–75.
2 Guillaume *Monachus* de La Ferté-Chevresis, possibly a son of Blihard, lord of La Ferté-Chevresis and Brémonde. Melleville, *DH*, vol. 1, 382.
3 Mesloy, comm. Chevresis-Monceau, https://dicotopo.cths.fr/places/P54953574.

Firmitate Bliardi,[4] miles qui dicitur Monachus, movit querelam adversus fratres Premonstratensis[5] ecclesie super quadam portione terre in territorio de Mesloi prope Walescourt[6,7] quam a canonicis Laudunensis ecclesie sub annuo censu prefati fratres se habere asserebant. Cum vero utrique in curia Laudunensis episcopi sepe convenissent, nec querela debito fine terminaretur, facta appellatione, venerunt in curiam nostram et, testibus ex utraque parte productis, prefate ecclesie contra predictum Willermum legitimorum testium sacramentis et judicio curie nostre eandem terram dirationaverunt. Verum quia idem Willermus alteram querelam habebat adversus prefatam ecclesiam super quadam portione terre de Lesbiis prope Walescourt quam fratres eiusdem ecclesie a domino Bliardo[8] de Firmitate ad quintam garbam acceperant, ex consilio personarum subscriptarum ecclesie nostre in hoc convenerunt idem Willermus et predicte ecclesie fratres, quod si Willermus eandem terram a domino Bliardo[9] quoquomodo recuperaret, debitum quod Bliardo[10] debebatur, Willermo ab ecclesia solveretur; interim vero dum Bliardus[11] eam teneret, Willermus prefatam ecclesiam super hoc inquietare non posset. Deo igitur cooperante, pacificati cum bona voluntate redierunt ad propria. Predictus igitur Willermus et Willermus, filius ipsius, sub fide sua spoponderunt quod deinceps super hiis[12] unde querela erat, predictam ecclesiam non inquietarent. Ut igitur ratum et inconvulsum permaneat sigillum nostrum apponi et auctoritate nostra corroborari fecimus et eorum nomina qui huius[13] terminationi interfuerunt, subnotari. Testes sunt: Milo[14] de Lageri qui vicem nostram in audiendis et terminandis querelis agebat, Leo[15] decanus, et ceteri.[16] Ne igitur super hoc prefatam ecclesiam aliquis inquietare presumat sub anathemate interdicimus. Actum anno incarnati verbi M° C° LX° V°. Datum Remis per manum magistri Roberti[17] cancellarii.

4 Blihardi *B*.

5 Premonstrate *B*.

6 Walescurt *B*.

7 Valécourt, comm. Chevresis-Monceau, https://dicotopo.cths.fr/places/P14207928.

8 Blihardo *B*.

9 Blihardo *B*.

10 Blihardo *B*.

11 Blihardus *B*.

12 his *B*.

13 *Om.* actionis *A*.

14 Milon de Lagery, canon of Reims, also appears in an 1168 act of Robert, an intermediary of the bishop of Amiens. Stein, *Cartulaire de l'ancienne abbaye de Saint Nicolas des Prés sous Ribemont*, 115.

15 Léon, dean of Reims, is attested in acts from 1130 to 1166.

16 *Add.* et ceteri *A*; Fulcho magister scolaris, Rogerus Suessionensis archidiaconus, magister Lietoudus, Petrus vicedominus, Tiebaudus Revelarz, Radulphus Lienredes *B*.

17 Robert, chancellor of Reims, is attested ca. 1153–ca. 1165. Marlot, *Histoire de la ville, cité et université de Reims, métropolitaine de la Gaule Belgique*, 685.

200

1170

Gautier [II],[1] bishop of Laon, makes known that Eustache de Montigny[2] transferred to the church of Prémontré what he held in the tithe of Valécourt, in exchange for the payment of an annual trecensus *of 9* modii *of grain (*frumentum*), 4* modii *of oats, and one* modius *of peas. Eustache's children Guillaume, Raoul, Guy, Jean, Marie, and Matilde consent, as does fief lord Bliard de La Ferté-Chevresis;[3] Brémunde, his wife; and their children Gobert, Ada, Marguerite, Luciane, and Magloire.*

A. Cartulary of Prémontré, fols. 49v–50r.

B[1]. Original (chirograph), AN, L 995, no. 34, previously sealed. In the right margin and beginning at the top, the bottom half of the letters that form the word CHYROGRAPHUM. (This charter belonged to Prémontré, based on dorsal annotations.)

B[2]. Original (chirograph), AN, L 995, no. 35, previously sealed. In the left margin and beginning at the top, the top half of letters that form the word CHYROGRAPHUM. (This charter also belonged to Prémontré, based on dorsal annotations.)

Karta episcopi Laudunensis de decima de Walescurs que fuit Eustachii, data ad trecensum IX modiorum bladi eidem ecclesiam.

[I]n nomine sancte et individue Trinitatis.[4] Ego Galterus, Dei gratia Laudunensis[5] episcopus, notum facimus universis tam futuris quam presentibus quod Eustacius[6] de Montiniaco quicquid habebat in decima de Walescourt[7,8] concessit in perpetuum ecclesie Premonstratensi ad trecensum IX[9] modiorum frumenti ad mensuram Firmitatis Castri, uno quoque galeto nummum unum meliori frumento minus valente, et quatuor modiorum avene et uno modio

1 Gautier de Mortagne was dean of Laon, ca. 1142–55, and bishop of Laon, 1155–74.

2 Perhaps lord of Montigny-sur-Crécy (cant. Crécy-sur-Serre, https://dicotopo.cths.fr/places/P41326438) in the 1170s. Melleville, *DH*, vol. 2, 131.

3 Bliard de La Ferté-Chevresis (cant. Ribemont, https://dicotopo.cths.fr/places/P35438398), son of Baudouin de Soupir and Cécile, and brother or half-brother of Guy de Soupir. Morelle, "Une charte nuptiale laonnoise de 1158 conservée en original," 222, fn. 64.

4 *Om.* amen *A*.

5 Laudunensium *B*[1], *B*[2].

6 Eustachius *B*[2].

7 Walescort *B*[1], *B*[2].

8 Valécourt, comm. Chevresis-Monceau, https://dicotopo.cths.fr/places/P14207928.

9 VIIII *B*[1], *B*[2].

pisorum ad eandem mensuram tunc currentem ita quod unusquisque habebit galetum suum ne possit augeri vel minui, et trecensus iste annuatim persolvetur usque ad festivitatem Sancti Martini hiemalis, conductus vecturis ecclesie usque ad domum Eustachii apud[10] Montiniacum vel apud[11] Firmitatem Castrum et, si terra casu aliquo depopulata fuerit, usque ad locum per leugam unam distantem a Walescourt[12] conducetur ubicumque Eustacius[13] vel eius heres voluerit. Quod si tempore determinato Eustachius vel heres eius[14] trecensum recipere noluerit, loco competenti ponetur sub testimonio et, si deinceps casu aliquo trecensus pejoraverit vel conbustus fuerit, qualiscumque fuerit, Eustachius vel heres eius[15] talem recipient et trecensum istum Eustacius[16] vel eius heres nec in elemosinam dare nec vendere nec invadiare alicui poterit nisi Premonstratensi ecclesie, si ipsa ei tantum facere voluerit quantum alia ecclesia; nec hoc Eustachio vel heredi suo facere licebit nisi assensu Bliardi[17] et heredum suorum a quo decima feodaliter descendit et hoc laudavit ipse Blihardus et uxor eius, Braimundis,[18] et filius eius, Gobertus, et filie eius Ada, Margarita, Luciana,[19] Magloria, et si Bliardus[20] predictam decimam saisierit, trecensum quem ecclesia Eustachio[21] persolvebat, Blihardo et eius heredi persolvet. Hoc laudaverunt filii Eustachii, Guillermus,[22] Radulphus,[23] Guido,[24] Johannes et filie eius Maria, Matildis. Hoc autem ut ratum et inconvulsum permaneat, sigilli nostri inpressione et testium subscriptione et cirographo[25] muniri fecimus. S. Galteri,[26] thesaurarii. S. Johannis,[27] decani de Marla et ceteri.[28] Actum anno incarnati verbi M° C° LXX°. Angotus cancellarius scripsit, relegit, et subscripsit.

10 aput *B*[1], *B*[2].
11 aput *B*[1], *B*[2].
12 Walescort *B*[1], *B*[2].
13 Eustacius *B*[1], *B*[2].
14 *Transp. A*; eius heres *B*[1], *B*[2].
15 *Transp. A*; eius here *B*[1], *B*[2].
16 Eustacius *B*[2].
17 Blihardi *B*[1], *B*[2].
18 Braymundis *B*[1], *B*[2].
19 Lucyana *B*[1], *B*[2].
20 Blihardus *B*[1], *B*[2].
21 Eustacio *B*[1], *B*[2].
22 Guylermus *B*[1], *B*[2].
23 Radulfus *B*[1], *B*[2].
24 Guydo *B*[1], *B*[2].
25 Cyrographo *B*[1], *B*[2].
26 Gautier, treasurer of Laon, ca. 1162–ca. 1173. Per AD Aisne, G 171, a nephew of Gautier de Mortagne, bishop of Laon.
27 Jean, dean of Marle, ca. 1170–ca. 1205. Desilve, "Analyse d'un cartulaire de l'abbaye de la Valroy," 164; Édouard de Barthélemy, *Analyse du cartulaire de l'abbaye de Foigny*, 89. He had a brother, Syger, and a nephew, Droard, also a priest. Barthélemy, *LDA*, 348, fn. 392.
28 *Add.* et ceteri *A*; S. Johannis, presbiteri de Firmitate. S. Stefani, presbiteri de Bois. S. Galteri, presbiteri de Moncellis. S. Mathei, clerici de Firmitate. S. Blihardi de Firmitate. S. Balduini de Loysi. S. Guidonis Cati, militum *B*[1], *B*[2].

201

1153

Abbot Gilbert[1] *of Saint-Nicolas-aux-Bois cedes to abbot Hugues [I]*[2] *and the brothers of Prémontré the part of the allods of Monceau-le-Neuf*[3] *that Rose, mother of Clarembaud, monk of Saint-Nicolas, had given to Saint-Nicolas, on the condition that Saint-Nicolas pay Prémontré two* solidi *annually from its* census *and that Prémontré undertake to say Mass for Rose; Arnoul Chauderon,*[4] *her brother; Clarembaud and Létaud, Rose's sons; and their father Geoffroi.*

A. Cartulary of Prémontré, fol. 50r.

B. Original, AN, L 995, no. 17, previously sealed. In the right margin, beginning at the top, the lower half of the word CHYROGRAPHUM.

Karta abbatis Sancti Nicholai de silva Vedogii de parte alodiorum de Moncellis super Penron.

[I]n nomine sancte et individue Trinitatis.[5] Ego Gillebertus, Sancti Nicholai de Silva Vedogii abbas dictus, et capitulum eiusdem loci Hugoni, abbati Premonstratensi,[6] et successoribus eius regulariter substituendis in perpetuum. Notum fieri volumus tam futuris quam presentibus quod abbati predicto et fratribus monasterii eius concessimus partem illam alodiorum de Moncellis super Penron quam tenuit hereditario jure Roza, mater Clarenbaldi, monachi nostri, et nobis in elemosinam de manu Roberti Muti vel heredum eius redimendam dimisit; partem etiam Arnulphi Chauderon[7] quam ipse prefate Roze, sorori sue, de manu supradicta dedit redimendam et ipsa Roza redimendam nobis dimisit pro anima ipsius Arnulphi[8] ea conditione ut ipsa Roza et Arnulphus,[9] Clarenbaldus quoque cum suo patre Godefrido et fratre Lietaldo in orationibus et benefactis Premonstrati habeantur et dies anniversariorum ipsorum ibidem scribantur sub assignatione duorum solidorum bone monete in festo Sancti Nicholai singulis annis censualiter nobis solvendorum. Huius rei testes sunt Lambertus, Mauricius et ceteri.[10] Actum anno incarnati verbi M° C° LIII°.

---

1 Gilbert, abbot of the Benedictine abbey of Saint-Nicolas-aux-Bois, 1134–ca. 1157. Duval, "Histoire de l'abbaye bénédictine de Saint-Nicolas-aux-Bois, diocèse de Laon, première partie," 181–96.

2 Hugues I de Fosses (ca. 1093–1164), first abbot of Prémontré.

3 Monceau-le-Neuf-et-Faucousis, cant. Sains, https://dicotopo.cths.fr/places/P93537665.

4 Arnoul Chauderon (d. bef. 1153), brother of Rose, also appears in the Cartulary of Saint-Martin de Laon in acts of 1137 and 1155. BM Laon, MS 532, fols. 26r, 26v–27r; Barthelemy, *LDA*, 523.

5 *Om.* amen *A*.

6 Premonstratensium *B*.

7 Arnulfi Calderon *B*.

8 Arnulfi *B*.

9 Arnulfus *B*.

10 *Add.* et ceteri *A*; item Lambertus Nicholaus Ado, Clarembaldus, Theodoricus, Gerardus *B*.

202

December, 1222. Laon.

Anselme,[1] *bishop of Laon,* magister *Baudouin,*[2] *archdeacon of Liège, and Jacques de Dinant,*[3] *canon of Laon, make known the agreement reached in their presence between the church of Prémontré and* magister *Raoul de Montigny, canon of Saint-Quentin, according to which the nine* modii *of grain (*frumentum*), measure of La Ferté, that Prémontré owed annually to Raoul will, during his lifetime, be valued at Laon by the people of Laon, and after Raoul's death, at La Ferté-Chevresis,*[4] *by the town councillors (*scabini*).*

A. Cartulary of Prémontré, fols. 50r–50v.

B. Original, AN, L 995, no. 71, previously sealed with three seals.

Other Manuscript Copies: Cartulary of Valécourt, BnF, nouv. acq. lat. 938, fol. 1r (partial, 13th c.).

REGISTER: *Studium Baldwin*, fiche 2388, 2434.

Karta episcopi Laudunensis et Leodiensis archidiaconi Balduini de compositione inter ecclesiam Premonstratensem et Radulphum de Montiniaco.

A[nselmus], Dei gratia Laudunensis episcopus, et magistri Balduinus Leodiensis archidiaconus et Jacobus de Dinant, canonicus Laudunensis, universis Christi fidelibus ad quos littere iste pervenerint salutem in Domino nostro Jesu Christo. Noverit universitas vestra quod, cum esset discordia inter ecclesiam Premonstratensem ex una parte et magistrum Radulphum de Montiniaco,[5] canonicum Sancti Quintini, ex altera super estimatione novem modiorum frumenti ad mensuram de Firmitate, quos eadem ecclesia dicto magistro reddere tenetur annuatim, secundum quod continetur in autentico instrumento felicis memorie Galteri,[6] quondam episcopi Laudunensis, et in nos a partibus fuisset compromissum sub pena viginti librarum Parisiensium quam partes sibi invicem reddere promiserunt, si dictum nostrum super hoc non servarent, tandem prefato magistro et fratre Johanne, procuratore dicte ecclesie habente speciale mandatum

1 Anselme de Mauny (or de Bercenay), bishop of Laon, 1215–38.

2 Baudouin de Vaux, canon of Saint-Lambert, 1218–ca. 1225, and archdeacon of Brabant, 1225–35. Renardy, *Les maîtres universitaires du diocèse de Liège*, 194.

3 *Magister* Jacques de Dinant (d. ca. 1259) was a canon of Laon from about 1218, and about 1230 became archdeacon of Thérouanne. Picó, "Membership in the Cathedral Chapter of Laon, 1217–1238," 16–17.

4 La Ferté-Chevresis, cant. Ribemont, https://dicotopo.cths.fr/places/P35438398.

5 Radulfum de Montigniaco *B*.

6 Walteri *B*.

ab abbate et conventu Premonstratensi ad componendum, ipsis se invicem de novo obligantibus sub pena quadraginta librarum Parisiensium quod subscriptam compositionem servabunt, coram nobis composuerunt in hunc modum, quod, quamdiu sepedictus magister vixerit, estimatio predicti frumenti fiet apud ~~Firmitatem Bliardi~~ Laudunum ab estimatoribus Laudunensibus; post decessum vero predicti magistri estimatio eiusdem frumenti fiet apud Firmitatem Bliardi[7] a scabinis eiusdem castri vel bonis viris in huiusmodi estimationibus edoctis. Ut igitur dicta conpositio perpetuam obtineat firmitatem et omnis controversia super hoc deinceps sopiatur, presens scriptum emisimus sigillorum nostrorum inpressionibus roboratum. Et ego[8] Laudunensis episcopus Anselmus[9] ad requisitionem partium eandem compositionem auctoritate pontificali confirmo. Actum Lauduni anno verbi incarnati M° CC° vicesimo II°,[10] mense decembri.

203

1189. Marle.

Raoul [I],[1] lord of Coucy, makes known that following a dispute, the Premonstratensian religious of Valécourt[2] will pay Gautier Discalciatus, *Alard Serians, and brothers Renier and Clarembaud, Raoul le Moine and Henri, the brothers Jean and Roger, and Jépuin, son of Marsille, 11* librae Laudunensium *in return for them renouncing all rights to the disputed goods.*

A. Cartulary of Prémontré, fol. 50v.

B. Original, AN, J 738, Soissons et Soissonnais, n° 1 *ter.*, previously sealed with a double strip of parchment.[3]

Other Manuscript Copies: Cartulary of Valécourt, BnF, nouv. acq. lat. 938, fols. 1r–1v (13th c.).

EDITION: Teulet et al, *Layettes du Trésor des chartes*, vol. 5, 33.

Karta Radulphi domini Couciaci de quadam compositione in territorio de Walescurs.

[E]go Radulphus, dominus Couciaci, notum omnibus volo fieri quod Walterus Discalciatus, Alardus Serjans et Renerus et Clarenbaldus, fratres eius,

7 Blihardi *B*.
8 *Om*. A. *A*.
9 *Add*. Anselmus *A*.
10 secundo *B*.

1 Raoul I, lord of Coucy (d. 1191), son of Enguerrand II, lord of Coucy, and Agnès de Beaugency.
2 Valécourt, comm. Chevresis-Monceau, https://dicotopo.cths.fr/places/P14207928.
3 Due to archival access restrictions in operation in 2020, the editors were unable to view this charter.

Radulphus monachus et Henricus fratres, Johannes et Rogerus fratres, et Jepuinus filius Marsilii, adversus fratres de Walescourt quasdam querelas habebant de quibus inter predictos homines et ipsos fratres pax et conpositio intercessit, que coram me et subscriptis testibus, presente et annuente utraque, parte recognita et confirmata fuit. Siquidem iidem fratres iam dictis hominibus, ex parte Premonstratensis, undecim libras Laudunenses pro bono pacis dederunt et ipsi homines quicquid juris habebant in omnibus querelis quas adversus prefatos fratres vel moverant vel movere poterant, Premonstratensi ecclesie in elemosinam dimiserunt et, renuntiatis omnibus rebus de quibus controversia oriri poterat, fide interposita spoponderunt se nullam amodo eidem ecclesie calumpniam vel molestiam illaturos sed prescriptam compositionis formam jugiter et inviolabiliter servaturos ita quod, si aliquis ecclesiam illam presumpserit molestare, supradicti homines contra omnes de quibus justicia haberi poterit, tenebuntur cum sumptibus predictorum fratrum eis warandiam exhibere. Ut autem hec conpositio firma et stabilis perseveret, eam presentium litterarum feci testimonio conmendari et tam sigilli mei munimine quam subscriptione testium roborari. S. Danielis. S. Ingelranni et ceteri. Actum apud Marlam, anno ab incarnatione Domini M° C° LXXX° IX°.

204

May, 1222.

Anselme,[1] *bishop of Laon, makes known that husband and wife Gérard Paillart de Parpeville*[2] *and Aelide, and their son Gobert, sold to the church of Prémontré three parcels of land located near the Premonstratensian* curtis *of Valécourt*[3] *for eleven* librae *and eight* solidi blancorum. *Aelide had held this land by right of* dotalicium, *and Gérard gave her a field at Montigny in compensation.*

A. Cartulary of Prémontré, fol. 50v.

B. Original, AD Aisne, H 773, previously sealed with a double strip of parchment.[4]

Other Manuscript Copies: Cartulary of Valécourt, BnF, nouv. acq. lat. 938, fols. 1v–2r (13th c.).

1 Anselme de Mauny (or de Bercenay), bishop of Laon, 1215–38.

2 Gerard Paillart (or Pallars) de Parpeville (cant. Ribemont, https://dicotopo.cths.fr/places/P82547248) also appears in **205** and in a 1225 act in a cartulary of the Cistercian abbey of Notre-Dame de Foigny. BM Reims, MS 1563 (N. Fonds), fol. 35r.

3 Valécourt, comm. Chevresis-Monceau, https://dicotopo.cths.fr/places/P14207928.

4 Due to conservation concerns, the original was not available to the editors.

Karta episcopi Laudunensis de terra quam vendidit Gerardus Paillars ecclesie Premonstratensi.

[A]nselmus, Dei gratia Laudunensis episcopus, universis tam presentibus quam futuris salutem in Domino. Scire volumus universos quod Gerardus, cognomento Pallars de Parpres, et Aelidis, uxor sua, et Gobertus, filius suus, in nostra presentia constituti, recognoverunt se vendidisse ecclesie Premonstratensi tres particulas terre site in Vaucello prope curtem de Walescourt, continentes sex galetas sementis, ad mensuram de Firmitate, parum plus vel parum minus pro undecim libris et octo solidis blancorum. Sciendum est autem quod quia eadem terra erat de dotalicio dicte Aelidis, ipsa publice recognovit quod venditionem istam gratam habet et acceptam, facta ei condigna ei sufficienti reconpensatione pro dotalicio suo a suo marito ad campum suum semite de Montigniaco et tam ipsa quam dictus maritus suus quam etiam prenominatus filius suus fidem corporaliter prestiterunt quod nec per se nec per alios reclamabunt ipsam terram vel facient reclamari nec aliquo modo pro eadem terra memoratam ecclesiam molestabunt. Preterea ipsi debent portare legitimam warandiam ecclesie Premonstratensi super eadem terra adversus omnes qui voluerint juri stare. Nos autem in testimonium huius recognitionis perpetuo valiture fecimus presentes litteras sigilli nostri munimine roborari. Actum mense maio, anno gratie M° CC° XX° II°.

205

May, 1224.

Jean [II],[1] *lord of Housset, makes known that he gave Gérard Paillart de Parpeville*[2] *the* modiagium *that the church of Prémontré owed Jean annually for land at Valécourt; in turn, Gérard gives this* modiagium *in alms to Prémontré.*

A. Cartulary of Prémontré, fol. 50v.

B. Original, AD Aisne, H 773, previously sealed with a double strip of parchment and a remaining fragment of a brown wax seal.[3]

Other Manuscript Copies: Cartulary of Valécourt, BnF, nouv. acq. lat. 938, fols. 2r–2v (13th c.).

1 Jean II, (d. bef. 1230) lord of Housset (cant. Sains, https://dicotopo.cths.fr/places/P27336521), son of Jean I and Marie (?). Barthelemy, *LDA*, 520–1.

2 Gerard Paillart (or Pallars) de Parpeville (cant. Ribemont, https://dicotopo.cths.fr/places/P82547248) also appears in **204** and in a 1225 act in a cartulary of the Cistercian abbey of Notre-Dame de Foigny. BM Reims, MS 1563 (N. Fonds), fol. 35r.

3 Due to conservation concerns, the original was not available to the editors.

Karta Johannis de Hussello de resignatione modiagii.

[E]go Johannes, dominus de Hussello, notum facio universis tam presentibus quam futuris quod illud modiagium quod ecclesia Premonstratensis michi debebat annuatim pro terra quadam sita ante domum de Walescourt, quam etiam terram tenebat de me et de patre meo tenuerat ecclesia memorata, resignavi et ipsum modiagium mandavi et precepi dari in perpetuum Gerardo, cognomento Pallart de Parpres, nec aliquid juris michi retinui vel in ipso modiagio vel in terra pro qua michi solvebatur modiagium prenotatum. Processu igitur temporis idem Gerardus, ductus devotione, quicquid ego feci eidem conferri ab ecclesia prenotata, sive in modiagio sive in terra, contulit in elemosinam ecclesie Premonstratensis perpetuo possidendum, nichil omnino sibi juris retinens vel in modiago vel in terra. Ego vero, tamquam superior dominus, elemosinam ipsam gratam habui et in perpetuum statui esse firmam nec jus aliquid vel in ipso modiagio vel in ipsa terra in perpetuum reclamabo. In cuius rei testimonium presentem kartam sigilli mei munimine roboravi. Actum mense maio, anno gratie M° CC° XX° quarto.

206

April, 1219.

Anselme,[1] *bishop of Laon, makes known that Guy de Monceau,*[2] *knight, upon his departure for the Albigensian crusade, gave to Anselme four-ninths of the minor tithe on Monceau-le-Vieil. Anselme now gives the tithe to abbot Gervais*[3] *and the brothers of Prémontré, who held the right of* patronatus.

A. Cartulary of Prémontré, fols. 50v–51r.

B. Original BnF, Coll. Picardie 290, no. 33, previously sealed.

Other Manuscript Copies: Cartulary of Valécourt, BnF, nouv. acq. lat. 938, fols. 2v–3r (13th c.).

EDITION: Slack, *Crusade Charters, 1138–1270*, 184–5.

1 Anselme de Mauny (or de Bercenay), bishop of Laon, 1215–38.

2 Guy de Monceau, knight, lord of Monceau-le-Vieil (comm. Chevresis-Monceau, https://dicotopo.cths.fr/places/P61634471), brother of Anselme, lord of Monceau-le-Neuf. Melleville, *DH*, vol. 2, 109.

3 Gervais, abbot of the Premonstratensian abbeys of Saint-Just-en-Chaussée, 1199–1205, Thenailles, 1205–9, and Prémontré, 1209–20, and bishop of Séez, 1220–8. *MP* II, 401, 527, 565; Cheney, "Gervase, Abbot of Prémontré."

Karta Laudunensis episcopi de elemosina Guidonis de Moncellis de novem portionibus minute decime Veteris Moncelli.

[E]go Anselmus, divina miseratione Laudunensis episcopus, omnibus in perpetuum. Notum facimus tam presentibus quam futuris quod cum Guido de Moncellis, miles, de novem portionibus minute decime Veteris Moncelli quasi hereditario jure quatuor reciperet portiones, crucesignatus pro succursu ecclesie Albigensis et cogitans de anime sue ~~sue~~ salute, personaliter ad presentiam nostram accessit et dictam partem quam habebat in prefata decima in manum nostram, intuitu Dei et nomine elemosine, resignavit ut Premonstratensis ecclesie que habebat jus patronatus ibidem, episcopali auctoritate[4] daretur. Nos autem recepimus resignationem ipsius et virum religiosum Gervasium, Premonstratensem abbatem, nomine ecclesie sibi commisse, investivimus de decima sepedicta. Ut igitur tam resignatio quam investitura per nos facta perpetuam habeat firmitatem, presens scriptum in memoriam rei geste sigilli nostri inpressione duximus roborandum. Actum mense aprili, anno gratie M° CC°[5] nonodecimo.

207

August, 1231.

Abbot Mathieu[1] *and the convent of Foigny make known that the church of Prémontré gave them the* terragium *and other rights to six separate pieces of land at Faucousis;*[2] *Prémontré held half of the tithe of one of these pieces of land and transfers this to Foigny, in exchange for an annual* census *of one* modius *of grain (*frumentum*), measure of Marle.*[3]

A. Cartulary of Prémontré, fol. 51r.

B. Original not found.

Other Manuscript Copies: Cartulary of Valécourt, BnF, nouv. acq. lat. 938, fols. 3r–4r (13th c.).

4 autoritate *B*.

5 millesimo ducentesimo *B*.

1 Matthieu I, abbot of the Cistercian abbey of Foigny, 1224–48. *GC* IX, col. 631.

2 Faucousis, comm. Monceau-le-Neuf, https://dicotopo.cths.fr/places/P08023812.

3 The companion act to this, issued by Conrad, abbot of Prémontré, is in two cartularies produced at Foigny. BM Reims 1563 (N. Fonds), fols. 21r–21v; BNF, MS lat. 18374, fol. 88v.

Karta abbatis Fusniaci de quitatione quam fecit ecclesia Premonstratensis in territorio de Foukauzies.

[E]go frater Matheus, dictus abbas, et conventus Fusniaci, notum facimus universis tam presentibus quam futuris quod ecclesia Premonstratensis quitavit et contulit nobis terragium et totum jus quod habebat in sex petiis terre sitis in territorio nostro de Foukouzies per loca diversa, videlicet in locis de Busignies, Es Vegars, in semita que tendit de Plancha ad Vilencel En Bergelin versus Tilloi; item En Bergelin, sicut strata ducit de Foucouzies ad Seont[4] per medium campum; que videlicet sex petie capiunt circiter quinque modios et quatuor galetos sementis ad mensuram de Firmitate; in quarum sexta petia, videlicet in fassia de Huquenies, dicta ecclesia habebat medietatem decime quam etiam contulit nobis cum predicto terragio sub annuo censu unius modii frumenti ad mensuram de Marla[5] currentem tempore huius scripti de meliori blado post sementem, quod crescet in territorio de Foucouzies; et solvetur a nobis eidem ecclesie idem modius bladi annuatim, non obstante aliquo defecteu vel tempestate vel guerra, singulis annis a festo Beati Remigii in octobri usque ad nativitatem Domini, quandocumque voluerimus infra istos duos terminos, ita tamen quod quando idem bladum trituratum fuerit, magister grangie nostre de Fouquozies nunciabit magistro grangie de Walescourt[6] ut veniat apud Fouquozies, vel mittat aliquem de fratribus suis qui dictum bladum videat, si sufficiens est, et mensuret illud et inponat vel inponi faciat super vecturam nostram in qua dictum bladum in grangiam de Walescurt deducetur et conducetur cum omni custu nostro, salvo eo quod si occasione ecclesie Premonstratensis vectura capta fuerit vel inpedita, non inputabitur nobis; si vero negligentes fuerimus de solvendo modio supradicto, predicta ecclesia ad sex petias terre predictas habebit sine aliqua contradictione recursum, donec eidem ecclesie fuerit de ipso modio satisfactum. In cuius rei testimonium et perpetuam firmitatem, presentem kartam eidem ecclesie dedimus sigilli nostri appensione et munimine roboratam. Actum anno gratie M° CC° XXX° I°, mense augusto.

208

June, 1227.

Jean,[1] abbot of Saint-Quentin, H., prior of Saint-Quentin, and Nicholas de Chambly,[2] canon of Beauvais, are tasked by Romano [Bonaventura], cardinal

4 Sons-et-Ronchères, cant. Marle, https://dicotopo.cths.fr/places/P19824727.

5 Marle, arr. Laon, https://dicotopo.cths.fr/places/P68626104.

6 Valécourt, comm. Chevresis-Monceau, https://dicotopo.cths.fr/places/P14207928.

1 Jean I d'Auteuil, abbot of the Augustinian abbey of Saint-Quentin de Beauvais, 1222–37. *GC* IX, cols. 822–3.

2 Nicolas de Chambly, canon of Beauvais, is also attested in a 1233 gift to the abbey of Froidmont. Deladreue, "Notice sur l'abbaye de Froidmont: 2e partie," 23.

deacon of Sant'Angelo [in Pescheria] with settling the dispute between the church of Prémontré and Thomas, priest of Sons,[3] *concerning the division of a tithe in the parish of Sons. Thomas acknowledged that Prémontré held the disputed rights and paid back to Prémontré what he had unduly received for four years. (See* ***209****.)*

A. Cartulary of Prémontré, fols. 51r–51v.

B. Original BnF, Coll. Picardie 290, no. 39, previously sealed.

Other Manuscript Copies: Cartulary of Valécourt, BnF, nouv. acq. lat. 938, fols. 4r–5r (13th c.).

Karta abbatis et prioris Sancti Quintini et Nicholaus de Cambliaco de causa inter ecclesiam et Thomam presbiterum de Sont.

[J]ohannes abbas, H., prior Sancti Quintini, et Nicholaus de Camliaco,[4] canonicus Belvacensis, universis tam presentibus quam futuris eternam in Domino salutem. Scire volumus universos quod cum reverendus pater Romanus Dei gratia, Sancti Angeli diaconus cardinalis, Apostolice Sedis legatus, nobis causam que inter Premonstratensem ecclesiam ex una parte et Thomam, presbiterum de Seont, ex parte altera super decimatione sita in parrochia de Seont in quibusdam campis qui inferius exprimentur, vertebatur, commisset fine debito[5] terminandam, tandem post multas altercationes habitas hinc inde prenominatus presbiter, in nostra presentia personaliter constitutus, recognovit spontanea voluntate quod nichil juris habebat vel habuerat in decimatione camporum ipsorum quorum nomina sunt hec: campus qui dicitur Sancti Vincentii retro Le Plois,[6] continens circiter tres galetas sementis; campus qui dicitur En Petainval, continens circiter galetam et dimidiam sementis; campus qui dicitur Ad Macerias, continens circiter duas galetas sementis; campus qui dicitur Ad Plantam, continens circiter quatuor galetas sementis; item campus qui dicitur Ad Plantam, continens circiter tres galetas sementis; campus qui dicitur Ad Diole, continens circiter galetam et dimidiam. Recognovit etiam idem presbiter quod in decimatione predictorum camporum nichil juris decetero reclamabit vel poterit reclamare sed ipsa ecclesia Premonstratensis decetero in perpetuum in pacifica possessione consistet decimationis predictorum camporum; recognovit nichilominus dictus presbiter quod super eo quod perceperat injuste per quatuor annos decimationem predictorum camporum, predicte Premonstratensis ecclesie plenarie satisfecit. Nos igitur recognitionem prenominati presbiteri conmisse nobis auctoritatis officio confirmantes, presentem paginam, ut robur

3 Sons-et-Ronchères, cant. Marle, https://dicotopo.cths.fr/places/P19824727.

4 Chambliaco *B*.

5 Canonico *B*.

6 Le Ploys *B*.

optineat perpetue firmitatis, sigillorum nostrorum duximus munimine roborandam. Actum mense junio, anno incarnationis dominice M° CC° vicesimo septimo.

209

July, 1227.

Gautier,[1] *abbot of Saint-Martin de Laon, and Guillaume,*[2] *abbot of Thenailles, after confirming by* vidimus *a 1227 act of Anselme,*[3] *bishop of Laon, judge that Prémontré holds the tithe on certain fields in the parish of Sons.*[4] *Having considered both sworn testimony and public consensus, Gautier and Guillaume also confirm by* vidimus *a charter in which bishop Anselme approved the decision of Thomas, priest of Sont, to agree to arbitration concerning his dispute with Prémontré.*[5] *(See **208**.)*

A. Cartulary of Prémontré, fols. 51v–52r.

B. Original not found.

Other Manuscript Copies: Cartulary of Valécourt, BnF, nouv. acq. lat. 938, fols. 5r–6v (13th c.).

Karta episcopi Laudunensis de compositione inter ecclesiam Premonstratensem et presbiterum de Sont.

[I]n nomine sancte et individue Trinitatis. Nos Walterus, Sancti Martini Laudunensis et Willermus, Thenoliensis Dei patientia dicti abbates, notum facimus universis tam presentibus quam futuris quod inter ecclesiam Premonstratensem ex una parte et Thomam, presbiterum de Seont, ex altera emersit controversia super decimatione quorumdam camporum sitorum in parrochia de Seont qui inferius sunt notati, videlicet campi qui dicitur Sancti Vincentii retro Le Plois[6] continentis circiter tres galetas sementis, campi qui dicitur En Petevial continentis circiter galetam et dimidiam sementis, quem campum tenebant Richardus et Willermus Haslez, campi qui dicitur Ad Macerias continentis circiter duas galetas sementis quem tenebant Stephanus Escorche et Rogerus

1 Gautier du Val-le-Roy, abbot of the Premonstratensian abbey of Saint-Martin de Laon. *MP* II, 512.

2 Guillaume, abbot of the Premonstratensian abbey of Thenailles, aft. 1220–30. *MP* II, 401.

3 Anselme de Mauny (or de Bercenay), bishop of Laon, 1215–38.

4 Sons-et-Ronchères, cant. Marle, https://dicotopo.cths.fr/places/P19824727.

5 The act of which this is a *vidimus* is AN, L 995, no. 73.

6 Plois, comm. Guise, https://dicotopo.cths.fr/places/P25085472.

Potions, campi qui dicitur Ad Plantam continentis circiter quatuor galetas sementis quem tenebant Ricardus Boquiaus et Renaldus filius Hugonis, item campi qui dicitur Ad Plantam continentis circiter tres galetas sementis quem tenuit Hugo Herboreis, campi qui dicitur Ad Diole continentis circiter galetam et dimidiam quem campum tenebat vir Radulphus nobilis, dominus de Seont, cum igitur partes super decimationem predictorum camporum et coram ordinario et coram delegatis judicibus diutius litigassent, tandem renuntiantes omnibus instrumentis et actis, compromiserunt de consilio bonorum virorum de conmuni consensu et spontanea voluntate in nos sub certa pena de omnibus controversiis que occasione predicte decimationis vel iam emerserant vel emergere poterant in futurum tali modo quod quicquid arbitraremur de controversiis iamdictis, ratum ab utraque parte in perpetuum haberetur et firmum et super rato habendo ipso arbitrio emanaverunt in hunc modum littere domini episcopi Laudunensis: Anselmus, Dei gratia Laudunensis episcopus, universis presentes litteras inspecturis salutem in Domino. Scire volumus universos quod Thomas, presbiter de Seont, in nostra presentia personaliter constitutus, recognovit quod de omnibus querelis que, occasione decimationis in parrochia sua site, inter ipsum et Premonstratensis ecclesiam vertebantur, conpromisit in venerabiles viros W[alterum], Sancti Martini Laudunensis, et W[illermum] Thenoliensis abbates, sub pena viginti librarum Parisiensium a parte que ab arbitrio resilierit solvendarum, ratum habiturus quicquid predicti abbates super eisdem querelis fuerint arbitrati. Recognovit etiam idem presbiter quod conpromiserit in eosdem de omnibus de quibus, occasione decimationis predicte, possent inter ipsum et prenominatam ecclesiam discordie suboriri. Nos autem, que premissa sunt quantum in nobis est, approbamus hoc modo quod dicti arbitri in arbitrio predicto vel etiam prolatione non procedant sine nostro vel curie nostre speciali consensu. Actum Lauduni mense junio anno gratie M° CC° vicesimo VII°. Nos igitur ad locum predicte decimationis personaliter accedentes, intelleximus tam per testes juratos quam per famam ville et vicinie de Seont decimationem omnium predictorum camporum ad ecclesiam Premonstratensem ab antiquo specialiter pertinere; unde, habito consilio, cum bonis viris et consensu speciali curie Laudunensis arbitrando pronuntiavimus ut dicta ecclesia Premonstratensis decetero in perpetuum in pacifica possessione consistat decimationis predictorum camporum, dicto Thomao et successoribus suis super ipsa decimatione perpetuum silentium inponentes. Ut autem hoc arbitrium nostrum de consensu curie Laudunensis et ad petitionem partium cum debita sollempnitate prolatum robur optineat perpetue firmitatis, presentem paginam duximus sigillorum nostrorum munimine roborandam. Actum mense julio, anno Domini M° ducentesimo XX° septimo.

210

September, 1231.

Abbot Conrad[1] *and the convent of Prémontré make known that Guy, priest of Monceau, gave them two pieces of land in perpetual alms, one near Valécourt,*[2] *the other near the fountain of* Aubrecies, *in return for which they will pay him annually one* modius *of grain (*bladus*), measure of Monceau. Prémontré gave Guy the minor tithes of Monceau-le-Vieil*[3] *and Monceau-le-Neuf,*[4] *together with the part of the tithes that Prémontré holds over the two churches there, in exchange for an annual* census *of 60* solidi Laudunensium, *valid for six years or until Guy's death, whichever happens first. (See* ***211****.)*

A. Cartulary of Prémontré, fol. 52r.

B. Original, AD Aisne, H 773, previously sealed.[5]

Other Manuscript Copies: Cartulary of Valécourt, BnF, nouv. acq. lat. 938, fols. 6v–7r (13th c.).

Karta Conradi abbatis et conventus Premonstratensis de elemosina presbiteri de Moncellis.

[U]niversis presentes litteras inspecturis Conradus, abbas et conventus Premonstratensis salutem in Domino. Noverit universitas vestra quod dilectus in Christo, Guido, presbiter de Moncellis, dedit nobis in perpetuam elemosinam duas petias terre quarum una sita est in valle ante portam domus nostre de Walescurt et alia sita est ad fontem a Aubrecies, a nobis perpetuo possidendas et nos in reconpensationem istius devotionis tenemur eidem presbitero, quamdiu vixerit, in uno modio bladi ad mensuram de Moncellis de meliori quem percipiemus in decima nostra de Moncellis, annuatim eidem Guidoni in nativitate Beate Marie Virginis persolvendo. Preterea dedimus et concessimus predicto Guidoni, presbitero de Moncellis, totam minutam decimam nostram de utraque villa de Moncellis et partem nostram oblationum quas habemus in utraque ecclesia de Moncellis tenendas et percipiendas a sepedicto Guidone a Pascha ultimo preterito usque ad sex annos, mediantibus sexaginta solidis Laudunensis monete quos idem Guido nobis annuatim reddere tenetur terminis subnotatis in nativitate Sancti Johannis Baptiste triginta solidos, et in festo Beati Remigii triginta solidios; verum si forte infra istos sex annos decesserit presbiter memoratus predicta minuta decima nostra ad nos libere et sine

1 Conrad the Swabian was prior of Weissenau, 1203–17, abbot of Valsecret, 1218–20, abbot of Prémontré, 1220–33, and abbot of Cuissy, aft. 1235–41. *MP* I, 89; *MP* II, 497, 527, 536.

2 Valécourt, comm. Chevresis-Monceau, https://dicotopo.cths.fr/places/P14207928.

3 Monceau-le-Vieil, comm. Chevresis-Monceau, https://dicotopo.cths.fr/places/P61634471.

4 Monceau-le-Neuf-et-Faucousis, cant. Sains, https://dicotopo.cths.fr/places/P93537665.

5 Due to conservation concerns, this original was not available to the editors.

contradictione aliqua revertetur et quam cito etiam decesserit, a solutione dicti modii bladi liberi erimus penitus et inmunes et nichilominus predicte due petie terre nobis in perpetuam elemosinam remanebunt. In cuius rei testimonium presentes litteras patentes emisimus sigilli nostri munimine roboratas. Actum anno gratie M° CC° tricesimo primo, mense septembri.

211

May, 1219.

Anselme [II],[1] *lord of Monceau-le-Neuf, approves as fief lord the alms that his brother Guy*[2] *gave to the church of Prémontré. (See **210**.)*

A. Cartulary of Prémontré, fol. 52r.

B. Original not found.

Other Manuscript Copies: Cartulary of Valécourt, BnF, nouv. acq. lat. 938, fol. 7r (13th c.).

NO RUBRIC.

[E]go Ansellus, dominus Moncelli Novi, notum facio universis tam presentibus quam futuris, qui viderint istud scriptum, quod Guido, frater meus, resignavit ecclesie Premonstratensi, nomine elemosine, totam illam partem minute decime quam tenebat de me in feodo in minuta decima Veteris Moncelli par manum domini Anselmi, episcopi Laudunensis. Ego autem elemosinam ipsam cui rationabiliter contradicere non poteram, laudavi et presentes litteras in testimonium perpetuum sigilli mei appensione munivi. Actum mense maio. Actum anno gratie M° CC° nono decimo.

212

1143–61.[1]

Samson,[2] *archbishop of Reims, makes known that Hugues Bouton, son of Guy de Chermizy,*[3] *renounced his suit concerning a gift that his father had made to*

1 Anselme II, lord of Monceau-le-Neuf (cant. Sains, https://dicotopo.cths.fr/places/P93537665), attested 1210s–20s; probably the son of Rénier de Monceau. Barthélemy, *LDA*, 525.

2 Guy de Monceau, knight, attested 1210s; probably the son of Rénier de Monceau. Barthélemy, *LDA*, 525.

1 This act must have been written after the original gift referred to here (1143) and before the end of the archiepiscopacy of Samson de Mauvoisin (1161). Dufour-Malbezin, *Actes*, 345–8.

2 Samson de Mauvoisin, son of Raoul III le Barbu de Mauvoisin, lord of Rosny-sur-Seine, and his first wife Odeline, was archdeacon and provost of Chartres, and archbishop of Reims, 1140–61.

3 Guy I, lord of Chermizy. Melleville, *DH*, vol. 1, 237. Chermizy, cant. Craonne, https://dicotopo.cths.fr/places/P58073186.

the church of Prémontré of the tithe of Vervins[4] *and the* terragium *of* Angeis. *Alexandre, brother of Hugues, consents, as do Alexandre's unnamed children.*

A. Cartulary of Prémontré, fol. 52r.

B. Original not found.

Other Manuscript Copies: Cartulary of Valécourt, BnF, nouv. acq. lat. 938, fol. 7v (13th c.).

Karta archiepiscopi Remensis de dono Guidonis de Chermisi et Hugonis Bouton.

[I]n nomine sancte et individue Trinitatis. Ego Sanson, divina miseratione Remorum archiepiscopus, universis Sancte Matris Ecclesie filiis tam presentibus quam futuris in perpetuum. ~~Ho~~ Onus curie pastoralis cogit nos pro aliis sollicitos esse et maxime ne quies contemplativorum aliquo incursu actionum secularium dissipetur, providere. Unde tam presentibus quam posteris notum esse volumus Hugonem Bouton, filium Guidonis de Chermisi, donum decime de Vervin et terragii de Angeiis quod pater eius, Guido, ipso approbante et fratre eius, Alexandro, prius fecerat ecclesie Premonstrate, postea calumpniatum esse; qui tamen Hugo, ad se rediens, omnem illam calumpniam penitus dimisit et tam decimam quam terragium per manum nostram ecclesie Premonstrate libere possidenda concessit, approbante hoc iterum Alexandro, fratre suo, et liberis suis. Quod ut a nemine mutari valeat litteris mandari easdemque literas sigilli nostri inpressione muniri precipimus et probabilium personarum testimonia adhiberi fecimus Boso[5] archidiaconus, Bartholomeus et ceteri. Robertus[6] cancellarius recognovit et scripsit.

213

September, 1202. Church of Notre-Dame de Vervins.

Jean [II],[1] *abbot of Clairefontaine, and Haimon, priest of Origny*[2] *– with the cooperation of Gobert,*[3] *abbot of Thenailles, and Jean,*[4] *dean of Vervins*[5] *– arbitrate*

---

4 Vervins, arr. Vervins, https://dicotopo.cths.fr/places/P65564790.

5 Boson, archdeacon of Reims, appears in a number of acts from the 1140s to the 1160s. He was a brother of Foulque d'Ecry (modern Asfeld, arr. Rethel). Marlot, *Histoire de la ville, cité et université de Reims, métropolitaine de la Gaule Belgique*, 640; Morelle, "Mariage et diplomatique," 268, fn. 7.

6 Robert, chancellor of Reims, is attested ca. 1153–ca. 1165. Marlot, *Histoire de la ville, cité et université de Reims, métropolitaine de la Gaule Belgique*, 685.

---

1 Jean II, abbot of the Premonstratensian abbey of Clairefontaine, 1201–18. *MP* II, 372.

2 Origny-Sainte-Benoîte, cant. Ribemont, https://dicotopo.cths.fr/places/P14935952.

3 Gobert, abbot of the Premonstratensian abbey of Thenailles, 1191–ca. 1202. *MP* II, 401.

4 A Jean, dean of Vervins, also appears as a witness in an 1190 charter of Raoul de Coucy. Herbomez, *Chartes de l'abbaye de Saint-Martin de Tournai*, vol. 1, 161.

5 Vervins, arr. Vervins, https://dicotopo.cths.fr/places/P65564790.

the dispute between the church of Prémontré and Robert de Autimont[6] *and Petreya de Vervins concerning the revenues of houses and gardens held within the boundaries of a certain* terragium *of Prémontré. For each garden without a house, Robert and Petreya will pay Prémontré a sixteenth part, and for each garden with a house, a twentieth part.*

A. Cartulary of Prémontré, fols. 52r–52v.

B. Original not found.

Other Manuscript Copies: Cartulary of Valécourt, BnF, nouv. acq. lat. 938, fols. 8r–8v (13th c.).

Karta abbatis Clarifontis de compositione inter ecclesiam Premonstratensem et Robertum de Autmont.

[J]ohannes, dictus abbas Clarifontis, et Haimo, presbiter de Origni, presentibus et futuris istam paginam inspecturis salutem presentem pariter et futuram. Universitati vestre huius scripti significatione notum facimus et testimonium perhibemus quod cum inter ecclesiam Premonstratensem et Robertum de Autimont simulque Petreyam de Vervin super quibusdam ortis et domibus ad terragia eiusdem ecclesie pertinentibus querela sepius mota fuisset et coram delegatis judicibus ventilata, tandem partes de assensu mutuo in nos conpromiserunt et, sufficienti cautione interposita, nos ipsius querele taliter arbitros elegerunt, quod quicquid conpositione vel judicio super hoc arbitraremur, ipse partes firmiter observarent. Litteris igitur de rato ab ecclesia Premonstratensi nobis exhibitis et a predictis Roberto et Petreia recepto date fidei sacramento, post rationes et allegationes hinc inde propositas, ad tractandum de pace laboravimus bona fide et cooperantibus nobiscum bonis viris, Goberto videlicet, abbate Thenoliensi, et Johanne, decano de Vervin, concordi voluntate partium inter eas amicabiliter composuimus in hunc modum. Siquidem de omnibus ortis et domibus quas prefati Robertus et Petreya sive ipsorum heredes infra terminos dictorum terragiorum tenuerint vel aliis tradiderint ad tenendum, hanc amodo et in perpetuum Premonstratensis ecclesia pro suis terragiis reconpensationem habebit quod, ubicumque fuerint horti sine domibus, pleno jure sexta decima pars, et ubi fuerint horti cum domibus, pro bono pacis, pars vicesima nummorum, caponum et quorumlibet aliorum proventuum eidem ecclesie per annos singulos sine contradictione solvetur, hoc proviso quod singuli capones sub certo sex nummorum precio redigentur omnibus aliis proventibus juxta quod valuerint annuatim in nummorum summam rationabiliter estimandis. Adjectum est denique de omnibus aliis qui domos vel hortos tenent aut tenuerint ad eadem terragia pertinentes sive aliis tradiderint ad tenendum quod quicumque ipsorum sextam decimam aut vicesimam partem, prout dictum est, solvere voluerint annuatim nominate

6 Perhaps Haution, cant. Vervins, https://dicotopo.cths.fr/places/P59639286.

pacis et conpositionis erunt participes. De hiis autem qui tenuerint solvere, Premonstratensis ecclesia justiciam querere poterit et adversus eos jus suum licite prosequetur. Quod ut ratum sit et ad memoriam perpetuo reducatur scriptum istud et sub particione cirographi et sub testimonio presentium sigillorum fecimus roborari. Actum in ecclesia Beate Marie de Vervin anno ab incarnatione Domini M° CC° secundo, mense septembri.

214

1138

Barthélémy,[1] bishop of Laon, notifies Hugues [I],[2] abbot of Prémontré, that Enguerrand [II],[3] son of Thomas of Marle, Robert[4] his brother, Mélisende[5] his mother, and Mélisende[6] his sister gave to the church of Prémontré certain revenues from lands in Vervins,[7] Angeis, *and Coucy-la-Ville. These monies are to support the annual general meeting of abbots, on the condition that each Premonstratensian church celebrates the anniversary of the donors and of Thomas their father and Alelme their brother.*

A. Cartulary of Prémontré, fol. 52v.

B. Original not found.

EDITION: Le Paige, *Bibliotheca*, 423–4; Hugo, *prob.* 1, col. xi; Florival, *Étude historique sur le XIIe siècle*, 361–2; Saint-Aymour, *La maison de Caix*, 33–5; Dufour-Malbezin, *Actes*, 283–4; *Chartae Galliae*, no. 208326, http://telma.irht.cnrs.fr/outils/chartae-galliae/charte208326/.

REGISTER: Bréquigny, *Table chronologique*, vol. 3, 18.

Karta Bartholomei episcopi Laudunensis de confirmatione elemosine quam Ingelrannus filius Thome de Marla contulit ecclesie Premonstrati.

[I]n nomine sancte et individue Trinitatis. Ego Bartholomeus, Dei patiencia Sancte Laudunensis ecclesie minister humilis, Hugoni, Premonstratensi ecclesie

1 Barthélemy de Jur (d. 1158), son of Conon, lord of Grandson and La Sarraz, and Ada de Roucy; first subdeacon and then treasurer of Reims, later bishop of Laon, 1113–51.

2 Hugues I de Fosses (ca. 1093–1164), first abbot of Prémontré.

3 Enguerrand II de Coucy (d. ca. 1149), son of Thomas de Marle, lord of Coucy, and his third wife, Mélisende de Crécy-sur-Serre.

4 Robert I, lord of Boves (d. 1191), son of Thomas de Marle, lord of Coucy, and Mélisende de Crécy.

5 Mélisende de Crécy (d. aft. 1147), daughter of Guy, lord of Crécy-sur-Serre.

6 Mélisende de Coucy, daughter of Thomas de Marle, lord of Coucy, and Mélisende de Crécy; married first Adelelme, castellan of Amiens, and second Hugues IV, lord of Gournay.

7 Vervins, arr. Vervins, https://dicotopo.cths.fr/places/P65564790.

abbati, eiusque successoribus canonice substituendis in perpetuum. Quia successu temporum facile subrepit preteritorum oblivio, res gestas paci futurorum memoratu necessarias scripto conmendare decrevit antiquitas. Ea propter Hugo, fili karissime, tam futuris quam presentibus volumus innotescere quod Enjorrannus, filius Thome de Marla, cum Roberto, fratre suo, et matre eorum, Milesende, et eiusdem nominis sorore sua, ob remedium animarum suarum tibi et ecclesie tue quosdam subternominandos contulerunt redditus hac quidem diffinitione ut in annuo colloquio coabbatum vestri ordinis apud vos celebrando ad eorum ponantur sumptus. Huius autem gratia beneficii primo post hanc attributionem colloquio coabbates talem illis constituerunt reconpensationem pietatis ut, audito ecclesiastico obitu singulorum ut prediximus, hanc elemosinam conferentium in omnibus ecclesiis huius ordinis tantum fiet pro eorum singulis quantum pro uniuscuiusque ecclesie fratribus et in perpetuum eorum anniversarius celebretur, anniversarius etiam Thome, ipsorum patris, et Alelmi, eorumdem fratris. Hii autem sunt reditus: terragium ~~etiam de Couci villa exceptis~~ de Vervinz cum decima et terragium de Angeis, sicut in dominio suo tenebat; terragium etiam de Couci Villa, exceptis duobus modiis hiemalis annone, qui persolvuntur ecclesie Beate Marie Nongenti; vivarium etiam, cum molendino, juxta eandem villam. Nos autem congaudentes et eorum saluti et vestris provectibus hoc donum in presentia mea factum coram legitimis testibus auctoritate nostra confirmamus scriptumque sigilli nostri impressione subsignamus. Si qua igitur in futurum ecclesiastica secularisve persona, hanc decreti nostri paginam sciens, hoc donum temerario ausu irritare temptaverit, secundo terciove commonita, nisi de contemptu episcopalis auctoritatis et injuria ecclesie satisfecerit, anathematis vinculo innodetur. Hii autem sunt testes: Arnaudus archidiaconus, Bruno abbas Sancte Marie Nongenti, et ceteri. Ad predictum etiam donum attinet decima et terragium de Ahemhi et molendinum de Raburees. Actum est hoc anno incarnationis dominice Mº Cº XXXº octavo, epacta VIIª, concurrente Vº, indictone XVª.

215

1188

Abbot Grégoire[1] *and the chapter of Thenailles make known that they received from the abbot [Hugues II]*[2] *and the brothers of Prémontré a field associated with the endowment of the altar of Murcy,*[3] *in exchange for an annual* census *of eight* galeti *of grain (*frumentum*), measure of Marle.*[4]

1 Grégoire, abbot of the Premonstratensian abbey of Thenailles, 1172–88. *MP* II, 401.

2 Hugues II de Douai, abbot of the Premonstratensian abbey of Cuissy, 1161–5, and abbot of Prémontré, 1174–89. *MP* II, 497.

3 Murcy, comm. Monceau-le-Neuf, https://dicotopo.cths.fr/places/P08613211.

4 Abbot Hugues II's act concerning the same agreement is in the cartulary of Thenailles. BnF, MS lat. 5649, fol. 30r.

A. Cartulary of Prémontré, fol. 52v–53r.
B. Original not found.

Karta abbatis Thenoliensis de dote altaris de Murci que accepimus sub annua pensione octo galetas frumenti.

[E]go Gregorius, abbas Thenolie, et capitulum nostrum ad omnium noticiam fecimus hic inscribi quod nos accepimus ab abbate et fratribus Premonstrati quendam campum terre de dote altaris de Murchi descendentem sub annua pensione octo galetorum frumenti melioris post sementem ad mensuram de Marla censualiter possidendum. Qui campus inter terram Thome de Sehon[5] et terram Sancte Marie Profunde situs est. Quod ut perpetue stabilitatis robur optineat, presens scriptum sub cyrographi divisione factum sigilli nostri munimine roborari et testes tam de ordine quam de ecclesia nostra fecimus annotari. S. Petri,[6] abbatis Buciliensis. S. Anfridi,[7] abbatis Clarifontis et ceteri. Actum anno gratie M° C° LXXX° octavo.

216

May, 1287.

Magister *Jean*[1] *de Leuse of the school of Saint-Étienne of Troyes and the cleric Jean de Ribemont arbitrate the dispute between Robert,*[2] *bishop of Laon, on the one hand, and the abbot and convent of Prémontré, on the other, in the court of the king [Philippe IV]. Prémontré retains its rights to cut wood within certain marked boundaries; Prémontré possesses the rights of* justicia *over the mill of Achery,*[3] *except for* fur *and* duellum*; Prémontré may acquire land to maintain the mill at Achery; Prémontré is to enjoy continued possession of all properties previously acquired; and the bishop will hold the fishing rights in the waters under the mill and the* pasturagium *of the pastures in front of their house at Achery. (See* ***217****.)*[4]

5 Likely Sons-et-Ronchères, cant. Marle, https://dicotopo.cths.fr/places/P19824727.

6 Pierre II (?), abbot of the Premonstratensian abbey of Bucilly, 1187–92. *MP* II, 366.

7 Anfridus, abbot of the Premonstratensian abbey of Clairefontaine, 1182–8. *MP* II, 372.

1 *Magister* Jean de Leuse of the school of the church of Saint-Étienne of Troyes. He appears in the late thirteenth-century obituary of the collegiate church of Saint-Étienne de Troyes on October 8, and in its late fourteenth-century obituary on March 3. Longnon, *Obituaires de la Province de Sens*, vol. 4, 473, 487.

2 Robert de Thourotte, son of Jean III, castellan of Thourotte and lord of Allibaudières, and Luce de Honnecourt, was first a canon of Reims and then bishop of Laon, 1285–97.

3 Achery, cant. La Fère, https://dicotopo.cths.fr/places/P61820808.

4 Robert, abbot of Prémontré, also issued an act confirming this agreement. AD Aisne, G 2, 244.

A. Cartulary of Prémontré, fol. 53r.
B. Original not found.
Other Manuscript Copies: AD Aisne, G 2, 246.

NO RUBRIC. LATER ADDITION.

Omnibus presentes litteras visuris magistri Johannes de Leusis, scolasticus ecclesie Sancti Stephani Trecensis, et Johannes de Ribemont, clericus, arbitri arbitratores seu amicabiles compositores in controversia mota in curia domini regis Francorum inter reverendum patrem dominum Robertum, Laudunensem episcopum, ex una parte et religiosos viros abbatem et conventum Premonstratenses ex altera, salutem in Domino. Noverint universi quod cum inter reverendum patrem dominum Robertum, Laudunensis episcopum predictum, et religiosos predictos super diversis articulis esset discordia suscitata, tandem bonorum et sapientum interveniente consilio de discordia predicta et tangentibus ipsam in nos compromiserunt, prout in litteris super hoc confectis a dictis partibus hinc et inde plenius continetur; nos igitur arbitri arbitratores seu amicabiles compositores predicti inspectis, auditis et intellectis diligenter rationibus, juribus partium earumdem, cartis seu privilegiis, dictis religiosis ab episcopis Laudunensis qui fuerunt pro tempore seu ab aliis quibuscumque concessis, facta insuper prius a nobis inquisitione diligenti per testes fide dignos et juratos et habito super hiis sapientium consilio, arbitrium, ordinationem seu arbitralem sentenciam nostram proferimus in hunc modum: In nomine Patris et Filii et Spiritus Sancti, amen. Primo ordinamus, et arbitraliter diffinimus et pronunciamus dominum Laudunensis episcopum in procliviis montium ad ecclesiam Premonstratensem pertinentium; que proclivia divisa sunt per bornas et distincta a forestis domini Couciaci; usuagium seu aliquod jus non habere ratione quacumque et, propter hoc quod nuper fecit dictus dominus episcopus per servientes suos scindi ligna in dictis procliviis et poni super quadrigas suas producendum quo vellet, pronunciamus et diffinimus ut supra, quod dictus dominus episcopus mittat aliquem ex parte sua qui abbatem et conventum Premonstratenses ressasiat nomine ipsius domine episcopi et emendet eisdem de huius modi forefacto. Secundo pronunciamus et arbitraliter diffinimus dominum episcopum predictum in molendinis dictorum abbatis et conventus de Acheriaco justiciam seu jus aliquod non habere sed ad dictos abbatem et conventum in ipsis molendinis totum jus et justiciam totam pertinere, exceptis solummodo fure et duello, prout in carta eisdem concessa plenius continetur. Tercio pronunciamus et diffinimus, ut supra, quod dicti abbas et conventus possunt accipere terram pro exclusis reparandis et aliis quibuscumque ~~neccis~~ necessitatibus dictorum molendinorum faciendis circa dicta molendina, exclusas seu in communi pasturagio et in omnibus aisansiis ville de Acheriaco. Quarto pronunciamus et diffinimus, ut supra, quod dicti abbas et conventus omnes acquestus quos acquisierunt usque in presentem diem in ducatu, comitatu, seu dominio dicti domini episcopi in feodis, retrofeodis seu domgmainis ipsius decetero, tamquam amortisatos a dicto domino episcopo tenebunt et habebunt pacifice et quiete. Item pronunciamus quod in recompensationem juris, si quod dictus episcopus habebat in predictis seu in aliquo predictorum dicti abbas et conventus quitant eidem domino episcopo piscationem quam habebant in aqua subtus molendina predicta, et pasturagium quod habebant in prato, quod est ante domum ipsius, quodmodo positum est in defenso, et hoc omnia et singula supradicta, prout in suis locis sunt expressa, ordinamus et arbitraliter diffinimus inter partes inviolabiliter et perpetuum observanda. Predictam siquidem arbitralem sentenciam seu ordinationem a nobis, ut dictum est, prolatam reverendus pater dominus Robertus, Dei gratia Laudunensis episcopus, et procuratores dictorum abbatis et conventus presentes coram nobis laudaverunt, approbaverunt et acceptaverunt et eam ratam, gratam et acceptam habuerunt. In quorum omnium testimonium sigilla nostra presentibus litteris duximus apponendum. Datum anno Domini millesimo ducentesimo octagesimo septimo, mense mayo.

217

May, 1287.

Robert,[1] *bishop of Laon, makes known that he accepts and approves the decision described in the previous act. (See* ***216****.)*

A. Cartulary of Prémontré, fol. 53r.
B. Original not found.[2]

NO RUBRIC. LATER ADDITION

Omnibus presentes litteras visuris Robertus miseratione divina Laudunensis episcopus salutem in Domino. Noveritis quod nos sentenciam seu ordinationem arbitralem de quam sint mentis in litteris quibus nostre presentes littere sunt annexe et omnia et singula in eisdem contenta laudamus approbamus [*margo:* et acceptamus] et ea rata et grata et accepta habemus. In super et acquestus de quibus sint mentis in eisdem litteris amortizamus et confirmamus et promittimus bona fide quod contra contenta in eisdem seu contra aliquid de contentis in ipsis per nobis vel per alium nullatenus decetero veniemus. In cuius rei testimonium sigillum nostrum presentibus litteris est appensum. Datum anno domini millesimo ducentesimo octuagesimo[3] septimo, mense mayo.

1 Robert de Thourotte, son of Jean III, castellan of Thourotte and lord of Allibaudières, and Luce de Honnecourt, was first a canon of Reims and then bishop of Laon, 1285–97.

2 Robert, bishop of Laon, also issued a longer act concerning this agreement in April 1287. AD Aisne, G 22.

3 *Sic A*.

TABLE OF CONTENTS: MERLIEU AND NOGENT

A. Cartulary of Prémontré, fol. 54r.

Incipiunt capitula[4] scriptorum curie de Merliu cum appenditiis suis, cum quibusdam kartis et compositionibus factis inter ecclesiam Premonstratensem et ecclesiam de Nongento.

Cyrographum inter ecclesiam Laudunensis[5] et ecclesiam Premontratensem super concordia et pace de communi decimagio de Merliu. **I**

Carta capituli maioris ecclesie Laudunensis de compositione et pace super decimis magnis et minutis in territorio de Merliu de Fouqueroles, de Valauregni, et de Montiermont. **II**

Carta officialis Laudunensis de XX solidorum datis in elemosinam super quandam vineam apud Challevoi. **III**

Littere officialis Laudunensis de quodam redditu viginti solidorum apud Challevoi. **IIII**

Carta curie Remensis super renuntiatione presbyteri de Merliu de novalibus parrochie sue. **V**

De concordia Premonstrate et Nongentine ecclesie.

Scriptum de quibusdam terrarum permutationibus inter Premonstratensem et Nongentinam ecclesiam. **VI**

De[6] quadam compromissione facta in abbatem Laudunensis et abbatem Vallis Secrete. **VII**

De quibusdam permutationibus vinagiorum inter ecclesiam Premonstrati et ecclesiam de Nongento. **VIII**

Quod ecclesia Premonstratensis et ecclesia de Nongento observabunt dictum abbatem Sancti Martini et Vallis Secrete sub pena C librarum Parisiensis. **IX**

Carta inter Premonstratensem et Nongentinam ecclesiam de quadam terra que dicitur ad vinetum. **X**

4 *Superscr. A.*
5 *Superscr. A.*
6 *Sic A.*

218

[June 5], 1229.[1]

Gautier,[2] dean of the chapter of Notre-Dame de Laon, abbot Conrad,[3] and the chapter of Prémontré approve the agreement reached through arbitration at Merlieux by Geoffroi l'Ainé, Colard de Coucy,[4] the brothers Gilbert and Rahier de Montarcène,[5] and Jean de Merlieux, carpenter, concerning a dispute over the major and minor tithes of Merlieux,[6] Fouquerolles, Valavergny,[7] and Monthiémont.[8] (See ***219****.)*

A. Cartulary of Prémontré, fols. 54r–55r.

B[1]. Original (chirograph), AN, L 731, no. 107, previously sealed with two seals. In the left margin and beginning at the top, the upper half of the letters that form the word CHYROGRAPHUM.

B[2]. Original (chirograph), BnF, Coll. Picardie 290, no. 40, previously sealed with two seals. In the right margin and beginning at the top, the lower half of the letters that form the word CHYROGRAPHUM.

Other Manuscript Copies: Cartulary of the Cathedral Chapter of Laon, AD Aisne, G 1850, fols. 212r–213r (13/14 c.).

Chirographum inter ecclesiam Laudunensem et ecclesiam Premonstratensem super concordia et pace de communi decimagio de Merlieu.

[E]go Galterus, decanus et capitulum maioris ecclesie Laudunensis, et ego Conradus, Premonstratensis abbas, et nostrum capitulum notum facimus universis tam presentibus quam futuris presentem paginam inspecturis quod, cum inter nos ad invicem pluries discordia suborta fuisset super decimis magnis et minutis in territorio de Merliu, de Foukeroles et de Valauregni et de Montiermont, tandem pro bono pacis, de communi assensu, compromisimus in viros bonos

1 While the cartulary scribe dates this to July 7 (*nonas julii*), both surviving original acts date this to June 5 (*nonas junii*).

2 Gautier de Chambly, dean of the cathedral chapter of Laon, ca. 1225–30. Picó, "Membership in the Cathedral Chapter of Laon, 1217–1238," 8.

3 Conrad the Swabian was prior of Weissenau, 1203–17, abbot of Valsecret, 1218–20, abbot of Prémontré, 1220–33, and abbot of Cuissy, aft. 1235–41. *MP* I, 89; *MP* II, 497, 527, 536.

4 A Colard de Coucy also appears in a 1224 act of Renaud II, lord of Magny. Tassus, "Notice historique sur la paroisse de Baboeuf," 83.

5 Montarcène, cant. Montbavin, https://dicotopo.cths.fr/places/P24202828.

6 Merlieux-et-Fouquerolles, cant. Anizy-le-Château, https://dicotopo.cths.fr/places/P92396813.

7 Valavergny, comm. Merlieux, https://dicotopo.cths.fr/places/P74214194.

8 Monthiémont, comm. Merlieux-et-Fouquerolles, https://dicotopo.cths.fr/places/P83003256.

Galfridum maiorem, Colardum de Couciaco, Gilebertum et Raherum[9] de Montarcenne, fratres, et Johannem de Merliu, carpentarium, dictum et ordinationem eorum, pro ut[10] statuissent, bona fide sub pena viginti librarum Parisiensium solvendarum parti adverse que a dicto vel ordinatione eorum resilisset, ratum et firmum habituri, ipsa etiam compromissione sigillo et litteris utriusque capituli confirmata. Die autem statuto, apud Merliu, presentibus bonis viris, videlicet domino Johanne Fabro,[11] canonico dicte ecclesie Laudunensis, qui ex parte eiusdem ecclesie presens erat, Petro etiam de Atichi[12] sacerdote, Wermundo diacono, canonicis Premonstratensis, Durando converso, magistro curtis de Merliu, qui ex parte Premonstratensis ecclesie ibi erant, et domino Johanne, presbitero de Merliu, et multis aliis qui presentes erant ibidem, prefati boni viri, dictum suum fideliter proferentes, taliter ordinarunt quod ecclesia Premonstratensis pro decimis vini quas accipiebat ecclesia Laudunensis in vineis ipsius ecclesie Premonstratensis, que in conmuni decimagio erant apud Merliu, restituit eidem ecclesie Laudunensis,[13] sicut superius est expressum. Prima quidem meta protenditur a Sambuco inter vineam Reneri et vineam Elizabeth[14] de Pontoir et a vinea illa ad Sambucum usque ad Firmitatem montis et iterum ab illa Sambuco ex parte altera protenditur recte ad semitam inter vineam Bovonis et vineam dicte Elizabeth,[15] et iterum sicut illa protenditur semita recte ad viculum conversorum. Hec omnes vinee que infra istos terminos continentur, usque ad vicum Del Chaperon que erant in communi decimagio, restitute sunt ab ecclesia Premonstratensis ecclesie Laudunensi in recompensationem et restaurationem decimarum quas accipiebat in vineis Premonstratensis apud Merliu, que in decimagio communi erant, ita quod in eisdem vineis totum decimagium integre accipiet eadem ecclesia Laudunensis et ecclesia Premonstratensis a solutione decimarum quas de suis vineis, que erant in communi decimagio, debebat dicte ecclesie Laudunensis, libera erit in perpetuum et inmunis, salva tamen eidem ecclesie Laudunensis, decima sua quam ei debet ecclesia Premonstratensis in proprio territorio et fundo eiusdem ecclesie Laudunensis, in qua partem non capiebat prius ecclesia Premonstratensis. De communi autem decimagio tam vinearum quam terrarum arabilium et minutarum decimarum prefati boni viri,

9 Raherium *B*[2].

10 prout *B*[2].

11 A Jean *Faber*, *officialis* of Laon, appears in an act of 1209 in the cartulary of Thenailles, while a Jean *Faber*, canon of Laon, is attested 1221–39. BnF, MS lat. 5649, fol. 43v; AD Aisne, G 1850, fols. 214v–215r, 233v–234r.

12 Atechi *B*[1], *B*[2].

13 *Om. and homeo.* vineas competentes in communi decimagio vinearum que restitutio taliter est expressa et hec sunt mete et divisiones illarum vinearum quas restituit ecclesia Premonstratensis ecclesie Laudunensis *A*. *This line appears as such in both B*[1] and *B*[2], *with the exception that in B*[1] *the phrase is* restitutio est taliter expressa.

14 Elyzabeth *B*[1], *B*[2].

15 Elyzabeth *B*[1].

tres partes facientes equales fideliter, sicut melius potuerunt, communi assensu taliter ordinarunt quod, jactatis fortibus fideliter hinc inde ecclesia Premonstratensis duas partes suas quas habebat in toto decimagio supradicto, acciperet in certis locis in parte seorsum. Ecclesia vero Laudunensis terciam partem suam quam similiter habebat in eodem toto decimagio, in certis locis, eodem modo acciperet in parte seorsum, ne de cetero inter ecclesias super partitione decimarum contentio vel discordia moveretur. Partes autem communis decimagii supradictas, communi consilio et assensu, distinxerunt in hunc modum fideliter. Prima pars assignata fuit apud Merliu et in illa parte comprehenduntur omnes campi in Monte de Montarcenne, ubi partem habebat ecclesia Premonstrati, exceptis campis illis qui sunt a quarreria de Merliu usque ad quarreriam de Lisiaco subtus viam. Vine~~eam~~ etiam que in ista parte comprehenduntur, taliter distinguntur: prima meta sive divisio protenditur a summitate vinee Oudardi[16] dou[17] Pontoir En Leschafout,[18] inter vineam Patrovillart[19] et vineam Reneri de Vaucellis,[20] usque ad domum Theoderici Lupi, minute vero decime sicut protenditur a loco qui dicitur Hardutristles[21] et Noire Wes, usque Ad Clari, ad partem de Merliu pertinent supradictam; secunda pars assignata fuit apud Valauregni in qua continetur omne residuum camporum in monte, sicut predictum est, videlicet a quarreria de Merliu usque ad quarreriam de Lisiaco subtus viam et les osches universe, excepta quarta parte earum que est versus furnum calcis, in ista parte secunda comprehenduntur. Vinea[22] autem in hac parte comprehense taliter dividuntur. Prima meta sive divisio protenditur a vico juxta domum Erenburgis la Moniere[23] usque ad montem, ad vineam presbiteri et iterum a domo Ade Diaboli secundum cursum rivuli et sicut idem rivulus protenditur usque ad quercetum et ab illo querceto usque in fluvium aquile, minute vero decime sicut protenditur a vico de La Saleuse usque ad vineam Oudardi[24] Coupele et ab eadem vinea usque ad rivulum et sicut idem rivulus protenditur usque in fluvium aquile in secunda parte de Valauregni continentur. Tercia pars assignata fuit apud Montiermont et in ista parte continetur omne residuum tam vinearum quam terrarum arabilium et minutarum decimarum que remanent de duabus supradictis partibus et que ad commune decimagium pertinebant, videlicet a vico de Valieres usque ad vicum de Montiermont, id est a domo La Molniere usque ad predictam vineam presbiteri in monte, sicut semita protenditur et distinguit et a Valauregni usque ad vicum Des Tasnieres[25] et quarta pars que remanet des osches, sicut predictum

16 Odardi B^1, B^2.
17 de B^1, B^2.
18 Leschefout B^1, B^2.
19 Patroullart B^1, B^2.
20 Vacellis B^1, B^2.
21 Hardritristles B^1, B^2.
22 Vinee B^1, B^2.
23 Molinere B^1, B^2.
24 Odardi B^1, B^2.
25 Taisnieres B^1, B^2.

est, versus furnum calcis in terra arabili similiter in ista parte tercia continetur et sciendum quod hec partitio supradicta facta est salvis decimis tam magnis quam minutis que sunt in dote altaris de Merliu que totaliter, ubicumque sint, pertinent ad dictam ecclesiam Laudunensem et remanent capitulo extra partem. Jactatis igitur ~~tam magnis quam minutis~~ sortibus a partibus fideliter ipso die prout dictum fuit et ordinatum a bonis viris predictis, ita contigit quod ecclesia Premonstratensis duas partes que pertinebant ad ipsam, sortita est in villis de Merliu et de Montiermont predictis, ecclesia vero Laudunensis similiter terciam partem pertinentem ad ipsam in villa predicta de Valauregni est sortita. Si autem post tempus presentium litterarum ecclesia Premonstratensis terras sive vineas apud Valauregni acquirat[18] in parte ecclesie Laudunensis, eadem ecclesia Laudunensis totam decimam, sicut in aliis, accipiet in eisdem. Et similiter ecclesia Premonstratensis totam decimam accipiet in hiis que in duabus partibus pertinentibus ad ipsam apud Merliu et apud Montiermont acquiret decetero ecclesia Laudunensis, non obstante privilegio aliquo hinc inde habito vel habendo. Ad pacem igitur utriusque ecclesie tam Laudunensis quam Premonstratensis fideliter et inviolabiliter in perpetuum conservandam, ut decetero omnis contentio et discordia sopiantur, nos ordinationem et dictum bonorum virorum predictorum divisiones partium, assignationem etiam metarum cum omnibus que superius continentur, sub cirographi[19] annotatione cuius una pars dicte ecclesie Laudunensis et altera pars[20] ecclesie Premonstratensis in perpetuam huius ordinationis memoriam remanebunt,[21] sigillorum nostrorum munimine duximus roborandum. Actum anno gratie M° CC°[22] vicesimo nono, nonas julii.[23]

219

June 1, 1229.

*Gautier,[1] dean, and the chapter of the cathedral of Laon declare that they and the church of Prémontré agree to arbitration to settle a dispute concerning the major and minor tithes of the territories of Merlieux,[2] Fouquerolles, Valavergny,[3] and Monthiémont.[4] (See **218**.)*

---

26 acquirat apud Valauregni *B*[2].
27 cyrographi *B*[1], *B*[2].
28 et pars altera *B*[2].
29 remanebit *B*[1], *B*[2].
30 millesimo ducentesimo *B*[1], *B*[2].
31 junii *B*[1], *B*[2].

---

1 Gautier de Chambly, dean of the cathedral chapter of Laon, ca. 1225–30. Picó, "Membership in the Cathedral Chapter of Laon, 1217–1238," 8.
2 Merlieux, cant. Anizy-le-Château, https://dicotopo.cths.fr/places/P92396813.
3 Valavergny, comm. Merlieux, https://dicotopo.cths.fr/places/P74214194.
4 Monthiémont, comm. Merlieux-et-Fouquerolles, https://dicotopo.cths.fr/places/P83003256.

A. Cartulary of Prémontré, fol. 55r.
B. Original, BnF, nouv. acq. lat. 2590, no. 54, previously sealed with three seals.

Karta capituli Laudunensis de compositione et pace super decimis magnis et minutis in territorio de Merliu de Fouqueroles.

[G]alterus,[5] Dei gratia decanus, et capitulum maioris ecclesie Laudunensis universis presentes litteras inspecturis salutem in Domino. Noverit universitas vestra quod, cum pluries discordia orta fuisset inter nos ex una parte et ecclesiam Premonstratensem ex altera super decimis magnis et minutis in territorio de Merliu, de Fouqueroles,[6] de Valauregni et de Montiermont, tam nos quam dicta ecclesia Premonstratensis pro bono pacis et pace mutuo conservanda compromisimus in Galfridum, Colardum, Gilebertum, Richerum de Montarcenne[7,8] et Johannem de Merliu, dictum eorum et ordinationem, prout statuerint bona fide sub pena viginti librarum Parisiensium parti adverse solvendarum, si a dicto eorum vel ordinatione resilierimus, ratum et firmum habituri sub presentium testimonio litterarum. Actum anno gratie M° CC°[9] vicesimo IX°,[10] kalendas junii.

220

January, 1227.

Jean de Buzancy,[1] *canon of Meaux and* officialis *of Laon, makes known that husband and wife Robert de Royaucourt,*[2] janitor *of the bishop of Laon, and Berthe, and Hugues their son gave to the church of Prémontré in perpetual alms 20* solidi Laudunensium censuales, *to be taken from a vineyard situated between Chailvet and Royaucourt.*

A. Cartulary of Prémontré, fol. 55r.
B. Original not found.

---

5 Walterus *B*.
6 Foukeroles *B*.
7 Montarcene *B*.
8 Montarcène, comm. Montbavin, https://dicotopo.cths.fr/places/P24202828.
9 millesimo ducentesimo *B*.
10 nono *B*.

---

1 Jean de Buzancy, canon of Meaux and *officialis* of Laon, by 1224–aft. May 1229. BM Reims 1563 (N. Fonds), fols. 55v–56r, 150r–150v; AD Ardennes, H 203, fols. 129v–130r.
2 Royaucourt-et-Chailvet, cant. Anizy-le-Château, https://dicotopo.cths.fr/places/P43149946.

Karta curie Laudunensis de XX^ti solidis datis in elemosinam ecclesie Premonstrato super quandam vineam de Chaillevoi.

[U]niversis presentes litteras inspecturis magister Johannes de Busenceio, canonicis Meldensis et officialis Laudunensis, in Domino salutem. Noverit universitas vestra quod, constituti in presentia nostra, Robertus de Rioucourt, janitor domini Laudunensis episcopi, Berta uxor eius, et Hugo filius eorum, recognoverunt se in elemosinam perpetuam contulisse, ob remedium animarum suarum, ecclesie Premonstratensi viginti solidos Laudunenses censuales assignatos super vineam unam, sitam Es Savelons inter Chaillevel et Rioucourt, singulis annis in perpetuum reddendos in Festo Beati Remigii. In cuius rei testimonium presentes litteras patentes emisimus sigillo curie Laudunensis roboratas salvo jure domini Laudunensis et alieno. Actum anno Domini M° CC° XX° VII°, mense januario.

221

January, 1227.

Jean de Buzancy,[1] *canon of Meaux and* officialis *of Laon, declares that in his presence Jean Holiers; Simon, son of Lierre de Chailvet;*[2] *and Robert Choques de Chailvet recognize that they owe the church of Prémontré an annual payment of 20* solidi Laudunensium *to be taken from a vineyard located between Chailvet and Royaucourt.*

A. Cartulary of Prémontré, fol. 55r.
B. Original, AD Aisne, H 820, previously sealed with double strip of parchment.

Item karta officialis Laudunensis de quodam redditu XX solidarum apud Chaillevoi.

[U]niversis presentes litteras visuris magister Johannes de Busenceio,[3] canonicus Meldensis, officialis domini[4] Laudunensis, in Domino salutem. Noverit universitas vestra quod, constituti in presentia nostra, Johannes Holiers,

1 Jean de Buzancy, canon of Meaux and *officialis* of Laon, by 1224–aft. May 1229. BM Reims 1563 (N. Fonds), fols. 55v–56r, 150r–150v; AD Ardennes, H 203, fols. 129v–130r.
2 Chailvet, comm. Royaucourt-et-Chailvet, https://dicotopo.cths.fr/places/P52087335.
3 Busenecio *B*.
4 *Add.* domini *A*.

Symon, filius Lierree de Chaillevel, et Robertus Coques[5] de Challevoi,[6] recognoverunt quod debent ecclesie Premonstratensis viginti solidos Laudunenses de redditu annuo in festo Beati Remigii persolvendos assignatos super vineam unam sitam Es Savelons inter Chaillevel et Rioucourt[7] quam ipsi tenent, sicut dicitur, quos dictus Johannes debet persolvere in dicto festo et, si defecerit in solutione eadem die, dicti R[oberti] Choques[8] et S[ymoni] illos prefate ecclesie solvent in crastino eiusdem festi et in partem dicti Johannis intrabunt tamquam in suam. Si autem dicti S[ymoni] et R[oberti] Coques[9] illos in dicto crastino non reddiderint, dicta ecclesia eandem vineam ex tunc intrabit tamquam in suam. De hiis etiam tenendis dicti J[ohannis], S[ymoni] et R[oberti] Coques[10] fidem interposuerunt corporalem. In cuius rei testimonium ad petitionem partium presentes litteras patentes emisimus, salvo jure domini Laudunensis et alieno sigillo curie Laudunensis roboratas. Actum anno Domini M° CC° XX° septimo,[11] mense januario.

222

1180s[1]

*Hugues [II],[2] abbot of Prémontré, and Hélie,[3] abbot of the Benedictine house of Nogent[-sous-Coucy], make known that they reached an agreement of association (*societas*) between their churches, aiming to settle their differences through a specified arbitration process and with each house undertaking to offer prayers and Masses for the other's members.*

A. Cartulary of Prémontré, fols. 55r–55v.

B. Original not found.

EDITION: Le Paige, *Bibliotheca*, 932–3; Hugo, *prob.* 1, cols. xxx–xxxii.

REGISTER: Bréquigny, *Table chronologique*, vol. 6, 14.

5 Chokes *B*.
6 Chaillevoi *B*.
7 Rioucort *B*.
8 Chokes *B*.
9 Chokes *B*.
10 Chokes *B*.
11 VII° *B*.

1 The cartulary act is undated. The only abbot Hélie of Nogent held office approximately 1183–8, while *GC*, vol. IX, 608, notes an 1184 agreement of fellowship made between Hélie and abbot Hugues II of Prémontré. That would seem to date this act to the 1180s. Hugo states that "huic chirographum curavimus annotari … anno Domini 1240" (Hugo, *prob.* 1, col. 31), but this could be understood as the date of a later confirmation of this act.

2 Hugues II de Douai, abbot of the Premonstratensian abbey of Cuissy, 1161–5, and abbot of Prémontré, 1174–89. *MP* II, 497.

3 Hélie, abbot of the Benedictine abbey of Nogent-sous-Coucy, bef. 1183–8. *GC* IX, col. 608.

Karta de compositione inter ecclesiam Premonstratensem et Nongentinam.

[I]n nomine sancte et individue Trinitatis. Ego Hugo, Dei gratia Premonstrati dictus abbas, nosterque conventus et ego Helias, eadem gratia de Nongento abbas, similiter dictus noster etiam conventus. Notum fieri volumus universis tam presentibus quam futuris quod pro bono conservande pacis atque intuitu perfectius habende et adimplende sancte caritatis, communi consilio atque laude decrevimus parique assensu statuimus, ut si qua, ut fieri solet, inter Premonstratensem et Nungentensem ecclesiam deinceps oborta, de qualibet re fuerit querela, nullatenus amodo vel ab abbatibus ipsarum ecclesiarum, vel a fratribus pro qualibet querimonia secularis ecclesiastice ve persone requiretur aut expetetur audientia, sed ipsi inter se de querelis suis ad invicem benigne, sicut decet sanctos sanctamque religionem professos, tractabunt, et ipso qui pax nostra est largiente, pro posse suo fideliter ac prudenter rem pacificabunt. Quod si grandis aliqua vel gravis causa inter utramque ecclesiam emerserit, que nec de facili aut leviter determinari vel pacificari possit, de singulis predictis ecclesiis duo eligentur fratres, de Premonstrato quidem duo canonici, de Nongento itidem duo monachi prudentes ac fideles servi Dei, quibus causa querele tractanda committetur, quatinus ab eis, vel concordi et justo moderamine, aut judiciaria diffinitione terminetur. Quod si fratres prefati penes se judicii nequiverint reperire certitudinem, alibi a doctioribus et in diffinitione judiciorum peritioribus sollicite inquirent judicii veritatem, et sic secundum id quod veritas judicii monstraverit, vel justicia dictaverit, ab ipsis querela terminabitur, et quicquid inde statuerint, hoc incunctanter atque inmobiliter perpetuis temporibus ab utraque ecclesia observabitur. Ad augendum autem adhuc et perplexius innodandum fortiusque perstringendum inter utramque ecclesiam sancte caritatis vinculum, hoc etiam statuimus, ut si una quelibet de hiis duabus ecclesia, vel per sui abbatis vel per alicuius fratris personam, Romanam expetierit curiam sedemque visitaverit apostolicam alterius ecclesie causam, si quam habuerit et eis commiserit proficiscentes illic pro posse suo sollicite procurabunt, fideliterque perficient sicut suam, nisi causa fuerit, vel contra aliquam ordinis nostri seu alterius ordinis ecclesiam nobis speciali dilectione conjunctam, vel etiam contra aliquam eminentem personam etque nobis venerabilem atque dilectam. Quod si quid hac de causa expenderint, ecclesia cuius hoc negotium fuerit, hoc eis voluntarie gratanterque restituere confestim curabit. Sic namque alterutrum onera portantes, et non que sua sunt tantum, sed et que aliorum querentes adimplebunt legem Christi, et ita efficientur filii Dei. Quoniam vero ista superius scripta caritative observando, temporalis pacis bonum procuramus obtinere; dignum multo magis esse judicamus, ut bona nostra spiritualia devote ad invicem communicando, et pro invicem suppliciter orando eterna pace mereamur feliciter gloriari et gaudere. Orationum itaque nostrarum omniumque bonorum spiritualium que quocumque modo facimus participium ad invicem modis omnibus et concedimus et communicamus. Illud etiam scripto huic approbamus annotandum, quod a predecessoribus nostris claret esse salubriter institutum, ut pro defunctis videlicet nostris plenarium tam in vigiliis novem lectionum quam in conmendatione et missa faciamus ad invicem servitium in conventibus nostris et hoc in crastina Sancti Clementis. Singuli etiam sacerdotes pro eisdem missam unam celebrabunt et quinquaginta psalmos dicent qui ad sacerdotium non fuerint promoti, et centies Pater Noster, laici qui conversi nostri sunt. Ut igitur hoc pacis et dilectionis bonum inconvulsis radicibus perpetuetur, et ab utraque ecclesia immobiliter observetur, huic cirographo curavimus annotari, sigillorumque utriusque capituli impressione muniri ac testium annotatione roborari. Sigillum Eustacii, tunc prioris. S. Egidii, subprioris. S. Haimonis, cantoris. S. Rainelmi, sacriste. S. Premonstratensium. S. Yvonis, tunc prioris. S. Fabiani, subprioris. S. Ade, sacriste. S. Theodorici, prepositi Nongenti.

223

November, 1228.

Abbot Gautier[1] *and the chapter of the Benedictine house of Nogent[-sous-Coucy] make known that an exchange took place between their community and Prémontré concerning fields at Coucy-la-Ville and at Rozières.*[2]

A. Cartulary of Prémontré, fols. 55v–56r.

B. Original, AD Aisne, H 777, previously sealed with two seals on a double strip of parchment.

De quibusdam permutationibus terrarum inter Premonstratensem et Nongentem ecclesiam.

[E]go Walterus, abbas de Nongento, et capitulum nostrum, notum facimus universis tam presentibus quam futuris quod cum haberemus apud Coucivillam[3] terras vicinas terris ecclesie Premonstratensis et ipsa ecclesia Premonstratensis haberet territorium apud Roserias vicinum quibusdam terris

1 Gautier, abbot of the Benedictine abbey of Nogent-sous-Coucy, ca. 1220–ca. 1239. *GC* IX, col. 608.

2 Rozières, cant. Oulchy-le-Château, https://dicotopo.cths.fr/places/P75685266.

3 Cocivillam *B*.

nostris nos, habita insimul amicabili collatione, de communi omnium nostrum assensu, conmutationem fecimus cum ipsa ecclesia Premonstrati tali modo quod nos quitavimus eidem ecclesie in perpetuum libere et absolute quatuor modiatas terre sitas inter domum de Roseriis et inter domum de Buin ab illa parte que respicit versus nigras macerias preter campum qui dicitur Au Bach. Nomina camporum quos tradidimus eidem ecclesie, sunt hec: campum qui dicitur Au Bach, cum terragio quod habebamus prope ipsum campum, campum qui dicitur Au Bos, campum qui dicitur A La Sabloniere, campum qui dicitur Ubi Stephanardus Mortuus Fuit, campum qui dicitur A Launel, campum contiguum campo Sancti Martini de Fraisnes, campum qui dicitur De Dote Altaris cuius decima est ipsius ecclesie Premonstratensis ab antiquo, campum qui dicitur Roberti Aguillon, campum contiguum campo domini Roberti de Vervino, campum subtus masuram Droini masuram Droini,[4] et campum contiguum ipsi masure. Preterea quitavimus eidem ecclesie in perpetuum illud terragium quod habebamus in campo qui dicitur Campus Domine Widele. Omnes istos campos tradidimus ecclesie sepedicte ab omni censu et terragio liberos et inmunes. Nomina vero camporum nobis ab ipsa ecclesia Premonstratensis[5] traditorum hec sunt: una petia terre que est in medio culture nostre de Walmont, campus qui fuit Johannis de Vernolio, de quo debet nobis ~~nobis~~ eadem ecclesia sex denarios Laudunenses, campus contiguus campo Radulphi[6] Caignon, campellus parvus qui dicitur Campellus Forestel, campus qui est in Honval, campus desuper Coucivillam,[7] quia vero terre quas tradidit nobis prenominata ecclesia Premonstrati, non erant ita bone sicut terre quas ei tradidimus, sciendum est quod quitavit nobis omnia terragia que debebamus eidem apud Coucivillam[8] tempore presentium litterarum. Et ut hec commutatio in perpetuum inviolabiliter observetur, presentem kartam de communi omnium nostrum assensu confectam et sigillatam, eidem ecclesie duximus conferendam, renuntiantes omni juris auxilio canonici et civilis et omnibus exceptionibus que possent produci contra hoc presens publicum instrumentum; ipsa nichilominus ecclesia Premonstratensis dedit nobis kartam suam commutationis huius seriem continentem. Actum mense novembri, anno incarnationis dominice millesimo ducentesimo vicesimo octavo.

---

4 *Superscr.* capitula *A.*

5 *Superscr.* Laudenensis *A.*

6 Radulfi *B.*

7 Cocivillam *B.*

8 Cocivillam *B.*

224

December, 1228.

Abbot Gautier[1] *and the chapter of the Benedictine house of Nogent make known that Barthélemy de Verneuil*[2] *and his associates owed Nogent and the church of Prémontré an annual 36* sextarii *of* vinagium *(26 to Nogent and 10 to Prémontré). Nogent and Prémontré agree that Nogent will keep the entire 36* sextarii, *and in exchange give up the nine and a half* sextarii *that Prémontré owes them on certain vineyards at Rochefort and at Verneuil.*

A. Cartulary of Prémontré, fol. 56r.

B. Original, AD Aisne, H 775. Previously sealed with two wax seals on a double strip of parchment.[3]

De quibusdam permutationibus vinagiorum inter ecclesiam Premonstratensem et Nongentem.

[E]go Walterus, abbas de Nogento, et nostrum capitulum notum facimus presentibus et futuris presentem paginam inspecturis quod cum Bartholomeus de Vernolio et comparticipes sui deberent nobis et ecclesie Premonstratensi de vinea sua que est contigua vinee Asceline, triginta sex sextarios vinagii, nobis videlicet viginti sex et ecclesie Premonstratensi decem, hereditarie in perpetuum persolvendos, tandem, amicabili conventione habita inter nos et ipsam ecclesiam Premonstrati, ita convenit inter nos et ipsam ecclesiam quod nos integre et in perpetuum recipiemus triginta sex sextarios vinagii supradictos et quia ipsa ecclesia Premonstratensis debebat nobis novem sextarios et dimidium vinagii, videlicet de vinea de Rochefort quatuor sextarios, de vinea Ad Quercum duos sextarios et de vinea que fuit Symonis Castellani in valle de Vernolio tres sextarios et dimidium, in recompensationem illorum decem sextariorum vinagii qui prenominati sunt, quos quitavit nobis ecclesia Premonstrati, quitavimus eidem ecclesie in perpetuum prenominatos novem sextarios et dimidium vinagii. Ut igitur commutatio ista perpetuam obtineat firmitatem, de communi assensu presentes litteras ecclesie Premonstratensi tradidimus sigillo nostro et nostri capituli communitas. Actum anno gratie M° CC° XX° octavo, mense decembri.

---

1 Gautier, abbot of the Benedictine abbey of Nogent-sous-Coucy, ca. 1220–ca. 1239. *GC* IX, col. 608.

2 Verneuil-sous-Coucy, cant. Coucy-le-Château, https://dicotopo.cths.fr/places/P85264680.

3 Due to conservation concerns, the original was not available to the editors. Françoise Muret described the first seal as depicting an abbot (obverse) and a fleur de lys (reverse), and the damaged second seal as depicting an image of the Virgin and Child (obverse) and a crowned head (reverse).

225

August, 1221.

Abbot Gautier[1] *and the chapter of Nogent make known that they agree to arbitration over their dispute with the church of Prémontré concerning the tomb of Mathilde de Coucy. Gautier,*[2] *abbot of Saint-Martin de Laon, and J[ean],*[3] *abbot of Valsecret, will arbitrate the question of burial of persons of Coucy who expressed, in their last wishes, the desire to be buried in the church of Prémontré. (See **226**.)*

A. Cartulary of Prémontré, fol. 56r.
B. Original not found.

Quod ecclesia Premonstratensis et ecclesia de Nongento observabunt dictam abbatum Sancti Martini et Vallis Secrete sub pena centum librarum.

[E]go Walterus, Dei patientia Nongentine ecclesie dictus abbas, et eiusdem loci conventus, notum facimus universis presentes litteras inspecturis quod cum inter Premonstratensem et nostram ecclesias super sepultura quondam Matildis de Couciaco controversia esset, tandem de consilio bonorum virorum in venerabiles viros W[alterum], Sancti Martini Laudunensis, et J[ohannem] Vallis Secrete abbates, super premissis compromisimus, ita quidem quod ipsi de plano in ipsius negotii decisione procedent, audituri testes et alia instrumenta que partes produxerint coram ~~istis~~ ipsis, si dicti arbitri viderint expedire. Ceterum ne super casu consimili possit inter partes in posterum questio agitari, compromissum est in eosdem super jure sepulture personarum Couciaci que apud Premonstratensem ecclesiam in extrema voluntate elegerint sepeliri. Adjectum est etiam quod si alterutra partium resiliret a compromissione premissa, solveret parti adverse centum libras Parisienses nomine pene ad cuius solutionem dicti arbitri compellerent per censuram ecclesiasticam partem resilientem cum utraque pars supposuerit se jurisdictioni ipsorum. Pronunciabunt autem ipsi arbitri dictum suum infra octavas Epiphanie, nisi dies de consensu partium fuerit prorogatus. Verum si contigerit, quod absit, quod dicti arbitri vel alter eorum in fata concesserint, antequam arbitrium sit prolatum, successores

1 Gautier, abbot of the Benedictine abbey of Nogent-sous-Coucy, ca. 1220–ca. 1239. *GC* IX, col. 608.
2 Gautier du Val-le-Roy, abbot of the Premonstratensian abbey of Saint-Martin de Laon. *MP* II, 512.
3 Jean II, abbot of the Premonstratensian abbey of Valsecret, ca. 1220–bef. 1224. *MP* II, 536.

eorum poterunt nichilominus super premissis arbitrari et eandem potestatem habebunt quam habuerunt ancessores eorum arbitri videlicet pretaxati. Actum mense augusto, anno gratie M° CC° XX° primo.

226

February, 1221.

Gautier[1] *and Jean,*[2] *abbots of Saint-Martin de Laon and Valsecret respectively, tasked with arbitrating the dispute between Prémontré and the Benedictine abbey of Nogent, ruled that Prémontré cease its claims against Nogent receiving the body of a woman of Coucy who desired to be buried at Prémontré, on the condition that the monks of Nogent cede to Prémontré half of what they received for her burial and that they no longer prevent the inhabitants of Coucy from being buried in the church of Prémontré if they so wish. This resolution will be made public to the parishioners of Coucy. (See* ***225****.)*

A. Cartulary of Prémontré, fols. 56r–56v.

B. Original, BnF, nouv. acq. lat. 2590, no. 51, previously sealed with two seals.

Dictum abbatum Sancti Martini et Vallis Secrete super quadam compromissione facta in ipsos.

[E]go Walterus, Sancti Martini Laudunensis, et ego Johannes, Vallis Secrete[3] Dei patientia dicti abbates, notum facimus universis tam presentibus quam futuris quod cum inter Premonstratensem et Nongentinam ecclesias super sepultura cuiusdam mulieris de Couciaci[4] Castro que in extrema voluntate posita elegerat, sicut dicebatur, in Premonstratensi ecclesia sepulturam, questio verteretur, abbates dictarum ecclesiarum, de assensu et beneplacito conventuum suorum, pro bono pacis compromiserunt in nos ut quod inde arbitraremur, firmum et stabile haberetur et servaretur bona fide ab ecclesiis memoratis et super hac compromissione tenenda litteras emiserunt in quibus comprehensa fuit certa pena qua pars resiliens ab arbitrio puniretur. Adjectum fuit preterea in litteris compromissionis datis ex utraque parte, de assensu abbatum et conventuum dictarum ecclesiarum ne possit inter

1 Gautier du Val-le-Roy, abbot of the Premonstratensian abbey of Saint-Martin de Laon. *MP* II, 512.

2 Jean II, abbot of the Premonstratensian abbey of Valsecret, ca. 1220–bef. 1224. *MP* II, 536.

3 Vallisecrete *B*.

4 Cociaci *B*.

dictas ecclesias in posterum super huius modi re discordia exoriri, quod similiter arbitraremur super jure transire volentium in extrema voluntate de castro predicto ad sepulturam in ecclesia Premonstrati. Nos autem de consilio bonorum virorum, presentibus partibus coram nobis, arbitrium nostrum protulimus in hunc modum: Ecclesie siquidem Premonstratensi imposuimus silentium super eo quod adversus ecclesiam de Nongento pro rehabendo cadavere dicte mulieris, quasi pro facta sibi injuria, litigabat, eo tenore quod medietatem omnium rerum quas receperunt pro muliere predicta, monachi de Nongento reddent ecclesie Premonstrati nec impedient decetero aliquas personas de Couciaco[5] quin libere eligant si voluerint, et habeant in Premonstratensi ecclesia sepulturam et hoc ipsum denuntiabunt[6] publice parrochianis de Couciaco[7] sub pena in compromissionis sue litteris comprehensa. Ut igitur arbitrium nostrum firmiter observetur, nos ipsum in scriptis redactum et sigillorum nostrorum appensione munitum tradidimus utrique parti, ita quod penes utramque ecclesiam litteras eiusdem forme et eiusdem tenoris censuimus deponendas et in perpetuum conservandas, statuentes ut alterutra pars, resiliens ab arbitrio predicto, solvat alteri parti penam in compromissionis sue litteris comprehensam et querela sit in eodem statu in quo erat, quando compromissio facta fuit. Actum mense februario, anno gratie M^o[8] ducentesimo vicesimo primo.

227

1173

Abbot Jean[1] *and the chapter of the Benedictine house of Nogent make known that following their dispute with the church of Prémontré, they ceded to it land called* Ad Vinetum, *in exchange for an annual payment of one* aissinus *of grain* (frumentum) *and one of oats, measure of Soissons.*

A. Cartulary of Prémontré, fols. 56v.

B. Original (chirograph), AD Aisne H 775, previously sealed with double strip of parchment. In the left margin and beginning on the top, the upper half of the letters that form the word CYROGRAPHUM.

---

5 Cociaco *B*.
6 denunciabunt *B*.
7 Cociaco *B*.
8 millesimo *B*.

---

1 Jean, abbot of the Benedictine abbey of Nogent-sous-Coucy, ca. 1164–ca. 1175. *GC* IX, col. 608.

Karta abbatis de Nongento et capituli de quadam terra que dicitur Ad Vinetum.

[E]go Johannes, Dei gratia Sancte Marie de Nongento dictus abbas, totumque capitulum nostrum notum fieri volumus tam futuris quam presentibus quod querela vertebatur inter nos et Premonstratensem ecclesiam de terra que dicitur Ad Vinetum. Mediantibus ergo honestis viris, ecclesia de Nongento Premonstrate ecclesie terram illam que dicitur Ad Vinetum pro qua querela orta est, perpetuo possidendam tali conditione concessit quod fratres de Premonstrato annuatim monachis de Nongento aissinum[2] unum de frumento et unum de avena ad mensuram Suessionensem persolvent etiam si terra illa pro qua conpositio[3] facta est, sterilis esset et curia cui adjacet destrueretur. Ut autem ratum sit et inconvulsum, sigillo nostro presens scriptum fecimus confirmari et monachorum nostrorum testimonio corroborari. S.[4] Theodrici, prioris. S.[5] Ade, supprioris.[6] S. Widonis, sacerdotis. S. Ogeri, prepositi. S. Ysenbardi.[7] S. Philippi. Actum anno incarnati verbi M° C° LXX° tercio.

228

June 12, 1222.

Magister *Guillaume,*[1] *canon and* officialis *of Reims, makes known that Jean, priest of Merlieux, brought suit against the church of Prémontré concerning the noval tithes in the parish of Merlieux.*[2] *Before a decision was rendered, Jean surrendered his claims over the tithes to Prémontré, which then withdrew its countersuit.*

A. Cartulary of Prémontré, fol. 56v.

B. Original not found.

REGISTER: *Studium Baldwin*, fiche 1619.

---

2 aiscinum *B*.

3 compositio *B*.

4 Signum *B*.

5 Signum *B*.

6 subprioris *B*.

7 Isenbardi *B*.

---

1 Guillaume, first canon of Langres and then of Reims, was *officialis* of Reims, ca. 1219–ca. 1222. Grandmottet, “Les officialités de Reims,” 94.

2 Merlieux-et-Fouquerolles, cant. Anizy-le-Château, https://dicotopo.cths.fr/places/P92396813.

Karta curie Remensis super renunciatione presbiteri de Merliu de novalibus parrochie sue.

[F]idelibus Christi universis presentes litteras inspecturis magistri Willermus et canonici et officialis Remenses salutem. Noverint universi quod, cum Johannes, presbiter de Merliu, Laudunensis diocesis, ecclesiam Premonstratensem super decimis novalium parrochie de Merliu per appellationem ad nos super hoc a curia Laudunensi factam et approbatam, coram nobis in jus vocari fecisset, tandem, antequam ad diffinitivam sententiam procederetur super premissis partibus coram nobis in jure constitutis, dictus presbiter quicquid juris habebat vel videbatur habere in predictis decimis, quitavit ecclesie memorate, promittens quod super ipsis, quam diu[3] parrochiam ipsam teneret, predictam ecclesiam non inquietaret. Ipsa quoque ecclesia omni actioni sive juri quod sibi competebat, vel videbatur competere, super expensis in lite factis, omnia renuntiavit. In cuius rei testimonium presentes litteras de utriusque partis assensu conscriptas sigillo Remensis curie fecimus sigillari. Datum quarta feria post dominicam qua cantatur Deus omnium, anno gratie M° CC° vicesimo secundo.

229

July, 1332.

Husband and wife Jean Curé de Penancourt[1] *and Marie la Bonne recognize in the presence of the mayor and council members of the Laonnois that they hold from the church and convent of Prémontré a vineyard located at Penancourt, at a place called* Au Molinet, *in exchange for an annual* cens *and* vinaige *of six* sols Parisis, *and have provided as guarantee of the payment their garden located below the Premonstratensian house at Penancourt.*

A. Cartulary of Prémontré, fols. 56v–57r.
B. Original not found.

3 *Sic A*.

1 Penancourt, comm. Anizy-le-Château, https://dicotopo.cths.fr/places/P36114519.

Panencourt.[2]

Sachent tout que l'an de grace mil trois cens trente et deus, ou mois de julet, vinrent en leurs propres persones par devant le maieur de Lannois et les eschevins ci desous nommés, Jehans Cures, de Panencourt et Marie la Bonne, sa femme, et reconnurent de leur plain gré et volenté, si comme il disoient, et especialment la dicte Marie dou congié et auctorité desou dit marit, qui congié et auctorité le donna et elle le rechut, que il le pour leur pourfit apparant avoient prinz a religieus hommes et honnestes, l'abbé et le couvent del eglize de Premonstré une vingne seant ou terroir de Panencourt, que on dist Au Molinet, tenant a la vingne de la Capelerie d'une part et a Jaquemart Langele d'autre part, a tenir la dicte vingne de la dicte eglize par les dessusdis Jehan et Marie, leur hoirs, leur succeseur ou cyaus qui d'iaus aroient cause a perpetuité parmi siz solz Parisis que li dessusdit leur hoir ou successeur ou cyus ou cil qui d'iaus avoient cause, en renderont et ~~parient~~ paieront chascun an a la dicte eglize a cause de cens ou de droit vinaige loy, au jour de le Saint Remy ou on chief de octembre; et a plus grans seureté des chozes dessus dictes yl ont obligié leur gardin, seant desous le maison de le dicte eglize, que on dit Panencourt, ainsi comme il se comporte, tenant d'une part ou fil maistre Aubry et as enfans Martigny d'autrepart et s'en sont devestu et mis en main de justice pour vendre et pour despendre et envestir celui ou ciaux a cui la dicte eglize aroit ledit gardin vendu, se li dis Jehans et Marie, leur hoir ou successeur ou cius ou cil qui d'iaus aroient cause, estoient en defaute de paier lezdis siz sols Parisis au dit jour en tout ou en partie, et renoncèrent expressement a exception de detenance et a toutes autres aides tant de droit comme de fait, tant generaus comme especiaus, et a toutes barres, cavillations, et defenses qui yaus, leur hoirs, leur successeur ou celui ou ciaus qui dyaus, de leur hoirs, ou de le successeur aroient cause en venant contre le teneur de ce cirographe, leur porroient aidier et au diz religieus ou au porteur de ce cirographe grever ou nuire la su, comme maires Gille Brunne de Lizy,[3] comme eschevin Ernoules li Tenurs de Lizy, Anciaus Pinars de Panencourt et Gerars Gaverné de Ursignicourt,[4] l'an et le mois deseurdit qui en eurent leurs drois.

2 This act is a later addition, and its rubric is in black rather than red ink.

3 Lizy, cant. Anizy-le-Château, https://dicotopo.cths.fr/places/P40948829.

4 Wissignicourt, cant. Anizy-le-Château, https://dicotopo.cths.fr/places/P16285342.

230

1330

Jean de Dercy,[1] baillius *of Ham, renders judgment in favour of the church of Prémontré and against the men of Béatrice*[2] *de Saint-Pol, lady of Nesle and Châ[tillon], concerning certain rights over the wood neighbouring the Premonstratensian house at Bonneuil.*[3]

A. Cartulary of Prémontré, fols. 57r–57v.[4]
B. Original not found.

NO RUBRIC. LATER ADDITION.

A tous ceulz qui ces presentes lettres verront et orront Jehan de Dercy, baillius de Hem, dame noble et poissant madame Beatrix de Saint-Pol, dame de Neelle et de Cha[illegible] salut. Comme pluseur debat et descort fuissent meu ou esperé a mouvoir entre la dame dessusdicte d'une part et religieux hommes et honestes l'abbé et le couvent de l'eglise de Premonstré d'autre part seur ce que ma dame dessusdicte ou ses gens disoient et maintenoient que en saisins estoient et avoient esté de mener ou faire mener pourchiaux et autres es bos appendans a la maison de Bonneul, maison des dis religieux pour mangier la p[aionage] et paistre l'erbe dou dit bos toutes fois que il leur plaisoit, les dis religieux disans et maintenans au contraire que en saisinne estoient de tel tamps et par tel tamps que memoire n'estoit dou contraire, ou au mains que il souffisoit a saisine avoir a[illegible] de avoir ou dit bos, conté, justice et signerie haute basse et moyenne seul et pour le [tout] et de tenir, warder et maintenir et goir franchement seul et pour le tout de tout le pourfis et yssues d'icelui et de tout paionage ou pasturage sans ce que ma dicte [dame] ou aultres quelconques y puissent mener ou faire mener aucunes bestes pour paioner, pasturer ou autre cause. Item sur ce que le dit religieux disoicnt et maintenoient que en saisine dessusdicte et par le tamps dessusdict estoient de chachier, haier et prendre toutes [illegible] de bestes sauvages en tous temps et a toutes manieres de las et d'engiens et en toutes saisons par yaulx, leurs sergens et veneurs et autres ayes et d'emporter lever et quier a leur pourfit toutes les bestes prinses en leur dit bos et ou bos monsigneur ~~de~~

1 Dercy, cant. Crécy-sur-Serre, https://dicotopo.cths.fr/places/P47810688.
2 Béatrice de Châtillon, daughter of Jacques I de Châtillon, lord of Leuze and governor of Flanders, and Catherine de Condé, lady of Carency and Duisant; wife of Jean de Flandre, lord of Termonde, Crèvecœur, and Nesle, and viscount of Châteaudun.
3 *MP* II, 484.
4 The right margin of this folio has been trimmed, and the bottom right corner badly smudged, and so several letters or words are missing or illegible.

~~Noyon~~ l'evesque de Noyon et les bos con dist le bos des parties nientmains Jehans alons et sergens a ma dame devant dicte avoec pluseurs ses complices et [illegible] ou grief, damage, vitupere et prejudices dez dis religieux avoit arresté un cerf que l[illegible]de la dicte eglise avoient prins es bos des parties et mist les main injurieusement audis sergens et as chevaux de la dicte eglise qui prins avoient ledit cerf et la venu esté pour emmener yceluy cerf a ledicte maison de Bonneul en tourbelant et empeschant les dis religieux en leur dicte saisine indeument et de nouvel. Item sur ce que li diz religieux disoient et maintenoient que en la saisine de susdicte estoient et avoient esté faire buisson es bos dessus dict toutesfois que pleu leur avoit et venu estoit a leur congnoissance que bestes avoit ou dit bos et buisson, detenir le buisson et au[illegible]paisible et sans ce que autres de par madame y peust ne deust cachier nientmoins Colars Bramons et Jehans Villes de Frann[illegible]ce marchant des Varennes ma dite dame aux heures et a commis pour leur volente ou grief, dommige et prejudice de l'eglise et contre la requeste des gens de la dicte eglise adfin qu'il cessaissent de cachier ou dit buisson a chiens, cors, crys et noise entrerent oudit buisson et les bestes encloses en yceluy buisson en chachierent et pour bien de p[illegible] et a cort eussent supplié li abbes de le dite église en sa personne et plusieurs autres a ma dite dame que des choses dessusdites elle se voulsist infourmer [illegible] et le droit de l'eglise warder et sur ce ma dite dame me eust commis et nommé que je a laissé sur le lieu contemptieux appelés avecques my son prevost, ses sergens et outres qui desdis debas et de son droit et dou droit et saisine de la dite dame peussent plainement infourmer. Sachent tout que pour acomplir la volenté et commandement de ma dite dame, je ne transportai es dis bos appeles avecques my le prevost de Frann[illegible]ce les sergens veneurs et autres plusieurs qui on dit bos longt tamps avoient repairie et encontre le sergent a l'abbé au prieux et au maistre de Bonneul ciquelz prieux, maistre et grande plenté de bonnes gens y vinrent offrant de grant instance my informer de leur droit et saisine dessusdite et la par les gens que mené y aviens je trouvay par la deposition de ceulx que mené y aviens que es dessusdit ma dite dame et ses gens avoient grevé l'eglise tourblée et mise en sa saisine et que faire ne poit par raison ce que fait avait esté ledit religieux fussent et eussent esté en le saisine dont il se ventoient pour quoy je, en conseil et deliberation sur les choses dessusdites, aux hommes de fief de ma dite dame fis amender s[illegible] dis religieux les choses par Pierre Brechart comme procureur de ma dite dame et resai les dis religieux des choses contemptieuses en jugement en la presence des hommes de fief de ma dite dame jugeans en sa court [illegible] noble homme monsigneur Gombaut de chevalier, Jehan escuyer le Rat et Pierre de [illegible]. En tesmoing desquelles choses jou y mis men seel a ces presentes lettres apres le Saint Valentin l'an de grace M. CCC. trente et dessus nomme jugans en de la dite dame ces lettres. En testmoing de ce nous avons mis nos scauls a ces presentes lettres avoecques le scel dou dit baillui. Ce fu fait l'an et le jour dessus dis.

231

March 31, 1355. Saint-Quentin.

Jean de Vaunoise,[1] baillius *of Vermandois, pronounces to the assizes of Saint-Quentin his confirmatory sentence concerning the transaction between Prémontré and husband and wife [Ingelger I,*[2] *lord of Amboise] and [Marie*[3] *de Flandres-Dampierre], lady of Nesle, concerning hunting (*garenne*), fishing (*peischa*), and* saisine de justice *of the woods of Bonneuil.*[4]

A. Cartulary of Prémontré, fol. 57v.

B. Original, AD Oise, Hs 1384, sealed with a double strip of parchment and a red wax seal, on one side a fleur de lys and on the other three fleurs de lys, surrounded by a mostly erased legend.

NO RUBRIC. LATER ADDITION.

A tous ceulz[5] qui ces presentes lettres verront et orront Jehans de Vennoise,[6] baillius de Vermendois salut. Sachent tout que, comparans en ces presentes assizes tenues par nous a Saint Quentin[7] le XXVIIIe jour de mars et les jours ensuivant l'an mil CCC LV,[8] le procureur des religieux abbé et couvent de Premonstré d'une part et le procureur de nobles et poissans personnes le singneur et dame d'Ambarde et de Neele d'autre part, apres ce que par lesdis procureurs fu congvenu[9] et confessé et acordé que les parties avoient jour audites assises en II[10] cas de nouvelleté et par II[11] complaintes piecha faites par les dis religieux pour la saisine de justice et de garenne[12] es bos de Bonneil[13] et de Vrelaines,[14] appendans a le maison de Bonnel, maison desdis religieux et que li uns des cas

1 Jean de Vaunoise, *bailli* of Vermandois, 1354–7, 1358–61. Waquet, *Le bailliage de Vermandois aux XIIIe et XIVe siècles*, 183–4.

2 Ingelger I "le Grand," lord of Amboise and Chevreuse (d. ca. 1373), son of Pierre I, lord of Amboise, and Jeanne, lady of Chevreuse. His first wife was Marie de Flandre, lady of Nesle.

3 Marie de Flandre, lady of Nesle (d. ca. 1355), was the daughter of Jean de Flandre, lord of Nesle and Crèvecoeur, and Beatrix de Châtillon.

4 Bonneuil, cant. Ham, https://dicotopo.cths.fr/places/P66750585.

5 chiaus *B*.

6 Vannoise *B*.

7 *Transp. A*; Saint-Quentin par nous *B*.

8 trois cens chainquante chuinq *B*.

9 congvenus *B*.

10 deux *B*.

11 deux *B*.

12 garesne *B*.

13 Bonneul *B*.

14 Vrelainnes *B*.

estoit piecha[15] meubs et pendans es dites assises et li autres estoit meues[16] a Chauny[17] sur Oise[18] en la court de tres haut et poissant singneur monseigneur[19] le duc[20] d'Orliens et estoit venus en ces presentes assises de Saint Quentin par vertu d'un rescript du roy contenant la forme[21] qui s'ensuit:[22] Johannes, Dei gratia et suie ainsy.[23] Datum Parisius, XXII[a] die januarii, anno Domini M[o] CCC[o] L[o] V[o24] in requestis hospitii. Li procureur des dites parties pour et en nom d'icelles parties congneurent ycelles[25] parties avoir esté et estre et par notre congie[26] en acord[27] sur[28] le fourme contenue en une cedule[29] baille par lesdis procureurs es

15 piech *B*.
16 meue *B*.
17 Chauny, arr. Laon, https://dicotopo.cths.fr/places/P32247131.
18 Chauni seur Oise *B*.
19 monsingneur *B*.
20 duk *B*.
21 fourme *B*.
22 ensuit *B*.
23 *Add.* et suie ainsy *A*; Francorum rex baillivo Viromandensi vel eius locum tenenti salutem. Sua nobis religiosi abbas et conventus ecclesie Premonstratensis gravi conquestione monstrarunt quod cum nuper postquam concessimus et contulimus karissimo germano nostro duci Aurelianensi castellania de Calniaco ad nos spectare ipsi conquerentes contra dilectum et fidelem nostram dominum de Ambardi militem et eius gentes coram preposito dicti germani nostri sue prepositure Calniacus in casu novitatis certa de causa conquesti fuissent in qua quidem causa partes predicte per certum tempus processerunt nichilominus dictus miles post predictum processum inceptum certus litteras a nobis seu a curia nostra dicitur impeccasse quarum pretextu se debere fore dicit exemptum a jurisdictione dicti germani nostri et super hoc pendet lis in nostra parlamenti curia inter dictum germanum nostrum ex un parte et dictum militem ex altera et huius occasione idem miles coram dicto preposito in causam predictam cum dictis conquerentibus procedere recusat propter quod jus quod ipsi conquerentes in causa huiusmodi se dicunt habere posset recordary nisi per nos eisiem super hoc de remedio provideatur gratoso ut asserunt. Hinc est quod nos attentus premissis tibi mandamus et ex causis predictis commitimus quatinus processibus super causa huiusmodi in curia de Calniaco predicta inter dictas partes factis et pendentibus in statu in quo sunt penes te resumptis quos tibi tradi volumus et mandamus tu secundum statum eorumdem in assisiis eius Sancti Quintini proximo venturis vocate que fuerunt evocandi in quibus assisiis prefatus miles habet ressortum prout fertur ratione castellanie sue de Nigella procedas dictas que partes procedere in eisdem facias exhibendo eisdem super hoc te leves justicie complementum quod eisdem conquerentur habita consideratione ad premissa concessimus et de gratia speciali concedimus per presentes si sit opus litteris subjectis in contrarium impetratis vel impetrandis non obstante quibuscumque *B*.
24 millesimo CCC[o] quinquagesimo quinte *B*.
25 icelles *B*.
26 congiet *B*.
27 accord *B*.
28 seur *B*.
29 cedulle *B*.

dites assises et laquelle[30] cedule[31] contenoit[32] le[33] fourme qui s'ensuit.[34] Sur[35] les debas meus ou esperes a mouvoir[36] entre les religieux abbé et couvent de l'eglise de Premonstré d'une part et nobles et poissants[37] personnes monseigneur, singneur d'Ambarde et de Neelle, comme bailli de ma dame Marie de Flandre, sa femme, et la dite dame comme héritière de la terre de Neelle d'autre part sur[38] ce que lidit conjoint es noms que dessus disoient et maintenoient a eulx[39] estre et avoir esté en possession et saisine de peure ou faire peure par eulx[40] ou leurs gens a cause de garenne toutes personnes de quelconque condition qu'il soient excepté les dis religieux ou leurs gens faisans maniere de cache en tous les bos de Bonnel et de Vrelain[41] appendans a le maison de Bonnel,[42] maison des dis religieux, et de traitier a amende yceulx[43] cachans, les dis religieux disans au contraire, c'est assavoir que a eulx[44] appartient la cache en tous les dis bos de Bonnel et de Vrelain, la prise et la garde de tous malfaiteurs et de traitier a amende sans ce que lidit noble y aient ou puissent avoir aucun garde ou prise en aucune maniere par aucun cause, traitiet est s'il plaist a la court entre les dites parties pour bien de pais et pour hoster toute matiere de descors que lidit conjoint comme en leur garenne[45] porroit chachier et haier[46] ou faire tendre, cachier,[47] hayer et fuister en tous les bos desdis religieux con dist[48] les bos de Bonnel et de Vrelain quant il leur plaira, mais quant lidis[49] religieux y vorrent cachier et il aront par eulx[50] ou leurs gens fait buisson celle journées[51] lidit conjoint n'y[52] porroit[53] cachier ne fustier ne mettre empeschement aucun par eulx[54]

30 le quelle *B.*
31 cedulle *B.*
32 et contient *B.*
33 ceste *B.*
34 *Add.* qui s'ensuit *A.*
35 seur *B.*
36 amouvoir *B.*
37 poissans *B.*
38 seur *B.*
39 euls *B.*
40 euls *B.*
41 Verlaine, cant. Ham, https://dicotopo.cths.fr/places/P23536505.
42 Bonniel *B.*
43 iceuls *B.*
44 euls *B.*
45 garene *B.*
46 ihaier *B.*
47 *Om.* et *A.*
48 condist *B.*
49 ledit *B.*
50 euls *B.*
51 journeé *B.*
52 n'i *B.*
53 pueroit *B.*
54 euls *B.*

ou leurs gens et aussi[55] se lidit conjoint y veillent cachier ou faire cachier et il y ont fait buisson[56] devant lesdis religieux lidit religieux celle journée ne leur porront briser leur buisson ne mettre empeschement aucun a leur cache et ce sera ceste maniere de cache de hayer et faire buissons sans fraude l'une partie envers l'autre et en tous les dis bos tant de Bonnel comme de Vrelain aront[57] lidit conjoint et leur successeur singneur de Nelle la garenne et toute la justice et sengneurie a cause d'icelle tant seulement toute aultre justice et signeurie es dis bos [illegible] religieux seulement et entierement et aussi toute la demainne de leurs dis bos desquels lidit religieux par eulx,[58] leurs gens ou marcheans porront user tant en coupant[59] poirier,[60] pruniers, melliers et autres arbres que on dit de garenne comme autrement et sus umbre de ledit[61] garenne[62] ou autrement ne se porront lidit conjoint ne leur successeur singneur de Neelle en saisiner d'aucun aultre justice es dis bos fors en cas de garenne[63] seulement et en[64] cas et en la maniere dessus dite pour quelconque[65] fais ou esplois de quelconque[66] temps que fait soient ja soit ce[67] que fait fussent de tel temps qu'il ne fust memoire du contraire et sanblablement[68] ne se porront lidit religieux sus umbre de leur justice autre que de garenne[69] ensaisiner contre lesdis conjoins ne leurs successurs de la dite garenne[70] ne de la dite justice a cause d'icelle fors en la maniere dessusdite pour quelconques fais ou explois de quelconques tamps que fait soient ja soit ce que fait fussent de tel tamps qu'il ne fut[71] ou soit memoire dou contraire. Item porront lidit religieux par eulx[72] et leurs gens et [illegible][73] et [illegible][74] et aultres menues gens empruntés non capables ou droit de justice de garenne[75] acquerir, cachier, tendre, hayer et faire buissons es di[76] bos pour leur propre pourfit tant seulement, sans fraude toutesfois qu'il leur plaira sans

55 aussy *B.*
56 buissons *B.*
57 auront *B.*
58 euls *B.*
59 caupant *B.*
60 poiriers *B.*
61 ladite *B.*
62 garene *B.*
63 garene *B.*
64 es *B.*
65 quelconques *B.*
66 quelconques *B.*
67 che *B.*
68 sanlablement *B.*
69 garene *B.*
70 garene *B.*
71 fust *B.*
72 euls *B.*
73 chiens *B.*
74 lyannas *B.*
75 garene *B.*
76 dis *B.*

empeschement estre mis des dis conjoins ou de leurs gens a cause de garenne[77] [damaged][78] les dis conjoins ou leurs gens y cachassent ou eussent fait buisson et se li chien des dis religieux ou li chien par eulx[79] empruntes passent oultre les mettes des dis bos de Bonnel et Vrelain sur[80] le terre et autre garenne des dis conjoins poursuivir les porront sans faire prise de beste, cry ne aultre fait malicieux sans pour ne[81] estre pris par les gens desdis conjoins et se prins estoient les gens des dis conjoins et leurs successeurs leur seroient tenu de rendre sans delay et sans frais quelconquez[82] si tost que requis en serront par la maistre de Bonnel ou les aultres gens des dis religieux et parmi cest accord toutes autres chartres et lettres faisans mention de garenne[83] ou de justice es dit bos de Bonnel et de Vrelain tant d'une partie comme d'autre demourront[84] en leur vertu sauf les poins contenus en cest[85] present accort lequel accort et traitier dessus dis par le[86] accord des dites parties, je Galchaus de Lailly[87] chevalier bailli dudit singneur et ma dame sa femme ay mis le scel de le baillie de Neelle avec le seel du prieux[88] de Premonstré, procureur desdis religieux en ceste partie a ce[89] present accord laquelle cedule[90] loueé[91] et accordeé nous du consentement des procureurs desdites parties avons loé et approuvé, loons et approuvons les choses dessus dites en tant comme nous poons[92] tant par notre commissaire ordinaire comme par vertu dou[93] rescript du roy notre sire dessusdit transcript et avons levé et levons les mains assises[94] as choses contempeiuses en tant comme mielx[95] poons au profit desdites parties selon[96] la teneur doudit[97] accord.[98] En tesmoing desquelle choses nous avons mis le seel de ledite baillie a ces presentes lettres qui furent

77 garene *B.*
78 ou autrement. Se ainssi n'estoit que *B.*
79 euls *B.*
80 seur *B.*
81 ce *B.*
82 quelconques *B.*
83 garene *B.*
84 demouront *B.*
85 ce *B.*
86 *Add.* par le *A.*
87 Luilly *B.*
88 prieus *B.*
89 che *B.*
90 cedulle *B.*
91 loué *B.*
92 peons *B.*
93 du *B.*
94 assizes *B.*
95 miex *B.*
96 selont *B.*
97 dudit *B.*
98 accort *B.*

faites et donneés en l'an et [illegible] assises dessus dites le jeudi darrain jour du mois de march.

232

1351–1418[1]

Raoul Joye, bailli *of Nesle, makes a judgment in favour of the religious of Prémontré in their dispute with the count of Dammartin, lord of Nesle, concerning certain rights over the woods of Bonneuil.*[2]

A. Cartulary of Prémontré, fol. 57v.
B. Original not found.

NO RUBRIC. LATER ADDITION.

A tous ceulx qui ces presentes lettres verront et orront Raoul Joye, bailli de Neelle, salut. Comme proces fust esperés a mouvoir entre religieuses personnes et honorables l'abbé et couvent de l'eglise de Premontré d'une part et notre tres redoubté seigneur monseigneur le cont de Dampmartin, signeur de Neelle d'autre part, sur ce que lez dis religieux se disoient estre tourblé et empesché en leur possession et saisine de ce que ja piecha no dit signeur ou ses gens avoient vendu a certains marchans le paissant des bos con dit les bos de Bonneil appartenans aux dis religieux et aussi des bos que on dit les bos de Brelain[3] pour par lesdis marchans maner ou faire mener en veux bos pour paistre leurs pourchiaux et de ce lez dis religieux se entendoient a pourcachier de ne dit signeur et de ses gens, sachent tout que pour esquieur toute matiere deplait et de discorde entre les dit religieux et no dit signeur et aussi pour ce qu'il nous est apparu par certaines lettres desquelles lesdis religieux nous ont fait apparoir que la dite vente ainsi faite par no dit signeur a esté et est faite contre et au préjudice desdis religieux et de leur eglise selonc la fourme et par la maniere qui contenu est es dites lettres nous pour et au nom de no dit signeur et a son commandement les choses dessusdites avons reputé et reputons pour nulx et comme s'il ne fuissent onques advenu sans ce qu'il porte ou puist porter prejudice aux dis religieux ne a leur dite église orec ou pour le tamps avenir et volons que les dites lettres desdis religieux demeurent en force et vertu selonc leur force et teneur.

1 Two men held both the title of count of Dammartin and of lord of Nesle: Charles de Trie, count of Dammartin, who ca. 1351 married Jeanne d'Amboise, lady of Nesle, daughter of Ingelger I, lord of Amboise, and Marie de Flandre, lady of Nesle; and Charles Bureau, lord of La Rivière, who ca. 1400 married Blanche de Trie, daughter of Charles and Jeanne.

2 Bonneuil, cant. Ham, https://dicotopo.cths.fr/places/P66750585.

3 Verlaine, cant. Ham, https://dicotopo.cths.fr/places/P23536505.

TABLE OF CONTENTS: HANAPPES

A. Cartulary of Prémontré, fol. 58r.

Incipiunt scripta de Hanapiis cum appenditiis suis.

Capitula I Karta episcopi Laudunensis de confirmatione curie de Hanapiis qua Albricus miles libera dedit.

II Karta Burchardi domini de Guisia et Godefridi fratris sui de alodio de Germania et de confirmatione territorii de Hanapiis et de ecclesia de Dorenc.

III Karta Audelvie de Guisia de confirmatione cuiusdam compromissionis.

IIII Karta domini Galteri de Avesnis de quadam compositione et de confirmatione elemosine patris sui.

V Karta Hugonis electi et decani Cameracensis de concordia inter ecclesiam Premonstrato et Prumensensem.

VI Karta episcopi Laudunensis de confirmatione alodii canonicorum de Guisia in territoria de Yrun que contulerunt ecclesie Premonstrati.

VII Karta domini Jacobi de Avesnis de confirmatione elemosine Audelvie.

VIII Karta domine Audelvie de confirmatione elemosine viginti solidorum quos dedit ad refectionem conventus.

IX Karta comitis Blesensis et uxoris eius de quadam compositione inter ecclesiam Premonstratensis et ipsos.

X Conpositione inter ecclesiam Premonstratensis et abbatem de Maricolis.

XI Littere testimoniales domini Buchardi super possessionibus Hanapiis.

XII Karta officialis Laudunensis de elemosina Godefridi militis de Flavigniaco.

XIII Item karta officialis de elemosina Philipi clerici de Tupigniaco.

XIIII Karta domine Ide de Yrun de medietate furni de Dorenc quam contulit in elemosinam ecclesie Premonstrati.

XV Karta curie Laudunensis de elemosina Godefridi de Seinz de tribus modiis bladi.

XVI Karta episcopi de XV denariis quos domus hospitalis de Ribodimonte tenetur reddere ecclesie de Dorenc.

XVII Karta Euberti militis de Ribodimonte de terragio de Yron nobis concesso.

XVIII Karta de mulierum quarundam possessione nobis adjudicata.

XIX Karta Hugonis Premontratensis abbatis de controversia molendini d'Yron.

XX Karta Stephani decani de Sancto Angesio de elemosina Wiardi Fabri et Alaidis uxoris eius.

XXI Item karta eiusdem decani de elemosina Elizabeth de Lescheriis.

XXII Karta de quadam compositione inter ecclesiam Premonstratensis et[1] Hugonem maiorem de Dorenc.

---

1 *Eras.* dominum *A.*

233

1139

Barthélemy,[1] *bishop of Laon, makes known that after their father's death, the brothers Pierre and Robert confirmed the gift of land at Hannape*[2] *made to the church of Prémontré by their parents Aubry,*[3] *knight of Nouvion, and Ermensendis. Fief lords Bouchard, lord of Lesquielles, and Geoffroi, his brother, consented to the gift. Barthélemy also makes known that Renier, miller of Hannape, with the consent of Eremburge his wife, Jean his son, and Marie and Bonesende his daughters, gave to Prémontré his part of the mill at Hannape in exchange for 20* solidi, *and that Nicolas, canon of Saint-Jean de Lesquielles,*[4] *gave the altar of Hannape and his parts of its tithe to Prémontré.*

A. Cartulary of Prémontré, fol. 58r.

B. Original, AD Aisne, H 797, previously sealed.

EDITION: Dufour-Malbezin, *Actes*, 301–2; *Chartae Galliae*, no. 208341, http://telma.irht.cnrs.fr/outils/chartae-galliae/charte208341/.

REGISTER: Florival, *Étude historique sur le XIIe siècle*, 364.

Karta Bartholomei episcopi de confirmatione curie de Hanapiis quam Albricus miles liberam dedit.

[I]n nomine sancte et individue Trinitatis. Ego Bartholomeus, Dei gratia Laudunensis episcopus, notum fieri volo futuris et presentibus quod Albricus, miles de Noviomo, et eius uxor Ermesendis,[5] concedentibus filiis suis Petro et Roberto, terram de Hanapia Premonstratensi[6] ecclesie pro sua et suorum salute libere concesserunt. Post mortem autem predicti Albrici, prememoratus Petrus et frater eius Robertus hoc donum, quod pater eorum fecerat, etiam ipsi fecerunt, sub hiis testibus: Gisleberto presbitero; Waszone, qui Stultus agnominatus est; Bartholomeo, filio Fulconis maioris, et Wiberto, fratre eius, et Pisello, qui et Vasles[7] dictus est, et Johanne de Genueri et Renero,[8] maiore de Bosor; Fulcone et Alelmo et Widone de Porta et Hugone Cossa. Postea vero concessum est a Burcardo,[9] domino Lesqueriarum,[10] atque a Godefrido, fratre

1 Barthélemy de Jur (d. 1158), son of Conon, lord of Grandson and La Sarraz, and Ada de Roucy; first subdeacon and then treasurer of Reims, later bishop of Laon, 1113–51.

2 Hannape, cant. Wassigny, https://dicotopo.cths.fr/places/P37303056.

3 Aubry, knight and lord of Nouvion-en-Thiérache. Melleville, *DH*, vol. 2, 172.

4 Lesquielles-Saint-Germain, cant. Guise, https://dicotopo.cths.fr/places/P39197714.

5 Ermensendis *B*.

6 Premonstrate *B*.

7 Vaslez *B*.

8 Rainero *B*.

9 Burchardo *B*.

10 Leskeriarum *B*.

suo, de quorum feodo pendebat. Huius rei testes sunt: canonici de Lescheriis[11] Walterus videlicet et Renaldus[12] presbiteri; Nicholaus[13] clericus; et de militibus predicti Burcardi,[14] Walterus dapifer et Rothardus[15] frater eius, Drogo[16] de Dulcilon, Robertus de Stabulis.[17] Decetero Renerus,[18] molendinarius de Hanapia, hereditatem, quam jure molendinarii in molendino de Hanapia possidebat, pro viginti[19] solidis Premonstratensis[20] ecclesie assensu conjugis sue, Erenburgis, et filii sui, Johannis, et filiarum suarum, Marie et Bonesendis, concessit et in manu domini Burchardi posuit idemque Burchardus supradicte ecclesie attribuit. Et super hoc testes sunt canonici et milites predicti. Nicholaus etiam canonicus Sancti Johannis de Lescheriis,[21] altare Hanapie cum partibus decime, quas in culturis indominicatis tenebat, et quicquid terrarum vel alterius portionis[22] in predicto fundo possidebat, annuentibus filiis suis, Johanne et Alberto, in manu nostra libere et canonice posuit, eo tenore ut liberum eidem Premonstratensis[23] ecclesie redderemus. Quod et fecimus. Huius rei testes sunt: Ernaudus[24] Laudunensis archidiaconus, Arnulphus[25] canonicus, Renaldus[26] et ceteri.[27] Quod ut ratum permaneat, tam sigilli quam scripti nostri auctoritate munivimus. Quisquis autem hec irrita facere presumpserit, usque ad condignam satisfactionem anathema sit. Actum anno incarnati verbi millesimo[28] C° XXX° VIIII°, indictione tercia,[29] epacta nulla, concurrente secundo.[30]

---

11 Leskeriis *B.*

12 Rainaldus *B.*

13 Nicholaus *B.*

14 Burchardi *B.*

15 Rohardus *B.*

16 A Dreux de Dulcelon (cant. Guise, https://dicotopo.cths.fr/places/P62286197) appears in an 1146 act concerning the abbey of Longpont. Waroquier, "La principauté de Vermandois, Valois et Montdidier au XIIe siècle," 703.

17 Étaves-et-Bocquiaux, cant. Bohain, https://dicotopo.cths.fr/places/P16456670. A Robert d'Etaves entered the Benedictine abbey of Homblières in the early 1150s. Newman, *Homblières*, 146–7.

18 Rainerus *B.*

19 XX[ti] *B.*

20 Premonstrate *B.*

21 Leskariis *B.*

22 *Om.* cum partibus decime, quas in culturis in dominicatis tenebat, et quicquid terrarum vel alterius portionis *A.*

23 Premonstrate *B.*

24 Ernaud, chancellor of Laon, 1133–41, and archdeacon of Laon, 1136/8–41. Dufour-Malbezin, *Actes*, 29.

25 Arnulfus *B.*

26 *Om.* subdecanus *A.*

27 *Add.* et ceteri *A*; Robertus, presbiter *B.*

28 M° *B.*

29 III[a] *B.*

30 II° *B.*

234

January 9, 1327. Saint-Quentin.

Jean,[1] *lord of Tupigny, swears in the presence of the* bailli[2] *of Vermandois the oath to uphold all the points of the charter of purchase concluded between Bautiers, his predecessor, and the religious of Prémontré.*

A. Cartulary of Prémontré, fols. 58r.[3]
B. Original not found.

NO RUBRIC. LATER ADDITION.

L'an de grace mil CCC et XXVII, le lundi apres les Rois jura messire Jehan sires de Thupigni, chevalier, a tenir tous les poins de la chartre lequele cil devancier jurerent et seellerent pour cause de licat que messire Bautiers, ses devanciers, fist a l'eglise de Premonstré et reconnut lidis messire Jehan le dite chartre estre scellée de ses devancier. A ce furent comme tesmoings [illegible] Neelle, Jehan de Thupigni escuiers, Mahieus de Folleville,[4] Jehan Curignes, Gerars Cuignes de Fariviller,[5] [illegible], Pierres de Fontainnes, Jaquemars de Muille,[6] Jehan le Bocheus, Florens de Nouviant et [illegible] le Roi a Ribemont, Jehan de Granart, Jehan Bosques de [illegible] freres, Herbers d'Amie [illegible] de Sens pladieres de prenommés et pluiser d'autre. Ce fu fait a l'Ostel de [illegible] a Saint-Quentin en le [illegible] de le maison l'an et le jour dessusdit le bailli de Vermendois en ledicte cause selon ces requestes.

235

1155–80[1]

Bouchard, lord of Guise, recounts in a single act the gifts of lands and rights at Hannape,[2] *Dorengt,*[3] *and Germaine*[4] *that he, his mother Adèle, his brother*

1 Jean I, lord of Tupigny (cant. Wassigny, https://dicotopo.cths.fr/places/P99706313), attested 1319–46; husband of Jeanne, widow of Tassard de Ribemont. Melleville, *DH*, vol. 2, 388.
2 Likely Henri de Genoilly. Waquet, *Le bailliage de Vermandois aux XIIIe et XIVe siècles*, 180.
3 This charter appears in the bottom margin of the folio.
4 Folleville, cant. Chauny, https://dicotopo.cths.fr/places/P57942146.
5 Likely Saint-André-Farivillers, cant. Froissy, https://dicotopo.cths.fr/places/P51274912.
6 Muille-Villette, cant. Ham, https://dicotopo.cths.fr/places/P77128677.

1 This act must have been composed after the time of the last gift mentioned (1155) and before Bouchard's death (1180).
2 Hannappe, cant. Wassigny, https://dicotopo.cths.fr/places/P37303056.
3 Dorengt, cant. Nouvion, https://dicotopo.cths.fr/places/P90882005.
4 Germaine, cant. Vermand, https://dicotopo.cths.fr/places/P36636067.

*Geoffroi, and vassals gave to the church of Prémontré between 1135 and 1155. (See **245**.)*

A. Cartulary of Prémontré, fols. 58v.
B. Original, AD Aisne, H 797, previously sealed.
EDITION: Slack, *Crusade Charters, 1138–1270*, 42.

Karta Burchardi domini de Guisia et Godefridi fratris suis de alodio de Germania [*margo:* et de confirmatione teritorii de Hanapiis et de ecclesia de Dorenc cum pertinentiis suis].

[Q]uia labili memorie hominum facile excidit rerum, gestarum cognitio, dignum est ut scripto tradantur que ad posterorum noticiam transmittenda judicantur. Iccirco ego Burchardus, Dei patientia dominus de Guisia, que in diebus meis Premonstratensis[5] ecclesie vel a me ipso vel ab hominibus meis, me concedente, collata sunt dignum duxi in unum conpingere ut nemini in posterum pateat super his locus contentionis aut calumpnie. Notum igitur esse volo tam futuris quam presentibus quod anno dominice incarnationis M° C° XXX° V° ego et frater meus, Godefridus, contulimus in elemosinam eidem Premonstratensis[6] ecclesie perpetuo possidendum alodium de Germania ab omni exactione liberum assensu matris nostre, Adeline, ob remedium anime nostrorum[7] et predecessorum nostrorum sub hiis[8] testibus: Hugone[9] abbate de Hunbleriis,[10] Roberto cognomine Muto, Renero[11] filio eius, Widone[12] de Uspais,[13] Widone de Biaumes,[14] Renero[15] de Romon,[16] Werrico[17] Havart. Anno quoque Domini M° C° XXX° VIII°. Albricus[18] miles de Noviomo, et filii eius, Petrus et Robertus, contulerunt in elemosinam eidem ecclesie territorium Hanapie quod a me in feodo tenebant, sicut predecessores eorum a predecessoribus meis tenuerant. Ego autem et frater meus totum ipsum territorium cum appenditiis suis libere concessimus

5 Premonstrate *B*.
6 Premonstrate *B*.
7 nostre *B*.
8 his *B*.
9 Hugues I, abbot of the Benedictine abbey of Homblières, 1132–43. Newman, *Homblières*, 18.
10 Humbleriis *B*.
11 Reinero *B*.
12 Likely Guy I, lord of Voulpaix. Melleville, *DH*, vol. 2, 470–1.
13 Uspaiz *B*.
14 Belors *B*.
15 Reinero *B*.
16 Roinon *B*.
17 Werricus Havars also appears in **320** and as a witness in an 1156 act of Geoffroi de Guise, Nicolas d'Avesnes, and Jacques d'Avesnes. BnF, MS lat. 17777, fol. 188r.
18 Aubry, knight and lord of Nouvion-en-Thiérache. Melleville, *DH*, vol. 2, 172.

sub hiis testibus:[19] Waltero et Renoldo[20] sacerdotibus, Nicholao clerico, Waltero dapifero et Rothardo fratre eius, Drogone[21] de Dulcilon, Roberto[22] de Stabulis. Interea quidam homo, Richerus nomine, villicationem Hanapie sibi vendicare contendebat qua tamen postea, me agente et fratre meo, recognovit et quiete ac libere remisit eidem Premonstratensis[23] ecclesie sub hiis[24] testibus: Gerardo decano, Waltero et Renaldo[25] sacerdote,[26] Nicholao clerico, Clarenbaldo et Rohardo et Odone de Waudencurt,[27,28] Hugone villico de Dorenc. Item alii duo Gaufridus et Arnulphus[29] terram et pratum in ipso territorio reclamantes tandem coram me et fratre meo in causam venerunt et quicquid calumpniabantur quiete dimittentes, super altare Sancti Johannis Baptiste eidem ecclesie in elemosinam posuerunt et pro hoc a fratribus in communionem orationum et beneficiorum suscepti sunt, astantibus et testantibus Gerardo decano qui etiam excommunicavit omnes qui hanc querelam deinceps resuscitarent, Waltero et Renoldo[30] sacerdote, Nicholao clerico, Sigero de Casteneriis, Balduino Furnel, Evrardo de Origni,[31] Clarenbaldo et Rohardo et Odone de Waudencurt.[32] Sub eodem tempore contuli prefate ecclesie capellam Sancti Nicholai apud Sanctum Quintinum liberam cum pertinentiis suis sub hiis testibus: Herberto sacerdote, Nicholao clerico, Guimundo laico, Hescelone[33] et Mainardo[34] conversis. Anno autem Domini M° C° XL° VII°[35] profecturus Jherosolimam, augere volens elemosinam, contuli eidem ecclesie, ubicumque extra castrum consistit, terram Segardi quam sicut alodium libere possidebam assensu conjugis mee, Adelidis

---

19 his *B.*

20 Reinoldo *B.*

21 A Dreux de Dulcelon (cant. Guise, https://dicotopo.cths.fr/places/P62286197) appears in an 1146 act concerning the abbey of Longpont. Waroquier, "La principauté de Vermandois, Valois et Montdidier au XIIe siècle," 703.

22 Étaves-et-Bocquiaux, cant. Bohain, https://dicotopo.cths.fr/places/P16456670. A Robert d'Etaves entered the Benedictine abbey of Homblières in the early 1150s. Newman, *Homblières*, 146–7.

23 Premonstrate *B.*

24 his *B.*

25 Reinoldo *B.*

26 sacerdotibus *B.*

27 Wadencurt *B.*

28 Vadencourt-et-Bohéries, cant. Guise, https://dicotopo.cths.fr/places/P32349545.

29 Guiffridus et Arnulfus *B.*

30 Reinoldo *B.*

31 Everardo de Orini *B.*

32 Wadencurt *B.*

33 Hezelone *B.*

34 Meinadro *B.*

35 M° C° XLVII° *B.*

et fratris mei Godefridi et ceteri.[36] Post hec vero anno Domini M° C° LV°, concessi etiam prefate ecclesie ecclesiam de Dorenc cum pertinentiis suis quam a me tenens in feodo Rogerus[37] castellanus cum fratribus[38] et matre eidem ecclesie contulerat, annuente uxore mea Adelide[39] et fratre meo Godefrido. Cuius concessionis testes sunt: Renoldus[40] decanus, Arnulphus[41] et Peterus clerici, Matheus de Sanctis,[42] Clarenbaldus, Drogo de Dulcilon, Werricus Havars. His omnibus testificandis et confirmandis sigillum meum apponere non incongruum judicavi.

236

December, 1210.

*Gautier [II],[1] lord of Avesnes and Guise, makes known that he and Marguerite[2] [de Blois], his wife, in partnership with the church of Prémontré, founded a free town at Hannape,[3] and enumerates the rights to be enjoyed by the town's inhabitants. (See **243**.)*

A. Cartulary of Prémontré, fols. 58v–59r.
B. Original not found.[4]
REGISTER: *Catalogue analytique des Chartes*, 59.

---

36 *Add.* et ceteri *A*; sub his testibus: Clarembaldo, Drogone de Dulcilon, Stephano de Sessi, Waltero Dulcet *B*.
37 Roger, castellan of Guise and lord of Dorengt. Melleville, *DH*, vol. 1, 344.
38 *Om.* suis *A*.
39 Adhelide *B*.
40 Reinoldus *B*.
41 Arnulfus *B*.
42 Possibly lord of Sains (arr. Vervins, https://dicotopo.cths.fr/places/P35898483), ca. 1120s–early 1150s. Melleville, *DH*, vol. 2, 305.

---

1 Gautier II, lord of Avesnes (d. ca. 1244), lord of Avesnes, Leuze, Condé, and Guise, son of Jacques I, lord of Avesnes, and Adèle, lady of Guise.
2 Marguerite, countess of Blois and Châteaudun (1170–1230), daughter of Thibaut V, count of Blois, and Alix of France. Gautier II, lord of Avesnes and Guise, was her third husband.
3 Hannape, cant. Wassigny, https://dicotopo.cths.fr/places/P37303056.
4 In the 1860s, the original charter for this act was in the collection of the Collège Héraldique et historique de France, Paris. Most of that body's collection was sold off in the 1930s, and it has not been possible to trace the original charter further. For the companion act to **236**, issued by abbot Gervais of Prémontré, see the cartulary of the lords of Guise, BnF, MS lat. 17777, fols. 54v–55v (Latin), fols. 55v–56r (French); Cocheris, *Notices et extraits des documents manuscrits conservés dans les dépôts publics de Paris et relatifs à l'histoire de la Picardie*, vol. 2, 525–7, 564–7. Melleville, *DH*, vol. 1, 445–6 (Melleville erroneously states that this act is in the cartulary of Prémontré).

Karta domini Galteri de Avesnis et eius uxoris Margarite de libertate ville de Hanapie et participatione.

[E]go Galterus, dominus de Avesnis et dominus Guisie, notum facio tam presentibus quam futuris quod cum ecclesia Premonstratensis haberet curtem que Hanapia dicebatur, que sine participe et socio sua propria erat, cum territorio adjacente, ipsa ecclesia, de mera voluntate sua, recepit me in participem et in socium ad liberam villam in eodem territorio faciendam hoc modo: Ecclesia tradet terram ad villam faciendam, tres scilicet aissinos terre singulis burgensibus qui tantum habere voluerint et non amplius, et illi aissini conplebuntur in villa vel extra villam, ita quod pro singulis aissinis dabuntur annuatim in festo Beati Remigii singuli galeti avene, et infra quatuor dies nativitatis dominice singuli capones et singuli panes, et singuli denarii, secundum quod alii plus, alii minus habebunt. Ad tradendas vero mansuras exponet ecclesia duas carrucatas terre, quadraginta scilicet duas modiatas terre, si opus fuerit; si qui autem recesserint, mansura relicta erit ecclesie ad faciendum inde commodum suum, donec burgensis venerit qui velit eam inhabitare et reddere debitum censum. Singuli etiam tam burgenses quam alii volentes manere in libertate ville, dabunt in festo Beati Remigii duodecim denarios pro burgoisia, et quatuor denarios pro thelonei libertate. Villa autem, sicut predictum est, libera erit, et conveniet in ea mercatum in die Jovis, et regetur tam villa quam mercatum secundum legem Lauduni, excepto quod domus non diruentur pro alicuius forisfacto, nec ego potero ducere homines ville ad torneamentum, vel in exercitum, vel in equitatum, nisi ad terram Guisie aut Viromandie defendendam; nec etiam potero capere gistum vel habere domum in ea. Erit enim villa ipsa communis inter me et ecclesiam in justicia, et in banno, et in redditibus, et in universis obventionibus que de villa provenient, et omnia possidebimus indivise, ita quod inter me et ecclesiam per medium partientur, ita quod ego nichil potero acquirere in villa sine ecclesia, nec ecclesia sine me, preter quedam que ecclesia sine partionaria sibi retinuit nominatim, videlicet: ecclesiam et atrium et managium eorum qui ibi habitabunt ex parte ecclesie, et totam decimam ville, et quicquid pertinet ad jus parrochiale, et aquas, et molendina, et furnos. Et ad ipsa molendina et furnos erunt homines bannales ville. Poterunt autem venire ad ipsam villam inhabitandam omnes qui non erunt de terra Guisie. Maior autem instituetur in villa per me et per ecclesiam, et singulis annis per communem assensum, tercio die Pasche, innovabitur et jurabit utrique fidelitatem, michi scilicet et ecclesie. Singulis etiam annis, innovabuntur scabini pariter et jurati. Si qua autem mansura vel domus data fuerit ecclesie in elemosinam, vendet eam infra annum et diem, si invenerit emptione, ut redeat in communitatem meam et suam. Ecclesia autem extra villam retinuit sibi duas carrucatas terre, et omnia prata sua, et viginti modiatas nemoris ad faciendam inde voluntatem suam. De reliquis vero terris et residuo nemoris ita convenit inter nos pro melioratione ville, quod ecclesia vendet eas hospitibus ville tenendas de ecclesia et excolendas ad rectum terragium, et ad rectam decimam, ita quod terragium et decima a serviente ecclesie insimul colligentur et in grangiam ecclesie ab agricolis adducentur. Nec aliquis poterit excolere terras ipsas qui non manserit in villa; inmo si villam reliquerit, perdet terram, salvo tamen eo quod si redierit infra annum et diem, reddet ecclesie debitum terre, si non fuerit aliunde receptum, et habebit eam. Si infra annum et diem non venerit, nichil juris poterit in ea vendicare. In toto autem territorio quod erit extra villam sive in nemoribus, sive in pratis, nichil omnino habebo nisi medietatem justicie contra quemcumque, sive scilicet contra ecclesiam de jure vel de redditibus suis vel contra alium fuerit forisfactum. Sane, si eadem villa aliquo, quod absit tempore vastaretur, ita quod non haberet habitatores, ad aliud dominium reverti non posset, quam ad dominium ecclesie. Ego autem de hiis omnibus que concessa sunt michi, nichil potero dare alicui in feodum, vel in elemosinam, vel quocumque alio modo, nisi termino ecclesie Premonstratensis; sed perpetuis temporibus quicumque erit dominus Guisie, erit sotius et partionarius ecclesie Premonstratensis de villa Hanapie. Et de hac conventione tenenda ecclesia similiter partem suam a se alienare non poterit sine assensu meo. Hoc autem juravi ego necnon et nobilis mulier Margareta, comitissa uxor mea, nos fideliter servaturos. Hoc etiam jurare tenebuntur heredes mei, domini Guisie, quando venient ad terram tenendam, infra quadraginta dies post summonitionem abbatis, si aliquid in villa habere voluerint. Ut igitur hec omnia futuris temporibus inviolabiliter observentur, ego et predicta uxor mea, Margarita, presens scriptum super hiis ~~scriptum~~ factum sigillorum nostrorum fecimus impressionibus communiri. Actum mense decembri anno incarnationis dominice M° CC° decimo.

237

1198

Adèle,[1] *lady of Guise, makes known the agreement reached between Abbot Pierre [I]*[2] *of Prémontré on the one hand, and Guyard d'Iron*[3] *on the other, following the resolution of a dispute concerning the* terragium *of Saint-Gervais de Guise. Guyard consents to this, as do Gila his wife, his sons Gérard and Philippe, and other unnamed children.*

1 Adèle, lady of Guise (d. aft. 1200), daughter of Bouchard, lord of Guise, and Adélaïde de Soupir.

2 Pierre I de Saint-Médard, abbot of the Premonstratensian abbeys of Saint-Just en Chaussée, 1184–95, Prémontré, 1195–1201, and Cuissy, 1210–17. *MP* II, 497, 527, 565.

3 Iron, cant. Guise, https://dicotopo.cths.fr/places/P04584610.

A. Cartulary of Prémontré, fols. 59r–59v.
B. Original, AN, L 995, no. 50, previously sealed.

Karta Domine Adelvie de Guisia de confirmatione cuiusdam conpromissionis in abbatem Premonstratensem.

[E]go Audeluia,[4] domina Guisie, omnibus presentem paginam inspecturis, notum facio quod cum inter ecclesiam Premonstrati et Guiardum de Yrun super quibusdam querelis esset discordia de quibus fuit coram me diutius litigatum, idem G[uiardus] et filius eius Philippus[5] conpromiserunt, me presente, in dominum Petrum, abbatem Premonstrati, propria voluntate fide interposita quod quicquid ipse abbas de jure prefate ecclesie et Guiardi testificaretur, ipse G[uiardus] et liberi sui sine contradictione tenerent et firmiter observarent. Postea vero abbate memorato die prefixa, in mea et hominum meorum astante presencia, pro parte ecclesie Premonstrati pars cuiusdam cyrographi sigillo domini Willelmi decani de Yrun sigillata ostensa fuit michi[6] et lecta que conventionem hactenus factam inter ecclesiam sepedictam et prescriptum G[uiardum] plenarie demonstrabat. Per lecto itaque cirographo memoratus abbas veraciter affirmavit jus ecclesie Premonstrati et G[uiardi] prenominati tale esse quale ipsius cyrographi narratio declarabat. Forma autem cyrographi talis erat quod de terragio Sancti Gervasii de Guisia quod tenet ecclesia Premonstrati unde Guiardus maior fuit, concesserunt abbas et fratres ipsius ecclesie Gerardo, filio eius, duos modios frumenti in grangia sua de Hanapiis singulis annis in festo Sancti Remigii ei solvendos de meliori post sementem conditione tali quod remisit ecclesie predicte omne jus quod habebat in[7] territorio predicto[8] et de propria terra de qua huc usque non dedit terragium amodo dabit. Sciendum tamen est quod Gerardus maioriam retinet assensu ecclesie per quam videlicet habet masuram suam liberam et pratum unum et de uno quoque[9] orte panem unum in festo Sancti Remigii solvendum cyrotecas[10] si aliquis in territorio illo masuram suam sive terram vendiderit. Terram etiam de Bucillies[11] sub trecensu duodecim nummorum in festo Sancti Remigii solvendorum. Si vero aliqua querimonia emerserit unde placitum nascatur. Idem Gerardus

4 Adeluia *B*.
5 *Transp. A*; Philippus filius eius *B*.
6 mihi *B*.
7 *Om.* eodem *A*.
8 *Add.* predicto *A*.
9 unoquoque *B*.
10 cyrotegas *B*.
11 Bucilly, cant. Hirson, https://dicotopo.cths.fr/places/P91269366.

diem debet prefigere et fratribus Hanapie ut diei intersint intimare ita quod fratres Premonstratenses[12] sicut domini idem placitum tenebuntur terminare. Sciendum est etiam quod de hac maioria est homo ecclesie et fidelitatem debet observare ita quod, si erga ecclesiam in aliquo forisfecerit, si monitus emendaverit, ecclesia eius emendationem recipiet. Si vero non emendaverit, ecclesia duos predictos modios retinebit donec forisfactum emendaverit. Hoc concessit predictus Guiardus et uxor eius, Gila, et Gerardus, filius eorum, qui maior est et ceteri eorum liberi. Ne igitur huiusmodi querelarum diffinitio in mea et hominum meorum presentia tam sollempniter facta aliquo tempore debeat retractari; presens scriptum sigilli mei inpressione confirmavi et testes ydoneos[13] qui presentes fuerunt volui hic inscribi. S. Galteri,[14,15] militis de Proisi.[16] S. Theoderici,[17] militis de Bosies et ceteri.[18] Actum anno dominice incarnationis M° C° nonagesimo octavo.

238

July, 1202.

Gautier [II],[1] *lord of Avesnes, confirms by* vidimus *the donation of the wood of Hannape*[2] *made by his father, Jacques [I],*[3] *lord of Guise and Lesquielles, to the church of Prémontré in 1186.*

A. Cartulary of Prémontré, fols. 59v–60r.

B. Original, AD Aisne, H 797.[4]

12 *Add.* Premonstratenses *A*.

13 idoneos *B*.

14 Walteri *B*.

15 Gautier, knight and lord of Proisy, attested 1195–1211. Melleville, *DH*, vol. 2, 237. He also appears in an 1195 act in the cartulary of Saint-Michel-en-Thierache. BnF, MS lat. 18375, fols. 196r–197r.

16 Proisy, cant. Guise, https://dicotopo.cths.fr/places/P06201832.

17 Possibly Thierry de Bousies, son of Gautier III, lord of Bousies, and Hildéarde de Berlaimont, who is attested in the 1170s. Dufrenelle, "La Maison française de Bousies," 176.

18 *Add.* et ceteri *A*; S. Morete, militis de Espinoit. S. Clarembaldi, militis de Leskieres. S. domini Haeri, abbatis Clarifontis. S. Stephani, clerici mei. S. Walteri Bertout. S. Arnulfi de Estrees. S. Johannis Nervart, servientium meorum *B*.

1 Gautier II, lord of Avesnes (d. ca. 1244), lord of Avesnes, Leuze, Condé, and Guise, son of Jacques I, lord of Avesnes, and Adèle, lady of Guise.

2 Hannape, cant. Wassigny, https://dicotopo.cths.fr/places/P37303056.

3 Jacques I, lord of Avesnes (d. 1191), son of Nicolas, lord of Avesnes, Leuze, Condé, and Guise, and Mathilde de La Roche.

4 The original charter is no longer available for consultation; variants noted here are from Françoise Muret's 1980s transcription.

Karta domini Galteri de Avesnis de compositione et confirmatione elemosine patris sui.

[E]go Galterus dominus de Avesnis presentibus et futuris. Notifico per hoc scriptum quod cum pie memorie pater meus, Jacobus, adhuc viveret, inter ipsum et ecclesiam Premonstratensem super quibusdam dampnis que per ipsum ecclesia passa fuerit, et specialiter super nemore Hanapie emerserunt querele de quibus conpositio facta fuit et redacta in scripto auctentico per hec verba: Eaque a fidelibus pro bono pacis gesta sunt, ne aliqua contradictionis vel calumpnie prejudicio possint in irritum revocari, memoriali scripto ad stabilitatem debent perpetuam commendari. Ea propter ego Jacobus, Guisie et Lescheriarum dominus, presentibus et futuris notifico per hoc scriptum quod[5] cum inter me et ecclesiam Premonstratensem querele super quibusdam dampnis que prefata ecclesia tempore hostilitatis per me et meos homines sustinuerat et super nemus Hanapie emersissent, ego et ipsius ecclesie abbas et fratres ad pacis reformationem sub hac compositionis forma[6] amicabiliter alterutro assensu processimus, videlicet quod ego Jacobus, Adeluya uxore mea, et liberis meis annuentibus, concessi iam dicte ecclesie nemus ipsum, sicut mete disterminant, libere et quiete perpetuo possidendum ita quod dare, vendere, extirpare et omnes commoditates suas memorate ecclesie fratres, sicut de suo proprio, facere poterunt nec licebit michi[7] vel[8] successoribus meis in eodem nemore aliquid reclamare nec hominibus meis quicquam in nemore ipso sive predictorum fratrum assensu accipere et si quam molestiam sepedicta ecclesia super ipso nemore passa fuerit, warandiam ei contra omnes homines exhibebo,[9] ad promerendas quoque orationes et benefacta[10] ordinis in quibus prefate ecclesie fratres me et uxorem meam et liberos meos[11] receperunt, omnes ipsius[12] ecclesie possessiones quas in terra mea tempore huius scripti habebat, recognovi, laudavi et sub defensione mea illesas mansuras accepi ita quod nec ego nec successores mei possessiones ipsas minuere poterimus, nec minui patiemur sed ad tuendas ipsius[13] ecclesie possessiones et jura promptus adjutor et defensor ero bonusque amicus et fidelis advocatus amodo permanebo. Quod ut stabile firmumque permaneat, sigilli mei[14] appensione roboravimus

---

5 notifico quod *B.*
6 *Transp. A*; forma compositionis *B.*
7 mihi *B.*
8 nec *B.*
9 omnes exhibere *B.*
10 beneficia *B.*
11 *Add.* meos *A.*
12 ipsi *B.*
13 ipsi *B.*
14 nostri *B.*

testiumque subscriptione confirmavimus. S. Willelmi decani de Yrun.[15,16] S. Oberti notarii. S.[17] Herberti clericorum meorum et ceteri.[18] Actum anno incarnationis dominice M° C° LXXX° VI°. Post mortem denique patris mei ego Galterus qui matri mee, Audelvye, ad huc viventi sperabar heres futurus et in dominatione Guisie et Lescheriarum jure primogeniti successurus requisitus a prefate ecclesie abbate et fratribus ipsam eandem compositionem sicut superius scripta est ratam habui et eam approbans confirmavi, specialiterque ipsum nemus Hanapie libere et quiete eisdem fratribus perpetuo possidendum concessi ita quod dare vendere, extirpare et omnes commoditates suas, sicut de suo proprio facere ipsis licebit. Ut autem concessio et confirmatio huiusmodi firma et stabilis perseveretur, presenti scripto in perpetuum valituro sigillum meum feci imprimi et apponi. Actum anno ab incarnatione Domini M° CC° II° mense julio.

239

November 6, 1198. Cloister of Notre-Dame de Cantimpré, Cambrai.

Hugues,[1] *bishop-elect of Cambrai, and Adam,*[2] *dean of Cambrai, make known the resolution of a dispute over property at Hannape between the Benedictine abbey of Prüm and Prémontré in favour of Prüm, following arbitration by* magister *Nicolas de la Ventries, canon of Cambrai, at the behest of Pope Innocent III. Gerhard,*[3] *abbot of Prüm, and Pierre [I],*[4] *abbot of Prémontré, agree that Prémontré will keep the disputed goods and pay 10* marci *annually to Prüm, each at the weight of 12* solidi Coloniensium.

A. Cartulary of Prémontré, fols. 60r–60v.

B. Original not found.

---

15 d'Irun *B*.

16 Iron, cant. Guise, https://dicotopo.cths.fr/places/P04584610.

17 *Om.* magistri *A*.

18 *Add.* et ceteri *A*; S. Drogonis de Tuponi. S. Radulfi de Vendories. S. Galteri Pasieres. S. Ligeri Rufi, militum. S. Gerardi senescalli Guisie *B*.

---

1 Hugues d'Oisy, son of Simon, lord of Oisy and Crèvecoeur, and Ada de Vermandois, lady of La Ferté-Gaucher, was elected bishop of Cambrai in 1198 but was never consecrated.

2 Adam, dean of Cambrai, ca. 1192–ca. 1219. Le Glay, *Cameracum Christianum ou histoire ecclésiastique du diocèse de Cambrai*, 96.

3 Gerhard von Vianden, son of Friedrich I, count of Vianden; abbot of the Benedictine abbey of Prüm, 1184–1212, and of Stavelot-Malmedy, 1193–1209.

4 Pierre I de Saint-Médard, abbot of the Premonstratensian abbeys of Saint-Just en Chaussée, 1184–95, Prémontré, 1195–1201, and Cuissy, 1210–17. *MP* II, 497, 527, 565.

Karta Hugonis electi et decani Cameracensis de concordia inter Premonstratensem et Prumiensem ecclesias.

[I]n nomine sancte et individue Trinitatis. Hugo Dei permissione electus, Adam, decanus Cameracensis, tam presentibus quam futuris in perpetuum. Noverint universi quod cum causa que inter Prumiensem et Premonstratensem ecclesias super bonis Hanapie diu et ab antiquis temporibus fuerat ventilata, nobis et magistro Nicholao de la Venties, canonico nostro, de assensu partium fuisset a venerabili patre nostro Innocentio Papa tercio delegata, etiam partes diu in nostra presentia disputassent de quadam sentencia que a Coloniensibus judicibus super possessione predictorum bonorum pro ecclesia Prumiensi fuerat auctoritate apostolica prolata, et testes, hinc ad probandam, inde ad reprobandam, eandem sentenciam producti fuissent, et attestationes eorum publicate, tandem dominus Gerardus Prumiensis et dominus Petrus Premonstratensis abbates in nostra presentia constituti, litteras conventuum suorum exhibuere de rato in quibus continebatur expressum quod, si ipsi abbates super predictis bonis aliquam transactionem vel compositionem inirent, ipsi conventus eam firmiter observarent. Ad nostram igitur anmonitionem et plurium personarum Cameracensis ecclesie que apud Cantipratum nobiscum convenerant, prefati abbates pro ecclesiis suis super premissis omnibus bonis de quibus erat controversia, in hunc modum, nobis mediantibus, transegerunt quod, possessione predictorum bonorum penes Premonstratensem ecclesiam pacifice remanente, eadem ecclesia singulis annis in perpetuum nuntio Prumiensis ecclesie, apud Hucheneiam, in Festo Beati Andree apostoli, decem marcas, ad pondus Coloniense XII solidos Coloniensibus pro marcis singulis computandis, nomine supradictarum Hanapie possessionum persolvet. Modus autem solutionis hic erit: Premonstratensis nuntius pecuniam memoratam apud Hucheneiam ~~should be struck through: in feste Beati Andree~~ preposito loci illius vel alii qui nuntius erit, ecclesie Prumiensi persolvet et ille qui pecuniam illam recipiet, litteras de solutione facta sigillo ad hoc deputato signatas conferet, et, si forte sigillum illud pre manibus non habuerit, coram bonis et honestis viris pecunia persolvetur qui, si aliquotiens necesse fuerit, possint de solutione ipsa testimonium perhibere. Si vero Premonstratensis ecclesia per mensem ultra dictum terminum vel amplius ab eiusdem pecunie solutione cessaret, penam unius marce ad idem pondus per singulos menses incurreret Prumiensi ecclesie nichilominus conferendam. Si autem cessaret per annum, a causa illa prorsus caderet que nobis fuerat auctoritate apostolica commissa, et possessionis predicte beneficio penitus privaretur. Adjectum est etiam quod quandocumque, sive tunc, sive in posterum Prumiensis ecclesie seu Premonstratensis ab istius transactionis observantia resiliret, resiliens a causa predicta et beneficio prenotato sine spe restitutionis caderet et totius cause sine diminutione aut dilatione qualibet incurreret detrimentum commodo possessionum que in controversia fuerant parti conpositionem servanti modis omnibus devoluendo. Dicti insuper abbates sponte se et ecclesias suas jurisdictioni nostre eatenus subdiderunt, ut tam ipsos quam ecclesias ipsas ita possemus conpellere ad observantiam omnium predictorum sicut ad observationem sententie, si quam super hoc tulissemus. Ipsi etiam clausulam illam que in litteris commissionis legebatur inserta, videlicet facientes quod exinde decreveritis statuendum per censuram ecclesiasticam inviolabiliter observari ita de hac transactione, nobis mediantibus, facta sicut de sentencia, si lata fuisset, intelligi voluerunt. Ne igitur temporis vetustate transactionis istius memoria deleatur vel recidivum patiatur questio tam sollempniter et rationabiliter iam sopita, auctoritate apostolica qua fungebamur transactionem huiusmodi confirmantes, eam presenti scripto et sigillorum nostrorum impressionibus duximus roborandam et subnotanda eorum nomina qui presentes fuerunt quorum quidam sua appenderunt sigilla et manu propria subscripserunt. S. Johannis,[5] Cameracensis prepositi. S. Herberti,[6] abbatis sancti Auberti. S. Mathei,[7] abbatis de Cantinprato et ceteri. Actum Cameraci in claustro de Cantinprato, anno verbi incarnati M° C° nonagesimo octavo, VIII° idus novenbris, anno primo pontificatus venerabilis patres nostri Innocentii Pape tercii.

240

1156. Laon.

Gautier [II],[1] bishop of Laon, makes known that the canons of Guise approve an agreement reached between them and Prémontré concerning the possession of the allod of Saint-Gervais at Guise, which at one time was held jointly by the canons of Guise and the monks of Fesmy.[2] Prémontré continues to hold half of the allod originally given to abbot Hugues [I][3] of Prémontré and the Premonstratensian brothers at Hannape[4] in exchange for an annual census *of four* modii *of grain (*frumentum*), measure of Guise.*

A. Cartulary of Prémontré, fol. 60v.

B. Original not found.

5 Jean, *prepositus* of Notre-Dame de Cambrai, ca. 1173–ca. 1198. BM Cambrai, MS 1041, fol. 208v; BnF, MS Lat 10968, fols. 69r–69v; 72r–73r.

6 Herbert, abbot of the Augustinian abbey of Saint-Aubert de Cambrai, ca. 1190–ca. 1200. *GC* III, col. 155.

7 Mathieu, abbot of the Victorine abbey of Notre-Dame de Cantimpré, ca. 1207–18. *GC* III, col. 162.

1 Gautier de Mortagne was dean of Laon, ca. 1142–55, and bishop of Laon, 1155–74.

2 The Benedictine abbey of Saint-Étienne de Fesmy.

3 Hugues I de Fosses (ca. 1093–1164), first abbot of Prémontré.

4 Hannape, cant. Wassigny, https://dicotopo.cths.fr/places/P37303056.

Karta episcopi Laudunensis de confirmatione alodii canonicorum de Guisia in territorio de Irun quod dederunt nobis.

[I]n nomine sancte et individue Trinitatis, amen. Ego Galterus, Dei gratia Laudunensis episcopus, notum fieri volumus universis tam futuris quam presentibus quod ecclesia Guisiacensis contulit censualiter Hugoni, Premonstratensi abbati, et fratribus eius qui in Hanapia commorantur, alodium Sancti Gervasii de Guisia, sicut ipsum libere tenebat, in territorio ville que dicitur Yrun,[5] in terris videlicet, aquis, pratis, hospitibus, silvis et omnibus appenditiis suis exceptis servis et ancillis, ita quod ab ipsis fratribus Premonstratensibus annuatim persolventur ecclesie de Guisia quatuor modii frumenti post sementem melioris ad mensuram Guisiacensem. Actum est hoc et definitum tempore illo quo monachi Fidemienses ecclesie Guisiacensis erant cum canonicis possessores et in eadem commorantes; remotis postmodum ab illa ecclesia monachis, canonici qui totam ecclesiam soli receperunt, contra fratres Premonstratenses de predicta pactione querimoniam moventes, quod factum fuerat, frustrare conati sunt sed, a viris prudentibus correcti, tandem sedati sunt et, ipsam pactionem in mea presentia concedentes, rem approbaverunt. Frumentum vero ab ipsis fratribus Hanapie commorantibus cum vecturis suis a festo Sancti Remigii usque ad festum Omnium Sanctorum ad Guisiam canonicis deducetur. Si qui vero fratres Premonstratenses super hoc inquietaverint, canonici Guiacenses de hiis qui justiciam exequi voluerint, guarandi eis erunt. Maior vero predicti alodii pro maioria sua, sicut a capitulo Guisiacensi affirmatur, masuram suam habet liberam et ortum unum et pratum ita tamen quod predictus maior grangiam fratribus Premonstratensibus pro rehautumno et stramine, quod inde habet, de suo providere debet. Ipsi vero fratres ibidem custodes suos, si eis placuerit, habebunt. Nos etiam predicte donationis pactionem presenti scripto renovantes ut rata et inconcussa in posterum permaneat, sigilli nostri impressione et sigilli utriusque ecclesie et testium subscriptione muniri fecimus. S. Lisiardi,[6] decani. S. Galteri,[7] abbatis Sancti Vincentii. S. Hugonis,[8] abbatis Sancti Nicholai de Bosco et ceteri. Actum Lauduni, anno incarnati verbi M° C° LVI° indictione IIII[a]. Angotus[9] cancellarius relegit, scripsit, et subscripsit.

5 Iron, cant. Guise, https://dicotopo.cths.fr/places/P04584610.

6 Lisiard, dean of Laon, ca. 1153–ca. 1168.

7 Gautier, abbot of the Benedictine abbey of Saint-Vincent de Laon, 1155/6–74. *GC* IX, col. 579; Wyard, *Saint-Vincent*, 416–21.

8 Hugues, abbot of the Benedictine abbey of Saint-Nicolas-aux-Bois, ca. 1156–ca. 1166. R. Duval, "Histoire de l'abbaye bénédictine de Saint-Nicolas-aux-Bois, diocèse de Laon, première partie," 196–8.

9 Angot, chancellor of Laon, ca. 1144–ca. 1170.

241

1180

Jacques [I][1] and Adèle[2] de Guise, lord and lady of Avesnes, and their unnamed children donate 20 solidi Viromandensium *to the church of Saint-Pierre de Dorengt[3] for oil to supply a permanently lit lamp. The payment is to be collected annually at Neuville[4] on the feast of St. John the Baptist.*

A. Cartulary of Prémontré, fols. 60v–61r.
B. Original not found.

Karta Jacobi de Avesnis de confirmatione elemosine domine Adelvie.

[I]n nomine sancte et individue Trinitatis, amen. Quoniam pie inchoata atque a bonis et bene consummata suo vetustatis nubilo recordationis noverca sepius infirmitati mortalium furata est oblivio, ob hoc filiorum Ade prudentia, sui non inmemor posteritatis, non oblita rerum gestarum seriem litterarum fideli conservatione perpetuare et in posteros transmittere non inconsulte curavit ut saltem eius instituta viverent, cuius vita moriendi conditionem effugere nequaquam poterat. Noverint igitur tam posteri quam moderni quod ego Jacobus de Avesnis cum uxore mea, Adeluya de Guisia, et liberis nostris, ecclesie Beati Petri de Dorenc ad usus comparandi oleum quod sufficiat uni lampadi in eadem ecclesia continue ardenti, XX solidos Viromandensis monete de duodennis nostris apud Novam Villam singulis annis et in festo Sancti Johannis Baptiste persolvendos assignavimus, mercedem ex eo cum illa paupercula vidua sperantes quam Dominus in evangelio pro duobus minutis missis in gazofilacium legitur commendasse.[5] Ut autem hoc tam venerabile institutum nullus de successoribus nostris ausu temerario presumat infringere, scripto mandare testium subscriptione roborare et tandem sigilli nostri impressione studuimus confirmare. S. Renaldi,[6] decani de Guisia et ceteri. Actum anno Domini M° C° LXXX°.

1 Jacques I, lord of Avesnes (d. 1191), son of Nicolas, lord of Avesnes, Leuze, Condé, and Guise, and Mathilde de La Roche.
2 Adèle, lady of Guise (d. aft. 1200), daughter of Bouchard, lord of Guise, and Adélaïde de Soupir.
3 Dorengt, cant. Nouvion, https://dicotopo.cths.fr/places/P90882005.
4 La Neuville-lez-Dorengt, cant. Nouvion, https://dicotopo.cths.fr/places/P68735093.
5 Luke 21:1–2.
6 Renaud, dean of Guise, is also attested in 1161 and 1174. BM Laon MS 532, fols. 1v–2r; BM Reims 1563 (N. Fonds), fols. 33r–33v.

242

1196

Adèle,[1] *lady of Guise, makes known that with the consent of her son Gautier [II,*[2] *lord of Avesnes] and her other unnamed children, she leaves to the church of Prémontré 20* solidi Viromandensium, *to be collected each year on All Saints' Day from the* vinagium *of Guise and Lesquielles.*[3,4]

A. Cartulary of Prémontré, fol. 61r.
B. Original not found.

Karta domine Adelvie de confirmatione elemosine XX solidorum quos dedit ad refectionem conventus.

[I]n nomine sancte et individue Trinitatis. Quoniam memorie labilis est humana fragilitas, quod priorum confirmat auctoritas necesse est litteris annotari et postere generationi transmitendum. Proinde ego Adeluya, domina Guisie, notum facio tam futuris quam presentibus quod, de voluntate et assensu Galteri, filii mei, ceterorumque liberorum meorum, pro remedio anime mee necnon et animarum tam domini et mariti mei, Jacobi de Avesnis, quam predecessorum meorum et heredum, reliqui viginti solidos monete Viromandensis ecclesie Premonstrati ex winagio Guisie et Escheliarum, in festivitate Omnium Sanctorum singulis annis persolvendos, et in die anniversarii mei ad refectionem conventus distribuendos. Ut hoc autem ratum et inconvulsum in perpetuum permaneat, sigilli mei sub ymaginatione et testium qui ibidem affuerunt astipulatione munire curavi. Et ut facilius plenum robur possit habere, cartam in qua tocius elemosine mee summa continetur, domini archiepiscopi et meao filorumque meorum Galteri et Jacobi sigillis communitam ecclesie Beate Marie Laudunensis in posterum reservandam commendavi. Huius rei testes sunt: Gislebertus,[5] abbas Fusniaci, et ceteri. Actum est hoc anno incarnati verbi millesimo centesimo XC° sexto.

1 Adèle, lady of Guise (d. aft. 1200), daughter of Bouchard, lord of Guise, and Adélaïde de Soupir.
2 Gautier II, lord of Avesnes (d. ca. 1244), lord of Avesnes, Leuze, Condé, and Guise, son of Jacques I, lord of Avesnes, and Adèle, lady of Guise.
3 Lesquielles-Saint-Germain, cant. Guise, https://dicotopo.cths.fr/places/P39197714.
4 In the same year and under almost the same terms, Adèle made a gift to the Premonstratensian abbey of Bucilly. BnF, MS Latin 10121, fol. 6r.
5 Gilbert, abbot of the Cistercian abbey of Foigny, 1186–1211/12. *GC* IX, col. 630.

243

April 21, 1219. Englancourt.

Gautier [II],[1] count of Blois, and Marguerite,[2] countess of Blois and Burgundy, jointly lord and lady of Avesnes and Guise, reach an agreement with the church of Prémontré concerning land outside of Hannape.[3] (See ***236****.)*

A. Cartulary of Prémontré, fol. 61r.
B. Original, AN, L 995, no. 67, previously sealed with two seals.

Karta comitis Blesensis et uxoris eiusdem de quadam compositione inter ipsos et ecclesiam.

[I]n nomine Patris et Filii et Spiritus Sancti, amen. Ego Walterus, comes Blesensis, dominus de Avesnis[4] et Guisie, et illustris mulier Margareta, uxor mea, comitissa Burgundie et Blesis, domina de Avesnis[5] et Guisie, notum facimus universis presentem paginam inspecturis quod cum nos et viri religiosi dominus Gervasius, abbas, et conventus Premonstratensis in territorio Hanapie quod erat ecclesie Premonstratensis, fecissemus olim villam de communi assensu sub quibusdam conditionibus que in aliis scriptis clarius sunt expresse, per quas ecclesia Premonstratensis totum nemus quod in eodem territorio Hanapie[6] habebat, exceptis viginti modiatis, venturis ad inhabitandam villam burgensibus vendere tenebatur, processu temporis pro utilitate utriusque partis, videlicet nostra et ville que erat iam facta, ita convenit inter nos et ecclesiam memoratam quod ecclesia Premonstratensis vendidit totam terram arabilem quam habebat extra villam Hanapie tempore huius scripti et retinuit sibi totum nemus quod habebat in territorio eodem[7] similiter tempore huius scripti, hoc adjecto quod de toto nemore quod sibi retinuit, poterit facere modis omnibus voluntatem suam, excepto quod in alienam manum illud ponere non poterit sine licentia nostra ita etiam quod si ecclesia vendiderit nemus ipsum, nec nos nec heredes nostri poterimus prohibere hominibus nostris aut aliis quin emant. Immo etiam emptoribus nemoris illius quod vendet ecclesia, sicut illis

1 Gautier II (d. ca. 1244), lord of Avesnes, Leuze, Condé, and Guise, son of Jacques I, lord of Avesnes, and Adèle, lady of Guise.

2 Marguerite, countess of Blois and Châteaudun (1170–1230), daughter of Thibaut V, count of Blois, and Alix of France. Gautier II, lord of Avesnes and Guise, was her third husband.

3 Hannape, cant. Wassigny, https://dicotopo.cths.fr/places/P37303056.

4 Avennis *B*.

5 Avennis *B*.

6 *Add.* Hanapie *A*.

7 *Transp. A*; in eodem territorio *B*.

qui ement, proprium nemus nostrum salvum per terram nostram tenebimur prestare conductum. Ne igitur commutatio ista futuris temporibus aliqua possit oblivione deleri eam fideliter hic inscribi et sigillorum nostrorum fecimus inpressione muniri. Actum apud Engleincourt,[8,9] XI kalendas maii, anno gratie M° CC° IX° decimo.[10]

244

1181. Bishop's palace, Cambrai.

Roger,[1] *bishop of Cambrai, Simon,*[2] *abbot of Saint-Sauveur d'Anchin, and Herbert,*[3] *abbot of Mont-Saint-Martin, make known the agreement reached between abbot Hugues [II] and the chapter of Prémontré and Nicholas, abbot of Maroilles,*[4] *concerning the wood and lands neighbouring the Premonstratensian* curtis *at Hannape.*[5]

A. Cartulary of Prémontré, fols. 61r–61v.
B. Original not found.

Compositio inter ecclesiam Premonstratensem et abbatem de Maricolis.

[I]n nomine sancte et individue Trinitatis. Ego Hugo, dictus abbas Premonstrati, et capitulum nostrum et ego frater Nicholaus, abbas de Maricolis, notum esse volumus tam presentibus quam futuris quod querela que diutius agitata est inter ecclesias nostras super quibusdam nemoribus et terris consistentibus juxta curtem de Hanapiis, mediantibus religiosis viris, sopita est. Convenimus quippe coram domino Rogero Cameracensi episcopo et domno Symone, Acquiscincti abbate et Herberto, abbate de Monte Sancti Martini, qui arbitri nostri erant, ex assensu utriusque partis et cum diu laboratum esset, ad pacem tandem, nutu gratie Dei, compositum est in hunc modum:

---

8 Engleincort *B*.
9 Englancourt, cant. La Capelle, https://dicotopo.cths.fr/places/ P68175313.
10 millesimo ducentesimo nonodecimo *B*.

---

1 Roger de Wavrin, son of Roger III, lord of Wavrin, and Mathilde (de Lens?), was first canon, 1169, archdeacon, 1177, and then bishop of Cambrai, 1178/9–91.
2 Simon I, abbot of the Benedictine abbey of Saint-Sauveur d'Anchin, 1174–1201. Gerzaguet, *L'Abbaye d'Anchin de sa fondation (1079) au XIVe siècle*, 136.
3 Herbert, abbot of the Premonstratensian abbey of Mont-Saint-Martin, 1174–96. *MP* II, 419.
4 The Benedictine abbey of Maroilles.
5 Hannape, cant. Wassigny, https://dicotopo.cths.fr/places/P37303056.

Ego Nicholaus, dictus abbas de Maricolis, et capitulum nostrum concessimus fratribus Premonstrati perpetuo possidenda nemora et terras infra metas sub testimonio quorundam circummanentium positas quemadmodum tempore domini Radulphi, predecessoris nostri, prefati fratres se dirationasse asserebant. Concessimus etiam eis quod in terra nostra que contigua est pomeriis, et hortis prefate curtis nec domum nobis ad inhabitandum construemus nec ab aliis construi permittemus, quia forte fratres aut sorores eorum tumultu inhabitantium inquietationem paterentur. Ego vero Hugo, dictus abbas Premonstrati, et capitulum nostrum pro bono pacis et in recompensatione predicte concessionis dedimus ecclesie de Maricolis tres modios frumenti ad minus mediocris ad mensuram de Guisia tunc temporis currentem in domo nostra de Hanapiis annuatim infra octavas Sancti Martini perpetuo eis solvendos. Ne igitur de omnibus hiis que pretaxavimus aliqua decetero questio oriatur, nos abbates sigillorum nostrorum inpressione et sigillorum utriusque capituli appositione presentem cartam sub cirographo dividendam munire curavimus sub annotatione personarum que huic compositioni apud castellum Cameracensis episcopi factem interfuerunt. Godefridus,[6] abbas de Viconia, Hugo[7] abbas de Brana et ceteri. Actum incarnati verbi anno M° C° LXXX° I°.

245

1155–60.[1]

Bouchard,[2] lord of Guise, writes to R[other],[3] abbot of Prüm, to attest that the land of Hannape was held in fief from him and his predecessors, for more than a century, until he ceded it to Prémontré, and to ask R[other] to take his wishes into consideration and no longer trouble Prémontré. (See ***235****.)*

A. Cartulary of Prémontré, fol. 61v.

B. Original, BnF, Coll. Picardie 290, no. 12, previously sealed.

EDITION: Le Paige, *Bibliotheca,* 972; Florival, *Étude historique sur le XIIe siècle,* 258–9.

6 Geoffroi de Tongres, abbot of the Premonstratensian abbey of Vicogne, 1177–84. *MP* II, 436.

7 Hugues, abbot of the Premonstratensian abbey of Braine, 1178–81. *MP* II, 486.

1 Bouchard was lord of Guise 1138–60, while Rother was installed as abbot of Prüm in 1155.

2 Bouchard, lord of Guise (d. aft. 1161), son of Guy, lord of Guise, and Adèle "Machania"; husband of Adèle de Soupir.

3 Rother von Malberg, abbot of the Benedictine abbey of Prüm, 1155–70.

Litere testimoniales domini Buchardi super possessionibus Hanapis.

Domino[4] et amico suo R[othero], Dei gratia Prumiensi abbati, Burchardus, qualiscunque dominus terre de Guisia, salutem et servitium. De possessione Hanapie pro qua inter vestram et Premonstratensem ecclesiam controversia agitur, coram celsitudine vestra, veraciter testimonium perhibeo quod tam meo quam predecessorum meorum tempore, a tercia etiam et quarta progenie par annos centum et amplius, legitimi et honesti viri libere et quiete eam in feodo a nobis tenuerunt et a predecessoribus nostris, sicut seniores terre nostre testantur, alii qui viderunt, alii qui a suis patribus audierunt, et cum ita esset, Premonstratensi ecclesie libere possidendam absque omni calumpnia tradiderunt et, ex quo ego ipse ad virilem etatem perveni, nullum ibi ex parte vestra vel vestrorum habitantem vel inde aliquid possidentem sed nec etiam aliquid reclamantem intellexi hoc quoque multi ex hominibus meis qui adhuc supersunt, si ad vos transire valerent, coram vobis constanter perhiberent. Unde humiliter obsecro ut hoc testimonium nostrum discretio vestra benigne accipiat et Premonstratensem ecclesiam sine causa vexare desistat. Quod siquis contraire et de hac possessione causari et tenentes in jus vocare temptaverit, volo, sicut et justum est, ut, me auctore, me tutore, me teste, causa tractetur et cum justicia judicium exeratur pro eo videlicet quia et possessor hereditario predecessorum meorum jure absque ulla calumpnia multis, ut prescriptum est, annis extiti et adhuc locum gero et personam advocati. Vale.[5]

246

1212

Magister *Prieur,*[1] *canon of Laon, and Guérin,*[2] *priest of Saint-Vincent,* officiales *of Laon, make known, at the request of Gervais,*[3] *abbot of Prémontré, that when Geoffroi,*[4] *knight of Flavigny, left for the Albigensian Crusade, he*

---

4 The initial letter has been added at a later, possibly post-medieval date, but the letter added ("A") is incorrect and should be "D."

5 Bene vale *B*.

---

1 Prieur, *officialis* of Laon, ca. 1210–ca. 1213. Wyard, *Saint-Vincent*, 36.

2 Guérin, priest of Saint-Vincent and *officialis* of Laon, is attested ca. 1212–ca. 1219. AD Aisne, G 1850, fols. 147v–148r; AD Aisne, H 874, fols. 242r–242v.

3 Gervais, abbot of the Premonstratensian abbeys of Saint-Just-en-Chaussée, 1199–1205, Thenailles, 1205–9, and Prémontré, 1209–20, and bishop of Séez, 1220–8. *MP* II, 401, 527, 565; Cheney, "Gervase, Abbot of Prémontré."

4 Geoffroi, knight of Flavigny-le-Grand (cant. Guise, https://dicotopo.cths.fr/places/P23628826). Melleville, *DH*, vol. 1, 391.

conceded that after his death and that of his wife, Prémontré would receive the three parts of the mill of Dorengt[5] *that he held, excepting two* modii *of grain (*frumentum*) for his sisters Emmeline and Elizabeth. (Emmeline is to receive 18* galeti *and Elizabeth six* galeti.*) The gift was later confirmed by Geoffroi and his wife Cécile* Domisons *in the presence of H.,*[6] *dean of Guise, and W.,*[7] *priest of Iron.*

A. Cartulary of Prémontré, fols. 61v–62r.
B. Original not found.
REGISTER: *Studium Baldwin*, fiche 2437.

Karta officialis Laudunensis de elemosine Godefridi militis de Flavigniaco.

[M]agister Prior, canonicus Laudunensis, et Garinus, presbiter Sancti Vincentii, officiales domini Laudunensis, universis inspectoribus huius carte in perpetuum. Noverit per hoc scriptum universitas vestra quod cum Godefridus, miles de Flavigniaco, in peregrinationem Albigensium profecturus, ea que subscripta sunt, sicut ipse in nostra presentia constitutus plenius recognovit, Premonstratensi ecclesie in elemosinam contulisse et vir venerabilis G[ervasius] abbas ipsius ecclesie, a nobis eadem confirmari per auctoritatem et sigillum Laudunensis curie postulasset, nos, ut ipsa confirmatio validioris esset momenti, assensum uxoris dicti G[odefridi], militis, per viros industrios et discretos H., decanum de Guisia, et W., presbiterum de Yrun, diligenter inquiri mandavimus et nobis fideliter remandari, ex quorum credibili testimonio nobis est exhibita plena fides, quod tam idem Godefridus, miles, quam ipsius, Cecilia, que cognominatur Domisons, coram ipsis presencialiter cognoverunt se dedisse in elemosinam Premonstratensi ecclesie tres partes quas habebant in molendino de Dorenc et pratum quod ad idem pertinet molendinum. Cognoverunt etiam se dedisse ecclesie memorate medietatem cuiusdam quarterii quod ipsa ecclesia modo possidet et iam diu possedit. Insuper et hoc fuit recognitum coram ipsis quod predictus Godefridus et uxor eius, quamdiu simul vixerint, vel alter eorum, fructus predicti molendini et prati integre percipient, excepta medietate iam dicti quarterii quam ecclesia diu possedit. Post decessum vero eorum quicquid possidebant in molendino et in prato, in jus ecclesie Premonstratensi cedet, excepto quod predicta ecclesia tenebitur, singulis annis in perpetuum, duos modios frumenti in predicto molendino solvere Enmeline

5 Dorengt, cant. Nouvion, https://dicotopo.cths.fr/places/P90882005.
6 An Henri, dean of Guise, is attested 1207–15. BM Laon, MS 532, fols. 7r, 8r.
7 Per Pécheur, he is Guillaume, priest of Iron (cant. Guise, https://dicotopo.cths.fr/places/P04584610). Pécheur, *Histoire de la ville de Guise et de ses environs*, vol. 1, 171–2.

et Elizabeth, sorori sue, et heredibus earum ita quod Enmelina inde habebit decem et octo galetas et Elizabeth sex galetas, tali conditione quod non licebit eis nec heredibus earum alicui vendere vel alienare predictum frumentum nisi ecclesie memorate, si ecclesia tantum voluerit reddere quantum aliis dare voluerit. Nos igitur officiales domini Laudunensis recognitionem prefate elemosine et donationis prius ab ipso Godefrido milite, coram nobis expressam et postmodum ab utroque videlicet eodem Godefrido et uxore sua, coram predictis H. decano et W. presbitero simul factam, redigi fecimus in hoc scripto ipsum perpetuis temporibus valiturum sigillo et auctoritate curie Laudunensis roborantes. Actum anno gratie M° CC° XII°.

247

April, 1212.

Magister *Prieur,*[1] *canon of Laon, and Guérin,*[2] *priest of Saint-Vincent,* officiales *of Laon, make known the gift made in their presence by Philippe, cleric of Tupigny,*[3] *to the church of Prémontré of half of his portion of the major and minor tithes of Neuville.*[4]

A. Cartulary of Prémontré, fol. 62r.
B. Original not found.

Karta officialis Laudunensis de elemosina Philipi clerici de Tupigni.

[M]agister Prior, canonicus Laudunensis, et Garenus, presbiter Sancti Vincentii, domini Laudunensis officiales, omnibus presentes litteras visuris salutem in Domino. Noverint universi quod Philippus, clericus de Tupigniaco, coram nobis in elemosinam contulit ecclesie Premonstratensi medietatem portionis sue in decima de Nova Villa, tam magna quam minuta, promittens se nunquam reclamaturum. In cuius rei testimonium presentes litteras patentes emisimus sigillo curie Laudunensis roboratas. Actum de assensu partium anno Domini M° CC° XII°, mense aprili.

1 Prieur, *officialis* of Laon, ca. 1210–ca. 1213. Wyard, *Saint-Vincent*, 36.
2 Guérin, priest of Saint-Vincent and *officialis* of Laon, is attested ca. 1212–ca. 1219. AD Aisne, G 1850, fols. 147v–148r; AD Aisne, H 874, fols. 242r–242v.
3 Tupigny, cant. Wassigny, https://dicotopo.cths.fr/places/P99706313.
4 Likely Neuville-lez-Dorengt, cant. Nouvion, https://dicotopo.cths.fr/places/P68735093.

248

1221

Ide,[1] *lady of Iron, widow of Eubert*[2] *de Ribemont, gives in perpetual alms to the church of Prémontré half of the oven of Dorengt*[3] *and the* terragium *of Bucilly*[4] *together with eight* galeti *of grain (*bladus*), measure of Guise, to be collected from the mill situated below Iron.*

A. Cartulary of Prémontré, fol. 62r.
B. Original not found.

Karta domine Ide de Yron de medietate furni de Dorenc quam contulit in elemosinam ecclesie Premonstrate.

[E]go Ida, domina de Yron, relicta viri nobilis Euberti de Ribodimonte, notum facio universis tam presentibus quam futuris quod ego libere et absolute dedi in perpetuam elemosinam ecclesie Premonstratensi medietatem furni de Dorenc quam ego et predictus dominus ac maritus meus acquisieramus. Dedi etiam eidem ecclesie in elemosinam omnia terragia que dicuntur terragia de Bucillies, inter Yron et Torchon, que terragia nos acquisivimus a liberis Wiardi, maioris de Yron, et a liberis Roberti de Frasnoi. Dedi insuper ipsi ecclesie octo galetos bladi ad mensuram Guisie accipiendos in perpetuum in molendino subtus Yron, a liberis Wiardi maioris predicti olim acquisitos. Et ut hec elemosina mea quam feci prenominate ecclesie ob remedium anime mee et predicti mariti mei ac antecessorum nostrorum, firma in perpetuum et irrevocabilis perseveret, ego feci presentem cartam in memoriam et testimonium huius rei confectam sigilli mei munimine roborari. Actum anno incarnationis dominice M° CC° XX° I°.

1 Ide, lady of Iron (d. bef. 1239), was first married to Eubert, lord of Ribemont, and widowed by 1221. By 1228, she was remarried to Gilles II, lord of Beaumetz (cant. Bertincourt, https://dicotopo.cths.fr/places/P35591263) and castellan of Bapaume. AN, S 4950B; "Commanderie des Templiers de Bertaignemont," 134; Stein, *Cartulaire de l'ancienne abbaye de Saint Nicolas des Prés sous Ribemont*, 64, 69, 74–5, 127.

2 Eubert (also referred to as Josbert, Hubert, or Albert), lord of Ribemont (d. 1220/1), son of Simon II, count of Ribemont, and Bertrade; first husband of Ide, lady of Iron. He and his wife also appear in the cartulary of the Benedictine abbey of Saint Nicolas des Prés sous Ribemont. Ibid., 64, 69.

3 Dorengt, cant. Nouvion, https://dicotopo.cths.fr/places/P90882005.

4 Bucilly, cant. Hirson, https://dicotopo.cths.fr/places/P91269366.

249

June, 1220. Laon.

Magister *Garnier,*[1] *canon and* officialis *of the bishop of Laon, attests that, on his departure for the Holy Land, Geoffroi,*[2] *lord of Sains, Agnès his wife, and their children Renier*[3] *and Elizabeth gave to Prémontré three* modii *and three* galeti *of grain (*frumentum*) that Prémontré owed them annually on the grange of Fontaine-Raimbaut.*[4] *In return, abbot Gervais*[5] *and the chapter of Prémontré give Geoffroi 60* librae blancorum *and promise to pray for his soul and those of his heirs.*

A. Cartulary of Prémontré, fols. 62r–62v.

B. Original not found.

REGISTER: *Studium Baldwin*, fiche 2300.

Karta curie Laudunensis de elemosina Godefridi de Seinz de tribus modii et tribus galetis bladi.

[M]agister Garnerus, canonicus et officialis domini Laudunensis, presentibus et futuris in perpetuum. Per hoc publicum instrumentum judiciaria potestate confectum ad omnium noticiam volumus pervenire quod vir nobilis Godefridus, dominus de Seinz, in nostra presentia constitutus, sollempniter recognovit quod cum profecturus esset in peregrinatione ~~in~~ transmarine terre quam Dominus pro ipso ibidem militantibus iam ex magna parte contulerat, ex devotione propria accessit personaliter ad ecclesiam Premonstrati ubi in capitulo, presente conventu tam canonicorum quam laicorum fratrum, ad humilem eius petitionem a viris religiosis domno Gervasio, eiusdem ecclesie abbate, et ab utroque eius conventu concesse fuerunt orationes ipsi G[odefrido] et heredibus suis ad animarum salutem perpetuo valiture. Cuius rei gratia hanc elemosinam duxit prefate ecclesie conferendam: Ecclesia siquidem prenominata debebat eidem Godefrido hereditarie et annuatim tres modios et tres galetos frumenti ad mensuram Guisie in grangia Rainbaldi Fontis accipiendos. Hoc igitur totum frumentum eidem ecclesie sibi retinendum et possidendum elemosine

1 Garnier, *officialis* of Laon, ca. 1219–ca. 1220. Wyard, *Saint-Vincent*, 37.

2 Geoffroi (d. by 1225), lord of Sains (arr. Vervins, https://dicotopo.cths.fr/places/P35898483); son of Renier de Guise, lord of Sains, and Sibille. BM Reims 1563 (N. Fonds), fol. 4r; Melleville, *DH*, vol. 2, 305.

3 Renier II, lord of Sains, son of Geoffroi, lord of Sains, and his first wife Marie de Ham, attested in the 1220s. BM Reims MS 1563 (N. Fonds), fol. 157v; Melleville, *DH*, vol. 2, 305.

4 Near La Ferté-Chevresis, cant. Ribemont, https://dicotopo.cths.fr/places/P15499504.

5 Gervais, abbot of the Premonstratensian abbeys of Saint-Just-en-Chaussée, 1199–1205, Thenailles, 1205–9, and Prémontré, 1209–20, and bishop of Séez, 1220–8. *MP* II, 401, 527, 565; Cheney, "Gervase, Abbot of Prémontré."

dono concessit, nobili muliere Agnete, uxore ipsius, assensum prebente et liberis eius, Renero videlicet et Elizabeth, annuentibus. Pro hac autem elemosina et pro subventione et auxilio peregrinationis dicti G[odefridi], Premonstratensis ecclesia, sicut sollempniter recognitum est coram nobis, reconpensavit ei in temporali beneficio certam summam pecunie numerate, videlicet sexaginta libras blancorum. Supradicta etiam uxor ipsius G[odefridi] coram nobis publice recognovit quod memoratum frumentum non erat de dotalicio suo et, ut hec elemosina rata in posterum perseveret, tam ipse G[odefridus] quam uxor sua A[gnes] et prefati liberi sui, R[einerus] et E[lizabeth], fidem corporaliter prebuerunt quod neque ipsi neque ex parte ipsorum alius aliquid in posterum super predicta elemosina reclamabunt ne ergo huiusmodi sollempnis recognitio quandoque oblivioni tradatur, ad petitionem sepedicti G[odefridi] et ad presentiam fratrum Premonstratensium in testimonium huius rei litteras istas emisimus auctentico sigillo Laudunensi curie roboratas. Actum Lauduni anno gratie M° CC° vicesimo, mense junio.

250

April, 1229.

Anselme,[1] *bishop of Laon, attests that Mathieu*[2] *de Parpeville obtained permission from the church of Prémontré and its dependent church of Dorengt*[3] *to sell to the* Domus Dei *of Ribemont land that he held at Thenailles*[4] *in exchange for an annual* census *of 15* denarii Parisiensium. *Marga, Mathieu's wife, from whose inheritance the land came, approves the sale.*

A. Cartulary of Prémontré, fol. 62v.
B. Original not found.

Karta episcopi Laudunensis de quindecim Parisiensium quos domus Dei de Ribodimonte tenetur reddere ecclesie de Dorenc.

[A]nselmus, Dei gratia Laudunensis episcopus, universis tam presentibus quam futuris eternam in Domino salutem. Scire volumus universos quod cum Matheus de Parpres teneret de ecclesia Sancti Petri de Dorenc, pertinente ad ecclesiam Premonstrati, circiter viginti galetos terre, site in territorio de Tenaille et preterea quartam

1 Anselme de Mauny (or de Bercenay), bishop of Laon, 1215–38.
2 Mathieu de Parpeville (d. 1281) and Marga (d. 1288?) are buried in the Benedictine abbey of Saint-Nicolas-des-Prés-sous-Ribemont. Gomart, *Essai historique sur la ville de Ribemont et son canton*, 227, 228, 358.
3 Dorengt, cant. Nouvion, https://dicotopo.cths.fr/places/P90882005.
4 Thenailles, cant. Vervins, https://dicotopo.cths.fr/places/P32092027.

partem unius falcate prati, quinque capones uno quarterio minus, quinque galetos avene integros, unum quarterium unius domus site apud Tenelle, item panes et vinum super masuras in villa de Tenaille usque ad valorem circiter trium solidorum Parisiensium sub annuo censu quindecim denariorum Parisiensium quos eidem ecclesie annuatim reddere tenebatur, tandem, intuitu Dei et ad preces bonorum virorum voluntarium prebuit assensum dicta ecclesia, et ecclesia similiter Premonstrati, quod idem Matheus tam predicta omnia quam quicquid tenebat tempore huius scripti apud Tenalle de ecclesia Premonstrati aut ecclesia de Dorenc sub censu predicto, vendidit domui Dei de Ribodimonte, salvo tamen in omnibus jure ecclesie de Dorenc predicte et tali etiam conditione apposita quod fratres dicte domus Dei tenentur reddere annis singulis quindecim denarios Parisienses in perpetuum annuatim fratribus de Dorenc aut nuntio eorum in festo Beate Benedicte apud Tenaille, alioquin legem debitam secundum consuetudinem patrie inde haberet ecclesia memorata. Hec omnia supradicta vendidit dictus Matheus dicte domui de Ribodimonte, fide prestita in manu nostra quod nichil decetero in predictis reclamabit aut faciet reclamari et quod super hiis legitimam warandiam portabit contra omnes qui juri et justicie parere voluerint. Hoc etiam laudavit Marga uxor dicti Mathei, de cuius hereditate hec movebant, promittens fide prestita quod nec jure hereditario nec alio titulo predicta decetero reclamabit. Ut autem de premissis in perpetuum memoria habeatur et reddatur census debitus dicte ecclesie Sancti Petri, presentem kartam episcopali auctoritate et sigilli nostri fecimus munimine roborari salvo jure nostro et alieno. Actum mense aprili, anno incarnationis dominice M° CC° XX° IX°.

251

June, 1208.

Eubert[1] *and Ide,*[2] *lord and lady of Ribemont, cede to the church of Prémontré the free possession of the* terragium *that they had acquired at Iron,*[3] *receiving in exchange the* census *that Prémontré possessed at Thenailles,*[4] *on the condition that Hubert and Ide not cede the* census *to anyone else, and that should Hubert die without heirs, the* census *will revert to Prémontré.*

1 Eubert (also attested as Josbert, Hubert, or Albert), knight and lord of Ribemont (d. 1220/1), son of Simon II, count of Ribemont, and Bertrade; first husband of Ide, lady of Iron. He and his wife also appear in the cartulary of the Benedictine abbey of Saint Nicolas des Prés sous Ribemont. Stein, *Cartulaire de l'ancienne abbaye de Saint Nicolas des Prés sous Ribemont*, 64, 69.

2 Ide, lady of Iron (d. bef. 1239), was first married to Eubert, lord of Ribemont, and widowed by 1221. By 1228, she was remarried to Gilles II, lord of Beaumetz (cant. Bertincourt, https://dicotopo.cths.fr/places/P35591263) and castellan of Bapaume. AN, S 4950B; "Commanderie des Templiers de Bertaignemont," 134; Stein, *Cartulaire de l'ancienne abbaye de Saint Nicolas des Prés sous Ribemont*, 64, 69, 74–5, 127.

3 Iron, cant. Guise, https://dicotopo.cths.fr/places/P04584610.

4 Thenailles, cant. Vervins, https://dicotopo.cths.fr/places/P32092027.

A. Cartulary of Prémontré, fol. 62v.
B. BnF, nouv. acq. lat. 2590, no. 41, previously sealed.

Karta Euberti militis de Ribodimonte de terragio de Yron.

[E]go Eubertus, miles de Ribodimonte,[5] tam futuris quam presentibus notum facio per hoc scriptum quod ego, assensu uxoris mee, Ide, concessi ecclesie Premonstrati liberum et perpetuo possidendum totum terragium quod ego et eadem uxor mea ex acquisitione[6] habuimus in territorio de Yron, pro qua videlicet concessione abbas et conventus Premonstratensis mihi in commutationem dederunt totum censum quem ipsi habebant in villa mea de Tenailles[7] cum his que ad ipsum censum pertinent ita tamen quod ex dicto censu non potero aliquid in elemosinam conferre alicui nisi tamen ecclesie Premonstrati et sciendum quod si ego Eubertus absque herede corporis mei decessero ex hac vita, memoratus census ad sepedictam ecclesiam libere revertetur. Actum anno gratie[8] M° CC°[9] octavo, mense junio.

252

1208

*Anselme, dean of Saint-Pierre of Soissons, R[enaud],[1] dean of Saint-Vaast of Soissons, and R., canon of Saint-Pierre of Soissons, make known the resolution of a dispute between the church of Prémontré on one hand, and Robert d'*Efferbisiaco, *and brothers Thierry and Robert on the other. The dispute concerns the status of certain women of* Aneio[2] *associated with the* Hospitium Dei*: Ada and her daughters Liégarde, Berte, Widèle, Ermengarde, and Amelina. The adjudicators decide that the women are under the authority of Prémontré (*possessionem ecclesie Premonstratensi*).*

---

5 Riboldi monte *B*.
6 adquisitione *B*.
7 Teneillis *B*.
8 *Add.* gratie *A*; incarnationis dominice *B*.
9 millesimo ducentesimo *B*.

---

1 Renaud, dean of Saint-Vaast de Soissons, attested 1203–18. Soissons, Archives hospitalières, 190, no. 1, fols. 1v, 11v; BM Laon, MS 532, fol. 58r.
2 Perhaps Any-Martin-Rieux, cant. Aubenton, https://dicotopo.cths.fr/places/P14804065.

A. Cartulary of Prémontré, fol. 62v.
B. Original not found.

Karta de quarundam mulierum possessione adjudicata ecclesie Premonstratensis.

[A]nselmus, decanus Sancti Petri, R[enaldus], decanus Sancti Vedasti et R., canonicus Sancti Petri Suessionensis, universis presentes litteras inspecturis salutem in Domino. Noverit universitas vestra quod cum causa que vertebatur inter ecclesiam Premonstratensem et Robertum de Efferbisiaco et Terricum et Robertum, fratrem eius, de hospitio Dei super quibusdam mulieribus de Aneio, scilicet Adda et filiabus eius Liegarde, Berta, Widela, Ermengarde, Amelina, nobis fuisset auctoritate apostolica commissa, tandem super possessione ipsarum lite sollempniter contestata, per recognitionem ipsarum mulierum nobis constitit evidenter quod se feminas ecclesie Premonstratensis recognoverunt, unde, de possessione ipsius ecclesie legitime cognoscentes, predictarum feminarum possessionem ecclesie Premonstratensi de prudentum virorum consilio adjudicavimus. Actum anno Domini M° CC° octavo.

253

1175

Hugues [II],[1] *abbot of Prémontré, makes known the resolution of the dispute between Prémontré and Dreux*[2] *[de Tupigny, lord of] Iron concerning the unauthorized mill that he and Elizabeth his wife had built on Prémontré's land at Iron.*[3] *Dreux and Elizabeth's sons Arnoul* Hoealdus *and Evrard consent to the resolution, and to a previous gift made to Prémontré by their parents of half of the prebend of the church of Dorengt.*[4]

A. Cartulary of Prémontré, fols. 62v–63r.
B. Original not found.

1 Hugues II de Douai, abbot of the Premonstratensian abbey of Cuissy, 1161–5, and abbot of Prémontré, 1174–89. *MP* II, 497.
2 Dreux, lord of Tupigny (cant. Wassigny, https://dicotopo.cths.fr/places/P99706313), ca. 1150–ca. 1175. Melleville, *DH*, vol. 2, 388.
3 Iron, cant. Guise, https://dicotopo.cths.fr/places/P04584610.
4 Dorengt, cant. Nouvion, https://dicotopo.cths.fr/places/P90882005.

Karta Hugonis Premonstratensis abbatis de controversia molendini de Yrun et de cursu aquis.

[E]go Hugo, Dei patientia dictus abbas Premonstrati, notum fieri volo tam futuris quam presentibus quod querela erat inter Premonstratensem ecclesiam et Drogonem de Yrun pro quodam molendino quod ipse Drogo ~~dedit eidem ecclesia~~ contra licitum et justiciam extruxerat super terram prefate ecclesie. Que videlicet querela, mediantibus honestis et prudentibus viris, ita sedata est quod ipse Drogo dedit eidem ecclesie culturam suam ad Dorenc perpetuo possidendam sub annuali trecensu IIII^{or} modiorum frumenti, quale in ipsa terra creverit, nec de peiori nec de meliori, ad mensuram Guisiacensem persolvendo a Festo Sancti Remigii usque ad Festum Omnium Sanctorum. Ecclesia autem Premonstratensis dimisit eidem Drogoni predictum molendinum pro modio frumenti annuatim persolvendo, quem videlicet modium idem Drogo assignavit predicte ecclesie in supradicto trecensu suo, ita quod ecclesia de trecensu illo modium unum pro molendino sibi retinebit cum alio modio quod idem Drogo ob remedium anime sue et conjugis sue, Elizabeth, apud Hanapias[5] quiescentis, Premonstratensi ecclesie dimisit et in predicto trecensu accipiendum assignavit. De molendino autem illo et de mansione eiusdem molendini et de cursu aque, qui vulgo Bez dicitur, ecclesie Premonstratensis debitam garandiam feret eidem Drogoni et heredibus eius contra omnes qui ad justiciam venire noluerint. Hoc autem concesserunt filii eiusdem Drogonis, Arnulphus, cognomine Hoealdus et Evrardus et sub hac conpositione laudaverunt etiam donum quod prius fecerat mater eorum, predicta Elizabeth, cum predicto Drogone Premonstratensi ecclesie de medietate prebendarum ecclesie de Dorenc et appenditiis eiusdem ecclesie. Cui concessioni interfuerunt et testes sunt: Renoldus[6] decanus ecclesie Guisiacensis, Willermus decanus de Yrun, Erebaudus[7] abbas Loci Restaurati et ceteri. Ut igitur hoc ratum et inconvulsum permaneat, presentem paginam cirographi conscriptione et sigilli nostri inpressione et personarum eiusdem capituli annotatione communiri fecimus. Actum anno Domini M^{o} C^{o} LXX° V^{o}. Et dictum et confirmatum quod de trecensu illo IIII^{or} modiorum ex quibus unus datus est sororibus Hanapie pro anniversario eiusdem Drogonis et conjugis sue faciendo, alter pro predicto molendino datus est eidem ecclesie, alii duo eidem Drogoni remanent, duos illos remanentes non poterit vendere neque invadiare neque elemosinam facere nisi ecclesie nostre, quantum ecclesia nostra voluerit rationabiliter pro illis facere sicut alius.

5 Hannape, cant. Wassigny, https://dicotopo.cths.fr/places/P37303056.

6 Renaud, dean of Guise, is also attested in 1161 and 1174. BM Laon MS 532, fols. 1v–2r; BM Reims 1563 (N. Fonds), fols. 33r–33v.

7 Erlebaud, abbot of the Premonstratensian abbey of Lieu-Restauré, 1172–9. *MP* II, 514.

254

1232

Étienne,[1] *dean of Saint-Algis, attests that in his presence the husband and wife Wiard* Faber *and Adèle*[2] *de Lesquielles undertake after their deaths to give to the church of Prémontré the house they have built in the town of Lesquielles.*[3] *(See* ***255****.)*

A. Cartulary of Prémontré, fol. 63r.
B. Original not found.

Karta Stephani decani de Sancto Angesio de elemosina Wiardi Fabri et Alaidis uxoris eius.

[S]tephanus, decanus de Sancto Angesio, universis fidelibus Christi presentes litteras inspecturis salutem in Domino. Noverint universi quod Wiardus Faber et Alaidis, uxor eius, de Lescheriis in nostra presentia personaliter constituti, recognoverunt se in perpetuam elemosinam contulisse, post decessum suum, ecclesie Premonstrati domum suam quam fecerunt de suo proprio, sitam apud Lescherias in media villa, ab ipsa ecclesia post decessum ipsorum amborum libere et pacifice perpetuo possidendam, hoc salvo quod siquis apparuerit post decessum eorum qui de jure velit, possit vel debeat clamare et redimere domum ipsam, quadraginta libras Parisienses ecclesie prenominate persolvet aut ipsa domus eidem ecclesie libera remanebit in pace. Ne autem ipsa Premonstratensis ecclesia de avaritia possit vel concupiscentia reprehendi, concessit eisdem Wiardo et Alaydi maxime cum status hominum de facili quandoque mutetur, quod si in tantam paupertatis penuriam ipsos labi contingat, quod non possit aliter eorum paupertati vel inopie provideri, de ipsa domo suam facient per omnia voluntatem, omni articulo alterius necessitatis quam note et probate paupertatis excepto penitus et excluso. Ceterum si post decessum eorum ita contingat quod ipsa ecclesia Premonstratensis in locando vel alio modo commodum suum fecerit de ipsa domo, quicquid inde receperit, sine contradictione aliqua suum erit et nichilominus quadraginta libras Parisienses integraliter persolvet eidem ecclesie, ob firmitatem elemosine supradicte, quicumque habere voluerit quocumque titulo domum ipsam, omni penitus exceptione cessante. Ut autem ista elemosina firma et stabilis in

1 Etienne, dean of Saint-Algis (cant. Vervins, https://dicotopo.cths.fr/places/P46995299) by 1226. Édouard de Barthélemy, *Analyse du cartulaire de l'abbaye de Foigny*, 34, 98.
2 Adèle, daughter of Elizabeth and Herbert de Lesquielles (**255**).
3 Lesquielles-Saint-Germain, cant. Guise, https://dicotopo.cths.fr/places/P39197714.

perpetuum perseveret, nos ad petitionem partium emisimus presentes litteras sigilli nostri appensione munitas. Actum mense februarii, anno Domini M° CC° trecesimo secundo.

255

1232

Étienne,[1] *dean of Saint-Algis, attests that Elizabeth, widow of Herbert de Lesquielles,*[2] *undertakes on her death to give in perpetual alms to the church of Prémontré a piece of land near Dorengt*[3] *able to hold about seven* galeti *of seed grain. During her life, Elizabeth will hold this land for an annual* census *of one* denarius. *Her children, Jean, Adèle, and Aude, and Adèle's husband, Wiard, consent to this. (See* ***254****.)*

A. Cartulary of Prémontré, fols. 63r–63v.
B. Original not found.

Karta decani de Sancto Angesio de elemosina Elizabeth de Lescheriis.

[S]tephanus, decanus de Sancto Angesio, universis fidelibus Christi presentes litteras inspecturis salutem in Domino. Noverint universi quod Elizabeth, relicta Herberti de Lescheriis, sue jurisdictionis existens in nostra presentia litera constituta personaliter, recognovit se in perpetuam elemosinam contulisse post decessum suum ecclesie Premonstratensi unam petiam terre sitam prope Dorenc, continentem circiter septem galetos sementis, ab ipsa ecclesia post decessum suum libere, quiete, pacifice et sine reclamatione aliqua perpetuo possidendum, annuentibus liberis suis, Johanne, Alayde, Oda et Wiardo, marito eiusdem Aelidis. Tenebit autem dicta Elizabeth ab ipsa ecclesia Premonstrati, quamdiu vixerit, ipsam terram sub annuo censu unius denarii bone monete in Festo Beati Remigii persolvendi et, post decessum eius, ipsa terra ad ecclesiam predictam libere devolvetur. Ut autem ista elemosina firma et stabilis in perpetuum perseveret, nos ad petitionem partium presentes litteras emisimus sigilli nostri appensione munitas. Actum anno incarnationis dominice M° CC° XXX° secundo.

---

1 Etienne, dean of Saint-Algis (cant. Vervins, https://dicotopo.cths.fr/places/P46995299) by 1226. Édouard de Barthélemy, *Analyse du cartulaire de l'abbaye de Foigny*, 34, 98.
2 Lesquielles-Saint-Germain, cant. Guise, https://dicotopo.cths.fr/places/P39197714.
3 Dorengt, cant. Nouvion, https://dicotopo.cths.fr/places/P90882005.

256

June 19, 1222.

Dean Guillaume and P., canons of Saint-Vaast of Soissons, confirm a resolution in favour of Prémontré following a dispute between Hugues, maior *of Dorengt,*[1] *and certain Premonstratensians, namely R., prior of the house of Dorengt, and the canon Thomas, over rights, payments, and properties concerning Dorengt.*[2]

A. Cartulary of Prémontré, fols. 63v–64r.
B. Original not found.

De compositione inter ecclesiam Premonstratensem et Hugonem maiorem de Dorenc.

[F]idelibus Christi universis presentes litteras inspecturis. Willermus, decanus, et P., canonici Sancti Vedasti Suessionensis, eternam in Domino salutem. Cum super quibusdam articulis inferius annotatis ecclesia Premonstratensis Hugonem, maiorem de Dorenc, coram nobis olim apostolica auctoritate fecisset in jus vocari tam super hiis quam super aliis inferius exprimendis, factam a partibus conpromissionem et arbitrium super ipsis prolatum conscribi fecimus secundum quod in cartula ipsorum arbitrorum contineri vidimus sub hiis verbis. Universis Christi fidelibus presentes litteras inspecturis frater R., dictus prior, et frater Thomas, canonici Premonstratenses, salutem in omnium salvatore. Noverit universitas vestra quod cum ecclesia Premonstratensis et Hugo, maior de Dorenc, varias haberent ad invicem hinc inde questiones peteretque ecclesia eadem ab ipso Hugone sexaginta decem solidos blancorum pro expensis scabinorum de Dorenc quas fecerunt querendo judicium apud Laudunum super querela que erat inter ipsum Hugonem et priorem de Dorenc, de qua convictus est idem Hugo calumpniose egisse contra ipsum priorem, peteret quoque ecclesia ipsa dampna sibi restitui usque ad valentiam triginta librarum blancorum; que quidem dampna ipsa ecclesia ~~constituit~~ sustinuit ex eo quod idem Hugo fundum ipsius ecclesie ingressus, homines et hospites ipsius bonis eorum spoliavit, peteret etiam satisfactionem ab Hugone de eo quod priorem de Dorenc et socios eius, canonicos Premonstratenses, scandalizavit et diffamavit, quantum in se erat, imponendo eis publice flagitiosa et enormia quedam, que nec fuerunt vera nec aliquo modo probata, esset que nichilominus ab ecclesia ipsa petita satisfactio de eo quod in unum ex fratribus ipsius ecclesie manus injecerat temere violentas, peteretque

1 Dorengt, cant. Nouvion, https://dicotopo.cths.fr/places/P90882005.
2 For a partial, paraphrased translation of this act into French, see Pécheur, *Histoire de la ville de Guise et de ses environs*, vol. 1, 190–2.

preterea ab Hugone viginti libras blancorum ex pena cuiusdam conpromissionis a cuius observatione ipse contumaciter recessit et propter hoc penam secundum formam compromissi incurrit; estimavit autem ipsa ecclesia injuriam predicte infamationis et violentie quadraginta marcas argenti, salva moderatione legitima super hoc facienda. Memoratus vero Hugo ex adverso assereret ecclesiam sibi existere injuriosam super detentione unius modiate terre quam pater ipsius Hugonis contulit in elemosinam ecclesie Premonstratensi et quatuor galetorum terre ex parte altera quam quondam Matheus, frater ipsius Hugonis, dimisit ipsi ecclesie pro remedio anime sue, necnon et super detentione cuiusdam gardini in quo dicebat, ratione propinquitatis et jure cognationis, se jus successionis habere, peteret quoque quadraginta libras blancorum pro expensis quas fecerat in lite contra ecclesiam ipsam et relaxari a terragio quarundam terrarum quas tenet de ecclesia in territorio de Dorenc. Tandem utraque pars super premissis omnibus in nos et nobilem virum Gobertum de Mailli, militem, sub pena triginta librarum conpromisit ita quidem quod a partibus ratum et perpetuum haberetur quicquid a nobis omnibus sive duobus nostrum si forte contingeret nos in unam sentenciam non convenire super premissis omnibus de plano pronuntiatum foret sive ordinatum. Cuius rei plegii sunt pro Hugone, Adam Enpirevile de Dorenc et Willermus Faber de Nova Villa[3] utraque videlicet in solidum de dicto secundum formam premissam observando ex parte ipsius Hugonis addito nichilominus predicte cautioni quicquid terrarum possidet. Idem Hugo sub ecclesia in territorio de Dorenc. Ecclesia vero per litteras suas ipsi Hugoni traditas ad ea que premissa sunt se obligavit. Cum igitur super premissis sufficienter essemus instructi domino Goberto de Mailli in sententia nobiscum non concordante pronuntiamus dictum nostrum in hunc modum. Licet Hugo, maior de Dorenc, in hiis que continentur in premissa petitione ecclesie de rigore viris esset merito condempnandus ex gratia tamen sola et toleratione ecclesie Premonstratensis absolvimus eum ab impetitione ecclesie super premissis excepto eo quod pro infamatione predicta et violenta manuum injectione in fratrem ipsius ecclesie dominica proxima post prolationem arbitrii nostri preparabit se idem Hugo exutis vestibus ad disciplinam coram omnibus qui fuerint ad missam in ecclesia de Dorenc. Et iterum semel preparabit se ad suscipiendum correptionem ubi garum apud Premonstratum nisi hoc remissum fuerit ab abbate Premonstra~~tra~~tensis. Inhibuimus etiam eidem Hugonem ne de cetero in territorio aut dominio Sancti Petri de Dorenc homines aut hospites ipsius ecclesie, absque assensu ipsius ecclesie aut servientum suorum, quos ad servandum justiciam de Dorenc deputaverit, audeat rerum ablatione suarum aut aliis quibuscumque modis inquietare. Absolvimus quoque ecclesiam Premonstratensem ab impetitione ipsius Hugonis super omnibus que in petitione sua sunt conprehensa, cum plena nobis facta sit fides quod predictas terras a patre et fratre ipsius Hugonis collatas ecclesia possit et debeat,

3 Likely La Neuville-lez-Dorengt, cant. Nouvion, https://dicotopo.cths.fr/places/P68735093.

nonobstante reclamatione ipsius, libere possidere et super terragio predicto fuerit ei alias inpositum silentium per diffinitivam sententiam judicum a domino Papa delegatorum et gardinum predictum quitaverit omnino ipsi ecclesie recepto juramento a Wiardo le Begue de Escheriis qui in dominium et proprietatem ipsius ecclesie transtulit ipsum gardinum, quod pro exheredando ipso Hugone malitiose non alienavit gardinum memoratum nec in petitione dictarum expensarum aliquid jus haberet cum in causis omnibus quarum occasione fecerat expensas illas in justam partem fovisset sicut de hiis et de premissis omnibus nobis per evidentia constitit documenta. Adjecimus quoque quod parte altera ab observatione omnium vel alicuius premissorum articulorum recedente et penam premissam triginta librarum blancorum propter hoc merito incurente reliqua pars et super petitione ipsius pene et super omnibus aliis questionibus supradictis poterit, si voluerit, coram decano Sancti Vedasti[4] Suessionensis et conjudicibus suis coram quibus ecclesia Premonstratensis super hiis que continentur in petitone premissa ipsum Hugonem fecerat ante conpromissionem predictam auctoritate apostolica in jus vocari contra partem adversam judiciario ordine experiri nec pars que resilierit decetero agendo super aliqua predictarum questionum audietur. Actum est hoc nonas junii anno incarnationis dominice M° CC° XX° secundo. Nos igitur ea que premissa sunt sicut rite facta auctoritate apostolica confirmantes litteras sigillorum nostrorum munimine fecimus roborari. Actum tertio decimo kalendas julii, anno gratie M° CC° XX° II°.

257

October 18, 1321. Saint-Quentin.

Jean [II],[1] *lord of Saillenay and* bailli *of Vermandois, passes sentence at the assizes of Saint-Quentin over a dispute between Prémontré and [Guy I],*[2] *count of Blois, concerning the rights of* justice *in the town of Dorengt.*[3] *Prémontré retains the right of* saisine, *while the count retains the rights of* justice *over the people in his territory.*

A. Cartulary of Prémontré, fols. 64r–64v.

B. Original not found.

Other Manuscript Copies: Cartulary of Guise, BnF, MS Latin 17777, 243v–244r (1327).

4 The collegiate church of Saint-Vaast de Soissons.

1 Jean de Saillenay was bailli of Vermandois, 1320–2. Waquet, *Le bailliage de Vermandois aux XIIIe et XIVe siècles*, 179.

2 Guy I de Châtillon, count of Blois (1298–1342), son of Hugues II, count of Blois, and Béatrice de Dampierre.

3 Dorengt, cant. Nouvion, https://dicotopo.cths.fr/places/P90882005.

NO RUBRIC. LATER ADDITION.

A tous chiaus qui ces presentes lettres verront et orront Jehans, sires de Sallenoy, chevaliers le Roy, garde de la baillie de Vermendois, salut. Comme debas fust meus en cas de saisine, dou temps de nos devanchiers baillius de Vermendois, entre religieux hommes l'abbé et le couvent de l'eglize de Premonstré d'une part et haut prince noble et puissant monseigneur le conte de Bloys d'autre seur le prinse de deus hommes que les gens dou dit monseigneur le conte avoient fait en justisant en le maison des dis religieus en le ville de Dorenc, en lequelle maison li dit homme estoient detenu pour cas criminel et les deus hommes mirrent les gens dou dit monseigneur le conte a execution, de laquelle prinse li dit religieux s'estoient dolu et complaint, disant euls estre en bonne et souffissant saisine de faire esplois de justice oudit liu en la ville de Dorenc et es apartenances et euls estre en saisine d'avoir la prince, la detention, la connoisse et le jugement des persones es dis lieus en cas criminel, et laquelle saisine les gens dou dit monseigneur le conte les avoient tourblés et empechiés indeuement et de nouvel en faisant la dite prinse, pour quoi il avoient requis que li dis messires li contes ou ses gens executant sa justice fuissent contraint a rendre et restablir as dis religieux les dis prisonniers audit liu et a amender. Le procureur dou dit monseigneur le conte opposent au contraire a fin de saisine et a le complainte des dis religieux eust esté la prinse remise au liu par les gens dou dit monseigneur le conte, les parties appelées et asemblées seur le liu, et par l'opposition des parties eust esté li debas prins en le main dou Roy comme en main souvrainne et jours assignés as parties es assizes apres ensivans, a St Quentin pour aler avant, si comme raisons seroit, ausquelles assizes comparurent en jugement les dites parties souffissamment fondées, entamerent plait seur les choses dessus dites, proposerent et baillierent par escript fais contraires en cas de saisine et les offrirent a prouver en cas criminel et mist en ni chascune partie le fait recevable de sa partie adverse, seur les quez faus auditeur furrent donné en assize homme le Roy pour enquerre de la verité. Par devant les quez auditeurs comparurent li procureur desdites parties souffissantement fondé, jurerent en la cause et[4] respondi chascunes des procureurs par son sairement aus articles de sa partie adverse, amenerent tesmoings a sentention prouver, liquel tesmoing jurerent, presens les dis procureurs, et deposerent et fu leur depositions mise en escript et reproches baillies de chascune partie enqueste faite et parfaite importée par les dis auditeurs avec tout le proces seelé de leur seaus, sachent tout que en nos presentes assizes comparurent li procureur des diz religieux d'une part et li procureur dou dit monseigneur le conte de Bloys d'autre, requerent a grant instance que la dite enqueste fust veue et jugié et que li drois leur fust fais seur ycelle, veue adonques la dite enquest rapportée aus arrez au conseil des hommes jugens en les dites assizes en jugement,

4 *Superscr.* et *A.*

veues les reproches proposées contre les tesmoings d'une part et d'autre, veu tout le proces et tout ce que chascune partie avoit volu proposer a obtention tant de fait comme de droit, dist fu part droit par le jugement des hommes jugens es dites assizes que li procureur des diz religieux en non d'eus et en non de la dite eglize a Muils prouve sentention es cas dessous diz de saisine par quoi li dit religieus demeurent en leur dite saisine et sera mis en leur main, comme en main de partie, ce qui estoit tenu en la main le Roy comme en main souvrainne, sauf ce que li dit religieux doivent livrer les personnes jugiés au dit monseigneur le conte ou a sa gent au chief de leur terroir, pour faire l'execution a se jugement faire et le firent comme homme maistres Nicoles[5] de Saint Just dyens[6] de l'eglize Saint Quentin, mesires Mahius[7] de la Motte canoines et cantres de la dite eglize, l'abbés de Humbelieres,[8] mesires Jehans,[9] sires de Waulaincourt, messires Oudars,[10] sires de Hem, messires Goulars,[11] sires de Moy, messires Robers,[12] sires de Gauchy, messires Tournes de Moy, messires Eustaces des Anes, messires Pierres Begues,[13] sires de Montaigny, messires Jehans de Clastres,[14] chevalier, Jehans de Tupaigny,[15] Mingot de Moy, Willaumes dou Foy,[16] Jehans de Bieurezis, Jehans Gautiers, Jehans Soiers, Quentins Cambellanis, Jehans de Tiergeville,[17] maistres

5 Nicolas de Saint-Just was appointed dean of Saint-Quentin in 1318, and grand master of the College of Navarre in Paris, ca. 1320. Colliette, *Mémoires pour servir à l'histoire ecclésiastique, civile et militaire de la province du Vermandois*, vol. 2, 749–50.

6 *Sic A.*

7 Mathieu de la Motte (or la Mothe), canon of Saint-Quentin, was cantor, 1320–30. Gomart, ed., *Extraits originaux d'un manuscrit de Quentin de la Fons intitulé histoire particulière de l'Église de Saint-Quentin*, vol. 1, 215; vol. 2, 183.

8 John II Coivrel was elected abbot of the Benedictine abbey of Homblières in 1306, though per Newman, *Homblières*, 19, it is "impossible to determine when John ceased being abbot, since there were several abbots by that name in the fourteenth century."

9 Jean III de Dours, lord of Walincourt (d. bef. 1338), son of Jean II and Marguerite de Hangest. Guiot, "Histoire genealogique et heraldique des seigneurs de la terre et baronnerie de Walincourt en Cambrésis," 164–7.

10 Oudard I (sometimes referred to as Eudes VI), lord of Ham. His relationship to the previous lords of Ham is not clarified in any known primary source, but he was likely a son of Jean II, lord of Ham (d. ca. 1285). By 1296, he was married to Dorée, daughter of Marie de Frianvile and Eustache, lord of Marteville. Pipon, ed., *Le chartrier de l'Abbaye-aux-Bois (1202–1341)*, 353.

11 Goulard (or Guy) VI (d. 1346), son of Goulard (or Guy) V, lord of Moy, and his second wife, Marie. Melleville, *DH*, vol. 2, 146.

12 Robert I, lord of Gauchy. Melleville, *DH*, vol. 1, 415.

13 Pierre Becquos (or Begues), lord of Montigny-Carotte. Melleville, *DH*, vol. 2, 127.

14 Jean II, lord of Clastres, 1310s–20s. Melleville, *DH*, vol. 1, 256.

15 Tupigny, cant. Wassigny, https://dicotopo.cths.fr/places/P99706313.

16 Possibly lord of Fay-le-Noyer (cant. Ribemont, https://dicotopo.cths.fr/places/P49852544). Melleville, *DH*, vol. 1, 374.

17 Jean de Tiergeville, notary royal at Saint-Quentin from 1318, and clerk and lieutenant of the *bailli* of Vermandois in the 1320s. Varin, *Archives administratives de la ville de Reims*, vol. 2, part 1, 377; Bouchot and Lemaire, *Le livre rouge de l'Hôtel de ville de Saint-Quentin*, 145, 156, 175.

Symons Riviere et pluseur autre. En tesmoingnaige des ques choses nous avons mis a ces presentes lettres le seels de le baillie de Vermandois avec les seaus des diz hommes et nous li homme dessous nommé faisons savoir a tous que nous au dit jugement faire et prononcier fimies comme homme et le feismes du conjurement dou dit baillif. En tesmoingnaige de ce nous avons mis a ces presentes lettres nos seaus avec le seel de la dite baillie. Donné en assizes a Saint Quentin le diemenche, jour de feste Saint Luc, l'an de grace mil CCC XXI.

258

February, 1317[?].

The king's notaries, Oudars Terudius, *the* prevost *of Pierrefonds,*[1] *and Adam* li Bons[2] *de Crépy*[3] *draw up an act establishing the conditions by which Marie de Vézaponin,*[4] *widow of Gérard de* Tringury, *gives Prémontré a mill and* courtillet *at Huet*[5] *in return for the payment of an annual* cens.

A. Cartulary of Prémontré, fol. 65r.[6]

B. Original not found.

EDITION: Martin-Marville, *Trosly-Loire ou le Trosly des conciles, ses chateaux, ses villas, ses fiefs et ses seigneurs*, 226–7.

NO RUBRIC. LATER ADDITION.

A tous ceulz qui ces presentes lettres verront et orront Oudars diz Terudius clers, a ce tamps garde dou seel de la prevosté de Pierrefons, et Adams, diz li Bons de Crespy, clers tabellions jurés de par notre seigneur le Roy es liés de la dite prevosté et dou ressort d'icelle, salut en nostre Signeur. Saichent tuit que par devant nous comme par devant justice pour y ce faire et accorder vint en sa propre personne damoysele Marie dou Wesaponin jadis feme Gerart de Tringury escuer, signeur de la dite ville du Wes et recognut et afferma en droit par devant nous de sa bonne volenté non contrainte que elle pour son grant pourfit clerement apparant, si comme elle disoit, avoit vu, prins, et receu a cense

1 Pierrefonds, cant. Attichy, https://dicotopo.cths.fr/places/P55680245.

2 Adam *li Bons* is also attested in the cartularies of the cathedral chapter of Soissons and of the Benedictine abbey of Notre-Dame de Morienval. AD Aisne, G 253, fol. 184v; BnF, MS lat. 9987, fol. 13v–15v, 15v–18r.

3 Crépy, cant. Laon, https://dicotopo.cths.fr/places/P85331504.

4 Vézaponin, cant. Vic-sur-Aisne, https://dicotopo.cths.fr/places/P00069317.

5 Huet, comm. Lizy, https://dicotopo.cths.fr/places/P74654387.

6 The right-hand side of this folio was trimmed at some point, resulting in the loss of part of the text.

a tous jours perpetuelment sans nul rappel, de religieus hommes et honnestes l'abbé et le couvent de Premonstré un molin que li dit religieus avoient seant en la dite ville dou Wes, avecques un courtillet joingnant a celli molin, et telle redevance comme yl avoient sur le maison de Fiourmentine es lius yl avoient toute signourie et justice et quelz liels yl tenoient et avoient tenu et possessé comme leur propre fons, demainne et heritaige de si lonc tamps que memoire n'estoit dou contraire, a tenir et a possesser ledit molin avecquez toutes les appartenances et apendances dessusdites par la dite damoiselle, par ces hoirs et par ces successeurs a tous jours perpetuelment parmi se qui s'ensuit, c'est as savoir trois aissins de terre ou environs, ainsi suit yl se comportent entre lez bonnes en la cousture de Loyre deles la Tonbele, item dels pieces de pré en la prée de Trocly, tenans l'une au pré Nostre Dame de Nongent d'une part et Bertram de Faillouel d'autre part et l'autre dessus la la[7] courtillet de Chauny de une part et de l'autre a Pierre Lefevre et a Pierre de Croy lezquels lieus dessusdis la dite damoiselle avoit pour le dit molin et appartenances restablis, donnés, quittiez, octroiez dou tout en tout et delaissiez perpetuelment et sans rappel as dis religieus a leurs successeurs et a leur dite eglise avecques VII livres de Parisis fort monnaie que elle, si hoir ou successeur, possesseur dou dit molin, sans nule desevance ne division faire entre eulz ou liquelz qui miels plaira des diz religieus d'iciaus possesseurs doudit molin renderont, deveront, et seront tenu a rendre et paier as devant dis religieus ou a leur certain commant en leur maison de Loirre chascun doit a tous jours perpetuelment la moitié de la Saint Martin d'iver et l'autre moitié a la Pasque close ensuivant chascun an perpetuelment, en telle maniere que ce le dite terre ~~ne~~ et prés n'estoient ou tamps advenir empeschiés dez dis religieus ou aucuns contredis mis que ne joissent lidit religieus a tousjours paisiblement d'iciaus et que li dessus dit sept livres de Parisis fussent entierement et sans quelcunque deffaite paiet chascun an a tous jours az lieu et jour dessus diz, le dite demoiselle, si hoir et se successeur, possesseur dudit molin, ou cuy, ou c'il encontre cuy ou lezquiels yl plairoit az dis religieus ceste presente lettre a monstrer, seroient en cheut en la main de le Roy pour tant de jours comme deffaute avoit en moy que ce fust pour chascun jour une amende et avecque ce en deus soulz de Parisis envers lez dis religieus pour chascun jour qu'avoient esté en deffaute en nom de painne sans estre point pour cela somme principal avueurie, dezquelles painnes li dit religieus povoient donner la moitiet a quelconque justice il leur plairoit pour lez dis deffaillans contraindre et ancore la dite damoiselle ou li possesseur dou dit molin sont et seront tenu et obligiet en rendre et restablir as diz religieus tous cous, frais, et demaiges telz comme leur procureur que l'on a juré par son serement qu'aroit fais en contens et tous ce que dessus est dit pour chacier sans autre pruesve traire et quant a toutes le choses dessus dites ensemble et chascune d'icelles tenir, garder et acomplir

7 *Sic A.*

fermement et entierement en la maniere que en ceste lettre sont contenuez, en obliga devant nous la dite damoiselle et lassa pour obligiez, envers lez religieus, leurs successeurs et ledit porteur son corps a mettre et a tenir en prison fermée de par notre signeur le Roy, ses hoirs, tous ces biens et lez biens de ses hoirs, de sez successeurs possesseurs doudit molin, meublés et non meublés, presens et advenir tous ensamble et chascun pour le tout ou qu'il soient et puissent estre trouvé et tous ses autres successeurs et hoirs a ce que ai[t] ou az quelz qu'il plaira miels au procureur des dis religieus il se puist traire pour faire contraindre a faire et acomplir tout ce que dedens est escript, est contenut ou tuit yl soient tenu et obligié sans riens dire encontre et avec ce elle obliga et establ[it] obligea especialment le di molin a touz jours et avecques lez possessions et heritaiges qui s'ensuivent c'est as savoir onze ayssins de terre au Butel tenant a Jeha[n] Tartier et a Jehan Joibert. Item IIII aissins qui furent le curé dou Wes tenant a la maladrer[ie]. Item onse aissins au Guoni tenant a Huart Maussion et a Simon le Clerc d'Oili. Item deus au Rigot de Servengny. Item dis sept aissins El Champ de Corblaincourt[8] tenant a Simon le [illegible] et a Huart Maussion. Item cinc aissins en Turel tenans a Jehan Tartier et a Thierry que elle tenoit et possessoit com siens propres en la justice et signourie de S. Mart d[e] Soissons, lez queles possessions et heretaiges dessus dis en nom de contrassent avec le dit [illegible] le dite damoiselle obliga et establi pour obligier envers lez diz religieus a ce que elle si h[oirs] ou si sussesseur[9] ou possesseur doudit molin deffaloient en aucun tamps ou année de paier, de warendir, de remplir ce qui dessus est escript li procureur dez dis religieus en nom d'ia[us] et pour iaus ce qui dessus est dit sans nul meffait par lui et sans nule autre justice appeller sans nul contredit de son auctorité puist entrer en dit molin et en [illegible] le dit contrassent et celli molin et contrassent[10] li dit r[eligieus] puissent tenir de la en avant comme leur propre fons, demainne et heritaige et faire dou tout leur pourfit, necessité et volenté paisiblement a tous jours. Item le dicte damoiselle recongnut que ledit molin elle doit retenir et maintenir en l'estat que yl estoi[t] quant faites furent ches lettres et que autres molins ne puet ne doit faire ne s[illegible] a faire en ledite ville. Item recognut la dite damoiselle que chacun an a tous jou[rs] li demourant en la dite maison ~~douoit~~ dou Loire ~~douvoiet~~ doivent avoir molut o[u][11] molin deus muis de blés sans point paier de moleture et renoncha la damoisselle a tout ce qui a ly et a sez hoirs porroit valoir et aidier contre se [illegible]. En tesmoingnaige de ce nous avons seellés ycelles dou seel de la dite dam[e] et dou dit tabellion sans tous drois. Ce fust fait en l'an de grace m[ille] [trois?] sens disept, en mois de frevier [erasure].

8 Comelancourt, comm. Morsain, https://dicotopo.cths.fr/places/P46673336.

9 *Sic A*.

10 *Sic A*.

11 *Sic A, read* au.

259

December, 1316. Paris.

Philippe [V] of France approves a decision made in 1313 by abbot Milon[1] *of Saint-Martin de Laon and canon Jean* Felix[2] *of Laon, which resolved the conflict between Gazon,*[3] *bishop of Laon, and Prémontré, concerning the possession of the mills of Liébuin*[4] *and Achéry, the quarries of* Resoulaloy, *and pasture rights at* Loroyencourt.[5]

A. Cartulary of Prémontré, fols. 65v–66r.
B. Original not found.

NO RUBRIC. LATER ADDITION.

Ph[ilippus], Dei gratia Francorum et Navarre rex, notum facimus universis tam presentibus quam futuris nos quasdam vidisse litteras tenorem qui sequitur continentes. In nomine Dei, amen. Cunctis tenore presentium appareat evidenter cum inter reverendum in Christo patrem dominum Gazonem, Dei gratia Laudunensem episcopum, ex una parte et religiosos viros abbatum et conventum Premonstratenses ex altera discordia esset mota super pluribus et diversis articulis videlicet super eo quod dicti religiosi dicebant et asserebant omnimodam justiciam in molendino de Liebuin et eiusdem pourprisio ad eos pertinere et quod aquam vivarii predicti molendino tenere poterant altam et bassam pro sue libito voluntatis, episcopo in contrarium dicente dictam justiciam ad ipsum pertinere et eum posse levare, auctoritate propria, aqualicia vivarii molendini predicti, quocienscumque molendinum dicti episcopi de Bourdel[6] aque sufficientia non habebat, item super eo quod dicti religiosi dicebant omnimodam justiciam in molendino suo quod habent apud Acheriacum[7] et eiusdem pourprisio ad eos pertinere, item quod poterant capere lapides in quarreria de Resoulaloy, quotiens sibi placeret, pro domibus suis omnibus in terra predicti episcopi situatis, dicto domino episcopo in contrarium dicente ipsos jus faciendi premissa non habere, item super eo quod dictus dominus episcopus se esse in saisina ducendi seu duci faciendi

---

1 Milon de Curigny, abbot of the Premonstratensian abbey of Saint-Martin de Laon, 1294–1324. *MP* II, 512.

2 Jean Félix, canon of Laon, ca. 1294–ca. 1314. Millet, *Les Chanoines du chapitre cathédral de Laon*, 513.

3 Gazon de Savigny (or de Champagne), bishop of Laon, 1297–1317.

4 Liébuin, comm. Brancourt, https://dicotopo.cths.fr/places/P25440726.

5 This act was confirmed by *vidimus* in 1316 by Henri de Taperel, *garde de la prévôté* of Paris. AD Aisne, G 38.

6 Barthel, comm. Lizy, https://dicotopo.cths.fr/places/P65460297.

7 Achery, cant. La Fère, https://dicotopo.cths.fr/places/P61820808.

animalia sua et animalia hominum suorum commorentium in villa de Loroyencourt ad pascendum, videlicet in loco qui dicitur Mailleval, in prato quod dicitur Wargemer et in campo contiguo dicto prato quod se extendit usque ad forestam, dictis religionis asserentibus contrarium et super quibusdam prisiis et violentiis factis hinc et inde in locis predictis super quibus omnibus in curia excellentissimi principis domini Philippi, Dei gratia regis Francorum, lite mota, tandem dicte partes nobis Miloni, Dei patiencia abbati Sancti Martini Laudunensis, et Johanni dicto Felis, canonico Laudunensi, causam super dictis discordiis obtinuerunt committi pace vel judicio terminandam, prout in litteris domini regis super hoc confectis plenius continetur quarum tenor talis est: Philippus, Dei gratia Francorum rex, dilectis suis abbati Sancti Martini Laudunensis, et magistro Johanni dicto Felis, canonico Laudunensi, salutem et dilectionem. Committimus vobis requirentes vos quatinus super prisiis et articulis quibuscumque molendinorum Liebuin et de Acheriaco justiciis et premissis tangentibus et super omnibus factis et querelis inter dilectum et fidelem nostrum episcopum Laudunensem ex una parte et abbatem et conventum Premonstratenses ex altera motis et maxime super hiis de quibus adjornamenta processerunt a nostra curia. Item super eo quod dictus episcopus se asserit de in saisina ducendi seu duci faciendi animalia sua et animalia hominum suorum degentium in villa de Lorencourt in locis inferius nominatis ad pascendum, videlicet in loco dicto Moilleval et in prato quod dicitur Wargemer in campo contiguo dicto prato quod se extendit usque ad forestam et ad molendinum dictum Renaut, partes ipsas ad concordiam pace vel judicio reducere studeatur. Quod si facere nequiverit debatum si quod inter partes ipsas fuerit ad manum nostram, tamquam superior, ponatis et loca resaisienda resaisiatis aut resaisiri faciatur per eandem manum nostram inquisituri postmodum vocatis evocandis super premissis et ea tangentibus cum diligentia veritatem et inquestam quam super hiis feceritis sub vestris clausam sigillis curie nostre mittatis ad futurum proximo parlamentum, si premissi pace vel judicio finem non duxerit imponendum. Actum Parisius de consensu procuratorum partium predictarum die vicesima nona novembris anno Domini millesimo CCC^{mo} duodecimo. Quarum auctoritate dictis partibus coram nobis sufficienter evocatis et legitime comparentibus, auditis omnibus que proponere et probare hinc et inde voluerunt et de jure dictarum partium in premissis, prout melius fieri potuit, informati supradictis discordiis, finem imposuimus in modum qui sequitur. De justicia in molendino Liebuin et pourprisio eiusdem quod ex parte inferiori usque ad rivum et ex parte superiori versus molendinum potenditur ultra rivum usque ad metas ibidem positas et ex parte opposita protenditur usque ad metas in clive montis positas, auditis confessionibus exquisitis et cognitis voluntatibus partium predictarum, ordinamus et pronunciamus quod alta justicia ad episcopum pertinet et pertinebit in futurum alia vero justicia de quibuscumque personis ad dictos religiosos necnon et alta justicia de manentibus in dicto molendino et de servientibus dictorum religiosorum undecumque sint et ubicumque morentur ad ipsos religiosos pertinet et pertinebit pro delictis tantummodo in dicto molendino et pourprisio eiusdem perpetratis; pronunciamus etiam quod exercitum alte justicie ad episcopum pertinentis fiet hoc modo et non aliter, videlicet quod de servientibus dictorum religiosorum laycis manentibus in dicto molendino unus quam episcopus ad hoc duxerit eligandum, semel faciet domino episcopo seu eius senescallo de Anisi juramentum quod deliquentes in dicto molendino et pourprisio eiusdem in casibus ad episcopum pertinentibus capiet et retinebit pro posse suo et, postquam capti fuerint et detenti, gentibus episcopi in domo episcopi commorantibus apud Anisiacum denunciabit malefactorem esse detentum et quod veniant vel mittant ad eum recipiendum, et, si veniant, tenebitur eum tradere et deliberare gentibus episcopi antedictis extra metas molendini et pourprisii et, si ad recipiendum dictum malefactorem venire differant, tenebitur eum custodire per unum diem naturalem et non ultra; si vero malefactorem non posset capere, seu captus et detentus sine culpa custodis evaserit, de hoc credetur ei per suum juramentum nichilque ultra ab eo exigi poterit; si vero contingat quod dictus juratus in premissis dolose egerit vel repertus fuerit culpabilis, alius serviens religiosorum subrogabitur in molendino manens qui simile faciet episcopo juramentum; de confugientibus ad dictum molendinum pro maleficiis extra perpetratis dictus juratus tenebitur facere illud, idem quod dictum est de delinquentibus in molendino in casu ad episcopum pertinente salvo quod denunciare non tenebitur episcopo nec etiam castellano; preterea si gentes episcopi furtas erigere velint, tenebuntur extra terras et possessiones eorumdem religiosorum illa facere ita longe a molendino quod habitantibus in molendino et pertinentiis eiusdem horror aut fetor inde venire non possint. Item ordinamus et pronunciamus quod in dicto vivario ante aqualicia fundabitur quoddam pilarium supra quod quiddam lapis cum ferro et plumbo sigillabitur altitudinem habens ad modum et mensuram per nos impositos, ad cuius lapidis altitudinem aqualicia dicti molendini fuerit nec fieri poterunt altiora et, si contingat aquam crescere ultra altitudinem aqualiciorum, aque super excrescentie cursum impedire non poterunt religiosi antedicti nec eam quoquomodo retinere, salvo quod ad retinendum pisces dicti vivarii dicti religiosi facere poterunt craticulam ferream seu ligneam aqualiciis altiorem poteruntque dicti religiosi dictum ~~in~~ vivarium in latum et profundum ampliare prout quando et quotiens sibi placuerit, dum tamen cursus aque super excrescentes ut dictum est, non impediatur; de justicia vero molendini de Acheriaco dicimus et pronunciamus quod ordinatio et pronunciatio per discretos viros magistros Johannem de Ribodimonte et Johannem de Leusis olim facte, tenebuntur et servabuntur et prisie et expleta justicie per gentes dicti episcopi ibidem facte ad statum debitum infra festum Omnium Sanctorum proximum reducentur. Item pronunciamus quod dicti religiosi possunt et poterunt capere lapides in lapidissina de Ronseloy pro domibus suis de Panencourt[8] et de Fontenillis[9] et de Merlieu[10] et molendini in Liebuin calceya et

8 Penancourt, comm. Anizy-le-Château, https://dicotopo.cths.fr/places/P36114519.

9 Fontenille, comm. Wissignicourt, https://dicotopo.cths.fr/places/P36537367.

10 Merlieux, cant. Anizy-le-Château, https://dicotopo.cths.fr/places/P92396813.

pertinentiis vivarii et molendini predictorum; super eo vero quod episcopus dicebat se esse in saisina ducendi seu duci faciendi animalia sua et animalia hominum suorum commorantium apud Loraiencourt ad pascendum in locis superius nominatis, dicimus et pronunciamus quod episcopus dictam saisinam de animalibus predictis non probavit et ideo animalia predicta ad pascendam in locis predictis ducere seu duci facere non poterit; de jure autem hominum suorum predictorum seu possessione in persona dictorum hominum residente, si quod habent nichil, per presentem ordinationem seu pronunciationem intendimus diffinire seu etiam ordinare; de prisiis autem et violentiis que facte hinc et inde dicebantur, nichil reperimus hinc inde sufficienter probatum et ideo super dictis prisiis et violentiis silentium perpetuum imposuimus partibus supradictis salvo quod illud quod factum dicitur pro gentis episcopi in molendino de Acheriaco, ad statum debitum reducet. Qua pronunciatione per nos Milonem et Johannem sic facta Guillermus de Barisiaco,[11] procurator, reverendi in Christo patris ac domini domini[12] Gazonis, Dei gratia Laudunensis episcopi predicti, et frater Adam de Bausignis,[13] procurator dictorum religiosorum in nostra presentia ad audiendam sententiam nostram seu pronunciationem personaliter constituti, dictam sententiam seu pronunciationem nomine procurationis ratam et gratam habuerunt et eandem emologaverunt expresse. In cuius rei testimonium nos Milo et Johannes predicti presentibus litteris sigilla nostra propria duximus opponenda. Datum anno Domini millesimo trecentesimo terciodecimo, die mercurii post festum nativitatis Beati Johannis Baptiste. Item quamdam aliam litteram sigillo dilecti et fidelis nostri episcopi Laudunensis sigillatam in littera superius scripta annexavi formam que sequitur continentem. Universis presentes litteras inspecturis Gazo, miseratione divina Laudunensis episcopus, salutem in Domino. Cum discordia orta esset inter nos ex una parte et religiosos viros abbatem et conventum Premonstratenses ex altera super pluribus et diversis articulis, causam quam super eadem discordia viro religioso domino Miloni, Dei patientia abbati ecclesie sancti Martini Laudunensis et venerabili et discreto viro magistro Johanni Felixi, canonico Laudunensis, nos et dicti religiosi obtinuerimus conjuncti pace vel judicio terminandam ab eisdem auctoritate, visis et inspectis diligenter rationibus et responsionibus nostris et religiosorum predictorum et habito super hoc bonorum consilio eidem dominus Milo et magister Johannes pronunciaverunt super dicta discordia secundum formam et tenorem litteraram hiis nostris presentibus annexarum; noverint universi quod nos dictam pronunciationem a predictis domino Milone et magistro Johanne super dicta discordia factam et omnia in predictis suis litteris hiis annexis contenta ratificamus, laudamus ac etiam approbamus, in cuius rei testimonium sigillum nostrum proprium hiis nostris presentibus litteris duximus apponendum. Datum anno Domini millesimo CCC^{o} tercio decimo, die mercurii post festum nativitatis Beati Johannis Baptiste. Nos vero predicta omnia et singula, prout superius sunt

11 Likely Barizis, cant. Coucy-le-Château, https://dicotopo.cths.fr/places/P70249408.

12 *Sic A*.

13 Likely Bancigny, cant. Vervins, https://dicotopo.cths.fr/places/P52650696.

expressa, rata et grata habentes ea volumus, laudamus, approbamus et ad requisitionem procuratorum dictarum partium tenore presentium confirmamus salvo in omnibus jure nostro et jure quolibet alieno. Quod ut firmum et stabile permaneat in futurum, presentibus litteris nostrum fecimus apponi sigillum. Actum Parisius anno Domini millesimo trecentesimo sexto decimo mense decembris. Constat nobis de rasura in verbis que sequantur: Sententiam nostram seu pronunciationem personaliter constituti dictam sentenciam seu pronunciationem nomine procuratoris ratam et gratam habuerunt. Actum Parisius anno et mense predictis.

260

February, 1269.

Gautier[1] *de Tupigny, lord of Iron,*[2] *Lavaqueresse,*[3] *and Torchon,*[4] *resolves a dispute with Prémontré by acknowledging that the abbey ceded to him the rights that it possessed in Iron, owing an annual payment of 30* livres Tournois.

A. Cartulary of Prémontré, fol. 66r.
B. Original not found.

NO RUBRIC. LATER ADDITION.

A tous ceulz qui ces lettres verront, je Wautiers de Tupigni chevaliers, sires de Yron de le Vakereche et du Torchon, salut en notre Signeur. Sachent tout que com descorde fust entre moy et l'eglise de Premontré de justices et de aultres choses que l'eglise tenoit en la ville et en terroir d'Iron, en la parfin par bien de pais et pour le preu de l'une partie et de l'autre, nous avons acordé en tel maniere de pais que l'eglize devant dite m'a otroué a tous jours a moy et a mes hoirs a tenir ce que elle avoit en la ville et en terroir d'Yron quitement et en pais en tel point comme elle le tenoit, soit en justices soit en terrages, ou en autres choses quelles que elles soient, fors la droiture telle comme l'eglise de Saint Pierre de Dorenc[5] y a qui n'est pas mise avoec ces choses par tele condition que je et mi hoir somme tenu a rendre a tous les jours du monde cascun an a l'eglise devant dite et as freres d'icelle eglise trente livres Tournois en leur maison de Hanappes,[6] lendemain de la Toussains, pour les choses devant dites par tel maniere que

1 Gautier I, lord of Tupigny (cant. Wassigny, https://dicotopo.cths.fr/places/P99706313), 1240s–60s. Melleville, *DH*, vol. 2, 388.
2 Iron, cant. Guise, https://dicotopo.cths.fr/places/P04584610.
3 Lavaqueresse, cant. Guise, https://dicotopo.cths.fr/places/P35390591.
4 Le Torchon, comm. Lavaqueresse, https://dicotopo.cths.fr/places/P03842443.
5 Dorengt, cant. Nouvion, https://dicotopo.cths.fr/places/P90882005.
6 Hannape, cant. Wassigny, https://dicotopo.cths.fr/places/P37303056.

se je ou mi hoir defaliens de paiement de tout ou de partie nous seriens tenu pour le defaute de cascun jour des le terme en avant a paier as freres de celle eglise trente sous Tournois par non de painne sans nul contredit et avoec tout ce pour ces XXX livres paier cascun an si comme il est dessus dit et pour le painne paier se jou ou mi hoir faliens de le paie je ay asené l'eglise et les freres de Premontré a quanque jay ou aurai ce villes dessusdites de Yron, de le Vakereche, et du Torchon soit en tailles ou enfrages ou en autres rentes et en toutes revenues de ches villes et si en oblege a l'eglize de Premontré et as freres dessusdis tous ciaulz que les choses des villes dessusdites receveront pour moy et pour mes hoirs se defaut avoit des paiemens et que cil receveur pourront estre contraint et seront tenu dou defaut des XXX livres et de la painne paier a ceulz de Premontré et tous les damages et les despens que cil de Premontré feroient ou recheveroient pour le defaut de le paie et de le painne. Je et mi hoir et cil receveur soens tenu a restablir et a rendre a la simple pere le d'un des prevues de Premontré ou dou maistre de Hanappes qui au temps seroient sans autre prevue et si fui tenus. Je et mi hoir a tenir le mairesse et le mairie de Yron et ses hoirs qui apres lui venront en tel franchise comme l'eglise de Premontré le devoit tenir et toutes ces coses. Je ay creantées et jurées a faire et a tenir en bonne foy et mi hoir qui apres mi venrent sont tenu aussi apres moy a paier tenir et remplir ces convenances et s'il avenoit que cil mien hoir qui apres mi venront et tout cil qui ma terre de Tupigni et des autres lius tenront apres moy ne veloient jurer ces convenances a tenir si com il est dessusdit je oblige y ciaulz miens hoirs et tous mes biens, catelz et meublez a paier I marc d'argent par non de painne pour le defaut de cascun jour dou sairement qui ne seroit fais de ces miens hoirs as freres de Premontré des le jour qu'il en seroient requis des freres dessusdis et se ma terre estoit aprés moi de partie cil freres de Premontré ne soit pas tenu a penre ces XXX livres sur cascunne partie mais les doivent penre et recevoir entierement de celui qui tenra le maison de Tupigni et Welz oblege a ce ces miens hoirs et tous mes biens, catelz et meubles envers l'eglise de Premontré en quelconques liu ou on les porroit trouver et que mesires li cuens de Blois ou cilz qui seroit sires de Guise au tamps, puist contraindre ces miens hoirs et cheulz qui la terre tenront et les receveurs des villes dessusdites, a paier ces XXX livres et les painnes des X sous et dou marc d'argent, se defaute y avoit de la paie ou dou sairement, sans nul amonnestement et sans meffaire et les damaiges et les damaiges[7] et les despens avoec seront il tenu a rendre a ceulz de Premontré, si comme il est dessus dit, et renonche a toutez chosez especialment et generaument qui porroient a moy ou a mes hoirs aidier et a ceulz de Premontré nuire; et pour ce que ce soit ferme chose et estable, je ay baillié a le dite eglise ces lettres seellées de mon seel. Ce fu fait en l'an de l'incarnation notre Signeur mil CC soissant nuef,[8] ou mois de fevrier.

7 *Sic A.*
8 *Sic A.*

261

April 3, 1344.

The officialis *of Soissons attests that in the presence of Colard de Cuffres,*[1] *sworn notary of the court of Soissons, husband and wife Jean* Cosses *de Vuillery*[2] *and Marie recognized that they had received land in Clamecy*[3] *from the religious of Prémontré in exchange for a* census *of 12* denarii Parisiensium.

A. Cartulary of Prémontré, fol. 66v.
B. Original not found.

NO RUBRIC. LATER ADDITION.

Universis presentes litteras inspecturis officialis Suessionensis salutem in Domino. Noverint universi quod coram fideli mandato nostro, videlicet Colardo de Cuffres, curie Suessionensis notario jurato, ad hec et consimilia a vobis deputato cuy fidem in et aliis maioribus indubiam adhibemus propter hoc personaliter constituti, Johannes dictus Cosses de Vilaribus juxta Clamecy et Maria, eius uxor, et specialiter dicta Maria de auctoritate, assensu et licensia dicti mariti sui quatinus ad subsequencia sibi prestantis recognoverunt et confessi fuerunt sua sponte legitime se ad annuam et perpetuum censum recipisse et accepisse a religiosis viris abbati et conventui Premonstratensibus quandam peciam terre harabilis in Savardum proprie hereditarie dicte ecclesie, sitam in Treffondo et territorio de Clamecy, in loco qui dicitur Engencier, continentem duodecim sextarios vel circiter contiguam ex uno latere vinee Gilonis de Bona et ex alio latere bosco Radulphi dicti Martin, prout se comportant et extendunt tenendos, habendos, excollandos, spoliandos et pacifice possidendos exnunc et in perpetuum a dictis conjugibus eorumque heredibus et successoribus et ab eis super hoc causam habentibus et habituris in futurum tanquam suam propriam, pacifice et quiete, mediantibus duodecim denariis Parisiensibus supracensus ex nunc et in perpetuum reddendis et solvendis nomine et perpetuo supracense dictis religiosis et quorum ecclesie aut eorum certo mandato seu etiam deputato ab eisdem quolibet anno ad Festum Sancti Martini hiemalis et una ad hoc predicti conjuges acquittabunt dominos Treffondales locy; voluerunt etiam dicti conjuges et in hoc se consentierunt quod, si contigeret, quod absit, ipsos defficere in solutione dictorum duodecim denariorum Parisiensium et acquitatione dicte terre vel dictam terram

1 Likely Cuffies, cant. Soissons, https://dicotopo.cths.fr/places/P52401664.
2 Vuillery, cant. Vailly, https://dicotopo.cths.fr/places/P30143836.
3 Clamecy, cant. Vailly, https://dicotopo.cths.fr/places/P24475745.

dimiterre in Savardum seu ex quacumque causa qua eidem religiosi possint et valeant reintrare et recipere dictam terram tanquam suam heredibus et successoribus causa labore seu chevagio in dicta causa seu alio quoquomodo et propremissis firmiter tenendis, solvendis, adimplendis dicti conjuges se heredes successores que suos ac omnia bona sua omnia et singula mobilia et inmobilia presentia et futura quecumque bonaque heredes et successores jure quicumque specialiter obligarunt et obligare super hoc corporaliter prestita et specialiter dicta Maria, de auctoritate assensu et lissensia dicti mariti sui, dictos duodecim denarios Parisienses predictos ad diem festivitatis Sancti Martini hyemalis nomine et perpetuo supracense dictis religiosis quolibet anno reddere et solvere et dictam peciam terre erga dictos dominos Treffondales locy quolibet anno et acquittare de omnibus reddibentiis, ut est dictum se et sua quantum ad hoc jurisdictione curie Suessionensis supponentes et renunciaverunt dicti conjuges in hoc facto penitus et expresse sub dicta fide sua et specialiter dicta Maria auctoritate qua supra omnibus exceptionibus doli, mali, fury, fraudis, lesionis, deceptionis et conventionis rey ita non geste juridictiony generalem renunciationem non valere exceptioni per quam subvenitur decepet ultra mediam partem iusti precii beneficio Vellyani et epistole dimidiani omni juri in favorem mulierum introducto omnibus graciis a quocumque principe impetratis et impetrandis et omnibus aliis exceptionibus, creationibus, cavillationibus et allegationibus tam juris quam facti que contra presens instrumentum possent abicy sive dicy ad destruendum premissa vel aliqua de premissis. In cuius rei testimonium hiis presentibus litteris sigilli curie Suessionensis duximus apponendum. Datum anno Domini millesimo CCC^{mo} quadragesimo quarto, die sabbaty post Ramos Palmarum.

Careat sigilli Colardus de Cuffres.

262

July, 1209.

Aymard,[1] *bishop of Soissons, mediates a dispute between Prémontré and the parish priest of Bieuxy*[2] *concerning certain tithes at Bieuxy, dependent on the Premonstratensian house of Valpriez.*[3]

A. Cartulary of Prémontré, fol. 66v.

B. Original not found.

1 Aymard de Provins, perhaps a descendant of the vicecomital family of Provins, was first a canon and cantor of Reims, and then bishop of Soissons, 1207–19. Bourquelot, *Histoire de Provins*, vol. 1, 217.

2 Bieuxy, cant. Vic-sur-Aisne, https://dicotopo.cths.fr/places/P16618416.

3 Valpriez, comm. Bieuxy, https://dicotopo.cths.fr/places/P64500821.

NO RUBRIC. LATER ADDITION.

In[4] nomine sancte et individue Trinitatis. Ego Haymuldus, Dei gratia Suessionensis episcopus omnibus in perpetuum. Notum facimus universis tam presentibus quam futuris quod querelam que inter ecclesiam Premonstratensem et presbiterum de Buici agitabatur pro decimis, coram nobis terminavimus et talis erat: prefatus presbiter decimam obtinere volebat in quadam partione terre dependentis a domo Vauldeperiers, pertinentis ad dictam ecclesiam Premonstratensem; fratres vero Premonstratenses hanc domum Vauldeperiers cum suis appendiciis sibi fuisse collatam in elemosinam sub obligatione qua obligabantur celebrare annuatim universarium et ultra mediam partem decimam de Buici sibi fuisse collatam a multis annis legitimorum testium assertionibus affirmabant. Inde est quod dicti querelam facientes me elegerint in arbitrium ut dictam querelam terminarem; assumptis igitur nobiscum religiosis et prudentibus discretisque personis atque auditis ex utraque parte rationibus ordinabimus et statuimus quod dicti fratres libere et pacifice gauderent hinc et in futurum dicta domo cum suis appenditiis et omnibus decimis tam grossis quam minutis cum pacto quod ultra non quererent decimas de Buici sed ipse presbiter libere et pacifice eas possideret et dicti querelam facientes hoc concordatum et pactum voluntarie acceptaverint et gratum habuerint. Testes sunt: Wirembaldus[5] monachus et propositus Sancti Crispini, Nivello prepositus, Engelbertus et Walterus Normanus presbiter, Reinoldus[6] miles de Terni,[7] Wilbertus de Sorni et ut hoc pactum et concordatum, ratum permaneat, sigilli nostri fecimus impressione muniri. Actum mense julio, anno dominice incarnationis M° CC° nono.

263

1182[1]

Abbot Hugues [II],[2] together with prior Eustache, subprior Roger, and the chapter of Prémontré, acknowledged that Thierry[3] de Beaurieux gave all his

---

4 The first word is preceded by a cross.

5 A *Wirembaldus* is also attested as prior of the Benedictine abbey of Saint-Crépin-le-Grand de Soissons in 1173. Lalanne, *Le cartulaire de Valpriez, 1135–1250*, 43.

6 A *Reinoldus miles de Terni* also appears as a witness in an 1173 act of Enguerrand, abbot of Saint-Médard de Soissons. Ibid.

7 Terny-et-Sorny, cant. Vailly, https://dicotopo.cths.fr/places/P98869464.

---

1 The copy of this act in the Valpriez cartulary dates it to 1182.

2 Hugues II de Douai, abbot of the Premonstratensian abbey of Cuissy, 1161–5, and abbot of Prémontré, 1174–89. *MP* II, 497.

3 Thierry, knight of Beaurieux (cant. Craonne, https://dicotopo.cths.fr/places/P20238442), attested ca. 1189–ca. 1210. Melleville, *DH*, vol. 1, 87.

tithe from land at Bieuxy[4] *to Prémontré in return for an annual payment of five* modii *of grain (*frumentum*). Adèle, his wife, and Albert, his son, consent, as do lord and lady Louis*[5] *[de Fressancourt] and Havide.*

A. Cartulary of Prémontré, fol. 66v.

B. Original not found.

Other Manuscript Copies: Cartulary of Valpriez, AD Aisne, H 753, fols. 12r–13r (13th c.).

EDITION: Lalanne, *Le cartulaire de Valpriez*, 37–8; *Chartae Galliae*, no. 211372, http://telma.irht.cnrs.fr/outils/chartae-galliae/charte211372/.

NO RUBRIC. LATER ADDITION.

Ego Hugo Dei gratia abbas, Eustachius prior, Rogerus supprior, et totum capitulum Premonstrati omnibus imperpetuum. Notum sit omnibus tam futuris quam presentibus quod Theodericus, miles de Belruco, assensu Adeline, uxoris sue, et Albrici, filii eius et domini Ludovici a quo tenebat et Hawidis, uxoris eiusdem Ludovici, totam decimam suam tam in blado quam in vino et ceteris omnibus ad decimam pertinentibus quam in territorio de Buici habebat, tractum etiam sicut ipse habere solebat et hautonnum et croinum et quicquid juris in eadem decima ad cum pertinebat ecclesie Premonstrati in perpetuum concessit, pro quod ecclesia predicta debet eidem Theoderico et heredi eius singulis annis dare quinque modios bladi quorum due partes hyemalis, tercia erit avene, ita etiam quod eidem hyemalis due partes ad minus frumentum tercia pars siligo esse debebit. Preterea sex aissinos pise eidem Theoderico et sex aissinos frumenti Sancte Marie Noienti singulis annis persolvet ecclesia Premonstrati de eadem decima. Erit autem mensura huius trecensus solvendi mensura Suessionensis currens tempore quo scriptum istud factum fuit. Si vero super eadem decima aliquis ecclesiam Premonstratensem vexaverit idem Theodericus in omnibus curiis garandiam octroyi legitimam feret, accipietur autem trecensus isto in domo nostra de Valledeperriers[6] et usque ad festum Sancti Andree solvetur et propriis ipsius Theoderici sive heredis eius vecturis ducetur nec ultra terminum illum, nisi de voluntate nostra fuerit, custodire tenebimur. Quod si postmodum aliquid de blado illo deperiret ecclesia non responderet ei. Huius rei testes sunt: dominus Hugo[7] de Martimont, Simon[8] de Sancto Medardo, Guerricus de Choisi, Philippus[9] Corsez et Robertus frater eius. Actum est hoc anno ab incarnatione Domini […][10]

4 Bieuxy, cant. Vic-sur-Aisne, https://dicotopo.cths.fr/places/P16618416.

5 Louis, lord of Fressancourt (cant. La Fère, https://dicotopo.cths.fr/places/P95117467), son of Pierre II, lord of Fressancourt. Melleville, *DH*, vol. 1, 410; Barthélemy, *LDA*, 173.

6 Valpriez, comm. Bieuxy, https://dicotopo.cths.fr/places/P64500821.

7 Hugues de Martimont appears as a witness in two acts of Conon, count of Soissons, 1178–80. Newman, *Seigneurs*, vol. 1, 167, 171.

8 Simon, lord of Saint-Mard? Melleville, *DH*, vol. 2, 74.

9 Philippe and Robert Cosset, son of Robert Cosset de Coucy. Newman, *Seigneurs*, vol. 2, 119–20.

10 Further text in this act is lost due to cropping of the folio and/or wear.

TABLE OF CONTENTS: SOISSONS

A. Cartulary of Prémontré, fol. 67r.

Incipiunt scripta possessionum ~~nostrarum~~ ecclesie Premonstratensis in episcopatu Suessionensis.

I Karta Joisleni episcopi de domo Suessionis.

II Karta Lisiardi episcopi Suessionensis de confirmatione elemosine Yvonis.

III Karta episcopi Suessionensis de elemosina Yvonis et Helvidis uxoris eius de vinea Perrisselle de Suessionensis.

IIII Karta Haimardi episcopi Suessionensis de permutatione quarundam vinearum inter Hugonem Aguillonem et ecclesiam Premonstratensem.

V Karta episcopi Suessionensis de elemosina Yvonis de Cathena et domo.

VI Karta episcopi Suessionensis de elemosina Ernaudi de Cathena et uxoris eius.

VII Karta episcopi Suessionensis de elemosina Matildis uxoris Berardi de Porta super quibusdam vineis.

VIII Karta episcopi Suessionensis de permutatione quarundam vinearum et vinagii.

IX Karta decani Suessionensis et capituli de compositione inter nos et ipsos.

X Karta decani Remensis et Suessionensis de quarundam conpositione inter ecclesiam Premonstratensis et Radulphum de Vauresio.

XI Karta Yvonis comitis Suessionensis de confirmatione doni et elemosine tam sue quam predecessorum suorum.

XII Karta episcopi Silvanectensis de confirmatione cuiusdam terre apud Suessionensem.

XIII Item carta Silvanectensis episcopi de confirmatione elemosine sue quam fecit ecclesie Premonstratensi.

XIIII Item karta eiusdem episcopi de vinea quam abbatis et conventus Premonstratensis concesserunt tenendam Nicholao ad vitam suam tantum.

XV Karta de quadam quitatione facta coram officialis Suessionensis.

XVI Karta officialis Suessionensis de eo quod Oda nobilis mulier devestivit se de dote sua coram nobis.

XVII Karta episcopi Suessionensis de venditione dimidii modii frumenti quam fecit Helvidis relicta Philipi ecclesie Premonstratensis.

XVIII Karta Silvanectensis episcopi de elemosina quorundam vinagiorum.

XIX Karta Radulfi comitis Suessionensis de elemosina domine Ade comitisse.

XX Karta archidiaconi Suessionensis de elemosina Symonis Albi de Ponte Sancti Medardi.

XXI Compositio inter ecclesiam Premonstratensis et Rogerum le Champanois.

XXII Karta de vinea Godefridi Cordeonarii.

XXIII Karta archidiaconi Suessionensis de elemosina Aelidis file Bernardi.

XXIIII Karta Jacobi thesaurarii Suessionensis terris Berengarii.

XXV Karta Suessionensis episcopi super quinque solidis nigrorum censualibus per conpositus.

XXVI Karta Garneri maioris archidiaconi Suessionensis de quadam compositione.

XXVII Karta de vinea de Boouton.

XXVIII Karta archidiaconi Suessionensis de elemosina Baiheri civis Suessionensis.

XXIX Karta Johannis comitis Suessionensis de confirmatione possessionum in episcopatu et etiam innovatione kartarum quas predecessores sui concesserunt ecclesie Premonstratensis.

Littera baillive episcopi Suessionensis de venditionibus domus contigue Stupis in loco qui dicitur En Bouton quam emit.[1]

264

1142

Joscelin,[1] *bishop of Soissons, cedes to abbot Hugues [I]*[2] *and the church of Prémontré a piece of land in front of Saint-Rémi; this land is to be used to construct a house free of* rotagium, foragium, *or* vinagium, *though the bishopric reserves the right of* justicia *and rights over merchants.*

A. Cartulary of Prémontré, fol. 67r.

B. Original, AD Aisne, H 825, previously sealed with a double strip of parchment.

REGISTER: Jacquemin, "Annales de la vie de Joscelin de Vierzi, 57e évêque de Soissons," 87.

Karta episcopi Suessoniensis de domo nostra eiusdem ville.

[I]n nomine sancte et individue Trinitatis, amen.[3] Goslenus, Dei patientia Suessorum vocatus episcopus, Hugoni, eiusdem gratia Premonstratensis ecclesie venerabili abbati, omnibusque successoribus eius canonice substituendis in perpetuum. Pontificalis amplitudinis est pauperum Deo servientium angustias dilatare

1 This entry is a later addition and a reference to **294**.

1 Joscelin de Vierzy, a *magister* at Bourges who was later bishop of Soissons, 1126–52.

2 Hugues I de Fosses (ca. 1093–1164), first abbot of Prémontré.

3 *Om.* amen *B*.

et in quibus inquietantur emendantis eorum quieti diligenter providere. Ea propter Hugo, abbas, fili karissime, tibi et Premonstratensi ecclesie cui Deo auctore prees, in posterum previdendo terram extra cathenam[43] ante Sanctum Remigium que in manu dominica nobis venerat ad mansionem statuendam tibi et posteris tuis in perpetuum ita contulimus ut nec ego nec aliquis successorum meorum episcoporum a fratribus religionis tue rotagium vel foragium sive vinagium in eternum accipiat. Verum consuetudines mercatorum inibi vendentium vel ementium et omnes justicias et infractiones terre episcopali sedi hac intentione retinuimus ut fratres religionis tue sub episcopali tutela quietius vivant et mali homines mansionem illam infringere vel aliquibus modis vexare vereantur qui vero eandem terram ante tenuerant ex habundanti eam prefate ecclesie fratribus concesserunt. Si qua igitur ecclesiastica secularisve persona hanc nostre auctoritatis paginam temere perturbare, minuere aut omnino inmutare temptaverit secundo terciove admonita nisi emendaverit ecclesiastica animadversione feriatur. Actum anno incarnati verbi M° C° XLII°, episcopatus vero nostri anno septimo decimo.[44] Signum mei ipsius Josleni,[45] episcopi. S. Brunonis,[46] Nongentine ecclesie abbatis. S. Theobaldi,[47,48] archidiaconi. S. Johannis, capellani. S. Hugonis de Marinis, canonici.

265

1124

*Lisiard,[1] bishop of Soissons, confirms the gift made by husband and wife Yves and Helvide, residents of Soissons, of their persons and all they possess in houses, vineyards, wine presses, and other things, to Norbert [of Xanten] and the brothers of the church of Prémontré. (See **268**.)*

A. Cartulary of Prémontré, fols. 67r–67v.

B. Original, AD Aisne, H 825.

EDITION: Le Paige, *Bibliotheca*, 457; Grauwen, "Twee onuitgegeven oorkonden over Norbert van Gennep," 286–7.

REGISTER: Bréquigny, *Table chronologique*, vol. 2, 526; Grauwen, "Lijst van oorkonden waarin Norbertus wordt genoemd," 146–7.

---

4 catenam *B*.

5 X° VII° *B*.

6 Gosleni *B*.

7 Bruno, abbot of the Benedictine abbey of Nogent-sous-Coucy, 1138–bef. 1157. *GC* IX, col. 607.

8 Teobaldi *B*.

9 Thibaut, archdeacon of Soissons, ca. 1122–ca. 1149. Newman, *Seigneurs*, vol. 1, 110, 115.

---

1 Lisiard de Crépy, son of Adam le Riche, lord of Nanteuil-le-Hardouin and castellan of Crépy, was bishop of Soissons, 1108–26.

Karta Lisiardi episcopi Suessonensis de confirmatione elemosine Yvonis.

In nomine sancte et individue Trinitatis. Ego Lisiardus Dei gratia Suessorum episcopus. Congratulandum nobis est et omnibus fidelibus, quoniam ea que promisit Deus omnia derelinquentibus et ipsum sequentibus, videlicet centuplum pro hiis[2] accipiendum et vitam eternam possidendam, etiam absque eo quod intrinsecus latet, iam in exterioribus ex parte impleri videmus. Ad servos enim Dei omnia derelinquentes et Christum sequentes ardenter concurritur eisque a bonis fidelibus bona et rerum suarum precia quasi ad pedes ponuntur, ut hiis[3] quibus est cor unum et anima una,[4] serviant et secundum illam apostolicam vitam unicuique, prout opus fuerit, distribuuntur. Notum igitur fieri volumus tam futuris quam presentibus quod Ivo, quidam parrochianus noster et civis, cum religiosa uxore sua, Helvide, divinitus affectus ut se et prolem suam suaque omnia Christo traderent; in presentia nostra sub testimonio personarum multarum in domo nostra episcopali reddiderunt se et sua[5] et quicquid possidebant tam in domibus quam in vineis, torcularibus et ceteris omnibus in manus domini Norberti, venerabilis et religiosi viri, et fratrum Premonstratensis[6] ecclesie. Hec autem in conspectu nostro ideo facta sunt ut maiorem evidentiam et firmitatem haberent. Nos itaque episcopali auctoritate sanctimus[7] et sub excommunicationis districtione confirmamus ne quisquam in perpetuum aliquid horum Premonstratensis[8] ecclesie auferre presumat, que eidem loco amore Deo ibidem servientium vidimus divina inspiratione conferri presentibus et nobiscum inde Deo gratias agentibus multis et magnis personis quorum nomina[9] duximus apponi. Signum Lisiardi, episcopi Suessionensis.[10] S. Bartholomei, Laudunensis episcopi et ceteri.[11] Actum[12] anno incarnationis dominice M°C°XX° IIII°, indictione III[a], epacta XIIII[a], concurrente III°.

2 his *B*.

3 his *B*.

4 Acts 4:32.

5 *Add.* et sua *A*.

6 Premonstrate *B*.

7 sancimus *B*.

8 Premonstrate *B*.

9 *Om.* dignum *A*.

10 *Add.* Suessionensis *A*.

11 *Add.* et ceteri *A*; S. Ansculfi, Suessionensis archidiaconi. S. Petri archidiaconi. Signum Ebali. S. Waleranni prepositi. S. Bernardi. S. Johannis sacerdotis. S. Engelberti, levite. S. Walteri, levite. S. Wiardi. S. Odonis. S. Theodorici. S. Herberti. S. Bernardi. S. Benedicti. S. Reinaldi, villici. S. Roberti, vicecomitis. S. Hatonis *B*.

12 *Add.* actum *A*.

266

1126–41[1]

Joscelin,[2] bishop of Soissons, confirms a gift that husband and wife Yves and Helvide made to the church of Prémontré upon entering the community there together with their unnamed sons. Joscelin also confirms gifts of more than a dozen other inhabitants of the town of Soissons, some of whom are related to Yves and Helvide. (See ***269, 289****.)*

A. Cartulary of Prémontré, fol. 67v.
B. Original, AD Aisne, H 825, previously sealed with a double strip of parchment.

Karta episcopi Suessoniensis de elemosina Yvonis et Helvidis uxoris eius de vinea Perrisselle.

[I]n nomine sancte et individue Trinitatis. Goslenus, Dei patientia Suessorum vocatus episcopus, Hugoni, eiusdem gratia Premonstratensium venerabili abbati, omnibusque successoribus eius canonice substituendis in perpetuum. Noverint omnes tam futuri quam presentes quod Yvo[3] Suessionensis et Helvidis uxor eius et eorum filii in Premonstratensi[4] ecclesia se et sua Deo obtulerunt et quicquid in prefata urbe habuerunt, litteris et sigillo domini Lisiardi, episcopi predecessoris mei, subsignatis testibus legitimis[5] conscripserunt. Nos vero tam eorum beneficia quam ceterorum fidelium in urbe nostra prefate ecclesie de Premonstrato fideliter collata litteris pariter et sigillo nostro sepefacte ecclesie[6] anathematis innodatione apposita confirmamus: vineam videlicet de Perroissella quam predictus Yvo[7] dedit in alodio. Quedam vero particula eiusdem vinee extra alodium solvit VI denarios census et quatuor deneratas cere. Dedit et vineam de Longuel pro qua solvitur modius unas et XVII sexteria et una gallina; vineam quoque de quarterum dedit solventem VI sextaria, vineam etiam in vivario que solvit dimidium

1 Joscelin de Vierzy was bishop of Soissons from 1126, and a gift made in this act is referenced in **271** dated 1141.
2 Joscelin de Vierzy, a *magister* at Bourges who was later bishop of Soissons, 1126–52.
3 Ivo *B*.
4 Premonstrata *B*.
5 *Transp. A*; legitimis testibus *B*.
6 *Om.* fratribus *A*.
7 Ivo *B*.

modium vini et gallinam unam, vineamque ad clos solventem XXXIX sextaria. Ernaudus de Cathena dedit eidem ecclesie vineam suam de Perroissella totam in alodio.[8]

Gislebertus, conversus qui vocabatur Escos,[9] vineam Perroisele[10] contiguam que solvit modium vini et gallinam unam. Matildis,[11] quondam uxor Berardi de Porta Episcopi, vineam in Laceveriis que solvit XVI sextaria et vineam in Larricio solventem XI sextaria vineamque de Mariun que solvit XV sextaria et dimidium. Dedit etiam ipsa Matildis[12] et Walterus clericus, filius eius, vineam de Warino que solvit XII sextaria, Ascelina,[13] soror Matildis,[14] masuram ad portam episcopi quam abbas et fratres commutaverunt Lisiardo, nepoti eius, pro vinea de Fossa. Lisiardus vero postea vineam suam de Savarz fratribus obtulit et vineam de Fossa recepit; hec itaque vinea de Savarz solvit modium vini et XVIII sextaria et gallinam unam et obolum; Gonfridus, qui dicitur Escos,[15] ad clos de Valbuin vineam que solvit XVI sextaria et unam gallinam et plantam ad pressorium de Baheta que solvit duos[16] nummos et medietatem eiusdem pressorii; Ivo, filius Ade, plantam ad fontem Ermengardis que solvit XVIII sextaria et unam gallinam; Manasses de Novo Vico vineam ad Bahetam que solvit VI sextaria et aliam ad Sanctum Crispinum que solvit XIII sextaria et unam gallinam; Huldeburs et Helvidis, soror eius, vineam ad Boetun[17] que solvit sex[18] sextaria et sex[19] nummos; Hugo, filius Erchenoldi, vineam ad Monmoilum[20] que solvit modium et III sextaria et unam gallinam; Amisardus de Cathena vineam ad Monmoilum[21] que solvit VI sextaria; Johannes Manez, vineam ad Escorcheveel que solvit IIII sextaria et dimidium; Natalis, frater Rogeri carpentarii plantam ad Macerias de Cufies[22] que solvit XXIII sextaria et vineam in Ameci.

8 This line break in the cartulary is also reflected in the original charter.
9 Escoz *B*.
10 Perroissele *B*.
11 Mathildis *B*.
12 Mathildis *B*.
13 Aszelina *B*.
14 Mathildis *B*.
15 Escoz *B*.
16 II *B*.
17 Boetum *B*.
18 VI *B*.
19 VI *B*.
20 Monmoilun *B*.
21 Monmoilun *B*.
22 Cufieiis *B*.

267

March 26, 1213.

Aymard,[1] *bishop of Soissons, gives notice of the exchange of vineyards between the church of Prémontré and Hugues Aguillon, a* civis *of Soissons.*

A. Cartulary of Prémontré, fols. 67v–68r.

B. Original, AD Aisne, H 825, sealed on green silk laces with a fragment of the seal in red wax.

Karta Haimardi episcopi Suessoniensis de permutatione quorundam vinearum inter Hugonem Aguillonem et ecclesiam Premonstratensem.

[E]go Haimardus,[2] Dei gratia dictus Suessionensis episcopus, omnibus in perpetuum. Notum facimus universis presentibus et futuris quod inter ecclesiam Premonstratensem et Hugonem Aguillon,[3] civem Suessionensem, talis quarumdam vinearum permutatio de assensu mutuo facta fuit et recognita coram nobis: ecclesia siquidem Premonstratensis vineam dicti Hugonis que est ad portam domus Premonstrati que dicitur Sancti Remigii, liberam ab aliena justicia et redditu in perpetuam hereditatem tenebit et ipse Hugo vineam quam habebat ecclesia Premonstrati in Ponvert,[4] sub ea consuetudine qua eam primitus tenebat ecclesia, similiter hereditarie possidebit et tam ipse Hugo ecclesie quam ecclesia ei super alterutra vinea portabunt ad invicem legitimam garandiam. Quod ut ratum sit et bona fide contracta permutatio stabilis habeatur perpetuo[5] presentem cartulam in memoriam et testimonium eiusdem permutationis confectam ad petitionem partium sigilli nostri munimine duximus roborandam. Actum in crastino Annuntiationis dominice intrante, anno gracie M° CC°[6] tertio decimo.

1 Aymard de Provins, perhaps a descendant of the vicecomital family of Provins, was first a canon and cantor of Reims, and then bishop of Soissons, 1207–19. Bourquelot, *Histoire de Provins*, vol. 1, 217.

2 Haymardus *B*.

3 Aguyllon *B*.

4 A *lieu-dit* on the Aisne where there was a bridge on the Roman road from Soissons to Amiens. Pécheur, "Noms des lieux mentionnés dans le cartulaire de Saint-Léger," 375.

5 *Transp. A*; perpetuo habeatur *B*.

6 millesimo ducentesimo *B*.

268

1149

Joscelin,[1] *bishop of Soissons, recounts the conditions agreed to concerning the entry of husband and wife Yves de Chaine and Helvide into Prémontré, together with their two sons and a daughter, and confirms an additional transaction which took place after Yves's death between Prémontré and Lisiard de Chaine in which two houses were exchanged for half of a vineyard. Helvide and Renaud, son of Yves and Helvide, confirm this transaction. (See* ***265****.)*

A. Cartulary of Prémontré, fols. 68r–68v.

B. Original, AD Aisne, H 761, previously sealed.

EDITION: Le Paige, *Bibliotheca*, 457–8 (partial).

REGISTER: Jacquemin, "Annales de la vie de Joscelin de Vierzi, 57e évêque de Soissons," 84–5, 125.

Karta episcopi Suessoniensis de elemosina Yvonis de Cathena et domo sua de Cathena.

[I]n nomine sancte et individue Trinitatis. Quoniam memorie hominum que facile labitur, plerumque temporum vetustas id quod minus caute agitur subripere consuevit, majorum sollers industria utilitati previdens posterorum rerum gestarum seriem literarum apicibus conservandam annotari decrevit. Quorum vestigia subsequutus nec ab eorum rectitudine discrepans. Ego Joislenus,[2] Dei gratia Suessorum episcopus, notum fieri volo tam futuris quam presentibus quod Yvo[3] de Cathena, voce veritatis anmonitus et unctione, omnibus que possidebat abrenuntians, in Premonstratensis[4] ecclesia quam plurimum dilexit, cum uxore sua et duobus filiis et filia iter religionis arripiens, Deo se serviturum devotus obtulit et, ut in numero trium virorum illorum quos solos Ezechiel[5,6] salvandos denuntiat, mereretur, aggregari sub Domini jugo, quod leve credidit, et suave voluit et didicit humiliari dedit itaque in elemosinam Premonstrate ecclesie ob remedium anime sue et uxoris sue et infantum et predecessorum suorum domum suam apud Cathenam cum hospitibus domui adjacentibus persolventibus annuatim XIIII[cim] solidos

1 Joscelin de Vierzy, a *magister* at Bourges who was later bishop of Soissons, 1126–52.

2 Goslenus *B*.

3 Ivo *B*.

4 Premonstrata *B*.

5 Iezechiel *B*.

6 Ezekiel 14:4.

obolum minus et sex[7] gallinas et domum unam altera parte vie subtus murum episcopi. Dedit preterea eidem ecclesie vineam unam sex arpennorum in alodio, que dicitur Petrosilla, et vineam alteram juxta Petrosillam solventem singulis annis IIII^or[8] nummatas cere thesaurario Beati Gervasii in die festivitatis eiusdem. Dedit etiam juxta vineam predictam, vineam aliam que dicitur Fortis Terra solventem singulis annis sex[9] denarios ecclesie Sancti Johannis et vineam Longuel[10] et torcularia juxta vineam et medietatem cuiusdam vinee ad Albanum, que dicitur Clausus, et vineam alteram, que dicitur Vivarius et campum unum in Pratella[11] in alodio et duos[12] sextarios vinatii in Brueriis et vineam unam in Couciaco[13] altera parte Longoil. Preterea dedit eidem ecclesie Helvidis, uxor eiusdem Yvonis, et Ascelina, soror predicte Helvidis, partes suas quas habebant apud Buciacum[14] in vinea quadam, que dicitur Daufoiart. Dedit etiam prefate ecclesie Gislebertus, nepos predicti Yvonis,[15] vineam unam subtus Petrosillam, que dicitur vinea Berneri. Actum est anno incarnationis dominice M° CC° XX° IIII°, epacta XXIII^a indictione III^a, concurrente III°, sicut in privilegio domini Lisiardi, predecessoris nostri, continetur.[16,17]

Optata vero diu et adepta religionis tranquillitate potitus, predictus Yvo[18] in consortio fratrum ibidem Deo servientium per aliquot annos laudabiliter conversatus de bono, ut credimus, inicio prosperos consecutus est exitus. Post decessum vero illius fratres Premonstrate ecclesie domum eiusdem Yvonis[19] cum hospitibus, ut supradictum est, domui adjacentibus et domum predictam subtus murum episcopi pro medietate cuiusdam vinee ad Albanum, que Clausus dicitur, cuius iam medietatem a predicto Yvone[20] in elemosinam acceperant, Lisiardo de Cathena commutaverunt. Et ut ista commutatio rata et certior haberetur in presentia nostra confirmaverunt. Postea ex petitione abbatis et

---

7 VI *B*.

8 quatuor *B*.

9 VI *B*.

10 Longoil *B*.

11 Presles, cant. Braine, https://dicotopo.cths.fr/places/P12121690.

12 II^os *B*.

13 Cociaco *B*.

14 Busciacum *B*.

15 Ivonis *B*.

16 Sub his testibus: S. Lisiardi episcopi. S. Bartholomei episcopi. S. Ansculfi archidiaconi. S. Petri, archidiaconi. S. Ebali. S. Waleranni, prepositi. S. Bernardi. S. Johannis, sacerdotis. S. Engelberti et Walteri, diaconorum. S. Wiardi. S. Odonis. S. Theoderici. S. Herberti. S. Berardi. S. Benedicti. Sig. Reinaldi, villici. S. Roberti, vicecomitis. S. Hatonis *B*.

17 This line break in the cartulary is also reflected in the original charter.

18 Ivo *B*.

19 Ivonis *B*.

20 Ivone *B*.

fratrum Premonstrate ecclesie et rogatu Helvidis, uxoris predicti Yvonis[21] et Renaldi,[22] filii eorum, a nobis innovatum et confirmatum est. Anno dominice incarnationis M° C° XL° IX°, epacta IX[a], indictione XII[a], concurrente V°. Sub his testibus: S. Ansculphi[23,24] prepositi. S. Nivelonis[25] archidiaconi et ceteri.[26] Ut autem presens scriptum firmitatis[27] robur obtineat, sigilli nostri auctoritate muniri precepimus prohibentes ne qua ecclesiastica secularisve persona hoc nostre institutionis decretum violare vel temerare presumat. Quod si fecerit, secundo terciove anmonita, nisi digne satisfecerit, anathemati subjacet. Ego Normannus, decanus et cancellarius, subscripsi.

269

1142

*Joscelin,[1] bishop of Soissons, makes known that husband and wife Ernaud de Chaine and Sibille gave to the church of Prémontré their vineyard called Perroiselle with the consent of their unnamed sons. (See **266**, **289**.)*

A. Cartulary of Prémontré, fol. 68v.

B. Original, AD Aisne, H 825, previously sealed with a double strip of parchment.

REGISTER: Jacquemin, "Annales de la vie de Joscelin de Vierzi, 57e évêque de Soissons," 87.

Karta episcopi Suessionensis de elemosina Ernaudi de Cathena et uxoris eius Sibille.

[I]n nomine sancte et individue Trinitatis. Goslenus, Dei patientia Suessorum vocatus episcopus, Hugoni, eiusdem gratia Premonstratensium[2] venerabili

21 Ivonis *B*.

22 Reinaldi *B*.

23 Ansculfi *B*.

24 Anscoul de Pierrefonds, son of Nivelon II, lord of Pierrefonds, and Hawide (de Montmorency?), was archdeacon of Soissons, 1101–25/9, *prepositus* of Soissons, 1129–52, and bishop of Soissons, 1152–8.

25 Nivelon I, archdeacon of Soissons, ca. 1129–ca. 1181. Newman, *Seigneurs*, vol. 1, 110, 115.

26 *Add* et ceteri, *A*; S. Radulfi archidiaconi. S. Willelmi archidiaconi. S. Johannis capellani. S. Rohardi, Harduini, Ingelberti, sacerdotum. S. Hathonis, Albrici, Crispin, diaconorum. S. Radulfi, Herluini, Galteri, subdiaconorum. S. Anselli de Septem Montibus. S. Widonis de Billiaco. S. Lisiardi de Porta. S. Philippi filii Wineberti *B*.

27 *Add.* scriptum firmitatis *A*; carte inviolatum *B*.

1 Joscelin de Vierzy, a *magister* at Bourges who was later bishop of Soissons, 1126–52.

2 Premonstratensis *B*.

abbati, omnibusque successoribus eius canonice substituendis in perpetuum. Christiane religionis sancta traditio docet post baptismi sacramentum secundam peccatorum abolitionem in elemosinarum largitione constare quia, sicut aqua ignis ardorem extinguit,[3] ita iniquitatis incendium refrigerat elemosinarum temperies, precedente penitencia cum confessione. Hinc est enim quod fideles iram judicis peccatis suis exasperatam amicos sibi de Manmona iniquitatis faciendo prevenire satagunt pauperum Christi indigentiam rerum suarum stipendiis relevantes. Huius rei gratia notum fieri volo tam futuris quam presentibus quod quidam civis noster Ernaudus, videlicet de Cathena, et Sibilla, uxor eius, quandam vineam suam, que Perroissella dicitur, concedentibus filiis suis et quibus hereditas accidere debuerat, Premonstratensi[4] ecclesie contulerunt peccatorum suorum penitudine simul et filiorum suorum amore quorum alter in prefata ecclesia sepultus fuerat, alter vero inibi servitiis Dei semetipsum mancipaverat; indignum enim judicaverunt eosdem filios suos qui se pro amore celestium seculo subtraxerant, bonorum suorum temporalium exsortes omnino remanere. Hoc autem actum est anno incarnationis dominice M° C° XL° II°, episcopatus vero nostri anno X° VII°, me presente et aliis honestissimis personis: Theobaldo[5,6] archidiacono et ceteri.[7] Siquis igitur hoc nostre institutionis[8] donum temere violare presumpserit secundo vel tercio admonitus, nisi resipuerit, divine animadversioni subjaceat.

270

1149

Joscelin,[1] bishop of Soissons, makes known that Mathilde, widow of Berard de la Porte, entered the religious community of Prémontré with her unnamed daughters and with the consent of her sons, the canon Gautier and Lisiard de la Porte, and Lisiard's unnamed wife and children. She gave Prémontré certain possessions to which the sons added their own gifts, including vineyards, lands, wine presses, and houses. Lisiard's gift was made for the support of his unnamed daughter who also entered the community at Prémontré.

---

3 This phrase, inspired by Ecclesiasticus (Sirach) 3:33, appears in many twelfth-century charters.

4 Premonstrate *B.*

5 Teobaldo *B.*

6 Thibaut, archdeacon of Soissons, ca. 1122–ca. 1149. Newman, *Seigneurs*, vol. 1, 110, 115.

7 *Add.* et ceteri *A*; Johanne capellano, Albrico diacono, Hugone subdiacono canonicis, Engelranno Matifart, Die de Valbuin, Johanne de Catena *B.*

8 confirmationis *B.*

---

1 Joscelin de Vierzy, a *magister* at Bourges who was later bishop of Soissons, 1126–52.

A. Cartulary of Prémontré, fol. 68v.
B. Original, AD Aisne, H 761.[2]
REGISTER: Jacquemin, "Annales de la vie de Joscelin de Vierzi, 57e évêque de Soissons," 126.

Karta Suessionensis episcopi de elemosina Matildis uxoris Berardi de Porta super quibusdam vineis.

[I]n nomine sancte et individue Trinitatis. Quoniam hominum brevis est vita labilisque memoria, res gestas custodie commendare litterarum maiorum decrevit auctoritas. Quorum sollertiam ego, Goslenus, Dei gratia Suessorum episcopus, ex multimoda utilitate approbans, notum fieri volo tam futuris quam presentibus quod Matildis, uxor quondam Berardi de Porta, post mortem ipsius Berardi ad religionem in ecclesia Premonstratensi cum filiabus suis se contulit eis ob remedium anime sue et anime mariti sui, Berardi et animarum predecessorum suorum, annuentibus filiis suis, Waltero, canonico, et Lisiardo de Porta et uxore eius cum filiis et filiabus suis, eidem ecclesie dedit in elemosinam vineas, clausum videlicet, larricium, marium et plantam, et medietatem cuiusdam torcularis ad Behetam et vineam vallis Drogonis ad Buci[3] quoque vineam de Murval et vineam dimidium modium vini solventem in Daufoiart, mansuram et vineam de viis furcatis et vineam de Abellai. Walterus, etiam, prefate Matildis filius, dedit in elemosinam ecclesie predicte, assensu Lisiardi, fratris sui, duas vineas post decessum suum, vineam videlicet Warini et vineam Berardi solventem sex sextarios vini cum pullo Silvanectensi episcopo. Lisiardus quoque de Porta, frater Walteri, sepefacte ecclesie dedit in elemosinam pro filia sua vineam in Monmoilum juxta vineas eiusdem ecclesie. Quandam vero mansuram de elemosina Helvidis et Asceline, materterarum ipsius Lisiardi, commutavit ecclesia Lisiardo pro duabus vineis quas habebat ipse Lisiardus ad Behetas, larricium Benscelini et vineam Roberti. Ut autem presens institutio inviolatum robur obtineat, presentem kartam sigilli nostri impressione munivimus, prohibentes ne qua ecclesiastica secularisve persona aliquando eam violare presumat. Siquis vero, quod absit, eam aliquando violare presumpserit, secundo terciove anmonitus nisi digne satisfecerit anathemati subjaceat. Actum anno incarnati verbi M° C° XLIX°. Signum Ansculphi et ceteri.

2 Due to conservation concerns, the original was not available to the editors.
3 Bucy-le-Long, cant. Vailly, https://dicotopo.cths.fr/places/P35759725.

271

1141

Joscelin,[1] *bishop of Soissons, makes known that abbot Hugues [I]*[2] *and the religious of Prémontré reached an agreement with Lisiard, son of Ernaud de Chaine, according to which the Premonstratensians acquired part of a vineyard that they had possessed with Lisiard and which had originally come from Lisiard's unnamed wife's* dotalicium. *In return Lisiard and his wife accepted a house which had been previously given to the Premonstratensians by husband and wife Yves de Chaine and Helvide, and their sons, which then became part of Lisiard's wife's* dos. *(See* ***284****.)*

A. Cartulary of Prémontré, fols. 68v–69r.

B. Original (chirograph), AD Aisne, H 825, previously sealed with a double strip of parchment. In the right margin and beginning at the top, the bottom half of letters that form the word CYROGRAPHUM.

REGISTER: Jacquemin, "Annales de la vie de Joscelin de Vierzi, 57e évêque de Soissons," 82.

Karta episcopi Suessionensis de quadam permutatione vinearum et vinagiorum.

[I]n nomine sancte et individue Trinitatis. Goslenus, Dei patientia Suessorum vocatus episcopus, Hugoni, eiusdem gratia Premonstratensis ecclesie venerabili abbati, omnibusque successoribus eius canonice substituendis in perpetuum. Quoniam hominum vita brevis est labilisque memoria res gestas custodie commendare litterarum decrevit antiquitas. Notum igitur sit omnibus quod domum quam ob remedium animarum suarum Ivo et Helvidis uxor eius et ipsorum filii Premonstratensi[3] ecclesie contulerunt, abbas et fratres eiusdem ecclesie eo quod usui ipsorum atque habitationi erat inconveniens ut pote in populari frequentia constituta, Lisiardo, filio Ernaudi de Cathena, commutaverunt pro parte vinee quam cum eis habebat ad Clos, qua parte vinee uxor eius dotata erat, in cuius dotis loco prefatam domum accepit. Hec igitur vinea XX^ti^ sex[4] sextaria de vinagio debebat, Petro de Veteri Foro XIII, et Hugoni Pichet de Sancto Medardo XIII; partem Petri ecclesia persolvet, Hugonis vero partem Lisiardus redemit et in feodo recepit, pro hoc scilicet servitio semel in anno iturus ad Sanctum Medardum et ad curiam episcopi pro prefati Hugonis

1 Joscelin de Vierzy, a *magister* at Bourges who was later bishop of Soissons, 1126–52.

2 Hugues I de Fosses (ca. 1093–1164), first abbot of Prémontré.

3 Premonstrate *B*.

4 VI^sex^ *B*.

negotio, si ab eo summonitus fuerit, quod servitium ab ecclesia nunquam exigetur sed a Lisiardo et ab eius heredibus semper persolvetur. Hospites etiam quos prefatus Ivo tenuerat, ecclesia Lisiardo concessit. Hoc autem factum est sub legitimis testibus anno incarnati verbi M° C° XL° I°, episcopatus vero nostri anno sexto decimo.[5] Quod ut ratum permaneat cirographi[6] conscriptione et sigilli nostri impressione necnon et anathematis innodatione roboramus. Inde sunt testes: Ingelrannus,[7] Johannes.[8]

272

October 22, 1209. Soissons.

Dean Guy[1] *and the cathedral chapter of Soissons conclude an agreement with the church of Prémontré which permits Prémontré to hold lands and vineyards that it has acquired in the territory of Soissons for as long as it wishes, regardless of the custom of the region. However, the cathedral chapter retains certain rights over the lands and vineyards in question.*

A. Cartulary of Prémontré, fols. 69r–69v.
B. Original, AN, L 995, no. 55, previously sealed.

Karta decani Suessionensis et capituli de compositione inter nos et ipsos.

[G]uido, decanus, totumque Suessionensis matris ecclesie capitulum omnibus in perpetuum. Noverint universi presentes pariter et futuri quod cum inter ecclesiam nostram et ecclesiam Premonstratensem super terris et vineis quas in territoriis nostris acquisierat, controversia verteretur quia volebamus ut non teneret eas nisi per annum, secundum consuetudinem regionis, tandem, ad preces bonorum virorum et favore ordinis, concessimus illi[2] ut terras illas sive vineas teneret quam diu vellet, quas tunc temporis possidebat, nec eas cogeretur a nobis ulterius alienare, salvo omni jure nostro tam in decimis reddendis quam vinagiis et aliis redditibus sive justiciis seu omni alio jure quod dominis conpetere potest aut solet in talibus evenire, hoc etiam expressim addito quod

---

5 XVI° *B*.
6 cyrographi *B*.
7 *Om.* Matifarz, Diez de Valbduin *A*.
8 *Om.* filius Lamberti prepositi *A*.

---

1 Guy I de Chézy, dean of Soissons, attested 1206–12. BnF, MS lat. 5528, fols. 18v–21r, 26v–27v.
2 *Add.* illi *A*; ei *B*.

si decetero terre vel vinee vel alii redditus qui sint in territoriis nostris, ad ecclesiam Premonstratensem per elemosinam vel alio modo devenirent, non teneret eos, nec illas ultra annum nisi per nostram[3] id fieret voluntatem ecclesia vero Premonstratensis quandam modicam decimam quam tunc temporis habebat apud Buciacum,[4,5] videlicet que appellatur decima vicecomitum, concessit nobis per amorem perpetuo possidendam. Hoc igitur retento quod de vineis illis quas infra decimationem illam tunc temporis tenebat, salvo omni alio jure nostro, sicut premissum est, tantum sibi decimas retinuit quarum nomina sunt: vinea Daufaiart[6] que solvit quinque modios vinagii duobus sextariis minus, vinea De Laruele que solvit decem et octo sextarios, vinea super Ruellam que solvit quatuor sextarios et dimidium, vinea Pagani que solvit viginti duos sextarios. Et si prefate vinee ad alienam manum devenirent, nobis decime redderentur. Similiter si ad partem colonus eas coleret, pro parte coloni decimas reciperemus vinearum autem et terrarum que decimas sive redditus cum omni alio jure nostro, sicut premissum est, nobis debent; nomina sunt hec: in territorio Suessionensis vinea de Rochemont,[7] vinea de Warin, larritium[8] Walteri, vinea de Marion, vinea de Houel, vinea Parvi Houel,[9] vinea Walteri, vinea de Escot, vinea de Prebendis, clausum memorie. In territorio de Buci:[10] vinea de Escot ad torcular de Abellay, vinea d'Escot supra viam, vinea de Murval, vinea Au Treu de Marval subtus viam, vinea Osanne, masura ad viam fulcatam, vinea Hugonis le Franc, vinea ad Alnetum, vinea ad ruellam Buticularii, vinea fratris Bernardi, campus ad Ulmum, campus supra ruellam, campus super larricium. In territorio de Clameci:[11,12] vinea ad[13] clausum Willeri. Adjectum est etiam quod ecclesia Premonstratensis non potest predictas terras vel vineas dare alii ad supercensum vel super vinagium vel ad alium redditum supercrescentem et, si faceret, possemus quicquid inde fieret in irritum revocare. Quod ut ratum perpetuis temporibus et inconcussum permaneat, presentem paginam sigilli nostri munimine fecimus roborari. Datum Suessione anno dominice incarnationis M° CC° nono, undecimo kalendas novembris.

3 *Om.* expressam *A.*
4 Bucyacum *B.*
5 Bucy-le-Long, cant. Vailly, https://dicotopo.cths.fr/places/P35759725.
6 de Aufaiart *B.*
7 Rochemont, comm. Pommiers, https://dicotopo.cths.fr/places/P44489607.
8 li larris *B.*
9 Hoel *B.*
10 Bucy *B.*
11 Clamecy *B.*
12 Clamecy, cant. Vailly, https://dicotopo.cths.fr/places/P24475745.
13 *Add.* ad *A*; infra *B.*

273

1183

Ralph,[1] *dean of Reims, and Guillaume, dean of Soissons, make known the resolution of the dispute between the religious of Prémontré and the siblings of one Lisiard (Raoul de Vauxrezis,*[2] *Robert, Baudouin, Huard, and Laure) concerning the 30* librae *that Lisiard left to Prémontré as an entry gift for his sister Mathilde to be taken from the revenues of the vineyard of Rochemont and a* census *and house in the neighbourhood of Chaine.*

A. Cartulary of Prémontré, fol. 69v.

B. Original, AD Aisne, H 825, previously sealed with a double strip of parchment.

EDITION: Lohrmann, *Papsturkunden in Frankreich. Neue Folge,* vol. 7, 561–2.

Karta decani Remensis et Suessionensis de compositione inter ecclesiam Premonstratensem et Radulphum de Vauresio.

[R]adulphus,[3] decanus Remensis, et Willermus, decanus Suessionensis, omnibus ad quos littere iste pervenerint in perpetuum. Notum sit tam futuris quam presentibus quod controversie que vertebantur inter fratres Premonstratenses et Radulphum[4] de Vaureseio et fratres eius nobis a domino Papa commisse fuerunt, remoto appellationis obstaculo justo fine terminande querele quas fratres Premonstratenses habebant contra Radulphum[5] et fratres eius, hee sunt: inpetebant enim eos de XXX^{ta} libris quas Lisiardus,[6] frater predicti R[adulphi], et aliorum fratrum suorum legaverat ecclesie Premonstratensi in elemosinam et de quibusdam redditibus vini quos debebant habere predicti fratres Premonstratenses pro Matilde,[7] sorore predictorum fratrum, quam receperant in conversam. Querele vero quas predictus Radulphus et fratres eius habebant contra ecclesiam Premonstratensem hee sunt: impetebant enim iamdictos fratres Premonstratenses de vinea de Rochemont[8] et de censu et domo que sunt in vico, qui dicitur Ad Cathenam, que omnia Lisiardus,[9] quando se ipsum

1 Ralph of Sarre (in Kent, England), a former clerk of Thomas Becket's. He was dean of Reims, 1176–95/6. Falkenstein, "Radulf von Sarre als päpstlicher Delegat und seine Mitdelegaten."

2 Vauxrezis, cant. Soissons, https://dicotopo.cths.fr/places/P18820270.

3 Radulfus *B.*

4 Radulfum *B.*

5 Radulfum *B.*

6 Lysiardus *B.*

7 Mathilde *B.*

8 Rochemont, comm. Pommiers, https://dicotopo.cths.fr/places/P44489607.

9 Lysiardus *B.*

dedit fratrem ecclesie Premonstratensi, in elemosinam eidem ecclesie contulerat, quorum omnium donum et elemosinam predictus Radulphus et sui fratres nitebantur extinguere et sibi omnia usurpare. Cum autem huiusmodi querele aliquotiens in presentia nostra ventilate fuissent, tandem mediante Theodrico Froissebos[5] et aliis amicis utriusque partis, inter eos ita transactum est quod predictus Radulphus[6] et fratres sui, videlicet Robertus, Balduinus, Huardus, et Lore, soror eorum, et Radulphus,[7] maritus eius, omnes querelas quas habebant adversus prefatam ecclesiam, quitas[8] clamaverunt ipsi ecclesie et, fide interposita, concesserunt quod contra omnes legitimam warandiam ferrent, qui vellent contra ipsam ecclesiam juste experiri de predictis querelis. Fratres vero Premonstratenses similiter suas querelas predicto Radulfo et fratribus eius quietas clamaverunt et, ne processu temporis aliqua predictarum querelarum in scrupulum contentionis quandoque deveniret, predictam transactionem presenti scripto commendavimus et ipsum scriptum sigillorum nostrorum inpressione communivimus. Actum anno incarnationis dominice[9] M° C° LXXX° III°.[10]

274

1172

*Yves [II],[1] count of Soissons and lord of Nesle, with the consent of his wife Yolande[2] [de Hainaut] and his nephew and successor Conon,[3] confirms that the church of Prémontré has free and peaceful possession of all its holdings in the territories of the count of Soissons and in the demesne of the castle of Nesle.[4] (See **293**.)*

---

5 Frussebos *B.*
6 Radulfus *B.*
7 Radulfus *B.*
8 quietas *B.*
9 Domini *B.*
10 M° C° LXXXIII° *B.*

---

1 Yves II de Nesle (d. ca. 1178), lord of Nesle and count of Soissons, son of Raoul, lord of Nesle, and Raintrude. Newman, *Seigneurs*, vol. 1, 61.

2 Yolande de Hainaut (d. aft. April 1202), daughter of Baudouin IV, count of Hainaut, and Alix de Namur. Yves II de Nesle, count of Soissons, was her first husband.

3 Conon de Nesle (d. 1180), first castellan of Bruges and then count of Soissons from 1178; son of Raoul II, lord of Nesle, and Gertrude, *neptis* of Thierry, count of Flanders. Newman, *Seigneurs*, vol. 1, 63–4.

4 This act was confirmed by *vidimus* in 1236 by Jean, count of Soissons. AN L 995, no. 83.

A. Cartulary of Prémontré, fols. 69v–70r.
B. Original, AD Somme, 20 H_SC_1, no. 1.[5]
EDITION: Newman, *Seigneurs*, vol. 2, 132–3; *Chartae Galliae*, no. 212842, http://telma.irht.cnrs.fr/outils/chartae-galliae/charte212842/.

Karta Yvonis comitis Suessionensis de confirmatione doni et elemosine tam sue quam predecessorum suorum.

[I]n nomine Patris et Filii et Spiritus sancti, amen. Ego Yvo, Suessorum comes et dominus Nigelle, presentibus et futuris. Ex doctrina veritatis anmonemur seminare carnalia ut metamus spiritualia dare temporalia ut recipiamus eterna. Huius rei gratia servorum Dei beneficiis et orationibus participari cupientes et eorum meritis celestia bona promereri confidentes, utile duximus et necessarium Premonstratensem ecclesiam diligere et honorare et, quantum in nobis est, confovere ut pote quam in diebus nostris manus Domini mirifice plantavit et quam pluribus bonis honorifice ampliavit. Proinde quicquid eadem Premonstratensis ecclesia tam in ditione comitatus Suessionensis quam in dominio Castri Nigellensis, sive ex predecessorum nostrorum, sive ex nostra, sive ex hominum nostrorum donatione, usque ad annum qui subscriptus est, possedisse disnoscitur, quiete et absque ulla calumpnia perpetuo possidendum eidem ecclesie concedimus et presentis scripti attestatione posterorum noticie commendamus. Sane quedam ex hiis propriis duximus exprimenda vocabulis: in comitatu Suessionensi domum de Buci,[6] ab omni consuetudine et exactione liberam cum vineis et terris et ceteris appenditiis suis, molendinum de Rupibus,[7] cum stagno et prato adjacenti et terram Odonis leprosi, terram Berengeri de Clameciaco,[8] vineam de Biart et vineam de Parco, torcular de Phillenis, ita liberum quod nemo aliud ibi torcular possit edificare; furnum etiam de Terni[9] ita quod nemo alium ibi possit edificare in dominio Nigellensi decimam de Falevi, partem decime de Divisa,[10] decimam de Ulmercourt,[11] decimam de Chisencourt,[12] terram de Betencourt,[13] terram de Allodiis et terram de Liencourt[14] que fuit Piselli, terram de Veroile que fuit Girberti et terram de

5 Due to conservation concerns, this original was not available to the editors.
6 Bucy-le-Long, cant. Vailly, https://dicotopo.cths.fr/places/P35759725.
7 Les Roches, comm. Bucy-le-Long, https://dicotopo.cths.fr/places/P20402237.
8 Clamecy, cant. Vailly, https://dicotopo.cths.fr/places/P24475745.
9 Terny-et-Sorny, cant. Vailly, https://dicotopo.cths.fr/places/P98869464.
10 Devise, cant. Ham, https://dicotopo.cths.fr/places/P85212875.
11 Omiécourt-Montréal, cant. Nesle, https://dicotopo.cths.fr/places/P59719870.
12 Cizancourt, cant. Nesle, https://dicotopo.cths.fr/places/P70322720.
13 Likely Béthencourt-sur-Somme, cant. Nesle, https://dicotopo.cths.fr/places/P85791062.
14 Likely Liancourt-Fosse, cant. Roye, https://dicotopo.cths.fr/places/P18767836.

Greuni[15] que fuit Enmeline senescalche, terram Milonis[16] de Voiana, terram et hospites, filii Ermenrici terram Radulphi Pulcri ad Haluns[17] et septem modios frumenti annuatim ad mensuram Nigellensem apud Walli,[18] duos modios frumenti ad mensuram Nigellensem quos annuatim accipiendos sororibus de Bonolio donavimus. Hec igitur et omnia alia que prefata ecclesia hactenus tenuit, ut supradictum est, firma et illibata in perpetuum eidem ecclesie permanere, annuente Jolende comitissa, censemus et tam sigilli nostri impressione quam domini Cononis, nepotis et successoris nostri, concessione cum sigilli sui appositione et legitimorum testium annotatione munire curavimus. Testes inde sunt: Ebroinus[19] diaconus, Johannes sacerdos et ceteri. Actum est hoc et confirmatum anno incarnati verbi M° C° LXX° II°, indictione quinta, epacta XX[a] III[a], concurrente VI[a].

275

February, 1216.

Guérin,[1] *bishop of Senlis, grants to the religious of Prémontré the authorization to hold from him and his successors lands and vineyards in the demesne of the bishops of Senlis in the territory of Soissons, owing the payment of an annual* census.

A. Cartulary of Prémontré, fol. 70r.

B. Original, AN, L 995, no. 65, previously sealed with three seals.

Karta Silvanectensis episcopi de confirmatione cuiusdam terre apud Suessionensem.

[E]go Garinus, divina miseratione Silvanectensis episcopus, omnibus in perpetuum. Notum facimus tam futuris et presentibus[2] quod cum, olim vocati ad anministrationem ecclesie Silvanectensis, cognovissemus quod fratres Premonstratenses tenerent terras arabiles et vineas in territorio Suessionensi sub nostro dominio constitutas, denunciavimus eis secundum consuetudinem qua utuntur

15 Grouches, cant. Roye, https://dicotopo.cths.fr/places/P04293263.

16 Milon de Voyennes (cant. Nesle, https://dicotopo.cths.fr/places/P32215646) also appears in acts **301** and **358.**

17 Hallon, cant. Ham, https://dicotopo.cths.fr/places/P04670263.

18 Likely Wailly, cant. Roye, https://dicotopo.cths.fr/places/P28127371.

19 Ebroin, dean of Saint-Pierre-au-Parvis de Soissons, ca. 1172–ca. 1180. BnF, Coll. Moreau, vol. 81, fol. 81r; vol. 83, fols. 215r, 217r.

1 Guérin, bishop of Senlis, ca. 1213–27, and chancellor of France, 1223–7.

2 tam presentibus quam futuris *B*.

ecclesie gallicane ut venderent terras memoratas et vineas pro eo quod de ipsis tenendis capituli nostri litteras non habebant. Verum cum innotuissent[3] nobis postmodum quod dicti fratres terras et vineas illas a militis retro temporibus tenuissent et quod ecclesie Silvanectensi nec multum acquireretur si a fratribus venderentur maxime cum quedam earum laboribus et expensis agriculture, sicut dicebatur, in fructu satis tenuiter responderent; de assensu tandem capituli nostri tam in favorem religionis quam ad preces bonorum virorum sustinuimus et concessimus fratribus ipsis[4] tres campos terre arabiles, circiter octo aissinos ad mensuram Suessionensem in semine capientes, quod ad terragium tenuerant prius, ad terragium similiter a nobis et a successoribus nostris teneant in futurum. De octo autem vineis de quibus consueverant solvere predecessoribus nostris quinque modios vinagii et XV sextarios[5] et octo gallinas et sex denarios annui census, solvet nobis et successoribus nostris amodo in perpetuum annuatim quinque modios vinagii et quindecim sextarios et octo gallinas et duodecim denarios censuales illius monete que currebat Suessione tempore huius scripti, salvo nichilominus dominio nostro necnon et justicia nostra tam in vineis quam in terris. Nomina autem vinearum hec sunt: vinea de Alneto, vinea de Malmarchie, vinea de Clausello, vinea de Labaate, vinea Petri Buirete, vinea Johannis Putenfant, vinea de Cailloue,[6] vinea que dicitur Trellia Magistri Gilleberti. Ne igitur dicti fratres super hac concessione nostra futuris possint temporibus ab aliquo molestari, presens scriptum continens ipsius concessionis formam sigilli nostri fecimus appensione muniri. Dilecti quoque nostri Robertus, decanus, et capitulum nostrum in testimonium assensus sui sigillum suum eidem, scripto similiter appenderunt. Actum anno gratie M° CC°[7] sexto decimo mense februarii.

276

1141

Pierre [I],[1] bishop of Senlis, grants to the church of Prémontré the remission of 10 sextarii *of wine from the 21* sextarii *of* census *that Prémontré owed to him annually for a piece of land situated in the territory of Soissons.*

A. Cartulary of Prémontré, fols. 70r–70v.

B. Original, AN, L 995, no. 10.

---

3 ignotuisset *B*.
4 *Om.* ut *A*.
5 *Add.* et XV sextarios *A*.
6 Cailloe *B*.
7 millesimo ducentestimo *B*.

---

1 Pierre I, bishop of Senlis, 1134–51.

Karta Silvanectensis episcopi de confirmatione elemosine sue quam contulit ecclesie.

[I]n nomine sancte et individue Trinitatis. Quoniam secundum Beati Job verba,[2] brevi in tempore irrevocabiliter transit et cito finietur dierum nostrorum qualiscunque paucitas nequaquam facile facta vel pactiones nostre in longam posteritatem nisi scripto commendentur, poterunt venire. Igitur ego Petrus, Dei gratia Silvanectensis episcopus, notum fieri volo tam futuris quam presentibus quod ecclesia Premonstratensis[3] terram quandam de manu nostra censualiter in territorio Suessionis tenebat, pro qua nobis singulis annis vini sextarios XXI solvere debebat, sed quia servorum Dei orationibus indigemus, quia etiam terram illam nisi sedulo excolatur predicte ecclesie non multum valere satis cognovimus, decem[4] sextarios de supradictis in perpetuum eis remittimus eo videlicet tenore ut residuos undecim[5] annuatim tam nobis quam successoribus nostris solvere non graventur. Ut autem hec constitutionis nostre pagina inviolatum munimen obtineat, auctoritate nostra confirmamus sigilli etiam nostri impressione subsignamus et ne quisquam presumptuosus hoc frustrare conetur sub anathemate interdicimus. Actum anno incarnationis dominice M° C° XL° I°,[6] epacta XI^{a},[7] indictione IIII^{a}, concurrente secundo.[8]

277

February, 1216. Senlis.

Guérin, bishop of Senlis, attests that Nicolas de Rosello, *canon of Saint-Quentin, requested that the vineyard he held for life at Soissons return to the church of Prémontré either upon his death or when he enters the monastic life.*

A. Cartulary of Prémontré, fol. 70v.

B. Original not found.

---

2 Job 14:5.

3 Premonstrata *B*.

4 X° *B*.

5 XI *B*.

6 M C XL I *B*.

7 XI *B*.

8 II° *B*. *Om.* sub his testibus Stephano, Landrico, Anselmo canonicis, Guidone decano de Crespi, Waltero maiore nostro, Roberto de Templo et conversis Godefrido et Rogero *A*.

Karta episcopi Silvanectensis de vinea quam abbas et conventus Premonstratensis [*margo:* contulerunt Nicholao ad vitam suam tantum.]

[G]arinus, Dei gratia Silvanectensis episcopus, omnibus ad quos littere presentes pervenerint, salutem in Domino. Noveritis quod vinea quam abbas et conventus ecclesie Premonstratensis, sitam in dominio nostro de Suessione, dederunt dilecto nostro Nicholao de Rosello, canonico Sancti Quintini, quamdiu vixerit pacifice possidendam, redibit sine contradictione alicuius ad manum ecclesie Premonstratensis quam cito viam universe carnis fuerat ingressus, vel quam cito religionem intraverit. In cuius rei memoriam presentes litteras ad petitionem dicti Nicholai fecimus sigillo nostro sigillari. Actum Silvanectum anno Domini M° CC° sexto X°, mense februarii.

278

November, 1222.

Eudes, dean of Vendeuil,[1] *informs Geoffroi,* officialis *of Soissons, that in Eudes's presence, Marie, wife of Guy de Hourges,*[2] *approved the sale made by Robert,*[3] *knight of Vauxrezis, and his wife Aude to the church of Prémontré of a vineyard relating to Marie's fief, contiguous to the house of Saint-Rémi de Soissons. (See **279**.)*

A. Cartulary of Prémontré, fol. 70v.

B. Original, AD Aisne, H 825, previously sealed with a double strip of parchment.

REGISTER: *Studium Baldwin*, fiche 2530.

Karta de quadam quitatione factam coram officiali Suessionensis.

[V]iro venerabili et discreto magistro Godefrido, officialis domini Suessionensis, et omnibus presentes litteras visuris Odo, decanus de Ventilaio, salutem in omnium salvatore. Noveritis quod Maria, uxor Guidonis de Hahourgiis, venditionem cuiusdam vinee pertinentis ad feodum suum, contigue domui Beati Remigii Suessionensis, factam Premonstratensi ecclesie a Roberto milite et Oda uxore sua de Valresi in nostra constituta presentia, marito suo presente, libera voluntate quitavit penitus et laudavit fide corporaliter prestita quod decetero non molestabit nec molestari faciet

1 Vendeuil, cant. Moy, https://dicotopo.cths.fr/places/P36797569.

2 Hourges, arr. Reims.

3 Robert, lord of Vauxrezis (cant. Soissons, https://dicotopo.cths.fr/places/P18820270), ca. 1199–ca. 1223. Melleville, *DH*, vol. 2, 407.

super dicta vinea ecclesiam memoratam. Inmo contra omnes qui voluerint stare juri, sicut domina feodi, portabit legitimam garandiam ecclesie supradicte. In cuius rei testimonium litteras presentes sigilli mei caractere roboravi. Actum anno gratie M° CC° XX°[1] secundo, mense novembri.

279

May, 1224.

Geoffroi,[2] *canon and* officialis *of Soissons, makes known that Aude, widow of Robert de Vauxrezis,*[3] *and her children Raoul, Elizabeth, Aelide, and Emmeline agree to surrender the vineyard near Saint-Remi that Aude held by right of* dos, *according to the terms of a transaction carried out by her late husband. The vineyard was first surrendered to Guy de Hourges,*[4] *fief lord, who then transferred it to Enguerrand,* prepositus *of Prémontré. (See **278**.)*

A. Cartulary of Prémontré, fol. 70v.

B. Original, AD Aisne, H 825, previously sealed with a double strip of parchment.

Karta officialis Suessionensis de resignatione dotis quam Oda nobilis mulier fecit coram nobis.

[E]go Godefridus, canonicus et officialis Suessionensis, omnibus presentibus et futuris notum volo fieri per hoc scriptum quod Oda, nobilis mulier, relicta Roberti de Valresi, devestivit se in manu nostra de dote sua quam habebat in quadam vinea sita juxta Sanctum Remigium et contigua domui Premonstratensi, quam vineam Robertus maritus suus, dum viveret, vendidit ecclesie Premonstrati. Liberi vero dictorum R[adulphi] et O[di], videlicet Radulphus,[5] Elizabeth,[6] Aelidis, Enmelina[7] in presentia nostra constituti, devestierunt se de eadem vinea in manu Guidonis de Hahourgiis de cuius feodo erat vinea nominata. Idem autem Guido, tamquam dominus feodi, et ego officialis revestivimus de dicta vinea Ingelrannum, prepositum Premonstratensem, pro ecclesia sua et tam mater quam predicti liberi fide plevita quitaverunt penitus vineam supradictum, adicientes quod per se nec per alios non reclamabunt

1 vicesimo *B.*

2 Geoffroi II, *officialis* of Soissons, ca. 1220–ca. 1239. Newman, *Seigneurs*, vol. 1, 282.

3 Robert, lord of Vauxrezis (cant. Soissons, https://dicotopo.cths.fr/places/P18820270), ca. 1199–ca. 1223. Melleville, *DH*, vol. 2, 407.

4 Hourges, arr. Reims.

5 Radulfus *B.*

6 Elizabet *B.*

7 Emelina *B.*

decetero prefatam vineam neque facient super hiis dictam ecclesiam molestari. In cuius rei testimonium presentes litteras sigilli mei appensione feci roborari. Actum anno Domini M° CC° XX° IIII°,[8] mense maio.

280

March 14, 1218. Septmonts.

Aymard,[1] *bishop of Soissons, makes known that out of necessity, Helvide, widow of the knight Philippe de Montgobert,*[2] *sells to the church of Prémontré a half* modius *of grain (*frumentum*), measure of Soissons, from the revenue that she received annually on the house of Valpriez.*[3] *Helvide's brothers Hugues (from whom the fief descends) and Eudes; her children Renier and Egline; and Egline's husband Raoul assent to the sale.*

A. Cartulary of Prémontré, fols. 70v–71r.
B. Original not found.
Other Manuscript Copies: Cartulary of Valpriez, AD Aisne, H 753, fols. 27v–28v (13th c.).
EDITION: Lalanne, *Le cartulaire de Valpriez*, 56–7; *Chartae Galliae*, no. 211386, http://telma.irht.cnrs.fr/outils/chartae-galliae/charte211386/.

Karta episcopi Suessionensis de venditione di modii midii frumenti quam fecit Helvidis ecclesie Premonstrate.

[E]go Haimardus, divina miseratione Suessionensis ecclesie minister humilis, omnibus in perpetuum. Notum facimus tam presentibus quam futuris quod Helvidis, relicta Philippi de Monte Gomberti militis, propter urgentissimam necessitatem suam vendidit ecclesie Premonstrati dimidium modium frumenti ad mensuram Suessionensem de redditu illo qui debebatur ei annuatim in domo de Vaudepriers, de assensu Hugonis et Odardi, fratrum suorum, necnon et Reneri, filii sui, et Egline filie, sed et Radulphi, mariti eiusdem Egline. Quin etiam ut venditio ipsa maiorem in posterum habeat firmitatem, devestivit se de eodem blado in manum dicti Hugonis, fratris sui, de cuius feodo movebat et Hugo in manum Ade de Vileirs cuius inde homo erat et Adam in manum nostram, ut Premonstratensis ecclesia per nos inde investiretur. Prenominati autem

8 vicesimo quarto *B*.

1 Aymard de Provins, perhaps a descendant of the vicecomital family of Provins, was first a canon and cantor of Reims, and then bishop of Soissons, 1207–19. Bourquelot, *Histoire de Provins*, vol. 1, 217.
2 Montgobert, cant. Villers-Cotterêts, https://dicotopo.cths.fr/places/P43060059.
3 Valpriez, comm. Bieuxy, https://dicotopo.cths.fr/places/P64500821.

omnes fidem dederunt corporaliter in manum nostram quod venditionem predictam ratam habeba̶unt nec aliquid per se vel per alios super hoc in dampnum ecclesie Premonstratensis machinabuntur; inmo adversus omnes qui voluerint juri stare, legitimam warandiam portabunt et super ipsa warandia portanda posuerunt in ostagium totum residuum bladi quod movet de eodem feodo in domo de Valdepriers. Nos itaque ad petitionem omnium prenominatorum investivimus fratrem. Ingelrannum, provisorem Premonstratensem, nomine ecclesie Premonstratensis de sepedicto blado in perpetuum tenendo. Ne igitur aliquid de supradictis cuiusquam in posterum possit malignitate mutari, presentem paginam super hiis que scripta sunt, episcopali auctoritate confectam sigilli nostri fecimus appensione muniri. Actum publice in domo nostra que dicitur de Septem Montibus pridie idus martii, anno gratie M° CC° octavo X°.

281

1183

Henri,[1] *bishop of Senlis, gives notice of an agreement reached between him and the church of Prémontré concerning the rights of* vinagium *over certain vineyards held by the bishopric of Senlis and the rights of* terragium *over certain fields.*

A. Cartulary of Prémontré, fol. 71r.
B. Original, AN, L 995, no. 44, previously sealed.

Karta Henrici Silvanectensis episcopi de elemosina quorumdam vinagiorum.

[H]enricus, Dei gratia Silvanectensis dictus episcopus. Noverint universi quod cum inter servientes nostros et fratres Premonstratenses super vinagio quod de vineis suis in territorio Suessioniensi sub nostro dominio constitu~~im~~tis ipsi Premonstratenses nobis reddere tenebantur, ortum esset jurgium et hinc inde super hoc litigarent, tandem in hunc modum pacis convenimus quod concessimus eisdem fratribus vineas istas in perpetuum possidendas quarum nomina subscripta sunt ad plenum vinagium secundum perticam legalem: vineam de Labahate, vineam Petri ~~de~~ Matifardi, vineam de Malo Foro, vineam de Alneto, clausum de Labahate, vineam Petri Buirete, vineam Magistri Gilleberti, vineam de Cailluel,[2] vineam Johannis Putenfant,[3] vineam d'Escorcheveel,[4] vineam del Larriz a[5] Labahate. Sciendum etiam quod vineas quas predicti fratres

1 Henri, bishop of Senlis, 1168/9–85.
2 Calluel *B*.
3 Puttefant *B*.
4 Scorcheveel *B*.
5 ad *B*.

sub annuo censu hucusque tenuerant, sub eodem censu in perpetuum a nobis tenendas concessimus vineam scilicet der[6] Larriz Bencelini pro duobus nummis et obolo Cathalaunensis et torcular quod subtus eandem vineam est, pro duobus nummis eiusdem monete et partem vinee Petri Matifart que dicitur in Walcheio, pro nummo monete currentis in civitate Suessionensi. Similiter concessimus tres[7] campos manu firma ad terragium, canpum[8] scilicet in Calluel[9] et canpum[10] super Escorcheveel[11] et campum juxta vineam de Malo Foro. Ne autem super[12] nos et supra memoratos fratres iterum questio suboriri vel factum istud valeat oblivione deleri presentem kartam[13] scribi fecimus et sigilli nostri munimine roborari.[14] Actum anno incarnati verbi M° C° LXXX° III°.

282

February, 1222.

Raoul[1] *and Ada,*[2] *count and countess of Soissons, make a gift in alms to Prémontré. (See duplicate* ***3, 496****.)*

A. Cartulary of Prémontré, fol. 71r.

B. Original BnF, Coll. Picardie 290, no. 35, previously sealed.

Karta Radulphi comitis Suessionensis de elemosina domine Ada comitisse.

[E]go Radulphus, comes Suessionensis, tam presentibus quam futuris, notum facio quod ego divine remunerationis intuitu et ob salutare remedium anime mee et illustris mulieris Ade, comitisse Suessionensis, uxoris mee, et antecessorum

6 del *B*.
7 III *B*.
8 *Sic A*.
9 Calleve *B*.
10 *Sic A*.
11 Scorcheveel *B*.
12 inter *B*.
13 cartam *B*.
14 *Om.* his videntibus et audientibus quorum nomina subscribantur. Signum Henrici archidiaconi nostri. S. fratris Alberici capellani nostri. S. Johannis Poete. S. Arnulfi canonici Sancti Reguli. S. Martini, clerici nostri. S. Frederici nepotis nostri. S. Durandi, camerarii nostri. S. Bertranni Cocci. S. Roberti castellani. S. Willelmi Normanni. S. Roberti Trepel. S. Hugonis de Lachaene *A*.

1 Raoul de Nesle, count of Soissons (d. 1235), son of Raoul, castellan of Nesle and Bruges, and Gertrude, *neptis* of Thierry, count of Flanders. Newman, *Seigneurs*, vol. 1, 64.
2 Ada d'Avesnes (d. aft. 1249), daughter of Jacques I, lord of Avesnes, Leuze, and Condé, and Adèle de Guise.

meorum necnon et liberorum meorum, ecclesie Premonstratensis quam sincera dilectione conplector, nomine elemosine concessi et dedi quod ipsa ecclesia de propriis vinis suis et propriis rebus suis cum propriis vecturis suis annuatim poterit ducere per wionagia mea usque ad summam sexaginta solidorum monete Suessionensis absque aliqua pedagii vel wionagii solutione et, si contigerit quod eadem ecclesia per wionagia mea de propriis vinis suis vel de propriis rebus suis duxerit plusquam summa prenotata sexaginta solidorum contineat, dicta ecclesia de super crescenti pedagium vel wionagium suum persolvet. Predictis siquidem est addendum quod memorata ecclesia michi et prenominate uxori mee divine pietatis mediante intuitu concessit anniversaria nostra annis singulis facienda. Quod ut ratum habeatur, presentem paginam sigilli mei[3] tradidi communitam. Actum anno gratie M° CC° XX°[4] secundo, mense februarii.

283

March, 1225.

Garnier,[1] *archdeacon (*maior archidiaconus*) of Soissons, makes known that in his presence husband and wife Simon* Albus, rusticus *of Pont-Saint-Mard,*[2] *and Béatrice recognized having given in perpetual alms to the church of Prémontré a half-*modius *of grain (*bladus*), measure of Coucy, that Prémontré owed them annually on the mill of Fay at Coucy-la-Ville.*

A. Cartulary of Prémontré, fol. 71r.
B. Original not found.

Karta archidiaconi Suessionensis de elemosina Symonis Albi de Porte Sancti Medardi.

[G]arnerus, maior archidiaconus Suessionensis, omnibus presentes litteras inspecturis in Domino salutem. Noverint universi quod Symon, cognomine Albus, rusticus de Ponte Sancti Medardi, et Beatrix, uxor eius, in presentia nostra constituti, recognoverunt se dedisse in perpetuam elemosinam ecclesie Premonstratensi dimidium modium bladi ad mensuram de Couci, quem dicta ecclesia eisdem debebat annuatim in molendino dou Fai de Coci Villa, fidem interponentes in manu nostra quod decetero memoratam ecclesiam super dicta elemosina non molestabunt vel facient molestari. Actum anno Domini M° CC° XX° quinto, mense martio. In cuius rei testimonium presentes litteras sigilli nostri munimine fecimus roborari.

3 *Om.* munimine *A*.
4 millesimo ducentesimo vicesimo secundo *B*.

1 Garnier, archdeacon of Soissons, ca. 1215–ca. 1232. Newman, *Seigneurs*, vol. 1, 111, 119.
2 Pont-Saint-Mard, cant. Coucy-le-Château, https://dicotopo.cths.fr/places/P93612418.

284

1206

The apostolic commissioners Osmand, Jean de Paris, and Germond, canons of Saint-Gervais de Soissons, make known the resolution of the dispute between the church of Prémontré, on the one hand, and husband and wife Roger le Champenois and Helvide; husband and wife Hugo Miedi and Pentecoste; and Adain, his unnamed wife, and their children, on the other hand, concerning the census *of a house in Chaine and a vineyard at Rochement.*[1] *The commissioners rule in favour of Prémontré in the presence of Pierre Escot, canon of Prémontré. (See* ***271****.)*

A. Cartulary of Prémontré, fols. 71r–71v.
B. Original, AN, L 995, no. 53, previously sealed.

Conpositione inter ecclesiam Premonstratensem et Rogerum le Champenois.

[E]go Osmundus, ego Johannes Parisiensis, ego Germundus, canonici Sancti Gervasii Suessionensis omnibus Christi fidelibus notum facimus per hoc scriptum et fidele perhibemus testimonium quod cum inter ecclesiam Premonstrati ex una parte et Rogerum le Champenois[2] et uxorem eius Helvidim,[3] et Hugonem Miedi et uxorem eius Pentecoste, et Adain, uxorem[4] earum necnon et liberos eorum ex altera querela verteretur super domo de Cathena, super quodam censu et super vinea de Rochemont, que omnia ecclesia Premonstratensis de elemosina Lisiardi longo tempore possederat pacifice, ipsa querela commissa nobis fuit auctoritate apostolica jure canonico terminanda, et cum in nostra presentia fuisset super hoc diutissime litigatum, tandem partes, de communi assensu et pari voluntate, compromiserunt in fratrem Petrum cognomento Escot, canonicum Premonstrati, abbate et fratribus Premonstratensibus qui presentes erant in veritate promittentibus, prefatis Rogeris et ceteris econtra fidem in manu nostra dantibus, quod ipsi bona fide quicquid iam dictus Petrus de ipsa querela diceret, utrinque firmiter et irretractabiliter observarent. Cum igitur ad audiendum dictum ipsius Petri, die prefixa, partes fuissent in nostra presentia constitute, dixit idem Petrus et assertive proposuit cunctis qui astabant audientibus quod prefati Rogeri et ceteri in domo memorata, censu et vinea nichil juris habebant. Quod dictum auctoritate apostolica confirmamus, prefatis R[ogeris] et ceteris, freti auctoritate eadem, sub pena excommunicationis districtius inhibentes ne de cetero litem

1 Rochemont, comm. Pommiers, https://dicotopo.cths.fr/places/P44489607.
2 Campenois *B*.
3 Helvidem *B*.
4 sororem *B*.

aliquando resuscitent super rebus memoratis adversus ecclesiam Premonstrati et, ut hoc omnibus certum appareret atque firmum, presentem paginam sigillorum nostrorum impressione voluimus roborari. Actum anno Domini M° CC° sexto.[5]

285

1203

Robert, prepositus, *J[ean],*[1] *dean, and the chapter of Soissons grant to the church of Prémontré the possession of the vineyard called* Godefridi Cordeonarii *in exchange for one and a half* modii *of* vinagium *and a hen, and of the vineyard called* Scoti *in exchange for a* modius *of* vinagium *and a hen.*

A. Cartulary of Prémontré, fol. 71v.

B. BnF, nouv. acq. lat. 2590, no. 40, previously sealed with a single seal.

Karta de vinea Godefridi Cordeonarii.

[R]obertus,[2] prepositus, J[ohannes], decanus totumque Suessionensis ecclesie capitulum omnibus in perpetuum. Notum esse volumus quod nos ecclesie Premonstratensis[3] concessimus in perpetuum possidendam vineam que dicitur G[odefridi][4] Cordoenarii pro uno modio vinatici et dimidio et unam gallinam[5] et vineam que dicitur Scoti pro uno modio vinagii[6] et una gallina.[7] Quod ut ratum permaneat sigilli nostri appositione roboravimus. Actum anno verbi incarnati M° CC°[8] tercio.[9]

286

February, 1219.

G[odefroi?], archdeacon of Soissons, makes known that, in his presence, Aelide, daughter of Bernard de la Rue Neuve, gave in perpetual alms to the

5 VI° *B*.

1 Jean, dean of the chapter of Soissons, is attested ca. 1190–1204. AD Aisne, G 253, fols. 121r, fol. 133r; BnF, MS lat. 11004, fols. 99v, 100v.

2 R. *B*.

3 Premonstratensi *B*.

4 This name has been expanded from G. in accordance with the cartulary rubric; the *B* version of the text states only "G."

5 *Sic A*; gaulinam *B*.

6 vinatici *B*.

7 gaulina *B*.

8 millesimo ducentesimo *B*.

9 III° *B*.

church of Prémontré a third part of a vineyard at Persoissons *which she had inherited from her father.*[1]

A. Cartulary of Prémontré, fol. 71v.
B. Original, AD Aisne, H 825, previously sealed with a double strip of parchment.

Karta archidiaconi Suessionensis de elemosina Aelidis filie Bernardi.

[G]odefridus,[2] archidiaconus Suessionensis, omnibus presens scriptum inspecturis in Domino salutem. Noverint universi quod Aelidis, filia Bernardi de Novo Vico, in presentia nostra constituta, dedit in puram et perpetuam elemosinam ecclesie Premonstratensi terciam partem cuiusdam vinee site in loco qui dicitur Persoissons que movebat de sua hereditate ex parte patris sui memorati. In cuius rei testimonium litteras istas sigilli nostri munimine fecimus roborari. Actum anno Domini M° CC° X° IX°,[3] mense februari.

287

1207

Jacques,[1] *treasurer of Soissons, abandons his dispute with the church of Prémontré over lands that had once belonged to Berenger de Villers, a* conversus *of Prémontré, because Prémontré had held the land for more than 40 years.*

A. Cartulary of Prémontré, fol. 71v.
B. Original not found.

---

1 In 1229, Garnier, archdeacon of Soissons, issued an act concerning this gift. Cartulary of Tinselve, SAHSS MS 193, fol. 9v.

2 The original charter reads "G.," not "Godefridus," and the expansion here seems to have been an independent act of the cartulary scribe. Newman, *Seigneurs*, vol. 1, 119, notes that no archdeacon by such a name existed during the relevant period, and suggests that the G. should rather be expanded to Galterus (archdeacon, d. June 1220) or to Garnerus (attested grand archdeacon in 1229, cartulary of Tinselve).

3 XIX° *B*.

---

1 Jacques de Bazoches (d. 1242), son of Nicolas I, lord of Bazoches, and Agnès de Chérisy, and nephew of Nivelon de Quierzy, bishop of Soissons, was first treasurer and then bishop of Soissons, 1219–42. Melleville, *DH*, vol. 1, 53.

Karta Jacobi thesaurarii Suessionensis de terris Berengarii.

[E]go Jacobus, thesaurarius Suessionensis, notum facio presentibus et futuris quod cum inter me et ecclesiam Premonstratensem super terris que fuerunt Berengarii de Vileirs, conversi predicte ecclesie, questio verteretur et ecclesia prenominata predictas terras titulo elemosine per quadraginta annos et amplius possedisse monstrasset, tandem jus ecclesia cognoscens, predicte liti ex toto renuntiavi, si quid juris habebam libere et absolute quitavi et in elemosinam concessi perpetuis temporibus pacifice possidendum. Ut autem hoc ratum permaneat presentem paginam sigilli mei caractere communivi. Actum anno incarnationis dominice M° CC° septimo.

288

September, 1226.

Jacques,[1] *bishop of Soissons, makes known the resolution of a dispute between him and the church of Prémontré concerning five* solidi nigrorum censualibus, *according to which the bishopric will receive the five* solidi *on a house located in Soissons in the bishop's quarter, to be paid by Manessès de Chaine and his brother-in-law Gilon de Septmonts.*[2]

A. Cartulary of Prémontré, fol. 71v.
B. Original not found.

Karta Suessionensis episcopi de compositione super quinque solidis nigrorum censualibus.

[J]acobus, Dei gratia Suessionensis episcopus, universis tam presentibus quam futuris salutem in Domino. Cum inter nos et ecclesiam Premonstratensem super quinque solidis nigrorum censualibus quos eadem ecclesia nobis annuatim debebat, discordia emersisset pro eo quod volebamus et requirebamus, ut exprimeretur nobis qua de causa deberentur nobis quinque solidi prenotati, tandem pro bono pacis ita convenit inter nos et ecclesiam memoratam quod ipsa ecclesia assignavit nobis et successoribus nostris in perpetuum dictos quinque solidos nigrorum accipiendos annuatim super domum Manasseri de Cathena et Gilonis, sororii sui, de Septem Montibus, que domus sita est in quarterio nostro in ipsa civitate Suessionensi. Inde autem solvet

1 Jacques de Bazoches (d. 1242), son of Nicolas I, lord of Bazoches, and Agnès de Chérisy, and nephew of Nivelon de Quierzy, bishop of Soissons, was first treasurer and then bishop of Soissons, 1219–42. Melleville, *DH*, vol. 1, 53.

2 Septmonts, cant. Soissons, https://dicotopo.cths.fr/places/P71270363.

idem Manasserus et heredes sui tres solidos et dimidium nigrorum, Gilo vero et heredes sui decem et octo denarios eiusdem monete. Sciendum vero quod nec nos nec successores nostri super censu predicto aliquam decetero movebimus questionem sed, si idem census non fuerit statuto tempore persolutus, nos et successores nostri habebimus ad prefatum assignamentum de defectu recursum. In quorum omnium perpetuam firmitatem presentes litteras tradidimus sigillo nostro munitas ecclesie supradicte. Actum mense septembri, anno incarnationis dominice M° CC° XX° VI°.

289

1219

Garnier,[1] *archdeacon (*maior archidiaconus*) of Soissons, arbitrates between the church of Prémontré on the one hand, and on the other hand the heirs of the late Lisiard de Chaine: clerics Jean Champenois and Enguerrand, Huard Miedi, Crispin Champenois, Berenger, Thibaud Le Chandelier, Jean* Ymaginarium, *and Pierre Hasle. Garnier makes known that the heirs will cede to Prémontré their rights over the vineyard of Rochemont*[2] *and the house in Chaine which Lisiard had given in alms to Prémontré; in return Prémontré will pay the heirs a modest sum of money and cover the procedural costs. Béatrice, Burea, and Odeline, Enguerrand's sisters, approve this, as do Isabelle and Emmeline, Thibaud's and Jean's wives. (See* ***266, 269****.)*

A. Cartulary of Prémontré, fol. 72r.
B. Original, AN, L 995 no. 54, sealed with a double strip of parchment.

Karta Garneri maioris archidiaconi Suessionensis de quadam compositione.

[U]niversis Christi fidelibus presentium litterarum noticiam habituris Garnerus, maior archidiaconus Suessionensis, perpetuam in Domino salutem. Noverit universitas vestra quod cum inter ecclesiam Premonstratensem ex una parte et Johannem Champenois[3] et Imorrannum,[4] clericos, Huardum Miedi, Crispinum Champenois,[5] Berengerum, Theobaldum Le Chandelier, Johannem Ymaginarium, Petrum Hasle, qui omnes gerebant se heredes quondam Lisiardi de Cathena ex parte altera, super vinea de Rochemont et domo de

1 Garnier, archdeacon of Soissons, ca. 1215–ca. 1232. Newman, *Seigneurs*, vol. 1, 111, 119.
2 Rochemont, comm. Pommiers, https://dicotopo.cths.fr/places/P44489607.
3 Champenoys *B*.
4 Iniorannum *B*.
5 Champenoys *B*.

Cathena quas idem Lisiardus dederat olim in elemosinam ecclesie Premonstratensi sub diversis judicibus fuisset diutius litigatum, tandem viri religiosi abbas et fratres Premonstratenses et memorati adversarii eorum, de consilio bonorum virorum, fide interposita et sub pena viginti librarum Parisiensium, supposuerunt se dicto nostro, sub eisdem obligationibus promittentes quod quicquid nos diceremus super prefata querela, firmiter observarent. Nos autem secundum ea que audieramus, indubitanter credentes quod sepedicti litigatores in elemosina iam dicta nichil aut parum juris haberent, precepimus eis ut renuntiarent omni juri et omni actioni que ipsis super iam dicta vinea et omnibus aliis que dictus Lisiardus ipsis in elemosinam contulerat, tempore huius scripti, conpetebat et quod eidem elemosine benigne suum prestarent assensum. Que cum ipsi sine contradictione fecissent, rogavimus dominum abbatem Premonstratensem ut de caritate ecclesie sue daret eis modicam et moderatam pecunie quantitatem, ne moleste ferrent dictam sui juris renuntiationem et expensas quas fecerant litem prosequendo. Abbas autem in hoc ipso nostro satis benigne consilio acquievit; prefatam autem renuntiationem approbaverunt et ratam habuerunt pro se Ysalel[6] et Enmelina,[7] dictorum Theobaldi et Johannis uxores, necnon et Beatrix, Burea et Odelina,[8] sorores predicti Ingeranni et tam viri memorati quam ipse mulieres, fide corporaliter prestita, firmaverunt quod nec per se nec per alios aliquam in posterum super premissis Premonstratensi[9] molestiam inferrent vel gravamen. Ut igitur ea que premissa sunt perpetuo inviolata permaneant, presens scriptum sigilli nostri munimine duximus roborandum. Actum anno Domini M° CC° nona decimo.

290

1126–64[1]

Abbot Hugues [I][2] and the convent of Prémontré cede the vineyard of Boetun *to ten inhabitants of Soissons for the construction of houses; each inhabitant pays a certain amount of* solidi *and hens for their plot. Garnier de la Rue Neuve and his wife Asceline assent to the arrangement.*

6 *Sic A.*
7 Emelina *B.*
8 Oedelina *B.*
9 *Om.* ecclesie *A.*

1 Dates refer to the abbacy of Hugues I, based on the family relationship noted in the witness lists. See Wacha, "La Puissance du Choix," 119.
2 Hugues I de Fosses (ca. 1093–1164), first abbot of Prémontré.

A. Cartulary of Prémontré, fol. 72r.

B. Original (chirograph), AN, L 995, no. 8, previously sealed. In the left margin and beginning at the top, the upper half of the letters of the word + CYROGRAPHUM +.

Karta de vinea de Bouton.

[I]n nomine sancte et individue Trinitatis. Ego Hugo, Dei gratia Premonstratensis abbas, totumque capitulum nostrum notum fieri volumus dedisse nos vineam nostram de Boetun hospitibus Suessionis ad masuras faciendas. Ex hiis[3] duas accepit Odo Pennelarius pro quibus dabit XIIII^{cim} solidos et quatuor[4] gallinas, Radulphus[5] unam pro qua dabit VII solidos et duas[6] gallinas, Ermenoldus unam pro qua dabit septem[7] solidos et duas[8] gallinas, Hugo tannator unam pro qua dabit novem[9] solidos et duas[10] gallinas, Henricus unam pro qua dabit septem[11] solidos et duas[12] gallinas, Frumoldus unam, Betherus unam, Hugo, nepos eius, unam, Odo, nepos Bosardi, unam, Jordanus unam; pro quibus dabunt singuli VII solidos et duas[13] gallinas. Persolvetur autem nobis de hoc censu medietas in Pascha et alia medietas in festo Sancti Remigii monete communis cursus usuariis civitatis. Ut autem hec constitutio rata permaneat cirographi[14] conscriptione et sigilli nostri capituli[15] impressione necnon et legitimorum testium annotatione munire curavimus. Testes inde sunt: Garnerus decanus et ceteri.[16] Factum est autem[17] hoc assensu et testimonio Garneri de Novo Vico et uxoris eius, Asceline, quibus inde sex[18] nummos bone monete annuatim debemus.

3 his *B*.
4 IIII^{or} *B*.
5 Radulfus *B*.
6 II^{as} *B*.
7 VII *B*.
8 II *B*.
9 IX *B*.
10 II^{as} *B*.
11 VII *B*.
12 II^{as} *B*.
13 II *B*.
14 cyrographi *B*.
15 *Transp. A*; capituli nostri *B*.
16 *Add.* et ceteri *A*; et sacerdos Sancti Martini, Guido maior communie, Gaufridus miles, frater eius, Hugo maior de Morcin, Johannes de Lauduneio, Havinus *B*.
17 *Add.* autem *A*.
18 VI *B*.

291

1232

Garnier,[1] *archdeacon (*maior archidiaconus*) of Soissons, makes known that Baiher,* civis *of Soissons, acknowledged that he had built a roof that sat atop the wall enclosing a house in Chaine belonging to the church of Prémontré without the right to do so.*

A. Cartulary of Prémontré, fol. 72r.
B. Original not found.

Karta archidiaconi Suessionensis de elemosina Baiheri, civis Suessioniensis.

[G]arnerus, maior archidiaconus Suessionensis, omnibus presentes litteras inspecturis in Domino salutem. Universitati vestre notum fieri volumus quod cum Baiherus, civis Suessionensis, tectum quoddam fecisset et posuisset super murum ecclesie Premonstratensis qui claudit domum ipsius ecclesie de Cathena Suessionensis, ipse postmodum in nostra presentia constitutus plenarie recognovit quod nichil juris habebat vel tunc habuerat in muro predicto, quando dictum tectum posuit super murum illum, sed ecclesia Premonstratensis, quandocumque voluerit et sicut ei placuerit, de dicto muro tamquam de proprio suam poterit facere voluntatem, non obstante tecto quod super positum est a predicto Baihero vel aliquo alio decetero ab eodem inponendo. In cuius rei testimonium presentes litteras sigilli nostri appensione fecimus ad petitionem partium roborari. Actum anno Domini M° CC° XXX° II°.

292

1172

The prepositus *Nivelon,*[1] *dean Guillaume, and the chapter of Soissons make known that Gautier de la Porte, canon of Soissons, gave certain vineyards to the church of Prémontré on the condition that, during his lifetime, Prémontré would celebrate the anniversary of his parents on July 25, and that after his death his anniversary would also be celebrated on the same date. On July 25, the brothers are to drink wine from those vineyards in the refectory.*

---

1 Garnier, archdeacon of Soissons, ca. 1215–ca. 1232. Newman, *Seigneurs*, vol. 1, 111, 119.

---

1 For a discussion of the career of Nivelon, variously archdeacon and *praepositus* of Soissons, see Newman, *Seigneurs*, vol. 1, 115.

A. Cartulary of Prémontré, fol. 72v.
B. Original, AD Aisne, H 825, previously sealed on strands of hemp.
REGISTER: *Studium Baldwin*, fiche 2535.

Karta Nevelonis prepositi et decani Suessionensis de elemosina Galteri de Porta.

[E]go Nevelo, prepositus, et Guillelmus, decanus, et capitulum Suessionensis ecclesie notum fieri volumus tam futuris quam presentibus quod Galterus de Porta, canonicus noster, dedit ecclesie Premonstrati ad Speculam vineam unam que dicitur vinea Berardi, ad Alnetum et alteram in Monte Toysiaco,[2] que dicitur vinea Garini, quas post decessum patris sui per XL[a] annos, nullo reclamante, et quiete possedit. Dedit etiam predicte ecclesie vineam unam subtus Petrosillam, que dicitur vinea Galteri, quam XX libris comparavit, ea scilicet conditione ut quamdiu ipse vixerit fiat anniversarium patris sui et matris sue X[o] kalendas augusti et post decessum suum eadem die fiet anniversarium eiusdem Galteri, licet alio tempore evenerit, et fratres Premonstratensis ecclesie tam clerici quam laici pro eisdem vineis habeant vinum in refectorio. Testes inde sunt Nevelo, Petrus et ceteri.[3] Actum est hoc anno incarnati verbi M[o] C[o] LXX[o] II[o].

293

May, 1236.

Jean [II],[1] count of Soissons, concludes an agreement with the church of Prémontré according to which he confirms possessions granted to it, including grants he previously contested, citing charters issued by him and his predecessors in 1172, 1214 (twice), and 1222. Jean and his wife Marie[2] further grant rights in their lands to the Premonstratensian houses of Bucy,[3] Soissons, and

2 Toisiaco *B*.
3 *Add.* et ceteri *A*; Symon, Rogerus, archidiaconi Radulfus thesaurarius, magister Gislebertus, Galterus, Albertus, Johannes, Hugo sacerdotes, Radulfus precentor, Garnerus succentor, Gaufridus, Herluinus, Lisiardus, Rainaldus diaconi, Radulfus de Brana, Guido, Odo, Bartholomeus subdiaconi *B*.

1 Jean II, count of Soissons (d. ca. 1270), son of Raoul I, count of Soissons, and his second wife Yolande. Newman, *Seigneurs*, vol. 1, 67–8.
2 Marie du Thour et du Chimay (d. ca. 1241), daughter of Roger I, lord of Chimay, and Agnès, lady of Thour. Newman, *Seigneurs*, vol. 1, 68.
3 Bucy-le-Long, cant. Vailly, https://dicotopo.cths.fr/places/P35759725.

Clamecy.[4] *In exchange, Prémontré pays Jean and Marie 120* librae Parisiensium. *Raoul,*[5] *brother of Jean, consents. (See* ***274.****)*

A. Cartulary of Prémontré, fols. 72v–73v.

B. Original, AN, L 995, no. 83, no evidence of seal as bottom has been damaged.

Karta Johannis comitis Suessionensis de confirmatione possessionum in episcopatu Suessionensis.

[I]n nomine Patris et Filii et Spiritus Sancti, amen. Ego Johannes, comes Suessionensis, notum facio universis tam presentibus quam futuris quod cum ecclesia Premonstratensis, domos, terras, vineas et res alias in comitatu Suessionensi possideret, quarum maiorem partem dominus Radulphus,[6] pater meus, et antecessores mei eidem ecclesie confirmaverant per scripta sua patientia que inspexi et legi in presentia mea feci, residuum vero sine sufficienti confirmatione, sicut michi videbatur, teneret vineam videlicet que fuit quondam domini Roberti[7] de Vaurresis militis, que est juxta Sanctum Remigium et contigua domui Premonstrati extra Suessionem, quam vineam dictus Robertus vendidit ecclesie Premonstrati, et quedam alia in comitatu Suessionensi noviter acquisita nec, ut michi videbatur, sufficienter vel rationabiliter confirmata, et ego dictam ecclesiam compellerem ad vendendum ea que illi vel per me vel per antecessores meos non fuerant confirmata et erant ab ipsa in comitatu Suessionensi et dominio meo noviter acquisita, tandem mediantibus bonis viris ita convenit inter me et ecclesiam memoratam quod ego cessavi eam compellere ad vendendum et volui et concessi ut quecumque in comitatu Suessionensi et dominio et feodo meo usque ad diem presentium litterarum emptione, donatione, elemosina, quocumque modo vel titulo acquisierat quiete, pacifice et libere in perpetuum possideret. Confirmavi etiam et innovavi cartas predecessorum meorum ecclesie memorate concessas, kartam[8] videlicet domini Yvonis,[9] quondam Suessionensis comitis et domini de Nigella, quam legi feci coram me et in qua verba inferius expressa[10] contineri audivi. Que quidem

4 Clamecy, cant. Vailly, https://dicotopo.cths.fr/places/P24475745.

5 Raoul de Soissons (d. bef. 1272), knight, son of Raoul I, count of Soissons, and his second wife Yolande. Newman, *Seigneurs*, vol. 1, 68.

6 Radulfus *B*.

7 Robert, lord of Vauxrezis (cant. Soissons, https://dicotopo.cths.fr/places/P18820270), ca. 1199–ca. 1223. Melleville, *DH*, vol. 2, 407.

8 cartam *B*.

9 Ivonis *B*.

10 *Transp. A*; expressa inferius *B*.

karta[11] sic incipit: In nomine Patris et Filii et Spiritus Sancti, amen. Ego Yvo,[12] Suessionensis comes et dominus Nigelle, presentibus et futuris ex doctrina veritatis anmonemur seminare carnalia ut metamus spiritualia dare tenporalia[13] ut recipiamus eterna. Proinde quicquid Premonstratensis ecclesia in ditione[14] comitatus Suessionensis sive ex predecessorum nostrorum sive ex nostra sive ex hominum nostrorum donatione usque ad annum qui subscriptus est possedisse dinoscitur, quiete et absque ulla calumpnia perpetuo possidendum eidem ecclesie concedimus et presentis scripti attestatione posterorum notitie commendamus sane quedam ex hiis propriis duximus exprimenda vocabulis: in comitatu Suessionensi domum de Buci ab omni consuetudine et exactione liberam, cum vineis, terris et ceteris appenditiis suis, terram Odonis leprosi, terram Berengeri de Clameciaco, vineam de Biart et vineam de Parco, torcular de Phillenis ita liberum quod nemo ibi aliud torcular possit edificare, furnum etiam de Terni ita quod nemo ibi alium possit edificare. Hec igitur et omnia alia que prefata ecclesia hactenus tenuit, ut supradictum est, firma et illibata in perpetuum eidem ecclesie permanere, annuente Iolende, comitissa, censemus. Actum est hoc et confirmatum anno incarnati verbi M^{o}[15] centesimo septuagesimo secundo. Confirmavi etiam quandam kartam[16] domini Radulphi[17] patris mei, ecclesie memorate concessam cuius tenorem esse talem audivi: Ego Radulphus,[18] Suessionensis comes, presentibus et futuris notifico per hoc scriptum quod quia locus ille subtus Buciacum in quo fratres Premonstratenses molendinum habebant, quod vocabatur Roques[19] cum quibusdam eorum possessionibus prope jacentibus michi et heredibus meis ad usus proprios oportunus[20] et utilis videbatur, talis inter me et eos nomine permutationis conventio facta fuit quod ego et heredes mei tenebimus in perpetuam possessionem molendinum predictum et ea que ipsi circa molendinum idem[21] habebant tempore huius scripti, videlicet vineam unam cum proximo sibi prato et duos campos terre arabilis divisim jacentes. Pro hiis autem omnibus reconpensavi et assignavi ecclesie Premonstratensi, in perpetuam similiter possessionem, quinque modios bladi in sexterlagio meo Suessionense ad mensuram ibi currentem tempore huius scripti hoc modo quod, annis singulis ab octavis Pasche et deinceps intrabit nuntius Premonstrati in saisinam totius sexterlagii et tenebit illud

11 carta *B.*
12 Ivo *B.*
13 temporalia *B.*
14 donatione *B.*
15 millesimo *B.*
16 cartam *B.*
17 Radulfi *B.*
18 Radulfus *B.*
19 vocatur Rokes *B.*
20 opportunus *B.*
21 *Transp. A*; idem molendinum *B.*

libere et integre, donec de blado tali quale veniet ad sexterlagium receperit dictos quinque modios sine ordeo quidem et avena sine pisa et faba, sine lente et vitia nec sexterlarius de collectione se interim intromittet nisi quod conpotum tenebit cum nuntio ecclesie et ipsi nuntio fidelitatem faciet annuatim quod nec per se nec per alium procurabit ut vel bladi solutio differatur vel solutionis bladium in aliquo peioretur et, quia de domino Suessionensi episcopo ipsum sexterlagium tenebam in feodum, posui dictum molendinum cum appenditiis suis in feodo eius pro excambio dictorum quinque modiorum id denique ad maiorem securitatem presenti scripto duxi de voluntate propria inserendum, quid si vel ego vel aliquis heredum meorum premissis conventionibus contrairet dictus episcopus et eius successores preter secularem justiciam qua tenebuntur ut principes defendere kartam[22] suam poterunt etiam in me et meos ecclesiasticam justiciam exercere modis omnibus quibus exercerent eam in nos si ecclesia teneret molendinum predictum et nos eius possessionem turbaremus. Ut autem hec omnia futuris temporibus firmiter observentur presentem kartam[23] utriusque partis assensu et approbatione confectam sigilli mei feci caractere confirmari. Actum anno ab incarnatione Domini M° CC°[24] quarto decimo. Confirmavi etiam aliam cartam dicti patris mei Radulphi[25] quam ipse dicte ecclesie concesserat in hec verba: Ego Radulphus,[26] Suessionensis comes, presentibus et futuris notifico per hoc scriptum quod pro remedio anime mee et antecessorum meorum et per devotionem quam habebam erga ecclesiam Premonstrati, concessi liberaliter et benigne ut vineam de Hardellieres quam bone memorie Radulphus,[27] archidiaconus Suessionensis, in elemosinam ei dedit et omnes alias vineas et terras quas ipsa ecclesia sub dominio meo acquisierat, tempore huius scripti, liceat ei tenere in perpetuum salvis redditibus meis et justicia mea in omnibus locis illis[28] in quibus vel redditum vel justiciam prius habebam. Ut autem elemosina et concessio ista perpetuam habeat firmitatem, presentem kartam[29] super hoc confectam feci sigilli mei caractere confirmari. Actum anno ab incarnatione Domini M° CC°[30] quarto decimo. Aliam siquidem cartam patris mei confirmavi continentem hec verba: Ego Radulphus,[31] comes Suessionensis, tam presentibus quam futuris notum facio quod ego nomine elemosine concessi et dedi ecclesie Premonstrati quod ipsa ecclesia de propriis vinis suis et propriis rebus suis cum propriis vecturis suis annuatim poterit ducere per

22 cartam *B*.
23 cartam *B*.
24 millesimo ducentesimo *B*.
25 Radulfi *B*.
26 Radulfus *B*.
27 Radulfus *B*.
28 *Transp. A*; illis locis *B*.
29 cartam *B*.
30 millesimo ducentesimo *B*.
31 Radulfus *B*.

wionagia mea usque ad summam sexaginta solidorum monete Suessionensis absque aliqua pedagii vel wionagii solutione; et si contigerit quod eadem ecclesia per wionagia mea de propriis vinis suis vel de propriis rebus suis duxerit plusquam summa prenotata sexaginta solidorum contineat, dicta ecclesia de super escrescenti[32] pedagium vel wionagium suum persolvet. Actum anno Domini M° CC° XX°[33] secundo mense februario. Preterea ego Johannes, comes Suessionensis, ex devotione adieci ut eidem ecclesie liceat habere in domo sua de Buci ducenta animalia lanam portantia et tres vaccas que liberum habebunt ingressum et egressum per omnia tam ad pascua quam ad alias aisentias que animalia eiusdem ville de Buci consueverunt aut debent habere in domo vero de Suessione totidem animalia atque vaccas que liberum habebunt ingressum per omnia et egressum tam ad pascua quam ad alias aisentias que animalia eiusdem ville [*margo et homeo.*: Suessionensis consueverunt aut debent habere. Similiter et in domo de Clameci totidem animalia atque vaccas que liberum habebunt ingressum per omnia et egressum tam ad pascua quam ad alias aisentias que animalia eiusdem ville] de Clameci consueverunt aut debent habere. Concessi etiam ecclesie sepefate per terram meam communes aisentias in chiminis et viis, ut valeat eis uti libere et quiete, sicut homines terre mee uti consueverunt eisdem et concessi etiam ut de premissis omnibus rebus suis tam ab antiquo quam de novo acquisitis ipsa ecclesia suum commodum et suam faciat voluntatem. Remisi autem eidem ecclesie omnes querelas et controversias que mote fuerant vel moveri poterant ex premissis vel occasione premissorum ~~ratione dotis vel alterius rei nichil penitus in posterum reclamabit. In quorum omnium recompensationem~~[34] usque ad tempus presentium litterarum et volui ut eadem ecclesia esset ab hiis penitus absoluta et hanc conventionem voluit, laudavit et approbavit Maria comitissa, uxor mea, sicut et ego ita quod ipsa in premissis omnibus vel occasione premissorum, ratione dotis alterius rei, nichil penitus in posterum reclamabit. In quorum omnium recompensationem centum et viginti libras Parisienses dedit nobis ecclesia memorata. Et ut omnia que superius sunt expressa efficatius et firmius in perpetuum observentur, promisi me et heredes meos bona fide omnia prenotata necnon et omnia predecessorum meorum scripta fideliter et firmiter servaturos ita quod nec ego nec dicta uxor mea nec heredum nostrorum aliquis predictam ecclesiam super dicta vinea que fuit dicti Roberti de Vaurresis, vel super aliquo de premissis omnibus vel aliis quibuscumque que tempore huius scripti in comitatu Suessionensis et dominio et feodo meo eadem ecclesia possidebat, inquietabimus nec inquietari faciemus aut sinemus sed eidem ecclesie portabimus legitimam warandiam adversus omnes qui voluerint juri stare et quos poterimus et debebimus cohercere,

32 supercrescenti *B*.

33 millesimo ducentesimo vicesimo *B*.

34 This struck-through section does not appear in *B*.

salvis in omnibus supradictis justicia mea et dominio meo ac redditibus meis ubi prius hec habebam et salvis etiam redditibus hominum meorum ubi prius eos habebant. In quorum omnium testimonium et perpetuam firmitatem ego et dicta Maria, uxor mea, presentem kartam[35] fecimus sigillorum nostrorum munimine roborari. Hec autem acta sunt de consensu et voluntate mei, Radulphi,[36] fratris dicti comitis, qui volui, laudavi et concessi conventionem et pacem confirmationes et innovationes predictas et promisi bona fide quod super hiis que dicta ecclesia possidebat tempore huius scripti in parte hereditatis mee que me contingit et in comitatu et in dominio Suessionnensi, ipsam ecclesiam nullatenus decetero molestabo nec permittam vel faciam molestari et pro hiis omnibus et singulis supradictis firmius observandis presenti karte[37] feci sigillum meum appendi. Actum anno gratie M° CC° tricesimo VI°,[38] mense maio.

294

January 4, 1332.

Richard le Boursier, baillius *of the bishop of Soissons, at the request of the church of Prémontré and after inquiry, recognizes that the rights of* gans *and* ventes *over a house in Soissons that he had given to the bishop actually belong to Prémontré.*

A. Cartulary of Prémontré, fol. 72v.

B. Original not found.

NO RUBRIC. LATER ADDITION.

A tous ciaus et cetera, Richars li Boursiers, baillius de Reverend pere en Diu monseigneur l'evesque de Soissons, salut. Sachent tout que comme nous eussions mis en la main dou dit reverend pere les gans et ventes d'une maison qui estoit gisée la Louveronne seant a Soissons ou liu que on dit en Bouton[1] lon li diz reverend pere a toute justice et signourie, tenant a la maison des Estuves de Bouton d'une part et a la maison Oede de Nully d'autre, li religieux de l'eglise de Premonstré disans que a euls appartenoient et devoient appartenir les diz gans et ventes, nous requirent que de ce nous vousissiens enfourmer

35 cartam *B.*

36 Radulfi *B.*

37 carte *B.*

38 millesimo ducentesimo tricesimo sexto *B.*

1 Bauton (Boetun or Boeton) was an area of Soissons in the Middle Ages which survives today as the rue de Bauton. Pécheur, "Les rues, boulevards et avenues de Soissons," 15.

et nous, oye leur requeste, nous enfourmemes bien et diligentment laquelle information seur ce faite et ew seur ce avis et deliberation, nous trouvames que as diz religieux appartenoient et devoient appartenir les dis gans et ventes et leur delivrames a plain. En tesmoingnaige desquez choses nous avons scelées ces presentes lettres dou seel de la baillie dou dit signeur qui furent faites et données le diemenche apres le Circoncision Notre Signeur, l'an de grace mil CCC XXX II. A ce furent comme tesmoing maistre Pierres d'Amigny,[2] maistre Jehans de Laon, freres Giles de Gournay,[3] Jehans Aloueste, Perrins de Coucy, Pierres de Faveroles,[4] Thierris li Kiveral, Herbers des Tyulles et plusieurs autres.

295

March, 1300.

Eudes [VI],[1] *lord of Ham, makes known that he cedes back to Prémontré all the* census *and rents at Ham which rightfully belonged to Prémontré, the total being valued at seven* livres, *12* sous, *and three* deniers, *following an inquiry concerning the issue.*

A. Cartulary of Prémontré, fols. 73v–74v.
B. Original not found.

NO RUBRIC. LATER ADDITION.

Jou Oudars, sires de Hem, chevaliers, fais savoir a tous chiaus qui ces presentes lettres verront et orront que comme descors fust meus entre mi d'une part et religieus hommes et honnestes l'abbé et le convent del eglize de Premonstré d'autre, sur chou que j'avoie fait saisin les cens et les rentes que la dicte eglise a la Hem en deniers, en chapons, en fouaches et en autres chozes appartenans a la maison de Bonoueil[2] qui est de la dicte eglize, duques a la value de cept livres XII sous et III deniers ou la entours, liquel sunt assené a prendre sus les iretages

2 Amigny, cant. Chauny, https://dicotopo.cths.fr/places/P65669952.
3 Likely Gournaye, comm. Soucy, https://dicotopo.cths.fr/places/P38968459.
4 Likely Faverolles, cant. Villers-Cotterêts, https://dicotopo.cths.fr/places/P76834043.

1 Oudard I (sometimes referred to as Eudes VI), lord of Ham. His relationship to the previous lords of Ham is not clarified in any known primary source, but he was likely a son of Jean II, lord of Ham (d. ca. 1285). By 1296, he was married to Dorée, daughter of Marie de Frianvile and Eustache, lord of Marteville. Pipon, ed., *Le chartrier de l'Abbaye-aux-Bois (1202–1341)*, 353.
2 The Premonstratensian *curtis* of Bonneuil. *MP* II, 484.

dessous nommés et les personnes desous nommés les doivent sur la maison qui fu Wautier le Fournier li oir Tieffane le Flevesse II sous, Maroie la Montdune I obole sur XXV setiers de terre a Rosemolin, Jehans de la Mote VII deniers et obole de sa maison en Chanterrainne, Wybers Foukeres III oboles sur la maison qui fu Jehan de Dury, li oir Coperon Sale II sous sur la maison qui fu maistre Jehan Faucille, li sires de Hem IX deniers sur la maison qui fu Gilon Houiguet, li ostelerie III deniers sur un pré assis a Mandompré, Aubris li Tonneliere III oboles sur la grange qui fu Baudri le Barbier, peches II sous et VI deniers sur la maison Richart le Marchier et sur un estal a truies en la fin des autres vers l'ostelerie, Maroie la Merchiere V sous sur les maisons qui furent le merchier dales le four des anes, Raherius li Leus IIII deniers de son curtil qui fu Colart Chaut pais dehors la porte Chaumoise, Philippes Chieves XII deniers de la maison Jehans Mouvart il sont la tresorie, Pierres Viediu VIII deniers de sa maison, li oir dame Flandrine VI deniers de leur maison desous la crois, de rechief VII Poitevins de la maison qui fu Agnes la Tuiliere, Colars Gossiaumes III Poitevins de celle maisme maison, Giles Doe les XV sous sur sa maison, Wautiers de Honnecort VI deniers sur la maison qui fu Widele Despeville, Thomas Delatre VI deniers de la maison qui fu Maroie Albete, Raus Godars III deniers de la maison qui fu Agnes de Neele, Jehans li Coriers VII deniers sur la maison qui fu Baudie et Jehan Lorfevre, Colars Noes VII deniers de ceste meisme maison, li abbés et li convens de Hem[3] V sous de leur maison qui est devant les molins de Hem, Maroie Audent V deniers de son curtil a Maudompré, Pierres Cendriers III sous et VI deniers de la maison qui fu Bauduyn Crahier, Symons li Fius [*et*] Huart le Fourmier III oboles de la maison qui fu Renaut la Justice, Jehans Ogiers li Jovenes II sous de la maison qui fu Colart Maledenrée devant Haironval,[4] Jehans Preudons III oboles de la maison qui fu Thomas le Sielier, li oir Jake dou Mouton XXXIII deniers et obole de leur pie en Chanteraine qui fu le Hubine, Maroie le Here et Jehans Hesselins [*et*] Grigoires Guedes IIII sous de la maison qui fu le Viel Machon, li oir Perron Chievet I obole sur un setier de terre assis a Rosemolin, Marge Baudescote IIII deniers de la maison qui fu Robert Domy, Druars Baudescos XXVI deniers de la maison qui fu Robin Betart dales le maison la Flevesse, Oudars de Muile[5] II sous de la maison Gilon l'oir de Muile, Renaus de Cramery III deniers de la maison qui fu le Viel Doien, li oir Jake de Bourgegnon III sous de la maison qui fu Mainsent Valiete dou lais qui fu ma dame Yzabel, mesires Oudars sires de Hem IIII sous de la maison qui fu Berte de Sommette[6] et Perron Guignon et ma dame Yzabel femme monsigneur Renaut de Hem chevalier, Maroie la Merchiere IIII deniers de la terre qui fu Aelis de Bourgignon, Robers Waignars et si frere II Tournois de la terre qui fu Aelis de

3 The Augustinian abbey of Notre-Dame de Ham.

4 Héronval, comm. Mondescourt, https://dicotopo.cths.fr/places/P76867184.

5 Muille-Villette, cant. Ham, https://dicotopo.cths.fr/places/P77128677.

6 Sommette-Éaucourt, cant. Saint-Simon, https://dicotopo.cths.fr/places/P82241903.

Bourgegnon entre Muile et les maladiaus dou fies de Muile, Maroie Heleguine XXVI deniers de la maison qui fu Jehan Agniel dehors la porte Chaumoyse et autant a Pasques dou lais ma dame Yzabel, Pierres Viediu VIII deniers de la maison qui fu Emmeline Levette, Thomas Delatre VI deniers de la maison qui fu Marie Labete, mesires Ganiars IIII deniers de la maison qui fu Robert de Oigny, Wybers Foukeres III oboles de la maison qui fu Marge Diaucourt, Symons li Fix [*et*] Huart le Fournier III oboles de la maison qui fu Jehan de Dury, li oir Dame Flandre VII Poitevins de la maison qui fu Agnes la Muliere, Colars Gossiaumes III Poitevins de ceste meisme maison, Jehans Preudons III oboles de la maison qui fu Marge Diaucourt, Mahuis li Leus IIII deniers dou curtil qui fu Colin Cautpain dehors la porte Chaumoise, mesires Oudars sires de Hem IX deniers de la maison qui fu Gilon Hoiguet, li maistres de la maladerie II deniers de la terre qui fu monsigneur Lever dales Muiles, Aubris li Tonneliers et Margue Castelaine III oboles de la grange qui fu Thomas dou Castiel, li Tonlius de Hem XII deniers, Jehans Rouges VI deniers de la maison qui fu Mahiu le Leu qui est a l'entrée de la rue dou Mes, Elies Bardous XII deniers sur son pré et sur sa maison que dame Biautrix dou Marchiet nous laissa, Thomas Delatre III capons de la maison Maroie Labette, Maroie Delatre II capons et II deniers de la maison Patin, Madame Biautrix la Castelaine III oboles de la maison qui fu Renaut Diaucourt, Ysabiaus Glace et Jehans Glace II chapons sur leur maison a Canesi, Jehans Daimery II sous et VI denier de sa maison ou marchiet, li abbés et li convens de Hem V sous des maisons les Morieles, de rechief ~~d.~~ XII deniers de la maison Agnes Doufer, Mahuies Floriette XII deniers de sa grange desous la crois, Symons li Fius [*et*] Huart le Fournier III oboles de la maison qui fu Jehan de Dury, Perres Peches I denier, I pain blanc et un chapon de sa maison a la portc dcs Scrumagcs, dc rcchicf ~~VI~~I dcnicr, I pain blanc I capon ct II sous ct VI deniers sur les maisons et l'estal qui furent Richart le Merchier, Giles Docles XV sous sur sa maison, Phillipes Chieves XII deniers sur la maison qui fu Jehan Monnart se soit le Tresoriere, Wybers Foukeres III oboles de la maison qui fu Jehan de Dury, Jehans Reviaumes II sous de la maison qui fu Yzabel la Merchiere, Jehans de la Mote VII deniers obole de sa maison en Chanteraine, Wautiers de Honnecourt VI deniers de sa maison qui fu Jehan Despeville, Jehans Preudons et si frere III oboles de la maison qui fu Jehan Diaucourt, Aubris li Tonneliers XII deniers de sa grange qui fu Baudry le Barbier, Margie Audent V deniers de son curtil a Maudompré, Gregoires Guedes IIII sous de la maison qui fu Maroie de Cannegny, Raus Godars III deniers de la maison qui fu Agnes de Marle, li oir Jake Mouton III oboles de sa grange en la rue Marcheande, Jehans li Coriers VII deniers de la maison qui fu Baudiere et Jehan Lorfevre, Colins Noes VII deniers de ceste meisme maison, Pierres Viediu IIII capons de la maison Emmeline Levete, li oir dame Flandrine VI deniers de leur maison desous la crois, de rechief VII Poitevins des maisons Agnes la Muliere, Colars Gossiaumes III Poitevins de celle meisme maison, li ostelerie III deniers de leur curtil a Mandompré, Estevenes Marcous ~~XX~~ XII deniers de la maison qui fu

Robert Rose-en-Mai, de rechief XII deniers de la maison qui fu Willaume Magne, Maroie la Merchiere XLV deniers des maisons Richart le Merchier dales le four des anes qui furent Jehan Diaucourt, de rechief XV deniers des ces meismes maisons, Druars Baudescos XXVI deniers de la maison qui fu Robert Betart et Thoumas Escaille Paste assize dales le maison Raul le Fil au marchiet, ~~Prieres Celid~~ Pierre Cendriers III sous et VI deniers de la maison qui fu trahier, Renaus de Cramery III deniers de la maison qui fu le Viel Doien, Symons Toukenfuies I capon de la maison et dou curtil Mahui le Bir, Maroie li Helekyne et si enfant X capons et II fouaches sur la maison Jehan Agnel dou lais madame Yzabel de Hem, mesires Oudars de Hem IIII sous de la maison qui fu Berte de Sommete et de la maison Perron Soirant et furent madame Yzabel femme Monsigneur Renaut de Hem chevalier, li oir Huet le Flament VI deniers de l'estel qui fu Jehan le Reloieur, demiselle Yzabiaus Taillebos XII deniers sur son curtil a le Saus, li oir Jaque dou Mouton XXXIII deniers et obole de son pré en Chanteraine qui fu le Hubine, Maroie le Here et Jehan Hesselin pour chou que il en avoient aquis partie puis XLVII ans en encha, si comme je disoie, se requeroie que il les ostassent hors de leur main et mesissent en main laic. Les devant dis religieus maintenans le contraire et disans que droit n'avoie d'iaus contraindre de mettre hors de leur main les chozes deseur dictes. Cum il l'eussent tenu tant de tamps que je ne les pooie ne devoie constraindre a mettre hors de leur main si comme il disoient. En la pardefin pour bien de pais et pour mius savoir la verité de la tenure de seur dite je m'en sui enformés diligeamment et en ai enquis bien et soufissamment a preudommes et a bonnes gens tré[7] aults par lequele enqueste jou ai trouvé que li dict religieus ont tenu les chozes deseur dictes par les passé de XLVII ans et plus de tamps ou tant que je ne les puis ne dois constraindre a mettre hors de leur main, aincois le puent maintenir comme en main morte a tous jours, pour coi je recongnois, grée, otrié et consens que doré en avant je, ne mi oir, ne mi successeur, ne autres qui aroit ou avoir porroit cause de mi ne les poons constraindre ne faire constraindre a mettre hors de leur main et weil, grée et otrié que doré en avant il aient, tengnent ou cil qui aront cause d'iaus pasiulement les choses de seur dictes perpetuelment a tous jours quitement et franchement, comme en main morte, des maintenant tant comme en mi, en mes oirs et en mes successeurs est et puet estres et appartenir a tenir a tous jours comme en main morte si comme dict est et proumes et ai encouvent loiaument en bonne foi que jamais en contre les chozes deseurdictes je ne venrai ne venir ferai en nulle maniere parmi ne par autrui et a che fermement tenir, oblege je moi et mes oirs et mes successeurs et tous chiaus qui aront ou avoir porront cause de mi tous mes biens presens et a venir et pour chou que se soit ferme choze et estable a tous jours jou ai ces presentes lettres scellées de mon seel qui furent faites du l'an de grace mil et trois cens, de moy de mars.

7 *Sic A, read* très.

296

1184

Raoul [I],[1] lord of Coucy, makes known that Louis,[2] knight of Fressancourt, with the consent of his wife, Havide, gave in alms to the church of Prémontré all that he possessed of the tithe of Bieuxy.[3] Raoul, lord of Coucy, and Pierre, knight of Bieuxy, consent.

A. Cartulary of Prémontré, fol. 74v.
B. Original not found.
Other Manuscript Copies: Cartulary of Valpriez, AD Aisne, H 753, fols. 16r–17r (13th c.).
EDITION: Lalanne, *Le cartulaire de Valpriez*, 40–1; *Chartae Galliae*, no. 211374, http://telma.irht.cnrs.fr/outils/chartae-galliae/charte211374/.

NO RUBRIC. LATER ADDITION.

Ego Radulphus, Dei gratia dominus de Cocy dictus, notum fieri volo tam futuris quam presentibus quod Ludowicus, miles de Frencencurt, laude et assensu Hawidis uxoris sue, dedit in elemosinam Premonstratensi ecclesie quicquid habebat in decima de Buici, id est quartam partem et totum decime tractum, de qua parte dabit singulis annis ecclesia Premonstratensis decem et octo aisinos frumenti ecclesie de Nungant, quos ipse et pater eius predicte ecclesie de Nungant pro animabus suis dederunt dabit etiam ecclesie de Frecencurt sex aisinos ad mensuram Suessionensem pro emendo Deo similiter et ecclesie de Buici, vel modium vini, vel, si hoc potius Premonstratensis ecclesia voluerit, quinque solidos dabit; fratres itaque Premonstratenses in quocumque voluerint loco totam decimam trahent et adunabunt, infra tamen ipsius parrochie terminum. Pro tractu autem ipsius decime habebunt de communi singulis diebus messionis gerbam de avena unam et in fine messionis tres aisinos frumenti; habebunt etiam stramen et paleam et lucrum et les hatons,[4] pars vero sacerdotis integra manebit ei et salva. Ut autem donum istud ratum perpetuo ei inconvulsum sit, Petrus, miles de Buici, a quod Ludovicus hanc decimam in feodo tenebat, hec concessit et laudavit. Ego etiam Radulphus, quia et ipsam decimam predictus Petrus de me in feodo habebat, hoc donum pariter laudavi et ad pacem perpetuam Premonstrate ecclesie sigilli mei impressione munivi. Prefatus etiam Ludovicus ex magna dilectione et devotione quam erga Premonstratensem

1 Raoul I, lord of Coucy (d. 1191), son of Enguerrand II, lord of Coucy, and Agnès de Beaugency.
2 Louis, lord of Fressancourt (cant. La Fère, https://dicotopo.cths.fr/places/P95117467), was the son of Pierre de Fressancourt and the brother of Pierre de Bieuxy. Barthélemy, *LDA*, 173.
3 Bieuxy, cant. Vic-sur-Aisne, https://dicotopo.cths.fr/places/P16618416.
4 *Sic A*, *read* les hautons.

ecclesiam habuit, elemosinam patris sui, id est terram XXX[ta] aisinos seminis capientem, ad immobile stabilitatis robur huic scripto inseri fecit. Huius rei testes sunt et fidejussores Simon de Coci, Wericus de Choisi et Robertus, frater eius, Robertus Rosed et Philippus, frater eius, Petrus[5] de Ponte Sancti Medardi et Simon, filius eius, H. de Martinmont,[6] Theodericus de Bello Rivo, Petrus de Buici, ipsius Ludowici patruus, et filii Radulphus et Petrus. Hanc etiam elemosinam postea predictus Petrus de Buici et Hawidis, uxor Ludowici, in ecclesia Premonstratensis coram Egidio tunc suppriore et aliis quam plurimis recongnoverunt [illegible] anno incarnationis dominice M° C° LXXX° IIII°.

297

August 1, 1346.

Pierre de Lunon[1] *establishes his powers as a representative of Jean, king of Bohemia and count of Luxembourg, in the regions of Faillouël*[2] *and Condren*[3] *through a* vidimus *of a letter of Jean's. Pierre also makes known that he ordered the arrest of Gilot Haimmart and Jean de Vertis in a house at La Férrole*[4] *belonging to the church of Prémontré. Subsequently the procurator of Prémontré proved to Pierre – by presenting a document dated December 1344 – that Prémontré possessed all rights of* justicia *and lordship in La Férrole, and accordingly Pierre released the men and recognized all of Prémontré's rights in La Férrole.*

A. Cartulary of Prémontré, fol. 75r.
B. Original not found.

NO RUBRIC. LATER ADDITION.

A tous ciaulz qui ces presentes lettres verront et orront, Pierres de Lunon garde et establis au gouvernment de la terre dite Foillowel et de Condren, des appartenances et dou ressort d'icelle salut. Comme nous par vertu des lettres de tres haut et excellent prince nostre tres chier et redoubté signeur nossigneur le roy de

5 Pierre de Pont-Saint-Mard (cant. Coucy-le-Château, https://dicotopo.cths.fr/places/P93612418) appears as a witness in acts associated with the Coucy family ca. 1163–ca. 1190. Newman, *Seigneurs*, vol. 2, 119.

6 Likely Martimont, comm. Croutoy, https://dicotopo.cths.fr/places/P77564093.

1 Possibly the same Pierre de Lunon who appears as a lieutenant of the *receveur de Vermandois* in a 1342 act. Gravier, *Essai sur les prévots royaux du XIe au XIVe siècle*, 119.

2 Faillouël, cant. Chauny, https://dicotopo.cths.fr/places/P41972474.

3 Condren, cant. Chauny, https://dicotopo.cths.fr/places/P28107866.

4 La Férolle, comm. Vouël, https://dicotopo.cths.fr/places/P51152055.

Boheme et conte de Lucembourt dont la teneur sensuit Jehans, par la grace de Dieu roys de Boheme et contes de Lucembourt, a tous ciaulz qui ces presentes lettres verront salut. Sachent tout que nous considerans et attendans la loyalté et la bonne diligence de notre amé et foyal Pierre de Lunon, faisons et establissons, avons fait et establit ycelui Pierre par la teneur de ces presents garde de toute notre terre de Foillowel et de Condren, des appartenances et dou ressort d'ycelle auquel nous donnons et avons donné franche poissance et mandement especial de faire et exercer pour nous et en notre non tous esplois de justice, de jurisdiction quel qu'il soient et faire droit et loy en tous cas laic yl appartenra par raison selonc les us et coustumes de notre dicte terre et dou pays, de gouverner nos hommes de fief et nos eschevins jugans en nostre court, se mestiers est, de jugier et sentencier et tenir lieu de juge en tous cas et tant pour nous comme contre nous, de demander et faire demandes pour nous en notre nom de nous et nos causes meutes et a movoir, defendre de faire cemandre, de convenir et enconvenir, de avouuer et desavouuer fais d'autruy, de entrer en garant et de demander garant, de demander et de requerir le retour de notre court, nos hommes, nos femmes, no subjes, soumanane et justissables, de faire et requerir ressaisine, restablissemens et venues de lieus, de faire et proposer pour nous propositions et articles, de respondre as fais et as articles proposées encontre nous, de produire et amener pour nous teismoings, lettres, instrumens et toutes maniers de prueuves, de dire contre les teismoins et contre leurs depositions, de jurer en l'ame de nous, se mestiers, en toutes manieres de savemens que ordre de plait requiert, de opposer et poursivir l'opposition de oir, drois et toutes manieres de sentence, de appeler et poursivir son appel ou appiaulz, de recevoir nos hommes de fief en fealté toutefois que li cas si offrira et de faire toutes autres choses que nous feriens, porriens faire et dire se nous y estiens presens ja soit ce que les choses requissent mandement especial et de faire [*margo*: et dire toute chose qui adviengne et garde de terre de seigneur et de haut justicier appartiennent, puvent et doivent appartenir, de substituer en lieu de luy] Jehan ou plusiers qui ait ou aient tout au tel pooir es choses dessus dictes comme li dit Pierres et de rappeler le pooir d'iceulz toutefois qu'il li plaira, prometans seur l'obligation de tous nos biens presens et avenir, de tenire et avoir ferme et estable tout ce qui par ledit Pierre ou par les substitus ou substitut de luy sera fait, dist et promet pour nous et en notre nom tant pour nous comme encontre nous et de paier le jugie se mestiers est en rappelant le pooir des establis que autres fois avons commis a garder notre dicte terre devant la date de ces presentes. En teismoing de ce nous avons fait seeller ces lettres de notre seel qui furent faites et données l'an de grace M CCC XLIIII ou mois de decembre le derrain jour, eussiemes fait penre de par notre dit signeur par Willaume Pilot, sergent doudit signeur en la maison et es termes et dedens la cloture de la Ferrole, maison de religieux hommes et honestes l'abbé et le couvent de l'eglize de Premontré, Gilot Haimmart et Jehan de Vertis demourans a Vowel pour ce qui yl se combattoient dedens les dis termes et enclos de la dite maison de la Ferrole et apres ce fust venus par devers nous li procureres desdis religieus en disant que li dis religieus estoient en bonne possession et saisine de si lonc tamps qu'il n'estoit memoire dou contraire, ou qu'il souffissoit a bonne saisine avoir acquise de avoir et exercer par yaus et par leurs gens a leur pourfit, publiquement et notoirement, la justice et signourie toute haute, moyenne et basse, seulz et pour le tout dedens les termes et l'encloture de la dite maison et que par la dite prise dez dis Gilot Haimmart et Jehan de Vercis que nous avions faite faire ou dit lieu les aviens tourblés et empeschiés en leur dite possession et saisine a tort et sans cause raisonable, indewement et, de nouvel supplians et requerans a nous que nous la dite prise et tout ledit esploit et tout ce qui s'en estoit ensivis vausissiens rappeler et mestre dou tout au nient et lesdits religieux laissier user et joir paisiblement de leur dite possession et saisine de la dite justice et offrans a nous enformer souffissamment dou droit de la dite possession et saisine desdis religieus, se nous la rappeliens en doubte, et pour ce que contre raison ne voliens grever ne empeschier les dis religieus en leur droit de la saisine de la dite justice, se droit y avoient, receumes ledit procureur a nous enfourmer, pour les dits religieux, des choses dessus dites et pour nous enfourmer seur ce, vismes plusieurs et grant quantité de tesmoins produis seur ce par ledit procureur, lesquels ois, jurés et diligamment examinés seur les choses dessudites et la deposition d'yceulz mise en escript et ycele information veue, a grant deliberation et elle consail seur ce tant au consail doudit signeur comme a autres, pour ce que par ladite information nous apparu lesdis religieus avoir souffissamment prouvé et monstré que yl avoient joy et usé par yaus et par leurs gens par le tamps dessudis es lieus dessusdit de la dite justice et que ycele avoient exercée et gouvernée et a leur pourfit publiquement et notoirement seulz et pour le tout, nous la dite prise des dessusdis Gilot et Jehan faite par notre dit sergant dedens les termes et cloture de la dite maison comme dist est, avons rappelée et mise au nient, rappelons et metons au nient dou tout et tout ce qui s'en est ensivi en ostant la dite main mise par ledit sergant as dits Gilot et Jehan ou dit lieu et tous les empeschemens dessusdis en restablissant lesdis religieus et le dit lieu dela prinse dessusdite et en yaus laissant joir paisiblement de leur dite possession et saisine de la dite justice. En teismoing de ce nous avons scellées ces presentes lettres de notre seel dou quel nous usons ou dit office, qui furent faites et données l'an de grace M CCC XLVI, le premier jour dou moys d'aoust.

TABLE OF CONTENTS: BONNEUIL

A. Cartulary of Prémontré, fol. 75v–76v.

Incipiunt scripta et confirmationes curie nostre de Bonolio Noviomensis dyocesis cum molendinis, decimis, pratis, pascuis, silvis, domibus, adjacentibus, et rebus aliis eidem domui pertinentibus.

I. Capitula. Karta Symonis Noviomensis episcopi de alodio Bonolii quod Alardus concessit ecclesie Premonstratensis miles de Ham.

II. Karta Symonis Noviomensis de elemosina Sancte Radegundis de Perrona.

III. Karta Noviomensis episcopi de elemosina Radulphi Pulchri quam contulit ecclesie Premonstrati.

IIII. Karta Noviomensis episcopi de elemosina militis de Wiana.

V. Karta episcopi Noviomensis de elemosina domine Adelidis uxoris Gervini de alodio de Sinicourt concesso ecclesie Premonstrati.

VI. Karta Walteri abbatis de Aroasia de quadam permutatione in territorio de Douilli inter canonicos de Aroasia et Premonstratensi.[1]

VII. Karta Reneri domini de Seinz de eo quod renunciavit quibusdam litteris concessis in maritagium filie sue.

VIII. Karta abbatis Premonstratensis de antecessoribus Mathei de Couci qui dederunt quasdam possessiones sub annuo censu decem modiorum frumenti.

IX. Karta Noviomensis episcopi de elemosina domini Hamensis super terra et nemore quod Colesiacum nuncupatur.

X. Karta Oberti abbatis ecclesie Premonstratensis de decima de Ulfois.

XI. Karta episcopi Noviomensis de conpositione inter fratres Premonstratenses et Petrum de Flavi.

XII. Karta episcopi Noviomensis de quadam compositione inter ecclesiam Premonstratem et dominum Renerum de Maigni.

XIII. De elemosina Walteri Arietis et de quatuor modiatis terre inter Hamem et cetera.

XIIII. Karta Noviomensis episcopi de elemosina Joie uxoris Roberti Morican quam contulit ecclesie Premonstrati.

XV. Karta Radulphi Sancti Eligii Noviomensis et abbatis de quadam compositione.

XVI. Karta Balduini fratris hospitalis Noviomi de annuo censu quinquaginta solidorum quos debent ecclesie Premonstrati pro jure parrochie.

XVII. Karta maioris et communie Noviomensis de dono parrochie Sancti Germani.

XVIII. Karta Balduini sacerdotis de XIII^{cim} libras Parisiensis quas Symon li Begues contulit in elemosinam hospitali Noviomensis.

XIX. Karta episcopi Noviomensis de elemosina furni Noviomi quem Basilla contulit ecclesie Premonstrati.

XX. Karta Stephani Noviomensis episcopi de permutatione furni Noviomensis pro quo recipit ecclesia Premonstratensis XII^{cim} denarios bone monete.

---

1 *Sic A.*

XXI. Karta episcopi Noviomensis de annuo censu hospitalis Noviomensis.
XXII. Karta domini Hugonis abbatis Premonstratensis de confirmatione hospitalis.
XXIII. Karta Symonis episcopi Noviomensis de confirmatione alodii de Germania.
XXIIII. Karta Noviomensis episcopi de terra quam Hugo Albus tenebat a Roberto Cane.
XXV. Karta episcopi Noviomensis de quadam compositione inter ecclesie Premonstratensis et castellanus de Couci.
XXVI. Karta Stephani Noviomensis episcopi de quadam conpositione inter ecclesiam Premonstratensem et Widelani et sex filios eius.
XXVII. Karta episcopi Noviomensis de literis Elizabeth Musarde de XIIcim modiis frumenti.
XXVIII. Karta episcopi Noviomensis de elemosina Elizabeth Musarde.
XXIX. Karta decani Christianitatis de confirmatione elemosine Elizabeth.
XXX. Karta ~~Egidii~~ Richardi prepositi Ambianensis de Egidio de Bapalmis.
XXXI. Karta officialis Noviomensis de elemosina Petri militis cognomento M[usart].
XXXII. Karta decani Christianitatis de confirmatione elemosine Elizabeth.
XXXIII. Karta episcopi Noviomensis de personatu altaris de Douci et de Germaniis.
XXXIIII. Karta Gaufridi militis domini de Douci, de Laurentio Passart, et Symone fratre eius quos dedit ecclesie Premonstrati.
XXXV. Karta abbatis Premonstrati et Sancti Theoderici de quadam compositione.
XXXVI. Karta episcopi Noviomensis de elemosina duarum partium decime de Canlencurt.
XXXVII. Karta episcopi Noviomensis de maiore decima de Falevi quam dedit Alardus miles de Hamo ecclesie Premonstrati.
XXXVIII. Karta Henricus Castellanus de Couciaco de confirmatione cuiusdam nemoris.
XXXIX. Karta Odonis Hamensis de confirmatione elemosine Lancelini.
XL. Karta Noviomensis episcopi de elemosina Ingeranni de Landovesin.
XLI. Karta Noviomensis episcopi de duabus partibus decime de Chisencurt et cetera.
XLII. Karta Noviomensis episcopi de duabus partibus decime de Gricourt quas et cetera.
XLIII. Karta castellani de Bapaumes de quadam elemosina quam fecit ecclesie Premonstrati in territorio de Douci et de Germaniis.
XLIIII. Karta abbatis Montis Sancti Quintini et decani Sancti Fursei de decima de Cartigni.
XLV. Karta Noviomensis episcopi de confirmatione maioris decime de Cartigni.
XLVI. Karta officialis Noviomensis de compositione inter ecclesiam Premonstratensem et Robertum Aginant.
XLVII. Karta Noviomensis episcopi de elemosina Berneri der Plaissie.
XLVIII. Karta Noviomensis episcopi de elemosina Odonis de Lanci filii Waldini.
XLIX. Karta Petri domini medietatis de Flavi de tribus sexterlatis terre.
L. Karta episcopi Noviomensis de elemosina Adelidis de Buscheavesnes.
LI. Karta abbatis Sancte Marie Hamensis et Odonis domini eiusdem castri de elemosina Radulphi domini de Flavi ac liberorum eius.
LII. Karta Gaufridi militis de Hamo de concordia inter Johannem de Lanci Patedoe et ecclesiam Premonstratensem super octava garba.

LIII. Karta Noviomensis episcopi de confirmatione doni quod fecerat Alaidis de Monci et cetera.

LIIII. Karta Noviomensis episcopi de quadam compositione inter ecclesiam Premonstratensem et Renaldum de Flavi.

LV. Karta officialis Noviomensis de elemosina Petri domini medietatis de Flavi.

LVI. Karta Symonis Noviomensis episcopi de elemosina Fulconis Obelin et de furno de Canlencurt.

LVII. Karta Odonis domini de Hamo de elemosina Elizabeth et de modiagio de Colesi.

LVIII. Karta domini Guidonis de Gontren et domini de Foilluel, de elemosina Gaufridi de Hamo et de manerio Remegii de Lanci.

LIX. Karta Gaufridi de Hamo et de elemosina mansi Martini de Estaliers siti apud Lanci.

LX. Karta domini de Seinz de pecunia eidem soluta peremptione modiagii.

LXI. Karta Noviomensis episcopi de confirmatione elemosine molendinorum de Escamli.

LXII. Karta prioris de Lihuns de molendinis de Escamli datis ecclesie Premonstrati sub annuo censu.

LXIII. Karta Noviomensis episcopi de canonicis Nigellensis qui dederunt nobis quicquid habebant in molendinis de Escamli pro XX modiis frumenti.

LXIIII. Karta Wiberti prioris Sancte Margarete de censu molendinorum de Escamli pro X modiis frumenti.

LXV. Karta Noviomensis episcopi de confirmatione tercie partis maioris decime de Ulfoiz.

LXVI. Karta Mathei de Duri militis de conventione molendini de Offois.

LXVII. Karta officialis Noviomensis de confirmatione et testimonio elemosine de Offoiz.

LXVIII. Karta abbatis Premonstratensis de elemosina de Offois et de mediatate calceate.

LXIX. Karta Noviomensis episcopi de elemosina septem modiorum bladi quos Beatrix dedit.

LXX. Karta officialis Noviomensis de venditione Symonis le Cat de Offois super duobus modiis bladi.

LXXI. Karta officialis Noviomensis super IIIIor sextariis frumenti et duobus pisorum.

LXXII. Karta abbatis Premonstratensis et capituli et abbatis Hamensis capituli super duobus modiis frumenti in molendinis de Espevilla nobis concessis.

LXXIII. Karta episcopi Noviomensis de concordia facta inter ecclesiam Premonstratem et dominum de Hamo super molendinis de Hamiaus.

LXXIIII. Karta Noviomensis episcopi de elemosina Johannis militis de Cremeri de molendinis de Hamiaus.

LXXV. Karta Odardi militis de Ponto de quitatione Goberti Arsi super tota terra de meo feodo descendente.

LXXVI. Karta officialis Noviomensis de venditione quam fecit Guido d'Estouilli ecclesie Premonstratensis in decima et in herbergagio d'Estouilli.

2 The scribe miscalculated the numbers on the table of contents here.

3 *Sic A*.

LXXXXVII. Karta de compositione inter ecclesiam Premonstratensem et ecclesie Vizelensem super quibusdam possessionibus de Bonolio.

LXXXXVIII. Karta Noviomensis episcopi de elemosina Hugonis de Ponte.

LXXXXIX. Karta Noviomensis episcopi de elemosina Fulconis maioris de Noviomo de decima de Muiles.

LXXXX.[4] Karta Noviomensis episcopi de elemosina domine Doe de Albigni de duabus partibus decime de Bruci.

CI.[5]

CII. Karta Noviomensis episcopi de elemosina Symonis Rati de novem denariis et quatuordecim ex alia parte.

CIII. Karta domini Philippi militis de Canlencort.

CIIII. Karta de furno eiusdem ville sub annuo censu quinque modii bladi.

CV. Karta Noviomensis episcopi de elemosina Johannis camerarii de parte decime de Muile.

CVI. Karta officialis Noviomensis de venditione duorum modiorum frumenti quos Hubertus vendidit.

CVII. Karta Gerardi de Ribercort de tribus areatis aque apud Beuni.

CVIII. Karta abbatis Sancti Remigii et decani Remensi de compositione inter ecclesiam Premonstratem et Hamensem.

CIX. Karta Noviomensi episcopi de quibusdam compositione inter nos et Galterum maiorem nostrum de Espevilla.

CX. Karta Stephani Meldensis episcopi de compositione inter ecclesiam Premonstratensem et ecclesiam Hamensem.

CXI. Karta Noviomensis episcopi de elemosina duorum molendinorum apud Espevile quam Hugo contulit.

CXII. Karta Johannis de Nigella de compostione inter ecclesiam Premonstratensem et Johannem de Partigni.

CXIII. Karta de eo quod ecclesia contulit domino Johanni potestatem capiendi gressios in gresseria.

CXIIII. Karta abbatis de Nongento de censu tredecim solidorum quos debemus ecclesie de Nongento.

CXV. Karta Yvonis comitis Suessionensis de elemosina Liegardis de Landovoisin.

CXVI. Karta abbatis Premonstratensis et Sancte Marie de Nongento de commutatione cuiusdam.

CXVII. Karta comitis Suessionensis et domini Nigellensis de elemosina Widele de Faiel et cetera.

CXVIII. Karta abbatis Premonstratensis de compositione cuiusdam terre inter monachos de Humbleriis.

CXIX. Karta archiepiscopi Remensis de compositione inter Hugonem Premonstrati et abbatem Hamensem.

---

4 *Sic A, read* LXXXXX.

5 *Sic A.*

CXX. Karta decani Christianitatis de venditione quam fecit Emmeline ecclesie Premonstratensis.

CXXI. Karta domini Hamensi de modiagio quod remisit ecclesie Premonstrati.

CXXII. Karta Noviomensi episcopi de venditione quam fecit Johannes de Flavi ecclesie Premonstrate.

CXXIII. Karta Simonis Noviomensis episcopi de patrimonio Odonis de Lanci quod contulit ecclesie Premonstratensis.

CXXIIII. Karta Noviomensis episcopi de elemosina Aelidis uxoris Simonis de Buscheavenes.

CXXV. Karta Noviomensis episcopi de elemosina Odonis militis de Falevi quam dedit ecclesie Premonstratensis.

CXXVI. Karta Reneri domini de Seinz de modiagio quod remisit ecclesie Premonstrate.

CXXVII. Karta decani Sancti Quintini de compositione nemoris de Colesiaco et cetera.

CXXVIII. Karta comitis Flandrensis de elemosina domini Hamensis super nemore.

CXXVIIII. Karta de recognitione Ermengardis de Biaumeis filie Aelidis et cetera.

CXXX. Karta officialis Noviomensis de elemosina et venditione cuiusdam terre de Flavi.

CXXXI. Karta officialis Noviomensis de venditione cuiusdam terre Johannis de Media Villa.

CXXXII. Karta Radulfi domini de Flavi de elemosina quam contulit ecclesie Premonstratensis.

CXXXIII. Karta decani Hamensis de venditione Petri domini de Flaviaco Lutoso et cetera.

CXXXIIII. Karta decani de Hamo de venditione nemoris episcopi quam fecit Elizabeth.

CXXXV. Karta Noviomensis episcopi de blado qui debetur burgensibus Sancti Quintini et cetera.

CXXXVI. Karta Remensis abbatis et decani de causa que erat inter Premonstratensem et Hamensem ecclesias.

CXXXVII. Karta Odonis de Olesi quod liceat ecclesie Premonstratensis relevare fossatum suum et cetera.

CXXXVIII. Karta abbatis Premonstratensis de annuo censu quinque solidorum quos Helinandus.

CXXXIX. Karta officialis Noviomensis de elemosina XII^{cim} denariorum quos Colardus contulit.

CXL. Karta abbatis Premonstratensis de annuo censu quod Radulphus tenet a Rogero.

CXLI. Karta cardinalis de quadam decima Simonis militis de Martisvilla.

CXLII. Karta domini Petri de Flavi super eo quod tenetur nobis in quinquaginta solidis.

CXLIII. Karta Odonis militis de Olesi super eo quod debet garantire et cetera.

CXLIIII. Karta officialis Noviomensis de eo quod Gerardus recognovit se debere quinque modios.

CXLV. Karta Noviomensis episcopi de elemosina Symonis qui dicitur Ratus super novem denariis.

CXLVI. Karta Noviomensis episcopi de elemosina domine Doe de Albigni de duabus partibus decime.

CXLVII. Karta Noviomensis episcopi de elemosina Fulconis maioris de Noviomo.

CXLVIII. Karta Philippi domini de Canlencort de furno eiusdem ville sub annuo censu.

CXLIX. Karta Noviomensi episcopi de elemosina Johannis de decima in territorio de Muile.

CL. Karta Gerardi de Ribercort de tribus areatis aqua apud Beuni.

CLI. Karta officialis Noviomensis de duobus modiis frumenti quos Hubertus de Marcel.

CLII. Karta decani Noviomensis de elemosina personatus de Douci.

CLIII. Karta Noviomensis episcopi de carruca in alodio apud Bolmunt quam dedit Richuera ecclesie.

CLIII.[6] Karta de pace facta inter Premonstratensem ecclesiam et Thieszonem de Voiz.

CLIIII. Karta de quadam compromissione inter ecclesiam Premonstratensem et Galfridum et Symonem fratres.

CLV. Karta Noviomensis episcopi de medietate furni de Calniaco quam Godo remisit ecclesie nostre.

CLVI. Karta officialis Noviomensis super eo quod Gaufridus recognovit se vendidisse quicquid habebat apud Calni.

CLVII. Karta Noviomensis episcopi de quodam excambio inter ecclesiam Premonstratensem et Hugonem mllltem.

CLVIII. Karta baillivi regis de eo quod maior de Vouel renunciavit omnibus que clamabat in Ferreola.

CLIX. Karta Noviomensis episcopi de confirmatione cuiusdam terre que fuit Willelmi.

CLX. Karta de quadam controversia inter ecclesiam Premonstratensem et Renaldum de Voue.

Karta[7] de eo quod Paschasius de Calni emendavit ecclesie Premonstratensis quod eruerat gressios.

Karta[8] Noviomensis episcopi de compositione inter ecclesiam Premonstratem et burgenses Calniacenses super gressia.

CLXI. Karta decani de Calniaci de eo quod Renoldus et Gerardus emerunt ab ecclesia gressios.

---

6 *Sic A.*

7 This entry has no number.

8 This entry has no number.

CLXII. Karta Hugoni domini de Guni de quitatione Cecile super duobus modiis bladi.

CLXIII. Karta decani de Calniaci de quadam compromissione in ipsum.

CLXIIII. Karta Noviomensis episcopi de elemosina Martelli de Abecourt.

CLXV. Karta episcopi Noviomensis de dono et elemosina Godonis filii Galteri de Viri.

CLXVI. Karta abbatis Premonstratensis de elemosina Iteri de Espaigni de terra de Mares.

CLXVII. Karta cuiusdam compositionis inter ecclesiam Premonstratensem et Johannem militem de Oisni.

CLXVII. Karta Noviomensis episcopi de compositione inter ecclesiam Premonstratensem et Gerardum de Arceio et Johannem de Truigni.

CLXIX. Karta abbatis Premonstratensi et decani Sancti Quintini de capella Sancti Nicholai apud Sanctum Quintinum.

CLXX. Karta Guidonis d'Estouilli de herbergagio decime d'Estouilli que pertinet ad ecclesie.

CLXXI. Karta Johannis de Montibus de quodam excambio inter ecclesiam Premonstratensem et dominum Simonem.

CLXXII. Karta decani et capituli Nigellensis de pace inter nos et ecclesiam Premonstratensem de campo Pouletiere.

CLXXIII. Karta Noviomensis episcopi de quitatione quam fecit Lambertus et filius eius super censu VII librorum.

CLXXIIII. Karta Noviomensis episcopi de quadam compostione inter ecclesiam Premonstratensem et Joibertum filium Egidii de Bretigny.

CLXXV. Karta Noviomensis episcopi de compositione inter ecclesiam Premonstratensem et dominum Nigellensem.

CLXXVI. Karta decani Christianitatis de elemosina Symonis de Martisvilla XL libras.

CLXXVII. Karta de compositione inter ecclesiam Premonstratensem et Symonem militem de Martisvilla.

CLXXVIII. Karta Noviomensis episcopi de elemosina Marthei filii Symonis Scabiosi de tribus modii bladi.

CLXXIX. Karta Symonis militis de Montibus de quitatione Balduini militis.

CLXXX. Karta domini Hugonis de Betencort de confirmatione elemosine filii mei.

CLXXXI. Karta domini Rogero de Faiel de compositione inter me et ecclesiam Premonstratensem.

CLXXXII. Karta domini Goberti de Cherisi de compositione inter ecclesiam Premonstratensem et ipsum.

CLXXXIII. Karta de forma pacis inter ecclesiam Premonstratensem et dominum Gobertum de molendino de Balluel.

CLXXXIIII. Karta Hugonis domini de Guni de quodam fossato per terram suam pro aisentia molendini.

298

1124. Noyon.

Simon [I],[1] bishop of Noyon and Tournai, at the request of Alard[2] de Ham, confirms the gift made by Alard, with the approval of his unnamed wife and children, of the allod of Bonneuil[3] to Norbert and the other religious of the church of Prémontré.

A. Cartulary of Prémontré, fol. 77r.

B. Original, AD Oise, H8 1368, sealed with partial red wax seal on leather strips.

EDITION: Lohrmann, *Papsturkunden in Frankreich. Neue Folge*, vol. 7, 269–70; Pycke and Vleeschouwers, *Actes*, 317–18; *Diplomata Belgica*, no. 6921, https://www.diplomata-belgica.be/charter_details_fr.php?dibe_id=6921.

REGISTER: Grauwen, "Lijst van oorkonden waarin Norbertus wordt genoemd," 146.

Karta Symonis Noviomensis episcopi de alodi Bonolli quod Alardus de Ham concessit ecclesie Premonstrate.

[I]n nomine sancte et individue Trinitatis. Ego Symon, Noviomorum atque Tornacensium Dei gratia presul, maiores nostri diligentissimi viri quod memorie

1 Simon I de Vermandois (d. 1148) was the son of Hugues I and Adélaïde, count and countess of Vermandois and Valois, and bishop of Noyon, 1123–42.

2 Alard I de Ham (or de la Porte), knight of Ham; husband of Helvide. He also appears in **91**, **334**, **385**, **415**, **452**, and **464**.

3 Bonneuil, cant. Ham, https://dicotopo.cths.fr/places/P66750585.

commendare volebant et in noticiam extendere posterorum ut assignaretur litteris usui tradiderunt eorum et nos, in hoc quoque prudentiam imitantes, Sancte Matris Ecclesie filiis tam futuris quam presentibus conscriptione presenti notificare decrevimus Alardum de Ham alodium suum quod Bonolii habebat, servo Dei Norberto ceterisque Premonstrate ecclesie fratribus, ob remedium anime sue tradidisse et ut idem nostra firmaretur auctoritate, sicut inferius continetur, a nobis summopere postulasse. Dedit quidem Alardus ipse nominate iam ecclesie totum alodium suum de Bonolio ut quicquid illud sit sive silva, sive pascua aut prata, seu terra culta, seu inculta predicti fratres et qui eis successerint integraliter habeant et, sicut ipse in vita patris sui, ex dono illius, multo tempore ac post mortem patris diutissime sine ulla contradictione illud tenuerat, isti quoque perpetua quiete possideant. Statutum est etiam ut medietatem ipsius alodii ad usus suos, si voluerit, in vita sua tantummodo, Alardus retineat sed post mortem eius totum ad ecclesiam revertatur. Preterea decime partem quam apud Letheri vadum habebat, in manum nostrum reddidit quam et nos, rogatu ipsius, predicte ecclesie concedimus. Laudavit hoc uxor eius et cum ipsa tota eorum que supererat soboles assensum prebuerunt. Hoc idem et nos insuper confirmamus et quicumque huic dono et institutioni huiusmodi adversari presumpserint, perpetuo nisi resipuerint, anathemate ex auctoritate Dei et ab ipso potestate nobis tradita condempnamus. Interfuerunt autem huic confirmationi Sancte Romane Ecclesie cardinales atque legati dominus Petrus Leonis[4] et dominus Gregorius[5] qui et ipsi tam excommunicationem nostram quam institutionem predictam astipulatione sua simul et auctoritate roboraverunt. Actum est hoc Noviomi anno dominice incarnationis M° centesimo vicesimo quarto. Huic autem tam confirmationi quam dono affuerunt non solum clerici sed et laici complures, quorum signa atque nomina inferius notata sunt. S. domni Symonis, episcopi. S. domni Ursionis,[6] abbatis Sancti Dionisii Remensis.[7] S. domni Leudonis,[8] abbatis Sancte Marie Hamensis.[9] S. domni Reinardi,[10] abbatis Sancti Bartholomei Noviomensis.[11] S. domni Walteri,[12] abbatis Sancti Martini

4 Pietro Pierleoni, cardinal priest of Santa Maria in Trastevere, 1120–30, and antipope as Anacletus II, 1130–8.

5 Gregorio Papareschi, cardinal deacon of Sant'Angelo in Pescheria, 1116–30, and pope as Innocent II, 1130–43.

6 Ursion (d. 1149/50), abbot of the Augustinian abbey of Saint-Denis de Reims, 1119–29, 1130s–49, and bishop of Verdun, 1129–31. *GC* IX, cols. 290–1.

7 *Superscr.* Sancti Dionisii Remensis *B*.

8 Leudon (or Huldo), abbot of the Augustinian abbey of Notre-Dame de Ham, 1108–32. *GC* IX, col. 1121.

9 *Superscr.* Sancte Marie Hamensis *B*.

10 Renaud (or Renier), abbot of the Augustinian abbey of Saint-Barthélemy de Noyon, 1123–bef. 1135. *GC* IX, col. 1116.

11 *Superscr.* Sancti Bartholomei Noviomensis *B*.

12 Gautier de Saint-Maurice was abbot of the Premonstratensian abbey of Saint-Martin de Laon, 1124–51, and bishop of Laon, 1151–3. *MP* II, 512.

Laudunensis.[13] S. Odonis[14] de Ham. S. Radulphi[15,16] de Nigella.[17] S. Hugonis[18] de Perrona. S. Yvonis,[19,20] castellani. Ego Hugo[21] cancellarius subscripsi. Ista karta habetur in duobus locis verbo ad verbum sigillata sed non scribitur nisi in uno loco.[22]

299

1138

Simon [I],[1] *bishop of Noyon, makes known that Mathieu de Péronne, about to enter Clairvaux, gives the tithe of the church of Sainte-Radegonde near Péronne to the church of Prémontré for the support of his wife Frédeburge*[2] Domez, *who had entered Prémontré as a* conversa. *His son Mathieu, daughter Adèle,*[3] *and son-in-law Simon de Bouchavesnes*[4] *consent.*

---

13 *Superscr.* Sancti Martini Laudunensis *B.*

14 Eudes II *Pes Lupi*, lord of Ham (d. aft. 1144).

15 Radulfi *B.*

16 Raoul I, lord of Nesle, son of Yves de Nesle and an unnamed daughter of Guillaume Busac, count of Eu, and Adèle, countess of Soissons. Newman, *Seigneurs*, vol. 1, 61.

17 Niella *B.*

18 A Hugues de Péronne appears in an 1139 act of the abbey of Ourscamp, also in the company of Roger de Thourotte. BnF, MS lat. 5473, fol. 130r.

19 Ivonis *B.*

20 Yves II, castellan of Noyon, attested 1124–30, brother of Guy I, castellan of Coucy and Noyon.Guyotjeannin, Episcopus, 212.

21 Hugues III de Roye, chancellor of Noyon-Tournai, ca. 1130–46, and of Noyon, 1146–63/6. Pycke, Le chapitre cathédral Notre-Dame de Tournai de la fin du XIe à la fin du XIIIe siècle, 64.

22 Add. Ista karta habetur in duobus locis verbo ad verbum sigillata sed non scribitur nisi in uno loco A. The editors believe that, here, the scribe may have been referring to another manuscript copy held at AD Oise, H 5987 (previously sealed), although this copy is not identical and contains phrases not found in B or in the cartulary.

---

1 Simon I de Vermandois (d. 1148) was the son of Hugues I and Adélaïde, count and countess of Vermandois and Valois, and bishop of Noyon, 1123–42.

2 The anniversary of Frédeburge *Domez* was celebrated at Prémontré on February 12. Van Waefelghem, *L'Obituaire de l'abbaye de Prémontré*, 47.

3 Adèle, daughter of Mathieu Strabo de Péronne and Frédeburge *Domez*. Her anniversary was celebrated at Prémontré on January 9. Ibid., 25. Adèle and her husband Simon de Bouchavesnes also gave the tithe of Courcelles to the Benedictine abbey of Notre-Dame d'Avesnes-lès-Bapaume, ca. 1142–7. Tock, ed., *Les chartes des évêques d'Arras: 1093–1203*, 110; Bougard and Delmaire, *Le cartulaire et les chartes de l'abbaye de femmes d'Avesnes-lès-Bapaume (1128–1337)*, 69–70.

4 According to de Cagny, the family of Bouchavesnes was a cadet branch of the seigneurial family of Péronne. Cagny, *Histoire de l'arrondissement de Péronne*, vol. 1, 182–3.

A. Cartulary of Prémontré, fols. 77r–77v.
B. Original, AD Somme, 20 H 15, no. 1, previously sealed on a double strip of leather.
EDITION: Pycke and Vleeschouwers, *Actes*, 421–3.

Karta Symonis Noviomensis episcopi de elemosina Sancte Radegundis de Perrona.

[I]n nomine sancte et individue Trinitatis. Ego Symon, sancte Noviomensis ecclesie minister humilis, Hugoni, abbati Premonstratensi eiusque successoribus canonice substituendis in perpetuum. Quia vite brevitate et presentium occupatione facile subrepit preteritorum oblivio, res gestas qualibet necessitate memorandas scripto commendari decretum est prudenti maiorum consilio. Ea propter notum fieri volumus presentibus et futuris quod Matheus de Perrona,[5] iturus ad conversionem Clarevallensis cenobii, reliquit uxorem suam nomine Fredeburgem, sed vulgo dictam Domez, in conversione ecclesie Premonstratensis. Ad sustentationem igitur prefate conjugis ceterorumque pauperum inibi Deo servientium contulit ipsi ecclesie Premonstratensi decimam cassii[6] ecclesie Sancte Radegundis juxta Perronam assensu filii sui, Mathei, et generis sui, Symonis de Buschesvennes,[7] et Adelidis, ipsius uxoris, reddens eam Yvoni,[8] Nigelle principi, a quo eam tenebat. Ipse vero domnus Yvo[9] reddidit eam Radulpho,[10] comiti Viromandensi, de cuius feodo descendebat et ipse comes michi sic legitime contradendam ecclesie Premonstratensi ob remedium animarum ipsam elemosinam conferen~~bat~~tium. Et[11] ipse ~~comes~~ autem Matheus inde separavit decimam solius cuiusdam vinee monachorum de Monte Sancti Quintini[12] quam in elemosinam dedit canonicis Sancte Marie de Ailcurt.[13] Hoc igitur donum, Hugo frater in Christo carissime, tibi et ecclesie tue attribui[14] et, ut ratum permaneat, scriptum et auctoritate mea confirmatum sigilli mei impressione subsignavi. Si qua igitur ecclesiastica secularisve persona hanc decreti nostri paginam sciens temerario ausu irritare temptaverit, secundo terciove commonita, si non emendaverit, anathemati subjaceat[15] donec et de turbatione ecclesie et contemptu auctoritatis nostre condigne satisfecerit. Huius

5 Perona *B*.
6 *Sic A*, *B*; *read* capsi.
7 Buzchesvennez *B*.
8 Ivoni *B*.
9 Ivo *B*.
10 Radulfo *B*.
11 *Add. A*.
12 The Benedictine abbey of Mont-Saint-Quentin.
13 The Augustinian abbey of Notre-Dame d'Eaucourt.
14 coenobii *B*.
15 sabiaceat *B*.

rei testes fuerunt: Hugo cancellarius,[16] Radulphus[17,18] de Helli, Aszo[19] medicus, Radulphus[20,21] castellanus de Nigella, Frumoldus[22] castellanus de Yprei, Engelrannus de Casneel,[23] Gerardus Pincerna, Petrus de Croisiles,[24,25] Guinemarus[26] Pincerna et[27] villicus de Athies.[28,29] Actum est hoc anno incarnationis dominice M° C° XXX° VIII°, epacta VII[a],[30] indictione prima,[31] concurrente V°.[32]

300

1152. Bonneuil.

Baudouin [II],[1] *bishop of Noyon, confirms the gifts in alms that Raoul* Pulcher[2] *made to the church of Prémontré: seven* modii *of grain (*frumentum*) at Waily*[3] *that he held in fief from Baudouin*[4] Rufus *de Péronne; the land of* Solente

---

20 Hugues III de Roye, chancellor of Noyon-Tournai, ca. 1130–46, and of Noyon, 1146–63/6. Pycke, *Le chapitre cathédral Notre-Dame de Tournai de la fin du XIe à la fin du XIIIe siècle*, 64.

21 Radulfus *B.*

22 Raoul d'Heilly, son of Thibault II, lord of Heilly, and his wife Mabille. Darsy, *Bénéfices de l'église d'Amiens, ou État général des biens, revenus et charges du clergé du diocèse d'Amiens en 1730, avec des notes*, vol. 1, 321, fn. 1.

23 A *medicus* called Aszo also appears as a witness in **397** and **443**. Wickersheimer, Beaujouan, and Jacquart, *Dictionnaire biographique des médecins en France au moyen âge*, vol. 3, 34.

20 Radulfus *B.*

21 Raoul I, castellan of Nesle (d. ca. 1139–46); married Adèle, sister of Guy II, castellan of Noyon and Coucy. Newman, *Seigneurs*, vol. 2, 211.

22 Either Fromold I, castellan of Ypres, son of Thibaut I, castellan of Ypres, or his son Fromold II, castellan of Ypres.

23 Likely Le Caisnel, comm. Villequier-Aumont, https://dicotopo.cths.fr/places/P21435178.

24 Chroisiles *B.*

25 Croisilles, arr. Arras, https://dicotopo.cths.fr/places/P85269058.

26 Guinemars *B.*

27 *Add.* Pincerna et *A.*

28 Atthies *B*; *Om* Radulfus miles de Atthies *A.*

29 Athies, cant. Ham, https://dicotopo.cths.fr/places/P98820850.

30 VII *B.*

31 I *B.*

32 V *B.*

---

1 Baudouin II de Boulogne, abbot of the Augustinian abbey of Saint-Eloi-Fontaine, ca. 1130–ca. 1139, and bishop of Noyon, 1148–67. *GC* IX, col. 1126.

2 Raoul *Pulcher*, brother of Hubert, appears also in **316**, **337**, **372**, and **436**, and is attested in acts to do with the lords of Nesle, 1150s–70s. Newman, *Seigneurs*, vol. 2, 59, 133.

3 Likely Wailly, cant. Roye, https://dicotopo.cths.fr/places/P28127371.

4 Baudouin *Rufus* de Péronne appears as a witness in acts concerning the lords of Nesle, 1150s–70s. His son, Jean, married Adèle, daughter of Raoul, castellan of Nesle. Newman, *Seigneurs*, vol. 2, 62, 149.

that he held in fief from Raoul, castellan of Nesle; and the land and meadow of Hallon[5] *that he held in* census *from Baudouin d'Ollezy.*[6] *Raoul* Pulcher*'s siblings Guy, Pierre, Aelide, and Beatrice and their unnamed mother consent to the second part of the gift, as does Raoul,*[7] *castellan of Nesle; Baudouin d'Ollezy consented to the third part of the gift. All of the gifts were consented to by Béatrice, wife of Raoul* Pulcher*, and their children Jean, Pierre, Elizabeth, Marge, and Marie.*

A. Cartulary of Prémontré, fol. 77v.

B. Original, AD Somme, 20 H 5, no. 1, previously sealed with a double strip of leather.

Karta Noviomensis episcopi de elemosina Radulphi Pulchri quam contulit ecclesie Premonstrati.

[I]n nomine sancte et individue Trinitatis. Quoniam memorie hominum que facile labitur plerumque temporum vetustas id quod minus caute agitur surripere consuevit, maiorum sollers[8] industria utilitati providens posterorum rerum gestarum seriem litterarum apicibus conservandam decrevit. Quorum vestigia subsecutus nec ab eorum rectitudine discrepans, ego Balduinus, Dei gratia Noviomensium episcopus, notum fieri volo tam futuris quam presentibus quod Radulphus,[9] cognomento Pulcher, contulit Premonstrate ecclesie in elemosinam ob remedium anime sue et predecessorum suorum quemdam[10] redditum septem modiorum frumenti ad Wali, concessu Balduini Rufi de Perrona, a quo ipsum in feodo tenebat. Ubi autem hoc donum fecit ipse Radulphus[11] Balduinusque feodum ecclesie concessit, fuerunt hii testes: Radulphus[12] Brumen, Johannes de Sali,[13] Hugo de Onella,[14] Radulphus[15] Pauper, Ursus de Anemens.[16] Itemque predictus Radulphus[17] aliud donum prenominate ecclesie

5 Hallon, cant. Ham, https://dicotopo.cths.fr/places/P04670263.

6 Ollezy, cant. Saint-Simon, https://dicotopo.cths.fr/places/P53765347.

7 Raoul II, castellan of Nesle, son of Raoul I, castellan of Nesle, and Adèle, sister of Guy II, castellan of Noyon and Coucy. Newman, *Seigneurs*, vol. 2, 211.

8 solers *B*.

9 Radulfus *B*.

10 quendam *B*.

11 Radulfus *B*.

12 Radulfus *B*.

13 Sailly-Saillisel, cant. Combles, https://dicotopo.cths.fr/places/P67749862.

14 Ognolles, cant. Guiscard, https://dicotopo.cths.fr/places/P57919721.

15 Radulfus *B*.

16 Ennemain, cant. Ham, https://dicotopo.cths.fr/places/P17633360.

17 Radulfus *B*.

contulit de quadam terra de Solenta, annuente Radulpho[18] castellano de Nigella, cum fratribus suis Widone et Petro, sororibusque suis Aalide et Beatrice una cum matre eorum. Ubi vero hoc donum Radulphus[19] fecit prenominatique de quorum feodo descendebat feodum ipsum, ecclesie concesserunt, fuerunt hii testes: Robertus de Espennecurt[20] et Robertus de Gardin et Drogo de Mainercurt et Odo, maior de Maisnil.[21,22] Rursumque ipse aliud donum predicte ecclesie fecit de quadam terra et quodam prato de Haluns[23] que censualiter tenebat de Balduino de Olesi pro censu XVIII°[24] nummorum obolorum que Balduinus[25] pro eodem censu concessit sub hiis testibus: Symone videlicet de Monstencurt[26] et Albrico[27] de Roia. Hec autem omnia dona una die facta sunt que quidem concesserunt Beatrix, uxor ipsius Radulphi,[28] et filii sui, Johannes et Petrus, filieque Elisabeth,[29] Marga et Maria, presentibus testibus istis Odone[30] Crasso de Diva et Odone de Bretul, Ingerranno[31] de Cella[32] et Ingerrano[33] de Landovesin.[34] Que omnia, ut rata inconvulsaque ecclesie permaneant, sigilli nostri impressione roboramus et ne quis in posterum ecclesie dampnum irroget, sub anathemate interdicimus testesque legitimos qui huic nostre confirmationi interfuerunt, supponimus, Hugonem[35] videlicet cancellarium, Reinerum et Alulfum capellanos. Actum anno incarnationis dominice M° C° LII°, apud Bonolium.

18 Radulfo *B.*
19 Radulfus *B.*
20 Epénancourt, cant. Nesle, https://dicotopo.cths.fr/places/P27455616.
21 Mainil *B.*
22 Probably Mesnil-Brunel, cant. Péronne, https://dicotopo.cths.fr/places/P62504714.
23 Hallon, cant. Ham, https://dicotopo.cths.fr/places/P04670263.
24 XVIII^to *B.*
25 *Om.* ecclesie *A.*
26 Likely Montécourt, cant. Ham, https://dicotopo.cths.fr/places/P29088475.
27 Aubry, lord of Roye and Becquigny, was the *dapifer* of Raoul, count of Vermandois in the 1130s/40s. He was the husband of one Mathilde, and brother of Wermond, lord of Cessoy. Tock and Milis, *Monumenta Arroasiensia*, 242–3; Guyotjeannin, *Episcopus*, 220; Newman, *Seigneurs*, vol. 2, 299; Newman, *Homblières*, 110. He is likely the same Aubry de Roye who appears in **371**, **398**, **442**, and **464**.
28 Radulfi *B.*
29 Elisabet *B.*
30 Perhaps the same Eudes *Crassus* who is attested in an act in the cartulary of Homblières, 1155–60. Newman, *Homblières*, 156.
31 Ingranno *B.*
32 Cenlla *B.*
33 Ingranno *B.*
34 Languevoisin, cant. Nesle, https://dicotopo.cths.fr/places/P00746276.
35 Hugues III de Roye, chancellor of Noyon-Tournai, ca. 1130–46, and of Noyon, 1146–63/6. Pycke, *Le chapitre cathédral Notre-Dame de Tournai de la fin du XIe à la fin du XIIIe siècle*, 64.

301

1140

Simon [I],[1] bishop of Noyon, makes known that Milon[2] de Voyennes and Jean, his nephew, gave all their goods to the church of Prémontré.

A. Cartulary of Prémontré, fol. 77v.
B. Original, AD Somme, 20 H_SC_19, no. 1, sealed.[3]
EDITION: Pycke and Vleeschouwers, *Actes*, 446.

Karta Noviomensis episcopi de confirmatione elemosine Milonis de Viana.

[I]n nomine sancte et individue Trinitatis. Ego Symon, Dei gratia Noviomensis episcopus, notum fieri volo tam futuris quam presentibus quod Milo de Viana et Johannes, nepos eius, contulerunt ecclesie Premonstrate, ob remedium anime sue et parentum suorum, omnem possessionem suam, in hereditate, in alodiis et manuum firmitate coram hiis testibus: domino Yvone[4] de Nigella et Drogone[5] et Radulpho,[6] fratribus suis, Herberto Cocco, Radulpho Paupere, Warnero de Haincurt, Roberto de Marcels, Johanne Lefrardo filio eius, Matheo de Calleincurt,[7] Odone nepote Roberti de Marcels, Petro filio eiusdem, Warnero Pelochin. Hoc autem donum fideliter et devote oblatum quisquis temeraria presumptione defraudare vel inminuere temptaverit anathema sit. Actum hoc anno incarnationis dominice M° C° XL°, epacta tricesima, indictione tercia, concurrente primo.

302

1155

Baudouin [II],[1] bishop of Noyon, makes known that when Adélaïde, widow of Gervin, entered Prémontré, she gave all her allod of Senicourt[2] to Prémontré.

---

1 Simon I de Vermandois (d. 1148) was the son of Hugues I and Adélaïde, count and countess of Vermandois and Valois, and bishop of Noyon, 1123–42.
2 Milon de Voyennes (cant. Nesle, https://dicotopo.cths.fr/places/P32215646) also appears in acts **274** and **358**.
3 Due to conservation concerns, the original was not available to the editors.
4 Yves II de Nesle (d. ca. 1178), lord of Nesle and count of Soissons, son of Raoul, lord of Nesle, and Raintrude. Newman, *Seigneurs*, vol. 1, 61.
5 Dreux de Nesle, knight (d. aft. 1146) son of Raoul, lord of Nesle, and Raintrude. Newman, *Seigneurs*, vol. 1, 62.
6 Raoul de Nesle, castellan of Nesle and of Bruges (d. ca. 1160), son of Raoul, lord of Nesle, and Raintrude. Newman, *Seigneurs*, vol. 1, 62–3.
7 Likely Caulaincourt, cant. Vermand, https://dicotopo.cths.fr/places/P02972526.

---

1 Baudouin II de Boulogne, abbot of the Augustinian abbey of Saint-Eloi-Fontaine, ca. 1130–ca. 1139, and bishop of Noyon, 1148–67. *GC* IX, col. 1126.
2 Likely Senicourt, cant. Chauny, https://dicotopo.cths.fr/places/P01572377.

Her sons Renier, Pierre, Hugues, and Robert consented to this. When Renier, the eldest, died after departing for Jerusalem, Hugues took back the allod, but recognized his transgression and returned it to Prémontré with Pierre and Robert's consent.

A. Cartulary of Prémontré, fol. 77v.
B. Original, AN, L 995, no. 23, previously sealed.

Karta episcopi Noviomensis de elemosina Adelidis uxoris Gervini de alodio de Sinicourt.

[I]n nomine sancte et individue Trinitatis. Ego B[alduinus], Dei gratia Noviomensium episcopus, notum volo fieri omnibus tam modernis quam futuris quod Adelidis, uxor Gervini, veniens ad conversionem, contulit in elemosinam ecclesie Premonstrati totum alodium suum de Sinicurt quod habebat tam in terris quam in pratis, annuentibus filius suis, Renero[3] et[4] Petro, Hugone et Roberto. Contigit autem ut Rainerus, qui maior erat natu, profectus Jerosolimam moreretur et resaisivit Hugo, frater eiusdem Reneri,[5] totam elemosinam, sed cum tandem penituisset multis corripientibus eum recognovit et reconcessit ecclesie Premonstrate predictam elemosinam, annuentibus iterum fratribus suis, Petro et Roberto. Concessit autem sub his testibus Balduino[6] decano, Gilleberto[7] decano, Hugone Furnero, Radulfo Stulto, Willelmo, Drogone, Theoderico, Matheo, Guidone Dieto conversis. Actum anno dominice incarnationis M° C° LV°.

303

1182

Abbot Gautier[1] *and the chapter of Arrouaise make known an exchange of land in the territory of Douilly*[2] *and Quivières*[3] *between the brothers at Margères*[4] *and the Premonstratensian brothers of Montizel.*[5]

---

3 Rainero *B*.
4 *Add.* et *A*.
5 Raineri *B*.
6 Baudouin, dean of Noyon, attested 1132–74. AD Oise, G 1984, fols. 71r, 78v–79v.
7 Gisleberto *B*.

---

1 Gautier de Cambrai, abbot of the Augustinian abbey of Saint-Nicolas d'Arrouaise, 1180–93. Franklin, *Dictionnaire des noms, surnoms et pseudonymes latins de l'histoire littéraire du Moyen-âge (1100 à 1530)*, col. 43.
2 Douilly, cant. Ham, https://dicotopo.cths.fr/places/P87195366.
3 Quivières, cant. Ham, https://dicotopo.cths.fr/places/P53835780.
4 The Arroasian priory of Margères.
5 Montizel, cant. Ham, https://dicotopo.cths.fr/places/P16235568.

A. Cartulary of Prémontré, fols. 77v–78r.
B. Original BnF, Coll. Flandres et Arras 183, pièce Arras no. 1, previously sealed.
EDITION: *Chartae Galliae*, no. 201287, http://telma.irht.cnrs.fr/outils/chartae-galliae/charte201287/; Tock and Milis, *Monumenta Arroasiensia*, 306–8.

Karta Walteri abbatis de Aroasia de quadam permutatione in territorio de Douilli inter canonicos de Aroasia et fratres Premonstratenses.

[I]n nomine Patris et Filii et Spiritus Sancti, amen. Ego Walterus, Aroasie dictus abbas et capitulum nostrum, notum fieri volumus presentibus et futuris quod fratres nostri de Margellis habebant quandam terram in territorio de Douilli,[6] similiter fratres de Monte Iselli habebant quandam terram in territorio de Kiveres. Quia igitur terra fratrum de Monte Iselli est contigua terre fratrum nostrorum de Margellis et terra fratrum de Margellis juncta est terre fratrum de Monte Iselli, communi consilio et assensu utriusque ecclesie, videlicet Sancti Nicholai de Aroasia et Premonstrate, fratres de Monte Iselli dederunt fratribus de Margellis XIcim sextariatas terre in territorio de Kiveres, quas ibidem habebant ex dono Waldonis de Lanci[7] liberas in perpetuam elemosinam, in campo videlicet juxta calciatam sex[8] sextariatas ~~quas iam dicti fratres~~ et dimidiam, in alio campo juxta semitam, unam sextariatam et tres[9] virgas, et in campo ad quartarios III sextaria et octo[10] virgas pro undecim[11] sexteriatis quas iam dicti fratres habebant in diversis locis adherentes campis fratrum de Monte Iselli, scilicet in Montfalcon sextariatam unam ex dono Roberti Pilosi, et in Caumaisnil III mencoldos et III virgas ex dono Roberti Creue, et in Civreres III sextariatas et dimidiam III virgas minus ex dono Hugonis Nigri de Montisel, et in Beeloi II sextariatas et X virgas et dimidiam et in valle Berte ex dono Alberici de Montisel III sextariatas et dimidiam III virgas et dimidia minus. Unaqueque autem ecclesia, alteri ecclesie terras quas contulit warantizare ab omni calumpnia et adquitare ab omni consuetudine et censu debebit. Quod ut firmum et stabile in perpetuum valeat permanere cirographi[12] divisione et utriusque matricis ecclesie sigilli appositione ac testium suppositione

6 Doilli *B*.
7 Lanchy, cant. Vermand, https://dicotopo.cths.fr/places/P51978975.
8 VI *B*.
9 III *B*.
10 VIIIto *B*.
11 XIcim *B*.
12 cyrographi *B*.

istud cambium placuit communire. Testes ex una parte Radulphus[13] prior de Margellis, Arnulphus[14,15] prepositus, Petrus, Robertus, Malgerus, conversi, Arnulphus[16] Colpesac,[17] Theobaldus de Haluns,[18] ~~de~~ Petrus Ligais, item Arnulphus.[19] Ex alia parte Gaufridus, magister de Bonolio,[20] Galterus canonicus, Wiardus, Rainoldus conversi, Bouderus de Oreoir,[21] Rainoldus de Lanci laici. Actum anno Domini M° C° LXXX° II°.

304

November, 1227.

Renier [II],[1] lord of Sains, renounces any claims to the modiagium *of Collezy[2] that his maternal grandfather Eudes [III],[3] lord of Ham, gave in* maritagium *to Renier's parents, Marie and Geoffroi, since he is unable to locate the relevant documents. (See* ***357****,* ***417****, and* ***422****.)*

A. Cartulary of Prémontré, fol. 78r.
B. Original, AD Somme, 20 H 6, no. 23, previously sealed on a double strip of parchment.

Karta Reneri domini de Seinz de eo quod renunciavit quibusdam litteris concessis in maritagium filie sue.

[E]go Renerus, dominus de Seins, notum facio universis tam presentibus quam futuris quod ego renunciavi ex toto litteris illis quas bone memorie Odo, dominus Hamensis Castri, avus meus, contulit in maritagium Marie, filie sue,

13 Raoul (II?) (d. 1206), prior of the Arroasian priory of Margères in the latter part of the twelfth century and briefly abbot of Saint-Nicolas d'Arrouaise ca. 1201. Josse, *Notice historique sur le village de Douilly et ses dépendances*, 94–6.
14 Ernulphus *B*.
15 Arnoul, prior of Arrouaise, ca. 1167–ca. 1182. Tock and Milis, *Monumenta Arroasiensia*, 255, 260, 272, 284, 285, 668.
16 Ernulphus *B*.
17 Perhaps a member of the Colpesac family, a prominent *bourgeois* family in Reims in the twelfth–thirteenth centuries. Schmugge, "Ministerialität und Bürgertum in Reims," 183–4.
18 Hallon, cant. Ham, https://dicotopo.cths.fr/places/P04670263.
19 Ernulphus *B*.
20 The Premonstratensian *curtis* of Bonneuil. *MP* II, 484.
21 Auroir, comm. Foreste, https://dicotopo.cths.fr/places/P79580266.

1 Renier II, lord of Sains (arr. Vervins, https://dicotopo.cths.fr/places/P35898483), son of Geoffroi, lord of Sains, and his first wife Marie de Ham, attested in the 1220s. BM Reims MS 1563 (N. Fonds), fol. 157v; Melleville, *DH*, vol. 2, 305.
2 Collezy, comm. Berlancourt, https://dicotopo.cths.fr/places/P68465476.
3 Eudes III, lord of Ham, son of Lancelin, lord of Ham, and Mathilde.

matri mee, cum Godefrido patre meo pro modiagio illo quod datum fuit ei in suo maritagio apud Colesi et volo quod sciant universi quod si ille littere, vel tempore meo, vel temporibus heredum et successorum meorum, producte vel ostense fuerint, quoquomodo non licebit mihi aut heredibus aut successoribus meis illis uti nec erunt alicuius valoris, immo de cetero sunt irrite penitus et inanes ac si nunquam facte fuissent. Juravit[4] insuper in sancta quod si ipsas litteras potuero invenire, vel eas karissimo avunculo meo Odoni, domino Hamensi Castri, restituam bona fide, vel eas coram ipso discerpam. In cuius rei testimonium presentes litteras sigilli mei munimine roboravi. Actum mense novembri, anno gratie M° CC° vicesimo VII°.[5]

305

July, 1232.

Abbot Conrad[1] *and the chapter of Prémontré make known that the agreement according to which they had paid Matthieu de Cressy*[2] *10* modii *of grain (*frumentum*), measure of Nesle, in recognition of the gift of land at Bonneuil*[3] *made by Matthieu's ancestors, is modified so that in future Prémontré will pay six* modii*, measure of Ham. Roger, abbot of Ham,*[4] *affixes his seal to the charter.*

A. Cartulary of Prémontré, fol. 78r.

B. Original (chirograph), AD Oise, H 6007, previously sealed with two seals on strips of parchment, one strip of which survives. In the left margin and beginning at the top, the lower half of the letters that form the word CYROGRAPHUM.

Karta Conradi abbatis Premonstratensis de antecessoribus Matthei de Creci qui dederunt quasdam possessiones sub annuo censu decem modiorum frumenti apud Bonolium.

[E]go Conradus, dictus abbas Premonstratensis, et capitulum nostrum notum facimus universis tam presentibus quam futuris quod cum antecessores Mathei de Cresci[5] possessiones quasdam olim dedissent in territorio Bonolii ecclesie

4 Juravi *B*.
5 septimo *B*.

1 Conrad the Swabian was prior of Weissenau, 1203–17, abbot of Valsecret, 1218–20, abbot of Prémontré, 1220–33, and abbot of Cuissy, aft. 1235–41. *MP* I, 89; *MP* II, 497, 527, 536.
2 Likely Cressy-Omancourt, cant. Roye, https://dicotopo.cths.fr/places/P62235034.
3 Bonneuil, cant. Ham, https://dicotopo.cths.fr/places/P66750585.
4 The Augustinian abbey of Notre-Dame de Ham.
5 Cressi *B*.

Premonstratensi et propter hoc solveremus eis annuatim decem modios frumenti ad mensuram Nigelle,[6] redacti sunt in sex modios ad mensuram Hamensem et eosdem sex modios debemus annuatim dicto Matheo solvere de decima quam habemus apud Cressi et, si minus ibi fuerit, de nostro supplebimus vecturis nostris usque ad[7] Nigellam vel usque Cressi deducendum, annuatim, infra festum Omnium Sanctorum ita quod tam idem Matheus quam heredes sui qui tenebunt dictos sex modios, tenebuntur facere hominium ecclesie nostre, hoc adiecto quod ipsos sex modios nec aliquem ipsorum poterunt dare vel vendere vel invadiare nisi ecclesie nostre, si tantum inde dare voluerimus quantum quilibet alius. Insuper sciant universi quod supradicti X^{cem}[8] modii qui erant olim ad mensuram Nigelle redacti sunt in sex modios ad mensuram Hamensem tam per venditionem quam per elemosinam. Quod ut firmiter observetur presenti scripto sigillum nostrum et sigillum venerabilis abbatis, Rogeri de Hamo, fecimus apponi. Actum anno incarnationis dominice M^o CC^o XXX° secundo, mense julio.

306

1177

Renaud,[1] *bishop of Noyon, gives notice that Eudes [III],*[2] *lord of Ham, gave lands and woods at Collezy*[3] *in alms to the churches of Prémontré and Ham to be cleared and cultivated. Elizabeth, Eudes's wife, his unnamed brothers, and unnamed sons promise to uphold the gift's terms, while Eudes's brother-in-law Rorigon*[4] *de Fayet and his wife Rotasia, husband and wife Jean*[5] *d'Athiès and Eustacie, and their children Manessès, Robert, Albert, and Eudes the cleric, also consent, as do Philippe and Elizabeth, count and countess of Flanders and Vermandois. (See* ***485****.)*

6 *Om.* Ita postmodum factum est inter nos et ipsos quod illi decem modii ad mensuram Nigelle *A*.
7 *Add.* Ad *A*.
8 decem *B*.

1 Renaud, bishop of Noyon, 1175–88.
2 Eudes III, lord of Ham, son of Lancelin, lord of Ham, and Mathilde.
3 Collezy, comm. Berlancourt, https://dicotopo.cths.fr/places/P68465476.
4 Rorigon, lord of Fayet (d. ca. 1199), and Simon (d. ca. 1187), sons of Aude, lady of Fayet. Newman, *Seigneurs*, vol. 2, 102.
5 Jean d'Athies, son of Robert *Rufus*, nephew of Mathieu and Bernier, and brother of Widèle and Adam. With his wife Eustacie, he was the father of Manassès, Robert, Aubry, and Eudes the cleric. With his brother Adam, knight and lord of Athies (cant. Ham, https://dicotopo.cths.fr/places/P98820850), he is attested in a number of acts ca. 1150–ca. 1188. Cagny, *Histoire de l'arrondissement de Péronne*, vol. 2, 259; Tock and Milis, *Monumenta Arroasiensia*, 251. He is also mentioned in **353**, **371**, **398**, **421**, **424**, and **442**.

A. Cartulary of Prémontré, fols. 78r–79r.
B. Original, AD Somme, 20 H_SC_6, no. 4.[6]

Karta Noviomensis episcopi de elemosina domini Hamensis super terra et nemore que Colesiacum nuncupatur [*margo*: Scripta de Colesi.]

[I]n nomine Patris et Filii et Spiritus Sancti, amen. Ego Rainaldus, Dei gratia episcopus Noviomensis, notum fieri volo tam futuris quam presentibus quod Odo, dominus Castri Hamensis, dedit totam terram et totum nemus quod Colesiacum nuncupatur ecclesie Premonstratensi et ecclesie Hamensi in elemosinam ad extirpandum et excolendum et omnimodum utriusque ecclesie commoditatem, pro suo earum arbitrio nichil in eadem terra vel nemore retinens preter subscriptum censum. Solvent predicte ecclesie ipsi Odoni et heredibus suis annuatim pro singulis terre modiatis singulos modios, duas partes frumenti, terciam partem avene; tale autem ei et heredibus suis solvetur frumentum quale creverit communiter in eadem terra; terminus huius solutionis est in festo Sancti Remigii, quod est kalendas octobris, ad mensuram Hami tempore huius donationis currentem, que sine diminutione vel augmentatione in utraque ecclesia servabitur et ligno ad lignum mensurabitur. Ipse autem prefatus Odo et heredes sui facient eundem censum per proprios suos ministros requiri vel per proprias suas vecturas duci quo voluerint; si eis sederit ut in grangiis fratrum servetur, servabunt usque ad Pascha et si interim, vel incendio, vel aliquo infortunio deperierit, et annona eorum simul non eis restituent a Pascha autem et deinceps non tenebuntur servare et, si ibi post Pascha predictum censum dimiserunt, quicquid inde contigerit non eis respondebunt. Excipiuntur ab huius ~~modi~~ census solutione decem modiate terre vel nemoris quas predictis ecclesiis dedit liberas ad faciendas curtes et domos construendas, ortos et virgulta sive etiam ad nemus reservandum vel ad aliud faciendum quod eis placuerit, ubi compententius sibi providerint. Quas curtes in perpetuum liberas et quitas esse concessit ab omni requisitione banni, sanguinis, latronis, rotagii, foragii, winagii et omnium consuetudinum et, ut nulli liceat ibi hominem capere pro qualicumque forisfacto vel aliquam violentiam inferre; quilibet etiam mercennarii eorum tutam habeant veniendi ad eos et redeundi potestatem. Siquis autem de familia eorum vel de aliquibus operariis ad eos pertinentibus in toto territorio de Colesi aliquod forisfactum fecerit adversus prefatum Odonem vel homines suos, cum per ipsum aut per ministros suos magistris curiarum innotuerit, aut facient emendari infra spacium quindecim dierum aut, si reus emendare noluerit, emittent eum et potestatem habebunt conducendi eum extra dominium Hamensis domini salvum cum rebus suis. Si

6 Due to conservation concerns, the original was not available to the editors.

quid ibi fratres vendiderint vel emerint, liberi erunt tam venditor quam emptor ab omni consuetudine et exactione, et emptor via qua volet, liber abibit excepto quod si voluerit per transversum eius transire, ibi dabit quod justum est; infra villam de Ham et de Estoilli et in omni loco dominationis eius de omnibus que ipsi fratres ducent, portabunt, vendent aut ement, liberos eos esse concessit ab omni consuetudine et winagio quod a ceteris ei reddi solet. Pascua etiam et aisentias et vicinitatis jura concessit eis per omnem terram libera. Sciendum preterea quod de predicto censu dedit in elemosinam in perpetuum ecclesie Sancti Quintini IIII[or] modios frumenti ad predictam mensuram Hami, in festo Sancti Remigii, cum suis propriis vecturis ducendos, quos assignavit annuatim accipiendos a predictis ecclesiis, duos videlicet modios a Premonstratensi et duos ab Hamensi de residuo autem censu ipse Odo vel heredes sui non poterunt quicquam dare vel elemosinam facere alii ecclesie nisi prefatis ecclesiis nec etiam vendere sive invadiare, si tantum inde facere voluerint quantum alius. Attamen filiis et fratribus et sorori sue dare vel vendere poterit, ita dumtaxat ut et ipsi et successores eorum teneantur sub predicta pactione. Has omnes pactiones promiserunt ipse et uxor eius, Elizabeth, et fratres eius et filii sub fidei sue sponsione se fideliter servaturos, assentientibus et laudantibus Rorigone, sororio suo, et uxore sua, Rotasia, Johanne etiam de Athies et uxore eius, Eustachia, et liberis, Manasse, Roberto, Albrico, Odone clerico. Insuper adversus omnes qui super hiis calumpniam moverint adversus predictas ecclesias legitimam garandiam portabunt infra Noviomensem episcopatum et Viromandensem comitatum ita sane quod, si deficerent a guarandia vel ab observantia pactionum resilirent predicte ecclesie censum pretaxatum retinerent donec pacem de omnibus haberent. Hanc igitur donationem cum prescriptis pactionibus ipse prefatus Odo et uxor eius, Elizabeth, et filii in manum nostram posuerunt et fratres etiam ipsius Odonis, et nos eandem donationem utrique ecclesie resignavimus. Et quia de feodo et hereditate Elizabeth, uxoris comitis Flandrensis et Viromandensis Philippi, predictum nemus et terra descendebat, pretaxatam ipsius Odonis donationem cum prescriptis pactionibus concesserunt et utrique prefate ecclesie litteris suis confirmaverunt. Huic igitur donationi coram nobis facte interfuerunt: Balduinus cancellarius noster, magister Ingelrannus et Tieszo, presbiteri et canonici ecclesie nostre, Rorigo de Faiel et Symon frater eius, Johannes de Athies et Adam[7] frater eius, Manasses et Robertus filii eiusdem Johannis, Balduinus de Olesi,[8] Odo[9] de Bonolio, Willermus

7 Adam, knight and lord of Athies (cant. Ham, https://dicotopo.cths.fr/places/P98820850), son of Robert Rufus, nephew of Mathieu and Bernier, and brother of Widèle and Jean. He attested a number of acts ca. 1150–ca. 1188. Cagny, *Histoire de l'arrondissement de Péronne*, vol. 2, 259; Tock and Milis, *Monumenta Arroasiensia*, 251. He also appears in **485**.

8 Ollezy, cant. Saint-Simon, https://dicotopo.cths.fr/places/P53765347.

9 Eudes de Bonneuil appears as a witness in acts dated 1140–78. Newman, *Seigneurs*, vol. 2, 119.

de Vileta,[10] Petrus[11] de Plessei, Walterus de Bruci,[12] Marcellus de Flavi. Ut igitur hec omnia perpetue stabilitatis robur optineant et utraque ecclesia scripti sui munimine fulciatur presentem paginam et cirographi conscriptione et proprii sigilli nostri impressione communire curavimus. Actum anno incarnati verbi M° C° LXX° VII°. Ego Balduinus[13] cancellarius Noviomensis legi.

307

1190. Prémontré.

Abbot Obert[1] *and the chapter of Prémontré make known the terms by which Raoul de Cartigny,*[2] *priest of Offoy,*[3] *undertakes to pay husband and wife Geoffroi, knight of* Tumbis, *and Béatrice the 42* librae Atrebatensium *that Prémontré had agreed to pay the couple for the acquisition of an annual seven* modii *of grain (*frumentum*), measure of Ham.*

A. Cartulary of Prémontré, fol. 79r.

B. Original (chirograph), BnF, Coll. Picardie 290, no. 17, previously sealed. In the left margin and beginning at the top, the upper half of the letters that form the word CHYROGRAPHUM.

Karta Oberti ecclesie Premonstratensis abbatis de decima de Ulfois.

[O]bertus ecclesie Premonstratensis abbas totumque capitulum universis presentibus et futuris in perpetuum. Noverint universi quod cum septem modios frumenti ad mensuram Hamensem qui Gaufrido, militi de Tumbis, et uxori eius, Beatrici, de decima de Ulfois a nobis pensione annua debebantur, ab eis eorumque liberis cum emptionis tum elemosine titulo acquisissemus, quoniam non sine multo detrimento et gravamine ad solutionem tante pecunie, videlicet quadraginta duarum librarum Atrebatensis[4] monete, domus nostra posset sufficere, dilectus noster Radulphus de Carteni, presbiter de Ulfois, ad petitionem

10 Villette, cant. Ham, https://dicotopo.cths.fr/places/P77128677.

11 Pierre du Plessis (Plessis-Patte-d'Oie, cant. Guiscard, https://dicotopo.cths.fr/places/P25690373) is a witness in **336**, **344**, and **485**.

12 Brouchy, cant. Ham, https://dicotopo.cths.fr/places/P33557845.

13 Baudouin, chancellor of Noyon, ca. 1172–ca. 1186. Stein, *Cartulaire de l'ancienne abbaye de Saint Nicolas des Prés sous Ribemont*, 62, 122.

1 Obert, abbot of the Premonstratensian abbey of Valsecret, 1186–9, 1192–1200, and abbot of Prémontré, 1189–91. *MP* II, 527, 536.

2 Cartigny, cant. Péronne, https://dicotopo.cths.fr/places/P86731604.

3 Offoy, cant. Ham, https://dicotopo.cths.fr/places/P14011159.

4 Attrebatensis *B*.

nostram predictam solvit pecuniam et nos ei annonam concessimus possidendam; in sartis quoque et novalibus nostris de Colesi[5] duos sextarios frumenti ad mensuram prenominatam acquisivit. Nos igitur pro septem modiis et duobus sextariis predictis sex modios frumenti ad mensuram Noviomensem, decem et septem mencoldis raso ad rasum mensuratis pro modio conputatis, frumento quidem duobus denariis tantum valente minus meliore eidem Radulfo annuatim tenemur solvere ac infra festum Sancti Remigii Noviomum, sumptibus et vehiculis nostris, intra muros ubicumque voluerit adducere. Post decessum autem eius ob salutem anime matris sue, que in domo nostra de Bonolio requiescit sepulta, pro sua quoque suorumque predecessorum animabus, unum modium et dimidium eidem domui aliumque modium et dimidium domui Premonstratensi in elemosinam in perpetuum contulit et concessit ea devotione quod in die anniversarii matris sue tam apud Premonstratum quam apud Bonolium servitium pro ipsa celebrabitur et utriusque domus conventus ipsa die plenius solito reficietur. Tres autem residuos modios, modo et tenore prescripto, cuicumque idem R[adulphus] assignaverit, nostra in perpetuum solvet ecclesia annuatim et post decessum eius quando ab his quibus illi modii fuerint assignati, requisiti fuerimus super hoc scriptum et sigillum nostrum conferemus. Siquis autem processu temporis super predicta annona ei calumpnia aut perturbationem aliquam moliretur inferre, nos ei et successoribus suis secundum formam et tenorem presentis pagine tenemur guarandire et inviolabiliter conservare. Ut igitur prescripta nullo posteritatis incursu perturbata roborentur firmitate perpetua presentis pagine testimonio ac sigilli nostri patrocinio cum astipulatione personarum que ascripte[6] sunt, memorato Radulpho tradidimus confirmata. S. Walteri,[7] abbatis Buciliensis. S. Renelmi, prioris nostri. S. Clarenbaldi, sacriste. S. Johannis, cellerarii. S. Raineri, camerarii. S. Gaufridi, prepositi. S. sacerdotum. S. Roberti de Duaco. S. Johannis de Sancto Paulo.[8] S. Radulphi[9] de Tilloi.[10] S. Hugonis Flandrensis. S. Lamberti,[11] Noviomensis diaconorum. S. Evrardi[12] de Hyrun.[13] S. Huberti de Perrona. S. Symonis Suessionensis. S. Herberti de Guisia. S. Hugonis de Nigella, subdiaconorum. S.

5 Collezy, comm. Berlancourt, https://dicotopo.cths.fr/places/P68465476.

6 subscripte *B.*

7 Gautier (d. 1195), abbot of the Premonstratensian abbey of Bucilly. *MP* II, 366.

8 Perhaps Saint-Paul-aux-Bois, cant. Coucy-le-Château, https://dicotopo.cths.fr/places/P45354298.

9 Radulfi *B.*

10 Thilloy, cant. Roye, https://dicotopo.cths.fr/places/P99200969.

11 A *Lambertus diaconus* appears as a witness in an 1185 charter of Adèle de Montepré, sister of Raoul, castellan of Nesle. *Chartae Galliae*, no. 201296, http://telma.irht.cnrs.fr/chartes/chartae-galliae/charte201296/.

12 Guerardi *B.*

13 Iron, cant. Guise, https://dicotopo.cths.fr/places/P04584610.

Bernardi de Fossis. S. Walteri de Hanapiis.[14] S. Nicholai de Atheci.[15,16] S. Hugonis de Cassel.[17] S. Johannis de Nigella, conversorum et fratrum Premonstrate ecclesie. S. Evrardi de Matheni.[18] S. Albrici de Plasseio. S. Walteri de Vilete[19] et Albrici fratrum. S. Rainaldi[20] de Flavi, militum. S. Manasse de Ulfois.[21] S. Mathei de Hunbleus.[22,23] S. Odonis le Creue. S. Roberti Pedis Lupis. S. Petri de Matheni.[24] Actum Premonstrati, anno incarnati verbi M° C° nonagesimo.

308

1164

Baudouin [II],[1] *bishop of Noyon, gives notice of the accord concluded between the Premonstratensians of Bonneuil*[2] *and husband and wife Pierre*[3] *de Flavy, knight, and Elizabeth concerning the pastures of Flavy and Bonneuil. Pierre also acknowledges a previous gift of alms made by his unnamed parents of six* modii *of grain (*frumentum*) from the mills of Eppeville.*[4]

A. Cartulary of Prémontré, fols. 79r–79v.

B. Original, AD Oise, H 5995, previously sealed on a double strip of white leather.

Karta Noviomensis episcopi de compositione inter fratres Premonstratenses et Petrum de Flavi.

[I]n nomine Patris et Filii et Spiritus Sancti. Ego Balduinus, Dei gratia Noviomensis episcopus, notum facio tam futuris quam presentibus quod

14 Hannape, cant. Wassigny, https://dicotopo.cths.fr/places/P37303056.

15 Atechi *B*.

16 Attichy, arr. Compiègne, https://dicotopo.cths.fr/places/P39233131.

17 Cassel, cant. Bailleul.

18 Matigny, cant. Ham, https://dicotopo.cths.fr/places/P92212887.

19 Villette, cant. Ham, https://dicotopo.cths.fr/places/P35405877.

20 Renaud, knight of Flavy, who was succeeded by his sister Marguerite, wife of Raoul, lord of Flavy-le-Meldeux (cant. Guiscard, https://dicotopo.cths.fr/places/P19622430). Newman, *Seigneurs*, vol. 2, 280–1.

21 Offoy, cant. Ham, https://dicotopo.cths.fr/places/P14011159.

22 Humbleus *B*.

23 Hombleux, cant. Nesle, https://dicotopo.cths.fr/places/P11898990.

24 Matigny, cant. Ham, https://dicotopo.cths.fr/places/P92212887.

1 Baudouin II de Boulogne, abbot of the Augustinian abbey of Saint-Eloi-Fontaine, ca. 1130–ca. 1139, and bishop of Noyon, 1148–67. *GC* IX, col. 1126.

2 The Premonstratensian *curtis* of Bonneuil. *MP* II, 484.

3 Perhaps a grandfather of Renaud, knight and lord of Flavy, and Marguerite, his sister and heir. A Pierre de Flavy appears in acts in the cartulary of Ourscamp, ca. 1140s–70s. BnF, MS lat. 5473, fols. 39v, 41r; Wacha, "La Puissance du Choix," 112.

4 Eppeville, cant. Ham, https://dicotopo.cths.fr/places/P94171781.

controversia emersit inter fratres de Bonolio et Petrum de Flavi, militem, pro pascuis eorum, que in presentia nostra hoc modo terminata est. Recognovit idem Petrus, recognoverunt et prefati fratres quod pascue de Flavi et de Bonolio ab antiquo solent et debent esse communes et ita concesserunt tam prefati fratres quam idem Petrus et uxor eius Elisabeth. De prato autem quod Reinberti Alnetum dicitur, et ceteris pratis de Bonolio statutum est quod, quamdiu fratres voluerint ea servare et sua ipsorum pecora vel animalia ab ingressu eorumdem pratorum cohibere, tam diu etiam poterunt pecoribus et animalibus Petri et hominum eius introitum prohibere; ex quo autem intrabunt animalia fratrum, intrare poterunt et animalia Petri et hominum eius. Pari modo dictum est et de pratis Petri de Flavi. Statutum est etiam quod si fratres de Bonolio ultra fossatum de Flavi domum aliquando fecerint, domus illa pascua de Flavi non habebit nisi eis Petrus vel heres eius concesserit. Similiter si Petrus vel heres aut homines eius ultra illud fossatum ex parte Bonolii domos aliquando fecerint, domus ille pascua Bonolii nisi licentia fratrum non habebunt. Concessit etiam ipse Petrus et recognovit elemosinam sex modiorum frumenti quam fecerat ipse et pater et mater eius ecclesie de Bonolio in molendinis de Espevile. Ut ergo ratum et inconvulsum permaneat, sigilli nostri auctoritate roborari et testium annotatione fecimus communiri. Signum Reneri,[5,6] abbatis Fontis Sancti Eligii. S. Drogonis, canonici et presbiteri. S. Johannis, capellani. S. Gaufridi,[7] cantoris. S. Symonis, cancellarii. S. Symonis canonici. Widonis,[8] castellani, S.[9] Symonis[10] de Mangi.[11] Wermundi[12] de Campania, Symonis de Monte[13] episcopi,[14] Hugonis de Morincourt[15,16] et Symonis fratris eius. Actum anno incarnati verbi M° C° LX° IIII°.

5 Reineri *B*.

6 Renier (d. 1191), abbot of the Arroasian Augustinian abbey of Saint-Éloi-Fontaine, 1162–ca. 1185. Poissonnier, "L'Abbaye de St-Éloi-Fontaine ou de Commenchon," 272–4.

7 A Geoffroi, cantor of Noyon, also appears in acts of Renaud, bishop of Noyon in 1176 and 1179. Peigné-Delacourt, *Cartulaire de l'Abbaye de Notre-Dame d'Ourscamp de l'ordre de Cîteaux, fondée en 1129 au diocèse de Noyon*, 174, 219.

8 Guy II, castellan of Coucy (d. 1165); husband of Théophanie. Barthélemy, *LDA*, 506–7.

9 *Om.* S. *A*.

10 Perhaps the same Simon de Magny who appears as a witness in **436**. A Simon de Magny also appears in acts dating 1181 in the cartulary of the cathedral chapter of Noyon, AD Oise, G 1984, fols. 92v–93r, 103r.

11 *Sic A*, *read* Magni.

12 A Vermond de Campagne appears in an 1166 act in the cartulary of the cathedral chapter of Notre-Dame de Noyon. AD Oise, G 1984, fol. 89r. Campagne, cant. Guiscard, https://dicotopo.cths.fr/places/P20414515.

13 Ponte *B*.

14 Pont-l'Évêque, cant. Noyon, https://dicotopo.cths.fr/places/P33255853.

15 Morincurt *B*.

16 Likely Muirancourt, cant. Guiscard, https://dicotopo.cths.fr/places/P50189896.

309

1195

Étienne,[1] *bishop of Noyon, makes known that Renier,*[2] *lord of Magny, relinquishes all the rights on the woods of Beaugies,*[3] *which he had claimed through his wife Mauduite,*[4] *in accordance with the terms stated in an act of 1141 issued by Simon [I],*[5] *bishop of Noyon, in which Mauduite's relation Roger*[6] *de Thourotte gave said rights to the brothers and sisters at Bonneuil.*[7] *Renier also relinquishes to Prémontré the three* modii *of grain (*frumentum*) which he took annually from the grange at Germaine.*[8] *In return Prémontré accords to Renier the usage rights of the dead wood taken at Beaugies. Mauduite assents to this act, as do Renier and Mauduite's children, Jean,*[9] *Arnoul,*[10] *Aelide, Aude,*[11] *Eustacie,*[12] *and Comitissa.*

A. Cartulary of Prémontré, fol. 79v.
B. Original, AD Oise, H 5998, previously sealed on a skein of pink silk.

Karta Stephani Noviomensis episcopi de conpositione inter Premonstratensem et Renerum dominum de Maigni.

[I]n nomine Patris et Filii et Spiritus Sancti, amen. Ego Stephanus, Dei gratia Noviomensis episcopus, notum facio tam futuris quam presentibus quod cum

1 Étienne de Villebéon (or de Nemours), son of Gautier de Villebéon, lord of La Chapelle-Gauthier and Nemours, and Aveline, was bishop of Noyon, 1188–1221.

2 Renier, lord of Magny (comm. Guiscard, https://dicotopo.cths.fr/places/P96954039), son of Simon, lord of Magny, and Agnès. Guyotjeannin, *Episcopus*, 274.

3 Beaugies-sous-Bois, cant. Guiscard, https://dicotopo.cths.fr/places/P02103056.

4 Mauduite, castellan of Coucy (d. bef. 1207), daughter of Guy II, castellan of Coucy, and Théophanie. Guyotjeannin, *Episcopus*, 273. She appears in the cartularies of the Cistercian abbeys of Ourscamp and Abbaye-aux-Bois. BnF, lat 5473, fols. 11r, 112v–113, 111v, 112r; Pipon, ed., *Le chartrier de l'Abbaye-aux-Bois (1202–1341)*, 120.

5 Simon I de Vermandois (d. 1148) was the son of Hugues I and Adélaïde, count and countess of Vermandois and Valois, and bishop of Noyon, 1123–42.

6 Roger *Filius Episcopi*, castellan of Thourotte and son of the lady Adèle and perhaps Teszo, castellan of Coucy. He entered Prémontré in 1141. Through his mother he was related to the castellans of Chauny. Guyotjeannin, *Episcopus*, 212–14, 273–4.

7 The Premonstratensian *curtis* of Bonneuil. *MP* II, 484.

8 Germaine, cant. Vermand, https://dicotopo.cths.fr/places/P36636067.

9 Jean de Magny, d. ca. 1198, son of Mauduite, castellan of Coucy and Renier, lord of Magny. Barthélemy, *LDA*, 512.

10 Arnoul de Magny, knight, son of Mauduite, castellan of Coucy and Renier, lord of Magny. Barthélemy, *LDA*, 512.

11 Aude de Magny, daughter of Mauduite, castellan of Coucy and Renier, lord of Magny; later wife of Jean I, lord of Condren. Barthélemy, *LDA*, 512.

12 Eustacie de Magny, daughter of Mauduite, castellan of Coucy and Renier, lord of Magny; later wife Geoffroi de Ham. Barthélemy, *LDA*, 512.

super silva de Bougies questio inter fratres Premonstratenses et Renerum[13] dominum de Maigni, coram nobis proposita verteretur, Renerus[14] jus dicte silve ex parte Malduitis, uxoris sue, clamabat, fratres vero Premonstratenses Rogerum de Torolta ipsam silvam preter quercum et fagum ad usus eorum ob remedium anime sue in elemosinam asserebant erogasse cuiusdam rescripti pie memorie domini Symonis, predecessoris nostri, quod etiam sigillo nostro roboratum et confirmatum fuerat, auctoritate nitentes,[15] cuius tenor hic erat: In nomine Patris et Filii et Spiritus Sancti. Ego Symon, Dei gratia Noviomensis episcopus, notum fieri volo tam posteris quam modernis quod Rogerus de Torolta qui cognominabatur Filius Episcopi, veniens ad conversionem in Premonstratense ecclesia, dedit fratribus et sororibus de Bonolio[16] quod habebat ad Bulgias, excepta fago et quercu; quod donum concesserunt Oda, soror sua, et Walterus et Thomas filii eiusdem Ode, qui idem nemus hereditario jure possidere debebant et idem donum altario in ecclesia Bonoliensi imposuerunt. Postea vero in presentiam mei de cuius feodo predictum nemus descenderat venientes, donum quod fecerant michi manifestaverunt, quod ego concessi et sigilli mei impressione confirmavi. Concesserunt autem hoc donum Gobertus[17] et Rogerus, frater eius, qui post prenominatos, Walterum videlicet et Thomam, hereditatem expectabant. Facta sunt hec anno dominice incarnationis M^{o} C^{o}[18] XL° I^{o}, indictione III^{a}, concurrente secundo,[19] epacta XI^{a}.[20] Huius rei testes sunt: Hugo cancellarius et Calo clericus, Adam filius Godini, Hugo de Aisei, Arnulphus[21] de Ooni, Tygerus, Hugo Poius, Rigaus, Burchardus[22] filius Litteri, Albertus frater eius, Robertus Encaseis, Walopinus, Robertus Cuisnels. Quicumque igitur hoc donum infregerit, anathema sit. Tandem, Deo annuente et prudentium virorum consilio mediante, lis tali modo sopita est. Prefatus Renerus[23] tres modios frumenti quos annuatim in grangia de Germaines accipiebat et duos alios quorum unum Guido, castellanus de Couciaco, pro remedio anime sue ecclesie Premonstratensi remisit, alter vero eidem ecclesie pro animabus filiorum dicti castellani, videlicet Renaldi[24],[25] de Cinceni, Petri Rubei et Roberti[26]

13 Reinerum *B.*
14 Reinerus *B.*
15 nittentes *B.*
16 *Om.* nemus *A.*
17 Goibertus *B.*
18 millesimo centestimo *B.*
19 II *B.*
20 VI *B.*
21 Arnulfus *B.*
22 Burcardus *B.*
23 Reinerus *B.*
24 Reinaldi *B.*
25 Renaud I de Coucy, lord of Sinceny (cant. Chauny, https://dicotopo.cths.fr/places/P29595722), son of Guy II, castellan of Coucy, and Théophanie. Barthélemy, *LDA*, 506.
26 Robert *Bove* (d. bef. 1192), son of Guy II, castellan of Coucy, and Theophanie. Barthélemy, *LDA*, 508, 510.

Bovis, ab heredibus eorum in elemosinam concessus fuerat, quitos clamavit et in posterum nunquam reclamandos cum omni jure alio in presentia nostra publice resignavit. Statutum est etiam ut ecclesia Premonstrati ad usus suos duos habeat summarios perpetuo, qualescumque[27] voluerit, ad cedenda ligna mortui nemoris et deducenda ita quod ipsi summarii, a Pascha usque ad festum Sancti Remigii, a domo Bonolii mittentur, a festo Sancti Remigii usque ad Pascha mittentur a grangia de Colisi vel a qualibet alia tunc ad ecclesiam Premonstrati spectante sepedicto Renero[28] salvum conductum per terram suam et per districtum suum prestante et adversus omnes qui juri et legi stare voluerint, warandiam[29] legitimam ecclesie prefate portante. Ductor autem summariorum Reinero presentabitur fidelitatem facturus quod nunquam in vivo nemore usque ad decem[30] denarios ipsum Reinerum dampnificabit[31] licebit tamen ductori retortas et alia ligna ad construendos summarios necessaria de quocumque[32] ligno voluerit sine forisfacto accipere. Quod si fidelitatem in cedendo non observare forte fuerit deprehensus ligna vivi nemoris deponentur sed Renerus[33] vel posteri eius super hoc forisfactum non habebunt. Ipse vero summularius nisi de premissione Reneri[34] in officio illo permanserit amovebitur et alius in loco ipsius substituetur. Sciendum est etiam quod universa que a Renero[35] super predictorum sunt pace concessa heredes et posteri eius integra et illesa observare debebunt. Hanc pactionem concessit atque laudavit Malduitis uxor Reneri[36] de Maigni, filia Guidonis castellani de Couci,[37] soror vero predictorum Renaldi[38] de Cinceni, Petri Rubei et Roberti Bovis que jus hereditarium in predicta silva clamaverat et filii eorum Johannes, Arnulphus[39] et filie, Aelidis, Auda, Eustachia et Comitissa. Ut autem hoc ratum permaneat et inconvulsum presentem paginam sigilli mei inpressione roboravi et fractis utriusque partis tam super nemore quam super predicto frumento munimentis prescripte pacis reformationem confirmavi. Quicumque[40] igitur hoc infregerit anathema sit. Actum est hoc anno incarnationis dominice M^{o}[41] centesimo nonagesimo quinto. Datum per manum Petri fratris et cancellarii nostri.

---

27 qualescunque *B.*
28 Reinero *B.*
29 warantiam *B.*
30 X *B.*
31 damnificabit *B.*
32 quocunque *B.*
33 Reinerus *B.*
34 Reineri *B.*
35 Reinero *B.*
36 Reineri *B.*
37 Coci *B.*
38 Reinaldi *B.*
39 Arnulfus *B.*
40 Quicunque *B.*
41 millesimo *B.*

310

1169

Gautier Aries *cedes to the church of Prémontré his land at Bonneuil*[1] *in return for four* modii *of land located between Ham and the bridge of Douilly,*[2] *and an annual payment of 10* modii *of grain (*frumentum*) and two* modii *of oats to be made at Bonneuil. Gautier's wife Agnès and unnamed children consent, as do the castellan Alelme*[3] *and the chapter of Prémontré.*

A. Cartulary of Prémontré, fols. 79v–80r.

B. Original (chirograph), AD Oise, H 5996, previously sealed.[4] In the left margin, beginning at the top, the upper half of the letters that form the word CYROGRAPHUM.

De elemosina Walteri Arietis et de quatuor modiatis terre inter Hamum et Pontem de Douilli.

[Q]uoniam posteritas pallio antiquitatis obfuscata[5] tum humana fragilitate tum illecebris mundi illaqueata lucem preteritorum modernis non accomodat. Ideo[6] ne quid scrupulosorum deliro assensu et suspecto interveniat scripti opus est evigilantia ut quod invidet animi ignorancia maturius commendet litterarum discussio. Notum sit itaque tam futuris quam presentibus quod Walterus Aries terram suam quam habebat in territorio Bonolii, Premonstratensi ecclesie concessit pro quatuor[7] modiatis terre inter Hamum et pontem Douilli[8] et pro decem modiis frumenti et duobus avene in uno quoque anno melioris in territorio Bonolii post sementem, secundam mensuram eiusdem temporis, ita quod ex utraque parte mensura recipiatur et continuo successu de tempore in tempus eadem servetur. Ita etiam dispositum est ut iste redditus usque ad crastinum diem sollempnitatis omnium sanctorum in hospitio suo persolvatur. Si contingat ut Walterus vel eius heres aliquo infortunio a patria procul pellatur, infra tres leugas cum salute rerum et secundum voluntatem omnia predicta ducentur. Item si aliquod impedimentum vel guerre vel alicuius infortunii interveniret, ne seges ista posset persolvi secundum termini considerationem nummi, quibus illa vendentur[9] in illo termino absque calumpnia tribuerentur. Item quatuor[10]

---

1 Bonneuil, cant. Ham, https://dicotopo.cths.fr/places/P66750585.

2 Douilly, cant. Ham, https://dicotopo.cths.fr/places/P87195366.

3 Alelme, castellan of Ham, brother of Pierre I, castellan of Péronne, and likely son of Roger I, castellan of Péronne. Gosse, *Histoire de l'Abbaye et de l'ancienne congrégation des chanoines réguliers d'Arrouaise, avec des notes critiques, historiques et diplomatiques*, 119–20, fn. c.

4 The original has been badly damaged, and much of the bottom half is illegible.

5 offuscata *B*.

6 Idcirco *B*.

7 IIII^or^ *B*.

8 Dolli *B*.

9 vendertur *B*.

10 IIII^or^ *B*.

modiate terre ab ecclesia Premonstratensi et a[11] curia Bonolii concesse a calumpnia omnium qui sub jure comprehendi poterunt liberabuntur ex alia parte a Waltero eadem deliberatio concessa est. Item si aliqua dissensio inter Walterum et castellanum dominium suum aliqua occasione vel defectu servitii vel alio incommodo ingruente it quod illa ad manum castellani reduceretur inculta permaneret modiatis terre ad ecclesiam Bonolii absque redditus solutione redactis donec confederatio fieret qua peracta priora prout disposuimus eodem modo sine restauratione utriusque partis restituerentur et hoc concensu[12] domini Alelmi castellani et si ita contingeret quod modiatio ista Bonolii deficeret Walterus vel eius heres in territorio Bonolii acciperet absque calumpnia octo modiatas terre jacentis inter pomerium novum et tumbam versus nemus. Hoc etiam factum est concessu Agnetis, uxoris ipsius Walteri, et infantium. Hiis testibus Drogonis de Oisni,[13] Waltero filio Evrardi, Symone de Broci,[14] Willermo[15] de Plaissie, Renero Verre, Petro[16] de Pieton. Hii fuerunt in consensu castellani Alelmi, in concessu uxoris Walteri et infantium. Hii sunt testes Walterus maior, Renerus[17] Verris, Gregorius et frater Petrus de Noviomo, Boscardus, Josbertus, Odo carnifex, Odo[18] medicus, Renerus Crisnons. Hoc actum est anno millesimo centesimo sexagesimo nono[19] verbi incarnati, Philippo existente abbate Premonstratensi assensu capituli sui.

311

1178

Renaud,[1] bishop of Noyon, makes known that Emmeline, called Joie, wife of Robert Morican,[2] together with their children Blavius, Dreux, Pierre, Havide, Basilie, and Helvide, confirm the gift of the oven[3] situated in front of the church of Saint-Martin de Noyon and of the cultivated field located near the mill of Saint-Barthélemy de Noyon which was made in alms by Emmeline's

---

11 ab *B.*

12 concessu *B.*

13 Ugny-l'Équipée, cant. Ham, https://dicotopo.cths.fr/places/P10325887.

14 Brouchy, cant. Ham, https://dicotopo.cths.fr/places/P33557845.

15 Willelmo *B.*

16 Pierre, lord of Pithon (cant. Saint-Simon, https://dicotopo.cths.fr/places/P56020430). Melleville, *DH*, vol. 2, 217.

17 Reinerus *B.*

18 Perhaps the same *medicus* Eudes attested in the Beauvaisis in the 1130s. Wickersheimer, Beaujouan, and Jacquart, *Dictionnaire biographique des médecins en France au Moyen Âge*, vol. 2, 70.

19 M° C° LXIX° *B.*

---

1 Renaud, bishop of Noyon, 1175–88.

2 On the Morican family, see Guyotjeannin, *Episcopus*, 205.

3 This oven was evidently located on the rue d'Wez in the parish of Saint-Germain. Ponthieux, "Notes sur l'ancien Noyon," xvi.

mother-in-law Basilie and her sisters-in-law Richilde and Emmeline. Eudes Havart, from whom the land descends, consents to this. (See ***316****.)*

A. Cartulary of Prémontré, fol. 80r.

B. Original, AD Oise, H 6053, previously sealed with a double strip of white leather.

REGISTER: *Studium Baldwin*, fiche 2080.

Karta Noviomensis episcopi de elemosina Joie uxoris Roberti Morican quam contulit ecclesie Premonstrati.

[I]n nomine sancte et individue Trinitatis. Quoniam cum lapsu temporum et fuga labitur et fugit hominum memoria, statuit[4] antiquitas ea litteris tradere quorum memoriam posteris volumus intimare. Antiquorum itaque vestigiis adherentes, ego Rainaldus, Dei gratia Noviomensis episcopus, notum fieri volo tam presentibus quam futuris quod Enmelina[5] que vocatur Joia, uxor Roberti Morican et liberi sui Blavius, Drogo, Petrus, Havidis, Basilia, Helvidis, elemosinam quam Basilia, mater predicti Roberti Morican, et filie sue Richaldis et Enmelina, ecclesie Premonstratensi fecerant, furnum scilicet qui est ante Sanctum Martinum Noviomi, et culturam que est juxta molendinum Sancti Bartholomei quam tenebat ab Odone Havart, predictus Robertus ad quintam garbam, in presentia nostra recognoverunt et in manus nostras reddiderunt et nos ecclesie Premonstratensi perpetuis temporibus possidenda concessimus. Huic concessioni et recognitioni interfuerunt testes: magister Ingelrannus, Tiezo, Lienardus[6,7] decanus, Johannes[8] de Nigella, Odo Havarz a quo terra illa descendebat qui etiam laudavit et testis est, Symon de Ponte, Radulphus[9] de Guni,[10] Rogerus Gloriosus milites, Ingelrannus decanus, Albricus maior communie, Drogo, frater Joie et, de Premonstrato, Eustachius[11] prior, Willelmus et Gaufridus canonici, Petrus conversus. Ut igitur hoc donum ab aliquo prevaricari non possit, sigilli nostri impressione presentem paginam munire curavimus. Actum est hoc anno ab incarnatione Domini M° C° LXX° VIII°. Ego Balduinus[12] cancellarius relegi et subscripsi.[13]

---

4 *Om.* provida *A*.

5 Emmelina *B*.

6 Lyenardus *B*.

7 An *Ansellus, nepos Leonardi decani olim nostri* appears in an 1180 act of Renaud, bishop of Noyon. BnF, nouv. acq. lat. 935, fol. 24r.

8 Likely Jean I, lord of Nesle and castellan of Bruges, son of Raoul, castellan of Bruges, and Gertrude. Newman, *Seigneurs*, vol. 1, 64.

9 Radulfus *B*.

10 Guny, cant. Coucy-le-Château, https://dicotopo.cths.fr/places/P88745448.

11 Eustatius *B*.

12 Baudouin, chancellor of Noyon, ca. 1172–ca. 1186. Stein, *Cartulaire de l'ancienne abbaye de Saint Nicolas des Prés sous Ribemont*, 62, 122.

13 suscripsi *B*.

312

1225

Raoul,[1] *abbot of Saint-Eloi de Noyon, Conrad,*[2] *abbot of Prémontré, and their respective chapters reiterate the terms of an agreement to exchange lands and rights made by their communities during the episcopacy of Étienne [I],*[3] *bishop of Noyon, subject to modifications.*

A. Cartulary of Prémontré, fols. 80r–80v.

B. Original, AD Oise, H 6004, previously sealed on threads of pink silk with two seals.

EDITION: Martin-Marville, *Trosly-Loire ou le Trosly des conciles, ses châteaux, ses villas, ses fiefs et ses seigneurs*, 235–8.

Karta Radulphi Sancti Eligii Noviomensis et Conradi Premonstratensis de quadam compositione.

[I]n nomine Patris et Filii et Spiritus Sancti.[4] Radulphus,[5] Sancti Eligii Noviomensis, et Conradus, Premonstratensis Dei patientia dicti abbates, et eorumdem locorum conventus omnibus in perpetuum. Notum esse volumus tam presentibus quam futuris quod olim inter ecclesia nostras pro communi utilitate ipsarum, de communi assensu et voluntate, mediante venerande memorie domino Stephano, Noviomensi episcopo, factam fuit quoddam excambium comprehensum in kartis ex utraque parte confectis cuius excambii verba in presenti karta duximus replicanda. Ecclesia Premonstratensis dedit et concessit tunc temporis ecclesie Sancti Eligii Noviomensis quandam partem mansure et aque quam habebat apud Landrimont[6] sicut distincta est et diversa metis pro suis aisentiis perpetuo possidendam. Preterea quitavit ecclesia Premonstratensis ecclesie Sancti Eligii Noviomensis sex denarios censuales quos debebat ei de domo de Alneto et novem denarios censuales quos debebat ei de vinea Roberti Le Franc ita quod nichil omnino juris vel consuetudinis retinuit sibi in omnibus supradictis, salvo eo quod ecclesia Sancti Eligii Noviomensis solvere

1 Raoul II, abbot of the Benedictine abbey of Saint-Éloi de Noyon, ca. 1197–1232.

2 Conrad the Swabian was prior of Weissenau, 1203–17, abbot of Valsecret, 1218–20, abbot of Prémontré, 1220–33, and abbot of Cuissy, aft. 1235–41. *MP* I, 89; *MP* II, 497, 527, 536.

3 Étienne de Villebéon (or de Nemours), son of Gautier de Villebéon, lord of La Chapelle-Gauthier and Nemours, and Aveline, was bishop of Noyon, 1188–1221.

4 *Om.* amen *A*.

5 Radulfus *B*.

6 Landrimont, comm. Noyon, https://dicotopo.cths.fr/places/P74301629.

debebat Havino[7] Cerario et eius heredibus[8] tres solidos et duos denarios Parisienses de superiori parte mansure sicut mete tunc posite proportabant, quos ecclesia Premonstratensis eidem Havino[9] solvere consueverat. Inferiorem vero partem mansure et aquam possidebit ecclesia Sancti Eligii Noviomensis ab omni consuetudine et ab omni redditu liberam et inmunem. Ecclesia vero Sancti Eligii Noviomensis in recompensationem huius concessionis et quitancie quitavit ecclesie Premonstratensi tres denarios Parisienses quos debebat ei de pressorio suo quod dicitur Bonolii et foragium et rotagium ipsius loci, salva tamen justicia ~~ecclesie Premonstratensis~~ sua. Remisit preterea ecclesia Sancti Eligii Noviomensis ecclesie Premonstratensi quatuor solidos et quinque denarios Parisienses quos solvebat ei annuatim de cultura Barlandi et sedecim denarios Parisienses quos solvebat ei annuatim pro vinea Amisardi. Obligavit se nichilominus ecclesia Sancti Eligii Noviomensis ad solvendum ecclesie Premonstratensi annuatim quinque modios bladi meditanei[10] aut minus ad[11] melioris ad mensuram Noviomensem apud Trosli.[12] Concessit quoque ecclesie Sancti Eligii Noviomensis ecclesie Premonstratensi pourprisum[13] quod est in circuitu communis grangie de Omercourt[14,15] tenendum de ecclesia Sancti Eligii sub annuo censu unius denarii Parisiensis solvendi, ibidem in festo Sancti Remigii annuatim, salvo communi introitu grangie qui erit exterius et quodam parvo posticio quod erit versus curtem Sancti Eligii, per quod ille qui erit in custodia grangie ex parte Sancti Eligii habebit ingressum, hoc tamen proviso quod salvitas grangie non periclitetur per posticium dum bladum commune fuerit in ea. Preterea ecclesia Premonstratensis pro usuario quod prioratus Sanctus Nicholai in Boscho,[16] pertinens ad ecclesiam Sancti Eligii Noviomensis, habebat in nemore apud Bonolium, quod dicitur Nemus Episcopi, assignavit et dedit eidem prioratui octo modiatas ipsius nemoris ad mensuram Hamensem perpetuo possidendas, salvo usuario quod hominibus de Espevilla[17] et de Vellenis in ipsis octo modiatis et in residuo totius nemoris est retentum secundum quod in auctentico[18] domini Noviomensis episcopi continetur expressum. Per hoc autem assignamentum et hoc donum ecclesia Sancti Eligii Noviomensis quitavit in perpetuum ecclesie Premonstratensi per manum dicti domini

7 Hawino *B*.
8 *Om.* annuatim *A*.
9 Hawino *B*.
10 medictanei *B*.
11 aut *B*.
12 Trosly-Loire, cant. Coucy-le-Château, https://dicotopo.cths.fr/places/P24780558.
13 porprisium *B*.
14 Omercort *B*.
15 Omiécourt-Montréal, cant. Nesle, https://dicotopo.cths.fr/places/P59719870.
16 bosco *B*.
17 Eppeville, cant. Ham, https://dicotopo.cths.fr/places/P94171781.
18 autentico *B*.

episcopi quicquid juris vel consuetudinis habebat idem prioratus Sancti Nicholai in residuo ipsius nemoris pro se vel pro alio. Omnes igitur conventiones, sicut superius sunt expresse, comprehense fuerunt in kartis super hoc ex utraque parte confectis. Sane processu temporis, habita iterum amicabili conventione inter ecclesias nostras de communi capitulorum nostrorum voluntate pariter et assensu pauca de premissis conventionibus mutata fuerunt. Ecclesia et enim Premonstratensis residuam partem mansure cum fundo mansure quam habebat apud Landrimont,[19] vendidit ecclesie Sancti Eligii Noviomensis, recepta inde certa pecunie portione, nec aliquid sibi retinuit in eadem mansura vel in fundo mansure ecclesia Premonstrati, salvo tamen eo quod ecclesia Sancti Eligii Noviomensis ecclesie Premonstratensi debebit solvere tres solidos et duos denarios Parisiensium quos solvere tenebatur supradicto Hawino Cerario et eius heredibus, sicut superius est expressum, de superiori parte mansure sicut mete dudum posite proportant et ecclesia Premonstratensis eosdem tres solidos et duos denarios Parisiensium sepedicto Hawino et eius heredibus solvere tenebitur annuatim. De quinque etiam modiis bladi meditanei[20] ad minus aut melioris quos ad mensuram Noviomensem ecclesie Premonstratensi solvere tenebatur apud Trosli ecclesia Sancti Eligii Noviomensis[21] ad mensuram predictam ecclesie vel nuntio Premonstratensi annuatim infra festum Omnium Sanctorum. Conventum est igitur firmiter ab utraque ecclesia et statutum ut tam inmutatio predictorum facta occasione venditionis predicte mansure quam cetere conventiones superius replicate firmiter in perpetuum teneantur. Ne autem ad kartas super articulis prioribus olim confectus[22] decetero habeatur recursus, karte ab utraque ecclesia exinde confecte de communi ecclesiarum earumdem assensu tamquam inutiles et superflue dilaniate fuerunt cum in presenti pagina contineatur, quod in kartis prioribus habebatur. Et ne aliqua de predictis aliquorum in posterum possint malignitate mutari, fecimus inde confici duo scripta eiusdem tenoris quorum alterum ecclesia Sancti Eligii tradidit ecclesie Premonstratensi sigillis abbatis et conventus signatum, reliquum vero tradidit ecclesia Premonstratensis ecclesie Sancti Eligii quia sigillum abbatis et conventus Premonstratensis erat commune et unicum sigillo unico sigillatum. Actum publice et receptum et sollempniter approbatum in utroque capitulo, anno incarnationis dominice millesimo ducentesimo vicesimo quinto.

19 Landrimont, comm. Noyon, https://dicotopo.cths.fr/places/P74301629.

20 medictanei *B*.

21 *Om.* in perpetuum annuatim ita inter ecclesiam utramque convenit quod ipsi quinque modii talis bladi, sicut superius est expressum solventur [illegible]tia Sancti Eligii Noviomensis *A*.

22 confectas *B*.

313

December, 1211.

The priest Baudouin, brother of the hospital of Saint-Jean de Noyon, makes known a modification, owing to a change in the value of currency, of the agreement made between his community and the religious of Prémontré, concerning the annual census *that the brothers of Saint-Jean owed to Prémontré for the rights on the parish of Saint-Germain in Noyon. (See **314**, **318**, and **319**.)*

A. Cartulary of Prémontré, fols. 80v–81r.
B. Original not found.[1]

Karta Balduini fratris hospitalis Noviomi de annuo censu quinquaginta solidorum quos debent ecclesie Premonstrati pro jure parrochie.

[I]n nomine Patris et Filii et Spiritus Sancti, amen. Balduinus presbiter, frater hospitalis Sancti Johannis Noviomi[2] eiusdemque domus fratres omnibus tam futuris quam presentibus in perpetuum. Per huius innovationem rescripti futuris et presentibus notum fiat quod cum bone memorie dominus Hugo, abbas et capitulum Premonstrati, jus illud quod eis in parrochia Sancti Germani Noviomensis quantum ad personatum sive donum altaris competebat, olim fratribus hospitalis Sancti Johannis, nomine elemosine, contulissent et collatum scripto auctentico[3] confirmassent, per eandem etiam confirmationem quicquid juris et commodi habebant in minutis decimis ipsius parrochie, concesserunt dictis fratribus perpetuo possidendum sub annuali censu quinquaginta solidorum talis monete, qualis in Noviomensi curreret civitate. Cum autem post primum scriptum prior moneta per annos plurimos legitimum cursum habens, in solutione census predicti data et recepta, sed postmodum in fortiorem monetam mutata fuisset, occasione ipsius mutationis, de mutanda etiam solutione census ~~predicti data et recepta~~ inter solventes et recipientes disceptatio mota fuit et tandem, de assensu et auctoritate partium, sic sopita, videlicet quod pro memorato censu solvetur a modo singulis annis, in crastino nativitatis Sancti Johannis Baptiste, maior argenti marcha continens tredecim solidos et quatuor denarios sterlingorum, qui tamen, si adsolvendum haberi nequiverint, de moneta publica secundum publicam et legitimam estimationem concambii Premonstratensibus satisfiet. Preterea quod in priori scripto erat adjunctum hoc etiam in isto pari est conventione insertum ut si casu aliquo vel eventu contigerit supradictam

1 Françoise Muret noted an original for this charter (AD Oise, H 6004) in the 1980s. The current editors could not locate it. Variants noted follow Muret's transcription.

2 Noviomensis *B*.

3 autentico *B*.

Sancti Johannis domum aut hospitalis vocabulum aut hospitalitatis officium non habere prefata Sancti Germani parrochia cum hiis que Premonstratenses prius ibidem habuerant, absolute revertetur ad ipsos et in eorum cedet pristinam potestatem. Ceterum si super hiis que fratres hospitalis prescripti a Premonstratensibus sive per elemosinam sive per censum tenent, eis fuerit illata molestia, ipsi Premonstratenses, salvis suis expensis, suam per omnia subventionem et auxilium interponent. Ut autem per renovatum hoc scriptum in quo fere eadem que in priori fuerant, continentur, prior quoque scripti auctoritas et perpetuitas renovetur ex utriusque partis diligentia est provisum ut hoc scriptum huic Premonstratensis ecclesie inde hospitalis Sancti Johannis Noviomensis sigillo habeatur et perpetuo conservetur munitum. Actum mense decembri, anno incarnationis dominice millesimo ducentesimo undecimo.

314

1188

Adon, maior, *and the* jurati *of the commune of Noyon make known that abbot [Hugues II]*[1] *of Prémontré, with the assent of his chapter, cedes to the new hospital of Noyon everything that Prémontré held in the parish of Saint-Germain in return for an annual* census *of 50* solidi. *(See **313**, **318**, and **319**.)*

A. Cartulary of Prémontré, fol. 81r.
B. Original not found.

Karta maioris Noviomensis communie de dono parrochie Sancti Germani.

[A]do, Noviomensis communie maior et jurati, omnibus ad quos pagina presens pervenerit salutem. Noverint universi quod dominus abbas Premonstratensis, tocius assensu capituli, quicquid habebant in parrochia Sancti Germani novo hospitali Noviomi sub annuo censu quinquaginta solidorum monete currentis in perpetuum habendum concesserunt, ita quod viginti quinque solidi de ipso censu in Natali Domini, et viginti quinque alii in nativitate Sancti Johannis Baptiste persolventur. Quod ut ratum sit et penitus inconvulsum tam presentes scripti patrocinio quam nostro decrevimus sigillo muniri. Actum anno incarnati verbi M° C° octogesimo octavo.

---

1 Hugues II de Douai, abbot of the Premonstratensian abbey of Cuissy, 1161–5, and abbot of Prémontré, 1174–89. *MP* II, 497.

315

July 18, 1215. Noyon.

The priest Baudouin, procurator, and the brothers of the new hospital of Noyon make known that Simon Bègues *left them in alms the revenue of two* modii *of oats, measure of Noyon, until that revenue reached 13* librae Parisiensium *in total. Since the revenue was taken from the tithe at Muile,*[1] *which was held by the church of Prémontré, and since abbot Gervais*[2] *and the convent of Prémontré did not wish for the brothers of Noyon to enter their fief, Prémontré gave Noyon 13* librae Parisiensium *so as to retain the two* modii *for itself until such time as the bequest has been paid out and the two* modii *returned to Simon's rightful heirs.*

A. Cartulary of Prémontré, fol. 81r.
B. Original, BnF, Coll. Picardie 290, no. 31, previously sealed.
EDITION: "Chronique," *Bibliothèque de l'École des chartes: Revue d'Érudition* 3 (1857): 570–1.

Karta Balduini sacerdotis de tredecim libris Parisiensium quas Symon cognomento Begues contulit hospitali Noviomensis.

[E]go Balduinus[3] presbiter et procurator novi hospitalis Noviomensis et eiusdem loci fratres, notum facimus universis presentes litteras inspecturis quod cum bone memorie quondam Symon,[4] cognomento Begues,[5] legasset domui nostre in elemosinam tredecim libras Parisiensium super duos modios avene ad mensuram Noviomensem, quos tenebat in feodo de ecclesia Premonstratensi et percipiebat eos annuatim in ea portione decime de Muile que ecclesiam Premonstratensem contingit viri venerabiles dominus Gervasius, abbas, et conventus Premonstratensis quia noluerunt ut in eorum feodum intraremus, dederunt nobis tredecim libras Parisiensium, ea conditione interposita quod tenebunt dictos duos modios donec ab herede legitimo redimantur et nos eis super hoc vel prestabimus warandiam, vel reddemus eis dictas tredecim libras quas recepimus ab eisdem. Actum Noviomi, XV° kalendas augusti, anni gratie M° CC°[6] quinto decimo.

1 Muille-Villette, cant. Ham, https://dicotopo.cths.fr/places/P77128677.
2 Gervais, abbot of the Premonstratensian abbeys of Saint-Just-en-Chaussée, 1199–1205, Thenailles, 1205–9, and Prémontré, 1209–20, and bishop of Séez, 1220–8. *MP* II, 401, 527, 565; Cheney, "Gervase, Abbot of Prémontré."
3 Baldewinus *B*.
4 Simon *B*.
5 Beges *B*.
6 millesimo ducentesimo *B*.

316

1148–75.[1]

Baudouin [II/III], bishop of Noyon, makes known that Basilie, wife of Adam[2] *Ballande, gives to the church of Prémontré the oven situated in front of the church of Saint-Martin de Noyon. Her children Robert, Richilde, Domesuns, and Emmeline consent to the gift. (See* ***311****.)*

A. Cartulary of Prémontré, fol. 81r.

B. Original, AD Oise, H 6053, previously sealed on a double strip of white leather.

Karta Balduini Noviomensis episcopi de elemosina furni Noviomi quam Basilla contulit ecclesie Premonstrati.

[I]n nomine sancte et individue Trinitatis. Quia successu defluentium temporum facile prolabimur in oblivionem preteritorum, que memoriter retineri volumus, scripto commendare solemus. Eapropter ego Balduinus, Dei gratia Noviomensis episcopus, notum fieri volo tam futuris quam presentibus quod Basilla, uxor Adam[3] Ballande, contulit Premonstrate ecclesie quendam furnum qui situs est ante Sanctum Martinum Noviomi, concedentibus ~~canonicis vero~~ Sancte Marie Noviomensis, a quibus ipsum censualiter pro IIIIor denariis per annum tenebat, eo videlicet modo ut Basilla furnum restitueret canonicis, canonici vero restituerent[4] illum ecclesie Premonstratensi perpetuo possidendum. Concesserunt etiam et hoc donum Robertus, filius eius et filie ipsius, Richoldis et Domesuns[5] et Enmelina.[6] Huic autem dono interfuerunt testes: Petrus[7] cantor, Arnulphus[8] tunc prepositus, Robertus celerarius, Wido capellanus, Robertus[9] Cardo, Liboldus[10] li Matras, Robertus filius Tivardi, Radulfus magnus, Ingelrannus[11] furnarius; ubi autem Robertus filius eius, concessit, interfuit[12] Albricus, sororius

---

1 Date based on the episcopacies of Baudouin II (1148–67) and Baudouin III (1167–74/5).

2 Adam Ballande (or de Batlande) gave land at Sempigny to the abbey of Ourscamp which was the subject of a dispute by his heirs in 1189. Peigné-Delacourt, *Cartulaire de l'Abbaye de Notre-Dame d'Ourscamp de l'ordre de Cîteaux, fondée en 1129 au diocèse de Noyon*, 243–4.

3 Adan *B*.

4 traderent *B*.

5 Domensuns *B*.

6 Emmelina *B*.

7 A Pierre, cantor of the chapter of Noyon, in also attested in acts of 1146. AD Oise, G 1984, fols. 70v–71r, 81r.

8 Arnulfus *B*.

9 A Robertus *Cardo* also appears in an undated act in the cartulary of Arrouaise. Tock and Milis, *Monumenta Arroasiensia*, 670–1.

10 Tiboldus *B*.

11 Ingolrannus *B*.

12 interfuerunt *B*.

eius, et Vivianus, armiger eius,[13] et Fulco li Defuleiz.[14] Ubi vero Domesuns, filia illius, concessit, interfuerunt Hubertus, frater Radulfi[15] Pulcri,[16] Ingelrannus[17] de Landovesin.[18] Verum post modum veniens predictus Robertus Bonolium, domum[19] prefatum inibi super altare posuit et interfuerunt Willelmus[20] de Pleissei, Petrus, filiaster eius, et Theoldus[21] armiger illius, et frater Hezelo et frater Johannes Judeus. Nos autem hoc donum sic legitime factum eidem ecclesie perpetuo possidendum sigilli nostri impressione confirmamus et ne quis eos inde ulterius inquietare presumat, sub anathemate interdicimus.

317

1196

Étienne [I],[1] bishop of Noyon, makes known that the brothers of Bonneuil, with the consent of the dean and chapter of Noyon and the abbot and chapter of Prémontré, cede to him the oven that they possess at Noyon in front of Saint-Martin, in exchange for an annual payment of 12 denarii Noviomensium *and exemption from customs and taxes on a quarter of a garden at Eppeville.*[2]

A. Cartulary of Prémontré, fols. 81r–81v.
B. Original not found.

Karta Stephani Noviomensis episcopi de permutatione furni Noviomensis pro quo recipit ecclesia Premonstratensis duodecim denarios bone monete.

[S]tephanus, Dei gratia Noviomensis episcopus, omnibus in perpetuum. Notum facimus universis presentibus pariter et futuris quod fratres Bonolii concesserunt nobis et successoribus nostris episcopis furnum quem habebant Noviomi ante Sanctum Martinum sub annua pensione duodecim denariorum monete

13 suus *B*.
14 Lidefuleth *B*.
15 Raoul *Pulcher*, brother of Hubert, appears also in **300**, **337**, **372**, and **436**, and is attested in acts to do with the lords of Nesle, 1150s–70s. Newman, *Seigneurs*, vol. 2, 59, 133.
16 Pulchri *B*.
17 Ingrannus *B*.
18 Languevoisin, cant. Nesle, https://dicotopo.cths.fr/places/P00746276.
19 donum *B*.
20 If this is the same Guillaume de Plessis who appears in acts **342**, **372**, and **401**, it would seem to imply a date in the late 1140s or early 1150s for this act.
21 Leoldus *B*.

1 Étienne de Villebéon (or de Nemours), son of Gautier de Villebéon, lord of La Chapelle-Gauthier and Nemours, and Aveline, was bishop of Noyon, 1188–1221.
2 Eppeville, cant. Ham, https://dicotopo.cths.fr/places/P94171781.

Noviomensis in festo Sancti Remigii solvendorum, assensu decani et capituli Noviomensis ad quos eiusdem furni fundus pertinet, abbate etiam et capitulo Premonstratensis laudante et concedente. Nos quoque quarterium unum cuiusdam orti qui est apud Espevillam ab omni consuetudine et exactione inmunem, salva dumtaxat justicia nostra, eisdem fratribus perpetuo habendum concessimus. Quod ut ratum et inconvulsum permaneat, presentem paginam nostro sigillo duximus roborare. Actum anno incarnati verbi M° C° nonagesimo sexto.

318

1188

Étienne,[1] *bishop of Noyon, makes known that abbot [Hugues II]*[2] *of Prémontré with the consent of his chapter cedes to the new hospital of Noyon everything that Prémontré held in the parish of Saint-Germain in return for an annual* census *of 50* solidi currentium. *The brothers of the hospital have 15 days to express any dissatisfaction with the agreement. (See* ***313****,* ***314****, and* ***319****.)*

A. Cartulary of Prémontré, fol. 81v.
B. Original, AD Oise, H 6055, previously sealed.

Karta episcopi Noviomensis de annuo censu hospitalis Noviomensis.

[S]tephanus, Dei gratia Noviomensis episcopus, omnibus ad quos pagina presens pervenerit, salutem et eternam beatitudinem. Quoniam rerum gestarum ordo a memoria hominum labitur, nisi scripto aut litteris commendetur, notum fieri volumus tam presentibus quam futuris quod dominus abbas Premonstratensis tocius capituli assensu quicquid habebant in parrochia Sancti Germani, novo hospitali Noviomi, sub annuo censu quinquaginta solidorum monete currentis in perpetuum habendum concesserunt ita quod viginti quinque[3] solidi de ipso censu in Natali Domini et XXV alii in nativitate Sancti Johannis Baptiste persolventur. Quod si fratres predicti hospitalis prefatum abbatem et ecclesiam suam super hoc contristaverint, infra XV dies post eorum summonitionem ecclesiastica censura reddere compellemus. Huius rei testes sunt: Matheus de Sancto Quintino, Symon de Sancto Quintino diaconi et canonici, Symon[4]

---

1 Étienne de Villebéon (or de Nemours), son of Gautier de Villebéon, lord of La Chapelle-Gauthier and Nemours, and Aveline, was bishop of Noyon, 1188–1221.

2 Hugues II de Douai, abbot of the Premonstratensian abbey of Cuissy, 1161–5, and abbot of Prémontré, 1174–89. *MP* II, 497.

3 XXV *B*.

4 Simon I *le Vieux* de Sermaize, lord of Béthencourt-sur-Somme (cant. Nesle, https://dicotopo.cths.fr/places/P85791062), likely a son or grandson of Hugues I de Sermaize, lord of Béthencourt-sur-Somme. Newman, *Seigneurs*, vol. 2, 99, 209; Guyotjeannin, *Episcopus*, 272.

de Betencourt,[5] Renerus[6,7] de Maigniaco[8] et Regnaldus[9] et Gervasius milites, Havinus. Hoc igitur ut ratum sit et penitus inconvulsum, tam presentis scripti patrocinio quam nostro decrevimus sigillo muniri. Actum anno incarnati verbi millesimo centesimo octogesimo octavo.

319

December, 1211.

A record of the agreement reached between the hospital at Noyon and abbot Gervais[1] *and the chapter of Prémontré concerning a modification of the annual* census *owed by the hospital to Prémontré due to changes in currency valuation; instead of paying 50* solidi Noviomensium, *the hospital brothers will instead pay one silver mark worth 13* solidi, *four* denarii sterlingorum. *(See* ***313****,* ***314****, and* ***318****.)*

A. Cartulary of Prémontré, fol. 81v.

B. Original, AD Oise, H 6055, previously sealed on a double strip of parchment.

Karta domini Hugonis abbatis Premonstratensis de confirmatione hospitalis.

[I]n nomine Patris et Filii et Spiritus Sancti.[2] Per huius innovationem rescripti futuris et presentibus notum fiat quod cum bone memorie dominus Hugo, abbas, et capitulum Premonstrati jus illud quod eis in parrochia Sancti Germani Noviomensis quantum ad personatum sive donum altaris competebat, olim fratribus hospitalis Sancti Johannis nomine elemosine, contulissent, et collatum scripto auctentico[3] confirmassent, per eandem etiam confirmationem quicquid juris et conmodi habebant in minutis decimis ipsius parrochie concesserunt dictis fratribus perpetuo possidendum sub annuali censu quinquaginta solidorum talis monete qualis in Noviomensi curreret civitate. Cum autem post primum scriptum prior moneta, per annos plurimos legitimum cursum habens, in solutione census predicti data et recepta, sed postmodum in fortiorem monetam mutata fuisset, occasione ipsius mutationis, de mutanda etiam solutione census inter

5 Bethencurt *B*.

6 Rainerus *B*.

7 Renier, lord of Magny, son of Simon, lord of Magny, and Agnès. Guyotjeannin, *Episcopus*, 274.

8 Mengniaco *B*.

9 Rainaldus *B*.

1 Gervais, abbot of the Premonstratensian abbeys of Saint-Just-en-Chaussée, 1199–1205, Thenailles, 1205–9, and Prémontré, 1209–20, and bishop of Séez, 1220–8. *MP* II, 401, 527, 565; Cheney, "Gervase, Abbot of Prémontré."

2 *Om.* amen *A*.

3 autentico *B*.

solventes et recipientes disceptatio[4] fuit et tandem, de assensu et auctoritate partium, sic sopita videlicet quod pro memorato censu solvetur amodo, singulis annis, in crastino nativitatis Sancti Johannis Baptiste, maior argenti marca continens tredecim solidos et quatuor denarios sterlingorum. Qui tamen, si ad solvendum haberi nequiverint, de moneta publica secundum publicam et legitimam estimationem concambii Premonstratensibus satisfiet. Preterea quod in priori scripto erat adjunctum hoc etiam in isto pari est conventione insertum ut, si casu aliquo vel eventu contigerit supradictam Sancti Johannis domum aut hospitalis ~~domum~~ vocabulum aut hospitalitatis officium non habere, prefata Sancti Germani parrochia cum hiis que Premonstratenses prius ibidem habuerant, absolute revertetur ad ipsos et in eorum cedet pristinam potestatem. Ceterum si super hiis que fratres hospitalis prescripti a Premonstratensibus sive per elemosinam sive per censum tenent eis fuerit illata molestia ipsi Premonstratenses salvis suis expensis suam per omnia subventionem et auxilium interponent. Ut autem per renovatum hoc scriptum in quo fere eadem que in priori fuerant, continentur, prior quoque scripti auctoritas[5] et perpetuitas renovetur ex utriusque partis diligentia est provisum ut hoc scriptum huic Premonstratensi ecclesie inde hospitalis Sancti Johannis Noviomensis sigillo habeatur et perpetuo conservetur munitum. Inde sunt testes dominus Gervasius abbas Premonstratensis, Joscelinus supprior, Ingelrannus[6] presbiter magister Bonolii, Balduinus et Helyas presbiteri fratres dicti hospitalis, Bartholomeus cognomento Filiolus capellanus altaris Sancti Thome. Actum mense decembri, anno incarnationis dominice M°[7] ducentesimo undecimo.

320

1135

Simon [I],[1] *bishop of Noyon, makes known that Bouchard*[2] *and Geoffroi*[3] *de Guise, having come of age, confirm the gift of the allod of Germaine*[4] *which their mother, Adèle* Machania,[5] *wife of Guy de Guise, had made when she*

4 *Om.* mora *A.*
5 autoritas *B.*
6 Ingerrannus *B.*
7 millesimo *B.*

1 Simon I de Vermandois (d. 1148) was the son of Hugues I and Adélaïde, count and countess of Vermandois and Valois, and bishop of Noyon, 1123–42.
2 Bouchard, lord of Guise (d. aft. 1161), son of Guy, lord of Guise, and Adèle "Machania"; husband of Adèle de Soupir.
3 Geoffroi de Guise (d. aft. 1155), son of Guy, lord of Guise, and Adèle "Machania."
4 Germaine, cant. Vermand, https://dicotopo.cths.fr/places/P36636067.
5 Adèle "Machania," possibly a daughter of Bouchard III, lord of Montmorency, and wife of Guy, lord of Guise.

entered the religious life at Prémontré at the time of Norbert [of Xanten]. This confirmation, with the assent of their brothers-in-law Reinier[6] *de Guise, Guy*[7] *de Voulpaix, and Anselme de Saint-Quentin, son of Oidard, was made in response to claims that Adèle's gift was invalid given that Bouchard and Geoffroi were minors at the time.*

A. Cartulary of Prémontré, fols. 81v–82r.

B. Original, AD Aisne, H 793, previously sealed with a double strip of parchment.

EDITION: Pycke and Vleeschouwers, *Actes*, 388–9.

REGISTER: Grauwen, "Lijst van oorkonden waarin Norbertus wordt genoemd," 163.

Karta Symonis episcopi Noviomensis de confirmatione alodii de Germania.

[I]n nomine sancte et individue Trinitatis. Quoniam que bene gesta sunt a fidelibus decrevit sanctorum patrum auctoritas scriptis commendare, ne hominum labili memoria oblivioni tradantur, ego Symon, Dei miseratione Noviomensis ecclesie minister indignus, notum fieri volumus tam futuris quam presentibus quod uxor Guidonis[8] de Guisia,[9] que proprio nomine Addelvia, sed vulgo dicebatur Machania, post obitum eiusdem mariti sui Guidonis,[10] venit ad ecclesiam Beate Marie et Sancti Johannis Baptiste Premonstrati, tempore domini Norberti, eiusdem ecclesie primi fundatoris, in presentia domini Bartholomei, Laudunensis episcopi, et ob remedium anime sue et predicti mariti sui sibique attinentium, tradidit eidem ecclesie jure perpetuo possidendum, in usum Deo famulantium, totum allodium ville que dicitur Germania, quicquid ibi proprii juris habebat, preter judiciariam potestatem feodatorumque suorum portionem, annuentibus duobus filiis suis Buchardo et Godefrido, tunc quidem adhuc parvulis. Ecclesia vero pro murmure quorumdam qui dicerent non legitime factum fuisse pro etate nondum discernentium puerorum non statim sibi vendicavit ipsum allodium, sperans si ex Deo esset quandoque provectis pueris quod melius confirmari posset. Factum est igitur postea, Deo disponente, predicti pueri scilicet Buchardus[11] iam diu miles et Godefridus pubescens armiger

6 Possibly the same Renier de Guise and his (step?)son Robert who are named as donors in an inventory of the abbey of Homblières dating to the 1130s/40s. Newman, *Homblières*, 97.

7 Guy I, lord of Voulpaix (cant. Vervins, https://dicotopo.cths.fr/places/P36863279). Melleville, *DH*, vol. 2, 470.

8 Gwidonis *B*.

9 Gusia *B*.

10 Gwidonis *B*.

11 Burchardus *B*.

cum duobus sororiis suis, Reinero de Guisia[12] et Guidone[13] de Uspaz, assensu etiam tercii, Anselmi videlicet de Sancto Quintino, filii Oidardi,[14] reversi sunt ad prefatam ecclesiam cum predicta matre sua et quod prius factum fuerat ipsis nondum discernentibus, renovaverunt et confirmaverunt, prefatis sororiis assentientibus et quod diu ante ipsa proposuerat sub habitu religionis in eadem ecclesia eorum mater, Addelvia scilicet, remansit. Huius rei testes sunt: Hugo[15] abbas de Humblieres,[16] Robertus[17] monachus qui dicitur Mutus, Renerus[18] de Gusia qui etiam Mutus dicitur, Guido[19] de Uspaz, Guido[20,21] de Belmes, Renerus[22] de Roinon, Wedericus[23] Havarz, Walderus[24] de Monciaus,[25] Joibertus[26] de Dorlet,[27] Radulfus de Landierfait,[28] Robertus[29] filius Petri Eschin. Quia igitur officii nostri est proprium tam precavendis adversitatibus quam corroborandis ecclesie provectibus operam dare, ut hoc ratum inconvulsumque maneret, perpetuo auctoritate[30] nostra decrevimus confirmari et scriptum sigillo nostro consignari. Si qua igitur ecclesiastica secularisve persona hoc legitime factum temerare presumpserit semel aut iterum commonita si non emendaverit auctoritate Dei et nostra a consortio fidelium segregata subiaceat anathemati donec ecclesie predicte pro illata injuria et pro contemptu episcopalis reverencie satisfaciat. Actum est hoc anno incarnationis dominice M° C° XXX° V°, epacta XXIII, indictione XII[a], concurrente septimo.[31]

12 Gusia *B.*
13 Gwidone *B.*
14 Oilardi *B.*
15 Hugues I, abbot of the Benedictine abbey of Homblières, 1132–43. Newman, *Homblières*, 18.
16 Humbliers *B.*
17 Rotbertus *B.*
18 Reinerus *B.*
19 Gwido *B.*
20 Gwido *B.*
21 Likely Guy de Beaumetz, lord of Beaumetz (cant. Bertincourt, https://dicotopo.cths.fr/places/P35591263) and castellan of Bapaume, son of Enguerrand de Beaumetz, lord of Beaumetz, and Marthe, lady of Bellancourt.
22 Reinerus *B.*
23 Werricus Havars also appears in **235** and as a witness in an 1156 act of Geoffroi de Guise, Nicolas d'Avesnes, and Jacques d'Avesnes. BnF, MS lat. 17777, fol. 188r.
24 Walterus *B.*
25 Munceil *B.*
26 Josbertus *B.*
27 Possibly Deuillet, cant. La Fère, https://dicotopo.cths.fr/places/P69846871.
28 Landerfait *B.*
29 Rotbertus *B.*
30 actoritate *B.*
31 VII *B.*

321

1158

Baudouin [II],[1] *bishop of Noyon, makes known that Hugues* Albus *gave to the church of Prémontré all the land that he held in* census *at Montizel*[2] *from Robert* Cane, *on the condition that, should Prémontré alienate any of this land in the future, Prémontré will return the rights of* justicia *and* districtum *to Robert. Matilde, wife of Robert, and their sons Albert, Robert, and Baudouin consent to this agreement.*

A. Cartulary of Prémontré, fol. 82r.

B. Original, BnF, nouv. acq. lat. 2309, no. 7, previously sealed.

REGISTER: Boghen, "Inventaire des actes épiscopaux originaux conservés à la Bibliothèque nationale (1121–1200)," 121.

Karta Noviomensis episcopi de terra quam Hugonis abbas tenebat a Roberto Cane dedit ecclesie Premonstrati.

[I]n nomine Patris et Filii et Spiritus Sancti.[3] Ego Balduinus, Dei gratia Noviomensis episcopus, scire volo tam presentes quam futuros quod Hugo, cognomine Albus, dedit Premonstrate ecclesie omnem terram illam quam censualiter tenebat a Roberto Cane apud Montisel, annuente eodem Roberto, cum uxore sua, Matilde, et filiis, Alberto et Roberto et Balduino; qui etiam ipse Robertus omnem justiciam et districtum predicte terre prefate ecclesie adeo libere dedit ut nichil in ea preter proprium censum retineret ea tamen pactione ut, siquis de eadem terra contra ecclesiam placitando aliquid adquirere posset, super terra illa acquisita[4] idem Robertus justiciam et districtum sibi retineret. Huic donationi Roberti sive pactioni interfuerunt testes: Symon[5] de Montescourt,[6] Symon Pincerna de Perona, Radulfus maior, Waiszo vicecomes de Monci,[7] frater Matheus et frater Petrus. Postea autem Balduinus, Roberti filius, qui tunc forte aberat, hoc idem concessit sub hiis testibus, videlicet Goiszone de

1 Baudouin II de Boulogne, abbot of the Augustinian abbey of Saint-Eloi-Fontaine, ca. 1130–ca. 1139, and bishop of Noyon, 1148–67. *GC* IX, col. 1126.

2 Montizel, cant. Ham, https://dicotopo.cths.fr/places/P16235568.

3 *Om.* amen *A*.

4 adquisita *B*.

5 Simon de Mondescourt (cant. Noyon, https://dicotopo.cths.fr/places/P60804459), son of Emmelot, appears as a witness in acts 1137–ca. 1183. Tock and Milis, *Monumenta Arroasiensia*, 143, 315.

6 Monteiscurt *B*.

7 Probably Monchy-Lagache, cant. Ham, https://dicotopo.cths.fr/places/P05686049.

Walluc[8,9] et Huberto, fratre eius, converso. Verum et hoc de censu eiusdem terre persolvendo determinatum fuit ut, si forte tanta guerra foret quod pro censu suo prefatus Robertus mittere non auderet pro libito suo, fratres ei deferrent sive apud Frameri villam sive apud Peronam. Si autem pax esset, Engelberto del[10] Pont daretur; ad ultimum autem si ex negligentia fratrum idem census in solvendo tardaretur per octo dies sive per quindecim, nulla inde calumpnia fieret sed absque controversia reciperetur. Hoc igitur donum legitime factum sigilli nostri impressione signamus et eorum qui interfuerunt astipulatione corroboramus. Signum Renaldi,[11,12] abbatis Hamensis. S. Alulfi,[13] Calniacensis abbatis. S. Reneri[14] capellani, S. Roberti, presbiterorum. S. Johannis, diaconi. S. Reneri,[15] canonici. Ne quis igitur in posterum hoc attemptare presumat sub anathemate interdicimus. Ego Hugo[16] cancellarius subscripsi et relegi. Actum anno incarnationis dominice M° C° quinquagesimo VIII°.[17]

322

1165

Baudouin [II],[1] *bishop of Noyon, makes known the resolution of a dispute between the church of Prémontré and husband and wife Guy [II],*[2] *castellan of Coucy, and Théophanie. In his presence, Guy and Théophanie cede to Prémontré their rights to the mill at Montizel,*[3] *a fishpond and its sluice, banks, and other appurtenances, in return for an annual payment of four* modii *of grain (*frumentum*), measure of Ham, to be taken annually at the grange of Germaine.*[4]

8 Walluch *B.*

9 Likely Hallu, cant. Rosières, https://dicotopo.cths.fr/places/P28843490.

10 de *B.*

11 Rainaldi *B.*

12 Renaud I, abbot of the Augustinian abbey of Notre-Dame de Ham, 1143–bef. 1160. *GC* IX, col. 1122.

13 Alulphe, previously archdeacon of Thérouanne and later abbot of the Arroasian Augustinian community of Sainte-Marie de Chauny, ca. 1135–ca. 1162. During his abbatiate, the brothers moved from Chauny to Saint-Éloi-Fontaine. Poissonnier, "L'Abbaye de St-Éloi-Fontaine ou de Commenchon," 271–2.

14 Raineri *B.*

15 Raineri *B.*

16 Hugues III de Roye, chancellor of Noyon-Tournai, ca. 1130–46, and of Noyon, 1146–63/6. Pycke, *Le chapitre cathédral Notre-Dame de Tournai de la fin du XIe à la fin du XIIIe siècle*, 64.

17 octavo *B.*

1 Baudouin II de Boulogne, abbot of the Augustinian abbey of Saint-Eloi-Fontaine, ca. 1130–ca. 1139, and bishop of Noyon, 1148–67. *GC* IX, col. 1126.

2 Guy II, castellan of Coucy (d. 1165); husband of Théophanie. Barthélemy, *LDA*, 506–7.

3 Montizel, cant. Ham, https://dicotopo.cths.fr/places/P16235568.

4 Germaine, cant. Vermand, https://dicotopo.cths.fr/places/P36636067.

Baudouin also states that on two separate occasions, Guy and Théophanie's children Renaud,[5] Robert,[6] Pierre,[7] and Béatrice consented to this arrangement.

A. Cartulary of Prémontré, fols. 82r–82v.

B. Original, BnF, Coll. Picardie 290, no. 10, previously sealed. In the right margin and beginning at the top, the bottom half of the letters that form the word CYROGRAPHUM.

REGISTER: Boghen, "Inventaire des actes épiscopaux originaux conservés à la Bibliothèque nationale (1121–1200)," 121; *Studium Baldwin*, fiche 2067.

Karta episcopi Noviomensis de quadam conpositione inter ecclesiam Premonstratem et castellanum de Couci.

[I]n nomine Patris et Filii et Spiritus Sancti, ego Balduinus, Dei gratia Noviomensis episcopus, notum facio tam presentibus quam futuris quod querela quedam emerserat inter ecclesiam Premonstratensem et dominum Widonem, castellanum de Couci,[8] que in presentia nostra terminata est in hunc modum: prefatus castellanus et uxor eius, Theophania,[9] ad cuius precipue hereditatem pertinebat, concesserunt predicte ecclesie possidendum perpetuo, libere et quiete, quicquid juris se habere asserebant in molendino de Montisel, in exclusa vivarii et vivario, in ripa vivarii, in feodo terre Fulconis[10] Obeline quam prefata ecclesia tenebat, et in terra Godefridi, maioris de Germania, apud Orvoir[11] districtum remisit et justiciam. Hec omnia libere possidenda concesserunt prefate ecclesie ita quod eadem ecclesia solvet eis et heredibus eorum, singulis annis infra octavas[12] Sancti Martini, IIII^or^ modios frumenti melioris post sementem in grangia Germanie, ad mensuram Hami, tunc temporis currentem, ita sane quod nec ipsi nec heredes eorum poterunt inde facere elemosinam nisi prefate ecclesie ~~ita quod eadem ecclesia solvet eis et heredibus eorum~~ neque vendere, neque invadiare si ecclesia tantum eis inde voluerit facere quantum alius. Ut igitur ratum et inconvulsum permaneat, sigilli nostri impressione corroboramus et testium qui interfuerunt nomina fecimus apponi; Gaufridus cantor, Symon

5 Renaud I de Coucy, lord of Sinceny, son of Guy II, castellan of Coucy, and Théophanie. Barthélemy, *LDA*, 506.

6 Robert *Bove* (d. bef. 1192), son of Guy II, castellan of Coucy, and Theophanie. Barthélemy, *LDA*, 508, 510.

7 Pierre, son of Guy II, castellan of Coucy, and Théophanie, also appears in **309**.

8 Coci *B*.

9 Teophania *B*.

10 Foulques Obelin is attested in acts from 1134–65. See **353**, **362**, **384**, **398**, and **442.**

11 Auroir, comm. Foreste, https://dicotopo.cths.fr/places/P79580266.

12 octabas *B*.

canonicus, Drogo capellanus, Tieszo decanus, Hugo magister, Wermundus miles, Renoldus[13] de Guni,[14] Johannes de Noviomo. Isti interfuerunt quando castellanus et filius eius, Renoldus,[15] et Robertus hanc concessionem coram nobis fecerunt. Ubi autem prefata uxor eius et filii eius, Robertus et Petrus, et filia Beatrix hoc concesserunt, interfuerunt Petrus presbyter de Pierremande,[16] Martinus presbyter, Hugo, clericus de Couci,[17] Ivo[18] filius castellani, Renaldus[19] de Guni, Johannes de Noviomo. Actum anno incarnati verbi[20] M° C° LX° V°.

323

1194. Bishop's palace, Noyon.

Étienne [I],[1] bishop of Noyon, approves the resolution of a dispute between Pierre [I],[2] abbot of Prémontré, and Adèle and her six sons – Pierre, Evrard, Robert, Baudric, Foulques, and Garnier – concerning six sextariatae *of land at Montizel,[3] and how the land is to be divided among the six brothers.*

A. Cartulary of Prémontré, fol. 82v.
B. Original, AN, L 995, no. 49, previously sealed.
REGISTER: *Studium Baldwin*, fiche 2131.

Karta Stephani Noviomensis episcopi de quadam conpositione inter ecclesiam Premonstratensem et Widelam et sex filios eius.

[S]tephanus, Dei gratia Noviomensis episcopus, presentibus et futuris litteras istas visuris in Domino salutem. Noverit universitas vestra quod cum inter ecclesiam Premonstratensem et Udelam et sex filios eius, videlicet Petrum, Evrardum, Robertum, Baldricum, Fulcheredum et Warnerum, super quadam hereditate quam in territorio de Montisel ad se pertinere dicebant, querela

13 Reinoldus *B*.
14 Guny, cant. Coucy-le-Château, https://dicotopo.cths.fr/places/P88745448.
15 Rainoldus *B*.
16 Pierremande, cant. Coucy-le-Château, https://dicotopo.cths.fr/places/P72978208.
17 Coci *B*.
18 Yves de Coucy, knight, son of Guy II, castellan of Coucy, and Theophanie, appears as a witness in acts 1165–ca. 1180. Barthélemy, *LDA*, 508.
19 Rainoldus *B*.
20 *Transp. A*; verbi incarnati *B*.

1 Étienne de Villebéon (or de Nemours), son of Gautier de Villebéon, lord of La Chapelle-Gauthier and Nemours, and Aveline, was bishop of Noyon, 1188–1221.
2 Pierre I de Saint-Médard, abbot of the Premonstratensian abbeys of Saint-Just en Chaussée, 1184–95, Prémontré, 1195–1201, and Cuissy, 1210–17. *MP* II, 497, 527, 565.
3 Montizel, cant. Ham, https://dicotopo.cths.fr/places/P16235568.

verteretur, tandem ad nostram curiam tracta fuit, et, presente utraque parte, nobis mediantibus, finem accepit. Dominus siquidem Petrus, predicte ecclesie abbas, causa pacis et compositionis, prefate mulieri et suis memoratis filiis sex sexterliatas terre ad domum de Montisel pertinentes in hereditatem donavit, ita quod unicuique eorumdem fratrum una sexterliata, metis positis disterminata, concorditer assignata fuit, addita tantummodo sexterliate Evrardi dimidia virga pro eo quod ipse Evrardus secus quandam viam suam sexterliatam accepit. Huius igitur assignationis et compositionis causa, supradicta mulier et eius sex filii, abjurata coram nobis ea hereditate quam proposuerant et, renuntiatis omnibus querelis quas adversus abbatem et fratres Premonstratenses juste sive injuste habuerant vel habere poterant, data prius fide super sancta, postea juraverunt se fideliter eandem compositionem in perpetuum servaturos, ita quod nullam amodo super cunctis possessionibus quas domus de Montisel tempore huius scripti tenebat, querelam vel molestiam occasione qualibet studebunt movere, nec eorum heredes aliquid ibi poterunt reclamare. Quod ut semper ad memoriam reducatur et firmum in tempus posterum habeatur scriptum istud appositione sigilli nostri et annotatione testium fecimus communiri. Actum publice in palatio nostro Noviomi anno incarnationis dominice M° C° nonagesimo quarto, presentibus eis quorum nomina subscripta sunt: domino videlicet Sigeberto,[4] domino Itero et magistro Theobaldo, canonicis Noviomensibus, Gileberto Louvet,[5] Thiezardo[6] marescaldo[7] et Berengario hostiario nostro.

324

January 2, 1231.

Nicolas,[1] bishop of Noyon, confirms by vidimus that Conrad, abbot of Prémontré, acknowledged the gift of 12 modii *of grain (*frumentum*), measure of Saint-Quentin, that Elizabeth* Musarde *and her son, the cleric Jacques, made to Prémontré in the presence of the dean of Saint-Quentin. Elizabeth and Jacques retain the use of the gift, originally purchased from Elizabeth's son the knight Pierre,[2] for life. (See **325**, **326**, **328**, and **329**.)*

A. Cartulary of Prémontré, fols. 82v–83r.

B. Original, AD Aisne, H 793, previously sealed with a double strip of parchment.

---

4 Sygeberto *B*.

5 Louet *B*.

6 Thiesardo *B*.

7 mareschaldo *B*.

---

1 Nicolas de Roye, son of the knight Pierre de Roye, was dean of Saint-Martin from 1216 and bishop of Noyon, 1228–39/40.

2 A Pierre *cognomento Musardus*, knight, appears in a 1241 act of Mont-Saint-Martin. BnF, MS lat. 5478, fol. 44v.

Karta Nicholai episcopi Noviomensis de literis Elizabeth Musarde et Jacobi fili sui de XII modiis frumenti.

[I]n nomine Patris et Filii et Spiritus Sancti, amen. Nicholaus, Dei gratia Noviomensis episcopus, universis presentem paginam inspecturis in Domino salutem. Noverint universi nos inspexisse litteras virorum religiosorum C[onradi] abbatis et conventus Premonstratensium quas tradiderunt Elizabeth, dicte Musarde, de Sancto Quintino, et Jacobo clerico filio eius, ad vitam eorum tantum modo valituras, sigillo dictorum abbatis et conventus sigillatas in hec verba: Ego Conradus, Premonstratensis abbas, et nostrum capitulum notum facimus universis presentem paginam inspecturis quod cum dilecta et familiaris nostra Elizabeth, dicta Musarde, de Sancto Quintino et Jacobus, clericus, filius eius, emissent et acquisissent quite[3] et libere duodecim modios frumenti sani et solubilis, ad mensuram Sancti Quintini nunc currentem, a Petro, milite, filio dicte Elizabeth, et eius heredibus ad quos dictum frumentum debebat post decessum prefate Elizabeth[4] jure hereditario devolvi, predicti Elizabeth[5] et Jacobus, filius eius, habentes ad novissima sua devota consideratione respectum, contulerunt in perpetuam elemosinam pro salute animarum suarum ecclesie nostre dictos duodecim modios frumenti quos jure hereditario ad grangiam nostram de Germaniis[6] habebant annis singulis assignatos, ita tamen quod sepedicti Elizabeth et Jacobus clericus, in quocumque statu sint, sive extra religionem, sive in religione erunt, in pacifica possessione duodecim modiorum frumenti predictorum a nobis quamdiu vixerint eisdem ad grangiam nostram predictam infra vicesimum die Natalis Domini annuatim integre solvendorum, ita quod si post diem predictum aliquod periculum de ipso frumento evenerit, ecclesia nostra non respondebit de periculo sive dampno. Sciendum est etiam quod quicumque ipsorum vel Elizabeth[7] Jacobus vel[8] prior decesserit, superstes nichilominus ipsos duodecim modios frumenti quamdiu vixerit, integre possidebit. Post decessum vero amborum, videlicet Elizabeth et Jacobi predictorum, sine contradictione aliquorum heredum presentium vel futurorum ipsius Elizabeth vel etiam ipsius Jacobi, si forte processu temporis ipsum liberos habere contigerit, duodecim modii prenotati ecclesie nostre in perpetuam elemosinam quite et libere remanebunt. Dictam vero elemosinam recognoverunt dicti Elizabeth et Jacobus, coram decano Christianitatis Sancti Quintini, ad hoc de mandato domini Noviomensis episcopis personaliter destinato, et petierunt dictam

3 *Sic A*, *read* quiete.
4 Elizabet *B*.
5 Elizabet *B*.
6 Germaine, cant. Vermand, https://dicotopo.cths.fr/places/P36636067.
7 Elizabet *B*.
8 *Transp. A*; vel Jacobus *B*.

elemosinam et recognitionem ab ipsis factam per auctenticum[9] instrumentum eiusdem episcopi confirmari. In cuius rei testimonium presentem paginam eisdem Elizabet[10] et Jacobo tradidimus sigilli nostri appensione munitam. Actum quarto idus januarii, anno Domini millesimo ducentesimo tricesimo primo.

325

January, 1231.

Nicolas,[1] *bishop of Noyon, confirms the gift that Elizabeth* Musarde *of Saint-Quentin and her son, the cleric Jacques, made in alms to Prémontré in his presence. (See* ***324****,* ***326****,* ***328****, and* ***329****.)*

A. Cartulary of Prémontré, fol. 83r.
B. Original, AD Aisne, H 793, previously sealed on a double strip of parchment.

Karta Noviomensis episcopi de elemosina Elizabeth Musarde et Jacobi filii sui.

[I]n nomine Patris et Filii et Spiritus Sancti, amen. Nicholaus, Dei gratia Noviomensis episcopus, universis tam presentibus quam futuris in Domino salutem. Noverint universi quod Elizabeth dicta Musarde, de Sancto Quintino, et Jacobus, clericus, filius eius in nostra presentia personaliter constituti, recognoverunt se divine pietatis intuitu, pro salute animarum suarum, irrevocabiliter contulisse in perpetuam elemosinam ecclesie Premonstratensi duodecim modios frumenti ad mensuram Sancti Quintini quos habebant, annis singulis apud Germanias,[2] curtem predicte ecclesie, assignatos, ita tamen quod predicti Elizabeth et Jacobus clericus vel alter eorum qui supervixerit recipient per totam vitam suam, in quocumque habitu fuerint, illos duodecim modios frumenti apud Germanias, locum predictum. Sed, ne post decessum eorum dictos duodecim modios ab aliquo reclamari vel ecclesiam predictam super hoc in posterum molestari contingat, et ne ipsius elemosine collatio possit vel personarum mutatione vel temporis diuturnitate deleri quominus ad ipsam ecclesiam Premonstratensem dicti duodecim modii frumenti post decessum amborum, videlicet Elizabet[3] et Jacobi predictorum, libere revertantur, nos in memoriam et perpetuam firmitatem ipsius elemosine, presentem kartam, ad petitionem partium sigilli nostri munimine fecimus roborari. Actum mense januario, anno gratis M° CC°[4] tricesimo primo.

9 autenticum *B*.
10 Elizabeth *B*.

1 Nicolas de Roye, son of the knight Pierre de Roye, was dean of Saint-Martin from 1216 and bishop of Noyon, 1228–39/40.
2 Germaine, cant. Vermand, https://dicotopo.cths.fr/places/P36636067.
3 Elizabeth *B*.
4 millesimo ducentesimo *B*.

326

January, 1231.

Robert,[1] decanus Christianitatis *of Saint-Quentin, makes known that, on the order of the bishop*[2] *of Noyon, Robert and Enguerrand, prepositus of Prémontré, met with Elizabeth* Musarde *and her son, the cleric Jacques, who reside in Robert's deanery, concerning their gift of 12* modii *of grain (*frumentum*) in alms to Prémontré. Robert and Enguerrand acknowledge the gift and Robert affixes his seal to this charter at the request of Elizabeth and Jacques. (See* ***324, 325, 328****, and* ***329****.)*

A. Cartulary of Prémontré, fol. 83r.

B. Original, AD Aisne, H 793, previously sealed on a double strip of parchment.

Karta decani Christianitatis de confirmatione elemosine Elizabeth et Jacobi filii sui.

[U]niversis presentem paginam inspecturis, R[obertus], decanus Christianitatis Sancti Quintini, salutem in Domino. Noverint universi quod cum nos, de mandato reverendi patris episcopi Noviomensis, personaliter accessissemus cum fratre Ingelranno[3] preposito Premonstratensi, ad Elizabeth[4] Musarde de Sancto Quintino, et Jacobum, clericum, filiusm eius, parrochianos nostri decanatus, ipsi Elizabeth et Jacobus clericus in presentia nostra constituti, divine pietatis intuitu, pro salute animarum suarum contulerunt in elemosinam perpetuam ecclesie Premonstratensi duodecim modios *frumenti apud Germanias*[5] *ad curtem predicte ecclesie assignatos quos habent singulis annis ad mensuram Sancti Quintini,*[6] ita tamen quod predicti Elizabeth[7] et Jacobus, clericus, vel alter eorum qui supervixerint, recipient per totam vitam suam, in quocumque habitu fuerint, illos duodecim modios frumenti apud Germanias, locum predictum. Post decessum vero amborum videlicet Elizabeth et Jacobi predictorum, dicti duodecim modii frumenti ad prefatam ecclesiam Premonstratensem libere et sine contradictione aliquorum heredum tam ipsius Elizabeth[8] quam etiam dicti Jacobi, si forte processu temporis ipsum liberos

1 Robert, *decanus Christianitatis* of Saint-Quentin, attested 1228–34. AD Aisne, H 1624, fols. 301r, 405r–407r.

2 Nicolas de Roye, son of the knight Pierre de Roye, was dean of Saint-Martin from 1216 and bishop of Noyon, 1228–39/40.

3 Ingelrrano *B*.

4 Elyzabet *B*.

5 Germaine, cant. Vermand, https://dicotopo.cths.fr/places/P36636067.

6 *For section in italics, read*: ad mensuram Sancti Quintini quos habent singulis annis apud Germanias curtem predicte ecclesie, assignatos *B*.

7 Elyzabeth *B*.

8 Elyzabet *B*.

habere contigerit, revertentur. In cuius rei testimonium presentem paginam ad petitionem dictorum Elizabeth[9] et Jacobi clerici sigilli nostri munimine duximus roborandum.[10] Actum mense januario, anno gratie M° CC° tricesimo primo.

327

March 7, 1212.

Richard,[1] prepositus *of Amiens, makes known that, in his presence, Étienne de Douchy*[2] *and the church of Prémontré resolve their dispute concerning the* trecensus *of lands and tithes associated with the altar of the church of Douchy, which had previously been given to Prémontré by Gilles [I],*[3] *castellan of Bapaume, and Gérard*[4] *de Ronssoy. Abbot Gervais*[5] *pays Étienne 40* librae Parisiensium *in return for renouncing his claims. Baudouin de Villevêque,*[6] *the knight Gautier* Loup, *and Étienne's maternal uncle Guy, mother Matilde, stepfather Franco, and brothers Oudard, Nicolas, and Geoffroi renounce the same claims. (See **340**.)*

A. Cartulary of Prémontré, fols. 83r–83v.
B. Original not found.

Karta Richardi prepositi Ambianensis de Egidio de Bapalmis et Gerardo de Roinsoi.

[E]go Richardus, prepositus Ambianensis, notum facio presentibus et futuris qui viderint istud scriptum quod, cum olim nobiles viri Egidius castellanus de Bapalmis et Gerardus de Roinsoi dedissent ecclesie Premonstratensi ad

9 Elyzabet *B*.
10 roboranda *B*.

1 Richard, *prepositus* of Amiens. Baldwin, *The Government of Philip Augustus*, 428.
2 Douchy, cant. Vermand, https://dicotopo.cths.fr/places/P84133506.
3 Gilles I, lord of Beaumetz (cant. Bertincourt, https://dicotopo.cths.fr/places/P35591263) and castellan of Bapaume (d. aft. 1214), son of Hugues, castellan of Bapaume and lord of Beaumetz, and Beatrix de Guines. He appears in a number of acts dating 1208–13 in the cartulary of the abbey of Avesnes-lès-Bapaume. Bougard and Delmaire, *Le cartulaire et les chartes de l'abbaye de femmes d'Avesnes-lès-Bapaume (1128–1337)*, 119–20, 121–2, 129–30.
4 Gérard, lord of Ronssoy (cant. Roisel, https://dicotopo.cths.fr/places/P97353507), husband of Jeanne de Thourotte; appears in acts ca. 1223–6. AD Aisne, H 1624, fols. 476r, 486r, 488r; BnF, MS lat. 5478, fols. 26v–27v, 111v–112r.
5 Gervais, abbot of the Premonstratensian abbeys of Saint-Just-en-Chaussée, 1199–1205, Thenailles, 1205–9, and Prémontré, 1209–20, and bishop of Séez, 1220–8. *MP* II, 401, 527, 565; Cheney, "Gervase, Abbot of Prémontré."
6 Villevêque, comm. Marteville, https://dicotopo.cths.fr/places/P98851080.

perpetuum trecensum quicquid possidebant in dote altaris de Douci, videlicet in terris et in decima et in tractu decime et in omnibus aliis pertinentiis eiusdem dotis altaris, Stephanus de Douci movit querelam adversus ecclesiam Premonstratensem super tractu decime et super terris quas dicebat se debere hereditarie excolere ad medietatem et propter hoc ipsam ecclesiam plurimum molestavit. Tandem vero cum querela ad hoc deducta fuisset quod predicti nobiles coram me debebant portare garandiam ecclesie Premonstratensi et Stephanus coram me jus facere et capere debebat apud Peronam, de consilio multorum proborum virorum, facta est inter partes pax et concordia in hac forma: Stephanus quitavit predictis nobilibus et ecclesie Premonstratensi quicquid juris clamabat vel clamare poterat quocumque modo in omnibus supradictis et fide plevivit ac juravit super sancta quod ecclesiam predictam super hiis per se vel per alium nunquam decetero molestaret aut scienter ab aliis permitteret molestari. Eandem vero quitanciam fecerunt Balduinus de Vilevesque, Walterus miles Lupus, et Egidius avunculi eius, Matilidis mater eius, et Franco victricus eius; Odardus, Nicholaus et Gaufridus, fratres eiusdem Stephani; et idem ipsi tam fide pleviverunt quam juramento firmaverunt quicquid predictus Stephanus presens pleniverat et firmaverat juramento. Ecclesia vero Premonstratensis de consilio meo per manum domini Gervasii, eiusdem ecclesie abbatis, quadraginta libras Parisiensium dedit sepedicto Stephano, non quia recognosceret ei jus aliquod in predictis, sed ut redimeret pacem suam. Per hanc autem conpositionem extincte sunt omnes querele que erant vel esse poterant inter ecclesiam Premonstratensem et predictam Stephanum de omnibus anteactis. Ut igitur compositio ista futuris temporibus inviolabiliter observetur, eam fideliter hic inscribi et sigilli mei feci impressione muniri. Inde sunt testes: nobiles viri Egidius[7] de Marchasio, Willermus et Hugo fratres eius, Johannes[8] de Liebermont, Gerardus de Staincourt[9] et Hugo de Alneto. Actum nonas martii, anno gratie M° CC° XII°.

328

December, 1231.

Magister *Hughes,*[1] *canon and* officialis *of Noyon, makes known that the knight Pierre* Musars, *with the consent of his wife Aelide and his children, Jean and*

7 Gilles I, lord of Marquaix. Newman, *Seigneurs*, vol. 2, 100.

8 A Jean de Libermont (cant. Guiscard, https://dicotopo.cths.fr/places/P88496451), knight, appears in two 1216 acts in the cartulary of the cathedral of Noyon. AD Oise G 1984, fols. 164r, 190r.

9 Possibly Equancourt, cant. Combles, https://dicotopo.cths.fr/places/P05599553.

1 *Magister* Hugues, canon and *officialis* of Noyon, ca. 1229–ca. 1236. AD Aisne, H 455, fol. 310v; AD Oise, G 1984, fols. 238v–239r.

Isabelle, sold to Elizabeth Musarde, *his mother, and to the cleric Jacques, her son, the 12* modii *of grain (*frumentum*) from an annual* census *that he had expected to inherit on his mother's death. Since this gift figured in Aelide's* dos, *she is compensated with* modii *from other places. (See* ***324****,* ***325****,* ***326****, and* ***329****.)*

A. Cartulary of Prémontré, fol. 83v.
B. Original not found.

Karta canonici officialis Noviomensis de elemosina Petri militis cognomento Musart.

[U]niversis presentes litteras inspecturis, magister H[ugo], canonicus et officialis Noviomensis salutem in omnium salutari. Noverint universi quod Petrus miles, cognominatus Musars, in nostra presentia constitutus, recognovit se vendidisse bene et legitime, de assensu et voluntate Aelidis, uxoris sue, et liberorum suorum, videlicet Johannis et Isabelle, Elizabeth la Musarde, matri sue et Jacobo clerico, filio eiusdem Elizabeth, duodecim modios frumenti quos idem Petrus habebat de annuo censu post decessum matris sue predicte apud Germanias,[2] curtem Premonstratensem, assignatos. Hanc venditionem creantavit prefatus P[etrus] miles, coram nobis fide interposita se firmiter in perpetuum observare. Prefata vero Aelidis, uxor predicti Petri, que dotata erat de medietate frumenti predicti, sicut asserebat, coram nobis, in propria persona, quitavit fide interposita omne jus dotis quod habebat in predictis duodecim modiis frumenti, recognoscens coram nobis in propria se habere plenariam restitutionem dotis predicte, asserens etiam se esse assignatam pro restitutione predicta ad medietatem novem modiorum et quinque sextariorum bladi apud Rikeval,[3] curtem Montis Sancti Martini,[4] assignatorum et ad tres modios bladi apud Oistricourt,[5] curtem prioratus de Quinsi, assignatos. Insuper prefati P[etri] miles et Aelidis, uxor eius, creantaverunt coram nobis, sicut dictum est, fide corporaliter prestita, quod prefatos Elizabeth dictam Musarde et Jacobum clericum, filium eiusdem, vel eorum successores quocumque modo succedant eisdem in duodecim modios frumenti prenotatis de predicta venditione et quitatione nullatenus vexare vel inquietare presument. In cuius rei testimonium

2 Germaine, cant. Vermand, https://dicotopo.cths.fr/places/P36636067.
3 Riqueval, comm. Bellicourt, https://dicotopo.cths.fr/places/P96970835.
4 Mont-Saint-Martin, comm. Gouy, https://dicotopo.cths.fr/places/P99793403.
5 Étricourt, comm. Nauroy, https://dicotopo.cths.fr/places/P13809640.

presentem paginam sigilli curie Noviomensis munimine fecimus roborari. Actum anno Domini M° CC° tricesimo primo, mense decembri.

329

January 2, 1231.[1] Saint-Quentin.

Robert,[2] decanus Christianitatis *of Saint-Quentin, recounts to Nicolas,*[3] *bishop of Noyon, the details of the gift made to Prémontré in his presence by Elizabeth* Musarde *of Saint-Quentin and by her son the cleric Jacques. (See* ***324****,* ***325****,* ***326****, and* ***328****.)*

A. Cartulary of Prémontré, fol. 83v.

B. Original, AD Aisne, H 793, previously sealed on a single strip.

Item karta decani Christianitatis de confirmatione elemosine Elizabeth Musarde.

[R]everendo patri ac domino N[icholao], Dei gratia Noviomensi episcopo, suus R[obertus] decanus Christianitatis Sancti Quintini, salutem et cum omni honore et reverentia paratam in omnibus obedientiam. Cum nos ad mandatum vestrum personaliter accessissemus cum preposito Premonstratensi ad Elizabeth[4] Musarde de Sancto Quintino et Jacobum, clericum filium eius, parrochianos nostri decanatus, ipsi Elizabeth[5] et Jacobus, clericus, in presentia nostra constituti, divine pietatis intuitu, pro salute animarum suarum, contulerunt in elemosinam perpetuam ecclesie Premonstratensi duodecim modios frumenti ad mensuram Sancti Quintini quos habent singulis annis apud Germanias,[6] curtem predicte ecclesie, assignatos, ita tamen quod predicti Elisabeth[7] et Jacobus, clericus, vel alter eorum qui supervixerit, recipient per totam vitam suam, in quocumque habitu fuerint, illos duodecim modios frumenti apud Germanias locum prenotatum; dictam vero collationem factam, sicut predictum est, paternitati vestre significamus. Actum apud Sanctum Quintinum, in crastino circumcisionis Domini, anno gracie M° CC° tricesimo,[8] mense januario.

---

1 The cartulary act is dated 1230, but the original charter is dated 1231.

2 Robert, *decanus Christianitatis* of Saint-Quentin, is attested 1228–34. AD Aisne, H 1624, fols. 301r, 405r–407r.

3 Nicolas de Roye, son of the knight Pierre de Roye, was dean of Saint-Martin from 1216 and bishop of Noyon, 1228–39/40.

4 Elisabet *B*.

5 Elisabet *B*.

6 Germaine, cant. Vermand, https://dicotopo.cths.fr/places/P36636067.

7 Elisabet *B*.

8 tricesimo primo *B*.

330

1196

Étienne [I],[1] bishop of Noyon, with the consent of the dean and the chapter of Noyon, gives in alms to the brothers of Bonneuil the benefices of the altars of Douchy[2] and Germaine[3] with their appurtenances save for episcopal rights. The brothers of Prémontré in return will celebrate an annual Mass for Étienne after his death.

A. Cartulary of Prémontré, fol. 83v.
B. Original not found.

Karta episcopi Noviomensis de personatum altaris de Douci et de Germaniis.

[S]tephanus, Dei gratia Noviomensis episcopus, omnibus in perpetuum. Noverint universi presentes pariter et futuri nos pro anima nostra et pro animabus antecessorum nostrorum, personatum altaris de Douci et de Germaniis cum pertinentiis suis fratribus Bonolii, salvo in omnibus jure episcopali, assensu decani et capituli Noviomensis, in elemosinam contulisse, ita quod abbas Premonstratensis per unum de fratribus suis canonicis qui, nobis ab ipso presentatus, curam suscipiat a nobis, ipsum altare de Douci et de Germaniis faciet procurari. Huius igitur beneficii nostri gratia, Premonstratensis ecclesia, post decessum nostrum anniversarium nostrum perpetuo celebrabit annuatim. Quod ut ratum penitus habeatur et inconvulsum, nos presentem paginam sigillo nostro roboravimus. Actum anno ab incarnatione Domini M° C° nonagesimo sexto.

331

June, 1219.

Geoffroi[1] de Ham, knight and lord of Douchy, releases his homines de corpore *Laurent Passart and his brother Simon from all* servagium, *and presents them to the altar of Saint-Médard de Douchy[2] in the presence of the priest Foulques, Geoffroi's elder [brother] Eudes, the* scabini *Rohard and Richard* Barbario, *and several others.*

---

1 Étienne de Villebéon (or de Nemours), son of Gautier de Villebéon, lord of La Chapelle-Gauthier and Nemours, and Aveline, was bishop of Noyon, 1188–1221.
2 Douchy, cant. Vermand, https://dicotopo.cths.fr/places/P84133506.
3 Germaine, cant. Vermand, https://dicotopo.cths.fr/places/P36636067.

---

1 Geoffroi de Ham, knight and lord of Douchy (cant. Vermand, https://dicotopo.cths.fr/places/P84133506), a brother of Eudes IV, lord of Ham, and a nephew of Guy de Condren, lord of Faillouel. He also appears in **349**, **355**, and **356**.
2 For the original donation of the altar of Saint-Médard de Douchy to Prémontré, see **340**.

A. Cartulary of Prémontré, fol. 83v.
B. Original not found.

Karta Gaufridi militis domini de Douci de Laurentio Passart et [*margo*: Simone fratre eius (illegible) ecclesie Premonstrati.]

[E]go Gaufridus de Hamo, miles et dominus de Douci, notum facio tam presentibus quam futuris quod ego Laurentium Passart et Symonem, fratrem eius, qui homines mei erant de corpore, de mea spontanea voluntate, misericordia Dei et bonorum virorum consilio, ab omni suo servagio quo mihi tenebantur quitavi et ipsos ad altare Sancti Medardi de Douchi obtuli coram fratre Fulcone, presbytero eiusdem ecclesie, et coram Odone, maiore meo, et Rohardo et Richardo Barbario, scabinis meis et pluribus aliis. Quod ut ratum permaneat in perpetuum et firmum, presentes litteras sigilli mei munimine roboratas eis tradidi in testimonium et munimen. Actum anno Domini M° CC° nonodecimo, mense junio.

332

1178

Abbot Hugues [II][1] *and the chapter of Prémontré, and the abbot Herbert*[2] *and the chapter of the Benedictine monastery of Saint-Thierry, record the agreement that resolved their dispute about the tithes of Athies,*[3] *Devise,*[4] *and* Excluvis. *Pierre, abbot of Saint-Rémi, Raoul, dean of the cathedral chapter of Reims, and Milon, canon of the cathedral of Reims, at the behest of Guillaume,*[5] *archbishop of Reims, mediated the agreement.*

A. Cartulary of Prémontré, fols. 83v–84r.
B. Original (chirograph), AM Metz, Salis II.243, no. 6, sealed with four seals, three of which remain intact. In the right margin and beginning at the top, the bottom half of the letters that form the word CIROGRAPHUM.
Other Manuscript Copies: Cartulary of Saint-Thierry-lès-Reims, BM Reims, 1602, fols. 190r–191v (13th c.).

---

1 Hugues II de Douai, abbot of the Premonstratensian abbey of Cuissy, 1161–5, and abbot of Prémontré, 1174–89. *MP* II, 497.
2 Herbert, abbot of Saint-Thierry, 1167–86.
3 Athies, cant. Ham, https://dicotopo.cths.fr/places/P98820850.
4 Devise, cant. Ham, https://dicotopo.cths.fr/places/P85212875.
5 Guillaume aux Blanches Mains (1135–1202), son of Thibaut II, count of Blois and Champagne, and Mathilde von Spanheim, was bishop of Chartres, 1164–76, archbishop of Sens, 1169–76 and archbishop of Reims, 1176–1202.

Karta abbatis Premonstratensis et abbatis Sancti Theoderici de quadam conpositione inter ipsos.

[I]n nomine Patris et Filii et Spiritus Sancti, amen. Servos Dei non oportet litigare,[6] quin potius servare unitatem spiritus in vinculo pacis et quia tenentur uni Domino servire, tenentur uni regi militare, etiam in dampnis temporalium debent retinere spiritus unitatem ne videantur in scissuris mentium extinxisse caritatem. Ea propter ego Hugo, Premonstrati dictus abbas, et capitulum nostrum, et ego Herbertus,[7] abbas Sancti Theoderici, et capitulum nostrum, notum fieri volumus tam presentibus quam futuris querelam que inter utramque ecclesiam nostram non ex proposito malignandi, sed potius ex ignorantia veritatis emerserat super quibusdam decimationibus, fraterna et amicabili compositione decisam esse. Sane decimationes de Athies que spectant ad monasterium Sancti Theoderici et decimationes de Divise et de Excluvis que spectant ad ecclesiam Premonstrati contigue sunt et invicem sibi coherentes adeo ut ipsa vicinitas non solum ministravit occasionem litigandi, sed etiam jus antique possessionis plerumque fecerit interrumpi. Cum igitur super decimatione duorum camporum quorum unus dicitur Waleri campus, alter campus Rome, questio sepius ventilata fuisset et quibus deberent in partem cedere ignoraretur a pluribus, ita ut occasione prefatorum camporum unaqueque partium in jus alienum transisset,[8] tandem mediantibus discretis et sapientibus viris, domino Petro, abbate Sancti Remigii, et Radulpho,[9] Sancte Marie Remensis decano, et Milone, eiusdem ecclesie canonico, ex parte domini archiepiscopi Guillelmi, voluntario utriusque partis assensu, hoc modo sopita conquievit: Assignata est decima Waleri campi monachis Sancti Theoderici perpetuo habenda; similiter et decima campi Rome Premonstratensibus cessit in portionem perpetuam et quicquid utraque predicta ecclesia possederat antequam litem intrarent super prefatis decimationibus, decetero in pace possidebit. Hoc enim modo interruptio possessionum que facta fuerat per ignorantiam, cassata est per venerabilium virorum industriam et unaqueque ecclesia rediit ad pristinam possessionem suam. Premonstratenses igitur ex beneficio reformate pacis et ex retentione predicti campi Rome solvent monachis Sancti Theoderici singulis annis duos modios frumenti nec de meliori, nec de peiori, in domo sua de Divise ad mensuram de Athies tempore huius scripti currentem, infra festum Omnium Sanctorum. Quod si ex negligentia fratrum Premonstrati infra eundem terminum soluti non fuerint propriis vecturis tenebuntur eos ducere ad grangiam monachorum de Athies, infra sequens festum Sancti Martini. Ut igitur hec compositio perpetue stabilitatis

6 2 Timothy 2:24.

7 Heribertus *B.*

8 *Transp. A*; transisset alienum *B.*

9 Radulfo *B.*

robur optineat presenti scripto fecimus eam annotari et sigillis nostris et capitulorum nostrorum roborari, sed et sigillum prefati abbatis Sancti Remigii et sigillum pretaxati decani qui huius compositionis mediatores in loco domini archiepiscopi fuerunt, fecimus apponi. Huius rei testes sunt: Ingelrannus[10] abbas Sancti Johannis Lauduni, Johannes[11] abbas Sancte Marie Novigenti, Guillelmus[12] abbas Sancti Nicholai de Silva, Bernerius[13] abbas Sancti Crispini, Herbertus[14] Vallis Serene abbas, Hugo[15] abbas de Brana, Guillelmus[16] de Cartovoro, Petrus prior Sancti Theoderici, Burchardus elemosinarius, Ebroinus camerarius, Warnerus, Galterus thesaurarius, Alemannus, Eustachius prior Premonstrati, Albinus subprior, Symon, Theobaldus prepositi, Haimo[17] cantor, Odo cellerarius. Actum anno Domini[18] M° C° LXX° VIII°.[19]

333

1137. Noyon.

Simon [I],[1] bishop of Noyon, confirms the gift that Agnès, wife of the late Bassin de Ham, and her son Mathieu made to Prémontré of two parts of the tithe of Caulaincourt[2] with the consent of Oilard, maior *of Saint-Quentin, and Anseau, his son, from whom the fief descends, and of their wives Havide and Aelide.*

A. Cartulary of Prémontré, fol. 84r.

B. Original, AN, L 995, no. 5.

EDITION: Pycke and Vleeschouwers, *Actes*, 400–1.

---

10 Enguerrand, abbot of the Benedictine abbeys of Nogent-sous-Coucy, 1157–ca. 1160, and of Saint-Jean de Laon, 1161–82. *GC* IX, col. 607; Taïée, "L'abbaye de Saint-Jean de Laon," 217.

11 Jean, abbot of the Benedictine abbey of Nogent-sous-Coucy, ca. 1164–ca. 1175. *GC* IX, col. 608.

12 Guillaume I, abbot of the Benedictine abbey of Saint-Nicolas-aux-Bois, ca. 1168–ca. 1180. Duval, "Histoire de l'abbaye bénédictine de Saint-Nicolas-aux-Bois, diocèse de Laon, première partie," 198–200.

13 Bernier (d. 1180), abbot of the Benedictine abbey of Saint-Crépin-le-Grand from 1164, cardinal bishop of Palestrina from 1179.

14 Herbert, abbot of the Premonstratensian abbey of Valsery, 1167–89. *MP* II, 538.

15 Hugues, abbot of the Premonstratensian abbey of Braine, 1178–81. *MP* II, 486.

16 Guillaume Hennepaix, abbot of the Premonstratensian abbey of Cuissy, 1170–4, of the Premonstratensian abbey of Bucilly, 1176–8, and of the Premonstratensian abbey of Chartreuve, 1178–85. *MP* II, 366, 494, 497.

17 Haymo *B*.

18 *Del.* Domini *B*.

19 M° C LXX VIII *B*; *om.* ab incarnatione Domini *A*.

---

1 Simon I de Vermandois (d. 1148) was the son of Hugues I and Adélaïde, count and countess of Vermandois and Valois, and bishop of Noyon, 1123–42.

2 Caulaincourt, cant. Vermand, https://dicotopo.cths.fr/places/P02972526.

Karta Symonis Noviomensis episcopi de elemosina duarum partium decime de Canlencourt [*margo*: Canlencurt.]

[I]n nomine sancte et individue Trinitatis. Ego Symon, Dei gratia Noviomensis episcopus, quod, nonnullis presentibus, est cognitum posterorum memorie nichilominus fore volo commendatum quorumdam animas tum devotis orationibus tum elemosinarum distributionibus esse redimendas nemo sane fidei qui dubitet. Igitur sub hac spe Agnes, uxor Basini de Hamo et Matheus, ipsorum filius, duas partes decime de Canlencourt Premonstrate ecclesie Sancte Marie et Sancte Johannis Baptiste post mortem Basini, ad ipsius et suorum predecessorum remedium, contulerunt, Oilardo maiore de Sancto Quintino et Ansello, eius filio, de quorum feodo pendebat, cum eorumdem uxoribus Havide[3] et Aelide hoc concedentibus et in manu nostra quod ibi habebant ponentibus sub hiis[4] testibus: Waltero[5] Laudunensi abbate Sancti Martini et abbate de Boini Oderanno,[6] Guidone[7] de Clastris, Guerrico[8] Gastel,[9] Nantero,[10] Guazone[11] qui Stultus agnominatus est, Radulpho[12,13] qui Aper est vocatus. Ego autem predictum donum sancte prenominate ecclesie perpetuo habendum concessi concessum sigilli nostri auctoritate confirmavi. Huic autem nostre concessioni quisquis irrationabiliter oblatrare, resistere et ipsam temerare voluerit, gladio anathematis subjaceat. Fiat. Fiat. Actum Noviomi, anno ab incarnatione Domini M° C° XXX°[14] septimo.[15]

---

3 Hawide *B.*

4 his *B.*

5 Gautier de Saint-Maurice was abbot of the Premonstratensian abbey of Saint-Martin de Laon, 1124–51, and bishop of Laon, 1151–3. *MP* II, 512.

6 Oderan, abbot of the Premonstratensian abbey of Bony (later Mont-Saint-Martin), 1137–40. *MP* II, 419.

7 Guy, lord of Clastres; son-in-law of Ricuère and Raimond of Clastres (**449**) through his marriage to their daughter Hawide. Melleville, *DH*, vol. 1, 256.

8 Wenric Vastel (or Guastel), brother of Renier de Roinon, is attested 1133–71. Newman, *Hombliѐres*, 166, fn. 2.

9 Guastel *B.*

10 Likely the Nanter de Saint-Quentin who appears as a witness in **345** and **419**, and therefore possibly the same Nanter, *bourgeois* of Saint-Quentin, who gave land to the Cistercian abbey of Notre-Dame de Longpont. Poquet, *Monographie de l'abbaye de Longpont, son histoire, ses monuments, ses abbés, ses personnages célèbres, ses sépultures, ses possessions territoriales*, 168.

11 Waszo *Stultus* of Saint-Quentin appears as a witness to episcopal charters, ca. 1137–ca. 1140 (**333**, **450**).

12 Radolfo *B.*

13 Raoul *Aper* also appears as a witness in **339**.

14 millesimo centesimo tricesimo *B.*

15 *Om.* epacta XX[a] VI[a], concurrente IIII, indictione XV. S. Teodorici, tesaurarii. S. Hugonis, cancellarii. S. Petri, cantoris. S. Rogeri, diaconi. S. Walberti, diaconi. S. Vidonis de Sancto Petro. S. Berlandi. S. Nihardi. S. Landrici. S. Roberti Cardun *A.*

334

1142

Simon [I],[1] bishop of Noyon, makes known that Alard[2] de la Porte, knight of Ham, gave the major tithe of Falvy[3] to Prémontré on Alard's sons Mathieu and Alard entering the community at Prémontré. Yves[4] [II, lord of] Nesle, from whom the fief descends, assents to the gift, as does Helvide, Alard's wife, and their other sons, Pierre[5] and Jean. Simon also makes known that Alard previously gave the minor tithe of Falvy to the priory of Villeselve.[6]

A. Cartulary of Prémontré, fol. 84v.

B. Original, AM Metz, Salis II.246, no. 1, sealed in brown wax on a single strip of parchment.

EDITION: Pycke and Vleeschouwers, *Actes*, 468–9.

Karta Noviomensis episcopi de maiore decime de Falevi quam dedit Alardus miles de Hamo.

[I]n nomine sancte et individue Trinitatis. Quia cum labente mundo labitur etiam hominum memoria ex officii nostri debito que a fidelibus bene gesta sunt, nostrum est et approbare et confirmare et scripto memorie commendare. Igitur ego Symon, Dei gratia Noviomensis episcopus, notum facio tam futuris quam presentibus quod Alardus, miles de Hamo, qui dicitur de Porta, contulit Premonstrate ecclesie totam majorem decimam de Falevi tam in tritico quam in siligine, avena, ordeo, faba, pisa, lenticula, vitia, vino, wasdio, ubicumque sive in hortis sive in agris creverit, ob remedium anime sue et predecessorum suorum et amore duorum filiorum suorum, Mathei scilicet et Alardi,[7] qui se ad eandem ecclesiam ad conversionem contulerunt, quibus in portione eandem

1 Simon I de Vermandois (d. 1148) was the son of Hugues I and Adélaïde, count and countess of Vermandois and Valois, and bishop of Noyon, 1123–42.

2 Alard I de Ham (or de la Porte), knight of Ham; husband of Helvide. He also appears in **91**, **298**, **385**, **415**, **452**, and **464**.

3 Falvy, cant. Nesle, https://dicotopo.cths.fr/places/P25248648.

4 Yves II de Nesle (d. ca. 1178), lord of Nesle and count of Soissons, son of Raoul, lord of Nesle, and Raintrude. Newman, *Seigneurs*, vol. 1, 61.

5 Pierre de la Porte, son of Alard I de Ham (or de la Porte), knight of Ham, and Helvide. He also appears in **353** and **388**.

6 The priory of Saint-Marie-Madeleine de Villeselve, dependant on Vézelay. Ponthieux, "Notice historique sur Villeselve et son ancien prieuré, Noyon."

7 Alhardi *B*.

decimam jure hereditario dederat. Hoc autem donum factum est assensu et voluntate Yvonis[8] de Nigella de cuius feodo Alardus eam habebat qui in nostra presentia in manu eiusdem Yvonis[9] eam reposuit, Yvo[10] autem in nostra. Nos vero, quia nostri juris erat, libere in perpetuum possidendam predicte ecclesie contradidimus. Acta sunt hec anno dominice incarnationis M° C° XLII°,[11] indictione tertia,[12] epacta undecima,[13] concurrente II°. Fuerunt autem huius rei testes: Hugo[14] cancellarius, Bartholomeus[15] abbas de Hamo, Matheus presbyter, vicarius episcopi de Perona, Rogerus custos de Noviomo, Yvo[16] dominus Nigelle, Odo[17] dominus de Ham,[18] annuente etiam uxore predicti Alardi, Helvide et filiis suis, Petro et Johanne. Nolumus etiam ignorari donum quod idem Alardus[19] prius fecerat per manum nostram ecclesie Sancte Marie Magdalene de Virziliaco ad usus monachorum de Villari Silva, que est cella eiusdem ecclesie, scilicet altare tantum cum oblationibus suis et minuta decima agnorum lane vitulorum et aliorum huiusmodi lini, canopi, cepe et aliorum holerum, ubicumque creverint. Concessit etiam eis de ipsorum vinea propria quam dedit eis Johannes, filius Balduini[20] de Nigella sive vinum ferat sive annonam; parrochiani etiam sacerdotis prebenda hec est IIII[or] modii tritici Nigellensis mensure et duo[21] avene et quarta[22] pars omnium fructuum hortorum. Et ut pax et concordia inter utramque ecclesiam et distinctio tam evidentis doni inconvulsa permaneat, placuit nobis ut eadem distinctio in privilegio Premonstratensi annotaretur. Siquis igitur contra hec aliquo modo venire temptaverit perpetuo anathemati subjaceat.

---

8 Ivonis *B.*
9 Ivonis *B.*
10 Ivo *B.*
11 M° C° XL° II° *B.*
12 III[a] *B.*
13 XI *B.*
14 Hugues III de Roye, chancellor of Noyon-Tournai, ca. 1130–46, and of Noyon, 1146–63/6. Pycke, *Le chapitre cathédral Notre-Dame de Tournai de la fin du XIe à la fin du XIIIe siècle*, 64.
15 Barthélémy, abbot of the Augustinian abbey of Notre-Dame de Ham, 1132–43. *GC* IX, cols. 1121–2.
16 Ivo *B.*
17 Eudes II *Pes Lupi*, lord of Ham (d. aft. 1144).
18 *Om.* Gerardus et Symon filii eius, Roubertus Rufus et Roubertus qui dicitur venator de Ham *A.*
19 Alhardus *B.*
20 Baldwini *B.*
21 II° *B.*
22 IIII[a] *B.*

335

November, 1225.

Henri and Aenor,[1] *castellans of Coucy, approve the sale made to Prémontré by Pierre,*[2] *lord of Flavy, of four* modiatae *of woods, measure of Ham, located between Bonneuil*[3] *and Flavy. The sale is consented to by Pierre's six siblings – Jean, Pierre, Robert, Isabelle, Mathilde, and Marie – and Herme, his wife, who gave up all rights, inclusive of* dotalicium, *over the woodland. Renaud, son of Aenor and stepson of Henri, also consents.*

A. Cartulary of Prémontré, fol. 84v.

B. Original, AD Oise, H 6002, previously sealed with two seals. This charter has been badly damaged and large parts of text are missing.

Karta Henrici castellani de Couciaco et uxoris eius de confirmatione cuiusdam nemoris venditi ecclesie Premonstrati.

[E]go Henricus, castellanus Couciaci[4] et Aenor, uxor mea, castellana, notum facimus universis tam presentibus quam futuris quod cum Petrus, dominus de Flavi, de assensu et beneplacito fratrum et sororum suarum, videlicet Johannis, Petri, Roberti, Ysabelle, Matildis et Marie necnon et Herme uxoris sue, vendiderit ecclesie Premonstrati quatuor modiatas nemoris ad mensuram Hamensis sitas in territorio inter Bonolium et Flaviacum libere in perpetuum possidendas, et idem Petrus teneret ipsum nemus de nobis, nos ad petitionem partium quitavimus ecclesie Premonstratensis dominium quod habebamus in ipso nemore et venditionem ipsam ratam et gratam habuimus. Quia vero Renaldus privignus noster, filius bone memorie Renaldi castellani de Cociaco, tamquam heres castellanie castellanus erat futurus, venditionem ipsam ratam habuit et fidem etiam prestitit corporalem. Quod cum ad ipsum terra possessio castellanie fuerit devoluta venditionem ipsam scripto suo confirmabit pariter et sigillo. Sciendum est autem quod idem Petrus portare tenetur ecclesie Premonstratensis legitimam warandiam de nemore pretaxato, fidem etiam prestitit corporalem ipse et fratres et sorores sue supradicte quod nec per

1 Aenor, castellan of Coucy (d. aft. 1231), married first Renaud II de Magny, castellan of Coucy, and second Henri de *Castello*, knight. Barthélemy, *LDA*, 512; Pipon, ed., *Le chartrier de l'Abbaye-aux-Bois (1202–1341)*, 134, 172–3.

2 Pierre (d. aft. 1247), lord of half of Flavy-le-Meldeux (cant. Guiscard, https://dicotopo.cths.fr/places/P19622430), son of Raoul, lord of Flavy-le-Meldeux, and Marguerite, sister and heir of Renaud, knight of Flavy. Newman, *Seigneurs*, vol. 2, 280–1.

3 Bonneuil, cant. Ham, https://dicotopo.cths.fr/places/P66750585.

4 Cociaci *B*.

se nec per alios repetent aut repeti facient ipsum nemus nec etiam molestabunt aut molestari facient ecclesiam Premonstratensis de nemore supradicto. Dicta autem Herma, uxor eiusdem Petri, spontanea voluntate sua resignavit quicquid juris tam nomine dotalicii quam alio modo habebat vel habere poterat in quatuor modiatis nemoris sepedicti. In quorum omnium memoriam et perpetuoum testimonium presentes litteras sigillis nostris duximus roborandas. Actum mense novembri, anno incarnationis dominice M° CC°[5] vicesimo quinto.

336

1177

Eudes [III],[1] lord of Ham, reiterates the agreement reached between his late father Lancelin and Prémontré concerning the gift of a woodland at Concis,[2] *in the territory of Golancourt,[3] as well as the additional rights Eudes himself negotiated with Prémontré concerning both the woods of* Concis *and another piece of land called the* terra Lamberti. *Elizabeth, Eudes's wife; his brothers Gérard, Simon, and the priest Lancelin; and Eudes and Elizabeth's sons, Eudes [IV] and Geoffroi, consented to the latter. Eudes also establishes the terms for future acquisitions by Prémontré.*

A. Cartulary of Prémontré, fols. 84v–85r.

B. Original, AD Oise, Hs 1388, sealed on a double strip of white leather, an equestrian seal in brown wax with damaged sides.

EDITION: Barbiche and Guyotjeannin, "Acte seigneurial," http://theleme.enc.sorbonne.fr/dossiers/notice80.php.

Karta Odonis domini Hamensis de confirmatione elemosine Lancelini.

[I]n nomine sancte et individue Trinitatis, amen. Ego Odo dominus Castri Hamensis, notum fieri volo presentibus et futuris quod ecclesia Premonstratensis quandam silvam habebat que vulgo Concis vocatur, in territorio de Gollencourt,[4] in qua sibi dominum Lancelinum patrem meum, associavit

---

5 millesimo ducentesimo *B*.

---

1 Eudes III, lord of Ham, son of Lancelin, lord of Ham, and Mathilde.

2 Perhaps Conchy, cant. Ressons-sur-Matz, https://dicotopo.cths.fr/places/P50611886.

3 Golancourt, cant. Guiscard, https://dicotopo.cths.fr/places/P75999303.

4 Gollencurt *B*.

ad quartum denarium, si eam aliquando vendere vellet prefata ecclesia. Post mortem vero eiusdem Lancelini ego Odo, filius eius, illum quartum denarium indulsi prefate ecclesie, et ipsam terram ad extirpandam et excolendam[5] in perpetuum ad nonam garbam, salva decima et secatione, eidem ecclesie reddidi assensu uxoris mee, Elizabeth,[6] et fratrum meorum, Gerardi, Symonis, Lancelini clerici et liberorum meorum, Odonis, Gaufridi, ita quod eadem ecclesia associavit me et heredes meos similiter ad nonam garbam in terra Lamberti in qua prius nichil habueram nec predecessores mei. Statutum est etiam quod si deinceps eadem ecclesia aliquam silvam in territorio de Gollencourt[7] adquisierit et extirpaverit, ibidem simili modo nonam garbam habebo. Sed in terra ab antiquo exculta, si eadem ecclesia eam adquisierit, nullum mihi jus vendicare potero. Cum autem secationis tempus advenerit, una die antequam secetur, nuntiabitur michi ut pro parte mea mittam servientem meum; quem si mittere noluero invitati[8] fratris qui messores custodierit vel famulo eiusdem fratris, si frater defuerit, debebo credere de partis mee quantitate. Quod si ipsum famulum de infidelitate suspectum habuero, eum ad juramentum super sancta potero conpellere et ab ipso vel a fratribus exinde nichil amplius exigere. Fratres etiam prefate ecclesie garbam meam ducent ad Gollencourt[9] si voluero vel si michi magis placuerit, in grangia sua Bonolii sub certo testimonio et certa computatione collocabunt et usque ad festum Omnium Sanctorum facient triturari et granum ducent Hamum, forragium sibi retinentes. Huic concessioni et donationi interfuerunt testes: Guillelmus de Vilete,[10] Rainerus de Mateni,[11] Symon[12] Ratus, Petrus[13] de Plaisse.[14] Ut igitur hec concessio et donatio rata permaneat et inconvulsa, presentem paginam sigilli nostri inpressione communire[15] curavi. Actum anno incarnati verbi M° C° LXX° VII°.[16]

5 extirpandum et excolendum *B*.

6 Elisabeth *B*.

7 Gollencurt *B*.

8 veritati *B*.

9 Gollencurt *B*.

10 Villette, cant. Ham, https://dicotopo.cths.fr/places/P35405877.

11 Matigny, cant. Ham, https://dicotopo.cths.fr/places/P92212887.

12 Simon *Ratus*, brother of Guillaume, also appears in **399** and **441**.

13 Pierre du Plessis is a witness in **306**, **344**, and **485**. Plessis-Patte-d'Oie, cant. Guiscard, https://dicotopo.cths.fr/places/P25690373.

14 del Pleissei *B*.

15 commure *B*.

16 M° C° LXX VII° *B*.

337

1156

Baudouin [II],[1] *bishop of Noyon, gives notice that husband and wife Enguerrand de Languevoisin*[2] *and Hesza gave Prémontré two parts of the tithe of Omiécourt*[3] *with the assent of Yves [II],*[4] *lord of Nesle and count of Soissons, from whom the fief descended.*

A. Cartulary of Prémontré, fol. 85r.
B. Original, AM Metz, Salis II.248, no. 3, previously sealed on a strip of leather.

Karta Balduini Noviomensis episcopi de elemosina Ingranni de Landovesin et Hesze uxoris eius.

[I]n nomine sancte et individue Trinitatis. Quoniam memorie hominum que facile labitur plerumque temporum vetustas id quod minus caute agitur subripere consuevit maiorum sollers industria utilitati providens posterorum rerum gestarum seriem litterarum apicibus conservandam decrevit. Quorum vestigia subsecutus nec ab eorum rectitudine discrepans ego Balduinus, Dei gratia Noviomensis episcopus, notum fieri volo tam futuris quam presentibus quod Ingrannus de Landovesin et Hesza, uxor eius, contulerunt Premonstrate ecclesie, pro remedio animarum suarum et predecessorum suorum, duas partes decime de Ulmecourt[5] quas ab antecessoribus suis longo tempore tenuerant et hereditario jure se tenere dicebant. Dederunt autem easdem duas partes decime, approbante et concedente Yvone,[6] Nigellensi domino et Suessionensi comite, de cuius feodo descendebat, quas quidem in manum ipsius Yvonis[7] comitis posuerunt prefate ecclesie concedendas. Sub hiis testibus: Theoderico[8] thesaurario fratre eiusdem comitis, Lamberto Rufo, Renoldo[9] clericis, Rogero[10]

1 Baudouin II de Boulogne, abbot of the Augustinian abbey of Saint-Eloi-Fontaine, ca. 1130–ca. 1139, and bishop of Noyon, 1148–67. *GC* IX, col. 1126.
2 Languevoisin, cant. Nesle, https://dicotopo.cths.fr/places/P00746276.
3 Omiécourt, cant. Nesle, https://dicotopo.cths.fr/places/P59719870.
4 Yves II de Nesle (d. ca. 1178), lord of Nesle and count of Soissons, son of Raoul, lord of Nesle, and Raintrude. Newman, *Seigneurs*, vol. 1, 61.
5 Ulmecurt *B*.
6 Ivone *B*.
7 Ivonis *B*.
8 Thierry de Nesle, son of Raoul, lord of Nesle, and Raintrude, was treasurer of Noyon, ca. 1134–ca. 1157, and archdeacon of Cambrai. In 1157, he participated in the translation of the relics of St Éloi. Mazière, "Annales Noyonnaises, première partie," 55–6.
9 Reinoldo *B*.
10 Roger the *justiciarius* is attested in acts of the lords of Nesle, 1142–75. Newman, *Seigneurs*, vol. 2, 37, 149.

justiciario, Radulpho[11,12] Pulchro, Petro filio dapiferi, Willelmo Naso, Alberico et Odone fratribus predicti Ingeranni. Postmodum vero idem comes easdem partes decime in manum meam posuit. Ego autem Premonstrate ecclesie ad usus suorum de Bonolio libere possidendas concessi. Huic concessioni nostre interfuerunt hii testes. Ipse Yvo[13] comes qui mox michi decimam ipsam adhuc astans reddiderat, Hugo[14] cancellarius, Renoldus[15,16] Hamensis abbas, Drogo prepositus, Renerus[17] capellanus, Leonardus, Hugo nepos cancellarii, Rogerus justiciarius, Radulphus[18] Bellus, frater Matheus. Quod ut ratum et inconvulsum permaneat, sigilli nostri inpressione[19] roboramus et ne quis in posterum ecclesie dampnum vel molestiam inferat sub anathemate interdicimus. Actum anno incarnati verbi M° C° LVI°, epacta XX[a] IIII[a],[20] indictione IIII[a], concurrente VII°.

338

1147

Simon [I],[1] bishop of Noyon, confirms that Eudes Awethart made a gift of two parts of the tithe of Cizancourt[2] to Prémontré with the assent of husband and wife Ogero de Cappy[3] and Herma, and Hugues,[4] castellan of Bapaumes, from whom the fief descended.

A. Cartulary of Prémontré, fol. 85r.

B. Original, AN, L 995, no. 14, previously sealed.

EDITION: Pycke and Vleeschouwers, *Actes*, 522.

---

11 Radulfo *B*.

12 Raoul *Pulcher*, brother of Hubert, appears also in **300**, **316**, **372**, and **436** and is attested in acts to do with the lords of Nesle, 1150s–70s. Newman, *Seigneurs*, vol. 2, 59, 133.

13 Ivo *B*.

14 Hugues III de Roye, chancellor of Noyon-Tournai, ca. 1130–46, and of Noyon, 1146–63/6. Pycke, *Le chapitre cathédral Notre-Dame de Tournai de la fin du XIe à la fin du XIIIe siècle*, 64.

15 Reinoldus *B*.

16 Renaud I, abbot of the Augustinian abbey of Notre-Dame de Ham, 1143–bef. 1160. *GC* IX, col. 1122.

17 Reinerus *B*.

18 Radulfus *B*.

19 impressione *B*.

20 XXIIII[a] *B*.

---

1 Simon I de Vermandois (d. 1148) was the son of Hugues I and Adélaïde, count and countess of Vermandois and Valois, and bishop of Noyon, 1123–42.

2 Cizancourt, cant. Nesle, https://dicotopo.cths.fr/places/P70322720.

3 Cappy, cant. Bray-sur-Somme, https://dicotopo.cths.fr/places/P43764512.

4 Hugues de Beaumetz (d. aft. 1173), lord of Beaumetz (cant. Bertincourt, https://dicotopo.cths.fr/places/P35591263) and castellan of Bapaume; married to Béatrice de Guines. He appears in the cartulary of Avesnes-lès-Bapaume, ca. 1146–ca. 1187. Bougard and Delmaire, *Le cartulaire et les chartes de l'abbaye de femmes d'Avesnes-lès-Bapaume (1128–1337)*, 64, 65, 85, 86, 103.

Karta Symonis Noviomensis episcopi de duabus partibus decime de Chisencourt que Odo Awethart dedit ecclesie Premonstrati.

[I]n nomine sancte et individue Trinitatis. Humana memoria quanto ad recipiendum paratior tanto ad obliviscendum est proclivior. Quanto enim maiora amplectitur tanto plura obliviscitur. Hoc autem solum medicinale adjuvenit scripto commendare quod in pluribus divisa non potuit tenere. Qua propter ego Symon, Dei gratia Noviomensis episcopus, notum fieri volo tam futuris quam presentibus quod Odo[5] Awethart contulit Premonstratensi ecclesie per manum nostram quicquid habebat in decima de Chisencourt,[6] videlicet duas partes eiusdem decime annuente Ogero de Cappi et uxore eius Herma necnon et Hugone, castellano de Bapalmes[7] de quorum feodo descendebat. Quod autem prefatus Odo hoc concesserit, testes sunt: Robertus de Hiencourt[8,9] et Gerardus Valii. Concessioni vero Herme uxoris Ogeri interfuerunt testes Robertus et Walterus de Hiencourt. Quod ut ratum et inconvulsum permaneat, sigilli nostri inpressione subsignamus et ne quis predicte ecclesie inde dampnum irroget, sub anathemate interdicimus testesque legitimos quorum hec nomina sunt apponimus Theodericus[10,11] thesaurarius, Balduinus[12] decanus, Theobaldus[13] Matras.[14] Concessioni quam fecit castellanus interfuerunt testes Wilelmus de Pieton,[15] Gerardus Valii, Robertus de Hiencourt,[16,17] Hugo. Actum anno incarnationis dominice M° C° XL° VII°, epacta XVII^{a}, indictione X^{a}, concurrente II°.

5 Eudes Awethart (or *Awaitars*), a seneschal of Nesle. Newman, *Seigneurs*, vol. 2, 62–3.

6 Chisencurt *B*.

7 Batpalmas *B*.

8 Hiencurt *B*.

9 Hyencourt-le-Grand, cant. Chaulnes, https://dicotopo.cths.fr/places/P87304652.

10 Teodericus *B*.

11 Thierry de Nesle, son of Raoul, lord of Nesle, and Raintrude, was treasurer of Noyon, ca. 1134–ca. 1157, and archdeacon of Cambrai. In 1157, he participated in the translation of the relics of St Éloi. Mazière, "Annales Noyonnaises, première partie," 55–6.

12 Baudouin, dean of Noyon, attested 1132–74. AD Oise, G 1984, fols. 71r, 78v–79v.

13 Teobaldus *B*.

14 Martus *B*.

15 Pithon, cant. Saint-Simon, https://dicotopo.cths.fr/places/P56020430.

16 Hiencurt *B*.

17 Hyencourt-le-Grand, cant. Chaulnes, https://dicotopo.cths.fr/places/P87304652.

339

1137

Simon [I],[1] *bishop of Noyon, confirms the donation made by husband and wife Renier de* Roinon[2] *and Aude, and Rogo, their son, to Prémontré of two parts of the tithe of Gricourt.*[3]

A. Cartulary of Prémontré, fols. 85r–85v.
B. Original, AN, L 995, no. 4, previously sealed.
EDITION: Pycke and Vleeschouwers, *Actes*, 421.

Karta Symonis Noviomensis episcopi de duabus partibus decime de Gricourt quas dedit Renerus et uxor eius ecclesie Premonstrate.

[I]n nomine sancte et individue Trinitatis. Qui sua ecclesiis inpendunt[4] beneficia, ne de libro viventium deleantur, ut in celebriori habeantur memoria ipsorum nomina et munera vivacitati scriptorum commendantur. Idcirco ego Symon Dei gratia Noviomensis episcopus quod presentibus est cognitum futuris etiam fore volo manifestum quod Rainerus de Roinon et uxor eius Oda et filius eius Rogo[5] duas partes decime de Gricourt[6] ad suum suorumque remedium Premonstrate ecclesie Sancte Marie et Sancti Johannis Baptiste, tempore Hugonis, eiusdem ecclesie abbatis, dederunt sub his testibus: Guerrico[7,8] Guastel, fratre predicti Raineri, Bartholomeo[9] de Monte Chavelon[10] genero eiusdem Raineri et Clareboldo, fratre eius, Guidone[11] de Clastris, Guazone[12] qui Stultus agnominatus est, Radulfo[13] qui Aper dictus est, Galtero[14] de Maihoc et filio eius,

1 Simon I de Vermandois (d. 1148) was the son of Hugues I and Adélaïde, count and countess of Vermandois and Valois, and bishop of Noyon 1123–42.
2 Renier de Roinon, brother of Wenric Vastel (or Guastel). Newman, *Homblières*, 166, fn. 2.
3 Gricourt, cant. Vermand, https://dicotopo.cths.fr/places/P68400511.
4 impendunt *B*.
5 Rorgo *B*.
6 Gricurt *B*.
7 Gwerrico *B*.
8 Wenric Vastel (or Guastel), brother of Renier de Roinon, is attested 1133–71. Newman, *Homblières*, 166, fn. 2.
9 Likely Barthélemy, lord of Bosmont, and Clarembaud, lord of Montchâlons, sons of Aubry, lord of Bosmont and Montchâlons. Melleville, *DH*, vol. 1, 131; vol. 2, 118.
10 Cavelon *B*.
11 Guy, lord of Clastres; son-in-law of Ricuère and Raimond of Clastres (**449**) through his marriage to their daughter Hawide. Melleville, *DH*, vol. 1, 256.
12 Waszo *Stultus* of Saint-Quentin appears as a witness to episcopal charters, ca. 1137–ca. 1140 (**333**, **450**).
13 Raoul *Aper* also appears as a witness in **333**.
14 Gautier (or Gilet), lord of Mayot. Melleville, *DH*, vol. 2, 90.

Rabodone de quorum feodo pendebat, Clareboldo[15] etiam de Vendolio et filiis suis, Drogone et Clareboldo, de quorum feodo ad predictum Galterum et filium eius, Rabodonem, descendebat. Idem concedentibus et quod suum ibi erat in manu nostra ponentibus sub his testibus: Odone Rufo et Herberto Mareschot, fratre eius, Hugone Captivo,[16] Hugone filio Guiardi, Matheo filio Richarii,[17] Mawart, Arnulpho[18] qui Brito dictus est, Galtero homine Sancti Petri, Guidone de Clastris et Guidone de Moi.[19] Ego autem predictum munus sancte Premonstrate ecclesie in perpetuum possidendum concessi et, ut firmum et inmobile permaneret, sigillo et privilegio meo roboravi. Quod quisquis cassum facere intenderit, anathema sit. Actum est hoc anno incarnationis dominice M° C° XXX° VII°, epacta septima,[20] concurrente quinto,[21] indictione prima. Signum Balduini,[22] abbatis Sancti Quintini de Insula. Signa Guarini[23,24] abbatis Sancti Prejecti, et Arnulphi[25,26] monachi Sancti Nichasii,[27] Gerardi[28] decani ecclesie maioris Sancti Quintini, Goffridi cantoris, Nevelonis, Odonis, Roberti, Raneri,[29] Clareboldi canonicorum ecclesie eiusdem Sancti Quintini. S. etiam Theoderici[30] Noviomensis ecclesie thesaurarii. Ego Hugo[31] cancellarius recensui.

---

15 Likely Clérembaud III, lord of Vendeuil, ca. 1130–ca. 1153. Newman, *Hombliéres*, 120, fn. 3; Melleville, *DH*, vol. 2, 412.

16 Hugues *le Captif* de Vendeuil; brother of Sarracin, castellan of La Fère and Laon, and Geoffroi de Condren, knight; husband of Ermengarde d'Ognolles. Newman, *Seigneurs*, vol. 2, 205.

17 Ricarii *B*.

18 Arnulfo *B*.

19 Guy II, lord of Moy (arr. Saint-Quentin, https://dicotopo.cths.fr/places/P53802372), son of Guy I, lord of Moy. Melleville, *DH*, vol. 2, 145.

20 VII[a] *B*.

21 V[to] *B*.

22 Baudouin II, abbot of the Benedictine abbey of Saint-Quentin-en-l'Isle, ca. 1136–64.

23 S. Gwarini *B*.

24 Guérin I, abbot of the Benedictine abbey of Saint-Prix de Saint-Quentin, ca. 1138–42. *GC* IX, col. 1095.

25 Arnulfi *B*.

26 Perhaps the Arnulphus who was abbot of the Benedictine abbey of Saint-Nicaise de Reims, 1138–9. Cossé-Durlin, *Cartulaire de Saint-Nicaise de Reims*, 45.

27 Nicasii *B*.

28 Gérard, dean of the chapter of Saint-Quentin, is attested from 1119. BnF, MS lat. 5478, fol. 98r–98v; BnF, MS lat. 11070, fols. 102r–103v.

29 Raineri *B*.

30 Thierry de Nesle, son of Raoul, lord of Nesle, and Raintrude, was treasurer of Noyon, ca. 1134–ca. 1157, and archdeacon of Cambrai. In 1157, he participated in the translation of the relics of St Éloi. Mazière, "Annales Noyonnaises, première partie," 55–6.

31 Hugues III de Roye, chancellor of Noyon-Tournai, ca. 1130–46, and of Noyon, 1146–63/6. Pycke, *Le chapitre cathédral Notre-Dame de Tournai de la fin du XIe à la fin du XIIIe siècle*, 64.

340

March, 1211.

Gilles,[1] castellan of Bapaume and lord of Beaumetz, with the consent of Agnès,[2] his wife, and witnessed by six local men – Gilles de Marquaix[3] and his brother Guillaume, Adam de Gomiecourt,[4] Barthélemy de Gonnelieu,[5] Jean de Villers,[6] and Anzelin de Wargnies[7] – cedes to Prémontré all his possessions in the areas of Douchy[8] and Germaine.[9] Gérard de Ronssoy makes an equivalent gift. Gilles's part of the land renders an annual pension of 12 modii *of grain (*frumentum*), measure of Saint-Quentin, which Gilles sells to Jean Musart of Saint-Quentin. (See **327**.)*

A. Cartulary of Prémontré, fol. 85v.
B. Original not found.

Karta castellani de Bapaumes de elemosina quam fecit ecclesie Premonstrati in territorio de Douci et de Germaniis.

[E]go Egidius, castellanus de Bapaumes et dominus de Biaumeis, futuros et presentes per hanc cartam certifico quod, presente et concedente uxore mea, Agnete, astantibus etiam nobilibus viris, Egidio de Marchais, Willelmo, fratre eius, Adam de Gomercourt, Bartholomeo de Goigneliu, Johanne de Vileirs, Anzelino de Waroignies, contuli ad firmam fratribus Premonstrati quicquid habebam infra parrochiam et territorium de Douci, sive de Germaniis, tam in terra dotis altaris quam in decima, oblationibus, hospitibus, caponibus ceterisque rebus sive redditibus pertinentibus ad altare, sive retentione qualibet possidendum sub annua pensione duodecim modiorum frumenti sani et solubilis ad mensuram Sancti Quintini, currentem eo tempore quo scriptum hoc factum fuit. Recognovit autem coram predictis astantibus viris eadem uxor mea, et ego

1 Gilles I, lord of Beaumetz (cant. Bertincourt, https://dicotopo.cths.fr/places/P35591263) and castellan of Bapaume (d. aft. 1214), son of Hugues, castellan of Bapaume and lord of Beaumetz, and Beatrix de Guines. He appears in a number of acts dating 1208–13 in the cartulary of the abbey of Avesnes-lès-Bapaume. Bougard and Delmaire, *Le cartulaire et les chartes de l'abbaye de femmes d'Avesnes-lès-Bapaume (1128–1337)*, 119–20, 121–2, 129–30.

2 Agnès de Coucy (d. aft. 1214), daughter of Raoul I, lord of Coucy, and Alix de Dreux.

3 Gilles I, lord of Marquaix (cant. Roisel, https://dicotopo.cths.fr/places/P34632361). Newman, *Seigneurs*, vol. 2, 100.

4 Gomiecourt, cant. Chaulnes, https://dicotopo.cths.fr/places/P21643469.

5 Gonnelieu, arr. Cambrai.

6 Likely Villers, cant. Crépy, https://dicotopo.cths.fr/places/P72234458.

7 Wargnies, cant. Domart, https://dicotopo.cths.fr/places/P88345782.

8 Douchy, cant. Vermand, https://dicotopo.cths.fr/places/P84133506.

9 Germaine, cant. Vermand, https://dicotopo.cths.fr/places/P36636067.

etiam publice confessus sum esse verum, quod nichil eorum omnium que predicta sunt, de dotalicio suo erat. Ceterum sciri debet quod totum predicte pensionis frumentum vendidi in perpetuam hereditatem Johanni Musart de Sancto Quintino et ipsi loco mei ab ecclesia Premonstratensi assignavi solvendum. Ita tamen quod idem Johannes vel heres eius sive quilibet alius qui frumentum illud tenuerit, nulli alii quam ecclesie Premonstratensi aut vendere ipsum poterit aut quolibet modo conferre. Ego vero et heredes mei, nichilominus ac si predictum reciperemus frumentum, rectam fratribus Premonstrati portabimus warandiam contra omnes qui adversus eos de hiis que premissa sunt, moverint questionem. Preterea et hoc etiam fieri notum volo quod dominus Gerardus de Ronseio totam suam partem quam in predictis omnibus equalem mecum habebat et a me tenebat in feodum, eisdem fratribus, me concedente, pari modo et sub simili pensione ad firmam contulit perpetuo possidendam. Qui Gerardus suos duodecim modios quos ecclesia Premonstrati tenetur ei solvere annuatim nomine pensionis, a me recepit in feodum sed nec ipse Gerardus nec heres eius alii quam ecclesie Premonstratensi ipsum frumentum aut vendere poterit aut quolibet modo conferre. Concessi etiam quod si ecclesia sepedicta aut totam pensionem quam prefato G[erardo] debet aut aliquam partem eius per elemosinam sive per emptionem seu per quemlibet legitimum modum acquisierit nullum inde mihi debebit servitium sed quicquid ab ipsa ecclesia interfuerit acquisitum a jure mei feodi erit penitus absolutum. Denique sciendum est quod et illi duodecim modii qui debentur Johanni Musart et illi duodecim modii qui debentur domino Gerardo, accipientur apud Germanias et ibidem solventur infra vicesimum diem natalis domini, ea conditione interposita quod, si post istum terminum aliquod periculum de utroque frumento evenerit, ex tunc ecclesia Premonstrati non respondebit de ipso periculo sive dampno. Quod ut ratum permaneat presentem kartam perpetuis temporibus valituram sigilli mei munimine confirmavi. Ego etiam Agnes, predicti castellani uxor, ad majorem confirmationem et assensum et sigillum meum apposui. Actum anno Domini M° CC° XI°, mense martio.

341

1170. The church of Notre-Dame, Ognon.

Hugues [I],[1] *abbot of Mont-Saint-Quentin, and Hugues [I],*[2] *dean of Saint-Fursy de Péronne, make known that Geoffroi,*[3] *canon of Saint-Fursy, son of the*

1 Hugues I de Péronne, abbot of the Benedictine abbey of Mont-Saint-Quentin, 1140–72; brother of Roger I, castellan of Péronne. *GC* IX, col. 1105.

2 Hugues I de Moreuil, dean of the collegiate church of Saint-Fursy de Péronne, ca. 1168–ca. 1209. Newman, *Charters of St-Fursy of Péronne*, 5.

3 Geoffroi, cantor of the collegiate church of Saint-Fursy de Péronne, ca. 1199–ca. 1205. Newman, *Charters of St-Fursy of Péronne*, 8.

*lady Adèle, renounced all claims to having inherited the tithe of Cartigny[4] from his mother and recognized that Prémontré held the tithe from Adèle. Geoffroi's brothers Pierre[5] and Mathieu,[6] as well as their maternal uncle, Mathieu de Buires,[7] consent. (See **342**, **347**, **420**, and **425**.)*

A. Cartulary of Prémontré, fols. 85v–86r.
B. Original not found.

Karta abbatis Montis Sancti Quintini et decani Sancti Fursei de decima de Cartigni.

[R]es gestas scripto mandare ad noticiam posterorum prudencia consuevit antiquorum. Ea propter ego Hugo Dei gratia Montis Sancti Quintini dictus abbas, ego Hugo, Peronensis ecclesie Sancti Fursei decanus, notum fieri volumus tam futuris quam presentibus quod Gaufridus, filius domine Adelidis, canonicus Sancti Fursei, calumpnia movit intulitque injuriam Premonstratensi ecclesie pro decima de Cartigni quam hereditario jure suam esse dicebat et econtra Premonstratensis ecclesia suam esse asserebat ut pote ex oblatione matris eiusdem Gaufridi iam vidue filiorumque suorum per manum venerabilis domni[8] Symonis, pie memorie Noviomensis episcopi, in elemosinam sibi datam ipsiusque sigillo confirmatam. Conperta vero tandem rei veritate supradictus Gaufridus nostro ceterorumque qui astabant propinquorum suorum consilio prefate Premonstratensi ecclesie suum jus recognovit et in manu domini Philippi,[9] Premonstratensis abbatis, predictam decimam, sicut idem abbas illam reclamabat, liberam reddidit, dampnum quod intulerat restituens et de illata injuria veniam et absolutionem requirens. Ex utraque ergo parte recognita pactio est ipsum videlicet Gaufridum, quamdiu vixerit in seculo et voluerit, decimam debere habere, postea vero quicquid in ea sui juris est Premonstratensibus provenire. Interim autem ipse Gaufridus annis singulis quatuor modios frumenti ad mensuram Peronensem Premonstratensibus pro recognitione investiture eiusdem decime dabit et conversum unum in collectione decime recipiet cui victus necessaria procurabit vel pro victus expensa XII^{cim} sextarios frumenti prebebit, data fide nonquam se deinceps super hac re Premonstratensibus injuriam facturum, immo quicquid decretum est fideliter observaturum concedentibus atque laudantibus amicis suis Mathon de Buires, avunculo suo,

4 Cartigny, cant. Péronne, https://dicotopo.cths.fr/places/P86731604.
5 Pierre de Bouchavesnes, son of Adèle de Péronne and Simon de Bouchavesnes.
6 Mathieu de Bouchavesnes, a canon at the Augustinian abbey of Arrouaise. Tock and Milis, *Monumenta Arroasiensia*, 182.
7 Mathieu de Buires, son of Mathieu *Strabo* de Péronne and Fredeburge *Domez*.
8 *Sic A*.
9 Philippe I de Reims, abbot of Prémontré, 1161–71.

et fratribus, Petro de Buscavesnes et Matheo, Sancti Nicholai de Aroasia canonico. Hoc igitur ut stabile sit firmumque permaneat ego Hugo, Montis Sancti Quintini abbas, sigilli mei impressione. Ego etiam Hugo Sancti Fursei decanus, meo sigillo et quorumdam qui presentes fuerunt virorum testatione presentem paginam corroborari decrevimus. Signum Goschuini. S. Roscelini. S. Gerardi Poiselart, Sancti Fursei canonicorum. S. domini Oldrici,[10] prioris de Margeles. S. domini Balduini de Monte Sancti Quintini,[11] monachi et presbyteri. S. Drogonis. S. Grinberti, presbyterorum. S. Heluini, diaconi. S. Walteri. S. Mathei. S. Alberti acolitorum. S. Petri, S. Clementis. S. Widonis, conversorum. S. Willelmi Germeir. S. Gregorii Rufi. S. Theobaldi Cretun. Actum apud Dognium in ecclesia Beate Marie, anno Dominice incarnationis M° C° LXX°.

342

1142

Simon [I],[1] bishop of Noyon, gives notice that Adèle de Péronne,[2] daughter of Mathieu Strabo *and widow of Simon de Bouchavesnes,[3] gave Prémontré two parts of the major tithe of Cartigny[4] that she possessed by hereditary right. Adèle's children, Pierre, Mathieu,[5] Ermengarde, and Iteburge, consent to this. (See **341**, **347**, **420**, and **425**.)[6]*

A. Cartulary of Prémontré, fol. 86r.

B. Original not found.

EDITION: Pycke and Vleeschouwers, *Actes*, 469–70.

---

10 An otherwise unattested prior of the Arroasian priory of Margelles (today Margères). Josse, *Notice historique sur le village de Douilly et ses dépendances*.

11 The Benedictine abbey of Mont-Saint-Quentin.

---

1 Simon I de Vermandois (d. 1148) was the son of Hugues I and Adélaïde, count and countess of Vermandois and Valois, and bishop of Noyon, 1123–42.

2 Adèle, daughter of Mathieu *Strabo* de Péronne and Frédeburge *Domez*. Her anniversary was celebrated at Prémontré on January 9. Van Waefelghem, *L'Obituaire de l'abbaye de Prémontré*, 25. Adèle and her husband Simon de Bouchavesnes also gave the tithe of Courcelles to the Benedictine abbey of Notre-Dame d'Avesnes-lès-Bapaume, ca. 1142–7. Tock, ed., *Les chartes des évêques d'Arras: 1093–1203*, 110; Bougard and Delmaire, *Le cartulaire et les chartes de l'abbaye de femmes d'Avesnes-lès-Bapaume (1128–1337)*, 69–70.

3 According to Cagny, the family of Bouchavesnes was a cadet branch of the seigneurial family of Péronne. Cagny, *Histoire de l'arrondissement de Péronne*, vol. 1, 182–3.

4 Cartigny, cant. Péronne, https://dicotopo.cths.fr/places/P86731604.

5 Mathieu de Bouchavesne, a canon at the Augustinian abbey of Arrouaise. Tock and Milis, *Monumenta Arroasiensia*, 182.

6 Hugues I de Fosses, abbot of Prémontré, also issued a charter confirming this gift. Beauvillé, *Recueil de documents inédits concernant la Picardie*, vol. 2, 5.

Karta Noviomensis episcopi de confirmatione maioris decime de Cartigni.

[I]n nomine sancte et individue Trinitatis. Sicut Spiritus Sancti gratia per fideles quosque fideliter agere et fideliter acta corroborare et si qua secus acta sint in melius novit commutare sic econtrario antiquus hostis per satellites suos prave gerere et prave gesta confirmare et si quo noverit bene agi quantum in se est consuevit perturbare. Hac de causa reverendis placuit predecessoribus nostris quatinus elemosine a fidelibus ecclesie Dei ad usus pauperum attribute ut inconvulse permanere valeant sigillo apostolico vel episcopali muniantur et legitimarum testimonio personarum approbentur. Ego igitur Symon, Dei gratia Noviomorum episcopus, notum facio tam futuris quam presentibus quod quedam nobilis mulier de Perona Adhelidis nomine, filia Mathei qui Strabo dictus est, uxor vero Symonis de Buscheavesnes, duas partes quas hereditario jure in maiori decima ad Cartigni possidebat que nulli feodata erat, ob remedium anime sue et predicti mariti iam defuncti et predecessorum suorum ecclesie Premonstrate ad sustentationem pauperum inibi Deo servientium per manus nostras, quia juris nostri erat, sub testimonio legitimorum virorum attribuit: Hugonis[7] cancellarii, Wiberti[8] capellani, Huberti de Felchers,[9] Walteri Marlier, Benedicti filii eius, Radulphi[10] fratris cancellarii, et hoc donum fideliter et devote oblatum concesserunt: filii predicte Adelidis, Petrus et Matheus et filie Ermengardis et Iteburgis sub hiis testibus: Hugone[11] abbate de Monte Sancti Eligii, Symone[12] abbate de Heolcor, Matheo et Thoma avunculis pueri Gelfridi, Radulfo Calvo de Morlens, Richardo famulo suo, Ricoldo de Perona, Roberto de Pint, Hugone de Bucelrue, Hengelberto de eadem villa, Willelmo der Plaissei.[13] Huius vero concessionis donum quicumque inminuere defraudare vel perturbare presumpserit, anathematis vinculo innodetur et nisi anmonitus resipuerit, divine ultioni subjaceat. Actum est hoc anno incarnationis dominice M° C° XLII°, epacta XXII^a^, indictione V^a^, concurrente III°.

7 Hugues III de Roye, chancellor of Noyon-Tournai, ca. 1130–46, and of Noyon, 1146–63/6. Pycke, *Le chapitre cathédral Notre-Dame de Tournai de la fin du XIe à la fin du XIIIe siècle*, 64.

8 Guibert, chaplain of the cathedral of Noyon, attested 1138–42. Pycke and Vleeschouwers, *Actes*, 415, 469.

9 Possibly Fluquières, cant. Vermand, https://dicotopo.cths.fr/places/P06908995.

10 Raoul *Buiaus*, brother of Hugues III de Roye, chancellor of Noyon-Tournai. He also appears as a witness in **407**.

11 Hugues, abbot of the Augustinian abbey of Mont Saint-Éloi, 1129–51.

12 Simon, abbot of the Augustinian abbey of Notre-Dame d'Eaucourt, ca. 1142–62.

13 Possibly the same Guillaume de Plessis as **316**, **372**, and **401**.

343

December, 1233.

Hugues,[1] *canon and* officialis *of Noyon, witnesses an act made by Robert* Aginant,[2] *lord of half of Flavy, in which Robert resolved a longstanding quarrel with Prémontré concerning its possession of various pieces of Bishop's Wood, namely three* modii *acquired from Robert's maternal uncle Renaud, five* modii *acquired from Robert's unnamed parents and descending from the fief of Simon* le Rogneux, *and four* modii *received in alms from Robert's brother, Pierre.*

A. Cartulary of Prémontré, fols. 86r–86v.
B. Original not found.[3]

Karta Hugonis officialis Noviomensis de conpositione inter ecclesiam Premonstratensis et Robertum Aginant.

[U]niversis presentes litteras inspecturis magister Hugo, canonicus et officialis Noviomensis, salutem in Domino. Universitati vestre notum facimus nos litteras Roberti dicti Aginant sigillo ipsius Roberti sigillatas inspexisse in hec verba: Ego Ego[4] Robertus dictus Aginans, dominus medietatis ville de Flavi, universis presentes litteras inspecturis notum facio quod cum inter me ex una parte et ecclesiam Premonstratensem ex altera diverse querele fuissent suborte pro eo quod eadem ecclesia quedam acquisierat absque consciencia mea et consensu meo, sicut dicebam, tam a domino Renaldo, quondam avunculo meo, quam a patre meo et matre mea, Petro etiam fratre meo, necnon et hominibus meis tam per elemosinam quam per emptionem et alias conventiones habitas inter eos de quibus michi prejudicium et injuria facta erant, sicut dicebam. Tandem mediantibus bonis viris, ob amorem quem habebam specialiter erga dictam ecclesiam, maxime propter patrem meum quem eadem ecclesia nuper propter Deum et de gratia ad conversionem recepit, de propria et bona voluntate mea pacem feci cum dicta ecclesia tali modo quod ego quitavi et remisi pacifice libere et quiete prefate ecclesie omnes querelas predictas et omnes etiam alias que mote erant vel moveri poterant inter me et ipsam ecclesiam usque ad tempus confectionis presentium litterarum. De quibus etiam omnibus quedam que quitavi et concessi eidem ecclesie libere et pacifice in perpetuum possidenda

1 *Magister* Hugues, canon and *officialis* of Noyon, ca. 1229–ca. 1236. AD Aisne, H 455, fol. 310v; AD Oise, G 1984, fols. 238v–239r.
2 Robert *Aginant* (d. aft. 1247), lord of half of Flavy-le-Meldeux (cant. Guiscard, https://dicotopo.cths.fr/places/P19622430), son of Raoul, lord of Flavy-le-Meldeux, and Marguerite de Flavy. Newman, *Seigneurs*, vol. 2, 280–1.
3 The charter of which this act contains a *vidimus* is AD Oise, H 6006.
4 *Sic A*.

nominatim censui exprimenda, videlicet tres modiatas nemoris de nemore quod dicitur Nemus Episcopi, quas olim dicta ecclesia a dicto Renaldo, avunculo meo, acquisierat, prout in cartis super hoc confectis continetur expressum; quinque etiam modiatas nemoris de eodem nemore quas ipsa ecclesia etiam a dictis patre meo et matre mea per emptionem legitimam acquisivit; nemus etiam quoddam situm ad foramina de Flavi contiguum nemori dicte ecclesie et quod tenebatur de Symone le Roigneuz, quod videlicet quod videlicet[5] nemus dicti pater meus et mater mea ipsi ecclesie similiter ғvendiderunt; item quatuor modiatas nemoris quas a dicto Petro, fratre meo, sepedicta ecclesia post modum per elemosinam acquisivit. Quas eidem ecclesie tenendas concessi sicut partite fuerunt et sicut eas tenet et mete posite pro portant. Hec omnia supradicta et alia etiam quecunque dicta ecclesia Premonstratensis acquisierat tempore huius scripti, tam in nemoribus quam in terris, pratis etiam pascuis, redditibus et rebus aliis tam a predicto Renaldo, avunculo meo, quam a dictis patre meo et matre mea, Petro etiam, fratre meo, necnon et hominibus meis que ad dominium meum vel hereditatem meam pertinebant vel pertinere poterant, remisi, quitavi et concessi dicte ecclesie in perpetuum possidenda libere, pacifice et quiete sicut hactenus possederunt et sicut vie et mete posite et apparentes proportant ita quicquid quod juris habebam vel habere poteram quocumque modo vel titulo in omnibus supradictis contuli, dedi, remisi, quitavi et concessi ecclesie sepedicte. Ad maiorem vero securitatem omnium predictorum promisi fideliter et firmiter, fide mea prestita corporali, me decetero omnia supradicta inviolabiliter servaturum et quod prefatam ecclesiam super premissis omnibus non molestabo decetero nec faciam molestari nec etiam premissa omnia vel eorum partem aliquam per me vel per alium repetam nec repeti faciam quoquomodo renuncians in hiis omnibus omni juris auxilio canonici et civilis et omni rei facto instrumento vel scripto que presentem kartam vel pacem predictam possent in posterum infirmare vel quomodolibet perturbare. In quorum omnium testimonium et perpetuam firmitatem presentem cartam sigilli mei roboravi. Actum anno dominice incarnationis M° CC° tricesimo tertio mense decembri. Dictus vero Robertus, postmodum in nostra presentia constitutus, omnes articulos superius contentos et tenorem tocius carte predicte laudavit et approbavit et spontaneus et non coactus, fide corporali in manu nostra prestita, firmiter creantavit quod omnia in karta predicta contenta tam fideliter quam firmiter in posterum observabit et quod numquam decetero dictam ecclesiam super aliquibus in hac presenti karta seu pagina contentis molestabit vel gravabit nec artem nec ingenium per se vel per alium queret per que eadem ecclesia possit vel debeat super eisdem in posterum molestari vel gravari. In cuius rei testimonium et perpetuam firmitatem presentem paginam ad petitionem dicti Roberti sigillo curie Noviomensis fecimus communiri. Actum anno gratie M° CC° tricesimo III°, mense decembri.

---

5 *Sic A.*

344

1163

Baudouin [II],[1] *bishop of Noyon, confirms that Bernier du Plaissy, with the consent of his wife Havide and of his heirs, and the consent of his fief lord Pierre du Plaissy,*[2] *gave the church of Bonneuil all the land he possessed around the spring of Saint-Crépin and beyond the* foramina *of Flavy, except for two gardens at Golancourt.*[3] *Once the land is productive, Prémontré will owe Bernier the fifth sheaf.*

A. Cartulary of Prémontré, fol. 86v.

B[1]. Original (chirograph), AM Metz, Salis II.241 no. 1, previously sealed. In the left margin and beginning at the top, the top half of the letters that form the word CYROGRAPHUM. (This charter is the right half of the chirograph and does not correspond to *B*[2].)

B[2]. Original (chirograph), AM Metz, Salis II.241 no. 2, sealed on a single strip of parchment with the episcopal seal mostly intact. In the left margin and beginning at the top, the top half of letters that form the word CYROGRAPHUM. (This charter is the right half of another set of chirographs and does not correspond to *B*[1].)

Karta Balduini Noviomensis episcopi de elemosina Berneri der Plaissie.

[I]n nomine Patris et Filii et Spiritus Sancti, amen. Ego Balduinus, Dei gratia Noviomensis episcopus, notum facio tam presentibus quam futuris quod Bernerus der[4] Plaissie dedit ecclesie Bonolii[5] totam terram quam habebat circa fontem Sancti Crispini et ultra foramina de Flavi excolendam manu firma ad quintam garbam, exceptis duobus ortis qui sunt apud Gollencourt,[6] annuente uxore sua, Havide,[7] et heredibus eius, concedente etiam Petro de Plaissie de cuius feodo descendebat. Statutum[8] est quod secationis tempore nuntiabunt fratres Bernero ad domum suam, si venerit, bene; sin autem, nichilominus secare facient et denuo nunciabunt ei ut pro suo terragio veniat; si non venerit, ducent illud ei ad Plaissie. Si conversus duxerit et Bernerus conquestus fuerit quod totum non habeat in veritate fratris se ponet et, si secularis duxerit, sacramento ei confirmabit quod totum habeat et hoc illi sufficiat.[9] Si vero conqueratur terram

1 Baudouin II de Boulogne, abbot of the Augustinian abbey of Saint-Eloi-Fontaine, ca. 1130–ca. 1139, and bishop of Noyon, 1148–67. *GC* IX, col. 1126.

2 Pierre du Plessis (Plessis-Patte-d'Oie, cant. Guiscard, https://dicotopo.cths.fr/places/P25690373) is a witness in **306**, **366**, and **485**.

3 Golancourt, cant. Guiscard, https://dicotopo.cths.fr/places/P75999303.

4 de *B*[1], *B*[2].

5 Bonoliensi *B*[1], *B*[2].

6 Gollencurt *B*[1], *B*[2].

7 Hauvide or Havuide *B*[1], *B*[2].

8 *Add.* vero *B*[1], *B*[2].

9 sufficiet *B*[1], *B*[2].

illam non bene excultam esse et inde fratres monuerit, ad domum eius ibunt et super terram ipsi et Bernerus convenient ubi judicio accolarum de Gollencourt[10] et de Plaissie fratres corrigent, siquid corrigendum fuerit. Si venire neglexerit decetero super hoc fratres non inquietabit. Ut ergo ratum et inconvulsum permaneat, sigilli nostri inpressione[11] confirmamus et eos qui contra hanc nostre subscriptionis paginam ire presumpserint, anathematis sentencia innodamus et de personis nostris testes subsignari fecimus et de eis qui huic concessioni interfuerunt quosdam annotari fecimus. S.[12] Drogonis et Johannis, capellanorum nostrorum. Testes sunt: Willelmus de Plaissie et Petrus de Plaissie, Johannes et Gerardus de Bellencourt.[13,14] Actum anno incarnati verbi M° C° LX° III°.

345

1137

Simon [I],[1] bishop of Noyon, makes known the decision taken by Yves [I], lord of Nesle, and by the nobles of the land, at the request of Raoul [I], count of Vermandois, to authorize Eudes de Lanchy,[2] his unnamed mother [Elizabeth], and his sister [Gersende],[3] who had entered the church of Prémontré, to leave to the said abbey only half of their inheritance, the rest of it going to Hescela, the sister of Eudes, and her husband Robert Creveiz. Guy[4] de Clastres and his daughters Adélaïde and Ricuère consent as fief lords, as do fief lords Raoul de Lille and Robert de Thenelles.[5] (See ***419****.)*

A. Cartulary of Prémontré, fols. 86v–87r.

B. Original, AD Aisne, H 802, previously sealed with a double strip of parchment.

EDITION: Pycke and Vleeschouwers, *Actes*, 408.

---

10 Gollencurt B^1, B^2.

11 impressione B^1, B^2.

12 Signum B^1, B^2.

13 Bellencurt B^1, B^2.

14 Berlancourt, cant. Guiscard, https://dicotopo.cths.fr/places/P39954495.

---

1 Simon I de Vermandois (d. 1148) was the son of Hugues I and Adélaïde, count and countess of Vermandois and Valois, and bishop of Noyon, 1123–42.

2 Eudes, lord of Lanchy (cant. Vermand, https://dicotopo.cths.fr/places/P51978975), son of Waldin/Baudouin and Elizabeth. Melleville, *DH*, vol. 1, 4.

3 Per **385**.

4 Guy, lord of Clastres (cant. Saint-Simon, https://dicotopo.cths.fr/places/P82112287); son-in-law of Ricuère and Raimond of Clastres (**449**) through his marriage to their daughter Hawide. Melleville, *DH*, vol. 1, 256.

5 Thenelles, cant. Ribemont, https://dicotopo.cths.fr/places/P63288757.

Karta Symonis Noviomensis episcopi de elemosina Odonis de Lanci, filii Waldini.

[I]n nomine sancte et individue Trinitatis. Ego Symon, Dei gratia Noviomensis episcopus, notum fieri volo tam futuris quam presentibus quod cum Odo de Lanci, filius Waldini, et mater sua et soror venissent ad conversionem ad Premonstratam ecclesiam, totam hereditatem suam eidem ecclesie dare voluerunt. Quod cum soror sua Hescela, que in seculo remanebat, vidisset et Robertus Creveiz,[6] maritus eius, noluerunt hoc concedere. Ob hoc Odo inpatiens[7] rediit ad seculum. Quod cum relatum esset comiti Radulfo, dixit quod partem posset dare sed non totam hereditatem et precepit Yvoni,[8] domino de Nigella, ut hanc rem componeret. Ipse vero precepit nobilibus illius terre quatinus hanc litem sedarent. Ex precepto vero ipsius congregati qui in fine scripti sunt, sic ab ei diffinitum est ut Odo et ecclesia medietatem de omnibus tam in districto quam in aliis acciperent et Hescela et heredes sui aliam partem. Hanc particionem concesserunt Wido de Clastris et filie sue Adelidis[9] et Richuera[10] quarum altera maritata erat, altera adhuc sub patre[11] custodia, ob remedium anime fratris sui Godefridi tunc noviter defuncti et aliorum predecessorum suorum et Radulfus de Insula et Robertus de Tenella de quorum feodis erat. Concessit etiam hoc Robertus Creveiz[12] et Hescela, uxor sua, legitimis viris astantibus et cooperantibus quorum subscripta sunt nomina: Wido de Clastris, Robertus Rufus,[13] Symon de Montescourt,[14,15] Werricus[16] Wastellus, Nanterus de Sancto Quintino,[17] Philippus de Pontruel,[18] Bernerus et Matheus frater eius, Radulphus,[19] Arnulphus,[20] Hermerus de Lanci. Quod quicumque ausu temerario infringere

6 Crevez *B*.
7 impatiens *B*.
8 Ivoni *B*.
9 Aleldis *B*.
10 Ricuera *B*.
11 patris *B*.
12 Crevez *B*.
13 Robert *Rufus*, brother of Mathieu and Bernier, and father of Adam, Jean, and Widèle, appears in **353**, **371**, **398**, **419**, and **442.**
14 Montescurt *B*.
15 Simon de Mondescourt (cant. Noyon, https://dicotopo.cths.fr/places/P60804459), son of Emmelot, appears as a witness in acts 1137–ca. 1183. Tock and Milis, *Monumenta Arroasiensia*, 143, 315.
16 Wenric Vastel (or Guastel), brother of Renier de Roinon, is attested 1133–71. Newman, *Homblières*, 166, fn. 2.
17 Nanter de Saint-Quentin appears as a witness in **419**, and likely in **333**. He is possibly the same Nanter, *bourgeois* of Saint-Quentin, who gave land to the Cistercian abbey of Notre-Dame de Longpont. Poquet, *Monographie de l'abbaye de Longpont, son histoire, ses monuments, ses abbés, ses personnages célèbres, ses sépultures, ses possessions territoriales*, 168.
18 Pontruet, cant. Vermand, https://dicotopo.cths.fr/places/P35872776.
19 Radulfus *B*.
20 Arnulfus *B*.

aut perturbare presumpserit, nisi resipuerit, anathemati subiaceat et in extremo examine a sanctorum consortio alienus fiat. Actum est hoc anno incarnationis dominice M° C° XXX° VII°, epactaVII^a, indictione I^a, concurrente IIII°.

346

February, 1231.

Pierre, lord of half of Flavy,[1] *with the consent of Herme, his wife, gives to Prémontré three and a half* sexterlatae, *less two* virgae, *of a piece of the assarted land of Flavy near the wood of Bonneuil.*[2] *Pierre reserves the ninth sheaf of grain (*bladus*), and both Pierre and Herme pledge never to dispute the arrangement.*

A. Cartulary of Prémontré, fol. 87r.
B. Original not found.

Karta Petri domini medietatis de Flavi de tribus sexterlatis terre et dimidio.

[E]go Petrus, dominus medietatis de Flavi, notum facio universis tam presentibus quam futuris quod ego intuitu Dei et ob remedium anime mee et antecessorum meorum, de assensu Hermetis uxoris mee, contuli in perpetuam elemosinam ecclesie Premonstratensi tres sexterlatas et dimidiam duabus virgis minus terre site in sartis de Flavi prope nemus de Bonolio. Retinui tamen michi et heredibus meis nonam garbam in prefata terra talis videlicet bladi quale super prefatam terram creverit. Tenebit itaque dicta ecclesia dictam terram de me et heredibus meis per prenominatam garbam. Sciendum est etiam quod super ista elemosina tenebor ego et heredes mei portare ipsi ecclesie legitimam warandiam adversus omnes qui juri et legi parere voluerint secundum usus et consuetudines patrie et tam ego quam Hermes, uxor mea, spontanei et non coacti fidem prestitimus corporalem quod dictam ecclesiam super dicta collatione per nos vel per alium decetero non molestabimus nec gravabimus nec artem nec ingenium queremus per que possit vel debeat in posterum molestari vel gravari. In cuius rei testimonium presentem cartam sigilli mei feci munimine roborari. Actum mense februario, anno incarnationis dominice M° CC° tricesimo primo.

1 Pierre (d. aft. 1247), lord of half of Flavy-le-Meldeux (cant. Guiscard, https://dicotopo.cths.fr/places/P19622430), son of Raoul, lord of Flavy-le-Meldeux, and Marguerite, sister and heir of Renaud, knight of Flavy. Newman, *Seigneurs*, vol. 2, 280–1.

2 Bonneuil, cant. Ham, https://dicotopo.cths.fr/places/P66750585.

347

March, 1204.

*Étienne [I],[1] bishop of Noyon, declares that he examined original documents written by his predecessors, Simon [I de Vermandois] and Baudouin [II de Boulogne], attesting to the gift that Adèle,[2] widow of Simon de Bouchavesnes,[3] made to Prémontré of two parts of the tithe of Cartigny.[4] Étienne states that Ermengarde, daughter of Adèle, and her children Gérard and Sara, acknowledged Adèle's gift and promised not to dispute further possession of the tithe with Prémontré. (See **341**, **342**, **420**, and **425**.)*

A. Cartulary of Prémontré, fol. 87r.
B. Original not found.

Karta Noviomensis episcopis Stephani de elemosina Adelidis quondam uxoris de Buschavesnes.

[S]tephanus, Dei gratia Noviomensis episcopus, omnibus in perpetuum. Notum fieri volumus quod nos inspeximus auctentica patrum et predecessorum nostrorum virorum venerabilium Symonis, pie recordationis, et bone memorie Balduini, episcoporum Noviomensium, quorum hic erat tenor quod nobilis mulier Adelidis, quondam uxor Symonis de Buscheavesnes, contulit ecclesie Premonstrati in elemosinam, pro anime sue et animarum antecessorum suorum remedio, duas partes quas de hereditate sua in decima de Cartigni habebat et jure perpetuo tenendas concessit. Cum igitur, sicut ex ipsis auctenticis accepimus, fratres Premonstratensis ecclesie illius decime diu fuissent legitima possessione gavisi, Ermengardis, filia videlicet prefate Adelidis, ipsam decimam postmodum reclamavit sed, prudentum[5] virorum usa consilio, tam ipsa quam Gerardus, filius eius, et Sarra filia in nostri presentia constituti, iam dicte Adelidis elemosinam legitime esse factam ecclesie Premonstrati recognoverunt unanimiter et devote ita quod, a sua injusta reclamatione desistentes, quicquid in prenominata decima se habere asserebant, in manus nostras sollempniter resignarunt et quitum omnimodis clamaverunt et quod ecclesie Premonstrati nullam

1 Étienne de Villebéon (or de Nemours), son of Gautier de Villebéon, lord of La Chapelle-Gauthier and Nemours, and Aveline, was bishop of Noyon, 1188–1221.

2 Adèle, daughter of Mathieu *Strabo* de Péronne and Frédeburge *Domez*. Her anniversary was celebrated at Prémontré on January 9. Van Waefelghem, *L'Obituaire de l'abbaye de Prémontré*, 25. Adèle and her husband Simon de Bouchavesnes also gave the tithe of Courcelles to the Benedictine abbey of Notre-Dame d'Avesnes-lès-Bapaume, ca. 1142–7. Tock, ed., *Les chartes des évêques d'Arras: 1093–1203*, 110; Bougard and Delmaire, *Le cartulaire et les chartes de l'abbaye de femmes d'Avesnes-lès-Bapaume (1128–1337)*, 69–70.

3 According to de Cagny, the family of Bouchavesnes was a cadet branch of the seigneurial family of Péronne. Cagny, *Histoire de l'arrondissement de Péronne*, vol. 1, 182–3.

4 Cartigny, cant. Péronne, https://dicotopo.cths.fr/places/P86731604.

5 *Sic A*, *read* prudentium.

deinceps inferrent molestiam, fide interposita, promiserunt. Nos itaque qui ex officio nostro ecclesiarum indempnitati pie tenemur et sollicite providere, ad petitionem etiam predictorum Ermengardis, Gerardi, filii sui, et Sarre, filie sue, elemosinam duarum partium decime de Cartigni, sicut canonice et religiose facta fuit, a nobili muliere Adelide prememorata, Premonstratensi ecclesie tam presenti scripto quam sigilli nostri testimonio in perpetuum confirmamus, statuentes et sub anathemate firmiter inhibentes ut nullus omnino hanc elemosinam perturbare seu nostre confirmationis paginam aliquatenus infringere presumat. Actum dominice incarnationis anno M° CC° quarto, mense martio.

348

August, 1220.

Roger,[1] *abbot of Notre-Dame de Ham, and Eudes [IV],*[2] *lord of Ham, attest that in their presence at Muille, husband and wife Raoul,*[3] *lord of Flavy, and Marguerite,*[4] *together with their children the cleric Pierre,*[5] *Robert,*[6] *and Jean, gave in perpetual alms to Prémontré five* modii *of woodlands and meadow at the place called Bishop's Wood and about four* sexterlatae *of woodlands at the* foramina *of Flavy in exchange for 52.5* librae Parisiensium.[7] *(See* ***428****.)*

A. Cartulary of Prémontré, fols. 87r–87v.
B. Original not found.

Karta Rogeri abbatis Sancte Marie Hamensis et Odonis domini eisdem castri de elemosina Radulphi domini de Flavi ac liberorum.

[U]niversis Christi fidelibus presentes litteras inspecturis, Rogerus, Dei patientia dictus abbas ecclesie Beate Marie Hamensis et Odo dominus eiusdem castri, salutem in omnium salvatore. Universitati vestre volumus esse notum et fidele testimonium prohibemus quod Radulfus, dominus de Flavi, et Margareta, uxor

1 Roger, abbot of the Augustinian abbey of Notre-Dame de Ham, ca. 1220–ca. 1226. Cagny, *Histoire de l'arrondissement de Péronne*, vol. 2, 219–20.

2 Eudes IV, lord of Ham (d. 1234), son of Eudes III, lord of Ham, and Elizabeth; husband of Elizabeth de Béthencourt.

3 Raoul, lord of Flavy-le-Meldeux (cant. Guiscard, https://dicotopo.cths.fr/places/P19622430) *iure uxoris*. Newman, *Seigneurs*, vol. 2, 280–1.

4 Marguerite de Flavy, sister and heir of Renaud, knight of Flavy. Newman, *Seigneurs*, vol. 2, 280–1.

5 Newman suggests that this *Petrus clericus* later left the clerical life and is the same person as Pierre, lord of half of Flavy-le-Meldeux (d. aft. 1247), son of Raoul, lord of Flavy-le-Meldeux, and Marguerite, sister and heir of Renaud, knight of Flavy. Newman, *Seigneurs*, vol. 2, 280–1.

6 Robert *Aginant*, lord of half of Flavy-le-Meldeux (d. aft. 1247), son of Raoul, lord of Flavy-le-Meldeux, and Marguerite de Flavy. Newman, *Seigneurs*, vol. 2, 280–1.

7 Raoul, lord of Flavy, issued a charter about the same transaction. AD Oise, H 6002.

eius necnon et liberi eorumdem, videlicet Petrus clericus, Robertus et Johannes, apud villam que dicitur Muile in nostra presentia constituti, recognoverunt se ecclesie Premonstratensi in perpetuum nomine elemosine contulisse ea que inferius duximus exprimenda. Dicti siquidem Radulfi et M[argareta] habebant quinque modiatas tam nemoris quam prati in nemore quod dicitur Nemus Episcopi et circiter quatuor alias sexterlatas nemoris que sunt ad foramina de Flavi que omnia tradiderunt ecclesie Premonstratensi in elemosinam perpetuo possidendam. Hanc autem elemosinam tam ipse Radulfus quam uxor sua M[argareta] de cuius hereditate hec omnia provenerunt, necnon et liberi ipsorum, videlicet Petrus Clericus, Robertus et Johannes, sub fidei corporalis interpositione laudaverunt et approbaverunt, renunciantes omni juri quod habebant vel habere poterant in omnibus supradictis, super quibus etiam tenebuntur portare legitimam warandiam secundum usus et consuetudines castellanie Hamensis adversus omnes qui voluerint juri stare preter quam adversus dominum episcopum Noviomensem et homines Espevile necnon et homines de Vellanis. Ecclesia vero Premonstratensis devotionem eorum attendens recompensavit et intuitu caritatis in temporali beneficio quinquaginta duas libras et dimidiam Parisiensis monete. Ut autem predicta omnia maiorem habere debeant firmitatem, litteras istas testimoniales emisimus sigillorum nostrorum munimine roboratas. Actum mense augusto, anno gratie millesimo CC° vicesimo.

349

1222

The knight Geoffroi,[1] *brother of Eudes [IV], lord of Ham, recounts the agreement reached between his man Jean* Patedoc *de Lanchy*[2] *and Prémontré concerning a dispute over rights and possession of lands in the territory of Lanchy,*[3] *and approves the gift that Jean leaves to Prémontré in his last will.*

A. Cartulary of Prémontré, fol. 87v.
B. Original not found.

Karta Gaufridi militis de Hamo de concordia inter Johannem de Lanci Patedoe et ecclesiam Premonstratem super octava garba.

[E]go Gaufridus, miles, frater illustris viri Odonis, domini de Hamo, notum facio universis tam presentibus quam futuris quod cum ecclesia

1 Geoffroi de Ham, knight and lord of Douchy, a brother of Eudes IV, lord of Ham, and a nephew of Guy de Condren, lord of Faillouel. He also appears in **331**, **355**, and **356**.
2 Jean, lord of Lanchy (cant. Vermand, https://dicotopo.cths.fr/places/P51978975), 1220s. Melleville, *DH*, vol. 2, 4.
3 Lanchy, cant. Vermand, https://dicotopo.cths.fr/places/P51978975.

Premonstratensis in quibusdam particulis territorii de Lanci octavam garbam et in quibusdam particulis eiusdem territorii perciperet quartam garbam et Johannes de Lanci Patedoe, homo meus, tam in octava garba octavam partem quam in quarta garba quartam partem haberet, unde inter ipsum et ecclesiam contingebat sepius discordiam exoriri, tandem mediantibus bonis viris, me quoque annuente, de quo tenebat in feodo dictus Johannes partes prenotatas, inter partes facta fuit conpositio in hunc modum quod Johannes sepedictus quitavit in perpetuum ecclesie partes predictas, et hospites quos habet ecclesia apud Lanci clamavit penitus quitos et ipsa ecclesia concessit eidem in perpetuum sex sexterlatas terre apud Lanci ad mensuram ipsius ville currentem tempore huius scripti et quartam garbam in quatuor sexterlatis terre et insuper unum modium frumenti ad mensuram Sancti Quintini recipiendum in grangia ecclesie Premonstratensis in perpetuum annuatim. Quia vero dictus Johannes in extrema voluntate, ductus propria devotione, remisit ecclesie sepedicte modium memoratum necnon et terciam partem vacui forragii quam habebat in decima de Lanci et quam tenebat de ecclesie sepedicta, ego tam ipsam elemosinam quam omnia supradicta benigne censui approbanda pariter et laudanda unde et presentes litteras sigilli mei munimine roboravi. Actum anno gratie M° CC° XX° II°.

350

1147

Simon [I],[1] bishop of Noyon, makes known that Simon d'Urvillers,[2] as fief lord, confirmed three sets of gifts made to Prémontré: the gift of Aelide, daughter of Baudouin de Monchy,[3] of land at Lanchy; the gift of Eudes de Lanchy,[4] of land; and gifts made by Simon's unnamed parents during their lifetime. Emma and Eva, sisters of Simon d'Urvillers, consented to this.

A. Cartulary of Prémontré, fol. 87v.

B. Original, AD Aisne, H 802, previously sealed on a double strip of white leather.

EDITION: Pycke and Vleeschouwers, *Actes*, 522–3.

---

1 Simon I de Vermandois (d. 1148) was the son of Hugues I and Adélaïde, count and countess of Vermandois and Valois, and bishop of Noyon, 1123–42.

2 Simon, lord of Urvillers (cant. Moy, https://dicotopo.cths.fr/places/P87012222), attested 1140s–60s. Melleville, *DH*, vol. 2, 389.

3 Monchy-Lagache, cant. Ham, https://dicotopo.cths.fr/places/P05686049.

4 Eudes, lord of Lanchy (cant. Vermand, https://dicotopo.cths.fr/places/P51978975), son of Waldin/Baudouin and Elizabeth. Melleville, *DH*, vol. 1, 4.

Karta Noviomensis episcopi de confirmatione doni quod fecerat Alaidis filia Balduini de Monci ecclesie Premonstratensi.

[I]n nomine sancte et individue Trinitatis.[5] Ego Symon, Dei gratia Noviomensis episcopus, notum fieri volo tam posteris quam modernis quod Symon de Urvileir concessit donum quod fecerat Alaidis, filia Balduini de Monci,[6] de terra de Lanci[7] Premonstrate ecclesie que de feodo suo descendebat. Concessit etiam donum quod fecerat Odo de Lanci[8] de terra sua quam tenebat de eo in feodum. Concessit quoque predicte ecclesie quicquid de hereditate sua pater suus et mater sua adhuc viventes ibidem concesserant. Quibus concessionibus predicti Symonis assenserunt sorores sue, Emme et Eva. Interfuerunt etiam hii[9] legitimi testes: Renerus[10] de Urvileir,[11] Symon de Montescort,[12,13] Robertus de Biacert, Matheus de Chamlencort,[14,15] Bernerus et Matheus frater eius. Ut autem firmum hoc inconvulsumque[16] perseveret, episcopali auctoritate sigillique nostri impressione communimus huicque nostre legitime constitutioni scienter contra ire presumentes anathematis vinculo innodamus. Actum anno incarnationis dominice M° C° XL° VII°, epacta XVII^{a}, indictione X, concurrente II°.

351

February, 1220.

Étienne [I],[1] bishop of Noyon, confirms that Marguerite,[2] sister of Renaud, knight of Flavy, transferred to Prémontré the five modiatae *of woodlands and*

5 *Om.* amen *A.*
6 Monchi *B.*
7 Lanchi *B.*
8 Lanchi *B.*
9 hi *B.*
10 Reinerus *B.*
11 Durvileir *B.*
12 Montescurt *B.*
13 Simon de Mondescourt (cant. Noyon, https://dicotopo.cths.fr/places/P60804459), son of Emmelot, appears as a witness in acts 1137–ca. 1183. Tock and Milis, *Monumenta Arroasiensia*, 143, 315.
14 Chamlencurt *B.*
15 Possibly Caulaincourt, cant. Vermand, https://dicotopo.cths.fr/places/P02972526.
16 inconcussumque *B.*

1 Étienne de Villebéon (or de Nemours), son of Gautier de Villebéon, lord of La Chapelle-Gauthier and Nemours, and Aveline, was bishop of Noyon, 1188–1221.
2 Marguerite de Flavy (cant. Guiscard, https://dicotopo.cths.fr/places/P19622430), sister and heir of Renaud, knight of Flavy. Newman, *Seigneurs*, vol. 2, 280–1.

meadow located in Bishop's Wood that Prémontré had conceded to Renaud in a previous agreement. Marguerite, who inherited the land on Renaud's death, undertook this transaction – part in alms, part as a sale – with the assent of her husband, Raoul, and of their heirs, and with the assent of bishop Étienne, from whom the fief descends.

A. Cartulary of Prémontré, fol. 87v.

B. Original, AD Oise, H 6000, sealed on a double strip of parchment, with a fragment of the bishop's seal in green wax.

Karta episcopi Noviomensis de quadam conpositione inter ecclesiam Premonstratensem et Renaldum de Flavi.

[S]tephanus, Dei gratia Noviomensis episcopus, omnibus presentes litteras inspecturis omnibus in perpetuum. Notum fieri volumus quod cum Renaldus, miles de Flavi, quondam homo noster, usuagium haberet in nemore ecclesie Premonstratensis versus Bonolium sito, quod dicitur Nemus Episcopi, tandem, assensu et voluntate nostra, dicti ecclesia Premonstratensis et R[enaldus] miles ad invicem in hunc modum conposuerunt[3] quod ipse R[enaldus] quinque modiatas illius nemoris, tam in nemore quam in prato, pro parte sua habuit et totum residuum ipsius nemoris ab usuagio quod in eo se habere dicebat, quitum[4] et liberum predicte ecclesie penitus clamavit. Post decessum vero ipsius Renaldi cum hereditas ipsius ad Margaretam, sororem suam, devoluta fuisset, ipsa M[argareta] assensu et voluntate Radulphi, mariti sui, et omnium heredum suorum cum ecclesia Premonstratensi spontanea, non coacta, sine vi et dolo hunc contractum iniit quod predictas quinque modiatas dicte ecclesie Premonstratensi partim ex elemosina partim ex venditione libere et absolute, assensu et voluntate nostra, qui domini feodi eramus, concessit. Dictus autem maritus ipsius M[argarete] et ipsa M[argareta] et omnes heredes eorum, fide corporaliter prestita, promiserunt quod nec per se nec per alios dictam ecclesiam super ipso contractu decetero molestabunt vel permittent aliquatenus molestari, immo etiam contra omnes qui juri et legi parere voluerint garandiam ferre tenentur. Nos autem ad utriusque partis petitionem in huius rei testimonium et munimine,[5] presentes litteras sigillo nostro fecimus roborari. Actum anno Domini M° CC°[6] vicesimo, mense februario. Datum per manum Philippi cancellarii.

3 composuerunt *B*.

4 *Sic A*, *read* quietum.

5 munimen *B*.

6 millesimo ducentesimo *B*.

352

March 6, 1231.

Magister *Hugues, canon and* officialis *of Noyon, makes known that in the presence of his representative Jean, dean of Ham, Pierre,*[1] *lord of half of Flavy, gave in alms to Prémontré three and a half* sextariatae *of land in the assarted land of Flavy near the wood of Bonneuil.*[2] *Herme, wife of Pierre, assented to this gift, and since the land formed part of her* dotalicium, *Herme received other land from Pierre in exchange.*

A. Cartulary of Prémontré, fols. 87v–88r.
B. Original, AD Somme, 20 H_SC_10, no. 3, sealed.[3]

Karta Hugonis officialis Noviomensis de elemosina Petri domini medietatis de Flavi super tribus sextariatis terre et dimidiam.

[O]mnibus hec visuris magister Hugo canonicus et officialis Noviomensis, salutem in Domino. Vobis notum facimus quod Petrus, dominus medietatis de Flavi, in presentia Johannis, decani nostri Hamensis, loco nostri, constitutus recognovit se contulisse in perpetuam elemosinam ecclesie Premonstratensis tres sexterariatas et dimidiam terre site in sartis de Flavi prope nemus de Bonolio ipsi ecclesie possidendas in perpetuum, Erma, uxore dicti Petri, presente dictam elemosinam laudante et approbante et recognoscente se sufficiens excanbium habere pro dotalicio quod habebat in dicta terra dicte ecclesie collata, videlicet in prato quod dicitur Ad Fossatum Angulorum ad quod pratum dictus Petrus eandem Ermam coram nobis pro dotalicio suo assignavit. Et per istud excambium quod in recompensationem dotalicii sui recepit a prefato Petro marito suo omne jus dotalicii quodcumque in dictis tribus sextariis et dimidio dicte ecclesie collatis habebat vel habitura erat, quocumque jure in manu dicti decani resignavit voluntate spontanea et non coacta et eidem penitus renunciavit. Et tam dictus Petrus quam ipsa Erma spontanea et non coacta fidem in manu nostra prestiterunt corporalem quod dictam ecclesiam per se vel per alium decetero super dicta elemosina non molestabunt nec gravabunt nec artem nec ingenium querent per que eadem ecclesia possit vel debeat super eadem elemosina in posterum molestari vel gravari. In cuius rei testimonium presentes litteras secundum tenorem litterarum dicti decani super eadem elemosina ad mandatum nostrum confectarum sigillo curie Noviomensis fecimus communiri. Actum anno Domini M° CC° tricesimo primo, in crastino Invocavit Me.

1 Pierre (d. aft. 1247), lord of half of Flavy-le-Meldeux (cant. Guiscard, https://dicotopo.cths.fr/places/P19622430), son of Raoul, lord of Flavy-le-Meldeux, and Marguerite, sister and heir of Renaud, knight of Flavy. Newman, *Seigneurs*, vol. 2, 280–1.

2 Bonneuil, cant. Ham, https://dicotopo.cths.fr/places/P66750585.

3 Due to conservation concerns, the original was not available to the editors.

353

1147

Simon [I],[1] *bishop of Noyon, gives notice that husband and wife Foulques*[2] *Obelin and Berthe gave the church of Prémontré land at Lanchy,*[3] *an oven at Caulaincourt,*[4] *and a house at Ham. Wibert, son of Foulques and Berthe, who is departing on pilgrimage to Jerusalem, promises not to claim his inheritance should he return but to enter the religious life at Prémontré. Foulques and Berthe's other children, Barthélemy and Erma; Jean,*[5] *son of Robert* Rufus, *from whom the fief descends; and Widela, sister of Jean, consent to the gift.*

A. Cartulary of Prémontré, fol. 88r.
B. Original not found.[6]
EDITION: Pycke and Vleeschouwers, *Actes*, 518–19.

Karta Symonis Noviomensis episcopi de elemosina Fulconis Obelin et de furno de Canlencurt.

[I]n nomine sancte et individue Trinitatis. Ego Symon, Dei gratia Noviomensium episcopus, notum fieri volo tam futuris quam presentibus quod Fulco, cognomento Obelin, et uxor sua, Berta, contulerunt Premonstrate ecclesie quandam terram suam que in territorio de Lanci adjacebat post obitum suum jure perpetuo possidendam et quendam furnum Canlencort et quandam masuram Hamo annuente hoc filio suo, Wiberto, atque suggerente cui hec omnia possidenda primitus jure hereditatis concesserant, qui etiam Wibertus Hierosolinam pergens sic semet ipsum cum predicta hereditate ecclesie reddidit ut, si forte Iherosolinam rediret, non solum hereditatem suam repeteret, verum nec ipse in seculo remaneret sed statim Premonstratum ad conversionem veniret. Concesserunt etiam hoc donum Bartholomeus frater suus et Erma soror sua, sed et Johannes, filius Roberti, de cuius feodo hec ipsa descendebant, benigne concessit et manu

1 Simon I de Vermandois (d. 1148) was the son of Hugues I and Adélaïde, count and countess of Vermandois and Valois, and bishop of Noyon, 1123–42.

2 Foulques Obelin is attested in acts from 1134–65. See **322**, **362**, **398**, and **442.**

3 Lanchy, cant. Vermand, https://dicotopo.cths.fr/places/P51978975.

4 Caulaincourt, cant. Vermand, https://dicotopo.cths.fr/places/P02972526.

5 Jean d'Athies, son of Robert *Rufus*, nephew of Mathieu and Bernier, and brother of Widèle and Adam. With his wife Eustacie, he was the father of Manassès, Robert, Aubry, and Eudes the cleric. With his brother Adam, knight and lord of Athies (cant. Ham, https://dicotopo.cths.fr/places/P98820850), he is attested in a number of acts ca. 1150–ca. 1188. Cagny, *Histoire de l'arrondissement de Péronne*, vol. 2, 259; Tock and Milis, *Monumenta Arroasiensia*, 251. He is also mentioned in **306**, **371**, **398**, **421**, **424**, and **442**.

6 In the 1980s, Françoise Muret described an original charter for this act (AD Aisne, H 764, sealed on a double strip of parchment with a partial surviving seal in brownish-red wax). For a detailed description of the original, see Pycke and Vleeschouwers, *Actes*, 518. However, the present editors could only locate a nineteenth-century transcription of this act under the same archival reference.

propria ecclesie contulit. Huius rei sunt testes: predictus Johannes filius Roberti Rufi, et Albericus cognomento Malus clericus, Robertus[7] de Sumet, Drogo de Plessei,[8] Petrus de Porta,[9] Robertus de Duaco. Ut autem hec firma et inconvulsa ecclesie permaneant, episcopali auctoritate sigillique nostri impressione communimus et ne quis hec irritare presumat, sub anathemate interdicimus. Acta sunt hec anno incarnationis dominice M° C° XL° VII°. Sed et hoc scire volumus omnes quod Widela, soror predicti Johannis, filia Roberti Rufi, concessit predicte ecclesie donum quod fecerat isdem frater suus Johannes de predicta terra et etiam quicquid in ea habebat aut habere expectabat. Huic concessioni interfuit ipsem et Johannes et Robertus de Oini[10] miles suus et frater Hescelo.

354

December, 1226.

Eudes [IV],[1] lord of Ham, concedes and guarantees the gift that his granddaughter Elizabeth[2] made in alms to La Valroy[3] of three modii *of grain (*frumentum*) from the* census *owed to Eudes at Collezy[4] by the churches of Prémontré and of Ham. The knight Renier,[5] Eudes's grandson and Elizabeth's brother, assents to the gift.*

A. Cartulary of Prémontré, fol. 88r.
B. Original, AD Somme 20 H 6, no. 17.[6]

Karta Odonis domini de Hamo de elemosina Elizabeth et de modiagio de Colesi.

[E]go Odo dominus de Hamo, notum facio universis tam presentibus quam futuris quod de elemosina Elizabeth, neptis mee, quam ipsa fecit ecclesie Vallis

7 Possibly the same Robert de Sommette (Sommette-Éaucourt, cant. Saint-Simon, https://dicotopo.cths.fr/places/P82241903) who appears in **384**.
8 Likely Le Plessis-Patte-d'Oie, cant. Guiscard, https://dicotopo.cths.fr/places/P25690373.
9 Pierre de la Porte, son of Alard I de Ham (or de la Porte), knight of Ham, and Helvide. He also appears in **334** and **388**.
10 Ugny-l'Équipée, cant. Ham, https://dicotopo.cths.fr/places/P10325887.

1 Eudes IV, lord of Ham (d. 1234), son of Eudes III, lord of Ham, and Elizabeth; husband of Elizabeth de Béthencourt.
2 Elizabeth, daughter of Geoffroi, lord of Sains (arr. Vervins, https://dicotopo.cths.fr/places/P35898483), and his second wife, Agnès or Elizabeth. Melleville, *DH*, vol. 2, 305.
3 The Cistercian abbey of La Valroy.
4 Collezy, comm. Berlancourt, https://dicotopo.cths.fr/places/P68465476.
5 Renier II, lord of Sains, son of Geoffroi, lord of Sains, and his first wife Marie de Ham, attested in the 1220s. BM Reims MS 1563 (N. Fonds), fol. 157v; Melleville, *DH*, vol. 2, 305.
6 Due to conservation concerns, the original was not available to the editors.

Regis, videlicet de modiagio de Colesi, tres modios frumenti de censu quem debent mihi apud Colesi Premonstratensis et Hamensis ecclesie ego concessi et quitavi eisdem ecclesiis in perpetuum possidendos et contra omnes qui ad jus et legem venirent, teneor garandire. In super etiam sciendum est quod hoc totum factum est de assensu et voluntate Reneri, nepotis mei, militis, fratris Elisabeth supradicte. In cuius rei testimonium feci presentes litteras sigilli mei munimine roborari. Actum anno incarnationis dominice M° CC° XX° VI°, mense decembri.

355

January, 1210.

Guy [I][1] *de Condren, lord of Faillouël, makes known that Geoffroi*[2] *de Ham, his nephew, gave in alms to the church of Prémontré all the rights of* justicia *over the* manerium *of Rémi de Lanchy*[3] *that Geoffroi held from Guy, save the right of* vavassorus.

A. Cartulary of Prémontré, fol. 88r.
B. Original not found.

Karta Guidonis de Condren et domini de Foilluel de elemosina Gaufridi de Hamo et de manerio Remigii de Lanci.

[E]go Guido de Condren et dominus Foilluel, notum facio tam presentibus quam futuris quod, cum vir nobilis Gaufridus de Hamo, nepos meus, haberet bannum et sanguinem et latronem et omnimodam aliam justiciam in manerio Remigii de Lanci, idem Gaufridus de assensu meo de quo tenebat hec eadem in feodo, dedit in elemosinam ecclesie Premonstrati quicquid juris habebat in ipso manerio vel in ipso Remigio vel in familia eius ita quod sibi nichil retinuit perpetuo possidendum, salvo tamen jure vavassorum ipsius Gaufridi qui pro defectu reddituum suorum qui debentur eis, de terris campestribus poterunt assignare ad ea que invenerint in domo vel in manerio ipsius Remigii donec ipsis de redditibus quos debebitur eis, idem Remigius vel eius heredes fuerit satisfactum. Ut igitur hec elemosina futuris temporibus conservetur integra et illesa presens scriptum super eadem concessione factum sigilli mei feci impressione muniri. Actum mense januarii, anno gratie M° CC° X°.

---

1 Guy I de Condren (cant. Chauny, https://dicotopo.cths.fr/places/P28107866), lord of Faillouël, son of Geoffroi de Condren, knight. Newman, *Seigneurs*, vol. 2, 203–4.

2 Geoffroi de Ham, knight and lord of Douchy, a brother of Eudes IV, lord of Ham, and a nephew of Guy de Condren, lord of Faillouël. He also appears in **331**, **349**, and **356**.

3 Lanchy, cant. Vermand, https://dicotopo.cths.fr/places/P51978975.

356

1231

Geoffroi[1] *de Ham, knight, gives in alms to Prémontré the* mansus *of Martin d'Estaliers located at Lanchy,*[2] *between the* mansus *of Dreux de Muile*[3] *and the* mansus *once belonging to Jean* Haitie. *Geoffroi and his heirs relinquish all rights to the property.*

A. Cartulary of Prémontré, fols. 88r–88v.
B. Original not found.

Karta Gaufridi de Hamo de elemosina mansi Martini de Estaliers siti apud Lanchi.

[E]go Gaufridus de Hamo, miles, omnibus presentibus et futuris notum facio quod ego pro animee mee, uxoris et antecessorum meorum remedio salutari, totum mansum Martini de Estaliers, manentis apud Monchi, situm apud Lanchi inter mansum Drogonis de Muile et mansum quondam Johannis dicti Haitie sub meo dominio in omni dominio et in omni justicia ecclesie Premonstratensi contuli in elemosinam et concessi. Hec ego et heredes mei supra dictum mansum aliquod dominium, justiciam censum, talliam vel aliquod aliud non possumus requirere vel debemus. Quod ut ratum sit et stabile presentes litteras sigilli mei munimine confirmavi. Actum anno Domini M° CC° tricesimo primo.

357

November, 1227.

Renier [II],[1] *lord of Sains, makes known that Prémontré paid in full the sum of money that it owed, having acquired from him the* modiagium *pertaining to its* grangia *at Collezy.*[2] *(See* ***304****,* ***417****, and* ***422****.)*

A. Cartulary of Prémontré, fol. 88v.
B. Original not found.

---

1 Geoffroi de Ham, knight and lord of Douchy, a brother of Eudes IV, lord of Ham, and a nephew of Guy de Condren, lord of Faillouël. He also appears in **331**, **349**, and **355**.
2 Lanchy, cant. Vermand, https://dicotopo.cths.fr/places/P51978975.
3 Muille-Villette, cant. Ham, https://dicotopo.cths.fr/places/P77128677.

---

1 Renier II, lord of Sains (arr. Vervins, https://dicotopo.cths.fr/places/P35898483), son of Geoffroi, lord of Sains, and his first wife Marie de Ham, attested in the 1220s. BM Reims MS 1563 (N. Fonds), fol. 157v; Melleville, *DH*, vol. 2, 305.
2 Collezy, comm. Berlancourt, https://dicotopo.cths.fr/places/P68465476.

Karta domini Reneri de Seins de pecunia eidem soluta pro emptione modiagii.

[E]go Renerus, dominus de Seins, notum facio universis presentes litteras inspecturis quod ecclesia Premonstratensis mihi plenarie solvit totam pecuniam quam michi debebat pro emptione modiagii quod a me in grangia sua de Colesi acquisivit. In cuius rei testimonium presentes litteras sigilli mei munimine roborari. Actum mense novembri, anno gratie M° CC° XX° VII°.

358

1144

Simon [I],[1] bishop of Noyon, confirms that the following gave their hereditary rights in alms over the mill of Canny[2] to the church of Prémontré in return for 16 modii *of grain (*frumentum*), measure of Nesle: husband and wife Henri and Richolde, with their children Evrard, Hersende, and Richolde; Ménard and his son Mathieu; Gautier and his son Waltème; husband and wife Eudes and Gontaux; husband and wife Gilbert and Marie; husband and wife Robert and Berthe; and husband and wife Eudes and Ermengarde.*

A. Cartulary of Prémontré, fol. 88v.

B. Original, BnF, Coll. Picardie 290, no. 4, previously sealed.

EDITION: Pycke and Vleeschouwers, *Actes*, 485–6.

REGISTER: Boghen, "Inventaire des actes épiscopaux originaux conservés à la Bibliothèque nationale (1121–1200)," 121.

Karta Noviomensis episcopi de confirmatione elemosine molendinorum de Escamli pro XVI modiis frumenti.

[I]n nomine sancte et individue Trinitatis. Ego Symon, Dei gratia Noviomensis episcopus, notum fieri volo tam futuris quam presentibus quod Henricus et Richoldis, uxor eius et Evrardus, filius eorum, Hersendis et Richoldis, filie eorum, item Menardus et Matheus filius,[3] Walterus et Waltelmus, filius eius, Odo et Gontaux, uxor eius, Gislebertus et Maria, uxor eius, Robertus et Berta,

1 Simon I de Vermandois (d. 1148) was the son of Hugues I and Adélaïde, count and countess of Vermandois and Valois, and bishop of Noyon, 1123–42.

2 Pycke and Vleeschouwers identify *Escamli* as Essenlis (comm. Chavonne, https://dicotopo.cths.fr/places/P65971619). Pycke and Vleeschouwers, *Actes*, 486. However, we concur with Dietrich Lohrmann that *Escamli* is Canny-lès-Voyennes (cant. Nesle, https://dicotopo.cths.fr/places/P44415541). Lohrmann, "Barrages et moulins sur la Somme au temps des chanoines réguliers (XIIe–XIIIe siècles)," 341, 345.

3 *Om.* eius *A.*

uxor eius, Odo et Ermengardis, uxor eius, concesserunt in elemosinam Premonstrate ecclesie quicquid hereditario molendinariorum jure habebant in molendinis de Escamli[4] pro XVI modiis frumenti Nigellensis mensure. Terminus autem persolvendi frumenti erit in nativitate Domini, frumentum autem tale dabitur quale in communi questu molendinorum accipi solet. Suprascripto vero Henrico et eius heredibus octo[5] modii dabuntur eo quod media pars hereditario jure eis proveniat; Menardo autem et aliis prenominatis atque eorum heredibus alii octo[6] modii persolventur tali siquidem conventione ut nec isti quos prefati sumus, nec aliquis subsequentium heredum ipsorum in futurum valeat aliquid in prefatis molendinis reclamare et quod legaliter coram ydoneis[7]testibus factum est et in elemosinam concessum perturbare. Hii autem sunt:[8] Richoldus[9] de Roi prepositus, Milo[10] maior de Voiana, Menardus cognomento Miles, Ansbertus Longus de Ulfoiz, Bertradus[11] Rufus, Rogerus filius Warneri prepositi de Parvo Roi, Robertus filius Aien, Hubertus filius Olrici, Wadinus de Berueci,[12,13] Paganus molendinarius, Johannes molendinarius. Ut igitur hec nostre constitutionis pagina inviolatum robur optineat,[14] sigilli nostri munimine apponere curavimus cum legitimorum virorum subscriptione et ne quis eam infringere presumat, prohibemus sub districta anathematis innodatione. Actum anno incarnati verbi M° C° XL IIII°,[15] indictione VI[a], epacta XIIII[a], concurrente IIII°.

359

1144

Dreux [II],[1] prior of the Cluniac house of Saint-Pierre de Lihons, with advice from Hugues[2] de Crécy, monk at Cluny, makes known that his priory cedes to

4 Escanli *B.*
5 VIII *B.*
6 VIII *B.*
7 idoneis *B.*
8 *Om.* testes *A.*
9 Richold, likely prior of the collegiate church of Saint-Florent de Roye (cant. Roye, https://dicotopo.cths.fr/places/P52439933).
10 Milon de Voyennes (cant. Nesle, https://dicotopo.cths.fr/places/P32215646) also appears in acts **274** and **301**.
11 Bertrandus *B.*
12 Beruerci *B.*
13 Likely Buverchy, cant. Nesle, https://dicotopo.cths.fr/places/P26244075.
14 obtineat *B.*
15 XL° IIII° *B.*

1 Dreux II, prior of the Cluniac priory of Saint-Pierre-et-Saint-Paul de Lihons-en-Santerre, 1140s. Du Cange, "Le Prieuré de Lihons en Santerre," 8.
2 Likely Hugues de Crécy (d. 1147), lord of Gometz and Chateaufort, later monk at Cluny; son of Guy II le Rouge, lord of Montlhéry and Adèle de Crécy.

Prémontré all the rights on a quarter part of the mills of Canny[3] *in exchange for eight* modii *of grain (*frumentum*), measure of Nesle, and a part of Prémontré's revenue from the tithe of Grouches.*[4] *This act, originally issued as a chirograph, was later confirmed by the addition of the seal of Pierre,*[5] *abbot of Cluny. (See* ***361****.)*

A. Cartulary of Prémontré, fol. 88v.

B. Original (chirograph), AM Metz, Salis II.245, no. 4, previously sealed with two seals, both on a double strip of parchment. In the right margin and beginning at the top, the bottom half of the letters that form the word CYROGRAPHUM.

Karta Drogonis prioris de Lihuns de molendinis de Escamli datis ecclesie Premonstrati sub annuo censu.

[I]n nomine sancte et individue Trinitatis. Ego Drogo, prior ecclesie Sancti Petri de Lihuns,[6] notum fieri volo quod in molendinis de Escamli[7] et in omnibus que ad ea pertinebant, in aqua, terra, transitu, justicia quartam partem habebat ecclesia nostra. Que, quia vetustate et negligentia adeo ad nichilum redacta erant ut nichil aut parum ex eis nobis proveniret, consilio et assensu fratrum ecclesie nostre, consilio etiam confratris nostri, Hugonis, monachi Cluniacensis, qui dicitur de Criciaco, Premonstrate ecclesie et Hugoni[8] abbati censualiter concessimus pro octo[9] modiis frumenti Nigellensis mensure. Frumentum vero tale erit quale in questu molendini accipietur et in festo Sancti Remigii persolvetur et nobis deducetur. Pro eo vero quod minus accipit ecclesia nostra quam ecclesia Sancte Margarete que similiter in eisdem molendinis quartam partem habebat, concessa est nobis pars quam habebat ecclesia Premonstrata in decima de Greuni, excepto quod ex ea persolvemus novem sextarios ecclesie de Bretenni quos per eadem decima debebat ei Premonstrata ecclesia. Et hoc determinatum et promissum est quod istud scriptum nostrum privilegio Cluniacensis ecclesie roboraretur, ne aliquis succedentium priorum posset infirmare quod nos ad tam evidens commodum ecclesie nostre studuimus

3 Pycke and Vleeschouwers identify *Escamli* as Essenlis (comm. Chavonne, https://dicotopo.cths.fr/places/P65971619). Pycke and Vleeschouwers, *Actes*, 486. However, we concur with Dietrich Lohrmann that *Escamli* is Canny-lès-Voyennes (cant. Nesle, https://dicotopo.cths.fr/places/P44415541). Lohrmann, "Barrages et moulins sur la Somme au temps des chanoines réguliers (XIIe–XIIIe siècles)," 341, 345.

4 Grouches, cant. Roye, https://dicotopo.cths.fr/places/P04293263.

5 Pierre the Venerable (or de Montboissier), son of Maurice de Montboissier and Raingarde de Semur, was abbot of Cluny, 1122–56.

6 Lehuns *B*.

7 Escanli *B*.

8 Hugues I de Fosses (ca. 1093–1164), first abbot of Prémontré.

9 VIII° *B*.

elaborare. Et ut hoc ratum et inconvulsum permaneat, cirographi[10] conscriptione et sigillorum nostrorum inpressione et legitimorum testium utriusque ecclesie Premonstrate scilicet et nostre confirmavimus annotatione. Testes ecclesie nostre sunt isti: ego Drogo prior, Azo supprior, Lambertus prepositus; Petrus, Jacobus de Maisieres,[11] Odo[12] castellanus, Gerardus monachi. Testes vero Premonstrate ecclesie isti sunt: Hugo abbas, Johannes prior, Erchenbertus supprior, Harduinus[13] cantor, Bertoldus cellerarius, Johannes, Radulphus, Alexander, Drogo sacerdotes, Hescelo,[14] Symon, Haimo, Gubertus,[15] Eustachius, Liebertus, Rogerus diaconi, Hugo, Johannes, Walterus, Balduinus,[16] Johannes subdiaconi, Matheus, Albericus, Johannes, Walterus, Lambertus accoliti. Actum est hoc anno incarnati verbi M° C° XLIIII°,[17] indictione VII^{a}, epacta XIIII^{a}, concurrente VI°. Ego frater Petrus, humilis Cluniacensis abbas hanc cartam, postquam facta est, vidi et sigilli mei impressione firmavi.

360

1144

Simon [I],[1] *bishop of Noyon, makes known that Thierry,* custos *of Notre-Dame de Nesle,*[2] *and certain of his fellow canons ceded to Prémontré all their land, mills, and rights at Canny*[3] *for an annual payment of 20* modii *of grain (*frumentum*), measure of Nesle, and seven* solidi obolorum.

A. Cartulary of Prémontré, fols. 88v–89r.

B[1]. Original (chirograph), AM Metz, Salis II.245, no. 7. Sealed with two seals on a single strip of parchment. The right one remains intact. In the left margin and beginning at the top, the top half of the letters that form the word CYROGRAPHUM. (This charter likely belonged to Prémontré.)

10 cyrographum *B*.
11 Likely Mézières, cant. Moreuil, https://dicotopo.cths.fr/places/P61459930.
12 Perhaps a castellan of Péronne, given that town's proximity to the priory of Lihons.
13 Hardewinus *B*.
14 Hezelo *B*.
15 Grinbertus *B*.
16 Baldewinus *B*.
17 M° C° XL° IIII° *B*.

1 Simon I de Vermandois (d. 1148) was the son of Hugues I and Adélaïde, count and countess of Vermandois and Valois, and bishop of Noyon, 1123–42.
2 The collegiate church of Notre-Dame-de-l'Assomption de Nesle.
3 Pycke and Vleeschouwers identify *Escamli* as Essenlis (comm. Chavonne, https://dicotopo.cths.fr/places/P65971619). Pycke and Vleeschouwers, *Actes*, 486. However, we concur with Dietrich Lohrmann that *Escamli* is Canny-lès-Voyennes (cant. Nesle, https://dicotopo.cths.fr/places/P44415541). Lohrmann, "Barrages et moulins sur la Somme au temps des chanoines réguliers (XIIe–XIIIe siècles)," 341, 345.

B[2]. Original (chirograph), AM Metz, Salis II.245, no. 8. Sealed with two seals on a single strip of parchment. The left one remains intact. In the right margin and beginning at the top, the bottom half of the letters that form the word CYROGRAPHUM. (This charter belonged to the church of Notre-Dame-de-Nesle, based on dorsal annotations.)

EDITION: Pycke and Vleeschouwers, *Actes*, 487–8.

Karta Noviomensis episcopi de canonicis Nigellensis qui dederunt nobis quicquid habebant in molendinis de Escamli pro XX modiis frumenti.

[I]n nomine sancte et individue Trinitatis. Quoniam brevitate vite hominum successu etiam temporum facile subrepit oblivio preteritorum, res gestas custodie commendare litterarum majorum decrevit auctoritas. Quorum sollertiam ex multimodi utilitate approbans, ego Symon, Dei gratia Noviomensis episcopus, notum fieri volo tam futuris quam presentibus quod dominus Theodericus, custos ecclesie Sancte Marie de Nigella, ceterique concanonici sui censualiter concesserunt Premonstrate ecclesie quicquid habebant apud Escamli[4] in molendinis, aqua, piscaria, terra, censu, transitu, justicia pro viginti modiis frumenti Nigellensis mensure et septem[5] solidis obolorum. Frumentum autem tale dabitur quale in primo foro Nigelle post Epiphaniam[6] melius vendetur, uno denario tantum[7] minus in sextario et usque ad Purificationem Beate Marie persolvetur et infra ambitum eiusdem castri ubi prepositus ipsorum canonicorum disposuerit, ducetur. Quod si eosdem viginti[8] modios molere voluerint, a festo Sancti Remigii usque ad Pascha ad nutum prepositi sine multura moletur, septem vero solidi obolorum duobus terminis persolventur, mediante maio tres solidi et sex nummi, et in festo Sancti Remigii tres solidi et sex nummi. Si vero aliquis aliquid eorum que superscripsimus, perturbare voluerit, hereditario jure proclamans ibi aliquid quamdiu justiciam sequi voluerit. Nigellenses canonici pro Premonstratensibus fratribus causam agent. Si autem causam eorum agere neglexerint vel per eorum negligentiam[9] fratres ibi perdiderint, quantum se perdidisse demonstraverint,[10] tantum de censu eorum retinebunt. Quod si fratres Premonstratenses predictum censum persolvere noluerint, Nigellenses canonici molendina sasientes tam diu reditum recipient donec universum debitum eis restituatur. Sed ne hoc in futurum duci valeat in irritum, presentium sigillorum

4 Escanli *B*[1], *B*[2].
5 VII *B*[1], *B*[2].
6 Epyphanum *B*[2].
7 *Transp. A*; tantum denario *B*[2].
8 XX *B*[1], *B*[2].
9 neggligentiam *B*[1], *B*[2].
10 demonstrare potuerint *B*[2].

inpressione[11] et cirographi[12] conscriptione necnon et subscriptorum testificatione confirmare studuimus. S.[13] Hugonis,[14] Premonstratensis abbatis. S. Johannis prioris. S. Johannis, presbiteri, et ceteri.[15] Actum anno incarnati verbi M°[16] C° XLIIII° regnante Ludovico et Yvone[17,18] Suessionensis[19] et Nigelle principante.

361

1144[?][1]

Wibert,[2] prior of the Cluniac house of Sainte-Marguerite [d'Elincourt], makes known that his priory cedes to Prémontré all its rights over a quarter part of the mills of Canny[3] in return for ten modii *of grain (*frumentum*), measure of Nesle, and two* solidi Viromandensium. *Hugues de Crécy[4] assents to this; originally issued as a chirograph, the act was later confirmed by the addition of the seal of Pierre,[5] abbot of Cluny. (See **359**.)*

A. Cartulary of Prémontré, fol. 89r.

B. Original (chirograph), AM Metz, Salis II.245, no. 1, previously sealed twice with one single strip of parchment remaining.

---

11 impressione *B*².

12 cyrographi *B*¹, *B*².

13 Signum *B*¹.

14 Hugues I de Fosses (ca. 1093–1164), first abbot of Prémontré.

15 *Add.* et ceteri *A*; S. Drogonis, diaconi. S. Simonis, diaconi. S. Mathei. S. Fulconis, canonicorum. S. Alardi de Bonolio. S. Bovonis et Thierzonis, conversorum. Item signum domini Theoderici custodis. S. Roberti, presbyteri et canonci. S. Hugonis et Radulfi. S. Johannis et Arnulfi. Signum Liethardi et Lamberti canonicorum. Item Signum Ivonis domini. Signum Radulfi, catellani. Signum Symonis de Maigni. S. Walteri Gerarth. S. Hugonis et Morrol. S. Walduini, filii Theobaldi Vasleth. S. Walteri, filii Geislini *B*¹, *B*².

16 millesimo *B*¹, *B*².

17 Ivone *B*¹, *B*².

18 Yves II de Nesle (d. ca. 1178), lord of Nesle and count of Soissons, son of Raoul, lord of Nesle, and Raintrude. Newman, *Seigneurs*, vol. 1, 61.

19 Suessioni *B*¹, *B*².

---

1 This act is undated; the date here is derived from the related act **359**.

2 A *Wifredus* is attested as the prior of Saint-Marguerite d'Elincourt in 1150. Morel, "Remarques sur la donation d'Hugues de Coudun à St-Hugues de Cluny et la Fondation du prieuré d'Elincourt-Sainte-Marguerite," 272.

3 Pycke and Vleeschouwers identify *Escamli* as Essenlis (comm. Chavonne, https://dicotopo.cths.fr/places/P65971619). Pycke and Vleeschouwers, Actes, 486. However, we concur with Dietrich Lohrmann that *Escamli* is Canny-lès-Voyennes (cant. Nesle, https://dicotopo.cths.fr/places/P44415541). Lohrmann, "Barrages et moulins sur la Somme au temps des chanoines réguliers (XIIe–XIIIe siècles)," 341, 345.

4 A monk of Cluny. See **359**.

5 Pierre the Venerable (or de Montboissier), son of Maurice de Montboissier and Raingarde de Semur, was abbot of Cluny, 1122–56.

Karta Wiberti prioris Sancte Margarete de censu molendinorum de Escamli pro X modiis frumenti.

[I]n nomine et cetera. Ego Wibertus,[6] prior ecclesie Sancte Margarete, notum fieri volo tam futuris quam presentibus quod in molendinis de Escamli[7] et in omnibus que ad ea pertinebant, in aqua, terra, transitu, justicia quartam partem habebat ecclesia nostra. Que quia vetustate et negligentia adeo ad nichilum redacta erant ut nichil aut parum ex eis nobis proveniret, consilio et assensu ecclesie nostre et Hugonis de Creciaco, Premonstrate ecclesie et Hugoni abbati censualiter concessimus pro X modiis frumenti Nigellensis mensure et duobus solidis Viromandensis monete. Frumentum vero tale erat quale in questu molendini accipietur et in festo Sancti Remigii persolvetur. Tali autem conventione factum est ut, si aliquis reditus in vicina nostra inveniretur, tantumdem valens acquirerent eum nobis. Si vero unum aut duos modios plus valeret ideo non remaneret. Si tamen rationabiliter emi posset et hoc determinatum et promissum est quod istud scriptum nostrum privilegio Cluniacensis ecclesie roboraretur ne aliquis succedentium priorum posset infirmare quod nos ad tam evidens commodum ecclesie[8] studium elaborare. Et ut hoc ratum et inconvulsum permaneat, cyrographi conscriptione et sigillorum nostrorum inpressione et legitimorum testium confirmavimus annotatione. S. mei ipsius.[8] S. Roberti supprioris, Richardi, Johannis, et ceteri.[10] Ego frater Petrus, humilis Cluniacensis abbas, hanc cartam postquam facta est, vidi et sigilli nostri impressione firmavi.

362

1137

Simon [I],[1] *bishop of Noyon, confirms that Guillaume de Ham, son of the* dapifer *Oudard, together with his wife, Ada, gave to Prémontré a third of the major tithe of Offoy.*[2] *Mathieu,*[3] *son of Basin, from whom the fief immediately*

6 Gwibertus *B.*
7 Escanli *B.*
8 *Om.* nostre *A.*
9 *Superscr.* Gerberti prioris *B.*
10 *Add.* et ceteri *A*; Roberti de Annai, sacerdotum. S. Evrardi diaconi. s. Evrardi conversi *B.*

1 Simon I de Vermandois (d. 1148) was the son of Hugues I and Adélaïde, count and countess of Vermandois and Valois, and bishop of Noyon, 1123–42.
2 Offoy, cant. Ham, https://dicotopo.cths.fr/places/P14011159.
3 Mathieu, son of Basin and Agnes of Ham, also appears in **333**.

descends, and Roger[4] *de Thourotte and his wife Havide,*[5] *from whom Mathieu held the fief, assent to this.*[6]

A. Cartulary of Prémontré, fol. 89r.
B. BM Louis Aragon, Legs Arthur de Marsy, 1005, no. 1.[7]
EDITION: Pycke and Vleeschouwers, *Actes*, 420.

Karta Symonis Noviomensis episcopi de confirmatione tercie partis maioris decime de Ulfoiz.

[I]n nomine et cetera. Sancte rectores ecclesie quanto ceteris dignitate et honore videntur preminere, tanto lucidius ac firmius que statuunt ac disponunt, debent diffinire. Igitur ego Symon Dei gratia Noviomensis episcopus, quod certum est modernis fore volo notum et posteris quod Guillelmus de Hamo, Odardi dapiferi filius, et uxor eius, Ada, terciam partem maioris decime de Ulfoiz, Premonstrate ecclesie Sancte Marie et Sancti Johannis Baptiste, tempore Hugonis abbatis, pro suo suorumque remedio contulerunt, Matheo, Basini filio, concedente de cuius feodo predictus Guillelmus illam habebat. Rogero etiam de Torota et Havide, uxore eius, de feodo quorum ad Matheum quem diximus descendebat, concedentibus et quod suum ibi erat, in manu nostra ponentibus, sub hiis testibus: clericis Soyhero de Wase, Rogero filio Roberti Cordubanarii, Terrico de Roi filio Bonardi de Mansais, et laicis Goisberto filio Adonis, Fulcone Obeline,[8] Galtero de Betencourt,[9] et ceteri. Ego autem illud donum sancte prememorate ecclesie perpetuo habendum concessi. Quod ut ratum ac stabile permaneret, tam sigilli quam privilegii mei firmitate munivi. Quod quisquis irritum facere conabitur, anathematis gladio feriatur. Actum est hoc anno incarnationis dominice M° C° XXX° VII°, epacta VII[a], concurrente V°, indictione prima. S. Balduini,[10] abbatis Sancti Quintini de Insula. S. Warini[11]

4 Roger *Filius Episcopi*, castellan of Thourotte and son of the lady Adèle and perhaps Teszo, castellan of Coucy. He entered Prémontré in 1141. Through his mother he was related to the castellans of Chauny. Guyotjeannin, *Episcopus*, 212–14, 273–4.

5 Havide (de Montmorency?) seems to have succeeded her husband Roger as castellan of Thourotte, 1143–70. Guyotjeannin, *Episcopus*, 214.

6 In the same year, Simon also confirms the gift of Raoul de Nesle to Prémontré of a third of the tithe of Offoy. BnF, nouv. acq. lat. 2590, no. 37; Poupardin, "Quatre Chartes anciennes d'Évêques de Noyon provenant de la Collection Phillipps," 219–20.

7 Due to archival access restrictions in operation in 2020, the editors were unable to access this charter.

8 Foulques Obelin is attested in acts from 1134–65. See **322**, **353**, **398**, and **442.**

9 Probably the same Gautier de Bethencourt who appears in **378** as a miller.

10 Baudouin II, abbot of the Benedictine abbey of Saint-Quentin-en-l'Isle, ca. 1136–64.

11 Guérin I, abbot of the Benedictine abbey of Saint-Prix de Saint-Quentin, ca. 1138–42.

abbatis Sancti Prejecti, et Arnulphi[12] monachi Sancti Nichasii, Gerardi[13] decani ecclesie maioris Sancti Quintini, Goffridi cantoris, Nivelonis, Odonis, Roberti, Raineri, Clareboldi canonicorum eiusdem ecclesie Sancti Quintini. S. etiam Theoderici,[14] Noviomensis ecclesie thesaurarii. Ego Hugo[15] cancellarius recensui.

363

April, 1224.

The knight Mathieu de Dury, son of Raoul [I], lord of Roye, confirms as fief lord the agreement reached between the brothers Roger Boutons and Garnier, millers of Offoy,[1] *and the church of Prémontré, by which the brothers relinquish any rights they may have to the mills of Offoy in exchange for an annual payment of nine* modii *of grain (*frumentum*). The charter also notes that Mathieu had previously approved the alms gift of Ermengarde, Pierre, and Simon de Offoy of the part of the mill that they held.*

A. Cartulary of Prémontré, fols. 89r–90r.
B. Original, BnF, Coll. Picardie 290, no. 37, previously sealed.[2]

Karta Mathei de Duri militis de conventione molendini de Offois.

[E]go Matheus de Duri, miles, filius domini Radulphi de Roia,[3] notum facio universis tam presentibus quam futuris quod Rogerus, cognomento Boutons[4] et Warnerus,[5] frater eius, molendinarii de Ouffois et eorum partionarii[6]

---

12 Perhaps the Arnulphus who was abbot of the Benedictine abbey of Saint-Nicaise de Reims, 1138–9. Cossé-Durlin, *Cartulaire de Saint-Nicaise de Reims*, 45.

13 Gérard, dean of the chapter of Saint-Quentin, is attested from 1119. BnF, MS lat. 5478, fol. 98r–98v; BnF, MS lat. 11070, fols. 102r–103v.

14 Thierry de Nesle, son of Raoul, lord of Nesle, and Raintrude, was treasurer of Noyon, ca. 1134–ca. 1157, and archdeacon of Cambrai. In 1157, he participated in the translation of the relics of St Éloi. Mazière, "Annales Noyonnaises, première partie," 55–6.

15 Hugues III de Roye, chancellor of Noyon-Tournai, ca. 1130–46, and of Noyon, 1146–63/6. Pycke, *Le chapitre cathédral Notre-Dame de Tournai de la fin du XIe à la fin du XIIIe siècle*, 64.

---

1 Offoy, cant. Ham, https://dicotopo.cths.fr/places/P14011159.

2 This charter is largely a reiteration of a charter issued in 1212 by abbot Gervais of Prémontré. See AN, L 995, no. 60.

3 Radulfi de Roya *B*.

4 Botons *B*.

5 Warinus *B*.

6 compartionarii *B*.

habebant sextum vasculum in molendino de Offois et propter hoc debebant facere magistram carpentariam molendini et contaxare materiam in nemore et scindere et excapulare et hec omnia debebant facere in conredio ecclesie Premonstratensis et partionariorum ipsius qui aliam non debebant eis inde mercedem. Coispelli autem et vetus materia molendini erant molendinariorum ipsorum. In domo autem molendini sive in ponte sive in calceata nichil ponebant molendinarii nec aliquid habebant, singulis septimanis habebant pro pane suo decem et octo boistellos in communi moltura molendini. Si tantum lucraretur et si tantum non lucraretur contenti erant eo quod lucraretur. Si quilibet molendinans adducebat bladum ad molendum, in eius erat voluntate ut aperirentur duo molendina vel unum et si duo aperta erant, molendinarii habebant de communi moltura duos boistellos pro apertura et si non apertum nisi unum, non habebant nisi unum boistellum, excepto quod si modius integer allatus esset insimul ad molendum sive ab uno molendino sive a duobus moleretur molendinarii habebant duos boistellos de communi pro apertura et quamdiu moleret de una apertura, molendinarii non habebant nisi quod uni convenit aperture. Pro molendinis aissantandis[7] debebant habere duos boistellos de communi, pellucum molendini poterant portare in domos suas sed in molendino nullum habere poterant nutrimentum, gallinam seu quodlibet animal; falcatio aque cista, ferrum, sepum, unctum et tota minuta materia tortre, cophini, vanni, boistelli, mencoldi et omnes mensure molendini providebantur de communi. Molendinarii habebant unam medietatem piscium et ponebant unam medietatem ingeniorum et ecclesia Premonstratensis cum suis partionariis aliam; molendinarii debebant hardinare cavetia molendinorum ita quod biga posset girare desuper et ecclesia et partionarii debebant ea cooperire marla. Si cavetium ruptum esset, ecclesia et partionarii debebant tradere palos et molendinarii debebant eos figere. Si aqua sclusanda esset pro reparatione molendinorum, ecclesia cum suis partionariis tradebat palos et molendinarii residuum faciebant. Molendinarii, si ecclesia vellet, ibant ad emendas molas et vivebant in eundo et redeundo in expensis ecclesie et partionariorum sine alia mercede et ponebant eas in opere sumptu suo, postquam adducte erant ab ecclesia et partionariis in plateam terre, ecclesia et partionarii dabant punctum aque per dominum Nigelle vel per eius famulum, et molendinarii debebant illum custodire et reddere dampna que eveniebant per defectum custodie. Ipsi debebant nocte et die custodire molendinum per se vel per ydoneum[8] servientem et serviens eorum debebat facere fidelitatem ecclesie et partionariis et custos qui erat in molendino ex parte ecclesie et custos qui erat in molendino faciebat fidelitatem molendinariis et tradebat eis jura sua. Bladum vero quod

7 aissattandis *B*.

8 idoneum *B*.

eos contingebat de lucro molendini, poterant molere ad disgranum, si volebant, antequam sustulissent illud de molendino sed, si sustulissent illud de molendino et reportarent ad molendinum, non molebatur eis nisi sicut extraneis venientibus aliunde. Omnem igitur jurisdictionem et omne jus et quicquid habebant vel habere poterant dicti Rogerus Boutons[9] et Warinus, frater eius, necnon et eorum conpartionarii in molendino de Offois, sive unum sive duo molendina dicantur, quitaverunt in perpetuum ecclesie Premonstrati sub annua modiatione novem modiorum frumenti talis quod recipietur de lucro molendini ipsius, reddendorum eis in perpetuum ab ecclesia predicta ad mensuram Hamensem currentem tempore huius scripti, hoc adiecto quod, siquid haberent quoquomodo in molendino predicto, quod non sit in presenti karta expressum, hoc ipsum eidem ecclesie in perpetuum quitaverunt nec ipsi aut heredes eorum in omnibus hiis que quitaverunt poterunt aliquid in posterum reclamare. Tenentur nichilominus super[10] predictis que ipsi ecclesie quitaverunt, portare eidem legitimam warandiam adversus omnes qui voluerint juristare. Ceterum cum dicti molendinarii Rogerus videlicet et Garinus et eorum conpartionarii omnia predicta de me tenerent, sub annuo censu quitationem, sicut superius facta est, ratam liberam et perpetuam esse volo pariter et concedo eo tenore quod nec ego nec heredes mei aliquomodo aliqua occasione pro aliquo defectu sive census mei quem michi debent ipsi molendinarii sive cuiuslibet alterius rei ipsum impediemus molendinum nec capiemus ferrum aut quelibet alia instrumenta que ad ipsum pertinuerint molendinum. Inmo si ipsi molendinarii sive alii qui sint homines mei de solvendo censu sive servitio meo defecerint, ego vel heredes mei non ad molendinum sed ad modiationem recurremus quam eis debet ecclesia sepedicta et ad partem etiam quam Petrus, filius domini Roberti de Sommete, in ipso habuerit molendino. Sciendum est preterea quod cum Ermengardis ac[11] Petrus et[12] Symon, filii eius, de Offois[13] partem illam quam habebant cum molendinariis sepedictis in molendino sepius nominato ecclesie predicte nomine elemosine contulissent, ego elemosinam ipsam amicabiliter approbavi concedens ut in perpetuum libere possideatur ab ecclesia sepedicta. Ut igitur premissa omnia futuris temporibus permaneant inconcussa presentem kartam sigilli mei munimine roboravi. Actum mense aprili, anno incarnationis dominice M° CC°[14] vicesimo quarto.

9 Botons *B.*
10 *Om.* omnibus *A.*
11 et *B.*
12 ac *B.*
13 Oiffois *B.*
14 millesimo ducentesimo *B.*

364

July 4, 1231.

Magister *Hugues,*[1] *canon and* officialis *of Noyon, confirms an agreement between Conrad, abbot of Prémontré, and the clerics and brothers Guy*[2] *and Nicholas* Tyson. *The two brothers cede to Prémontré all their rights over the territories of Offoy,*[3] *Canny,*[4] *and Voyennes*[5] *for an annual census of three* modii *of grain (*bladus*) and a half* modius *of peas, measure of Noyon. Guy and Nicholas's other brother, Louet, consents to this agreement as fief lord.*

A. Cartulary of Prémontré, fol. 90r.
B. Original, BnF, Coll. Picardie 290, no. 42, previously sealed.

Karta canonici Noviomensis et officialis de confirmatione et testimonio elemosine de Offois de Escamli de Wiane.

[U]niversis presentes litteras inspecturis, magister Hugo, canonicus et officialis Noviomensis, salutem in Domino. Noveritis nos litteras virorum venerabilium et religiosorum abbatis et conventus Premonstratensis inspexisse in hec verba. In nomine Patris et Filii et Spiritus Sancti.[6] Ego Conradus, Dei patientia dictus abbas et conventus Premonstratensis, notum facimus universis tam presentibus quam futuris quod Guido et Nicholaus, clerici, fratres, dicti Tyson,[7] contulerunt et concesserunt nobis in perpetuum, libere et pacifice possidendum quicquid juris, dominii, census, possessionis et redditus et quocumque alio titulo in territoriis de Offois, de Escamli[8] et de Voiane[9]

1 *Magister* Hugues, canon and *officialis* of Noyon, ca. 1229–ca. 1236. AD Aisne, H 455, fol. 310v; AD Oise, G 1984, fols. 238v–239r.
2 Guy Tyson, cleric, also appears in a 1233 act in the cartulary of the cathedral chapter of Noyon. AD Oise, G 1984, fols. 205r–205v.
3 Offoy, cant. Ham, https://dicotopo.cths.fr/places/P14011159.
4 Pycke and Vleeschouwers identify *Escamli* as Essenlis (comm. Chavonne, https://dicotopo.cths.fr/places/P65971619). Pycke and Vleeschouwers, *Actes*, 486. However, we concur with Dietrich Lohrmann that *Escamli* is Canny-lès-Voyennes (cant. Nesle, https://dicotopo.cths.fr/places/P44415541). Lohrmann, "Barrages et moulins sur la Somme au temps des chanoines réguliers (XIIe–XIIIe siècles)," 341, 345.
5 Voyennes, cant. Nesle, https://dicotopo.cths.fr/places/P32215646.
6 *Om.* amen *A*.
7 Tison *B*.
8 Eskanli *B*.
9 Voienne *B*.

habebant sub annuo censu trium modiorum bladi dictorum territoriorum et dimidii modii pisorum ad mensuram Noviomensem currentem tempore huius scriptis, eisdem Guidoni et Nicholao et eorum heredibus annuatim infra festum Omnium Sanctorum apud Noviomum ad quamcumque domum voluerint a nobis integre solvendorum tali modo quod dictus Nicholaus clericus cognomine Tysons, frater eiusdem Guidonis, de dicto blado debet habere, unum modium annuatim quem modum acquisivit cum tribus obolis annuis de censu ab heredibus Guidonis[10] de Canduerre,[11] sicut idem Nicholaus asseruit coram nobis, ita quod idem Nicholaus dictum modium bladi, cuicumque voluerit, poterit assignare tam in vita sua quam post decessum suum non tamen ducendum a nobis extra Noviomum. Et si forsitan, aliquo anno, territoria predicta non sufficerent ad dictum modiagium persolvendum, nos tenemur eisdem reddere dictum modiagium de blado mediocri vel meliori. Et si nos forsitan deficeremus de dicto modiagio statuto termino persolvendo, ipsi possunt capere super dicta territoria sine aliquo forisfacto et retinere ~~eas~~ res nostras, donec eis de dicto modiagio plenarie fuerit satisfactum, ita etiam quod non possunt a nobis propter hoc aliquam emendam exigere vel clamare. Fidem etiam dicti fratres prestiterunt corporaliter quod nos super predictis per se vel per alios nullatenus molestabunt nec artem vel ingenium querent per que valeamus molestari, inmo nobis legitimam ferent garandiam secundum usus et consuetudines patrie adversus omnes qui juri et legi parere voluerint, renuntiantes omni juris auxilio canonici et civilis et etiam consuetudinarii et etiam omnibus exceptionibus, si que forsitan possent produci contra possessionem nostram omnium predictorum et etiam exceptioni de deceptione ultra medietatem justi precii. Et hec omnia facta sunt de assensu et bona voluntate Loueti, fratris eorumdem, de quo dictus Guido clericus tenebat in feodum dictos duos modios bladi et dimidium modium pisorum supradictos[12] anno gratie M° CC° tricesimo primo mense julio quarto nonarum eiusdem. Nos igitur ad petitionem partium contractum factum, sicut in eorumdem abbatis et conventus Premonstratensis litteris presentibus continetur auctoritate ordinaria confirmamus. Et in perpetuam memoriam confirmationis ipsius presentem cartam fecimus sigillo Noviomensis curie sigillari. Actum anno Domini M° CC° tricesimo primo, mense julio quarto nonarum eiusdem.

10 *Om.* domini *A*.

11 Candor, cant. Lassigny, https://dicotopo.cths.fr/places/P48793595.

12 *Om.* actum *A*.

365

1178

Hugues [II],[1] abbot of Prémontré, makes known that with the consent of his sister Ada, Manessès, son of Robert d'Offoy, gave to Prémontré the mill of Offoy[2] with its fishing rights, half of the causeway, and nine denarii obolorum *to be collected each year from the garden at the* grangia *of Offoy. Manessès also confirmed as fief lord a certain Lambert's gift to the Premonstratensian church at Bonneuil,[3] namely what Lambert held in fief near Golancourt,[4] in exchange for an annual payment of 15* modii *of grain (*frumentum*). Should Lambert be unable to fulfil his duties of* servitium *to Manessès, Manessès can claim part of the 15* modii *as recompense.*

A. Cartulary of Prémontré, fol. 90r.

B[1]. Original (chirograph), AN, L 995, no. 38, previously sealed with a double strip of leather. In the left margin and beginning at the top, the top half of the letters that form the word CHYROGRAPHUM. (This charter belonged to Prémontré, based on dorsal annotations.)

B[2]. Original (chirograph), AN, L 995, no. 39, previously sealed with a double strip of leather. In the right margin and beginning at the top, the lower half of the letters that form the word CHYROGRAPHUM. (This charter likely belonged to Manessès d'Offoy.)

Karta abbatis Premonstratensis de elemosina de Oufois et de medietate calceate.

[E]go H[ugo], Dei gratia Premonstrati abbas et capitulum nostrum notum fieri volumus tam futuris quam presentibus quod Manasses, filius Roberti de Olfois,[5] contulit ecclesie nostre in elemosinam perpetuo, concedente Ada, sorore sua, molendinum de Holfois cum piscatione que sui juris erat et medietatem calceate et IX denarios obolorum quos accipiebat singulis annis de horto ubi grangia nostra nunc sita est. Et concessit nobis hoc quod Lambertus ecclesie nostre Bonolii contulerat juxta Gollencourt[6] quod de feodo ipsius erat, pro quibus omnibus singulis annis debemus solvere ipsi et heredibus suis XV modios frumenti ad mensuram Hami, tempore huius concessionis currentem, que sine diminutione vel augmentatione ab utraque parte servabitur. Tale autem

1 Hugues II de Douai, abbot of the Premonstratensian abbey of Cuissy, 1161–5, and abbot of Prémontré, 1174–89. *MP* II, 497.

2 Offoy, cant. Ham, https://dicotopo.cths.fr/places/P14011159.

3 The Premonstratensian *curtis* of Bonneuil. *MP* II, 484.

4 Golancourt, cant. Guiscard, https://dicotopo.cths.fr/places/P75999303.

5 Holfois *B*[1], *B*[2].

6 Gollencurt *B*[1], *B*[2].

frumentum solvetur quale in molendino provenerit et si ibi non suffecerit in grangia nostra de Holfois supplebitur. Solvetur autem frumentum istud hiis[7] terminis V[que] modii in festo Sancti Remigii, V[que] in Natali Domini, V[que] in Pascha, quos propria sua vectura ex tunc deducet quo voluerit et si illud vel aliud frumentum in predicto molendino molere voluerit, molturam persolvet sicut et alii. Si vero Lambertus servitium quod debet Manasse, non impleverit, Manasses pro forisfacto accipiet duos modios frumenti quos ecclesia de Bonolio solvere solet Lamberto. Siquis autem de hiis que predicta sunt, ecclesiam inquietare voluerit, prefatus Manasses legitimam garandiam[8] se ferre promisit. Huic donationi et conventioni interfuerunt et testes sunt: Rogerus de Hunbleus,[9] Willelmus[10] de Vilete, Walterus de Bruci[11] et Symon frater eius, Johannes de Espeville,[12] Teobaldus de Pin,[13] Eustachius[14] prior, Johannes filius Alardi, Godebertus, Walcherus, Gaufridus canonici, Petrus, Evrardus[15] conversi. Actum anno incarnationis dominice M° C° septuagesimo octavo.[16]

366

1188–9[1]

Étienne [I],[2] bishop of Noyon, makes known that husband and wife Geoffroi, knight of Tumbis, *and Béatrice, and their children Pierre, Jean, Robert, Simon, Gerard, and Marie, ceded to Prémontré seven* modii *of grain* (frumentum) *from the tithe of Offoy,[3] part of Béatrice's inheritance, in return for 42* librae Attrebatensium. *The gift was assented to by the fief lord, Eudes de Vieuville.[4]*

7 his *B*[1].
8 guarandiam *B*[1], *B*[2].
9 Hombleux, cant. Nesle, https://dicotopo.cths.fr/places/P11898990.
10 A Guillaume de Villette also appears as a witness in **405**.
11 Brouchy, cant. Ham, https://dicotopo.cths.fr/places/P33557845.
12 Eppeville, cant. Ham, https://dicotopo.cths.fr/places/P94171781.
13 Le Pin, cant. Nesle, https://dicotopo.cths.fr/places/P67675587.
14 Eustacius *B*[1], *B*[2].
15 Everardus *B*[1], *B*[2].
16 *Add.* octavo *A* (*in a later hand*); LXX VIII *B*[1], *B*[2].

1 The cartulary dates this to 1180, but Étienne only becomes bishop in 1188, suggesting that the cartulary date is a scribal error, with the final *octo* (for 1188) or *nono* (for 1189) accidentally omitted.
2 Étienne de Villebéon (or de Nemours), son of Gautier de Villebéon, lord of La Chapelle-Gauthier and Nemours, and Aveline, was bishop of Noyon, 1188–1221.
3 Offoy, cant. Ham, https://dicotopo.cths.fr/places/P14011159.
4 Perhaps La Viéville, comm. Porquéricourt, https://dicotopo.cths.fr/places/P01985742.

A. Cartulary of Prémontré, fols. 90r–90v.
B. Original not found.

Karta Stephani Noviomensis de elemosina septem modiorum Beatricis quos contulit ecclesie Premonstrate.

[Q]uia ex varietate rerum et temporum plerumque subrepit oblivio preteritorum, ego Stephanus, Dei gratia Noviomensis episcopus, notum facio tam futuris quam presentibus quod Gaufridus, miles de Tumbis, et uxor eius, Beatrix, simul etiam eorum liberi, videlicet Petrus, Johannes, Robertus, Symon, Gerardus et Maria contulerunt in elemosinam, sicut in nostra et subscripturarum personarum presentia recognitum est et concessum, septem modios frumenti ecclesie Premonstratensis qui ad hereditatem predicte Beatricis pertinebant et quos fratres Premonstratenses de decima de Ulfoiz per annos singulos exsolvebant. Hec autem elemosina de consensu Odonis de Veteri Villa, ad cuius feodum frumentum illud spectabat, facta fuit et tam ipso Odone quam Gaufrido et Beatrice et eorum liberis qui suprascripti sunt eandem elemosinam et quicquid in ea habebant in manum nostram resignantibus et ex toto werpientibus, nos ipsam memorate Premonstratensis ecclesie jure perpetuo possidendam reddidimus. Sciendum vero quod ex istius beneficii gratia ipsius concessores quadraginta et duas libras Attrebatensium de Premonstratensis ecclesia caritatis intuitu habuerunt et tam Odo, dominus feodi, quam Gaufridus et Beatrix fidem dederunt quod nullo deinceps tempore super iam dicta elemosina Premonstratensis ecclesie nec per se nec per alios calumpniam inferent vel inferri permittent. Ut igitur huius donationis concessio ex nostrarum litterarum testimonio perpetue stabilitatis robur optineat, presenti pagine sigillum nostrum apponi et testes qui huic concessioni interfuerunt fecimus annotari. S. Hugonis, decani. S. Hugonis, archidiaconi Noviomensis ecclesie. S. Renoldi,[5] Sancti Eligii. S. Guidonis,[6] Ursicampi. S. Johannis,[7] Sancti Bartholomei. S. Johannis,[8] Sancte Marie Hami. S. Willermi,[9] Sancte Marie Viromandensis. S. Gerardi,[10] Sancti Prejecti abbatum. Actum anno incarnationis dominice M° CC° octogesimo.

5 Renaud I, abbot of the Benedictine abbey of Saint-Éloi de Noyon from ca. 1179.
6 Guy, abbot of the Cistercian abbey of Ourscamps, 1170–95, and abbot of Clairvaux, 1193–6.
7 Jean I, abbot of the Augustinian abbey of Saint-Barthélemy de Noyon, ca. 1187–ca. 1200. *GC* IX, cols. 1116–17.
8 Jean I, abbot of the Augustinian abbey of Notre-Dame de Ham, ca. 1185–ca. 1200. *GC* IX, col. 1122.
9 Likely Guillaume, abbot of the Premonstratensian abbey of Vermand, ca. 1190. *MP* II, 427.
10 Gérard, abbot of the Benedictine abbey of Saint-Prix de Saint-Quentin, 1180s.

367

June 27, 1233.

Hugues,[1] *canon and* officialis *of Noyon, makes known that Simon* li Caz *d'Offoy*[2] *sold to Prémontré two* modii *of grain (*bladus*), measure of Ham, that Prémontré had owed him annually during his lifetime.*

A. Cartulary of Prémontré, fol. 90v.

B. Original, AN, L 995, no. 81, previously sealed on a double strip of parchment.

Karta officialis Noviomensis de venditione Symonis le Cat de Offois super duobus modiis bladi.

Omnibus[3] hec visuris magister Hugo, canonicus et officialis Noviomensis, salutem in domino. Vobis notum facimus quod Symon li Caz de Offois, in nostra presentia constitutus, recognovit se vendidisse ecclesie Premonstratensis duos modios bladi ad mensuram Hamensem in quibus eadem ecclesia ei tenebatur annuatim ad festum Beati Remigii, dum viveret idem Symon, et fide data in manu nostra creantavit quod dictam ecclesiam super dicto blado decetero non molestabit nec gravabit nec artem nec ingenium per se vel per alium queret per que dicta ecclesia possit vel debeat super eodem vendagio in posterum[4] molestari vel gravari. Renunciavit etiam coram nobis spontaneus et non coactus et predicta fidei datione omni privilegio quod habebat contra dictam ecclesiam de habendo bladum predictum ad vitam suam quocumque modo illud habebat vel habere debebat.[5] In cuius rei testimonium presentes litteras ad petitionem dicti Symonis sigillo curie Noviomensis fecimus communiri. Actum anno Domini M° CC° tricesimo tertio, feria secunda post nativitatem Beati Johannis Baptiste.

368

January, 1231.

Magister *H[ugues],*[1] *canon and* officialis *of Noyon, makes known that Simon* li Caz *d'Offoy*[2] *sold to Prémontré 15* solidi Parisiensium *of annual* census, *four* sextariae *of grain (*frumentum*), and two* sextariae *of peas, measure of Ham.*

1 *Magister* Hugues, canon and *officialis* of Noyon, ca. 1229–ca. 1236. AD Aisne, H 455, fol. 310v; AD Oise, G 1984, fols. 238v–239r.

2 Offoy, cant. Ham, https://dicotopo.cths.fr/places/P14011159.

3 The initial letter has been added at a later, post-medieval date.

4 imposterum *B*.

5 Here the original charter has "et eidem penitus resignavit," struck through.

1 *Magister* Hugues, canon and *officialis* of Noyon, ca. 1229–ca. 1236. AD Aisne, H 455, fol. 310v; AD Oise, G 1984, fols. 238v–239r.

2 Offoy, cant. Ham, https://dicotopo.cths.fr/places/P14011159.

A. Cartulary of Prémontré, fol. 90v.
B. Original, BnF, Coll. Picardie 290, no. 43, previously sealed.

Item karta eidem officialis de venditione Simonis le Cat ecclesie Premonstrate super quatuor sextarios frumenti et duobus pisorum.

Omnibus[3] hec visuris magister H[ugo], canonicus et officialis Noviomensis, salutem in domino. Notum vobis facimus quod Symon li Caz[4] de Ouffois, constitutus coram nobis, recognovit se vendidisse ecclesie Premonstratensis bene et legitime quindecim solidos Parisiensium de annuo censu, quatuor sextarios frumenti et duos sextarios pisorum ad mensuram Hamensem. Que omnia dicta ecclesia eidem Symoni,[5] quamdiu viveret, singulis annis in festo Sancti Remigii solvere tenebatur. Promisit etiam idem Symon,[6] fide et sacramento corporaliter prestitis, quod dictam ecclesiam Premonstratensem super dicta venditione coram ecclesiastico vel seculari judice decetero per se vel per alium non trahet in causam nec trahi procurabit. In cuius rei testimonium presentes litteras sigillo curie Noviomensis ad petitionem et instanciam dicti Symonis[7] fecimus roborari. Actum anno Domini M° CC° tricesimo I°,[8] mense januarii.[9]

369

1155

*Hugues [I],[1] abbot of Prémontré, and Renaud [I],[2] abbot of Notre-Dame de Ham, make known that their abbeys reached an agreement concerning the possession of certain revenues held at Eppeville,[3] Golancourt,[4] Lanchy,[5] Flamicourt,[6] and Bonneuil.[7] Baudouin [II],[8] bishop of Noyon, assents to this. (See **370**.)*

3 The initial letter has been added at a later, post-medieval date.
4 Simon li Cas *B*.
5 Simoni *B*.
6 Simon *B*.
7 Simonis *B*.
8 primo *B*.
9 januario *B*.

1 Hugues I de Fosses (ca. 1093–1164), first abbot of Prémontré.
2 Renaud I, abbot of the Augustinian abbey of Notre-Dame de Ham, 1143–bef. 1160. *GC* IX, col. 1122.
3 Eppeville, cant. Ham, https://dicotopo.cths.fr/places/P94171781.
4 Golancourt, cant. Guiscard, https://dicotopo.cths.fr/places/P75999303.
5 Lanchy, cant. Vermand, https://dicotopo.cths.fr/places/P51978975.
6 Flamicourt-lès-Ham, cant. Ham, https://dicotopo.cths.fr/places/P00189975.
7 Bonneuil, cant. Ham, https://dicotopo.cths.fr/places/P66750585.
8 Baudouin II de Boulogne, abbot of the Augustinian abbey of Saint-Eloi-Fontaine, ca. 1130–ca. 1139, and bishop of Noyon, 1148–67. *GC* IX, col. 1126.

A. Cartulary of Prémontré, fols. 90v–91r.

B. Original (chirograph), AD Oise, H 5993, previously sealed with two seals. In the right margin, and beginning at the top, is the bottom half of the word CYROGRAPHUM in red ink.

Karta abbatis Premonstratensis et capituli ~~de concessione~~ et abbatis Hamensis et capituli super duobus modiis frumenti in molendinis de Espevilla nobis concessis.

[I]n nomine Patris et Filii et Spiritus Sancti.[9] Ego Hugo Premonstratensis ecclesie abbas totumque capitulum nostrum, ego etiam Renaldus,[10] Hamensis ecclesie abbas, simulque capitulum nostrum, omnibus tam futuris quam presentibus in perpetuum. Quia servi Dei que Dei sunt, maxime concordiam fratrum et amorem proximorum, debent querere, pactum quod pro bono pacis inter nos ad invicem statutum est huic cartule studuimus inserere ut siquis deinceps inter nos presumpserit violare caritatem, ad vinculum pacis reducatur per memoratam scripti veritatem. Rainaldus itaque, Hamensis ecclesie abbas, totumque capitulum suum Premonstratensi ecclesie in perpetuum concessit duos modios frumenti quos in molendinis de Expetivilla habebat et dimidium quem in terra eorum de Lanci possidebat. Partes quoque alodiorum de Gollencourt[11] quas ibi habebat, eis concessit, quas videlicet[12] distinguendo ita divisit: medietas decime totius territorii de Bonolio, exceptis hortis et dotalicio altaris et terragia terre quam excolit Laherus in unum collecta in quinque partibus dividebantur ex quibus duas portiones Hamensis ecclesia libere possidebat et in tercia duas partes in quarta etiam quartam partem habebat. Quatuor etiam sextarios frumenti quos de eisdem alodiis Hamensi ecclesie singulariter singulis annis. Idem Laherus persolvebat et hominium ipsius Laheri et quicquid aliud possessionis sive juris in eisdem alodiis habebat Premonstratensi ecclesie concessit terram etiam Walteri pueri quam sub statuto censu ab eis Guiardus Rufus tenet et partem prati quod est juxta bullonem Bonolii. Siquis autem super his Premonstrate ecclesie calumpniam moverit, Hamensis ecclesia secundum jus ecclesiasticam disrationabit. Pro his vero omnibus predictus abbas Hugo suique successores persolveret annuatim in perpetuum Hamensi ecclesie in festo Sancti Remigii octo[13] modios frumenti et duos[14] et dimidium avene ex agricultura sua Bonolii ad mensuram que tunc erat Hami et propriis expensis ad horreum suum Hami perducent. Hortulum etiam quem apud Framercort[15]

9 *Om.* amen *A.*

10 Rainaldus *B.*

11 Gollencurt *B.*

12 *Om.* partes *A.*

13 VIII^{to} *B.*

14 II^{os} *B.*

15 Framecurt *B.*

habebant, eidem ecclesie liberum concesserunt. Statutum est etiam ut quod laici tenentes per manum episcopi utrique contulerunt ecclesie, utraque ecclesia teneat in pace. Ex concessione autem utriusque ecclesie definitum est ut nulla inter eos subito oriatur controversia sed et si nata fuerit fratrum Bonolii sive canonicorum Hami sive abbatum Premonstratensis et Hamensis sive capitulorum pacificabitur caritate et benivolentia nec maiorum ab alterutra requiretur audientia donec in alterutra fraterna deficiat justicia sed et si clamor inter predictas ecclesias ad episcopum factus fuerit, una queque[16] ecclesia hoc quod ante clamorem tenuit, donec ei abjudicetur, quiete possidebit quod ergo in hoc scripto continetur nos ambo personarum nostrarum testimonio, cyrographo quoque et sigillis ecclesiarum nostrarum alternatim confirmavimus sed et auctoritate et sigillo venerabilis Balduini Noviomensis episcopi corroboravimus. Signum Rainaldi abbatis. S. Radulfi prioris. S. Gerardi, Odonis, diaconorum, et ceteri.[17] Ego autem Balduinus, Dei gratia Noviomensis episcopus, nobisque assistentes hanc concordiam unitatis et vinculum pacis audientes laudavimus et auctoritate nostra et sigillo insignivimus. Actum anno incarnati verbi M° C° LV°,[18] indictione III[a].[19]

370

1146

*Hugues [I],[1] abbot of Prémontré, and Renaud [I],[2] abbot of Ham, make known that their abbeys reached an agreement. The scribe refers the reader to the previous page. (See **369**.)*

A. Cartulary of Prémontré, fol. 91r.

B. Original not found.

Karta ista in precedenti pagina habetur verbo ad verbum et ideo non scripsi illam et habemus duas kartas super his confectas.

[I]n nomine sancte et cetera. Ego Hugo ecclesie Premonstratensis abbas totumque capitulum nostrum, ego etiam Rainaldus Hamensis ecclesia abbas, simulque capitulum nostram omnibus tam presentibus quam futuris in perpetuum. Totum ut supra antea.

16 una queque *B*.

17 *Add.* diaconorum, et ceteri *A*; David, diaconorum. Helye, Drogonis presbiterorum. S. Raineri, Rabbodi, Johannis, Roberti diaconorum. S. Johannis, Mathei, Evurardi subdiaconorum *B*.

18 millesimo centestimo quinquagesimo V° *B*.

19 tertia *B*.

1 Hugues I de Fosses (ca. 1093–1164), first abbot of Prémontré.

2 Renaud I, abbot of the Augustinian abbey of Notre-Dame de Ham, 1143–bef. 1160. *GC* IX, col. 1122.

371

Athies. 1146.

Simon [I],[1] bishop of Noyon, makes known that Raoul [I],[2] count of Vermandois, and Yves [II],[3] count of Soissons and lord of Nesle, restored the peace between the church of Prémontré and Gérard,[4] lord of Ham, after disputes concerning the possession of the mills of Hamel.[5]

A. Cartulary of Prémontré, fols. 91r–91v.
B. Original, AD Somme, 20 H 9, no. 3, sealed.[6]
EDITION: Pycke and Vleeschouwers, *Actes*, 499–501.

Karta episcopi Noviomensis de concordia facta inter ecclesiam Premonstratem et dominum de Ham super molendinum de Hamiaus.

[I]n nomine sancte et individue Trinitatis. Ego Symon, Dei gratia Noviomensis episcopus, notum fieri volo tam futuris quam presentibus quod Radulfus, comes Viromandensis et Yvo, comes Suessionensis et Nigelle dominus, fecerunt concordiam de quadam querela que erat inter Premonstratensem ecclesiam et Gerardum dominum de Ham. Querela siquidem hec erat: Odo, pater prenominati Gerardi, contradicebat fratribus Bonolii, qui sunt de Premonstrata ecclesia, molendina de Hamels que juste acceperant a Johanne de Cremeri,[7] sive de Pin, cuius erant hereditario jure, sed ipse Odo infra contradictionem mortuus est. Successit vero predictus Gerardus filius eius et eandem contradictionem quam pater eius fecerat, iterans affligebat ecclesiam, plurima dampna inferens ita ut nullatenus posset sustinere dampnosam eius inportunitatem. Venientes igitur ecclesie fratres ad prefatum comitem Yvonem, precabuntur ut propter Deum pacem quereret eis de tanta inquietatione et dampno quod Gerardus inferebat eis, sperantes quod hoc facere posset eo quod esset ei junctus in amicicia ex matrimonio matris sue quam ei conjunxerat. Ipse vero pacem Yvo componere studens, persuasit fratribus molendina Gerardi censualiter accipere ut sic illa querela et alia de molendinis de Espevile[8] que

1 Simon I de Vermandois (d. 1148) was the son of Hugues I and Adélaïde, count and countess of Vermandois and Valois, and bishop of Noyon, 1123–42.
2 Raoul I, count of Vermandois, Amiens, and Valois (d. 1152), was the son of Hugues I le Grand, count of Vermandois and Valois, and Adélaïde de Vermandois, and served as seneschal of France, 1131–51.
3 Yves II de Nesle (d. ca. 1178), lord of Nesle and count of Soissons, son of Raoul, lord of Nesle, and Raintrude. Newman, *Seigneurs*, vol. 1, 61.
4 Gérard, lord of Ham by 1144, son of Eudes II, lord of Ham. Newman, *Homblières*, 115–16.
5 Hamel-lès-Corbie, cant. Corbie, https://dicotopo.cths.fr/places/P37197765.
6 Due to conservation concerns, the original was not available to the editors.
7 Crémery, cant. Roye, https://dicotopo.cths.fr/places/P44909124.
8 Eppeville, cant. Ham, https://dicotopo.cths.fr/places/P94171781.

occasione illa orta fuerat, in pace sopiretur. Sed et ab ecclesia X libras accepit Gerardus et consiliarii eius XL solidos ea conditione ut quicquid in dominio suo habebat ecclesia, in pace conservaret et, si alius inpugnaret, pro posse suo justiciam faceret et, ut hoc firmiter teneretur, ipse Gerardus fidem suam dedit et prefatus Yvo, sicut fidejussor, in manu accepit. Parvo itaque intervallo facto Gerardus, rursus malis consiliis usus, pactum rupit, silvas que juris fratrum erant, eis prohibuit, jumentum unum eis abstulit, molituram que ad molendinum suum venire debebat, vendidit, sclusam molendini ecclesie rupit et, requisitus tertio corrigere, noluit. Fratres igitur, cum tantam injuriam pati non possent, accedentes rogaverunt prefatum Yvonem ut illud corrigeret, sicut in manu acceperat. Sed cum Gerardus compositionem factam tenere nollet, ipse Yvo de fidejussoria se exposuit et fratres, eius consilio, Gerardo molendina sua reddiderunt. Ob quam causam multa mala intulit eis et abstulit de bonis ecclesie XV modios frumenti et duos avene et molendina sua non permisit molere per IIII[or] menses. Unde cum iterum querimoniam faceret abbas prefatis comitibus Radulfo et Yvoni, cum gravis esset inter abbatem et Gerardum contentio, vix obtinuerunt ut in eorum compositione se ponerent. Hec igitur fuit compositio. Gerardus de dampnis ecclesie illatis ex preceptorum prefatorum comitum veniam petiit, et abbas, eorum consilio, dampnum quod intulerat et peccatum quantum in se erat, remisit et, si alter eorum alteri aliquid addere deberet, in ipsorum comitum dispositione remansit, excepto quod molendina Gerardi ecclesia censualiter amplius non acciperet. Sed pro diuturne pacis reformatione viginti libras obolorum ecclesia Gerardo dedit et fidejussores fuerunt sepefati comites quod de omnibus his querelis Gerardus ecclesiam ulterius non inquietaret. Factum est hoc Athies in palatio, multis astantibus et testimonium perhibentibus ex quibus quorumdam nomina subscripsimus: Robertus[9] cancellarius comitis Radulfi, Burchardus de Guisia,[10] Albricus de Roia,[11] Rogerus castellanus de Perona,[12] Petrus castellanus de Roia,[13] Ingelrannus Oisuns,

9 Robert, chancellor of Raoul, count of Vermandois, also appears in an 1146 charter of the cartulary of Notre-Dame d'Homblières. BnF, MS lat. 13911, fols. 46r–46v.

10 Bouchard, lord of Guise (d. aft. 1161), son of Guy, lord of Guise, and Adèle "Machania"; husband of Adèle de Soupir.

11 Aubry, lord of Roye and Becquigny, was the *dapifer* of Raoul, count of Vermandois in the 1130s/40s. He was the husband of one Mathilde, and brother of Wermond, lord of Cessoy. Tock and Milis, *Monumenta Arroasiensia*, 242–3; Guyotjeannin, *Episcopus*, 220; Newman, *Seigneurs*, vol. 2, 299; Newman, *Homblières*, 110. He is likely the same Aubry de Roye who appears in **300**, **398**, **442**, and **464**.

12 Roger, castellan of Péronne (d. bef. 1158); brother of Hugues I, abbot of the Benedictine abbey of Mont-Saint-Quentin. *GC* IX, col. 1105.

13 Pierre, castellan of Roye, also appears in **372**. A Pierre, castellan of Roye, son of Guerry, castellan of Roye and Aude, appears in an act of 1102 in the cartulary of Ourscamp, and in an 1103 act of Adèle, countess of Vermandois. Peigné-Delacourt, *Cartulaire de l'Abbaye de Notre-Dame d'Ourscamp de l'ordre de Cîteaux, fondée en 1129 au diocèse de Noyon*, 148; Pycke and Vleeschouwers, *Actes*, 176.

Johannes[14] filius Roberti Rufi, Matheus patruus eius, Wermundus frater Alberici de Roia, Rogo de Faiel,[15] Petrus Cramals. Quod ut ratum permaneat, sigilli nostri ac prefatorum comitum attestatione roboravimus et siquis infringere presumpserit, anathematis eum vinculo innodamus. Actum anno incarnati verbi M° C° XL° VI°, epacta VI°, indictione IX^a, concurrente primo.

372

1140

Simon [I],[1] bishop of Noyon, makes known and approves as fief lord that Jean, knight of Crémery,[2] gave Prémontré certain mills at Hamel.[3] Jean's relative Pérégrin de Roye[4] also concedes, with the approval of his son Thomas and the assent of their lord, the knight Pierre de Roye.[5] The brother millers Raoul and Renier also relinquished their rights over these mills.

A. Cartulary of Prémontré, fol. 91v.

B. Original, AD Somme, 20 H 9, no. 1, sealed with brownish red wax on a double strip of parchment.

EDITION: Pycke and Vleeschouwers, *Actes*, 445–6.

Karta Noviomensis episcopi de elemosina Johannis militis de Cremeri de molendinis de Hamiaus.

[I]n nomine sancte en̶t individue et cetera.[6] Quicquid legitimarum testimonio personarum perhibetur, licet satis firmitatis habere videatur tamen quasi quodam

---

14 Jean d'Athies, son of *Robert Rufus*, nephew of Mathieu and Bernier, and brother of Widèle and Adam. With his wife Eustacie, he was the father of Manassès, Robert, Aubry, and Eudes the cleric. With his brother Adam, knight and lord of Athies (cant. Ham, https://dicotopo.cths.fr/places/P98820850), he is attested in a number of acts ca. 1150–ca. 1188. Cagny, *Histoire de l'arrondissement de Péronne*, vol. 2, 259; Tock and Milis, *Monumenta Arroasiensia*, 251. He is also mentioned in **306**, **353**, **398**, **421**, **424**, and **442**.

15 Rorigon I, lord of Fayet, son of Aude, lady of Fayet. Newman, *Seigneurs*, vol. 2, 102.

---

1 Simon I de Vermandois (d. 1148) was the son of Hugues I and Adélaïde, count and countess of Vermandois and Valois, and bishop of Noyon 1123–42.

2 Crémery, cant. Roye, https://dicotopo.cths.fr/places/P44909124.

3 Hamel-lès-Corbie, cant. Corbie, https://dicotopo.cths.fr/places/P37197765.

4 Roye, https://dicotopo.cths.fr/places/P52439933.

5 Pierre, castellan of Roye, also appears in **371**. A Pierre, castellan of Roye, son of Guerry, castellan of Roye and Aude, appears in an act of 1102 in the cartulary of Ourscamp, and in an 1103 act of Adèle, countess of Vermandois. Peigné-Delacourt, *Cartulaire de l'Abbaye de Notre-Dame d'Ourscamp de l'ordre de Cîteaux, fondée en 1129 au diocèse de Noyon*, 148; Pycke and Vleeschouwers, *Actes*, 176.

6 *Add.* et cetera *A*; Trinitatis *B*.

vallo munitur id quod episcopalis auctoritatis assertione confirmatur. Idcirco ego Symon, Dei gratia Noviomensis episcopus, notum fore volo tam posteris quam modernis quod Johannes, miles de Cremeri, ob remedium anime sue et predecessorum suorum, contulit Premonstrate ecclesie quedam molendina que dicuntur de Hameals, que quidem hereditario jure possederat. Fecit autem hoc donum per manum nostram de cuius feodo predicta molendina descendebant. Peregrinus quoque de Roia, cognatus eius, assensu domini sui, Petri de Roia castellani, quicquid in prefatis molendinis habebat, concessit, annuente filio suo Thomas;[7] similiter Radulfus et Rainerus, frater eius, molendinarii, quicquid juris in predictis molendinis habebant, ob remedium animarum suarum prenominate ecclesie contulerunt. Hii sunt testes tam de concessione Johannis quam molendinariorum: Robertus Venator,[8] Radulfus Brumans,[9,10] Willelmus de Pleissei,[11] Arnulphus[12] Vasles,[13,14] Gregorius de Ham. Hii vero sunt testes quod episcopus concesserit: Hugo,[15] cancellarius, Radulphus,[16,17] frater domini Yvonis de Nigella,[18] Johannes de Marceals,[19] Johannes de Aissei.[20] Hoc autem donum quisquis temeraria presumptione violare vel inmutare presumpserit, anathema sit. Actum est hoc anno incarnationis dominice M° C° XL°, epacta XXX[a],[21] indictione III[a],[22] concurrente primo. Hii autem sunt testes quod

---

7 Thoma *B*.

8 Robert Venator de Ham also appears as a witness in **388** and in an 1145 act of Gerard, lord of Ham, and was the *maior communiae* of Ham in the same year. La Fons, *Une cité picarde au Moyen-Age, ou Noyon et la noyonnais aux XIVe et XVe siècles*, 251; Newman, *Homblières*, 116.

9 Brusmauns *B*.

10 Raoul Brumans, knight of Péronne, appears in acts concerning the abbey of Arrouaise, 1150s–70s. Tock and Milis, *Monumenta Arroasiensia*, 124, 281.

11 Possibly the same Guillaume de Plessis as in **316**, **342**, and **401**.

12 Arnulfus *B*.

13 Vaslet *B*.

14 Arnoul Vallet appears as a witness in an 1145 act of Gerard of Ham. Tock and Milis, *Monumenta Arroasiensia*, 108.

15 Hugues III de Roye, chancellor of Noyon-Tournai, ca. 1130–46, and of Noyon, 1146–63/6. Pycke, *Le chapitre cathédral Notre-Dame de Tournai de la fin du XIe à la fin du XIIIe siècle*, 64.

16 Radulfus *B*.

17 Raoul de Nesle, castellan of Nesle and of Bruges (d. ca. 1160), son of Raoul, lord of Nesle, and Raintrude. Newman, *Seigneurs*, vol. 1, 62–3.

18 Ivonis *B*.

19 Marcels *B*.

20 Possibly the Jean *de Asseio* discussed by Guyotjeannin, *Episcopus*, 191.

21 XXX *B*.

22 III *B*.

Peregrinus concesserit: Drogo de Nigella,[23] Radulphus[24] Bellus,[25] Rogerus justiciarius,[26] Odo de Amii,[27] Odo de Bonolio,[28] Symon[29] de Montiscort,[30,31] Liudo de Roia.

373

October, 1229.

Oudard, knight of Pont, consents to and makes known that his man Gobert Arsus *relinquished to the church of Prémontré what he held in fief from Oudard at Eppeville*[1] *and which Prémontré had previously held from Gobert, in exchange for an annual payment of three and a half* modii *of grain (*bladus*) and two* modii *of oats, measure of Ham.*

A. Cartulary of Prémontré, fol. 91v.

B. Original, AM Metz, Salis II.244, no. 9, previously sealed with pink silk thread.

Karta Odardi militis de Ponte de quitatione Goberti Arsi super tota terra de meo feodo descendente.

[E]go Odardus, miles de Ponte, notum facio omnibus presentes litteras inspecturis quod Gobertus Arsus, homo meus, quitavit, me concedente et laudante, in perpetuum ecclesie Premonstratensi per subscriptam modiationem totam terram de meo feodo descendentem quam ecclesia Premonstratensis tenebat de eodem Goberto juxta Espevillam ad manum firmam et ad quartam garbam et quicquid juris vel consuetudinis vel justicie vel quocumque alio modo habebat in terra ipsa, excepto quod si modiatio de qua convenit inter dictam ecclesiam et Gobertum pro hac quitatione non fuerit ei soluta, poterit sine forisfacto

23 Dreux de Nesle, knight (d. aft. 1146), son of Raoul, lord of Nesle, and Raintrude. Newman, *Seigneurs*, vol. 1, 62.

24 Radulfus *B*.

25 Raoul *Bellus*, brother of Mathieu, also appears in **396** and is attested as a witness in acts for the lords of Nesle, 1133–59. Newman, *Seigneurs*, vol. 2, 35.

26 Roger the *justiciarius* is attested in acts of the lords of Nesle, 1142–75. Newman, *Seigneurs*, vol. 2, 37, 149.

27 Probably Amy, cant. Lassigny, https://dicotopo.cths.fr/places/P93748797.

28 Eudes de Bonneuil appears as a witness in acts dated 1140–78. Newman, *Seigneurs*, vol. 2, 119.

29 Simon *B*.

30 Montoiscurt *B*.

31 Mondescourt, cant. Noyon, https://dicotopo.cths.fr/places/P60804459.

1 Eppeville, cant. Ham, https://dicotopo.cths.fr/places/P94171781.

capere in terra ipsa donec solvatur. Modiatio autem talis est. Debet ecclesia Premonstratensis eidem Goberto et heredibus eius[2] solvere annuatim tres modios et dimidium bladi sani et solubilis et duos modios avene in Hamensi Castro currentem tempore huius scripti. Hoc adjecto quod si mensura aliquo tempore retalliata fuerit in futurum ita quod modius crescat vel decrescat usque ad unum mencoldum, modiatio crescet vel decrescet usque ad eandem mensuram. Ipse autem Gobertus et eius heredes tenebuntur recipere modiationem predictam quacumque die fuerit eis oblata, ab uno festo Sancti Remigii ad aliud et fratres predicte ecclesie debent eam ducere ad domum suam Hami et ibidem tradere ad mensuram prefatam. Ego vero nichil potero saisire in feodo nisi modiationem tantum ita quidem quod si ipsi fratres post factam a me saisinam reservabunt penes se dictam modiationem denuntiaturi dicto[3] Goberto vel heredi eius apud domum suam Hami ut infra quadraginta dies saisine michi satisfaciat quod si interim non satisfecerit ex tunc tenebuntur fratres michi respondere de modiatione solvenda sed nonquam[4] de soluta nec etiam tenebuntur fratres respondere Goberto vel eius heredibus de aliquo quod contingat infra tempus saisine donec fecerit eam absolute quitari et tunc etiam fratres erunt penitus absoluti ab eo quod ego inventus fuero recepisse. De hiis omnibus tenetur Gobertus vel eius heredes ecclesie Premonstratensi portare legitimam garandiam. In cuius rei firmitatem presentes litteras sigilli mei munimine roboravi. Actum[5] anno Domini M° CC°[6] vicesimo nono, mense octobri.

374

March, 1232.

Magister *Hugues,*[1] *canon and* officialis *of Noyon, makes known that in the presence of the dean of Ham and the knight Guy, lord of Estouilly,*[2] *with the assent of his wife Philippa, he sold to Prémontré all his rights to the tithe of Estouilly, for which Philippa received compensation, since the rights sold were part of her* dotalicium.

A. Cartulary of Prémontré, fols. 91v–92r.

B. Original not found.

---

2 suis *B*.

3 eidem *B*.

4 numquam *B*.

5 *Add.* Actum *A*.

6 millesimo ducentesimo *B*.

---

1 *Magister* Hugues, canon and *officialis* of Noyon, ca. 1229–ca. 1236. AD Aisne, H 455, fol. 310v; AD Oise, G 1984, fols. 238v–239r.

2 Estouilly, cant. Ham, https://dicotopo.cths.fr/places/P96663971.

Karta officialis Noviomensis de venditione quam fecit Guido d'Estoulli ecclesie Premonstratensis in decima et in herbergagio.

[O]mnibus hec visuris magister Hugo, canonicus et officialis Noviomensis, salutem in Domino. Vobis notum facimus quod dominus Guido de Estouilli, miles, in presentia decani Hamensis, cui vices nostras super hoc specialiter commisimus, constitutus, recognovit se vendidisse ecclesie Premonstratensi quicquid juris habebat in decima de Estolli vel habere poterat, quocumque modo tam in herbergagio eiusdem decime quam in eius stramine et grano, Philippa uxore dicti Guidonis, presente, dictam venditionem volente, laudante et approbante et recognoscente se sufficiens excambium habere per dotalicio quod in dicta decima et in rebus venditis habebat, videlicet in duobus modiis frumenti ad mensuram Hamensem singulis annis in festo Sancti Remigii ad molendinos dicti Guidonis de Estoilli capiendis ad quos dictus Guido pro dotalicio quod in dictis rebus venditis habebat quocumque modo spontanea et non coacta in manu dicti decani resignavit et eidem fide data penitus renunciavit et tam dictus Guido quam ipsa Philippa spontanei et non coacti fidem in manu dicti decani prestiterunt corporalem quod dictam ecclesiam super dicto vendagio decetero non molestabunt nec gravabunt nec artem nec ingenium per se vel per alium querent per que dicta ecclesia possit vel debeat super eodem vendagio in posterum molestari vel gravari. In cuius rei testimonium presentes litteras sigillo curie Noviomensis fecimus communiri. Actum anno Domini M° CC° tricesimo secundo, mense martio.

375

August, 1207.

Étienne [I],[1] *bishop of Noyon, makes known that he mediated a quarrel between Jean [II],*[2] *lord of Nesle, castellan of Bruges, and the church of Prémontré concerning property that two* conversae *of Bonneuil,*[3] *Adélaïde and Elizabeth, had inherited on the death of their brother Robert, knight of Châteaufort.*[4] *Prémontré ceded the property to Jean and his heirs with the consent of Adélaïde and Elizabeth. In return, the sisters will receive six* modii *of grain (*frumentum*), measure of Nesle, annually for the rest of their lives; after their deaths, this will be paid to Bonneuil. (See near-duplicate* ***474****.)*

---

1 Étienne de Villebéon (or de Nemours), son of Gautier de Villebéon, lord of La Chapelle-Gauthier and Nemours, and Aveline, was bishop of Noyon, 1188–1221.

2 Jean II, castellan of Bruges and lord of Nesle (d. 1239), son of Jean I, lord of Nesle and castellan of Bruges, and Elizabeth van Peteghem.

3 The Premonstratensian *curtis* of Bonneuil. *MP* II, 484.

4 Perhaps the *lieu-dit* of Chateau-Fort, comm. Languevoisin-Quinquery, https://dicotopo.cths.fr/places/P45423225.

A. Cartulary of Prémontré, fol. 92r.
B. Original, AD Oise, H 5999, previously sealed on a double strip of parchment.
EDITION: Newman, *Seigneurs*, vol. 2, 194–5; *Chartae Galliae*, no. 212890, http://telma.irht.cnrs.fr/outils/chartae-galliae/charte212890/.

Karta Stephani Noviomensis episcopi de conpositione inter ecclesiam Premonstratem et dominum Johannem Nigellensis.

[E]go Stephanus, Dei gratia Noviomensis episcopus, tam presentibus quam futuris notum facimus per hoc scriptum et fidele testimonium perhibemus quod cum inter nobilem virum Johannem, dominium Nigelle, castellanum Brugie, et ecclesiam Premonstratensem super hereditate conversarum Bonolii, Adelidis et Elizabeth, que ad ipsas ex morte fratris ipsarum, Roberti, militis de Castello Forti, fuerat devoluta, questio verteretur, tandem, me ipso mediante, inter dictum dominum Johannem et abbatem ac capitulum ecclesie memorate talis compositio facta fuit quod idem abbas et capitulum de assensu et concessione dictarum conversarum, ipsi domino Johanni et heredibus suis terram illam concesserunt perpetuo possidendam sub ea tamen conditione et lege quod ipse dominus Johannes et heredes sui in perpetuum annuatim in festo Sancti Remigii solvent dictis sororibus, quamdiu vixerint, sex modios frumenti ad mensuram Nigellensem ex horreo suo Nigellensi; post decessum vero dictarum conversarum prefati sex modii frumenti singulis annis in perpetuum ad eundem terminum ecclesie Bonolii solventur. Erit autem frumentum quod solvi debet in valore et precio melioris tribus denariis minus. Ut ergo hec compositio futuris temporibus rata permaneat et illesa, presentem paginam conscribi fecimus sigilli nostri testimonio roboratam pariter et munitam. Actum anno domini M° CC° VII°,[5] mense augusto.

376

November, 1231.

Eudes [IV],[1] *lord of Ham, acknowledges that abbot Conrad*[2] *and the convent of Prémontré allowed him to include in his wood at Douilly*[3] *approximately six* sextariae *of land, measure of Ham, that had belonged to Prémontré. In return,*

5 millesimo ducentesimo septimo *B*.

1 Eudes IV, lord of Ham (d. 1234), son of Eudes III, lord of Ham, and Elizabeth; husband of Elizabeth de Béthencourt.
2 Conrad the Swabian was prior of Weissenau, 1203–17, abbot of Valsecret, 1218–20, abbot of Prémontré, 1220–33, and abbot of Cuissy, aft. 1235–41. *MP* I, 89; *MP* II, 497, 527, 536.
3 Douilly, cant. Ham, https://dicotopo.cths.fr/places/P87195366.

Eudes ceded to Prémontré two modii *of grain (*bladus*), measure of Ham, that it owed him annually on the mills of Eppeville.*[4] *Elizabeth, wife of Eudes, consents, as does fief lord Nicolas,*[5] *bishop of Noyon. (See* ***379****.)*

A. Cartulary of Prémontré, fol. 92r.

B. Original, AM Metz, Salis II.244, no. 13, sealed with brown wax on a single strip of parchment.

Karta Odonis domini Hamensis de quadam restitutione facta ab ipso ecclesie Premonstratensis et conpositione.

[E]go Odo, dominus Hamensis Castri, notum facio universis tam presentibus quam futuris quod ego de consensu et voluntate dilectorum meorum C[onradi], abbatis, et conventus Premonstratensis, inclusi in meo nemore de Douilli sex sextarios terre vel ea circiter ad mensuram Hamensem ad dictam ecclesiam Premonstratensem jure hereditario pertinentis. Quam terram dicta ecclesia mihi et meis heredibus in perpetuum quitavit. Et ego tam in recompensationem illius terre quam pro anime mee remedio salutari dicte ecclesie, Elizabeth, dilecta uxore mea, spontanea concedente, duos modios bladi ad mensuram Hamensem quos dicta ecclesia mihi debebat in perpetuum ad eiusdem ecclesie molendinos singulis annis capiendos, scilicet apud Espevile, de propria voluntate venerabilis in Christo patris Nicholai, episcopi Noviomensis, a quo dictum bladum tenebam in feodum, contuli in perpetuum et concessi ita quod ego terram predictam mihi collatam in feodum dicti domini mei episcopi Noviomensis, loco bladi predicti, ad ipsius episcopi instantiam restitui. In cuius rei perpetuam firmitatem presentem kartam feci sigilli mei munimine roborari. Actum mense novembri, anno gratie M° CC° tricesimo primo.

377

1171

Hugues [II],[1] *abbot of Prémontré, Renaud [II],*[2] *abbot of Notre-Dame de Ham, and their respective chapters confirm and accept the resolution that*

4 Eppeville, cant. Ham. https://dicotopo.cths.fr/places/P94171781.

5 Nicolas de Roye, son of the knight Pierre de Roye, was dean of Saint-Martin from 1216 and bishop of Noyon, 1228–39/40.

1 Hugues II de Douai, abbot of the Premonstratensian abbey of Cuissy, 1161–5, and abbot of Prémontré, 1174–89. *MP* II, 497.

2 Renaud II, abbot of the Augustinian abbey of Notre-Dame de Ham, ca. 1168–88. *GC* IX, col. 1122.

Étienne,[3] bishop of Meaux, Henri,[4] bishop of Senlis, and Yves [II],[5] abbot of Saint-Denis, put forth to resolve the dispute between Prémontré and Ham concerning the mills of Hamel.[6]

A. Cartulary of Prémontré, fol. 92r.
B. Original, AD Somme, 20 H_SC_9, no. 9, sealed.[7]

Karta abbatis Premonstratensis et Renaldi abbatis Hamensis super querela terminata molendinorum de Hamiaus.

[I]n nomine sancte et individue Trinitatis. Ego Hugo, Dei gratia Premonstrati dictus abbas totumque capitulum nostrum et ego Rainaldus, eiusdem gratia Hamensis abbas simulque capitulum nostrum, presentibus et futuris in perpetuum salutem. Mota iam pridem querela inter Premonstratensem ecclesiam et Hamensem super molendinis de Hameals per venerabiles viros Stephanum Meldensem et Henricum Silvanectensem episcopos et Yvonem, abbatem Sancti Dyonisii, a domino Papa super eadem causa judices constitutos, tali compositione sedata est. Statutum est, mediantibus predictis judicibus et assensu Premonstratensis capituli et Hamensis confirmatum, quod Premonstratenses ad molendina sua de Hameals recipient omnes molere volentes de ultra pontem de Alemane,[8] citra vero versus Hamum nominem recipient ad molendina illa. Decretum est etiam quod si custos predictorum molendinorum contra tenorem presentis scripti aliquem molentem reciperet, abbas Premonstratensis et capitulum ita hoc emendaret quod emendatum esse pateret et questus moliture contra conpositionem istam recepte in usus pauperum cederet. Ut autem ratum et inconvulsum permaneat, sigillis utriusque, Premonstratensis videlicet et Hamensis presens cyrographum fecimus confirmari et legitimarum testimonio personarum corroborari. S. Johannis, prioris de Premonstrato. S. Grinberti, subprioris. S. S.[9] Drogonis. S. Clarembaldi, et ceteri. Actum anno verbi incarnati M° C° LXX° I°.

3 Étienne de la Chapelle, son of Josselin II de Villemomble, lord of Beaumont, and Herceline de Villebéon was bishop of Meaux, 1162–71, and archbishop of Bourges, 1171–3.
4 Henri, bishop of Senlis, 1168/9–85.
5 Yves II, abbot of the Benedictine abbey of Saint-Denis, ca. 1169–ca. 1172.
6 Hamel-lès-Corbie, cant. Corbie, https://dicotopo.cths.fr/places/P37197765.
7 Due to conservation concerns, the original was not available to the editors.
8 Le Pont-d'Allemagne, cant. Ham, https://dicotopo.cths.fr/places/P01242205.
9 *Sic A*.

378

1142

Simon [I],[1] bishop of Noyon, makes known the resolution of a dispute between the brothers of the Premonstratensian house of Bonneuil and the Knights Templar concerning the ownership of the mills of Hamel[2] and Canisy.[3]

A. Cartulary of Prémontré, fols. 92r–92v.
B. Original not found.

Karta Noviomensis episcopi de conpositione inter ecclesiam Premonstratensem et milites Templi de molendinis de Hamiaus et de Chanesi.

[I]n nomine sancte et cetera. Ego Symon Dei gratia Noviomensis episcopus, scire volo tam futuros quam presentes quendam querimoniam fuisse inter fratres Bonolienses et Templi milites pro molendinis de Hameals et molendinis de Canesi, militibus Templis facientibus exclusam suam jungere excluse de Hameals invitis fratribus de Bonolio atque contradicentibus. Cum autem Templi milites Bonolientibus nollent assentire ut, secundum antiquam consuetudinem, exclusam suam facerent fratres de Bonolio patrocinium nostrum adierunt et ut justiciam eis veluti de elemosina mea tenerem, petierunt. Quorum petitioni libenter annuens, statui diem utrisque super molendina et ut circa manentes molendinarii ceterique qui molendinorum antiquum morem noverant, adessent precepi. Et cum die statuta omnes convenissent, ipse quoque cum Odone de Ham affui et ut circa manentes veritatem de statu antiquo molendinorum preferrent sub anathematis comminatione mandavi. Illi autem veritatem proferentes testificati sunt nullam prorsus exclusam a Hameals usque ad eum locum qui dicitur Vetus Summa, esse debere nisi tantummodo planitiem paludis. Quod si planities ipsa aliquo eventu interrumperetur, solum wasonem ponendum qui planitiei paludis equaretur. Ac igitur, veritate comperta, precepi ut nemo in posterum amplius aliqua inportunitate molendina de Hameals que elemosine mee erant, ex hac causa amplius impediret nec eorum qui tunc erant possidentes molendina nec aliquis successorum in perpetuum. Ut autem hoc firmum omni tempore perseveret episcopali auctoritate sigillique nostri impressione communimus huicque nostre institutioni legitime contraire presumentes excommunicationis vinculo innodamus testesque legitimos qui huic cause interfuerunt subsignavimus: Odo de Ham,[4]

1 Simon I de Vermandois (d. 1148) was the son of Hugues I and Adélaïde, count and countess of Vermandois and Valois, and bishop of Noyon, 1123–42.
2 Hamel-lès-Corbie, cant. Corbie, https://dicotopo.cths.fr/places/P37197765.
3 Canisy, cant. Nesle, https://dicotopo.cths.fr/places/P34153509.
4 Eudes II *Pes Lupi*, lord of Ham (d. aft. 1144).

Hugo cancellarius,[5] Hugo, Robertus maior,[6] Evrardus de Douilli,[7] Johannes de Cremeri,[8] Albricus molendinarius, Galterus molendinarius de Betencourt,[9] Balduinus molendinarius de Tuine.[10] Actum est hoc anno M° C° XL° II° incarnationis dominice.

379

November, 1231.

Nicolas,[1] bishop of Noyon, as fief lord approves the agreement reached between husband and wife Eudes [IV, lord of][2] Ham and Elizabeth, and the church of Prémontré, to exchange two modii *of grain (*bladus*) at the mill of Eppeville[3] for six* sextariatae *of land at Douilly.[4] (See* ***376****.)*

A. Cartulary of Prémontré, fol. 92v.

B. Original, AM Metz, Salis II.244, no. 10, previously sealed with a single strap of parchment.

Karta Noviomensis episcopi de excambio facto inter ecclesiam Premonstratensem et dominum Odonem de Hamo.

[N]icolaus, permissione divina Noviomensis episcopus, omnibus hec visuris salutem in Domino. Noverint universi quod nos excambium et collationem factam a domino Odone de Hamo et Elizabeth[5] uxore sua ecclesie Premonstratensi, sicut in literis eiusdem Odonis inde confectis plenius apparet, de duobus scilicet modiis bladi quos de nobis in feodum tenebat idem Odo in molendinis de Espevile[6] et de de[7] sex sexteriatis terre, site apud Douilliacum que ad dictam pertinebant ecclesiam, volumus et approbamus et sciendum

5 Hugues III de Roye, chancellor of Noyon-Tournai, ca. 1130–46, and of Noyon, 1146–63/6. Pycke, *Le chapitre cathédral Notre-Dame de Tournai de la fin du XIe à la fin du XIIIe siècle*, 64.

6 A Robert, mayor of Ham, appears in **401**, **421**, and **445**.

7 Douilly, cant. Ham, https://dicotopo.cths.fr/places/P87195366.

8 Crémery, cant. Roye, https://dicotopo.cths.fr/places/P44909124.

9 Probably the same Gautier de Bethencourt (Bethencourt-sur-Somme, cant. Nesle, https://dicotopo.cths.fr/places/P85791062) who appears in **362**.

10 Tugny-et-Pont, cant. Saint-Simon, https://dicotopo.cths.fr/places/P85639589.

1 Nicolas de Roye, son of the knight Pierre de Roye, was dean of Saint-Martin from 1216 and bishop of Noyon, 1228–39/40.

2 Eudes IV, lord of Ham (d. 1234), son of Eudes III, lord of Ham, and Elizabeth; husband of Elizabeth de Béthencourt.

3 Eppeville, cant. Ham. https://dicotopo.cths.fr/places/P94171781.

4 Douilly, cant. Ham, https://dicotopo.cths.fr/places/P87195366.

5 Helysabeth *B*.

quod, sicut dicti duo modii bladi de nobis in feodum tenebantur, ita dictus Odo et eius heres dictas sex sextariatas terre de nobis in feodum tenebunt. In huius vel igitur rei testimonium presentes litteras sigilli nostri fecimus appensione muniri. Actum anno gratie M° CC°[8] trecesimo[9] primo, mense novembri.

380

1195[1]

Étienne [I],[2] bishop of Noyon, makes known that husband and wife Eudes Surdo *and Oburge, and Marie, mother of Oburge, received 24* solidi Parisiensis *from the Premonstratensian brothers of Bonneuil.[3] This payment was for the remittal of one and a half of the two and a half* sextariae *of grain (*frumentum*), measure of Ham, owed to Oburge and Marie annually by hereditary right on the mill of Hamel.[4] Oburge promises that unless she buys back the one and a half* sextariae *within a year and a day of becoming a widow, it will remain permanently the property of the church of Bonneuil.*

A. Cartulary of Prémontré, fol. 92v.

B. Original, AD Oise, H 6000, previously sealed on a double strip of parchment.

Karta episcopi Noviomensis episcopi[5] de XX[ti] IIII[or] solidis Parisiensium quos fratres Premonstratensis commodaverint Oburgi.

[S]tephanus, Dei gratia Noviomensis episcopus, omnibus ad quos pagina presens pervenerit salutem. Notum fieri volumus quod fratres Bonolienses, ante nostram constituti presentiam, commodaverint[6] Odoni Surdo et uxori eius, Oburgi et matri eiusdem Oburgis, Marie, XXIIII[or] solidos Parisiensium et unum sextarium frumenti super duo sextaria frumenti et dimidium ad mensuram Hamensem, que ipsi in molendino predictorum fratrum apud Hameaus, jure

6 Espeville *B.*
7 *Sic A*; *om. B.*
8 decentesimo *B.*
9 *Eras. B.*

1 While the cartulary copy is dated to 1125, the original charter is dated to 1195. It would appear that the cartulary scribe misread *XC* as *XX*.
2 Étienne de Villebéon (or de Nemours), son of Gautier de Villebéon, lord of La Chapelle-Gauthier and Nemours, and Aveline, was bishop of Noyon, 1188–1221.
3 The Premonstratensian *curtis* of Bonneuil. *MP* II, 484.
4 Hamel-lès-Corbie, cant. Corbie, https://dicotopo.cths.fr/places/P37197765.
5 *Sic A.*
6 commodaverunt *B.*

hereditario, percipiebant annuatim, et quia frumentum illud ad prefatam Oburgem[7] ex parte matris sue, Marie, jure pertinebant hereditatis, concessit quod nisi frumentum illud infra annum unum et diem unum postquam vidua fuerit redemerit a fratribus predictis, liberum ecclesie Bonoliensi in perpetuum remaneat et quietum. Nos igitur in huius rei testimonium presentem paginam nostro fecimus sigillo communiri. Actum anno Domini M° C° vicesimo[8] V°.[9]

381

April 17, 1218. Bonneuil.

Eudes, priest of Eppeville[1] and dean of Ham, makes known that he made amends to the abbot and church of Prémontré for having taken two quadrigatae *of flour and some iron tools from one of their mills.*

A. Cartulary of Prémontré, fol. 92v.

B. Original, AM Metz, Salis II.244, no. 5, previously sealed on a single parchment strip.

Karta decani Hamensis de emenda quam fecit ecclesie Premonstratensis super dampnis.

[E]go Odo presbiter de Espevile,[2] dictus decanus Hamensis, notum facio universis presentes literas inspecturis quod emendavi domino abbati et ecclesie Premonstratensi dampna et injurias quas feci eis super hoc quod cepi duas quadrigatas farine sue et ferros unius molendinorum ~~mo~~ suorum et detinui hec predicta per aliquot dies. Super hac autem emendi[3] prosequenda dedi eis plegios viros venerabiles et amicos meos Johannem de Douilli[4] et Soibertum de Estoilli[5] presbiteros et presentes etiam literas sigilli mei appensione munitas emisi quod prosequitur emendam predictam ad voluntatem et summonitionem abbatis. Actum Bonolii XV°[6] kalendas maii sub testibus inferius annotatis: Joscelino priore Bonolii, Wiberto[7] quondam abbate de Doa, Ingelranno provisore Premonstratensi, Nicholao magistro Bonolii, Fulcardo[8] curato de Douci,[9,10] et

7 Oburgim *B*.
8 XC° *B*.
9 quinto *B*.

1 Eppeville, cant. Ham. https://dicotopo.cths.fr/places/P94171781.
2 Espeville *B*.
3 emenda *B*.
4 Doilli *B*.
5 Estouilly, cant. Ham, https://dicotopo.cths.fr/places/P96663971.
6 XV *B*.

Guidone de Cociaco canonicis Premonstratensis. Anno gratie M° CC° VIII° X°.[11]

382

1175

Renaud,[1] bishop of Noyon, makes known that Eustache de Froissy[2] gave in alms to Prémontré his part of the major and minor tithes of Devise.[3] This gift was made with the consent of his fief lord, Raoul le Gentil,[4] and of Yves [II],[5] count of Soissons, from whom the fief descended. Other consenters included Ada, Eustache's wife, their children Lambert and Wiger, and Eustache's siblings: Jean, Raoul, Sara, Sauvide, and Fredesende. (See ***386****.)*

A. Cartulary of Prémontré, fols. 92v–93r.

B. Original, AM Metz, Salis II.243, no. 3, sealed on braided leather with seal intact.

REGISTER: *Studium Baldwin*, fiche 2040.

Karta Renaldi Noviomensis episcopi de elemosina decime magne et minute de Devise.

Quoniam[6] instant tempora periculosa et ecclesiarum jura et possessiones frequenter injuste calumpniantur et libentius et avidius rapiuntur aliena quam propria largiantur[7] dignum judicamus litteris annotari quod memoriter et stabiliter et absque calumpnia volumus retineri legitimum enim judicatur et magis auctenticum quod litteris episcoporum atque sigillis constat confirmatum.

---

7 Wibert, an otherwise unattested abbot of the Premonstratensian abbey of Doue. *MP* III, 150; Pontvianne, *Recherches historiques sur l'Abbaye de Doue*, 51.

8 Folcardo *B*.

9 Doci *B*.

10 Douchy, cant. Vermand, https://dicotopo.cths.fr/places/P84133506.

11 millesimo ducentesimo octavodecimo *B*.

---

1 Renaud, bishop of Noyon, 1175–88.

2 Froissy, arr. Clermont, https://dicotopo.cths.fr/places/P14479148.

3 Devise, cant. Ham, https://dicotopo.cths.fr/places/P85212875.

4 Raoul le Gentil appears in acts associated with the counts of Soissons in the latter half of the 1170s. Newman, *Seigneurs*, vol. 2, 149–50, 155, 163.

5 Yves II de Nesle (d. ca. 1178), lord of Nesle and count of Soissons, son of Raoul, lord of Nesle, and Raintrude. Newman, *Seigneurs*, vol. 1, 61.

6 The initial letter has been added at a later, post-medieval date.

7 tribuatur *B*.

Ego igitur Renaldus,[8] Dei gratia Noviomensis episcopus, notum fieri volumus tam futuris quam presentibus quod Eustachius de Froischies dedit in elemosinam Premonstrate ecclesie totam partem decime magne et minute quam tenebat apud Devise,[9] concedente Radulfo cognomine Legentisl de cuius feodo descendebat et propter hoc de beneficio ecclesie predicte habuit, sicut inter ipsum Eustachium et ecclesiam prefatam convenit. Sciens autem idem Eustachius ut pote miles quod dampnabiliter decimam iamdictam tenebat, ad nos venit et in presentia nostra predicto Radulfo Legentil de quo eam tenebat, reddidit, qui in manu nostra, annuente Eustachio, posuit et nobis penitus resignavit et nos, ecclesiarum jura conservare volentes et eidem[10] disponere[11] consulentes,[12] abbati et ecclesie Premonstrati decimam ipsam reddidimus et perpetuo possidere concessimus. Factum est hoc assensu domini Yvonis, Suessionensis comitis, in cuius dominio decima prefata erat. Concessit etiam hoc uxor Eustachii iamdicti, Ada, et liberi eorum, Lambertus et Wigerus, et fratres ipsius Eustachii, Johannes et Radulphus, et sorores eius, Sarra,[13] Sauvidis,[14] Fredesendis, et super altare de Bonolio coram abbate et fratribus eiusdem loci decimam predictam obtulerunt et absolute ecclesie Premonstrati dimiserunt. Quia vero virtutem semper insequitur invidia et equitatem subvertere conatur injuria et nos, utilitati iamdicte ecclesie in posterum providere curantes, volumus ut predictam decimam de Devise[15] ecclesia Premonstrati quiete et pacifice teneat et ne qua exinde amodo controversia oriatur, presenti pagine sigillum nostrum apposuimus et astipulationem subscriptorum testium muniri fecimus. S.[16] Joiffridi, cantoris. S. magistri Ingelranni. S. magistri Gerardi, et ceteri.[17] Actum anno verbi incarnati M° C° LXX° V°. Ego Balduinus cancellarius legi et subscripsi.

---

8 Rainoldus *B*.

9 Divise *B*.

10 eisdem *B*.

11 consulere *B*.

12 disponentes *B*.

13 Sara *B*.

14 Sawidus *B*.

15 Divise *B*.

16 Signum *B*.

17 *Add.* et ceteri *A*; S. Johannis, capellani. S. Odonis de Compendio. S. Roberti de Luzarches. S. magistri Rorici, S. Mauricii, magistri de Bonoli, S. Petri, sacerdotium. S. Evrardi, S. Heberti, S. Petri, conversorum *B*.

383

1156

Baudouin,[1] *dean of the chapter of Noyon, makes known the resolution of a dispute between his chapter and the brothers of the Premonstratensian house at Bonneuil*[2] *concerning certain tithes on land between Matigny*[3] *and Falvy.*[4]

A. Cartulary of Prémontré, fol. 93r.
B. Original not found.

Karta decani Noviomensis de querelis terminatis inter ecclesiam Premonstratem per ipsum.

[E]go Balduinus, Dei gratia Noviomensis ecclesie decanus et capitulum, notum fieri volumus tam futuris quam presentibus quod de querelis ex quibusdam decimis inter nos et fratres de Bonolio dudum exagitatis et emersis unde causa sepius extiterat nec ad finem deducta sed appellatio apud dominum Sansonem, archiepiscopum Remensem, facta in presentia eiusdem archiepiscopi apud Sanctum Quintinum per venerabilem patrem nostrum Balduinum Noviomensem episcopum, conpositio facta fuit. Sane inter nos et predictos fratres querela fuerat de quadam decima adjacente inter Mateni et Falevi unde ex nostra et illorum concessione et virorum circummanentium approbata attestatione, mete sunt apposite designantes quod ab eis metis ex parte Mateni decima nostra est et erit. Ex altera autem parte est quidam campus cuius ab antiquo decima nostra sine calumpnia fuit et erit. Decima vero de territorio Sancti Nicholai de Nemore que nostra extitit sed ipsi eam clamabant ut pertinentem ad Espevile ab eis nostra esse concessa est et recognita. Nos vero donum de nemore quod dicitur Nemus Episcopi et quod dominus episcopus ecclesie de Bonolio perpetuo censualiter habendum dedit eis in perpetuum possidendum, benigne concedimus eo tenore quod de sartis illius nemoris decima nostra est et erit. Pro hiis igitur querelis sopiendis ne ulterius possint moveri, consilio predictorum dominorum archiepiscopi et episcopi nostri et aliorum virorum bonorum, statutum est pro bono pacis quod in grangia nostra de Mateni in augusto unum modium frumenti ad mensuram Nigellensem, nec de meliori nec de peiori, predicti fratres singulis annis accipient ita quod sextarius qui modo currit, nec augmentari poterit nec minui et ligno ad lignum radetur frumentum. Preterea cognitum est de alodio quod fuit fratris Petri et quod ad conversionem proficiscens in duas partes divisit quod illa pars quam Drogoni de Plaisi dedit ecclesie nostre sex denarios debet de censu et foragium et veritas. Altera vero pars nullum debet censum sed libera est et alodium fratrem de Bonolio. Ut hoc igitur

1 Baudouin, dean of Noyon, attested 1132–74. AD Oise G 1984, fols. 71r, 78v–79v.
2 The Premonstratensian *curtis* of Bonneuil. *MP* II, 484.
3 Matigny, cant. Ham, https://dicotopo.cths.fr/places/P92212887.
4 Falvy, cant. Nesle, https://dicotopo.cths.fr/places/P25248648.

ratum maneat et inconvulsum, presenti scripto et cyrographo in duas partes diviso atque utrique parti sigillis domini videlicet Balduini episcopi, et nostro cum Premonstratensi appositis firmamus et tam clericorum quam laicorum subscriptorum testimonio corroboramus. Hii sunt testes: Balduinus decanus, Theodericus[5] thesaurarius, Hugo[6] cancellarius, Hugo, et ceteri. Actum anno dominice incarnationis M° C° LVI°.

384

1134

Simon [I],[1] bishop of Noyon, confirms that Albert de Sommette, as he lay dying, gave the church of Prémontré the tithe of Sommette. Robert,[2] son of Albert, confirms his late father's gift with the consent of Ermena, his mother.

A. Cartulary of Prémontré, fol. 93r.

B. Original, AN, L 995, no. 3, previously sealed.

EDITION: Pycke and Vleeschouwers, *Actes*, 376–7.

REGISTER: Jacquemin, "Annales de la vie de Joscelin de Vierzi, 57e évêque de Soissons," 38.

Karta Noviomensis episcopi de elemosina decime de Sumete quam Albertus contulit ecclesie Premonstrati.

[I]n nomine et cetera.[3] Quoniam decrevit antiquitas res gestas commendare litteris ne hominem labili memoria et vite brevitate tradantur oblivioni, ego Symon, per Dei patientiam Noviomensis ecclesie minister indignus, notum fieri volumus tam futuris quam presentibus quatinus Albertus de Sumete in infirmitate, qua et defunctus est, ob remissionem peccatorum suorum in ecclesia Beate Marie Premonstrati conversus, eidem ecclesie contulit decimam prefate ville scilicet Sumete, sicut eam obtinuerat de manu domini[4] Odonis, principis de Ham, qui dicitur Pes Lupi. Ut autem hoc[5] legitime posset fieri, Robertus, filius eiusdem Alberti, annuente matre sua Ermena, ipsam decimam

5 Thierry de Nesle, son of Raoul, lord of Nesle, and Raintrude, was treasurer of Noyon, ca. 1134–ca. 1157, and archdeacon of Cambrai. In 1157, he participated in the translation of the relics of St Éloi. Mazière, "Annales Noyonnaises, première partie," 55–6.

6 Hugues III de Roye, chancellor of Noyon-Tournai, ca. 1130–46, and of Noyon, 1146–63/6. Pycke, *Le chapitre cathédral Notre-Dame de Tournai de la fin du XIe à la fin du XIIIe siècle*, 64.

1 Simon I de Vermandois (d. 1148) was the son of Hugues I and Adélaïde, count and countess of Vermandois and Valois, and bishop of Noyon, 1123–42.

2 Possibly the same Robert de Sommette (Sommette-Éaucourt, cant. Saint-Simon, https://dicotopo.cths.fr/places/P82241903) who appears in **353**.

3 *Add.* et ceteri *A*; sancte et individue Trinitatis *B*.

4 domni *B*.

reddidit domno Odoni a quo eam tenebat in mea presentia et ipse dominus Odo ob remedium anime sue et predecessorum suorum ad opus prefate ecclesie Premonstrati in manu mea quia de feodo meo erat, ego vero eam reddidi Hugoni, ipsius ecclesie abbati. Quod ut ratum et inconvulsum permaneat commendatum scripto sigilli nostri inpressione subsignavimus et legitimorum testium subsignatione confirmavimus. Siqua igitur ecclesiastica secularisve persona contra hanc decreti nostri paginam contraire[6] temptaverit, semel atque iterum commonita, si non emendaverit, auctoritate Dei et nostra a consortio fidelium segregata divine ultioni subjaceat donec satisfactione congrua peniteat. Huius rei sunt testes: Goislenus[7] venerabilis Suessorum episcopus, Bliardus[8,9] cantor Laudunesis, Hugo[10] cancellarius et ceteri.[11] Actum est hoc anno incarnationi dominice M° C° XXX° IIII°, epacta XXª IIIª, indictione XII, concurrente VII°.[12]

385

1134

Simon [I],[1] bishop of Noyon, confirms that Eudes[2] de Lanchy made a gift of half of the tithe of Devise[3] and Excluis. *This was at the request of Elizabeth, his mother and widow of Waldin de Lanchy, who had entered the community of Prémontré together with Gersende, her daughter.*

A. Cartulary of Prémontré, fols. 93r–93v.

B. Original, AD Somme, 20 H_SC_7, no. 1, sealed.[4]

EDITION: Pycke and Vleeschouwers, *Actes*, 377–8.

5 *Transp. A*; hoc autem *B*.

6 inire *B*.

7 Joscelin de Vierzy, a magister at Bourges who was later bishop of Soissons, 1126–52.

8 Blihardus *B*.

9 Bliard, cantor of Laon, attested ca. 1113–ca. 1135. BM Reims, MS 1843 (N. 863), fols. 13r, 24v; BM Laon MS 532, fols. 24v–25r, 36r–37r; Wyard, *Saint-Vincent*, 37.

10 Hugues III de Roye, chancellor of Noyon-Tournai, ca. 1130–46, and of Noyon, 1146–63/6. Pycke, *Le chapitre cathédral Notre-Dame de Tournai de la fin du XIe à la fin du XIIIe siècle*, 64.

11 *Add.* et ceteri *A*; Noviomensis, Andreas, Odo qui dicitur Pes Lupi, Wido de Belmeis, Reinerus de Roinun, Nanterus de Sancto Quintino, Watso de Duilli, Everardus nepos eius, Fulco qui dicitur Obelin, et Hugo de Perona, Johannis nepos eius, item Hugo nepos eius, Thietsardus de Noviomo *B*.

12 epacta XX° III°, indictione XII, concurrente VII *B*.

1 Simon I de Vermandois (d. 1148) was the son of Hugues I and Adélaïde, count and countess of Vermandois and Valois, and bishop of Noyon, 1123–42.

2 Eudes, lord of Lanchy (cant. Vermand, https://dicotopo.cths.fr/places/P51978975), son of Waldin/Baudouin and Elizabeth. Melleville, *DH*, vol. 1, 4.

3 Devise, cant. Ham, https://dicotopo.cths.fr/places/P85212875.

4 Due to conservation concerns, the original was not available to the editors.

Karta Symonis Noviomensis episcopi de elemosina decime de Devise quam Elizabeth contulit ecclesie.

[I]n nomine sancte et individue et cetera. Quoniam decrevit antiquitas res gestas commendare litteris, ne hominum labili memoria et vite brevitate tradantur oblivioni, ego Symon, per Dei patientiam Noviomensis ecclesie minister indignus, notum fieri tam futuris quam presentibus quatinus Elisabeth, uxor Waldini de Lanci, eodem suo marito iam diu defuncto, ad agendam penitentiam peccatorum suorum in ecclesia Beate Marie Premonstrati cum filia sua, Gersendi, discipline regulari se subiciens, impetravit a filio suo Odone qui manu tenens erat sue hereditatis ut mediam partem decime tocius parrochie in villa que dicitur Devisa et alia que dicitur Excluis, que media pars tantum erat sue possessionis, eidem prefate ecclesie Premonstrati conferret jure perpetuo in usus ibidem Deo servientium. Ille vero petitioni patris[5] et sororis benignus assentiens, in presentia mea, ipsam decimam in manu Alardi[6] de Porta de Ham a quo eam tenebat reposuit. Item ipse Alardus domino Yvoni, principi de Noiella, a quo et ipse eam habebat, reddidit. Ipse autem dominus Yvo mihi quia de feodo meo erat ad opus sepefate ecclesie Premonstrate et ego eam Hugoni, eiusdem ecclesie abbati, dedi. Quod ut ratum et inconvulsum permaneat commendatum scripto sigilli nostri impressione subsignavimus et legitimorum testium subsignatione confirmavimus. Si qua igitur ecclesiastica secularisve persona contra hanc decreti nostri paginam inire temptaverit, semel atque iterum commonita, si non emendaverit, auctoritate Dei et nostra a consortio fidelium segregata divine ultioni subjaceat, donec satisfactione congrua peniteat. Huius rei sunt testes: Goislenus[7] Suessorum venerabilis episcopus, Blihardus[8] cantor Laudunensis, Hugo[9] cancellarius Noviomensis, Theodericus[10] thesaurarius, Vuido, et ceteri. Actum est hoc anno incarnationis dominice M° C° XXX° IIII°, epacta XXIII[a], indictione XII, concurrente VII°.

---

5 *Sic A, read* matris.

6 Alard I de Ham (or de la Porte), knight of Ham; husband of Helvide. He also appears in **91**, **298**, **334**, **415**, **452**, and **464**.

7 Joscelin de Vierzy, a magister at Bourges who was later bishop of Soissons, 1126–52.

8 Bliard, cantor of Laon, attested ca. 1113–ca. 1135. BM Reims, MS 1843 (N. 863), fols. 13r, 24v; BM Laon MS 532, fols. 24v–25r, 36r–37r; Wyard, *Saint-Vincent*, 37.

9 Hugues III de Roye, chancellor of Noyon-Tournai, ca. 1130–46, and of Noyon, 1146–63/6. Pycke, *Le chapitre cathédral Notre-Dame de Tournai de la fin du XIe à la fin du XIIIe siècle*, 64.

10 Thierry de Nesle, son of Raoul, lord of Nesle, and Raintrude, was treasurer of Noyon, ca. 1134–ca. 1157, and archdeacon of Cambrai. In 1157, he participated in the translation of the relics of St Éloi. Mazière, "Annales Noyonnaises, première partie," 55–6.

386

1175[1]

Yves [II],[2] count of Soissons and lord of Nesle, makes known that Eustache de Froissy[3] gave to the church of Prémontré his part of the major and minor tithes of Devise.[4] Consenters include Raoul le Gentil, fief lord; Ada, Eustache's wife; Eustache's siblings Jean, Raoul, Sara, Sauvide, and Fredesende; and Eustache and Ada's children Lambert and Wiger. (See ***382****.)*

A. Cartulary of Prémontré, fol. 93v.

B. Original, AM Metz, Salis II.243, no. 5, previously sealed on braided leather strip.

EDITION: Newman, *Seigneurs*, vol. 2, 149–50; *Chartae Galliae*, no. 212854, http://telma.irht.cnrs.fr/outils/chartae-galliae/charte212854/.

Karta Yvonis comitis Suessionensis de confirmatione decime magne et minute de Devise.

[Q]uia tempore labente labitur hominum memoria, scripto memorie opus est commendare quod a fidelibus bene gestum cognoscitur. Propterea ego Yvo,[5] Suessorum comes et dominus Nigelle, notum facio futuris et presentibus quod Eustachius de Froischies dedit ecclesie Premonstrati me annuente, concessu Radulfi le Gentil de cuius feodo descendebat, totam partem decime magne et minute quam habebat apud Devise.[6] Habuit quoque propter hoc idem Eustachius de beneficio ecclesie prefate centum et sexaginta[7] libras. Nos autem de manu predicti Eustachii et Radulfi le Gentil de quo eam tenebat, decimam ipsam recepimus et ecclesie Premonstrati reddidimus. Hoc totum concesserunt uxor ipsius Eustachii, Ada, et fratres eius, Johannes et Radulfus, et sorores,[8] Sarra,[9] Sauvidis,[10] Fredesendis filii quoque eiusdem Eustachii, Lambertus et

1 This date is derived from **382**, which concerns the same transaction and is dated 1175. Original charters survive for both **382** and **386**, and given their similar sealing with braided leather, were likely made at the same time.

2 Yves II de Nesle (d. ca. 1178), lord of Nesle and count of Soissons, son of Raoul, lord of Nesle, and Raintrude. Newman, *Seigneurs*, vol. 1, 61.

3 Froissy, arr. Clermont, https://dicotopo.cths.fr/places/P14479148.

4 Devise, cant. Ham, https://dicotopo.cths.fr/places/P85212875.

5 Ivo *B*.

6 Divise *B*.

7 XL *B*.

8 *Om.* eius *A*.

9 Sara *B*.

10 Sawidis *B*.

Wigerus. Huius rei testes sunt: Iolendis[11] comitissa, Radulfus[12] castellanus de Nigella, Robertus[13] de Chilli, Albricus Gigas,[14,15] Petrus Guiserez filius Rogeri Mufle. Ne qua autem exinde in posterum calumpnia oriatur, sigilli mei impressione hoc factum testificor et confirmo.

387

July 31, 1215.

Étienne [I],[1] bishop of Noyon, describes his predecessor Baudouin [II]'s[2] gift of the Bishop's Wood and associated rights to the church of Prémontré, together with the authorization to acquire others' rights to the same woods. Étienne also makes known that Prémontré reached an agreement with the priory of Saint-Nicolas-aux-Bois, the knights Renaud[3] de Flavy and Mathieu[4] d'Eppeville, and the inhabitants of Eppeville and Vellenas *concerning the acquisition of those rights.*

A. Cartulary of Prémontré, fols. 93v–94r.
B. Original, AD Oise, H 6000, previously sealed.

Karta Noviomensis episcopi de Nemore Episcopi que tenemus sub annuo censu dimidie marce argenti.

[E]go Stephanus, divina miseratione dictus Noviomensis episcopus, omnibus in perpetuum. Notum esse volumus tam presentibus quam futuris quod, cum

11 Yolande de Hainaut (d. aft. April 1202), daughter of Baudouin IV, count of Hainaut, and Alix de Namur. Yves II de Nesle, count of Soissons, was her first husband.

12 Raoul II, castellan of Nesle, son of Raoul I, castellan of Nesle, and Adèle, sister of Guy II, castellan of Noyon and Coucy. Newman, *Seigneurs*, vol. 2, 211.

13 A Robert de Chilly (Chilly, cant. Rosières, https://dicotopo.cths.fr/places/P80391731), knight, also appears as a witness in acts 1160s–80s. Newman, *Seigneurs*, vol. 2, 94.

14 Gygas *B*.

15 Aubry *Gigas/Gaiant*, knight of Nesle and son of Robert *Gaianz*, appears as a witness in acts dated 1142–78. Newman, *Seigneurs*, vol. 2, 119.

1 Étienne de Villebéon (or de Nemours), son of Gautier de Villebéon, lord of La Chapelle-Gauthier and Nemours, and Aveline, was bishop of Noyon, 1188–1221.

2 Per **383**, this must be Baudouin II rather than Baudouin III. Baudouin II de Boulogne, abbot of the Augustinian abbey of Saint-Eloi-Fontaine, ca. 1130–ca. 1139, and bishop of Noyon, 1148–67. *GC* IX, col. 1126.

3 Renaud, knight of Flavy, who was succeeded by his sister Marguerite, wife of Raoul, lord of Flavy-le-Meldeux (cant. Guiscard, https://dicotopo.cths.fr/places/P19622430). Newman, *Seigneurs*, vol. 2, 280–1.

4 Mathieu d'Eppeville (cant. Ham. https://dicotopo.cths.fr/places/P94171781), knight, nephew of Jean, lord of Eppeville. Cagny, *Histoire de l'arrondissement de Péronne*, vol. 3, 128.

venerande memorie quondam Balduinus,[5] Noviomensis episcopus, predecessor noster, nemus quoddam apud Bonolium, quod dicitur Nemus Episcopi, et quicquid juris in eo habebat, Premonstratensi ecclesie sub annuo censu dimidie marce argenti ad Noviomense pondus in crastino Beati Johannis Baptiste sibi et suis successoribus persolvende dedisset, hoc adiecto quod ecclesia Premonstratensis quicquid alii tenebant de episcopo memorato, posset libere adipisci, tandem quia prioratus Sancti Nicholai in Boscho,[6] pertinens ad ecclesiam Sancti Eligii Noviomensis, et Renaldus de Flavi et Matheus de Espevilla, milites, necnon et homines manentes apud Espevillam et apud Vellenas usuarium habebant in nemore supradicto, unde nemus ipsum deveniebat ad nichilum, pro bono pacis et pro utilitate partium coram nobis et a nobis facta fuit et recepta a partibus ordinatio inferius, exprimenda, ecclesia Premonstratensis assignavit et dedit prioratui Sancti Nicholai in Boscho[7] octo modiatas ipsius nemoris ad mensuram Hamensem perpetuo possidendas, Renaldo autem de Flavi dedit octo modiatas similiter de quibus tres modiate ad ecclesiam Premonstratensem post eius obitum revertentur et quinque modiate suis heredibus remanebunt, Matheo vero de Espevilla dedit eadem ecclesia Premonstratensis hereditarie possidendos omnes census et omnes capones quod habebat apud Espevillam tempore huius scripti tenendos de nobis cum alio feodo suo et duas modiatas terre et dimidiam apud Muile[8] tenendas de ecclesia Premonstratensi et[9] feodo ad placitum et ad curiam tribus diebus in anno apud Bonolium, quem feodum Premonstratensis ecclesia tenebit de nobis sub annuo censu sex denariorum qui nobis et successoribus nostris in crastino Beati Johannis Baptisti solventur. Preterea dedit ei quadraginta et octo sexterlatas terre quas tenebat ecclesia Premonstratensis ad manum firmam de Roberto cognomento Arso et eius heredibus ad quartam garbam quas et ipse Matheus in eodem puncto tenebit de ecclesia Premonstratensi hoc adiecto quod et de ipsa manu firma erit homo abbatis ~~abbatis~~ Premonstratensis cum alia terra predicta. Per hoc autem assignamentum et hoc donum tam abbas et conventus Sancti Eligii quam Renaldus et Matheus milites supradicti quitaverunt in perpetuum ecclesie Premonstratensi per manum nostram quicquid juris vel consuetudinis quocumque modo habebant in residuo ipsius nemoris pro se vel pro alio. De hominibus autem manentibus apud Espevillam et apud Vellenas in justicia et in districto nostro recognitum fuit et dictum quod habebunt per totum nemus ipsum hoc quod appellatur Mortuum Nemus ad ardendum et

5 Baldewinus *B*.

6 bosco *B*.

7 bosco *B*.

8 Muille-Villette, cant. Ham, https://dicotopo.cths.fr/places/P77128677.

9 *Add.* et *A*; in *B*.

ad claudendum terras que sunt in eadem justicia et in eadem districto nostro et hoc quod appellatur vivum nemus ad edificandum secundum approbatam consuetudinem comitatus Noviomensis. Hoc autem usuarium habebunt tam in nemore quod remanet ecclesie Premonstrati quam in illis portionibus que sunt assignate prioratui Sancti Nicholai et Renaldo de Flavi et quia Matheus de Espevilla habebat conductum hominum ipsorum in nemus quando capiebant ad edificandum. Sciendum quod singuli dominorum habebunt eundem conductum in portionibus[10] quia vero constabat quod supradictus predecessor noster contulerat ecclesie Premonstratensi quicquid juris habebat in toto nemore et potestatem acquirendi hoc quod alii tenebant de ipso, recognovimus eidem ecclesie justiciam et custodiam et omnia alia in perpetuum integre possidenda que ad nos in ea portione quam retinuit sive in transfundo, sive in superfacto poterant quomodolibet pertinere, ita quod cum voluerit abbas Premonstratensis poterit vendere superfactum salvo annuo censu dimidie marce argenti que nobis antea solvebatur. Nos etiam quancumque conventionem vel commutationem ecclesia Premonstratensis potuerit facere cum hominibus memoratis de usuario quod eis remanet tenebimus secundum quod statuit predecessor noster sine contradictione aliqua[11] approbare. Hoc etiam adiectum fuit quod si abbas Premonstratensis et fratres[12] voluerint vel ad tollendum violentiam vel diligentiorem[13] custodiam eiusdem nemoris facere advocatum vel perpetuo vel ad tempus non poterunt alium quam nos et successores nostros donec eis defuerimus evocare. Et si defuerimus eis, quod absit, non poterunt recurrere ad alium quam ad dominum regem Francorum vel eius baillivos. Ceterum quia querela erat inter nos et ipsos fratres de falcatione herbe in fluvio Somane ad expediendum cursum aque supra et subtus molendina de Espevilla[14] et de Hameals[15,16] cum didicissemus per liberos homines nostros quod ipsi fratres poterant eam de jure falcare, recognovimus eis jus suum et concessimus quod possint falcare subtus et supra quandocumque voluerint. Ut igitur hec omnia futuris temporibus inviolabiliter observentur, ea fideliter hic inscribi et sigilli nostri fecimus appensione muniri. Actum pridie kalendas augusti, anno gratie M° CC°[17] quinto decimo.

10 *Om.* suis *A.*
11 qualibet *B.*
12 *Om.* Premonstratenses *A.*
13 *Om.* ad *A.*
14 Eppeville, cant. Ham. https://dicotopo.cths.fr/places/P94171781.
15 Hamels *B.*
16 Hamel-lès-Corbie, cant. Corbie, https://dicotopo.cths.fr/places/P37197765.
17 millesimo ducentesimo *B.*

388

1148–60[1]

Baudouin [II],[2] bishop of Noyon, makes known the agreement reached between the church of Prémontré and Lancelin,[3] lord of Ham, concerning two woods which had been given to Prémontré: one by Robert Gaianz *and his son Aubry[4] when an unnamed daughter of Robert's entered the monastery, the other by Thierry de Hombleux.[5]*

A. Cartulary of Prémontré, fol. 94r.
B. Original not found.

Karta episcopi Noviomensis de concessione nemoris quod Robertus Gaianz et R. Albricus filius eius contulerunt ecclesie Premonstrate.

[I]n nomine et cetera. Quoniam memorie hominum que facile labitur plerumque temporum vetustas id quod minus caute agitur surripere consuevit, maiorum sollers industria utilitati providens posterorum rerum gestarum seriem litterarum apicibus conservandam decrevit. Quorum vestigia subsecutus nec ab eorum rectitudine discrepans, ego Balduinus, Dei gratia Noviomensium episcopus, notum fieri volo tam futuris quam presentibus quod Robertus Gaianz et Albricus, filius eius, contulerunt quoddam nemus Premonstrate ecclesie pro quadam filia sua quam inibi ad conversionem posuerunt. Dedit etiam Theodericus de Humblos aliud quoddam nemus juxta prefatum prenominate ecclesie pro censu septem solidorum per annum. Hec ergo nemora dicebat Lanzelinus, Hamensis dominus, sui feodi esse suumque jus hoc esse ut quando venderet Colesi[6] nemus suum, venderet etiam prefata nemora ut sua. Verum quicquid illud esset, totum ecclesie concessit tam feodum quam omnia quecumque clamare poterat ea videlicet pactione quod, cum ecclesia nemora ipsa vendere voluerit, ipse Lancelinus quartum denarium habebit nec tamen venditio in ditione ipsius Lancelini erit sed in libera ecclesie voluntate. Interdum vero ecclesia in nemore illo accipiet quicquid inde necesse habuerit preter fagum et quercum et pomerium et pirum et escularium; fratres custodient nemora nec alii custodes apponentur nec in custodia nec in venditione. Sed nec servi Lancelini occasiones querent aliquas adversus fratres in aliqua querela sed omnia in

1 This date is based on the tenures of Baudouin, bishop of Noyon (1148–67) and of Lancelin, lord of Ham (1148–60).

2 Baudouin II de Boulogne, abbot of the Augustinian abbey of Saint-Eloi-Fontaine, ca. 1130–ca. 1139, and bishop of Noyon, 1148–67. *GC* IX, col. 1126.

3 Lancelin, lord of Ham, son of Eudes II, lord of Ham.

4 Aubry *Gigas/Gaiant*, knight of Nesle and son of Robert *Gaianz*, appears as a witness in acts dated 1142–78. Newman, *Seigneurs*, vol. 2, 119.

5 Hombleux, cant. Nesle, https://dicotopo.cths.fr/places/P11898990.

6 Collezy, comm. Berlancourt, https://dicotopo.cths.fr/places/P68465476.

fratrum veritate conquiescent tam in venditione quam in custodia. Decetero erat quedam querimonia inter Lancelinum et ecclesiam pro quadam domo de Bruci[7] et pro quodam vivario de Montisel,[8] et concessit Lancelinus ut ipsi domus de Bruci haberet omnes aesias quascumque necesse haberet in districtu suo tam in pascuis quam in ceteris quibus indigeret, excepto quod terram que ad ipsum pertineret, sine licentia ipsius non acciperet. Vivarium vero liberum ecclesie contulit et quicquid emendationis in illud facere possent, concessit et, si quid calumpnie exinde oriretur, pro suo posse auxilium ecclesie ferre promisit. Hiis concessionibus et donis interfuerunt testes: Symon[9] de Montescourt, Robertus[10] Venator, Petrus[11] de Porta, Odo filius Herli, Evrardus, Galterus filius eius, Grinbertus, frater Matheus, frater Petrus. Hec autem omnia ut rata inconvulsaque ecclesie permaneant, sigilli nostri impressione roboramus et, ne quis in posterum ecclesie dampnum irroget, sub anathemate interdicimus testesque legitimos qui huic nostre confirmationi interfuerunt supponimus.

389

July, 1223.

The knight Jean[1] *de Béthencourt gives to the church of Prémontré all his rights, including that of* garbam, *over certain lands at Bonneuil*[2] *which Prémontré had previously held of Jean and of Hugues du Plessis.*[3] *In exchange for this gift, Prémontré gave Jean and his family the right to fish once a week below the roadway of Canny.*[4] *Jean's father Hugues consents.*[5]

---

7 Brouchy, cant. Ham, https://dicotopo.cths.fr/places/P33557845.

8 Montizel, cant. Ham, https://dicotopo.cths.fr/places/P16235568.

9 Simon de Mondescourt (cant. Noyon, https://dicotopo.cths.fr/places/P60804459), son of Emmelot, appears as a witness in acts 1137–ca. 1183. Tock and Milis, *Monumenta Arroasiensia*, 143, 315.

10 Robert Venator de Ham also appears as a witness in **372** and in an 1145 act of Gerard, lord of Ham, and was the *maior communiae* of Ham in the same year. La Fons, *Une cité picarde au Moyen-Age, ou Noyon et la noyonnais aux XIVe et XVe siècles*, 251; Newman, *Homblières*, 116.

11 Pierre de la Porte, son of Alard I de Ham (or de la Porte), knight of Ham, and Helvide. He also appears in **334** and **353**.

---

1 Jean (d. aft. October 1248), lord of Béthencourt-sur-Somme (cant. Nesle, https://dicotopo.cths.fr/places/P85791062), son of Hugues II, lord of Béthencourt-sur-Somme. Newman, *Seigneurs*, vol. 2, 209–10.

2 Bonneuil, cant. Ham, https://dicotopo.cths.fr/places/P66750585.

3 Likely Le Plessis-Patte-d'Oie, cant. Guiscard, https://dicotopo.cths.fr/places/P25690373.

4 Pycke and Vleeschouwers identify *Escamli* as Essenlis (comm. Chavonne, https://dicotopo.cths.fr/places/P65971619), Pycke and Vleeschouwers, *Actes*, 486. However, we concur with Dietrich Lohrmann that *Escamli* is Canny-lès-Voyennes (cant. Nesle, https://dicotopo.cths.fr/places/P44415541). Lohrmann, "Barrages et moulins sur la Somme au temps des chanoines réguliers (XIIe–XIIIe siècles)," 341, 345.

5 The abbot of Prémontré issued an act about the same transaction. See AD Oise, H 6003.

A. Cartulary of Prémontré, fols. 94r–94v.
B. Original, AM Metz, Salis II.245, no. 11, previously sealed on a single strip of parchment.

Karta Johannis militis de Betencort de concessione cuiusdam terre ecclesie.

[E]go Joannes de Betencourt[6] miles notum facio universis tam presentibus quam futuris quod cum ego, de assensu et voluntate patris mei, domini Hugonis, garbam et quicquid juris habebatm in quibusdam terris sitis in territorio Bonolii quas ecclesia Premonstratensis tenebat de me et olim tenuerat de domino Hugone de Plaisseto, eidem ecclesie in perpetuam elemosinam contulissem ita quod ego et heredes mei debemus portare ipsi ecclesie super ipsam elemosinam[7] legitimam warandiam adversus omnes qui voluerint juri stare, prenominata ecclesia habens ad meam liberalitatem devota consideratione respectum aquam suam subtus calceatam de Escamli[8] mihi et heredibus contulit ad piscandum tali modo quod ego et heredes mei poterimus piscari in eadem aqua singulis septimanis, uno die tantum et non pluribus, cum reti et instrumento, quod vulgariter dicitur tramail[9] et botoir, nec aliis instrumentis uti poterimus ad piscandum. Ecclesia similiter piscari poterit singulis septimanis in eadem aqua, uno die tantum et non pluribus, cum reti et instrumento, quod dicitur tramail et botoir, nec aliis instrumentis uti poterit ad piscandum, nisi in eo quod retinuit sibi jus piscandi in bordel et penchons molendini nec ego aut heredes mei aliquid habebimus ibidem. Hanc siquidem piscationem tenetur michi et heredibus meis ipsa ecclesia warandire adversus omnes, qui voluerint juri stare. Sciendum est autem quod piscatores mei et heredum meorum, cum piscabuntur, deferent medietatem piscium captorum in domum ecclesie Premonstratensis de Escanli,[10] qui etiam piscatores facient fidelitatem ecclesie memorate. Similiter piscatores ecclesie facient fidelitatem michi et heredibus meis et cum piscabuntur deferent medietatem piscium captorum in domum meam de Betencourt.[11] Preterea ecclesia sepedicta retinuit sibi omnem justiciam et omnes aisentias. In quorum omnium testimonium feci presentes litteras sigilli mei munimine roborari. Actum mense julio, anno gratie M° CC°[12] vicesimo tercio.

---

6 Betencort *B*.
7 elemosina *B*.
8 Eskanli *B*.
9 tramal *B*.
10 Eskanli *B*.
11 Betencort *B*.
12 millesimo ducentesimo *B*.

390

January, 1228.

In the presence of Jacques,[1] officialis *of Noyon, husband and wife Gautier d'Eppeville*[2] *and Marie,*[3] *sister of the knight Gobert*[4] *d'Apilly, acknowledge that they possess no rights over the Bishop's Wood except for the right of* cerke, *which they may exercise for 15 days either side of Christmas. (See **392**.)*

A. Cartulary of Prémontré, fol. 94v.

B. Original, AD Oise, Hs 1380, sealed on a double strip of parchment, surviving fragment of brown wax seal.

Karta officialis Noviomensis de illa consuetudine que vulgo dicitur cerque quam Walterus de Espevilla dicebat se habere in nostro nemore.

[J]acobus, sedis Noviomensis officialis, omnibus presentes litteras inspecturis salutem in domino. Universitati vestre notum facimus quod cum Walterus de Espevilla et Maria, uxor eius, soror Goberti de Apilli militis, haberent in bosco ecclesie Premonstratensis, quod dicitur Nemus Episcopi, unam consuetudinem que vulgariter dicitur cerke et occasione illius consuetudinis dicerent se debere habere in ipso nemore alias consuetudines et exactiones quas ecclesia Premonstratensis non recognoscebat et super hoc mota esset discordia inter dictos W[alterum] et M[ariam] uxorem eius, ex una parte et dictam ecclesiam ex altera, tandem prenominati Walterus et Maria, uxor eius, in nostra presentia personaliter constituti bonorum virorum consilio mediante, recognoverunt spontanei non coacti quod nullas consuetudines, nullas exactiones nec etiam aliquid jus habebant nec umquam[5] habuerunt in nemore supradicto nisi tantummodo illam consuetudinem que dicitur cerke sic intelligendam et sic restringendam videlicet custodiam quindecim diebus ante nativitatem Domini et quindecim diebus post nativitatem a malefactoribus et extraneis salvo dicte ecclesie usu et possessione ita quod si preter voluntatem et commodum ecclesie prenominate vel fratrum Bonolii aliquid forisfacti fieret in eodem nemore quindecim diebus

1 Jacques, *officialis* of Noyon, also appears in a 1229 act in the cartulary of the cathedral chapter of Noyon. AD Oise, G 1984, fols. 250r–250v.

2 Eppeville, cant. Ham. https://dicotopo.cths.fr/places/P94171781.

3 Marie d'Appilly, daughter of Jean d'Appilly, knight, and Pétronille de Coucy. Ponthieux, "Notes historiques sur Appilly," 15.

4 Gobert d'Appilly (cant. Noyon, https://dicotopo.cths.fr/places/P38602761), knight and husband of Mathilde, son of Jean d'Appilly, knight, and Pétronille de Coucy. He also appears in some 1230 acts in the cartulary of the cathedral chapter of Noyon. Ibid.; AD Oise, G 1984, fols. 76r, 200r–200v, 226r.

5 unquam *B*.

ante nativitatem Domini et quindecim diebus post nativitatem dicti Walterus et Maria, uxor sua, super hoc haberent emendam. Hanc autem compositionem prefati Walterus et Maria uxor sua, fide corporaliter prestita, promiserunt se ratam et gratam in perpetuum habituros ita quod super hoc vel occasione huiusmodi decetero per se vel per alium dictam ecclesiam nullatenus molestabunt nec facient molestari nec artem nec ingenium querent per que prenominata ecclesia possit vel debeat in perpetuum molestari. In cuius rei testimonium presentes literas ad instantiam et petitionem dictorum Walteri et Marie, uxor eius, sigillo curie Noviomensis ecclesie prenominate tradidimus roboratas. Actum mense januario, anno gratie M° CC° vicesimo VIII°.[6]

391

1189. Ham.

Obert,[1] abbot of Prémontré, recognizes that husband and wife Alard de Cressy[2] and Mauduite, daughter of Ermenrice, ceded to the church of Prémontré all Mauduite's inheritance related to the mills of Canisy,[3] owing an annual census *payment of six* modii *of grain (*seges*) during Mauduite's lifetime, to be reduced to two* modii *after her death.*

A. Cartulary of Prémontré, fol. 94v.

B. Original (chirograph), AD Aisne, H 763, sealed on a double strip of parchment with damaged brown wax seal showing an effigy of the abbot. In the left margin and starting at the the top, the upper half of the letters that form the word CHYROGRAPHUM.

Karta Oberti abbatis Premonstratensis de concessione Alardi de Cresci et uxoris eius de sede molendinorum de Chanesi.

[Q]uia per litteras facilius ea que facta sunt ad memoriam solent reduci, ego Obertus, abbas Premonstrati, et capitulum nostrum ad omnium noticiam fecimus hic inscribi quod Alardus de Cresci[4] et uxor eius Malducta, filia Ermenrici, conventione nobiscum habita, concesserunt in perpetuam possessionem ecclesie nostre quicquid habebant in sede molendinorum de Chanesi que erat de hereditate ipsius Malducte sub annuo censu sex modiorum segetis qualem unum molendinorum nostrorum circumiacentium lucrabitur, qui sex modii

6 octavo *B*.

1 Obert, abbot of the Premonstratensian abbey of Valsecret, 1186–9, 1192–1200, and abbot of Prémontré, 1189–91. *MP* II, 527, 536.

2 Likely Cressy-Omancourt, cant. Roye, https://dicotopo.cths.fr/places/P62235034.

3 Canisy, cant. Nesle, https://dicotopo.cths.fr/places/P34153509.

4 Cressi *B*.

Malducta vivente, per singulos annos usque ad festum Omnium Sanctorum solventur. Post decessum autem eius quatuor modii de predicto censu ob remedium anime sue in elemosinam nostre ecclesie remanebunt et illi qui post ipsam ad tenendam hereditatem legitima successione accesserint duos reliquos modios habebunt. Hec autem conventio primum facta fuit apud Espevillam,[5] presentibus ex parte ecclesie nostre: Waltero de Yrun,[6] preposito nostro et Willermo priore Bonolii,[7] et Waltero, converso de Hanapia,[8] et ex parte Alardi presentibus tam ipso et fratre eius Radulpho,[9] quam uxore eius[10] Malducta et fratre eius, Gerardo, ad quem hereditas pertinebat, qui hanc conventionem et elemosinam concessit pariter et laudavit. Postea vero hec eadem conventio quemadmodum superius dicta est, apud Hamum coram subscriptis testibus recognita ab utraque parte fuit, quam nos etiam ad maiorem stabilitatem presenti scripto cum appositione sigilli nostri et eorumdem testium annotatione sub divisione cirographi[11] fecimus commendari. S. Balduini,[12] prepositi de Ham et officialis comitis Flandrensis. S. Walteri de Bruchi,[13] S. Mathei[14] de Espevilla, militum. S. Albrici[15] Gigantis. Actum anno ab incarnatione Domini, M° C° octogesimo nono.

392

January, 1228.

*The knight Gobert[1] d'Apilly as fief lord confirms the agreement reached between his sister Marie,[2] her husband, Gautier d'Eppeville,[3] and the church of Prémontré. (See **390**.)*

---

5 Eppeville, cant. Ham. https://dicotopo.cths.fr/places/P94171781.
6 Iron, cant. Guise, https://dicotopo.cths.fr/places/P04584610.
7 The Premonstratensian *curtis* of Bonneuil. *MP* II, 484.
8 Hannape, cant. Wassigny, https://dicotopo.cths.fr/places/P37303056.
9 Radulfo *B*.
10 sua *B*.
11 chirographi *B*.
12 Bolduini *B*.
13 Brouchy, cant. Ham, https://dicotopo.cths.fr/places/P33557845.
14 Mathieu d'Eppeville, knight, nephew of Jean, lord of Eppeville. Cagny, *Histoire de l'arrondissement de Péronne*, vol. 3, 128.
15 Aubry *Gigas/Gaiant*, knight of Nesle and son of Robert *Gaianz*, appears as a witness in acts dated 1142–78. Newman, *Seigneurs*, vol. 2, 119.

---

1 Gobert d'Appilly (cant. Noyon, https://dicotopo.cths.fr/places/P38602761), knight and husband of Mathilde, son of Jean d'Appilly, knight, and Pétronille de Coucy. He also appears in some 1230 acts in the cartulary of the cathedral chapter of Noyon. Ponthieux, "Notes historiques sur Appilly," 15; AD Oise, G 1984, fols. 76r, 200r–200v, 226r.
2 Marie d'Appilly, daughter of Jean d'Appilly, knight, and Pétronille de Coucy. Ponthieux, "Notes historiques sur Appilly," 15.
3 Eppeville, cant. Ham. https://dicotopo.cths.fr/places/P94171781.

A. Cartulary of Prémontré, fols. 94v–95r.
B. Original, AD Oise, Hs 1500, sealed on a double strip of parchment with surviving seal that shows a crown bearing a cross.

Karta domini Goberti de Apilli de confirmatione doni Walteri de Espevilla de consuetudine que dicitur cerke.

[E]go Gobertus de Apilli miles notum facio universis tam presentibus quam futuris quod cum Walterus de Espevilla et Maria soror mea, uxor eiusdem Walteri, haberent in nemore Premonstratensis ecclesie, quod dicitur Nemus Episcopi, unam consuetudinem que vulgariter dicitur cerke, quam consuetudinem de me tenent, et occasione illius consuetudinis dicerent se habere debere in ipso nemore alias consuetudines et exactiones quas ecclesia Premonstratensis predicta non recognoscebat et super hoc orta esset discordia inter ipsos et ecclesiam memoratam, tandem inter partes de communi assensu facta fuit conpositio[4] in hunc modum: quod dictus Walterus et prenominata Maria soror mea, uxor eiusdem Walteri, de qua hec hereditas descendebat, spontanea voluntate recognoverunt quod nullas consuetudines, nullas exactiones, nullum denique jus habuerunt vel habebant in nemore supradicto, nisi tantum modo consuetudinem illam que dicitur cerke sic intelligendam et sic restringendam, videlicet custodiam in ipso nemore quindecim diebus ante nativitatem Domini et quindecim diebus post nativitatem Domini a malefactoribus et extraneis ita quod, si preter voluntatem et commodum ecclesie Premonstratensis vel fratrum Bonolii[5] aliquid fieret in ipso nemore quod forisfactum esset quantum ad nemus quindecim diebus ante nativitatem Domini et quindecim diebus post inde haberent emendam. Hanc conpositionem idem W[alterus] et M[aria] uxor sua, fide corporaliter prestita, promiserunt se ratam et gratam in perpetuum habituros ita quod super hoc vel occasione huius[6] ipsam ecclesiam nec molestabunt nec dampnificabunt nec facient molestari. Ut igitur conpositio[7] ista perpetuam optineat firmitatem, ego tamquam dominus ipsam compositionem ratam et gratam habui et approbavi et presentem kartam super hoc confectam sigilli mei munimine roboravi. Actum mense januario, anno incarnationis dominice M° CC° XX° VIII°.[8]

---

4 compositio *B*.
5 The Premonstratensian *curtis* of Bonneuil. *MP* II, 484.
6 *Om.* modi *A*.
7 compositio *B*.
8 millesimo CC° vicesimo octavo *B*.

393

March 17, 1216. Saint-Barthélemy, Noyon.

Étienne [I],[1] *bishop of Noyon, makes known the accord concluded in his presence between the church of Prémontré on the one part and the bishop's men of Eppeville*[2] *and* Vellenis *on the other, concerning a meadow established by the Premonstratensians at the border of the Bishop's Wood at Bonneuil.*[3]

A. Cartulary of Prémontré, fol. 95r.

B. Original, AD Oise, H 6000, previously sealed on pink silk threads.

EDITION: Fossier, *Chartes de coutume en Picardie*, 337–8; *Chartae Galliae*, no. 211251, http://telma.irht.cnrs.fr/outils/chartae-galliae/charte211251/.

Karta Stephani Noviomensis episcopi inter ecclesiam Premonstrate et homines de Espevilla.

[E]go Stephanus, divina permissione Noviomensis episcopus, omnibus in perpetuum. Notum facimus tam presentibus quam futuris quod cum inter ecclesiam Premonstratensem ex una parte et homines nostros de Espevilla et de Vellenis ex parte altera questio verteretur super quodam prato quod fratres Premonstratenses fecerant in extremitate nemoris quod dicitur Nemus Episcopi, apud Bonolium, abbas tandem Premonstratensis et dicti homines ad nostram presentiam accesserunt et fecerunt pacem ac concordiam, nobis mediantibus in hac forma: dicti homines quitaverunt predictum pratum ecclesie Premonstratensi eo tenore quod fratres Premonstratenses decetero non poterunt sartare in nemore illo ad dampnum hominum predictorum sive ipsorum assensu vel nisi nemus vel aliqua pars nemoris ad hoc devenerit quod ad usuarium ardendi et edificandi inutile sit omnino secundum estimationem abbatis Ursicampi[4] qui tempore illo erit; scindetur autem ipsum nemus tam a fratribus Premonstratensibus quam ab hominibus sepedictis ad blancham talliam et ad rectum talliam et servabunt fratres tallicia ab omni genere animalium usque ad quadriennium ad minus etiam a suis animalibus propriis. Si autem animalia in talliciis capta fuerint, eo ducantur quo duci debebunt de jure ad judicium liberorum hominum Noviomensis comitatus. Ut igitur ista conpositio[5] futuris temporibus debitam firmitatem eam fideliter hic inscribi et sigilli nostri fecimus impressione muniri salvo in omnibus aliis jure ecclesie Premonstratensis et hominum predictorum secundum quod in nostro auctentico[6] quod est penes ecclesiam Premonstratensem expressius est

1 Étienne de Villebéon (or de Nemours), son of Gautier de Villebéon, lord of La Chapelle-Gauthier and Nemours, and Aveline, was bishop of Noyon, 1188–1221.

2 Eppeville, cant. Ham. https://dicotopo.cths.fr/places/P94171781.

3 Bonneuil, cant. Ham, https://dicotopo.cths.fr/places/P66750585.

4 The Cistercian abbey of Notre-Dame d'Ourscamp.

5 compositio *B*.

6 autentico *B*.

notatum. Actum Noviomi apud Sanctum Bartholomeum, sexto decimo kalendas aprilis, anno incarnationis dominice M° CC°[7] sextodecimo.

394

November, 1230. Noyon.

Magister *Hugues,*[1] *canon and* officialis *of Noyon, makes known the accord concluded between the church of Prémontré and Gautier, priest of Devise,*[2] *that increased the value of Gautier's benefice, which he had found to be insufficient.*

A. Cartulary of Prémontré, fol. 95r.

B. Original, AD Somme, 20 H_SC_7, no. 3, sealed.[3]

Karta officialis Noviomensis de compositione inter ecclesiam Premonstratem et presbiterum de Devisa.

[U]niversis Christi fidelibus presentes literas inspecturis magister Hugo, canonicus et officialis Noviomensis salutem in Domino. Vobis notum facimus quod cum discordia esset inter Walterum, presbyterum de Divisa, ex una parte, et ecclesiam Premonstratensem ex altera super hoc quod idem presbyter petebat ab ea quod beneficium suum quod erat de donatione ipsius, facerent sufficiens cum esset insufficiens, ut dicebat. Tandem de bonorum virorum consilio intervenit pax amicabiliter inter eos quod idem presbyter habebit singulis annis in grangia de Divisa octo modios frumenti ad mensuram d'Aties.[4] Habebit etiam terciam partem decime feni eiusdem parrochie et totam decimam minutam infra interclausuram ville et omnes oblationes altaris sui, preterquam in die Purificationis et in die Parascenes in quibus diebus ecclesia terciam partem habebit. Recognovit autem presbyter sibi esse satisfactum omnino et promisit in verbo Domini quod dictam ecclesiam decetero super augmentatione dicti beneficii nullatenus molestabit sed contentus erit de premissis. Promisit etiam de verbo Domini quod dicte ecclesie deserviet et quod non recedet ab ea in anno plusquam per quindecim dies ad plus non nisi de licentia sui superioris sed moram continuam faciet in eadem. Quod si contra premissa vel aliquid premissorum venerit idem presbyter ex tunc ipso facto ex toto privabitur eadem. Et extunc licebit Premonstratensi ecclesie persone ydonee ecclesiam conferre eandem. In cuius rei testimonium presentes literas sigillo curie Noviomensis fecimus sigillari. Datum Noviomi anno gratie M° CC° XXX°, mense novembri.

7 millesimo ducentesimo *B*.

1 *Magister* Hugues, canon and *officialis* of Noyon, ca. 1229–ca. 1236. AD Aisne, H 455, fol. 310v; AD Oise, G 1984, fols. 238v–239r.

2 Devise, cant. Ham, https://dicotopo.cths.fr/places/P85212875.

3 Due to conservation concerns, the original was not available to the editors.

4 Athies, cant. Ham. https://dicotopo.cths.fr/places/P98820850.

395

1180.[1] Vézelay.

Abbot Gérard[2] *of the Benedictine abbey of Vézelay confirms the agreement reached between Abbot Hugues [II] of Prémontré and brother Barthélemy of Vézelay, according to which Vézelay relinquishes to Prémontré all the rights and revenues which its dependent house of Vilerselve had formerly claimed at Bonneuil,*[3] *together with two* modii *of grain (*frumentum*) taken annually at the mill of Canisy.*[4] *In return, Prémontré relinquishes to Vézelay the tithe of Golancourt.*[5]

A. Cartulary of Prémontré, fol. 95r.
B. Original, AD Oise, Hs 1369, with fragments of two seals, the bishop's and abbot's seals, on two double threads of hemp.
EDITION: Cherest, "Étude Historique sur Vézelay," 470–1.

Karta de conpositione inter ecclesiam Premonstratensem et ecclesiam Vizelensem super quibusdam possessionibus de Bonolio.

[V]enerabili domino confratri et amico Hugoni, Dei gratia Premonstratensi abbati, atque sancto eiusdem ecclesie capitulo, Gerardus, Vizellensis abbas, et universis eiusdem loci conventus salutem et orationum suffragia. Transmutationes quas ecclesie in vicem pro bono pacis et sine detrimento earum frequenter faciunt, tanto debent in posterum esse firmiores quanto rationis et utilitatis consideratione sunt fortiores. Pro vitando igitur seditionis scandalo et discordie seminario quod non nunquam religiosis etiam parit ~~in~~ obprobrium, de communi consensu, in perpetuum dimittimus et renunciamus illi juri et redditibus quos prior abbatie de Villari Silva et domus sibi commissa habent in territoriis atque culturis fratrum vestrorum de Bonooculo et duobus modiis frumenti quos pro sede molendini de Chanesiaco predicti fratres quotannis solvere debebant, sicut inter vos et dilectum fratrem nostrum Bartholomeum, prescripte abbatie priorem, bona fide contractum et ordinatum est. Vos quoque in perpetuum dimittitis et renunciatis toti decime terre nostre de Goslencort[6] que recipit semen duodecim[7] modi~~a~~orum. Ut autem hec transmutatio perpetuam

1 Per *B*. The cartulary copy erroneously gives the date as 1130.
2 Gérard d'Arcy, abbot of the Benedictine abbey of Vézelay, 1171–98.
3 Bonneuil, cant. Ham, https://dicotopo.cths.fr/places/P66750585.
4 Canisy, cant. Nesle, https://dicotopo.cths.fr/places/P34153509.
5 Golancourt, cant. Guiscard, https://dicotopo.cths.fr/places/P75999303.
6 Guoslencort *B*.
7 XII^{cim} *B*.

utrinque[8] optineat firmitatem presens scriptum exinde factum sigillorum nostrorum munimine confirmamus; ex parte vero vestra cartam[9] similia dicentem et continentem atque sigillatam habere debemus. Actum est hoc Vizeliaci, anno ab incarnatione Domini M° C°[10] tricesimo.[11]

396

1157. Nesle.

Baudouin [II],[1] *bishop of Noyon, gives notice that Hugues du Pont, with the consent of Yves [II],*[2] *count of Soissons, gave the church of Prémontré his part of the tithe of Devise.*[3]

A. Cartulary of Prémontré, fols. 95r–95v.
B. Original, AM Metz, Salis II.243, no. 1, sealed on alum-tawed leather strap with partial seal intact.

Karta Noviomensis episcopi de elemosina Hugonis de Ponte de decima de Devisa.

[I]n nomine sancte et cetera.[4] Ego B[alduinus], Dei gratia Noviomensium episcopus, notum facio omnibus tam futuris quam presentibus quod Hugo de Ponte concessit dono Premonstrate ecclesie hoc quod habebat in decima de Divisa. Fecit autem hoc assensu comitis Yvonis,[5] et comes Yvo[6] reposuit in manu nostra et ego reddidi ecclesie Premonstrate mittens in manu Hugonis, eiusdem ecclesie abbatis. Hoc autem donum Hugonis de Ponte factum est in curia comitis Yvonis[7] apud Nigellam, presente domino Radulfo[8] de Cusdum et

---

8 utrincque *B.*
9 chartam *B.*
10 *Om.* L *A.*
11 LXXX° *B.*

---

1 Baudouin II de Boulogne, abbot of the Augustinian abbey of Saint-Eloi-Fontaine, ca. 1130–ca. 1139, and bishop of Noyon, 1148–67. *GC* IX, col. 1126.
2 Yves II de Nesle (d. ca. 1178), lord of Nesle and count of Soissons, son of Raoul, lord of Nesle, and Raintrude. Newman, *Seigneurs*, vol. 1, 61.
3 Devise, cant. Ham, https://dicotopo.cths.fr/places/P85212875.
4 *Add.* et cetera *A*; et individue Trinitatis *B.*
5 Ivonis *B.*
6 Ivo *B.*
7 Ivonis *B.*
8 Raoul, lord of Coudun (cant. Ressons, https://dicotopo.cths.fr/places/P96692478). He confirmed a donation to the Premonstratensian abbey of Braine in 1151, and made a gift to the Cistercian abbey of Ourscamp in 1166. Peigné-Delacourt, *Cartulaire de l'Abbaye de Notre-Dame d'Ourscamp de l'ordre de Cîteaux, fondée en 1129 au diocèse de Noyon*, 395–6; Guyotjeannin et al., *Le chartrier de l'abbaye prémontrée de Saint-Yved de Braine (1134–1250)*, 282.

Radulfo,[9] castellano de Nigella, Radulfo[10] etiam bello, Rogero[11] justiciario, Widone joculatore. Actum est hoc anno dominice incarnationis M° C° L°[12] septimo.

397

1137. Noyon.

*Simon [I],[1] bishop of Noyon, makes known and approves that husband and wife Foulques,[2] mayor of Noyon, and Berthe, and their sons Barthélemy and Guibert, gave to the church of Prémontré half of the major tithe and a third of the minor tithe of Muille.[3] Hugues[4] de Béthencourt, from whom the fief descended, consented. (See near-duplicate **443**.)*

A. Cartulary of Prémontré, fol. 95v.
B. Original, BnF, Coll. Picardie 290, no. 1, sealed on a single strip of leather in brown wax.
EDITION: Pycke and Vleeschouwers, *Actes*, 401–2.
REGISTER: Boghen, "Inventaire des actes épiscopaux originaux conservés à la Bibliothèque nationale (1121–1200)," 120.

Karta Symonis Noviomensis episcopi de elemosina Fulconis, maioris de Noviomo, de decima de Muiles.

[I]n nomine sancte et cetera. Quoniam defluentibus annis multa solent in oblivione defluere, que memoriter retinere volumus, scriptis solemus annotare. Quapropter ego Symon, Dei gratia Noviomensis episcopus, tam posteris quam

9 Raoul II, castellan of Nesle, son of Raoul I, castellan of Nesle, and Adèle, sister of Guy II, castellan of Noyon and Coucy. Newman, *Seigneurs*, vol. 2, 211.
10 Raoul *Bellus*, brother of Mathieu, also appears in **372** and is attested as a witness in acts for the lords of Nesle, 1133–59. Newman, *Seigneurs*, vol. 2, 35.
11 Roger the *justiciarius* is attested in acts of the lords of Nesle, 1142–75. Newman, *Seigneurs*, vol. 2, 37, 149.
12 millesimo centesimo quinquagesimo *B*.

1 Simon I de Vermandois (d. 1148) was the son of Hugues I and Adélaïde, count and countess of Vermandois and Valois, and bishop of Noyon, 1123–42.
2 Foulques, mayor of Noyon, 1120s–30s.
3 Muille-Villette, cant. Ham, https://dicotopo.cths.fr/places/P77128677.
4 Likely Hugues I de Sermaize, lord of Béthencourt-sur-Somme (cant. Nesle, https://dicotopo.cths.fr/places/P85791062), a father or grandfather of Simon *le Vieux* de Sermaize, lord of Béthencourt-sur-Somme. See Newman, *Seigneurs*, vol. 2, 99, 209–10; Guyotjeannin, *Episcopus*, 272.

modernis notum facio quod Fulco, maior de Noviomo, et uxor eius, Bertha, cum filiis suis, Bartholomeo et Guiberto, dimidiam partem maioris decime et terciam minute de Muiles[5] tam pro suo quam pro suorum remedio Premonstrate ecclesie Sancte Marie et Sancti Johannis Baptiste dederunt, Hugone de Betencourt[6] ad cuius feodum decima pertinebat, concedente et quod suum in ea erat, in manu nostra ponente sub his testibus: Hugone, cancellario, magistro Azone[7] medico, Gilleberto monacho, Rogero[8] de Torota, Hugone[9] de Perona, Johanne de Axcei, Yvone[10] de Sancto Petro. Ego autem predicte ecclesie decimam illam omni tempore obtinendam concessi et, ne ullatenus cassum fieri posset, scripto et sigillo nostro roboravi. Quisquis inde ecclesie cui data est, nocere intenderit, anathema sit. Actum Noviomi anno ab incarnatione Domini M° C° XXX° VII°, epacta VII^a, concurrente IIII°, indictione I^a. S. Theoderici,[11] thesaurarii. S. Hugonis,[12] cancellarii. S. Petri, cantoris. S. Rogeri, diaconi. S. Walberti, diaconi. S. Widonis[13] de Sancto Petro. S. Berlandi. S. Richardi.[14] S. Landrici. S. Roberti Cardun.[15]

398

1163

Baudouin [II],[1] bishop of Noyon, makes known that Doa d'Aubigny[2] had previously conceded to the church of Prémontré two parts of the tithe of Brouchy[3]

5 Muvles *B.*

6 Bethencurt *B.*

7 A *medicus* called Aszo also appears as a witness in **299** and **443.** Wickersheimer, Jacquart, and Beaujouan, *Dictionnaire biographique des médecins en France au moyen âge*, vol. 3, 34.

8 Roger *Filius Episcopi*, castellan of Thourotte and son of the lady Adèle and perhaps Teszo, castellan of Coucy. He entered Prémontré in 1141. Through his mother he was related to the castellans of Chauny. Guyotjeannin, *Episcopus*, 212–14, 273–4.

9 A Hugues de Péronne appears in an 1139 act of the abbey of Ourscamp, also in the company of Roger de Thourotte. BnF, MS lat. 5473, fol. 130r.

10 Ivone *B.*

11 Thierry de Nesle, son of Raoul, lord of Nesle, and Raintrude, was treasurer of Noyon, ca. 1134–ca. 1157, and archdeacon of Cambrai. In 1157, he participated in the translation of the relics of St Éloi. Mazière, "Annales Noyonnaises, première partie," 55–6.

12 Hugues III de Roye, chancellor of Noyon-Tournai, ca. 1130–46, and of Noyon, 1146–63/6. Pycke, *Le chapitre cathédral Notre-Dame de Tournai de la fin du Xie à la fin du XIIIe siècle*, 64.

13 Vidonis *B.*

14 Rihardi *B.*

15 Carclun *B.*

1 Baudouin II de Boulogne, abbot of the Augustinian abbey of Saint-Eloi-Fontaine, ca. 1130–ca. 1139, and bishop of Noyon, 1148–67. *GC* IX, col. 1126.

2 Aubigny-Planche, cant. Ham, https://dicotopo.cths.fr/places/P23943075.

3 Brouchy, cant. Ham, https://dicotopo.cths.fr/places/P33557845.

with the consent of her sons Mathieu and Paganus; Aelide, fief lord and wife of Doa's unnamed brother; Aelide's children; and Aubry[4] *de Roye. Later, Jean Bruer, husband of Doa's daughter Aelide, claimed damages against the church but then recognized and conceded Doa's gift. Jean's wife Aelide, her sisters Marie and Emmeline, and their husbands, Jean and Aubert, assent to this renunciation. (See near-duplicate* ***442****.)*[5]

A. Cartulary of Prémontré, fol. 95v.

B. Original, BnF, Coll. Picardie 290, no. 8, no evidence of a seal as the bottom has been damaged.

REGISTER: Boghen, "Inventaire des actes épiscopaux originaux conservés à la Bibliothèque nationale (1121–1200)," 121.

Karta Balduini Noviomensis episcopi de elemosina domine Doe de Albigni de duabus partibus decime de Bruci.

[I]n nomine sancte et cetera.[6] Beneficia servorum Dei episcopali debent auctoritate communiri, ne cum occasu temporum cadat et memoria rerum gestarum. Ea propter ego Balduinus, Dei gratia Noviomensis ecclesie minister, notum fieri volo tam futuris quam presentibus quod domina Doa de Albigni,[7] sicut in litteris domini Symonis, predecessoris nostri, repperimus, concessit Premonstrate ecclesie duas partes decime de Bruci perpetuo possidendas, concedentibus heredibus suis, Matheo videlicet filio suo, et Pagano, fratre suo, concedentibus etiam illis de quorum feodo descendebat decima, Aelide uxore fratris Doe, cum filiis suis et Albrico de Roia. Hii[8] omnes decimam istam per manus prefati episcopi supra memorate ecclesie contulerunt sub hiis testibus: Bonefacio, archidiacono; Hugone, cancellario; Johanne Rufo, Drogone de Plaissei.[9] Quod autem Albricus de Roia, Doa et filiis eius, Aelidis et eius filii, hoc concesserint. Testes sunt: Bernerus frater Roberti Rufi,[10]

---

4 Aubry, lord of Roye and Becquigny, was the *dapifer* of Raoul, count of Vermandois in the 1130s/40s. He was the husband of one Mathilde, and brother of Wermond, lord of Cessoy. Tock and Milis, *Monumenta Arroasiensia*, 242–3; Guyotjeannin, *Episcopus*, 220; Newman, *Seigneurs*, vol. 2, 299; Newman, *Homblières*, 110. He is likely the same Aubry de Roye who appears in **300**, **398**, **442**, and **464**.

5 Doa's original gift is detailed in an 1147 act of Simon, bishop of Noyon. BnF, nouv. acq. lat. 2390, no. 5.

6 *Add.* cetera *A*; individue Trinitatis. *B*.

7 Albingni *B*.

8 Hi *B*.

9 Plaisei *B*.

10 Robert *Rufus*, brother of Mathieu and Bernier, and father of Adam, Jean, and Widèle, appears in **345**, **353**, **371**, **419**, and **442.**

Fulcho, Symon filius eius, Fulcho[11] Obeline, Bartholomeus de Parrona. Succedente vero tempore Johannes Bruers qui primogenitam filiam prefate Doe uxorem duxerat, movit calumpniam super eadem decima Premonstrate ecclesie sed tandem donum illud quod eadem Doa predicte ecclesie fecerat, recognovit et concessit ipse et Aelidis, uxor eius. Hoc etiam laudaverunt et concesserunt Maria et Enmelina,[12] filie eiusdem Doe et mariti earum Johannes, ~~filius~~ decani famulus, et Autbertus.[13] Huius donationis testes sunt: Tieszo decanus noster, qui loco nostro interfuit et vice nostra elemosinam de manu eorum suscepit, Petrus de Duaco, Robertus frater eius, Bartholomeus[14] filius Fulconis Obeline, Wibertus frater eius, Arnulphus[15] Persez, Robertus de Froemont, Rogerus de Warentruz. Ut autem hoc donum prefate ecclesie firmum inconcussumque permaneat, episcopali auctoritate communimus et sigilli nostri impressione corroboramus et eos qui super prefata decima supra memoratam ecclesiam inquietare scienter deinceps presumpserint, anathematis vinculo innodamus. Actum anno incarnati verbi Mº Cº LXº IIIº, epacta XIIII[a].

399

1163

Baudouin [II],[1] *bishop of Noyon, makes known that Simon*[2] Ratus *and his brother Guillaume gave to the church of Prémontré revenues and rights in the territory of Golancourt.*[3] *Guillaume and Simon also concede all their rights as fief lords on the share of the* garba *that Jean de Camas*[4] *gave to Prémontré. Marie, sister of Simon and Guillaume, and her unnamed sons consent to this. (See near-duplicate* ***441****.)*

A. Cartulary of Prémontré, fols. 95v–96r.

B. Original, AD Oise, H 6038, previously sealed on two strips of white leather.

---

11 Foulques Obelin is attested in acts from 1134–65. See **322**, **353**, **362**, and **442.**

12 Emmelina *B*.

13 Aubertus *B*.

14 Barthélemy and Wibert, sons of Foulques Obelin and Berthe, also appear in **353**.

15 Ernulphus *B*.

---

1 Baudouin II de Boulogne, abbot of the Augustinian abbey of Saint-Eloi-Fontaine, ca. 1130–ca. 1139, and bishop of Noyon, 1148–67. *GC* IX, col. 1126.

2 Simon *Ratus*, brother of Guillaume, also appears in **336** and **441**.

3 Golancourt, cant. Guiscard, https://dicotopo.cths.fr/places/P75999303.

4 Camas, comm. Jussy. https://dicotopo.cths.fr/places/P27501164.

Karta Balduini Noviomensis episcopi de elemosina Symonis cognomento Rati de novem denariis et quatuordecim ex alia parte.

[I]n nomine sancte et cetera.[5] Ego Balduinus, Dei gratia Noviomensis dictus episcopus, notum fieri volo tam futuris quam presentibus quod Symon dicitur[6] Ratus et Willermus, frater eius, dederunt Premonstrate ecclesie per manum nostram in elemosina novem denarios obolorum censualiter singulis annis quos in terra Enmeline[7] reclamabant et quatuordecim[8] denarios et obolum eiusdem monete pari modo prefate ecclesie concesserunt quos accipiebat[9] in terra Gisleberti de Gollencurt[10] singulis annis et duas[11] corvatas quas eadem terra eis debebat, prefate ecclesie remiserunt eo tenore quod si prefatus G[islebertus] predicte ecclesie daret aliam terram quam sibi retinuerat, ipsi censum haberent. Concesserunt etiam prefate[12] duodecim[13] denarios obolorum quod reclamabant de terra Odonis qui dicitur Cum Barba, ita quod in omnibus supradictis nec districtum nec justiciam sibi retinuerunt in omnibus que ad prefatam ecclesiam pertinerent. Donum etiam quod Johannes de Kamac fecerat prefate ecclesie de quadam terra sua ad sextam garbam[14] perpetuo que de feodo eorum descendebat, concesserunt et liberam fecerunt ab omni districto et justicia fratribus prefate ecclesie et omnibus que ad ipsos pertinent ea conditione quod si prefatus Johannes feodum suum non deserviret, garbam[15] que eum contingebat, seisire possent, sed terra ecclesie libera remaneret. Hanc tamen seisinam non debent facere infra quinque annos instantes quia inter predictos milites et prefate ecclesie fratres ita terminatum est. Concesserunt etiam prefate ecclesie libere in perpetuum possidere et sine omni districto et justicia in omnibus que ad ecclesiam pertinent, quicquid in die conscriptionis huius habebat in territorio de Gollencourt[16] tam in terris quam in nemoribus quod erat juris eorum ea conditione quod si de omnibus predictis aut aliquo horum ecclesia predicta inquietaretur, aut aliquis super hoc reclamaret, ecclesia non haberet inde respondere

5 *Add.* cetera *A*; et individue Trinitatis *B*.
6 *Om.* qui *A*.
7 Emmeline *B*.
8 XIII[cim] *B*.
9 accipiebant *B*.
10 Golleincurt *B*.
11 II[as] *B*.
12 *Om.* ecclesie *A*.
13 XII[cim] *B*.
14 karbam *B*.
15 karbam *B*.
16 Golleincurt *B*.

nisi coram ecclesiastica justicia. Huius concessionis testes sunt: Renerus[17,18] abbas de Calniaco, Rabodus frater eorum, Johannes[19] de Nigella, Confridus[20] capellanus, Willermus camerarius noster frater,[21] Gerardus clericus, Petrus, Henricus, laici. Coram his testibus werpierunt hec predicta in manu nostra et soror eorum Maria[22] laudavit et filii eius. Actum anno incarnati verbi M° C° LX° III°, epacta XIIII[a].

400

March 25, 1224.

The knight Philippe [II],[1] *lord of Caulaincourt, recognizes that the church of Prémontré gave him an oven at Caulaincourt to be held in return for an annual* census *of five* modii *of grain (*frumentum*),*[2] *measure of Saint-Quentin, payable at the Premonstratensian house at Chauvigny. Adèle called* Sarracena, *Philippe's wife, and their children, Gérard and Raoul, assent to the transaction. (See near-duplicate* ***444****.)*

A. Cartulary of Prémontré, fol. 96r.

B. Original, BnF, Coll. Picardie 290, no. 36, previously sealed.

Karta domini Philippi militis de Canlencort de furno eisdem ville sub annuo censu quinque modii bladi.

[E]go Philippus, miles, dominus de Canlencort, notum facio per hoc scriptum universis tam presentibus quam futuris quod ecclesia Premonstratensis furnum suum de Canlencort tradidit mihi tenendum a me fideliter cum eodem pondere et cum eodem modo quo eadem ecclesia tenuerat ipsum furnum et a me et

---

17 Reinerus *B*.

18 Renier, abbot of the Arroasian Augustinian abbey of Sainte-Marie de Chauny, 1162–ca. 1185. Poissonnier, "L'Abbaye de St-Éloi-Fontaine ou de Commenchon," 272–4.

19 A canon Jean de Nesle also appears in acts of Renaud, bishop of Noyon, in the 1180s. Peigné-Delacourt, *Cartulaire de l'Abbaye de Notre-Dame d'Ourscamp de l'ordre de Cîteaux, fondée en 1129 au diocèse de Noyon*, 219–20; Bouchot, "Chartes du XIIe siècle relatives aux anciennes abbayes de Fervaques, d'Ourscamp et de Saint-Quentin-en-l'Isle," 348–9.

20 Gonfridus *B*.

21 fratres *B*.

22 Marga *B*.

---

1 Philippe II, lord of Caulaincourt (cant. Vermand, https://dicotopo.cths.fr/places/P02972526), attested ca. 1217–ca. 1224. Melleville, *DH*, vol. 1, 189.

2 While the act states the *census* is of *frumentum*, the rubric states that it is of *bladum*.

ab heredibus meis perpetuo possidendum sub annuo censu quinque ~~solidorum~~ modiorum frumenti ad mensuram Sancti Quintini quod erit pagabile atque sanum et tam ego quam heredes mei solvemus annuatim in perpetuum eidem ecclesie dictos quinque modios in domo sua de Cauvigni[3] in festo Omnium Sanctorum. Quitavi nichilominus prenominate ecclesie omnes census quos mihi debebat quocumque modo tempore huius scripti, hoc faciens de meorum liberorum assensu. Sciendum est autem quod si vel ego, vel heredes mei dictos quinque modios censuales vel non solveremus termino constituto aut forte non solveremus, tale frumentum quod esset pagabile atque sanum feci eidem ecclesie assignamentum ad molendinum meum de Canlencort meum et etiam ad furnum mihi et heredibus meis ab ipsa ecclesia traditum et concessum ut de proventibus utriusque molendini videlicet atque furni tamen sine contradictione et sine obstaculo possit capere quod ei vel nuntiis suis de defectu sit plenarie satisfactum. Hiis siquidem omnibus superius expressis tam uxor mea, Adeluia,[4] que et Sarracena dicebatur, quam liberi mei, Gerardus videlicet et Radulphus,[5] amicabiliter et sine contradictione suum prebuerunt assensum rata habentes omnia que in presenti pagina continentur. Et ego de eorum consciencia et voluntate ob perpetuam firmitatem presentem kartam sigilli mei munimine roboravi. Actum mense martio, in Annunciatione dominica intrante. Anno gratie M° CC°[6] vicesimo quarto.

401

1147

Simon [I],[1] bishop of Noyon, approves as fief lord the gift made by Jean, called bishop's chamberlain, and his unnamed wife to the church of Prémontré of their part of the tithe on the territory of Muille[2] that renders an annual census *of 10* sextariae *of grain (*triticum*) and two* sextariae *of peas, measure of Ham. (See near-duplicate* ***445****.)*

3 Cauveigni *B.*
4 Adeluya *B.*
5 Radulfus *B.*
6 millesimo ducentesimo *B.*

1 Simon I de Vermandois (d. 1148) was the son of Hugues I and Adélaïde, count and countess of Vermandois and Valois, and bishop of Noyon, 1123–42.
2 Muille-Villette, cant. Ham, https://dicotopo.cths.fr/places/P77128677.

A. Cartulary of Prémontré, fol. 96r.
B. Original, AM Metz, Salis II.247, no. 1, sealed in brown wax on a single strip of parchment.
EDITION: Pycke and Vleeschouwers, *Actes*, 524–5.

Karta Noviomensis episcopi de elemosina Johannis Camerarii de portione decime de Muile.

[I]n nomine sancte et cetera.[3] Ego Symon, Dei gratia Noviomensis ecclesie minister, notum fieri volo tam futuris quam presentibus quod Johannes qui dicitur episcopi camerarius et uxor eius contulerunt per manum meam Premonstrate ecclesie in perpetuum quicquid habebant decime in territorio de Muile[4] pro censu decem sextariorum[5] tritici et duorum sextariorum pise Hamensis tunc currentis mensure annuatim in festo Sancti Remigii Noviomi sive Landrimont[6] persolvendum. Frumentum vero tale erit quale in eadem decima accipietur ea tamen conditione quod predictum censum nulli ecclesie vel alicui hominum dare aut vendere absque prenominate ecclesie assensu licebit. Hoc autem factum est me annuente de cuius feodo descendebat et eundem feodum ecclesie penitus condonante eo scilicet modo ut si aliqua pactione predictum censum possent sibi conparare liberam ab omni exactione decimam possiderent. Huius rei testes sunt: Hugo[7] cancellarius, Odo decanus de Ham, Willermus[8,9] de Plaissei,

3 *Add.* cetera *A*; individue Trinitatis. *B*.
4 Muille *B*.
5 cestariorum *B*.
6 Landrimont, comm. Noyon, https://dicotopo.cths.fr/places/P74301629.
7 Hugues III de Roye, chancellor of Noyon-Tournai, ca. 1130–46, and of Noyon, 1146–63/6. Pycke, *Le chapitre cathédral Notre-Dame de Tournai de la fin du XIe à la fin du XIIIe siècle*, 64.
8 Willelmus *B*.
9 Possibly the same Guillaume de Plessis as **316**, **342**, and **372**.

Robertus[10] maior de Ham, Robertus de Duaco. Ut autem hec pactio firma omni tempore perseveret episcopali auctoritate sigillique nostri impressione communimus. Et ne quis eam irritare presumat sub anathemate interdicimus. Actum est hoc anno incarnationis dominice M° C° XL° VII°.

402

March 28, 1226.

Magister *Milon,*[1] officialis *of Noyon, makes known that the knight Hubert de Marcel recognizes having sold to the church of Prémontré two* modii *of grain (*frumentum*) that he had held from Prémontré in fief and that he had received annually on the grange of Omiécourt.*[2] *Emmeline, Hubert's wife, their children Oudard and Ricalde, and their granddaughter Agnès consent to the sale. (See near-duplicate* ***447****.)*

A. Cartulary of Prémontré, fol. 96r.

B. Original, AM Metz, Salis II.248, no. 9, previously sealed.

Karta officialis Noviomensis de venditione duorum modiorum frumenti quos Hubertus Marciaus vendidit ecclesie Premonstrate.

[M]agister Milo, officialis Noviomensis, omnibus hec visuris salutem in Domino. Vobis notum facimus quod Hubertus de Marcel, miles, coram nobis recognovit se vendidisse bene et legitime in perpetuum ecclesie Premonstratensi duos modios frumenti quos de dicta ecclesia tenebat in feodum et percipiebat annis singulis annis in grangia dicte ecclesie de[3] Omercort, quos etiam a dicta ecclesia receperat in excambium pro tractu et questu decime d'Omercort et pro duodecim sextariis bladi quos in eadem decima amavit[4] percipiebat et etiam

10 A Robert, mayor of Ham, appears in **378**, **421**, and **445**.

1 *Magister* Milon, *officialis* of Noyon, ca. 1224–ca. 1228. AD Oise, G 1984, fol. 189r; AD Aisne, H 455, fol. 311r.

2 Omiécourt-Montréal, cant. Nesle, https://dicotopo.cths.fr/places/P59719870.

3 apud *B*.

4 annuatim *B*.

vacuo stramine et procuratione et omni alio jure quod in dicta grangia habere se dicebat sicut in literis ipsius Huberti militis vidimus contineri. Hanc autem venditionem laudaverunt et concesserunt coram nobis Enmelina, uxor dicto Huberti militis, Odardus et Ricaldis liberi ipsius, necnon et Agnes, neptis eius, fidem corporalem prestantes coram nobis tam dictus Hubertus miles quam Enmelina, uxor eius, necnon liberi et neptis predicta, quod contra predictam venditionem decetero per se vel per alium nullatenus venerunt[5] nec venire facient nec dictam ecclesiam super dictis duobus modiis frumenti venditis deinceps aliquatenus molestabunt nec artem nec ingenium quereret per quod possit dicta ecclesia molestari. Actum anno Domini M° CC° vicesimo sexto, sabbato post Oculi Mei.

403

April, 1231.

Gérard[1] *de Ribécourt, knight, acknowledges that he holds three* areatae *of water at Buny*[2] *from the church of Prémontré, in return for an annual* census *of seven and a half* solidi Parisiensium. *(See duplicate* ***446****.)*

A. Cartulary of Prémontré, fol. 96r.
B. Original, AD Oise, H 6005, previously sealed on a double strip of parchment.

Karta Gerardi de Ribercourt de tribus areatis aque apud Beuni quam tenet sub annuo censu septem solidorum.

[E]go Gerardus de Ribercort, miles, notum facio universis tam presentibus quam futuris quod teneo ab ecclesia Premonstratensi tres areatas aque apud Beuni sub annuo censu septem solidorum et dimidium Parisiensis monete solvendorum singulis annis eidem ecclesie in medio martii. Si vero forte contingeret quod ego vel heres meus qui tenebit aquam ipsam non solveremus censum predictum in termino constituto, teneremur ad emendam super hoc ecclesie prenominate secundum legem patrie et ecclesie nichilominus Premonstratensis posset saisire ipsam aquam donec esset satisfactum eidem. In cuius rei testimonium et perpetuam

5 venient *B*.

1 Gérard de Ribécourt (arr. Compiègne, https://dicotopo.cths.fr/places/P45097454) appears in charters as early as 1220. Édouard de Barthélemy, *Analyse du cartulaire de l'abbaye de Foigny*, 88. On his possible familial connections, see Mazière, "Notice historique sur Ribécourt," 88–9.

2 Buny, cant. Nesle, https://dicotopo.cths.fr/places/P07807251.

firmitatem presentes litteras eidem ecclesie dedi sigilli mei munimine roboratas. Actum mense aprilis, anno gratie M° CC° tricesimo primo.[3]

404

1170

*Pierre,[1] abbot of Saint-Remi and Foulques,[2] dean of Reims, on the request of Pope Alexander [III], and with the assistance of certain other abbots and priors, resolve the dispute between Prémontré and the Augustinian abbey of Notre-Dame de Ham concerning a causeway and certain mills at Eppeville.[3] (See **406**, **432**.)[4]*

A. Cartulary of Prémontré, fols. 96r–96v.

B. Original, AD Somme, 20 H 9, no. 7, sealed on a strip of parchment.

EDITION: Ramackers, *Papsturkunden in Frankreich*, vol. 4, 258–9; *Chartae Galliae*, no. 210481, http://telma.irht.cnrs.fr/outils/chartae-galliae/charte210481/.

Karta abbatis Sancti Remigii et decani Remensis ecclesie de conpositione inter Premonstratensem ecclesiam et Hamensem.

[P]etrus, humilis abbas Sancti Remigii et Fulco, decanus ecclesie Remensis, universis fidelibus. Noverint omnes, quod accepto mandato domini Pape Alexandri, ut de causa, que inter Premonstratensems ecclesiam et Hamensem vertebatur super quadam calceata et quibusdam molendinis, cognosceremus et mediante justicia eam terminaremus, accessimus ad locum non semel neque sine multo labore neque soli, sed frequenter cum multis religiosis et discretis viris et peritis aque, ut quam fidelius possemus preceptum eius executioni mandaremus. Circumspectis ergo omnibus cum abbatibus Petro[5] Humiliarensi[6] et Sancti Vincentii Silvanectensis[7] et prioribus Symone[8] de Monte Dei et Engelberto[9] de Valle Sancti Petri et quibusdam aliis, relectis etiam litteris ab eius

3 millesimo ducentesimo *B*.

1 Pierre de Celle, abbot of the Benedictine abbey of Montier-la-Celle, 1145–61/2, abbot of the Benedictine abbey of Saint-Remi de Reims, 1161/2–81, and bishop of Chartres, 1181–3.

2 Foulques, dean of Reims, ca. 1170–ca. 1176. AD Ardennes, H 203, fols. 76r–77r.

3 Eppeville, cant. Ham. https://dicotopo.cths.fr/places/P94171781.

4 For the initial commission of Pope Alexander III, see JL no. 11671; BnF, Coll. Moreau, vol. 76, fol. 209r.

5 Pierre I, abbot of the Benedictine abbey of Homblières, 1163–75. Newman, *Homblières*, 18.

6 Humulariensi *B*.

7 Hugues II, abbot of the Augustinian abbey of Saint-Vincent de Senlis, ca. 1163–89. *GC* X, col. 1496.

sanctitate missis cum autentico scripto episcoporum B[alduini][10] Noviomensis et M[ilonis][11] Morinensis calceatam, de qua principaliter agebatur, a Premonstratensibus destructam penitus juxta auctenticum[12] scriptum episcoporum invenimus. Instabant tamen Hamenses et conquerebantur de quadam congestione palorum et glebarum, quam contra auctenticum[13] scriptum episcoporum dicebant esse factam a Premonstratensibus. Premonstratenses vero in hoc se nichil fecisse contra auctenticum[14] scriptum episcoporum asserebant, quia non esset de calceata. Sed ad hoc tantummodo id efficiebant, ut solidior esset antiqua ripa et ne tota aqua exinde elaberetur nullum habens repagulum. Nichil enim aque aut nimis parum remaneret suis molendinis, si omnem licentiam evagandi aqua haberet etsi non liceret eis saltem firmare ripam. Appenso tamen et librato saltu molendinorum tam Hamensium quam Premonstratensium deprehensum est habere molendinos Hamenses pene trium pedum saltum, Premonstratenses vero non nisi IIII^{or} digitorum. Cum autem ex hac congestione nichil obstaculi videremus habere molendinos Hamenses, ne tamen Premonstratenses in posterum dolo vel fraude aliqua possent adversus eos malignari stipitem in medio aque jussimus defigi, ut hoc signo disnosceretur si umquam aliquo modo aliquo tempore a Premonstratensibus ad impedimentum Hamensis aliquid supponeretur. Preterea ad auferendum omne impedimentum soleas ligneas digito uno inferiores ipsa ripa apponi jussimus, ne quid supra soleas liceat Premonstratensibus apponere, hoc tamen retento ut infra soleas Premonstratensibus liceat soliditatem ripe conservare. Hamensis vero non adquieverunt, sed contumaciter domini Pape audientiam appellaverunt. Nos tamen ipsius domini Pape freti auctoritate, qua omnis appellatio interdicta fuerat, nichilominus consilio sapientum et religiosorum, sicut etiam in literis domini Pape continebatur, ex sentencia eis silentium inposuimus.[15] Huius rei testes sunt: Leo[16] abbas Sancti Gisleni,[17] Pontius capellanus abbas Sancti Remigii, Nicholaus canonicus Remensis, Richardus frater, Magister Johannis[18] de Salesburgia et alii multi. Actum anno verbi incarnati M^{o} C^{o} LXX°.

---

8 Simon, prior of the charterhouse of Mont-Dieu, 1160–84. Gillet, *La chartreuse de Mont-Dieu au diocèse de Reims, avec pièces justificatives inédites*, 131, 171.

9 Likely Engelbert, prior ca. 1160–ca. 1180 of the charterhouse of Val-Saint-Pierre. Marchand, *Essai historique sur la Chartreuse du Val Saint-Pierre, située dans l'ancien diocèse de Laon, 1140–1789*, 25.

10 Either Baudouin II de Boulogne, bishop of Noyon, 1148–67, or Baudouin III de Beuseberg, bishop of Noyon, 1167–74/5.

11 Milon II, bishop of Thérouanne, 1159–69.

12 autenticum *B*.

13 autenticum *B*.

14 autenticum *B*.

15 imposuimus *B*.

16 Léon, abbot of the Benedictine abbaye of Saint-Ghislain, ca. 1166–ca. 1170. Berlière, *Monasticon belge*, vol. 2, 255.

17 Gilleni *B*.

18 John of Salisbury, bishop of Chartres, 1176–80.

405

1178

Renaud,[1] *bishop of Noyon, makes known that abbot Hugues [II] and the brothers of Prémontré, and Gautier,* maior *of Eppeville,*[2] *reached an agreement concerning rights over Bishop's Wood and the mills of Hamel*[3] *and Eppeville. Gautier consents to this, as does his unnamed wife, and their children Mathieu, Egide, Agnès, and Hesza.*

A. Cartulary of Prémontré, fols. 96v–97r.

B. Original, AD Oise, Hs 1370, sealed on a double strip of parchment with a fragment of the surviving seal in brown wax.

REGISTER: *Studium Baldwin*, fiche 2081.

Karta Noviomensis episcopus de quadam conpositione inter nos et Galterum maiorem nostrum de Espevilla.

[I]n nomine sancte et cetera.[4] Renaldus, Dei gratia Noviomensis episcopus, dilectis in Christo filiis, Hugoni, abbati et fratribus Premonstrati et eorum successoribus in perpetuum. Ea que ad memoriam posterorum volumus transmittere, scripto solemus commendare. Ea propter, dilecti in Christo filii, notum fieri volumus tam futuris quam presentibus quod inter vos et Gualterum, maiorem nostrum de Espevile, longa fuerit[5] concertatio de nemore episcopi quod predecessor noster Balduinus[6] de Bolonia pie memorie contulit vobis sub annuo censu dimidie marce argenti ad usus tantum modo Bonoliensis curie, que tandem, Deo auxiliante, hoc modo sopita fuit per nostrum laborem. Recognovit siquidem Gualterus et concessit in presentia nostra et personarum ecclesie nostre quod eam libertatem quam prefatus Balduinus episcopus dedit vobis in eodem nemore vos habere debitis et habebitis sine omni contradictione et sine denariorum vel obolorum solutione ita tamen quod nec sartare nec dare alicui vobis inde licebit. Verum si nemus illud vobis vendere placuerit, habebit Galterus[7] et successor eius qui maioriam[8] nostram tenuerit de singulis

1 Renaud, bishop of Noyon, 1175–88.

2 Eppeville, cant. Ham. https://dicotopo.cths.fr/places/P94171781.

3 Hamel-lès-Corbie, cant. Corbie, https://dicotopo.cths.fr/places/P37197765.

4 *Add.* cetera *A*; et individue Trinitatis. *B*.

5 fuerat *B*.

6 Baudouin II de Boulogne, abbot of the Augustinian abbey of Saint-Eloi-Fontaine, ca. 1130–ca. 1139, and bishop of Noyon, 1148–67. *GC* IX, col. 1126.

7 Gualterus *B*.

8 *Sic A*.

carris denarium et de singulis caretis obolum et post venditionem tamen cuparios venditi nemoris per annum usuagium[9] quoque suum habebit Gualterus et successor eius in nemore, sicut eius antecessores habuerunt ita sane quod nec dare nec vendere aliquid eis licebit, vos etiam quicquid volueritis de nemore asportabitis omni tempore ad usus tantummodo Bonoliensis curie omnibus aliis domibus, exclusis custodietisque illud tam vos quam villicus. Preterea concessit idem Gualterus quod ad molendina vestra de Hamel et de Espevile libere accipiatis wasonem et hardinam ad reficiendas sive innovandas exclusas vestras et habeatis omnimodam piscationem apud Hamel supra et subtus quantum jactus martelli vobis donabit. Similiter apud Espevile superius et sub molendinis quantum latitudo domus molendinorum comprehenderit ita ut propter ingenia piscationis vestre viam vadi non obstruatis nec impedientem clausuram inibi faciatis, viam etiam vobis concedit ad molendina vestra quietam et liberam ita quod si una careta alteri occurrerit, utraque sine forisfacto transibit. De campo vero Johannis vavassoris de quo solvitis XII denarios, non poterit vos querelare Galterus[10] nec heredes eius de omnibus itaque supradictis non poterunt vos perturbare amodo vel querelare ipse vel heredes ipsius sed si cognoverint quod alicubi dampnum nobis faciatis notificabunt nobis et successoribus nostris et ad nos pertinebit emendatio. Hanc pacem concesserunt Gualterus et uxor eius et filii, Matheus et Egidius, filie quoque Agnes et Hezsa. Ut igitur hec rata et inconvulsa permaneant, presentium litterarum cautione et sigilli nostri impressione et testium annotatione fecimus roborari. Dominus Rainaldus[11] abbas Sancti Eligii, Johannes decanus Sancte Marie Noviomi, Johannes capellanus, magister Ingelrannus, Robertus de Lusarches,[12,13] Syrotus,[14] Albricus, Odo de Coisi[15] canonici Sancte Marie, Willelmus de Vilete,[16,17] Adam,[18] Galterus[19] de Bruci,[20] Symon[21] frater eius, Hugo Lupus milites suprascripte compositionis testes existunt. Actum anno domini M° C° LXX° VIII°.

9 usagium *B*.

10 Gualterus *B*.

11 Rainaud I, abbot of the the Benedictine abbey of Saint-Éloi de Noyon, early 1170s–1189. *GC* IX, cols. 1067–8.

12 Lusarces *B*.

13 Possibly Luzarches, arr. Sarcelles.

14 Sirotus *B*.

15 Coisy, cant. Villers-Bocage, https://dicotopo.cths.fr/places/P48118901.

16 Villette, cant. Ham, https://dicotopo.cths.fr/places/P35405877.

17 A Guillaume de Villette also appears as a witness in **365**.

18 *Om.* de Erciu *A*.

19 Gualterus *B*.

20 Brouchy, cant. Ham, https://dicotopo.cths.fr/places/P33557845.

21 Simon *B*.

406

1170–1[1]

*Étienne,[2] bishop of Meaux, Henri,[3] bishop of Senlis, and Yves [II],[4] abbot of Saint-Denis, confirm the resolution of a dispute between Prémontré and the Augustinian abbey of Notre-Dame de Ham about the mills of Eppeville[5] mediated by Robert, bishop of Amiens, Pierre, abbot of Saint-Remi, and Foulques, dean of Reims. (See **404**, **432**.)*

A. Cartulary of Prémontré, fol. 97r.

B. Original, AD Somme, 20 H 9, no. 4, originally sealed with three seals on double strips of leather, two of which survive in fragmentary condition.

EDITION: Ramackers, *Papsturkunden in Frankreich*, vol. 4, 268–9; *Chartae Galliae*, no. 210488, http://telma.irht.cnrs.fr/outils/chartae-galliae/charte210488/.

Karta Stephani Meldensis episcopi de conpositione inter Premonstratenses et Hamenses.

[E]go Stephanus, Dei gratia Meldensis episcopus et ego Henricus, eiusdem clementia Silvanectensis episcopus, ego quoque Yvo,[6] Dei ordinatione Sancti Dyonisii[7] abbas, presentibus et futuris salutem in perpetuum. Querelam calceate quorumdam molendinorum, qui dicuntur de Espevile, que vertebatur inter Premonstratenses et Hamenses, venerabili R[oberto], quondam Ambianensi episcopo, et P[etro], abbati Sancti Remigii et F[ulco], decano Remensi a domino Papa ad terminandam commissam episcopo predicto de medio sublato, duo reliqui, abbas videlicet et decanus terminaverunt. Sed eorum sententiam ad se delatam cum dominus Papa confirmare noluisset, propter quod in registro suo non invenit duobus causam fuisse commissam, si tertius interesse non posset, sententiam eorum, quemadmodum ab eis prolata fuerat, auctoritate apostolica confirmaremus et eam inviolabiliter observari preciperemus. Convocata itaque ante presentiam nostram utraque parte et allatis litteris domini Pape; de quibus nobis mandaverat, invenimus in eisdem literis duobus causam fuisse commissam, si tertius interesse non posset, et sententiam eorum quemadmodum ab ipsis prolata fuit, auctoritate apostolica confirmavimus et eam

1 Date based on **404** (1170) and the episcopal tenure of Étienne, bishop of Meaux (1162–71).

2 Étienne de la Chapelle, son of Josselin II de Villemomble, lord of Beaumont, and Herceline de Villebéon, was bishop of Meaux, 1162–71, and archbishop of Bourges, 1171–3.

3 Henri, bishop of Senlis, 1168/9–85.

4 Yves II, abbot of the Benedictine abbey of Saint-Denis, ca. 1169–ca. 1172.

5 Eppeville, cant. Ham. https://dicotopo.cths.fr/places/P94171781.

6 Ivo *B*.

7 Dionisii *B*.

inviolabiliter observari precepimus et calceatam, de qua principaliter causa orta est, sicut memorati judices statuerant, Premonstrate ecclesie adjudicavimus et sigillorum nostrorum impressione presens scriptum muniri fecimus.

407

1142

Simon [I],[1] *bishop of Noyon, gives notice that Thomas* de Feria *d'Ognolles; Hugues*[2] *and Ermengarde, his children; and Hugues*[3] Captivus, *husband of Ermengarde, gave Prémontré two mills at Eppeville*[4] *in exchange for 45* librae. *The fief lord Enguerrand [II],*[5] *lord of Coucy, assented to the gift.*

A. Cartulary of Prémontré, fol. 97r.

B. Original, AM Metz, Salis II.244, no. 1, sealed on a double strip of parchment with red wax.

~~Ego~~ Karta Noviomensis episcopi de elemosina duorum molendinorum apud Espevile quam Hugo contulit.

[I]n nomine et cetera.[6] Quia juxta veritatis testimonium elemosina extinguit peccatum[7] confert patrocinium amplificat premium sanum profecto est et commodum ut devotio principum seu quorumcumque fidelium ecclesiam Dei oblationibus erigat, elemosinis foveat et spe celestium temporalia impertiri non abnuat. Et ne cui in posterum bene gesta fideliter oblata legitime concessa fraudulenter infestare liceat et cassare ex antiqua patrum decretum est traditione ut quod ecclesie Dei de exteriorum provenit beneficio episcopali muniatur privilegio vel apostolico.[8] Hac igitur de causa ego Symon,[9] Dei gratia

1 Simon I de Vermandois (d. 1148) was the son of Hugues I and Adélaïde, count and countess of Vermandois and Valois, and bishop of Noyon 1123–42.

2 Hugues, lord of Ognolles, is attested as late as 1194, and is likely dead by 1206. Leroy-Morel, *Recherches généalogiques sur les familles nobles de plusieurs villages des environs de Nesle, Noyon, Ham et Roye, et recherches historiques sur les mêmes localités*, 104; Pipon, ed., *Le chartrier de l'Abbaye-aux-Bois (1202–1341)*, 103.

3 Hugues *le Captif* de Vendeuil; brother of Sarracin, castellan of La Fère and Laon, and Geoffroi de Condren, knight; husband of Ermengarde d'Ognolles. Newman, *Seigneurs*, vol. 2, 205.

4 Eppeville, cant. Ham. https://dicotopo.cths.fr/places/P94171781.

5 Enguerrand II de Coucy (d. ca. 1149), son of Thomas de Marle, lord of Coucy, and his third wife, Mélisende de Crécy-sur-Serre.

6 *Add.* cetera *A*; sancte et individue Trinitati *B*.

7 This phrase, inspired by Ecclesiasticus (Sirach 3:33), appears in many twelfth-century charters.

8 *Transp. A*; vel apostolico muniatur privilegio *B*.

9 Simon *B*.

Noviomensis episcopus, notificari volo tam futuris quam presentibus quod Thomas de Uniole, qui et De Feria dicitur, et Hugo, filius eius, et alter Hugo, gener eius, qui Captivus cognominatur, et Ermengardis, filia predicti Thome, uxor vero eiusdem Hugonis ~~Hugonis~~ Captivi, contulerunt Premonstrate ecclesie, salvo districtu nostro, per manum nostram de cuius feodo primitus descendebant, duo molendina que hereditario jure apud Espevile[10] possidebant, tum pro remedio animarum suarum tum pro aliquo beneficio quod eis dedit ecclesia XL videlicet et quinque libris. Ingelrannus vero de Couci de cuius feodo hec eadem molendina post nos descendebant, hoc donum fideliter et devote oblatum voluntarius concessit. Hii sunt testes tam de primo dato quam de concessione episcopi et Ingelranni: Wido[11] castellanus de Coci, Addo de Guni,[12] Witerus[13] frater eius, Bonefacius prepositus, Lambertus Gruas, Gerardus Auris,[14] Macharius[15] de Vernul, Radulphus[16,17] de Helli decanus de Ammiens, Hugo[18] cancellarius, Odo Balam,[19] Renaldus[20] decanus de Sancto Eligio, Andreas de Sancto Petro, magister Lambertus de Sancto Quintino, Rogerus clericus, filius Roberti corduonarii, Nicholaus de Tornai, Robertus de Ham, Matheus filius Hugonis de Perona, Symon[21] de Burguus de Bethencourt,[22] Galterus[23] frater eius, Radulfus[24] Buiaus[25] frater cancellarii, Robertus Masuers,

10 Hespevile *B.*

11 Guy II, castellan of Coucy (d. 1165); husband of Théophanie. Barthélemy, *LDA*, 506–7.

12 Adon de Guny (cant. Coucy-le-Château, https://dicotopo.cths.fr/places/P88745448), son of Guy I, lord of Guny, and Elisabeth, and nephew of Guy II, castellan of Coucy. Newman, *Seigneurs*, vol. 2, 96; Barthélemy, *LDA*, 150–5.

13 Itier de Guny, son of Guy I, lord of Guny, and Elisabeth, and nephew of Guy II, castellan of Coucy. Newman, *Seigneurs*, vol. 2, 96; Barthélemy, *LDA*, 150–5.

14 Gérard *l'Oreille* was part of the seigneurial family of Housset (cant. Sains, https://dicotopo.cths.fr/places/P27336521), and frequently appeared in charters issued by the Coucy family in the 1130s–60s. Barthélemy, *LDA*, 521.

15 Possibly lord of Verneuil-sous-Coucy (cant. Coucy-le-Château, https://dicotopo.cths.fr/places/P85264680), 1140s–60s. Macaire appears as a witness in an act of Hugues I de Fosses, abbot of Prémontré, in 1152. Melleville, *DH*, vol. 2, 425; Lalanne, *Le cartulaire de Valpriez, 1135–1250*, 30–1.

16 Radulfus *B.*

17 Raoul d'Heilly, son of Thibault II, lord of Heilly, and his wife Mabille. Darsy, *Bénéfices de l'église d'Amiens, ou État général des biens, revenus et charges du clergé du diocèse d'Amiens en 1730, avec des notes*, vol. 1, 321, fn. 1.

18 Hugues III de Roye, chancellor of Noyon-Tournai, ca. 1130–46, and of Noyon, 1146–63/6. Pycke, *Le chapitre cathédral Notre-Dame de Tournai de la fin du XIe à la fin du XIIIe siècle*, 64.

19 Eudes Balam also appears as a witness in an 1146 act of Simon, bishop of Noyon. Pycke and Vleeschouwers, *Actes*, 511.

20 Reinoldus *B.*

21 Simon *B.*

22 Bethencurt *B.*

Hugo de Nemore, Ricerus armiger eius, Walters de Maioc.[26] Siquis autem hoc Dei donum legitime factum temere violare presumpserit, bis vel ter ammonitus nisi resipuerit anathematis, gladio feriatur. Actum est hoc anno incarnationis dominice M° C° XL° II°,[27] epacta XXII[a28] indictione quinta, concurrente III°.

408

May, 1220.

The brothers Jean [II],[1] lord of Nesle and castellan of Bruges, and Raoul[2] confirm the resolution of a dispute between the church of Prémontré and Jean de Pertain[3] reached by Pope Honorius III, concerning the possession of 20 modii *of grain (*frumentum*) from the tithe of Falvy.[4]*

A. Cartulary of Prémontré, fol. 97r.

B. Original, AD Somme, 20 H_SC_10, no. 1, sealed.[5]

EDITION: Newman, *Seigneurs*, vol. 2, 221–2; *Chartae Galliae*, no. 212911, http://telma.irht.cnrs.fr/outils/chartae-galliae/charte212911/.

Karta domini Johannis de Nigella de conpositione inter ecclesiam Premonstratensem et Johannem de Partigni.

[E]go Johannes, dominus Nigelle, castellanus Brugii et Radulfus, frater meus, notum facimus presentibus et futuris quod cum inter ecclesiam Premonstratensem

23 Likely the Gautier de Bethencourt, miller, who appears in **362** and **378**.

24 Raoul *Buiaus*, brother of Hugues III de Roye, chancellor of Noyon-Tournai. He also appears as a witness in **342**.

25 Buials *B*.

26 Likely Mayot, cant. La Fère, https://dicotopo.cths.fr/places/P54209066.

27 XL II° *B*.

28 XXII *B*.

1 Jean II, lord of Nesle and castellan of Bruges (d. 1239/40), son of Jean I, lord of Nesle and castellan of Bruges, and Elizabeth; husband of Eustacie de Saint-Pol. Jean and Eustacie founded the Cistercian abbey of Abbaye-aux-Bois in 1202 and feature prominently in that house's cartulary. Newman, *Seigneurs*, vol. 1, 71–2; Pipon, ed., *Le chartrier de l'Abbaye-aux-Bois (1202–1341)*, 42–3.

2 Raoul de Nesle, lord of Flavy (d. bef. 1226), son of Jean I, lord of Nesle and castellan of Bruges, and Elizabeth; husband of Adèle de Roye. Newman, *Seigneurs*, vol. 1, 72.

3 Pertain, cant. Nesle, https://dicotopo.cths.fr/places/P94420761.

4 Falvy, cant. Nesle, https://dicotopo.cths.fr/places/P25248648.

5 Due to conservation concerns, the original was not available to the editors.

ex una parte et Johannem de Partigni ex altera super viginti modiis frumenti quos idem Johannes petebat in decima de Falevi, quos etiam dicebat se tenere de nobis in feodum, questio mota fuisset et terminata per dominum Honorium, Papam, tertium secundum quod in eius auctentico nobis exhibito intelleximus contineri, tandem, inspectis aliis munimentis, que a bone memorie Ivone, comite Suessionensi domino Nigelle et comite Conone[6] eius nepote ecclesia Premonstratensis habebat, illos viginti modios frumenti et totum residuum maioris decime quod eadem ecclesia habebet apud Falevi nominatim et generaliter omnia alia que tenuerat usque ad tempus huius scripti in dominio Nigellensi pietatis intuitu et ob nostrarum remedium animarum quiete et absque calumpnia eidem ecclesie perpetuo concessimus et sicut in predecessorum nostrorum Yvonis,[7] comitis Suessionensis, domini Nigelle et comitis Cononis, nepotis sui, cartula continetur, nostrorum munimine sigillorum confirmavimus et consilium necnon et auxilium sine nostro mittendo contra omnes malefactores qui per nos poterunt rationabiliter coherceri ipsi ecclesie promisimus bona fide. Actum mense maio, anno gratie M° CC° XX°.

409

January, 1237.

Jean [II],[1] *lord of Nesle, in thanks for rights which the abbot and convent of Premontré had granted to him in the woods of La Perriole, gave to Premontré two and a half* jornalia *of woods adjacent to Premontré's woodland between La Perriole and Flavy,*[2] *which he had acquired from Robert* Aguinant.[3]

A. Cartulary of Prémontré, fols. 97r–97v.
B. Original not found.

6 Conon de Nesle (d. 1180), first castellan of Bruges and then count of Soissons from 1178; son of Raoul II, lord of Nesle, and Gertrude, *neptis* of Thierry, count of Flanders. Newman, *Seigneurs*, vol. 1, 63–4.

7 Yves II de Nesle (d. ca. 1178), lord of Nesle and count of Soissons, son of Raoul, lord of Nesle, and Raintrude. Newman, *Seigneurs*, vol. 1, 61.

1 Jean II, lord of Nesle and castellan of Bruges (d. 1239/40), son of Jean I, lord of Nesle and castellan of Bruges, and Elizabeth; husband of Eustacie de Saint-Pol. Jean and Eustacie founded the Cistercian abbey of Abbaye-aux-Bois in 1202 and feature prominently in that house's cartulary. Newman, *Seigneurs*, vol. 1, 71–2; Pipon, ed., *Le chartrier de l'Abbaye-aux-Bois (1202–1341)*, 42–3.

2 Flavy-le-Meldeux, cant. Guiscard, https://dicotopo.cths.fr/places/P19622430.

3 Robert *Aguinant* (d. aft. 1247), lord of half of Flavy-le-Meldeux (cant. Guiscard, https://dicotopo.cths.fr/places/P19622430), son of Raoul, lord of Flavy-le-Meldeux, and Marguerite, sister and heir of Renaud, knight of Flavy. Newman, *Seigneurs*, vol. 2, 280–1.

EDITION: Newman, *Seigneurs*, vol. 2, 279–80; *Chartae Galliae*, no. 212963, http://telma.irht.cnrs.fr/outils/chartae-galliae/charte212963/.

Karta domini Johannis Nigellensis super eo quod ecclesia contulit et potestatem capiendi gressios in gresseria.

[O]mnibus presentes litteras inspecturis Johannes, dominus Nigelle, salutem. Quoniam abbas et conventus Premonstratensis michi ex gratia concesserunt et contulerunt potestatem findendi et capiendi gressios in nemore suo quod dicitur Le Perriole, et eosdem per terram suam educendi, ego ob remedium animee mee et antecessorum meorum et ob quedam dampna que feceram in hiis ~~ecclesie~~ ecclesie Premonstratensis restitui et reddidi eidem ecclesie duo jornalia et dimidium jornale nemoris ad mensuram Nigelle de illo nemore quod acquisivi a Roberto dicto Aguinant libere et pacifice in perpetuum possidendi que videlicet duo jornalia et dimidium jornale sunt contigua nemori memorate ecclesie sito inter La[4] Perriole et Flavi.[B] [5] Ne autem super hac restitutione per me vel heredes meos seu aliquem alium possit in posterum calumpnia suboriri presentem kartam ad maiorem istius restitutionis stabilitatem sigilli mei feci munimine roborari. Actum mense januario anno incarnationis dominice Mº CCº XXXº VIIº et ipsam terram teneor warantire ad usus et consuetudines patrie videlicet per annum et diem.[A] Ne autem et cetera.

410

1129

André,[1] *abbot of Nogent, cedes to the church of Prémontré his allod of Bonneuil* [2] *in exchange for an annual* census *of 13* solidi Vermandensium.

4 *Sic A.*

5 The scribe's inclusion of superscript letters A and B in the cartulary text suggest that for a correct reading, the "B" sentence should be moved to the end of the act after the "A" sentence but before "Ne autem et cetera."

1 André, abbot of the Benedictine abbey of Nogent-sous-Coucy, aft. ca. 1124–bef. ca. 1138. *GC* IX, col. 607.

2 Bonneuil, cant. Ham, https://dicotopo.cths.fr/places/P66750585.

A. Cartulary of Prémontré, fol. 97v.

B. Original (chirograph), AD Oise, H 5990, previously sealed on a double strip of parchment. In the bottom margin, the top half of the letters that form the word CYROGRAPHUM.

EDITION: Guibert of Nogent, *Venerabilis Guiberti abbatis B. Mariae de Novigento Opera omnia*, 627.

REGISTER: Bréquigny, *Table chronologique*, vol. 2, 565.

Karta abbatis de Nongento de censu tredecim solidorum quos debebit ecclesie de Nongento pro quadam terra apud Bonolium.

[I]n nomine sancte et cetera.[3] Sciant omnes presentes et futuri quod ego Andreas, abbas Sancte Marie Nongenti,[4] concessu capituli nostri, concessi ecclesie Premonstrate omnem terram alodii nostri quod possidebamus apud Bonolium per censum tredecim solidorum monete Vermendensis omni anno persolvendum ad Purificationem Sancte Dei Genitricis Marie. Et hoc ratum et firmum attestatione sigilli nostri confirmamus et inconvulsum permanere decernimus, ut ipsas res ita bene et quiete et pacifice ipsa ecclesia teneat, sicut nos aliquando melius et quietius tenuimus. Huius concessionis testes sunt: Godefridus, monachus et cantor Nongenti,[5] Bernardus elemosinarius, Adelardus monachus, Adelelmus secretarius, Albricus[6] prepositus, Herbertus Cellerarius, Fulco puer, Iterius puer et ceteri et de eadem Premonstrata ecclesia Hugo,[7] tunc temporis abbas, Gerardus prior, Harduinus[8] cantor, Petrus diaconus, Amolricus diaconus, Adam, Tiebaldus[9] subdiaconi, Rainaldus, Johannes pueri. Anno incarnationis dominice[10] M° C° XX° IX°,[11] indictione VII[a], epacta XXVIII[a], concurrente primo.[12]

3 *Add.* cetera *A*; individue Trinitatis. *B*.
4 Nogenti *B*.
5 Nonigenti *B*.
6 Albericus *B*.
7 Hugues I de Fosses (ca. 1093–1164), first abbot of Prémontré.
8 Harduwinus *B*.
9 Tibaldus *B*.
10 Domini *B*.
11 VIIII *B*.
12 I *B*.

411

1178

Yves [II],[1] *count of Soissons and lord of Nesle, makes known that Liégarde de Languevoisin*[2] *gave to Prémontré a piece of land that holds eight* sextariae *of seed grain at* Delleincourt.[3] *This gift was assented to by Liégarde's two daughters, both called Agnès. Eustache*[4] *de Martinsart, from whom the fief descended, together with his wife Agnès and their sons, Eustache and Baudouin, also consented and received 10* librae blancorum.

A. Cartulary of Prémontré, f. 97v.

B. Original, AD Oise, H 6031, previously sealed.

EDITION: Newman, *Seigneurs*, vol. 2, 163; *Chartae Galliae*, no. 212863, http://telma.irht.cnrs.fr/outils/chartae-galliae/charte212863/.

Karta Yvonis comitis Suessionensis et domini Nigellensis de elemosina Liegardis de Landovesinus de octo sextariis terre.

[I]n nomine et cetera.[5] Ego Ivo, Dei gratia comes Suessorum et dominus Nigelle, notum fieri volo presentibus et futuris quod Liegardis de Landovesin dedit in elemosinam ecclesie Premonstratensi terram octo sextarios sementis capientem ad Delleincourt[6] concessu duarum filiarum suarum que utreque eodem vocantur nomine, scilicet Agnes. Ibi fuerunt et inde testes sunt Odo de Landoveisin et Albricus frater eius et frater Evrardus de Monci. Hoc etiam donum predicta Liegardis posuit super altare Bonolii presentibus fratribus eiusdem ecclesie et aliis viris quampluribus. Hoc autem concesserunt Eustachius de Martinsart et Agnes, uxor eius de quorum feodo descendebat cum liberis suis, Eustachio et Balduino et pro hac concessione habuerunt, de beneficio eiusdem ecclesie, decem libras blancorum. Hec concessio coram nobis facta est sub his testibus: Radulfo[7]

---

1 Yves II de Nesle (d. ca. 1178), lord of Nesle and count of Soissons, son of Raoul, lord of Nesle, and Raintrude. Newman, *Seigneurs*, vol. 1, 61.

2 Languevoisin, cant. Nesle, https://dicotopo.cths.fr/places/P00746276.

3 Possibly Dreslincourt, cant. Roye, https://dicotopo.cths.fr/places/P84324274.

4 Eustache I de Martinsart (cant. Albert, https://dicotopo.cths.fr/places/P32127661), lord of Buverchy, attested 1175–95. Newman, *Seigneurs*, vol. 2, 145, 182.

5 *Add.* cetera *A*; Domini, amen. *B*.

6 Delleincurt *B*.

7 Raoul II, castellan of Nesle, son of Raoul I, castellan of Nesle, and Adèle, sister of Guy II, castellan of Noyon and Coucy. Newman, *Seigneurs*, vol. 2, 211.

castellano, Odone[8] de Bonolio, Albrico[9] Gaiant, Radulfo[10] le Gentil, Huberto de Voiane.[11] Nos ergo similiter quia de feodo nostro descendit, pro remedio anime nostre et predecessorum nostrorum, eandem terram in perpetuum prefate ecclesie libere et quiete possidendam concessimus et sigilli nostri inpressione[12] communire curavimus. Actum anno incarnationis dominice[13] M° C° LXX° VIII°.

412

1147

Abbot Bruno[1] *of Nogent cedes to Abbot Hugues [I]*[2] *and the church of Prémontré all the land his community possesses at Bonneuil,*[3] *which pays an annual* census *of 13* solidi. *Bruno also makes arrangements concerning lands and rights at Loire,*[4] *Trosly,*[5] Berolcourt, *Pont-Saint-Mard,*[6] *and Coucy-la-Ville.*

A. Cartulary of Prémontré, fol. 97v.
B. Original not found.
EDITION: Martin-Marville, *Trosly-Loire ou le Trosly des conciles, ses chateaux, ses villas, ses fiefs et ses seigneurs*, 225–6.

Karta abbatis Premonstratensis et Sancte Marie de Nongento de commutatione cuiusdam terre apud Bonolium.

[I]n nomine et cetera. Ut gestarum rerum in posterum maneret veritas, scripto eas commendare consuevit antiquitas. Notum sit igitur ~~igitur~~ tam futuris quam presentibus quod ecclesia Sancte Marie de Noiant concessit Premonstrate

8 Eudes de Bonneuil (cant. Ham, https://dicotopo.cths.fr/places/P66750585) appears as a witness in acts dated 1140–78. Newman, *Seigneurs*, vol. 2, 119.
9 Aubry *Gigas/Gaiant*, knight of Nesle and son of Robert *Gaianz*, appears as a witness in acts dated 1142–78. Newman, *Seigneurs*, vol. 2, 119.
10 Raoul le Gentil appears in acts associated with the counts of Soissons in the latter half of the 1170s. Newman, *Seigneurs*, vol. 2, 149–50, 155, 163.
11 Voyennes, cant. Nesle. https://dicotopo.cths.fr/places/P32215646.
12 impressione *B*.
13 Domini *B*.

1 Bruno, abbot of the Benedictine abbey of Nogent-sous-Coucy, 1138–bef. 1157. *GC* IX, col. 607.
2 Hugues I de Fosses (ca. 1093–1164), first abbot of Prémontré.
3 Bonneuil, cant. Ham, https://dicotopo.cths.fr/places/P66750585.
4 Loire, cant. Coucy-le-Château, https://dicotopo.cths.fr/places/P25342398.
5 Trosly-Loire, cant. Coucy-le-Château, https://dicotopo.cths.fr/places/P24780558.
6 Pont-Saint-Mard, cant. Coucy-le-Château, https://dicotopo.cths.fr/places/P93612418.

ecclesie quicquid terre habebat apud Bonolium perpetuo possidendum sub censu XIII[cim] solidorum bone monete, scilicet obolorum in Purificatione Beate Marie persolvendorum commutavit etiam eadem ecclesia de Noiant quasdam terras quas habebat circa curias de Premonstrato videlicet Loirre, Trosli in Valle et Toiri,[7] capientes XX[ti] II[os] modios sementis ad mensuram de Olmencurt, pro terra quam apud eandem villam habebat Premonstrata ecclesia de elemosina Hugonis de Sailli, item ecclesia de Noiant commutavit mediam partem cuiusdam campi cum suo censu, id est tribus denariis quem tenebat cum Hugone de Juvigni[8] apud Berolcourt, censum etiam trium solidorum quem de minuta decima capiebat apud Rosieres[9] et Bolmunt[10] pro hiis omnibus que secum partiebatur Premonstrata ecclesia in villa que Pons Sancti Medardi nuncupatur de elemosina sororis Riche de Chaum[11] et filie sue Ermengardis. Item ecclesia Nonjantina terram quam habebat apud Cocivillam, XI[cim] aissinos sementis capientem commutavit cum predicta Premonstrata ecclesia pro terra ad serendos XVI aissinos, sufficiente excepto terragio IIII[or] aissinorum in terra que fuit fratris Harduini. Quod ut ratum deinceps atque inconvulsum permaneat ego Hugo, Premonstrate ecclesie abbas, et generalis capituli nostri conventus, ego quoque Bruno quoque Nonjantine ecclesie abbatis, et generalis capituli nostri conventus presenti cirographo roboramus et sigillis nostris imponamus. Signum Hugonis, Premonstratensis abbatis. S. prioris, Radulfi. S. Rainaldi, suprioris. S. Grinberti, diaconi. S. Simonis, subdiaconi. S. Fulconis, cellerarii et ceteri. Actum est hoc anno dominice incarnationis M[o] C[o] XLVII[o] indictione VIII[a], concurrente primo, epacta septima.

7 Thury, comm. Marest-Dampcourt, https://dicotopo.cths.fr/places/P84789655.
8 Juvigny, cant. Soissons, https://dicotopo.cths.fr/places/P97496070.
9 Rozières, cant. Oulchy-le-Château, https://dicotopo.cths.fr/places/P75685266.
10 Likely Beaumont-en-Beine, cant. Chauny, https://dicotopo.cths.fr/places/P18685379.
11 Champs, cant. Coucy-le-Château, https://dicotopo.cths.fr/places/P17397889.

413

1146–78[1]

Yves [II],[2] count of Soissons and lord of Nesle, makes known that Widèle,[3] first wife of Rorigon[4] [I, lord of] Fayet, gave in alms to the sisters of Bonneuil[5] two modii *of grain (*frumentum*) to be taken each year from Rorigon's grange at Offoy and used to pay for clothes for the aforesaid sisters. This gift was assented to by Rorigon, Widèle's husband; Gobert[6] de Ribemont, brother of Widèle; Gobert, son of Widèle; and Simon, brother of Rorigon.*

A. Cartulary of Prémontré, fols. 97v–98r.

B. Original not found.

EDITION: Newman, *Seigneurs*, vol. 2, 101; *Chartae Galliae,* no. 212818, http://telma.irht.cnrs.fr/outils/chartae-galliae/charte212818/.

Karta comitis Suessionensis et domini Nigellensis de elemosina Widele de Faiel de duobus modiis frumenti.

[E]go Yvo, Dei gratia Suessorum comes et dominus Nigelle, notum fieri volo tam futuris quam presentibus quod Widela, prima uxor Rorigani de Faiel, ob remedium anime sue dedit in elemosinam sororibus de Bonolio duos modios frumenti, concedente Goberto, fratre suo, de Ribodimonte quos singulis annis accipient in grangia ipsius Rorigani de Faiel apud Offois in Festo Sancti Remigii, nec in alios usus deputabuntur nisi tantum ad vestes ipsarum sororum acquirendis. Hoc donum concessit Roriganus de Faiel, maritus ipsius Widele, et Gobertus, ipsorum filius et Symon frater predicti Rorigani. Nos etiam quia prefati modii frumenti de feodo nostro erant, ipsum donum concessimus et presenti cartule ne qua exinde controversia oriatur, sigillum nostrum cum subscriptis testibus apposuimus.

1 This date is based on the tenure of Yves, count of Soissons (1146–78). Newman dates this act to 1161–78 based on possible, though unconfirmed, familial relationships. Newman, *Seigneurs*, vol. 2, 101.

2 Yves II de Nesle (d. ca. 1178), lord of Nesle and count of Soissons, son of Raoul, lord of Nesle, and Raintrude. Newman, *Seigneurs*, vol. 1, 61.

3 Widèle, daughter of Simon I, lord of Ribemont. Melleville, *DH*, vol. 2, 277.

4 Rorigon, lord of Fayet (d. ca. 1199), and Simon (d. ca. 1187), sons of Aude, lady of Fayet. Newman, *Seigneurs*, vol. 2, 102.

5 The Premonstratensian *curtis* of Bonneuil. *MP* II, 484.

6 Gobert I, lord of Ribemont, son of Simon I, lord of Ribemont. Melleville, *DH*, vol. 2, 277.

414

1143–50[1]

Hugues [I],[2] abbot of Prémontré, concludes an agreement with the Augustinian abbey of Notre-Dame de Ham, the Benedictine abbey of Notre-Dame de Homblières, the priory of Notre-Dame de Villeselve, and Gautier[3] de Trosly. The parties agree on an exchange of lands in and around Bonneuil[4] to consolidate their respective holdings.

A. Cartulary of Prémontré, fol. 98r.

B. Original (chirograph), AD Oise, Hs 1373, previously sealed with two seals on a double strip of parchment, one of which survives in brown wax. In the right margin, beginning at the top, the bottom half of the letters that form the word CYROGRAPHUM.

EDITION: Martin-Marville, *Trosly-Loire ou le Trosly des conciles, ses chateaux, ses villas, ses fiefs et ses seigneurs*, 255; Newman, *Homblières*, 133–4.

Karta abbatis Premonstratensis de conpositione cuiusdam terre inter monachos de Humblieriis.

[I]n nomine sancte et cetera.[5] Ego Hugo, Dei patientia Premonstrate ecclesie abbas vocatur, eiusdemque loci fratrum conventus omnibus tam futuris quam presentibus notum fieri volumus quoniam fratres Sancte Marie Hamensis et monachi Sancte Marie ~~Hamensis~~ de Humbleriis et monachi Sancte Marie de Vileselva et quidam Galterus de Trosli quasdam terras nostris terris interjacentes et admixtas et curie nostre Bonolii propinquas habebant. Nos vero communi assensu tam nostro quam predictarum ecclesiarum, quam etiam Galteri, ut dissensiones, litigationes in futuro inter nos evitaremus, terras predictas hoc modo acquisivimus quod quasdam alias terras singulariter nostras et proprias pro acquisitis ecclesiis predictis obtinere et possidere in perpetuum concessimus. Huiusmodi autem conventio inter nos et predictas ecclesias sic instituta est, ut, si forte ex viris secularibus de predictis terris calumpnia exorta fuerit, ad hoc ut terra in pace teneri non potuerit, nos illis et ipsi nobis invicem restaurabimus. Hoc igitur ut ratum et inconvulsum habeatur, tam nostre ecclesie quam

1 This date range is based on the abbacies of Hugues [I], abbot of Prémontré, 1128–56, Renaud, abbot of Ham, 1143–?, and Hugues [I/II], abbot of Homblières, 1132–43 or 1143–50.

2 Hugues I de Fosses (ca. 1093–1164), first abbot of Prémontré.

3 Possibly a lord of Trosly (cant. Coucy-le-Château, https://dicotopo.cths.fr/places/P24780558). Martin-Marville, *Trosly-Loire, ou le Trosly des conciles, ses chateaux, ses villas, ses fiefs et ses seigneurs*, 189.

4 Bonneuil, cant. Ham, https://dicotopo.cths.fr/places/P66750585.

5 *Add.* cetera *A*; in nomine sancte et individue Trinitatis *B*.

predictarum ecclesiarum sigillorum impressione et cyrographorum distributione communi assensu et auctoritate in posterum volumus confirmari et confirmando corroborari. S.[6] Hugonis, Premonstrate ecclesie abbatis. S. Radulfi, prioris eius. S. totius capituli. S. Renoldi,[7] Hamensis abbatis. S. prioris eius.[8] S. totius capituli. S. Hugonis[9] abbatis de Humbleriis. S. prioris eius. S. totius capituli. S. Macharii et Theobaldi[10] et Alexis et Guillelmi[11,12] priorum Sancte Marie de Vileselva.

415

1153

Samson,[1] archbishop of Reims, makes known the resolution of a dispute between Hugues [I],[2] abbot of Prémontré, and Renaud [I], abbot of Ham, concerning certain allods situated at Omiécourt[3] and the minor tithe of Flamicourt.[4]

A. Cartulary of Prémontré, fol. 98r.

B. Original (chirograph), AM Metz, Salis II.248, no. 1, previously sealed with two seals, each on a single strip of leather. The seal on the left remains intact. In the left margin and beginning at the top, the top half of the letters that form the word + CYROGRAPHUM.

Karta archiepiscopi Remensis de quadam conpositione inter Hugonem Premonstratensem et Renoldum Hamenses abbates.

[I]n nomine sancte et cetera.[5] Sanson, Dei gratia Remorum archiepiscopus, omnibus tam presentibus quam futuris in perpetuum. Sicut ad nostrum pertinet

6 Signum *B*.
7 Renaud I, abbot of the Augustinian abbey of Notre-Dame de Ham, 1143–bef. 1160. *GC* IX, col. 1122.
8 *Om*. Odonis *A*.
9 Hugues II, first prior of the Benedictine abbey of Saint-Jean de Laon and later abbot of the Benedictine abbey of Homblières, 1143–50. Newman, *Homblières*, 18.
10 Teobaldi *B*.
11 Guilelmi *B*.
12 Guillaume, prior of the Benedictine priory of Saint-Marie-Madeleine de Villeselve, ca. 1150. Ponthieux, "Notice historique sur Villeselve et son ancien prieuré, Noyon," 237.

1 Samson de Mauvoisin, son of Raoul III le Barbu de Mauvoisin, lord of Rosny-sur-Seine, and his first wife Odeline, was archdeacon and provost of Chartres, and archbishop of Reims, 1140–61.
2 Hugues I de Fosses (ca. 1093–1164), first abbot of Prémontré.
3 Omiécourt-Montréal, cant. Nesle, https://dicotopo.cths.fr/places/P59719870.
4 Flamicourt-lès-Ham, cant. Ham, https://dicotopo.cths.fr/places/P00189975.
5 *Add*. cetera *A*; individue Trinitatis *B*.

officium altercationibus finem omnimodam imponere ita nobis quoque necesse est easdem pacificatas tam presentibus quam futuris scripto notificare, ne bonum pacis oblivione decedentium in dissensionis[6] malum aliquatenus possit ~~in~~resurgere. Unde per hoc scriptum notificamus quod quedam altercatio inter Hugonem Premonstratensem et Renoldum[7] Hamensem abbates, prius in curia fratris nostri Balduini, Noviomensis episcopi, et postea in nostra diu agitata, hoc modo terminata est: Renoldus,[8] Hamensis abbas, quedam alodia de Homercourt que adversus Premonstratensem reclamabat et XII^{cim} assignationis nummos quos ex dono Alardi[9] de Ham et filie eius, Ide,[10] diu tenuerat, in presentia nostra predictique venerabilis Noviomensis nostrarumque personarum, Premonstratensi ecclesie dimisit et concessit suique capituli assensu hoc idem confirmavit. Abbas quoque Premonstratensis minutam decimam de Framercurt quam adversus Hamensem reclamabat pro recompensatione et bono pacis omnino liberam Hamensi ecclesie dimisit sed et medietatem decime que ad eum pertinebat in duabus carrucatis terre arabilis que eidem curti tam de propria Hamensis ecclesie quam de aliena propinquior designabitur, omnino liberam indulsit et hoc ipsum capituli sui assensu scriptoque firmavit. Nos quoque[11] geminam utriusque abbatis concessionem in presenti cirographo[12] nostro pariter et Noviomensis sigillo corroboramus nostrarumque personarum que interfuerunt, nomina subscripsimus. S. Bartholomei.[13] S. Bosonis,[14] archidiaconorum. S. Drogonis, prepositi. S. Leonis,[15] decani. S. Odonis,[16] abbatis. S. Dionisii. S. Gisleberti,[17] abbatis Viromandensis. S. Hugonis,[18] cancellarii

6 dissensioris *B*.

7 Reinoldum *B*.

8 Reinoldus *B*.

9 Alard I de Ham (or de la Porte), knight of Ham; husband of Helvide. He also appears in acts **91**, **298**, **334**, **385**, **452**, and **464**.

10 Ide, daughter of Alard I de Ham (or de la Porte), knight of Ham, and Helvide.

11 *Om.* hanc *A*.

12 cyrographo *B*.

13 Barthélemy de Montcornet (d. 1175), son of Hugues de Montcornet and Béatrice de Reynel, was archdeacon of Laon from 1133, treasurer of Laon from 1137, and chancellor of Laon, 1141–4; later archdeacon of Reims; and bishop of Beauvais, 1162–75. Guyotjeannin, *Episcopus*, 131; Dufour-Malbezin, *Actes*, 30.

14 Boson, archdeacon of Reims, appears in a number of acts from the 1140s to the 1160s. He was a brother of Foulque d'Ecry (modern Asfeld, arr. Rethel). Marlot, *Histoire de la ville, cité et université de Reims, métropolitaine de la Gaule Belgique*, 640; Morelle, "Mariage et diplomatique," 268, fn. 7.

15 Léon, dean of Reims, is attested in acts from 1130 to 1166. Marlot, *Histoire de la ville, cité et université de Reims, métropolitaine de la Gaule Belgique*, 636–7.

16 Likely Eudes, abbot of the Augustinian abbey of Saint-Denis de Reims, 1150s–60s. *GC* IX, col. 291.

17 Gilbert I, abbot of the Premonstratensian abbey of Vermand, 1152–66. *MP* II, 427.

18 Hugues III de Roye, chancellor of Noyon-Tournai, ca. 1130–46, and of Noyon, 1146–63/6. Pycke, *Le chapitre cathédral Notre-Dame de Tournai de la fin du XIe à la fin du XIIIe siècle*, 64.

Noviomensis. Robertus[19] cancellarius recognovit scripsit. Actum anno incarnationis Domini M° C° LIII°.

416

December, 1228.

Thomas,[1] *dean of the church of Péronne, and Jean,*[2] decanus Christianitatis *of Péronne, make known that husband and wife Renier de Clary*[3] *and Emmeline sold to the church of Prémontré the three* modii *of grain (*frumentum*), measure of Ham, that they held in fief from Jean,* prepositus *of* Montibus. *Emmeline quitclaimed her rights of* dotalicium *to the three* modii. *Gilona, daughter of Emmeline and Renier, and the* prepositus *Jean also consented. (See* ***486****.)*

A. Cartulary of Prémontré, fols. 98r–98v.

B. Original, AD Oise, H 6002, previously sealed with two seals on a double strip of parchment.

Karta decani Christianitatis de venditione quam fecit Emmelina ecclesie Premonstrati.

[M]agister Th[omas] Peronensis ecclesie decanus, Johannes,[4] decanus Christianitatis Peronensis, omnibus presentes litteras inspecturis in Domino salutem. Ad universitatis vestre noticiam volumus pervenire quod, constituti in presentia nostra, Renerus de Clari et Enmelina,[5] uxor eius, recognoverunt se in perpetuum vendidisse ecclesie Premonstratensi et exinde plenariam solutionem recepisse, tres modios frumenti ad mensuram Hamensem

19 Robert, chancellor of Reims, is attested ca. 1153–ca. 1165. Marlot, *Histoire de la ville, cité et université de Reims, métropolitaine de la Gaule Belgique*, 685.

1 Thomas de Provins, dean of Péronne, 1223–30. Newman, *Charters of St-Fursy of Péronne*, 5.

2 Jean, *decanus Christianitatis* of Péronne, is attested 1228–30. AD Somme, 14 G 1, fol. 30r; Loisne, "Le Cartulaire de la Commanderie d'Éterpigny," 190, 192.

3 Clary, comm. Merlieux, https://dicotopo.cths.fr/places/P10581161. This family was perhaps related to Robert de Clari (fl. 1200), son of Gilon de Clari, given the shared toponymic and use of the name Gilon(a). Boudon, "Robert de Clari en Aminois, chevalier auteur d'une chronique de la IVe croisade (1200–1216)," 704–8.

4 *Om.* et *A*.

5 Emelina *B*.

ita tamen quod prefati R[eneri] et E[nmeline], uxor eius, in manu Johannis, prepositi de Montibus, domini fundi de quo prefatos tres modios frumenti tenebant, in feodum reddiderunt, hoc salvo quod dictus Johannes, dominus fundi, ecclesiam Premonstratensem prenotatam de predictis tribus modiis frumenti saisivit tali tenore adjuncto quod dicta ecclesia prefatos tres frumenti modios, contradictione aliquorum non valitura, possidebit in perpetuum. Quitavit etiam dicta Enmelina[6] fide media si quod habebat vel habere poterat in predictis tribus modiis frumenti ratione dotalicii. Creantaverunt insuper Renerus et Enmelina[7] sepedicti, fide[8] juramento corporaliter prestitis, venditionem prenotatam, ut predictum est, bene et legitime tenendam. Hanc autem venditionem de assensu et voluntate Johannis supradicti domini fundi factam, Gilona, dictorum Reneri et Enmeline[9] uxoris eius filia, in nostra presentia constituta, laudavit et per fidei interpositionem approbavit. Promiserunt etiam Renerus, Enmelina,[10] uxor eius, et Gilona, eorumdem filia, prenotati, fide et sacramento corporaliter prestitis, quod dictam ecclesiam Premonstratensem super premissis aliquo modo coram ecclesiastico judice vel mundano decetero non molestabunt et renunciaverunt omni juri pariter canonico et civili et omnibus aliis que possunt vel poterunt obici tam contra premissa quam contra instrumentum de premissis contentum. Quod ut ratam et debitam obtineat stabilitatem, ne de cetero super premissis questio possit suboriri, ad petitionem utriusque partis presentem kartam[11] sigillorum nostrorum munimine confirmamus. Actum anno Domini M° CC° XX° VIII°,[12] mense decembri.

6 Emelina *B.*
7 Emelina *B.*
8 *Om.* et *A.*
9 Emeline *B.*
10 Emelina *B.*
11 cartam *B.*
12 vicesimo octavo *B.*

417

November, 1227.

Eudes [IV],[1] *lord of Ham, approves the sale made to the church of Prémontré by Renier [II]*[2] *de Sains, his grandson. (See* ***304****,* ***357****, and* ***422****.)*

A. Cartulary of Prémontré, fol. 98v.
B. Original, AD Somme, 20 H 6, no. 25, previously sealed on pink silk threads.

Karta domini Odonis Hamensis de modiagio quod remisit ecclesie Premonstrati.

[E]go Odo, dominus Hamensis Castri, notum facio universis tam presentibus quam futuris quod cum ecclesia Premonstratensis deberet patri meo modiagium quod percipiebat annuatim in grangia dicte ecclesie de Colesi[3] juxta Hamum et idem pater meus de illo modiagio contulisset viro nobili Godefrido, domino de Seins, in maritagium cum Maria, sorore mea, viginti duos modios ad mensuram Hamensem quos idem dominus Godefridus de eodem patre meo sub annuo censu duodecim denariorum tenebat et, dictis domino Godefrido et Maria, uxore sua, de medio sublatis, cum dicta ecclesia de assensu et voluntate mea de illis viginti duobus modiis unum modium et dimidium acquisisset et reliquos viginti modios et dimidium teneret Renerus miles, filius eorumdem et heres de me sub censu predicto, ipse Renerus post modum de assensu et voluntate mea eosdem viginti modios et dimidium vendidit dicte ecclesie et ipsam ecclesiam et dictam grangiam sine curtem de Colesi de illis in perpetuum quitavit, fidem exhibens corporalem quod nec per se nec per alium repetet vel repeti faciet ipsum bladum vel super hoc ipsam ecclesiam decetero molestabit vel faciet molestari. Et cum, sicut predictum est, predictum bladum moveret et esset de dominio et censu meo, ego dictam venditionem laudavi et approbavi et venditionem ipsius bladi. Ego, tamquam[4] dominus qui recipit censum, warandire tenebor in perpetuum eidem ecclesie adversus omnes qui voluerint juri stare secundum usus et consuetudines Viromandesie sub annuo censu sex denariorum solvendorum annuatim in Festo Sancti Remigii sive infra octavas eiusdem ita quod, si infra octavas ipsius non fuerint persoluti, potero capere de

1 Eudes IV, lord of Ham (d. 1234), son of Eudes III, lord of Ham, and Elizabeth; husband of Elizabeth de Béthencourt.

2 Renier II, lord of Sains (arr. Vervins, https://dicotopo.cths.fr/places/P35898483), son of Geoffroi, lord of Sains, and his first wife Marie de Ham, attested in the 1220s. BM Reims, MS 1563 (N. Fonds), fol. 157v; Melleville, *DH*, vol. 2, 305.

3 Collezy, comm. Berlancourt, https://dicotopo.cths.fr/places/P68465476.

4 tanquam *B*.

rebus ecclesie ubi liceret michi capere de rebus ipsius. Si ipsa ecclesia deficeret de solutione modiagii quod michi debet, sciendum autem est quod ego omne jus et dominium quod in dicto blado ratione feodi vel alio modo vel titulo habebam in perpetuum quitavi ecclesie sepedicte renuncians omnibus conventionibus habitis inter me et dictam ecclesiam super dicto blado et omnibus kartis, litteris et instrumentis super eodem confectis et omni auxilio mihi super hoc competenti salvo eo quod residuum modiagii supradicti michi solvet ecclesia sepedicta. Et ut premissa omnia rata in perpetuum habeantur, ego presentem kartam sigilli mei feci munimine roborari. Actum mense novembri, anno gracie M° CC° vicesimo septimo.

418

October 24, 1231.

Hugues,[1] *canon and* officialis *of Noyon, makes known that Jean de Nesle de Flavy sold to the church of Prémontré around four* sextariatae *of land situated at Flavy-le-Meldeux.*[2] *Isabelle,*[3] *wife of Jean, recognizes having been compensated for her rights of* dotalicium.

A. Cartulary of Prémontré, fol. 98v.
B. Original not found.

Karta officialis Noviomensis de venditione quam fecit Johannes de Nigella de Flavi ecclesie Premonstrati.

[O]mnibus hec visuris magister Hugo, canonicus et officialis Noviomensis, salutem in Domino. Vobis notum facimus quod Johannes de Nigella de Flavi in nostra presentia constitutus, recognovit se vendidisse ecclesie Premonstratensi circiter quatuor sextariatas terre site in territorio de Flavi le Merdeus in duobus locis videlicet in Grandicampo circiter tres mancoldatas et circiter duas mancoldatas et dimidiam in campo A Le Fosse juxta terram dicte ecclesie, ipsi ecclesie in perpetuum possidendas, Isabella, dicti uxoris Johannis, presente, dictam venditionem laudante et approbante et recognoscente se sufficiens excambium habere pro dotalicio quod habebat in dicta terra dicte ecclesie vendita, videlicet in residuo terre quam habebat maritus suus habet in dicto campo A Le Fosse ad quod residuum dictus Johannes eandem

1 *Magister* Hugues, canon and *officialis* of Noyon, ca. 1229–ca. 1236. AD Aisne, H 455, fol. 310v; AD Oise, G 1984, fols. 238v–239r.

2 Flavy-le-Meldeux, cant. Guiscard, https://dicotopo.cths.fr/places/P19622430.

3 Isabelle, daughter of Raoul, lord of Flavy-le-Meldeux, and Marguerite, sister and heir of Renaud, knight of Flavy. Wacha, "La Puissance du Choix," 124.

Isabellam coram nobis pro dotalicio suo assignavit. Et per istud excambium quod in recompensationem dotalicii sui recepit a prefato Johanne marito suo, omne jus dotalicii quodcumque in dictis quatuor sextariis dicte ecclesie venditis habebat vel habitura erat quocumque jure, in ~~jure~~ manu nostra resignavit voluntate spontanea et non coacta et eidem penitus renunciavit. Et tam dictus Johannes quam ipsa Isabella, spontanea et non coacta, fidem in manu nostra prestiterunt corporalem quod dictam ecclesiam per se vel per alium decetero super dicto vendagio non molestabunt nec gravabunt nec artem nec ingenium querent per que eadem ecclesia possit vel debeat super eodem in posterum molestari vel gravari. In cuius rei testimonium presentes literas ad petitionem dictorum Johannis et Isabelle sigillo curie Noviomensis fecimus communiri. Actum anno Domini M° CC° tricesimo primo, feria sexta post festum Beati Luce Evangeliste.

419

1137

Simon [I],[1] *bishop of Noyon, makes known that at the request of Raoul [I], count of Vermandois, Yves [III], lord of Nesle, and other nobles, siblings Eudes*[2] *de Lanchy and Hescela settle their differences over the family inheritance. Eudes gives half of the inheritance to Prémontré on entering the church there together with his unnamed mother and his sister. The other half goes to Hescela and Robert Creveiz, her husband. (See* ***345****.)*

A. Cartulary of Prémontré, fols. 98v–99r.

B. Original, AD Aisne, H 802, previously sealed on a double strip of parchment.

EDITION: Pycke and Vleeschouwers, *Actes*, 406–7.

Karta Symonis Noviomensis episcopi de patrimonio Odonis de Lanci qui contulit ecclesie Premonstrati.

[I]n nomine et cetera.[3] Bona et possessiones que Deo famulantibus traduntur in remissionem peccatorum et animarum redemptionem, tunc in perpetuum

1 Simon I de Vermandois (d. 1148) was the son of Hugues I and Adélaïde, count and countess of Vermandois and Valois, and bishop of Noyon, 1123–42.

2 Eudes, lord of Lanchy (cant. Vermand, https://dicotopo.cths.fr/places/P51978975), son of Waldin/Baudouin and Elizabeth. Melleville, *DH*, vol. 1, 4.

3 *Add.* cetera *A*; sancte et individue Trinitatis *B*.

ipsorum usibus pro futura quiete conservantur, cum auctoritate episcoporum[4] roborantur et sigilli impressione commendantur. Idcirco ego Symon, Dei gratia Noviomensis episcopus, notum fieri volo tam futuris quam presentibus quod Odo de Lanci, filius Waldini, quando Premonstratum conversionis gratia cum matre et sorore sua venit, patrimonium suum, scilicet terram quam de Guidone[5] de Clastris et eam terram quam de Radulfo de Insula eamque quam de Roberto de Tenella[6] in feodo tenebat, cum cetera hereditaria possessione et domo paterna, ecclesie Premonstrate in elemosinam optulit. Quod cum soror eius, Heszela, et maritus eius Robertus Creveiz,[7] contradicerent et nullatenus acquiescere vellent ipsa etiam ecclesia hoc donum renueret eo quod populus et jus regionis injustum esse illud acclamaret; ille idem Odo ob hoc inpatiens abiectis vestibus, et totum regulare propositum resumpsit seculariter totam prefatam hereditatem suam et mansit, ut prius, in seculo. Cum autem hoc factum populus admirans detestaretur et relatum fuisset ad aures Radulfi, comitis Viromandensis, et Yvonis,[8] domini de Nigella, precepit idem comes eidem Ivoni ut hanc controversiam componi faceret qui precepit eiusdem regionis nobilibus quibus res nota erat, quatinus utrisque convocatis, Odone videlicet et Heszela, hanc contentionem sedarent. Et determinatum est ab eis ut tota hereditas districtus etiam in duas partes divideretur, preter portionem illam quam in matrimonio prefata Heszela acceperat, et mediam partem ecclesia predicta in elemosinam perpetuo possideret, mediam vero Heszela et Robertus maritus[9] eius haberet. Hanc particionem legitime concesserunt Robertus Crevez et eius uxor, Heszela, et ceteri heredes concesserunt etiam hoc supradicti viri de quorum feodis terra illa pendebat. Hanc concordiam fecerunt legitimi viri ex precepto domini Yvonis[10] quorum subscripta sunt nomina et ipsimet testes positi, videlicet Guido de Clastris, Robertus[11] Rufus, Symon[12] de Montescours,[13]

4 episcopali *B*.

5 Guy, lord of Clastres (cant. Saint-Simon, https://dicotopo.cths.fr/places/P82112287); son-in-law of Ricuère and Raimond of Clastres (**449**) through his marriage to their daughter Hawide. Melleville, *DH*, vol. 1, 256.

6 Thenelles, cant. Ribemont, https://dicotopo.cths.fr/places/P63288757.

7 Crevez *B*.

8 Ivonis *B*.

9 *Transp. A*; maritus Robertus *B*.

10 Ivonis *B*.

11 Robert *Rufus*, brother of Mathieu and Bernier, and father of Adam, Jean, and Widèle, appears in **345**, **353**, **371**, **398**, and **442**.

12 Simon de Mondescourt (cant. Noyon, https://dicotopo.cths.fr/places/P60804459), son of Emmelot, appears as a witness in acts 1137–ca. 1183. Tock and Milis, *Monumenta Arroasiensia*, 143, 315.

13 Montescurz *B*.

Werricus[14] Gastellus, Nanterus[15] de Sancto Quinto, Philippus de Montruel,[16,17] Bernerus et Matheus, fratres eius, Radulfus, Arnulphus,[18] Hermerus de Lanci. Quod ut ratum et inconvulsum permaneat, sigilli nostri impressione subsignavimus et quicumque ausu temerario infringere aut perturbare presumpserit, nisi resipuerit, anathemati subjaceat et in extremo examine a sanctorum consortio alienus fiat. Actum est hoc anno incarnationis dominice[19] M° C° XXX° VII°, epacta VII^a, indictione prima,[20] concurrente quarto.[21]

420

March, 1201.

Étienne [I],[1] *bishop of Noyon, confirms both the gift by Adèle [de Péronne],*[2] *widow of Simon de Bouchavesnes, of two parts of the tithe of Cartigny in alms to the church of Prémontré, and the later recognition of that gift by Adèle's son, Geoffroi,*[3] *the cantor of Péronne, as he prepared to leave for Jerusalem. (See* ***341****,* ***342****,* ***347****, and* ***425****.)*

A. Cartulary of Prémontré, fol. 99r.

B. Original not found.

---

14 Wenric Vastel (or Guastel), brother of Renier de Roinon, is attested 1133–71. Newman, *Homblières*, 166, fn. 2.

15 Nanter de Saint-Quentin appears as a witness in **345**, and likely in **333**. He is possibly the same Nanter, *bourgeois* of Saint-Quentin, who gave land to the Cistercian abbey of Notre-Dame de Longpont. Poquet, *Monographie de l'abbaye de Longpont, son histoire, ses monuments, ses abbés, ses personnages célèbres, ses sépultures, ses possessions territoriales*, 168.

16 Pontruel *B*.

17 Pontruet, cant. Vermand, https://dicotopo.cths.fr/places/P35872776.

18 Arnulfus *B*.

19 Domini *B*.

20 I^a *B*.

21 IIII° *B*.

---

1 Étienne de Villebéon (or de Nemours), son of Gautier de Villebéon, lord of La Chapelle-Gauthier and Nemours, and Aveline, was bishop of Noyon, 1188–1221.

2 Adèle, daughter of Mathieu Strabo de Péronne and Frédeburge *Domez*. Her anniversary was celebrated at Prémontré on January 9. Van Waefelghem, *L'Obituaire de l'abbaye de Prémontré*, 25. Adèle and her husband Simon de Bouchavesnes also gave the tithe of Courcelles to the Benedictine abbey of Notre-Dame d'Avesnes-lès-Bapaume, ca. 1142–7. Tock, ed., *Les chartes des évêques d'Arras*, 110; Bougard and Delmaire, *Le cartulaire et les chartes de l'abbaye de femmes d'Avesnes-lès-Bapaume (1128–1337)*, 69–70.

3 Geoffroi, cantor of the collegiate church of Saint-Fursy de Péronne, ca. 1199–ca. 1205. Newman, *Charters of St-Fursy of Péronne*, 8.

Karta Stephani Noviomensis episcopi de elemosina Aelidis uxoris Symonis de Buscheavesnes.

[S]tephanus, Dei gratia Noviomensis episcopus, omnibus in perpetuum. Notum fieri volumus quod nos inspeximus auctentica scripta patrum et predecessorum nostrum virorum venerabilium, Symonis, pie recordationis et bone memorie Balduini qui primus ei successit, episcoporum Noviomensium, quorum hic erat tenor quod nobilis mulier Aelidis, quondam uxor Symonis de Buscheavesnes, contulit ecclesie Premonstratensi in elemosinam, pro anime sue et antecessorum suorum remedio, duas partes quas de hereditate sua in decima de Cartigni habebat, et jure perpetuo tenendas concessit. Gaufridus itaque cantor Peronensis, filius eiusdem Aelidis, qui decimam prescriptam tenebat, ad Jherosolimitane peregrinationis iter accinctus, ad nostram devote accessit presentiam et ipsam elemosinam recognoscens, humiliter postulavit a nobis ut eam ratam haberemus et tam scripti nostri auctoritate quam sigilli nostri appensione confirmaremus. Recognovit etiam quod nomine elemosine et concessionis illius ecclesie Premonstratensi IIII^or^ modii frumenti ex eadem decima reddere tenebatur annuatim. Nos quoque postulationem eius, quoniam rationabilis visa est, benigne suscipientes et ecclesie Premonstratensi indemnitati volentes providere, elemosinam ipsam et pensionem sepedictam sicut eam idem Gaufridus cantor recognovit, laudavimus et tam presenti scripto quam sigilli nostri testimonio confirmavimus. Statuentes et sub anathemate firmiter inhibentes ut nullus omnino hanc elemosinam perturbare seu nostre confirmationis paginam aliquatenus infringere presumat. Actum anno incarnationis dominice M° CC° I°, mense martio. Datum per manum Willelmi, fratris et cancellarii nostri.

421

1165

Baudouin [II],[1] *bishop of Noyon, makes known that Eudes de Falvy*[2] *gave to the church of Prémontré and the Augustinian abbey of Saint Nicolas d'Arrouaise his part of the major and minor tithes of Lanchy,*[3] *worth 100* librae Provinensium. *Eudes [III],*[4] *lord of Ham and fief lord, consents to the gift,*

1 Baudouin II de Boulogne, abbot of the Augustinian abbey of Saint-Eloi-Fontaine, ca. 1130–ca. 1139, and bishop of Noyon, 1148–67. GC IX, col. 1126.

2 Falvy, cant. Nesle, https://dicotopo.cths.fr/places/P25248648.

3 Lanchy, cant. Vermand, https://dicotopo.cths.fr/places/P51978975.

4 Eudes III, lord of Ham, son of Lancelin, lord of Ham, and Mathilde.

as do Mathilde, his mother, and Gérard, his brother.[5] *Helissende, Eudes de Falvy's wife, and Elizabeth, his sister, also consent.*

A. Cartulary of Prémontré, fol. 99r.

B. Original, BnF, Coll. Picardie 290, no. 11, previously sealed. In the right margin and beginning at the top, the bottom half of the letters that form the word CYROGRAPHUM.

Other Manuscript Copies: Cartulary of Saint-Nicolas d'Arrouaise, BM Amiens, MS 1077, fols. 85v–86r (12th c.).

EDITION: Tock and Milis, *Monumenta Arroasiensia*, 218–19; *Diplomata Belgica*, no. 11155, https://www.diplomata-belgica.be/charter_details_en.php?dibe_id=11155; *Chartae Galliae*, no. 201231, http://telma.irht.cnrs.fr/outils/chartae-galliae/charte201231/.

REGISTER: Michel, "Inventaire sommaire du cartulaire d'Arrouaise," 266; Boghen, "Inventaire des actes épiscopaux originaux conservés à la Bibliothèque nationale (1121–1200)," 121; *Studium Baldwin*, fiche 2041.

Karta Balduini Noviomensis episcopi de elemosina Odonis militis de Falevi quam dedit ecclesie Premonstrate et ecclesie de Aroasia.

[I]n nomine et cetera.[6] Ego Balduinus, Dei gratia Noviomensis episcopus, notum facio tam futuris quam presentibus quod Odo, miles de Falevi, dedit Premonstrate ecclesie et ecclesie Sancti Nicholai de Aroasia quicquid habebat in maiori decima et in minuta de Lanci, excepta decima terre sue quam ibi propriam tempore huius concessionis possidebat; utraque vero prefata ecclesia simul dederit predicto Odoni respectu huius doni centum libras Provinensis monete. Concesserunt autem hoc donum et laudaverunt uxor predicti Odonis, Helissendis, et soror eiusdem Elizabeth, presentibus Radulpho,[7] priore de Marzeles, Radulpho, maiore de Athies,[8] Pagano et Dyonisio,[9] genero eius, Amisardo, Ascelino, Petro. Ut igitur hoc donum utrique prefate ecclesie ratum absque ulla reclamatione permanent, predictus Odo assensum domini Odonis,

5 Gérard (d. aft. 1177), son of Lancelin, lord of Ham, and Mathilde. Charles Gomart, "Les seigneurs et gouverneurs de Ham," *Mémoires de la Société des antiquaires de Picardie*, Second Series, 8 (1861), 329.

6 *Add.* et cetera *A*; *om.* sancte et individue Trinitatis *B*.

7 Raoul (d. 1206), prior of the Arroasian priory of Margères, ca. 1160s–ca. 1200, briefly abbot of Saint-Nicolas d'Arrouaise, ca. 1201. Josse, *Notice historique sur le village de Douilly et ses dépendances*, 94–6.

8 Athiis *B*.

9 Dionisio *B*.

Hamensis domini, et matris sue Matildis,[10] et fratris sui Gerardi, quesivit, quia de feodo eiusdem Odonis descendebat et obtinuit ea tamen conditione quod in feodo ipsius quinquaginta libras predicte monete poneret ne feodum domini sui deperiret. Assensit igitur predictus dominus eius Odo et mater et frater eius presentibus, Radulpho priore de Marzeles, et Matheo Premonstratensi canonico, Johanne[11] de Athiis milite, Symone[12] de Montescourt, Roberto[13] maiore Hamensi, Radulfo[14] maiore de Athiis, Radulfo[15,16] maiore de Monci, et Symone filio eius. Postmodum autem uterque predictus Odo ad nostram presentiam venerunt et in manu nostra hoc ordine werpierunt, Odo de Falevi in manu alterius Odonis, Hamensis domini, dominus vero Hamensis in manu nostra et nos utrique prefate ecclesie predictam decimam contulimus perpetuo possidendam. Ut igitur ratum et inconvulsum permaneat sigilli nostre auctoritate confirmari et nomina personarum ecclesie nostre fecimus subnotari. Signum Balduini, decani. S. Gaufridi,[17] cantoris. S. magistri Roberti. S. magistri Autberti.[18] S. Radulfi,[19] sacerdotis. S. Henrici et ceteri.[20] Quicumque igitur huic nostre et ceteri.[21] Actum anno incarnati verbi M° C° sexagesimo[22] V°.

---

10 Mathildis *B.*

11 Jean d'Athies, son of *Robert Rufus*, nephew of Mathieu and Bernier, and brother of Widèle and Adam. With his wife Eustacie, he was the father of Manassès, Robert, Aubry, and Eudes the cleric. With his brother Adam, knight and lord of Athies (cant. Ham, https://dicotopo.cths.fr/places/P98820850), he is attested in a number of acts ca. 1150–ca. 1188. Cagny, *Histoire de l'arrondissement de Péronne*, vol. 2, 259; Tock and Milis, *Monumenta Arroasiensia*, 251. He is also mentioned in **306**, **353**, **371**, **398**, **424**, and **442**.

12 Simon de Mondescourt (cant. Noyon, https://dicotopo.cths.fr/places/P60804459), son of Emmelot, appears as a witness in acts 1137–ca. 1183. Tock and Milis, *Monumenta Arroasiensia*, 143, 315.

13 A Robert, *maior* of Ham, appears in **378**, **401**, and **445**.

14 Radulpho *B.*

15 Radulpho *B.*

16 Raoul, *maior* of Monchy, appears as a witness in acts 1153–65. Tock and Milis, *Monumenta Arroasiensia*, 144.

17 Geoffroi, cantor of the cathedral chapter of Noyon, appears as a witness in acts ca. 1152–82. Tock and Milis, *Monumenta Arroasiensia*, 282, 299, 313.

18 Auberti *B.*

19 Radulphi *B.*

20 *Add.* et cetera *A*; *om.* Petri diaconorum. S. Symonis, Balduini subdiaconorum *A.*

21 *Add.* et cetera *A*; *om.* confirmatione ausu temerario obviare temptaverit nisi resipuerit anathema sit *A.*

22 LX° *B.*

422

November, 1227.

The knight Renier [II],[1] *lord of Sains, makes known that he sold 22* modii *of grain (*bladus*), measure of Ham, to the church of Prémontré. Elisende, his wife, approves. (See* ***304****,* ***357****, and* ***417****.)*

A. Cartulary of Prémontré, fol. 99v.

B. Original, AD Somme, 20 H 6, no. 19, previously sealed on a double strip of parchment.

Karta Reneri domini de Seins de modiagio que remisit ecclesie Premonstrati.

[E]go Renerus, miles, dominus de Seins,[2] notum facio universis tam presentibus quam futuris quod cum bone memorie Odo, dominus Hamensis Castri, de modiagio illo quod percipiebat annuatim in grangia Premonstratensis ecclesie apud Colesi, contulisset in maritagium Marie, filie sue, matri mee cum Godefrido, patre meo, viginti duos modios bladi ad mensuram Hamensem et ego, tanquam heres eorumdem, perciperem viginti duos modios supradictos, ego, postmodum habita amicabili conventione inter me et ecclesiam memoratam, vendidi eidem Premonstratensis ecclesie predictos viginti duos modios et ipsos eidem ecclesie et predicte grangie in perpetuum quitavi renuncians omnibus conventionibus, literis, kartis, instrumentis super eodem blado confectis et omni auxilio mihi[3] super hoc conpetenti[4] et nichil omnino michi retinui in eisdem. Hanc etiam venditionem Elisendis, uxor mea, approbavit penitus et laudavit et quitavit in perpetuum ipsi ecclesie quicquid vel ratione dotis, vel alio modo habebat vel habere poterat in eisdem et tam ego quam predicta uxor mea fidem prestitimus corporalem quod nec per nos, nec per alium ipsum bladum aliquatenus repetemus vel repeti faciemus nec aliquo modo molestabimus ecclesiam sepedictam. Ut autem predicta venditio maneat in perpetuum inconcussa, ego presentem kartam feci sigilli mei munimine roborari. Actum mense novembri, anno gratie M° CC° XX°[5] septimo.

---

1 Renier II, lord of Sains (arr. Vervins, https://dicotopo.cths.fr/places/P35898483), son of Geoffroi, lord of Sains, and his first wife Marie de Ham, attested in the 1220s. BM Reims, MS 1563 (N. Fonds), fol. 157v; Melleville, *DH*, vol. 2, 305.

2 Seyns *B*.

3 michi *B*.

4 competenti *B*.

5 vicesimo *B*.

423

1178

Guerry,[1] *dean of Saint-Quentin, and Eudes [III],*[2] *lord of Ham, reach an agreement concerning the rights that the chapter of Saint-Quentin claimed over the wood of Collezy.*[3]

A. Cartulary of Prémontré, fol. 99v.
B. Original, AD Somme, 20 H_SC_6, no. 13, sealed.[4]
REGISTER: *Studium Baldwin*, fiche 2042.

Karta decani Sancti Quintini de conpositione nemoris de Colesiaco et de jure eisdem.

[I]n nomine et cetera. Ego Werricus, ecclesie Sancti Quintini maioris decanus, totumque capitulum notum fieri volumus omnibus tam presentibus quam futuris quod super jure quod in nemore de Colesiaco reclamabamus inter nos et Hamensem dominum, Odonem, qui diu et antecessores sui nemus idem possederant, ita convenitur ut IIII^{or} modios frumenti annuatim solvendos in grangiis ecclesie Premonstrati et ecclesie Hamensis quibus idem nemus sub annuo censu ad perpetuo excolendum collatum erat, quem acciperemus de censu, prefato Odoni dicte ecclesie solvere tenebantur; solventur autem nobis eodem modo et eadem mensura, scilicet Hamensi, qua domino Odoni et successoribus eius solvi debebant. Que conpositio ita facta est quod omne jus quod in prefato nemore reclamabamus, supradictis ecclesiis perpetuo tenendum remisimus, ipsum eundem Odonem et antecessores eius absolventes ab offensa, si quam adversus nos super sepedicto nemore contraxerant. Super qua concessione vel remissione ne qua de cetero litigandi suscitetur occasio sigilli nostri appositione et subscriptorum testium annotatione fecimus muniri. Testes itaque sunt: Thomas cancellarius, Wenzio cantor, magister Winbertus, Guido capellanus, Bernardus, Hugo sacerdotes, magister Gerardus, magister Evrardus, Johannes, Petrus diaconi, Walterus, Judeus, Evrardus pincerna, Symon filius Nivelonis, Thomas de Belleneglise[5] subdiaconi. Actum anno incarnati verbi M^{o} C^{o} LXX° VIII°.

1 Guerry, dean of Saint-Quentin, is attested 1165–81. BnF, MS lat. 11069, fols. 2v–3r, 4r–5r; BnF, MS lat. 5478, fols. 98v–99v.
2 Eudes III, lord of Ham, son of Lancelin, lord of Ham, and Mathilde.
3 Collezy, comm. Berlancourt, https://dicotopo.cths.fr/places/P68465476.
4 Due to conservation concerns, this original was not available to the editors.
5 Bellenglise, cant. Catelet, https://dicotopo.cths.fr/places/P65342481.

424

1177. Nesle.

Philippe [I][1] and Elizabeth,[2] count and countess of Flanders and Vermandois, make known that Eudes [III],[3] lord of Ham, gave the land and woods of Collezy[4] to the churches of Prémontré and Ham to be cleared and exploited, in return for his receiving an annual census *of grain (*annona*). Philippe and Elizabeth approve this and concede their rights as fief lords over these lands and woods.*

A. Cartulary of Prémontré, fol. 99v.
B. Original, AD Somme, H_SC_6, no. 7, sealed.[5]

Karta comitis Flandrensis et uxoris eiusdem de elemosina domini Hamensis super nemore que Colesiae dicitur.

[I]n nomine Patris et Filii et cetera. Ego Philippus, Dei gratia comes Flandrensis et Viromandensis, ego quoque Elisabeth, Flandrensis et Viromandensis comitissa, notum facimus presentibus et futuris quod Odo, dominus Hamensis, per manum nostram contulit ecclesie Premonstratensi et ecclesie Hamensi totam terram et totum nemus quod Colesiacum nuncupatur, ad extirpandum et excolendum et omnimodam utriusque ecclesie utilitatem. Nos igitur donationem terre illius et nemoris, quia de feodo nostro descendit, sub annuali censu annone inter ipsum Odonem et predictas ecclesias constituto, ad petitionem predicti Odonis pro remedio animarum nostrarum et predecessorum nostrorum predictis ecclesiis in perpetuum concedimus cum omni libertate et omnibus aisentiis quas prefatus Odo utrique ecclesie concessit, sicut in litteris predicti Odonis sigillo ipsius confirmatis continetur. Ut autem hec donatio utrique predicte ecclesie per nos facta, rata et inconvulsa permaneat, ego et comitissa presentem paginam sigillorum nostrorum impressione et testium subscriptione communiri fecimus et ipse prefatus Odo nos obsides dedit utrique ecclesie quod si in aliquo deviaverint, ipse vel heredes eius a pactionibus inter se constitutis et confirmatis nos et heredes nostri, vel monendo eos, ad pacem et concordiam revocabimus, vel ad corrigendum arbitrio curie nostre conpellemus. Ideo autem presens scriptum sub cyrographo distinctum est, ut utraque ecclesia penes se partem suam habeat

1 Philippe I d'Alsace (1143–1191), count of Flanders, son of Thierry d'Alsace, count of Flanders, and his second wife Sibylle d'Anjou.

2 Elizabeth de Vermandois, countess of Vermandois and Valois (d. 1183), daughter of Raoul I, count of Vermandois and Valois, and Pétronille d'Aquitaine; first wife of Philippe I d'Alsace, count of Flanders.

3 Eudes III, lord of Ham, son of Lancelin, lord of Ham, and Mathilde.

4 Collezy, comm. Berlancourt, https://dicotopo.cths.fr/places/P68465476.

5 Due to conservation concerns, the original was not available to the editors.

et contra adversantes prolata nostre concessionis auctoritate perpetue tuitionis robur obtineat. Actum Nigelle anno incarnationis dominice M° C° LXX° VII°, astantibus et testantibus legitimis et honestis personis: domino Conone[6] de Petrefonz, Willermo de Medo, Waltero de Locris,[7] Waltero de Atrebato, Rorigone[8] de Faiel et Symone fratre eius, Johanne[9] de Athies et Manasse filio eius, Sawalone[10] cognomento Hukedeu, Odone Malin. S. Gerardi[11] notarii et sigillarii nostri.

425

March 21, 1204. Bishop of Noyon's house, Péronne.

Guillaume Pastez,[1] *Pierre d'Amiens,*[2] *and Renaud de Béthisy,*[3] prepositi *and* bailli *of the king, make known that in their presence, Ermengarde*[4] *de*

6 Conon de Nesle (d. 1180), first castellan of Bruges and then count of Soissons from 1178; son of Raoul II, lord of Nesle, and Gertrude, *neptis* of Thierry, count of Flanders. He was lord of Pierrefonds through his marriage to Agathe, lady of Pierrefonds. Newman, *Seigneurs*, vol. 1, 63–4.

7 Loker, comm. Heuvelland.

8 Rorigon, lord of Fayet (d. ca. 1199), and Simon (d. ca. 1187), sons of Aude, lady of Fayet. Newman, *Seigneurs*, vol. 2, 102.

9 Jean d'Athies, son of *Robert Rufus*, nephew of Mathieu and Bernier, and brother of Widèle and Adam. With his wife Eustacie, he was the father of Manassès, Robert, Aubry, and Eudes the cleric. With his brother Adam, knight and lord of Athies (cant. Ham, https://dicotopo.cths.fr/places/P98820850), he is attested in a number of acts ca. 1150–ca. 1188. Cagny, *Histoire de l'arrondissement de Péronne*, vol. 2, 259; Tock and Milis, *Monumenta Arroasiensia*, 251. He is also mentioned in **306**, **353**, **371**, **398**, **421**, and **442**.

10 Sauwalon Huchedieu, son of Henri Huchedieu and Aude, *maior* of Arras in the late twelfth century. Guesnon, "Les origines d'Arras et de ses institutions," 228.

11 Gérard de Messines was notary and *sigillarius comitis* of the count of Flanders 1169–81 and *prepositus* of Lille, ca. 1183–ca. 1191. Reusens, "Les chancelleries inferieures en Belgique depuis leur origins jusqu'au XIIIe siècle," 111; Verhulst and de Hemptinne, "Le chancelier de Flandre sous les comtes de la maison d'Alsace (1128–1191)," 308.

1 Guillaume Pastez (or Pasté), knight, king's *bailli*, 1200–17. Bouquet and Delisle, eds., *Recueil des historiens des Gaules et de la France*, vol. 24, part 1, 53–7; Baldwin, *The Government of Philip Augustus*, 131, 431.

2 Pierre de Béthisy, king's *bailli* and *prévôt* at Amiens, ca. 1186–1216, with a sphere of activity extending to Péronne, Abbeville, Roye, and Bapaume. He was brother of the *bailli* Renaud de Béthisy and husband of Luciane. Bouquet and Delisle, eds., *Recueil des historiens des Gaules et de la France*, vol. 24, part 1, 53–7; Baldwin, *The Government of Philip Augustus*, 130, 428, 431.

3 Renaud de Béthisy, king's *bailli*, worked principally at Compiègne and Montdidier, ca. 1196–1221, with a sphere of influence extending to Péronne, Beauvais, Senlis, and Meaux. He was brother of the *bailli* Pierre de Béthisy, and husband of Emmeline, lady of Houdancourt. Bouquet and Delisle, eds., *Recueil des historiens des Gaules et de la France*, vol. 24, part 1, 53–7; Baldwin, *The Government of Philip Augustus*, 130, 431.

4 Ermengarde de Bapaumes, daughter of Adèle de Péronne and Simon de Bouchavesnes.

Bapaumes, daughter of Adèle[5] *and sister of Geoffroi,*[6] *cantor of Péronne, renounced in favour of the church of Prémontré her claim to two parts of the tithe of Cartigny*[7] *that her mother Adèle had given in alms to the monastery. Gérard, Ermengarde's son, consented to this. (See **341**, **342**, **347**, and **420**.)*

A. Cartulary of Prémontré, fols. 99v–100r.

B. Original not found.

EDITION: Delisle, *Recueil des historiens des Gaules et de la France*, vol. 24, part 1, 272.

Karta de recognitione Ermengardis de Biaumeis filie Aelidis de Boischavesne.

[E]go Willelmus Pastes et Petrus Ambianensis et Renaldus de Bestesi, prepositi et ballivi domini regis, omnibus sacro Christi caractere signatis salutem in perpetuum. Notum esse volumus universis quod Ermengardis de Biaumeis, filia Aeldis de Boischavesne, soror domini Gaufridi, cantoris de Perona, recognovit in presentia nostra, coram hominibus domini regis apud Peronam, die sessionis, elemosinam quam mater sua delegavit ecclesie Premonstrati, duas videlicet partes decime de Cartigni et siquid juris in predicta elemosina prefata Ermengardis habebat vel habere debebat, coram nobis renuntiavit, werpivit et ecclesie memorate in elemosinam, assensu, voluntate et concessu filii sui, Gerardi, perpetuo dimisit. Et ut istud predicta ecclesia sine cuiusdam molestia vel inquietatione in omni modo melius sibi competenti decetero firmius possideret, tam mater quam filius in presentia nostra coram domini regis hominibus et multis militibus fidei sacramento se obligaverunt. Ut autem iam dicta elemosina recognita coram nobis et facta maneat inconvulsa perpetuumque robur obtineat, scriptum presens, hominibus qui interfuerunt annotatis, sigilli nostri caractere dignum duximus insigniri: S. castellani de Perona.[8] S. castellani de

5 Adèle, daughter of Mathieu Strabo de Péronne and Frédeburge *Domez*. Her anniversary was celebrated at Prémontré on January 9. Van Waefelghem, *L'Obituaire de l'abbaye de Prémontré*, 25. Adèle and her husband Simon de Bouchavesnes also gave the tithe of Courcelles to the Benedictine abbey of Notre-Dame d'Avesnes-lès-Bapaume, ca. 1142–7. Tock, ed., *Les chartes des évêques d'Arras*, 110; Bougard and Delmaire, *Le cartulaire et les chartes de l'abbaye de femmes d'Avesnes-lès-Bapaume (1128–1337)*, 69–70.

6 Geoffroi, cantor of Péronne, son of Adèle de Péronne and Simon de Bouchavesnes.

7 Cartigny, cant. Péronne, https://dicotopo.cths.fr/places/P86731604.

8 Pierre II, castellan of Péronne and lord of Bray, attested ca. 1200–ca. 1205. Cagny, *Histoire de l'arrondissement de Péronne*, vol. 1, 474.

Biaumes.[9] S. Hellini de Wauri, Egidii[10] de Marcais. S. Johannis de Perona. S. Galteri de Gonguelin. S. Goifridi de Cartigni et ceteri. Actum apud Peronam, in domo episcopi[11] Noviomensis, feria secunda post Letare Jherusalem, ipsa die Beati Benedicti abbatis, anno gratie M° CC° IIII°.

426

February 22, 1231.

Hugues,[1] *canon and* officialis *of Noyon, makes known in the presence of his representative Jean, dean of Ham, that Raoul, a taverner of Flavy,*[2] *acknowledged having sold to Prémontré six* sextariatae *of land situated in the essarts of Flavy near the woods of Bonneuil.*[3] *Marie, wife of Raoul, approved of this gift, and received in exchange, as her rights of* dotalicium, *a house at Flavy.*

A. Cartulary of Prémontré, fol. 100r.
B. Original not found.

Karta officialis Noviomensis de elemosina et venditione cuiusdam terre Radulfi tabernarii de Flavi.

[O]mnibus hec visuris magister Hugo, canonicus et officialis Noviomensis, salutem in Domino. Vobis notum facimus quod Radulfus, tabernarius de Flavi, in presentia Johannis, decani nostri Hamensis, loco nostri, constitutus recognovit se vendidisse ecclesie Premonstratensi sex sextariatas terre site in sartis de Flavi prope nemus de Bonolio, ipsi ecclesie in perpetuum possidendas, Maria, uxore dicti Radulfi, presente, dictam venditionem laudante et approbante et recognoscente se sufficiens excambium habere pro dotalicio quod habebat in dicta terra dicte ecclesie vendita, videlicet quoddam mansum quod dictus

9 Gilles I, lord of Beaumetz (cant. Bertincourt, https://dicotopo.cths.fr/places/P35591263) and castellan of Bapaume (d. aft. 1214), son of Hugues, castellan of Bapaume and lord of Beaumetz, and Beatrix de Guines. He appears in a number of acts dating 1208–13 in the cartulary of the abbey of Avesnes-lès-Bapaume. Bougard and Delmaire, *Le cartulaire et les chartes de l'abbaye de femmes d'Avesnes-lès-Bapaume (1128–1337)*, 119–20, 121–2, 129–30.

10 Gilles I, lord of Marquaix. Newman, *Seigneurs*, vol. 2, 100.

11 Étienne de Villebéon (or de Nemours), son of Gautier de Villebéon, lord of La Chapelle-Gauthier and Nemours, and Aveline, was bishop of Noyon, 1188–1221.

1 *Magister* Hugues, canon and *officialis* of Noyon, ca. 1229–ca. 1236. AD Aisne, H 455, fol. 310v; AD Oise, G 1984, fols. 238v–239r.

2 Flavy-le-Meldeux, cant. Guiscard, https://dicotopo.cths.fr/places/P19622430.

3 Bonneuil, cant. Ham, https://dicotopo.cths.fr/places/P66750585.

Radulfus habet apud Flavi, ad quod ipse eandem Mariam coram dicto decano pro dotalicio suo assignavit et per istud excambium quod in recompensationem dotalicii sui recepit a prefato Radulfo, marito suo, omne jus dotalicii sui quodcumque in dictis sex sextariatis dicte ecclesie venditis habebat vel habitura erat quocumque jure, in manu dicti decani resignavit voluntate spontanea et non coacta et eidem penitus renunciavit. Et tam dictus Radulfus quam ipsa Maria, spontanea et non coacta, fidem in manu dicti decani prestiterunt corporalem quod dictam ecclesiam per se vel per alium decetero super dicto vendagio non molestabunt nec gravabunt nec artem nec ingenium querent per que eadem ecclesia possit vel debeat super eodem in posterum molestari vel gravari. In cuius rei testimonium presentes literas secundum tenorem literarum dicti decani ad mandatum nostrum super dicto vendagio confectarum sigillo nostre curie fecimus roborari. Actum anno Domini M° CC° tricesimo primo, in crastino Invocavit Me et cetera.

427

March, 1231.

Hugues,[1] *canon and* officialis *of Noyon, makes known that Jean de Moyenville*[2] *de Flavy recognized that he had sold to the church of Prémontré four* sextariatae *of land at Flavy in two separate places. Mathilde, wife of Jean, approves the sale and, in exchange, receives rights of* dotalicium *over three* sextariatae *of land at the* foramina *of Flavy.*

A. Cartulary of Prémontré, fol. 100r.
B. Original, AD Somme, 20 H_SC_10, no. 5.[3]

Karta officialis Noviomensis de venditione cuiusdam terre Johannis de Media Villa.

[O]mnibus hec visuris magister Hugo, canonicus et officialis Noviomensis, salutem in Domino. Vobis notum facimus quod Johannes de Media Villa, videlicet de Flavi, in presentia nostra constitutus, recognovit se vendidisse ecclesie Premonstratensi quatuor sextariatas terre site in territorio de Flavi in duobus locis, videlicet in sartis de Flavi juxta nemus de Bonolio duas sextariatas et juxta fossatum illud castellani duas sextariatas, ipsi ecclesie in perpetuum

1 *Magister* Hugues, canon and *officialis* of Noyon, ca. 1229–ca. 1236. AD Aisne, H 455, fol. 310v; AD Oise, G 1984, fols. 238v–239r.

2 Likely Moyenville, cant. Saint-Just-en-Chaussée, https://dicotopo.cths.fr/places/P11933165.

3 Due to conservation concerns, the original was not available to the editors.

possidendas, Matilde uxore Johannis presente, dictam venditionem laudante et approbante et recognoscente se sufficiens excambium habere pro dotalicio quod habebat in dicta terre dicte ecclesie vendita, videlicet in tribus sextariatis terre quas maritus suus habet ad foramina de Flavi ad quas dictus Johannes eandem Matildem coram nobis pro dotalicio suo assignavit et per istud excanbium quod in recompensationem dotalicii sui recepit a prefato Johanne marito suo omne jus dotalicii quodcumque in dictis IIII^or sextariatis dicte ecclesie venditis habebat vel habitura erat, quocumque jure, in manu nostra resignavit voluntate spontanea et non coacta et eidem penitus renunciavit. Et tam dictus Johannes quam ipsa Matildis spontanea et non coacta, fidem in manu nostra prestiterunt corporalem. Quod dictam ecclesiam per se vel per alium decetero super dicta vendagio non molestabunt nec gravabunt, nec artem nec ingenium querent per que eadem ecclesia possit vel debeat super eodem in posterum molestari vel gravari. In cuius rei testimonium presentes litteras ad petitionem dictorum Johannis et Matildis sigillo curie Noviomensis fecimus roborari. Actum anno Domini M° CC° tricesimo primo, mense martio.

428

August, 1220.

Raoul,[1] *lord of Flavy, and Marguerite,*[2] *his wife, give in alms to the church of Prémontré five* modiatae *of wood and meadow at Bishop's Wood and about four other* sexterlatae *of wood at the* foramina *of Flavy; in return, they receive 52.5* librae Parisiensium. *Their six children – the cleric Pierre,*[3] *Robert,*[4] *Jean, Elizabeth, Mathilde, and Marie – consent to this. (See* ***348****.)*

A. Cartulary of Prémontré, fol. 100r.

B. Original, AD Oise, H 6000, previously sealed with two seals on strips of parchment.

REGISTER: *Studium Baldwin*, fiche 2285.

1 Raoul, lord of Flavy-le-Meldeux (cant. Guiscard, https://dicotopo.cths.fr/places/P19622430) *iure uxoris*. Newman, *Seigneurs*, vol. 2, 280–1.

2 Marguerite de Flavy, sister and heir of Renaud, knight of Flavy. Newman, *Seigneurs*, vol. 2, 280–1.

3 Newman suggests that this *Petrus clericus* later left the clerical life and is the same person as Pierre, lord of half of Flavy-le-Meldeux (d. aft. 1247), son of Raoul, lord of Flavy-le-Meldeux, and Marguerite, sister and heir of Renaud, knight of Flavy. Newman, *Seigneurs*, vol. 2, 280–1.

4 Robert Aguinant, lord of half of Flavy-le-Meldeux, son of Raoul, lord of Flavy-le-Meldeux, and Marguerite, sister and heir of Renaud, knight of Flavy. Newman, *Seigneurs*, vol. 2, 280–1.

Karta Radulfi domini de Flavi et uxoris eiusdem de elemosina quam contulit ecclesie Premonstrati.

[E]go Radulfus, dominus de Flavi, et Margareta, uxor mea, notum facimus tam futuris quam presentibus per hoc scriptum quod nos, saluti nostre providere volentes, elemosinam que subscripta est duximus Premonstratensi ecclesie in perpetuum concedendum. Nos siquidem habebamus quinque modiatas tam nemoris quam prati in nemore quod dicitur Nemus Episcopi et circiter quatuor alias sexterlatas nemoris que sunt ad foramina de Flavi, que omnia tradidimus ecclesie Premonstratensi in elemosinam perpetuo possidenda. Hanc autem elemosinam tam ego R[adulfus] quam predictam uxor mea, M[argaretam], de cuius hereditate hec omnia provenerunt necnon et liberi nostri, videlicet Petrus clericus, Robertus et Johannes, Elizabeth, Matildis et Maria, sub fidei corporalis interpositione laudavimus et approbavimus, renunciantes omni juri quod habebamus vel habere poteramus in omnibus supradictis, super quibus etiam tenebimur portare legitimam warandiam secundum usus et consuetudines castellanie Hamensis adversus omnes qui voluerint juri stare preter quam adversus dominum episcopum Noviomensem et homines Espevile[5,6] necnon et homines de Vellanis. Ecclesia vero Premonstratensis, devotionem nostram attendens, recompensavit nobis intuitu caritatis in temporali beneficio quinquaginta duas libras et dimidiam Parisiensis monete. Huius autem elemosine traditioni presentes fuerunt vir religiosus Rogerus,[7] abbas ecclesie Beate Marie Hamensis, vir nobilis Odo[8] dominus Hamensis, Hugo de Alneto et Johannes milites, Robertus prior, Symon[9] et Ingelrannus prepositi, necnon et Nicholaus magister Bonolii, et Hugo canonici ecclesie Premonstratensis. Ut autem predicta elemosina futuris temporibus firmiter teneatur, nos emisimus presentes litteras in testimonium huius rei confectas sigillorum nostrorum appensione munitas. Actum mense augusto, anno gratie M°[10] ducentesimo vicesimo.

5 Espeville *B*.

6 Eppeville, cant. Ham. https://dicotopo.cths.fr/places/P94171781.

7 Roger, abbot of the Augustinian abbey of Notre-Dame de Ham, ca. 1220–ca. 1226. Cagny, *Histoire de l'arrondissement de Péronne*, vol. 2, 219–20.

8 Eudes IV, lord of Ham (d. 1234), son of Eudes III, lord of Ham, and Elizabeth; husband of Elizabeth de Béthencourt.

9 Simon *B*.

10 millesimo *B*.

429

December, 1225.

Raoul, representing the dean of Ham, makes known that Pierre[1] *and Herme, lord and lady of Flavy-le-Meldeux, sold to the church of Prémontré four* modiatae *of wood at Flavy-le-Meldeux. In exchange, Herme receives rights of* dotalicium *over four different* modiatae *of land at Flavy-le-Meldeux.*

A. Cartulary of Prémontré, fols. 100r–100v.

B. Original, AD Oise, H 6035, previously sealed on a double strip of parchment.

Karta decani Hamensis de venditione ~~elemosina~~ Petri domini de Flaviaco Lutoso super IIII^{or} modiatis nemoris.

[R]adulfus gerens vices decani Hamensis omnibus presentes litteras inspecturis in perpetuum. Noverint universi quod Petrus, dominus de Flaviaco Lutoso vendidit ecclesie Premonstratensi quatuor modiatas nemoris sitas apud Flaviacum Lutosum jure hereditario in perpetuum possidendas, Erma, uxore sua, volente, concedente et laudante, spontanea nec coacta, et dotalicium quod dicta Erma dicebat se habere in eodem nemore, in manu nostra resignavit ad dictam ecclesiam saisiendam tali conditione quod dictus Petrus, maritus eius, in recompensatione dicti dotalicii alibi ad voluntatem dicte Erme sufficiens dedit excanbium,[2] videlicet quatuor modiatas terre sitas in territorio de Flaviaco Lutoso. Creantaverunt etiam coram nobis tam dictus Petrus quam Erma, uxor eius, per fidei interpositionem quod dictam ecclesiam super eadem venditione per se vel per alios decetero non presument in aliquibus molestare. In cuius rei testimonium presens scriptum sigillo curie Hamensis fecimus roborari. Actum anno Domini M^{o} CC^{o} XX° V^{o},[3] mense decembri.

1 Pierre (d. aft. 1247), lord of half of Flavy-le-Meldeux (cant. Guiscard, https://dicotopo.cths.fr/places/P19622430), son of Raoul, lord of Flavy-le-Meldeux, and Marguerite, sister and heir of Renaud, knight of Flavy. Newman, *Seigneurs*, vol. 2, 280–1.

2 excambium *B*.

3 quinto *B*.

430

1231

Jean, decanus Christianitatis *of Ham, makes known that Elizabeth, widow of Renaud, lord of Flavy,*[1] *sold to the church of Prémontré all the rights she held by right of* dotalicium *or otherwise at the Bishop's Wood, on a contiguous meadow, and on the two* modiatae *acquired by the abbey from her kinsmen, the lords of Flavy. Elizabeth also gave about four* sextariae *of wood situated at the* foramina *of Flavy, contiguous to the land and woods of Bonneuil.*[2]

A. Cartulary of Prémontré, fol. 100v.
B. Original, AD Oise, H 6006, previously sealed on a double strip of parchment.

Karta decani Christianitatis de Hamo de venditione quam fecit Elizabeth relicta domini de Flavi ecclesie Premonstrati de Nemore Episcopi.

[E]go Johannes, decanus Christianitatis de Hamo, notum facio tam presentibus quam futuris quod nobilis mulier Elizabeth,[3] relicta domini Renaldi de Flavi, in mea presentia personaliter constituta, recognovit se vendidisse ecclesie Premonstratensi totum jus quod habebat vel habere poterat ratione dotalicii vel alio modo in nemore quod dicitur Nemus Episcopi et in prato adjacenti, contiguo eidem nemori, et in duabus modiatis aliis quas eadem ecclesia Premonstratensis acquisivit ab heredibus, dominis de Flavi. Recognovit etiam se eidem ecclesie in perpetuam elemosinam contulisse circiter IIII^{or}[4] sextarios nemoris sitos in loco qui dicitur ad foramina de Flavi, contiguos territorio et nemori de Bonolio et fidem prestitit corporalem quod nec per se nec per aliquem super omnibus antedictis dictam ecclesiam molestabit nec faciet aliquatenus molestari nec queret artem nec ingenium per quod eadem ecclesia possit in posterum molestari. In cuius rei testimonium presentem kartam feci sigilli mei munimine roborari. Actum anno gratie M^{o} CC^{o}[5] tricesimo primo.[6]

1 Flavy-le-Meldeux, cant. Guiscard, https://dicotopo.cths.fr/places/P19622430.
2 Bonneuil, cant. Ham, https://dicotopo.cths.fr/places/P66750585.
3 Elyzabeth *B*.
4 quatuor *B*.
5 millesimo ducentesimo *B*.
6 *Om.* mense augusto *A*.

431

1193

Étienne [I],[1] *bishop of Noyon, makes known that the churches of Prémontré and Ham agree to pay at Collezy*[2] *to the burghers of Saint-Quentin the grain (*bladus*) that they had previously owed to Eudes [III],*[3] *lord of Ham, and his brother Simon.*[4] *Guy*[5] *de [Condren, lord of] Faillouël, Jean*[6] *de Condren, the unnamed castellan of Ham, and Jean d'Ollezy*[7] *pledge to guarantee the sale for Eudes, E[lisabeth] his wife, and their children Eudes*[8] *and Geoffroi.*

A. Cartulary of Premontré, fol. 100v.

B. Original, AD Somme, 20 H 6, no. 15, previously sealed.

Karta Noviomensis episcopi de blado qui debetur burgensibus Sancti Quintini pro domino Odone de Hamo.

[E]go Stephanus Dei gratia Noviomensis episcopus scire volumus universis quod presentibus Odonis domini de Ham, qui homo noster est obnixius, rogavimus Premonstratensis et Hamensis ecclesias quatinus bladi[9] quod debent ei et fratri suo Symoni debebant cuius puerorum ab presens prenominatus O[do] tutor est, burgensibus Sancti Quintini quibus vendiderat, tribus annis apud Colesi persolverent. Tandem prefate ecclesie precibus nostris et ~~precibus~~ ipsius O[doni] annuentes concesserunt. Ipse autem O[do] et uxor sua E[lizabeth] et liberi sui Odo et Gaufridus in manu nostri fidem dederunt et plegios Guidonem de Foilluel[10] et Johannem de Condiem[11] et castellanum[12] de Ham

1 Étienne de Villebéon (or de Nemours), son of Gautier de Villebéon, lord of La Chapelle-Gauthier and Nemours, and Aveline, was bishop of Noyon, 1188–1221.

2 Collezy, comm. Berlancourt, https://dicotopo.cths.fr/places/P68465476.

3 Eudes III, lord of Ham, son of Lancelin, lord of Ham, and Mathilde.

4 Simon de Ham, son of Lancelin, lord of Ham, and Mathilde.

5 Guy I, knight and lord of Faillouël, son of Geoffroy de Condren (cant. Chauny, https://dicotopo.cths.fr/places/P28107866); husband of Mathilde de Bussu. Newman, *Seigneurs*, vol. 2, 203–4.

6 Jean I, knight and lord of Condren and Montescourt, son of Geoffroy de Condren; husband of Aude de Magny. Newman, *Seigneurs*, vol. 2, 203–4.

7 Ollezy, cant. Saint-Simon, https://dicotopo.cths.fr/places/P53765347.

8 Eudes IV, lord of Ham (d. 1234), son of Eudes III, lord of Ham, and Elizabeth; husband of Elizabeth de Béthencourt.

9 bladum *B*.

10 Folluel *B*.

11 Condran *B*.

12 Either Algrin (attested 1188) or his son Gautier (attested 1202), both castellans of Ham. Gomart, *Ham, son château et ses prisonniers*, 304.

et Johannem de Olesi constituerunt et etiam totum feodum de Doulli[13,14] quod tenent a nobis in contraplegiam ipsis plegiis ad petitionem ipsius O[donis] et uxoris eius et liberorum nobis concedentibus assignaverunt. Plegii quo simili modo fiduciaverunt quod si predicte ecclesie de blado illo alicuius violentia dampnum incurrerent ipsi communiter restituerent vel apud Sancti Quintini[15] ad voluntatem ecclesiarum donec dampnum restitueretur captionem teneretur.[16] Licebit autem ipsis plegiis de rebus domini O[doni] vel ad Doulli[17] vel ubi potuerint pro restitutione dampnorum suorum et ecclesiarum capere. Ut autem ist~~u~~ad[18] conventio usque ad prefinitum tempus rata et inconvulsa permaneat tradidimus ecclesiis presentem paginam sigillo nostro confirmatam. Actum anno incarnationis dominice M° C° nonagesimo III°.

432

1170–81[1]

Pierre,[2] abbot of Saint-Remi de Reims, and magister *Foulques,[3] dean of Reims, report to Pope Alexander [III] concerning the inquiry that he asked them to conduct into the dispute between the abbey of Prémontré and the church of Ham about a dam, mills, and water rights. (See **404**, **406**.)*

A. Cartulary of Prémontré, fols. 100v–101r.

B. Original AM Metz, Salis II.244, no. 3, sealed with two seals each on a single strip of parchment. One seal remains intact.

EDITION: *Chartes originales conservées en France (1121–1220)*, no. 760, http://telma.irht.cnrs.fr/outils/originaux2/charte268315/.

13 Dolli *B*.

14 Douilly, cant. Ham, https://dicotopo.cths.fr/places/P87195366.

15 Sanctum Quintinum *B*.

16 tenerent *B*.

17 Dolli *B*.

18 ista *B*.

1 Date based on **404** (1170), **406** (1170–1), and the papal tenure of Alexander III (1159–81.) *Chartae Galliae* (http://telma.irht.cnrs.fr/outils/originaux2/charte268315/) dates this charter to 1175, but neither the original nor the cartulary copy is dated.

2 Pierre de Celle, abbot of the Benedictine abbey of Montier-la-Celle, 1145–61/2, abbot of the Benedictine abbey of Saint-Remi de Reims, 1161/2–81, and bishop of Chartres, 1181–3.

3 Foulques, dean of Reims, ca. 1170–ca. 1176. AD Ardennes, H 203, fols. 76r–77r.

Scriptum abbatis Sancti Remigii et decani Remensis ad domum propriam de causa que erat inter Premonstratensis et Hamensis ecclesias.

[D]omino et Patri A[lexandri], universali pape, frater P[etrus], humilis abbas Sancti Remigii, et magister F[ulcanus], decanus Remensis ecclesie salutem et omnem obedientiam. Accepto, Domine Pater, a vobis mandato ut de causa que inter Premonstratensem ecclesiam et Hamensem vertebatur super quadam calceata et quibusdam molendinis, cognosceremus et mediante justicia eam terminaremus; accessimus ad locum non semel neque sine multo labore neque soli sed frequenter cum multis religiosis et discretis viris et peritis aque ut quam fidelius possemus preceptum vestrum executioni mandaremus. Circumspectis ~~discretis viris et peritis aque~~ ergo omnibus cum abbatibus Humiliarensi.[4,5] et Sancti Vincentii Silvanectensis[6] et prioribus Kartuariensis ordinis, de Monte Dei[7] et Valle Sancti Petri[8] et quibusdam aliis, relectis etiam litteris a vestra sanctitate missis cum auctentico[9] scripto episcoporum B[alduini][10] Noviomensis et M[ilonis][11] Morinensis, calceatam[12] de qua principaliter agebatur, a Premonstratensibus destructam penitus juxta auctenticum[13] scriptum episcoporum invenimus. Instabant tamen Hamenses et conquerebantur de quadam congestione palorum et glebarum quam contra auctenticum[14] scriptum episcoporum ~~invenimus~~ dicebant esse factam a Premonstratensibus. Premonstratenses vero in hoc se nichil fecisse contra auctenticum[15] scriptum episcoporum asserebant, quia non esset de calceata. Sed ad hoc tantummodo id efficiebant ut solidior esset antiqua ripa et ne tota aqua exinde elaberetur, nullum habens repagulum. Nichil enim aque aut nimis parum remaneret suis molendinis, si omnem licentiam evagandi aqua haberet etsi non liceret eis saltem firmare

4 Humulariensi *B.*

5 Either Pierre I (1163–75) or Hubert (1176–92), abbots of the Benedictine abbey of Homblières. Newman, *Homblières*, 18–19.

6 Hugues II, abbot of the Augustinian abbey of Saint-Vincent de Senlis, ca. 1163–89. *GC* X, col. 1496.

7 Simon, prior of the charterhouse of Mont-Dieu, 1160–84. Gillet, *La chartreuse de Mont-Dieu au diocèse de Reims, avec pièces justificatives inédites*, 131, 171.

8 Likely Engelbert, prior ca. 1160–ca. 1180 of the charterhouse of Val-Saint-Pierre. Marchand, *Essai historique sur la Chartreuse du Val Saint-Pierre, située dans l'ancien diocèse de Laon, 1140–1789*, 25.

9 autentico *B.*

10 Either Baudouin II de Boulogne, bishop of Noyon, 1148–67, or Baudouin III de Beuseberg, bishop of Noyon, 1167–74/5.

11 Milon II, bishop of Thérouanne, 1159–69.

12 calceata *B.*

13 autenticum *B.*

14 autenticum *B.*

15 autenticum *B.*

ripam. Appenso tamen et librato saltu molendinorum tam Hamensium quam Premonstratensium, deprehensum est habere molendinos Hamensibus[16] pene trium pedum saltum Premonstratensium vero non nisi quatuor digitorum. Cum autem ex hac congestione nichil obstaculi habere videremus molendinos Hamensium, ne tamen Premonstratensis in posterum dolo vel fraude aliqua possent adversus eos malignari, stipitem aque in medio[17] fecimus defigi ut hoc signo dinosceretur si umquam aliquod modo aliquo tempore a Premonstratensibus ad inpedimentum Hamensium aliquid superponeretur. Preterea ad auferendum omne inpedimentum, soleas ligneas digito uno inferiores ipsa ripa apponi fecimus nequid supra soleas liceat Premonstratensibus apponere. Hoc tamen retento ut infra soleas Premonstratensibus liceat soliditatem ripe conservare. Hamenses vero non acquieverunt sed contumaciter vestram audienciam appellaverunt. Nos tamen freti auctoritate vestra qua omnis appellatio interdicta fuerat, nichilominus consilio sapientum et religiosorum, sicut etiam in literis vestris continebatur, ex sentencia eis silentium inposuimus. Provideat itaque discretio vestra paci ecclesiarum et ne improbitate aliquorum recidivus labor resuscitetur et supervacuis sumptibus religiosa monasteria afficiantur. Placuit etiam paternitati vestre mandare nobis per literas vestras quatinus[18] rei veritatem inquireremus et inquisitam vobis remandaremus super molendinis de Hameals[19] de quibus controversia erat inter Premonstratenses predictos[20] et Hamenses. Quod igitur super hoc scire possumus tam scriptis auctenticis quam verbis eorum qui nobis fidem facere poterant, vestre paternitati remandamus et ad singulas inquisitiones quas fieri mandastis singula vobis responsa remittimus. Precepistis nobis inquirere de conpositione inter Premonstratenses et Hamenses facta et invenimus compositionem illam sigillo bone memorie B[alduini],[21] Noviomensis episcopi, et sigillis utriusque capituli munitam in qua continebatur quod utraque ecclesia in pace possideret quicquid per manum episcopi a laicis habebat. Hec conpositio inter eos facta est infra quindecim annos et Premonstratenses viginti quinque annis et eo amplius molendina predicta in pace tenuerunt, Hamensibus videntibus nec reclamantibus. De donatione vero quam inquiri precepistis, invenimus quod quidam miles qui adhuc superstes est, donavit Premonstrate ecclesie molendina illa in elemosinam per manum Symonis,[22] Noviomensis episcopi, de cuius feodo erant,[23] sicut ipsi

16 Hamenses *B*.

17 *Transp. A*; in medio aque *B*.

18 quatenas *B*.

19 Hamel-lès-Corbie, cant. Corbie, https://dicotopo.cths.fr/places/P37197765.

20 *Transp. A*; predictos Premonstratenses *B*.

21 Either Baudouin II de Boulogne, bishop of Noyon, 1148–67, or Baudouin III de Beuseberg, bishop of Noyon, 1167–74/5.

22 Simon I de Vermandois (d. 1148) was the son of Hugues I and Adélaïde, count and countess of Vermandois and Valois, and bishop of Noyon, 1123–42.

23 See **407**.

perspeximus in literis sigillo eius confirmatis. Nos autem conpositionis inter eos facte et donationis sigillo episcopi confirmate transcriptum vobis mittimus. Preterea molendina illa, sicut accepimus, tunc temporis quando data sunt Premonstratensibus, non molebant sed tamen sedes eorum apparent. Super hoc autem quod Hamenses proponunt ex concessione Premonstratensis abbatis non debere ibi esse nisi unum molendinum et quod moleret tantum frumentum Premonstratensium invenimus in Romanis privilegiis non molendinum sed molendina de Hameals Premonstrate ecclesie confirmata similiter et in scripto prefati episcopi non molendinum sed molendina Premonstratensibus data. Insuper dominus Hugo, Premonstratensis abbas, negavit se concessionem illam fecisse nec Hamenses aliquid inde scriptum ostendere potuerunt vel munimentum. Quod vero de consuetudine terre precepistis inquiri accepimus non esse contra consuetudinem terre antiqua molendina reparare. Vestra igitur interest supplere quod minus fecimus et utrique ecclesie ius suum conservare.

433

May, 1231.

Eudes[1] *and Béatrice, lord and lady of Ollezy, grant Prémontré permission to remake the ditch surrounding the meadow at Montizel*[2] *whenever the brothers desire to do so. They also cede to Prémontré the free possession of that which they hold, including all rights, in the* villa *and territory of Auroir.*[3]

A. Cartulary of Prémontré, fol. 101r.

B. Original, AN, L 995, no. 75, no evidence of seal as bottom has been damaged.

Karta domini Odonis de Olesi et uxoris eius quod liceat ecclesie Premonstratensis relevare fossatum suam circa pratum de Montisel.

[I]n nomine Patris et cetera.[4] Ego Odo, dominus de Olesi, et Beatrix, uxor mea, notum facimus universis tam presentibus quam futuris quod nos, ex mera voluntate nostra, ob remedium animarum nostrarum, recognovimus et concessimus ecclesie Premonstratensi ut, quandocumque voluerit et quocienscumque voluerit, prout ei placuerit, liceat eidem ecclesie et fratribus eiusdem reficere et relevare fossatum suum quod est circa pratum suum apud Montisel ita etiam

1 Eudes (or Oudard), knight and lord of Ollezy (cant. Saint-Simon, https://dicotopo.cths.fr/places/P53765347), husband of Béatrice. Melleville, *DH*, vol. 2, 180.

2 Montizel, cant. Ham, https://dicotopo.cths.fr/places/P16235568.

3 Auroir, comm. Foreste, https://dicotopo.cths.fr/places/P79580266.

4 *Add.* cetera *A*; Filii et Spiritus Sancti, amen *B*.

quod in girum prati ipsius ex omni et utraque parte poterunt facere fossatum ipsum viginti pedum ad minus versus pascua et terram et limum qui extrahentur de fossato poterunt jactare in quamcumque partem[5] sive versus pratum sive versus pascua libere et sine omni contradictione mea vel hominum meorum vel quorumlibet aliorum. Preterea concessimus eidem ecclesie libere et pacifice possidendum et ab omni consuetudine et exactione penitus absolutum quicquid eadem ecclesie tenet in villa et in toto territorio de Oroir sub dominio et potestate nostra tam in terris quam in redditibus et aliis omnibus et dedimus et quitavimus ipsi ecclesie quicquid juris vel dominii habebamus vel habere poteramus in omnibus supradictis tam nos quam heredes nostri ita etiam quod nos et heredes nostri tenemur portare legitimam warandiam eidem ecclesie tam de fossato predicto sicut expressum est faciendo quam de aliis omnibus supradictis que recognovimus, concessimus, dedimus et quitavimus ecclesie sepedicte adversus omnes qui voluerint juri stare, promittentes etiam interposita fide nostra corporali quod omnia supradicta tenebimus et servabimus bona fide nec eandem ecclesiam super premissis omnibus per nos vel per alium molestabimus nec faciemus aliquatenus molestari et renunciamus omni juris auxilio tam canonici quam civilis quam etiam consuetudinarii et omnibus exceptionibus que possent obici contra hoc instrumentum. In cuius rei testimonium presentem kartam fecimus sigillorum nostrorum munimine roborari. Actum mense maio, anno gratie M° CC° tricesimo primo.

434

1185

Abbot Hugues [II][1] *and the chapter of Prémontré make known that they conceded to Elinaud du Pont certain revenues in return for an annual* census *of five* solidi. *If the value of Elinaud's revenues increases, his* census *payment to Prémontré will also increase.*

A. Cartulary of Prémontré, fol. 101r.

B. Original (chirograph), SAHSS, *casier* 2, no. 16, sealed on a double strip of leather with a damaged seal partially depicting a doe. In the left margin and beginning at the top, the upper half of the word CYROGRAPHUM.

---

5 *Om.* voluerint *A*.

---

1 Hugues II de Douai, abbot of the Premonstratensian abbey of Cuissy, 1161–5, and abbot of Prémontré, 1174–89. *MP* II, 497.

Karta Hugonis abbatis Premonstratensis de annuo censu quinque solidorum quos Helinandus de Ponte tenetur reddere ecclesie.

[Q]uoniam decedente et succedente rerum et temporum mutabilitate antiquitas oblivionem oblivio confusionem confusio litem solet parere, ego Hugo, Premonstrati abbas, et eiusdem ecclesie capitulum universitati fidelium notum facimus quod Helinandus de Ponte tenebat a nobis quosdam redditus quos eidem et heredibus suis in perpetuum habendos concessimus sub annuali censu quinque solidorum bone monete in medio mensis martii solvendorum. Sane si ipse[2] vel successores eius de predicte ecclesie redditibus aliquid amplius acquisierint quam eo tempore quo scriptum hoc factum est, tenuisse dinoscitur, secundum augmentationem reddituum census annualis capiet augmentum. Quod ut perpetue stabilitatis robur optineat id ipsum sigilli nostri appositione et cyrographi divisione curavimus confirmare. Actum est hoc incarnationis dominice anno M° C° LXXX° V°.

435

May, 1223.

Magister *Simon,*[1] *canon and* officialis *of Noyon, makes known that Colard*[2] *de Berlancourt*[3] *gave in alms to the Premonstratensian house at Bonneuil*[4] *12* denarii *of the* census *that Bonneuil owed to him annually.*

A. Cartulary of Prémontré, fols. 101r–101v.

B. Original, AD Oise, H 6003, previously sealed on a single strip of parchment.

REGISTER: *Studium Baldwin*, fiche 2128.

---

2 *Om.* Helinandus *A*.

---

1 Simon de Douai was first canon and then *officialis* of Noyon, before serving as *scolasticus*, ca. 1230–ca. 1250. Coüard-Luys, "L'Ecolâtre de Noyon et les écoles de cette ville jusqu'au milieu du XIIIe siècle," 279–80; AD Oise, G 1984, fols. 198v–199v, 342v–343v, 346v–347v.

2 The essart of Colard de Berlancourt is mentioned in a 1230 act in the cartulary of the cathedral chapter of Noyon. AD Oise, G 1984, fol. 226r.

3 Berlancourt, cant. Guiscard, https://dicotopo.cths.fr/places/P39954495.

4 The Premonstratensian *curtis* of Bonneuil. *MP* II, 484.

Karta officialis Noviomensis de elemosina XIIcim denariorum quos Colardus de Bellencourt contulit domui de Bonolio.

[M]agister S[imon] canonicus et officialis Noviomensis, omnibus presentes litteras inspecturis salutem in Domino. Noverint universi presentes pariter et futuri quod Colardus de Bellencourt,[5] in presentia nostra constitutus, recognovit se contulisse in elemosinam domui de Bonolio duodecim denarios de censu quos ipsa domus annuatim de censu habebat[6] eidem; promisit etiam coram nobis per fidei interpositionem quod super elemosina illa per se vel per alios dictam domum decetero nullatenus molestabit. In cuius rei testimonium presentes litteras sigillo curie Noviomensis fecimus roborari, anno Domini M° CC° XX° III°,[7] mense maio.

436

1159

Hugues [I],[1] *abbot of Prémontré, makes known that Raoul* Bellus *conceded to Prémontré three pieces of land totalling eight* sexterlatae, *on the condition that Prémontré undertakes to pay to Roger Warentrut an annual* census *of a* modius *of grain (*frumentum*) on a certain piece of land at* Albini Pontem.[2] *Roger then cedes this* census *to Prémontré in return for 12* librae Proveniensium, *with the consent of his sisters, Ermène and Ansgarde.*[3]

A. Cartulary of Prémontré, fol. 101v.
B. Original not found.

Karta abbatis Premonstratensis de annuo censu quod Radulphus optinet a Rogero.

[E]go H[ugo], Dei gratia Premonstrate ecclesie abbas, scire volo universos fratres meos tam futuros quam modernos quod Radulfus, cognomento

5 Bollencort *B*.
6 debebat *B*.
7 vicesimo tercio *B*.

1 Hugues I de Fosses (ca. 1093–1164), first abbot of Prémontré.
2 Possibly Aubigny, cant. Vermand, https://dicotopo.cths.fr/places/P34524600.
3 The charter concerning the original cession is AD Oise, H 5994.

Bellus, optinet a Rogero Warentrut quandam terram apud Albini Pontem sub annuo censu modii frumenti uno denario minus valentis a meliori ad mensuram Noviomensem, frumenti autem modius crastina die post festum Omnium Sanctorum vel usque Epiphaniam, pro eodem Radulfo, prefato Rogero a nobis persolvetur et ad domum suam Noviomi a fratribus de Omencourt vel de Bonolio conducetur. Si vero acciderit, quod absit, ut supradictum frumentum statuto termino persolvi negligatur, prefatus Rogerus a domo Landrimontis[4] tantumdem valens sine forisfacto accipiet et nos ei sine placito vel lege persolvemus. Pro annuo vero frumenti modio quem pro ipso Radulfo persolvimus et pro quodam prato quod ei concessimus, contulit nobis idem Radulphus particulas terre tres, octo sexterlatas terre continentes, unam versus Barastre, duas versus Herci adjacentes. Huius rei testes sunt: Symon[5] de Maigni, Symon[6] de Betencourt, ipse Radulfus Bellus, Robertus[7] de Fromont, Lambertus, filius domine Enmelot. Quod pro communi pace inter nos et ipsos perpetuo conservanda sigilli nostri impressione signare curavimus. Actum est hoc ab incarnatione Domini M° C° quinquagesimo nono. Contigit autem postea non multo tempore eiusdem ~~anministratis~~ eiusdem[8] anni transacto quod isdem supradictus Rogerus eundem modium frumenti ecclesie Premonstrati in elemosinam concessit, annuentibus sororibus suis Ermena et Ansgarde, XII libris Proveniensis monete ex beneficio ecclesie ab eodem Rogero susceptis et huic denique concessioni interfuerunt testes Gislebertus sacerdos, Rainerus filius Symonis de Maigni, Dudo[9] de Genueri, Wibertus filius maioris, frater Petrus, frater Alricus.

4 Landrimont, comm. Noyon, https://dicotopo.cths.fr/places/P74301629.

5 Perhaps the same Simon de Magny who appears as a witness in **308**. A Simon de Magny also appears in acts dating 1181 in the cartulary of the cathedral chapter of Noyon, AD Oise, G 1984, fols. 92v–93r, 103r.

6 Simon I *le Vieux* de Sermaize, lord of Béthencourt-sur-Somme (cant. Nesle, https://dicotopo.cths.fr/places/P85791062), likely a son or grandson of Hugues I de Sermaize, lord of Béthencourt-sur-Somme. Newman, *Seigneurs*, vol. 2, 99, 209; Guyotjeannin, *Episcopus*, 272.

7 Robert de Frémont also appears in **442**. Possibly Frémont, cant. Nesle, https://dicotopo.cths.fr/places/P77307649.

8 *Sic A*.

9 Possibly the same Dude who appears in the witness list in **489**. Genvry, cant. Noyon, https://dicotopo.cths.fr/places/P86438840.

437

February 16, 1212–17.[1] Tournai.

Robert,[2] cardinal priest of Santo Stefano al Montecelio, legate of the Holy See, instructs Gervais,[3] abbot of Prémontré, to accept from the knight Simon[4] de Marteville the tithe which Simon had inherited and wished to give to the church.

A. Cartulary of Prémontré, fol. 101v.
B. Original not found.

Scriptum cardinalis de quadam decima Symonis militis de Martis Villa.

[R]obertus, servus crucis Christi divina miseratione tituli Sancti Stephani in Monte Celio presbyter cardinalis, Apostolice Sedis legatus, dilecto filio Gervasio, abbati Premonstrati, salutem in omnium salvatore. Accessit ad nos nuper vir nobilis Symon de Martis Villa, miles, asserens quod quandam decimam possideret, ad se hereditarie devolutam, de qua ita liberari petebat eo quod eandem teneret injuste ut in subsidium inopie sue vel sibi vel alicui suorum aliquod ex ea provideretur commodum temporale. Quia igitur de discretione ac devotione tua minime dubitamus, tibi plenarie, vices nostras committimus in hac parte, discretione tue legationis qua fungimur auctoritate mandantes quatinus de eadem decima ita ordinare procures ut hereditaria successione sublata vel ad illam ecclesiam ad quam spectat de jure vel ad aliam aliquo tempore revertatur. Datum Tornaci, XIIII° kalendarum martii.

1 Date based on the period between Robert of Courson's appointment as cardinal in 1212 and his departure on the Fifth Crusade in 1217.
2 Robert of Courson (d. 1219) was appointed a canon of the cathedral chapter of Noyon in 1204, a canon of the cathedral chapter of Paris in 1209, and cardinal priest of Santo Stefano al Monte Celio in 1212.
3 Gervais, abbot of the Premonstratensian abbeys of Saint-Just-en-Chaussée, 1199–1205, Thenailles, 1205–9, and Prémontré, 1209–20, and bishop of Séez, 1220–8. *MP* II, 401, 527, 565; Cheney, "Gervase, Abbot of Prémontré."
4 Simon I, lord of Marteville (cant. Vermand, https://dicotopo.cths.fr/places/P05099925), attested 1202–31. Melleville, *DH*, vol. 2, 84.

438

May, 1233.

Pierre,[5] *lord of Flavy, acknowledges that he owes the Premonstratensians of Bonneuil*[6] *the sum of 50* solidi Parisiensium *that it loaned him when he was in great need. In recompense, he cedes to Bonneuil his share of the crop from the five and a half* sexterlatae *that Bonneuil holds from him in the assarts of Flavy, next to the wood of* Courel, *until the debt is repaid.*

A. Cartulary of Prémontré, fol. 101v.
B. Original not found.

Karta domini Petri de Flavi super eo quod tenetur nobis in quinquaginta solidis Parisiensium.

[E]go Petrus, dominus de Flavi, notum facio omnibus presentibus et futuris quod ego debeo ecclesie Bonolii quinquaginta solidos Parisiensium quos in magno necessitatis articulo michi commodavit dicta ecclesia ea tamen conventione intermedia. Dicta ecclesia tenet de me quinque sexterlatas terre et dimidiam in sartis de Flavi juxta nemus de Courel in quibus habeo garbam talis bladi quale super eandem terram creverit, quam siquidem garbam concessi dicte ecclesie annuatim percipiendam donec de ea receperit memoratam pecuniam nisi ei aliunde persolvatur. In cuius rei testimonium presens scriptum sigilli mei appensionem munivi. Actum anno gratie millesimo ducentesimo tricesimo tercio mense maio.

439

1231

Eudes,[1] *knight and lord of Ollezy, with the consent of his wife Béatrice, guarantees the church of Prémontré and its* curtis *at Montizel*[2] *the possession of its*

---

5 Pierre (d. aft. 1247), lord of half of Flavy-le-Meldeux (cant. Guiscard, https://dicotopo.cths.fr/places/P19622430), son of Raoul, lord of Flavy-le-Meldeux, and Marguerite, sister and heir of Renaud, knight of Flavy. Newman, *Seigneurs*, vol. 2, 280–1.

6 *MP* II, 484.

---

1 Eudes (or Oudard), knight and lord of Ollezy (cant. Saint-Simon, https://dicotopo.cths.fr/places/P53765347), husband of Béatrice. Melleville, *DH*, vol. 2, 180.

2 Montizel, cant. Ham, https://dicotopo.cths.fr/places/P16235568.

goods at Houroit[3] *against any claims from Gautier de Pontruet,*[4] burgensis *of Saint-Quentin.*

A. Cartulary of Prémontré, fol. 101v.
B. Original, BnF, Coll. Picardie 290, no. 48, previously sealed.

Karta domini Odonis, militis de Olesi, super eo quod debet guarantire curiam nostram de Montisel.

[E]go Odo, miles, dominus de Ollesi, notum facio presentibus et futuris quod de assensu et voluntate uxoris mee, Beatricis, teneor guarantire et indempnem omnimodis conservare ecclesiam Premonstratensem et curtem eiusdem ecclesie de Montisel de omnibus rebus generaliter quas dicta curtis habet apud Houroit et circa dictam villam ita quod si Galterus de Pontruel,[5] burgensis Sancti Quintini, vel alius ex parte ipsius, fratres dicte ecclesie occasione illarum rerum quas in villa possident memorata vel circa[6] dictum est molestaverit, perturbaverit vel aliquam vexationem intulerit sive dampnum qualecumque, ego pro dicta ecclesia respondebo et plene satisfaciam et conservabo indempnem in hunc modum quod dicta ecclesia omnes res superius memoratas liberrime et pacifice possidebit; hoc tamen adiecto quod si tractu temporis dictus Galterus de Pontruel[7] prefatam ecclesiam absolverit et quitaverit de illa justicia sive redditibus quos in villa possidet sepedicta, fratres Premonstratenses presentem kartam[8] mihi reddent, cui, ut valeat et firma sit, sigillum meum apposui. Actum anno Domini M° CC° tricesimo primo.

440

March 11, 1232.

Hugues,[1] *canon and* officialis *of Noyon, makes known that in his presence the knight Gérard*[2] *de Caulaincourt acknowledged that he owed the church of*

3 Possibly Auroir, comm. Foreste, https://dicotopo.cths.fr/places/P79580266.
4 Pontruet, cant. Vermand, https://dicotopo.cths.fr/places/P35872776.
5 Pontrueil *B*.
6 *Om.* ut *A*.
7 Pontrueil *B*.
8 cartam *B*.

1 *Magister* Hugues, canon and *officialis* of Noyon, ca. 1229–ca. 1236. AD Aisne, H 455, fol. 310v; AD Oise, G 1984, fols. 238v–239r.
2 Gérard, lord of Caulaincourt (cant. Vermand, https://dicotopo.cths.fr/places/P02972526), attested ca. 1229–ca. 1238, son of Philippe II, lord of Caulaincourt, and Adèle "Sarracine." Melleville, *DH*, vol. 1, 189.

Prémontré an annual revenue of five modii *of grain (*bladus*), and that he was in arrears. Prémontré is to collect the arrears either at Gérard's mill or on his oven of Caulaincourt.*

A. Cartulary of Prémontré, fols. 101v–102r.
B. Original not found.

Karta officialis Noviomensis de eo quod Gerardus de Canlencort recognovit se debere ecclesie quinque modios bladi.

[O]mnibus hoc visuris magister Hugo, canonicus et officialis Noviomensis, salutem in Domino. Vobis notum facimus quod dominus Gerardus de Canlencort, miles, recognovit coram nobis se debere ecclesie Premonstratensi quinque modios bladi de annuo redditu ad mensuram Sancti Quintini et quinque modios de arreragiis et assignavit eandem ecclesiam coram nobis ad capiendum dictum bladum de arreragio ad molendinum suum de Canlencort ad proventus suos de eodem molendino ita quod hoc instanti sabbato ante Oculi Mei eosdem proventus capere incipiet et continue eosdem proventus percipiet donec de toto blado quinque modiorum pro arreragio predicto eidem ecclesie plenarie fuerit satisfactum et de hoc molendinarius eidem ecclesie de assensu dicti Gerardi militis facere debet fidelitatem et servientem suum ipsa ecclesia in eodem molendino ponere poterit, si voluerit, ad maiorem securitatem et hoc quolibet anno si dictum bladum idem Gerardus solvere retinuerit termino statuto et omni eodem modo debet eos assignare ad furnum suum de Canlencort pro dicto redditu si hoc continetur in karta quam ipsa ecclesia habet de eodem Gerardem quod hoc facere debeat. Datum anno Domini M° CC° tricesimo secundo, feria sexta ante Oculi Mei.

441

1163

Baudouin [II],[1] *bishop of Noyon, makes known that the brothers Simon*[2] Ratus *and Guillaume gave to the church of Prémontré revenues and rights in the territory of Golancourt.*[3] *Guillaume and Simon also concede all their rights as fief lords on the share of* garba *that Jean de Camas*[4] *gave to Prémontré. Marie, sister of Simon and Guillaume, with her unnamed sons, consents to this. (See near-duplicate **399**.)*

---

1 Baudouin II de Boulogne, abbot of the Augustinian abbey of Saint-Eloi-Fontaine, ca. 1130–ca. 1139, and bishop of Noyon, 1148–67. *GC* IX, col. 1126.

2 Simon *Ratus*, brother of Guillaume, also appears in **336** and **399**.

3 Golancourt, cant. Guiscard, https://dicotopo.cths.fr/places/P75999303.

4 Camas, comm. Jussy, https://dicotopo.cths.fr/places/P27501164.

A. Cartulary of Prémontré, fol. 102r.
B. Original, AD Oise, H 6038, previously sealed on a double strip of white leather.

Karta Noviomensis episcopi de elemosina Symonis qui dicitur Ratus super[5] novem denariis obolorum.

[I]n nomine sancte et individue Trinitatis. Ego Balduinus, Dei gratia Noviomensis dictus episcopus, notum fieri volo tam futuris quam presentibus quod Symon, qui dicitur Ratus, et Willermus, frater eius, dederunt Premonstrate ecclesie per manum nostram in elemosina novem denarios obolorum censualiter singulis annis quos in terra Enmeline[6] reclamabant et tredecim[7] denarios et obolum eiusdem monete pari modo prefate ecclesie concesserunt quos accipiebant in terra Gisleberti de Gollencourt[8] singulis annis, et duas[9] corvatas quas eadem terra eis debebat, prefate ecclesie remiserunt eo tenore quod si prefatus G[islebertus] predicte ecclesie daret aliam terram quam sibi retinuerat, ipsi censum haberent. Concesserunt etiam prefate ecclesie duodecim[10] denarios obolorum quos reclamabant de terra Odonis, qui dicitur Cum Barba, ita quod in omnibus supradictis nec districtum nec justiciam sibi retinuerunt in omnibus que ad prefatam ecclesiam pertinent. Donum etiam quod Johannes de Kamac fecerat fecerat[11] prefate ecclesie de quadam terra sua ad sextam garbam[12] perpetuo que de feodo eorum descendebat, concesserunt et liberam fecerunt ab omni districto et justicia fratribus prefate ecclesie et omnibus que ad ipsos pertinent ea conditione quod si prefatus Johannes feodum suum non deserviret, garbam[13] que eum contingebat, seisire possent sed terra ecclesie libera remaneret. Hanc tamen seisinam non debent facere infra quinque annos instantes, quia inter predictos milites et prefate ecclesie fratres ita terminatum est. Concesserunt etiam prefate ecclesie libere in perpetuum possidere et sine omni districto et justicia in omnibus que ad ecclesiam pertinent, quicquid in die conscriptionis huius habebat in territorio de Gollencort[14] tam in terris quam in nemoribus, quod erat juris eorum, ea conditione quod si de omnibus predictis aut aliquo horum ecclesia predicta inquietaretur aut aliquis super hoc reclamaret, ecclesia non haberet inde respondere nisi coram ecclesiastica justicia.

5 *Superscr.* super *A*.
6 Emmeline *B*.
7 XIII[cim] *B*.
8 Golleincurt *B*.
9 II[as] *B*.
10 XII[cim] *B*.
11 *Sic A*.
12 karbam *B*.
13 karbam *B*.
14 Golleincurt *B*.

Huius concessionis testes sunt: Renerus[15,16] abbas de Calniaco, Rabodus frater eorum, Johannes[17] de Nigella, Gonfridus capellanus, Willermus camerarius noster frater,[18] Gerardus clericus, Petrus, Henricus laici. Coram hiis testibus werpierunt hec predicta in manu nostra et soror eorum Maria[19] laudavit et filii eius. Actum anno incarnati verbi M° C° LX° III°, epacta XIIII[a].

442

1163

*Baudouin [II],[1] bishop of Noyon, makes known that Doa d'Aubigny[2] had previously conceded to the church of Prémontré two parts of the tithe of Brouchy[3] with the consent of Mathieu and Paganus, her sons; Aelide, fief lord and wife of Doa's unnamed brother; Aelide's children; and Aubry[4] de Roye. Later, Jean Bruer, husband of Doa's daughter Aelide, claimed damages against the church but then recognized and conceded Doa's gift. Jean's wife Aelide, her sisters Marie and Emmeline, and their husbands, Jean and Aubert, assent to this renunciation. (See near-duplicate **398**.)*[5]

A. Cartulary of Prémontré, fol. 102r.

B. Original, BnF, Coll. Picardie 290, no. 8, no evidence of a seal as the bottom has been damaged.

---

15 Reinerus *B*.

16 Renier, abbot of the Arroasian Augustinian community of Sainte-Marie de Chauny, 1162–ca. 1185. Poissonnier, "L'Abbaye de St-Éloi-Fontaine ou de Commenchon," 272–4.

17 A canon Jean de Nesle also appears in acts of Renaud, bishop of Noyon, in the 1180s. Peigné-Delacourt, *Cartulaire de l'Abbaye de Notre-Dame d'Ourscamp de l'ordre de Cîteaux, fondée en 1129 au diocèse de Noyon*, 219–20; Bouchot, "Chartes du XIIe siècle relatives aux anciennes abbayes de Fervaques, d'Ourscamp et de Saint-Quentin-en-l'Isle," 348–9.

18 fratres *B*.

19 Marga *B*.

---

1 Baudouin II de Boulogne, abbot of the Augustinian abbey of Saint-Eloi-Fontaine, ca. 1130–ca. 1139, and bishop of Noyon, 1148–67. *GC* IX, col. 1126.

2 Aubigny-Planche, cant. Ham, https://dicotopo.cths.fr/places/P23943075.

3 Brouchy, cant. Ham, https://dicotopo.cths.fr/places/P33557845.

4 Aubry, lord of Roye and Becquigny, was the *dapifer* of Raoul, count of Vermandois in the 1130s/40s. He was the husband of one Mathilde, and brother of Wermond, lord of Cessoy. Tock and Milis, *Monumenta Arroasiensia*, 242–3; Guyotjeannin, *Episcopus*, 220; Newman, *Seigneurs*, vol. 2, 299; Newman, *Homblières*, 110. He is likely the same Aubry de Roye who appears in **300**, **398**, **442**, and **464**.

5 Doa's original gift is detailed in an 1147 act of Simon, bishop of Noyon. BnF, nouv. acq. lat. 2390, no. 5.

Karta Noviomensis episcopi de elemosina domine Doe de Albigni de duabus partibus decime de Bruci.

[I]n nomine sancte et cetera.[6] Beneficia servorum Dei episcopali debent auctoritate communiri ne cum occasu temporis cadat et memoria rerum gestarum. Ea propter ego Balduinus, Dei gratia Noviomensis ecclesie minister, notum fieri volo tam futuris quam presentibus quod domina Doa de Albigni,[7] sicut in literis domni Symonis predecessoris nostri, repperimus, concessit Premonstrate ecclesie duas partes decime de Bruci perpetuo possidendas, concedentibus heredibus suis, Matheo videlicet filio suo, et Pagano, fratre suo, concedentibus etiam illis de quorum feodo descendebat decima, Aelide uxore fratris Doe, cum filiis suis et Albrico de Roia. Hii[8] omnes decimam istam per manus prefati episcopi supra memorate ecclesie contulerunt sub hiis testibus: Bonefacio[9] archidiacono, Hugone[10] cancellario, Johanne Rufo, Drogone de Plaissie.[11] Quod autem Albricus de Roia, Doa et filii eius, Aelidis et eius filii hoc concesserint. Testes sunt: Bernerus frater Roberti Rufi, Fulcho, Symon filius eius, Fulcho[12] Obeline, Bartholomeus de Parrona. Succedente vero tempore, Johannes Bruers, qui primogenitam filiam prefate Doe uxorem duxerat, movit calumpniam super eadem decima Premonstrate ecclesie sed tantum donum illud quod eadem Doa predicte ecclesie fecerat, recognovit et concessit ipse et Aelidis, uxor eius. Hoc etiam laudaverunt et concesserunt Maria et Enmelina,[13] filie eiusdem Doe et mariti earum, Johannes, famulus decani[14] et Autbertus.[15] Huius donationis testes sunt: Tieszo decanus noster, qui loco nostro interfuit et vice nostra elemosinam de manu eorum suscepit, Petrus de Duaco, Robertus frater eius, Bartholomeus[16] filius Fulchonis Obeline, Wibertus frater eius, Ernulphus Persez, Robertus[17] de Fromont,[18] Rogerus Warentruz. Ut autem hoc

6 *Add.* cetera *A*; individue Trinitatis *B*.

7 Albingni *B*.

8 Hi *B*.

9 Boniface, archdeacon of Noyon (d. ca. 1190), son of Bonifazio del Vasto, margrave of Savona, and Agnès de Vermandois.

10 Hugues III de Roye, chancellor of Noyon-Tournai, ca. 1130–46, and of Noyon, 1146–63/6. Pycke, *Le chapitre cathédral Notre-Dame de Tournai de la fin du XIe à la fin du XIIIe siècle*, 64.

11 Plaisei *B*.

12 Foulques Obelin is attested in acts from 1134–65. See **322**, **353**, **362**, and **398.**

13 Emmelina *B*.

14 *Transp. A*; decani famulus *B*.

15 Aubertus *B*.

16 Barthélemy and Wibert, sons of Foulques Obelin and Berthe, also appear in **353**.

17 Robert de Frémont also appears in **436**. Possibly Frémont, cant. Nesle, https://dicotopo.cths.fr/places/P77307649.

18 Froemont *B*.

donum prefate ecclesie firmum inconcussumque permaneat, episcopali auctoritate communimus et sigilli nostri inpressione ~~communimus~~ corroboramus et eos qui super prefata decima supra memoratum ecclesiam inquietare scienter deinceps presumpserint, anathematis vinculo innodamus. Actum anno incarnati verbi Mº Cº LXº IIIº, epacta XIIIIª.

443

1137.[1] Noyon.

*Simon [I],[2] bishop of Noyon, makes known and approves that husband and wife Foulques,[3] mayor of Noyon, and Berthe; and their sons Barthélemy and Guibert gave to the church of Prémontré half of the major tithe and a third of the minor tithe of Muille.[4] Hugues[5] de Béthencourt, from whom the fief descended, also consented. (See near-duplicate **397**.)*

A. Cartulary of Prémontré, fols. 102r–102v.

B. Original, BnF, Coll. Picardie 290, no. 1, sealed on a single strip of leather in brown wax.

EDITION: Pycke and Vleeschouwers, *Actes*, 401–2.

REGISTER: Boghen, "Inventaire des actes épiscopaux originaux conservés à la Bibliothèque nationale (1121–1200)," 120; *Studium Baldwin*, fiche 2049.

Karta Symonis Noviomensis episcopi de elemosina Fulconis, maioris de Noviomo.

[I]n nomine sancte et individue et cetera. Quoniam defluentibus annis multa solent in oblivionem defluere que memoriter retineri[6] volumus, scriptis solemus annotare. Quapropter ego, Symon, Dei gratia Noviomensis episcopus, tam posteris quam modernis, notum facio quod Fulcho,[7] maior de Noviomo, et

1 The cartulary incorrectly dates this to 1177, but both the original charter and the near-duplicate act **397** date it to 1137.

2 Simon I de Vermandois (d. 1148) was the son of Hugues I and Adélaïde, count and countess of Vermandois and Valois, and bishop of Noyon, 1123–42.

3 Foulques, mayor of Noyon, 1120s–30s.

4 Muille-Villette, cant. Ham, https://dicotopo.cths.fr/places/P77128677.

5 Likely Hugues I de Sermaize, lord of Béthencourt-sur-Somme (cant. Nesle, https://dicotopo.cths.fr/places/P85791062), a father or grandfather of Simon *le Vieux* de Sermaize, lord of Béthencourt-sur-Somme. See Newman, *Seigneurs*, vol. 2, 99, 209–10; Guyotjeannin, *Episcopus*, 272.

6 Retinere *B*.

7 Fulco *B*.

uxor eius, Berta,[8] cum filiis suis, Bartholomeo et Guiberto, dimidiam partem maioris decime et terciam minu~~ta~~te de Muiles[9] tam pro suo quam pro suorum remedio Premonstrate ecclesie Sancte Marie et Sancti Johannis Baptiste dederunt, Hugone de Bethencort[10] ad cuius feodum decima pertinebat, concedente, et quod suum in ea erat in manu nostra ponente sub hiis[11] testibus: Hugone,[12] cancellario, magistro Aszone[13,14] medico, Gilleberto monacho, Rogero[15] de Torota, Hugone[16] de Perona, Johanne de Acxei, Ivone de Sancto Petro. Ego autem predicte ecclesie decimam illam omni tempore obtinendam concessi et ne ullatenus cassum fieri posset, scripto et sigillo nostro roboravi. Quisquis inde ecclesie cui data est nocere intenderit, anathema sit. Actum Noviomi, M° C° LXXVII°.[17]

444

March 25, 1224.

The knight Philippe [II],[1] *lord of Caulaincourt, recognizes that the church of Prémontré gave him an oven at Caulaincourt to be held in return for an annual* census *of five* modii *of grain (*frumentum*), measure of Saint-Quentin, payable at the Premonstratensian house at Chauvigny. Adèle called* Sarracena,

8 Bertha *B.*
9 Muvles *B.*
10 Bethencurt *B.*
11 his *B.*
12 Hugues III de Roye, chancellor of Noyon-Tournai, ca. 1130–46, and of Noyon, 1146–63/6. Pycke, *Le chapitre cathédral Notre-Dame de Tournai de la fin du XIe à la fin du XIIIe siècle*, 64.
13 Azone *B.*
14 A *medicus* called Aszo also appears as a witness in **299** and **397.** Wickersheimer, Jacquart, and Beaujouan, *Dictionnaire biographique des médecins en France au moyen âge*, vol. 3, 34.
15 Roger *Filius Episcopi*, castellan of Thourotte and son of the lady Adèle and perhaps Teszo, castellan of Coucy. He entered Prémontré in 1141. Through his mother he was related to the castellans of Chauny. Guyotjeannin, *Episcopus*, 212–14, 273–4.
16 A Hugues de Péronne appears in an 1139 act of the abbey of Ourscamp, also in the company of Roger de Thourotte. BnF, MS lat. 5473, fol. 130r.
17 Actum Noviomi anno ab incarnatione Domini M. C. XXX. VII, epacta VII, concurrente IIII, indictione I. S. Teoderici, thesSararii. S. Hugonis, cancellarii. S. Petri, cantori. S. Rogeri, diaconi. S. Walberti, diaconi. S. Vidonis de Sancto Petro. S. Berlandi. S. Nihardi. S. Landrici. S. Roberti Carclun *B.*

1 Philippe II, lord of Caulaincourt (cant. Vermand, https://dicotopo.cths.fr/places/P02972526), attested ca. 1217–ca. 1224. Melleville, *DH*, vol. 1, 189.

*Philippe's wife, and their children, Gérard and Raoul, assent to the transaction. (See near-duplicate **400**.)*

A. Cartulary of Prémontré, fol. 102v.

B. Original, BnF, Coll. Picardie 290, no. 36, previously sealed.

Karta Philippi domini de Canlencort de furno de Canlencort quem accepi ab ipsa ecclesia sub annuo censu quinque modiorum.

[E]go Philippus, miles, dominus de Canlencort, notum facio per hoc scriptum universis tam presentibus quam futuris quod ecclesia Premonstratensis furnum suum de Canlencort tradidit michi tenendum a me fideliter cum eodem pondere et cum eodem modo quo eadem ecclesia tenuerat ipsum furnum et a me et ab heredibus meis perpetuo possidendum sub annuo censu quinque modiorum frumenti ad mensuram Sancti Quintini, quod erit pagabile atque sanum et tam ego quam heredes mei solvemus annuatim in perpetuum eidem ecclesie dictos quinque modios in domo sua de Cauvigni[2] in festo Omnium Sanctorum. Quitavi nichilominus prenominate ecclesie omnes census quos michi debebat quocumque modo tempore huius scripti, hoc faciens de meorum liberorum assensu. Sciendum est autem quod si vel ego vel heredes mei dictos quinque modios censuales vel non solveremus termino constituto aut forte non solveremus, tale frumentum quod esset pagabile atque sanum feci eidem ecclesie assignamentum ad molendinum de Canlencort meum[3] et etiam ad furnum michi et heredibus meis ab ipsa ecclesia traditum et concessum ut de proventibus utriusque molendini videlicet atque furni tantum sine contradictione et sine obstaculo possit capere quod ei vel nuntiis suis de defectu sit plenarie satisfactum. Hiis siquidem omnibus superius expressis tam uxor mea, Adeluya, que et Sarracena dicebatur, quam liberi mei, Gerardus videlicet et Radulfus, amicabiliter et sine contradictione suum prebuerunt assensum, rata habentes omnia que in presenti pagina continentur. Et ego de eorum consciencia et voluntate ob perpetuam firmitatem presentem kartam sigilli mei munimine roboravi. Actum mense martio in Annunciatione dominica intrante, anno gratie M° CC° XX° IIII°.[4]

---

2 Cauveigni *B*.

3 *Transp. A*; ad molendinum meum de Canlencort *B*.

4 millesimo ducentesimo vicesimo quarto *B*.

445

1147[1]

Simon [I],[2] bishop of Noyon, approves as fief lord the gift made by Jean, called bishop's chamberlain, and his unnamed wife to the church of Prémontré of their part of the tithe on the territory of Muille[3] that renders an annual census *of 10* sextariae *of grain (*triticum*) and two* sextariae *of peas, measure of Ham. (See near-duplicate **401**.)*

A. Cartulary of Prémontré, fol. 102v.
B. Original, AM Metz, Salis II.247, no. 1, sealed in brown wax on a single strip of parchment.
EDITION: Pycke and Vleeschouwers, *Actes*, 524–5.

Karta Symonis Noviomensis episcopi de elemosina Johannis et uxoris eius de decima in territorio de Muile.

[I]n nomine sancte et individue Trinitatis. Ego Symon, Dei gratia Noviomensis ecclesie minister, notum fieri volo tam futuris quam presentibus quod Johannes qui dicitur episcopi camerarius et uxor eius contulerunt per manum meam Premonstrate ecclesie in perpetuum quicquid habebant decime in territorio de Muile[4] pro censu decem sextariorum[5] tritici et duorum sextariorum pise Hamensis tunc currentis mensure, annuatim in festo Sancti Remigii Noviomi sive Landrimont[6] persolvendum. Frumentum vero tale erit quale in eadem decima accipietur ea tamen conditione quod predictum censum nulli ecclesie vel alicui hominum dare aut vendere absque prenominate ecclesie assensu licebit. Hoc autem factum est me annuente de cuius feodo descendebat et eundem feodum ecclesie penitus condonante eo scilicet modo ut si aliqua pactione predictum censum possent sibi comparare, liberam ab omni exactione decimam possiderent. Huius rei testes sunt: Hugo[7] cancellarius, Odo decanus de

1 The cartulary dates this as 1148, but the original is 1147, as is the near-duplicate **401**.
2 Simon I de Vermandois (d. 1148) was the son of Hugues I and Adélaïde, count and countess of Vermandois and Valois, and bishop of Noyon, 1123–42.
3 Muille-Villette, cant. Ham, https://dicotopo.cths.fr/places/P77128677.
4 Muille *B*.
5 cestariorum *B*.
6 Landrimont, comm. Noyon, https://dicotopo.cths.fr/places/P74301629.
7 Hugues III de Roye, chancellor of Noyon-Tournai, ca. 1130–46, and of Noyon, 1146–63/6. Pycke, *Le chapitre cathédral Notre-Dame de Tournai de la fin du XIe à la fin du XIIIe siècle*, 64.

Ham, Willermus[8] de Plaissie,[9] Robertus[10] maior de Ham, Robertus de Duaco. Ut autem hec pactio firma omni tempore perseveret, episcopali auctoritate sigillique nostri impressione communimus. Et ne quis eam irritare presumat, sub anathemate interdicimus. Actum est hoc anno incarnationis dominice M° C° XL° VIII°.

446

April, 1231.

Gérard[1] *de Ribécourt, knight, acknowledges that he holds three* areatae *of water at Buny*[2] *from the church of Prémontré, in return for an annual* census *of seven and a half* solidi Parisiensium. *(See duplicate* ***403****.)*

A. Cartulary of Prémontré, fol. 102v.

B. Original, AD Oise, H 6005, previously sealed on a double strip of parchment.

Karta Gerardi de Ribercort de tribus areatis aque apud Beuni.

[E]go Gerardus de Ribercort, miles, notum facio universis tam presentibus quam futuris quod teneo ab ecclesia Premonstratensi tres areatas aque apud Beuni sub annuo censu septem solidorum et dimidiam Parisiensis monete solvendorum singulis annis eidem ecclesie in medio martii. Si vero forte contingeret quod ego vel heres meus qui tenebit aquam ipsam non solveremus censum predictum in termino constituto, teneremur ad emendam super hoc ecclesie prenominate secundum legem patrie et ecclesia nichilominus Premonstratensis posset saisire ipsam aquam donec esset satisfactum eidem. In cuius rei testimonium et perpetuam firmitatem, presentes literas eidem ecclesie dedi sigilli mei munimine roboratas. Actum mense aprilis, anno gratie M° CC° XXX° I°.[3]

---

8 Willelmus *B*.

9 Plessei *B*.

10 A Robert, *maior* of Ham, appears in **378**, **401**, and **421.**

---

1 Gérard de Ribécourt (arr. Compiègne, https://dicotopo.cths.fr/places/P45097454) appears in charters as early as 1220. Édouard de Barthélemy, *Analyse du cartulaire de l'abbaye de Foigny*, 88. On his possible familial connections, see Mazière, "Notice historique sur Ribécourt," 88–9.

2 Buny, cant. Nesle, https://dicotopo.cths.fr/places/P07807251.

3 millesimo ducentesimo tricesimo primo *B*.

447

March 28, 1226.

Magister *Milon,*[1] officialis *of Noyon, makes known that the knight Hubert de Marcel recognizes having sold to the church of Prémontré two* modii *of grain* (frumentum*) that he had held from Prémontré in fief and that he had received annually on the grange of Omiécourt.*[2] *Emmeline, Hubert's wife, their children Oudard and Ricalde, and their granddaughter Agnès consent to the sale. (See near-duplicate* ***402****.)*

A. Cartulary of Prémontré, fol. 102v.
B. Original, AM Metz, Salis II.248, no. 9, previously sealed.

Karta officialis Noviomensis de duobus modiis frumenti quos Hubertus de Marcel vendidit ecclesie.

[M]agister Milo, officialis Noviomensis, omnibus hec visuris salutem in Domino. Vobis notum facimus quod Hubertus de Marcel, miles, coram nobis recognovit se vendidisse bene et legitime in perpetuum ecclesie Premonstratensi duos modios frumenti quos de dicta ecclesia tenebat in feodum et percipiebat singulis annis in grangia dicte ecclesie apud Omercort, quos etiam de[3] dicta ecclesia receperat in excambium pro tractu et questu decime d'Omercort et pro duodecim sextariis bladi quos in eadem decima annuatim percipiebat et etiam vacuo stramine et procuratione et omni alio jure quod in dicta grangia habere se dicebat, sicut in literis ipsius Huberti militis vidimus contineri. Hanc autem[4] laudaverunt et concesserunt coram nobis, Enmelina, uxor dicti Huberti militis, Odardus et Richaldis liberi ipsius, necnon et Agnes, neptis eius, fidem corporalem, prestantes coram nobis tam dictus H[ubertus] miles quam Enmelina, uxor eius, necnon liberi et neptis predicta, quod contra predictam venditionem decetero per se vel per alium nullatenus venient nec venire facient nec dictam ecclesiam super dictis duobus modiis frumenti venditis deinceps aliquatenus molestabunt nec artem nec ingenium querent per quod possit dicta ecclesia molestari. Actum anno Domini M° CC° vicesimo sexto, sabbato post Oculi Mei.

1 *Magister* Milon, *officialis* of Noyon, ca. 1224–ca. 1228. AD Oise, G 1984, fol. 189r; AD Aisne, H 455, fol. 311r.
2 Omiécourt-Montréal, cant. Nesle, https://dicotopo.cths.fr/places/P59719870.
3 a *B*.
4 *Om.* venditionem *A*.

448

1191

Hugues,[1] *dean, and the chapter of Noyon approve the gift made in alms to Bonneuil*[2] *by Étienne [I],*[3] *bishop of Noyon, of the* personatus *of Douchy*[4] *and of Germaine,*[5] *as well as the remission of the custom on a quarter of the garden of Eppeville.*[6] *They also approve the agreement reached between the brothers of Bonneuil and bishop Étienne concerning the* census *owed on the oven situated in front of Saint-Martin.*

A. Cartulary of Prémontré, fols. 102v–103r.
B. Original not found.

Karta decani Noviomensis de elemosina personatus de Douci.

[E]go Hugo, Noviomensis ecclesie decanus, totumque nostrum capitulum notum facimus universis presentem paginam inspecturis quod nos ex communi assensu elemosinam personatus de Duci et de Germaniis a venerabili patre nostro Stephano, Noviomensi episcopo, ecclesie de Bonolio collatam simulque remissionem consuetudinis in quartero cuiusdam orti de Espevilla et etiam conventionem census inter predictum episcopum et fratres Bonolii super furno ante Sanctum Martinum cuius fundus ad nos spectat habitam eo tenore qui in auctenticis eiusdem episcopi continetur, laudamus, approbamus et presentis scripti patrocinio confirmamus. Actum anno incarnati verbi M° C° nonagesimo primo.

1 Hugues de Coucy, son of Guy II, castellan of Coucy, and Théophanie; dean of the chapter of Noyon, ca. 1186–ca. 1210. Barthélemy, *LDA*, 510; AD Oise, G 1984, fols. 116r, 129v–130r.
2 The Premonstratensian *curtis* of Bonneuil. *MP* II, 484.
3 Étienne de Villebéon (or de Nemours), son of Gautier de Villebéon, lord of La Chapelle-Gauthier and Nemours, and Aveline, was bishop of Noyon, 1188–1221.
4 Douchy, cant. Vermand, https://dicotopo.cths.fr/places/P84133506.
5 Germaine, cant. Vermand, https://dicotopo.cths.fr/places/P36636067.
6 Eppeville, cant. Ham. https://dicotopo.cths.fr/places/P94171781.

449

1120s–30s[1]

Simon [I],[2] bishop of Noyon, makes known that Ricuère,[3] wife of Raimond de Clastres, entered the religious life at Prémontré and gave the community there a carruca *of land from an allod she held at Bolmont. Guy de Clastres, Ricuère's son-in-law, gave the rest of the allod to Prémontré after the death of his wife Havide, daughter of Ricuère. Guy and Havide's children, Geoffroi, Ricuère, and Alaide, assent to this.*

A. Cartulary of Prémontré, fol. 103r.
B. Original not found.
EDITION: *AASS*, October 11, 52 (partial); Colliette, *Mémoires pour servir à l'histoire de la province de Vermandois*, vol. 2, p. 155; Pycke and Vleeschouwers, *Actes*, 395–6.
REGISTER: Grauwen, "Lijst van oorkonden waarin Norbertus wordt genoemd," 141.

Karta Simonis Noviomensis episcopi de carruca alodii apud Bolmunt quam Richuera dedit.

[I]n nomine sancte et cetera. Quia labente annorum curriculo labitur etiam plerumque rerum gestarum memoria, saniori predecessorum consilio sancitum est ut beneficia que ecclesie Dei a fidelibus contribuuntur, veracis pagine memorie commendentur. Hac igitur de causa, ego Symon, Dei gratia Noviomensis episcopus, notum fieri volo tam futuris quam presentibus quod eo tempore quo domnus Norbertus, vir admirande religionis, in Premonstratum locum cum suis ad serviendum Deo se recepit, quedam nobilis mulier, Rikuera nomine, uxor Rainmundi de Clastris, in predictum locum conversionis gratia se contulit et ad sustentationem fratrum eiusdem loci carrucam alodii quam Bolmunt habebat, libere possidendam tradidit. Post non multum vero temporis defuncta filia sua, Haudewide nomine, quam Guido de Clastris duxerat uxorem, maritus eius, Guido scilicet, totam reliquam partem alodii quod a Bolmunt cum eadem uxore sua acceperat, pro remedio anime eiusdem et cunctorum parentum suorum, concedentibus ~~parentibus~~ heredibus suis, Godefrido videlicet, filio suo, et filiabus suis Rikuera et Alaide, sicut liberam possidebat, ita

1 While this charter is dated 1121, this is improbable, as Simon was only elected bishop in 1123. Pycke and Vleeschouwers date the charter to 1123–36.
2 Simon I de Vermandois (d. 1148) was the son of Hugues I and Adélaïde, count and countess of Vermandois and Valois, and bishop of Noyon, 1123–42.
3 Ricuère, lady of Clastres (cant. Saint-Simon, https://dicotopo.cths.fr/places/P82112287). *AASS*, October 13, 51–3; Melleville, *DH*, vol. 1, 256.

liberam perpetuo habendam supradicte ecclesie donavit, districto tantum secularium retento. Concessit etiam quod siquis in eodem districto terram, silvam pascuamve haberet quam dare in elemosinam vellet vel vendere sine requisitione aliqua posset eidem ecclesie dare vel vendere et ecclesia accipere. Et de supradicto alodio, siquis mansionarius aliquid teneret, non posset dare alicui commutare vel vendere nisi supradicte ecclesie. Et ne quis hoc donum temeritatis vel cupiditatis ausu in futurum violare presumat, sigilli nostri impressione subsignavimus et in perturbatores, nisi resipuerint, anathematis sentenciam proferimus. Actum est hoc anno incarnationis dominice M° C° XXI° indictione XIIII[a], epacta nulla, concurrente quinto.

450

1140

Hugues [I],[1] *abbot of Prémontré, makes known the agreement reached between the abbey of Prémontré and Thieszo* Villicus *de Vois*[2] *following a dispute concerning the possession and partition of a* mansus *and its associated revenues. This agreement was reached with the consent of Erenburge, wife of Thieszo; their children Amisars, Guillaume, Albericus, Foulques, and Emmeline; and their son-in-law Gelbert.*

A. Cartulary of Prémontré, fol. 103r.
B. Original not found.

De quadam pace facta inter Premonstratensem ecclesiam et Thiesconem de Voiz tempore Hugonis abbatis.

[I]n nomine sancte et cetera. Ego Hugo, abbas, et fratres Premonstrate ecclesie notum fieri volumus omnibus tam futuris quam presentibus quod de controversia habita inter Premonstratam ecclesiam et Thieszonem de Vooiz, qui dicitur Villicus, post plures inde factas retractiones hoc modo tandem stabilita fuit concordia: Tieszo quicquid de terra occupaverat, ecclesie recognovit et reddidit preter tres quartas partes unius mansi que equali dimensione et censu dividuntur ad terram Petri de Vooiz. Harum trium partium una tantum cedit ei jure hereditario patrimonii et inde censum dabit ecclesie; de altera habere debet reditum pro feodo suo quicumque villicus ecclesie fuerit; de tercia autem, quia eam ad ipsum feodum villicationis Tieszo pertinere dicebat, examinandum

1 Hugues I de Fosses (ca. 1093–1164), first abbot of Prémontré.
2 Forest of Vois, https://dicotopo.cths.fr/places/P93994197.

remansit. Ubi, si non attineat ecclesia habebit reditum terram vero et secunde et tercie partis qui jure hereditario optinere debebit. Quod si forte non fuerit villicus nec duas predictas nec earum reditus quendam etiam campum trium sextariorum et alium ~~dimi~~ dimidii sextarii et hortum unum concessit ecclesia eidem Tieszoni hac quidem conditione ut, si ipse Tieszo quandoque recognoverit hoc se injuste possidere, absque contradictione heredum suorum reddet ecclesie. Hec igitur sic definita sunt assensu uxoris eius, Erenburgis, et filiorum suorum, qui vulgo Amisars, Willelmus, Alberici, Fulconis, et generis sui, Gelberti, et filie sue, Enmeline. Et quod perpetuo sic observabunt nec inde dampnum ecclesie facient vel pacientur fieri in quantum avertere possint, data fide et jurandi sacramento, confirmaverunt tam ipsi quam propinqui eorum quorum nomina subscripta sunt: Walterus, villicus de Viri, et eius filiis[3] G[onfridus]. Si vero ipse Tieszo aut unus vel plures heredum suorum huius pacti transgrediantur diffinitionem propinqui qui cum ipsis juraverunt, ad satisfactionem eos cogere debebunt. Quod si non fecerint, ego Hugo et successor meus vel fratres ecclesie ab Ingelranno vel ab eo qui dominium Ferie post eum obtinebit, requiremus justiciam secundum fidem quam inde fecerant Milesendi, matri ipsius, Ingelranni in precedenti eiusdem rei tractacione ipse Tieszo et filius eius, Willelmus et Walterus villicus de Viri, et ipsius filius Gonfridus similiter pro eadem concordia fidem dantes ut si eius concordie pactum transgrederentur ad ammonitionem principis Ferie vel emendarent vel in captivitate Coceii vel Ferie se redderent transgressores vel ipsis nolentibus, si eos cogere non possent, se ipsos in captivitate ponerent. Si autem et hoc ipsum omnes contradicerent, concesserunt supradicte domine ut se ipsos et sua, ubi posset, diriperet, donec ad satisfacionem redirent. Huic actioni interfuerunt hii testes: Wido[4] de Clastris, Waszo[5] Stultus de Sancto Quintino, Guido[6] de Moy, Albricus miles de Feria, Bunardus[7] antiquus prepositus, Willelmus Cornars, Willelmus[8] de Gontran, Paganus villicus de Tanni, Hugo de Duri,[9] Tieszo, et ceteri. Acta sunt hec anno Domini M° C° XL°, indictione secunda, epacta nulla, concurrente primo. Quod si predictam satisfactionem subterfugerint, apostolice excommunicationi subjacere se sciant que sic se habet ut reos se divino judicio esse cognoscant.

3 *Sic A*, *read* filius.

4 Guy, lord of Clastres; son-in-law of Ricuère and Raimond of Clastres (**449**) through his marriage to their daughter Hawide. Melleville, *DH*, vol. 1, 256.

5 Waszo *Stultus* of Saint-Quentin appears as a witness to episcopal charters, ca. 1137–ca. 1140 (**333, 339**).

6 Guy II, lord of Moy and castellan of Saint-Quentin, son of Guy I (or Gilles), lord of Moy. Melleville, *DH*, vol. 2, 145.

7 Bonard, *prepositus* of La Fère, appears in episcopal acts 1133–49. Dufour-Malbezin, *Actes*, 243, 430.

8 Guillaume, lord of Condren (cant. Chauny, https://dicotopo.cths.fr/places/P28107866). Melleville, *DH*, vol. 1, 273.

9 Dury, cant. Saint-Simon, https://dicotopo.cths.fr/places/P78356002.

451

December, 1214.

At the request of Étienne [I],[1] bishop of Noyon, Guy,[2] abbot of Saint-Nicolas-aux-Bois, and Simon [I],[3] abbot of Saint-Eloi-Fontaine, resolved the dispute between the brothers Geoffroi and Simon de Condren[4] and the church of Prémontré concerning lands at the curtis *of La Férolle,[5] in favour of the brothers of Prémontré. Elizabeth, Geoffroi and Simon's sister, promises to uphold the terms of the agreement.*

A. Cartulary of Prémontré, fol. 103v.
B. Original not found.

Scriptum de quadam compromissione inter ecclesiam Premonstratem et Galfridum et Simonem fratres de Gondram super quibusdam terris.

[G]uido, Sancti Nicholai in Boscho, et S[imon], de Sancti Eligii Fonte Dei patientia dicti abbates, omnibus presentibus et futuris in perpetuum. Notum sit omnibus presentem paginam inspecturis quod cum Galfridus et Symon, fratres de Gondran, laici, super quibusdam terris ad curtem de Ferreola pertinentibus adversus Premonstratensem ecclesiam querelam movissent, adtendentes tandem sue non expedire saluti ut de terris eisdem in quibus se jus aliquid habere certi non erant, memoratam ecclesiam ulterius molestarent, in nos conpromissionem fecerunt, ratum habituri quicquid nos de ipsa querela ordinaremus vel per nostram inquisitionem legitimam faciendam de plano vel proprii nostri arbitrii motu et hoc ipsum coram reverendo patre Stephano, Noviomensi episcopo, presentialiter constituti fide interposita pleniverunt. Eandem quoque conpromissionem creantavit tenendam Elizabeth, soror ipsorum, pro parte sua coram me S[ymone], abbate de Sancti Eligii Fonte, qui vice dicti episcopi et de mandato ipsius accepi super hec ab ea fidei sacramentum. Nos igitur ad petitionem virorum venerabilium abbatis et fratrum Premonstratensium qui noluerunt reddere se suspectos de retinendo jure conquerentium predictorum,

1 Étienne de Villebéon (or de Nemours), son of Gautier de Villebéon, lord of La Chapelle-Gauthier and Nemours, and Aveline, was bishop of Noyon, 1188–1221.

2 Guy, abbot of the Benedictine abbey of Saint-Nicolas-aux-Bois, ca. 1206–ca. 1230. Duval, "Histoire de l'abbaye bénédictine de Saint-Nicolas-aux-Bois, diocèse de Laon, première partie," 208–14.

3 Simon I, abbot of the Augustinian abbey of Saint-Éloi-Fontaine, 1202–28. Per Poissonier, "L'abbaye de Saint-Eloi-Fontaine ou de Commenchon," 275–6.

4 Condren, cant. Chauny, https://dicotopo.cths.fr/places/P28107866.

5 La Férolle, comm. Vouël, https://dicotopo.cths.fr/places/P51152055.

inquisivimus de plano super predictis diligentissime veritatem. Cumque tam ex inquisitione facta quam ex confessione dictorum G[alfridi] et S[ymoni] invenissemus Premonstratensem ecclesiam predictas terras per quadraginta annos et eo amplius tenuisse et cum dictis conquerentibus qui alias super hoc moverant questionem pacem factam fuisse ratione prescriptionis qua Premonstratensis ecclesia tueri se posset necnon et pacis que facta fuerat cum conquerentibus sepedictis adjudicavimus arbitrando Premonstratensis ecclesie possessionem et proprietatem terrarum deductarum in litem et imposuimus eisdem conquerentibus perpetuum silencium in hac parte ne vel ipsi vel aliqui ex parte ipsorum querelam super memoratis terris sollempniter terminatam suscitare presumerent vel in posterum aliquatenus reclamarent. In huius igitur rei testimonium arbitrarie jurisdictionis auctoritate perpetuo valiturum, presens scriptum emisimus sigillorum nostrorum impressione munitum. Actum mense decembri, anno incarnationis dominice M° CC° X° IIII°.

452

1142

Simon [I],[1] bishop of Noyon, makes known that Godon,[2] son of Gautier de Viry, gave to abbot Hugues [I][3] and the church of Prémontré the half of the oven that he possessed at Chauny[4] upon his entry into the religious life at Prémontré. Raoul, son of Yobert de Sommete,[5] Godon's heir and relative; Gautier de Viry and his sons, Robert and Gonfrid; and Roger de Thourotte,[6] from whom the fief descended, all consented to the gift.[7]

A. Cartulary of Prémontré, fol. 103v.

B. Original, AD Aisne, H 769, previously sealed on a double strip of parchment.

EDITION: Pycke and Vleeschouwers, *Actes*, 465–7.

---

1 Simon I de Vermandois (d. 1148) was the son of Hugues I and Adélaïde, count and countess of Vermandois and Valois, and bishop of Noyon, 1123–42.

2 Godon, son of Gautier de Viry, also made a gift of half of the oven he possessed at Cannectancourt (cant. Lassigny, https://dicotopo.cths.fr/places/P56289764) to the Premonstratensian abbey of Cuissy. Hugo, *prob.* I, col. 72. His anniversary was celebrated at Premontre on March 9. Van Waefelghem, *L'Obituaire de l'abbaye de Prémontré*, 64.

3 Hugues I de Fosses (ca. 1093–1164), first abbot of Prémontré.

4 Chauny, arr. Laon, https://dicotopo.cths.fr/places/P32247131.

5 Sommette-Éaucourt, cant. Saint-Simon, https://dicotopo.cths.fr/places/P82241903.

6 Roger *Filius Episcopi*, castellan of Thourotte and son of the lady Adèle and perhaps Teszo, castellan of Coucy. He entered Prémontré in 1141. Through his mother he was related to the castellans of Chauny. Guyotjeannin, *Episcopus*, 212–14, 273–4.

7 The 1140 act which this act confirms is also in folder AD Aisne, H 769.

Karta Symonis Noviomensis episcopi de medietate furni de Calniaco quam Godo remisit.

[I]n nomine sancte et individue Trinitatis. Docet veritas elemosinas fidelium esse redemptiones animarum cum dicit: "Date elemosinam et omnia munda sunt vobis"[8] et sicut aqua extinguit ignem, ita elemosina peccatum.[9] Quas episcoporum est ex officii debito et conservare et memorie commendare. Ea propter ego Symon, Dei gratia Noviomensis episcopus, notum fieri volo tam futuris quam presentibus quod Godo, filius Walteri de Viri, dedit ecclesie Premonstrate et Hugoni, abbati et fratribus ibidem Deo servientibus, ob remedium anime sue et predecessorum suorum, dimidietatem cuiusdam furni quem habebat Chalni et se ipsum conversum reddidit. Quod donum concessit Radulphus,[10] filius Yoberti[11] de Sumete, qui propinquior eius erat heres,[12] quia heredem corporis sui non habebat et Walterus de Viri et filii eius, Robertus et Gonfridus. Quorum alter, videlicet Gonfridus, quod factum erat voluit contradicere et inde apud Calniacum facto clamore et responso ex precepto Radulphi[13] comitis de Perona coram Albrico de Roia et multis aliis; cum se in judicio deficere presentiret quicquid in predicto furno se habere dicebat, perpetuo prefate ecclesie[14] possidendum concessit statimque judicatum est quod ecclesia eundum furnum sine ipsius vel cuiuslibet heredum suorum contradictione liberum a modo possideat. Hoc judicium fecit Walbertus castellanus, Alardus de Porta,[15] Robertus Vitulus,[16] Godinus de Plaissie,[17] Helgot de Calni, Radulphus[18] Stultus, Hugo[19] filius Thome de Feria, et multi alii. Concessit etiam hoc donum Rogerus de Torota de cuius feodo descendebat. Quod vero factum sit hoc donum legitime et evidenter legitimorum virorum testimonium appositum est. Affuerunt testes

---

8 Luke 11:41.

9 This phrase, inspired by Ecclesiasticus (Sirach) 3:33, appears in many twelfth-century charters.

10 Radulfus *B*.

11 Yolberti *B*.

12 *Transp. A*; heres erat *B*.

13 Radulfi *B*.

14 *Transp. A*; prefate ecclesie perpetuo *B*.

15 Alard I de Ham (or de la Porte), knight of Ham; husband of Helvide. He also appears in **91**, **298**, **334**, **385**, **415**, and **464**.

16 Robert *Vitulus* (or le Veau), a knight of Coucy, also appears in **4** and **184**. Barthélemy, *LDA*, 155–6.

17 Le Plessis-Patte-d'Oie, cant. Guiscard, https://dicotopo.cths.fr/places/P25690373.

18 Radulfus *B*.

19 Hugues, lord of Ognolles (cant. Guiscard, https://dicotopo.cths.fr/places/P57919721), is attested as late as 1194, and is likely dead by 1206. Leroy-Morel, *Recherches généalogiques sur les familles nobles de plusieurs villages des environs de Nesle, Noyon, Ham et Roye, et recherches historiques sur les mêmes localités*, 104; Pipon, ed., *Le chartrier de l'Abbaye-aux-Bois (1202–1341)*, 103.

ubi Radulfus, Yoberti[20] filius concessit: Walbertus castellanus,[21] Johannes presbyter, frater prefati Godonis et Yvo,[22] canonici ecclesie Calniaci, Radulfus Stultus, Helgoz, Robertus de Vadis, Robertus Beles. Quod Walterus de Viri et Robertus, filius eius, concesserunt, testes sunt: Walbertus castellanus, Godinus de Plaissie, Robertus Desgueiz.[23] Concessit etiam prefatus comes Radulfus in cuius manus post mortem Rogeri de Torota feodum devenit. Ut vero ratum permaneat, auctoritate episcopali sanctimus et quicumque ausus fuerit hanc elemosinam perturbare, minuere vel auferre, anathematis vinculo subjaceat et in extremo examine a sacratissimo corpore et sanguine Domini nostri Jhesu Christi alienus fiat et, nisi anmonitus satisfecerit, in ultione divina sentenciam dampnationis incurrat. Actum est hoc et confirmatum anno incarnationis dominice M° C° XL° II°, epacta III[a], indictione quinta,[24] concurrente III°. Ego Hugo[25] cancellarius relegi.

453

October, 1233.

Magister *Hugues,*[1] *canon and* officialis *of Noyon, makes known that for the sum of 12* librae Parisiensium, *Geoffroi de Senicourt*[2] *sold to the church of Prémontré 15* solidi Parisiensium *and six capons from the annual* supercensus *he received from a residence at Chauny.*[3] *Eremburge, mother of Geoffroi, and Helvide, his wife, approved this sale, and in exchange for ceding their rights of* dotalicium, *they received from Geoffroi 19* aissini *of grain (*bladus*) annually from land at Laffaux.*[4]

A. Cartulary of Prémontré, fols. 103v–104r.

B. Original, AD Aisne, H 769, previously sealed on a double strip of parchment.

---

20 Yolberti *B*.

21 Galbert, castellan of Thourotte, also appears in an 1140 act of Simon, bishop of Noyon. Pycke and Vleeschouwers, *Actes*, 444.

22 Ivo *B*.

23 Desguez *B*.

24 V *B*.

25 Hugues III de Roye, chancellor of Noyon-Tournai, ca. 1130–46, and of Noyon, 1146–63/6. Pycke, *Le chapitre cathédral Notre-Dame de Tournai de la fin du XIe à la fin du XIIIe siècle*, 64.

---

1 *Magister* Hugues, canon and *officialis* of Noyon, ca. 1229–ca. 1236. AD Aisne, H 455, fol. 310v; AD Oise, G 1984, fols. 238v–239r.

2 Senicourt, comm. Genvry, https://dicotopo.cths.fr/places/P98155849.

3 Chauny, arr. Laon, https://dicotopo.cths.fr/places/P32247131.

4 Laffaux, cant. Vailly, https://dicotopo.cths.fr/places/P16868587.

Karta officialis Noviomensis super eo quod Gaufridus recognovit se vendidisse quicquid habebat apud Calni.

[O]mnibus hec visuris magister Hugo, canonicus et officialis Noviomensis, salutem in Domino. Vobis notum facimus quod Gaufridus de Seniscort, in nostra presentia constitutus, recognovit se vendidisse pro duodecim libris Parisiensium ecclesie Premonstratensis quindecim solidos Parisiensium et sex capones quos habebat de annuo supercensu apud Calniacum super quadam masura de retro domum ipsius ecclesie quam habet apud Calniacum, inter aquam scilicet et dictam domum sita, dicte ecclesie in perpetuum possidendos, Erenburgi,[5] matre dicti Gaufridi, et Helvide,[6] uxore eiusdem, presentibus, dictam venditionem volentibus, laudantibus et approbantibus et recognoscentibus quod sufficiens excambium a dicto G[aufrido] receperant pro dotalicio quod in dicto supercensu habebant, videlicet decem et novem aissinos[7] bladi de annuo redditu super terra ipsius G[aufridi] quam habet apud Lafou[8] in Suessionensi dyocesi. Et per istud excanbium ad quod ipsas E[renburgem] et H[elvidem] coram nobis assignavit pro suo dotalicio predicto eo modo quo dotate erant de dicto supercensu una quidem post alteram omne jus quod habebant vel habere debebant tam jure dotalicii quam alio titulo in dicto supercensu, spontanee et non coacte in manu nostra resignaverunt et eidem supercensui fide data penitus renunciaverunt. Et tam dictus Gaufridus spontaneus et non coactus quam etiam dicte E[renburgis] et H[elvidis] spontanee et non coacte fidem in manu nostra prestiterunt corporalem quod dictam ecclesiam super dicto vendagio decetero non molestabunt nec gravabunt nec artem nec ingenium per se vel per alium querent per que possit vel debeat super eodem vendagio in posterum[9] molestari vel gravari. Recognovit insuper dictus Gaufridus coram nobis se de dicta pecunia plenariam recepisse solutionem. Actum anno Domini M° CC° XXX° III°,[10] mense octobri.

5 Eremburgi *B.*
6 Helevide *B.*
7 assinos *B.*
8 Laffou *B.*
9 imposterum *B.*
10 tricesimo tercio *B.*

454

1217

Étienne [I],[1] bishop of Noyon, makes known that the convent of Prémontré ceded to the knight Hugues[2] de Ribécourt a field near Hugues's house at Voyenne, in exchange for Hugues's cession of two fields at Mares *and* Lescalete *that the bishop holds in fief. The bishop renounces his rights over those two fields, on the condition that the field acquired by Hugues at Voyenne becomes an episcopal fief.*

A. Cartulary of Prémontré, fol. 104r.

B. Original, AD Somme, 20 H 19, no. 3, previously sealed on red silk threads.

Karta Stephani episcopi Noviomensis de quodam excambio inter ecclesiam Premonstratem et Hugonem militem.

[E]go Stephanus, divina permissione Noviomensis episcopus omnibus in perpetuum. Notum facimus tam presentibus quam futuris quod frater Nicholaus, canonicus Premonstratensis, litteris communitus[3] abbatis et conventus,[4] et Hugo de Ribercort, miles, in nostra presentia constituti, recognoverunt Premonstratensem ecclesiam et ipsum Hugonem fecisse quoddam excambium in hac forma: ecclesia Premonstratensis dedit ei quendam campum terre quem habebat juxta domum ipsius Hugonis extra Voianam cum honeribus suis hereditarie et integre possidendum; ipse autem Hugo dedit ecclesie Premonstratensi duos campos terre quorum unus dicitur Ad[5] Mares, alter A Lescalete, sicut disterminati sunt metis, ab omni honere etiam a decime solutione liberos et inmunes.[6] Et quia idem Hugo prefatos campos cum decima in feodo tenebat de nobis vice versa posuit in feodo nostro campum terre quem recepit ab ecclesia Premonstratensi et nos quitavimus eidem ecclesie quicquid juris quocumque modo habebamus in campis illis quos ecclesia ipsa a sepedicto Hugone recepit. Ne igitur excanbium[7] istud de assensu nostro factum futuris temporibus aliqua

1 Étienne de Villebéon (or de Nemours), son of Gautier de Villebéon, lord of La Chapelle-Gauthier and Nemours, and Aveline, was bishop of Noyon, 1188–1221.

2 Perhaps a son of Roger Tyrel, knight and lord of Ribécourt (arr. Compiègne, https://dicotopo.cths.fr/places/P45097454) in the late twelfth century. Cuvillier-Morel-d'Acy, *Histoire généalogique et héraldique sur la maison des Tyrel, sires, puis princes de Poix*, 40.

3 *Transp. A*; abbatis et conventus litteris communitus *B*.

4 *Om.* Premonstratensis *A*.

5 Al *B*.

6 immunes *B*.

7 excambium *B*

possit vel malicia vel oblivione mutari presens scriptum super hoc confectum sigilli nostri fecimus appensione muniri. Actum anno incarnationis dominice M° CC° XVII°.[8]

455

December, 1239. Chauny.

André[1] Juvenis, *the king's* baillivus *of Vermandois, gives notice that Jean,* maior *of Vouël,*[2] *renounced his claim on a house at La Férrole*[3] *and acknowledged that it belonged to the church of Prémontré.*

A. Cartulary of Prémontré, fol. 104r.
B. Original not found.

Karta ballivi regis de eo quod maior de Vouel renunciavit omnibus que clamabunt in domo de la Ferrole.

[A]ndreas juvenis, ballivus domini regis in Viromandia, universis tam presentibus quam futuris presentes litteras inspecturis salutem in Domino. Noveritis quod cum Johannes, dictus maior de Vouel aliquam consuetudinem in domo de la Ferrole que est ecclesie Premonstrati, diceret se habere, quamquam, sicut idem maior dicebat, nec ipse nec pater ipsius umquam in eodem domo aliquam consuetudinem habuissent, tandem maior prefatus in nostra presentia constitutus et ductus consilio saniori renuntiavit omnia in perpetuum omni consuetudini, si quam ipse vel progenitores ipsius umquam habuerint vel habere debuerint in domo prefata, nec ipse nec heredes nec successores ipsius poterunt decetero in eadem domo de la Ferrole occasione aliqua juris aliquid vel consuetudinis reclamare et dedit temporaliter fidei sacramentum quod super premissis vel occasione premissorum per se vel per alium domum dictam de la Ferrole vel ecclesiam Premonstratensem nullatenus decetero molestabit nec faciet aliquatenus molestari. In cuius rei testimonium presentes literas emisimus sigilli nostri munimine roboratas. Actum Calniaci anno gratie M° CC° XXX° nono, mense decembri.

---

8 millesimo ducentesimo septimodecimo *B*.

---

1 André le Jeune, *bailli* of Vermandois, 1236–45. Bouquet and Delisle, eds., *Recueil des historiens des Gaules et de la France*, vol. 24, part 1, 67–8.
2 Vouël, cant. La Fère, https://dicotopo.cths.fr/places/P57123769.
3 La Férolle, comm. Vouël, https://dicotopo.cths.fr/places/P51152055.

456

1132

Simon [I],[1] *bishop of Noyon, confirms the gift made to the church of Prémontré by Guillaume Coenarz of as much land as is needed to build a house with* curia *in the parish of Ferrières.*[2] *Clérembaud*[3] *de Vendeuil, from whom the fief descends, consents to the gift, as do Guillaume li Ors, Guillaume de Viri, and Gérard, son of Hugues, the tithe holders.*

A. Cartulary of Prémontré, fol. 104r.
B. Original not found.
EDITION: Pycke and Vleeschouwers, *Actes*, 363–4.

Karta Simonis Noviomensis episcopi de confirmatione cuiusdam terre que fuit Willermi Cornart

[I]n nomine sancte et cetera. Symon, Noviomensium episcopus, notum fieri volumus tam futuris quam presentibus quod Guillelmus Coenarz fratribus Premonstrate ecclesie tantum terre ubi domus cum curia possit fieri, in parrochia de Feriris, pro remedio anime sue dedit, concedente Clarenbaldo de Vendolio de cuius feodo descendebat. Huius rei testes sunt: Hugo de Silva et Odo Rufus. Eiusdem vero loci decimam qui eam tenebant predicte ecclesie concesserunt, Guillelmus li Ors, testibus hiis: Tizone, villico de Vouel, et Guillelmo de Viri; Gerardus Hugonis filius, testibus his: et ceteri. Et ut hoc ratum et inconvulsum sit, sigilli nostri impressione confirmamus. Signum Goiffridi,[4] abbatis Sancti Medardi, et Anselmi[5] abbatis Sancti Vincentii, et Hugonis[6] cancellarii. Actum anno incarnationis dominice M° C° XXX° II, epacta XX^{a}, concurrente III°.

1 Simon I de Vermandois (d. 1148) was the son of Hugues I and Adélaïde, count and countess of Vermandois and Valois, and bishop of Noyon, 1123–42.
2 Ferrières, comm. La Ferté-Chevresis, https://dicotopo.cths.fr/places/P96262032.
3 Likely Clérembaud III, lord of Vendeuil, ca. 1130–ca. 1153. Newman, *Homblières*, 120, fn. 3; Melleville, *DH*, vol. 2, 412.
4 Geoffroi I Col-de-Cerf was abbot of the Benedictine abbey of Saint-Médard de Soissons, 1120–31, and bishop of Châlons, 1131–42. The 1132 date of this charter therefore suggests a discrepancy between old style and new style dates. Poquet, *Pélerinage à l'ancienne abbaye de Saint-Médard-lès-Soissons*, 41.
5 Anselme, abbot of the Benedictine abbey of Saint-Vincent de Laon, 1128–ca. 1145.
6 Hugues III de Roye, chancellor of Noyon-Tournai, ca. 1130–46, and of Noyon, 1146–63/6. Pycke, *Le chapitre cathédral Notre-Dame de Tournai de la fin du Xie à la fin du XIIIe siècle*, 64.

457

1198–1216[1]

Cantor R. and P. d'Orgeval,[2] canons of Saint-Quentin, at the request of Pope Innocent [III], make known the resolution of a dispute between the Premonstratensians and Renaud de Vouël[3] concerning the tithe of the essart of La Férolle.[4,5]

A. Cartulary of Prémontré, fols. 104r–104v.
B. Original not found.

Scriptum de quadam controversia inter ecclesiam Premonstratem et Renaldum de Voue.

[E]go R. cantor et P. de Orgival, canonici Sancti Quintini, universos presentes literas inspecturos nosse volumus quod cum querela que inter Premonstratenses ex una parte et Renaldum de Vouel ex altera super decimatione sarti de la Ferrole vertebatur a domino Papa Innocentio nobis commissa fuisset cognoscenda et sine debito terminanda, nos duo predicti, videlicet cantor et P. de Orgival, juris peritorum freti, consilio servato juris ordine in cognitione cause ad diffinitionem processimus in hunc modum. Convocatis partibus et coram nobis in jure constitutis ipsis Premonstratensibus proponentibus debitam sibi decimationem sarti predicti a iamdicto R. injuste detineri et eam sibi reddi debere, econtra Renaldo pro se respondente sarti illius decimationem ipsi jure hereditario contingere, ipsi Premonstratenses constanter asserentes se jus habere in decimatione sarti memorati et eam diutius possedisse ac recepisse, id per legitimos testes indubitanter se probaturos promiserunt. Nos igitur huic probationi diem prefiximus. Productis vero testibus ex parte Premonstratensium coram nobis die sibi prefixa Renaldus ibidem presens, data sibi copia dicendi in ipsos testes si vellet, nichil in eos dixit. Testibus autem receptis sub forma juramenti expressa examinatis diligenter et auditis eorumque attestationibus redactis in scriptum die statuto partibus ad publicandas attestationes presentibus tam Premonstratensibus quam Renaldo coram positis attestationibus, cum interrogaremus Renaldum utrum in eas

1 A Pierre d'Orgeval was a canon of Saint-Quentin in 1226 (AD Aisne, H 1654), so this act likely dates to the papacy of Innocent III.

2 Orgeval, cant. Laon, https://dicotopo.cths.fr/places/P49065943.

3 Vouël, cant. La Fère, https://dicotopo.cths.fr/places/P57123769.

4 La Férolle, comm. Vouël, https://dicotopo.cths.fr/places/P51152055.

5 At the bottom of the first column on fol. 104r, a note has been added by a fourteenth-century hand. It states: "Quere novam kartam de justicia domus nostre de le Ferrole ante intitulationem kartaram Bonolii ad tale signum." See also pp. 67–9.

dicere vellet, ipso nolente eas audire sed ad Sedem Apostolicam appellante et ita a nobis discedente et indignanter abeunte. Nos publicatis attestationibus lectis diligenter et recitatis in publico accito juris peritorum consilio sepedicte decimationis possessionem Premonstratensi ecclesie apostolica freti auctoritate adjudicavimus firmiter statuentes ut ipsi eadem libere gaudeant et quiete.

458

1216. Chauny.

Gilles de Versailles,[1] *Guillaume des Châtelliers,*[2] *Renaud de Béthisy,*[3] *and Soibert,*[4] *the king's* ballivi, *attest that at the assizes of Chauny, Paschase,* bourgeois *of Chauny,*[5] *paid 22.5* solidi Parisiensium *as compensation for having taken sandstone from Thury*[6] *both for uses other than the construction of a fortress or the communal way of Chauny and without the prior authorization of abbot Gervais*[7] *of Prémontré.*

A. Cartulary of Prémontré, fol. 104v.
B. Original not found.

Karta de eo quod Paschasius de Calni emendavit ecclesie Premonstrati id quod eruerat gressios sine licentia.

[N]os Gilo de Versaliis, Willermus de Castellario, Renaldus de Bestiaco, Soibertus Laudunensis domini regis Francie ballivus notum facimus universis presentibus pariter et futuris quod Paschasius, burgensis Calniaci, emendavit in

1 Gilles de Versailles, a member of the family of the lords of Versailles, was a king's *bailli*, 1207–33. Bouquet and Delisle, eds., *Recueil des historiens des Gaules et de la France*, vol. 24, part 1, 57–8.
2 Guillaume des Châtelliers, a *bailli* of the king, 1214–27. Ibid., 59.
3 Renaud de Béthisy, king's *bailli*, worked principally at Compiègne and Montdidier, ca. 1196–1221, with a sphere of influence extending to Péronne, Beauvais, Senlis, and Meaux. He was brother of the *bailli* Pierre de Béthisy, and husband of Emmeline, lady of Houdancourt. Ibid., 53–7; Baldwin, *The Government of Philip Augustus*, 130, 431.
4 Soibert, *bourgeois* of Laon, was a king's bailli from 1216. Bouquet and Delisle, eds., *Recueil des historiens des Gaules et de la France*, vol. 24, part 1, 53–6; Baldwin, *The Government of Philip Augustus*, 131, 133.
5 Chauny, arr. Laon, https://dicotopo.cths.fr/places/P32247131.
6 Thury, arr. Laon, https://dicotopo.cths.fr/places/P84789655.
7 Gervais, abbot of the Premonstratensian abbeys of Saint-Just-en-Chaussée, 1199–1205, Thenailles, 1205–9, and Prémontré, 1209–20, and bishop of Séez, 1220–8. *MP* II, 401, 527, 565; Cheney, "Gervase, Abbot of Prémontré."

assisia Calniaci coram multis viro religioso Gervasio, abbati Premonstratensi, quod eruerat gressios in territorio de Toiri, invito abbate, pro alio faciendo quam fortericia et communi calciata Calniaci. Dixerunt autem milites subscripti qui presentes fuerunt per estimationem non judicum faciendo quod emenda illius infracture valebat viginti et duos solidos et dimidium Parisiensium. Idem vero abbas ad petitionem nostram quitavit illam emendam Paschasio. Inde sunt testes: viri nobiles Renaldus,[8] castellanus Couciaci, Johannes de Bretigniaco,[9] Marcellus[10] de Abbatis Curte, Johannes de Pleisseio, milites, Gilebertus Cornez, Johannes de Nigella, Petrus de Gloa[11] Noviomensis, et multi alii, presentibus etiam maiore et juratis Calniaci. Actum Calniaci publice anno incarnationis dominice M° CC° X° VI°.

459

August, 1212.

Étienne [I],[1] bishop of Noyon, makes known that Éléonore,[2] countess of Vermandois and Valois, and the bourgeois *of Chauny[3] reached an agreement with the church of Prémontré concerning the sandstone quarries at Thury.[4]*

A. Cartulary of Prémontré, fol. 104v.
B. Original, AN, L 995, no. 62, previously sealed.

Karta Stephani Noviomensis episcopi de compositione inter ecclesiam Premonstratem et burgensium Calniacum super gresseria.

[S]tephanus, divina miseratione Noviomensis episcopus omnibus in perpetuum. Scire volumus tam posteros quam presentes quod cum olim inter

---

8 Renaud II, castellan of Coucy, son of Mauduite, castellan of Coucy, and Renier, lord of Magny. Guyotjeannin, *Episcopus*, 274.

9 A Jean, lord of Brétigny, appears in acts of the abbey of Ourscamp in 1204, while a Jean de Bretigny, knight, d. ca. 1235, was buried at Ourscamp. Peigné-Delacourt, *Cartulaire de l'Abbaye de Notre-Dame d'Ourscamp de l'ordre de Cîteaux, fondée en 1129 au diocèse de Noyon*, 361, 505; Bouchot, *Inventaire des dessins exécutés pour Roger de Gaignières et conservés aux Départements des estampes et des manuscrits*, vol. 1, 307.

10 Marcel, knight and lord of Abbécourt, ca. 1200–ca. 1216. Melleville, *DH*, vol. 1, 2.

11 Possibly La Glaue, comm. Dommiers, https://dicotopo.cths.fr/places/P24687810.

---

1 Étienne de Villebéon (or de Nemours), son of Gautier de Villebéon, lord of La Chapelle-Gauthier and Nemours, and Aveline, was bishop of Noyon, 1188–1221.

2 Éléonore, countess of Vermandois (d. 1213), daughter of Raoul I, count of Vermandois and Valois, and Pétronille d'Aquitaine.

3 Chauny, arr. Laon, https://dicotopo.cths.fr/places/P32247131.

4 Thury, arr. Laon, https://dicotopo.cths.fr/places/P84789655.

illustrem mulierem Elienor, comitissam Viromandie et Valesie, necnon et burgenses Calniaci ex parte una et ecclesiam Premonstratensem ex parte altera super gresseria de Toyri coram nobis questio verteretur, terminata fuit controversia inter eos habita in hac forma: licitum erit dicte comitisse et successoribus eius, dominis Calniaci, in territorio de Toiri,[5] extra clausuram domus, sumere lapides pro forticia et calciata Calniaci facienda ita tamen quod dampna que facta fuerint in terra inbladiata pro ervitione et eductione gressiorum restituere et fossas replere ad terram coequare tenebuntur. Ecclesia vero Premonstratensis a calciagio solvendo ibidem erit in perpetuum libera et inmunis. Burgenses vero sine licentia ecclesie nec gressios nec aliud ibidem capere poterunt vel debebunt. Postmodum autem cum post aliquot annos querela super hoc ipso esset iterum suscitata et predicta comitissa cum consilio suo ex parte una et abbas Premonstratensis cum fratribus suis ex parte altera apud Noviomum in nostra essent presencia constituti, prefata conpositio que de assensu partium facta fuerat, coram nobis recordata fuit iterum et fuit a partibus creantatum quod decetero servaretur. Actum mense augusto, anno ab incarnatione domini M° CC° XII°.[6]

460

April, 1236. Chauny.

Dean Pierre of Chauny affixes his seal to the agreement reached between Renaud Audent[1] *and Gérard de Haironval,*[2] bourgeois *of Chauny,*[3] *on the one part, and Égide and Vermond,* prepositi *of Prémontré, on the other part, concerning Renaud and Gérard's acquisition and quarrying of 2000 pieces of sandstone each from the quarry at Thury.*[4]

A. Cartulary of Prémontré, fol. 104v.

B. Original not found.

---

5 Toyri *B*.

6 duodecimo *B*.

---

1 A Renaud Audent (or Odent) was mayor of Chauny, ca. 1230. Capaumont, *Notice historique sur la ville de Chauny*, 39.

2 A Gérard de Haironval (comm. Mondescourt, https://dicotopo.cths.fr/places/P76867184) also appears in a revenue list from the town of Chauny, 1260. Teulet et al, *Layettes du Trésor des chartes*, vol. 3, 524.

3 Chauny, arr. Laon, https://dicotopo.cths.fr/places/P32247131.

4 Thury, arr. Laon, https://dicotopo.cths.fr/places/P84789655.

Karta decani de Calniaci de eo quod Renoldus et Gerardus emerunt ab ecclesia gressios.

[P]etrus, decanus Calniaci, universis presentes literas inspecturis salutem in Domino. Cum Renoldus Au Dent et Gerardus de Haironval, burgenses Calniaci, necesse haberent gressos accipere et extrahere in domo de Thoiri que est ecclesie Premonstratensis, ipsi emerunt a prepositis ecclesie predicte, Egidio videlicet et Wermundo, quilibet eorum duo scilicet milia gressorum accipiendorum in domo predicta de Thoiri et de precio satisfecerunt eisdem prepositis ad voluntatem eorum. Inde quoniam dicta domus de Thoiri adeo libera est quod nullus ibidem gressios accipere possit vel extrahere absque licentia ecclesia supradicte, ne eidem ecclesie super libertate sua in posterum propter hoc prejudicium generetur, presentes literas in testimonium predicte emptionis ad petitionem tam dictorum prepositorum quam dictorum Renoldi Audent et Gerardi sigilli nostri fecimus munimine roborari. Datum Calniaci, mense aprili, anno Domini M° CC° XXX° VI°.

461

1217

Hugues,[1] *lord of Guny, makes known that his sister Cécile,*[2] *widow of Renaud de Magny, gave to Prémontré two* modii *of grain (*frumentum*) that she receives annually at the house of Thury,*[3] *in exchange for a meadow that Prémontré held near the* villa *of Varesnes.*[4] *Hugues consents as fief lord as does Renaud de Magny, Cécile's son, while Hugues accepts in exchange rights as fief lord over the newly acquired meadow.*

A. Cartulary of Prémontré, fols. 104v–105r.

B. Original, BnF, nouv. acq. lat. 2590, no. 49, previously sealed with two seals.

Karta Hugonis domini de Guni de eo quod Cecilia quitavit ecclesie Premonstrate II modios bladi.

[E]go Hugo, dominus de Guni,[5] notum facio tam presentibus quam futuris quod nobilis mulier Cecilia, soror mea, relicta quondam nobilis viri Renaldi

---

1 Hugues, lord of Guny (cant. Coucy-le-Château, https://dicotopo.cths.fr/places/P88745448), son of Guy II, lord of Guny, and Elizabeth d'Oulchy. Newman, *Seigneurs*, vol. 2, 98.

2 Cécile, daughter of Guy II, lord of Guny, and Elizabeth d'Oulchy, married Renaud de Magny (cant. Guiscard, https://dicotopo.cths.fr/places/P96954039), *avocatus* of Baboeuf. Newman, *Seigneurs*, vol. 2, 98.

3 Thury, arr. Laon, https://dicotopo.cths.fr/places/P84789655.

4 Varesnes, cant. Noyon, https://dicotopo.cths.fr/places/P62882188.

5 Guini *B*.

de Magniaco, dedit et quitavit in perpetuum ecclesie Premonstratensi duos modios frumenti quos percipiebat annuatim in domo de Thoiri[6] et recepit in excambium ipsorum duorum modiorum totum pratum quod habebat ecclesia Premonstratensis, tempore huius scripti, ante villam de Varennes hereditarie possidendum. Hoc autem excambium factum est de assensu meo de cuius feodo dicti duo modii descendebant et de assensu Renaldi de Magniaco, filii predicte sororis mee, eo siquidem tenore quod ego et idem Renaldus cum sepedicta sorore mea quitavimus in perpetuum quicquid juris habebamus vel habere poteramus quocumque modo in duobus modiis supradictis. Sciendum quoque quod sepedicta soror mea necnon et Renaldus, filius eius, posuerunt in feodo meo pratum illud quod a Premonstratensis ecclesia in excambium receperunt. In testimonium igitur huius rei ego et idem Renaldus presens scriptum super hoc factum sigillorum nostrorum appensione duximus roborandum. Actum anno incarnationis dominice M° CC° X° VII°.[7]

462

1212

Pierre, dean of Chauny, gives notice that the abbot and convent of Prémontré reached a compromise with Gobert de Dampcourt[1] following a dispute concerning the house and dependances of Thury.[2] Pierre, Soibert,[3] canon of Noyon, and Gautier Wasteblei mediated the dispute.

A. Cartulary of Prémontré, fol. 105r.

B. Original, BnF, Coll. Picardie 290, no. 28, previously sealed.

Karta decani Calniacensis de quadam compromissione in ipsum.

[E]go Petrus, decanus Calniacensis, notum facio universis presentes literas[4] inspecturis quod cum abbas et conventus Premonstratenses[5] ex una parte et Gobertus de Daencourt[6] ex parte altera super quadam querela que erat inter eos de domo et pertinentiis de Thoiri conpromisissent in me et dominum Soibertum,[7]

6 Toiri *B*.
7 millesimo ducentesimo septimodecimo *B*.

1 Dampcourt, arr. Laon, cant. Chauny, https://dicotopo.cths.fr/places/P76396213.
2 Thury, comm. Marest-Dampcourt, https://dicotopo.cths.fr/places/P84789655.
3 A Soibert, canon of Noyon, also appears in an act of 1191. AD Oise, G 1874.
4 Litteris *B*.
5 Premonstrati *B*.
6 Daencurt *B*.
7 Soybertum *B*.

canonicum Noviomensis, et Walterum Wasteblei[8] sub pena sexaginta librarum Parisiensium solvendarum parti adverse ab eo qui ab arbitrio resiliret, nos, habito consilio, diximus dictum nostrum et precepimus sub pena predicta ut hinc inde satisfacerent sibi ad invicem de quibusdam mobilibus que secundum dictum nostrum alterutrum debebantur infra quindecim dies a die prolati arbitrii proxime secuturos. Elapsis vero quindecim diebus et amplius, ad conquestionem predicti abbatis, citavi Gobertum, qui apud Noviomum in presentia mea conparens,[9] confessus est in jure quod non satisfecisset eidem abbati et conventui memorato secundum quod tenebatur infra tempus a me et a meis coarbitris constitutum et super hoc fecit emendam abbati tam ipse Gobertus quam Johannes[10] de Appelli miles qui cum aliis erat plegius pro Goberto. Abbas vero ad meas et aliorum preces posuit solutionem predicte pene insuff~~ic~~erentia salvo eo quod si petere vellet eum in posterum Gobertus per testes aliquos quos produceret, non posset convincere abbatem de solutione vel de quitantia facta, nisi frater Hugo, tunc temporis provisor Premonstrati, et frater Ingelrannus, tunc temporis magister Bonolii, de solutione vel de quitancia testimonium perhiberent. Ne igitur de hoc facto possit in posterum dubitari, presentes litteras super hoc[11] factas emisi sigilli mei inpressione munitas. Actum anno incarnationis dominice M° CC° XII°.[12]

463

1157

Baudouin [II],[1] bishop of Noyon, makes known that Martel[2] d'Abbécourt gave in alms to the Premonstratensian brothers of Thury[3] the use of all the pastures pertaining to his territory and woods, as well as the use of his curtis *and adjacent mill. Prémontré then concedes to Martel the use of its pastures at Thury.*

A. Cartulary of Prémontré, fol. 105r.

B. Original not found.

---

8 Wasteble *B*.

9 comparens *B*.

10 Jean, lord of Appilly (cant. Noyon, https://dicotopo.cths.fr/places/P38602761), knight (d. bef. 1231), possibly the son of Robert, lord of Appilly, and Emmeline. Ponthieux, "Notes historiques sur Appilly," 15.

11 hac *B*.

12 millesimo ducentesimo duodecimo *B*.

---

1 Baudouin II de Boulogne, abbot of the Augustinian abbey of Saint-Eloi-Fontaine, ca. 1130–ca. 1139, and bishop of Noyon, 1148–67. *GC* IX, col. 1126.

2 Geoffroi Martel, knight and lord of Abbécourt (cant. Chauny, https://dicotopo.cths.fr/places/P64472484), 1154–7. Melleville, *DH*, vol. 1, 2.

3 Thury, arr. Laon, https://dicotopo.cths.fr/places/P84789655.

Karta Balduini Noviomensis episcopi de elemosina Martelli de Abecourt.

[I]n nomine sancte et cetera. Quia labili hominum memorie facile rerum gestarum subrepit oblivio necessario mos inolevit ut scripto tradantur que ad posterorum noticiam transmittenda judicantur. Iccirco ego Balduinus, Dei gratia Noviomorum dictus episcopus, notum fieri volo tam futuris quam presentibus quod Martellus de Abecourt contulit in elemosinam Premonstrate ecclesie ad usus fratrum commorantium ad Thoiri omnia pascua ad districtum suum pertinencia et nemora sua, ad omnimodos usus eiusdem curtis et molendini adjacentis. Concessit etiam ut omnes qui illic ad molendum venire voluerint, libere et licite et sine omni inpedimento venire possint viam quoque suam propter aisiamenta curtis et molendini facta inter Thoiri et Mares[4] omnino liberam et ab omni exactione quietam, omnia etiam aisiamenta ad districtum de Abecourt pertinencia excepta piscatura. Ecclesia vero Premonstratensis concessit eidem Martello ad usus suos et hominum suorum ad Abecourt commanentium omnia pascua de Toiri ita tamen quod fratribus si voluerint in pascuis suis prata facere licebit similiter et Martello in susis. Factum est hoc assensu et concessione filiorum suorum Martelli et Radulphi sub his testibus Alulfo[5] abbate Calniacensi, Petro priore, Johanne fratre Martelli, Hugone de Unnolia, Jacobo de Calmont, Werrico armigero predicti Johannis, Adone clerico, Renero filio Udonis, Waszone qui cognominatus est Pater, Odone filio Mensendis, Balduino et Hugone conversis. Quod ne ulla in posterum valeat perturbatione cassari, sigilli nostri impressione presentem paginam communimus. Et in perturbatores nisi resipuerint anathematis sentenciam promulgamus. Actum anno incarnati verbo M° C° L° VII°, epacta VII^a^, indictione V^a^.

4 Marest-Dampcourt, cant. Chauny, https://dicotopo.cths.fr/places/P37392982.

5 Alulphe, previously archdeacon of Thérouanne and later abbot of the Arroasian Augustinian community of Sainte-Marie de Chauny, ca. 1135–ca. 1162. During his abbatiate, the brothers moved from Chauny to Saint-Éloi-Fontaine. Poissonnier, "L'Abbaye de St-Éloi-Fontaine ou de Commenchon," 271–2.

6 Simon I de Vermandois (d. 1148) was the son of Hugues I and Adélaïde, count and countess of Vermandois and Valois, and bishop of Noyon, 1123–42.

7 Thury, comm. Marest-Dampcourt, https://dicotopo.cths.fr/places/P84789655.

464

1137

Simon [I],[1] *bishop of Noyon, makes known the circumstances of a dispute concerning land at Thury*[2] *that Gaubert de Laon held in fief from the lord Aubry*[3] *de Roye. Gaubert had subinfeudated the land at Thury without Aubry's permission. Godon,*[4] *son of Gautier* Grossus *de Viry, who held the land and its appurtenences (including a woman named Hersende, her children, a mill, meadows, pastureland, and all pertinent rights of* justicia*) from Gaubert, sold half of the territory to Adon*[5] *de Guny, who in turn, thinking his purchase legitimate, ceded half of the land he had acquired to his son-in-law, Jean Gobart. To resolve the resulting dispute, the land and appurtenances at Thury were given in alms to Prémontré, and in return Godon, Adon, and Jean received a* census *of eight* modii *of grain (*frumentum*), measure of Chauny,*[6] *to be divided between the three men.*

A. Cartulary of Prémontré, fols. 105r–105v.
B. Original, AD Aisne, H 807, previously sealed.
EDITION: Pycke and Vleeschouwers, *Actes*, 405–6.

Karta Symonis Noviomensis episcopi de dono et elemosina Godonis filii Galteri de Viri.

[I]n nomine sancte et individue Trinitatis. Quicquid legitimarum personarum testimonio perhibetur licet satis firmitatis habere videatur tamen quodam quasi vallo munitur id quod episcopalis auctoritatis assertione confirmatur. Idcirco ego Symon, Dei gratia Noviomensis episcopus, notum fore volo tam posteris quam modernis quod Godo, filius Galteri de Viri, qui Grossus agnominabatur, territorium de Thoiri super Ysaram et mulierem unam, scilicet Hersendem, cum

1 Simon I de Vermandois (d. 1148) was the son of Hugues I and Adélaïde, count and countess of Vermandois and Valois, and bishop of Noyon, 1123–42.

2 Thury, comm. Marest-Dampcourt, https://dicotopo.cths.fr/places/P84789655.

3 Aubry, lord of Roye and Becquigny, was the *dapifer* of Raoul, count of Vermandois in the 1130s/40s. He was the husband of one Mathilde, and brother of Wermond, lord of Cessoy. Tock and Milis, *Monumenta Arroasiensia*, 242–3; Guyotjeannin, *Episcopus*, 220; Newman, *Seigneurs*, vol. 2, 299; Newman, *Homblières*, 110. He is likely the same Aubry de Roye who appears in **300**, **398**, **442**, and **464**.

4 Godon de Viry's wife and children must have all died (or entered the church?) between 1137 and 1142, when per **452** his heir is Raoul de Sommete.

5 Adon, lord of Guny (cant. Coucy-le-Château, https://dicotopo.cths.fr/places/P88745448), son of Guy I, lord of Guny, and Elizabeth. He married a sister of Sarracin, castellan of La Fère. Newman, *Seigneurs*, vol. 2, 95–7.

6 Chauny, arr. Laon, https://dicotopo.cths.fr/places/P32247131.

progenie sua et molendinum, prata et pascua, ipsius etiam loci justiciam et cetera ad ipsum locum pertinentia a Walberto de Lauduno, Radulphi[7] dapiferi filio, in feodum tenebat cuius partem dimidiam, sine assensu predicti Walberti, Adoni de Guni vendidit, hac conditione inter se habita quod Ado a Godone eam in feodum teneret; ipse autem Ado sue partis dimidie dimidiam partem Johanni Gobart,[8] filio Fulconis Rufi de Breteni,[9,10] pro sua filia quam ei in uxorem dederat, concessit. Hac de causa orta contentione inter predictum Walbertum et prememoratum Godonem et prenominatum Adonem, Walbertus illud quod in predicto territorio habebat, domino Albrico de Roy[11] concessit eo pactionis vinculo quod ipse Walbertus ab eodem Albrico idipsum quod ibi habuerat, in feodum reciperet et teneret. Tandem pro pace facienda et pro redemptione animarum suarum consequenda Premonstrate ecclesie Sancte Marie et Sancti Johannis Baptiste predictum territorium et omnia ad ipsum pertinentia tempore Hugonis, eiusdem ecclesie abbatis, predictus Godo prenominatus,[12] Ado prenominatus etiam, Johannes Gobarz in perpetuum habenda censualiter contulerunt scilicet pro octo modiis frumenti singulis annis secundum Calniacensem mensuram ita quod Godo pro sua dimidia parte quatuor inde modios recipiet de alia dimidia parte, Ado duos modios et Johannes Gobarz duos modios. Hoc autem factum est, concedente Walberto a cuius feodo ipsum territorium ad Godonem descendebat, concedente Walberto a cuius feodo ipsum territorium ad Godonem descendebat.[13] Concedente etiam Albrico cui Walbertus illud quod suum in eo erat dederat et id ipsum ab eodem in feodo tenendum receperat sub his testibus affuit Alardus[14] de Porta, Petrus et Matheus, ipsius filii, Hugo Furnerus, Marcellus filius Manasses, Marcellus filius Marcelli, Robertus Cretinz, Hoherus Senex, Hergoldus de Calniaco et eius frater Eustachius, Albricus[15] Pellez, Baldricus de Crespini[16] et eius frater Gunfridus. Hoc autem quisquis temeraria presumptione violare vel inmutare intenderit, anathema sit. Actum est hoc anno incarnationis dominice M° C° XXX° VII°, epacta VII^{a}, concurrente III°.[17]

---

7 Radulfi *B*.

8 Gobarz *B*.

9 Bretenni *B*.

10 Brétigny, cant. Noyon, https://dicotopo.cths.fr/places/P36981434.

11 Roi *B*.

12 prememoratus *B*.

13 *Add.* concedente Walberto a cuius feodo ipsum territorium ad Godonem descendebat *A*.

14 Alard I de Ham (or de la Porte), knight of Ham; husband of Helvide. He also appears in **91**, **298**, **334**, **385**, **415**, and **452**.

15 Aubry Pellez de Chauny also appears in an 1137 act of Joscelin, bishop of Soissons. Guyotjeannin et al., *Le chartrier de l'abbaye prémontrée de Saint-Yved de Braine (1134–1250)*, 162–3.

16 Crépigny, comm. Caillouël-Crépigny, https://dicotopo.cths.fr/places/P31528875.

17 *Om.* I° *A*; IIII°, indictione 1^{a} *B*.

465

1164

Philippe [I],[1] *abbot of Prémontré, makes known that lord Itier*[2] *d'Épagny gave Prémontré all the land that he possessed inside the stream at Moulin-Chevreux,*[3] *Marest,*[4] *and Abbécourt*[5] *for them to cultivate as they wished, reserving only part of the harvest and tithe.*

A. Cartulary of Prémontré, fol. 105v.
B. Original, AN, L 995, no. 30, previously sealed.

Karta Philipi, abbatis Premonstratensis, de elemosina Iteri de Espaigni de terra de Mares et Habecurt.

[I]n nomine Patris et cetera.[6] Ego Philippus, Dei gratia Premonstrate ecclesie dictus abbas, notum facio tam futuris quam presentibus quod dominus Iterus de Espaigni[7] dedit ecclesie nostre omnem terram quam habebat intra rivum de Molinseurous et Mares et Habecourt excolendam firma manu ad terciam partem, excepta parte messoris et decime. Quando vero fructus de terra colligentur, ducentur ad domum nostram de Thoiri et post triturationem mensurabuntur ad sextarium et habebit vas tercium et ducetur ei ad domum suam de Calni vel apud Meinencamp.[8] Si famulus eius in domo nostra fuerit in messe, de suo vivet. Si non fuerit in messe mandabitur in partitione que fiet post triturationem. Si inducendo auferretur[9] segetes eius conducentibus causa ipsius non restauraremus ei. Si sue cum nostris deperirent aliquo casu non restauraremus ei. Si communis fuerit guerra in regione ut in vicino excoli non possint terre nostre et aliorum et sua exculta non fuerit, non querelabit inde ecclesia[10] nec poterit illud vendere, in vadium ponere nisi prefate ecclesie, si ecclesia inde dare voluerit quantum alius nec elemosinam inde faciet nisi ecclesie nostre.

---

1 Philippe I de Reims, abbot of Prémontré, 1161–71.
2 Itier, lord of Épagny (Épagny, cant. Vic-sur-Aisne, https://dicotopo.cths.fr/places/P39948319); husband of Elizabeth. Melleville, *DH*, vol. 1, 353; Newman, *Seigneurs*, vol. 2, 120.
3 Le Moulin-Chevreux, comm. Ognes, https://dicotopo.cths.fr/places/P67319306.
4 Marest-Dampcourt, cant. Chauny, https://dicotopo.cths.fr/places/P37392982.
5 Abbécourt, cant. Chauny, https://dicotopo.cths.fr/places/P64472484.
6 *Add.* cetera *A*; Filii et Spiritus Sancti, amen *B*.
7 Espangi *B*.
8 Meinencanp *B*.
9 auferrentur *B*.
10 ecclesiam *B*.

Huius rei testes sunt: Gerardus de Marisel,[11] Robertus de Crespigni,[12,13] maior Iteri, Radulphus[14] filius eius, Geroldus de Habecourt, Hulduinus de Mares, Aubertus Faber, Lorinus filius eius, de fratribus eius[15] Waudinus et Robertus. Actum anno verbi incarnati M° C° sexagesimo[16] IIII°.

466

1221

The apostolic delegates Raoul [II][1] *and R., abbot and prior respectively of Saint-Éloi de Noyon, together with Adam*[2] *de Paris, canon of Noyon, mediate the dispute between the abbot and convent of Prémontré and Jean d'Ognes.*[3] *The dispute concerns the boundaries and rights of their respective properties in the marshland between Marest and Dampcourt, and of the ditches which enclose the cultivated lands at Marest,*[4] *Dampcourt, and the Premonstratensian house of Thury.*[5]

A. Cartulary of Prémontré, fol. 105v.
B. Original, AN, L 995, no. 69, previously sealed with three seals.

Karta cuiusdam conpositionis inter ecclesiam Premonstratensem et Johannem militem de Oisni super quodam marisco.

R[adulphus], Sancti Eligii Noviomensis dictus abbas, et R., eiusdem loci dictus prior, omnibus presentes litteras inspecturis volumus esse notum quod cum querela que erat inter viros religiosos abbatem et conventum Premonstratensem ex parte una et nobilem virum Johannem de Oisni militem ex parte altera

11 Marizelle, comm. Bichancourt, https://dicotopo.cths.fr/places/P06012580.
12 Crespengi *B*.
13 Crépigny, comm. Caillouël-Crépigny, https://dicotopo.cths.fr/places/P31528875.
14 Radulfus *B*.
15 nostris *B*.
16 LX° *B*.

1 Raoul II, abbot of the Benedictine abbey of Saint-Éloi de Noyon, ca. 1197–1232. *GC* IX, col. 1068.
2 An "Adam de Parisius, dictus Magister, canonicus Noviomensis" also appears in a 1222 act in the cartulary of Ourscamp. Peigné-Delacourt, *Cartulaire de l'Abbaye de Notre-Dame d'Ourscamp de l'ordre de Cîteaux, fondée en 1129 au diocèse de Noyon*, 25.
3 Ognes, cant. Chauny, https://dicotopo.cths.fr/places/P68696739.
4 Marest-Dampcourt, cant. Chauny, https://dicotopo.cths.fr/places/P37392982.
5 Marest-Dampcourt, cant. Chauny, https://dicotopo.cths.fr/places/P37392982.

super quodam marisco qui est inter villas de Mares et de Doencourt[6] et fossata que claudunt agriculturas ipsarum villarum ex una parte et inter fossata que claudunt agriculturas domus de Thoiri ex parte altera, nobis et viro discreto D. de Cardolio, scolastico Noviomensi auctoritate apostolica commissa fuisset, tandem pro bono pacis, de consilio proborum virorum, partes de communi assensu in nos et virum prudentem magistrum Adam de Parisius, canonicum Noviomensem, conpromiserunt tali modo quod, inquisita veritate a testibus hinc inde productis et habito prudentem virorum consilio, arbitrium nostrum pronunciaremus, de plano jus ecclesie disterminantes a jure domini Johannis. Sed arbitrio nostro nondum[7] prolato, mediantibus bonis viris coram nobis duobus, amicabilis conpositio[8] inter partes intercessit in hunc modum quod a poncello qui dicitur de La Cloiete usque ad salicem que est in fine clausure domus de Thoiri versus villam de Mares recta linea, sicut metis positis disterminatum est, ex parte fossatarum que claudunt agriculturas de Thoiri, erit mariscus ecclesie Premonstratensis cum omni districtu et jurisdictione ita quod quicquid voluerint, fratres ecclesie facere poterunt ibidem, nec reclamare aut contradicere poterit dominus Johannes nec heredes ipsius aut homines sui. Si vero fuerit ibi communis pastura, dictus Johannes et eius heredes necnon et homines sui animalia sua in eadem pastura libere ponent nec licebit ecclesie ipsos prohibere. Mariscus qui a metis premissis protenditur versus villas de Mares et de Doencourt[9] erit domini Johannis cum omni districtu et jurisdictione ita quod ipse et heredes sui facere poterunt in eo quicquid voluerint nec predicti fratres Premonstratenses reclamare poterunt aut contradicere, sed si fuerit ibidem communis pastura, fratribus iamdictis licebit animalia sua sine difficultate qualibet ponere in eadem, nec prohibere eos poterunt dominus Johannes aut heredes ipsius nec etiam homines eorum. Adjectum est insuper de communi partium assensu quod siquis de predicto marisco adversus ecclesiam premissam questionem moveret, dominus Johannes aut eius heredes eum non juvabunt in prejudicium et gravamen ecclesie. Similiter ecclesia nullum juvabit de predicto marisco contra sepedictum J[ohannem] militem aut eius heredes. De tenenda igitur conpositione[10] ista abbas Premonstratensis asseruit et affirmavit in verbo veritatis pro se et conventu suo quod eam ratam et firmam haberet et dominus Johannes per fidem corporaliter prestitam ad hoc ipsum se astrinxit. Per istam etiam conpositionem[11] sopite sunt et quitate

6 Doencort *B.*
7 nundum *B.*
8 compositio *B.*
9 Doencort *B.*
10 compositio *B.*
11 compositionem *B.*

omnes lites[12] et controversie que, occasione huius litis,[13] antea mote fuerant. Sciendum est etiam quod magister Adam de Parisius, canonicus Noviomensis, qui fuit tercius coarbiter noster conpositionem[14] istam gratam habuit et acceptam et sigillum suum apposuit litteris istis cum nostris que in perpetuam huius conpositionis[15] memoriam presentibus literis fecimus apponi. Actum anno gratie millesimo ducentesimo vicesimo primo.

467

August, 1212.

Étienne [I],[1] bishop of Noyon, makes known that abbot G[ervais][2] and the brothers of Prémontré reached an agreement with the knights Gérard d'Arcy and Jean[3] de Trugny concerning lands situated in the diocese of Noyon that the Premonstratensian brothers at Thury[4] claimed to have received previously for their own cultivation, together with a third of the land's revenue.

A. Cartulary of Prémontré, fol. 106r.
B. Original, BnF, Coll. Picardie 290, no. 29.

Karta Stephani Noviomensis episcopi de conpositione inter ecclesiam Premonstratem et Gerardum de Arceio et Johannem de Truigni.

[S]tephanus, Dei gratia Noviomensis episcopus, presentibus et futuris in perpetuum. Quia scriptum ordinarii judicis super hiis que coram ipso vel gesta vel recognita sunt, in jure solet et debet ad perpetuam facti memoriam et ad perhibendum veritati testimonium tam in proprio quam in alieno foro per se sufficere. Idcirco[5] per hoc autenticum et publicum instrumentum, notum fieri

12 littes *B*.
13 littis *B*.
14 compositionem *B*.
15 compositionis *B*.

1 Étienne de Villebéon (or de Nemours), son of Gautier de Villebéon, lord of La Chapelle-Gauthier and Nemours, and Aveline, was bishop of Noyon, 1188–1221.
2 Gervais, abbot of the Premonstratensian abbeys of Saint-Just-en-Chaussée, 1199–1205, Thenailles, 1205–9, and Prémontré, 1209–20, and bishop of Séez, 1220–8. *MP* II, 401, 527, 565; Cheney, "Gervase, Abbot of Prémontré."
3 A Jean de Trugny appears in the cartulary of Ourscamp in acts dated 1203. BnF, MS lat. 5473, fols. 54v, 139r, 139v.
4 Thury, arr. Laon, https://dicotopo.cths.fr/places/P84789655.
5 iccirco *B*.

volumus universis quod cum inter religiosos viros G[ervasium], abbatem et fratres Premonstratenses ex una parte et Gerardum de Arceio simulque Johannem de Truigni, milites, ex altera super quibusdam terris infra nostram dyocesim constitutis quas idem abbas et fratres ad terciam partem et ad firmam se olim excolendas suscepisse dicebant, quod tamen ipsi milites denegabant, aliquamdiu controversia mota fuisset postmodum assensu mutuo et de consilio bonorum virorum amicabiliter inter ipsos conpositione[6] formata tandemque ratione rei de qua agebatur, partibus in nostra presencia constitutis, utrinque fuit recognitum sollempniter in jure quod terre ille que dicebantur Castellanorum et quas fratres Premonstratenses apud curtem de Thoiri manentes diu ad terciam partem excoluerant, reddite sunt absolute ab eisdem abbate et fratribus militibus supradictis; ipsi quoque milites tam pro bono pacis quam in donum elemosine de terris eisdem dederunt ecclesie Premonstratensi undecim sexterliatas ad mensuram Calniaci libere et sine qualibet consuetudinis vel juris retentione perpetuo et proprie possidendas. Ut igitur huius modi tam conpositio[7] quam elemosina cum debita sollempnitate coram nobis recognita episcopalis auctoritatis et inconcusse perpetuitatis obtineat firmitatem, scriptum istud huius rei causa confectum sigilli nostri munimine fecimus roborari. Actum mense augusto, anno Domini M° CC° XII°.[8]

468

1174–89.[1]

Hugues [II],[2] abbot of Prémontré, makes known the agreement reached between Prémontré and dean Werry and the chapter of Saint-Quentin whereby they agree to share possession of the chapel of Saint-Nicolas.

A. Cartulary of Prémontré, fol. 106r.

B. Original not found.

Other Manuscript Copies: Cartulary of the Chapter of Saint-Quentin, BnF, Latin 11070, fols. 98r–99r (14th c.).

6 compositione *B*.

7 compositio *B*.

8 millesimo ducentesimo duodecimo *B*.

1 Based on the dates of Hugues II's abbatial tenure.

2 Hugues II de Douai, abbot of the Premonstratensian abbey of Cuissy, 1161–5, and abbot of Prémontré, 1174–89. *MP* II, 497.

Karta abbatis Premonstratensis et decani Sancti Quintini de capella Sancti Quintini ad Sanctem Nicholaum.

[I]n nomine sancte et cetera. Ego Hugo, Dei gratia Premonstrati dictus abbas totumque capitulum nostrum et ego Werricus eiusdem clementia Sancti Quintini decanus simulque capitulum nostrum presentibus et futuris salutem in perpetuum. Plerumque calumpniam in rebus bene gestis movet oblivio et idcirco dignum duximus cyrographi scripto commendari quod notum fieri volumus future posteritati. Igitur orta fuit quondam querela inter ecclesiam Premonstratensem et ecclesiam Sancti Quintini de capella Sancti Nicholai. Ut autem inter predictas ecclesias discordiarum turbo penitus sopiretur et pax atque dilectio inter eas a modo reformaretur, presentibus B[artholomeo],[3] Belvacense et Stephano,[4] Meldense episcopis et F., decano Remensi, a domino Papa super eadem querela judicibus delegatis, inter prefatas ecclesias conpositio talis intercessit quod Premonstratensis ecclesia medietatem capelle Sancti Quintini[5] et ecclesia Sancti Quintini aliam medietatem eiusdem capelle possidebit. Consona autem diffinitione decretum est quod, assensu utriusque capituli, Premonstratensis scilicet et Sancti Quintini, sacerdos in predicta capella inponetur et exponetur de utrique partibus, vicariam accipiens et quicquid capelle collatum fuerit vel sacerdoti oblatum vel etiam dimissum per medium partietur et unaquaque ecclesia, Premonstrati videlicet et Sancti Quintini, medietatem suam sortietur et si quid in eadem capella restaurandum vel reedificandum fuerit, communiter de utrisque partibus reficietur et siquid ad restaurationem vel ornatum capelle in elemosinam datum fuerit, soli capelle remanebit. Si autem capellanus proprium capelle catallum subtraxerit vel furtive abstulerit justicie abbatis et decani subjacebit. Preterea statutum est quod Premonstratenses annuatim in festo Sancti Remigii canon~~es~~icis Sancti Quintini XVII solidos et VI denarios persolvent et pro decima de Germaniis quam canonici Premonstratensibus liberam concesserunt XX[ti] modios frumenti, modio VI nummos minus valente, meliore frumento ad mensuram que erat apud Sanctum Quintinum anno verbi incarnati M° C° LXX° I° ipsis canonicis Premonstratensibus singulis annis similiter dabunt et propria vectura apud Sanctum Quintinum a kalendis septembris usque ad festum Sancti Martini conducent

3 Barthélemy de Montcornet (d. 1175), son of Hugues de Montcornet and Béatrice de Reynel, was archdeacon of Laon from 1133, treasurer of Laon from 1137, and chancellor of Laon, 1141–4; later archdeacon of Reims; and bishop of Beauvais, 1162–75. Guyotjeannin, *Episcopus*, 131; Dufour-Malbezin, *Actes*, 30.

4 Étienne de la Chapelle, son of Josselin II de Villemomble, lord of Beaumont, and Herceline de Villebéon, was bishop of Meaux, 1162–71, and archbishop of Bourges, 1171–3.

5 *Sic A, read* Nicholai.

nec huic censure Premonstratenses renuntiare poterunt nec canonici eos infestare. Censum etiam de Germaniis XL[ta] et octo solidos capellano Sancti Nicholai antiquitus deputatum a modo canonici non reclamabunt. Ut autem rata et irrefragabilis permaneat ista conpositio, sigillis utriusque capituli eam muniri fecimus et legitimarum testimonio personarum corroboravimus. S. Yvonis,[6] abbatis Sancti Dyonisii. S. Symonis de Sancto Dyonisio. S. Johannis, prioris de Premonstrato. S. Grinberti, subprioris. S. Leodegarii. S. Clarenbaldi, sacerdotum. S. Stephani. S. Hugonis. S. Willelmi, diaconi. S. Gerardi. S. Wiberti. S. Albodi, subdiaconi. S. canonicorum Sancti Quintini. S. Bernardi. S. Hugonis. S. Gerardi, sacerdotum. S. Wentonis. S. Thome. S. Grinbaldi, diaconi. S. Raineri. S. Udonis. S. Walteri. S. Evrardi.

469

February, 1232.

Guy, lord of Estouilly,[1] *makes known that following a dispute with the church of Prémontré, he gave Prémontré his rights on the tithe of Estouilly, of which two-thirds belonged to Prémontré and a third to Saint-Barthélemy of Noyon. Philippa, wife of Guy, in exchange for ceding her rights of* dotalicium, *received two* modii *of grain (*bladus*) from the mill at Estouilly.*

A. Cartulary of Prémontré, fols. 106r–106v.
B. Original not found.

Karta Guidonis domini de Estouilli de herbergagio decime de Estouilli que pertinet ad ecclesiam Premonstratem.

[I]n nomine sancte et cetera. Ego Guido, dominus de Estouilli, notum facio universis tam presentibus quam futuris quod cum discordia inter me ex una parte et Premonstratensem ecclesiam ex altera emersisset pro eo quod clamabam herbergagium decime de Estouilli cuius due partes ad ipsam Premonstratensem ecclesiam et tercia pars ad ecclesiam Sancti Bartholomei Noviomensis pertinere noscuntur, in qua videlicet decima percipiebam annuatim jure hereditario duos

6 Yves II, abbot of Saint-Denis (d. 1173). The discrepancy between the attested date of Yves's death and the beginning of Hugues's abbacy may indicate a conflict between old and new dating styles.

1 Estouilly, cant. Ham, https://dicotopo.cths.fr/places/P96663971.

modios bladi eiusdem decime et quadraginta gelimas straminis de communi; tandem ductus consilio saniori quitavi in perpetuum eidem Premonstratensi ecclesie quicquid in predicta decima seu duobus modiis antedictis seu stramine sine herbergagio seu etiam quolibet alio modo habebam vel habere poteram, laudante et spontanea voluntate consentiente Philippa, uxore mea, et quitante jus dotalicii quod habebat in premissis, facta sibi recompensatione condigna et sufficiente de dotalicio suo ad duos modios bladi in molendino meo de Estoulli et fidem prestiti corporalem quod nec per me nec per alium ipsam ecclesiam super premissis omnibus decetero molestabo nec queram artem vel ingenium per quod ista quitatio infringi possit aliquatenus vel rescindi. In cuius rei testimonium et perpetuam firmitatem presentem kartam predicte Premonstratensi ecclesie tradidi sigilli mei munimine commutniani.[2] Actum mense februario, anno gratie M° CC° tricesimo secundo.

470

January, 1218.

Jean des Monts, fief lord, makes known that the church of Prémontré reached an agreement with his kinsman, the knight Simon des Monts. Simon cedes to Prémontré all his rights over the land at Bonneuil[1] *that he had acquired from the late Jean de Villiers; and in return, Simon receives 22* sexterlatae *of land at Golancourt.*[2] *(See* ***478****.)*

A. Cartulary of Prémontré, fol. 106v.
B. Original not found.

Karta Johannis de Montibus de quodam excambio inter ecclesiam Premonstratensem et dominum Symonem in territorio Bonolii.

[E]go Johannes de Montibus notum facio tam futuris quam presentibus per hoc scriptum quod cum Symon de Montibus, miles, consanguineus et homo meus, haberet olim terragium in novem modiatis terre et dimidia Parisiensis plus minusve in territorio Bonolii quod acquisierat per excambium a bone memorie domino Johanne de Vileirs, milite, ecclesia Premonstratensis et idem Symon

2 *Sic A, read* communivi.

1 Bonneuil, cant. Ham, https://dicotopo.cths.fr/places/P66750585.
2 Golancourt, cant. Guiscard, https://dicotopo.cths.fr/places/P75999303.

pro bono pacis et pro utilitate utriusque partis et ad tollendum hinc inde peccatum, fecerunt quoddam excambium in hac forma: ecclesia Premonstratensis dedit et contradidit dicto Symoni viginti et duas sexterlatas terre in territorio de Gollencourt hereditario in perpetuum jure tenendas; ipse autem Symon de assensu meo de quo tenebat dictum terragium in feodo dedit et quitavit ecclesie memorate quicquid juris habebat vel in ipso terragio vel in fundo vel in justicia terre de qua terragium solvebatur perpetuo jure tenendum ita quod nec ipse nec ego nec heredes nostri in terra predicta vel in aliquibus pertinentibus ad terram ipsam aliquid poterimus reclamare. Et ut hoc excambium firmiter teneretur, sepedictus Symon posuit terram quam recepit ab ecclesia Premonstratensis in feodo meo de quo tenebat terragium et ego dedi ecclesie Premonstratensis literas meas de confirmatione excambii et ecclesia dedit Symoni literas sigillo suo signatas. Super hoc autem excambio tenetur ecclesia Premonstratensis Symoni et Symon ipsi ecclesie portare legitimam warandiam secundum quod lex portabit. Actum mense januario, anno gratie M° CC° octavo decimo.

471

1208

Étienne,[1] *dean, and the chapter of the church of Nesle resolve their dispute with the brothers of the church of Prémontré concerning the possession of a field called* Pouletière. *The* magister hospitalarii *will pay the church of Prémontré one* sextaria *of grain (*frumentum*) each year, while the church of Nesle will retain possession of the land.*

A. Cartulary of Prémontré, fol. 106v.
B. Original, AD Oise, Hs 1376, sealed on a double strip of parchment with a fragment of the surviving seal in brown wax.

Karta decani et capituli Nigellensis de pace inter nos et ecclesiam Premonstratem de campo qui dicitur Pouletiere.

[E]go Stephanus, decanus, et capitulum ecclesie Nigellensis omnibus notum facimus per hoc scriptum quod cum querela esset inter nos ex una parte et fratres ecclesie Premonstratensis ex altera super quandam terram que campus Pouletiere dicitur[2] tandem talis inter nos et ipsos fratres concordia intervenit quod

1 Étienne, dean of the chapter of Nesle, by 1191–aft. 1208.
2 nominatur *B*.

de assensu et voluntate nostra magister hospitalarie unum sextarium frumenti ad mensuram eiusdem ville annis singulis in festo Sancti Remigii perpetuo solvere ipsis fratribus tenebitur et ipsa terra de qua querela erat, nobis possidenda in perpetuum remanebit. Quod si forte in huius[3] solutione prefatus magister defecerit, ipsum sextarium frumenti eisdem fratribus nichilominus persolvemus. Ut autem hoc ratum permaneat atque firmum, presentem paginam sigilli nostri impressione volumus roborari. Actum anno Domini M° CC° VIII°.

472

1203

Étienne [I],[1] *bishop of Noyon, makes known that Lambert Matons and his son Thierry gave to the Premonstratensian house of Bonneuil the* serganteria *of Bonneuil, seven* solidi *of* census, *and all rights that they held over the same house, in return for which the brothers of Bonneuil give them annually five* modii *of grain (*frumentum*), measure of Collezy.*[2]

A. Cartulary of Prémontré, fol. 106v.

*B*¹. Original (chirograph), AD Oise, H 5999, previously sealed. In the right margin and beginning at the top, the bottom half of the letters of the word CYROGRAPHUM. (This charter likely belonged to Lambert Matons and his son Thierry.)

*B*². Original (chirograph), AD Oise, H 5999, previously sealed on a double strip of parchment. In the left margin and beginning at the top, the upper half of the letters of the word CYROGRAPHUM. (This charter likely belonged to Prémontré, based on dorsal annotations.)

Karta Stephani Noviomensis episcopi de quitatione quam fecit Lambertus Matonis et filius eius super serganteria et VII solidos.

[S]tephanus, Dei gratia Noviomensis episcopus, omnibus ad quos litere iste pervenerint, notum fieri volumus quod Lambertus cognomine Matons, et Terricus, filius eius, in presentia nostra constituti serganteriam et septem solidos de censu et quicquid habebant juris in domo Bonolii quitaverunt et quod decetero nil in eadem domo reclamarent fide interposita concesserunt ita tamen quod,

3 huiusmodi *B*.

1 Étienne de Villebéon (or de Nemours), son of Gautier de Villebéon, lord of La Chapelle-Gauthier and Nemours, and Aveline, was bishop of Noyon, 1188–1221.

2 Collezy, comm. Berlancourt, https://dicotopo.cths.fr/places/P68465476.

singulis annis, fratres de Bonolio eis quinque modios frumenti de meliori post sementem in festo Beati Remigii ad mensuram qua redditur modiagium de Colesi, reddent et infra Castrum Hamensis propriis sumptibus ubicumque ipsi voluerint adducent. In huius rei testimonium presens scriptum nostro fecimus sigillo roborari. Actum anno Domini M° CC°[3] tercio.

473

April, 1209.

Étienne [I],[1] *bishop of Noyon, makes known that Joubert, son of the knight Gilles*[2] *de Brétigny, upon the advice of his uncle, the knight Jean*[3] *de Brétigny, recognizes that the church of Prémontré owes him only three* modii *of grain (*bladus*), measure of Ham, on the land at Golancourt*[4] *that it had held from his ancestors, rather than the four* modii *that Joubert had claimed. This was assented to and approved by Joubert's brother, Nicolas, from whom the fief descended.*

A. Cartulary of Prémontré, fols. 106v–107r.

B. Original (chirograph), AD Oise, Hs 1390, sealed on a double strip of white leather with the brown wax seal of the bishop. In the upper margin and beginning at the left, the bottom half of the letters of the word CYROGRAPHUM.

Karta Noviomensis episcopi de quadam conpositione inter ecclesiam Premonstratem et Joibertum filium Egidii de Bretigni.

[E]go Stephanus, Dei gratia Noviomensis episcopus, omnibus in perpetuum. Notum facimus universis presentes litteras inspecturis quod, cum inter

3 millesimo ducentesimo *B*[1], *B*[2].

1 Étienne de Villebéon (or de Nemours), son of Gautier de Villebéon, lord of La Chapelle-Gauthier and Nemours, and Aveline, was bishop of Noyon, 1188–1221.

2 Gilles de Brétigny appears as a witness in an 1177 act of Conon, count of Soissons. Newman, *Seigneurs*, vol. 2, 162.

3 A Jean, lord of Brétigny (cant. Noyon, https://dicotopo.cths.fr/places/P36981434), appears in acts of the abbey of Ourscamp in 1204, while a Jean de Brétigny, knight, d. ca. 1235, was buried at Ourscamp. Peigné-Delacourt, *Cartulaire de l'Abbaye de Notre-Dame d'Ourscamp de l'ordre de Cîteaux, fondée en 1129 au diocèse de Noyon*, 361, 505; Bouchot, *Inventaire des dessins exécutés pour Roger de Gaignières et conservés aux Départements des estampes et des manuscrits*, vol. 1, 307.

4 Golancourt, cant. Guiscard, https://dicotopo.cths.fr/places/P75999303.

Premonstratensem ecclesiam ex una parte et Joibertum[5] filium quondam Egidii de Bretigni[6] militis, ex parte altera, verteretur questio super eo quod idem Joisbertus dicebat sibi deberi a Premonstratensi ecclesia quatuor modios bladi de terris quas ecclesia tenuerat de antecessoribus suis et tenere debebat de ipso apud Gollencourt,[7] et ecclesia diceret ex adverso quod non debebat ei nisi tres modios tantum, tandem idem Joisbertus, de consilio Johannis de Bretigni[8] militis, avunculi sui, in presentiam nostram, venit et recognovit quod ecclesia ipsa non debebat ei nisi tres modios tantum solvendos ei et heredibus suis, annis singulis, ad mensuram Hami currentem tempore huius scripti, infra nativitatem Domini, in grangia Bonolii de residuo sementis, si residuum ibi inventum fuerit, cum nuncius eius venerit, vel, si residuum sementis ibi non fuerit, nuncio veniente, de meliori blado post sementem secundum estimationem grangiarii adjurati in ordine suo, quod verum dicet. Huic autem recognitioni interfuit et assensit Nicholaus, frater eiusdem Joisberti, de quo tenebat ipsam pensionem in feodo. Ecclesia autem ex una parte per nuncios suos et dicti Nicholaus et Joisbertus ex parte altera omnes querelas que erant vel esse poterant inter eos de omnibus anteactis, in presentia nostra, mutuo quitaverunt. Ut autem predicta omnia firmiter observentur, ad partium preces cyrographum[9] presens super hiis factum sigilli nostri fecimus impressione muniri. Actum mense aprili, anno incarnationis dominice M° CC° IX°.[10]

474

August, 1207.

Étienne [I],[1] *bishop of Noyon, makes known that he mediated a quarrel between Jean [II],*[2] *lord of Nesle and castellan of Bruges, and the church of Prémontré concerning property that two* conversae *of Bonneuil,*[3] *Adélaïde and Elizabeth,*

5 Joisbertum *B.*
6 Bretegni *B.*
7 Goullencort *B.*
8 Bretegni *B.*
9 cirographum *B.*
10 millesimo ducentesimo nono *B.*

1 Étienne de Villebéon (or de Nemours), son of Gautier de Villebéon, lord of La Chapelle-Gauthier and Nemours, and Aveline, was bishop of Noyon, 1188–1221.

2 Jean II, lord of Nesle and castellan of Bruges (d. 1239/40), son of Jean I, lord of Nesle and castellan of Bruges, and Elizabeth; husband of Eustacie de Saint-Pol. Jean and Eustacie founded the Cistercian abbey of Abbaye-aux-Bois in 1202 and feature prominently in that house's cartulary. Newman, *Seigneurs*, vol. 1, 71–2; Pipon, ed., *Le chartrier de l'Abbaye-aux-Bois (1202–1341)*, 42–3.

3 The Premonstratensian *curtis* of Bonneuil. *MP* II, 484.

inherited on the death of their brother Robert, knight of Châteaufort.[4] *Prémontré ceded the property to Jean and his heirs with the consent of Adélaïde and Elizabeth. In return, the sisters will receive six* modii *of grain (*frumentum*), measure of Nesle, annually for the rest of their lives. After their deaths, this will be paid to Bonneuil. (See near-duplicate **375**.)*

A. Cartulary of Prémontré, fol. 107r.

B. Original, AD Oise, H 5999, previously sealed on a double strip of parchment.

EDITION: Newman, *Seigneurs*, vol. 2, 194–5; *Chartae Galliae*, no. 212890, http://telma.irht.cnrs.fr/outils/chartae-galliae/charte212890/.

Karta Noviomensis episcopi de compositione inter ecclesiam Premonstratensem et dominum Nigellensis.

[E]go Stephanus, Dei gratia Noviomensis episcopus tam presentibus quam futuris notum facimus per hoc scriptum et fidele testimonium perhibemus quod cum inter nobilem virum Johannem, dominum Nigelle, castellanum Brugie, et ecclesiam Premonstratensem super hereditate conversarum Bonolii, Adelidis et Elisabeth,[5] que ad ipsas ex morte fratris ipsarum Roberti, militis de Castello Forti, fuerat devoluta, questio verteretur, tandem, me ipso mediante, inter dictum dominum Johannem et abbatem ac capitulum ecclesie memorate talis compositio facta fuit quod idem abbas et capitulum de assensu et concessione dictarum conversarum, ipsi domino Johanni et heredibus suis terram illam concesserunt perpetuo possidendam sub ea tamen conditione et lege quod ipse dominus Johannes et heredes sui in perpetuum annuatim in festo Sancti Remigii solvent dictis sororibus, quamdiu vixerint, sex modios frumenti ad mensuram Nigellensem ex horreo suo Nigellensi; post decessum vero dictarum conversarum prefati sex modii frumenti singulis annis in perpetuum ad eundem terminum ecclesie Bonolii solventur. Erit autem frumentum quod solvi debet in valore et precio melioris tribus denariis minus. Ut ergo compositio hec[6] futuris temporibus rata permaneat et illesa, presentem paginam conscribi fecimus sigilli nostri testimonio roboratam parit[7] et munitam. Actum anno Domini M° CC°[8] septimo, mense augusto.

4 Perhaps the *lieu-dit* of Château-Fort, comm. Languevoisin-Quinquery, https://dicotopo.cths.fr/places/P45423225.

5 Elizabeth *B*.

6 *Transp. A*; hec compositio *B*.

7 *Sic A*; pariter *B*.

8 millesimo ducentesimo *B*.

475

June 4, 1231. Bonneuil.

Jean,[1] decanus Christianitatis *of Ham, declares to the abbot [Eudes III]*[2] *of Essômes and to his papally appointed co-judges, in the presence of the canons and sisters of Bonneuil, that Simon,*[3] *lord of Marteville, renounced his claim to 11.5* solidi Parisiensium *drawn annually from the revenues of Montizel*[4] *and acknowledged that Bonneuil should rightfully receive it each year on the feast of Saint Remi. (See **476**.)*

A. Cartulary of Prémontré, fol. 107r.
B. Original not found.

Karta decani Christianitatis de elemosina Symonis de Martisvilla XI solidorum.

[V]iris venerabilibus et discretis abbati Sosmensis et conjudicibus suis J[ohannus] decanus Christianitatis Hamensis, salutem et peratam ad beneplacita voluntatem. Discretioni vestre presentibus litteris significamus quod dominus Symon, miles de Martisvilla, in nostra presentia constitutus feria quarta ante festum Beati Medardi in ecclesia de Bonolio, presentibus canonicis et sororibus eiusdem loci, spontanea voluntate recognovit elemosinam undecim solidorum et dimidii Parisiensium super qua lis erat mota coram nobis auctoritate apostolica inter ecclesiam Premonstratensem ex una parte et dictum Symonem ex altera, pro anima patris ipsius, Symonis, sororibus ecclesie de Bonolio et canonicis legitime esse factam et accipiendam singulis annis in festo Sancti Remigii ad redditus memorati Symonis apud Montisel. Preterea iamdictus Symon predictam elemosinam per manuum suarum appositionem super altare coram nobis et coram canonicis et sororibus ecclesie et etiam coram multis aliis humiliter et devote presentavit et hoc nobis et procuratori ecclesie Premonstratensis significamus. Datum feria IIII[a] ante festum Beati Medardi, anno Domini M° CC° XXX° primo.

1 Name per **430**.
2 Eudes III of the Augustinian abbey of Essômes. *GC* IX, col. 462.
3 Simon I, lord of Marteville (cant. Vermand, https://dicotopo.cths.fr/places/P05099925), attested 1202–31. Melleville, *DH*, vol. 2, 84.
4 Montizel, cant. Ham, https://dicotopo.cths.fr/places/P16235568.

476

September, 1231.

Baudouin,[1] *abbot of Essômes, an unnamed prior of Essômes, and J., priest of Château-Thierry, were appointed by the pope to resolve the dispute between the church of Prémontré and Simon,*[2] *lord of Marteville. They ruled in favour of Prémontré, deciding that Simon or his heirs pay Prémontré 11.5* solidi Parisiensium *annually. (See* ***475****.)*

A. Cartulary of Prémontré, fol. 107r.

B. Original, AD Oise, H 6006, previously sealed with two seals, each on a single strip of parchment.

De conpositione inter ecclesiam Premonstratensem et Symonem militem de Martisvilla.

B[alduinus], Dei patientia dictus abbas, prior Sosmensis et J., presbyter de Castro Theoderici, omnibus in perpetuum. Ventilata coram nobis auctoritate apostolica quadam causa que inter ecclesiam Premonstratensem ex una parte et dominum Symonem, militem de Martisvilla ex altera vertebatur, tandem, productis testibus, attestationibus publicatis, auditis quoque et intellectis rationibus et confessionibus hinc et inde, adjudicavimus ecclesie Premonstrati undecim illos solidos et dimidium Parisiensium de quibus coram nobis actum fuerat inter partes, condempnantes prefatum militem ad solutionem pecunie memorate annis singulis in festo Sancti Remigii a prefato milite vel eius heredibus faciendam et in expensis legitimis[3] quas de jure probare poterit prefata ecclesia Premonstrati. Et ut hoc ratum permaneat atque firmum sigilla nostra presenti sentencie duximus apponenda. Actum anno Domini M° CC° XXX°[4] primo, mense septembri.

1 Baudouin, abbot of the Augustinian abbey of Essômes, ca. 1231–49. *GC* IX, col. 463.

2 Simon I, lord of Marteville (cant. Vermand, https://dicotopo.cths.fr/places/P05099925), attested 1202–31. Melleville, *DH*, vol. 2, 84.

3 legittimis *B*.

4 millesimo ducentesimo tricesimo *B*.

477

1213

Étienne [I],[1] *bishop of Noyon, gives notice that Mathieu* Scabiosi, *son of the late Simon, with the consent of Eustacie, his wife, and Agnès, his sister, gave in alms to the church of Prémontré three* modii *of grain (*bladus*), measure of Ham, that he received annually from the grange of Bonneuil, in return for which the Premonstratensians at Bonneuil*[2] *gave Mathieu 28.5* librae Parisiensium. *This transaction was approved by the knight Hugues du Plessis,*[3] *from whom the fief descended. Hugues also bequeathed to Prémontré a* modius *of grain (*bladus*), measure of Ham, to be taken annually at Plessis.*

A. Cartulary of Prémontré, fol. 107r.

B. Original, AD Oise, Hs 1375, sealed on a double strip of parchment with partial seal of brown wax.

Karta Noviomensis episcopi de elemosina Mathei filii Simonis cognomento Scabiosi de tribus modiis bladi.

[S]tephanus, Dei gratia Noviomensis episcopus, omnibus in perpetuum. Notum facimus tam presentibus quam futuris qui viderint istud scriptum quod Matheus, filius quondam Symonis, cognomento Scabiosi, laude et assensu Eustachie[4] sue et Agnetis, sororis sue uxoris[5] dedit in elemosinam ecclesie Premonstratensi tres modios bladi ad mensuram Hamensem quos percipiebat in grangia Bonolii annuatim. Ecclesia autem in recompensationem elemosine sibi facte dedit ei viginti et octo libras et dimidiam Parisienses; et quia idem Matheus tenebat illos tres modios de Hugone de Plesseio milite in feodo, sciri volumus quod idem ipse Hugo et Matheus cum uxore et sorore sua venerunt in presentiam nostram et recognoverunt ac laudaverunt elemosinam supradictam esse liberam ecclesie Premonstratensi. Nos autem intuitu Dei et ecclesie Premonstratensi quam diligebamus, ad petitionem sepedicti Hugonis et aliorum supradictorum, ipsam[6] laudavimus et presentibus litteris sigillo nostro munitis confirmavimus perpetuo duraturam. Preterea volumus nichilominus ut ad noticiam veniat posterorum quod prefatus Hugo legavit

1 Étienne de Villebéon (or de Nemours), son of Gautier de Villebéon, lord of La Chapelle-Gauthier and Nemours, and Aveline, was bishop of Noyon, 1188–1221.

2 The Premonstratensian *curtis* of Bonneuil. *MP* II, 484.

3 Likely Le Plessis-Patte-d'Oie, cant. Guiscard, https://dicotopo.cths.fr/places/P25690373. Guyotjeannin, *Episcopus*, 224.

4 *Om.* uxoris *A*; Eustacie *B*.

5 *Add.* uxoris *A*.

6 *Om.* elemosinam *A*.

ecclesie Bonolii, pro anima matris sue Agnetis, unum modium bladi in elemosinam ad mensuram Hamensem recipiendum in perpetuum annuatim apud Pleisseium. Eandem quoque elemosinam recognovit et laudavit coram nobis ipse Hugo et nos ad petitionem ipsius ut perpetuo duraret eam presenti scripto censuimus inserendam. Actum anno incarnationis dominice M° CC°[7] tercio decimo.

478

June, 1217.

The knight Simon des Monts makes known that his man Baudouin, knight of Ham, left to the church of Prémontré all his rights of justicia *and share of* garba *on land at Bonneuil*[1] *and Golancourt*[2] *descending from Simon's fief, which in turn descends from Simon de Camas.*[3] *In exchange, the church of Prémontré owes two* modii *of grain (*frumentum*) and one* modius *of oats, both measure of Ham. (See* ***470****.)*

A. Cartulary of Prémontré, fols. 107r–107v.

B. Original, AD Oise, Hs 1378, previously sealed with two seals on double strips of leather.

Karta Symonis militis de Montibus de quitatione Balduini militis super jure suo de territorio Bonolii.

[E]go Symon de Montibus, miles, notum facio omnibus hec visuris quod Balduinus, miles de Hamo, homo meus, quitavit ecclesie Premonstratensis in perpetuum per subscriptam modiationem quicquid juris vel consuetudinis vel justicie vel garbe vel quocumque alio modo habebat in tota terra de meo feodo descendente que fuit Symonis de Camach et sita est in territorio Bonolii et de Gollencourt;[4] ecclesia autem predicta debet ei et eius heredibus pro hac quitancia solvere annuatim duos modios frumenti sani et solubilis et unum modium avene ad mensuram in Hamensi Castro currentem tempore huius scripti. Ipse vero Balduinus tenetur de predictis eidem ecclesie portare

7 millesimo ducentesimo *B*.

1 Bonneuil, cant. Ham, https://dicotopo.cths.fr/places/P66750585.

2 Golancourt, cant. Guiscard, https://dicotopo.cths.fr/places/P75999303.

3 Camas, comm. Jussy, https://dicotopo.cths.fr/places/P27501164.

4 Gollencort *B*.

legitimam garandiam. Si autem eundem Balduinum aut eius heredes unico servitio deficere contigerit nichil in terra ipsa nisi modiationem tantum potero saisire. In cuius rei firmitatem ego et Balduinus predictus homo meus presentem paginam sigillorum nostrorum appensione fecimus roborari. Actum anno Domini M° CC° XVII°,[5] mense junio.

479

July, 1223.

Hugues [II],[1] lord of Béthencourt, makes known and approves that his son Jean gave in alms to the church of Prémontré a sheaf of grain and all rights over certain lands at Bonneuil[2] that Prémontré held from Hugues, and that it had previously held from lord Hugues de Plaissey.[3]

A. Cartulary of Prémontré, fol. 107v.

B. Original, AD Oise, H 6003, previously sealed on a double strip of parchment.

Karta Hugonis domini de Betencort de confirmatione elemosine filii mei.

[E]go Hugo, dominus de Betencourt, notum facio universis tam presentibus quam futuris quod elemosinam quam Johannes, filius meus, fecit ecclesie Premonstratensi de garba et de omni jure quod habebat in quibusdam terris sitis in territorio Bonolii quas ipsa ecclesia tenebat de ipso et olim tenuerat de domino Hugone de Plaisseto, benigne laudavi. Actum mense julio, anno gratie M°[4] CC° vicesimo tercio.

5 millesimo ducentesimo septimo decimo *B*.

1 Hugues II de Sermaize (d. bef. 1228), lord of Béthencourt-sur-Somme (cant. Nesle, https://dicotopo.cths.fr/places/P85791062), son of Simon de Sermaize, lord of Béthencourt-sur-Somme, and Emeline. Newman, *Seigneurs*, vol. 2, 99, 209–10; Guyotjeannin, *Episcopus*, 272.

2 Bonneuil, cant. Ham, https://dicotopo.cths.fr/places/P66750585.

3 Likely Le Plessis-Patte-d'Oie, cant. Guiscard, https://dicotopo.cths.fr/places/P25690373. Guyotjeannin, *Episcopus*, 224.

4 millesimo *B*.

480

September, 1231.

Rorigon [II],[1] *lord of Fayet, makes known that he resolves a dispute with the church of Prémontré concerning the gift he had made in perpetual alms of a piece of land and its associated rights in the territory of* Kaisnoi.[2]

A. Cartulary of Prémontré, fol. 107v.
B. Original not found.

Karta Domini Rogonii de Faiel de conpositione inter me et ecclesiam Premonstratensem.

[E]go Rogonius, dominus de Faiel, notum facio universis tam presentibus quam futuris quod cum inter me ex una parte et ecclesiam Premonstratensem ex altera super quadam petia terre que sita est in territorio del Kaisnoi, contigua campo Stephani, cognomento Latomi, lis mota fuisset, hinc et inde lite sopita pax inter nos ita fuit amicabiliter reformata quod totam dictam petiam terre necnon et totum jus quod habebam vel habere poteram in eadem dedi et concessi in perpetuam elemosinam ecclesie supradicte et, fide interposita, juravi quod per me vel per alium super eadem elemosina dictam ecclesiam nullatenus molestabo aut faciam molestari; immo adversus omnes qui voluerint juri stare, tenebor eam legitime warandire. Et ne ista elemosina possit in posterum occasione aliqua perturbari vel per aliquorum maliciam revocari, presentem kartam feci sigilli mei munimine roborari. Actum anno gratie M° CC° XXX° primo, mense septembri.

481

September, 1216.

Gobert,[1] *lord of Quierzy, and the brothers of Prémontré conclude an agreement concerning the upkeep of the course of the river Oise on the length of their lands from the mill of* Bailluel *towards* Loillier.[2]

---

1 Rorigon II, lord of Fayet (d. aft. 1242), son of Eudes, lord of Fayet, and Havide. Newman, *Seigneurs*, vol. 2, 103.
2 Possibly Quesnoy-en-Santerre, cant. Rosières, https://dicotopo.cths.fr/places/P25322369.

---

1 Gobert de Chérisy, lord of Quierzy (d. ca. 1250), son of Gérard III de Chérisy and Gila.
2 Likely Leullier, comm. Mélicocq, https://dicotopo.cths.fr/places/P05748697.

A. Cartulary of Prémontré, fol. 107v.
B. Original, AN, L 995, no. 64, previously sealed.

Karta domini Goberti de Cherisi de conpositione inter ecclesiam Premonstratensem et ipsum.

Ego[3] Gobertus, dominus Chirisiaci, notum facio tam presentibus quam futuris quod inter me et fratres Premonstratenses facta est conpositio in hunc modum: Ego dedi et concessi ipsis fratribus plenam licentiam ut omnes rupturas quas fluvius Ysare fecerat ante tempus huius scripti vel in posterum faciet in terra mea, a molendino de Balloel[4] versus Loillier, quod est in terra domini Hugonis[5] de Guini, et omnes aperturas fossatorum per quas idem fluvius ab alveo suo in terram meam poterat divertere et pro retinenda vel prendenda aqua, licebit eis quindecim pedibus super ripam in latum et quantum opus fuerit in longum, superius et inferius quantum terra mea durat, terram et glebas accipere. Concessi preterea ut ipsi fratres viam navium que facta fuerat tempore huius scripti et a terra domini Hugonis de Guini descendebat in terram meam, dilatent in tantum ut habeat in latum, quando facta erit, tres thesias ad thesiam domini regis et duos pedes ad pedem manus quantum terra mea durat et duobus pedibus approfundent ad plumbum in ea parte in qua via est profundior et ad mensuram illius profunditatis ducant illam viam per totum. Concessi etiam ut in eadem via dilatent fratres cursum aque in tribus locis duodecim pedibus ad pedem manus ad profunditatem alterius et ad plumbum ex una parte qua maluerint propter occursus navium, et illa dilatatio habebit in longum decem thesias ad thesiam regis. Verum si molendinum de Bailluel[6] aliquo tempore fuerit reparandum ita quod propter hoc oporteat aquam ante molendinum sclusari, fratres poterint rumpere sclusam illam que est propinquior molendino ut aqua exeat per eam donec molendinum fuerit reparatum et post reparationem molendini licebit fratribus iterum obstruere rupturam illam et, secundum quod superius dictum est, accipere terram et glebas in terra mea super ripam quindecim pedibus in latum et quantum opus fuerit in longum superius et inferius. Hec autem que predicta sunt tam ego quam heredes mei infra terram dominii nostri semper warandiabimus adversus omnes qui ad jus et ad placitum venire voluerint, nec abbas aut fratres poterunt a me plus requirere per hanc conventionem quam quod superius est expressum. Actum mense septembri, anno incarnationis dominice M° CC° XVI°.[7]

3 The initial letter has been added at a later, post-medieval date.
4 Bailloel *B*.
5 Hugues, lord of Guny, son of Guy II, lord of Guny, and Elizabeth d'Oulchy. Newman, *Seigneurs*, vol. 2, 98.
6 Bailloel *B*.

482

September 5, 1225.

The text of an agreement mediated by Raoul,[1,2] *abbot of Saint-Jean-des-Vignes, and concluded between the church of Prémontré and lord Gobert*[3] *de Chérisy concerning the possession of the mill of* Bailluel.

A. Cartulary of Prémontré, fols. 107v–108r.
B. Original, AN, L 995, no. 72, previously sealed with two seals.

De forma pacis inter ecclesiam Premonstratensem et dominum Gobertum de Cherisi de molendino de Bailluel.

[H]ec est forma concordie inter ecclesiam Premonstratensem et dominum Gobertum de Cherisiaco. Pons qui factus est subtus molendinum de Bailluel[4] cuius pes respiciens versus villam de Marez[5] est in districto ecclesie Premonstratensis, decetero remanebit sine contradictione in loco in quo est, propter aisentias domini Goberti et hominum suorum, eo tenore quod ecclesia et fratres ecclesie Premonstratensis habebunt in perpetuum aisentias suas ad locandam materiam ligneam et lapideam et alias commoditates suas ad molendinum sine faciendis fossatis aut fossis in pratello quod adjacet ventallis molendini de Bailluel,[6] ita tamen quod ex eo tempore quo fenata fuerint fena et in Messlis posita usque ad medium martium quo fiunt inhibitiones de pratis, poterunt ibidem habere aisentias suas, sicut predictum est, et ex eo tempore quo fiunt inhibitiones de pratis in medio martio, sicut predictum est, usque dum fenata fuerint fena; si necessitas urgeat ecclesiam vel fratres Premonstratenses, poterunt ibidem nichilominus[7] habere aisentias suas, sicut supradictum est, ita tamen quod ecclesia et fratres restituant domino Goberto dampnum de herba vel feno et hoc nichilominus retinuit sibi ecclesia Premonstratensis quod infra quindecim pedes immo quantum quindecim pedes se extendunt quos habet eadem ecclesia

7 millesimo ducentesimo sexto decimo *B*.

1 *GC* IX, col. 458.
2 Raoul de Chézy, abbot of the Augustinian abbey of Saint-Jean-des-Vignes de Soissons, ca. 1201–34/5.
3 Gobert de Chérisy, lord of Quierzy (d. ca. 1250), son of Gérard III de Chérisy and Gila.
4 Bailloel *B*.
5 Marest-Dampcourt, cant. Chauny, https://dicotopo.cths.fr/places/P37392982.
6 Bailloel *B*.
7 *Om.* ibidem *A*.

ultra ventalla molendini[8] si opus fuerit. Hoc etiam conductum est inter ecclesiam Premonstratensem et dominum Gobertum quod dominus Gobertus pro predicto pratello quod adjacet ventallis molendini de Bailluel,[9] quod debebat esse ecclesie Premonstratensi, debet restituere dominus Gobertus in pratis suis que sunt non longe ab ipso molendino in ripa Ysare pratum eiusdem quantitatis et valoris cuius est pratellum predictum ad arbitrium bonorum virorum, videlicet domini Gerardi[10] de Viri et fratris Goscewini, magistri de Thoiri,[11] qui hoc fide interposita tenentur facere infra instans festum Beate Marie Magdalene ita etiam quod inter ecclesiam Premonstratensem et dominum Gobertum de Cherisiaco salve erunt aisentie utrique parti in utroque prato in educendo feno et herba, hoc etiam proviso quod dominus Gobertus tenebitur warandire pratum ipsum quod restituet, sicut supradictum est, ecclesie Premonstrati adversus dominum suum: In quorum omnium perpetuam memoriam vir venerabilis R[adulphus] abbas Sancti Johannis in Vineis Suessionensis huius concordie mediator et predictus dominus Gobertus presenti pagine sua sigilla fecerunt appendi. Actum est hoc feria sexta proxima post festum Beati Johannis Baptiste, anno gratie M° CC° XX°[12] quinto.

483

December, 1216.

Hugues,[1] lord of Guny, authorizes the brothers of Prémontré to use wood, stones, and earth whenever necessary to make repairs to the canal that they had constructed across his land as far as the land of Gobert[2] de Chérisy to improve the mill of Bailluel, *and to allow for passage of boats up and down the river Oise.*

A. Cartulary of Prémontré, fol. 108r.
B. Original, BM Louis Aragon, Amiens, Legs Arthur de Marsy, 1005, no. 2.[3]
REGISTER: *Catalogue analytique des Chartes*, 60.

8 *Homeo. A*; *om.* poterit ecclesia dilatare ventalla *A*.
9 Bailloel *B*.
10 Perhaps the same Gérard who was *advocatus* of Viry (cant. Chauny, https://dicotopo.cths.fr/places/P15709172) in the early thirteenth century. Colliette, *Mémoires pour servir à l'histoire ecclésiastique, civile et militaire de la province du Vermandois*, vol. 1, 638.
11 Thury, comm. Marest-Dampcourt, https://dicotopo.cths.fr/places/P84789655.
12 millesimo ducentesimo vicesimo *B*.

1 Hugues, lord of Guny (cant. Coucy-le-Château, https://dicotopo.cths.fr/places/P88745448), son of Guy II, lord of Guny, and Elizabeth d'Oulchy. Newman, *Seigneurs*, vol. 2, 98.
2 Gobert de Chérisy, lord of Quierzy (d. ca. 1250), son of Gérard III de Chérisy and Gila.
3 Due to archival access restrictions in operation in 2020, the editors were unable to access this charter.

Karta Hugonis domini de Guni de quodam fossato per terram suam pro aisentia molendini de Bailluel.

Ego[4] Hugo, dominus de Guni, notum facio tam presentibus quam futuris quod fratres Premonstratenses de licentia et de assensu meo pro aisentia molendini sui de Bailluel et pro via navium ascendentium et descendentium per fluvium Ysare, fecerunt quoddam fossatum per terram meam usque in terram domini Goberti de Cherisiaco quod habuit in latitudine, quando factum fuit, tres thesias ad thesiam domini regis et duos pedes ad pedem manus. Verum si aliquo tempore vel per violentiam aque vel aliquo alio casu contigerit fossatum dilatari, concessi fratribus supradictis ut liceat eis restringere fossatum ipsum ad suam primam mensuram tam in introitu quam inferius quantum terra mea durat ligno, lapide, atque terra et aliis que necessaria erunt cum opus fuerit. Hec autem que predicta sunt tam ego quam heredes mei infra terram dominii nostri semper warandiabimus adversus omnes qui voluerint juri stare et ad placitum venire. Actum mense decembri, anno incarnationis dominice M° CC° XVI°.

484

1158

Abbot Hugues [I][1] *and the chapter of Prémontré conclude an agreement with abbot Guérin*[2] *and the chapter of Homblières, according to which Homblières gives Prémontré what it held in lands and vineyards in the territories of Bonneuil*[3] *and Golancourt*[4] *in return for an annual* census *of one and a half* modii *of grain (*frumentum*) and another* modius *of oats, measure of Ham.*

A. Cartulary of Prémontré, fol. 108r.

B. Original (chirograph), AD Oise, H 5989, previously sealed with a double strip of parchment. In the top left margin and beginning at the top, the upper part of the letters that form the word CYROGRAPHUM.

EDITION: Newman, *Homblières*, 150–1; *Chartae Galliae*, no. 212283, http://telma.irht.cnrs.fr/outils/chartae-galliae/charte212283/.

4 The initial letter has been added at a later, post-medieval date.

1 Hugues I de Fosses (ca. 1093–1164), first abbot of Prémontré.

2 Guérin I, abbot of the Benedictine abbey of Homblières, 1150/1–59/60. Newman, *Homblières*, 18.

3 Bonneuil, cant. Ham, https://dicotopo.cths.fr/places/P66750585.

4 Golancourt, cant. Guiscard, https://dicotopo.cths.fr/places/P75999303.

Karta abbatis et conventus Premonstratensis et Humolariensis super quadam permutatione in territorio Bonolii.

[I]n nomine sancte et cetera.[5] Ego Hugo, Premonstrate ecclesie abbas, totumque capitulum nostrum. Ego etiam Garinus,[6] Humolariensis abbas, simulque capitulum nostrum omnibus tam futuris quam presentibus in perpetuum. Quia servi Dei que Dei sunt, maxime concordiam fratrum et amorem proximorum, debent querere pactum quod pro bono pacis inter nos ad invicem statutum est, huic cartule studuimus inserere, ut, siquis deinceps inter nos presumperserit violare caritatem, ad vinculum pacis reducatur per memoratam scripti veritatem. Garinus itaque, Humolariensis abbas, totumque capitulum suum Premonstrate ecclesie in perpetuum censualiter concessit quicquid in territorio Bonolii et Gollencurtis possidebat, tam in terra quam in decima, pro modio et dimidio frumenti et modio uno avene ad mensuram Hamensem, que eo tempore Hami erat; qui census annuatim in festo Sancti Remigii persolvetur, quem Humolarienses in curia Bonolii accipient. Ne quis ergo pactum hoc quod pro pacis concordieque gratia pro utrorumque commodo factum est, in posterum violare valeat, nos ambo personarum nostrarum testimonio cyrographo quoque et sigillis ecclesiarum nostrarum alternatim confirmavimus, sed et auctoritate et sigillo venerabilis Balduini,[7] Noviomensis episcopi, corroboravimus testesque capitulorum qui huic pactioni interfuerunt, subsignamus. S. Huberti prioris. S. Renaldi,[8] S. Harduini, S. Rogeri[9] sacerdotum. S. Henrici. S. Anselmi. S. Petri, diaconorum. S. Symonis. Rainoardi. S. Richardi, subdiaconorum. S. Reneri.[10] S. Bonardi. S. Haimonis, monachorum. S. Hugonis, Premonstrati prioris. S. Johannis. S. Goschuini,[11] sacerdotum. S. Ade. S. Johannis. S. Rainardi, diaconorum. S. Richardi. S. Ligeri. S. Osmundi, subdiaconorum. S. Fulconis. S. Mathei. S. Lamberti,[12] canonicorum. Actum anno incarnationis dominice[13] M° C° LVIII°.

5 *Add.* cetera *A*; individue Trinitatis *B*.

6 Gaurinus *B*.

7 Baudouin II de Boulogne, abbot of the Augustinian abbey of Saint-Eloi-Fontaine, ca. 1130–ca. 1139, and bishop of Noyon, 1148–67. *GC* IX, col. 1126.

8 Rainaldi *B*.

9 Rotgeri *B*.

10 Raineri *B*.

11 Goszuini *B*.

12 Lantberti *B*.

13 *Transp. A*; incarnationis dominice anno *B*.

485

1177

Eudes [III],[1] *lord of Ham, makes known that he gave to the churches of Prémontré and Ham land and woodland at Collezy*[2] *to clear and cultivate. Prémontré and Ham will pay a* census *consisting of one* modius *of grain (*annona*) for each* modiata *of land in the first year, with the rate of payment to increase annually for five years as the amount of land under cultivation increases to reach a total of 200* modiatae, *worth 50* librae obolorum. *At the end of five years, the payment will be reassessed. (See* ***306****.)*

A. Cartulary of Prémontré, fols. 108r–108v.

B. Original, AD Somme, 20 H_SC_6, no. 9, sealed.[3]

Karta domini Hamensis de elemosina nemoris que Colesiacum nuncupatur.

[I]n nomine Domini, ego Odo, dominus Castri Hamensis, notum fieri volo tam futuris quam presentibus dedisse me ecclesie Premonstratensi et ecclesie Hamensi totam terram et nemus quod Colesiacum nuncupatur ad extirpandum et excolendum et ad omnimodam utriusque ecclesie commoditatem sub annuali censu annone inter me et prefates ecclesias constituto, videlicet singulis modiis annone pro singulis modiatis terre, sicut in aliis litteris sigillo meo confirmatis plenius continentur. Qui siquidem census ita mihi persolvendus est ut in primo anno XL modii, in secundo LXXX, in III° C° XX°, in IIII° CLX, in quinto anno ducenti modii persolvantur. De quibus omnibus due partes frumenti, tercia pars avene reddentur. In quinto igitur anno terra metietur et si plures modiate terre invente fuerint, deinceps crescet census secundum quantitatem modiatarum. Si autem minus, minuetur census. Ego autem de caritate utriusque ecclesie pro hoc habui quingentas libras obolorum, videlicet pro singulis modiatis terre quinquaginta solidos de quibus constitutum est quod cum ventum fuerit ad predictum quinti anni terminum, si plures modiate invente fuerint predicte ecclesie plus mihi persolvent pecunie, donec recipiam quinquaginta solidos pro singulis modiatis terre. Si autem minus, de censu mihi debito retinebunt donec rehabeant quod mihi plus justo dederunt. Sciendum etiam quod uxor mea et fratres mei et alii amici et familiares mei et alii amici et familiares mei habuerunt de caritate utriusque ecclesie LXVI libras obolorum pro concessionibus eorum que prescripta sunt. Ne igitur prefatis ecclesiis aliquod in futurum

1 Eudes III, lord of Ham, son of Lancelin, lord of Ham, and Mathilde.

2 Collezy, comm. Berlancourt, https://dicotopo.cths.fr/places/P68465476.

3 Due to conservation concerns, the original was not available to the editors.

de his omnibus gravamen proveniat prescriptam pactionem presenti scripto commendare et tam testium annotatione quam sigilli mei impressione communire curavi. Testes hii sunt: Rorigo[4] de Faiel et Symon, frater eius; Johannes de Athies et Adam,[5] frater eius; Manasses et Robertus, filii eiusdem Johannis; Willermus de Vilete;[6] Odo[7] de Bonolio; Petrus de Plaissie;[8] Walterus de Bruci.[9] Actum anno incarnati verbi M° C° LXX° VII°.

486

December, 1228.

Jean, prepositus *of* Montibus,[1] *relinquishes his rights as fief lord to the three* modii *of grain (*frumentum*), measure of Ham, that Renier de Clary*[2] *and his wife Emmeline sold to the church of Prémontré. (See* ***416****.)*

A. Cartulary of Prémontré, fol. 108v.
B. Original, AD Oise, H 6002, previously sealed with a double strip of parchment.

Karta Johannis prepositi de Montibus de venditione trium modiorum bladi quam fecit Renerus.

[E]go Johannes, prepositus de Montibus, notum facio universis tam presentibus quam futuris quod cum Renerus de Clari et Enmelina, uxor sua, vendidissent ecclesie Premonstratensis in perpetuum tres modios frumenti ad mensuram Hamensem quos ipsa ecclesia Premonstratensis debebat eisdem et ipsi tres modii essent de feodo meo, ego ad petitionem partium ipsam venditionem gratam et ratam habui et in perpetuum approbavi et quicquid juris habebam ratione feodi in ipsis tribus modiis eidem ecclesie intuitu Dei et salutis

4 Rorigon, lord of Fayet (d. ca. 1199), and Simon (d. ca. 1187), sons of Aude, lady of Fayet. Newman, *Seigneurs*, vol. 2, 102.
5 Adam, knight and lord of Athies (cant. Ham, https://dicotopo.cths.fr/places/P98820850), son of Robert Rufus, nephew of Mathieu and Bernier, and brother of Widèle and Jean. He attested a number of acts ca. 1150–ca. 1188. Cagny, *Histoire de l'arrondissement de Péronne*, vol. 2, 259; Tock and Milis, *Monumenta Arroasiensia*, 251. He also appears in **306**.
6 Villette, cant. Ham, https://dicotopo.cths.fr/places/P35405877.
7 Eudes de Bonneuil appears as a witness in acts dated 1140–78. Newman, *Seigneurs*, vol. 2, 119.
8 Pierre du Plessis (cant. Guiscard, https://dicotopo.cths.fr/places/P25690373) is a witness in **306**, **336**, and **344**.
9 Brouchy, cant. Ham, https://dicotopo.cths.fr/places/P33557845.

1 Perhaps Mons-en-Laonnois, cant. Anizy-le-Château, https://dicotopo.cths.fr/places/P73499722.
2 Clary, comm. Merlieux-et-Fouquerolles, https://dicotopo.cths.fr/places/P10581161.

proprie resignavi. Ut autem que premissa sunt perpetuam habeant firmitatem presentem kartam super hoc confectam sigilli mei munimine roboravi. Actum mense decembri, anno gratie M° CC° XXVIII°.[3]

487

July, 1218.

Dean Renaud, cantor R., and Pierre de Neuville, canon of Saint-Vaast[1] *de Soissons, make known that after a dispute, Oudard de Saint-Simon and Mathieu, his son by the late Marie* Venatrix, *conceded and approved the gift Marie had made to the church of Prémontré of whatever rights she held over certain pieces of land, and promised not to dispute the gift further. (See* ***490****.)*

A. Cartulary of Prémontré, fol. 108v.
B. Original not found.

Karta de conpositione inter ecclesiam Premonstratensem et Odardum de Sancto Symone et Matheum filium eius.

[E]go Renaldus, decanus, et R. cantor, et ego Petrus de Novo Vico, canonicus Sancti Vedasti Suessionensis, notum facimus universis presentes litteras inspecturis quod cum inter ecclesiam Premonstratensem ex una parte et Odardum de Sancto Symone ac Matheum, filium eius, quem suscepit de bone memorie Maria Venatrice, ex parte altera, super quadam elemosina quam olim fecerat eidem ecclesie memorata Maria, questio verteretur, auctoritate apostolica coram nobis tandem predicti Odardus et Matheus in nostra presencia constituti recognoverunt quod dicta Maria dederat in elemosinam ecclesie Premonstratensi quicquid juris habebat in masura que dicebatur Reneri prepositi et in masura Marie Veelete et in campo super plancham qui fuit Reneri Restorei, videlicet masueriam, justiciam, et districtum et ipsam elemosinam. Laudaverunt et quitaverunt omnino interposito fidei sacramento quod nunquam decetero super ea movebunt per se vel per alios eidem ecclesie questionem. Nos igitur

3 millesimo ducentesimo vicesimo octavo *B*.

1 The collegiate church of Saint-Vaast de Soissons.

tam elemosinam quam quitanciam supradictam auctoritate nobis commissa duximus confirmanda supponentes excommunicationis sententie omnes illos qui secundo tertiove commoniti eam presumpserint aliquo tempore perturbare. Actum mense julio, anno gratie M° CC° XVIII°.

488

1199

Étienne [I],[1] *bishop of Noyon, makes known that his baker Werry gave the Premonstratensian church of Bonneuil*[2] *a* modius *of grain (*frumentum*) to be taken annually at Ercheu,*[3] *on the condition that if Werry should join a community of lepers, the Premonstratensian church of Bonneuil would return to him his* modius *of grain (*frumentum*).*

A. Cartulary of Prémontré, fol. 108v.

B. Original, AD Oise, H 6034, previously sealed with a strip of parchment.

Karta Noviomensis episcopi de elemosina Werrici panetarii super uno modio frumenti.

[S]tephanus, Dei gratia Noviomensis episcopus, omnibus ad quos littere iste pervenerint. Notum fieri volumus quod Werricus, panetarius noster, contulit ecclesie de Bonolio unum modium frumenti assensu nostro in feodo nostro quem de nobis tenet apud Erciacum percipiendum annuatim. Ita scilicet quod si eundem Werricum leprosum fore et ad leprosorum domum transire et cum eis manere contigerit, ecclesia Bonoliensis modium illum frumenti ei restituet, leprosis cum quibus manserit conferendum. In huius igitur rei testimonium presens scriptum tradidimus sigillo nostro communitum. Actum anno Domini M° C° nonagesimo nono.[4]

1 Étienne de Villebéon (or de Nemours), son of Gautier de Villebéon, lord of La Chapelle-Gauthier and Nemours, and Aveline, was bishop of Noyon, 1188–1221.

2 *MP* II, 484.

3 Ercheu, cant. Roye, https://dicotopo.cths.fr/places/P67904398.

4 M° centesimo XC° nono *B*.

489

1163

Baudouin [II],[1] bishop of Noyon, makes known the agreement reached between the Premonstratensian church of Bonneuil[2] and Pierre du Plessis[3] concerning land held in fief by a certain Freeburge, which had been the subject of a prior dispute.

A. Cartulary of Prémontré, fols. 108v–109r.

B. Original (chirograph), AD Oise, H 5994, previously sealed with a double strip of parchment. In the left margin, beginning at the top, the upper half of the letters that form the word CYROGRAPHUM.

Karta Noviomensis episcopi de conpositione inter ecclesiam Bonoliensis et Petrum de Plaissie de terra Freeburgis.

[I]n nomine patris et cetera.[4] Ego Balduinus, Dei gratia Noviomensis ecclesie dictus episcopus, notum fieri volo tam futuris quam presentibus quod contentio erat inter ecclesiam Bonoliensem et Petrum de Plaissie de terra quam tenebat Freeburgis in feodo a predicto Petro. Facta est autem concordia hoc modo: concessit Petrus ut ecclesia Bonoliensis terram illam excolat in perpetuum ad sextam garbam sic tamen quod si de cultura terre postmodum querimoniam ipse vel heres eius fecerit, ecclesia inde respondebit ei super terram judicio accolarum patrie; verum in terra illa ipse nec super ecclesie fratres nec super eorum operarios neque super res eorum districtum habebit vel justiciam de alienis habebit. Statutum etiam est quod si per elemosinam vel per emptionem acquirere poterit ecclesia partem terre vel totam, cuius participes modo sunt quamplures, ea garba et ea libertate possidebit qua partem supradictam excolit sed et de hac terra nusquam faciet elemosinam nisi ad ecclesiam Bonolii; quando fratres ibi metere voluerint, nuntiabunt Petro ad Plaissie; si non venerit vel non miserit, secabunt et nuntiabunt ei ut pro terragio mittat. Si non miserit, ducent ei ad Plaissie. Si dixerit quod totum non habeat, si conversus duxerit, verbo eius credetur; si secularis, juramento firmabit[5] et Petro sufficiet. Concessit etiam terram Odonis, qui dicitur Cum Barba, prefate ecclesie in pace possidere. Ut igitur ratum et inconvulsum permaneat, sigilli nostri impressione

1 Baudouin II de Boulogne, abbot of the Augustinian abbey of Saint-Eloi-Fontaine, ca. 1130–ca. 1139, and bishop of Noyon, 1148–67. *GC* IX, col. 1126.

2 *MP* II, 484.

3 Le Plessis-Patte-d'Oie, cant. Guiscard, https://dicotopo.cths.fr/places/P25690373.

4 *Add.* cetera *A*; Filii et Spiritus Sancti, amen *B*.

5 confirmabit *B*.

confirmamus et eos qui contraire temptaverint, anathematis sententia innodamus et nomina quorumdam qui huic concessioni interfuerunt annotavimus: Symon de Maigni[6,7] et Renerus[8] filius eius, Willermus de Plaissie, Dudo de Juveri,[9,10] Johannes et Gerardus de Bellencourt.[11,12] Actum anno incarnati verbi M° C° LX° III° et coram nobis recognitum.

490

1218

Mathieu de Saint-Simon approves the alms gift his mother Marie Venatrix *made to the church of Prémontré and promises not to dispute it further. (See **487**.)*

A. Cartulary of Prémontré, fol. 109r.
B. Original not found.

Karta Mathei de Sancto Symone de elemosina Marie Venatricis.

[I]n nomine Patris et Filii et cetera. Ego Matheus de Sancto Symone notum facio tam presentibus quam futuris quod bone memorie Maria, dicta Venatrix, mater mea, dederit in elemosinam ecclesie Premonstrati quicquid juris habebat in masura que dicitur Reneri prepositi et in masura Marie Veelete et in campo super planchiam qui fuit Reneri cognomento Restorei, videlicet masueriam, justiciam et districtum. Post decessum vero matris mee cum ego, tanquam juvenis et iniquo ductus consilio, prefatam elemosinam intenderem revocare et possessionem in quam missa fuerat Premonstratensis ecclesia, perturbarem, viri religiosi G[ervasii][1] abbas, et fratres Premonstratenses traxerunt me in causam coram venerabilibus viris Renaldo, decano Sancti Vedasti[2] Suessionensis, et eius conjudicibus a Sede Apostolica delegatis. Coram quibus

6 Simon de Magni *B*.
7 Magny, comm. Guiscard, https://dicotopo.cths.fr/places/P96954039.
8 Reinerus *B*.
9 Jenuri *B*.
10 Possibly the same Dude who appears in the witness list of **436**. Genvry, cant. Noyon, https://dicotopo.cths.fr/places/P86438840.
11 Bellencurt *B*.
12 Berlancourt, cant. Guiscard, https://dicotopo.cths.fr/places/P39954495.

1 Gervais, abbot of the Premonstratensian abbeys of Saint-Just-en-Chaussée, 1199–1205, Thenailles, 1205–9, and Prémontré, 1209–20, and bishop of Séez, 1220–8. *MP* II, 401, 527, 565; Cheney, "Gervase, Abbot of Prémontré."
2 The collegiate church of Saint-Waast de Soissons.

cum querela fuisset diutius ventilata, ego tandem meliori consilio ductus, intuitu Dei et ob remedium anime matris mee in presentia judicium predictorum memoratam elemosinam recognovi et laudavi et quitavi, omnino interposito fidei sacramento quod nunquam decetero super ea per me vel per alium Premonstratensem ecclesiam molestabo. Ut igitur recognitio et quitancia ista perpetuam habeant firmitatem, presentem kartam sigilli mei appensione munivi. Actum anno incarnationis dominice M° CC° octavo decimo.

491

January, 1233.

Colard[1] *[II] de Commenchon, with the assent of Aelide, his wife, gives in alms to the church of Prémontré the 12* denarii Parisiensium *that it had paid him annually on his house at Bonneuil,*[2] *and receives in return from Prémontré a lump sum of 20* solidi Parisiensium. *Aelide also renounces what she held by right of* dos *in the above gift.*

A. Cartulary of Prémontré, fol. 109r.

B. Original, AD Oise, H 6008, previously sealed on a double strip of parchment.

Karta Colardi de Caumenchon de elemosina duodecim denariorum Parisiensium quos remisit ecclesie Premonstrate.

[E]go Colardus de Caumencon notum facio omnibus presentes litteras inspecturis quod ego ob remedium anime mee, de consensu et bona voluntate Aelidis, uxoris mee, contuli et remisi in perpetuam elemosinam ecclesie Premonstratensis duodecim denarios Parisienses quos in domo sua de Bonolio michi et heredibus meis, annis singulis, in perpetuum reddere tenebantur. Et ut elemosina ista stabilior perseveret tam ego quam dicta Aelidis, uxor mea, fidem dedimus corporalem quod dictam elemosinam non repetemus decetero nec repeti faciemus nec ipsam ecclesiam super eadem elemosina molestabimus nec faciemus modo aliquo molestari. Renunciavit etiam prefata uxor mea omni juri quod habebat vel habere poterat tam nomine dotis quam alio jure vel titulo in elemosina supradicta. Ecclesia vero Premonstratensis, ad huiusmodi beneficium habens respectum, de gratia et bona voluntate sua viginti solidos Parisienses mihi dedit. Ut autem elemosina ista firma sit et stabilis in perpetuum

---

1 Colard II, lord of Commenchon (cant. Chauny, https://dicotopo.cths.fr/places/P45903373). Leducq, *Commenchon*, 53.

2 Bonneuil, cant. Ham, https://dicotopo.cths.fr/places/P66750585.

presentem kartam ad petitionem dicte uxoris mee sigilli mei munimine roboravi. Actum anno gratie M° CC° XXX° III°,[3] mense januario.

492

1318

Jean,[1] dean, and the chapter of Noyon, upon the advice of Pierre[2] de Hattencourt and Jean de Châtillon,[3] reach an agreement with the abbot [Adam I][4] of Prémontré following a dispute about the tithes of the lands, meadows, and other cultivated areas concerning the Premonstratensian house at Thury.[5]

A. Cartulary of Prémontré, fol. 109r.
B. Original, AN, L 995, no. 149, previously sealed.

NO RUBRIC. LATER ADDITION.

[U]niversis presentes litteras inspecturis J[ohannes], decanus et capitulum Noviomensis[6] salutem in Domino sempiternam. Dudum inter nos ex una parte et religiosos viros abbatem et conventum ecclesie Premonstratensis ex altera orta controversia super decimis terrarum pratorum et aliorum[7] culturarum pertinentium ad domum dictorum religiosorum de Thoiry,[8] nobis asserentibus et dicentibus quociens et quando dicta domus fuit vel est in manibus eorumdem et dicte terre, prata seu appenditie predicte per eosdem seu eorum nomine coluntur seu culte fuerant, fuisse et esse in possessione percipiendi et levandi decimas de terris, pratis seu appenditiis predictis, sicut quando domum predictam cum terris et appenditiis colonis extraneis a[9] censam seu firmam tradiderunt et

3 millesimo ducentesimo tricesimo tertio *B*.

1 Jean d'Ercheu (cant. Roye, https://dicotopo.cths.fr/places/P67904398), attested as dean of the chapter of Noyon from 1297 to the 1310s and founder of the hospital at Ercheu ca. 1309. *GC* IX, col. 1034; Colliette, *Mémoires pour servir à l'histoire ecclésiastique, civile et militaire de la province du Vermandois*, vol. 2, 743.
2 Pierre de Hattencourt, canon of Noyon, was involved in the translation of relics of St Éloi in 1306. Le Vasseur, *Annales de l'Eglise Cathédrale de Noyon*, 1050.
3 Likely Jean de Châtillon, who was first prior and then abbot of Prémontré, ca. 1333–40. *GC* IX, col. 653.
4 Adam I de Crécy, abbot of Prémontré, 1304–27. *MP* II, 527.
5 Thury, arr. Laon, https://dicotopo.cths.fr/places/P84789655.
6 *Om.* ecclesie *A*.
7 aliarum *B*.
8 Thoiri *B*.
9 ad *B*.

quod pro minutis decimis in eadem contingentibus tres solidos in ecclesia parrochiali de Mares singulis annis in nativitate Beati Johannis Baptiste tenebantur et tenentur nobis solvere religiosis[10] predicti,[11] dictis religiosis ex adverso dicentibus et asserentibus per speciale privilegium a prestatione decimarum huiusmodi se exemptos, tandem nos pacem totis conatibus affectantes super totis[12] decimis et tota controversia, mediantibus discretis viris, magistris Petro de Hatencourt,[13] scolastico nostro, utriusque juris doctore, et Johanne de Castellione, doctore in decretis, fratre et canonico dicte Premonstratensis ecclesie, cum religiosis predictis compromisimus[14] in hunc modum, videlicet quod ipsi nobis seu nostro nontio[15] singulis annis in nativitate Domini solum unum modium bladi cum dimidio ad mensuram Calniacensem talis scilicet qualis in territorio domus predicte crescet, in grangia[16] domus assumendum quando et quociens domum predictam in suis manibus tenebunt et possessiones ad eamdem pertinentes aut ipsorum partem aliqualem propriis manibus aut sumptibus excoli facient. Item pro minutis decimis in clausura dicte domus tres solidos in nativitate[17] Beati Johannis et in ecclesia parrochiali predictis solvere tenebuntur; si vero domum et possessiones predictas ad firmam seu censam in toto vel in parte dederint religiosi predicti aut colantur sumptibus alienis, nos decimas percipiemus et levabimus integre, prout hactenus consuevimus, de possessionibus predictis[18] salvis in omnibus aliis utriusque partis juribus et privilegiis quibus propter compositionem premissam in ceteris nolumus in aliquo derogari seu prejudicium generari. Compositionem autem predictam promittimus bona fide inviolabiliter observare nos et successores nostros[19] bona nostra mobilia et immobilia ad observationem omnium premissorum efficaciter obligantes. In cuius et ceteri.[20] Datum anno Domini M° CCC° XVIII°.[21]

---

10 religiosi *B*.

11 supradicti *B*.

12 dictis *B*.

13 Hatencurt *B*.

14 composuimus *B*.

15 nuntio *B*.

16 *Om.* dicte *A*.

17 termino nativitatis *B*.

18 supradictis *B*.

19 nostros *B*.

20 *Add.* ceteri *A*; rei testimonium sigillum nostri capituli litteris presentibus duximus apponendum *B*.

21 millesimo trecentesimo decimo octavo, mense octobris *B*.

493

July, 1313.

Oudard [I],[1] *lord of Ham, following a dispute with the abbot and convent of Prémontré about the rights of* haute justice *and* basse justice *on the ponds in the vicinity of the Premonstratensian house of Bonneuil,*[2] *puts in place boundary markers to delimit each party's respective lands. (See **494**.)*

A. Cartulary of Prémontré, fol. 109v.
B. Original not found.

NO RUBRIC. LATER ADDITION.

A tous chiaus qui ches presentes lettres verront et orront, jou Oudars, escuiers, sires de Hem, salut. Comme descors fust meus entre religieus hommes et honnestes l'abbé et le couvent de Premonstré d'une part et moi Oudart devantdit d'autre part seur chau que jou disoie et maintenoie que toute li justice haute et basse des mares qui sont entour le maison de Bonnuel estoit mine dusques as fosses qui sont entour les gardins, les ortaus, les aires et le pourpris de le maison de Bonnueil devantdite et que en saisine en estoie les devantdiz abbé et couvent disant au contraire que toute li justiche haute et basse apparetenoit et appartient a yaus et en saisine en sont et estoient dusques au cours del yawe qui vient devers l'annoy de Gaulencourt,[3] ainsi que li vies kemins de Bonneil se porte, qui va parmi le mares droit a Ham. Sachent tout que je par le conseil de bonnes gens veu et consideré et mi en fourme par bonne gent digné de foy, du droit et de la saisinne des devantdiz religieus et du mien, pour bien de pais, reconnois que je me sui acordés et acordé que pour hoster tous descors dore en avant, bonnes seront ~~bonnes seront~~ assises en le menniere qui sensuit. Ch'est a savoir a mouvoir du kemin qui va a Gaulencourt tout selonc les fosses dusques a le fontainne qu'on dist a le Sanch ou assaria bonnes qui seront deus verges en sus des fosses qui cloent le maison les ortans, les aires de Bonniel, si comme dit est, et d'endroit chele fontainne tout entour les fosses des devantdiz lius, si con dit est, entour le mares ou assaria, bonnes a une vergne pres des fosses, tout entour ainsi que li fosse se portent, dusques au vies garding et dusques as pres et as terres et dusques a ycheles bonnes; je m'acorde et otrie que li dit religieus

1 Oudard I (sometimes referred to as Eudes VI), lord of Ham. His relationship to the previous lords of Ham is not clarified in any known primary source, but he was likely a son of Jean II, lord of Ham (d. ca. 1285). By 1296, he was married to Dorée, daughter of Marie de Frianvile, and Eustache, lord of Marteville. Pipon, ed., *Le chartrier de l'Abbaye-aux-Bois (1202–1341)*, 353.

2 *MP* II, 484.

3 Golancourt, cant. Guiscard, https://dicotopo.cths.fr/places/P75999303.

puissent prendre, ~~justische~~ justichier et esploitier a tous jours toute fois que quelconques cas si offerra et widier le bourbe de leur fosses et jeter dusques as dites bonnes sans les ~~des~~ devantdiz fosses a larguir en tele maniere que le dit religieus par cest acort ne porront dore en avant justichier ne demander justiche entre les dites bonnes ne je dore en avant justiche ne seignerie dedans les dites bonnes ne porrai ne devrai demander et est chius acors fais sans prejudice porter a chiaus qui avoient leur pasture au mares au chois que les bonnes fussent assises; liquel porront pasturer dedens les dites bonnes dusques as fosses et dehors toutes les fois qu'il leur plaira. De rekief il est acordé entre les devantdiz religieus et mi Oudart devandit que je veul loé, grée et otrié que, entre le mares et le kemin qui va de Bonnuel a le mote, bonnes seront assises par devers le mares ainsi que li fosses anchiens se porte entre le mares et le mares[4] et le kemin et pour che je ai entendu et sui enfourmés que li devantdit religieus fisent les fosses ainsi com il s'aperent quant il furent autrefois fais. Je veul greé et otrié et acordé que li dit religieus puissent, les fosse~~us~~ ainsi com il s'aprerent et monstrent faire, reparier et widier dusques as bonnes toutes fois quantes fois il leur plaira a tous jours et jeter le terre par devers le kemin pour le kemin amender. Et se ou temps qui est avenir aucuns empeschement estait mis as devantdis religieus a che qu'il ne gassent paisivlement de toutes les choses deseure devisées ou d'aucunnes d'icheles, je, mi hoir et chil qui aront cause de mi seriens tenut as dis religieus warandis et delivrer toutes les choses devant dites et a hoster l'empeeschement sancun en iavoit horsmis et exepté le fait du Roy men seignoir, ses hoirs, ses successeurs, et a rendre tous cous, frais et damaiges qui pour l'occasion de che leur porroient venir. Et veul que li porteres de ches lettres en soit creus par son serment sans autre preuve traire. Et s'il estoit ainsi que ja n'aviegne, que je, mi hoir et chil qui aront cause de mi, fussiens endefaute trouvé de warandir as dis religieus toutes les choses dessus dites ou auccunes d'icheles, je, mi hoir et chil qui aront cause de mi seriens tenu as dis religieus en trente livres Parisi pour cause de painne avoec les cous, et les frais, si com dit est, et pour che ne demouront mie que toutes les choses devandites ne fussent et demourassent fermes et estaules a tous jours, et a toutes les chosses dessus dites de point en point fermement tenir, warder et acomplir, obliger jou, mi, mes hoirs tous chiaus qui aront cause de mi et tous mes biens et les biens de mes hoirs meules et non meules, presens et a venir, pour penre, saisir, vendre et despendre dusques a plainne satisfation de toutes les choses dessus dites et de chascune d'eles et a plus grant seurté de tenir et d'acomplir toutes les choses devant dites, si com dit est, jou ai suppliet et supplie encore a tres excellent prinche haut et poissant nostre seigneur le Roy de France que il les choses dessus dites et chascune d'eles veule graer, loer, otrier, approver, et confirmer par ses lettres pendans scelées de son seel en le fourme

4 *Sic A.*

et en[5] le maniere qu'il est contenu en ches presentes lettres. Et pour chou que che soit ferme chose et estaule a tous jours ju ai ches presentes lettres seelés de mon seel qui furent faites en l'an de grace mil CCC et treze, ou mois de jungnet.

494

July 20, 1313.

*Oudard [I],[1] lord of Ham, designates his procurer Arnoul le Barbier de Golancourt[2] to mark out the agreed-upon boundaries between the lands of Oudard and that of the Premonstratensian house of Bonneuil.[3] (See **493**.)*

A. Cartulary of Prémontré, fol. 110r.

B. Original, AD Oise, Hs 1385, previously sealed on a single strip of parchment with fragment of surviving seal in brown wax.

NO RUBRIC. LATER ADDITION.

Jou Oudars, sirez de Hem, escuiers, fas savoir a tous que comme jou aie fait acort a l'eglise de Premonstré de metre bonnes au depert de me justiche[4] entour leur maison de Bonniol,[5] si comme li acorz est contenuz en mes letres et je et li dit religieus avons assis bonnes[6] puis[7] le desenre de le fontaine au tonnel par devers Gaulencourt dusques a le Sanch et miz ~~estas~~ estes[8] ou les bonnes[9] doivent estre ~~pour~~ puis[10] le fontaine a le Sanch dusques au vies[11] gardin, je

5 *Superscr.* en *A*.

1 Oudard I (sometimes referred to as Eudes VI), lord of Ham. His relationship to the previous lords of Ham is not clarified in any known primary source, but he was likely a son of Jean II, lord of Ham (d. ca. 1285). By 1296, he was married to Dorée, daughter of Marie de Frianvile, and Eustache, lord of Marteville. Pipon, ed., *Le chartrier de l'Abbaye-aux-Bois (1202–1341)*, 353.

2 Golancourt, cant. Guiscard, https://dicotopo.cths.fr/places/P75999303.

3 *MP* II, 484.

4 justice *B*.

5 Bonoel *B*.

6 bonnez *B*.

7 puiz *B*.

8 *Superscr*. estes *B*.

9 bonnez *B*.

10 *Superscr*. puis *B*.

11 viez *B*.

estaulis[12] Ernoul le Barbier de Gaulencourt procureur pour mi pour assir les dites bonnes,[13] si comme il est contenu en l'acort es lieus li estoc sont fakié et li doiens[14] pooir et mandement especial de ce faire et de garder les dites bonnes[15] contre tous exepté le Roi monseigneur et ses gens[16] et tenrai tout ce qu'il en fera sus obligations[17] de mes biens,[18] aussi comme se je l'avoie fait. Au tesmoing de ce je ai ces letres[19] scelées de mon seel. Ce fut fait le venredi devant le Magdelainne, l'an de grace mil CCC et treze.

495

June 17, 1327. Corbeil.

Brother Simon le Rat,[1] prior of the Knights Hospitaller in France, makes known the resolution of a dispute between his order on the one hand, and abbot [Adam I/II][2] and the convent of Prémontré and abbot [Hugues II][3] and the abbey of Notre-Dame de Ham on the other, concerning the tithes of Offoy[4] and Buny.[5] Simon relinquishes to Prémontré and Ham the rights that the Hospitallers claimed to possess on these tithes, in exchange for an annual payment of four muids *of grain (*blé*), measure of Ham.*

A. Cartulary of Prémontré, fol. 110r.

B. Original not found.

---

12 estauliz *B*.
13 bonnez *B*.
14 doins *B*.
15 ditez bonnez *B*.
16 genz *B*.
17 l'obligation *B*.
18 mez bienz *B*.
19 letrez *B*.

---

1 Simon le Rat was marshal of the Knights Hospitaller, 1299, 1303, and 1306–10, and preceptor of that order in Cyprus, 1303, before becoming its prior in France in 1313. However, Jochen Burgtorf notes a reference in a letter of Pope John XXII to Simon's death in March 1327; this discrepancy in dating may be the result of conflicting old style and new style dates. Burgtorf, *The Central Convent of Hospitallers and Templars*, 655–6.

2 Adam I de Crécy, abbot of Prémontré, 1304–27 or Adam II de Wassignies, abbot of Prémontré, 1327–33. *MP* II, 528.

3 Hugues II, abbot of the Augustinian abbey of Notre-Dame de Ham, 1310s/20s. *GC* IX, col. 1123.

4 Offoy, cant. Ham, https://dicotopo.cths.fr/places/P14011159.

5 Buny, cant. Nesle, https://dicotopo.cths.fr/places/P07807251.

NO RUBRIC. LATER ADDITION.

A tous chiaus qui ces presentes lettres verront et orront frere Simon le Rat de la sainte maison de l'ospital Saint Jehan de Jherusalem, humele prieur en France, salut en Nostre Signeur. Comme debas et descors fust mus entre relegieus hommes et honnet l'abbé et le convent de Premonstré, de l'esveschié de Laon, l'abbé et le convent de Nostre Dame de Hem, de l'eveschié de Noyon, d'une part et nous et nos freres d'autre part seur che que li dit abbé et convent disoient et maintenoient que il avoient et avoir devoient et a aus apartenoit et apartenir devoit toutes les dimes des terres seans es terrois d'Ouffois et de Beuni, excepté siz vins sestiers de terre ou environ, es queles nous, a cause de la petite dime, aviens la moitié et partissians a le dite dime de ces siz vins sestiere de terre: encontre les dis abbés et convens. Et de se disoient avoir goy, usé et possessé de tel tamps et per tel tamps et si lonc qu'il n'estoit memoire dou contraire et qui devoit souffire a saisine avoir acquise. Nous proposans et maitenans au contraire et disans que a nous apartenoient et apartenir devoient les dimes de pluseurs autreschaus seans es dis terrois et que de ce estions nous en saisine de tel tamps et per tel tamps qu'il devoit souffire a droit et saisine avoir acquise. Sachent tout que nous en la pardefin et par le conseil et assentement de nos freres et pour le grant pourfit de nostre maison et par le conseil d'autres bonnes gens, pour bien de pais et d'acort avons acordé amiablement avoec les devant dis abbés et convens en la maniere qui s'en suit. C'est a savoir que li devant dit abbé et convent doivent goir paisuimlement a tous jours mais et avoir pour jaus tele partie de dimes comme nous avions ou poions avoir en toutes les dimes des terrois desus dis. Et avons transporté et transportons es dis abbés et convens et a leurs esglises tout le droit et l'action que nous avions ou poions avoir es dites dimes par quelconque maniere que ce fust, et parmi se et en recompensation des dites dimes li dit abbé et convent nous doivent rendre et paier a tous jours mais chascun an a Ouffois au terme de Noel quatre muis de blé a la mesure de Hem. Et en paiers chascun abbé selonc sa porcion sur les dites dimes et dou de la dime et a plus grant seurté de nous rendre et paier la soume dou blé dessus dit chascun an au terme en la fourme et en la maniere qu'il est par dessus dit et devisé, ont li dit abbé et convent obligiet et aloiet, obligent et aloient tout le pourfit des dites dimes pour prendre, lever et arester jusques a plaine satisfacion des quatre muis de blé desus dis. Sainsi estoit qu'il fussent en defaute de paier les quatre muis de blé que ja n'aviengne avoec tous cous, frais et despens que nous y arions ou porrions avoir par le deffaute de lor paiement. Et nous proumetons en bonne foi as dis abbes et convens que contre ceste pais et ordenanche si comme il est par devant dit et devisé, ne venrons ne venir ne ferons par nous ne par autre en aucunne maniere. En tesmongnage de la quele chose nous avons ceste presente lettre seelée dou seel de nostre prioure de Franche. Donné en men general capitre a Corbeuill, le merquedi apres la feste Saint Barnabe apostre, l'an de grace mil CCC et vint et VII.

496

July 27, 1325.

Jean de Soissons,[1] *lord of Ostel,* prévôt *of the church of Reims, and dean of Laon, adds an emendation to a pre-existing agreement between abbot [Adam I]*[2] *and the convent of Prémontré and the counts of Soissons concerning the* winaige *and* pedaige *in the lands of the counts of Soissons. Jean lowers the limit above which the Premonstratensians must pay the* winaige *from 60 to 20* sols de Soissons. *(See **3**, **282**.)*

A. Cartulary of Prémontré, fol. 110v.

B. Original, AN, L 995, no. 152, previously sealed with a double strip of parchment.

Winaiges d'Ostel.[3]

A tous ciaus qui ces presentes lettres verront et orront Jehans de Soissons, sires[4] d'Ostel, prevos de l'eglize de Rains et doyens de Laon salut. Sachent[5] tout que comme li abbés[6] et li convens de l'eglize de Premonstré soient[7] privilegié[8] et chartré[9] des contes[10] de Soissons que il puissent mener leur[11] propres vins et leur[12] propres choses a leur[13] propres voitures chascun an par les winaiges[14] de le[15] conte de Soissons sans paier winaige[16] jusques[17] a le[18] somme de soissante solz chascun an de le[19] monnoie de Soissons c'on dist[20] noires et se il avenoit que il menassent plus de leur[21] propres choses par les winaiges[22] de Soissons, dont li winaiges[23] montast

---

1 Jean de Nesle (d. 1330), son of Jean III de Nesle, count of Soissons, and Marguerite de Montfort, was dean of Laon from 1323. Millet, *Les Chanoines du chapitre cathédral de Laon*, 423–4.

2 Adam I de Crécy, abbot of Prémontré, 1304–27. *MP* II, 528.

3 This act is a later addition, and its rubric is in black rather than red ink.

4 sirez *B*.

5 Scachent *B*.

6 abbez *B*.

7 soyent *B*.

8 privilegiet *B*.

9 chartret *B*.

10 contez *B*.

11 leurs *B*.

12 leurs *B*.

13 leurs *B*.

14 winage *B*.

15 la *B*.

16 winage *B*.

17 jusquez *B*.

18 la *B*.

19 la *B*.

20 qu'on dist *B*.

21 leurs *B*.

22 winages *B*.

23 winages *B*.

plus que la dite summe[24] des LX[25] solz, il paieroient pedaige[26] ou winaige[27] dou souscrois et li dit winaige[28] soient adpresent[29] divisé[30] et [illegible]tit[31] par freraige[32] et nous entaingnons[33] partie a Hostel[34] pour bien de pais, acordé[35] est entre les dis religieus d'une part et nous d'autre que li dit religieus porront mener leur[36] propres choses a leur[37] propres voitures par le dit winaige[38] d'Ostel chascun an sans paier winaige[39] jusques a le[40] somme des vint solz de la dite monnoie et, se plus menoient de leur[41] propres choses a leur[42] propres voitures par le dit winaige[43] chascun an, dont li winaiges[44] montast plus de la dite somme des vint solz, il paieroient winaige[45] dou seurplus. Laquelle[46] composition et acort nous prometons[47] a tenir loialment[48] en bonne foy et a ce oblegons[49] nous, nos hoirs et nos successeurs et tous[50] les biens de nous, de nos hoyrs[51] et de nos successeurs. En tesmoingnaige[52] de la quel[53] chose[54] nous avons ces presentes lettres seelées de nostre propre seel qui furent faites l'an de grace mil CCC[55] vint et cinc,[56] le samedi apres la Magdelainne.[57]

---

24 somme *B.*
25 soissante *B.*
26 pedage *B.*
27 winage *B.*
28 winage *B.*
29 a present *B.*
30 divisiet *B.*
31 partit *B.*
32 frerage *B.*
33 en taingnons *B.*
34 Ostel *B.*
35 acordet *B.*
36 leurs *B.*
37 leurs *B.*
38 winage *B.*
39 winage *B.*
40 la *B.*
41 leurs *B.*
42 leurs *B.*
43 winage *B.*
44 winages *B.*
45 winage *B.*
46 Laquele *B.*
47 proumettons *B.*
48 loyalment *B.*
49 obligons *B.*
50 touz *B.*
51 hoirs *B.*
52 tesmoingnage *B.*
53 des quelz *B.*
54 choses *B.*
55 trois cens *B.*
56 cuinc *B.*
57 Mazelainne *B.*

497

October 11, 1142.

The Cistercians and Premonstratensians, represented by Raynaud,[1] *abbot of Cîteaux, and Hugues [I],*[2] *abbot of Prémontré, respectively, conclude a treaty, agreeing that their houses should be situated at a certain minimum distance from one another – depending on the region and whether the house is a house of brothers or sisters – and that they will pray once a year for the deceased members of the other order. (See* ***498****.)*[3]

A. Cartulary of Prémontré, fol. 111r.

B. Original (chirograph), AN, L 995, no. 6, previously sealed. In the left margin and beginning at the top, the upper half of the letters that form the word CYROGRAPHUM.

Other Manuscript Copies: AD Haute-Marne, 4 H 18, previously sealed (12th c.); "Liber usuum Cisterciensis ordinis," KBR, MS II 1059, fol. 1r (12/13th c.); Cartulary of Grimbergen Abbey, Abdij van Grimbergen Oud Archief, Klas II, 1, fol. 9r (13th c.); Cartulary of Park Abbey, Archief van de Abdij van Park te Heverlee, Cartulary B ("Liber ruber"), fol. 142r (13th c.); "Institutiones patrum Premonstratensis ordinis," BnF, MS lat. 9752, fol. 29r (13th c.); Cartulary of Floreffe Abbey, Archives de l'État à Namur, Arch. Eccl., no. 3288, fol. 181r (late 13th c.); Cartulary of Averbode Abbey, Archief van de abdij van Averbode, Sectie I, Reg. 2, fol. 19r (1380); "Privilegia a Romanis Pontificibus ordini Praemonstratensi concessa," BnF, MS lat. 4394, fol. 87r–89r (14th c.); Bayerische Staatsbibliothek München, Clm 9903, fol. 1r–1v (14th c.); "Liber statutorum necnon et de institutione sive de origine candidi ordinis scilicet Premonstratensis," Koninklijke Bibliotheek van Nederland, MS 128 G 21, fols. 76–76v (1445); Archief van de Abdij van Park te Heverlee, MS VII, 14, fol. 65v–66r (15th c.); Archief van de Abdij van Park te Heverlee, MS VII, 40, fol. 91v–92r (15th c.)

EDITION: Le Mire, *Ordinis Praemonstratensis chronicon*, 110–12; Le Paige, *Bibliotheca*, 322–3; Manrique, *Cistercienses seu verius ecclesiasticae annales a condito Cistercio*, vol. 1, 432–3; Kuen, *Collectio Scriptorum Rerum Historico-Monastico Ecclesiasticarum Variorum Religiosorum Ordinum*, vol. 6, 28; Canivez, *Statuta Capitulorum Generalium Ordinis Cisterciensis ab Anno 1116*

---

1 Raynaud de Bar, son of Milon II, count of Bar-sur-Seine, and Mathilde de Noyers, abbot of Cîteaux, 1134–50.

2 Hugues I de Fosses (ca. 1093–1164), first abbot of Prémontré.

3 This act was confirmed twice by *vidimus* in 1257. See Peigné-Delacourt, *Cartulaire de l'abbaye de Morienval*, 70; Verlaguet, *Cartulaire de l'abbaye de Bonnecombe*, vol. 1, 140–1, fn. 2. It was also confirmed by *vidimus* in 1259. See Klosterarchiv Merherau, no. 8.

ad Annum 1786, vol. 1, 35–7; Gerits, "Les actes de confraternité de 1142 et de 1153 entre Cîteaux et Prémontré," 201–3; Spahr, "Zum Freundschaftsbündnis zwischen Cisterciensern und Prämonstratensern," 14–16; Valvekens, "Actus Confraternitatis Inter Ordinem Praemonstratensem et Ordinem Cisterciensem," 329–30; Waddell, "The Myth of Cistercian Origins," 351–2; Abadie, "Un temporel monastique dans l'espace médiéval gascon," vol. 2, 22.

REGISTER: Weissthanner, *Die Urkunden und Urbare des Klosters Schäftlarn*, 256–7.

Confirmatio societatis et pacis inter Cistercienses et Premonstratenses.

[I]n nomine sancte et cetera.[4] Confirmatio societatis et pacis inter Cistercienses[5] et Premonstratenses. Igitur ad custodiam pacis et karitatis, utriusque capituli assensu, inter utrumque ordinem constitutum et confirmatum est ut nullus Cistercensium[6] canonicum vel novicium seu conversum Premonstratensis ordinis, nullus Premonstratensium monachum, vel novitium seu conversum Cisterciensis[7] ordinis nisi ex pari consensu, recipiant. Nullus in utroque ordine locum ad abbatiam edificet circa alterius ordinis abbatiam infra quatuor[8] leugas ad mensuram uniuscuiusque provincie preter quod in Anglia due leuge pro una computentur et in Longobardia duo miliaria pro una leuga, nisi forte antiqua loca sint, quorum redditus[9] et possessiones ad tenendum conventum sufficiant de grangia ad grangiam sive de grangia ad abbatiam ad minus semper una sit[10] leuga, mansio vero sororum ab abbatia distet duabus leugis. Verum tamen terre ille que ante annum incarnationis et diem qui suscriptus[11] est suscepte fuerant sub hac lege non tenebuntur siquidem singule terre ad integram carrucam suffecerint vel ad edificandam abbatiam suscepte fuerint. Nullus in utroque ordine alter ab altero tam de nutrimentis quam de laboribus decimas exiget vel accipiet. Si aliquis in utroque ordine de qualibet re emenda vel acquirenda[12] loco suo prius tractare vel alique convenire inceperit, antequam sponte dimiserit, nullus de altero ordine

4 *Om.* cetera *A*; individue Trinitatis, Patris et Filii et Spiritus Sancti, amen *B*.
5 Cystercienses *B*.
6 Cystercensium *B*.
7 Cysterciensis *B*.
8 IIII^or *B*.
9 reditus *B*.
10 intersit *B*.
11 subscriptus *B*.
12 adquirenda *B*.

sibi usurpare vel inpedire presumat. Si forte in aliquibus locis inter aliquos utriusque ordinis aliquid querimonie emerserit et inter eos familiariter per aliquos religiosos mediatores componi non poterit, sine maiori audientia differetur et ad audientiam alterutrius generalis capituli referetur quisquis in eodem capitulo reus esse claruerit quod intulit dampnum prius restituat et postmodum in capitulum abbatis que offendit veniens usque ad satisfactionem ante pedes eius[13] humiliet reliquum vero penitencie in dispositione generalis capituli sui ordinis permaneat commemorationem et plenarium officium pro omnibus defunctis suis singulis annis invicem facient. Quod ut firmum deinceps et in eternum quamdiu utriusque ordinis status viguerit inconvulsum permaneat. Ego Renaldus,[14] Cisterciensis[15] abbas, et generalis nostri capituli conventus, ego quoque Hugo, Premonstratensis abbas, et generalis nostri capituli conventus presenti karitatis cyrographo firmamus et sigillis nostris pariter consignamus. S. Renaldi,[16] Cisterciensis[17] abbatis. S. Bartholomei,[18] abbatis de Firmitate. S.[19] domini Bernardi,[20] Clarevallensis abbatis. S. Wichardi,[21] Pontiniacensis abbatis. S.[22] Hugonis, Premonstratensis abbatis. S. Walteri,[23] Laudunensis abbatis. S. Gerlandi,[24] Florefiensis[25] abbatis. S. Henrici,[26] Vivariensis abbatis. Actum est hoc anno incarnationis dominice M° C° XLII°, epacta XX[a],[27] indictione quinta,[28] concurrente III°, V° idus octobris.

13 *Om.* se *A.*
14 Reinaldus *B.*
15 Cysterciensis *B.*
16 Signum Reinaldi *B.*
17 Cysterciensis *B.*
18 Barthélemy I, abbot of the Cistercian abbey of La Ferté-sur-Grosne, 1132–71.
19 Signum *B.*
20 Bernard, abbot of Clairvaux, 1115–53.
21 Guichard de Pontigny, abbot of the Cistercian abbey of Pontigny, 1137–65, and later archbishop of Lyon, 1165–81.
22 Signum *B.*
23 Gautier de Saint-Maurice was abbot of the Premonstratensian abbey of Saint-Martin de Laon, 1124–51, and bishop of Laon, 1151–3. *MP* II, 512.
24 Gerland, abbot of the Premonstratensian abbey of Floreffe, 1134–73. *MP* II, 377.
25 Floreffiensis *B.*
26 Henri, abbot of the Premonstratensian abbey of Viviers (later moved to Valséry), ca. 1125–ca. 1153. *MP* II, 538.
27 XX[a] II[a] *B.*
28 V[a] *B.*

498

1153

*Abbot Hugues [I][1] of Prémontré and [Goswin],[2] abbot of Cîteaux, following certain disputes, urge the members of their respective orders to respect the treaty previously concluded between the Premonstratensian and Cistercian Orders. (See **497**.)*[3]

A. Cartulary of Prémontré, fol. 111r.

B. Original (chirograph), AN, L 995, no. 16, previously sealed. In the right margin and beginning at the top, the lower half of letters that form the word CIROGRAPHUM.

Other Manuscript Copies: "Liber usuum Cisterciensis ordinis," KBR, MS II 1059, fol. 1r (12/13th c.); Cartulary of Grimbergen Abbey, Abdij van Grimbergen Oud Archief, Klas II, 1, fol. 9r–9v (13th c.); Cartulary of Park Abbey, Archief van de Abdij van Park te Heverlee, Cartulary B ("Liber ruber"), fol. 138r (13th c.).

EDITION: Le Paige, *Bibliotheca*, 323; Hugo, *prob.* 2, col. xliii; Gerits, "Les actes de confraternité de 1142 et de 1153 entre Cîteaux et Prémontré," 204–5; Abadie, "Un temporel monastique dans l'espace médiéval gascon," vol. 2, 23.

Item karta abbatis Premonstratensis et Cisterciensis de quadam conpositione.

[I]n nomine Domini. Nos, abbates Premonstratensis et Cisterciensis ordinis, pariter congregati querelas quasdam que inter fratres nostros emerserant, fraterne caritatis zelo[4] et rationabili consideratione terminavimus; quocirca utriusque ordinis auctoritate statuimus que ibidem sunt diffinita irretractabiliter utrinque teneri secundum recognitionem personarum quarum arbitrio diffinita noscuntur sed et hoc quoque utriusque ordinis auctoritate statuimus et firmamus ut conpositio et societas inter utrumque ordinem

1 Hugues I de Fosses (ca. 1093–1164), first abbot of Prémontré.

2 Goswin, abbot of the Cistercian abbey of Bonnevaux, 1141–ca. 1151, and of Cîteaux, ca. 1151–5.

3 This act was confirmed by *vidimus* in 1257. Cartulary of Lieu-Restauré, AD Oise, H 5733, fol. 24v–25r.

4 xelo *B*.

olim firmata ita deinceps irrefragabiliter observetur, ut null~~u~~is vestrum liceat inde aliquid dispensare vel aliquid contra formam illam sibi invicem indulgere absque communi assensu generalis capituli Premonstratensis et Cisterciensis. Quicquid autem contra illam compositionem presumptum fuerit, penitus amittatur et qui presumpserit, graviter puniatur. Anno ab incarnatione Domini M° C° LIII°, hoc statuimus et vice utriusque capituli generalis firmavimus nos abbates. Ego Hugo Premonstratensi. Ego Garinus[5] Sancti Martini Laudunensis. Ego Gillebertus[6] Viromandensis. Ego Philippus[78] de Sancti Petrimonte. Ego Johannes[9] de Septem[10] Fontibus. Ego Balduinus[11] de[12] Basso Fonte.[13] Ego quoque Wicardus[14] Pontinus. Ego Robertus[15] Clarevallis. Ego Lambertus[16] Morimundensis. Ego Willermus[17,18] de Fonteneto. Ego Robertus[19] de Fusniaco cum multis aliis utriusque ordinis.

5 Guérin, abbot of the Premonstratensian abbey of Saint-Martin de Laon, 1151–71. *MP* II, 512.

6 Gilbert I, abbot of the Premonstratensian abbey of Vermand, 1152–66. *MP* II, 427.

7 Phyllipus *B*.

8 Philippe, abbot of the Premonstratensian abbey of Bucilly, 1153–6. *MP* II, 366.

9 Jean, abbot of the Premonstratensian abbey of Septfontaines-en-Thiérache. *MP* II, 399.

10 VII *B*.

11 Baudouin, abbot of the Premonstratensian abbey of Basse-Fontaine, 1148–58. *MP* II, 480.

12 *Superscr.* de *B*.

13 Baiso Fonte *B*.

14 Guichard de Pontigny, abbot of the Cistercian abbey of Pontigny, 1137–65, and later archbishop of Lyon, 1165–81.

15 Robert de Bruges, first abbot of the Cistercian abbey of Notre-Dame des Dunes, 1139–53, and abbot of Clairvaux, 1153–7.

16 This conflicts with the accepted chronology of the abbots of Morimond, as laid out in Bouchard, *Sword, Miter, and Cloister*, 421, which states that Lambert was abbot of the Cistercian abbeys of Clairefontaine, 1133–54, of Morimond, 1154–5, and of Cîteaux, 1155–61. This discrepancy in dating may be the result of conflicting old style and new style dates.

17 Willelmus *B*.

18 Guillaume d'Épiry, abbot of the Cistercian abbey of Fontenay, ca. 1126–ca. 1154.

19 Robert I (de Coucy?), abbot of the Cistercian abbey of Foigny, 1148–69. *GC* IX, col. 630.

499

1128–56[1]

Abbot Pierre of Cluny declares that, each year, all Cluniac abbeys will celebrate an office and a general Mass for deceased Premonstratensians, as well as a Low Mass said by each priest of the order; in return, abbot Hugues [I] of Prémontré undertakes the same obligation on behalf of the Premonstratensians for the deceased of the Cluniac Order.[2]

A. Cartulary of Prémontré, fols. 111r–111v.
B. Original not found.
EDITION: Le Paige, *Bibliotheca*, 321–2 (variant).

Item karta conpositionis inter Premonstratenses et Cluniacenses.

[C]um fidelium omnium una sit expectatio, una leticia Christus Dominus qui ipsum desiderant, audiant dicentem: "Hoc est preceptum meum ut diligatis invicem."[3] Hec est caritas que in hac vita operibus sanctis et affectibus exercetur in alia quibusdam iam purgatis diu desiderata conpletur; quibusdam vero veniam sperantibus et purgandis complenda desideratur. Quorumdam peccata elemosinis et salutaribus hostiis redimere quam pium et utile sit viventibus ipsa caritas liquido edocet que quanto ceteris virtutibus prestantior tanto eius merces apparebit in fine gloriosior. Qua propter ego frater P[etrus], Cluniacensis abbas indignus, recogitans orationes religiosorum michi et nostris fore necessarias, concessi karissimo fratri nostro H[ugoni], abbatis de Premonstrato, et omnibus abbatibus ac prepositis eiusdem congregationis ut defunctis eorum officium et missa generalis singulis annis, crastina Sancti Vincentii, in nostris conventibus celebretur et ab uno quoque sacerdote missa privata eis persolvatur eo videlicet tenore ut et eorum congregationes nostris hoc idem persolvant defunctis. Ut autem rata permaneat hec constitutio litteris nostris et sigillo firmitatem eorum annunciamus congregationibus, orantes ut de eorum assensu litteris et sigillo reddamur certiores. Concedimus etiam ut nullum de eorum professis nisi abbatis sui permissione ulterius recipiamus quamdiu in huius prepositi rigore permanserint ne karitatis lese querela inter nos et ipsos

1 Pierre the Venerable (or de Montboissier) was abbot of Cluny, 1122–56; Hugues I de Fosses was abbot of Prémontré, 1128–61.

2 Le Paige's version of this act includes a clause dating it to 1140, something which is omitted in the copy in the cartulary of Prémontré. The final two sentences in the cartulary copy are omitted from Le Paige's copy. Gerits accepts the 1140 date. Gerits, "Les actes de confraternité de 1142 et de 1153 entre Cîteaux et Prémontré," 194, fn. 4.

3 John 15:12.

aliquando oriatur. Supplicamus karissimi domini, caritatem vestram ut per omnes congregationes vestras tricenarium vestrum michi concedatis et audito obitu nostro, persolvi faciatis, scientes quia orationes vestre in sinum vestrum convertentur.

500

1150s–60s[1]

The cathedral chapter of Le Puy-en-Velay writes to Hugues [I], abbot of Prémontré, asking to affiliate its church at Doue[2] to the Premonstratensian order.

A. Cartulary of Prémontré, fol. 111v. (Cancellation of charter indicated with red X placed upon the entire entry.)

B. Original not found.

EDITION: Le Paige, *Bibliotheca*, 418–19.

NO RUBRIC.

[R]everendo patri et amico, H[ugoni] Dei gratia Premonstratensis ecclesie abbati et venerabili eiusdem ecclesie conventui, Sancte Aniciensis ecclesie conventus salutem et sinceram in Christo dilectionem. Vestri fama ordinis et laudabilis eminentia sanctitatis ad nos usque perveniens voluntatem nobis inmisit ac desiderium ut nostram ecclesiam vestre ecclesie in Christi gratiam et consortium sociaremus pium desiderium quod super hoc diu habuimus, annuente Domino, intendimus perducere ad effectum. Ecclesiam siquidem quadam nostre ecclesie, que Doa dicitur, communi assensu tocius nostri capituli, ecclesie vestre concedimus ut secundum modum vestre religionis et ordinis instruatur et secundum tenorem vestri ordinis qui in ea servierint, dedicentur, salvo tamen jure nostre ecclesie ut predicta ecclesia annuum ipsi persolvat canonem pro quibusdam terris que disnoscuntur ad jurisdictionem nostre ecclesie specialiter pertinere, salva etiam obedientia que debetur nostro capitulo et confirmatione electionis abbatis ipsius

1 This act must date to the abbacy of Hugues I of Prémontré or shortly thereafter. The abbey of Saint-Jacques de Doue was founded ca. 1138 as a community of canons regular and is traditionally stated to have been given to the Premonstratensian Order by Pierre de Solignac, bishop of Puy (1159–90). The obituary of Prémontré states "Fratri Petri, Anicensis episcopi, qui ecclesiam de Doa nostro contulit ordini." Van Waefelghem, *L'Obituaire de l'abbaye de Prémontré (XIIe s., ms. 9 de Soissons)*, 41. Pierre Cubizolles states that this transfer occurred around 1162. *MP* III, 149; Cubizolles, *Le diocèse du Puy-en-Velay des origines à nos jours*, 125.

2 *MP* III, 149.

loci post factam electionem, ut assensus nostri capituli requiratur. Cum autem ob habendam in Christo ecclesie vestre societatem hoc factum sit, volumus ut memorata ecclesia ad ecclesiam vestram tanquam ad matrem filia, specialiter pertineat, nulla alia ecclesia mediante. Discretionem igitur vestram in Domino exoramus ut pro abbate virum discretum religiosum et litteratum ad nos mittatis et viros secum qui ecclesie vestre cedant ad gloriam et ad honorem et tales sint in quibus vestra ecclesia honoretur. Istud in quantum poteritis festinate; mora enim in distractione bonorum ipsius concesse ecclesie ad se traheret periculum. Vale.

501

1182[1]

Hugues [II],[2] abbot of Prémontré, and other abbots present at the General Chapter write to the abbots of the English and Scottish houses of Newsham, Sulby, Welbeck, Barlings, Croxton, Beeleigh, Lavendon, Tupholme, and Dryburgh informing them of decisions made at the General Chapter. These abbots are reminded of their obligation to attend the annual General Chapter at Prémontré, but in recognition of the difficulty of long-distance travel, only a certain number of them need attend each year on a four-year rotating basis.

A. Cartulary of Prémontré, fol. 111v.

B. Original not found.

EDITION: Holstenius, *Codex regularum monasticarum et canonicarum*, vol. 5, 294.

Conpositio inter ecclesiam Premonstratensem et Anglicos quo anno debent accedere ad capitulum generale.

H[ugonis], Dei patientia dictus abbas Premonstrati, et ceteri generalis capituli abbates, dilectis fratribus coabbatibus de Nehus,[3] de Welleford,[4] de Wellebech,[5]

---

1 The text states that the English and Scottish abbots will be obliged to attend the General Chapter from the following year, 1183, implying that this was written in 1182.

2 Hugues II de Douai, abbot of the Premonstratensian abbey of Cuissy, 1161–5, and abbot of Prémontré, 1174–89. *MP* II, 497.

3 Gervais(?), abbot of the Premonstratensian abbey of Newhouse/Newsham at the end of the twelfth century. *MP* II, 68.

4 Adam(?), abbot of the Premonstratensian abbey of Sulby, ca. 1200. *MP* II, 74.

5 Adam(?), abbot of the Premonstratensian abbey of Welbeck, 1180s/90s. *MP* II, 83.

de Berlinc,[6] de Krostun,[7] de Mandunensi,[8] de Lawedensi,[9] de Lupehosem,[10] de Drieford,[11] salutem. De circatione singulis annis inter nos facienda et qualiter annuatim ad capitulum venire debeatis quid in commune statuimus vobis scribendo innotescimus et inviolabiliter observandum in posterum presenti cyrographo communimus. Generali itaque omnium nostrum institutione sancitum est ut vos novem in una sitis circatione et duo ex vobis singulis annis veniant ita ut quarto anno veniant tres. Qui autem simul circationem facere et ad capitulum simul debeant venire nominatim exprimimus. Primo igitur anno proximo prout scilicet post hanc institutionem qui est annus M° C° LXXX° III° ab incarnatione domini circatores sint et ad capitulam veniant de Welleford et de Crokestun. Secundo anno de Neheus et de Thopeholem. Tercio de Drieford et de Maudim. Quarto anno de Wellebec et de Berling et de Leweden. Nobis ergo omnibus auctoritate ordinis in vi obedientie iniungimus ut institutionem hanc sicut hic expressa est absque omni contradictione observetis. Et unusquisque nostram harum litterarum transcriptum habeat. Scriptum vero sigillatum in domo de Nehus maneat. Si vero contigerit ut usque ad portum de Dovre venientes vel regia prohibitione vel tenpestate transfretare nequiveritis obsistente illud nobis et circationem vestram aliquo modo innotescentes ita excusabiles habeamus ac si illo anno ad capitulum proveniretis. Ad plenam huius scripti confirmationem et ad devitandam oblivionem medietas huius scripti in Premonstratensi ecclesia habetur.

502

1132. Cambrai.

Liétard,[1] bishop [of Cambrai,] decrees that should the abbot of a Premonstratensian community in the diocese of Cambrai commit an error, deviate from the order's rule, or fail in his stewardship, the abbot of Prémontré together with other Premonstratensian abbots should warn the erring abbot; and should the abbot persist in his error, he will be referred to the bishop and chapter of Cambrai for further discipline.

6 David(?), abbot of the Premonstratensian abbey of Barlings before 1189. *MP* II, 35.
7 William(?), abbot of the Premonstratensian abbey of Croxton, ca. 1177. *MP* II, 49.
8 Robert(?), abbot of the Premonstratensian abbey of Beeleigh. *MP* II, 40.
9 The Premonstratensian abbey of Lavendon. *MP* II, 64.
10 Ralph or Yvo, abbot of the Premonstratensian abbey of Tupholme. *MP* II, 81.
11 Gerard, abbot of the Premonstratensian abbey of Dryburgh, 1177–84. *MP* II, 102.

1 Liétard, bishop of Cambrai, 1131–5, when he was deposed at a council of Reims.

A. Cartulary of Prémontré, fol. 111v. (Cancellation of charter indicated with red X placed upon the entire entry. The word *vacat* is written in red on both left and right sides of the act with the *va* and *cat* separated by an elongated vertical line.)

B. Original not found.

EDITION: Evers, "Kamerijk en Premonstreit in 1132," 89–90; *DiplomataBelgica*, no. 3864, https://www.diplomata-belgica.be/charter_details_fr.php?dibe_id=3864.

NO RUBRIC.

~~[I]n nomine sancte et~~ individue Trinitatis,[2] tam futuris quam presentibus in perpetuum. Quoniam ex officii nostri sollicitudine commonemur ut que plantanda sunt plantemus, que eradicanda eradicemus, communicato capituli nostri consilio, Premonstrate ecclesie ad eradicandas infructuose plantationis arbores concessimus ut si in episcopatu nostro quilibet sui ordinis abbas peccaverit et a tenore prepositi ordinis deviare voluerit, videlicet si fuerit criminosus, contemptor ordinis vel destructor regule, bonorum temporalium dissipator, vel negligens aut remissus in cura sibi commissa, abbas Premonstrate ecclesie ~~per se suggerat~~[3] et si forte eorum incuria eius excessus incorrectus remanserit, tunc abbas, assumptis duobus coabbatibus suis, episcopo conveniant factoque clamore super reo sine dilatione infra quadraginta dies, prout dictaverint, rei judicium terminetur absque invitatione maioris audientie et, si depositus fuerit, ad illud de quo prodiit monasterium revertatur. Quod si noluerit ab ipso episcopo et ab ipsis abbatibus cum his qui cum eo consenserint, excommunicetur et alius ydoneus consilio eorumdem abbatum a fratribus eiusdem loci eligatur et episcopali benedictione substituatur. Ad arcendas igitur quorumlibet inportunitates data conservatoribus pace in prevaricatores, quo ad resipuerint, excommunicationis sententiam proferimus atque canonica subsignatione nostra quoque sub ymaginatione huius nostri decreti paginam confirmamus. S. mei ipsius Lietardi episcopi et ceteri. Actum est hoc Cameraci, anno incarnationis dominice,[4] secundo, indictione Xª, presulatus domini[5] primo.

---

2 *Eras.* Lietardus Dei gratia Cameracensis episcopus *A*.

3 *Eras.* aut per suum priorem semel bis et tercio quod si incorrigibilis fuerit episcopo et toti capitulo Cameracensis ecclesie *A*.

4 *Eras.* Mº Cº XXXº secundo *A*.

5 *Eras.* Lietardi *A*.

503

1135

Thibaut [IV],[1] *count of Blois, makes known that after the death of Guy, lord of Braine, Aelide, his widow, gave all the* census *that she held below both the castle of Braine and the* villa *of Branelle to Prémontré, with the assent of Guy's parents, André de Baudement*[2] *and Agnès de Braine;*[3] *his brother, Waleran,*[4] *abbot of Ourscamp; and his sisters Helvide*[5] *and her husband, Guy [I, lord] of Dampierre, and Humbeline*[6] *and her husband Gautier, count of Brienne. Prémontré then gave this* census *to the Premonstratensian church of Braine in exchange for a certain tithe Braine held on its grange at Trosly. Since the church of Braine was dissatisfied with that particular* census, *Prémontré repurchased it for 35* librae, *with which Braine purchased a more convenient* census. *Thibaut, from whose fief the land descended, consented to this.*

A. Cartulary of Prémontré, fol. 112r.

B. Original, AN, K22[C], no. 8[5(1)], previously sealed.

EDITION: Du Chesne, *Histoire généalogique de la maison royale de Dreux, de Bar-le-Duc, de Luxenbourg et de Limbourg, du Plessis de Richelieu, de Broyes et de Chasteauvillain*, 233–4; Prioux, *Histoire de Braine et de ses Environs*, 335; Martin-Marville, *Trosly-Loire ou le Trosly des conciles, ses châteaux, ses villas, ses fiefs et ses seigneurs*, 223–4; Guyotjeannin et al., *Le chartrier de l'abbaye Prémontrée de Saint-Yved de Braine*, 353–5.

REGISTER: Tardif, *Monuments Historiques*, 230; Jacquemin, "Annales de la vie de Joscelin de Vierzi, 57e évêque de Soissons," 47.

1 Thibaut II, count of Champagne (IV of Blois and Chartres) (d. 1152), son of Étienne II, count of Blois, and Adèle of Normandy.

2 André de Baudement (d. ca. 1146), lord of Baudement and La Fère-en-Tardenois, was the seneschal of Thibaut II, count of Champagne.

3 Agnès I, lady of Braine (d. aft. 1144), entered the Premonstratensian community at Fontenille.

4 Waleran, son of André de Baudement and Agnès I, lady of Braine, first abbot of the Cistercian abbey of Ourscamp, 1129–42.

5 Helvide (d. 1165), daughter of André de Baudement and Agnès I, lady of Braine; married first Hugues de Chacenay, lord of Montréal, and second Guy I, lord of Dampierre.

6 Humbeline (d. ca. 1166), daughter of André de Baudement and Agnès I, lady of Braine; married Gautier II, count of Brienne.

De quadam permutationem inter ecclesiam Premonstratensem et ecclesiam de Brana.

[I]n nomine sancte et cetera.[7] Ego Theobaldus Blesencium comes notum fieri volo tam futuris quam presentibus quod Aelaidis, uxor Widonis domini de Brana, post mortem viri sui ipsius, videlicet Widonis, omnes census quos juste habebat infra ambitum Brane Castri et Branelle ville dedit Premonstrate ecclesie possidendos, ob remedium anime viri sui et ob amorem fratris Theobaldi[8] prefati Widonis, ibidem conversi, annuente patre eorum Andrea de Baldimento et matre eorum Agnete et ipsorum fratre Waleranno, Urscampi abbate, et sororibus eorum Helvide et Hubelina et earum maritis, Waltero comite de Brienna et Widone de Dampierre, ceterisque heredibus et ipsius castri nobilibus, de quibus in testimonio subscripsimus quosdam.[9] Hos census Premonstratensis ecclesia ecclesie Branensi commutavit pro quadam decima quam habebat in grangia sua de Trosli, ab episcopo Suessionensi Goisleno sibi collata. Hanc vero commutationem postea Branenses quia non satis equam approbabant ecclesia Premonstrata predictos census XXX[a] quinque[10] libris redemit unde illi alios redditus commodiores sibi emerunt. Ecclesia vero Premonstrata census suos recepit, me concedente et volente, quia de feodo meo descendebat, assensu etiam et testimonio domini Goisleni, prefati Suessionensis episcopi, et Walteri, comitis de Brienna,[11] Widonis de Dampierre,[12] Odonis Canpenois, Widonis filii Raineri et fratrem eius Bartholomei et Pagani de Brana. Quod ut ratum permaneat sigilli mei inpressione et prefatorum testium annotatione roborari feci. Actum est hoc donum anno incarnationis dominice M[o] C[o] XXX[o] V[o] et confirmatum anno incarnationis M[o] C[o] XL[o] V[o], epacta XXV[a], indictione VIII[a], concurrente VII[o].

---

7 *Add.* cetera *A*; individue Trinitatis *B*.

8 *Transp. A*; Theobaldi, fratris *B*.

9 *Transp. A*; quosdam subscripsimus *B*.

10 V[que] *B*.

11 Briena *B*.

12 Dampiere *B*.

504

October 6, 1147. Chaumont.

Hugues [III],[1] *archbishop of Rouen, writes to abbot Hugues [I]*[2] *and the convent of Prémontré at the request of husband and wife Hugues [IV, lord of] Gournay*[3] *and Mélisende [de Coucy]*[4] *to confirm that the couple gave 25* solidi Belvacensium *in* census *to Prémontré at Gaillefontaine.*[5]

A. Cartulary of Prémontré, fol. 112r.
B. Original not found.

Karta de confirmatione elemosine Hugonis de Gornaio.

H[ugo] Dei gratia Rothomagensis archiepiscopus, karissimis filiis et fratribus Hugoni venerabili abbati et conventui Pratimonstrati in perpetuum. Que ad honorem Dei et utilitatem ecclesie juste petuntur, merito debent exaudiri et prompta devotione conpleri; quidem que juste postulatis qua karitate a nobis confirmari requiritis volumus in eternum firma stabilitate rata manere et robur proprium nostre concessionis in posterum obtinere. De quibus igitur pro vobis nos requirit filius noster, karissimus Hugo de Gornaio, et uxor eius, Milesendis, ut que vobis apud Goisleni Fontem dederunt, videlicet XXV solidos Belvacenses in festo Sancti Remigii in censibus ipsius ville, vos concedimus et sub testamento Sancte Dei ecclesie nostra qua preminemus episcopali auctoritate deinceps habendos confirmamus. Siquis autem hanc elemosinam auferre vobis aut demere presumpserit, excommunicationem quam pro sua presumptione incurrerit, confirmamus et, nisi digne emendare citius satagerit, penam pro merito transgressionis patiatur. Datum apud Calvum Montem pridie nonas octobris, anno quo rex illustris Ludovicus perrexit Jherosolimam.

---

1 Hugues III d'Amiens, first abbot of the Cluniac abbey of Reading, 1123–30, and archbishop of Rouen, 1130–64.

2 Hugues I de Fosses (ca. 1093–1164), first abbot of Prémontré.

3 Hugues IV (d. 1180), lord of Gournay (arr. Dieppe, https://dicotopo.cths.fr/places/P73099768), son of Gérard de Gournay and Edith de Warenne.

4 Mélisende de Coucy (d. 1181), daughter of Thomas de Marle, lord of Coucy, and Mélisende de Crécy-sur-Serre; second wife of Hugues IV, lord of Gournay.

5 Gaillefontaine, cant. Forges-les-Eaux, https://dicotopo.cths.fr/places/P96391296.

505

1121[1]

Louis [VI], king of France, confirms all gifts made by Barthélemy,[2] bishop of Laon, to Norbert and his companions as well as all past and present gifts pertaining to the royal right of regalia. *(See **506**.)*

A. Cartulary of Prémontré, fol. 112r.

B. Original, SAHSS, *casier* 1, no. 4, previously sealed with a double strip of parchment and monogram of the king.

EDITION: Le Paige, *Bibliotheca*, 374, 760; Florival, *Étude historique sur le XIIe siècle*, 239–40; Bautier and Dufour, *Recueil des actes de Louis VI, roi de France (1108–1137)*, vol. 1, 375–7.

REGISTER: Bréquigny, *Table chronologique*, vol. 2, 501; Luchaire, *Louis VI le Gros*, 259; Grauwen, "Lijst van oorkonden waarin Norbertus wordt genoemd," 142.

Karta domini Ludovici regis de confirmatione donorum que pertinent ad regalia.

[I]n nomine sancte et individue Trinitatis. Ego Ludovicus Dei gratia Francorum[3] notum fieri volo cunctis fidelibus tam futuris quam et instantibus quod quicquid Bartholomeus, venerabilis Laudunensium episcopus domno Norberto et cum eodem famulantibus dedit et daturus et[4] quicquid etiam quilibet alii quod ad regalia pertineat illis dederunt vel daturi sunt nos et volumus et approbamus et regia auctoritate[5] nostra in perpetuum confirmamus. Quod ne valeat[6] oblivione deleri scripto commendari et sigilli nostri auctoritate[7] et nominis nostri karactere subterfirmari precepimus. Datum per manum Stephani cancellarii.[8]

1 The charter is undated, but Robert-Henri Bautier and Jean Dufour estimate its date to be approximately August 1121. See Bautier and Dufour, *Recueil des actes de Louis VI, roi de France (1108–1137)*, vol. 1, 375–6.

2 Barthélemy de Jur (d. 1158), son of Conon, lord of Grandson and La Sarraz, and Ada de Roucy; first subdeacon and then treasurer of Reims, later bishop of Laon, 1113–51.

3 *Om.* rex *A*.

4 est *B*.

5 actoritate *B*.

6 *Om.* ac *A*.

7 actoritate *B*.

8 Etienne de Garlande (d. 1150), son of Guillaume I, lord of Garlande-en-Brie, and Havoise, was bishop of Beauvais, 1099–1103 and seneschal of France, 1108–27 and 1132–7.

506

1136. Laon.

Louis [VI], king of France, with the approval of his son Louis [VII], confirms all past and future gifts made by Barthélemy,[1] *bishop of Laon, or anyone else, to the church of Prémontré. (See* ***505****.)*[2]

A. Cartulary of Prémontré, fol. 112r.

B. Original, SAHSS, *casier* 1, no. 4, previously sealed with a double strip of parchment and with the monogram of the king.

EDITION: Le Paige, *Bibliotheca*, 424–5; Hugo, *prob.* 1, cols. x–xi; Pardessus, *Ordonnances des rois de France de la troisième race: Supplément*, 239; Florival, *Étude historique sur le XIIe siècle*, 240–1; Bautier and Dufour, *Recueil des actes de Louis VI, roi de France (1108–1137)*, vol. 2, 296–7.

REGISTER: Bréquigny, *Table chronologique*, vol. 2, 631; Luchaire, *Louis VI le Gros*, 259.

Item privilegium domini regis Ludovici de confirmatione omnium que episcopus Laudunensis dedit vel daturus est ecclesie sive alii de his que pertinent ad regnum.

[I]n nomine sancte et individue Trinitatis, amen. Ego Ludovicus,[3] Dei gratia rex Francorum, notum fieri volumus cunctis fidelibus tam futuris, quam instantibus, quod quicquid Bartholomeus, venerabilis Laudunensium episcopus ecclesie de Premonstrato et fidelibus ibi Deo famulantibus dedit et daturus est et[4] quicquid etiam quilibet alii, quod ad regalia pertineat, illis dederunt vel daturi sunt, nos et volumus et concedimus et approbamus et regia auctoritate nostra, annuente filio nostro Ludovico[5] iam in regem coronato, in perpetuum confirmamus. Quod ne valeat oblivione deleri, scripto commendavimus et ne possit a posteris infirmari sigilli nostri auctoritate et nominis nostri karactere subterfirmavimus. Actum Lauduni publice, anno incarnati verbi M° C° XXX° VI°, regni nostri vicesimo nono, Ludovico[6] filio nostro in regem coronato anno quarto, astantibus in palatio nostro quorum[7] subtitulata et signa sunt. Signum

---

1 Barthélemy de Jur (d. 1158), son of Conon, lord of Grandson and La Sarraz, and Ada de Roucy; first subdeacon and then treasurer of Reims, later bishop of Laon, 1113–51.

2 This act was confirmed by *vidimus* in 1442 by Gilbert Fournet, canon of Laon. SAHSS, *casier* 1.

3 Lucdovicus *B*.

4 *Superscr.* et *A*.

5 Lucdovico *B*.

6 Lucdovico *B*.

7 *Om.* nomina *A*.

Radulfi[8] Viromandorum, comitis et dapiferi nostri. S. Guillelmi, buticularii.[9] S. Hugonis, constabularii.[10] S. Hugonis,[11] camerarii.[12] Data per manum Stephani cancellarii.[13]

507

July, 1231. Saint-Germain-en-Laye.

Louis [IX], king of France, informs his baillivi *and* prepositi *of his esteem for the church of Prémontré, and instructs them to protect Premonstratensian properties and rights.*

A. Cartulary of Prémontré, fol. 112r.

B. Original not found.

EDITION: Secousse et al., *Ordonnances des roys de France de la troisième race, recueillies par ordre chronologique*, vol. 8, 433–4.

Karta domini Ludovici regis de rebus nostris manutenendis et custodiendis sicut sua propria.

Ludovicus,[1] Dei gratia Francorum rex, amicis et fidelibus suis, ballivis et prepositis suis, omnibus ad quos iste littere pervenerint salutem. Noverit universitas vestra nos ecclesiam ~~nostram~~ Premonstratensem affectuosius diligere et eam ad nostram specialius spectare custodiam, unde vobis mandamus, et sub optentu gratie nostre requirimus quatinus eius res, sicut nostras proprias, custodiatis et cum ab aliquo eam inhabitantium requisiti fueritis, jus ipsius ad posse vestrum manuteneatis. Actum apud Sanctum Germanum in Laya anno domini M° CC° tricesimo primo, mense julio.

---

8 Raoul I, count of Vermandois, Amiens, and Valois (d. 1152), was the son of Hugues I le Grand, count of Vermandois and Valois, and Adélaïde de Vermandois, and served as seneschal of France, 1131–51.

9 Guillaume le Loup de Senlis, knight and lord of Chantilly and Ermenonville, son of Guy de la Tour de Senlis, lord of Chantilly and Ermenonville, and Berthe, butler of France, ca. 1130–47. Voillemier, "Note sur la maison des Bouteiller de Senlis," 36–7.

10 Hugues *Strabo*, viscount of Chaumont-en-Vexin, likely son of Enguerrand de Chaumont, and constable of France, 1108–ca. 1138.

11 Hugues du Puy-du-Fou, son of Guillaume du Puy-du-Fou and Adèle de Beaumont-sur-Oise, and chamberlain of France in the 1130s. Bouquet and Delisle, eds., *Recueil des historiens des Gaules et de la France*, vol. 12, 409.

12 chamerarii *B*.

13 Etienne de Garlande (d. 1150), son of Guillaume I, lord of Garlande-en-Brie, and Havoise, was bishop of Beauvais, 1099–1103, and seneschal of France, 1108–27 and 1132–7.

---

1 The initial letter has been added at a later, post-medieval date.

508

April, 1240.

Hugues [III],[1] *abbot of Prémontré, makes known the decisions of a General Chapter meeting concerning the modes of dress, work, and discipline to be adopted by the sisters of the Premonstratensian house of Bonneuil.*[2] *No more than 20 women are to live there at any one time; and the female head of the community is to call herself a* magistra *rather than a* priorissa. *Both* magister *and* magistra *are forbidden from claiming the* cura animarum.

A. Cartulary of Prémontré, fol. 112v.
B. Original, AD Oise, H 6009, previously sealed with two seals.
EDITION: Le Paige, *Bibliotheca*, 932.

NO RUBRIC. LATER ADDITION.

Universis presentes litteras inspecturis Hugo, Dei patientia abbas Premonstratensis et eiusdem loci conventus, salutem in Domino. Cum de communi consensu capituli generalis, causa pietatis, concessum fuerit et preceptum, ut processu temporis in domo nostra de Bonolio recipiantur sorores, ne ipsarum numerus ad nichilum redigatur, volentes ut tam receptis quam recipiendis ibidem sororibus secundum facultates[3] domus sufficienter et honeste valeat provideri, de receptione numero et modo vivendi earum de communi nostro consensu, ita duximus statuendum scilicet ut cum aliqua recipienda fuerit in sororem, recipiatur de abbatis, prioris, supprioris et aliquorum maiorum ecclesie nostre qui pro tempore fuerint, communi consilio et assensu, hoc proviso quod tam recepte, quam recipiende in eadem domo sorores vicesimum numerum aliquatenus non excedant nec possint in posterum ibi esse, sive vestite, seu vestiende plus quam viginti sorores, que in vestitu, victu et aliis observantiis ordinis, prout potuerint, se ad invicem conformantes, in communi refectorio comedant, nisi sint in infirmitorio pro egritudine manifesta, uno pane et eodem potu, eisdem que pulmentis vescantur communiter vestiantur in communi et pro communi laborentur, quicquid laboraverunt, quicquid habuerint sive redditus, seu alia bona, totum redigantur[4] in commune et omnia sub communi et certa custodia reserventur ad preceptum abbatis, ut pro

1 Hugues III d'Hirson, perhaps a descendant of the lords of Hirson and/or a relative of the lords of Guise, was abbot of Prémontré, 1238–42. Le Long, *Histoire ecclésiastique et civile du diocèse de Laon, et de tout le pays contenu entre l'Oise et la Meuse, l'Aisne et la Sambre*, 516; *GC* IX, cols. 649–50; Goovaerts, *Ecrivains, artistes et savants de l'ordre de Prémontré*, vol. 3, 129–30.

2 *MP* II, 484.

3 facultes *B.*

4 redigant *B.*

dispositione ipsius et secundum ordinem, de hiis et aliis necessaria eisdem sororibus ministrentur; et si alique rebelles fuerint in hac parte ad observationem premissorum, per censuram ecclesiasticam compellantur et puniantur, prout abbati visum fuerit expedire; verum quoniam sepe multiloquium gignit peccatum et perturbat affectum devotionis ac impedit intentionem orandi, statuimus et volumus firmiter observari ut eedem sorores infra monasterium, claustrum, refectorium et dormitorium, silentium teneant secundum ordinis instituta, transgredientibus secundum statuta eadem puniendis; et si aliqua voluerit cuiquam loqui, non vadat ad portam nisi de licentia magistre ipsarum et cum custodia deputata, et illa que habebit, ad mandatum abbatis, magisterium, post ipsum abbatem super omnes sorores non dicatur vel vocetur priorissa decetero sed magistra, cum nec ipsa magistra nec etiam magister domus illius curam habeant animarum annexam. Ut autem premissa omnia tam a nobis quam a receptis et recipiendis sororibus, bona fide, et firmiter observentur, presentes litteras fecimus sigillorum nostrorum munimine roborari. ~~Act~~ Actum anno Domini M° CC°[5] quadragesimo, mense aprili.

509

April, 1334. Ourscamp.

Philippe [VI], king of France, gives to the abbot [Jean III][1] *and convent of Prémontré a perpetual exemption from tax on the equivalent of 30* livres *of land or perpetual annual rent in the* bailli *of Vermandois. In return, Prémontré will offer a Mass for his soul each week during his lifetime, and a Requiem Mass once a year after his death.*

A. Cartulary of Prémontré, fol. 112v.
B. Original not found.

Carta domini regis super amortisatione triginta libratarum terre seu annui reditus acquisitarum seu acquisitendarum a tempore dicte subsequentes.[2]

Phelippes, par la grace de Diu roys de France, savoir faisons a tous presenz et avenir que pour le salu de nostre ame et de grace especial nous avonz otroié a religieus hommes nos ames en Diu, l'abbé et le couvent de Premonstré que trente livrées de terre ou de rente annuel et perpetuel acquisés ou a[3] acquerré

5 millesimo ducentesimo *B*.

1 Jean de Châtillon, first prior and then abbot of Prémontré, ca. 1333–40. *GC*, IX, col. 653.
2 This is a rubric-like sentence, indented from the rest of the charter, in black rather than red ink.
3 *Superscr.* a *A*.

sans fié et sanz justice dedens lez termes de nostre baillie de Vermendois et du ressort yl puissent tenir perpetuelment et pasiblement sanz ce que il soient ou puissent estre constrains a lez vendre ou mettre autrement hors de leur main et de leur moustier et sanz en paier jamais financé, quele que elle soit, la quelle nous pour nous et pour nos successeurs leur avons quitté et quittons de nostre dicte grace et de leur humilité yl nous ont ottroié une messe du Saint Esperit chascune septmainne tant comme nous vivronz, et apres nostre decés une messe sollemnel de requiem chascun an touz temps. En tesmoing de laquelle chose et que elle soit ferme et estable a touz jours nous avons fait mettre en ces lettres nostre seel, sauve nostre droit en autres choses et l'autrui droit en toutes. Donné a Oscamps, l'an de grace mil trois cens trente quatre, en mois d'avril.

APPENDICES

APPENDIX 1: OTHER MANUSCRIPTS POSSIBLY HELD OR MADE AT PRÉMONTRÉ IN THE THIRTEENTH CENTURY

Soissons, Bibliothèque municipale

MS 3: Eustache de Lens, *Cosmographia Moysi*, 13th century.
MS 4: *Divine hystorie abbreviatio*, 13th century.
MS 8: Letter formulary, usage of Prémontré, 12th/13th century.
MS 9: Obituary and martyrology of Prémontré, 13th–17th centuries.
MS 10: Statutes and Ordinary of Prémontré, late 13th century.
MS 11: Extracts of saints' lives, 13th century.
MS 12: Saints' lives and sermons, 12th/13th century.
MS 14: Herman of Tournai, *Miracula sanctae Mariae Laudunensis*, 13th century.
MS 22: Guillaume Péraud, *Summa de viciis*, 13th century.
MS 23: Guillaume Péraud, *Summa de virtutibus*, 13th century.
MS 48: Collection of medical treatises, 13th century.
MS 55: Tancred of Bologna, *Ordo judicarius*, 13th century.
MS 66: Psalter, usage of Prémontré, 13th century.
MS 69: Commentary on the Psalms (fragment), 13th century.
MS 72: *Esdras, Nehemias, cum glossa ordinaria* (fragment), 13th century.
MS 75: Commentary on the Old Testament and the Song of Songs, 12th century.
MS 76: Bernard of Clairvaux, *Sermones super Cantica Canticorum*, 12th century.
MS 78: Gospel of Luke with glosses, 12th century.
MS 80: Gilbertus Porretanus, *In epistolas S. Pauli*, 12th century.
MS 83: Peter Lombard, *Sentences*, 13th century.
MS 97: Ordinary, usage of Prémontré, late 13th/early 14th century.
MS 103: Breviary, usage of Prémontré, 13th century.

MS 104: Liturgical miscellany, 13th/14th century.
MS 115: Extracts from Augustine of Hippo, 12th century.
MS 116: Collection of theological works, 13th/14th century.
MS 117: Augustine of Hippo, *Contra Faustum Manichaeum*, 12th century.
MS 118: Gregory the Great, *Dialogues*, 12th century.
MS 119: Origen, *Homilies*, 12th century.
MS 120: Works of Hugues de Saint-Victor, 12th century.
MS 121: Hugo de Folieto, Basilius Caesariensis, 12th century.
MS 125: Collection of theological works, 13th–15th century.
MS 129: Bible commentary, fragments, 12th/13th century.
MS 131: Petrus Comestor, *Sermons*, 13th century.
MS 137: Collection of theological works, fragments, 13th century.
MS 143: Collection of theological works, 12th century.

APPENDIX 2: SELECT LATIN GLOSSARY[1]

Agricultural Produce

These terms are used in the manuscript to describe various types of or mixtures of grain, but their use is not necessarily consistent.

Annona
Bladus
Frumentum
Seges, segetis
Sementis
Triticum

Weights and Measurements

These terms are used in the manuscript to describe various measurements of area and produce, sometimes interchangeably.

Areata, *areatae* (measurement of water)
Assinus, *assini* (grain or land)
Carrucata, *carrucatae* (plough land)
Carruca, *carrucae* (plough land)
Dolium, *dolia* (usually liquid)
Falca, *falce* (meadow)
Galetus, *galeti* (grain and land)
Garba, *garbae* (sheaf or sheaves)
Jornalius, *jornalia* (measure of daily labour)
Modiata, *modiatae* (see *modius*)
Modius, *modii* (grain and liquid)
Quadrigata, *quadrigatae* (cartload)
Sextaria, *sextariae* (land and rights over land)
Sextariata, *sexteriatae*, variant *sexterlata*, *sexterlatae* (see *sextaria*)
Virga, *virgae* (land)

Monies

Denarius, *denarii*
Libra, *librae*

---

1 For a further discussion of these units, many of which varied in use according to location, see Doursther, *Dictionnaire universel des poids et mesures anciens et modernes, contenant des tables des monnaies de tous les pays*; Zupko, *French Weights and Measures before the Revolution*.

Marcus, marci
Nummus, nummi
Obolus, oboli
Solidus, solidi

Rights

Advocatus
Altarie
Calceiagium
Quercum (cerke) (likely the right to glean from oaks)
Consuetudine
Districtum
Duellum
Foragium
Fur
Justicium
Maritagium
Modiagium
Naulum
Passagium
Pasturagium
Patronatus
Pedagium
Personatus
Regalia
Rotagium
Servagium
Terragium
Theoloneum
Traversum
Vavassorus
Vinagium (or winagium)
Wionagium

Payments and Revenues

Assisia
Censuales (after ca. 1208, an adjectival form of census used with specific measurements)
Census

Supercensus
Tallia
Trecensus

People, Professions, and Places

Ballivus
Burgensis
Civis, civis
Communitas
Conversus, conversi, conversa, conversae
Cura animarum
Curia, curiae
Curtis, curtes
Custos
Dapifer
Domus Dei
Feminae de corpore
Foramina
Grangia, grangiae
Homines de corpore
Hospitium Dei
Janitor
Juratus, jurati
Laudunesio (Laonnois)
Leprosarium
Magister
Magister hospitalarii
Magistra
Maior
Manerium, maneria
Mansus, mansi
Masura
Ministeriales
Officialis, officiales
Princeps
Prepositus, prepositi
Priorissa
Procurator
Scabinus, scabini
Serganteria

Tabernarius
Vidame
Vidimus
Villa, villae

APPENDIX 3: SELECT FRENCH GLOSSARY[1]

Agricultural Produce

Blé

Weights and Measurements

Muid, muid
Piece (of wine)
Septier

Monies

Denier, deniers
Livre, livres
Sols, variant *sous*

Rights

Gans
Garenne
Justice (haute justice and basse justice)
Pedaige
Peishca
Saisine
Vente
Vinaige (see Latin Vinagium)
Winaige (see Latin Wionagium)

Payments and Revenues

Cens

People, Professions, and Places

Baillius, bailli
Court
Courtillet

1 See Doursther, *Dictionnaire universel des poids et mesures anciens et modernes, contenant des tables des monnaies de tous les pays*; Zupko, *French Weights and Measures before the Revolution*.

APPENDIX 4: LIST OF ABBOTS OF PRÉMONTRÉ

This list of abbots spans the period 1128–1250, roughly the period between the election of the first abbot of Prémontré and the completion of the cartulary. Those abbots whose names are highlighted in **bold** are the principal or co-principal of an act in the cartulary. Those abbots whose names are *italicized* are the recipient of, are witness to, or are otherwise named in an act in the cartulary.

1128–61: Hugues I de Fosses
1161–71: Philippe I de Reims
1171: Jean I de Brienne
1171–4: Eudes
1174–89: Hugues II
1189–91: Robert I
1191–5: Gautier
1195–1201: Pierre I de Saint-Médard
1201–3: Baudouin
1203–4: Vermond
1204–6: Guillaume I de Saint-Omer
1206–9: Robert II
1209–20: Gervais
1220–33: Conrad Suève
1233–8: Guillaume II d'Angles
1238–42: Hugues III d'Hirson
1242–7: Conon
1247–69: Jean II de Rocquigny

APPENDIX 5: BISHOPS OF LAON, NOYON, AND SOISSONS

This list of bishops spans the period 1120–1250, roughly the period between the foundation of the abbey and the completion of the cartulary. Those bishops whose names are highlighted in **bold** are the principal or co-principal of an act in the cartulary. The cartulary includes some later charter additions from the fourteenth century, two of which are issued by bishops whose names are included in this list.

Laon

1113–51: Barthélemy de Jur
1151–3: Gautier I de Saint Maurice
1153–74: Gautier II de Mortagne
1175–1207: Roger de Rosoy
1207–10: Renaud Surdelle
1210–15: Robert de Châtillon
1215–38: Anselme de Mauny/de Bercenay
1238–49: Garnier de Laon
1249–61: Itier de Mauny

Noyon

1114–22: Lambert
1123–48: Simon I de Vermandois
1148–67: Baudoin II de Boulogne
1167–74/5: Baudoin III de Beuseberg
1175–88: Renaud
1188–1221: Étienne I de Nemours
1222–8: Gérard de Bazoches
1228–40: Nicolas de Roye
1240–9: Pierre I Charlot
1250–72: Vermond de la Boissière

Soissons

1108–26: Lisiard de Crépy
1126–52: Joscelin de Vierzy
1152–8: Anscoul de Pierrefonds
1158–75: Hugues II de Champfleury
1176–1207: Nivelon I de Quierzy/de Chérisy
1207–19: Aymard de Provins

1219–42: Jacques de Bazoches
1242–5: Raoul de Coudun
1245–50: Guy III de Château-Porcien
1331–49: Pierre de Chappes
1362–1404: Simon de Bucy

APPENDIX 6: LIST OF POPES

This list of popes spans the period 1120–1250, roughly the period between the foundation of the abbey and the completion of the cartulary. Those popes whose names are highlighted in **bold** are the principal or co-principal of an act in the cartulary.

February 1119–December 1124: Callixtus II
December 1124–February 1130: Honorius II
February 1130–September 1143: Innocent II
September 1143–March 1144: Celestine II
March 1144–February 1145: Lucius II
February 1145–July 1153: Eugene III
July 1153–December 1154: Anastasius IV
December 1154–September 1159: Adrian IV
September 1159–August 1181: Alexander III
September 1181–November 1185: Lucius III
November 1185–October 1187: Urban III
October 1187–December 1187: Gregory VIII
December 1187–March 1191: Clement III
March 1191–January 1198: Celestine III
January 1198–July 1216: Innocent III
July 1216–March 1227: Honorius III
March 1227–August 1241: Gregory IX
October 1241–November 1241: Celestine IV
June 1243–December 1254: Innocent IV

APPENDIX 7: LIST OF ACTS IN CHRONOLOGICAL ORDER

Year	Date	Act Number
1121		71
1121		72
1121		505
1124		140
1124		265
1124		298
1125	June 28	13
1125	October 13	73
1125		150
1126	February 16	52
1126–41		266
1126–64		290
1128–56		499
1129		410
1120s–30s		449
1132		74
1132		456
1132		502
1133		106
1134	August 25	107
1134	August 25	111
1134		384
1134		385
1135		112
1135		320
1135		503
1136		123
1136		506
1137		333
1137		339
1137		345
1137		362
1137		397
1137		419

Year	Date	Act Number
1137		443
1137		464
1138		5
1138		95
1138		151
1138		214
1138		299
1138–40	December 21	40
1138–43		29
1138–43	December 21	34
1139		233
1140		99
1140		301
1140		372
1140		450
1141		96
1141		141
1141		161
1141		271
1141		276
1142		91
1142		98
1142		264
1142		269
1142		334
1142		342
1142		378
1142		407
1142		452
1142	October 11	497
1143	December 6	49
1143		178
1143–50		414
1143–61		212
1144		137

(Continued)

(Continued)

Year	Date	Act Number
1144		358
1144		359
1144		360
1144?		361
1145		160
1145		179
1146		169
1146		370
1146		371
1146–78		413
1147	May 17	50
1147		184
1147		338
1147		350
1147		353
1147		401
1147		412
1147		445
1147	October 6	504
1148		164
1148–60		388
1148–75		316
1149		170
1149		268
1149		270
1150s–60s		500
mid-12th century		185
1151		76
1152		300
1152–97		116
1153		198
1153		201
1153		415
1153		498
1153–8	Before September	75
1154	January 3	51

Year	Date	Act Number
1155		302
1155		369
1155–60		245
1155–80		235
1156		139
1156		181
1156		240
1156		337
1156		383
1157		396
1157		463
1158	May 30	47
1158		77
1158		125
1158		321
1158		484
1159		196
1159		436
1160–81	March 9	65
1162		113
1163		138
1163		142
1163		344
1163		398
1163		399
1163		441
1163		442
1163		489
1164		197
1164		308
1164		465
1164–71	February 13	60
1165		199
1165		322
1165		421

(*Continued*)

(Continued)

Year	Date	Act Number
1166		97
1166		156
1169		310
1170		200
1170		341
1170		404
1170–1		406
1170–81		432
1171		377
1172		162
1172		274
1172		292
1173	August 21	33
1173	June 15	61
1173		79
1173	October	92
1173		118
1173		227
1174		122
1174–8	February 28–9	66
1174–89		468
1174–1207		163
1175		126
1175		253
1175		382
1175		386
1175–81		63
1176–81	March 14	62
1177		306
1177		336
1177		424
1177		485
1178		4
1178		78
1178		124

Year	Date	Act Number
1178		311
1178		332
1178		365
1178		405
1178		411
1178		423
1180		241
1180		395
1180s		222
1181		244
1182		12
1182		182
1182		191
1182		263
1182		303
1182		501
1183		273
1183		281
1184		183
1184		296
1185		19
1185		434
1186	July 21	64
1186		114
1186		192
1187	June 10	68
1188	April 1	48
1188	March 17	70
1188		215
1188		314
1188		318
1188–9		366
1189		203
1189		391
1190	August	2

(*Continued*)

(Continued)

Year	Date	Act Number
1190	August	7
1190		173
1190		307
1191		93
1191		448
1193	September 9	127
1193		431
1194		323
1195		309
1195		380
1196		242
1196		317
1196		330
1198	August 27	24
1198	May 13	39
1198	May 12	67
1198	June 22	69
1198		237
1198	November 6	239
1198?	May 25	37
1198–1216		159
1198–1216		457
1199		488
12th century		104
12th century		168
after ca. 1200		22
1200		193
1201	January 20	27
1201	March	420
1202	March	1
1202	September	213
1202	July	238
1203		285
1203		472
1204		195

Year	Date	Act Number
1204	March	347
1204	March 21	425
1206	January 2	121
1206	February 15	157
1206		284
1207		80
1207		86
1207		88
1207		175
1207	August	180
1207		287
1207	August	375
1207	August	474
1208	February 27	115
1208	June	251
1208		252
1208		471
1208–34		105
1209		155
1209		174
1209	July	262
1209	October 22	272
1209	April	473
1210	April 17	83
1210	December	236
1210	January	355
1211	December 26	110
1211		194
1211	December	313
1211	December	319
1211	March	340
1211–15	After December 26	136
1212	July	89
1212	July	102
1212		152

(Continued)

(Continued)

Year	Date	Act Number
1212		246
1212	April	247
1212	March 7	327
1212	August	459
1212		462
1212	August	467
1212–17	February 16	437
1213	July 25	176
1213	March 26	267
1213		477
1214	October 5	167
1214	December	451
1215	June	120
1215	September	172
1215	July 18	315
1215	July 31	387
1216	February	275
1216	February	277
1216	March 17	393
1216		458
1216	September	481
1216	December	483
1217	December	90
1217	December 22	108
1217	December 22	117
1217	December	128
1217		454
1217		461
1217	June	478
1218	June	101
1218	March 14	280
1218	April 17	381
1218	January	470
1218	July	487
1218		490

Year	Date	Act Number
1219	February 18	41
1219	March 5	54
1219	February 18	55
1219	April	206
1219	May	211
1219	April 21	243
1219	February	286
1219		289
1219	June	331
1220	July 14	36
1220	July 21	56
1220	February	100
1220	April 29	103
1220	June	249
1220	August	348
1220	February	351
1220	May	408
1220	August	428
1221	July	81
1221	April 6	166
1221	August	190
1221	August	225
1221	February	226
1221		248
1221		466
1222	February	3
1222	May 22	38
1222	December	202
1222	May	204
1222	June 12	228
1222	June 19	256
1222	November	278
1222	February	282
1222		349
1223	July 20	9

(Continued)

(Continued)

Year	Date	Act Number
1223	July	389
1223	May	435
1223	July	479
1224	April	10
1224	December 1	14
1224	May	205
1224	May	279
1224	April	363
1224	March 25	400
1224	March 25	444
1225	July 24	31
1225	April 19	53
1225		165
1225	March	283
1225		312
1225	September 5	482
1225	November	335
1225	December	429
1226	April	130
1226	September	288
1226	December	354
1226	March 28	402
1226	March 28	447
1227	December	94
1227	June	208
1227	July	209
1227	January	220
1227	January	221
1227	November	304
1227	November	357
1227	November	417
1227	November	422
1227–40		8
1228	March 16	30
1228	June	85

Year	Date	Act Number
1228	November	223
1228	December	224
1228	January	390
1228	January	392
1228	December	416
1228	December	486
1229	April	11
1229	February	119
1229	June 1	219
1229	June 5	218
1229	April	250
1229	October	373
1230	February 7	32
1230	January	109
1230	November	394
1231		6
1231	January 25	35
1231	August	187
1231	February	189
1231	August	207
1231	September	210
1231	January 2	324
1231	January	325
1231	January	326
1231	December	328
1231	January 2	329
1231	February	346
1231	March 6	352
1231		356
1231	July 4	364
1231	January	368
1231	November	376
1231	November	379
1231	April	403
1231	October 24	418

(*Continued*)

(Continued)

Year	Date	Act Number
1231	February 22	426
1231	March	427
1231		430
1231	May	433
1231		439
1231	April	446
1231	June 4	475
1231	September	476
1231	September	480
1231	July	507
1232	June 6	26
1232	May 23	57
1232	May	82
1232	May	84
1232	November	132
1232	After Christmas	133
1232		134
1232	After Christmas	135
1232	April	186
1232	Octave of Christmas	188
1232		254
1232		255
1232		291
1232	July	305
1232	March	374
1232	March 11	440
1232	February	469
1233	January 7	44
1233	January 16	58
1233	March	131
1233	July	154
1233	December	343
1233	June 27	367
1233	May	438
1233	October	453

Year	Date	Act Number
1233	January	491
1233–4	January 27	25
1234	January 17	28
1234	January 26	42
1234	February 19	43
1234	January 16	45
1234	February 20	46
1234	September 5	59
1234	June	153
1235	March	171
1236	June	129
1236	May	293
1236	April	460
1237	January	409
1239	October 5	15
1239	October	16
1239	October	17
1239	October	18
1239	December	455
1240	April	508
1250	January 7	143
1250	January	144
1250	December	145
1250	March	146
1264	April	87
1269	February	260
1287	May	216
1287	May	217
1290	December	148
1300	March	295
1311	September	147
1313	July	493
1313	July 20	494
1316	June	23
1316	December	259

(*Continued*)

(Continued)

Year	Date	Act Number
1317?	February	258
1318		492
1321	October 18	257
1325	July 27	496
1327	January 9	234
1327	June 17	495
1330		230
1332	July	229
1332	January 4	294
1334	April	509
1335	March 31	231
1338	March 27	20
1344	April 3	261
1346	August 1	297
1349	August	177
1351–1418		232
1363	January 1	21
1586	July 11	149
Undated		158

BIBLIOGRAPHY

MANUSCRIPT PRIMARY SOURCES ASSOCIATED WITH PRÉMONTRÉ

Amiens, Archives départementales de la Somme

20 H_SC_1, no. 1
20 H_SC_6, no. 4
20 H_SC_6, no. 7
20 H_SC_6, no. 9
20 H_SC_6, no. 13
20 H_SC_7, no. 1
20 H_SC_7, no. 3
20 H_SC_9, no. 9
20 H_SC_10, no. 1
20 H_SC_10, no. 3
20 H_SC_10, no. 5
20 H_SC_19, no. 1
20 H 5, no. 1
20 H 6, no. 15
20 H 6, no. 17
20 H 6, no. 19
20 H 6, no. 23
20 H 6, no. 25
20 H 9, no. 1
20 H 9, no. 3
20 H 9, no. 4
20 H 9, no. 7
20 H 15, no. 1
20 H 19, no. 3

Amiens, Bibliothèque municipale Louis Aragon

Legs Arthur de Marsy, 1005, no. 1
Legs Arthur de Marsy, 1005, no. 2

Beauvais, Archives départementales de l'Oise

H 5987
H 5989
H 5990
H 5993
H 5994
H 5995
H 5996
H 5998
H 5999

H 6000
H 6002
H 6003
H 6004
H 6005
H 6006
H 6007
H 6008
H 6009
H 6031
H 6034
H 6035
H 6038
H 6053
H 6055
Hs 1368
Hs 1369
Hs 1370
Hs 1373
Hs 1375
Hs 1376
Hs 1378
Hs 1380
Hs 1385
Hs 1388
Hs 1384
Hs 1390
Hs 1500

Laon, Archives départementales de l'Aisne

H 121
H 741
H 745
H 753 (Cartulary of Valpriez)
H 761
H 763
H 767
H 769
H 773
H 775
H 777
H 782
H 791
H 793
H 797
H 800
H 802
H 806
H 807
H 818
H 819
H 820
H 825
H 826
H 841
H 845
H 1654

Laon, Bibliothèque municipale

MS 518

Metz, Archives municipales

Salis II.241 no. 1
Salis II.241 no. 2
Salis II.242, no. 3
Salis II.243, no. 1
Salis II.243, no. 3
Salis II.243, no. 5
Salis II.243, no. 6
Salis II.244, no. 1
Salis II.244, no. 3
Salis II.244, no. 5
Salis II.244, no. 9
Salis II.244, no. 10
Salis II.244, no. 13
Salis II.245, no. 1
Salis II.245, no. 4
Salis II.245, no. 7
Salis II.245, no. 8
Salis II.245, no. 11
Salis II.246, no. 1
Salis II.247, no. 1
Salis II.248, no. 1
Salis II.248, no. 3
Salis II.248, no. 9

Montigny-le-Bretonneux, Archives départementales des Yvelines

46 H1

Paris, Archives nationales de France

K22^{C}, no. 8$^{5(1)}$
K 22, no. 9 (4)
K 22, no. 13
L 995, no. 1
L 995, no. 3
L 995, no. 4
L 995, no. 5
L 995, no. 6
L 995, no. 8
L 995, no. 9
L 995, no. 10
L 995, no. 13
L 995, no. 14
L 995, no. 16
L 995, no. 17
L 995, no. 18
L 995, no. 19
L 995, no. 22
L 995, no. 23
L 995, no. 24
L 995, no. 26
L 995, no. 27
L 995, no. 29
L 995, no. 30
L 995, no. 33
L 995, no. 34
L 995, no. 35
L 995, no. 38
L 995, no. 39
L 995, no. 40
L 995, no. 42
L 995, no. 43
L 995, no. 44
L 995, no. 45
L 995, no. 49
L 995, no. 50
L 995, no. 51
L 995, no. 53
L 995, no. 54
L 995, no. 55
L 995, no. 57
L 995, no. 58
L 995, no. 60
L 995, no. 62
L 995, no. 64
L 995, no. 65
L 995, no. 67
L 995, no. 69
L 995, no. 71
L 995, no. 72
L 995, no. 73
L 995, no. 75
L 995, no. 79
L 995, no. 80
L 995, no. 81
L 995, no. 83
L 995, no. 84
L 995, no. 105
L 995, no. 145
L 995, no. 149
L 995, no. 152

Paris, Bibliothèque nationale de France

Coll. Flandres et Arras 183, pièce Arras no. 1
Coll. Picardie 290, no. 1
Coll. Picardie 290, no. 2

Coll. Picardie 290, no. 3
Coll. Picardie 290, no. 4
Coll. Picardie 290, no. 5
Coll. Picardie 290, no. 8
Coll. Picardie 290, no. 9
Coll. Picardie 290, no. 10
Coll. Picardie 290, no. 11
Coll. Picardie 290, no. 12
Coll. Picardie 290, no. 13
Coll. Picardie 290, no. 17
Coll. Picardie 290, no. 18
Coll. Picardie 290, no. 21
Coll. Picardie 290, no. 22
Coll. Picardie 290, no. 23
Coll. Picardie 290, no. 24
Coll. Picardie 290, no. 26
Coll. Picardie 290, no. 28
Coll. Picardie 290, no. 29
Coll. Picardie 290, no. 31
Coll. Picardie 290, no. 32
Coll. Picardie 290, no. 33
Coll. Picardie 290, no. 34
Coll. Picardie 290, no. 35
Coll. Picardie 290, no. 36
Coll. Picardie 290, no. 37
Coll. Picardie 290, no. 39
Coll. Picardie 290, no. 40
Coll. Picardie 290, no. 42
Coll. Picardie 290, no. 43
Coll. Picardie 290, no. 48
Coll. Picardie 290, no. 49
lat. 17062, no. 1
nouv. acq. lat. 938 (Cartulary of Valécourt)
nouv. acq. lat. 2309, no. 2
nouv. acq. lat. 2309, no. 7
nouv. acq. lat., 2590, no. 37
nouv. acq. lat., 2590, no. 37bis
nouv. acq. lat. 2590, no. 40
nouv. acq. lat. 2590, no. 41
nouv. acq. lat., 2590, no. 42
nouv. acq. lat., 2590, no. 45
nouv. acq. lat., 2590, no. 46
nouv. acq. lat. 2590, no. 49
nouv. acq. lat. 2590, no. 51
nouv. acq. lat. 2590, no. 54

Soissons, Bibliothèque municipale de Soissons

7 (Cartulary of Prémontré)
9 (Obituary of Prémontré)

Soissons, Société archéologique, historique, et scientifique de Soissons

Dossier 1
Dossier 2
Dossier 4
Dossier 5
Dossier 7
Dossier 8
Dossier 10
Dossier 13
Dossier 16
Dossier 19
Dossier 193 (Cartulary of Tinselve)
Dossier 194, no. 1–15

OTHER MANUSCRIPT PRIMARY SOURCES

Amiens, Archives départementales de la Somme

14 G 1

Amiens, Bibliothèque municipale Louis Aragon

1077 (Cartulary of Saint-Nicolas d'Arrouaise)

Antwerp, Rijskarchief te Antwerpen-Beveren

Fonds S. Michiels in Antwerpen, no. 2

Averbode, Archief van de abdij van Averbode

Sectie I, Reg. 2 (Cartulary of Averbode Abbey)
Sectie IV, no. 109 (Cartulary of Averbode Abbey)

Beauvais, Archives départementales de l'Oise

G 1874
G 1984 (Cartulary of the Cathedral Chapter of Noyon)
H 5733 (Cartulary of Lieu-Restauré)
H 6074

Bologna, Real Colegio de España

Cod. 275 ("Formulae curiae")

Bregenz, Klosterarchiv Merherau

Klosterarchiv, no. 8

Brussels, KBR

1251
4132 (Cartulary of Saint-Augustin-lès-Thérouanne)
II 1059 ("Liber usuum Cisterciensis ordinis")

Cambrai, Bibliothèque municipale

1041

Chamarandes-Choignes, Archives départementales de la Haute-Marne

4 H 18
F 523

Charleville-Mézières, Archives départementales des Ardennes

H 203 (Cartulary of Signy)

Düsseldorf, Hauptstaatsarchiv Düsseldorf

Steinfeld, no. 5

Ghent, Rijksarchief te Gent

K9–8 (Cartulary of Drongen Abbey)
K9–9 (Cartulary of Drongen Abbey)

Grimbergen, Abdij van Grimbergen

Oud Archief, Klas II, 1 (Cartulary of Grimbergen)

The Hague, Koninklijke Bibliotheek

128 G 21 ("Liber statutorum ordinis Praemonstratensis")

Heverlee, Archief van de Abdij van Park

"Liber Ruber" (Cartulary of Park Abbey)
VII 14 (Cartulary of Park Abbey)
VII 24 (Cartulary of Park Abbey)
VII 26 (Cartulary of Park Abbey)
VII 31 (Cartulary of Park Abbey)
VII 35 (Cartulary of Park Abbey)
VII 40 (Cartulary of Park Abbey)

Innsbruck, Stiftsarchiv Wilten

Lade 8 M

Laon, Archives départementales de l'Aisne

G 2 (*Grand Cartulaire* of the Bishops of Laon)
G 38
G 171
G 253 (Cartulary of the Cathedral Chapter of Soissons)
G 706

G 1850 (Cartulary of the Cathedral Chapter of Laon)
H 325 (Cartulary-Chronicle of Nogent-sous-Coucy)
H 375
H 455 (Cartulary of Saint-Crépin-le-Grand de Soissons)
H 659
H 826
H 873 (Cartulary of Saint-Martin de Laon)
H 874
H 1624 (Cartulary of Fervaques)
H 1654

Laon, Bibliothèque municipale de Laon

532 (Cartulary of Saint-Martin de Laon)

Liège, Bibliothèque du Séminaire Episcopal

G IV 7 (Cartulary of Beaurepart)

Lille, Archives départementales du Nord

36 H 335
59 H 95 (Cartulary of Vicoigne)

London, British Library

Add. 37769 (Cartulary of Cockersand Abbey)
Egerton 2827 (Cartulary of Easby Abbey)
Cotton Vespasian E. XIV (Cartulary of Leiston Abbey)

Magdeburg, Landeshauptsarchiv Sachsen-Anhalt

Abt. Magdeburg, U 4a Stifter und Klöster im Erzstift Magdeburg, Kloster Gottesgnaden, no. 18

Mechelen, Archives de l'Archevêché de Malines-Bruxelles

Fonds Prémontrés Ninove, MS 1 (Cartulary of Ninove)

Munich, Bayerische Hauptstaatsarchiv

Clm 9903 (Book of Privileges of Osterhofen Abbey)
Literalien des Klosters Schäftlarn, no. 2

Munich, Bayerische Staatsbibliothek

Clm 17174 ("Statuta Praemonstratensia")

Namur, Archives de l'État

Arch. Eccl., no. 3288 (Cartulary of Floreffe Abbey)

Oxford, Bodleian Library

Ashmole 1519 (Register of Richard Redman)

Paris, Archives nationales de la France

J 738, Soissons et Soissonnais, no. 1 ter.
JJ 46
JJ 62
K 21 no. 1/11
LL 1015 (Cartulary of Saint-Nicolas-des-Près-de-Ribemont)
LL 1583 (Cartulary of Saint-Yved de Braine)

Paris, Bibliothèque nationale de France

Coll. Baluze, 51
Coll. Moreau, 76
Coll. Moreau, 81
lat. 4169 ("Liber Cancellariae Apostolicae")
lat. 4394 ("Privilegia a Romanis Pontificibus ordini Praemonstratensi concessa")
lat. 5473 (Cartulary of Ourscamp)
lat. 5478 (Cartulary of Mont-Saint-Martin)
lat. 5528 (Cartulary of the Cathedral of Meaux)
lat. 5649 (Cartulary of Thenailles)
lat. 9752 ("Institutiones patrum Premonstratensis ordinis")
lat. 9904 (Cartulary of Igny)
lat. 9987 (Cartulary of Morienval)
lat. 10121 (Cartulary of Bucilly)

lat. 10968 (Cartulary of the Cathedral of Cambrai)
lat. 11059 (Cartulary of Silly)
lat. 11004 (Cartulary of Saint-Jean-des-Vignes)
lat. 11069 (Cartulary of Vermand)
lat. 11070 (Cartulary of the Chapter of Saint-Quentin)
lat. 11073 (Cartulary of Vauclair)
lat. 13911 (Cartulary of Homblières)
lat. 17777 (Cartulary of the Lords of Guise)
lat. 18375 (Cartulary of Saint-Michel-en-Thiérache)
nouv. acq. lat. 935 (Cartulary of Ourscamp)
nouv. acq. lat. 2390, no. 5

Paris, Institut de recherche et d'histoire des textes

Le Cartulaire de Saint-Jean-Baptiste de Prémontré: Les Transcriptions de Mme. Françoise Muret d'après Soissons, Bm Ms 7. Boîtes bleues I and II.
IHRT-section diplomatique. "Cartulaire de l'abbaye Notre-Dame et Saint-Jean-Baptiste de Prémontré [1] (Notice)." 2015.

Reims, Bibliothèque municipale

1563 (N. Fonds) (Cartulary of Foigny)
1602 (Cartulary of Saint-Thierry-lès-Reims)
1843 (N. 863) (Cartulary of Saint-Nicaise de Reims)

Soissons, Archives hospitalières

190, no. 1

Tongerlo, Archief van de abdij van Tongerlo

35

Troyes, Archives départementales

1 H 5, no. 1

Verdun, Bibliothèque municipale

751 (Cartulary of Saint-Paul de Verdun)

Wrocław, Archiwum Państwowe we Wrocławiu

Rep. 67, no. 2 (3)
Rep. 136 D 90 a (Cartulary of Wincentego na Ołbinie we Wroclawiu)

PRIMARY SOURCES IN PRINT

Amt, Emilie, ed. *The Latin Cartulary of Godstow Abbey*. Records of Social and Economic History. Oxford: Oxford University Press, 2014.

Antry, Theodore J., and Carol Neel, eds. *Norbert and Early Norbertine Spirituality*. Classics of Western Spirituality. New York: Paulist Press, 2007.

Auvray, Lucien, ed.. *Les registres de Grégoire IX: Recueil des bulles de ce pape*. Vol. 1 of 4 vols. Paris, 1896.

Baluze, Étienne, ed.. *Epistolarum Innocentii III Romani Pontificis*. 2 vols. Paris, 1682.

Barthélemy, Édouard de. "Cartulaire de l'abbaye de Bucilly." *Annales de la Société historique et archéologique de Château-Thierry*, 1881, 109–67.

Bautier, Robert-Henri, and Jean Dufour, eds. *Recueil des actes de Louis VI, roi de France (1108–1137)*. 4 vols. Chartes et diplômes relatifs à l'histoire de France. Paris: Diffusion de Boccard, 1992.

Beaurain, Georges, ed. *Le cartulaire de l'abbaye de Selincourt 1131–1513*. Mémoires de la Société des antiquaires de Picardie 40. Paris: Picard, 1925.

Beauvillé, Victor de, ed.. *Recueil de documents inédits concernant la Picardie*. 5 vols. Paris, 1860–82.

Benton, John, and Michel Bur, eds. *Recueil des actes d'Henri le Libéral, comte de Champagne, 1152–1181*. 2 vols. Chartes et diplômes relatifs à l'histoire de France. Paris: Diffusion de Boccard, 2009.

Berger, Élie, ed. *Les registres d'Innocent IV, publiés ou analysés d'après les manuscrits originaux du Vatican et de la Bibliothèque nationale*. 4 vols. Paris, 1884–1920.

Bouchot, Henri, and Emmanuel Lemaire, eds. *Le livre rouge de l'Hôtel de ville de Saint-Quentin*. Saint-Quentin, 1881.

Bougard, Pierre, and Bernard Delmaire, eds. *Le cartulaire et les chartes de l'abbaye de femmes d'Avesnes-lès-Bapaume (1128–1337)*. Atelier de recherche sur les textes médiévaux 19. Turnhout: Brepols, 2014.

Bouquet, Martin, and Léopold Delisle, eds. *Recueil des historiens des Gaules et de la France*. New ed. 24 vols. Paris, 1869–1904.

Bretonnier, Barthélemy-Joseph, ed. *Oeuvres de M. Claude Henrys*. Vol. 1 of 4 vols. Paris, 1772.

Canivez, Joseph-Marie, ed. *Statuta capitulorum generalium ordinis Cisterciensis ab anno 1116 ad annum 1786*. 8 vols. Bibliothèque de la Revue d'histoire ecclésiastique 9. Louvain: Bureaux de la Revue, 1933–41.

"Chronique." *Bibliothèque de l'École des chartes: Revue d'Érudition* 3 (1857): 570–1.

Cocquelines, Charles, ed. *Bullarium privilegiorum ac diplomatum romanorum pontificum amplissima collectio.* 14 vols. Rome, 1733–62.

Cossé-Durlin, Jeannine, ed. *Cartulaire de Saint-Nicaise de Reims.* Paris: Éditions du CNRS, 1991.

Desilve, I. "Analyse d'un cartulaire de l'abbaye de la Valroy." *Bulletin de la Société académique de Laon* 22 (1875): 111–252.

Dufour-Malbezin, Annie, ed. *Actes des évêques de Laon des origines à 1151.* Paris: CNRS Editions, 2001.

Erler, George, ed.. *Der Liber Cancellariae Apostolicae vom Jahre 1380: und der Stilus palatii abbreviatus.* Leipzig, 1888.

Evers, Julius. "L'obituaire de l'Abbaye de Prémontré (XIIe S. – Ms. 9 de Soissons) – 2me partie." *Analecta Praemonstratensia* 1 (1925).

Farrer, William, ed.. *The Chartulary of Cockersand Abbey of the Premonstratensian Order; Printed from the Original in the Possession of Thomas Brooke.* 3 vols. Manchester, 1898.

Fawtier, Robert, ed. *Registres du trésor des chartes.* 3 vols. Inventaires et documents. Paris: Imprimerie Nationale, 1958.

Fejér, György, ed. *Codex diplomaticus Hungariae ecclesiasticus ac civilis, studio et opera.* 11 vols. Buda, 1829.

Fossier, Robert, ed. *Chartes de coutume en Picardie: XIe–XIIIe siècle.* Collection de documents inédits sur l'histoire de France: Section de philologie et d'histoire jusqu'à 1610 10. Paris: Bibliothèque nationale, 1974.

Gassies, Georges, ed. *Les Chartes de la commune de Meaux, 1179–1222.* Meaux: Société historique et littéraire de la Brie, 1900.

Gaubin, Joachim. *Abbaye de La Case-Dieu, monastère de l'ordre des chanoines réguliers prémontrés de Saint-Norbert, depuis la fondation (1135) jusqu'à nos jours.* Toulouse: J. Fournier, 1903.

Gilbert, John T., ed. *Chartularies of St. Mary's Abbey, Dublin: With the Register of Its House at Dunbrody, and Annals of Ireland.* 2 vols. London, 1884.

Gomart Charles, ed. *Extraits originaux d'un manuscrit de Quentin de la Fons intitulé histoire particulière de l'Église de Saint-Quentin.* 2 vols. Saint-Quentin, 1854–6.

Grünhagen, Colmar, ed. *Codex Diplomaticus Silesiae.* Vol. 7. Breslau, 1884.

Guibert of Nogent. *A Monk's Confession: The Memoirs of Guibert of Nogent.* Trans. Paul J. Archambault. University Park: Pennsylvania State University Press, 1996.

– *Venerabilis Guiberti abbatis B. Mariae de Novigento Opera omnia.* Paris, 1602.

Guyotjeannin, Olivier, et les élèves de l'École nationale des chartes, eds. *Le chartrier de l'abbaye Prémontrée de Saint-Yved de Braine (1134–1250).* Mémoires et documents de l'École des chartes 49. Paris: École des Chartes, 2000.

Hageneder, Othmar, and Anton Haidacher, eds. *Die Register Innocenz' III.* 10 vols. Graz: Verlag Hermann Böhlaus Nachfolger, 1964.

Haigneré, Daniel. "Les chartes de Notre-Dame de Licques, 1078–1311." *Mémoires de la Société académique de l'arrondissement de Boulogne-sur-Mer* 15 (1889): 4–166.

Heinemann, Otto von, ed. *Codex diplomaticus Anhaltinus*. 6 vols. Dessau, 1867.

Herbomez, Armand Auguste d', ed. *Chartes de l'abbaye de Saint-Martin de Tournai*. 2 vols. Brussels, 1898.

Herman of Tournai. "De miraculis Laudunensis de gestis venerablilis Bartholomaie episcopi et S. Norberti." *PL* 156, cols. 961–1018.

– *Les miracles de Sainte Marie de Laon*. Ed. Alain Saint-Denis. Sources d'Histoire Médiévale 36. Paris: CNRS, 2008.

Hertel, Gustav, ed. *Urkundenbuch des Klosters Unser Lieben Frauen zu Magdeburg*. Halle, 1878.

Holstenius, Lucas, ed. *Codex regularum monasticarum et canonicarum*. 6 vols. Augsburg, 1759.

Honorius III. *Honorii III Romani Pontificis Opera Omnia*. Ed. César Auguste Horoy. 5 vols. Bibliotheca Patristica Medii Aevi. Paris, 1879–82.

Hugo, Charles-Louis. *Sacrae antiquitatis monumenta historica, dogmatica, diplomatica, notis illustrata*. 2 vols. Saint-Dié-des-Vosges, 1725.

– *Sacri et Canonici Ordinis Praemonstratensis annales, probationes*. 2 vols. Nancy, 1734–6.

Joester, Ingrid, ed. *Urkundenbuch der Abtei Steinfeld*. Publikationen der Gesellschaft für Rheinische Geschichtskunde 60. Cologne: Hanstein, 1976.

Joinville, Jean de, and Geoffroy de Villehardouin. *Chronicles of the Crusades*. Trans. Margaret R.B. Shaw. New York: Penguin, 1963.

Klempin, Robert, ed. *Pommersches Urkundenbuch*. Vol. 1 of 11 vols. Stettin, 1868.

Kuen, Michael, ed. *Collectio Scriptorum Rerum Historico-Monastico Ecclesiasticarum Variorum Religiosorum Ordinum*. 6 vols. Ulm, 1755.

Lalanne, J.-M., ed. *Le cartulaire de Valpriez, 1135–1250*. Paris: Editions du C.T.H.S., 1990.

Lalore, Charles, ed. *Collection des principaux cartulaires du diocèse de Troyes: Cartulaire de l'Abbaye de Basse-Fontaine*. Vol. 3. Paris: E. Thorin, 1878.

– *Collection des principaux cartulaires du diocèse de Troyes: Cartulaire de l'Abbaye de la Chapelle-aux-Planches*. Vol. 4. Paris: E. Thorin, 1878.

Launoy, Jean de, ed. *Opera Omnia*. Vol. 3, part 1, of 5 vols. Geneva, 1732.

Lecocq, Georges, ed. *Histoire de l'abbaye Notre-Dame de Vermand*. Saint-Quentin: Impr. Ch. Poette, 1875.

Lefèvre, Placide F., ed. *Les statuts de Prémontré réformés sur les ordres de Grégoire IX et d'Innocent IV au XIIIe siècle*. Louvain: Bureaux de la Revue, Bibliothèque de l'Université, 1946.

Lefèvre, Placide F., and Wilfrid M. Grauwen, eds. *Les Statuts de Prémontré au milieu du XIIe siècle*. Bibliotheca Analectorum Praemonstratensium 12. Averbode: Praemonstratensia, 1978.

Le Long, Nicolas. *Histoire ecclésiastique et civile du diocèse de Laon, et de tout le pays contenu entre l'Oise et la Meuse, l'Aisne et la Sambre.* Seneuze, 1783.
Le Paige, Jean. *Bibliotheca Praemonstratensis ordinis.* 2 vols. Paris, 1633.
Le privilège pour les dixmes novalles, concedé, maintenu et conservé. Paris, 1669.
Lohrmann, Dietrich, ed. *Papsturkunden in Frankreich, Neue Folge: Nördliche Ile-de-France und Vermandois.* Vol. 7 of 9 vols. Abhandlungen der Akademie der Wissenschaften in Göttingen. Philologisch-Historische Klasse. Göttingen: Vandenhoeck & Ruprecht, 1976.
Longnon, Auguste, ed. *Obituaires de la Province de Sens.* 4 vols. Paris: Imprimerie nationale, 1902–23.
Melleville, Maximilien. "Une charte où une femme, vassale d'un seigneur, est appelée *Homo mea.*" *Bulletin de la Société Académique de Laon* 4 (1855): 539–40.
Middendorp, Jacob, ed. *D. Innocentii Pontificis Maximi Eivs Nominis III.* 2 vols. Cologne, 1575.
Migne, J.-P., ed. *Patrologiae cursus completus, series Latina.* 221 vols. Paris, 1844–64.
Minon, René, ed.. *L'abbaye et le cartulaire de Fesmy (Aisne) près du Cateau (Nord).* Avesnes: Impr. Dubois-Viroux, 1902.
Monumenta Boica. Vol. 21. 60 vols. Munich, 1813.
Monumenta Germaniae Historica. 77 vols. Munich, 1826–present.
Morel, Émile, ed. *Cartulaire de l'abbaye de Saint-Corneille de Compiègne.* 3 vols. Compiègne: Imprimerie Henry Lefebvre, 1894–9.
Morel, Émile, and Louis Carolus-Barré, eds. *Cartulaire de l'abbaye de Saint-Corneille de Compiègne.* 3 vols. Montdidier, Paris: J. Bellin, Nouvelles Éditions Latines, 1904–77.
Mortimer, Richard, ed. *Leiston Abbey Cartulary and Butler Priory Charters.* Ipswich: Boydell Press, 1979.
Nanglard, Jean, ed. *Cartulaire de l'église d'Angoulême.* Angoulême: Imprimerie G. Chasseignac, 1900.
Newman, William Mendel. *The Cartulary and Charters of Notre-Dame of Homblières.* Ed. Theodore Evergates and Giles Constable. Cambridge, MA: Medieval Academy of America, 1990.
– *Charters of St-Fursy of Péronne.* Cambridge, MA: Medieval Academy of America, 1977.
Pardessus, Jean-Marie, ed. *Ordonnances des rois de France de la troisième race. Supplément.* Paris, n.d.
Pécheur, Louis-Victor. "Cartulaire de Tinselve." *Bulletin de la Société archéologique de Soissons*, 2nd series, 5 (1875): 212–46.
Peigné-Delacourt, Achille, ed. *Cartulaire de l'abbaye de Morienval.* Senlis, 1876.
– *Cartulaire de l'Abbaye de Notre-Dame d'Ourscamp de l'ordre de Cîteaux, fondée en 1129 au diocèse de Noyon.* Amiens, 1865.

Philip of Harvengt. "Philippi de Harveng inclyti Monasterii Bonae Spei Abbatis Epistolae." *PL* 203, cols. 1–188.

Pichler, Isfried, ed. *Urkundenbuch des Stiftes Schlägl: die Rechts- und Geschichtsquellen der Cisterce Slage und des Prämonstratenserchorherrenstiftes Schlägl von den Anfängen bis zum Jahr 1600.* Schlägler Schriften 12. Schlägl: Stift Schlägl, 2003.

Pipon, Brigitte, ed. *Le chartrier de l'Abbaye-aux-Bois (1202–1341).* Mémoires et documents de l'École des chartes. Paris: École nationale des chartes, 1996.

Poupardin, René. "Cartulaire de Saint-Vincent de Laon (Arch. Vatican. Misc. arm. x. 145). Analyse et pièces inédites." *Mémoires de la Société de l'Histoire de Paris et de l'Ile-de-France* 29 (1902): 173–267.

– "Quatre Chartes anciennes d'Évêques de Noyon provenant de la Collection Phillipps." *Comptes rendus et mémoires lus aux séances de la Comité archéologique de Noyon* 22 (1910): 214–22.

Pycke, Jacques, and Cyriel Vleeschouwers, eds. *Les actes des évêques de Noyon-Tournai (7e siècle–1146/48).* Episcopalis officii sollicitudo I. Louvain-la-Neuve: CIACO, 2015.

Ramackers, Johannes, ed. *Papsturkunden in den Niederlanden (Belgien, Luxemburg, Holland und Französisch-Flandern).* 2 vols. Abhandlungen der Akademie der Wissenschaften in Göttingen. Philologisch-Historische Klasse. Berlin: Weidmannsche Buchhandlung, 1933.

– *Papsturkunden in Frankreich.* Vol. 4. Abhandlungen der Akademie der Wissenschaften in Göttingen. Philologisch-Historische Klasse. Göttingen: Vandenhoeck & Ruprecht, 1942.

Redford, Jill, ed. *The Cartulary of Alvingham Priory.* Kathleen Major Series of Medieval Records. Woodbridge: Boydell & Brewer, 2018.

Riedel, Adolph Friedrich, ed. *Codex diplomaticus Brandenburgensis: Sammlung der Urkunden, Chroniken und sonstigen Quellenschriften für die Geschichte der Mark Brandenburg und ihrer Regenten.* 41 vols. Berlin, 1838.

Rodríguez de Diego, José Luis, ed. *Colección Diplomática de Santa María de Aguilar de Campoo (852–1230).* Salamanca: Junta de Castilla y León, 2004.

Saulnier, Charles, ed. *Statuta candidi et canonici ordinis Praemonstratensis renovata ac anno 1630.* 2nd ed. Étival, 1725.

Secousse, Denis-François, et al. *Ordonnances des rois de France de la troisième race.* 21 vols. Paris, 1723–1849.

Sirleto, Guglielmo, ed. *Innocentii tertii, pontificis maximi decretalium, atque aliarum epistolarum tomus.* Rome, 1543.

Slack, Corliss Konwiser, ed. *Crusade Charters, 1138–1270.* Tempe: Arizona Center for Medieval and Renaissance Studies, 2001.

Smet, Joseph Jean de, ed. *Corpus chronicorum Flandriae.* 4 vols. Brussels, 1837.

Society of Bollandists. *Acta Sanctorum quotquot toto orbe coluntur.* 68 vols. Brussels, 1643–present.

Spottiswoode, John, ed. *Liber S. Marie de Dryburgh: registrum cartarum abbacie premonstratenis de Dryburgh.* Bannatyne Club Publications 83. Edinburgh, 1847.

Stein, Henri, ed. *Cartulaire de l'ancienne abbaye de Saint Nicolas des Prés sous Ribemont (diocèse de Laon).* Saint-Quentin, 1884.

Tangl, Michael, ed. *Die päpstlichen Kanzleiordnungen von 1200–1500.* Innsbruck, 1894.

Teulet, Alexandre, et al., eds. *Layettes du Trésor des chartes.* 5 vols. Paris, 1863–1909.

Tock, Benoît-Michel, ed. *Les chartes des évêques d'Arras: 1093–1203.* Collection de documents inédits sur l'histoire de France 20. Paris: Comité des travaux historiques et scientifiques, 1991.

Tock, Benoît-Michel, and Ludo Milis, eds. *Monumenta Arroasiensia: Textes narratifs et diplomatiques de l'abbaye d'Arrouaise.* Corpus Christianorum. Continuatio mediaevalis 175. Turnhout: Brepols, 2000.

Valvekens, Johannes B., ed. *Acta et Decreta Capitulorum Generalium Ordinis Praemonstratensis. Vol. 1: Saeculis 12–15.* Averbode: Praemonstratensia, 1966.

– "Actus Confraternitatis Inter Ordinem Praemonstratensem et Ordinem Cisterciensem." *Analecta Praemonstratensia* 42 (1966): 326–30.

Van der Velden, Gregorius Maria. "Documenten betreffende de orde van Prémontré, verzameld door Merselius van Macharen in 1445." *Analecta Praemonstratensia* 58 (1982): 35–95.

Van Waefelghem, Raphaël, ed. *L'Obituaire de l'abbaye de Prémontré (XIIe s., ms. 9 de Soissons).* Louvain: Impr. de P. Smeesters, 1913.

– "Les premiers statuts de l'Ordre de Prémontré. Le Clm. 17.174 (XIIe siècle)." *Analectes de l'Ordre de Prémontré* 9 (1913): 1–74.

Varin, Pierre, ed.. *Archives administratives de la ville de Reims: collections de pièces inédites pouvant servir à l'histoire des institutions dans l'intérieur de la cité.* 5 vols. Paris, 1839–48.

Verein für Mecklenburgische Geschichte und Alterthumskunde. *Mecklenburgisches Urkundenbuch.* 25 vols. Schwerin, 1863.

Verlaguet, P.-A., ed. *Cartulaire de l'abbaye de Bonnecombe.* 2 vols. Rodez: Imprimerie P. Carrère, 1925.

"Vita Norberti archiepiscopi Magdeburgensis." *Monumenta Germaniae Historica, Scriptorum* 12, ed. Roger Wilmans. Hanover, 1956.

"Vita S. Norberti auctore canonico Praemonstrantensi coaevo." *PL* 170, cols. 1257–1343.

Weissthanner, Alois, ed. *Die Urkunden und Urbare des Klosters Schäftlarn.* Quellen und Erörterungen zur bayerischen Geschichte 10:2. Munich: Beck, 1957.

Wiederhold, Wilhelm, ed. "Papsturkunden in Frankreich." *Nachrichten von der Gesellschaft der Wissenschaften zu Göttingen.* Philologisch-Historische Klasse 7 (1913): 1–202.

Wölfing, Günther, ed. *Das Prämonstratenserkloster Veßra: Urkundenregesten 1130–1573; mit einem Verzeichnis der weiteren archivalischen Quellen.* Böhlau Verlag. Veröffentlichungen des Hennebergischen Museums Kloster Veßra 15. Cologne, 2010.

ARCHAEOLOGICAL REPORTS

Galmiche, Thierry, et al. Unpublished Prémontré excavation reports:
Code Patriarche: 9414
Code Patriarche: 9596
Code Patriarche: 10007
Code Patriarche: 10038

ONLINE RESOURCES

Annuaire prosopographique: la France savante. 2006. https://cths.fr/an/savant.php.

Barbiche, Jean-Marie, and Olivier Guyotjeannin, eds. "Acte seigneurial." THELEME, 2006. http://theleme.enc.sorbonne.fr/dossiers/notice80.php.

Bibliothèque virtuelle des manuscrits médiévaux. 2013. https://bvmm.irht.cnrs.fr/.

CartulR: Répertoire des cartulaires médiévaux et modernes. 2012. https://telma-repertoires.irht.cnrs.fr/cartulr/page/presentation.

Chartae Galliae. 2012. http://telma.irht.cnrs.fr//outils/chartae-galliae/index/.

Chartes originales conservées en France (1121–1220). 2012. http://telma.irht.cnrs.fr/outils/originaux2/index/.

Dictionnaire topographique de la France, 2020. https://dicotopo.cths.fr/.

Diplomata Belgica. 2015. https://www.diplomata-belgica.be/.

"Independent Crusaders Project." 2017. https://independentcrusadersproject.ace.fordham.edu/.

Studium Baldwin, 2018. http://studium-baldwin.lamop.fr.

SECONDARY SOURCES

Abadie, Stéphane. "Un temporel monastique dans l'espace médiéval gascon: l'abbaye prémontrée de la Casedieu (Gers), XIIe–XVIe s." PhD dissertation, University of Toulouse-Jean Jaurès, 2016.

Alcina-Rossello, Lorenzo. "Les Prémontrés en Espagne au XVIe siècle: réforme et sécession." In *Les Prémontrés et la Lorraine, XIIe–XVIIIe siècle*, ed. Dominique-Marie Dauzet and Martine Plouvier, 63–85. Bibliothèque Beauchesne Religion Société Politique 33. Paris: Beauchesne, 1998.

Ardura, Bernard. *Abbayes, prieurés et monastères de l'ordre de Prémontré en France des origines à nos jours: dictionnaire historique et bibliographique*. Nancy; Pont-à-Mousson: Presses universitaires de Nancy; Centre culturel des Prémontrés, 1993.

– "De conciles en réformes, les Prémontrés et leurs interprétations du charisme de saint Norbert (XVe–XXe siècles)." In *Écrire son histoire: les communautés religieuses régulières face à leur passé: actes du 5e colloque international du CERCOR, Saint-Etienne, 6–8 novembre 2002*, ed. Nicole Bouter, 221–55. Saint-Etienne: Université de Saint-Etienne, 2005.

– *The Order of Prémontré: History and Spirituality.* Trans. Edward Hagman. De Pere, WI: Paisa Publications, 1995.

Attal, Robert. "Les Riches Heures de La Société." Société archéologique, historique et scientifique de Soissons. Accessed July 1, 2020. http://www.sahs-soissons.org/menu/cadre.php?page=orgh_histo&som=org&tpg=tp&PHPSESSID=8dead31e749b0bef0731e3c52fbb4f24.

Backmund, Norbert. *Monasticon Praemonstratense id est, Historia circariarum atque canoniarum candidi et canonici Ordinis Praemonstratensis.* 3 vols. Straubing: Cl. Attenkofersche Buchdruckerei, 1949.

– "Ordo Praemonstratensis in Italia. Circaria Tusciae et Calabriae." *Brundisii res* 9 (1977): 3–44.

Baldwin, John W. *The Government of Philip Augustus: Foundations of French Royal Power in the Middle Ages.* Berkeley: University of California Press, 1991.

Barthélemy, Dominique. *Les deux âges de la seigneurie banale: pouvoir et société dans la terre des sires de Coucy, milieu XIe–milieu XIIIe siècle.* Université de Paris IV, Série Histoire Ancienne et Médiévale 12. Paris: Publications de la Sorbonne, 1984.

– "Monachisme et aristocratie au XIIe siècle: les bénédictins de Nogent-sous-Coucy face à la concurrence et à l'exemple de Prémontré." In *Sous la Règle de saint Benoît: structures monastiques et sociétés en France, du Moyen Âge à l'époque moderne*, 185–98. Hautes études médiévales et modernes 47. Geneva: Droz, 1982.

Barthélemy, Édouard de. *Analyse du cartulaire de l'abbaye de Foigny.* Vervins, 1879.

– "Le cartulaire de l'abbaye d'Andecy." *Mémoires de la Société d'agriculture, commerce, sciences et arts du département de la Marne*, 1883, 89–138.

Bautier, Robert-Henri. "Les 'courts' de l'Ordre de Prémontré au XIIe siècle: Formation et premiers développements." In *L'Espace cistercien*, ed. Michel Pressouyre, 216–25. Mémoires de la Section d'Archéologie et d'Histoire de l'Art 5. Paris: Léon, 1994.

Beach, Alison I. *Women as Scribes: Book Production and Monastic Reform in Twelfth-Century Bavaria.* Cambridge Studies in Palaeography and Codicology 10. Cambridge: Cambridge University Press, 2004.

Becquet, Jean. "Abbayes et Prieurés. Tome XVII. Diocèse de Soissons (Province de Reims)." *Revue Mabillon*, no. 303/4 (1986): 161–252.

Bergin, Joseph. *Cardinal Richelieu: Power and the Pursuit of Wealth.* New Haven: Yale University Press, 1985.

Berkhofer, Robert. *Day of Reckoning: Power and Accountability in Medieval France.* The Middle Ages Series. Philadelphia: University of Pennsylvania Press, 2004.

– "Inventaires de biens et proto-comptabilités dans le nord de la France (XIe–début XIIe siècle)." *Bibliothèque de l'École des chartes* 155, no. 1 (1997): 339–49.

Berlière, Ursmer. *Monasticon belge: Province de Namur et de Hainaut.* 2 vols. Maredsous, 1897.

Berman, Constance Hoffman. "Later Monastic Economies." In *The Cambridge History of Medieval Monasticism in the Latin West*, ed. Alison I. Beach and Isabelle Cochelin, 2:831–47. Cambridge: Cambridge University Press, 2020.

Bertrand, Paul, and Xavier Hélary. "Constructions de l'espace dans les cartulaires." In *Construction de l'espace au Moyen Âge: Pratiques et représentations; XXXVIIe congrès de la SHMES, Mulhouse, 2–4 juin 2006*, ed. Thomas Lienhard, 193–208. Histoire ancienne et médiévale 96. Paris: Publications de la Sorbonne, 2007.

Blanton, Virginia, Veronica M. O'Mara, and Patricia Stoop, eds. *Nuns' Literacies in Medieval Europe: The Antwerp Dialogue*. Medieval Women 28. Turnhout: Brepols, 2018.

– eds. *Nuns' Literacies in Medieval Europe: The Hull Dialogue*. Medieval Women 26. Turnhout: Brepols, 2013.

– eds. *Nuns' Literacies in Medieval Europe: The Kansas City Dialogue*. Medieval Women 27. Turnhout: Brepols, 2015.

Boghen, Jeannine. "Inventaire des actes épiscopaux originaux conservés à la Bibliothèque nationale (1121–1200)." In *À propos des actes d'évêques. Hommage à Lucie Fossier*, ed. Michel Parisse, 79–138. Nancy: Presses Universitaires de Nancy, 1991.

Böhmer, Johann Friedrich, and Ulrich Schmidt. *Regesta Imperii IV. Lothar III. und ältere Staufer 1125–1197, 4. Papstregesten 1124–1198*. Vol. 4. Cologne: Böhlau Verlag, 2014.

Bond, C.J. "The Premonstratensian Order: A Preliminary Survey of Its Growth and Distribution in Medieval Europe." In *In Search of Cult: Archaeological Investigations in Honour of Philip Rahtz*, ed. Martin Carver, 153–85. Woodbridge: Boydell Press, 1993.

Bonde, Sheila, and Clark Maines. "Note sur la fouille de l'église de saint Norbert à Prémontré: son importance pour la première architecture cistercienne." *Cîteaux* 38 (1987): 100–1.

Bondéelle-Souchier, Anne. *Bibliothèques de l'Ordre de Prémontré dans la France d'Ancien Régime: Répertoire des abbayes*. Vol. 2 of 2 vols. Documents, études et répertoires, publiés par l'IRHT 58. Paris: CNRS Éditions, 2000.

Bonnet, Philippe. *Les constructions de l'ordre de Prémontré en France aux XVIIe et XVIIIe siècles*. Bibliothèque de la Société française d'archéologie 15. Geneva: Librairie Droz, 1983.

Bouchard, Constance Brittain. "Monastic Cartularies: Organizing Eternity." In *Charters, Cartularies, and Archives: The Preservation and Transmission of Documents in the Medieval West; Proceedings of a Colloquium of the Commission Internationale de Diplomatique (Princeton and New York, 16–18 September 1999)*, 22–32. Papers in Mediaeval Studies 17. Toronto: Pontifical Institute of Mediaeval Studies, 2002.

– *Rewriting Saints and Ancestors: Memory and Forgetting in France, 500–1200*. The Middle Ages Series. Philadelphia: University of Pennsylvania Press, 2014.

– *Sword, Miter, and Cloister: Nobility and the Church in Burgundy, 980–1198*. Ithaca: Cornell University Press, 1987.

Bouchot, Henri. "Chartes du XIIe siècle relatives aux anciennes abbayes de Fervaques, d'Ourscamp et de Saint-Quentin-en-l'Isle." *Mémoires de la Société académique des sciences, arts, belles-lettres, agriculture et industrie de Saint-Quentin*, 4th series, 3 (1880): 344–55.

– *Inventaire des dessins exécutés pour Roger de Gaignières et conservés aux Départements des estampes et des manuscrits.* 2 vols. Paris, 1891.

Boudon, Georges. "Robert de Clari en Aminois, chevalier auteur d'une chronique de la IVe croisade (1200–1216)." *Bulletin de la Société des antiquaires de Picardie* 19 (1897): 700–34.

Bourquelot, Félix. *Histoire de Provins.* 2 vols. Provins, 1839.

Bréquigny, Louis-George de, et al. *Table chronologique des diplômes, chartes, titres et actes imprimés concernant l'histoire de France.* 8 vols. Paris, 1769–1876.

Brun, Felix. "Note sur les Simon de Bucy et le vieux château de Bucy-le-Long." *Bulletin de la Société archéologique, historique et scientifique de Soissons* 14 (1907): 359–405.

Brunel, Clovis. "Les parchemins de la collection Salis aux archives historiques de la ville de Metz." *Bibliothèque de l'École des chartes* 75, no. 1 (1914): 345–53.

Brunel, Ghislain. "Agriculture et équipement agricole à Prémontré (XIIe–XIIIe s.)." In *Monachisme et technologie dans la société médiévale du Xe au XIIIe siècle: Actes du colloque scientifique international de Cluny, 4–6 septembre 1991*, ed. Charles Hetzlen and René de Vos, 123–50. Cluny: École nationale supérieure d'arts et métiers, 1994.

Burgtorf, Jochen. *The Central Convent of Hospitallers and Templars: History, Organization, and Personnel (1099/1120–1310).* Leiden: Brill, 2008.

Caffiaux, Philippe-Joseph. *Trésor généalogique, ou extraits de titres anciens qui concernent les maisons & familles de France & des environs, connus en 1400 ou auparavant.* Paris, 1777.

Cagny, Paul de. *Histoire de l'arrondissement de Péronne.* 3 vols. Amiens, 1869 87.

Capaumont, L. *Notice historique sur la ville de Chauny; suivie d'un Traité sur les mesures locales nouvelles et anciennes.* Noyon, 1840.

Cárcel Ortí, María Milagros, ed. *Vocabulaire international de la diplomatique.* Collecció Oberta 28. València: Universitat de València, 1994.

Catalogue analytique des chartes, documents historiques, titres nobiliaires, etc: composant les archives du Collège héraldique et historique de France, première partie: Picardie. Paris, 1866.

Caviness, Madeline H. "Writing Women: Problematics of History and Language." *Reframing Medieval Art: Difference, Margins, Boundaries*, 2000. http://dca.lib.tufts.edu/caviness/chapter1.html.

Chastang, Pierre. *Lire, écrire, transcrire: le travail des rédacteurs de cartulaires en Bas-Languedoc (XIe–XIIIe siècles).* CTHS Histoire 2. Paris: Éditions du CTHS, 2001.

Cheney, Christopher R. "Gervase, Abbot of Prémontré: A Medieval Letter-Writer." *Bulletin of the John Rylands Library* 33, no. 1 (1950): 25–56.

– "The Office and Title of the Papal Chancellor, 1187–1216." *Archivum Historiae Pontificiae* 22 (1984): 369–76.

Cheney, Christopher R., and Mary G. Cheney. *The Letters of Pope Innocent III (1198–1216) Concerning England and Wales*. Oxford: Clarendon Press, 1967.

Cherest, Aimé. "Étude Historique sur Vézelay." *Bulletin de la Société des sciences historiques et naturelles de l'Yonne* 16 (1862): 209–525.

Clemens, Raymond, and Timothy Graham. *Introduction to Manuscript Studies*. Ithaca: Cornell University Press, 2007.

Cocheris, Hippolyte. *Notices et extraits des documents manuscrits conservés dans les dépôts publics de Paris et relatifs à l'histoire de la Picardie*. 2 vols. 1854–8.

Colliette, Louis-Paul. *Mémoires pour servir à l'histoire ecclésiastique, civile et militaire de la province du Vermandois*. 3 vols. Cambrai, 1771–2.

Colvin, H.M. "The Internal History of Dale Abbey." *Derbyshire Archaeological Journal* 62 (1941): 31–57.

"Commanderie des Templiers de Bertaignemont." *La Thiérache: recueil de documents* 1 (1849): 131–8.

Constable, Giles. *The Reformation of the Twelfth Century*. Cambridge: Cambridge University Press, 1996.

– *Three Studies in Medieval Religious and Social Thought: The Interpretation of Mary and Martha, the Ideal of the Imitation of Christ, the Orders of Society*. Cambridge: Cambridge University Press, 1998.

Coüard-Luys, Émile. "L'Écolâtre de Noyon et les écoles de cette ville jusqu'au milieu du XIIIe siècle." *Mémoires de la Société des antiquaires de Picardie*, 3rd series, 10 (1899): 267–92.

Crenshaw, Kimberlé. *On Intersectionality: Essential Writings*. New York: New Press, 2017.

Cubizolles, Pierre. *Le diocèse du Puy-en-Velay des origines à nos jours*. Nonette: Editions Creer, 2005.

Cuvillier-Morel-d'Acy, Marie-Joseph. *Histoire généalogique et héraldique sur la maison des Tyrel, sires, puis princes de Poix …* Paris, 1869.

Cyrus, Cynthia J. *The Scribes for Women's Convents in Late Medieval Germany*. Toronto: University of Toronto Press, 2009.

Darras, Joseph Épiphane. "Observations sur le cartulaire de Prémontré (XIIIe siècle)." *Bulletin de la Société archéologique et scientifique de Soissons* 10 (1856): 12–14.

Darsy, François-Irénée. *Bénéfices de l'église d'Amiens, ou État général des biens, revenus et charges du clergé du diocèse d'Amiens en 1730, avec des notes*. 2 vols. Amiens, 1869–71.

David-Roy, Marguerite. "Les granges monastiques en France aux XIIe et XIIIe siècles." *Archeologia* 58 (1973): 53–62.

Davis, Adam Jeffrey. *The Holy Bureaucrat: Eudes Rigaud and Religious Reform in Thirteenth-Century Normandy*. Ithaca: Cornell University Press, 2006.

Deladreue, Louis-Eudore. "Notice sur l'abbaye de Froidmont: 1re partie." *Mémoires de la société académique d'archéologie, sciences et arts du département de l'Oise* 7 (1868): 469–624.

– "Notice sur l'abbaye de Froidmont: 2e partie." *Mémoires de la société académique d'archéologie, sciences et arts du département de l'Oise* 8 (1871): 11–78.

Delancy, Jean. *Historia Fusniacensis Coenobii, Ordinis Cisterciensis*. Laon, 1671.

De Laprairie, Jules. "Notes sur le village de Soupir." *Bulletin de la Société historique et archéologique de Soissons* 17 (1863): 254–7.

Delcambre, Étienne. *Servais de Lairuelz et la réforme des prémontrés*. Bibliotheca Analectorum Praemonstratensium 5. Averbode: Praemonstratensia, 1964.

Delisle, Léopold. *Le cabinet des manuscrits de la Bibliothèque nationale: étude sur la formation de ce dépôt, comprenant les éléments d'une histoire de la calligraphie, de la miniature, de la reliure et du commerce des livres à Paris avant l'invention de l'imprimerie*. Vol. 2 of 3 vols. Paris, 1874.

– "Mémoire sur les actes d'Innocent III." *Bibliothèque de l'École des chartes* 19, no. 1 (1858): 1–73.

Demay, Germain. *Inventaire des sceaux de l'Artois et de la Picardie: recueillis dans les dépôts d'archives, musées et collections particulières des départements du Pas-de-Calais, de l'Oise, de la Somme et de l'Aisne*. Paris, 1877.

De Paermentier, Els, and Steven Vanderputten. "Aristocratic Patronage, Political Networking and the Shaping of a Private Sanctuary: Countess Clemence of Flanders and the Early Years of Bourbourg Abbey (*c* .1103–21)." *Journal of Medieval History* 42, no. 3 (26 May 2016): 317–37.

Dereine, Charles. "Les origines de Prémontré." *Revue d'histoire ecclésiastique* 42 (1947): 352–78.

– "Le premier ordo de Prémontré." *Revue Bénédictine* 58 (1948): 84–92.

– "Saint-Ruf et ses coutumes au XIe et XII siècles." *Revue Bénédictine* 59 (1949): 170–4.

Desnoyers, Jules. "Topographie ecclésiastique de la France: Pendant le Moyen Âge et dans les temps modernes jusqu'en 1790." *Annuaire historique pour l'année ...* 27 (1863): 601–806.

Despy, Georges. "Les richesses de la terre: Cîteaux et Prémontré devant l'économie de profit aux XIIe et XIIIe siècles." *Problèmes d'histoire du christianisme* 5 (1975): 58–80.

Dobenecker, Otto. *Regesta diplomatica necnon epistolaria historiae Thuringiae*. 4 vols. Jena, 1895.

Doursther, Horace. *Dictionnaire universel des poids et mesures anciens et modernes*. Brussels, 1840.

Dubal, Francisco. *Vida apostólica, muerte y translacion de N.P. y Patriarca S. Norberto, fundador del orden cándido y canónico premonstratense*. Madrid, 1667.

Du Cange, Charles Dufresne. "Le Prieuré de Lihons en Santerre." In *Mélanges historiques sur la Picardie*, ed. Arthur Demarsy, 3–9. Amiens, 1870.

Du Chesne, André. *Histoire généalogique de la maison royale de Dreux et de quelques autres familles illustres, qui en sont descenduës par Femmes: le tous justifié par chartes de diverses églises, tiltres, arrests, histoires et autres bonnes preuvęs*. Paris, 1631.

– *Histoire généalogique des maisons de Guines, d'Ardres, de Gand, et de Coucy, et de quelques autres familles illustres qui y ont été alliées: le tout illustré par chartes de diverses églises, tiltres, histoires anciennes et autres bonnes preuves*. Paris, 1631.

Dufrenelle, Henri. "La Maison française de Bousies." *Mémoires de la fédération des sociétés savantes de l'Aisne* 16 (1970): 170–89.

Duval, R. "Histoire de l'abbaye bénédictine de Saint-Nicolas-aux-Bois, diocèse de Laon, première partie." *Mémoires de la Société académique des sciences, arts, belles-lettres, agriculture et industrie de Saint-Quentin*, 4th series, 12 (1893): 153–258.

École nationale des chartes. "Missions et projets." 1 April 2015. http://www.chartes.psl.eu/fr/rubrique-ecole/missions-et-projets.

Elm, Kaspar, ed. "Hugo von Fosses, Erster Abt von Prémontré und Organisator des Prämonstratenserordens." In *Studien zum Prämonstratenserorden*, ed. Irene Crusius and Helmut Flachenecker, 35–55. Veröffentlichungen des Max-Planck-Instituts für Geschichte 185. Göttingen: Vandenhoeck & Ruprecht, 2003.

– *Norbert von Xanten: Adliger, Ordensstifter, Kirchenfürst*. Cologne: Wienand, 1984.

Evergates, Theodore. *Aristocracy in the County of Champagne, 1100–1300*. The Middle Ages Series. Philadelphia: University of Pennsylvania Press, 2007.

– *Henry the Liberal: Count of Champagne, 1127–1181*. The Middle Ages Series. Philadelphia: University of Pennsylvania Press, 2016.

– *Littere Baronum: The Earliest Cartulary of the Counts of Champagne*. Toronto: University of Toronto Press, 2003.

– *Marie of France: Countess of Champagne, 1145–1198*. The Middle Ages Series. Philadelphia: University of Pennsylvania Press, 2019.

Evers, J.J. "Kamerijk en Premonstreit in 1132." *Analecta Praemonstratensia* 2 (1926): 88–90.

Évrard, Jean-Pol. "Écrire à Verdun au XIIIe siècle. Le cartulaire de l'abbaye prémontrée Saint-Paul de Verdun. Approche codicologique et paléographique." In *L'écrit et le livre peint en Lorraine, de Saint-Mihiel à Verdun (IXe–XVe siècles): Actes du colloque de Saint-Mihiel (25–26 octobre 2010)*, ed. Anne-Orange Poilpré and Marianne Besseyre, 193–228. Culture et société médiévales 27. Turnhout: Brepols, 2014.

Falkenstein, Ludwig. "Radulf von Sarre als päpstlicher Delegat und seine Mitdelegaten." In *Grundlagen des Rechts. Festschrift für Peter Landau zum 65. Geburtstag*, ed. Richard Henry Helmholz, Paul Mikat, Jorg Müller, and Michael Stolleis, 301–32. Paderborn: De Gruyter, 2000.

Florival, Adrien de. *Étude historique sur le XIIe siècle. Barthélemy de Vir, évêque de Laon*. Laon, 1877.

Fossier, Robert. "La Société Picarde au Moyen Âge." In *Histoire de la Picardie*, ed. Robert Fossier, 135–76. Univers de la France et des pays francophones. Toulouse: Privat, 1974.

– "Première exploitation des ressources picardes." In *Histoire de la Picardie*, ed. Robert Fossier. Univers de la France et des pays francophones. Toulouse: Privat, 1974.

Framond, Martin de. "Chartes et notices relatives à la fondation de Saint-Sauveur de Séverac et sa donation à Saint-Chaffre-du-Monastier: réécritures utilitaires au XIIe et au XVIIe siècles." In *Écrire son histoire. Les communautés régulières face à leur passé*. Actes du 5e colloque international du C.E.R.C.O.R., Saint-Étienne, 6–8 novembre 2002, 555–71. Saint-Étienne: L'Université de Saint-Étienne, 2005.

François, Jean Luc. "Trois granges médiévales méconnues dans le canton de Crépy-en-Valois (Oise)." *Revue archéologique de Picardie* 20, no. 1 (1980): 17–20.

Franklin, Alfred. *Dictionnaire des noms, surnoms et pseudonymes latins de l'histoire littéraire du Moyen-âge (1100 à 1530)*. Paris, 1875.

Froese, Walter. "The Early Norbertines on the Religious Frontiers of Northeastern Germany." PhD dissertation, University of Chicago, 1978.

Galmiche, Thierry, and Vincent Buccio. "Les ardoises gravées de l'abbaye de Prémontré (Aisne), un support de notation musicale aux XVe–XVIe siècles." *Archéologie médiévale*, no. 46 (1 December 2016): 123–34.

Gaztambide, José Goñi. "La reforma de los Premonstratenses españoles del siglo XVI." *Hispania Sacra* 13 (1960): 6–96.

Geary, Patrick. "Entre Gestion et Gesta." In *Les cartulaires. Actes de la table ronde organisée par l'École nationale des chartes et le G.D.R. 121 du C.N.R.S.*, ed. Olivier Guyotjcannin, Laurent Morelle, and Michel Parisse, 13–26. Mémoires et documents de l'École des Chartes 39. Paris: École nationale des chartes, 1993.

– *Phantoms of Remembrance: Memory and Oblivion at the End of the First Millennium*. Princeton: Princeton University Press, 1994.

Gercken, Philipp Wilhelm. *Ausführliche Stifts-Historie von Brandenburg*. Wolffenbüttel, 1766.

Gerits, Trudo. "À propos de l'organisation des bibliothèques médiévales de l'Ordre de Prémontré en Angleterre et en Allemagne." *Analecta Praemonstratensia* 37 (1961): 75–84

– "Les actes de confraternité de 1142 et de 1153 entre Cîteaux et Prémontré." *Analecta Praemonstratensia* 40 (1964): 192–205.

Gerzaguet, Jean-Pierre. *L'Abbaye d'Anchin de sa fondation (1079) au XIVe siècle: Essor, vie et rayonnement d'une grande communauté bénédictine*. Villeneuve d'Ascq: Presses Universitaires Septentrion, 1997.

Gillet, Joseph. *La chartreuse de Mont-Dieu au diocèse de Reims, avec pièces justificatives inédites*. Reims, 1889.

Goethals, F.V. *Généalogie de la famille de Roye, originaire de Picardie*. Brussels, 1851.

Gomart, Charles. *Essai historique sur la ville de Ribemont et son canton*. Saint-Quentin, 1869.

– *Ham, son château et ses prisonniers*. Ham, 1864.

– "Les seigneurs et gouverneurs de Ham." *Mémoires de la Société des antiquaires de Picardie*, 2nd series, 8 (1861): 325–58.

Goovaerts, Léon. *Écrivains, artistes et savants de l'ordre de Prémontré*. 4 vols. Brussels: Société Belge de Librarie, 1899–1920.

Gosse, Antoine Alexandre. *Histoire de l'Abbaye et de l'ancienne congrégation des chanoines réguliers d'Arrouaise, avec des notes critiques, historiques et diplomatiques*. Lille, 1786.

Grandmottet, Odile. "Les officialités de Reims." *Revue d'Histoire des Textes* 4 (1956): 77–106.

Grauwen, Wilfried M. "Lijst van oorkonden waarin Norbertus wordt genoemd." *Analecta Praemonstratensia* 51 (1975): 139–82.

– *Norbertus, aartsbisschop van Maagdenburg (1126–1134)*. Brussels: Koninklijke Academie voor Wetenschappen, Letteren en Schone Kunsten van België, 1978.

– "Twee onuitgegeven oorkonden over Norbert van Gennep." *Analecta Praemonstratensia* 64 (1988): 273–87.

Gravier, Henri. *Essai sur les prévots royaux du XIe au XIVe siècle*. Paris: LaRose et Tenin, 1904.

Green, Johanna M.E. "Digital Manuscripts as Sites of Touch: Using Social Media for 'Hands-On' Engagement with Medieval Manuscript Materiality." *Archive Journal*, September 2018. http://www.archivejournal.net/?p=7795.

Gribbin, Joseph A. *The Premonstratensian Order in Late Medieval England*. Studies in the History of Medieval Religion 16. Woodbridge: Boydell Press, 2000.

Griffin, Appleton Prentiss Clark. *List of Cartularies (Principally French) Recently Added to the Library of Congress with Some Earlier Accessions*. Washington, DC: Government Printing Office, 1905.

Guesnon, Adolphe. "Les origines d'Arras et de ses institutions." *Mémoires de l'Académie d'Arras*, 2nd series, 26 (1895): 183–258.

Guiot, Léon. "Histoire genealogique et heraldique des seigneurs de la terre et baronnerie de Walincourt en Cambrésis." *Mémoires de la Société d'émulation de Cambrai* 54 (1900): 103–252.

Gullick, Michael. "How Fast Did Scribes Write?: Evidence from Romanesque Manuscripts." In *Making the Medieval Book: Techniques of Production. Proceedings of the Fourth Conference of the Seminar in the History of the Book to 1500, Oxford, July 1992*, ed. Linda L. Brownrigg, 39–58. London: Red Gull Press, 1995.

Guyotjeannin, Olivier. *Episcopus et comes: affirmation et déclin de la seigneurie épiscopale au nord du royaume de France (Beauvais-Noyon, Xe–début XIIIe siècle)*. Mémoires et documents 30. Genève: Librairie Droz, 1987.

– "La fabrique du Cartulaire Blanc." *Bibliothèque de l'École des chartes* 172, no. 1/2 (2014): 277–99.
– "La tradition de l'ombre: Les actes sous le regard des archivistes médiévaux (Saint-Denis XIIe–XVe)." In *Charters, Cartularies, and Archives: The Preservation and Transmission of Documents in the Medieval West*, ed. Adam J. Kosto and Anders Winroth, 81–112. Toronto: Pontifical Institute of Mediaeval Studies, 2002.
Guyotjeannin, Olivier, Laurent Morelle, and Michel Parisse, eds. *Les cartulaires. Actes de la table ronde organisée par l'École nationale des chartes et le G.D.R. 121 du C.N.R.S.* Mémoires et documents de l'École des Chartes 39. Paris: École nationale des chartes, 1993.
Hagemans, Gustave. *Histoire du pays de Chimay*. 2 vols. Brussels, 1866.
Hanegraaf, Cornelius. *Compendio della vita, miracoli, et instituto del glorioso patriarcha S. Norberto*. Rome, 1632.
Heidecker, Karl. "30 June 1047: The End of Charters as Legal Evidence in France?" In *Strategies of Writing: Studies on Text and Trust in the Middle Ages*, ed. P. Schulte, M. Mostert, and I. van Renswoude, 85–94. Turnhout: Brepols, 2008.
Hennezel d'Ormois, Jehan. *Les bibliophiles du pays Laonnois: leurs ex-libris et fers de reliure*. Vol. 1 of 3 vols. Paris: Société française des collectionneurs d'ex-libris, 1914.
Herbomez, Armand Auguste d'. *Histoire des châtelains de Tournai de la maison de Mortagne*. 2 vols. Tournai, 1895.
– "Une charte des chatelains de Tournai." *Annales de la Société historique et archéologique de Tournai* 10, part 1 (1906): 14–15.
Hertoghe, Cornelius Polycarpus de. *Religio canonicorum ordinis Praemonstratensis*. Antwerp, 1663.
Hidé, Charles. "L'administration et la juridiction municipale de la commune de Bruyères, du XIIe au XVIIIe siècle." *Bulletin de la Société Académique de Laon* 11 (1861): 44–75.
Hugo, Charles Louis. *La vie de S. Norbert, Archevêque de Magdebourg*. Luxembourg, 1704.
– *Sacri et Canonici Ordinis Praemonstratensis annales*. 2 vols. Nancy, 1734–6.
– *Vita Sancti Norberti, Sacri Ordinis Praemonstratensium Canonicorum Regularium Patriarchae*. Prague, 1732.
Jacquemin, Louis. "Annales de la vie de Joscelin de Vierzi, 57e évêque de Soissons (1126–1152)." In *Quatrièmes mélanges d'histoire du Moyen Âge*, ed. Achille Luchaire, 1–161. Paris: Alcan, 1905.
Jaffé, Philipp. *Regesta Pontificum Romanorum ab condita ecclesia ad annum post Christum natum MCXCVIII*. Berlin, 1851.
Jaffé, Philipp, and Samuel Löwenfeld. *Regesta Pontificum Romanorum ab condita ecclesia ad annum post Christum natum MCXCVIII*. 2nd ed. 2 vols. Leipzig, 1885–8.
Jordan, William Chester. *The Apple of His Eye: Converts from Islam in the Reign of Louis IX*. Princeton: Princeton University Press, 2019.

Josse, Hector. *Notice historique sur le village de Douilly et ses dépendances: Margères, ancien prieuré obédiencier d'Arrouaise, puis de Corbie; Forest et Montizelle*. Amiens, 1888.

Jubainville, Henri d'Arbois de. *Histoire des ducs et des comtes de Champagne, depuis le VIe siècle jusqu'à la fin du XIe*. Vol. 3 of 8 vols. Paris, 1861.

Ker, Neil R. "From "above Top Line" to "below Top Line": A Change in Scribal Practice." *Celtica* 5 (1960): 13–16.

Knowles, David. *The Religious Orders in England: The End of the Middle Ages*. Vol. 2 of 3 vols. Cambridge: Cambridge University Press, 1940.

Kosto, Adam J. *Making Agreements in Medieval Catalonia: Power, Order, and the Written Word, 1000–1200*. Cambridge: Cambridge University Press, 2007.

La Fons, Alexandre de. *Une cité picarde au Moyen-Age, ou Noyon et la noyonnais aux XIVe et XVe siècles*. Noyon, 1841.

Lalou, Elisabeth. *Itinéraire de Philippe IV le Bel (1285–1314)*. 2 vols. Mémoires de l'Académie des inscriptions et belles-lettres 37. Paris: Académie des inscriptions et belles lettres, 2007.

Lamy, Hugues. *Vie du bienheureux Hugues de Fosses: premier abbé de Prémontré (1164)*. Charleroi: Éditions de "La terre Wallonne," 1925.

Larive, André. *Essai historique sur la commune de Vendeuil*. La Fère, 1899.

La Roncière, Charles Bourel de, Joseph de Loye, Pierre de Cenival, and Auguste Coulon. *Les registres d'Alexandre IV; recueil des bulles de ce pape publiées ou analysées d'après les manuscrits originaux des archives du Vatican*. 3 vols. Paris: A. Fontemoing, 1902–59.

Leducq, Victor. *Commenchon (Canton de Chauny, Aisne)*. Chauny: Imprimerie Richez, 1931.

Lefèvre, Placide. "Deux bulles pontificales inédites du XIIe siècle relatives à l'Ordre de Prémontré." *Analecta Praemonstratensia* 12 (1936): 67–70.

– "L'ancienne bibliothèque de l'abbaye d'Averbode d'après les sources d'Archives." *Analecta Praemonstratensia* 36 (1960): 62–112, 317–36.

Le Glay, André. *Cameracum Christianum ou histoire ecclésiastique du diocèse de Cambrai*. Lille, 1849.

Le Mire, Aubert. *Ordinis Praemonstratensis Chronicon*. Cologne, 1613.

Leroy-Morel. *Recherches généalogiques sur les familles nobles de plusieurs villages des environs de Nesle, Noyon, Ham et Roye, et recherches historiques sur les mêmes localités*. Amiens, 1867.

Leson, Richard A. "'Partout la figure du lion': Thomas of Marle and the Enduring Legacy of the Coucy Donjon Tympanum." *Speculum* 93, no. 1 (January, 2018): 27–71.

Le Vasseur, Jacques. *Annales de l'Église Cathédrale de Noyon*. Paris, 1633.

Lewis, Andrew W. "The Career of Philip the Cleric, Younger Brother of Louis VII: Apropos of an Unpublished Charter." *Traditio* 50 (1995): 111–27.

– "Fourteen Charters of Robert I of Dreux (1152–1188)." *Traditio* 41 (1985): 145–79.

Linehan, Peter, and Martin Bertram. "Bermerkungen zu einer Extravagante Gregors IX. und zu ihrer Verwendung im Lorvão-Prozeß." In *Honos alit artes: studi per il settantesimo compleanno di Mario Ascheri*, ed. Paola Maffei and Gian Maria Varanini, 1:355–78. Florence: Firenze University Press, 2014.

Lohrmann, Dietrich. "Barrages et moulins sur la Somme au temps des chanoines réguliers (XIIe–XIIIe siècles)." In *L'hydraulique monastique. Milieux, réseaux, usages*, ed. Bonis Armelle et al., 337–47. Grâne: Créaphis, 1996.

– "Évolution et organisation interne des cartulaires rhénans du Moyen Âge." In *Les cartulaires. Actes de la table ronde organisée par l'École nationale des chartes et le G.D.R. 121 du C.N.R.S.*, ed. Olivier Guyotjeannin, Laurent Morelle, and Michel Parisse, 79–90. Mémoires et documents de l'École des Chartes 39. Paris: École nationale des chartes, 1993.

– *Kirchengut im nördlichen Frankreich. Besitz, Verfassung und Wirtschaft im Spiegel der Papstprivilegien des 11.–12. Jahrhunderts.* Pariser Historische Studien 20. Bonn: Ludwig Röhrscheid, 1983.

– "Répartition et création de nouveaux domaines monastiques au XIIe siècle: Beauvaisis, Soissonnais, Vermandois." In *Villa – Curtis – Grangia. Landwirtschaft zwischen Loire und Rhein von der Römerzeit zum Hochmittelalter. Economie rurale entre Loire et Rhin de l' epoque gallo-romaine au 12.–13. siècle*, ed. Walter Jansen and Dietrich Lohrmann, 242–59. Beihefte der Francia 11. Munich: Bayerische Staatsbibliothek, 1983.

Loisne, Auguste de. "Le Cartulaire de la Commanderie d'Éterpigny." *Bulletin de la société des antiquaires de Picardie* 25 (1911): 150–213.

Luchaire, Achille. *Histoire des institutions monarchiques de la France sous les premiers Capétiens (mémoires et documents). Études sur les actes de Louis VII.* Paris, 1885.

– *Louis VI le Gros. Annales de sa vie et de son règne.* Paris, 1890.

– *Remarques sur la succession des grands officiers de la couronne qui ont souscrit les diplômes de Louis VI et de Louis VII (1108–1180).* Paris, 1881.

Mabire La Caille, Claire. "Château, bourg castral, Villeneuve. La genèse d'une agglomération secondaire, Coucy-le-Château (XIIe–XIIIe siècles)." *Revue archéologique de Picardie*, no. 1/2 (2005): 161–72.

Madelaine, Godefroid. *L'abbaye de Prémontré en 1882.* Caen, 1882.

– *Histoire de saint Norbert, fondateur de l'ordre de Prémontré et archevêque de Magdebourg.* Lille, 1886.

Maguire, Laurie E. "Feminist Editing and the Body of the Text." In *A Feminist Companion to Shakespeare*, ed. Dympna Callaghan, 2nd ed., 75–97. Blackwell Companions to Literature and Culture. Chichester: John Wiley & Sons, 2016.

Manrique, Ángel. *Cisterciensium seu verius ecclesiasticorum annalium a condito Cistercio.* 4 vols. Lyon, 1642.

Marchand, Lucien. *Essai historique sur la Chartreuse du Val Saint-Pierre: située dans l'ancien diocèse de Laon, 1140–1789.* Chateau-Thierry: M. Marchand, 1952.

Marlot, Guillaume. *Histoire de la ville, cité et université de Reims, métropolitaine de la Gaule Belgique*. Reims, 1843.

Martinet, Suzanne. "Elinand, évêque de Laon méconnu (1052–1098)." *Mémoires de la Fédération des sociétés d'histoire et d'archéologie de l'Aisne* 36 (1991): 58–78.

– "Un évêque bâtisseur: Gautier de Mortagne." *Mémoires de la Fédération des Sociétés d'histoire et d'archéologie de l'Aisne* 8 (1961/2): 81–92.

Martin-Marville, C.P.H. *Trosly-Loire, ou le Trosly des conciles, ses châteaux, ses villas, ses fiefs et ses seigneurs: mémoires historiques*. Noyon, 1870.

Matton, Auguste. *Inventaire sommaire des Archives départementales antérieures à 1790: Archives ecclésiastiques. Séries G et H*. 3 vols. Laon, 1885.

Mazière, Léon. "Annales Noyonnaises, première partie." *Comptes rendus et mémoires lus aux séances de la Société archéologique et historique de Noyon* 12 (1896): 1–331.

– "Notice historique sur Ribécourt." *Comptes rendus et mémoires lus aux séances de la Société archéologique et historique de Noyon* 5 (1874): 61–195.

McIntosh, James C. "Public Libraries in France." *University of Illinois Library School Occasional Papers* 41 (February 1955): 1–28.

Melleville, Maximilien. *Dictionnaire historique du département de l'Aisne*. 2nd ed. 2 vols. Laon, 1865.

Ménage, Gilles, and Auguste François Jault. *Dictionnaire etymologique de la langue françoise*. 2 vols. Paris, 1750.

Mennesson, Eugène. "Les chartes de Vervins." *La Thiérache: bulletin de la Société archéologique de Vervins* 13 (1889): 1–94.

Michel, Henri. "Inventaire sommaire du cartulaire d'Arrouaise." *Bulletin de la société des antiquaires de Picardie* 28 (1919): 251–73.

Millet, Hélène. *Les Chanoines du chapitre cathédral de Laon. 1272–1412*. Rome: École française de Rome, 1982.

Mol, Johannes A. "The Cistercian Model? The Application of the Grange System by the Various Religious Orders in the Frisian Coastal Area, 1150–1400." *The Medieval Low Countries* 1 (2014): 205–32.

Molinier, Auguste. *Catalogue général des manuscrits des bibliothèques publiques de France: Départements*. Vol. 3. Paris, 1885.

Morel, Émile. "Remarques sur la donation d'Hugues de Coudun à St-Hugues de Cluny et la Fondation du prieuré d'Elincourt-Sainte-Marguerite." *Bulletin de la Société Historique de Compiègne* 7 (1888): 268–72.

Morelle, Laurent. "Mariage et diplomatique: autour de cinq chartes de douaire dans le Laonnois-Soissonnais, 1163–1181." *Bibliothèque de l'École des chartes* 146, no. 2 (1988): 225–84.

– "Une charte nuptiale laonnoise de 1158 conservée en original." *Bibliothèque de l'École des chartes* 168, no. 1 (2010): 209–24.

Mülverstedt, George Adalbert von. *Regesta archiepiscopatus Magdeburgensis: Sammlung von Auszügen aus Urkunden und Annalisten zur Geschichte des Erzstifts und Herzogthums Magdeburg*. 3 vols. Magdeburg, 1876.

Neel, Carol. "The Premonstratensian Project." In *A Companion to Medieval Rules and Customaries*, ed. Krijn Pansters, 193–224. Brill's Companions to the Christian Tradition 93. Leiden: Brill, 2020.

Nerini, Felix. *De templo et coenobio sanctorum Bonifacii et Alexii Historica Monumenta*. Rome, 1752.

Newman, William Mendel. *Les seigneurs de Nesle en Picardie (XIIe–XIIIe siècle), leurs chartes et leur histoire; étude sur la noblesse régionale ecclésiastique et laïque*. 2 vols. Memoirs of the American Philosophical Society 91. Philadelphia: American Philosophical Society, 1971.

Oberste, Jörg. "Règle, coutumes et statuts: le système normatif des prémontrés aux XIIe–XIIIe siècles." In *Regulae – consuetudines – statuta; studi sulle fonti normative degli ordini religiosi nei secoli centrali del Medioevo; atti del I e del II Seminario internazionale di studio del Centro italo-tedesco di storia comparata degli ordini religiosi*, ed. Cristina Andenna. Münster: LIT, 2005.

Omont, Henri Auguste. *Catalogue des manuscrits latins et français de la collection Phillipps acquis en 1908 pour la Bibliothèque nationale*. Paris: Ernest Leroux, 1909.

Ott, John S. "'Both Mary and Martha': Bishop Lietbert of Cambrai and the Construction of Episcopal Sanctity in a Border Diocese around 1100." In *The Bishop Reformed: Studies of Episcopal Power and Culture in the Central Middle Ages*, ed. John S. Ott and Anna Trumbore Jones, 137–60. New York: Routledge, 2016.

Palaude, Stéphane. "La politique de défrichement de la terre par le verre. Les religieux et les territoires du verre en Thiérache XVe et XVIe siècles." *Revue du Nord* 94, no. 295 (2012): 435–55.

Parisse, Michel. "Les cartulaires. Copies ou sources originales?" In *Les cartulaires. Actes de la table ronde organisée par l'École nationale des chartes et le G.D.R. 121 du C.N.R.S.*, edited by Olivier Guyotjeannin, Laurent Morelle, and Michel Parisse, 503–12. Mémoires et documents de l'École des Chartes 39. Paris: École nationale des chartes, 1993.

Paulin Paris, Alexis, ed. *Histoire littéraire de la France*. New ed. Vol. 10 of 46 vols. Paris, 1868.

Pearson, John B. *Pope Innocent III: A Tabular Index to His Letters, Briefs and Instructions A.D. 1198–1214*. Cambridge: n.p., 1911.

Pécheur, Louis-Victor. *Histoire de la ville de Guise et de ses environs: de ses seigneurs, comtes, ducs, etc.* 2 vols. Vervins, 1851.

– "Les rues, boulevards et avenues de Soissons." *Bulletin archéologique, historique et scientifique de Soissons*, 3rd series, 7, part 2 (1899): 1–121.

– "Noms des lieux mentionnés dans le cartulaire de Saint-Léger." *Bulletin de la Société historique et archéologique de Soissons*, 2nd series, 10 (1868): 371–7.

Petit, François. *La spiritualité des Prémontrés aux XIIe et XIIIe siècles*. Études de théologie et d'histoire de la spiritualité 10. Paris: Librairie Philosophique J. Vrin, 1947.

– "Pourquoi saint Norbert a choisi Prémontré." *Analecta Praemonstratensia* 40 (1964): 5–16.

– *Spirituality of the Premonstratensians: The Twelfth and Thirteenth Centuries*. Ed. Carol Neel. Trans. Victor Szczurek. Collegeville, MN: Liturgical Press, 2011.
Pfaff, Volkert. "Papst Clemens III. (1187–1191). Mit einer Liste der Kardinalsunterschriften." *Zeitschrift der Savigny-Stiftung für Rechtsgeschichte: Kanonistische Abteilung* 66 (1980): 261–316.
Picó, Fernando. "Membership in the Cathedral Chapter of Laon, 1217–1238." *Catholic Historical Review* 61, no. 1 (1975): 1–30.
Piolin, P. *Gallia Christiana in Provincias Ecclesiasticas Distributa*. 16 vols. Paris, 1715–65.
Plouvier, Martine. "L'abbaye de Prémontré (Aisne)." In *Congrès archéologique de France. 148e session, 1990, Aisne méridionale*, 2:509–48. Paris: Société française d'archéologie, 1994.
– *L'Abbaye de Prémontré aux XVIIe et XVIIIe siècles: histoire d'une reconstruction*. Bibliotheca Analectorum Praemonstratensium 16. Louvain: Commission historique de l'Ordre de Prémontré, 1985.
– *L'abbaye de Prémontré: du service de Dieu au soin des hommes*. Amiens: Association pour la généralisation de l'Inventaire régional en Picardie, 2007.
Poissonnier, J. "L'Abbaye de St-Éloi-Fontaine ou de Commenchon." *Comptes rendus et mémoires du Comité archéologique de Noyon* 5 (1874): 269–303.
Ponthieux, Alfred. "Notes historiques sur Appilly." *Comptes rendus et mémoires. Comité archéologique de Noyon* 20 (1906): 1–41.
– "Notes sur l'ancien Noyon: La paroisse Saint-Germain." *Comité archéologique et historique de Noyon: Comptes-rendus et mémoires lus aux séances* 21 (1908): xv–xvi.
– "Notice historique sur Villeselve et son ancien prieuré, Noyon." *Comptes rendus et mémoires. Comité archéologique de Noyon* 15 (1898): 211–94.
Pontvianne, Régis. *Recherches historiques sur l'Abbaye de Doue: et sur les prieurés qui en dépendaient (1162–1789)*. Le Puy: Imprimerie Catholique, 1900.
Poquet, Alexandre. *Monographie de l'abbaye de Longpont, son histoire, ses monuments, ses abbés, ses personnages célèbres, ses sépultures, ses possessions territoriales*. Paris, 1869.
– *Pélerinage à l'ancienne abbaye de Saint-Médard-lès-Soissons*. 2nd ed. Paris, 1849.
Posner, Ernst. "Some Aspects of Archival Development since the French Revolution." *American Archivist* 3, no. 3 (July 1940): 159–72.
Potthast, August. *Regesta Pontificum Romanorum inde ab anno post Christum natum 1198 ad annum 1304*. 2 vols. Berlin, 1874–5.
Prioux, Stanislas. *Histoire de Braine et de ses environs*. Paris, 1846.
– *Monographie de l'ancienne abbaye royale Saint-Yved de Braine, avec la description des tombes royales et seigneuriales renfermées dans cette église*. Paris, 1859.
Pycke, Jacques. *Le chapitre cathédral Notre-Dame de Tournai de la fin du XIe à la fin du XIIIe siècle: son organisation, sa vie, ses membres*. Recueil de Travaux d'Histoire et de Philologie 30. Louvain: Nauwelaerts, 1986.

Radini, Anita, M. Tromp, A. Beach, E. Tong, C. Speller, M. McCormick, J.V. Dudgeon, et al. "Medieval Women's Early Involvement in Manuscript Production Suggested by Lapis Lazuli Identification in Dental Calculus." *Science Advances* 5, no. 1 (2019), https://doi.org/10.1126/sciadv.aau7126.

Renardy, Christine. *Les maîtres universitaires du diocèse de Liège: répertoire biographique, 1140–1350*. Paris: Librairie Droz, 1981.

Reusens, Edmond. "Les chancelleries inférieures en Belgique depuis leur origine jusqu'au XIIIe siècle." *Analectes pour servir à l'histoire ecclésiastique de la Belgique* 26 (1896): 20–206.

Robinson, I.S. *The Papacy, 1073–1198: Continuity and Innovation*. Cambridge: Cambridge University Press, 1990.

Rothe, Katrin. "Zwischen *contemplatio* und *vita apostolica*. Aspekte der Identität des frühen Prämonstratenserordens." In *Die Orden im Wandel Europas. Historische Episoden und ihre globalen Folgen*, ed. Petrus Bsteh, Brigitte Proksch, and Cosmas Hoffman, 46–60. Spiritualität im Dialog 5. Berlin: Lit Verlag, 2013.

Saint-Aymour, Amédée Caix de. *La maison de Caix: rameau mâle des Boves-Coucy*. Paris, 1895.

Saint-Denis, Alain. *Apogée d'une cité: Laon et le Laonnois aux XIIe et XIIIe siècles*. Nancy: Presses universitaires de Nancy, 1994.

– "Maires et jurés de Laon aux premiers temps de la commune (1128–1297)." *Mémoires de la Fédération des Sociétés d'histoire et d'archéologie de l'Aisne* 54 (2009): 153–78.

Sanders, Antoon. *Chorographia sacra Brabantiae*. 3 vols. The Hague, 1726.

Schmugge, Ludwig. "Ministerialität und Bürgertum in Reims. Untersuchungen zur Geschichte der Stadt im 12. und 13. Jahrhundert." *Francia* 2 (1974): 152–212.

Seale, Yvonne. "Handlist of Premonstratensian Cartularies." November 28, 2019. https://yvonneseale.org/blog/2019/11/28/handlist-of-premonstratensian-cartularies/.

– "'Ten Thousand Women': Gender, Affinity, and the Development of the Premonstratensian Order in Medieval France." PhD dissertation, University of Iowa, 2016.

– "Well-Behaved Women? Agnès of Baudement and Agnès of Braine as Mediators and Patrons of the Premonstratensian Order." *Haskins Society Journal: Studies in Medieval History* 28 (2016): 101–17.

Seale, Yvonne, and Heather Wacha. "Spare No Scrap: A Piece of Binder's Waste as Evidence for Institutional Development at the Abbey of Prémontré in the Thirteenth Century." *Revue d'histoire ecclésiastique* 116 (May/June, 2021): 5–31.

Shortell, Ellen. "An Image of the Abbey Church of Prémontré under Construction." *Gesta* 29, no. 2 (1990): 234–8.

Spahr, Kolumban. "Zum Freundschaftsbündnis Zwischen Cisterciensern und Prämonstratensern." *Cistercienser Chronik* 73 (1966): 10–17.

Steger, Michelle. "L'église de Saint-Jean-Baptiste de Prémontré est-elle l'église construite en 1121 sous la direction de saint Norbert?" In *Actes officiels du*

12e Colloque du Centre d'études et de recherches prémontrées, Averbode 1986, ed. Martine Plouvier, 30–8. Reims: Centre d'études et de recherches prémontrées, 1987.

Stein, Henri. *Bibliographie générale des cartulaires français ou relatifs à l'histoire de France*. Paris: A. Picard et fils, 1907.

Stucky Skinner, Pamela. "The Cartulary of Clairmarais, a Monastery of Cistercian Nuns at Reims, France, c. 1220–1460: Edition and Commentary." PhD dissertation, University of Iowa, 2005.

Suckling, Alfred. *The History and Antiquities of the Hundreds of Blything and Part of Lothingland in the County of Suffolk*. London, 1847.

Taïée, Charles. "L'abbaye de Saint-Jean de Laon." *Bulletin de la Société académique de Laon* 21 (1876): 175–309.

– "Prémontré. Étude sur l'abbaye de ce nom et sur l'ordre." *Bulletin de la Société académique de Laon* 19 (1872): 93–262.

Tanner, Heather J., ed. *Medieval Elite Women and the Exercise of Power, 1100–1400: Moving beyond the Exceptionalist Debate*. The New Middle Ages. Chur: Palgrave Macmillan, 2019.

Tardif, Jules. *Monuments historiques: Cartons des rois, 528–1789*. Paris, 1866.

Tassus, E. "Notice historique sur la paroisse de Baboeuf." *Comité Archéologique et Historique de Noyon. Comptes-Rendus et Mémoires* 21 (1908): 10–230.

Tétart, Jean-Louis. "Barthélemy, évêque de Laon, moine cistercien de Foigny." *Mémoires de la Fédération des Sociétés d'Histoire et d'Archéologie de l'Aisne* 46 (2001): 7–20.

Thomas, A.H. "Une version des statuts de Prémontré au début du XIIIe siècle." *Analecta Praemonstratensia* 55 (1979): 153–70.

Tucker, Joanna. *Reading and Shaping Medieval Cartularies: Multi-Scribe Manuscripts and Their Patterns of Growth.* Studies in Celtic History 41. Woodbridge: Boydell & Brewer, 2020.

– "Understanding Scotland's Medieval Cartularies." *Innes Review* 70, no. 2 (1 November 2019): 135–70.

Valvekens, Emile. "Le chapitre général de Prémontré et les nouveaux statuts de 1505." *Analecta Praemonstratensia* 14 (1938): 53–94.

Van Bavel, Bas J.P. "Schakels tussen abdij en stad. De stadshoven van de norbertijner abdijen in de Nederlanden (ca. 1250–ca. 1600)." *Analecta Praemonstratensia* 76 (2000): 133–57.

Van de Perre, Dirk. "Die ältesten Klostergesetzgebungen von Prémontré, Oigny, Cîteaux, Klosterrath und Arrouaise und ihre Beziehungen zueinander." *Analecta Praemonstratensia* 76, no. 1–4 (2000): 29–69.

Van Engen, John. "Norbert of Xanten: Preaching to the People, Converting the Clergy." In *Reclaiming Our Norbertine Heritage: Lectures Presented in Honor of the 100th Anniversary of the Norbertine Presence in the Green Bay Diocese*, ed. Roman R. Vanasse, 95–111. De Pere, WI: St. Norbert Abbey, 1995.

– *Rupert of Deutz*. Publications of the Center for Medieval and Renaissance Studies 18. Berkeley: University of California Press, 1983.

Van Dijck, Leo. "L'état général de l'ordre de Prémontré au XVIe siècle." In *Les Prémontrés et la Lorraine, XIIe–XVIIIe siècle*, ed. Dominique-Marie Dauzet and

Martine Plouvier, 44–61. Bibliothèque Beauchesne Religion Société Politique 33. Paris: Beauchesne, 1998.

Vieillard, Françoise, and Olivier Guyotjeannin. *Conseils pour l'édition des textes médiévaux, Fascicule 1*. Paris: CTHS, 2005.

Venarde, Bruce L. "Making History at Fontevraud: Abbess Petronilla de Chemillé and Practical Literacy." In *Nuns' Literacies in Medieval Europe: The Antwerp Dialogue*, ed. Virginia Blanton, Veronica M. O'Mara, and Patricia Stoop, 19–32. Medieval Women: Texts and Contexts 28. Turnhout: Brepols, 2018.

Verhulst, Adriaan, and Thérèse de Hemptinne. "Le chancelier de Flandre sous les comtes de la maison d'Alsace (1128–1191)." *Bulletin de la Commission royale d'Histoire* 141, no. 1 (1975): 267–311.

Voillemier, Jean-Baptiste-Marie-Joseph. "Note sur la maison des Bouteiller de Senlis." *Comité Archéologique de Senlis: Comptes-rendus et Mémoires* 3 (1865): 28–56.

Wacha, Heather. "The Cartulary of the Abbey of Prémontré: A Story of Conflict and Resolution." *Essays in Medieval Studies* 31, no. 1 (30 September 2016): 125–42.

– "La Puissance du Choix: Women's Economic Activity in Twelfth- and Thirteenth-Century Picardy." PhD dissertation, University of Iowa, 2016.

Waddell, Chrysogonus. "The Myth of Cistercian Origins: C.H. Berman and the Manuscript Sources." *Cîteaux: Commentarii Cistercienses* 51 (2000): 299–386.

Waquet, Henri. *Le bailliage de Vermandois aux XIIIe et XIVe siècles: étude d'histoire administrative*. Paris: É. Champion, 1919.

Waroquier, Roman. "La principauté de Vermandois, Valois et Montdidier au XIIe siècle: formation et physionomie d'un espace politique." *Revue du Nord* 101 (2019): 679–705.

Wauters, Alphonse. "Exploration de chartes et de cartulaires belges existants à la Bibliothèque Nationale à Paris." *Compte-rendu des Séances de la Commission royale d'Histoire*, 4th series, 2 (1876): 78–198.

Wernimont, Jacqueline. "Whence Feminism? Assessing Feminist Interventions in Digital Literary Archives." *Digital Humanities Quarterly* 7, no. 1 (2013). http://digitalhumanities.org:8081/dhq/vol/7/1/000156/000156.html.

Wichmans, Augustinus. *Brabantia Mariana Tripartita*. Antwerp, 1632.

Wickersheimer, Ernest, Guy Beaujouan, and Danielle Jacquart. *Dictionnaire biographique des médecins en France au Moyen Âge*. 3 vols. Hautes études médiévales et modernes. Geneva: Librairie Droz, 1979.

Wolbrink, Shelley Amiste. "Noble Pursuits: Family, Power, and Gender in the Premonstratensian Monasteries of Northwestern Germany, 1120–1250." PhD dissertation, University of Cincinnati, 1998.

Wyard, Robert. *Histoire de l'abbaye de Saint-Vincent de Laon*. Saint-Quentin, 1858.

Wymans, Gabriel. *Inventaire des archives de l'abbaye de Saint-Feuillien du Roeulx*. Brussels: Archives générales du Royaume, 1975.

Zupko, Ronald Edward. *French Weights and Measures before the Revolution: A Dictionary of Provincial and Local Units*. Bloomington: Indiana University Press, 1978.

INDEX

www.ingramcontent.com/pod-product-compliance
Lightning Source LLC
LaVergne TN
LVHW010354080826
844660LV00015B/962/J

* 9 7 8 1 4 8 7 5 4 4 8 3 6 *